MODERN AMERICA 1914 to 1945

Ross Gregory

Richard Balkin
General Editor

Facts On File, Inc.

For

Shirley

Modern America, 1914–1945

Facts On File, Inc.
132 West 31st Street
New York NY 10001

Library of Congress Cataloging-in-Publication Data
Gregory, Ross.
    Modern America, 1914–1945 / Ross Gregory.
      p.   cm. — (Almanacs of American life)
    Includes bibliographical references and index.
    ISBN 0-8160-2532-0
    1. United States—History—1913–1921.   2. United States—
    History—1919–1933.   3. United States—History—1933–1945.
    4. United States—Social life and customs—1918–1945.   I. Title.
    II. Series.
    E766.G67   1995
    973.9—dc20   94-4168

Facts On File books are available at special discounts when purchased in
bulk quantities for businesses, associations, institutions, or sales promotions.
Please call our Special Sales Department in New York at 212/967-8800 or
800/322-8755.

You can find Facts On File on the World Wide Web at
http://www.factsonfile.com

Text design by F. C. Pusterla
Maps on pages 2, 102, 255, 273, 320, 379 by Dale Williams

Printed in the United States of America

VB BVC 10 9 8 7 6 5

This book is printed on acid-free paper.

CONTENTS

LIST OF MAPS

PREFACE

This almanac offers a multidimensional approach to the history of the United States from 1914 to 1945. It seeks to interweave various compilations of statistics with discussion through introductory essays, personality profiles, selected highlighted topics, and other special coverage, although the basic foundation of the volume is to be found in the data. A second objective is to combine the broad-based coverage of the contemporary almanac with the approach of historical almanacs, most of which have been given over to a year-by-year listing of developments. The result, hopefully, is a happy marriage of the two: a volume offering the breadth of a yearly almanac and the depth and perspective of a historical volume.

Any presentation of history is by nature a process of selection. The rule applies especially to coverage of a general period of history and to material involved in extensive use of detail. What topics should an almanac cover and in how much detail? The process of selection for this volume grew largely out of four considerations:

1. Information that was most reflective of the period under consideration—that is, the years 1914–45. This was the most important factor. The information might or might not be intriguing, depending upon one's point of view (I found that most of it was), but it was necessary for a description of the era.

2. Information that was most meaningful from a contemporary perspective—that is, topics that attract more popular attention in the present generation than they did at the time under consideration. Minority groups and women, as examples, fall into this category.

3. Information for which sufficient data was available. A better way to make the point might be in reverse fashion: for some topics adequate data did not exist to permit development of the theme. There was no systematic accounting of the economic status of black people; Mexican Americans as a rule were not even counted as a separate entity. Many social trends of the first half of the twentieth century were not measured as carefully as they would be in the second half.

4. Information that caught the eye of the author. Baseball received a good measure of attention because it was an important reflector of culture in this period (and good baseball data existed) but also because I like baseball, especially as played in those years before a .250 hitter could become a multimillionaire.

A few words are in order with respect to ground rules. Publications from another era sometimes carried labels appropriate to that time but out of step with terminology preferred many years later. The best examples are *Negro* or *colored,* the most polite and accepted terms for reference to black people in the years before 1945. As a rule I have allowed the original labels to stand. Otherwise the term *black* is used interchangeably with *African American* and the term *Indian* with *Native American.* Statistics come in many forms and styles of arrangement, including those from the most important source of information for this publication: the government of the United States. Some government agencies arrange historical numbers forward—from oldest to the most recent—and others do it in reverse. Although I occasionally have turned tables around to conform with straight chronological change, the numbers usually appear in this volume as they appeared in the sources—both forward and backward. There is something to be said for either approach.

The period itself should require no introduction, no elaborate explanation of why it merited attention. It perhaps could not match the superlative numbers of the time that followed—in gross national product, for example, or in personal income—but no period of American history could surpass the ups and downs, twists and turns of the time from the start of the First World War until the end of the Second World War. In scarcely more than thirty years the country experienced two world wars, its most severe depression, and a short interlude in between. Warren Harding called the interlude a time of "normalcy," but in fact nothing was normal about the 1920s or any other part of the era. If the period produced segregation and other ghastly treatment of racial minorities, the great flu pandemic, vast wartime destruction, and the production of the atomic bomb, it also brought forth penicillin, the V-8 engine, air-conditioning, *Gone With the Wind,* and two grand experiments designed to preserve peace. It is, of course, not possible to obtain a full account of this part of the American past from charts, tables, or any formulation of figures alone, but it is impossible to receive a clear picture without them.

In the preparation of this manuscript I received advice, suggestions, and various types of assistance from numerous friends, students, and colleagues. They deserve my thanks but otherwise for the most part will remain nameless. The Burnham-MacMillan Fund at Western Michigan University provided funds that facilitated the acquisition of photographs and illustrations. Charles Johnson helped with my many searches for information. Steve Cartwright did diligent and careful work in several aspects of the process of preparing the manuscript. Special thanks should go to two people. My wife, Shirley, was a steady source of encouragement, a close friend, and perceptive adviser. Richard Balkin has been a wise and patient editor, prompt with guidance yet open to different ideas and recommendations.

Ross Gregory
Kalamazoo, Michigan

NOTE ON PHOTOS

Many of the illustrations and photographs used in this book are old, historical images. The quality of the prints is not always up to modern standards, as in many cases the originals are from glass negatives or the originals are damaged. The content of the illustrations, however, made their inclusion important despite problems in reproduction.

CHAPTER 1 The Americans: Population and Immigration

The American Population

The United States was unusual in the sense that it had two major sources of population change: the standard relationship between the birth and death rates, and immigration. Already one of the world's largest and most populous nations, the United States continued to grow in population during the period from 1914 to 1945. The changes came in proportion to the changing state of national and international affairs. Upheaval abroad, notably in Europe, produced the prospect of immigration surges so threatening—or so people of that era perceived them—that the government moved to reduce immigration sharply. Changes in the domestic condition manifested themselves in population change most clearly in the 1930s, the time of the Great Depression. An increase that had been running at 15–16% per decade dropped to approximately 7% during the 1930s. The years 1940–45, during the Second World War, produced a modest increase in the growth of population, but perhaps more im-portant, they laid a foundation for the great surge that would follow the war, what would become known as the "baby boom."

Characteristics of the population stood out in the government's periodic census reports. Males continued to outnumber females—partly a consequence of immigration—but females had almost caught up by the year 1945. Americans increasingly were city dwellers. The urban population had passed the rural by 1920 (it was 51.2% in that year). By 1940 it had changed to 56.5%. During the years 1941–45 the farms experienced an additional loss of nearly three million. The change often was more of location than of attitude. Although the Census Bureau classified any place with more than 2,500 people as urban, there was some doubt that residents of the villages and small towns truly were city folk. Many genuine city dwellers as well retained close ties to their former residence in the countryside.

TABLE 1.1   ESTIMATED POPULATION OF THE UNITED STATES, BY SEX, COLOR

Year	Total	Sex		Color		Males per 100 Females	
		Male	Female	White	Nonwhite	Total	Foreign Born
1914	99,118,000	50,889,000	48,229,000	88,483,000	10,635,000	. . .	. . .
1915	100,549,000	51,572,000	48,977,000	89,850,000	10,699,000	. . .	. . .
1916	101,966,000	52,238,000	49,728,000	91,202,000	10,764,000	. . .	. . .
1917	103,266,000	52,786,000	50,481,000	92,437,000	10,829,000	. . .	. . .
1918	103,203,000	51,968,000	51,234,000	92,354,000	10,849,000	. . .	. . .
1919	104,512,000	53,107,000	51,405,000	93,681,000	10,831,000	. . .	. . .
1920	106,466,000	54,295,000	52,171,000	95,511,000	10,955,000	104	122.9
1921	108,541,000	55,292,000	53,250,000	97,417,000	11,124,000	. . .	. . .
1922	110,055,000	55,891,000	54,164,000	98,768,000	11,287,000	. . .	. . .
1923	111,950,000	56,864,000	55,086,000	100,511,000	11,438,000	. . .	. . .
1924	114,113,000	57,987,000	56,126,000	102,513,000	11,601,000	. . .	. . .
1925	115,832,000	58,820,000	57,012,000	104,065,000	11,767,000	. . .	. . .
1926	117,399,000	59,590,000	57,809,000	105,469,000	11,930,000	. . .	. . .
1927	119,038,000	60,402,000	58,636,000	106,939,000	12,099,000	. . .	. . .
1928	120,501,000	61,100,000	59,401,000	108,245,000	12,256,000	. . .	. . .
1929	121,770,000	61,684,000	60,086,000	109,385,000	12,385,000	. . .	. . .
1930	123,077,000	62,297,000	60,780,000	110,559,000	12,518,000	102.5	116.6
1931	124,040,000	62,726,000	61,314,000	111,433,000	12,606,000	. . .	. . .
1932	124,840,000	63,070,000	61,770,000	112,154,000	12,686,000	. . .	. . .
1933	125,579,000	63,384,000	62,195,000	112,815,000	12,764,000	. . .	. . .
1934	126,374,000	63,726,000	62,648,000	113,527,000	12,847,000	. . .	. . .
1935	127,250,000	64,110,000	63,140,000	114,309,000	12,941,000	. . .	. . .
1936	128,053,000	64,459,000	63,594,000	115,022,000	13,031,000	. . .	. . .
1937	128,825,000	64,790,000	64,035,000	115,706,000	13,118,000	. . .	. . .
1938	129,825,000	65,235,000	64,590,000	116,592,000	13,233,000	. . .	. . .
1939	130,880,000	65,713,000	65,166,000	117,524,000	13,355,000	. . .	. . .
1940	132,122,000	66,352,000	65,770,000	118,629,000	13,494,000	100.7	111.8
1941	133,402,000	66,920,000	66,482,000	119,731,000	13,671,000	. . .	. . .
1942	134,860,000	67,597,000	67,263,000	120,992,000	13,868,000	. . .	. . .
1943	136,740,000	68,546,000	68,194,000	122,605,000	14,134,000	. . .	. . .
1944	138,398,000	69,378,000	69,020,000	124,009,000	14,388,000	. . .	. . .
1945	139,928,000	70,035,000	69,893,000	125,266,000	14,662,000	. . .	. . .

Note: Estimates for 1940–45 are as of July 1. Estimates for 1917–19 do not include armed forces overseas; estimates for 1940–45 do include armed forces overseas. The term *Nonwhite* included Negro (African Americans), Indian, Chinese, Japanese, and "all other."
Source: Bureau of the Census, *Historical Statistics of the United States, Colonial Times to 1957* (Washington, D.C., 1960), 8.

TABLE 1.2 POPULATION, BY RACE AND NATIVITY, WITH INDIVIDUAL MINOR RACES: 1910 TO 1940

Class	1910	1920	1930	1940
All classes	91,972,266	105,710,620	122,775,046	131,669,275
White	81,731,957	94,820,915	110,286,740	118,214,870
Negro	9,827,763	10,463,131	11,891,143	12,865,518
Indian	265,683	244,437	332,397	333,969
Chinese	71,531	61,639	74,954	77,504
Japanese	72,157	111,010	138,834	126,947
All other[a]	3,175	9,488	50,978	50,467
Native (all races)	78,456,380	91,789,928	108,570,897	120,074,379
Foreign-born (all races)	13,515,886	13,920,692	14,204,149	11,594,896
Native white	68,386,412	81,108,161	96,303,335	106,795,732
Foreign-born white	13,345,545	13,712,754	13,983,405	11,419,138
Percent of total	100.0	100.0	100.0	100.0
White	88.9	89.7	89.8	89.8
Negro	10.7	9.9	9.7	9.8
Indian	.3	.2	.3	.3
Chinese	.1	.1	.1	.1
Japanese	.1	.1	.1	.1
All other[a]	b	b	b	b
Native (all races)	85.3	86.8	88.4	91.2
Foreign-born (all races)	14.7	13.2	11.6	8.8
Native white	74.4	76.7	78.4	81.1
Foreign-born white	14.5	13.0	11.4	8.7

Class	1910	1920	1930	1940
Increase over preceding census:[c]				
All classes	15,977,691	13,738,354	17,064,426	8,894,229
Percent	21.0	14.9	16.1	7.2
White	14,922,761	13,088,958	15,465,825	7,928,130
Percent	22.3	16.0	16.3	7.2
Negro	993,769	635,368	1,428,012	974,375
Percent	11.2	6.5	13.6	8.2
Indian	28,487	−21,246	87,960	1,572
Percent	12.0	−8.0	36.0	.5
Chinese	−18,332	−9,892	13,315	2,550
Percent	−20.4	−13.8	21.6	3.4
Japanese	47,831	38,853	27,824	−11,887
Percent	196.6	53.8	25.1	−8.6
All other[a]	3,175	6,313	41,490	−511
Percent	. . .	198.8	437.3	−1.0
Native (all races)	12,803,081	13,333,548	16,780,969	11,503,482
Percent	19.5	17.0	18.3	10.6
Foreign-born (all races)	3,174,610	404,806	283,457	−2,609,253
Percent	30.7	3.0	2.0	−18.4
Native white	11,791,033	12,721,749	15,195,174	10,492,397
Percent	20.8	18.6	18.7	10.9
Foreign-born white	3,131,728	367,209	270,651	−2,564,267
Percent	30.7	2.8	2.0	−18.3

[a]Comprises Filipinos, Hindus, Koreans, Hawaiians, Malays, Siamese, Samoans, and Maoris.
[b]Less than one-tenth of 1 percent.
[c]A minus sign (−) denotes a decrease.
Source: Bureau of the Census, *Statistical Abstract of the United States, 1946* (Washington, D.C., 1946), 18.

Population Density, 1940

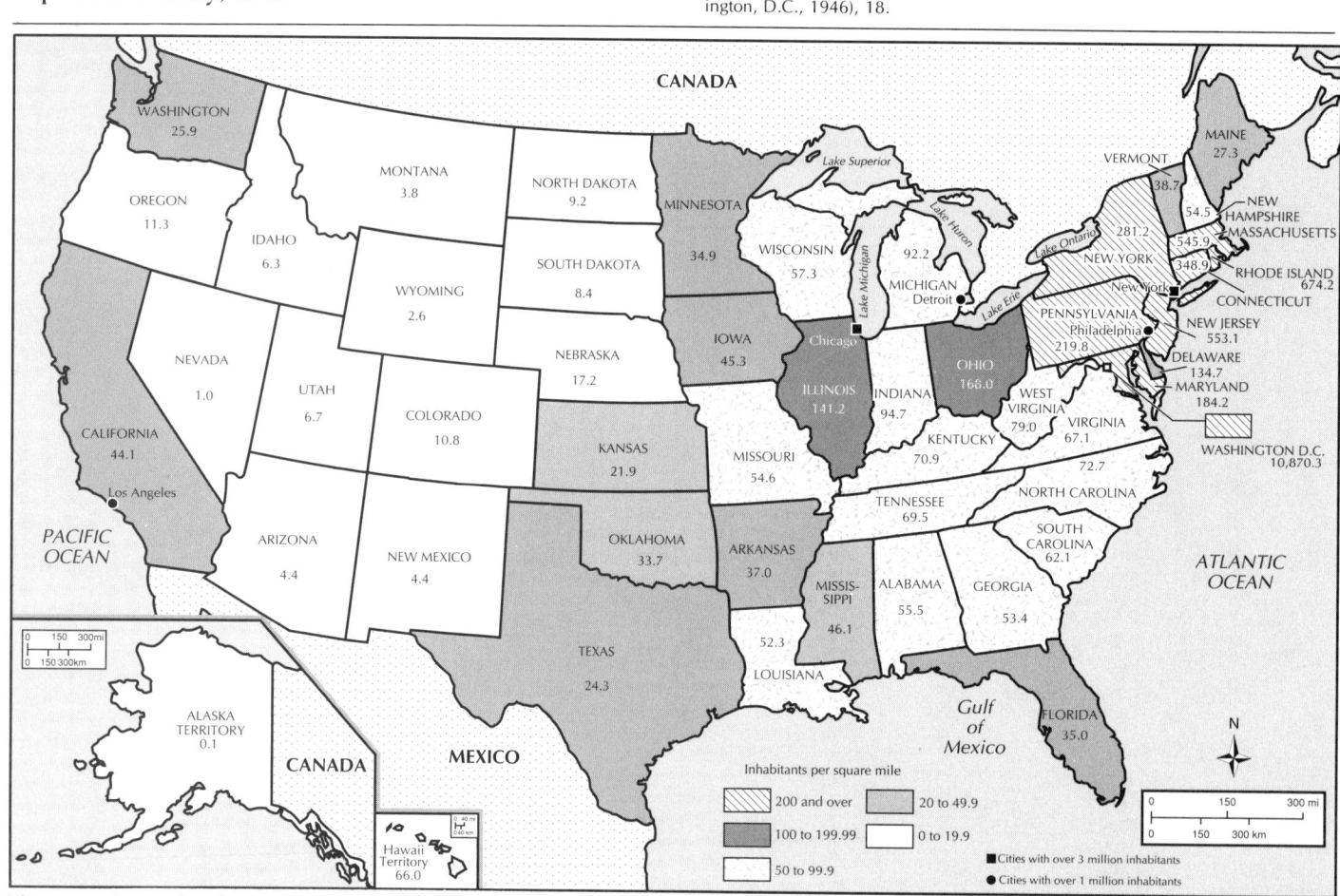

This map indicates that the American population during 1914–45 continued to be concentrated in the northeast and east north central states—the area east of the Mississippi River. The greatest density was in New Jersey, Rhode Island, and Massachusetts, all small states, and even in West Virginia the density was nearly twice that of California. The center of population was in Indiana, and it had been slowly nudging westward within the state for some time. The move to the West was only hinted at in the somewhat larger numbers for California and Texas—statistics that were considerably softened by the fact that these were the nation's two largest states.

TABLE 1.3 POPULATION, URBAN AND RURAL, BY STATES: 1910 TO 1940

Division and State	1910 Urban	1910 Rural	1920 Urban	1920 Rural	1930 Urban	1930 Rural	1940 Urban	1940 Rural	Percent Urban 1910	1920	1930	1940
Continental U.S.	42,166,120	49,806,146	54,304,603	51,406,017	68,954,823	53,820,223	74,423,702	57,245,573	45.8	51.4	56.2	56.5
New England	**4,998,082**	**1,554,599**	**5,865,073**	**1,535,836**	**6,311,976**	**1,854,365**	**6,420,542**	**2,016,748**	**76.3**	**79.2**	**77.3**	**76.1**
Maine	262,248	480,123	299,569	468,445	321,506	475,917	343,057	504,169	35.3	39.0	40.3	40.5
N.H.	255,099	175,473	279,761	163,322	273,079	192,214	283,225	208,299	59.2	63.1	58.7	57.6
Vt.	98,917	257,039	109,976	242,452	118,766	240,845	123,239	235,992	27.8	31.2	33.0	34.3
Mass.	3,125,367	241,049	3,650,248	202,108	3,831,426	418,188	3,859,476	457,245	92.8	94.8	90.2	89.4
R.I.	524,654	17,956	589,180	15,217	635,429	52,068	653,383	59,963	96.7	97.5	92.4	91.6
Conn.	731,797	382,959	936,339	444,292	1,131,770	475,133	1,158,162	551,080	65.6	67.8	70.4	67.8
Middle Atlantic	**13,723,373**	**5,592,519**	**16,672,595**	**5,588,549**	**20,394,707**	**5,866,043**	**21,147,543**	**6,391,944**	**71.0**	**74.9**	**77.7**	**76.8**
N.Y.	7,185,494	1,928,120	8,589,844	1,795,383	10,521,952	2,066,114	11,165,893	2,313,249	78.8	82.7	83.6	82.8
N.J.	1,907,210	629,957	2,474,936	680,964	3,339,244	702,090	3,394,773	765,392	75.2	78.4	82.6	81.6
Pa.	4,630,669	3,034,442	5,607,815	3,112,202	6,533,511	3,097,839	6,586,877	3,313,303	60.4	64.3	67.8	66.5
East North Central	**9,617,271**	**8,633,350**	**13,049,272**	**8,426,271**	**16,794,908**	**8,502,277**	**17,444,359**	**9,181,983**	**52.7**	**60.8**	**66.4**	**65.5**
Ohio	2,665,143	2,101,978	3,677,136	2,082,258	4,507,371	2,139,326	4,612,986	2,294,626	55.9	63.8	67.8	66.8
Ind.	1,143,835	1,557,041	1,482,855	1,447,535	1,795,892	1,442,611	1,887,712	1,540,084	42.4	50.6	55.5	55.1
Ill.	3,476,929	2,161,662	4,403,153	2,082,127	5,635,727	1,994,927	5,809,650	2,087,591	61.7	67.9	73.9	73.6
Mich.	1,327,044	1,483,129	2,241,560	1,426,852	3,302,075	1,540,250	3,454,867	1,801,239	47.2	61.1	68.2	65.7
Wis.	1,004,320	1,329,540	1,244,568	1,387,499	1,553,843	1,385,163	1,679,144	1,458,443	43.0	47.3	52.9	53.5
West North Central	**3,873,716**	**7,764,205**	**4,727,372**	**7,816,877**	**5,556,181**	**7,740,734**	**5,993,124**	**7,523,866**	**33.3**	**37.7**	**41.8**	**44.3**
Minn.	850,294	1,225,414	1,051,593	1,335,532	1,257,616	1,306,337	1,390,098	1,402,202	41.0	44.1	49.0	49.8
Iowa	680,054	1,544,717	875,495	1,528,526	979,292	1,491,647	1,084,231	1,454,037	30.6	36.4	39.6	42.7
Mo.	1,398,817	1,894,518	1,586,903	1,817,152	1,859,119	1,770,248	1,960,696	1,823,968	42.5	46.6	51.2	51.8
N. Dak.	63,236	513,820	88,239	558,633	113,306	567,539	131,923	510,012	11.0	13.6	16.6	20.6
S. Dak.	76,673	507,215	101,872	534,675	130,907	561,942	158,087	484,874	13.1	16.0	18.9	24.6
Neb.	310,852	881,362	405,306	891,066	486,107	891,856	514,148	801,686	26.1	31.3	35.3	39.1
Kans.	493,790	1,197,159	617,964	1,151,293	729,834	1,151,165	753,941	1,047,087	29.2	34.9	38.8	41.9
South Atlantic	**3,092,153**	**9,102,742**	**4,338,792**	**9,651,480**	**5,698,122**	**10,095,467**	**6,921,726**	**10,901,425**	**25.4**	**31.0**	**36.1**	**38.8**
Del.	97,085	105,237	120,767	102,236	123,146	115,234	139,432	127,073	48.0	54.2	51.7	52.3
Md.	658,192	637,154	869,422	580,239	974,869	656,657	1,080,351	740,893	50.8	60.0	59.8	59.3
D.C.	331,069	. . .	437,571	. . .	486,869	. . .	663,091	. . .	100.0	100.0	100.0	100.0
Va.	476,529	1,585,083	673,984	1,635,203	785,537	1,636,314	944,675	1,733,098	23.1	29.2	32.4	35.3
W. Va.	228,242	992,877	369,007	1,094,694	491,504	1,237,701	534,292	1,367,682	18.7	25.2	28.4	28.1
N.C.	318,474	1,887,813	490,370	2,068,753	809,847	2,360,429	974,175	2,597,448	14.4	19.2	25.5	27.3
S.C.	224,832	1,290,568	293,987	1,389,737	371,080	1,367,685	466,111	1,433,693	14.8	17.5	21.3	24.5
Ga.	538,650	2,070,471	727,859	2,167,973	895,492	2,013,014	1,073,808	2,049,915	20.6	25.1	30.8	34.4
Fla.	219,080	533,539	355,825	612,645	759,778	708,433	1,045,791	851,623	29.1	36.7	51.7	55.1
East South Central	**1,574,229**	**6,835,672**	**1,994,207**	**6,899,100**	**2,778,687**	**7,108,527**	**3,165,356**	**7,612,869**	**18.7**	**22.4**	**28.1**	**29.4**
Ky.	555,442	1,734,463	633,543	1,783,087	799,026	1,815,563	849,327	1,996,300	24.3	26.2	30.6	29.8
Tenn.	441,045	1,743,744	611,226	1,726,659	896,538	1,720,018	1,027,206	1,888,635	20.2	26.1	34.3	35.2
Ala.	370,431	1,767,662	509,317	1,838,857	744,273	1,901,975	855,941	1,977,020	17.3	21.7	28.1	30.2
Miss.	207,311	1,589,803	240,121	1,550,497	338,850	1,670,971	432,882	1,750,914	11.5	13.4	16.9	19.8
West South Central	**1,957,456**	**6,827,078**	**2,970,829**	**7,271,395**	**4,427,439**	**7,749,391**	**5,203,401**	**7,861,124**	**22.3**	**29.0**	**36.4**	**39.8**
Ark.	202,681	1,371,768	290,497	1,461,707	382,878	1,471,604	431,910	1,517,477	12.9	16.6	20.6	22.2
La.	496,516	1,159,872	628,163	1,170,346	833,532	1,268,061	980,439	1,383,441	30.0	34.9	39.7	41.5
Okla.	320,155	1,337,000	539,480	1,488,803	821,681	1,574,359	879,663	1,456,771	19.3	26.6	34.3	37.6
Tex.	938,104	2,958,438	1,512,689	3,150,539	2,389,348	3,435,367	2,911,389	3,503,435	24.1	32.4	41.0	45.4
Mountain	**947,511**	**1,686,006**	**1,214,980**	**2,121,121**	**1,457,922**	**2,243,867**	**1,771,742**	**2,378,261**	**36.0**	**36.4**	**39.4**	**42.7**
Mont.	133,420	242,633	172,011	376,878	181,036	356,570	211,535	347,921	35.5	31.3	33.7	37.8
Idaho	69,898	255,696	119,037	312,829	129,507	315,525	176,708	348,165	21.5	27.6	29.1	33.7
Wyo.	43,221	102,744	57,348	137,054	70,097	155,468	93,577	157,165	29.6	29.5	31.1	37.3
Colo.	404,840	394,184	453,259	486,370	519,882	515,909	590,756	532,540	50.7	48.2	50.2	52.6
N. Mex.	46,571	280,730	64,960	295,390	106,816	316,501	176,401	355,417	14.2	18.0	25.2	33.2
Ariz.	63,260	141,094	117,527	216,635	149,856	285,717	173,981	325,280	31.0	35.2	34.4	34.8
Utah	172,934	200,417	215,584	233,812	266,264	241,583	305,493	244,817	46.3	48.0	52.4	55.5
Nev.	13,367	68,508	15,254	62,153	34,464	56,594	43,291	66,956	16.3	19.7	37.8	39.3
Pacific	**2,382,329**	**1,809,975**	**3,471,483**	**2,095,388**	**5,534,881**	**2,659,552**	**6,355,909**	**3,377,353**	**56.8**	**62.4**	**67.5**	**65.3**
Wash.	605,530	536,460	748,735	607,886	884,539	678,857	921,969	814,222	53.0	55.2	56.6	53.1
Oreg.	307,060	365,705	391,019	392,370	489,746	464,040	531,675	558,009	45.6	49.9	51.3	48.8
Calif.	1,469,739	907,810	2,331,729	1,095,132	4,160,596	1,516,655	4,902,265	2,005,122	61.8	68.0	73.3	71.0

Source: Bureau of the Census, *Statistical Abstract of the United States, 1940* (Washington, D.C., 1941), 8, and *1947* (Washington, D.C., 1947), 16.

The American population was overwhelmingly white—nearly 90% throughout the period—and immigration policy helped keep it so. The largest nonwhite group by far was black Americans, who remained at approximately 10% of the population. Other racial minority groups, mostly Native Americans, Japanese, and Chinese, were tiny, together less than 1% of the population. Except for the African Americans, when one spoke of multiculturalism during 1914–45, one mostly referred to cultural differences between Poles, Irish, Italians, Jews, Germans, and other white ethnic groups.

The connection of Americans to foreign countries remained strong. Although the percentage of foreign-born residents steadily decreased—from approximately 14% in 1914 to less than 9% in 1940—it still was substantial. The same can be said about what the Bureau of the Census called "Foreign White Stock": whites who were either foreign-born or of foreign or mixed parentage. Even though the percentage in the total population declined from almost 35% in 1920 to 26% in 1940, these numbers indicate that a large number of people had close ties to another land. In nearly all cases the land was a European country. The large influx of such people as Hispanics and Asians remained for the years to come. Except for the large number of black people, Americans in this era were mostly transplanted Europeans.

Internal Migration

The fact that Americans always had been a people on the move was doubtless fostered by their living in a spacious land that offered varied opportunities and living conditions. The first half of the twentieth century produced both general and specific reasons for accelerating the internal movement. The specific reasons included a large depression that inspired people to move around, to escape poverty and hopefully find a better economic situation, and two world wars, which provided more reasons to move, such as entering military service or seeking out booming industrial centers that offered the prospect of work. The general factors involved an extension of the old trend of Americans leaving the farm and rural areas for life in the city, and a steady movement, which was as old as the Republic, from east to west. Except for one year, 1933, the farm population declined annually between 1920 and 1945, the largest losses coming during 1942–45. A population of nearly thirty-two million in 1920 had dropped by 1945 to slightly more than twenty-five million. Traveling around was most pronounced during the period of the Second World War. A survey taken in 1945 indicated that 15,330,000 people were living in a different county than in December 1941. During the same period some 7,670,000 people had moved from one state to another. The big losers of population were much of New England, the Plains states and especially the South, with the exceptions of Florida and Texas. The major gains were in New York, New Jersey, select industrial states of the Midwest, notably Michigan and Ohio, and also Washington, D.C., and Florida, but the biggest gains were in the Pacific Coast states, especially California, which became a virtual mecca for the nation.

TABLE 1.4 ESTIMATED NET INTERCENSAL MIGRATION OF TOTAL POPULATION SURVIVING FROM THE PRECEDING CENSUS DATE, BY STATES

[In thousands]

State	1940 to 1950	1930 to 1940	1920 to 1930	1910 to 1920
Total Population				
New England				
Maine	−35.8	−1.2	−39.3	−8.3
N.H.	−9.1	9.1	−10.2	−3.6
Vt.	−23.8	−18.7	−20.6	−17.6
Mass.	−29.5	−69.5	22.1	192.2
R.I.	2.7	−2.3	11.4	12.8
Conn.	89.5	39.2	64.1	122.1
Middle Atlantic				
N.Y.	83.8	396.3	1,062.1	467.4
N.J.	200.7	−28.2	442.3	278.2
Pa.	−447.2	−301.0	−252.9	51.9
East North Central				
Ohio	151.6	−56.6	214.7	499.4
Ind.	56.7	10.6	−0.9	16.0
Ill.	−22.1	−60.8	414.0	255.6
Mich.	251.4	17.1	549.6	465.2
Wis.	−95.1	−10.9	−17.9	37.6
West South Central				
Minn.	−160.9	36.0	−106.2	59.1
Iowa	−178.8	−73.4	−167.2	−18.3
Mo.	−168.6	−20.8	−98.7	−134.7
N. Dak.	−109.4	−105.8	−76.3	−46.0
S. Dak.	−71.2	−101.4	−45.0	−31.2
Nebr.	−123.0	−139.5	−78.1	−34.5
Kans.	−86.8	−163.8	−83.1	−74.5

State	1940 to 1950	1930 to 1940	1920 to 1930	1910 to 1920
South Atlantic				
Del.	14.5	16.0	−3.5	5.1
Md.	213.3	87.0	10.2	43.1
D.C.	78.5	157.8	27.3	97.0
Va.	152.0	0.2	−231.6	−27.7
W. Va.	−210.8	−73.6	−53.8	−1.7
N.C.	−202.8	−85.4	−7.9	−74.3
S.C.	−172.4	−102.5	−256.9	−80.9
Ga.	−224.3	−134.1	−414.9	−98.1
Fla.	510.9	280.3	297.6	101.6
East South Central				
Ky.	−319.2	−93.5	−206.1	−167.1
Tenn.	−102.8	−14.9	−113.8	−131.2
Ala.	−271.0	−165.3	−149.2	−113.9
Miss.	−349.9	−90.3	−101.6	−199.3
West South Central				
Ark.	−320.4	−128.8	−191.3	−74.7
La.	−112.1	5.7	−23.2	−64.7
Okla.	−356.1	−269.4	−51.8	62.4
Tex.	132.9	−72.8	243.5	114.3
Mountain				
Mont.	−42.2	−19.3	−72.9	90.1
Idaho	−29.6	20.5	−50.6	37.3
Wyo.	−4.6	−0.1	−1.2	20.7
Colo.	32.4	1.0	−16.6	39.8
N. Mex.	9.8	18.6	−22.9	−20.2
Ariz.	117.4	−3.5	23.5	75.4
Utah	6.4	−30.5	−30.8	−0.2
Nev.	28.8	12.5	6.9	−6.4
Pacific				
Wash.	351.3	109.2	81.6	97.5
Oreg.	244.0	94.1	96.5	56.0
Calif.	2,399.1	974.6	1,695.2	804.1

Source: Bureau of the Census, *Historical Statistics of the United States, Colonial Times to 1957*, 44–45.

A tenant farmer from Tennessee with all his belongings takes to the road in a Model T truck. (Arthur Rothstein, *The Depression Years As Photographed by Arthur Rothstein* [New York: Dover Press, 1978])

The African-American population remained generally steady in proportion to the rest of the population in the first half of the twentieth century, hovering around 10% throughout the period. If there was a slight proportionate decline, it was due less to birth and death statistics than to the fact that there was virtually no black immigration to the United States. Most black people continued to live in the South, the segregated South—a fact that suggested important information about the status and living conditions of African Americans. An important trend that had been established was the steady movement of black people out of the South and border states. The movement was continuous since the start of the twentieth century, if not slightly before, but it was most pronounced at the time of the Second World War. Although the most persistent target of the black migration was the industrial cities of the North, in the 1940s a new theme surfaced with stepped-up movement to the Pacific West. The state that scored the largest gain in black—as well as white—population in the 1940s was California. Even so, more than 70% of black people still lived in the South at the end of the period. Blacks followed the national course in another theme: urbanization. Whereas scarcely one-third of southern blacks lived in urban areas in 1914, by the 1940s more than 50% did. The African American population in the North had long been overwhelmingly urban, and it continued so as the period moved along. When blacks left the South, they mostly went to such places as Detroit, Chicago, New York, and, in the 1940s, the cities of California.

TABLE 1.5 BLACK POPULATION BY DECADE, AS PERCENT OF TOTAL POPULATION

Year	Black Population	Percent of Total Population
1910	9,828,000	10.7
1920	10,463,000	9.9
1930	11,891,000	9.7
1940	12,866,000	9.8

Source: Bureau of the Census, *Statistical Abstract of the United States, 1947*, 19.

TABLE 1.7 RATIO OF BLACKS TO TOTAL POPULATION BY PLACE OF RESIDENCE

Decennial Year	Percent Black by—								
	Region					Residence			
								Rural	
	Total	North-east	North Central	South	West	Urban	Total	Non-farm	Farm
1910	10.7	1.9	1.8	29.8	0.7	6.3	14.5	. . .	. . .
1920	9.9	2.3	2.3	26.9	0.9	6.6	13.4	9.0	16.3
1930	9.7	3.3	3.3	24.7	1.0	7.5	12.4	8.5	15.5
1940	9.8	3.8	3.8	23.8	1.2	8.4	11.6	7.8	14.9

Source: Bureau of Labor Statistics, *The Negroes in the United States: Their Economic and Social Situation* (Washington, D.C., 1966), 66.

TABLE 1.6 BLACK POPULATION BY REGION

Year	Northeast		North Central		South		West	
	Number	Percent of Black Pop.	Number	Percent of Black Pop.	Number	Percent of Black Pop.	Number	Percent of Black Pop.
1910	483,176	5.0	543,498	5.5	8,749,427	89.0	50,662	0.5
1920	679,204	6.5	793,075	7.6	8,912,231	85.0	78,591	0.8
1930	1,146,985	9.6	1,262,234	10.6	9,361,577	78.7	120,347	1.0
1940	1,369,875	10.6	1,420,318	11.0	9,904,619	76.9	170,706	1.0

Source: Bureau of the Census, *Statistical Abstract of the United States, 1940*, 14–15, *1947*, 20.

TABLE 1.8 PROPORTION OF BLACKS AND WHITES IN URBAN AREAS

Year	Percent Urban					
	United States		South		North and West	
	Black	White	Black	White	Black	White
1910	27	49	21	23	77	57
1920	35	53	27	29	84	62
1930	44	58	32	35	88	66
1940	49	59	37	37	89	67

Source: Bureau of Labor Statistics, *Negroes in the United States,* 67.

TABLE 1.9 ESTIMATED NET INTERCENSAL MIGRATION OF BLACKS, BY REGION

(Numbers in thousands. Plus sign (+) denotes net in-migration; minus sign (−) denotes net out-migration)

Intercensal Period	South	North				West
		Total	North-east	North Central		
1910–1920	−454	+426	+182	+244		+28
1920–1930	−749	+713	+349	+364		+36
1930–1940	−347	+299	+171	+128		+49
1940–1950	−1,599	+1,081	+463	+618		+339

Source: Department of Commerce, *The Social and Economic Status of the Black Population in the United States, 1790–1978* (Washington, D.C., 1979), 15.

Rest rooms were integrated (the alternative was to provide four), but the water cooler was segregated. Oklahoma City, 1939. (Library of Congress)

Hispanics in the United States in the first half of the twentieth century largely meant people of Mexican origin, and there existed much uncertainty about the number involved. How many people were of Mexican origin, and how many entered the country each year? Officials at the Census Bureau persisted for many years in classifying them in the large category of "whites," rather than providing the sort of separate identity—as with blacks and Indians—that in terms of social and economic status they probably deserved. Policy changed in the census of 1930, when the bureau determined that there were 1,422,533 "Mexicans" in the country, a number that was commonly regarded as too low. Thereafter the government reverted to the practice of leaving the number obscure.

People in the immigration service provided more regular statistics on Mexicans entering the country. It was widely accepted, however, that the statistics were far from correct, that there were many more people entering the country than the government reported. Illegal immigration was already an issue. When Congress debated the immigration laws in the 1920s, there was some sentiment for applying restrictions to immigration from Mexico. However, pressure from groups that needed Mexican labor and an assumption that Mexicans were only temporary immigrants apparently carried the day. The quotas were not applied to Mexico. During the 1920s labor was needed in the Southwest, and Mexico was in a state of upheaval, and so legal Mexican immigration constituted more than 10% of total immigration to the United States. The situation was in some measure reversed in the 1930s. Many fewer Mexicans crossed the border during the years of the depression, and there was a concerted effort to return illegal immigrants to Mexico. The drives evidently caught up some individuals who were American citizens. The period of the Second World War produced another labor shortage and another shift in the attitude toward Mexican immigration. In the Bracero Program, which started in 1942, the American government openly courted Mexican laborers to come to the United States. That there existed a deep local prejudice against Mexican immigrants and Mexican Americans as well was made clear in the "zoot-suit" riots in 1943–44 in Los Angeles and other cities of California, in which whites openly attacked people identified as being Latinos. The considerable Latin-American influence in that day—much of it Mexican—could be seen in place-names and foods as well as movies, dances, and popular music. "South of the Border (Down Mexico Way)" was a part of the repertoire of such varied singers as Gene Autry, Bing Crosby and, later, Frank Sinatra.

TABLE 1.10 MEXICAN IMMIGRANTS TO THE UNITED STATES

Year	Number
1914	14,614
1915	12,340
1916	18,425
1917	17,869
1918	18,524
1919	29,818
1920	52,361
1921	30,758
1922	19,551
1923	63,768
1924	89,336
1925	32,964
1926	43,316
1927	67,721
1928	59,016
1929	40,154
1930	12,703
1931	3,333
1932	2,171
1933	1,936
1934	1,801
1935	1,560
1936	1,716
1937	2,347
1938	2,502
1939	2,640
1940	2,313
1941	2,824
1942	2,378
1943	4,172
1944	6,598
1945	6,702

Source: Bureau of the Census, *Historical Statistics of the United States, Colonial Times to 1957*, 58.

TABLE 1.11 MEXICAN AND TOTAL IMMIGRATION

Year	Immigrants		Percentage Mexican
	Mexicans	All Countries	
1911–20	219,004	5,735,811	3.8
1921–30	459,287	4,107,209	11.2
1931–40	22,319	528,431	4.2
1941–50	60,589	1,035,039	5.9

Source: Immigration and Naturalization Service, *Annual Reports* (Washington, D.C., 1976), 87.

Native Americans

With the end of the wars in the West and with the United States growing and expanding its interests and concerns, the issue of Native Americans faded more and more into obscurity. The number at any time was approximate, largely based on the propensity of individuals to identify themselves as American Indians. The government's statistics for good reason underwent frequent revision. Native Americans represented a tiny portion of the population of the United States. In the early twentieth century the number dropped below 250,000, and there was some concern about the ability of Indians to sustain themselves as a group. Although the numbers began a significant revival in the 1920s, by the end of the Second World War the proportion of Indians to whites remained about the same as it had been in 1890. The bulk of Native Americans lived in rural areas, mostly on reservations, the largest of which were in Arizona and Oklahoma. Wherever they lived, Indians faced living conditions that were exceptionally harsh—hardship that could be documented with high rates of unemployment, alcoholism, and several diseases, such as tuberculosis.

Among the changes that occurred was the granting of American citizenship in 1924 to those Indians who did not have it, a move that many individuals doubtless saw as an empty gesture. In 1933 John Collier became commissioner of Indian Affairs, the person charged with administering the New Deal for Indians. On Collier's urging, Congress in 1934 ended the policy, known as allotment, of breaking reservation land into individual plots and provided for a restoration of tribal ownership and tribal authority. Native Americans entered the armed forces of the United States in the two world wars. More than 25,000 served in various military branches during the Second World War, although there were some who refused to go. Unlike black people and in some cases Japanese Americans, Indians in the armed forces were not segregated. The most famous In-

Substandard conditions under which reservation Indians lived are clear in this picture of Mescalero Apache boys. (Library of Congress)

dian servicemen were approximately 300 Navajo code talkers in the Marine Corps in the Pacific theater who communicated frontline military information in their native tongue to prevent the Japanese from reading the messages. At war's end the Indians who had served in the armed forces probably returned to the demoralizing, dead-end existence they had left behind. The condition of Native Americans continued to stand as a considerable blot on the record of the society and government of the United States.

TABLE 1.12 INDIAN POPULATION OF THE UNITED STATES AND ALASKA AT THE DECENNIAL CENSUS

	United States (except Alaska)	Alaska Natives[a]	Total	Percentage Change
1910	265,683	25,331	291,014	+9.1
1920	244,437	26,558	270,995	−6.9
1930	332,397	29,983[b]	362,380	+33.7
1940	333,969	32,458[c]	366,427	+1.1

[a] Includes Eskimos, Aleuts, and Indians living in Alaska.
[b] Census of 1929.
[c] Census of 1939.
Source: Paul Stuart, Nations within a Nation: Historical Statistics of American Indians (New York, 1987), 54.

TABLE 1.13 PERCENTAGE OF THE UNITED STATES INDIAN POPULATION WHO WERE URBAN

Year	Percentage
1910	4.5
1920	6.1
1930	9.9
1940	7.2

Source: Russell Thornton, The American Indian: Holocaust and Survival (Norman, Okla., 1987), 227.

TABLE 1.14 NATIVE AMERICAN POPULATION BY STATES, INCLUDING ALASKA AND WASHINGTON, D.C.

State	1910	1920	1930	1940
Ala.	909	405	465	464
Alaska	11,244	9,918?	10,955	11,283
Ariz.	29,201	32,989	43,726	55,076
Ark.	460	106	408	278
Calif.	16,371	17,360	19,212	18,675
Colo.	1,482	1,383	1,395	1,360
Conn.	152	159	162	201
Del.	5	2	5	14
D.C.	68	37	40	190
Fla.	74	518	587	690
Ga.	95	125	43	106
Idaho	3,488	3,098	3,638	3,537
Ill.	188	194	469	624
Ind.	279	125	285	223
Iowa	471	529	660	733
Kans.	2,444	2,276	2,454	1,165?
Ky.	234	57	22	44
La.	780	1,066	1,536	1,801
Me.	892	839	1,012	1,251
Md.	55	32	50	73

State	1910	1920	1930	1940
Mass.	688	555	874	769
Mich.	7,519	5,614	7,080	6,282
Minn.	9,053	8,761	11,077	12,528
Miss.	1,253	1,105	1,458	2,134
Mo.	313	171	578	330
Mont.	10,745	10,956	14,798	16,841
Nebr.	3,502	2,888	3,256	3,401
Nev.	5,240	4,907	4,871	4,747
N.H.	34	23	64	50
N.J.	168	100	213	211
N. Mex.	20,573	19,512	28,941	34,510
N.Y.	6,046	5,503	6,973	8,651
N.C.	7,851	11,824	16,579	22,546
N. Dak.	6,486	6,254	8,387	10,114
Ohio	127	151	435	338
Okla.	74,825	57,337	92,725	63,125
Oreg.	5,090	4,590	4,776	4,594
Pa.	1,503	337	523	441
R.I.	234	110	318	196
S.C.	331	304	959	1,234
S. Dak.	19,137	16,384?	21,833	23,347
Tenn.	216	56	161	114
Tex.	702	2,109	1,001	1,103
Utah	3,123	2,711	2,869	3,611
Vt.	26	24	36	16
Va.	539	824	779	198
Wash.	10,997	9,061	11,253	11,394
W. Va.	36	7	18	25
Wis.	10,142	9,611	11,548	12,265
Wyo.	1,486	1,343	1,845	2,349

Source: Thornton, American Indian, 162–163.

TABLE 1.15 INDIAN LANDS, BY STATE AND TYPE, 1936 (ACRES)

State	Tribal	Allotted[a]	Total
Ariz.	18,915,802	172,800	19,088,602
Calif.	507,865	60,683	568,548
Colo.	396,143	39,440	435,583
Fla.	26,741	. . .	26,741
Idaho	57,369	460,513	517,882
Iowa	3,480	. . .	3,480
Kans.	863	37,195	38,058
Mich.	683	12,952	13,635
Minn.	565,003	177,854	742,857
Miss.	2,609	. . .	2,609
Mont.	958,758	5,096,050	6,054,808
Nebr.	7,317	60,630	67,947
Nev.	1,024,382	15,066	1,039,448
N. Mex.	5,385,122	354,327	5,739,449
N.C.	63,211	. . .	63,211
N. Dak.	117,142	3,067,574	3,184,716
Okla.	78,543	2,803,160	2,881,703
Oreg.	1,197,192	375,600	1,572,792
S. Dak.	661,775	4,162,053	4,823,828
Tex.	3,071	. . .	3,071
Utah	1,583,280	83,408	1,666,688
Wash.	749,135	975,204	1,724,339
Wis.	273,574	146,178	419,752
Wyo.	525,000	194,789	719,789
Total	33,104,050	18,295,476	51,399,526

[a] Allotted pertains to land previously distributed to individuals, as opposed to land under tribal control.
Source: Stuart, Nations within a Nation, 24.

TABLE 1.16 POPULATION OF SELECTED RESERVATIONS, BIA[a]: SELECTED YEARS

	1915 (BIA)	1925 (BIA)	1932 (BIA)	1943 (BIA)
Blackfeet (Mont.)	2,724	3,244	3,812	4,904
Cherokee (N.C.)	2,211	2,611	3,230	3,665
Cheyenne River (S. Dak.)	2,708	2,964	3,168	3,751
Crow (Mont.)	1,699	1,781	1,987	2,424
Flathead (Mont.)	2,302	2,719	2,929	3,349
Ft. Apache (Ariz.)	2,388	2,602	2,705	3,103
Ft. Peck (Mont.)	1,943	2,273	2,552	3,079
Gila River (Ariz.)	. . .	5,691	4,588	5,095
Hopi (Ariz.)	2,455	2,719	6,038	3,558
Laguna (N. Mex.)	. . .	1,927	2,191	2,686
Menominee (Wis.)	1,730	1,890	1,988	2,454
Navajo (Ariz.- N. Mex.-Utah)	29,421	31,985	38,605	49,373
Northern Cheyenne (Mont.)	1,456	1,408	1,508	1,694
Papago (Ariz.)	6,990	. . .	4,914	5,684
Pine Ridge (S. Dak.)	7,240	7,628	8,220	9,774
Red Lake (Minn.)	1,486	1,698	1,881	2,406
Rosebud (S. Dak.)	5,519	5,700	6,215	7,150
San Carlos (Ariz.)	2,608	2,533	2,715	3,290
Standing Rock (N. Dak.-S. Dak.)	3,434	3,610	3,708	4,210
Turtle Mountain (N. Dak.)	3,123	4,043	5,527	7,330
Wind River (Wyo.)	1,705	1,808	2,097	2,579
Yakima (Wash.)	3,146	3,001	2,908	3,001
Zuni (N. Mex.)	1,603	1,932	1,991	2,320

[a]Bureau of Indian Affairs.
Source: Stuart, Nations within a Nation, 60.

TABLE 1.17 POPULATION OF SELECTED TRIBES AT THE CENSUSES OF 1910, 1930

	1910	%	1930	%
Apache	4,973	1.7	6,537	1.8
Arapaho	1,419	0.5	1,241	0.3
Blackfeet	2,367	0.8	3,145	0.9
Chemhuevi	355	0.1	. . .	. . .
Cherokee	31,489	10.8	45,238	12.5
Cheyenne	3,055	1.0	2,695	0.7
Chickasaw	4,204	1.4	4,745	1.3
Chippewa	20,214	6.9	21,549	5.9
Choctaw	15,917	5.5	17,757	4.9
Colville	785	0.3	. . .	. . .
Commanche	1,171	0.4	1,423	0.4
Creek	7,341	2.5	9,083	2.5
Crow	1,799	0.6	1,674	0.5
Delaware	985	0.3	971	0.3
Flathead	486	0.2	. . .	. . .
Iroquois[a]	8,190	2.8	7,219	2.0
Kaw	238	0.1	318	0.1
Kiowa	1,126	0.4	1,050	0.3
Lumbee	6,195	2.1	12,975	3.6
Menominee	1,422	0.5	1,969	0.5
Navajo	22,455	7.7	39,064	10.8
Omaha	1,105	0.4	1,103	0.3
Osage	1,373	0.5	2,344	0.6
Paiute	5,631	1.9	5,060	1.4
Papago	3,798	1.3	5,205	1.4

	1910	%	1930	%
Pima	4,236	1.5	4,382	1.2
Ponca	875	0.3	939	0.3
Potawatomie	2,440	0.8	1,854	0.5
Pueblo	10,843	3.7	12,047	3.3
Quapaw	231	0.1	222	0.1
Seminole	1,729	0.6	2,048	0.6
Shoshone	3,840	1.3	3,994	1.1
Sioux (Dakota)	22,778	7.8	25,934	7.2
Stockbridge	533	0.2	. . .	. . .
Tlingit-Haida	. . .	. . .	5,050	1.4
Ute	2,244	0.8	1,980	0.5
Winnebago	1,820	0.6	1,446	0.4
Yakima	1,362	0.5	. . .	. . .
Yuman	4,267	1.5	4,537	1.3

[a]Includes Cayuga, Mohawk, Oneida, Onondaga, Seneca, Tuscarora, and Wyandotte tribes.
Source: Stuart, Nations within a Nation, 58.

The Case of the Japanese Americans

Although the number of people of Japanese origin in the United States remained tiny, these people continued to be victims of discrimination and racial prejudice. Members of the first generation of Japanese in America, the Issei, were not permitted citizenship, and in many states they faced various other restrictions. In the immigration law of 1924, Japan received no regular quota, although the minimum number of 100 was applied to Japanese immigration. To the deep racial prejudice that existed, especially in the states of the Pacific Coast, where most Japanese Americans lived (California alone

TABLE 1.18 POPULATION OF JAPANESE IN AMERICA

	Mainland United States				Total Mainland and Hawaii	Total as Percentage of U.S. Population
Year	Issei	Nisei	Total Main- land	In Hawaii		
1910	67,655	4,502	72,157	79,675	151,832	0.1
1920	81,338	29,672	111,010	109,284	220,294	0.2
1930	70,477	68,357	138,834	139,631	278,465	0.2
1940	47,305	79,642	126,947	157,905	284,852	0.2

Sources: Bureau of the Census, Statistical Abstract of the United States, 1947, 19; Bill Hosokawa, Nisei: The Quiet Americans (New York: 1969), 151.

TABLE 1.19 JAPANESE IMMIGRATION TO THE UNITED STATES, 1901–1950

1901–10	129,797
1911–20	83,837
1921–30	33,462
1931–40	1,948
1941–50	1,555

Source: Bureau of the Census, Historical Statistics of the United States, Colonial Times to 1957, 58.

TABLE 1.20 WAR RELOCATION CENTERS FOR JAPANESE AMERICANS DURING WORLD WAR II

(Listed in order of their establishment)

Name of Center	Location	Opening Date	Closing Date	Peak Resident Population
Manzanar	Manzanar, Inyo County, Calif.	Mar. 21, 1942	Nov. 21, 1945	10,046
Colorado River	Poston, Yuma County, Ariz.	May 8, 1942	Nov. 28, 1945	17,814
Tule Lake	Newell, Modoc County, Calif.	May 27, 1942	Mar. 20, 1946	18,789
Gila River	Rivers, Pinal County, Ariz.	Jul. 20, 1942	Nov. 10, 1945	13,348
Minidoka	Hunt, Jerome County, Idaho	Aug. 10, 1942	Oct. 28, 1945	9,397
Heart Mountain	Heart Mountain, Park County, Wyo.	Aug. 12, 1942	Nov. 10, 1945	10,767
Granada	Amache, Prowers County, Colo.	Aug. 27, 1942	Oct. 15, 1945	7,318
Central Utah	Topaz, Millard County, Utah	Sep. 11, 1942	Oct. 31, 1945	8,130
Rohwer	McGehee, Desha County, Ark.	Sep. 18, 1942	Nov. 30, 1945	8,475
Jerome	Denson, Drew and Chicot Counties, Ark.	Oct. 6, 1942	Jun. 30, 1944	8,497

Source: War Relocation Authority, *The Evacuated People: A Quantitative Description* (Washington, D.C., 1946), 17.

TABLE 1.21 AMERICAN OPINION ON JAPANESE-AMERICAN RELOCATION: QUESTIONS ASKED BY POLLSTERS

(Mar. 28, 1942) Do you think we are doing the right thing in moving Japanese aliens (those who are not citizens) away from the Pacific coast?

Yes 93%   No 1%   Don't know 6%

(Mar. 28, 1942) How about the Japanese who were born in this country and are United States citizens, do you think they should be moved?

Yes 59%   No 25%   Don't know 16%

(Mar. 28, 1942) For those Japanese who are moved from the Pacific coast, do you think they should be kept under strict guard as prisoners of war, or do you think they should be allowed to go about fairly freely in their new community?

Strict guard	65%
Go about fairly freely	28
Don't know	7

(Dec. 2, 1942) Do you think the Japanese who were moved inland from the Pacific coast should be allowed to return to the Pacific coast when the war is over?

	Yes, Would Allow All	No, Would Not Allow Any	Would Allow Only Japanese Who Are Citizens to Return	No Opinion
National total	35%	17%	26%	22%

(Dec. 2, 1942) What should be done with them [the Japanese who were moved inland from the Pacific coast during the war]? Asked of a national cross-section of those who thought the Japanese who were moved inland from the Pacific coast should not be allowed to return to the Pacific coast when the war was over. 17% of the sample is represented.

Kill them; wipe them off the map; destroy them	7%
Put them out of this country; deport them	13
Send them back to Japan	50
If a citizen, keep here; if not, send back to Japan	4
Leave them where they are	10
Keep them inland; keep in some place allotted to them after the war	4
Other answers	3
No opinion	9
(of those questioned)	100%

Source: Hadley Cantril, ed., *Public Opinion, 1935–1946* (Princeton University Press: Princeton, 1951), 380–381.

had nearly 75% of the population), there was added in 1941 a great fear of attack in the aftermath of the Japanese assault on Pearl Harbor. It was widely assumed that Japanese living in the vulnerable coastal area would lend support to the land of their ancestral origin, not to the land of their residence or even their birth. Faced with cries for action from many quarters, especially in California, the government yielded to expediency and undertook the placement of virtually the entire Japanese-American population in internment camps in the interior of the country. The major focus of this undertaking was the second-generation Japanese, the Nisei. Although born in the United States and thus American citizens, they too were subjected to involuntary removal and the subsequent loss of rights and privileges. Most Japanese Americans stayed in the camps until the end of the war.

Eventually the army began to accept Japanese-American volunteers; later young Nisei men were drafted. Approximately 33,000 Nisei served in the armed forces, and some of them made up one of the most famous units of the Second World War. The 442d Regimental Combat Team (which included the 100th Infantry Battalion), formed entirely of Japanese Americans, distinguished itself for valor, determination, and willingness to take risks. In several campaigns in Europe, the 442d took nearly 9,500 casualties—more than three times the original strength—and received in excess of 18,000 decorations, including 9,500 Purple Hearts. The performance of Nisei soldiers only confirmed what a terrible mistake the wartime treatment of Japanese Americans had been.

Having packed their belongings, Japanese Americans are being moved out by the army. Bainbridge Island, Washington, March 30, 1942. (Museum of History and Industry, Seattle, Washington)

America: A Melting Pot or Salad Bowl or Neither or Both?

The idea of the United States as a multiethnic nation was made in no place more clear than in New York City. The landing place of most people newly arriving in the United States and the stopping place for many of them, New York was an immigrant city; most of the city's citizens were first- or second-generation immigrants. To no small extent it also was a Jewish city. Jewish people made up the largest ethnic group, and more than one-third of the nation's Jews lived in New York. The fact that nearly 90% of Americans were white had not stood in the way of suspicion, rivalry, and even conflict between the white ethnic groups. The members of each ethnic group mostly lived in their own neighborhoods, produced their own newspapers (often in the native language), and pursued to varying degrees their ethnic interests. Politics often formed around ethnic boundaries, New York City again supplying the best example.

The degree of separation and hostility, however, was subject to change. Suspicion between groups was not as sharp in 1940 as it had been in 1915, the ethnic communities not as insular. The Second World War fostered the mixing of peoples even more as Americans moved around the country in large numbers. There was no more powerful force of amalgamation than the American armed forces. If white America remained more a salad bowl than a melting pot, the salad at least was taking on more common characteristics. If Jewish people remained something of an exception, the object of most suspicion among the white groups, the wartime experience of the Holocaust would call these feelings into question as well.

TABLE 1.22 PERCENTAGE DISTRIBUTION OF FOREIGN-BORN POPULATION OF THE UNITED STATES, 1940, BY COUNTRIES OF BIRTH

Country of Birth		Percentage
Northwestern Europe		**24.8**
England and Wales	5.8	
Irish Free State	5.0	
Scotland	2.5	
Norway	2.3	
Sweden	3.9	
All Others	5.3	
Central Europe		**30.5**
Germany	10.8	
Poland	8.7	
Czechoslovakia	2.8	
Austria	4.2	
Hungary	2.6	
Yugoslavia	1.4	
Eastern Europe		**12.9**
Russia (U.S.S.R.)	9.1	
All Others	3.8	
Southern Europe		**16.6**
Italy	14.2	
All Others	2.4	
Canada and Newfoundland		**9.3**
All Others		**5.9**
Total		100.0

Source: William S. Bernard, ed., *American Immigration Policy: A Reappraisal* (Port Washington, N.Y., 1969), 168.

TABLE 1.23 ATTITUDES TOWARD ETHNIC AND RACIAL GROUPS: OPINION POLLS, 1942, 1945

(Nov. 1942) A national cross section of high-school students were asked: Which of the following groups would be your last choice as a roommate; which, if any, of those groups would you refuse to work with side by side in a position of equality and, which, if any, would you refuse to marry?

	Last Choice Roommate	Would Not Work With	Would Not Marry
Swedes	5%	. . .	9%
Protestants	4	. . .	9
Negroes	78	21%	92
Catholics	9	1	16
Jews	45	7	51
Irish	3	. . .	5
Chinese	38	5	73
Makes no difference	5	69	1
Don't know	3	3	2
	190%[a]	106%[a]	258%[a]

[a]Since the respondents were asked to name more than one group if they wished, percentages add to more than 100.

(Nov. 1942) Are there any on the list [Protestants, Catholics, Jews, Negroes] that you would not consider marrying? Asked of a national cross section of high school students.

Protestants

Negroes	91.6%
Chinese	71.9
Jews	51.6
Catholics	19.9
Swedes	7.7
Irish	4.7
Protestants	1.8
Makes no difference	1.3
Don't know	1.6
	252.1%

Catholics

Negroes	92.8%
Chinese	75.5
Jews	58.8
Protestants	25.2
Swedes	9.3
Irish	2.8
Catholics	1.0
Makes no difference	1.0
Don't know	1.4
	267.8%

Jews

Negroes	95.0%
Chinese	80.0
Catholics	28.8
Protestants	27.5
Swedes	9.3
Irish	23.8
Jews	1.3
Makes no difference	1.3
Don't know	3.8
	270.8%

Negroes

Jews	57.8%
Chinese	54.1
Swedes	45.0
Irish	42.2
Catholics	29.4
Protestants	22.0
Negroes	1.8
Makes no difference	13.8
Don't know	12.8
	278.9%

(Nov. 1942) A national cross section of factory workers were asked: Which of the following groups would you least like to see move into your neighborhood?

Swedes	3%
Protestants	2
Negroes	72
Catholics	4
Jews	42
Irish	2
Chinese	28
Makes no difference	13
Don't know	5
	171%[a]

[a]Since the respondents were asked to name more than one group if they wished, percentages add to more than 100.

(Jun. 12, 1945) Do you favor or oppose a law in this state which would require an employer to hire a person if he is qualified for the job, regardless of his race or color?

	Favor	Oppose	No Opinion
National total	43%	44%	13%

Source: Cantril, *Public Opinion*, 431, 477.

Mandy's giving us another chance

since we changed to silence!

1 **"I'se quittin'," announces Mandy** heatedly one day last month. "Can't sleep nights on account of the rumbling of that ol' refrigerator. Then just when I'se makin' ice cream, it stops en-tirely!" "John," warns my wife, "if Mandy leaves, we're sunk. We need a new refrigerator . . . *right away!*"

2 **"I know one that can't make a noise,"** she continues. And with that she rushes me downtown to the Servel showroom. There I see a refrigerator . . . *without machinery* . . . with only a tiny gas flame doing the work. Naturally, it's always silent. And having no moving parts, there's nothing to wear.

3 **Among folks who've had experience,** Servel is winning more friends every year. And no wonder. Survey after survey shows that the things people wisely look for in their *second* refrigerator are permanent silence . . . lasting dependability . . . continued low operating cost. And Servel Electrolux is the only automatic that offers all these big advantages.

4 **"Lor-dy, it sure is quiet!"** Mandy's happy and so are we. Servel's saving us enough on food alone to pay the installments. And we always have plenty of ice cubes. "You know," smiles Mandy the other day, "las' place I worked they had one of these gas refrigerators that was 'most ten years old. Looks like me and Servel are goin' to be with you a mighty long time!"

Stays silent...lasts longer

SERVEL
ELECTROLUX
Gas
REFRIGERATOR

The condition of nonwhite minority groups was another story. There was no melting here, or almost none, and the marks of discrimination were easy for all to observe. Native Americans were not only segregated but also plagued by some of the nation's worst social and economic maladies. Long the object of discrimination, Japanese Americans in the 1940s were subjected to special racial hatred and wartime treatment. America's Chinese were tolerated because they were allies, but their status otherwise did not change.

African Americans were a special case, even within the broader concept of racial prejudice. The fact that black people were by far the most numerous nonwhite group helped make discrimination more profound and easier to detect. The prejudice against blacks was broadest and most deeply rooted. The images, stereotypes, the racial terminology reached across the entire United States, extending in some cases even to the way blacks referred to themselves. There were studies of the problem, recognition of the need for better treatment of African Americans and appeals for tolerance. But beside some evidence of change—and there was some—must be placed the facts that during 1914–45 segregation remained the law of the land in the South, that de facto segregation and city slums remained the fact of life in the North, that the American army was as segregated

in 1941–45 as it had been in 1917–18, and that in so many ways racial prejudice remained strong. Any change that had come to the status of black people by 1945 only demonstrated how far the country had to go.

Immigration

Immigration was of course one of the oldest themes of America and one of the great distinguishing marks of the United States as a nation. Justly or not, American immigration policy at any time was considered in light of the concept of America as a potential home for the homeless, a beacon to those people wishing for a new start. During the years 1914–45 immigration fluctuated in accordance with changes in world conditions, economic conditions in the United States, and domestic American social currents. Ellis Island, the 27-acre landfill south of Manhattan, continued throughout the period to be the primary receiving station of incoming people, but its busi-

TABLE 1.24   NET CHANGE IN POPULATION BY ADMISSION AND DEPARTURE OF ALIENS

Year Ending June 30	Aliens Admitted			Aliens Departed			Net Increase or Decrease
	Immigrant[a]	Non-immigrant	Total	Emigrant	Non-emigrant	Total	
1914	1,218,480	184,601	1,403,081	303,338	330,467	633,805	769,276
1915	326,700	107,544	434,244	204,074	180,100	384,174	50,070
1916	298,826	67,922	366,748	129,765	111,042	240,807	125,941
1917	295,403	67,474	362,877	66,277	80,102	146,379	216,498
1918	110,618	101,235	211,853	94,585	98,683	193,268	18,585
1919	141,132	95,889	237,021	123,522	92,709	216,231	20,790
1920	430,001	191,575	621,576	288,315	139,747	428,062	193,514
1921	805,228	172,935	978,163	247,718	178,313	426,031	552,132
1922	309,556	122,949	432,505	198,712	146,672	345,384	87,121
1923	522,919	150,487	673,406	81,450	119,136	200,586	72,820
1924	706,896	172,406	879,302	76,789	139,956	216,745	262,557
1925	294,314	164,121	458,435	92,728	132,762	225,490	232,945
1926	304,488	191,618	496,106	76,992	150,763	227,755	268,351
1927	335,175	202,826	538,001	73,366	180,142	253,508	284,493
1928	307,255	193,376	500,631	77,457	196,899	274,356	226,275
1929	279,678	199,649	479,327	69,203	183,295	252,498	226,829
1930	241,700	204,514	446,214	50,661	221,764	272,425	173,789
1931	97,139	183,540	280,679	61,882	229,034	290,916	−10,237
1932	35,576	139,295	174,871	103,295	184,362	287,657	−112,786
1933	23,068	127,660	150,728	80,081	163,721	243,802	−93,074
1934	29,470	134,434	163,904	39,771	137,401	177,172	−13,268
1935	34,956	144,765	179,721	38,834	150,216	189,050	−9,329
1936	36,329	154,570	190,899	35,817	157,467	193,284	−2,385
1937	50,244	181,640	231,884	26,736	197,846	224,582	7,302
1938	67,895	184,802	252,697	25,210	197,404	222,614	30,083
1939	82,998	185,333	268,331	26,651	174,758	201,409	66,922
1940	70,756	138,032	208,788	21,461	144,703	166,164	42,624
1941	51,776	100,008	151,784	17,115	71,362	88,477	63,307
1942	28,781	82,457	111,238	7,363	67,189	74,552	36,686
1943	23,725	81,117	104,842	5,107	53,615	58,722	46,120
1944	28,551	113,641	142,192	5,669	78,740	84,409	57,783
1945	38,119	164,247	202,366	7,442	85,920	93,362	109,004
Totals	7,628,652	4,686,662	12,315,314	2,757,286	4,776,289	7,533,575	4,781,739

[a] An immigrant alien was a person admitted to the United States for permanent residence. A nonimmigrant alien was an alien resident returning from temporary visit abroad, or a nonresident entering the country for a temporary period—such as a student, official, visitor, or merchant.
Source: National Industrial Conference Board, *The Economic Almanac for 1950* (New York, 1950), 10–11.

est times were in the past. The year 1914 was the last year that more than one million immigrants entered the United States. Movement to America then was slowed by the First World War. When immigration threatened to resume massive proportion after the war, the U.S. government adopted the first quantitative restrictions, designed to keep the numbers down as well as screen the ethnic and racial characteristics of the people seeking to enter.

The coming of the depression drastically reduced immigration in the 1930s, and in fact for each year from 1931 to 1936 the United States had a net loss in population movement. The Second World War produced another exceptional situation that served to keep both immigration and emigration in small numbers. The character of the war, especially in Europe, also created new pressures for the government to rethink its policy, continuous since the 1920s, of restricting and screening on racial and ethnic terms the people allowed to resettle in the United States.

Between 1914 and 1945 the origin of immigration was overwhelmingly Europe, and the immigrants mostly were white. While the legislation of the 1920s helped to filter the people entering the country, an absence of the laws of 1921 and 1924 probably would not have caused vastly different results with respect to race. Immigration otherwise likely would have been less northern European more than it would have been less white.

It is striking to note how large a portion of immigration, starting in 1934, was made up of Jewish people. By 1939 and 1940 Jews made up more than 50% of all immigrant aliens admitted. The percentage remained high until 1944—the time of the "Final Solution"—when the number dropped so low that it no longer occupied a separate category.

TABLE 1.25   IMMIGRANTS, BY COUNTRY: EUROPE

| Year | All Countries | Total Europe | Northwestern Europe | | | | Central Europe | | | Eastern Europe | | Southern Europe | |
			Great Britain	Ireland	Scandinavia	Other Northwestern	Germany	Poland	Other Central	U.S.S.R. and Baltic States	Other Eastern	Italy	Other Southern
1945	38,119	5,943	3,029	427	224	365	172	195	206	98	97	213	917
1944	28,551	4,509	1,321	112	281	619	238	292	316	157	109	120	944
1943	23,725	4,920	974	165	239	1,531	248	394	206	159	54	49	901
1942	28,781	11,153	907	83	371	5,622	2,150	343	396	197	117	103	864
1941	51,776	26,541	7,714	272	1,137	9,009	4,028	451	786	665	299	450	1,730
1940	70,756	50,454	6,158	839	1,260	7,743	21,520	702	3,628	898	491	5,302	1,913
1939	82,998	63,138	3,058	1,189	1,178	5,214	33,515	3,072	5,334	1,021	620	6,570	2,367
1938	67,895	44,495	2,262	1,085	1,393	3,352	17,199	2,403	5,195	960	542	7,712	2,392
1937	50,244	31,863	1,726	531	971	2,512	10,895	1,212	3,763	629	533	7,192	1,899
1936	36,329	23,480	1,310	444	646	1,745	6,346	869	2,723	378	424	6,774	1,821
1935	34,956	22,778	1,413	454	688	1,806	5,201	1,504	2,357	418	453	6,566	1,916
1934	29,470	17,210	1,305	443	557	1,270	4,392	1,032	1,422	607	347	4,374	1,461
1933	28,068	12,383	979	338	511	1,045	1,919	1,332	981	458	352	3,477	991
1932	35,576	20,579	2,057	539	938	1,558	2,670	1,296	1,749	636	592	6,662	1,882
1931	97,139	61,909	9,110	7,305	3,144	4,420	10,401	3,604	4,500	1,396	1,192	13,399	3,438
1930	241,700	147,438	31,015	23,445	6,919	9,170	26,569	9,231	9,184	2,772	2,159	22,327	4,647
1929	279,678	158,598	21,327	19,921	17,379	9,091	46,751	9,002	8,081	2,450	2,153	18,008	4,435
1928	307,255	158,513	19,958	25,268	16,184	9,079	45,778	8,755	7,091	2,652	1,776	17,728	4,244
1927	335,175	168,368	23,669	28,545	16,860	9,134	48,513	9,211	6,559	2,933	1,708	17,297	3,939
1926	304,488	155,562	25,528	24,897	16,818	8,773	50,421	7,126	6,020	3,323	1,596	8,253	2,807
1925	294,314	148,366	27,172	26,650	16,810	8,546	46,068	5,341	4,701	3,121	1,566	6,203	2,186
1924	706,896	364,339	59,490	17,111	35,577	16,077	75,091	28,806	32,700	20,918	13,173	56,246	9,150
1923	522,919	307,920	45,759	15,740	34,184	12,469	48,277	26,538	34,038	21,151	16,082	46,674	7,008
1922	309,556	216,385	25,153	10,579	14,625	11,149	17,931	28,635	29,363	19,910	12,244	40,319	6,477
1921	805,228	652,364	51,142	28,435	22,854	29,317	6,803	95,089	77,069	10,193	32,793	222,260	76,409
1920	430,001	246,295	38,471	9,591	13,444	24,491	1,001	4,813	5,666	1,751	3,913	95,145	48,009
1919	141,132	24,627	6,797	474	5,590	5,126	52	a	53	1,403	51	1,884	3,197
1918	110,618	31,063	2,516	331	6,506	3,146	447	a	61	4,242	93	5,250	8,471
1917	295,403	133,083	10,735	5,406	13,771	6,731	1,857	a	1,258	12,716	369	34,596	45,644
1916	298,826	145,699	16,063	8,639	14,761	8,715	2,877	a	5,191	7,842	1,167	33,665	46,779
1915	326,700	197,919	27,237	14,185	17,883	12,096	7,799	a	18,511	26,187	2,892	49,688	21,441
1914	1,218,480	1,058,391	48,729	24,688	29,391	25,591	35,734	a	278,152	255,660	21,420	283,738	55,288

aDuring these years Poland was included with Austria-Hungary, Germany, and Russia.
Source: Bureau of the Census, Historical Statistics of the United States, Colonial Times to 1957, 56.

TABLE 1.26 IMMIGRANTS, BY COUNTRY: ASIA, AMERICAS

Year	Asia Total	Turkey in Asia	China	India	Japan	Korea[a]	Philippines	Other Asia	Americas Total	Canada and New-foundland	Mexico	West Indies	Other America
1945	461	13	71	103	1	. . .	19	254	29,646	11,530	6,702	5,452	5,962
1944	231	15	50	41	4	. . .	4	117	23,084	10,143	6,598	3,198	3,145
1943	342	36	65	71	20	. . .	8	142	18,162	9,761	4,172	2,312	1,917
1942	615	31	179	36	44	. . .	51	274	16,377	10,599	2,378	1,599	1,801
1941	1,971	16	1,003	94	289	. . .	170	399	22,445	11,473	2,824	4,687	3,461
1940	2,050	7	643	52	102	. . .	137	1,109	17,822	11,078	2,313	2,675	1,756
1939	2,281	15	642	36	102	. . .	119	1,367	17,139	10,813	2,640	2,231	1,455
1938	2,492	11	613	34	93	. . .	116	1,625	20,486	14,404	2,502	2,110	1,470
1937	1,149	13	293	47	132	. . .	84	580	16,903	12,011	2,347	1,322	1,223
1936	793	20	273	13	91	. . .	72	324	11,786	8,121	1,716	985	964
1935	682	31	229	32	88	. . .	b	302	11,174	7,782	1,560	931	901
1934	597	22	187	28	86	. . .	. . .	274	11,409	7,945	1,801	861	802
1933	552	27	148	44	75	. . .	. . .	258	9,925	6,187	1,936	862	940
1932	1,931	43	750	87	526	. . .	. . .	525	12,577	8,003	2,171	1,029	1,374
1931	3,345	139	1,150	123	653	. . .	. . .	1,280	30,816	22,183	3,333	2,496	2,804
1930	4,535	118	1,589	110	837	. . .	. . .	1,881	88,104	65,254	12,703	5,225	4,922
1929	3,758	70	1,446	103	771	. . .	. . .	1,368	116,177	66,451	40,154	4,306	5,266
1928	3,380	80	1,320	102	550	. . .	. . .	1,328	144,281	75,281	59,016	4,058	5,926
1927	3,669	73	1,471	102	723	. . .	. . .	1,300	161,872	84,580	67,721	4,019	5,552
1926	3,413	37	1,751	93	654	. . .	. . .	878	144,393	93,368	43,316	3,222	4,487
1925	3,578	51	1,937	65	723	. . .	. . .	802	141,496	102,753	32,964	2,106	3,673
1924	22,065	2,820	6,992	183	8,801	. . .	. . .	3,269	318,855	200,690	89,336	17,559	11,270
1923	13,705	2,183	4,986	257	5,809	. . .	. . .	470	199,972	117,011	63,768	13,181	6,012
1922	14,263	1,998	4,406	360	6,716	. . .	. . .	783	77,448	46,810	19,551	7,449	3,638
1921	25,034	11,735	4,009	511	7,878	. . .	. . .	901	124,118	72,317	30,758	13,774	7,269
1920	17,505	5,033	2,330	300	9,432	. . .	. . .	410	162,666	90,025	52,361	13,808	6,472
1919	12,674	19	1,964	171	10,064	. . .	. . .	456	102,286	57,782	29,818	8,826	5,860
1918	12,701	43	1,795	130	10,213	. . .	. . .	520	65,418	32,452	18,524	8,879	5,563
1917	12,756	393	2,237	109	8,991	. . .	. . .	1,026	147,779	105,399	17,869	15,507	9,004
1916	13,204	1,670	2,460	112	8,680	. . .	. . .	282	137,424	101,551	18,425	12,027	5,421
1915	15,211	3,543	2,660	161	8,613	. . .	. . .	234	111,206	82,215	12,340	11,598	5,053
1914	34,273	21,716	2,502	221	8,929	. . .	. . .	905	122,695	86,139	14,614	14,451	7,491

[a] No record of immigration from Korea during this period.
[b] Prior to 1936 the Philippines were included in "All Other Countries."
Source: Bureau of the Census, Historical Statistics of the United States, Colonial Times to 1957, 58.

TABLE 1.27 IMMIGRANTS, BY COUNTRY: AFRICA, AUSTRALASIA

Year	Africa Total	Australasia Total	Australia and New Zealand	Other Pacific Islands	All Other Countries Total
1945	406	1,663	1,625	38	. . .
1944	112	615	577	38	. . .
1943	141	160	120	40	. . .
1942	473	163	120	43	. . .
1941	564	255	194	61	. . .
1940	202	228	207	21	. . .
1939	218	222	213	9	. . .
1938	174	248	228	20	. . .
1937	155	174	145	29	. . .
1936	105	165	147	18	. . .
1935	118	141	132	9	63
1934	104	147	130	17	3
1933	71	137	122	15	. . .
1932	186	303	291	12	. . .
1931	417	652	616	36	. . .
1930	572	1,051	1,026	25	. . .
1929	509	636	619	17	. . .
1928	475	606	578	28	. . .
1927	520	746	712	34	. . .
1926	529	591	556	35	. . .
1925	412	462	416	46	. . .
1924	900	679	635	44	58
1923	548	759	711	48	15
1922	520	915	855	60	25
1921	1,301	2,281	2,191	90	130
1920	648	2,185	2,066	119	702
1919	189	1,310	1,234	76	46
1918	299	1,090	925	165	47
1917	566	1,142	1,014	128	77
1916	894	1,574	1,484	90	31
1915	934	1,399	1,282	117	31
1914	1,539	1,446	1,336	110	136

Source: Bureau of the Census, Historical Statistics of the United States, Colonial Times to 1957, 58.

Closing the Door: Immigration in the 1920s

Until the 1920s the United States had allowed generally open immigration from nations abroad (exclusion of Chinese was an em-barrassing special case), imposing late in the period only a few quali-tative restrictions. In the turmoil that followed the First World War, the government moved to change this policy substantially. Influenced

TABLE 1.28   QUOTAS ALLOTTED AND QUOTA ALIENS ADMITTED, 1921, 1924–1945

Country or Region	Under Immigration Act of 1921, Annual Quota[a]	Under Immigration Act of 1924							
		Annual Quota, 1925–1929	Admitted, 1925–1929, Total	Annual Quota, 1930 to 1945	Admitted				
					1935–1939, Total	1940–1944, Total	1943	1944	1945
All countries	357,803	164,667	761,622	153,879[b]	168,540	121,253	9,045	9,394	11,623
Europe	356,061	161,422	749,911	150,501[b]	162,243	115,338	8,240	8,017	8,949
Albania	228	100	472	100	482	109	3	10	5
Belgium	1,563	512	2,652	1,304	1,154	2,357	203	127	79
Bulgaria	302	100	509	100	383	236	8	20	9
Czechoslovakia	14,357	3,073	14,668	2,874	8,464	5,019	362	323	276
Danzig, Free City of	301	228	1,065	100	336	168	6	9	6
Denmark	5,619	2,789	13,114	1,181	1,078	916	131	106	98
Estonia	1,348	124	612	116	239	233	18	27	16
Finland	3,921	471	2,363	569	1,349	857	99	63	53
France	5,729	3,954	17,730	3,086	2,980	4,324	492	210	159
Germany	67,607	51,227	242,363	}27,370[c]	74,337[c]	46,617	1,276	1,324	1,190
Austria	7,342	785	4,213						
Greece	3,063	100	737	307	1,773	1,365	301	287	218
Hungary	5,747	473	2,445	869	3,702	2,675	163	212	117
Ireland (Eire)[d]	. . .	28,567	132,715	17,853	3,633	1,777	196	123	232
Italy	42,057	3,845	18,383	5,802	15,082	4,864	67	159	268
Latvia	1,540	142	754	236	600	584	62	62	43
Lithuania	2,629	344	1,828	386	1,324	862	117	93	78
Luxemburg	92	100	495	100	69	231	23	2	11
Netherlands	3,607	1,648	7,708	3,153	1,804	2,809	192	208	99
Norway	12,202	6,453	30,335	2,377	1,718	1,282	102	176	100
Poland	30,977	5,982	29,000	6,524	15,517	13,834	1,533	1,338	1,122
Portugal	2,465	503	2,449	440	1,541	1,513	261	377	418
Rumania	7,419	603	3,783	377[b]	1,854	1,487	220	230	215
Soviet Union (Russia)	24,405	2,248	10,018	2,712[b]	3,970	4,696	391	383	341
Spain	912	131	805	252	1,263	1,160	255	240	182
Sweden	20,042	9,561	44,849	3,314	1,305	981	94	80	57
Switzerland	3,752	2,081	9,683	1,707	1,725	1,778	121	46	52
Turkey	2,654	100	431	226	281	350	38	106	73
United Kingdom[d]	77,342	34,007	148,660	65,721	10,888	10,738	1,377	1,461	3,182
Yugoslavia	6,426	671	3,081	845	2,735	1,253	90	167	177
Other Europe	353	500[e]	1,991[f]	500[e]	657[f]	263[f]	39[f]	48[f]	73[f]
Asia	1,261	1,424[e]	4,927[f]	1,528[e]	2,980[f]	2,387[f]	302[f]	293[f]	473[f]
Africa	122	1,200[e]	1,667[f]	1,200[e]	523[f]	665[f]	71[f]	56[f]	90[f]
Australia, New Zealand, and Pacific islands	359	621[e]	1,470[f]	650[e]	975[f]	876[f]	101[f]	169[f]	144[f]
American colonies of European countries	. . .	[e]	3,647[f]	[e]	1,819[f]	1,987[f]	331[f]	859[f]	1,967[f]

[a]Quota for 1924; revisions from 1922 or 1923 allotments for certain countries were made due to changes in boundaries or other adjustments. Quota immigrants admitted, 1922 to 1924, are as follows: 1922, 243,953; 1923, 335,480; 1924, 357,643. For admissions by countries see the 1934 and previous issues of the *Statistical Abstract*.
[b]Quota 1934 to Feb. 8, 1944, was 153,774. The Act of Dec. 17, 1943, repealing the Chinese Exclusion Laws authorized a quota for Chinese. This quota of 105 was allotted on Feb. 8, 1944, increasing the maximum quota from 153,774 to 153,879. The total quota for 1930 and 1931 was 153,714; for 1932 and 1933, 153,831; the Soviet Union's quota was 2,784 for 1930 and 1931, and 2,701 for 1932 and 1933; Rumania's, 295 prior to 1934. There were also changes in 1932 and 1933 for certain countries included in "Other Europe," Asia, and Pacific islands.
[c]Austria included with Germany beginning with 1938.
[d]All Ireland included with United Kingdom prior to 1925; thereafter, Northern Ireland only.
[e]Annual quotas for colonies, dependencies, or protectorates in "Other Europe," Asia, Africa, Pacific islands, and America are included in the annual quotas of the European countries to which they belong.
[f]Includes quota immigrants born in colonies, dependencies, or protectorates of European countries.
Source: Bureau of the Census, Statistical Abstract of the United States, 1946, 112.

by a strong nativist movement, fearful of radical political currents from abroad, persuaded—as many people were—that native culture was going to be undermined by foreigners, by the "wrong" kind of foreigners, the nation adopted restrictive policies. The law of 1921 limited immigration of any nationality to 3% of the number of foreign-born persons of that nationality living in the country in the year 1910. The harsher law of 1924—the National Origins Act—reduced the percentage to 2 and changed the year of demarcation to 1890. The effect, and indeed the purpose, of the legislation was to reduce the amount of immigration and modify its racial and ethnic characteristics. The laws favored white northern European countries and

plicant for the first paper must be at least 18 years old and may take out the first paper at any time after arrival as a permanent resident and at any place.

When applying for the first paper, an applicant must fill out Form N-300. After the Government receives and checks the Form N-300, the applicant is notified as to when and where to get the first paper. The clerk of the court fills out the first paper, using the information the applicant gave in Form N-300. The applicant must sign the first paper before the clerk of the court and swear that the statements in it are true. The applicant pays $3 to the clerk of the court for the declaration of intention.

TABLE 1.29   IMMIGRANT ALIENS ADMITTED—PERCENTAGES, BY RACE OR NATIONALITY: YEARS ENDED JUNE 30, 1936 TO 1945

Race or People	1936	1937	1938	1939	1940	1941	1942	1943	1944	1945
Total	100.0	100.0	100.0	100.0	100.0	100.0	100.0	100.0	100.0	100.0
Dutch and Flemish	1.6	1.5	1.2	0.9	1.5	2.6	1.3	1.6	1.5	1.1
English	9.9	9.8	8.4	6.1	6.9	11.8	13.2	15.3	14.4	18.7
French	4.5	4.5	4.1	2.7	3.3	6.3	8.2	7.4	5.5	5.6
German	12.9	12.6	11.4	6.7	5.0	4.2	2.8	2.1	3.6	3.6
Greek	2.8	2.0	1.7	1.2	1.5	0.8	0.9	1.6	1.3	0.9
Hebrew	17.2	22.6	29.1	52.4	52.2	45.8	36.9	19.8	a	a
Irish	4.3	4.5	4.9	3.6	3.6	3.7	5.9	6.4	5.3	5.6
Italian	19.6	15.2	12.3	8.1	7.8	1.3	0.5	0.6	0.9	1.1
Magyar	1.4	1.3	1.4	0.7	0.8	0.5	0.5	0.4	0.6	0.3
Polish	1.3	1.5	1.6	1.0	0.7	1.3	1.5	1.8	2.9	2.8
Russian	1.0	1.0	1.0	1.0	0.9	1.8	0.9	0.9	1.3	1.2
Scandinavian[b]	2.5	2.8	2.9	1.9	2.1	2.6	2.1	2.6	2.3	1.6
Scotch	4.1	4.4	3.6	2.4	2.8	3.6	5.7	5.8	5.2	5.1
Slovak	2.1	2.7	3.5	1.2	0.5	0.3	0.4	0.5	0.5	0.3
Spanish	1.2	0.9	0.8	0.5	0.6	0.9	1.0	1.7	1.4	1.1
Spanish-American	1.8	1.6	1.3	1.0	1.3	2.2	3.9	6.1	8.9	11.4
Other peoples { [c]	3.6	3.6	2.8	2.6	2.5	3.7	7.4	16.3	22.9	} 39.6
[d]	8.2	7.6	8.0	6.1	5.9	6.5	6.8	8.9	21.5	

[a]Included with appropriate national group or "Other peoples."
[b]Norwegians, Danes, and Swedes.
[c]Chiefly natives of Mexico.
[d]Other than those for which percentages are given.
Source: Bureau of the Census, Statistical Abstract of the United States, 1941 (Washington, D.C., 1942), 111, and 1946, 111.

were prejudicial against all other places. The bias was conspicuous in the treatment of Italy, a major target of the legislation. More than two million Italians immigrated to the United States between 1901 and 1910 and more than one million in the decade that ended in 1920. Italy's quota in the law of 1921 was approximately 42,000 per year, and in 1924 it was reduced to 3,845. The law of 1924 placed the quota for all Asian countries combined at 1,424. Germany's quota for one year was 51,227. Beginning in 1929, the law introduced a different, complicated system of establishing quotas, still based on national origin. The ethnic and racial flavor of the measure remained the same.

A Brief Summary of Naturalization Requirements and Procedure

An applicant for naturalization must have been lawfully admitted to the United States for permanent residence.

The first step toward becoming a citizen is to make a declaration of intention, commonly called taking out the first paper. An ap-

The procedure for filing a petition for naturalization and becoming a citizen is commonly called taking out the second paper, Form N-400.

An applicant must be at least 20 years old to file a declaration of intention with the petition. An alien filing under a section not requiring a declaration of intention may file a petition upon reaching the age of 18.

An applicant must be able to carry on an ordinary conversation in English and to sign his name (unless physically unable to talk or to write). Some courts require that an applicant for a second paper must be able to read English; the applicant should find out whether the court in his district has such a requirement.

An applicant must have lived continuously in the United States for the number of years required by law; for aliens who are required to have a first paper, that is five years; they must have lived at least the last six months of that five-year period in the state where they apply for the second paper. For wives and husbands of citizens of the United States and some of the other aliens who do not need a first paper it means one, two, or three years, depending on the date of marriage or other facts of the case.

The applicant will be notified by the Immigration and Naturalization office when and where to come for his first hearing. The applicant must take with him two citizen witnesses to this hearing. A naturalization examiner questions them separately to make sure the applicant meets the requirements of the naturalization laws. If the examiner is satisfied that the applicant does, he helps him file a petition for naturalization. At this time the applicant pays $8 to the clerk of the court for the petition and the certificate of naturalization.

Not less than thirty days after the petition was filed, the applicant is notified to appear in the naturalization court for a final hearing to renounce allegiance to the foreign government and to take an oath of allegiance to the United States.

The examiner may recommend that an application for citizenship be granted, denied, or put off until the applicant is better prepared. If the examiner recommends that the petition be denied, notice of this recommendation is sent to the applicant before the case is put on the court calendar for final hearing. The applicant may ask to be examined by the judge in court if he feels that the examiner's recommendation is not just.

Source: Immigration and Naturalization Service, as summarized by *Information Please Almanac, 1948* (New York, 1948), 270.

TABLE 1.30 NATURALIZATION, 1910–1945

Period or Year Ended Jun. 30—	Declarations Filed[a]	Petitions Filed[b]			Aliens Naturalized[c]		
		Total	Civilian	Military	Total	Civilian	Military
1910–1914, total	925,929	446,006	446,006	. . .	345,147	354,147	. . .
1915–1919, total	1,631,252	772,396	580,068	192,328	636,590	444,262	192,328
1920–1924, total	1,597,667	919,189	822,834	96,355	825,016	728,661	96,355
1925–1929, total	1,348,285	1,070,669	1,059,790	10,879	956,475	946,392	10,083
1930–1934, total	460,880	619,441	609,629	9,812	676,504	667,741	8,763
1935–1939, total	767,201	852,795	837,151	15,644	776,077	765,969	10,108
1940–1944, total	807,487	1,602,164	1,510,997	91,167	1,543,830	1,451,234	92,596
1914	214,104	124,475	124,475	. . .	104,145	104,145	. . .
1915	247,958	106,399	106,399	. . .	91,848	91,848	. . .
1916	209,204	108,767	108,767	. . .	87,831	87,831	. . .
1917	440,651	130,865	130,865	. . .	88,104	88,104	. . .
1918	342,283	169,507	105,514	63,933	151,449	87,456	63,993
1919	391,156	256,853	128,523	128,335	217,358	89,023	128,335
1920	299,076	218,732	166,760	51,972	177,683	125,711	51,972
1921	303,904	195,534	177,898	17,636	181,292	163,656	17,636
1922	273,511	162,638	153,170	9,468	170,447	160,979	9,468
1923	296,636	165,168	158,059	7,109	145,084	137,975	7,109
1924	424,540	177,117	166,947	10,170	150,510	140,340	10,170
1925	277,218	162,258	162,258	. . .	152,457	152,457	. . .
1926	277,539	172,232	172,107	125	146,331	146,239	92
1927	258,295	240,339	235,298	5,041	199,804	195,493	4,311
1928	254,588	240,321	235,328	4,993	233,155	228,006	5,149
1929	280,645	255,519	254,799	720	224,728	224,197	531
1930	62,138	113,151	111,209	1,942	169,377	167,637	1,740
1931	106,272	145,474	142,249	3,225	143,495	140,271	3,224
1932	101,345	131,062	131,043	19	136,600	136,598	2
1933	83,046	112,629	110,604	2,025	113,363	112,368	995
1934	108,079	117,125	114,524	2,601	113,669	110,867	2,802
1935	136,524	131,378	131,378	. . .	118,945	118,945	. . .
1936	148,118	167,127	165,559	1,568	141,265	140,784	481
1937	176,195	165,464	157,670	7,794	164,976	162,923	2,053
1938	150,673	175,413	169,131	6,282	162,078	158,142	3,936
1939	155,691	213,413	213,413	. . .	188,813	185,175	3,638
1940	203,536	278,028	276,840	1,188	235,260	232,500	2,760
1941	224,123	277,807	277,807	. . .	277,294	275,747	1,547
1942	221,796	343,487	341,979	1,508	270,364	268,762	1,602
1943	115,664	377,125	338,885	38,240	318,933	281,459	37,474
1944	42,368	325,717	275,486	50,231	441,979	392,766	49,213
1945	31,195	195,917	172,905	23,012	231,402	208,707	22,695

Sex	1940	1941	1942	1943	1944	1945	
Aliens Naturalized[c]							
Males	132,406	136,348	112,040	157,663	202,698	116,691	
Females	102,854	140,946	158,324	161,270	239,281	114,711	

[a] Declaration of intention to become citizen.
[b] Petition for naturalization.
[c] Certificates of naturalization issued.
Source: Bureau of the Census, *Statistical Abstract of the United States, 1947*, 114.

TABLE 1.31   ALIENS DEBARRED AND DEPORTED: 1910 TO 1945

Period or Year Ended Jun. 30	Debarred	Deported	Deportable Aliens Required to Depart	Indigent Aliens Returned at Their Request[a]
1910–1914, total	115,655	16,010	. . .	. . .
1915–1919, total	74,929	11,835	. . .	. . .
1920–1924, total	90,208	21,694	. . .	. . .
1925–1929, total	102,661	56,594	. . .	. . .
1930–1934, total	35,952	82,943	. . .	. . .
1935–1939, total	35,198	43,820	. . .	. . .
1940–1944, total	13,199	26,456	. . .	. . .
1933	5,527	19,865	. . .	. . .
1934	5,384	8,879	. . .	. . .
1935	5,558	8,319	7,978	114
1936	7,000	9,195	8,251	80
1937	8,076	8,829	8,788	40
1938	8,066	9,275	9,278	1,070
1939	6,498	8,202	9,590	1,825
1940	5,300	6,954	8,594	1,151
1941	2,929	4,407	6,531	152
1942	1,833	3,709	6,904	30
1943	1,495	4,207	11,947	5
1944	1,642	7,179	32,270	4
1945	2,341	11,270	69,490	12

[a]Does not include 157 Filipinos returned at their own request in 1936, 580 in 1937, 502 in 1938, 392 in 1939, 425 in 1940, and 134 in 1941.
Source: Bureau of the Census, *Statistical Abstract of the United States, 1946,* 108.

CHAPTER 2 Weather and Climate

The basic structure of weather and climate did not change during the first half of the twentieth century, but the United States found new ways to learn more about it. The development of radio and travel by air assisted in the acquisition of knowledge and in its communication. The fighting of two world wars contributed a major incentive for learning as much as possible about weather; other knowledge emerged by accident from devices developed for other wartime purposes. Bomber pilots during the Second World War identified the existence of a jet stream high in the sky, the significance of which was yet to be learned. The same war prompted the development of radar for military purposes, and by war's end radar was being used as a tool in the discovery of weather.

Fortunately for the well-being of the people and for the nation's wealth and power, the United States is situated mostly in an area of moderate climate and weather. The nation's vast size, however, does permit wide extremes, ranging in the first half of the century from the highest recorded temperature of 134°F at Death Valley, California, to the lowest temperature of −68 at Yellowstone Park, Wyoming, on February 9, 1933. The wettest state, Louisiana, had annual rainfall of nearly 50 inches; the driest, Nevada, averaged barely 9. If one took into account the possessions of the United States, from Alaska to the islands in the Pacific, there would have been even greater variations of weather and climate.

Climate

TABLE 2.1   MEAN TEMPERATURES

[Average of daily maximum and minimum temperatures][a]

	Station	Jan.	Feb.	Mar.	Apr.	May	Jun.	Jul.	Aug.	Sep.	Oct.	Nov.	Dec.	Annual
Ala.	Mobile	52.0	54.4	59.6	66.8	74.1	80.3	81.8	81.6	78.2	68.8	59.1	53.2	67.5
	Montgomery	48.9	51.5	58.1	65.3	73.2	80.0	81.7	80.9	77.0	66.6	56.1	49.6	65.8
Ariz.	Phoenix	52.0	55.8	60.7	67.6	75.7	85.1	90.4	88.7	83.3	71.4	60.1	52.6	70.3
Ark.	Little Rock	42.0	44.8	53.4	62.4	70.0	78.0	81.2	80.4	74.6	63.8	52.1	44.0	62.2
Calif.	Fresno	46.2	51.4	55.4	61.0	67.6	75.3	82.1	80.4	73.7	64.8	54.8	46.8	63.3
	Los Angeles	55.5	56.3	58.1	60.2	62.7	66.4	70.5	71.4	69.7	65.8	62.0	57.3	63.0
	San Francisco	50.1	52.8	54.4	55.7	57.1	58.9	58.9	59.4	61.5	60.8	56.8	51.5	56.5
Colo.	Denver	30.6	32.9	39.2	47.6	56.8	66.8	72.5	71.4	62.8	50.9	40.5	32.5	50.4
D.C.	Washington	35.0	35.4	44.8	54.2	64.8	72.7	77.2	75.2	69.2	57.7	46.7	36.9	55.8
Fla.	Jacksonville	55.4	58.0	62.6	68.7	75.0	79.9	82.1	81.7	78.3	71.1	62.2	56.3	69.3
	Miami	67.7	68.1	71.1	73.8	77.4	80.3	81.8	82.2	81.1	77.7	72.5	68.8	75.2
Ga.	Atlanta	42.5	45.3	52.0	61.1	70.8	76.7	79.1	78.0	72.8	62.7	51.5	44.2	61.4
Idaho	Boise	28.7	36.2	41.6	50.1	57.0	62.8	74.4	72.2	62.4	54.2	39.2	32.7	51.0
Ill.	Chicago	24.9	26.9	36.1	47.1	57.5	67.5	73.3	72.0	65.3	53.9	40.2	29.2	49.5
Ind.	Indianapolis	28.4	31.1	40.0	52.1	62.9	71.6	75.7	73.7	66.9	55.7	42.3	32.2	53.0
Iowa	Des Moines	20.1	23.7	35.9	50.1	61.3	70.6	75.4	73.1	65.6	53.4	38.4	26.0	49.5
Kans.	Wichita	32.1	35.0	45.2	56.4	65.1	74.9	80.1	79.3	71.3	59.4	45.4	35.0	56.6
Ky.	Louisville	34.8	36.8	45.8	56.2	66.2	74.8	78.6	77.0	70.7	59.0	46.5	37.3	57.0
La.	New Orleans	54.8	57.3	63.2	69.0	75.4	81.1	82.6	82.6	79.6	71.4	62.0	55.9	69.6
Maine	Eastport	20.9	21.4	29.8	38.9	47.8	55.1	60.4	60.7	56.0	47.6	37.3	25.6	41.8
Mass.	Boston	27.9	28.8	35.6	46.4	57.1	66.5	71.7	69.9	63.2	53.6	42.0	32.5	49.6

(continued)

TABLE 2.1 (continued)

[Average of daily maximum and minimum temperatures][a]

Station		Jan.	Feb.	Mar.	Apr.	May	Jun.	Jul.	Aug.	Sep.	Oct.	Nov.	Dec.	Annual
Mich.	Detroit	24.9	25.2	33.9	46.1	57.9	67.7	72.7	70.6	63.9	52.3	39.3	29.1	48.6
	Sault Ste. Marie	12.1	11.4	20.6	36.5	48.2	57.5	62.7	60.8	54.0	43.0	30.4	18.8	38.0
Minn.	Minneapolis	12.7	15.9	29.6	46.4	57.7	67.5	72.3	69.9	61.4	48.9	32.4	19.6	44.5
Miss.	Vicksburg	48.2	51.8	58.5	65.6	72.9	79.0	81.3	80.8	76.6	66.7	56.6	50.0	65.6
Mo.	Kansas City	29.9	32.3	43.4	55.1	64.8	74.3	79.3	77.7	70.0	58.6	44.6	33.5	55.3
	St. Louis	31.1	34.8	44.1	56.1	67.0	75.0	78.8	77.5	70.5	58.8	45.4	34.9	56.2
Mont.	Helena	18.7	21.6	31.7	43.5	51.6	59.2	65.7	64.6	55.4	43.8	31.8	22.7	41.5
	Miles City	17.1	19.4	31.8	47.0	56.9	66.9	74.3	71.7	60.4	48.0	33.6	22.3	45.9
Nebr.	North Platte	23.9	27.5	36.9	49.0	59.0	68.7	75.0	73.1	63.9	51.5	37.4	27.6	49.5
	Omaha	22.2	26.1	37.6	51.6	62.5	72.0	77.5	75.1	66.6	54.7	39.1	27.3	51.1
Nev.	Winnemucca	28.1	33.4	40.1	47.0	54.8	63.2	71.9	69.6	59.6	48.9	37.9	30.3	48.8
N.J.	Atlantic City	32.5	33.6	38.6	47.8	58.1	66.6	72.1	72.5	66.8	56.9	45.6	36.4	52.3
N. Mex.	Albuquerque	34.1	40.5	45.9	54.0	63.3	72.6	76.7	73.9	67.9	56.6	43.3	34.5	55.3
N.Y.	Albany	23.6	24.5	33.8	46.8	59.2	68.3	72.4	70.6	62.8	50.8	39.3	28.0	48.3
	New York	30.9	31.3	37.7	49.4	60.6	68.8	73.8	73.1	66.8	56.3	44.2	35.0	52.3
	Rochester	24.9	24.3	32.5	44.6	56.8	66.3	71.3	69.2	62.8	50.3	39.3	28.9	47.7
N.C.	Asheville	35.4	38.5	44.9	53.9	62.6	68.7	71.7	70.5	65.0	55.3	45.1	37.8	54.1
	Raleigh	41.1	43.2	50.2	59.4	68.5	75.7	78.8	76.9	71.1	62.0	51.0	43.0	60.1
N. Dak.	Bismarck	6.3	8.5	21.9	40.4	53.0	62.9	69.4	66.7	57.3	43.6	26.5	12.8	39.1
Ohio	Cleveland	24.7	26.3	34.5	46.2	58.1	67.7	71.9	70.2	63.8	52.7	39.0	29.1	48.7
Okla.	Oklahoma City	37.5	40.4	50.2	60.0	67.9	77.0	81.3	81.2	74.0	62.5	49.6	39.6	60.1
Oreg.	Portland	39.4	42.1	46.9	51.8	56.9	62.4	66.7	66.7	61.7	54.2	46.8	41.2	53.1
Pa.	Harrisburg	29.0	30.2	38.9	50.9	61.8	70.3	74.8	72.6	65.8	54.8	42.8	32.7	52.1
	Pittsburgh	30.9	31.4	39.9	50.7	62.0	70.4	74.4	72.4	66.6	54.9	43.0	33.8	52.5
S.C.	Charleston	50.1	52.4	57.4	64.5	72.7	78.9	81.4	81.0	76.6	67.8	58.1	51.7	66.0
S. Dak.	Huron	11.3	14.3	28.9	45.1	56.4	66.2	71.8	69.4	61.3	47.7	31.5	18.7	43.6
Tenn.	Nashville	39.2	41.6	49.7	59.2	68.2	76.3	79.4	78.2	72.2	61.0	49.0	41.0	59.6
Tex.	Amarillo	33.1	36.1	45.3	53.8	62.1	71.4	75.9	74.6	67.8	55.8	43.8	35.5	54.6
	El Paso	43.6	48.6	54.9	62.3	70.0	78.0	79.7	78.0	72.3	63.5	51.1	43.7	62.1
	Fort Worth	46.2	48.4	57.5	64.9	72.5	80.7	83.9	84.4	77.9	67.7	56.5	47.4	65.6
	Houston	53.5	56.4	62.8	69.3	75.2	81.2	83.2	83.3	79.0	70.9	61.5	54.7	69.2
Utah	Salt Lake City	26.0	32.1	40.6	49.8	58.5	66.8	76.8	74.5	64.1	53.0	38.3	30.7	50.9
Vt.	Burlington	18.8	19.4	29.1	43.3	56.5	65.7	70.3	67.9	60.3	49.2	36.3	24.4	45.1
Va.	Norfolk	41.6	42.3	48.8	57.1	66.7	74.8	78.5	77.4	72.4	62.0	51.8	43.4	59.7
	Richmond	37.9	39.6	47.2	56.6	66.5	74.1	78.5	76.5	70.5	59.6	48.3	39.8	57.5
Wash.	Seattle	40.5	42.3	45.6	50.4	55.5	60.1	64.3	64.1	59.1	53.0	46.3	42.3	52.0
	Spokane	27.4	31.4	40.2	48.6	56.3	62.8	70.4	68.8	59.3	49.1	37.5	30.9	48.6
W. Va.	Parkersburg	33.4	33.8	43.0	53.2	63.4	71.9	75.4	73.8	69.2	56.0	44.3	35.6	54.3
Wis.	Madison	17.5	20.1	31.2	45.6	57.7	67.4	72.5	70.2	62.3	50.2	35.2	22.9	46.1
Wyo.	Cheyenne	25.5	27.3	33.1	40.9	50.3	60.4	66.7	65.6	57.0	44.8	34.8	28.5	44.6
Alaska	Juneau	28.1	30.2	33.9	40.9	47.9	54.3	56.7	55.4	50.5	43.5	36.0	31.2	42.4
Hawaii	Honolulu	71.5	71.5	71.7	73.1	74.9	76.6	77.6	78.3	78.2	77.2	75.0	73.2	74.9
P.R.	San Juan	74.9	74.9	75.5	76.7	78.7	70.7	80.0	80.5	80.5	80.0	78.3	76.4	78.0

[a]While the Census Bureau failed to identify the period being measured, it ranged from 19 years in Salt Lake City to 77 in Madison, Wisconsin. For most sites it was between 50 and 74 years.
Source: Bureau of the Census, *Statistical Abstract of the United States, 1947* (Washington, D.C., 1947), 146.

TABLE 2.2 AVERAGE DAILY MAXIMUM TEMPERATURES

[Averages for period of record, including 1945]

	Station	Length of Record (yrs.)	Jan.	Feb.	Mar.	Apr.	May	Jun.	Jul.	Aug.	Sep.	Oct.	Nov.	Dec.	Annual
Ala.	Mobile	74	60.4	62.7	67.1	75.1	82.5	88.3	89.6	89.4	86.3	77.8	68.1	61.9	75.8
	Montgomery	74	57.8	60.7	68.0	75.5	83.4	89.8	90.9	89.9	86.4	76.7	66.2	58.4	75.3
Ariz.	Phoenix	50	65.1	69.0	74.5	82.3	91.1	101.0	103.6	101.4	97.3	86.4	74.8	65.6	84.3
Ark.	Little Rock	66	50.2	53.5	62.7	71.9	79.1	87.1	90.4	89.6	84.1	73.9	61.3	52.0	71.3
Calif.	Fresno	58	54.3	61.2	66.4	74.0	81.9	91.1	99.1	97.3	89.3	78.6	66.5	55.2	76.3
	Los Angeles	68	64.9	65.5	67.3	69.5	71.9	76.1	81.1	82.0	80.5	76.3	72.7	67.0	72.9
	San Francisco	71	55.1	58.5	60.7	62.1	63.4	65.5	65.0	65.2	68.5	67.8	62.9	56.5	62.6
Colo.	Denver	74	42.7	44.7	51.2	59.6	68.9	80.0	85.6	84.3	76.5	64.7	52.7	44.5	63.0
D.C.	Washington	50	42.6	43.6	54.1	64.3	75.2	82.4	86.7	84.4	78.8	67.6	55.5	44.4	65.0
Fla.	Jacksonville	75	64.1	66.9	71.6	77.5	83.5	87.9	90.2	89.5	85.4	78.5	70.6	65.0	77.6
	Miami	48	74.5	75.4	78.0	80.5	83.6	86.3	87.7	88.2	86.9	83.4	78.4	75.6	81.5
Ga.	Atlanta	67	51.4	54.1	62.1	70.6	79.1	85.9	87.4	86.2	82.1	71.9	60.7	52.3	70.3
Idaho	Boise	6	36.0	44.2	52.3	62.0	70.0	75.9	90.1	88.0	76.5	66.9	47.5	39.6	62.4
Ill.	Chicago	73	31.8	33.7	43.0	54.4	65.4	75.2	80.6	78.7	72.5	61.1	47.0	35.6	56.6
Ind.	Indianapolis	74.	35.8	39.0	48.4	61.3	74.1	81.2	85.5	83.3	76.7	64.9	50.1	39.1	61.6
Iowa	Des Moines	67	29.0	32.8	45.2	60.2	71.5	81.3	85.7	83.4	75.9	63.6	47.4	34.1	59.1
Kans.	Wichita	57	41.3	45.0	56.1	67.0	75.1	85.1	90.8	90.2	82.1	70.0	55.4	44.0	66.9
Ky.	Louisville	73	42.5	45.0	54.8	65.7	75.9	84.1	88.1	86.4	80.5	69.0	54.8	44.6	66.0
La.	New Orleans	72	62.5	65.1	71.1	76.8	83.1	88.4	89.6	89.5	86.3	78.6	69.7	63.4	77.0
Maine	Eastport	72	28.8	28.7	36.3	45.4	55.2	63.4	68.8	68.4	62.8	53.7	43.0	32.4	48.9
Mass.	Boston	59	35.8	36.6	43.4	54.5	65.6	75.2	80.1	77.8	71.2	61.6	49.3	39.6	57.6
Mich.	Detroit	70	31.4	32.1	41.5	54.9	67.3	76.9	82.0	79.5	72.6	60.2	45.8	35.1	56.6
	Sault Ste. Marie	55	19.8	20.3	29.2	45.0	58.2	68.3	73.2	70.3	62.5	50.1	36.0	25.2	46.5
Minn.	Minneapolis	54	22.2	24.7	38.1	55.5	68.0	77.3	82.9	80.2	71.7	58.6	40.5	27.1	53.9
Miss.	Vicksburg	71	56.6	60.5	67.7	74.9	82.2	88.3	90.0	89.7	86.0	76.6	66.1	58.3	74.7
Mo.	Kansas City	57	38.2	41.1	53.0	64.6	74.0	83.4	88.7	87.2	79.6	68.4	53.4	41.1	64.4
	St. Louis	75	38.7	43.0	52.9	65.1	75.9	83.6	87.4	86.4	79.5	67.5	53.5	42.5	64.7
Mont.	Helena	66	27.0	30.4	41.2	54.1	62.5	70.7	79.2	72.9	67.3	55.9	41.6	32.8	53.4
	Miles City	50	27.2	29.9	42.4	58.7	68.7	79.0	87.8	85.7	73.6	60.3	44.0	32.0	57.4
Nebr.	North Platte	71	35.9	39.8	49.6	61.6	71.1	80.8	87.6	86.0	77.7	65.8	50.6	39.5	62.2
	Omaha	73	31.0	35.1	47.1	61.6	72.3	81.7	87.4	84.9	76.8	65.0	48.2	35.4	60.6
Nev.	Winnemucca	67	39.0	44.4	52.8	61.2	69.7	79.1	89.7	88.3	77.8	65.7	52.2	41.7	63.5
N.J.	Atlantic City	72	39.5	40.4	45.2	54.5	64.6	73.0	78.1	78.2	73.6	63.6	52.5	43.2	58.9
N. Mex.	Albuquerque	53	47.6	54.5	60.6	69.2	78.7	88.6	90.7	87.6	82.0	71.3	57.5	47.8	69.9
N.Y.	Albany	72	31.4	32.0	41.6	55.7	69.0	77.8	82.6	80.2	72.7	60.5	46.8	35.1	57.1
	New York	46	37.4	38.4	45.4	67.2	68.5	77.0	81.7	80.1	73.7	63.7	51.0	41.2	59.6
	Rochester	74	31.7	31.4	39.8	53.0	66.2	76.0	80.7	78.2	71.9	59.3	45.8	34.9	55.7
N.C.	Asheville	43	44.6	49.1	55.1	64.8	73.3	78.8	81.8	80.1	75.0	66.4	55.5	46.9	64.3
	Raleigh	58	50.0	52.3	60.3	70.0	78.8	85.4	88.1	86.0	80.4	71.7	60.5	51.7	69.6
N. Dak.	Bismarck	71	16.4	19.2	31.7	51.4	65.0	75.0	82.2	80.2	70.3	55.5	36.9	22.9	50.6
Ohio	Cleveland	79	32.0	34.3	43.0	56.3	69.3	78.9	83.5	81.3	74.7	62.6	46.8	35.6	58.2
Okla.	Oklahoma City	55	47.3	51.0	61.6	70.8	77.8	87.0	91.8	92.2	84.9	73.4	60.1	48.9	70.6
Oreg.	Portland	71	44.3	48.0	54.3	60.8	66.4	72.0	77.5	77.5	71.3	62.0	52.5	45.9	61.1
Pa.	Harrisburg	56	35.5	37.1	46.7	59.9	71.2	79.7	84.0	81.4	74.7	63.4	49.7	38.8	60.3
	Pittsburgh	72	38.4	39.5	48.7	60.5	72.1	80.2	84.1	82.1	76.3	64.2	50.5	40.6	61.4
S.C.	Charleston	72	59.5	60.0	65.2	72.0	79.8	85.4	89.8	87.3	81.8	74.7	66.0	59.2	73.1
S. Dak.	Huron	63	21.6	26.1	39.3	57.1	68.5	78.8	84.2	82.8	74.0	60.4	42.4	28.7	55.3
Tenn.	Nashville	75	47.4	50.2	59.1	69.1	78.1	85.9	88.8	87.8	82.4	71.6	58.3	49.1	69.0
Tex.	Amarillo	54	45.5	48.9	59.0	67.3	74.6	83.8	87.8	86.6	80.0	68.2	56.3	47.1	67.1
	El Paso	58	56.2	61.3	69.4	76.0	83.5	91.5	94.4	89.5	84.2	76.5	64.2	55.5	74.9
	Fort Worth	47	56.5	59.3	68.5	75.4	82.3	90.7	94.0	94.7	88.1	78.4	66.3	57.1	75.9
	Houston	55	62.1	65.0	71.8	77.9	84.2	90.2	92.2	92.4	88.1	81.0	70.7	63.3	78.2
Utah	Salt Lake City	17	35.1	40.9	50.8	62.0	72.0	81.6	92.4	89.7	79.0	66.3	49.1	39.7	63.2
Vt.	Burlington	55	27.0	27.7	37.1	51.8	65.9	74.9	79.4	76.9	69.0	51.2	42.8	31.3	53.4
Va.	Norfolk	71	49.3	50.4	57.7	66.1	75.6	83.3	86.8	84.8	79.6	69.6	59.5	50.8	67.7
	Richmond	47	47.8	48.7	58.2	67.3	77.4	84.0	87.7	85.8	80.6	70.4	58.9	48.7	68.0
Wash.	Seattle	55	44.9	47.6	52.1	58.1	63.5	68.5	73.6	73.1	67.0	59.0	51.1	46.6	58.8
	Spokane	65	33.3	38.7	49.3	59.5	67.9	74.7	84.4	83.1	72.1	59.9	44.2	36.2	58.6
W.Va.	Parkersburg	57	40.7	42.5	53.3	63.1	74.9	81.9	85.9	84.2	78.2	66.9	52.8	42.5	64.0
Wis.	Madison	77	24.8	27.7	38.6	54.0	66.6	76.0	81.3	78.7	70.6	58.0	41.9	29.1	53.9
Wyo.	Cheyenne	73	36.3	38.4	44.3	52.7	52.5	73.9	80.5	79.3	71.0	57.5	46.2	39.2	56.8
Alaska	Juneau	45	32.0	34.8	38.8	47.1	55.4	62.2	63.6	61.7	56.4	48.1	40.1	34.6	47.9
Hawaii	Honolulu	40	76.3	76.4	76.6	77.7	79.6	81.2	82.2	82.9	82.9	82.0	79.7	77.8	79.6
P.R.	San Juan	47	80.0	80.2	80.8	81.9	83.8	84.6	84.7	85.3	85.8	85.5	83.4	81.3	83.1

Source: Bureau of the Census, *Statistical Abstract of the United States, 1947*, 147.

TABLE 2.3 AVERAGE DAILY MINIMUM TEMPERATURES

[Averages for period of record, including 1945]

	Station	Length of Record (yrs.)	Jan.	Feb.	Mar.	Apr.	May	Jun.	Jul.	Aug.	Sep.	Oct.	Nov.	Dec.	Annual
Ala.	Mobile	74	43.6	46.2	52.0	58.5	65.7	72.3	74.0	73.7	70.2	59.7	50.1	44.6	59.2
	Montgomery	74	40.0	42.3	48.3	55.3	63.1	70.3	72.4	71.9	67.5	56.4	46.1	40.9	56.2
Ariz.	Phoenix	50	38.9	42.7	47.0	52.9	60.3	69.1	77.2	76.5	69.3	56.4	45.4	39.5	56.2
Ark.	Little Rock	66	33.7	36.2	44.0	53.0	60.8	68.8	72.0	71.1	65.2	53.8	42.9	35.9	53.1
Calif.	Fresno	58	38.1	41.6	44.5	48.0	53.2	59.6	65.0	63.5	58.1	51.0	43.0	38.4	50.3
	Los Angeles	68	46.2	47.2	48.8	50.8	53.6	56.7	59.9	60.8	58.9	55.3	51.2	47.9	53.1
	San Francisco	71	44.9	47.1	48.4	49.4	50.8	52.3	52.9	53.5	54.8	53.8	50.7	46.6	50.4
Colo.	Denver	74	18.6	21.1	27.2	35.5	44.6	53.5	59.4	58.3	49.2	38.4	27.8	20.6	37.8
D.C.	Washington	50	27.3	27.3	35.5	44.0	54.4	63.0	67.8	66.0	59.6	47.8	37.9	29.4	46.7
Fla.	Jacksonville	71	46.7	49.1	53.6	59.9	66.5	71.9	74.0	73.9	71.2	63.7	53.8	47.6	61.0
	Miami	48	60.7	60.7	64.1	67.1	71.2	74.4	75.8	76.1	75.3	72.1	66.3	62.1	68.8
Ga.	Atlanta	67	35.4	37.0	43.3	51.4	60.0	67.2	69.7	69.0	64.5	53.7	43.4	36.7	52.6
Idaho	Boise	6	21.4	28.2	30.9	38.2	44.0	49.7	58.7	56.4	48.3	41.4	31.0	25.9	39.5
Ill.	Chicago	73	17.9	20.0	29.2	39.6	49.6	59.7	66.0	65.3	58.3	46.9	33.8	23.4	42.5
Ind.	Indianapolis	74	21.0	23.2	31.6	42.9	51.7	62.0	65.9	64.1	57.1	46.5	34.5	25.3	44.4
Iowa	Des Moines	67	11.2	14.6	26.6	40.0	51.1	60.8	65.0	62.8	55.3	43.2	29.5	17.9	39.8
Kans.	Wichita	57	22.8	24.9	34.3	45.7	55.2	64.8	69.5	68.5	60.5	48.7	35.5	26.1	46.4
Ky.	Louisville	73	27.1	28.7	36.9	46.7	56.5	65.5	69.1	67.5	61.0	49.2	38.3	29.4	48.1
La.	New Orleans	72	47.2	49.5	55.2	61.3	67.8	73.8	75.5	75.6	72.9	64.2	54.4	48.4	62.2
Maine	Eastport	72	13.1	14.1	23.2	32.5	40.5	46.9	32.0	33.0	49.2	41.5	31.4	18.7	34.7
Mass.	Boston	59	20.0	21.0	27.8	38.3	48.6	57.8	63.3	62.0	55.2	45.5	34.8	25.4	41.6
Mich.	Detroit	70	18.6	18.3	26.5	37.4	48.6	58.5	63.5	61.8	55.4	44.4	33.1	23.6	40.8
	Sault Ste. Marie	55	4.4	2.4	12.0	28.0	38.3	46.7	52.2	51.4	45.5	35.9	24.8	12.5	29.5
Minn.	Minneapolis	54	5.5	8.1	21.6	36.6	48.2	58.4	63.3	60.7	52.5	40.7	25.6	12.4	36.1
Miss.	Vicksburg	72	39.9	43.2	49.3	56.3	63.6	70.3	72.6	71.9	67.3	56.8	47.1	41.7	56.7
Mo.	Kansas City	57	21.7	23.7	33.8	45.7	55.6	65.2	69.9	68.2	60.5	48.9	35.8	25.7	46.2
	St. Louis	75	23.4	26.6	35.3	47.0	56.2	66.4	70.2	68.6	61.5	50.1	37.3	27.3	47.7
Mont.	Helena	66	10.4	12.8	22.2	32.9	40.6	47.7	52.2	51.2	43.5	35.4	24.3	17.0	32.5
	Miles City	50	7.0	8.9	21.2	35.2	45.1	54.8	60.8	57.7	47.2	35.6	23.2	12.6	34.1
Nebr.	North Platte	71	11.8	15.4	24.2	36.3	46.9	56.7	62.4	60.3	50.2	37.1	24.2	15.7	36.8
	Omaha	73	13.5	17.0	28.1	41.6	52.7	62.4	62.5	65.3	56.5	44.5	30.1	19.3	41.5
Nev.	Winnemucca	67	17.2	22.5	27.4	32.9	54.7	47.3	54.0	50.9	41.2	32.1	23.7	18.8	34.0
N.J.	Atlantic City	72	25.5	26.7	31.9	41.1	51.6	60.2	66.1	66.8	60.0	50.2	38.8	29.6	46.5
N. Mex.	Albuquerque	53	20.6	26.5	31.2	38.7	47.9	56.7	62.8	60.2	53.8	42.0	29.1	21.2	40.9
N.Y.	Albany	72	15.5	15.6	25.5	37.3	48.9	58.1	62.9	60.8	53.8	42.5	32.6	21.0	39.5
	New York	46	24.5	24.2	30.2	41.6	52.6	60.5	65.9	66.2	59.8	49.0	37.3	28.8	45.0
	Rochester	74	18.2	16.9	25.2	36.2	47.4	56.8	61.9	60.2	53.8	42.9	32.9	22.9	39.6
N.C.	Asheville	43	26.1	30.0	34.7	43.1	51.9	58.6	61.7	61.0	55.0	44.2	34.7	28.7	44.1
	Raleigh	58	32.2	34.1	40.1	48.8	58.2	66.0	69.5	68.0	61.8	52.3	41.5	34.3	50.6
N. Dak.	Bismarck	71	− 3.8	− 2.2	12.1	29.4	41.0	50.8	56.6	53.2	44.3	31.7	16.1	2.7	27.7
Ohio	Cleveland	70	17.4	18.3	26.0	36.1	46.9	56.5	60.3	59.2	52.9	42.8	31.3	22.6	39.2
Okla.	Oklahoma City	55	27.7	29.9	38.8	49.2	58.1	66.9	70.8	70.2	63.2	51.5	39.2	30.2	49.6
Oreg.	Portland	71	34.4	36.1	39.4	42.8	47.4	52.8	55.8	55.9	52.1	46.5	41.0	36.5	45.1
Pa.	Harrisburg	56	22.4	23.3	31.1	41.9	52.3	60.9	65.6	63.8	56.9	48.2	35.9	26.6	44.1
	Pittsburgh	72	23.4	23.4	31.1	40.9	51.8	60.6	64.6	62.8	56.9	45.6	35.5	26.9	43.6
S.C.	Charleston	72	42.3	44.9	49.7	57.0	65.8	72.4	75.0	74.6	70.8	60.8	50.7	44.2	59.0
S. Dak.	Huron	63	1.0	4.0	18.5	33.1	44.3	55.4	59.5	57.3	47.9	35.0	20.6	8.7	32.9
Tenn.	Nashville	75	30.9	32.9	40.3	49.5	58.3	66.7	70.0	68.7	62.1	50.3	39.8	32.9	50.2
Tex.	Amarillo	54	20.8	23.3	31.6	40.4	49.6	58.9	64.0	62.6	55.5	43.3	31.2	23.9	42.1
	El Paso	56	30.9	35.9	40.4	48.6	56.5	64.6	68.0	66.6	60.4	50.5	38.0	31.9	49.4
	Fort Worth	47	36.0	37.4	46.5	54.4	62.7	70.7	73.8	74.0	67.7	57.0	46.7	37.7	55.4
	Houston	55	44.5	46.9	53.5	60.0	66.3	72.2	74.1	74.2	70.2	61.2	52.0	45.9	60.1
Utah	Salt Lake City	17	16.9	23.4	30.3	37.7	44.9	52.0	61.3	59.3	49.2	39.7	27.5	21.7	38.7
Vt.	Burlington	55	10.5	11.2	21.1	34.8	47.1	56.5	61.2	58.9	51.6	41.3	29.8	17.4	36.8
Va.	Norfolk	71	33.9	34.2	40.1	48.1	57.7	66.2	70.5	70.1	65.5	54.7	44.3	36.1	51.8
	Richmond	47	30.0	29.9	37.5	45.6	55.8	64.2	68.5	67.2	61.2	49.3	38.8	31.3	48.3
Wash.	Seattle	55	36.0	37.0	39.2	42.7	47.4	51.8	55.0	55.2	51.8	47.0	41.5	38.1	45.2
	Spokane	65	21.6	24.2	31.3	37.7	44.7	50.9	56.3	54.5	46.6	38.5	31.0	25.8	38.7
W.Va.	Parkersburg	57	24.3	25.8	32.4	43.8	52.6	61.0	64.9	63.5	57.1	45.3	34.7	27.8	44.6
Wis.	Madison	77	10.1	12.5	23.7	37.2	48.9	58.9	63.9	61.8	54.1	42.3	28.5	16.6	38.2
Wyo.	Cheyenne	73	14.7	16.2	21.9	29.1	38.1	46.9	52.9	51.9	43.0	32.1	23.4	17.8	32.3
Alaska	Juneau	44	23.9	26.2	29.1	34.7	40.4	46.5	50.1	49.4	44.6	39.0	31.7	26.9	36.9
Hawaii	Honolulu	40	68.7	66.6	66.8	68.5	70.2	72.0	73.1	73.7	73.5	72.4	70.4	68.6	70.2
P.R.	San Juan	47	69.9	69.6	70.2	71.5	73.5	74.8	75.3	75.6	75.2	74.5	73.2	71.5	72.9

Source: Bureau of the Census, *Statistical Abstract of the United States, 1947,* 148.

TABLE 2.4 AVERAGE RELATIVE HUMIDITY

[For period of record, including 1945]

Station		Length of Record (yrs.)	Jan.	Feb.	Mar.	Apr.	May	Jun.	Jul.	Aug.	Sep.	Oct.	Nov.	Dec.	Annual
Ala.	Mobile	48	74	73	73	71	71	72	68	76	74	70	71	77	72
	Montgomery	46	70	67	64	62	62	64	70	72	67	64	66	71	67
Ariz.	Phoenix	42	48	47	39	31	25	23	35	41	38	38	43	50	38
Ark.	Little Rock	46	69	67	63	62	66	66	66	67	67	65	66	70	66
Calif.	Fresno	50	76	69	62	52	44	36	31	33	39	49	61	76	52
	Los Angeles	49	56	61	61	64	68	68	67	67	64	61	51	54	62
	San Francisco	44	75	72	70	70	72	74	79	80	74	70	69	74	73
Colo.	Denver	48	52	52	49	49	49	44	44	45	44	46	48	52	48
D.C.	Washington	36	66	63	61	59	65	69	71	70	71	71	66	68	67
Fla.	Jacksonville	54	74	72	69	67	69	72	74	75	77	75	74	75	73
	Miami	30	73	72	70	69	71	74	73	73	75	74	71	73	73
Ga.	Atlanta	38	72	69	66	63	64	67	73	74	71	67	67	72	69
Idaho	Boise	6	83	76	60	55	53	52	38	36	46	54	75	81	59
Ill.	Chicago	27	75	73	70	66	66	67	65	68	70	67	70	76	69
Ind.	Indianapolis	54	75	71	67	61	60	61	59	63	64	64	69	74	66
Iowa	Des Moines	50	79	77	72	65	65	68	66	70	72	70	73	78	71
Kans.	Wichita	54	70	65	59	58	63	61	57	57	60	60	64	70	62
Ky.	Louisville	48	72	69	65	61	61	62	62	64	65	63	67	71	65
La.	New Orleans	47	75	73	71	70	69	70	74	74	73	70	72	75	72
Maine	Eastport	48	74	74	73	74	76	79	82	81	80	77	77	75	77
Mass.	Boston	31	68	66	65	65	67	67	68	71	71	68	70	68	68
Mich.	Detroit	42	84	85	74	68	66	66	62	64	68	71	76	81	71
	Sault Ste. Marie	33	84	82	78	70	68	70	73	75	79	79	82	84	77
Minn.	Minneapolis	42	79	76	68	60	58	63	60	62	66	66	72	78	64
Miss.	Vicksburg	46	74	70	68	70	72	74	78	79	76	73	72	74	73
Mo.	Kansas City	38	72	69	65	63	65	66	61	64	66	63	66	72	66
	St. Louis	46	71	68	64	61	62	62	59	62	64	62	65	71	64
Mont.	Helena	57	68	66	58	53	52	50	43	44	51	57	64	68	56
	Miles City	50	75	73	68	57	53	54	47	48	54	61	70	75	61
Nebr.	North Platte	48	70	67	61	57	59	61	58	58	60	58	63	70	62
	Omaha	38	75	74	68	62	63	66	63	66	66	63	69	75	67
Nev.	Winnemucca	38	76	70	58	49	60	40	30	29	37	49	62	74	52
N.J.	Atlantic City	57	74	73	73	72	75	77	78	78	76	73	72	73	75
N. Mex.	Albuquerque	21	60	52	44	39	36	33	45	49	50	49	51	61	47
N.Y.	Albany	38	75	74	70	66	65	69	70	72	76	74	74	75	72
	New York	47	68	64	63	61	63	65	69	70	70	67	68	67	65
	Rochester	46	74	74	69	63	61	63	62	64	68	69	72	74	68
N.C.	Asheville	40	71	68	65	61	63	68	72	75	72	68	66	70	68
	Raleigh	57	73	71	69	66	68	72	76	79	78	74	71	74	72
N. Dak.	Bismarck	56	76	75	69	59	57	61	57	56	60	63	72	76	66
Ohio	Cleveland	52	59	58	59	58	61	64	65	66	66	66	58	59	61
Okla.	Oklahoma City	36	71	68	62	63	68	68	62	62	64	66	66	71	66
Oreg.	Portland	48	81	77	71	65	64	63	60	62	66	74	80	81	70
Pa.	Harrisburg	56	68	65	62	56	58	63	63	65	66	66	64	65	64
	Pittsburgh	49	73	73	67	62	61	64	63	65	66	67	70	77	67
S.C.	Charleston	52	70	65	63	65	65	78	78	78	77	77	72	78	72
S. Dak.	Huron	56	78	77	69	61	58	62	58	59	60	62	70	77	66
Tenn.	Nashville	38	75	70	66	62	66	67	68	71	70	67	69	73	69
Tex.	Amarillo	52	60	57	50	49	56	54	52	54	57	58	57	61	55
	El Paso	55	44	38	30	25	25	28	41	45	44	42	43	48	38
	Fort Worth	34	67	66	59	62	64	61	58	58	61	63	64	69	63
	Houston	33	75	74	72	73	74	73	74	73	74	70	71	75	73
Utah	Salt Lake City	11	80	76	63	54	47	44	38	38	43	55	70	77	57
Vt.	Burlington	38	80	81	77	72	70	73	75	77	81	79	79	81	77
Va.	Norfolk	8	73	69	68	67	71	74	77	77	77	74	71	72	73
	Richmond	47	72	67	64	61	64	67	70	72	72	69	67	71	68
Wash.	Seattle	39	81	80	73	68	67	66	66	69	72	79	82	82	73
	Spokane	54	82	75	62	52	49	47	38	40	50	62	78	83	60
W. Va.	Parkersburg	37	76	74	68	64	67	72	71	74	74	72	72	76	72
Wis.	Madison	37	81	79	73	65	64	67	64	67	70	70	76	82	71
Wyo.	Cheyenne	41	55	58	57	58	56	53	48	49	49	50	51	55	53
Alaska	Juneau	26	77	74	70	69	70	70	78	81	81	82	77	77	76
Hawaii	Honolulu	35	70	70	68	67	67	66	66	67	67	68	69	71	68
P.R.	San Juan	47	81	80	77	76	77	77	78	78	79	79	81	81	79

Source: Bureau of the Census, *Statistical Abstract of the United States, 1947*, 156.

TABLE 2.5 AVERAGE PRECIPITATION, INCHES

[Data adopted as "normals"] [a]

Station		Jan.	Feb.	Mar.	Apr.	May	Jun.	Jul.	Aug.	Sep.	Oct.	Nov.	Dec.	Annual
Ala.	Mobile	4.76	5.09	6.32	4.91	4.34	5.61	7.25	6.42	5.05	3.51	3.56	4.94	61.76
	Montgomery	4.89	5.35	6.30	4.77	3.62	4.09	4.76	4.10	3.08	2.33	3.22	4.82	51.33
Ariz.	Phoenix	.80	.84	.71	.42	.13	.06	1.02	.97	.86	.45	.67	.92	7.85
Ark.	Little Rock	4.76	3.82	4.59	5.08	4.74	3.68	3.37	3.48	3.06	2.75	4.01	4.18	47.52
Calif.	Fresno	1.75	1.58	1.59	.91	.37	.11	.01	.01	.17	.58	.86	1.56	9.50
	Los Angeles	3.04	3.39	2.76	1.05	.37	.08	.01	.03	.21	.63	1.08	2.89	15.54
	San Francisco	4.75	3.81	3.08	1.55	.68	.15	.01	.02	.29	.97	2.45	4.42	22.18
Colo.	Denver	.43	.56	1.07	2.06	2.28	1.31	1.60	1.40	1.03	1.01	.59	.65	14.01
D.C.	Washington	3.32	2.88	3.45	3.30	3.36	3.91	4.37	4.42	3.64	2.91	2.46	3.09	41.11
Fla.	Jacksonville	2.80	2.97	2.91	2.38	4.02	5.33	6.71	5.81	7.35	4.46	1.98	3.02	49.75
	Miami	2.70	2.04	2.57	3.37	6.57	7.11	5.97	6.24	8.99	8.75	2.73	1.92	58.96
Ga.	Atlanta	5.03	5.06	5.41	3.72	3.42	3.94	4.84	4.70	3.04	2.69	3.11	4.79	49.75
Idaho	Boise	1.14	1.49	1.16	1.54	1.50	1.34	.13	.12	.45	.98	1.34	1.47	12.66
Ill.	Chicago	1.92	1.88	2.66	2.80	3.61	3.52	3.13	3.20	3.21	2.58	2.37	1.93	32.81
Ind.	Indianapolis	2.95	2.73	3.93	3.62	3.89	3.62	3.34	3.31	3.40	2.78	3.35	2.98	39.90
Iowa	Des Moines	1.07	1.12	1.78	2.91	4.56	4.76	3.50	3.52	3.67	2.50	1.43	1.22	32.04
Kans.	Wichita	.78	1.21	1.75	3.11	4.44	4.38	3.08	3.11	3.33	2.35	1.57	1.07	30.26
Ky.	Louisville	3.97	3.34	4.47	3.90	3.69	3.94	3.63	3.26	2.69	2.62	3.37	3.61	42.49
La.	New Orleans	4.59	4.41	5.03	5.31	4.86	5.79	6.71	6.05	5.31	3.56	3.53	4.64	59.81
Maine	Eastport	3.56	3.14	3.70	2.79	2.88	3.04	3.10	2.98	3.14	3.65	3.41	3.43	38.82
Mass.	Boston	3.61	3.37	3.57	3.34	3.18	2.89	3.49	3.62	3.14	3.15	3.33	3.45	40.14
Mich.	Detroit	2.13	2.11	2.42	2.55	3.27	3.41	3.23	2.75	2.72	2.35	2.32	2.28	31.53
	Sault Ste. Marie	2.02	1.43	1.75	2.13	2.64	2.71	2.69	2.70	3.54	3.09	3.01	2.23	29.94
Minn.	Minneapolis	.86	.95	1.42	2.23	3.67	4.22	3.73	3.12	3.13	2.08	1.27	.98	27.66
Miss.	Vicksburg	5.37	4.82	5.57	5.19	4.32	3.99	4.53	3.46	2.87	2.77	3.71	5.33	51.93
Mo.	Kansas City	1.31	1.55	2.47	3.36	4.87	4.74	3.60	4.00	4.29	2.68	2.06	1.39	36.32
	St. Louis	2.25	2.41	3.47	3.78	4.47	4.40	3.46	3.43	3.19	2.84	2.81	2.47	38.98
Mont.	Helena	.56	.37	.79	1.12	1.98	2.04	1.14	.77	1.25	.61	.45	.47	11.55
	Miles City	.66	.49	.86	1.12	2.24	2.66	1.54	1.08	1.04	.90	.57	.63	13.79
Nebr.	North Platte	.40	.48	.82	2.21	2.72	3.10	2.59	2.27	1.53	1.03	.46	.52	18.13
	Omaha	.70	.87	1.31	2.56	3.60	4.60	3.69	3.16	3.09	2.07	1.16	.91	27.72
Nev.	Winnemucca	1.10	.96	.93	.83	.85	.68	.23	.18	.35	.65	.76	1.02	8.56
N.J.	Atlantic City	3.49	3.36	3.60	2.99	3.05	3.04	3.93	4.49	2.65	3.20	2.82	3.94	40.56
N. Mex.	Albuquerque	.40	.32	.45	.60	.60	.49	1.41	1.24	.82	.81	.46	.41	8.01
N.Y.	Albany	2.51	2.38	2.74	2.72	3.29	3.82	3.90	3.64	3.36	3.14	2.90	2.52	36.92
	New York	3.66	3.82	3.64	3.23	3.24	3.33	4.24	4.33	3.39	3.53	2.96	3.62	42.99
	Rochester	2.78	2.26	2.97	2.20	2.80	2.94	2.99	2.78	2.48	2.74	2.54	2.65	32.76
N.C.	Asheville	3.10	3.15	3.97	3.02	3.43	3.93	4.30	4.16	3.04	2.75	2.23	3.20	40.28
	Raleigh	3.66	3.92	3.87	3.47	3.81	4.39	5.40	5.41	3.61	2.86	2.28	3.58	46.26
N. Dak.	Bismarck	.45	.44	.89	1.52	2.32	3.35	2.24	1.82	1.23	.94	.57	.57	16.34
Ohio	Cleveland	2.51	2.51	2.71	2.44	3.12	3.12	3.45	2.77	3.33	2.78	2.64	2.44	33.82
Okla.	Oklahoma City	1.28	1.17	2.12	3.34	4.82	3.91	2.53	2.81	3.15	2.86	2.07	1.59	31.65
Oreg.	Portland	6.60	5.36	3.91	2.87	2.19	1.52	.61	.64	1.98	3.12	6.10	6.72	41.62
Pa.	Harrisburg	3.09	2.96	3.04	2.69	3.44	3.59	3.83	4.04	3.05	2.93	2.26	3.02	37.94
	Pittsburgh	2.96	2.53	3.22	3.02	3.25	3.74	4.13	3.33	2.67	2.55	2.34	2.79	36.53
S.C.	Charleston	3.02	2.98	3.02	2.53	3.00	4.59	6.89	6.53	4.53	3.27	2.14	2.72	45.22
S. Dak.	Huron	.56	.54	.91	2.24	2.98	3.79	3.16	2.46	1.57	1.28	.59	.57	20.65
Tenn.	Nashville	4.59	4.11	5.11	4.20	3.75	4.13	3.98	3.45	3.25	2.46	3.40	3.97	46.11
Tex.	Amarillo	.51	.71	.71	1.83	2.79	2.84	2.84	3.08	2.30	1.66	.92	.80	20.99
	El Paso	.46	.42	.36	.26	.33	.58	1.99	1.70	1.25	.80	.50	.52	9.17
	Fort Worth	1.86	1.89	2.35	3.76	4.52	3.21	2.23	2.28	2.59	2.82	2.22	2.10	31.87
	Houston	3.62	2.95	3.23	3.44	4.60	4.28	4.29	3.88	4.09	3.55	3.64	4.38	45.95
Utah	Salt Lake City	1.19	1.34	1.54	1.70	1.21	.91	.59	.90	.65	1.19	1.15	1.08	13.45
Vt.	Burlington	1.76	1.57	2.04	2.15	2.85	3.38	3.50	3.37	3.48	2.97	2.66	1.88	31.61
Va.	Norfolk	3.18	3.38	3.31	3.32	6.67	4.24	5.81	5.30	3.76	3.09	2.45	3.24	45.25
	Richmond	3.21	3.17	3.68	3.49	3.79	3.90	4.73	4.42	3.25	2.88	2.21	3.29	42.02
Wash.	Seattle	4.81	3.70	3.11	2.28	1.82	1.36	.61	.70	1.71	2.82	4.80	5.56	33.28
	Spokane	2.01	1.62	1.23	1.06	1.29	1.27	.54	.58	.88	1.19	1.97	2.15	15.79
W.Va.	Parkersburg	3.58	3.13	3.49	3.19	3.38	4.00	4.29	3.51	2.76	2.48	2.57	3.03	39.41
Wis.	Madison	1.52	1.41	2.02	2.49	3.60	3.85	3.57	3.22	3.75	2.28	1.92	1.54	31.15
Wyo.	Cheyenne	.42	.64	1.02	1.99	2.43	1.61	2.10	1.55	1.20	.96	.52	.55	14.99
Alaska	Juneau	7.33	5.53	5.56	5.41	5.14	4.06	5.18	7.46	10.16	11.68	9.21	7.70	84.42
Hawaii	Honolulu	4.00	2.52	3.01	1.83	1.09	.74	.84	1.11	1.38	2.09	2.47	3.89	24.97
P.R.	San Juan	4.36	2.60	2.77	4.19	6.05	5.36	5.77	6.16	6.08	5.60	6.72	5.10	53.54

[a]While the Bureau of the Census failed to identify the period being measured, for most sites it was between 50 and 75 years.
Source: Bureau of the Census, *Historical Abstract of the United States, 1947,* 151.

TABLE 2.6   AVERAGE SNOWFALL, INCHES

[For period of record, including 1945. T denotes trace]

Station		Length of Record (yrs.)	Jan.	Feb.	Mar.	Apr.	May	Jun.	Jul.	Aug.	Sep.	Oct.	Nov.	Dec.	Annual
Ala.	Mobile	65	0.1	0.1	T	0	0	0	0	0	0	0	0	T	0.2
	Montgomery	74	.2	.2	T	T	0	0	0	0	0	0	T	0.3	.7
Ariz.	Phoenix	50	T	T	T	0	T	0	0	0	0	0	T	T	T
Ark.	Little Rock	61	1.9	1.3	.5	T	0	0	0	0	0	T	.1	.9	4.7
Calif.	Fresno	58	.1	T	T	0	0	0	0	0	0	0	T	T	.1
	Los Angeles	68	T	T	0	0	0	0	0	0	0	0	T	T	T
	San Francisco	75	T	.1	T	0	0	0	0	0	0	0	0	.1	.2
Colo.	Denver	64	5.5	7.8	10.6	9.8	1.9	T	0	0	.7	4.1	6.1	8.4	54.9
D.C.	Washington	58	6.2	5.5	4.0	.4	T	0	0	0	0	.1	.7	3.3	20.2
Fla.	Jacksonville	75	0	0	0	0	0	0	0	0	0	0	0	0	0
	Miami	58	0	0	0	0	0	0	0	0	0	0	0	0	0
Ga.	Atlanta	61	.9	.9	.2	T	0	0	0	0	0	T	T	.3	2.3
Idaho	Boise	6	5.6	3.4	1.0	T	T	0	0	0	0	T	1.2	3.8	15.0
Ill.	Chicago	61	9.2	8.5	6.0	1.0	.1	0	0	0	0	.1	1.8	6.7	33.4
Ind.	Indianapolis	61	5.8	4.9	3.5	.7	.1	0	0	0	0	T	1.3	4.5	20.8
Iowa	Des Moines	60	8.5	7.3	5.4	1.1	T	0	0	0	T	.3	2.2	7.1	31.9
Kans.	Wichita	57	2.9	3.7	2.9	.4	T	0	0	0	T	.1	.7	3.0	13.7
Ky.	Louisville	61	4.0	3.7	2.0	.2	T	0	0	0	0	.1	.4	3.1	13.5
La.	New Orleans	75	.1	.2	T	0	0	0	0	0	0	0	0	T	.3
Maine	Eastport	61	15.9	17.6	12.8	6.5	.2	. . .	. . .	. . .	. . .	.2	4.3	12.0	69.5
Mass.	Boston	75	11.9	12.6	7.4	2.0	T	0	0	0	0	T	1.6	7.6	43.1
Mich.	Detroit	59	10.5	9.6	7.2	2.0	.1	0	0	0	0	.1	2.7	8.6	40.8
	Sault Ste. Marie	55	18.6	13.4	10.2	3.5	.6	0	0	0	T	2.3	12.6	18.1	79.3
Minn.	Minneapolis	54	9.1	7.8	8.4	3.0	.2	0	0	0	T	.5	4.4	7.2	40.9
Miss.	Vicksburg	55	.9	.4	T	0	0	0	0	0	0	0	T	.3	1.6
Mo.	Kansas City	57	4.7	5.8	4.0	1.0	T	0	0	0	T	.2	1.3	4.4	21.4
	St. Louis	61	4.4	5.0	3.4	.4	.1	0	0	0	0	.1	.9	3.4	17.7
Mont.	Helena	65	10.1	8.3	9.2	5.3	1.8	T	T	T	.8	3.9	6.6	8.6	54.6
	Miles City	50	6.2	4.2	6.8	2.2	1.7	0	0	0	.1	1.5	3.8	5.7	32.2
Nebr.	North Platte	62	3.7	4.9	6.4	1.9	.3	0	0	0	T	1.1	2.7	3.8	24.8
	Omaha	61	6.4	6.8	5.8	.8	.1	0	0	0	0	.5	2.2	5.4	28.0
Nev.	Winnemucca	67	7.6	5.2	4.0	1.6	.5	.1	T	0	T	.5	2.0	6.2	27.7
N.J.	Atlantic City	62	4.2	5.2	2.3	.3	0	0	0	0	0	T	.6	2.8	15.4
N. Mex.	Albuquerque	53	1.6	1.5	1.2	.3	T	0	0	0	T	T	.8	1.9	7.3
N.Y.	Albany	61	12.6	12.9	9.6	2.0	.1	0	0	0	0	T	3.4	9.0	49.6
	New York	61	7.9	9.7	5.9	1.1	0	0	0	0	0	T	1.1	5.9	31.6
	Rochester	61	18.2	18.6	13.3	3.7	.2	0	0	0	0	.3	6.3	15.1	75.7
N.C.	Asheville	40	2.9	2.7	1.9	.3	0	0	0	0	0	.1	.4	2.0	10.3
	Raleigh	58	2.0	2.8	1.2	.4	0	0	0	0	0	T	T	1.3	7.7
N. Dak.	Bismarck	60	5.5	5.3	7.6	3.0	.7	T	0	0	.2	1.1	5.0	6.1	34.5
Ohio	Cleveland	60	10.6	10.0	5.6	1.8	T	0	0	0	0	.2	4.0	9.2	41.4
Okla.	Oklahoma City	55	2.4	1.9	1.2	.1	0	0	0	0	0	T	.3	1.7	7.6
Ore.	Portland	61	5.7	3.1	.6	.1	T	0	0	0	0	T	.4	3.0	12.9
Pa.	Harrisburg	56	9.0	9.1	6.4	.9	T	0	0	0	0	.1	1.1	5.3	31.9
	Pittsburgh	61	8.6	7.7	6.1	3.0	T	0	0	0	T	.1	1.7	6.7	33.8
S.C.	Charleston	55	T	.2	T	0	0	0	0	0	0	0	0	.1	.3
S. Dak.	Huron	63	6.0	5.2	6.0	2.1	.1	0	0	0	T	.6	3.2	5.0	28.2
Tenn.	Nashville	61	2.4	2.5	1.3	T	T	0	0	0	0	T	.3	1.5	8.0
Tex.	Amarillo	54	3.3	4.8	3.2	1.1	.2	0	0	0	0	.4	2.3	4.8	20.1
	El Paso	67	.8	.4	.1	T	T	0	0	0	0	T	.3	.7	2.3
	Fort Worth	47	.9	.5	.4	T	0	0	0	0	0	T	.2	.4	2.4
	Houston	49	.1	T	T	0	0	0	0	0	0	0	0	.1	.2
Utah	Salt Lake City	17	12.2	9.6	7.7	2.4	.1	T	0	0	T	.2	5.8	8.7	46.7
Vt.	Burlington	60	14.8	14.0	13.6	4.1	.1	0	0	0	0	.4	6.6	12.2	65.8
Va.	Norfolk	75	2.5	2.7	1.7	T	0	0	0	0	0	T	.2	2.0	9.1
	Richmond	47	3.7	3.5	2.2	.4	0	0	0	0	0	T	.5	2.7	13.0
Wash.	Seattle	55	4.8	3.6	.8	.1	T	0	0	0	0	T	.8	1.5	11.6
	Spokane	61	11.4	8.1	2.8	.4	T	T	0	0	T	.1	4.2	8.8	35.8
W. Va.	Parkersburg	54	6.5	6.5	4.4	.8	T	0	0	0	0	.1	1.4	4.8	24.5
Wis.	Madison	62	9.5	8.0	7.7	1.8	.2	0	0	0	T	.3	3.0	7.2	37.7
Wyo.	Cheyenne	62	5.2	7.9	11.3	12.0	3.6	.3	0	0	.6	3.9	5.7	6.2	56.7
Alaska	Juneau	26	26.3	23.2	16.4	4.0	.1	0	0	0	T	1.6	9.8	26.3	107.7
Hawaii	Honolulu	40	0	0	0	0	0	0	0	0	0	0	0	0	0
P.R.	San Juan	47	0	0	0	0	0	0	0	0	0	0	0	0	0

Source: Bureau of the Census, Statistical Abstract of the United States, 1947, 153.

Stormy Weather

Storms of various kinds are products of nature, of course, but their consequences can be greatly influenced by what humankind has or has not done. A variety of forces—many of them traceable to the behavior, or absence of behavior, of people—combined during the years 1914–45 to produce some of the most deadly and costly storms of modern time.

Tropical Storms

The term *tropical cyclone* generally refers to storms that originate over water in the tropics. In the Northern Hemisphere the winds circulate counterclockwise. If the winds reach 39 miles per hour, the storm is classified as a tropical storm; if winds reach 74 miles per hour, the storm is called a hurricane in the Atlantic Ocean. The same storm is called a typhoon in the Pacific and a cyclone in the Indian Ocean. The trouble develops when these moving sea-bred storms come upon land or vessels at sea. The United States has been threatened largely by hurricanes on the Atlantic and Gulf coasts in late summer and early autumn, when the water is of sufficient temperature to enhance their development. Nothing could have been done to combat these storms, but the absence of a sophisticated warning system during 1914–45 probably meant that in some cases casualties and to a lesser extent property damage were greater than later would have been the case. In some instances, warnings were given consistent with the means of detection and communication available at that time.

TABLE 2.7 NORTH ATLANTIC TROPICAL STORMS (INCLUDING HURRICANES) REACHING THE U.S. COAST

Year	Total	Hurricanes Only	Lives Lost in the United States
1914	1	. . .	. . .
1915	4	3	600
1916	8	6	107
1917	1	1	5
1918	2	1	34
1919	2	1	287
1920	3	2	2
1921	2	2	5
1922	1	. . .	. . .
1923	4	2	. . .
1924	3	2	2
1925	2	1	6
1926	4	4	269
1927	1	. . .	. . .
1928	3	2	1,836
1929	2	2	3
1930	1	. . .	. . .
1931	2	. . .	. . .
1932	5	2	. . .
1933	7	5	63
1934	5	3	17
1935	2	2	414
1936	7	3	9
1937	4	. . .	. . .
1938	4	2	600
1939	3	1	3
1940	3	2	51
1941	4	2	10
1942	3	2	8
1943	4	1	16
1944	4	3	64
1945	5	3	7

Source: Ben J. Wattenberg, *Statistical History of the United States* (New York, 1976), 448.

TABLE 2.8 MAJOR NORTH ATLANTIC HURRICANES, 1914–1945

Date	Areas Hardest Hit	Land Stations with Highest Wind Speed	Deaths (U.S. Only)	Est. Damage (Millions)	Remarks
1915, Aug. 5–23	East Texas and Louisiana	Galveston, Tex. (120 mph)	275	50	Water 5–6 ft deep in Galveston business district. 90% of homes demolished. Warnings issued well ahead of time.
1915, Sept. 22–Oct. 1	Mid-Gulf Coast	Burrwood, La. (140 mph)	275	13	Many casualties due to persons insiting on staying in low-lying areas despite warnings.
1919, Sept. 2–15	Florida, Louisiana, and Texas	Sand Key, Fla. (84ª mph)	287	22	488 persons drowned at sea.
1926, Sept. 11–22	Florida and Alabama	Miami, Fla. (138 mph)	243	112	Most deaths were in Miami area. Said to have been one of most destructive storms of century.
1928, Sept. 6–20	Southern Florida	Lake Okeechobee, Fla. (75ª mph)	1,836	25	1,870 injured. Nearly all deaths were in Lake Okeechobee area. Winds estimated as high as 160 mph caused Lake to overflow into populated areas.

Date	Areas Hardest Hit	Land Stations with Highest Wind Speed	Deaths (U.S. Only)	Est. Damage (Millions)	Remarks
1935, Aug. 29–Sept. 10	Southern Florida	Tampa, Fla. (86 mph)	408	6	Sustained winds over Florida Keys est. 150–200 mph. Remembered as "Labor Day Storm."
1938, Sept. 10–22	Long Island and Southern New England	Blue Hills Obs., Mass. (183 mph)	600	306	Unusually destructive. Storm center moved as fast as 56 mph at times. 1,754 injured.
1944, Sept. 9–16	North Carolina to New England	Cape Henry, Va. (150[a] mph)	46	100	344 deaths at sea. Shipping lanes were crowded with wartime activity.
1944, Oct. 12–23	Florida	Dry Tortugas Is. (120 mph)	18	100	About 300 were killed in Cuba area before storm reached U.S. Evacuation of thousands from threatened areas in Fla. prevented higher toll.

[a]Wind measuring equipment disabled at speed indicated.
Source: *Information Please Almanac, Atlas and Yearbook, 1988* (Boston, 1988), 652.

Tornadoes: The Great Tristate Tornado of 1925

Tornadoes are land-based storms that are associated with cumulonimbus clouds of severe thunderstorms. The winds rotate in a counterclockwise direction around a hollow cavity and can be exceptionally violent—reaching interior speeds of up to 300 miles per hour—and therefore deadly and destructive. Tornadoes usually cover a small area and last a short period of time. In the United

TABLE 2.9   NUMBER OF TORNADOES REPORTED IN THE UNITED STATES, TORNADO DAYS, AND RESULTING LOSSES BY YEARS, 1916–1945

(Compiled by the U.S. Weather Bureau)

Year	Number Reported	Number Tornado Days	Total Loss of Life	Most Deaths in a Single Tornado	Total Reported Property Losses	Number of Tornadoes Causing Losses of $100,000	Number of Tornadoes Causing Losses of $1,000,000
1916	90	36	150	30	$ 2,264,500	6	1
1917	121	38	509	101	15,007,700	22	5
1918	81	45	135	36	7,431,150	19	1
1919	65	36	206	59	6,861,500	9	2
1920	87	50	498	87	15,007,500	24	7
1921	106	56	202	61	5,456,300	13	1
1922	108	61	135	16	6,880,000	20	0
1923	102	59	109	23	2,968,725	8	0
1924	130	58	376	85	26,072,350	25	6
1925	119	64	794	689	24,039,900	29	1
1926	111	56	144	23	4,323,950	16	0
1927	164	61	540	92	43,455,650	28	7
1928	203	76	92	14	13,235,600	25	4
1929	197	75	274	40	10,112,400	30	1
1930	192	72	179	41	12,289,100	28	3
1931	94	57	36	6	3,215,900	7	1
1932	152	67	394	37	8,888,525	11	1
1933	260	96	362	34	16,190,640	31	5
1934	147	77	47	6	4,424,950	9	0
1935	182	77	70	11	4,661,430	15	0
1936	159	74	552	216	26,228,550	17	6
1937	148	76	29	5	3,155,875	11	0
1938	220	78	183	32	8,793,457	18	3
1939	155	74	87	27	5,891,930	10	2
1940	128	65	65	18	6,015,320	9	1
1941	118	57	53	25	4,492,650	15	0
1942	170	68	384	65	15,268,950	32	3
1943	155	62	58	5	12,198,400	25	4
1944	173	67	275	100	21,594,150	34	7
1945	126	68	210	69	22,069,800	25	8

Source: Snowden D. Flora, *Tornadoes of the United States* (Norman, Okla., 1954), 32.

States the area most threatened by tornadoes has been the midwestern and southern states of the interior in the spring: the place and time suited to clashing weather systems. Before 1945 the number of tornadoes reported each year usually ranged between 100 and 200. After the National Weather Service developed a more advanced system of forecasting and reporting, the number increased substantially. Better methods of communication and detection would have increased the number of storms reported during 1914–45, and they also surely would have reduced the costs in lives and property.

The great tristate tornado of 1925 stood out not merely because it was the most destructive on record but also because it broke many of the rules believed to be associated with the behavior of these storms. It began in Missouri at 1:00 P.M. on March 18, drove straight across southern Illinois, and ran out a few miles beyond Princeton, Indiana, at 4:18. It thus was on the ground not a few minutes but more than three hours, traveling 219 miles with ground speeds of up to 68 miles per hour and interior speeds of up to 260. People did not see a funnel cloud that hopped and skipped but a continuous boiling black mass. It destroyed four small towns and damaged others, killed 689, and caused property damage of nearly $17 million, measured in values of that day, despite the fact that it did not strike any large cities. Had it entered a city such as St. Louis, as did another tornado in 1927, there would have been numbers of much greater magnitude.

TABLE 2.10 STATES HAVING THE GREATEST NUMBER OF TORNADOES PER UNIT AREA

(Based on number reported to Weather Bureau during 1916–49. States arranged in order of frequency per unit area)

State	Area (Square Miles)	Average Annual Number	Average Annual Number per Unit Area of 10,000 Square Miles
Iowa	56,280	15.6	2.8
Kansas	82,276	17.0	2.1
Arkansas	53,102	8.9	1.6
Oklahoma	69,919	10.3	1.5
Mississippi	47,716	6.0	1.3
Alabama	51,609	5.5	1.1
Missouri	69,674	6.7	1.0
Indiana	36,291	3.4	0.9
Illinois	56,400	4.9	0.9
Ohio	41,222	3.2	0.8
Georgia	58,876	4.4	0.8
Texas	267,339	13.5	0.5
District of Columbia	69	0.12	26.5[a]

[a] The high relative frequency credited to the District of Columbia is due to the fact that its area is only 69 square miles and 4 tornadoes have occurred there during the period under consideration.
Source: Flora, Tornadoes, 33.

Floods

Americans could not control the rainfall, but they could influence what happened to the rain once it reached the ground. By engaging in unwise methods of farming and generally pursuing an environmentally careless lifestyle, the people contributed to a condition that they would condemn as the wrath of nature, or of God. Americans cut down the trees; they cultivated the land wherever they found it—including on the hillsides—and often left the soil without vegetation for part of the year. They drained the swamps and wetlands that had helped hold the water in place to make room for more farming and more living space. The water as a result had nothing to do but run off quickly. The streams ran into rivers; the small rivers ran into large ones, and their banks could not control the flow. One could count on the floods virtually every spring in the years before the Second World War. Although almost any stream could flood almost any year in the eastern half of the nation, the territory most frequently plagued by floods was the area of the Ohio and Mississippi Rivers and their vast tributaries.

With the floods came death, destruction of property, loss of income, and demoralization, especially during the 1930s, which was a time of hardship for other reasons. There also was the permanent problem of water erosion, leaving land that was virtually useless for agriculture. Floods came every year in some places, but most harmful

TABLE 2.11 EFFECTS OF FLOODS, 1925–1945

Year	Lives Lost	Property Loss ($1,000)
1925	36	9,923
1926	16	23,468
1927	423	347,656
1928	15	44,611
1929	89	68,098
1930	14	15,850
1931	. . .	2,808
1932	11	10,295
1933	33	36,679
1934	88	10,362
1935	236	127,127
1936	142	282,549
1937	142	440,738
1938	180	101,098
1939	83	13,834
1940	60	40,467
1941	47	39,524
1942	68	98,507
1943	107	199,732
1944	33	101,079
1945	91	165,798

Source: Wattenberg, Statistical History, 448.

were the floods of 1927 in the Mississippi Valley, which killed more than 400 and left 700,000 homeless, and the annual floods of 1935–38. The great flood of 1937 in the Ohio and Mississippi Valleys killed nearly 150 and set a record for damage to property. For good reason the administration of Franklin D. Roosevelt gave much attention in the 1930s to the issues of soil conservation, flood control, and river development, of which the Tennessee Valley Authority was the best example.

High waters in the Ohio Valley cover Cincinnati's Coney Island Amusement Park in 1937. (The Cincinnati Historical Society)

Examples of damage caused by the great flood in the Ohio and Mississippi Valleys in 1937 are these overturned houses near Shawneetown, Illinois. (Library of Congress)

TABLE 2.12   MAJOR AMERICAN DAMS

One method of reducing floods was to hold back waters on the great rivers and their tributaries by building dams and thus creating lakes. Flood control was not the only factor behind the construction of the following dams (generation of electric power also was a major factor), but it was an important reason for many of them.

Capacity, Thousands of Acre Feet	Name	Location	Maximum Height, Feet	Date Completed
31,142	Hoover	Colorado River, Ariz.-Nev.	726	1936
19,412	Fort Peck	Missouri River, Mont.	250	1940
9,517	Grand Coulee	Columbia River, Wash.	550	1942
6,100	Kentucky	Tennessee River, Ky.	160	1944
6,089	Wolf Creek	Cumberland River, Ky.	242	a
5,825	Denison	Red River, Okla.-Tex.	165	1944
4,500	Shasta	Sacramento River, Calif.	602	1945
3,000	Salt Springs	North Fork, Mokelumne River, Calif.	345	1931
2,567	Norris	Clinch River, Tenn.	265	1936
2,300	Saluda	Saluda River, S.C.	208	1930

Floods and lack of protective vegetation left land that was often useless, as in this case in Alabama, 1937. (Arthur Rothstein, *The Depression Years*)

Capacity, Thousands of Acre Feet	Name	Location	Maximum Height, Feet	Date Completed
2,219	Elephant Butte	Rio Grande, N. Mex.	301	1916
2,092	Center Hill	Canev Fork River, Tenn.	240	a
2,000	Kingsley	North Platte River, Nebr.	162	1941
1,997	Osage (Bagnell)	Osage River, Mo.	148	1931
1,983	Norfolk	North Fork River, Ark.	230	1944
1,975	Pensacola	Grand River, Okla.	152	1940
1,934	Marshall Ford (Mansfield)	Colorado River, Tex.	270	1941
1,820	Davis	Colorado River, Ariz.-Nev.	200	a
1,706	Dale Hollow	Obey River, Tenn.-Ky.	183	1943
1,704	American Falls	Snake River, Idaho-Wyo.	92	1927
1,565	Cherokee	Holston River, Tenn.	212	1942
1,560	Sardis	Little Tallahatchie River, Miss.	117	1940
1,540	Douglas	French Broad River, Tenn.	160	1943
1,450	Fontana	Little Tennessee River, N.C.	470	1944
1,400	Roosevelt	Salt River, Ariz.	280	1911

[a] Under construction, 1945.
Source: Information Please Almanac, 1948 (New York, 1948), 631.

Norris Dam, here being completed in 1936, was part of the Tennessee Valley Authority, a major purpose of which was to hold back rivers and reduce floods. (Franklin D. Roosevelt Library)

Dust Storms of the 1930s

The great dust storms of the years 1932–40 were products of nature that were substantially worsened by practices of people who lived on the Great Plains. The high winds were aided by the level terrain and by the absence of trees to slow them down. That the winds became dust storms was attributable to a lack of rainfall and to the farmers' practice of destroying permanent vegetation, to their loosening the soil and leaving it vulnerable to the winds. The area involved stretched from Texas to Canada and from the Rocky Mountains to the western reaches of the Mississippi Valley. The states most affected were Texas, Oklahoma, Kansas, and Colorado. The large storms started coming in January 1932. The great black blizzard of November 11, 1933, darkened the sky from Texas to Canada. The storms of May 10–11, 1934, carried 300 million tons of soil from Texas and Oklahoma to New York City and Washington, D.C., and as far as 500 miles out to sea. The black blizzard of April 14, 1935,

that turned day into night all along the Great Plains was perhaps the most devastating of them all. Other major storms struck in May, June, and October 1937. The immediate loss of life was not as large as from other types of hazardous weather, but there were deaths of human beings and more of livestock (many of them from eating dirt mixed in with the feed), and the long-range consequences of dust storms rivaled that of other acts of nature. Millions of tons of priceless and virtually irreplaceable topsoil was lost, creating the great dust bowl in Oklahoma, Texas, Kansas, and the Dakotas. The will of a generation of people was tested, if not broken. Many of these families left farming, left the area for new territory, which in many cases turned out to be California. Although they departed from several states, including Oklahoma, as a group they were known as the Okies.

The "black blizzards" of the mid-1930s were perhaps as devastating as the floods. This storm of August 14, 1935, approaches Spearman, Texas. (Franklin D. Roosevelt Library)

Daylight Saving Time

If Americans could not manipulate the weather or the seasons, they did attempt to arrange the sun and the hours of daylight to suit their purposes. They introduced something called Daylight Saving Time to prolong the hours of light during spring and summer by advancing the clocks an hour. Daylight time was observed first in New York City in 1918, during the First World War, and in 1923 it was established, apparently permanently, with its institution to start at 2:00 A.M. on the last Sunday of April. Many American states, much of Canada, and several European and South American countries observed the change. Daylight Saving Time was replaced during the years 1942–45 by national War Time, to be observed throughout the nation from February 9, 1942, to September 30, 1945, at which point Standard Time was to be resumed. War Time called for moving the clocks ahead one hour during the prescribed hours, and it was to be the law of the land. There were, however, those individuals—surely die-hard Republicans—who were convinced in the 1930s and 1940s that Franklin D. Roosevelt was trying to change everything, from the economy and foreign policy to the date of Thanksgiving Day, and now he even was changing "God's Time." Rather than submit to an imposition of "Roosevelt's Time," they kept their clocks the way they were. Of course they would have to remember to start an hour before the rest of the people.

CHAPTER 3 Chronological Events, 1914–1945

The Period of the First World War

January 5, 1914 Henry Ford announces a revolutionary policy of paying workers $5.00 a day, up from $2.30 and approximately double what other auto manufacturers were paying.

January 14, 1914 The first complete endless-chain conveyor is installed at the Ford plant at Highland Park, Mich., making it possible to assemble a Model T in ninety-three minutes, one-eighth the previous time.

February 13, 1914 Music professionals organize the American Society of Composers, Authors, and Publishers (ASCAP) in New York City with Victor Herbert as director.

April 19, 1914 President Woodrow Wilson asks for authority to use force in response to the arrest of American sailors in Tampico, Mexico, and to deal with dictator Victoriano Huerta.

April 21, 1914 U.S. ships shell Veracruz, Mexico. Marines land.

May 7, 1914 Congress passes a bill stipulating that the second Sunday in May be designated Mother's Day.

June 28, 1914 Archduke Francis Ferdinand, heir apparent to the throne of Austria-Hungary, is assassinated, setting in motion events that will lead to the First World War.

July 15, 1914 Huerta, the object of Wilson's scorn, resigns the presidency of Mexico.

August 4, 1914 Britain declares war on Germany, a move that means that all major powers of Europe now have become engaged. Wilson proclaims U.S. neutrality in the war.

August 6, 1914 Ellen Axson Wilson, the president's wife, dies.

August 19, 1914 The Panama Canal opens to shipping.

August 19, 1914 Wilson unrealistically asks Americans to respond to the war in Europe by being neutral "in thought as well as in action."

September 5, 1914 A German offensive is stopped at the Battle of the Marne. A long stalemate then ensues on the Western front.

September 10, 1914 A new five-member Federal Trade Commission to regulate certain business practices becomes law.

October 15, 1914 Congress passes the Clayton Antitrust Act to assist in the battle against monopoly.

October 22, 1914 Congress passes the first income tax permissible under the new Sixteenth Amendment. Incomes over $3,000 are taxed.

November 2, 1914 Britain declares the North Sea a military zone. This and other British measures complicate U.S. efforts to trade with belligerents.

November 23, 1914 The United States withdraws troops from Veracruz, but strained relations with Mexico continue.

Other events of 1914 Yale Bowl, the first full-sized football stadium with almost 80,000 seats, opens in New Haven, Conn.

Edgar Rice Burroughs produces his first "Tarzan" book, *Tarzan of the Apes;* twenty-four more will follow.

Other publications include Joyce Kilmer's "Trees," Booth Tarkington's *Penrod,* and Robert Frost's first book, *North of Boston.*

January 25, 1915 The first transcontinental telephone call is made by Alexander Graham Bell in New York to Thomas A. Watson in San Francisco. As in 1876, Bell said, "Mr. Watson, come here, I want you."

January 26, 1915 Congress creates Rocky Mountain National Park in Colorado.

January 28, 1915 Congress creates the U.S. Coast Guard.

February 8, 1915 The first full-length film (twelve reels), D. W. Griffith's *Birth of a Nation,* opens in Los Angeles.

February 23, 1915 Nevada adopts a measure that reduces residency requirement for divorce to six months.

March 30, 1915 Wilson protests British blockade of German ports.

April 5, 1915 Jess Willard knocks out Jack Johnson in the twenty-sixth round to win the heavyweight boxing championship.

May 1, 1915 A German submarine torpedoes the U.S. tanker *Gulflight.* Germany apologizes.

May 7, 1915 The Cunard passenger liner *Lusitania* is sunk by a German submarine, a shocking deed that kills nearly 1,200 people, 124 of them Americans. The United States is outraged.

May 13, 1915 Wilson sends the first *Lusitania* note, a protest and list of demands made on Germany. The Germans proceed to haggle.

June 9, 1915 Wilson sends the second *Lusitania* note to Germany. Believing the message too harsh, William Jennings Bryan resigns as secretary of state.

July 21, 1915 Dissatisfied with the German response, Wilson sends a third *Lusitania* note, warning that further hostile submarine action would be deemed "deliberately unfriendly."

The Supreme Court invalidates the "grandfather clause," a device for preventing black people from voting in the southern states.

July 24, 1915 The steamer *Eastland* capsizes at Chicago pier; 852 perish.

July 28, 1915 U.S. Marines land at Port-au-Prince, Haiti, after political upheaval on that island. Haiti later becomes an American protectorate.

August 10, 1915 A military camp for civilians opens in Plattsburgh, N.Y. Other camps follow, based on the Plattsburgh model.

August 17, 1915 Leo Frank, a Jew convicted of murdering a white woman, is lynched in Marietta, Ga., after the governor had reduced his sentence to life imprisonment.

August 19, 1915 In seeming indifference to American opinion, a German submarine sinks the British liner *Arabic,* killing two Americans. U.S. threats eventually lead Germany to promise not to sink passenger ships.

October 19, 1915 The United States recognizes Venustiano Carranza as Mexico's president.

November 7, 1915 In Chicago 40,000 men march to protest closing saloons on Sunday.

November 14, 1915 Black leader Booker T. Washington dies in Tuskegee, Ala.

November 25, 1915 The Ku Klux Klan is revived in a ceremony at Stone Mountain, Ga., by William J. Simmons and fourteen others.

December 4, 1915 Henry Ford, who wants to end the war by Christmas, embarks on his "peace ship" for Europe.

December 18, 1915 President Wilson, a widower since August 1914, marries Edith Bolling Galt.

Other events of 1915 Edgar Lee Masters's *Spoon River Anthology* is published.

Ty Cobb sets the major-league base-stealing record at ninety-six.

Auto owners learn that pedestrians will pay for an intercity ride—thus the taxicab arrives on the scene. The cost is five cents.

January 1, 1916 The first permanent Rose Bowl game is played between Brown and Washington State Universities.

January 28, 1916 Wilson appoints Louis D. Brandeis, the first Jewish justice, to the United States Supreme Court.

February 28, 1916 World-known author Henry James dies at seventy-two.

February 29, 1916 South Carolina passes landmark legislation raising the minimum age for children working in mines, mills, and factories from twelve to fourteen.

March 9, 1916 The Mexican revolutionary leader Pancho Villa raids Columbus, N. Mex., killing seventeen. U.S. troops cross into Mexico, seeking out Villa's forces.

March 24, 1916 A German submarine strikes the French channel steamer *Sussex,* seemingly breaking previous promises. Americans are aboard but none die.

April 10, 1916 The first professional golf tournament is held in Bronxville, N.Y., by the Professional Golfers Association of America.

May 4, 1916 In reply to Wilson's threat to break relations over the *Sussex* incident, Germany promises to not attack cargo ships without warning.

June 3, 1916 A National Defense Act increases the standing army to 175,000, the National Guard to 450,000.

June 7, 1916 The Progressive Party nominates Theodore Roosevelt for the presidency, but he refuses to accept.

June 7–10, 1916 The Republicans meet and nominate Charles Evans Hughes and Charles W. Fairbanks for the presidential ticket.

June 14–16, 1916 The Democrats renominate Wilson and Vice President Marshall.

June 15, 1916 The Boy Scouts of America is incorporated by law.

June 17, 1916 Mexican officials threaten combat unless U.S. troops under John Pershing are withdrawn.

July 11, 1916 Wilson signs the Good Roads Bill, allocating $5 million to the states to build roads.

July 17, 1916 A Federal Farm Loan Act provides government loans for needy farmers.

July 18, 1916 Britain publishes a blacklist of U.S. firms that are to be denied British business because of their alleged dealing with the enemy. Many Americans, including Wilson, are angry.

July 22, 1916 James Whitcomb Riley, the "Hoosier poet," dies at age sixty-six.

July 30, 1916 German spies blow up ammunition supplies near Jersey City, N.J.

August 4, 1916 The United States signs a treaty to purchase the Virgin Islands from Denmark.

August 25, 1916 The organization that eventually becomes the National Park Service is established by law.

September 3, 1916 The president signs the Adamson Act, calling for the eight-hour day for workers on interstate railroads.

October 16, 1916 The first birth-control clinic is opened by Margaret Sanger in Brooklyn. She is later arrested for keeping a "public nuisance."

November 7, 1916 Riding on the slogan "He kept us out of war," Wilson defeats Hughes in a close election, although it takes three more days to determine the outcome. Democrats now control Congress.

November 22, 1916 Author Jack London commits suicide at age forty.

November 29, 1916 Political unrest leads the United States to impose military occupation on the Dominican Republic.

December 18, 1916 Wilson asks European belligerents to state their war aims, hoping thereby to create an opening for peace negotiations.

Other events of 1916 Carl Sandburg's *Chicago Poems* is published.

John Dewey proposes a "progressive" education in *Democracy and Education.*

What is deemed the Original Dixieland Jazz Band opens in Chicago.

Grover Cleveland Alexander pitches a record sixteen shutout games.

General John T. Thompson invents a submachine gun, to be known thereafter as the "Tommy gun."

January 22, 1917 Wilson tries again to end the war by calling for belligerents to accept "peace without victory."

January 28, 1917 Pershing's troops are recalled from Mexico after a long, futile search for Pancho Villa.

January 29, 1917 Wilson vetoes a bill that required a literacy test for immigrants; Congress later repasses the measure over the veto.

January 31, 1917 In an ominous move, Germany announces that unrestricted submarine warfare will resume the following day. All previous concessions are canceled.

February 3, 1917 Wilson breaks relations with Germany, normally a prelude to war.

February 5, 1917 A law excluding Asian laborers passes over a presidential veto.

March 1, 1917 The U.S. government allows publication of the Zimmermann telegram, a German document that outlines a secret conspiracy against the United States—a clear provocation.

March 2, 1917 Passage of the Jones Act makes Puerto Rico a territory and its people citizens of the United States.

Typical of the "hate the enemy" message of 1917–18, this poster urged people to buy government bonds and crush German bestiality. (National Archives)

March 4, 1917   With war on the horizon, Wilson is inaugurated for a second term.

March 8, 1917   The Senate adopts a cloture rule establishing conditions for ending debate.

March 12, 1917   The United States begins to arm its merchant vessels.

March 15, 1917   Americans are encouraged with news that the Russian Revolution has overthrown the despotic czarist regime.

March 18, 1917   The United States learns that Germany has been true to its threat and submarines have torpedoed three American ships.

April 2, 1917   Wilson delivers an eloquent war message to a special session of Congress.

Elected in 1916, Jeannette Rankin (R, Mont.) becomes the first woman member of the House.

April 6, 1917   By a vote of 82 to 6 in the Senate and 373 to 50 in the House, the United States declares war on Germany. Congresswoman Rankin votes no.

April 14, 1917   A government propaganda agency, the Committee on Public Information, is created. George Creel becomes its director.

April 24, 1917   Passage of a Liberty Loan Act establishes one means of raising money for the war. Liberty bonds go on sale.

May 18, 1917   Congress passes the Selective Service Act, starting a process of conscription. Young men aged twenty-one to thirty are to be affected.

June 14, 1917   Gen. John J. Pershing arrives in Paris to command U.S. forces. A token force arrives within two weeks.

June 15, 1917   Congress passes an Espionage Act to discourage opposition to the war effort.

July 24, 1917   Congress appropriates money to develop military aviation. A force of 4,500 aviators is anticipated. The first training field is at Rantoul, Ill.

August 10, 1917   Congress passes the Lever Food and Fuel Law, facilitating the creation of a wartime economy.

August 19, 1917   The first baseball game is played in the Polo Grounds, the National League park in New York. The managers of New York and Cincinnati are later arrested for violating a law prohibiting playing baseball on Sunday.

August 28, 1917   Women petitioning for the vote—the suffragettes—are arrested in front of the White House. Four will receive six-month sentences.

September 5, 1917   The offices of the Industrial Workers of the World are raided in twenty-four cities because of suspicion of antiwar activity.

October 3, 1917   Congress passes a War Revenue Act, increasing many kinds of taxes.

October 6, 1917   Passage of the Trading with the Enemy Law increases government authority over foreign trade and mail.

November 11, 1917   The constitution of the state of New York is changed to permit women to vote. The move provides a huge boost for the suffragette movement.

November 13, 1917   To save electricity, the National Fuel Administration orders electric advertising signs turned off on Thursdays and Sundays.

November 30, 1917   Members of the 42d ("Rainbow") Division, with soldiers from every state, begin to arrive in France.

December 7, 1917   The United States declares war on Austria-Hungary.

December 18, 1917   Congress sends to the states a proposed amendment that will prohibit the sale of alcoholic beverages.

The wartime Railroad Administration gives the government control over most railroads.

Other events of 1917   The Columbia School of Journalism announces its plan to begin offering Pulitzer Prizes in various areas of publication.

George M. Cohan writes his rousing, confident war song "Over There."

Bobbed hair for women takes hold in the United States.

January 8, 1918   President Wilson speaks to Congress on the issue of a settlement at the end of the war. He lists fourteen points as a basis for a just peace.

January 10, 1918   The House passes a woman suffrage amendment. The measure, however, eventually fails in the Senate.

January 26, 1918   Herbert Hoover, head of the Food Administration, calls for two wheatless, two porkless, and one meatless days each week.

February 8, 1918   The first edition of the army newspaper, *Stars and Stripes*, appears.

February 12, 1918   All Broadway theaters close to save coal.

The first keel is laid at Hog Island, Philadelphia, as part of the government's speeded-up program of building ships.

March 3, 1918   Russia, now under a radical Bolshevik government, signs a separate peace with Germany. Collapse of the Russian front places great pressure on the war in the West.

March 4, 1918   Bernard Baruch becomes head of the powerful War Industries Board.

March 7, 1918   Wilson authorizes the army to award a Distinguished Service Medal.

March 19, 1918   Congress authorizes advancing the clock one hour during March through October, a new system later called Daylight Saving Time.

April 8, 1918   The War Labor Board is created to handle labor disputes.

April 14, 1918   Having shot down five German aircraft, Lt. Douglas Campbell becomes the first American-trained ace.

May 15, 1918   The first airmail service begins between New York and Washington, D.C. Army pilots fly the planes.

May 16, 1918   Passage of a Sedition Act broadens the power of the government to act against criticism of the war.

June 3, 1918   U.S. troops participate in heavy fighting at Chateau-Thierry and later at Belleau Wood in France.

The Supreme Court in *Hammer v. Dagenhart* strikes down a national child labor law.

July 14, 1918   Quentin Roosevelt, Theodore's youngest son, dies in an air battle.

July 18, 1918   U.S. troops begin participation in a two-week Second Battle of the Marne, helping to stop a large German advance.

July 30, 1918,   Joyce Kilmer, thirty-one, author of "Trees" and other poems, dies in combat in France.

September 11, 1918   The Boston Red Sox defeat the Chicago Cubs 2–1 to win the World Series 4–2, ending a season shortened one month by the war. Babe Ruth pitched a shutout in the series' first game.

September 14, 1918   Pershing's troops capture the St. Mihiel salient.

Eugene V. Debs, Socialist labor leader and presidential candidate, is sentenced to prison for violation of the Sedition and Espionage Acts.

September 26, 1918   U.S. troops begin fighting in the area of the Meuse-Argonne. By the time the fighting stops, 1.2 million Americans will have served at the front.

October 1, 1918   Vote in the Senate fails by two to win necessary two-thirds majority to pass the woman suffrage amendment.

October 5, 1918   Prince Max of Baden, Germany's new chancellor, asks Wilson to arrange peace on the basis of his fourteen points. Wilson forwards the terms to the Allies.

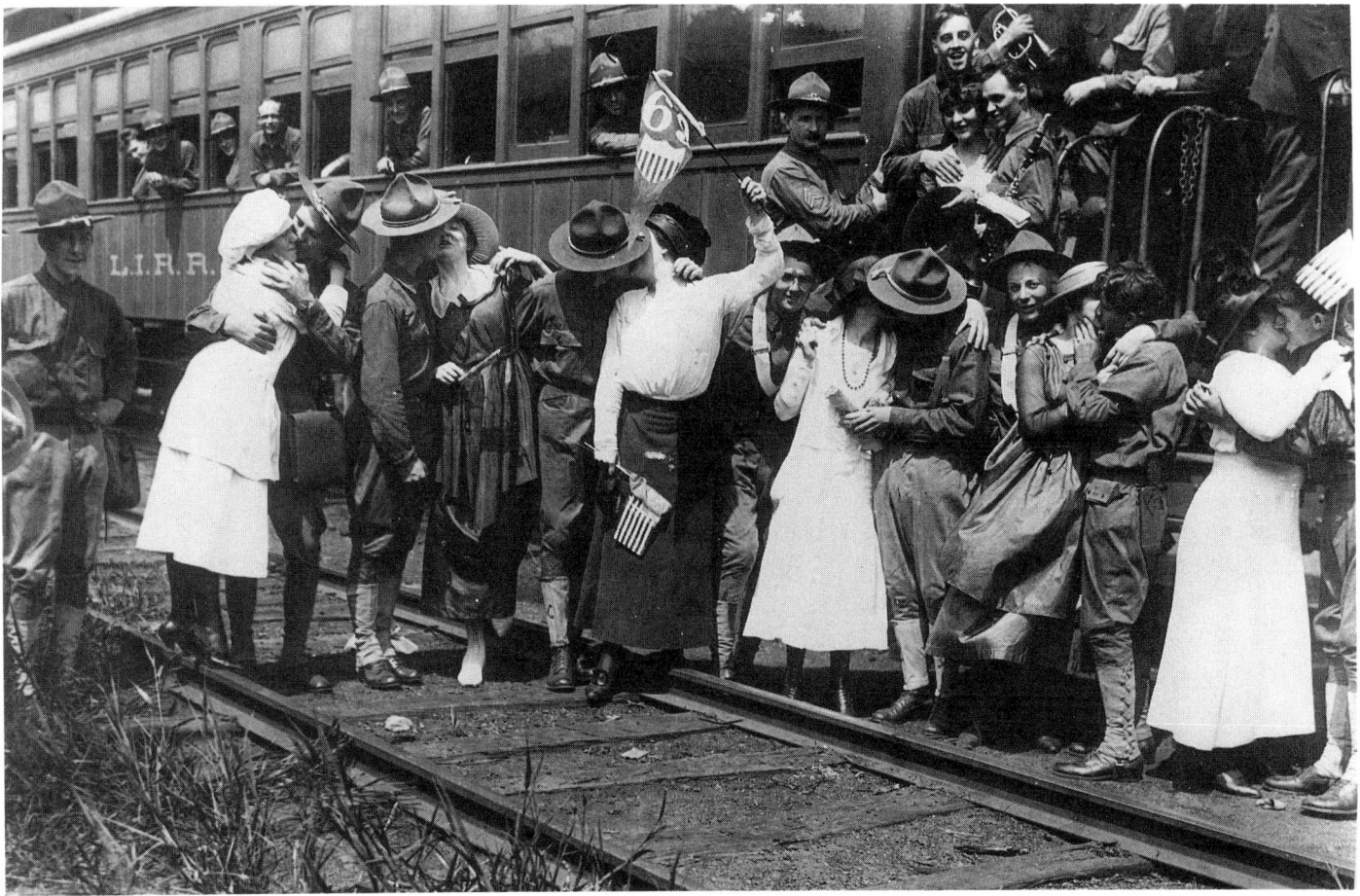

Amidst much hoopla and fond farewells, soldiers depart on a journey that will take them to the battlefields of France, 1918. (National Archives)

October 13–15, 1918 Forest fires in Wisconsin and Minnesota kill approximately 1,000.

November 2, 1918 Derailment of five subway cars in Brooklyn, N.Y., kills nearly 100.

November 4, 1918 Austria-Hungary surrenders and orders demobilization.

November 5, 1918 In national elections, Republicans gain twenty-six seats in the House, six in the Senate, and take control of both houses, further weakening the president's ability to formulate foreign policy.

November 7, 1918 Premature reports of peace spark wild demonstrations in New York.

November 9, 1918 Kaiser Wilhelm of Germany abdicates and flees the country.

November 11, 1918 The armistice is signed; the Great War is over and celebrations truly begin. The date will become a national holiday known as Armistice Day, later changed to Veterans Day.

November 18, 1918 Wilson announces that he will attend the peace conference in Paris personally. Many are critical of this decision.

November 21, 1918 Wilson signs a law prohibiting the sale of intoxicants from June 30, 1919, until the troops are demobilized.

December 4, 1918 With a large delegation of advisers, Wilson departs for France aboard the liner *George Washington* to begin participation in a momentous conference.

Other events of 1918 A gigantic influenza epidemic spreads to forty-six states, reaching a peak by the autumn. It kills between 400,000 and 500,000 and causes panic in many cities.

January 6, 1919 Former president Theodore Roosevelt dies at age sixty-one.

January 18, 1919 The peace conference—a negotiation between the victors—starts in Paris. Germany is not represented.

January 29, 1919 Nebraska accepts the Eighteenth Amendment on Jan. 16, and the prohibition amendment is ratified. Prohibition will go into effect on Jan. 16, 1920.

February 15, 1919 Wilson interrupts peace negotiations and returns home to handle national business. He returns to Paris approximately a month later.

March 4, 1919 As a foretaste of difficult times ahead for the president, Sen. Henry Cabot Lodge circulates a statement signed by thirty-seven senators saying that the League of Nations is unacceptable.

March 10, 1919 In the *Schenck* case the Supreme Court upholds the Espionage Act; Justice Oliver Wendell Holmes, Jr.'s "clear and present danger" doctrine explains that freedom of speech is not absolute.

March 15, 1919 Members of U.S. military units meet in Paris and form the American Legion.

June–July 1919 Twenty-five incidents of racial violence erupt during "Red Summer," leaving many dead and hundreds injured, notably in Washington, D.C., and Chicago, where thirty-eight die.

June 4, 1919 Congress adopts woman suffrage and sends a proposed Nineteenth Amendment to the states.

June 28, 1919 The long Paris Peace Conference ends with the signing of the controversial Treaty of Versailles, which contains

Members of the 105th Field Artillery in France celebrate the Armistice of November 11, 1918. (National Archives)

Wilson's League of Nations.

July 1, 1919 The first daily airmail service is established between Chicago and New York.

July 4, 1919 Jack Dempsey, twenty-four, becomes heavyweight boxing champion with a technical knockout of Jess Willard, thirty-seven, who is 6′ 6 1/2″ and weighs 243.

July 21, 1919 "Wingfoot," a balloon owned by Goodyear, crashes in downtown Chicago, killing twelve, injuring twenty-eight.

August 31, 1919 The American Communist Party is formed in Chicago. "Workers of the world unite" is the motto.

September 3, 1919 Wilson begins a speaking tour on behalf of his Treaty of Versailles, which has become the object of intense debate because of the League of Nations.

September 9, 1919 Most of Boston's police go on strike. Gov. Calvin Coolidge hires new police and issues a statement condemning the strike that makes him famous.

September 25, 1919 Troubled and very tired, Wilson collapses in Pueblo, Colo., suffers a stroke, and nearly dies. He partially recovers but is much weakened in his struggle for the League of Nations.

October 9, 1919 Cincinnati defeats the Chicago White Sox 10–4 to win the World Series 5–3. Eight Chicago players, the infamous "Black Sox," are later banned for life for fixing the series.

October 28, 1919 Congress passes the Volstead Act over Wilson's veto. Enforcing the Eighteenth Amendment, it defines an alcoholic beverage as anything containing more than 0.5% alcohol.

November 19, 1919 The Senate fails to ratify the Treaty of Versailles in two separate votes.

December 22, 1919 Atty. Gen. A. Mitchell Palmer organizes a series of raids against leftists and alleged disloyal people, as part of a large "Red Scare."

Other events of 1919 Booth Tarkington receives a Pulitzer Prize for *The Magnificent Ambersons.*

Henry Adams publishes *The Education of Henry Adams,* Sherwood Anderson *Winesburg, Ohio.*

Father Divine, a fundamentalist religious leader and spokesman for racial equality, receives national attention for his activities in Long Island.

Henry Ford opens his enormous River Rouge assembly plant at Dearborn, Mich.

The 1920s

January 16, 1920 Prohibition starts.

February 13, 1920 A partially ill Wilson discharges Secretary of State Robert Lansing; Bainbridge Colby replaces him.

February 28, 1920 Congress passes the Esch-Cummins Act, which returns railroads to private hands.

March 19, 1920 The Senate votes for a third and final time on the Treaty of Versailles. The vote is 49 to 35, short of the necessary two-thirds majority. The United States never joins the League of Nations.

April–September 1920 The United States dominates the Olympic Games in Antwerp, held after an eight-year interruption. Finland finishes a distant second.

May 5, 1920 Two Italian immigrants, Nicola Sacco and Bartolomeo Vanzetti, are arrested for murder in Braintree, Mass., touching off a long and emotional civil rights case.

May 8, 1920 The Socialist Party nominates Eugene Debs for the presidency despite the fact that he is still in national prison.

June 8–10, 1920 The Republican National Convention meets. After a deadlock between Leonard Wood and Frank O. Lowden, the Republicans choose Warren G. Harding of Ohio with Calvin Coolidge as the running mate.

June 28–July 6, 1920 A divided Democratic convention in San Francisco turns to James Cox as a compromise, with Franklin D. Roosevelt the vice presidential candidate.

August 26, 1920 The Nineteenth Amendment is ratified and women have the vote—barely in time for the presidential election.

September 8, 1920 Airmail service is established between New York and San Francisco.

October 30, 1920 A large parade of the Ku Klux Klan in Jacksonville, Fla., attracts much attention in the press.

November 2, 1920 The ticket of Harding and Coolidge trounces the Democrats, winning more than 60% of the popular vote. The first regular radio broadcast begins when KDKA (Pittsburgh) carries the election results.

November 8, 1920 Judge Kenesaw Mountain Landis becomes commissioner of baseball—part of the effort to clean up the tarnish on the game.

December 10, 1920 Woodrow Wilson receives the Nobel Peace Prize.

Other events of 1920 Life expectancy in the United States reaches 54.09 years, a gain of almost five years since 1901. For the first time the urban population exceeds the rural population.

F. Scott Fitzgerald's *This Side of Paradise* helps touch off the Jazz Age.

The Department of War officially adopts a shoulder patch to distinguish one army unit from another.

Baseball player Babe Ruth is sold by the Boston Red Sox to the New York Yankees for $125,000. When the Curtis Candy Company introduces a candy bar named Baby Ruth, the Babe sues for a part of the royalties. Curtis wins the case by arguing that the candy was named after Ruth Cleveland, the first child born to a president in the White House.

The Palace Hip Dancers in Seattle prove that in the 1920s showing a little ankle went a long way. (Museum of History and Industry, Seattle, Washington)

Detroit introduces a system of traffic lights, borrowing the signal colors from railroads.

January 3, 1921   Despite a provision in the Clayton Act, the Supreme Court refuses to exempt labor unions from antitrust prosecution.

March 4, 1921   Warren Harding is inaugurated as the twenty-ninth president of the United States.

April 20, 1921   The Senate ratifies a treaty that pays Colombia $25 million for the loss of Panama in 1903.

May 3, 1921   President Harding transfers naval petroleum reserves at Teapot Dome and two other sites to the Department of the Interior, laying the foundation for a monumental scandal that will follow.

May 19, 1921   Congress passes a law that bases immigration on a quota system: 3% of each given nationality in the United States in 1910 can immigrate.

June 3, 1921   Cloudbursts cause flooding of the Arkansas River, leading to $25 million in losses, near destruction of Pueblo, Colo., and 1,500 killed or missing.

June 10, 1921   The office of comptroller general and the Bureau of the Budget are created in the Treasury Department.

June 30, 1921   Harding appoints William Howard Taft chief justice of the Supreme Court.

July 2, 1921   Congress declares that war with Germany and Austria-Hungary is now over.

Jack Dempsey defeats Georges Carpentier of France in boxing's first million-dollar gate.

July 14, 1921   Gen. Billy Mitchell suggests the capabilities of bombing from the air with a test attack on condemned battleships.

October 5, 1921   Station WJZ in Newark offers—during the World Series—the first broadcast of a baseball game.

November 2, 1921   America's first Birth Control League is formed in New York under the leadership of Margaret Sanger.

November 11, 1921   The first Armistice Day as a legal holiday is celebrated with a ceremony at the Tomb of the Unknown Soldier in Arlington, Va.

November 12, 1921   The Washington Conference on naval disarmament opens. It meets until Feb. 6, 1922, and produces several treaties.

December 15, 1921   Harding pardons Eugene Debs.

Other events of 1921   By year's end women's skirts reach knee length and are still going up.

February 6, 1922   A Five-Power Pact is signed at the Washington Conference, limiting possession of battleships for the signatories (Britain, the United States, Japan, Italy, France).

February 21, 1922   The airship *Roma* strikes wires at Hampton Roads, Va., exploding and killing thirty-four of the crew.

April 1, 1922   Coal miners begin a long strike against wage reduction and other company practices. Conflict follows, notably in Herrin, Ill., on June 22.

May 12, 1922   A 20-ton meteor falls near Blackton, Va., creating a crater of more than 400 square feet.

May 23, 1922   *Abie's Irish Rose,* an ethnic-oriented play that will run more than five years, opens in New York.

May 30, 1922   The Lincoln Memorial is dedicated in Washington, D.C.

August 28, 1922   Radio station WEAF in New York broadcasts the first commercially sponsored program.

September 4, 1922   James H. Doolittle sets a record with a transcontinental flight in less (fifteen minutes less) than twenty-four hours.

September 12, 1922   Bishops of the Protestant Episcopal Church

vote 36–27 to remove "obey" from the marriage ceremony.

September 21, 1922   The Fordney-McCumber Tariff imposes record high duties on manufactured goods and farm products.

September 22, 1922   The Cable Act stipulates that women will no longer lose citizenship if they marry aliens.

October 3, 1922   Mrs. W. H. Felton of Georgia becomes the first woman to serve in the United States Senate when, in a token gesture, she is selected to fill out the term of her husband, who had died. She served one hour before the newly elected senator took over.

November 7, 1922   In congressional elections, the Republicans lose seventy seats in the House, seven in the Senate, but still control both chambers.

Other events of 1922   Louis Armstrong, brilliant coronetist from New Orleans, moves to Chicago to join Joseph "King" Oliver's jazz band.

Herbert T. Kalmus makes the first successful use of Technicolor, although it would not be put into general use until later.

Reader's Digest, founded by DeWitt Wallace, begins publication.

January 4, 1923   Emile Coue, French psychologist and creator of the Coue System of well-being through mental suggestion, is mobbed by admirers on arrival in New York.

January 23, 1923   Harding orders U.S. occupation troops withdrawn from Germany.

March 4, 1923   Congress passes a law establishing special banks to handle agricultural loans.

March 5, 1923   Montana and Nevada pass laws granting the nation's first old-age pensions.

March 13, 1923   Dr. Lee de Forest introduces "phonofilm," a new process for producing motion pictures with sound.

March 15, 1923   Charles F. Cramer, an official in the Veterans Bureau and member of Harding's "Ohio Gang," commits suicide as the story of high-level scandal proceeds to unfold.

March 23, 1923   A lively new newsmagazine entitled *Time,* the work of two young former Yale students, Henry R. Luce and Briton Fadden, makes its appearance.

April 18, 1923   Yankee Stadium opens in New York, becoming the home park for the Yankee baseball team of the American League.

May 9, 1923   A federal judge rules that prohibition does not limit prescriptions for whiskey written by doctors.

August 2, 1923   Tired and troubled, President Harding dies in San Francisco of somewhat mysterious causes. He was fifty-eight.

August 3, 1923   Calvin Coolidge is sworn in as thirtieth president by his father in Plymouth, Vt.

September 14, 1923   In a heavyweight title match, Jack Dempsey knocks out Luis Firpo in the second round, ending a bout marked with eleven knockdowns, including one that drove Dempsey out of the ring.

September 15, 1923   Activities of the Ku Klux Klan become so threatening in Oklahoma that Gov. J. C. Walton places the state under martial law.

November 6, 1923   Col. Jacob Schick is awarded a patent for an electric "dry" shaver.

December 6, 1923   In the first official presidential message on radio, Coolidge supports prohibition, low taxes, and the World Court but remains detached from a League of Nations.

Other events in 1923   DuPont begins manufacture of cellophane film through the purchase of a Swiss patent.

William Jennings Bryan spearheads a fundamentalist opposition to modernists who endorse the doctrine of evolution and its teaching in the schools.

New York installs a block signal stoplight system.

The hit of Broadway is the musical comedy *No, No, Nanette.*

February 3, 1924 Woodrow Wilson dies at his house on S Street in Washington, D.C.

February 12, 1924 George Gershwin's composition "Rhapsody in Blue" is first played by Paul Whiteman's orchestra.

March 31, 1924 The Supreme Court rules that Oregon cannot force school-age children to attend public school (as opposed to a parochial school)—a decision that in effect challenges the Klan.

April 9, 1924 The Dawes Plan, authored by an American banker, is presented and later accepted by Germany as a means of easing tension over reparations payments.

May 19, 1924 Congress passes, over a presidential veto, the Soldiers' Bonus Bill, providing annuities for most veterans of the First World War.

May 21, 1924 The Presbyterian Church officially rejects Charles Darwin's theory of evolution.

May 26, 1924 Congress passes the National Origins Act, which tightens the quota system to impose more stringent restrictions on immigration. It is an overt attempt to keep the population predominantly of northern European stock.

June 2, 1924 Congress passes a proposed amendment regulating child labor. The measure fails to receive approval by the states.

June 10, 1924 Henry Ford announces production of his ten millionth car. Ford lowers the price of a Model T this year to $290.

June 12, 1924 Meeting in Cleveland, the Republicans pick Coolidge and Charles G. Dawes for the presidential ticket.

June 30, 1924 Former secretary of the interior Albert Fall and others are indicted in the Teapot Dome scandal.

July 1, 1924 Congress passes the much-needed Rogers Act to reform and professionalize the American foreign service.

July 4, 1924 The Progressive Party nominates Robert M. LaFollette for the presidency and Burton K. Wheeler of Montana for the vice presidency.

July 9, 1924 Meeting in New York, the Democrats, after 103 ballots and sheer exhaustion, nominate John W. Davis of West Virginia and Charles W. Bryan of Nebraska for the presidential ticket.

July 21, 1924 A sensational trial comes to an end with the sentencing (life imprisonment) of Nathan Leopold and Richard Loeb for the "thrill-killing" of young Bobby Franks.

August 24, 1924 An Agriculture Credits Act is passed to help stave off farm bankruptcy—further evidence of the woes of farmers in the 1920s.

November 4, 1924 The Republican scandals have no effect as Coolidge trounces Davis 15,725,016 to 8,385,503. LaFollette the Progressive receives more than half as many votes as the Democrat.

November 9, 1924 Henry Cabot Lodge, Wilson's opponent and opponent of Wilson's League of Nations, dies at seventy-four.

Other events of 1924 Congress passes the Citizenship Act, granting citizenship to all Native Americans (although some states still withhold the right to vote).

The year sees the production of *The Student Prince* by Sigmund Romberg, *Rose Marie* by Rudolf Friml, and *All God's Chillun Got Wings* by Eugene O'Neill.

Notre Dame University's football team, coached by Knute Rockne, wins all nine games and is declared national champion.

Crossword puzzles, introduced in 1913, and now a national craze, appear in book form. Mah Jong is another national fad.

January 5, 1925 Completing her dead husband's term, Nellie Tayloe Ross becomes the first woman governor (of Wyoming) in the United States.

January 21, 1925 George Washington Cable, noted black novelist, dies at eighty.

January 24, 1925 Coolidge appoints Harlan F. Stone to the Supreme Court.

February 2, 1925 Relays of dog teams reach Nome, Alaska, with serum to combat a diphtheria epidemic. Gunnar Kasson, driver of the last leg, arrives blind and almost frozen. (This route later becomes that of the Iditarod dog sled race.)

February 26, 1925 Spelunker Floyd Collins dies still stuck in a cave in Kentucky, bringing a sad end to a national vigil of seventeen days.

March 4, 1925 Calvin Coolidge is inaugurated for his first full term. Characteristically, his speech deals with contentment.

March 18, 1925 Deadly tornadoes in five states of the Midwest and border states destroy thirty-five towns, kill 800, and injure 3,000.

May 13, 1925 Florida passes a measure requiring reading from the Bible in all public schools.

June 18, 1925 Robert M. LaFollette, perhaps the most important progressive leader, dies at seventy.

July 10, 1925 The trial of John T. Scopes—the "Monkey Trial"—begins in Dayton, Tenn. Scopes will be convicted of breaking a state law that forbade teaching evolution. The case highlights the growing controversy between fundamentalists and modernism and pits two famous, but poorly matched, attorneys against each other: William Jennings Bryan and Clarence Darrow.

July 26, 1925 Bryan, veteran of many campaigns, including three races for the presidency, dies in Dayton, Tenn., after a less than brilliant effort in his last crusade: the Scopes trial.

September 1925 Henry Ford reports that his Fords, previously all black, now also would be available in "deep channel green" and "rich Windsor maroon."

September 3, 1925 The army's dirigible *Shenandoah* crashes in a storm at Ava, Ohio—fourteen die.

October 28–December 17, 1925 Col. Billy Mitchell, army champion of air power who charged the military with incompetence and "criminal negligence," is court-martialed for insubordination. Found guilty and suspended, he resigns from the army.

November 3, 1925 James J. Walker—Beau James, as he is later called—is elected mayor of New York by a large margin.

December 10, 1925 Vice President Dawes receives the Nobel Peace Prize for his work in Europe's reparations controversy.

December 29, 1925 Trinity College in Durham, N.C., becomes Duke University in order to receive $40 million from the estate of tobacco producer James Buchanan Duke.

Other events of 1925 The year sees publication of *An American Tragedy,* by Theodore Dreiser, *Manhattan Transfer,* by John Dos Passos, *The Great Gatsby,* by F. Scott Fitzgerald.

The *New Yorker* magazine makes its first appearance.

A Nashville radio station begins broadcasting the "WSM Barn Dance," later renamed the Grand Old Opry.

In developing a masking tape to assist painting new cars, the 3M Company produces one with such little adhesive that a critic condemned it as "Scotch" tape.

January 27, 1926 The Senate approves U.S. participation, under certain conditions, in the Permanent Court of International Justice at The Hague.

February 9, 1926 The Board of Education in Atlanta prohibits the teaching of evolution in the public school system.

February 28, 1926 Coolidge approves a Revenue Act that reduces several kinds of taxes—a central theme of policy in the 1920s.

March 7, 1926 The first transatlantic conversation by radiotelephone is held between London and New York.

May 5, 1926 Sinclair Lewis rejects the Pulitzer Prize for his novel *Arrowsmith* on grounds that the prize inhibits creativity.

May 9, 1926 Richard E. Byrd and Floyd Bennett make the first flight over the North Pole.

May 10, 1926 U.S. Marines return to Nicaragua to quiet domestic unrest. They stay until June 5.

May 18, 1926 The apparent kidnapping of evangelist Aimee Semple MacPherson in California attracts national attention. She mysteriously reappears a few days later.

June 20, 1926 The First International Eucharistic Congress opens in Chicago.

July 2, 1926 Congress creates the Army Air Corps. The Distinguished Flying Cross is created for heroism in flight. In 1927 Charles A. Lindbergh will be the first recipient.

July 10, 1926 Lightning strikes a naval ammunition depot in New Jersey, killing thirty-one.

August 5, 1926 What is billed as the first "talking movie," *Don Juan,* with John Barrymore, opens in New York. Sound comes from a separate synchronized phonograph record.

August 6, 1926 Gertrude Ederle of New York becomes the first woman to swim the English Channel.

September 18, 1926 A hurricane sweeps Florida and the lower South, killing 372, injuring 6,000.

September 23, 1926 Gene Tunney defeats Jack Dempsey to become heavyweight champion as 120,000 watch in Philadelphia.

October 25, 1926 The Supreme Court rules that the president can remove executive officers without Senate approval, thus invalidating—somewhat belatedly, perhaps—a law of 1866 that had sparked the impeachment of Andrew Johnson.

Other events of 1926 The United States reaches agreement on war debts owed by several European countries—scaling down the amount and extending payment over many years.

Ernest Hemingway's *The Sun Also Rises* is published.

The Book-of-the-Month Club begins operations.

Innovator Henry Ford acts again, this time introducing the eight-hour day and five-day week for his workers.

The radio show "Sam and Henry" first airs. Changed to "Amos 'n' Andy," it will be one of the most popular ever, broadcast weekdays 7–7:15, P.M. until 1943, when it becomes weekly; later the show moves to television.

January 7, 1927 The first commercial telephone service opens between New York and London.

February 23, 1927 Congress passes a measure that creates a

Henry Ford in 1927 abandoned the reliable Model T and began producing the Model A. Ford and son Edsel here pose with the 1928 Model A. (From the Collections of Henry Ford Museum and Greenfield Village)

board to regulate radio. It later will be called the Federal Communications Commission.

March 3, 1927 A Prohibition Bureau is established within the Department of the Treasury.

March 7, 1927 In *Nixon v. Herndon* the Supreme Court invalidates a law in Texas that prevented black people from voting in primary elections.

April 7, 1927 The first successful demonstration of television takes place in New York. Herbert Hoover in Washington appears on the screen.

April 17, 1927 Gov. Al Smith of New York, a potential candidate for the presidency, denies that his Catholic faith would interfere with exercise of the presidential duties.

April–May 1927 Floods devastate the lower Mississippi River area. Hundreds drown, and more than 600,000 are left homeless. Herbert Hoover calls it the nation's "greatest peacetime calamity."

May 16, 1927 The new Academy of Motion Picture Arts and Sciences meets at the Roosevelt Hotel in Hollywood to present its first annual awards, to be known as "Oscars."

May 20–21, 1927 Charles A. Lindbergh makes the first solo nonstop transatlantic flight. In the *Spirit of St. Louis* he flies from New York to Paris, 3,600 miles in thirty-three hours, thirty-nine minutes; 100,000 greet him in France. He stood, perhaps, as the nation's foremost hero of the decade.

June 28, 1927 Two army pilots, Lester Maitland and Albert Hegenberger, fly from San Francisco to Hawaii.

July 29, 1927 The first electric respirator—the "iron lung"—is used at Bellevue Hospital in New York City.

August 2, 1927 President Coolidge says, surprisingly and somewhat ambiguously, that he does "not choose" to run for reelection the next year.

August 27, 1927 Sacco and Vanzetti are executed in Massachusetts.

September 27, 1927 Babe Ruth hits his sixtieth home run for the season, in Yankee Stadium—a new record and one that will stand for many years.

September 29, 1927 A tornado of only five minutes' duration kills eighty-seven and injures 1,500 in St. Louis.

October 6, 1927 The first true "talkie" movie, with soundtrack on the film—*The Jazz Singer,* with Al Jolson—is released in New York.

October 10, 1927 The Supreme Court invalidates Albert Fall's lease of Teapot Dome Oil Reserve on the grounds that it was fraudulent.

November 19, 1927 The first underwater vehicular tunnel—the Holland Tunnel, 1.8 miles under the Hudson River from New York to New Jersey—opens to commercial traffic.

December 2, 1927 Henry Ford's new multicolored automobile, the Model A, is introduced to the public.

December 17, 1927 The American submarine S-4 sinks after striking a destroyer. Divers hear but cannot respond to pleas for help inside the vessel that last three days. The entire crew of forty perishes.

December 27, 1927 The musical *Showboat,* produced by Flo Ziegfeld with music by Jerome Kern and Oscar Hammerstein II, opens on Broadway. From a book by Edna Ferber, the show introduces "Ol' Man River" and several other notable songs.

Other Events of 1927 John D. Rust develops the first mechanical cotton picker.

The Brookings Institution is established in Washington, D.C.

January 16, 1928 The Pan-American Conference opens in Havana, Cuba. President Coolidge calls for cooperation and peace among the nations of the Western Hemisphere.

February 6, 1928 The United States and France sign an arbitration treaty on the 150th anniversary of the Treaty of Alliance of 1778.

February 10, 1928 The Senate adopts a resolution strongly critical of a president's serving more than two terms.

Radiotelephone service begins between the United States and Germany.

February 21, 1928 Oilman Harry F. Sinclair is sentenced to six months in prison for contempt of court as part of the Teapot Dome scandal.

March 4, 1928 A group of 274 men depart Los Angeles, determined to walk to New York City; fifty-five make it.

March 9, 1928 The House rejects an amendment to change the president's inauguration from March to January.

March 13, 1928 A dam breaks north of Los Angeles, flooding Santa Clara Valley and killing 450.

May 3, 1928 Congress passes for a second time the McNary-Haugen bill, designed to have the government help shore up farm prices. Coolidge will veto the measure for a second time.

May 11, 1928 Station WGY in Schenectady, N.Y., begins scheduled television broadcasts.

May 25, 1928 Amelia Earhart becomes the first woman to fly the Atlantic, as a passenger. In 1932 she does it again but as the pilot.

June 11–15, 1928 The Republicans meet in Kansas City, Mo., and nominate Herbert Hoover for the presidency and Charles Curtis for the vice presidency.

June 26–29, 1928 The Democrats assemble in Houston, Tex., and nominate Alfred E. Smith and Joseph T. Robinson for the presidential ticket.

July 29–Aug. 12, 1928 The ninth Olympic Games take place in the Netherlands. The United States leads the way in medals with twenty-four gold, twenty-one silver, seventeen bronze.

July 30, 1928 To a select audience in Rochester, N.Y., George Eastman gives a first exhibition of color motion pictures.

August 27, 1928 After several months of discussion, mostly by the United States and France, fifteen countries sign the Kellogg-Briand Pact, which outlaws war. Eventually sixty-two nations will sign, but, alas, the treaty has no provision for enforcement.

September 27, 1928 The United States recognizes the Nationalist regime in China, the government of Chiang Kai-shek.

November 6, 1928 After a campaign marked with reference to Al Smith's Roman Catholic faith, Hoover and Curtis score a large presidential victory, carrying forty of forty-eight states.

The *New York Times* installs the first moving electric sign at Times Square. Not surprisingly, the sign carries the election returns.

November 12, 1928 Notre Dame upsets the Army football team 12–6. Before the game, coach Knute Rockne reportedly urges his players to remember a deceased teammate and "win one for the Gipper."

November 16, 1928 The New York Stock Exchange reports record trading of 6,641,250 shares. The great bull market moves on.

November 19, 1928 President-elect Hoover departs for a South American tour aboard the battleship *Maryland.* Police in Argentina will foil an attempt to assassinate him.

Other events of 1928 George Gershwin composes "An American in Paris."

Walt Disney releases the first animated sound film, *Steamboat Willie,* which introduces what will become Mickey Mouse to the public.

The Depression and the New Deal

January 12, 1929 An eight-mile railroad tunnel through the Cascades, the longest in the United States, opens in Washington State.

January 15, 1929 The Senate approves the Kellogg-Briand Pact—which seeks to outlaw war—by a vote of 85–1.

February 2, 1929 In an effort to cool off speculation on Wall Street, the Federal Reserve Board forbids member banks to loan money to buy stocks on margin.

February 11, 1929 An American, Owen Young, leads an international team that reduces and revises reparation demands made on Germany.

February 13, 1929 In a move that perhaps suggests a new arms race, Congress authorizes the construction of nineteen new cruisers and one aircraft carrier.

February 14, 1929 Members of Al Capone's underworld organization, dressed as police, line six members of the rival gang of Buggsy Moran against a wall in a garage in Chicago and shoot them down. The incident becomes known as the "St. Valentine's Day Massacre."

March 4, 1929 Herbert Hoover is inaugurated as the thirty-first president of the United States.

April 4, 1929 The police commissioner of New York City reports that there are 32,000 speakeasies (illegal saloons) in the city and that prohibition had caused a great increase in crime.

April 10, 1929 Tornadoes kill fifty-six and injure more than 200 in Arkansas.

May 17, 1929 Mobster Al Capone pleads guilty to carrying a concealed weapon and receives a one-year prison sentence.

May 27, 1929 Hoover appoints a special commission chaired by George Wickersham to study the effects of prohibition.

The Supreme Court upholds the constitutionality of the presidential "pocket veto."

Charles Lindbergh marries Anne Morrow, daughter of the U.S. ambassador to Mexico.

June 15, 1929 An Agricultural Marketing Act assists in the creation of farm cooperatives, a tactic meant to increase prices for farm goods.

July 10, 1929 New paper currency, smaller than the old, begins circulation.

September 24, 1929 Gen. James Doolittle makes the first airplane flight at Mitchell Field in New York flying "blind," that is, using only instruments.

October 7, 1929 Ramsay MacDonald becomes the first British prime minister to speak before Congress. He supports naval disarmament.

October 22, 1929 Although some people are concerned about the large withdrawal of capital from the United States and the steady slide in stock prices, the president of National City Bank expresses confidence in the stock market and American business.

October 24, 1929 Prices fall sharply; thirteen million shares change hands on this "Black Thursday," and efforts by Rockefeller, Morgan, and others cannot stop the fall.

October 29, 1929 Thereafter known as "Black Tuesday," the market faces the worst day in its history as sixteen million shares are sold and the bottom drops out of prices. The collapse sets in motion events that lead to the Great Depression.

November 11, 1929 Ambassador Bridge, linking Detroit and Windsor, Ontario, is dedicated.

November 21, 1929 Hoover meets separately with leaders of business and trade unions, to promote national assurance and seek out general goals.

November 29, 1929 Richard E. Byrd and Bernt Balchen make the first airplane flight over the South Pole.

December 2, 1929 Secretary of State Henry Stimson urges Russia and China to settle peacefully their armed dispute over Manchuria.

December 3, 1929 In the annual message to Congress Hoover asserts that confidence in the nation's business climate has been restored.

December 17, 1929 An explosion in a coal mine in Oklahoma kills fifty-nine.

Other events of 1929 Thomas Wolfe's first novel, *Look Homeward, Angel,* and Ernest Hemingway's *Farewell to Arms* are published.

Acting on a complaint from the Daughters of the American Revolution, police raid Margaret Sanger's birth-control clinic in New York and arrest several people.

Miniature golf becomes a fad.

The New York Yankees try a new practice of putting numbers on the back of players' uniforms, assigning numbers in accordance with the place in the batting order. Because he batted third, Ruth earned number 3; Gehrig batted fourth.

February 3, 1930 Hoover appoints Charles Evans Hughes to replace ailing William Howard Taft as chief justice. Taft will die on March 8.

February 10, 1930 A federal grand jury indicts thirty-one corporations and 158 people for participating in a bootleg ring that sold seven million gallons of illegal whiskey.

March 4, 1930 The Coolidge Dam on the Gila River in Arizona is dedicated by the former president.

March 13, 1930 The Lowell Observatory in Flagstaff, Ariz., announces identification of a new planet named Pluto.

April 6, 1930 Frank Hawks completes the first cross-country flight in a glider towed by a biplane. The journey took eight days.

April 21, 1930 A fire in the vastly overcrowded state penitentiary at Columbus, Ohio, causes the death of 318 prisoners.

May 11, 1930 The Adler Planetarium, first in the United States, opens in Chicago.

May 20, 1930 The Senate, having turned down the nomination of John J. Parker for the Supreme Court, now confirms Owen J. Roberts for the judicial seat.

June 12, 1930 Max Schmeling of Germany becomes heavyweight boxing champion after being fouled by Jack Sharkey.

June 17, 1930 Hoover signs the highly protective Smoot-Hawley Tariff, even though many economists urge him to veto the measure.

July 3, 1930 Congress creates the Veterans Administration.

August 1930 The lower Midwest and South experience severe drought, adding more woes for a depression-stricken land.

September 3, 1930 Two French pilots end their flight across the Atlantic in New York, reversing Lindbergh's journey.

Thomas Edison's electric passenger train makes a first run on the Lackawanna Railroad in New Jersey.

September 27, 1930 Bobby Jones becomes the first golfer to win the four most important tournaments in one year.

November 4, 1930 The Democrats win several seats and take control of the House of Representatives. While Democrat gains in the Senate are also impressive, the Republicans retain a one-seat edge.

November 5, 1930 Fire and explosions kill seventy-nine in a coal mine in Ohio.

Sinclair Lewis receives the Nobel Prize in literature for *Babbitt,* the first American to be so honored.

December 11, 1930 The Bank of the United States in New York, with sixty branches and 400,000 depositors, closes, the largest bank failure in American history. Two weeks later the Chelsea Bank and Trust in New York also closes.

December 20, 1930 With unemployment estimated at seven million, Congress passes an appropriation of $116 million for work projects.

December 28, 1930 The state capitol in Bismarck, N. Dak., burns to the ground.

Other events of 1930 The Institute for Advanced Study is established at Princeton University.

A painting that catches the public eye is *American Gothic* by Grant Wood.

A copy of James Joyce's novel *Ulysses,* arriving at a New York publisher from Paris, is deemed obscene and seized by the Bureau of Customs.

A new soft drink labeled Bib-Label Lithiated Lemon-Lime Soda hits the market. Later it will be renamed 7-Up.

January 19, 1931 A report of the Wickersham Commission suggests that prohibition cannot be enforced. Even so, the report does not recommend repeal of the Eighteenth Amendment.

February 7, 1931 Pilot Amelia Earhart marries publisher George Putnam.

February 19, 1931 Congress passes a law permitting veterans to borrow on their bonus certificates. Shortly afterward, the measure is repassed over a presidential veto.

February 23, 1931 Congress authorizes the operation of power and fertilizer plants at Muscle Shoals on the Tennessee River, a forerunner of the Tennessee Valley Authority. Hoover vetoes the measure, thus killing the project.

March 3, 1931 "The Star-Spangled Banner" is officially adopted as the national anthem.

March 13, 1931 The legislature in Massachusetts urges Congress to move to repeal the Eighteenth (prohibition) Amendment.

March 20, 1931 Gambling becomes legal in Nevada.

March 25, 1931 Nine young black men (one only twelve years old) are arrested in Scottsboro, Ala., for raping a white woman. The case of the "Scottsboro boys" becomes one of the most lengthy and celebrated episodes in the history of racial relations in the United States.

May 1, 1931 The Empire State Building opens in New York City. It remains the world's tallest building for more than forty years.

June 20, 1931 Aware of troubles in international economics, Hoover proposes a one-year moratorium on reparations and war debts payments.

September 18, 1931 Japan invades Manchuria, a major first step toward a major war (a branch of the Second World War) in Asia.

September 22, 1931 The United States Steel Corporation announces a 10% reduction in wages for 220,000 workers.

October 1931 By the end of this month more than 800 banks will have closed in two months. Panic sets in and people start to hoard gold.

October 5, 1931 Hugh Herndon and Clyde Pangborn arrive in Wenatchee, Wash., after completing the first nonstop flight across the Pacific Ocean—4,860 miles.

October 17, 1931 Mobster Al Capone is convicted of income tax evasion and receives a prison sentence of eleven years.

October 18, 1931 Thomas Alva Edison, a giant of American technology, dies at eighty-four in New Jersey.

October 25, 1931 The George Washington Bridge, a suspension bridge linking New York and New Jersey, opens to traffic.

December 7, 1931 Hundreds of "hunger marchers" arrive in Washington and are turned away as they attempt to petition the White House for a program of employment.

December 8, 1931 Hoover's message to Congress requests more taxes to eliminate a deficit of nearly $1 billion.

Other events of 1931 William Faulkner's *Sanctuary* is published, as is Pearl Buck's *The Good Earth,* a novel about China that will be a runaway best-seller.

The *New York World,* long a popular newspaper, shuts down in February.

Two Americans, Jane Addams and Nicholas Murray Butler, share the Nobel Peace Prize.

Babe Ruth earns $80,000 playing for the Yankees. When someone pointed out that he made more than President Hoover (who received $75,000), the Babe replied: "Why not? I had a better year."

January 7, 1932 Secretary of State Henry Stimson protests Japan's invasion of Manchuria by refusing to recognize any change in the status of northeast China. This position becomes known as the Stimson Doctrine.

January 22, 1932 The Reconstruction Finance Corporation (RFC) is established to loan money to banks and other institutions, in tune with a "trickle down" theory of easing the effects of the depression.

January 31, 1932 Managers and employees of most railroads agree to lower wages 10% for the following year.

February 4, 1932 Gov. Franklin D. Roosevelt of New York opens the winter Olympic Games at Lake Placid, N.Y.

February 27, 1932 Congress passes the Glass-Steagall Act, giving the Federal Reserve more control over interest rates and authorizing the government to release gold into the market.

March 1, 1932 Baby Charles Lindbergh, Jr., age 1½, is kidnapped.

March 3, 1932 The Twentieth Amendment is sent to the states for ratification. This "lame duck" amendment moves the president's inauguration from March 4 to Jan. 20.

March 21, 1932 Tornadoes in five southern states kill 360.

March 23, 1932 Organized labor applauds the passage of the Norris-LaGuardia Act, which limits use of injunctions and other devices against union activity.

May 12, 1932 Charles Lindbergh, Jr., is found dead despite a ransom payment of $50,000. An outraged public induces several states to adopt the death penalty for such crimes. From prison Al Capone offers a $10,000 reward. More than two years later Bruno Richard Hauptmann will be apprehended and later executed for the crime.

May 14, 1932 Demonstrators in Detroit, New York, and other cities march for ten hours demanding the sale of beer.

May 20, 1932 Amelia Earhart becomes the first woman to fly the Atlantic solo, albeit following a shorter route than Lindbergh—from Newfoundland to Ireland.

May 29, 1932 Members of the "Bonus Army" arrive in Washington: veterans who demand immediate payment of bonuses. Congress fails to agree. Later, troops commanded by Douglas MacArthur drive them from encampment near the Capitol.

June 14–16, 1932 Republicans meet in Chicago to renominate the ticket of Hoover and Curtis.

June 21, 1932 Jack Sharkey returns the heavyweight boxing championship to the United States, winning a fifteen-round decision over Max Schmeling.

June 27–July 2, 1932 Democrats meet in Chicago and nominate Franklin D. Roosevelt and John Nance Garner of Texas. Accepting the nomination in person, Roosevelt promises a "new deal" for the country.

July 15, 1932   Amidst evidence of a deepening depression, Hoover announces an intent to reduce his salary by 20%.

July 18, 1932   Canada and the United States agree to build the St. Lawrence Seaway, linking the Great Lakes to the Atlantic Ocean.

July 30, 1932   The games of the Tenth Olympiad open in Los Angeles.

September 1, 1932   Besieged by charges of corruption, Mayor James Walker of New York resigns.

September 9, 1932   The steamer *Observation* blows up in the East River in New York City, killing seventy and injuring many more.

November 8, 1932   Roosevelt defeats Hoover by more than seven million votes, carrying all but seven states. The Democrats also dominate Congress by large margins.

November 11, 1932   The Tomb of the Unknown Soldier is dedicated at Arlington National Cemetery.

December 5, 1932   Renowned scientist Albert Einstein comes to the United States from Germany. He begins work at Princeton's Institute for Advanced Study.

December 27, 1932   Radio City Music Hall opens at Rockefeller Center in New York City.

In the depths of the Great Depression in 1932, the army routs veterans of the First World War who had come to Washington to demand payment of a bonus. (National Archives)

Other events of 1932   Wheat prices drop to $0.32 a bushel this year, as compared with $2.33 in 1920. The Department of Agriculture reports that the average farmer cleared $341 in 1931, compared with $847 in 1929. Unemployment reaches thirteen million. For good reason a popular song is "Brother, Can You Spare a Dime?"

January 4, 1933   At a farm foreclosure sale in Iowa, a mob threatens to lynch an agent of a life insurance company if he does not bid enough to cover the farm's mortgage. He does.

January 5, 1933   Calvin Coolidge, age sixty, dies in Massachusetts.

January 30, 1933   The radio show "The Lone Ranger" begins on station WXYZ in Detroit.

February 6, 1933   The Twentieth Amendment—which moves the start of the new presidential term to Jan. 20—becomes part of the Constitution.

February 15, 1933   An assassin fires at President-elect Roosevelt in Miami, Fla. Although Roosevelt is uninjured, shots hit several people, including Mayor Anton Cermak of Chicago, who will die three weeks later.

February 20, 1933   Congress votes to repeal the prohibition amendment. The proposed Twenty-first Amendment goes to the states for ratification.

February 25, 1933   America's first aircraft carrier, the *Ranger,* enters naval service.

March 4, 1933   Roosevelt is inaugurated as the thirty-third president. In this time of economic catastrophe, he projects an air of hope, saying, "The only thing we have to fear is fear itself."

March 5, 1933   Roosevelt declares a bank holiday until March 9, halts export of hard currency, and calls Congress into special session. Congress validates most of these moves on March 9.

March 10, 1933   Earthquakes in Los Angeles kill 120 and injure many more.

March 13, 1933   Banks start to reopen; by month's end approximately 75% of them are operating.

March 20, 1933   Roosevelt signs a measure reducing veterans' benefits and government salaries (by 15%).

March 22, 1933   Congress passes a new Volstead Act, legalizing sale of 3.2% beer and wine and placing a tax on such beverages.

March 31, 1933   Congress creates the Civilian Conservation Corps (CCC) to employ men aged eighteen to twenty-five on useful conservation projects.

April 4, 1933   The navy's dirigible *Akron* sinks in the Atlantic with loss of seventy-two of the crew.

April 19, 1933   Roosevelt takes the United States off the gold standard; currency is no longer redeemable in gold.

May 1–5, 1933   Tornadoes in the lower South kill ninety-nine and do much damage.

May 12, 1933   Congress establishes the Federal Emergency Relief Administration. Under Harry Hopkins, it assists the states in aiding the poor and hungry. Congress creates the Agriculture Adjustment Act (AAA) to subsidize farmers and raise prices for farm goods by limiting production.

May 18, 1933   Building on the Muscle Shoals idea, Congress creates the Tennessee Valley Authority (TVA), a broad project for revitalizing the entire Tennessee River valley.

May 27, 1933   Congress approves policing of the stock exchanges, a job to be undertaken by the Federal Trade Commission.

June 6, 1933   The first drive-in theater opens in Camden, N.J.

June 13, 1933   The Home Owner Loan Corporation is established to refinance mortgages of homes about to be foreclosed.

June 16, 1933   On this final day of Roosevelt's "hundred days," Congress passes what is heralded as the most important depression-fighting measure: the National Industrial Recovery Act (NIRA or NRA), the symbol of which is the Blue Eagle. The same law establishes a Public Works Administration (PWA) to funnel money into work-relief projects. Congress also passes the Glass-Steagall Act, which creates a Federal Deposit Insurance Corporation to protect bank deposits.

June 21, 1933   Enormous Primo Carnera (6′ 6″, 260 lbs.) defeats Jack Sharkey to become world heavyweight boxing champion.

June 22, 1933   The Illinois Ship Canal opens to link the Great Lakes with the Gulf of Mexico.

July 6, 1933   In the first all-star baseball game, the American League defeats the National League 4–2 at Comiskey Park in Chicago.

July 29, 1933   Gov. Gifford Pinchot mobilizes the militia to keep order in the strike-ridden coal fields of Pennsylvania.

August 5, 1933   Roosevelt creates a National Labor Board to police labor provisions of the NIRA.

September 13, 1933   More than 250,000 march in New York in support of the Blue Eagle and the NIRA.

November 7, 1933   Fiorello LaGuardia is elected mayor of New York City, ending a long rule by Tammany Hall and beginning a long tenure in office by the "Little Flower."

November 8, 1933   Congress creates the Civil Works Administration to provide work relief for some four million.

November 11, 1933   An enormous dust storm, the "great black blizzard," darkens the sky from Texas to Canada, carrying soil hundreds of miles to the east.

November 16, 1933   The United States and the Soviet Union formally establish diplomatic relations, ending a sixteen-year period of no relations with the Communist government.

December 4, 1933   *Tobacco Road,* from an earthy novel by Erskine Caldwell, begins a long, long run on Broadway.

December 5, 1933   Prohibition ends as national policy. Utah becomes the thirty-sixth state to ratify the Twenty-first Amendment. The states now control the sale of alcohol.

December 17, 1933   In Chicago the Chicago Bears defeat the New York Giants 23–21 to win the first National Football League championship.

Other events in 1933   The nation observes a splurge of depression-fighting legislation, much of it passed during the period from March to June, the so-called Hundred Days. The measures belong to Roosevelt's New Deal.

Frances Perkins, secretary of labor, becomes the first woman cabinet member.

January 1, 1934   Dr. Francis Townsend of California unveils his simplistic "Old Age Revolving Pensions Plan" that attracts many supporters.

January 7–10, 1934   Fighting breaks out as farmers try to prevent delivery of milk to Chicago. They hope that an embargo on supply will cause prices to rise.

January 31, 1934   Using power under the Gold Reserve Act, Roosevelt devalues the dollar to 59.06 cents.

January 31, 1934   Congress passes a Farm Mortgage Refinancing Act to help prevent loss of individual farms.

February 2, 1934   The Export-Import Bank of the United States is created by executive order.

February 9, 1934   Amidst charges of bribery paid by private airlines, Roosevelt orders the army to start carrying airmail.

March 13, 1934   Henry Ford restores the practice of paying five dollars a day to most of his company's workers.

March 24, 1934   The Tydings-McDuffee Act guarantees independence to the Philippine Islands ten years after the Philippines approve (they do so in 1934).

April 12, 1934   A Senate committee, chaired by Gerald P. Nye, begins an inquiry into profiteering, especially by arms manufacturers, during the First World War.

April 18, 1934   The legislature in Puerto Rico requests statehood.

May 10–11, 1934   Dust storms on the Great Plains remove 300 million tons of topsoil, some of it carried as far east as the Atlantic Ocean. Fostered by drought and unwise farming practices, the series of storms creates a dust bowl.

May 23, 1934   Gangsters Clyde Barrow and Bonnie Parker are killed by police in a shootout in Louisiana. Brutal but colorful, the couple even was regarded as glamorous. Clyde once had written the Ford Motor Company to praise the "dandy" car, saying he always chose a Ford when he "could get away with one."

May 28, 1934   Americans take extraordinary interest in the birth in Canada of the Dionne quintuplets—all girls. The Dionne farm in lower Ontario will become a major tourist attraction.

June 6, 1934   Congress creates a new Securities and Exchange Commission, to police the stock market.

June 12, 1934   A Reciprocal Trade law permits the president to negotiate lower tariffs with other nations.

June 19, 1934   Congress creates the Federal Communications Commission to regulate radio and other communications.

June 28, 1934   A law creates the Federal Housing Authority, to facilitate construction and repair of private dwellings.

July 16, 1934   Longshoremen strike in San Francisco, only one of many work stoppages this year.

July 22, 1934   Gangster John Dillinger, public enemy number one and almost a folk hero, is gunned down by the FBI outside the Biograph Theater in Chicago.

September 8, 1934   Fire aboard the cruise ship *Morro Castle* off the coast of New Jersey leads to the death of 130.

October 22, 1934   Fugitive Charles "Pretty Boy" Floyd is killed by federal agents at a farm in Ohio.

October 25, 1934   A train of the Union Pacific sets a speed record traveling from Los Angeles to New York City in fifty-seven hours.

November 6, 1934   In national elections, the Democrats add nine seats in the House and nine in the Senate to an already substantial majority in Congress. Harry S. Truman of Missouri is one of the new senators.

Other events of 1934   The Legion of Decency of the Roman Catholic Church begins reviewing and classifying all films as to their suitability for Catholic viewing.

The first Soapbox Derby, for boys aged eleven to fifteen, takes place in Dayton, Ohio.

Alcatraz prison opens in San Francisco Bay.

January 4, 1935   Roosevelt's message to Congress sets the tone of policy for the new year by stressing reform and security, especially for the needy.

April 8, 1935   Congress appropriates approximately $5 billion for various forms of relief.

April 27, 1935   To deal with massive soil erosion plaguing parts of the United States, Congress creates the Soil Conservation Service.

May 1, 1935   Roosevelt establishes the Resettlement Administration to relocate farm families. The RA also will construct from scratch some "green-belt" towns.

May 6, 1935   Congress creates a new type of work relief agency, the Works Progress Administration. Under Harry Hopkins the WPA employs artists, actors, writers, and many others with special skills. By 1943, 8.5 million will have been affected.

May 11, 1935   Roosevelt creates the Rural Electrification Administration to help bring electricity to the countryside.

May 24, 1935   The Cincinnati Reds play the Phillies in the first major league night game, at Crosley Field in Cincinnati. The Reds win 2–1.

May 27, 1935   As a sign of things to come, the Supreme Court in the *Schechter* case invalidates the New Deal's most ambitious measure, the NIRA.

June 10, 1935   Four alcoholics join together in New York City to organize Alcoholics Anonymous.

June 13, 1935   Jim Braddock becomes heavyweight boxing champion, beating Max Baer in fifteen rounds.

July 5, 1935   The president signs the National Labor Relations Act, also known as the Wagner Act. Probably the most important labor legislation ever, it places the power of the national government behind the principle of unionism.

August 14, 1935   Roosevelt signs the Social Security Act. Designed to deal with unemployment, the unemployable, and retirement, it will be one of the farthest-reaching laws in American history.

August 26, 1935   The Wheeler-Rayburn Act becomes law, giving the government more power to regulate utility companies.

August 30, 1935   Congress passes a new Revenue Act, sometimes referred to as the "Soak the Rich" tax law; it does impose some higher taxes.

August 31, 1935   The first Neutrality Act becomes law. It is designed to prevent war for the United States by forbidding the sale of arms and munitions.

September 8, 1935   Huey Long, charismatic senator from Louisiana, populist, and potential presidential candidate, is shot. He dies two days later.

October 5, 1935   Roosevelt applies the neutrality law after Italy's attack on Ethiopia. The conflict becomes a first step in Europe's movement toward a second world war.

October 10, 1935   George Gershwin's opera *Porgy and Bess,* from a novel by DuBose and Dorothy Heyward, opens in New York.

November 9, 1935   John L. Lewis of the United Mine Workers becomes head of a new labor movement, the Committee for Industrial Organizations. In time the CIO will break with and challenge the parent American Federation of Labor (AFL).

Other events of 1935   Male swimmers in Atlantic City, N.J., are arrested for wearing topless bathing suits.

Parker Brothers introduces a new board game called Monopoly.

Babe Ruth retires as a player at age forty.

January 6, 1936   In the *Butler* decision, the Supreme Court strikes down another major piece of New Deal legislation, the Agriculture Adjustment Act (AAA).

January 24, 1936   For a second time Roosevelt vetoes a measure giving veterans cash payment for bonus certificates. This time Congress overrides the veto.

February 17, 1936   The Supreme Court upholds the constitutionality of the TVA.

February 29, 1936   Partly to compensate for destruction of the AAA, Congress passes the Soil Conservation Act.

March 1936   Heavy rains cause flooding in the East, leading to 171 deaths.

March 2, 1936   In a treaty with Panama, the United States relinquishes a special "protectorate" relationship, although the Americans keep control of the canal.

June 1, 1936   The Supreme Court invalidates a minimum-wage law for women and children in New York.

June 1936   Margaret Mitchell's 1,037-page novel *Gone with the Wind* is published. It becomes an immediate sensation, selling a million copies in six months.

June 9–12, 1936   The Republicans meet in Cleveland and nominate Alfred M. Landon of Kansas for the presidency and Frank Knox of Illinois for the vice presidency.

June 23–27, 1936 The Democrats meet in Philadelphia and renominate the ticket of Roosevelt and Garner.

June 30, 1936 Passage of the Walsh-Healey Act requires companies doing business with the government to maintain certain wage and hours standards.

July 11, 1936 The government reports that drought has ruined agriculture in more than 300 counties.

August 3, 1936 The Department of State warns Americans to leave Spain and thus avoid that nation's civil war.

October 9, 1936 Boulder Dam, later renamed Hoover Dam, is completed on the Colorado River, creating Lake Mead and a huge capacity for hydroelectric power.

November 3, 1936 Roosevelt and Garner score an overwhelming victory, with 523 electoral votes to 8, carrying all states but two. Both houses of Congress also are heavily Democrat.

November 23, 1936 The first issue (reissue) of the pictorial magazine *Life* is published by Henry Luce, and it sells 500,000 copies.

December 11, 1936 Americans are fascinated by the news that King Edward VIII of Britain has abdicated the throne in order to wed an American divorcee, Wallis Warfield Simpson.

Other events of 1936 Cunard's *Queen Mary,* a massive new liner, arrives in New York in June on its maiden voyage.

Dr. Alexis Carrel introduces an artificial heart called a perfusion pump.

Eugene O'Neill receives the Nobel Prize for literature.

The Baseball Hall of Fame is created in Cooperstown, N.Y.

African-American track star Jesse Owens arrives home from the summer Olympic Games in Berlin with four gold medals, adding much to an ongoing world dispute about race.

January 20, 1937 Roosevelt is inaugurated for a second term. His address speaks of "one third of a nation ill-housed, ill-clad, ill-nourished."

January–February 1937 Huge floods along the valleys of the Ohio and Mississippi Rivers affect half a million homes; some 900 are left dead.

February 4, 1937 A shipping strike of more than three months ends on the West Coast.

February 5, 1937 Troubled by recent judicial decisions, Roosevelt sends to Congress a proposal to reorganize the Supreme Court, better known as the "Court-Packing Plan."

February 11, 1937 A long sit-down strike at General Motors in Michigan ends with the company accepting—agreeing to bargain with—the United Auto Workers of the new CIO.

March 2, 1937 United States Steel and Carnegie Illinois Steel agree to bargain with the United Steel Workers, marking another victory for the CIO and John L. Lewis.

March 17, 1937 A taxi strike in downtown Chicago turns violent, with many wrecks and clashes with the police.

March 18, 1937 The Supreme Court upholds a minimum-wage law for the state of Washington, in virtual contradiction of an earlier Court decision.

April 12, 1937 In another ruling that suggested a shifting majority, the Court upholds the Wagner labor law.

April 22, 1937 A large peace demonstration takes place in New York City. Participants insist that they will not support any further war for the United States.

May 1, 1937 Roosevelt signs another neutrality act that extends and adds to earlier measures designed to assure that the United States will not be drawn into another war.

May 6, 1937 The German dirigible *Hindenburg* burns at its mooring on arriving at Lakehurst, N.J., killing thirty-six. The disaster virtually ends commercial travel for this type of airship.

May 18, 1937 Willis Van Devanter, one of the "nine old men" on the Supreme Court, announces his retirement—signaling a

possible change in future Court decisions.

May 24, 1937 In a critical decision for Roosevelt and the New Deal, the Supreme Court upholds the Social Security Act.

May 27, 1937 The Golden Gate Bridge, the longest suspension bridge in the world, opens in California.

May 30, 1937 A bitter and violent strike at Republic Steel in Chicago leaves ten dead.

June 22, 1937 Knocking out James Braddock in the eighth round, Joe Louis becomes heavyweight champion. Only the second black man to hold the title, he will be in the judgment of many the best champion ever.

July 2, 1937 Flier Amelia Earhart vanishes over the Pacific Ocean, leaving mystery and speculation but no trace of her fate.

July 11, 1937 Composer George Gershwin dies at age thirty-eight.

July 22, 1937 Congress in effect kills Roosevelt's court-packing plan.

August 12, 1937 At last able to choose a nominee for the High Court, Roosevelt picks Hugo L. Black of Alabama, who is later confirmed but not without controversy.

September 28, 1937 Bonneville Dam on the Columbia River is dedicated.

October 5, 1937 With an eye toward conflict in the world, especially the clash between Japan and China, Roosevelt speaks of a "quarantine" of aggression. The response is not encouraging.

December 12, 1937 As an outgrowth of the war in China, Japanese aircraft sink the American gunboat *Panay* on the Yangtze River. Japan apologizes and promises reparation.

Other events of 1937 John Dos Passos's *U.S.A.* trilogy is published, as is John Steinbeck's *Of Mice and Men.*

I'd Rather Be Right, a musical comedy by George Kaufman and Moss Hart, opens on Broadway.

January 5, 1938 Worried by continuing economic troubles, labor and business leaders confer with the president.

February 16, 1938 Congress passes the second Agriculture Adjustment Act, calling for restrictions on marketing and payments to participating farmers.

March 2, 1938 Floods and landslides kill 144 in southern California.

March 30, 1938 Tornadoes in the Midwest kill thirty-six and virtually destroy South Rekin, Ill.

April 12, 1938 New York becomes the first state to require medical tests for marriage licenses (to prevent the spread of syphilis).

May 26, 1938 What will become the infamous House Committee on Un-American Activities is formed (HUAC or the Dies Committee), chaired by Martin Dies of Texas.

June 15, 1938 John VanderMeer of the Cincinnati Reds becomes the only pitcher to pitch two consecutive no-hit baseball games.

June 17, 1938 A train crashes in Montana while passing over a weakened bridge, killing forty-seven.

June 22, 1938 In a fight with much international political and racial implication, Joe Louis avenges an earlier defeat and knocks out Max Schmeling of Germany in the first round.

June 23, 1938 Congress creates the Civil Aeronautics Authority to police nonmilitary air traffic.

June 25, 1938 The president signs the landmark Fair Labor Standards Act, calling for minimum wages and maximum hours for covered workers.

June 1938 Superman is born. The creation of writer Jerry Siegal and artist Joseph Shuster, the Man of Steel first appears in *Action Comics.*

July 17, 1938 Denied permission to fly the Atlantic, Douglas Corrigan takes off from New York and lands in Ireland, claiming that he thought he was heading for California. He forever will be known as "Wrong-way Corrigan."

August 18, 1938 The Thousand Islands Bridge over the St. Lawrence connecting the United States and Canada opens to traffic.

September 21, 1938 A hurricane strikes New York and New England, causing enormous damage and perhaps 700 deaths.

September 26, 1938 Roosevelt proposes arbitration of a critical European dispute over Hitler's claim of the Sudetenland in Czechoslovakia.

September 30, 1938 Americans applaud the agreement signed at Munich over the Sudeten crisis, thinking that it will preserve peace. As with many others, they will be misled.

October 30, 1938 Orson Welles's realistic radio broadcast of *War of the Worlds* causes panic among thousands of listeners.

November 8, 1938 Although Democrats still control both houses of Congress, the Republicans score striking gains (eighty-one in the House, eight in the Senate) in off-year national elections.

November 14, 1938 To protest anti-Jewish policy in Nazi Germany, especially the events of *Kristallnacht,* Roosevelt recalls the U.S. ambassador in Berlin.

November 18, 1938 The Congress of Industrial Organizations officially becomes a separate union. The leader of the CIO is John L. Lewis.

Other events of 1938 A new synthetic fiber called nylon is developed. The first nylon product will be a toothbrush, made by DuPont.

The self-propelled combine appears on the American market.

The Era of the Second World War

January 4, 1939 Roosevelt's message to Congress warns of totalitarianism and threats to peace. He later will ask for a defense budget of nearly $1.4 billion.

January 26, 1939 Physicists Enrico Fermi and Niels Bohr meet in Washington to discuss a process called fission, an initial step toward development of an atomic weapon.

February 27, 1939 The Supreme Court rules that the sit-down strike is illegal.

March 14, 1939 In a move that is ominous for the future, Germany invades Czechoslovakia.

April 30, 1939 The World's Fair opens in Queens, N.Y. The theme is the wonders of science and technology, including television.

May 5, 1939 John L. Lewis's United Mine Workers strike the bituminous mines, the source of much of the nation's fuel and energy.

May 5–13, 1939 Three main branches of the Methodist Church unite, bringing together eight million members.

May 16, 1939 The first food stamp program for people on public relief starts in Rochester, N.Y.

May 23, 1939 The submarine *Squalus* sinks off the coast of New Hampshire. Rescuers save thirty-three of the crew, but twenty-six perish.

June 7, 1939 King George VI and Queen Elizabeth of Great Britain arrive to a grand reception in Washington, D.C.

June 28, 1939 Pan American's Clipper departs New York on the first regular passenger air service to Europe.

June 30, 1939 As a sign of an ongoing depression, Congress appropriates $1.5 billion for the WPA.

August 2, 1939 The Hatch Act prohibits Federal Civil Service workers from participating in political campaigns for office.

August 17, 1939 The film fantasy *The Wizard of Oz,* destined to be a classic, opens in New York.

September 1, 1939 After signing a nonaggression pact with Russia, Hitler attacks Poland.

September 3, 1939 Britain and France declare war on Germany. The Second World War has started. Although he proclaims U.S. neutrality, Roosevelt makes no secret of his support for the Allies. He soon will ask for a change in previous neutrality policies.

October 21, 1939 Inspired by a letter of Albert Einstein to the president, a committee of scientists meet in Washington to probe the idea of an atomic bomb.

October 25, 1939 The first nylon stockings go on sale in the United States.

November 4, 1939 Prompted by Roosevelt's wish to aid Britain and France, Congress amends the neutrality law to permit the sale of arms on a "cash and carry" basis.

December 15, 1939 The long-awaited premier of *Gone with the Wind* takes place in Atlanta, with such international stars as Clark Gable, Vivien Leigh, and Laurence Olivier in attendance. It will be perhaps the most famous movie of all time.

Other events of 1939 John Steinbeck's story of the "Okies," *The Grapes of Wrath,* is published.

Refused permission by the Daughters of the American Revolution to sing at Constitution Hall, black opera singer Marian Anderson gives a free open concert at the Lincoln Memorial.

The American Tobacco Company makes its Pall Mall cigarettes longer than the rest and then issues a claim that the length makes them milder.

Seeking a more precise fitting for its brassieres, the Warner Company introduces a new measurement called "cup sizes."

January 3, 1940 In the annual message to Congress, Roosevelt requests $1.8 billion for defense.

February 29, 1940 For her supporting role in *Gone with the Wind,* Hattie McDaniel becomes the first black person to win an Academy Award.

March 4, 1940 Congress creates the Kings Canyon National Park in California.

April 7, 1940 The Socialist Party picks Norman Thomas to run for the presidency. It is his fourth candidacy.

April 12, 1940 Roosevelt signs a measure that extends the Reciprocal Trade policy another three years.

April 29, 1940 The Supreme Court upholds the government's power to establish minimum wages for firms doing government work.

May 15, 1940 An experimental helicopter, the work of Igor Sikorsky, flies for the first time.

May 20, 1940 British forces flee the Continent from Dunkirk. The miracle of escape cannot cloak the devastation of defeat at German hands.

May 31, 1940 Roosevelt requests $1.3 billion in additional funds for military goods. He wants 50,000 airplanes built each year.

June 3, 1940 The United States agrees to sell surplus arms to the Allies.

June 21, 1940 France surrenders, meaning in essence that Germany has conquered western Europe. Britain stands alone.

June 24–28, 1940 The Republicans hold an emotion-packed convention in Philadelphia and pick for the presidency a former Democrat, Wendell L. Willkie, and for the vice presidency Sen. Charles L. McNary.

June 28, 1940 Congress passes the Alien Registration Act, better known as the Smith Act, which makes it illegal to seek to overthrow the government forcibly.

July 4, 1940   An American Negro Exposition in Chicago celebrates the Emancipation Proclamation.

July 10, 1940   Roosevelt asks Congress for yet more money—$4.8 billion more—for defense.

July 15–19, 1940   The Democrats meet in Chicago and nominate Roosevelt for an unprecedented third term. The convention reluctantly accepts Roosevelt's choice of Henry A. Wallace as running mate.

August 29, 1940   Peter C. Goldmark demonstrates color television in New York.

September 3, 1940   Roosevelt arranges to send Britain fifty warships (destroyers) in exchange for leases on British bases.

September 1940   Determined to resist Roosevelt's policy toward the war, opponents—commonly called isolationists—organize the America First Committee.

September 16, 1940   Congress passes the Selective Service Act, to draft selected young men into military service for one year.

October 24, 1940   The forty-hour week goes into effect for workers covered under the labor law of 1938.

October 25, 1940   A bitter foe of the president, John L. Lewis promises to resign as head of the CIO if Roosevelt is reelected.

October 29, 1940   The numbers are chosen to determine who first will be drafted under the recent law.

November 5, 1940   Roosevelt defeats Willkie by a margin of 449 electoral college votes to 82.

November 7, 1940   The Tacoma Narrows suspension bridge, also known as Galloping Gertie, falls into Puget Sound during a storm, only four months after it opened.

November 21, 1940   Lewis quits the CIO; Philip Murray takes over as president.

December 21, 1940   F. Scott Fitzgerald, novelist and symbol of another era, dies at age forty-four.

December 29, 1940   In an ending fitting to this fateful year, Roosevelt promises all possible aid to Britain—now fighting Germany alone—and to make America the "arsenal of democracy."

Other events of 1940   The center of population continues to nudge west, now reaching Sullivan County, Ind. Life expectancy reaches sixty-four. A survey shows that thirty million homes have radio.

Significant publications include *Native Son* by Richard Wright, *You Can't Go Home Again* by Thomas Wolfe, and *For Whom the Bell Tolls* by Ernest Hemingway.

January 6, 1941   In his message to Congress Roosevelt proposes a bold new program of aid for Britain called Lend-Lease; he also identifies his "four freedoms." He later requests almost $11 billion for defense.

January 20, 1941   Roosevelt is inaugurated for a third term.

February 3, 1941   The Supreme Court upholds the Fair Labor Standards Act of 1938.

March 11, 1941   After intense debate, Congress passes the Lend-Lease bill, which in essence allows the United States government to give arms to nations fighting Hitler.

March 19, 1941   The National Gallery of Art opens in Washington, D.C.

March 22, 1941   The Grand Coulee Dam on the Columbia River begins generating electricity.

March 31, 1941   Lewis orders bituminous miners out of the pits. Lasting about a month, the strike slows economic recovery and rearmament.

April 1, 1941   Workers strike the mammoth River Rouge plant of the Ford Motor Company. Ford still refuses to bargain with unions.

April 11, 1941   An Office of Price Administration (OPA) is created to deal with possible price and wage controls.

April 28, 1941   Charles A. Lindbergh, an isolationist, responds to criticism from Roosevelt by resigning from the Army Air Force Reserve.

May 15, 1941   Joe DiMaggio of the New York Yankees fails to get a base hit in a game in Cleveland, bringing his batting streak to an end. DiMaggio nonetheless will be left with a remarkable record of hitting safely in fifty-six consecutive games.

May 20, 1941   Roosevelt returns Thanksgiving Day to the last Thursday in November after a two-year experiment with the next-to-last Thursday.

May 27, 1941   Roosevelt proclaims a state of unlimited national emergency.

May 31, 1941   *Tobacco Road* finally closes on Broadway, after 3,180 performances.

June 2, 1941   Lou Gehrig, superb baseball player of the New York Yankees, holder of a record of playing in 2,130 consecutive games, dies of a rare paralysis that thereafter will bear his name.

June 9, 1941   The army occupies North American Aviation, a bomber plant in California, because of a strike.

June 18, 1941   Joe Louis wins a very close boxing match with Billy Conn in thirteen rounds, Louis's seventh fight of the year. Before 1941 ends, Louis will have defended his title nineteen times.

June 20, 1941   The Ford Motor Company becomes the last of the Big Three auto makers to accept unionism by signing a contract with the United Auto Workers (the UAW).

June 24, 1941   Two days after Hitler invades Russia, Roosevelt promises Lend-Lease aid to the Soviet Union.

June 25, 1941   Roosevelt creates the Fair Employment Practices Commission to appease black leaders and head off a threatened demonstration by black people in Washington, D.C.

July 7, 1941   U.S. Marines land in Iceland to deter a possible German invasion.

July 25, 1941   Trouble with Japan intensifies. After Japanese troops occupy French Indochina, Roosevelt freezes all Japanese assets. The next day he nationalizes the armed forces of the Philippine Islands, with Douglas MacArthur in command.

August 3, 1941   A gasoline curfew ordered in seventeen eastern states closes filling stations from 7 P.M. to 7 A.M.

August 9–12, 1941   Roosevelt meets secretly with Prime Minister Winston Churchill of Great Britain off the coast of Newfoundland. There the two leaders pledge cooperation to defeat Hitler and sign the Atlantic Charter.

August 18, 1941   To the chagrin of the draftees, Congress extends the term of military service (originally one year) an additional eighteen months.

September 5, 1941   Elaborate military maneuvers, "war games" involving nearly half a million men, begin in Louisiana. Col. Dwight D. Eisenhower will distinguish himself.

September 11, 1941   After a clash between a German submarine and a U.S. destroyer (the *Greer*), Roosevelt orders the navy to shoot at all German ships on sight.

September 20, 1941   Designed to help pay for military costs, a new law sharply increases many kinds of taxes.

October 27, 1941   Roosevelt proclaims that "the shooting has started," in reference to the torpedoing of a destroyer, the *Kearney*, ten days earlier.

John L. Lewis calls a strike in the "captive" coal mines, one of several stoppages he will order in the year.

October 30, 1941   A German submarine sinks the U.S. destroyer *Reuben James;* 100 Americans die.

November 1, 1941 Rainbow Bridge just below Niagara Falls opens to traffic.

November 7, 1941 Congress authorizes U.S. merchant ships to enter war zones; the ships also can be armed.

November 17, 1941 Japan and the United States engage in intense negotiations to head off a clash. They eventually deadlock, largely over Japan's position in China.

November 21, 1941 Convicted murderer Ethel Spinelli becomes the first woman to face the death penalty in California.

November 24, 1941 The Supreme Court strikes down a California law designed to keep such "undesirable" people as Okies from entering the state.

December 3, 1941 Japanese consulates in the United States start burning confidential material.

December 7, 1941 Japanese aircraft from six carriers execute a surprise attack at the Pearl Harbor naval base in Oahu, Hawaii, sinking or damaging eight battleships and several other vessels; 162 airplanes are destroyed; 2,403 are killed.

December 8, 1941 Reminded by the president of the "date which will live in infamy," Congress declares war on Japan by a vote of 82–0 in the Senate, 388–1 in the House (only Jeannette Rankin said no). "Remember Pearl Harbor" becomes a rallying cry for years to come.

December 10, 1941 Japanese forces invade the Philippine Islands.

December 11, 1941 Germany and Italy declare war on the United States. Congress reciprocates immediately.

December 17, 1941 Chester Nimitz replaces Husband Kimmel as commander of the disabled Pacific Fleet; an investigation into the Pearl Harbor disaster soon begins.

December 22, 1941 Despite impressive resistance from 400 Marines, Japanese forces conquer Wake Island.

December 27, 1941 The OPA announces rationing of rubber, including tires. Civilian consumption of rubber must decline by 80%.

January 1, 1942 The government decrees a ban on the sale of new passenger cars and trucks.

January 6, 1942 Roosevelt calls for vast amounts of war materiel. Of a budget of nearly $59 billion he submits, more than $52 billion is earmarked for military purposes.

January 16, 1942 The War Production Board (WPB) is created by executive order. The first head is Donald Nelson.

Actress Carole Lombard, wife of Clark Gable, dies in a plane crash on return from a war bond drive.

January 28, 1942 The Office of Civil Defense is created to organize various defense activities on the home front.

February 9, 1942 Daylight Saving Time takes effect for the duration of the war. A few die-hard Republicans, preferring "God's time" to "Roosevelt's time," refuse to change their clocks.

The interned French liner *Normandie,* being converted to a

This shot-up Packard, bodies still inside, fell victim not to Japanese strafing but to errant shells from American warships. (National Archives)

troop ship, burns and rolls over in New York Harbor.

February 20, 1942 Roosevelt issues the order for the internment of virtually all Japanese Americans in the United States, most of them American citizens. Most will spend the war in the camps.

A carrier pilot, Edward "Butch" O'Hare, shoots down five Japanese aircraft in the South Pacific. He will later receive the Medal of Honor and then be killed in action. Chicago names an airport in his honor.

March 11, 1942 On Roosevelt's order, General MacArthur slips out of the doomed Philippine Islands. On arrival in Australia, he promises in grandiose fashion, "I shall return."

March 17, 1942 The AFL and CIO offer a "no-strike" pledge to last for the duration of the war.

April 8, 1942 The WPB orders a halt to all construction not essential to the war effort.

April 9, 1942 The bulk of U.S. and Philippine troops on Bataan Peninsula on Luzon (some 78,000) surrender to the Japanese. They soon embark on the Bataan Death March, more than 80 miles; some 14,000 will lose their lives.

April 18, 1942 Sixteen B-25 bombers commanded by Gen. James Doolittle fly off the aircraft carrier *Hornet* for a surprise bombing attack on Tokyo. It is a symbolic move, to boost American morale.

April 28, 1942 A section of the Atlantic Coast begins blackouts at night to make operations more difficult for German submarines.

The OPA imposes national controls on rent for property, including residences.

May 4–8, 1942 Naval air forces engage the Japanese in the Battle of Coral Sea near Australia. The Americans lose the carrier *Lexington;* Japanese losses are at least as great.

May 5, 1942 The rationing of sugar begins in the United States.

May 7, 1942 The final U.S. forces on tiny Corregidor Island in the Philippines, commanded by Gen. Jonathan Wainwright, surrender to the Japanese.

May 14, 1942 Congress creates a women's volunteer army force, the Women's Army Corps (WAC). Oveta Culp Hobby is the first commander.

May 15, 1942 Gasoline rationing begins in seventeen eastern states. The standard allocation is 3 gallons per week unless there is a compelling reason for more.

June 4–6, 1942 The United States scores a smashing air naval victory near the Midway Islands in the central Pacific. The Americans lose the carrier *Yorktown* but destroy four Japanese carriers, nearly 300 aircraft, and many of the best Japanese pilots.

June 13, 1942 The Office of War Information is created, as is the Office of Strategic Services (OSS), the predecessor to the CIA.

June 15, 1942 On Roosevelt's urging, Americans begin a huge drive to collect scrap rubber.

June 22, 1942 The first lightweight V-mail is sent abroad—to London.

June 25, 1942 Maj. Gen. Dwight D. Eisenhower becomes commander of U.S. troops in the European theater.

June 30, 1942 Congress appropriates nearly $43 billion for military purposes. The CCC is allowed to die.

July 16, 1942 In what becomes known as the "Little Steel Formula," the War Labor Board allows certain workers to have a 15% wage increase.

July 23, 1942 The government authorizes a barge canal to be constructed across northern Florida.

July 30, 1942 Congress creates a women's unit of the naval reserve, to become known as the WAVES.

August 1942 Paramount releases *Holiday Inn,* with Bing Crosby.

The film introduces Irving Berlin's "White Christmas," a song with exceptional (and lasting) appeal because of so many people being away from home.

August 7, 1942 U.S. forces land on Guadalcanal in the Soloman Islands in the southwest Pacific. The landing touches off a complex struggle for the island and represents the first step in a long American counteroffensive.

September 10, 1942 A special commission warns of a crisis because of a shortage of rubber. Purchases from South America help, but the answer rests with development of a synthetic product.

October 2, 1942 Bell Aircraft tests the first American jet airplane, the XP-59A.

October 21, 1942 Congress passes a new revenue law that includes a Victory Tax of 5% on all incomes over $624.

November 3, 1942 The Republicans gain several seats in both houses, but the Democrats continue to control Congress. The election of Thomas E. Dewey as governor of New York makes him a presidential front-runner.

November 7–8, 1942 U.S. and Allied forces land on the coast of North Africa.

November 12–15, 1942 A U.S. fleet inflicts heavy damage on the Japanese in the continuing Guadalcanal operation. American losses in the costly engagement include the cruiser *Juneau,* taking to their deaths five brothers of the Sullivan family.

November 13, 1942 The minimum draft age is lowered from twenty-one to eighteen.

November 27, 1942 Warner Brothers releases a timely film with Humphrey Bogart and Ingrid Bergman called *Casablanca.*

November 28, 1942 The rationing of coffee goes into effect in the United States.

Fire in the Coconut Grove nightclub in Boston kills 487.

December 1, 1942 Gasoline rationing takes effect over all the United States. A system of coupons goes into operation.

December 4, 1942 Roosevelt officially closes down the depression-era Works Progress Administration (WPA).

December 30, 1942 Crooner Frank Sinatra opens at the Paramount Theater in New York City. A girl in the audience swoons; others follow suit and a new craze starts.

January 5, 1943 Scientist George Washington Carver, born a slave, dies at age seventy-eight.

January 12–24, 1943 Roosevelt meets with Churchill at Casablanca, Morocco, to plan strategy for the European war.

January 25, 1943 Construction on the Pentagon in Arlington, Va., heralded as the world's largest office building, is completed.

February 7, 1943 The rationing of shoes begins. Each person gets three pairs per year.

February 9, 1943 Roosevelt announces that all defense factories must work at least forty-eight hours a week.

February 13, 1943 Congress creates a women's branch for the Marine Corps.

March 1, 1943 Rationing extends to all canned goods and at the end of the month to meats, fats, and cheese. The system utilizes rationing books with points for each coupon.

March 2–5, 1943 U.S. forces score a substantial victory over the Japanese at Bismarck Sea; 15,000 Japanese soldiers drown.

March 7, 1943 The Manpower Commission eliminates the 4-H deferment, making men thirty-eight to forty-five eligible for the draft.

March 30, 1943 *Oklahoma,* a sparkling musical stressing traditional American culture, with many popular songs by Rodgers and Hammerstein, opens on Broadway. It will run for 2,212 performances.

UNITED STATES OF AMERICA
OFFICE OF PRICE ADMINISTRATION

61 069 **AE**

WAR RATION BOOK No. 3

Void if altered

Identification of person to whom issued: PRINT IN FULL

George J. Howell

(First name)   (Middle name)   (Last name)

Street number or rural route *#2   Bx 103*

City or post office *Bangor*   State *Michigan*

AGE	SEX	WEIGHT	HEIGHT	OCCUPATION
51	*Male*	*185* Lbs.	*5* Ft. *8* In.	*Sandblaster*

NOT VALID WITHOUT STAMP

SIGNATURE --
(Person to whom book is issued. If such person is unable to sign because of age or incapacity, another may sign in his behalf.)

WARNING

This book is the property of the United States Government. It is unlawful to sell it to any other person, or to use it or permit anyone else to use it, except to obtain rationed goods in accordance with regulations of the Office of Price Administration. Any person who finds a lost War Ration Book must return it to the War Price and Rationing Board which issued it. Persons who violate rationing regulations are subject to $10,000 fine or imprisonment, or both.

OPA Form No. R-130

LOCAL BOARD ACTION

Issued by --
(Local board number)   (Date)

Street address --

City ------------------------------------   State -------------

----
(Signature of issuing officer)

This illustration shows the cover of a ration booklet. The original booklet measured 5½″ × 4½″. (Courtesy John T. Houdek)

April 1943 Wendell Willkie's volume *One World,* calling for American participation in future world affairs, is published. It sells more than a million copies in two months.

April 8, 1943 The president orders that salaries, wages, and prices be frozen where they stand.

April 13, 1943 Roosevelt presides over the dedication of the Jefferson Memorial in Washington, D.C.

April 27, 1943 The War Manpower Commission freezes twenty-seven million workers on the job they currently hold.

May 1–2, 1943 Roosevelt orders government seizure of coal mines in eastern Pennsylvania struck by the United Mine Workers (the UMW.)

May 5, 1943 A postal-zone system of numbering—a forerunner of the zip code—starts in 176 cities.

May 11, 1943 U.S. forces begin the reconquest from the Japanese of Attu and a few weeks later of Kiska in the Aleutian Islands near Alaska.

May 13, 1943 With the surrender of large numbers of Italian and German soldiers, the North African campaign comes to an end. Hitler's Afrika Korps ceases to exist.

May 27, 1943 Roosevelt forbids racial discrimination in any work that involves government contracts.

June 4–8, 1943 The "zoot-suit" riots occur as servicemen attack blacks and Mexican Americans in Los Angeles.

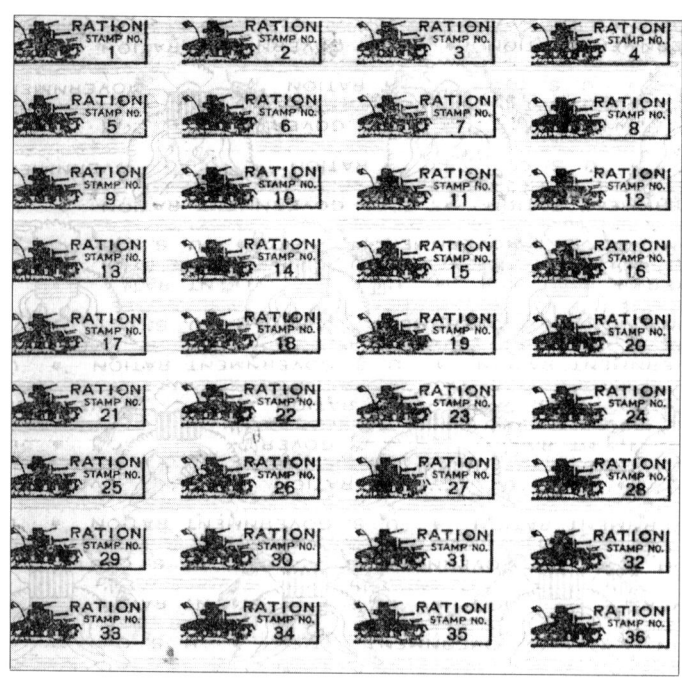

Shown in this photo are sample coupons (or stamps) used to purchase food-stuffs or other scarce commodities. (Courtesy John T. Houdek)

June 10, 1943 The president signs the Withholding Tax Act, which inaugurates a "pay-as-you-go" system of deducting taxes from paychecks.

June 14, 1943 In a case involving Jehovah's Witnesses, the Supreme Court rules that school children cannot be forced to salute the flag.

June 16, 1943 Film giant Charlie Chaplin, fifty-four, marries Oona O'Neill, eighteen, daughter of playwright Eugene O'Neill.

June 20, 1943 Fed by rumor, overcrowding, and hatred, a vicious race riot strikes Detroit, leaving thirty-four dead and hundreds injured.

June 25, 1943 Passage (over presidential veto) of the Smith-Connally Act authorizes government seizure of any war industry subjected to a strike.

July 10, 1943 Allied forces, including George Patton's 7th Army, begin conquest of Sicily. Mussolini is eventually captured by Italian partisans.

July 19, 1943 The longest pipeline, the "Big Inch," which stretches from Texas to Pennsylvania, opens to service.

August 1943 Although injured himself, Lt. (j.g.) John F. Kennedy helps rescue part of his crew when his PT boat is rammed by a Japanese destroyer.

August 2, 1943 The Manpower Commission announces that fathers are now eligible for conscription.

September 3, 1943 Allied forces begin invasion of Italy. Italy soon surrenders, but heavy fighting continues against the Germans in Italy. Mussolini is eventually rescued by German soldiers.

November 20, 1943 After defeating Japanese naval forces at Rabaul, the Americans land at Tarawa in the Gilbert Islands.

November 22–26, 1943 Roosevelt, Churchill, and Chiang Kai-shek meet in Cairo and demand unconditional surrender from Japan. The vessel on which the president traveled to the conference, the new battleship *Iowa*, was almost struck by a torpedo accidentally launched by a U.S. destroyer.

November 28–December 1, 1943 Roosevelt, Churchill, and Stalin meet in Teheran, Iran, in the first meeting of the Big Three, to discuss plans for the war against Germany.

December 16, 1943 A train collision and derailment near Rennert, N.C., kills sixty-two.

December 17, 1943 Congress repeals the old Chinese Exclusion Act and in its stead awards China an annual quota of 105.

December 24, 1943 Roosevelt announces that Eisenhower will be supreme commander of Allied forces planning an invasion of Europe.

Other events of 1943 Radar goes into widespread use in U.S. military forces.

Discovery of a mold on a cantaloupe in Peoria, Ill., speeds up the production of penicillin, discovered earlier in Britain, by approximately tenfold. It will become a wonder drug, effective against infections and a growing number of diseases.

Significant publications of the year include Ernie Pyle, *This Is Your War;* Richard Tregaskis, *Guadalcanal Diary;* Robert L. Scott, Jr., *God Is My Copilot;* Ted Lawson, *Thirty Seconds over Tokyo;* and Betty Smith, *A Tree Grows in Brooklyn.* Willkie's *One World* is the publishing sensation.

January 22, 1944 Allied forces land at Anzio as part of the difficult contest over Italy. Surrounded by the Germans, they withstand a four-month siege.

January 31, 1944 U.S. troops attack and in three weeks capture the Marshall Islands from Japan.

February 20–27, 1944 In what is later known as "Big Week," hundreds of U.S. bombers raid German aircraft industries. Losses are heavy on both sides.

March 6, 1944 More than 600 bombers and 800 fighter planes participate in the first U.S. air raid on Berlin.

April 3, 1944 The Supreme Court in *Smith v. Allwright* in effect invalidates the white primary in Texas—a person cannot be denied participation in elections because of color.

April 4, 1944 In a quest for a second presidential nomination, Wendell Willkie experiences a devastating defeat in the Wisconsin primary. He eventually withdraws from the race and dies a few months later.

April 26, 1944 When Montgomery Ward and Company refuses an order to deal with the union, the government seizes the company. Soldiers physically carry chairman Sewell Avery from the firm's offices.

April 30, 1944 Gen. Douglas MacArthur announces that he will not accept the Republican presidential nomination.

May 3, 1944 Except for certain kinds of beef, meat rationing comes to an end.

Robert Woodward and William Doering announce the development of a synthetic quinine, vital in combating malaria.

June 1, 1944 Allied troops finally break out at Anzio. Within a week Rome is captured.

June 6, 1944 On D-Day, Allied armies launch the long-awaited Operation Overlord, the invasion of the European continent along the Normandy coast of France. Americans land at two places labeled Omaha Beach and Utah Beach.

June 19–20, 1944 The Japanese are soundly defeated in the Battle of the Philippine Sea. The naval battle is part of the U.S. conquest of the Mariana Islands, which include Guam, Tinian, and Saipan.

June 22, 1944 Roosevelt approves the Serviceman's Readjustment Act—creating a GI Bill of Rights and promising future benefits for veterans.

June 28, 1944 Republicans meet in Chicago and nominate Thomas E. Dewey and John Bricker of Ohio.

July 6, 1944 The main tent of the Ringling Brothers circus catches fire in Hartford, Conn., killing 168 and injuring 250.

July 17, 1944 An explosion of an ammunition ship kills 300 at Port Chicago, Calif.

July 20, 1944 Hitler escapes major injury in an assassination plot at his headquarters in East Prussia.

July 21, 1944 The Democrats meet in Chicago, pick Roosevelt for a fourth term, and nominate for the vice presidency a relative newcomer, Harry S. Truman of Missouri.

August 12, 1944 Joseph P. Kennedy, Jr., dies when his B-24 bomber explodes over the English Channel. If Joe had lived, younger brother John would say, he (John) never would have run for office.

August 14, 1944 The government permits resumption of production of some consumer appliances, such as electric ranges.

August 21, 1944 Allied diplomats meet at Dumbarton Oaks, near Washington, D.C., to work on a future United Nations organization.

August 25, 1944 French soldiers enter Paris as the Germans depart without a fight. Eisenhower and the Americans arrive two days later.

September 14, 1944 A large hurricane sweeps the northeast coast, killing more than 400 on shore and at sea.

October 20, 1944 U.S. troops land at Leyte, beginning the reconquest of the Philippine Islands, honoring MacArthur's promise to return.

October 23–26, 1944 U.S. fleets destroy much of the remaining Japanese navy at Leyte Gulf, the largest naval battle of this, or any other, war.

November 7, 1944 Roosevelt wins for a fourth time, defeating Dewey by 25.6 million votes to 22 million.

November 24, 1944 B-29 bombers launch the first massive air raid on Tokyo from bases in the Mariana Islands.

December 15, 1944 Congress bestows the title of General of the Army on Marshall, Eisenhower, MacArthur, and "Hap" Arnold. Marked with five stars, the rank is the equivalent of field marshal.

December 16, 1944 U.S. forces in Belgium are surprised by a German offensive, starting the ten-day Battle of the Bulge.

December 17, 1944 The army lifts the exclusion of Japanese Americans from the West Coast.

December 24, 1944 Glenn Miller, popular big-band leader and a major in the army's special services, disappears on a flight from Paris to London.

December 31, 1944 A train wreck near Ogden, Utah, leads to the death of forty-eight.

January 15, 1945 To conserve fuel, especially coal, a nationwide "dim-out" is ordered.

January 25, 1945 Grand Rapids, Mich., becomes the first city to add fluoride to its water supply to combat tooth decay.

February 4–12, 1945 Roosevelt, Churchill, and Stalin meet at the Yalta Conference in the Crimea to discuss postwar political settlements. Many controversial decisions are made.

February 7, 1945 MacArthur enters Manila, signaling the liberation of the Philippine capital from the Japanese.

February 14, 1945 In what at the time appears as a colorful, minor footnote to history, Roosevelt meets with Saudi Arabia's King Ibn Saud aboard the American cruiser *Quincy*.

February 19, 1945 U.S. forces invade tiny Iwo Jima, beginning a costly engagement that lasts nearly a month.

March 7, 1945 U.S. armored units begin crossing the Rhine River at Remagen.

March 9–10, 1945 Nearly 300 B-29 bombers participate in a firebombing raid of Tokyo. The resultant firestorm causes more than 100,000 to perish.

April 1, 1945 U.S. troops begin the two-month battle for Okinawa in the Ryuku Islands. Only 350 miles from Japan, the island is projected as the last target before an invasion of Japan itself.

April 12, 1945 Complaining about a "terrific headache," Roosevelt, age sixty-three, dies at Warm Springs, Ga., eighty-three days into his fourth term. Harry Truman is sworn in as president.

April 15, 1945 Fifty nations meet in San Francisco to draw up a charter of the United Nations.

April 18, 1945 Popular and respected war correspondent Ernie Pyle is killed in action at Ie Jima, a tiny island near Okinawa.

April 25, 1945 U.S. and Soviet troops link up at the Elbe River, marking the virtual end of Nazi Germany.

April 28, 1945 U.S. forces overrun Nazi concentration camps at Buchenwald and later at Dachau.

May 7, 1945 This is V-E—Victory in Europe—Day. At Eisenhower's headquarters in Reims, Germany surrenders, ending the war in Europe and ending the Third Reich of Adolf Hitler. Hitler had already committed suicide.

May 10, 1945 The War Production Board orders resumption of the manufacture of seventy-three consumer items.

The military establishes a point system to determine priorities for demobilization of troops.

May 25, 1945 The government orders a 25% reduction in the production of military aircraft.

June 27, 1945 The Federal Communications Commission allocates thirteen channels to be used for commercial television.

July 16, 1945 An atomic device is tested for the first time at Alamogordo, New Mexico. It works.

July 17–August 2, 1945 A new "Big Three," Truman, Stalin, and Churchill (who will be replaced by Clement Atlee), meet at Potsdam, Germany, to discuss disposition of Germany and other problems. Stalin hears about a special bomb.

July 28, 1945 The Senate ratifies a United Nations Charter by 89–2. On this foggy Saturday morning, a twin-engine B-25 bomber crashes into the seventy-eighth and seventy-ninth floors of the Empire State Building. Three crew members and ten people on the streets below are killed.

August 6, 1945 A B-29 bomber, the *Enola Gay,* drops the first atomic bomb on Hiroshima, Japan. At least 80,000 die.

August 8, 1945 The Soviet Union declares war on Japan.

August 9, 1945 The Americans drop a second atomic bomb, "Fat Man," on Nagasaki, Japan, killing perhaps 40,000. Five days later Japan transmits its wish to surrender.

August 18, 1945 Truman orders restoration of civilian production and of other nonmilitary market conditions.

August 25, 1945 Capt. John M. Birch, Baptist missionary and army officer, is killed by local Communists in China. Certain Americans, notably one Robert Welch, will give Birch's name to a right-wing society.

September 2, 1945 MacArthur and other officers accept the formal surrender of Japan aboard the battleship *Missouri* in Tokyo Bay. The Second World War is over.

October 10, 1945 In a World Series that some sports writers speculated that neither team would win, Detroit defeats the Chicago Cubs 9–3 to win the series 4 games to 3. The series would mark the last appearance of the Cubs in the fall classic for a long, long time.

October 30, 1945 Shoe rationing ends, soon to be followed by the end of rationing on all meat and butter and, on Dec. 20, limits on tires.

November 20, 1945 War crimes trials for Nazi leaders begin in Nuremberg, Germany.

November 21, 1945 The United Auto Workers begin a strike of all General Motors plants.

December 14, 1945 John D. Rockefeller, Jr., donates $8.5 million to purchase land along the East River in New York to erect the headquarters of the United Nations.

December 15, 1945 Truman sends George Marshall to China to try to resolve a growing conflict between the Communists and the Nationalists.

December 21, 1945 Gen. George S. Patton dies of injuries received in an automobile accident near Heidelberg, Germany.

Other events of 1945 In a move fateful for this unique baseball franchise, the Brooklyn Dodgers are purchased in August by a group of businessmen that includes Walter O'Malley.

CHAPTER 4 The American Economy

The power and operations of the American economy during the years 1914–45 might be suggested by the example of steel. The fact that the United States produced more than half the world's steel in most of these years indicated that there was but one economic giant in the world. The American economy was most productive in time of war. The steel industry operated at more than 90% capacity for two years during the First World War, and during the Second World War it did even better. In 1943 the steel industry came remarkably close to working at 100% capacity. Even a giant can have problems, however, and in 1932 the steel industry did not function at 20% of what it was capable of doing.

The example of steel indicated that this era was a time of striking ups and downs for the world's most dynamic economy. The period of the First World War was a time of high employment, high profits, and productivity, sparked largely by the war itself. The end of the war produced a sharp but brief recession that was followed in 1922 by an upturn that lasted until 1929. These years gave an identity to the 1920s as a period of optimism, high investment, high production, and high living. The "Roaring Twenties," however, lasted only seven years. The economic statistics of that era—which were impressive—had the effect of hiding or at least obscuring such weaknesses in the economy as an unstable banking system and persistent hard times in many aspects of agriculture.

If the Great Depression was sparked by the stock market crash of 1929, it was in a broader sense caused by economic weaknesses that the managers of the 1920s chose to ignore, if indeed they spotted or understood them. The depression reached its worst point in 1932–33. Its effects can be seen in the sharp reduction in gross national product, profits, wages, stock prices—almost every statistic but unemployment and bank failures, both of which increased markedly. The depression lasted some twelve years. Its impact was softened modestly by measures introduced in the administration of Franklin D. Roosevelt starting in 1933—the New Deal—but the hoped-for recovery was unsteady and agonizingly slow. The New Deal thus failed in its original objective.

The genuine turnabout occurred, of course, because of the start of another war. During the years 1939–41 the war in Europe produced new demand for American goods—both for European armies and for a fledgling American rearmament effort. After December 1941, the American economy was given over to the production of as much war-related materials as the government felt was necessary. The result was another boom, this one longer and much larger than during the First World War. By 1944 the gross national product was more than double the nation's previous record, set in 1929. Old companies were running at nearly full capacity; they expanded and new ones formed for the occasion. Many people who previously could not get a job now were working. There were many people, and some economists, who feared that because the boom grew out

of extraordinary circumstances, it would end with the end of war. The bubble would burst. These individuals failed to recognize that by saving huge sums of money, by opening new avenues of production, and by building up demand for goods that they could not buy during the war, Americans were laying the foundation for a new period of sustained economic growth.

TABLE 4.1 GROSS NATIONAL PRODUCT, TOTAL IN BILLIONS OF DOLLARS AND PER CAPITA[a]

1945	211.9	1,515
1944	210.1	1,518
1943	191.6	1,401
1942	157.9	1,171
1941	124.5	934
1940	99.7	754
1939	90.5	691
1938	84.7	651
1937	90.4	701
1936	82.5	643
1935	72.2	567
1934	65.1	514
1933	55.6	442
1932	58.0	465
1931	75.8	611
1930	90.4	734
1929	103.1	847
1928	97.0	805
1927	94.9	797
1926	97.0	826
1925	93.1	804
1924	84.7	742
1923	85.1	760
1922	74.1	673
1921	69.6	641
1920	91.5	860
1919	84.0	804
1918	76.4	740
1917	60.4	585
1916	48.3	473
1915	40.0	398
1914	38.6	389

[a]In current prices. Gross national product is the total value of a nation's output in goods and services and the standard device for measuring the economy.
Source: Ben J. Wattenberg, *The Statistical History of the United States* (New York, 1976), 224.

TABLE 4.2 INDUSTRIAL PRODUCTION INDEXES, BY GROUPS[a]

[1935–39 average = 100]

Item	1919	1926	1929	1932	1939	1940	1941	1943	1944	1945
Durable manufactures										
Iron and steel	84	115	133	32	114	147	186	208	206	183
Machinery	. . .	102	130	43	104	136	221	443	439	343
Transportation equipment	. . .	109	134	38	103	145	245	735	719	487
Nonferrous metal and products	. . .	113	136	52	113	139	191	267	259	204
Lumber and products	. . .	148	146	51	106	116	134	129	125	109
Stone, clay and glass products	50	105	110	51	114	124	162	173	164	163
Total	84	114	132	41	109	139	201	360	353	274
Nondurable manufactures										
Textiles and products	73	84	94	71	112	114	152	153	148	146
Leather and products	94	90	95	76	105	98	123	114	113	117
Manufactured food products	77	87	101	79	108	113	127	145	152	150
Alcoholic beverages	. . .	. . .	. . .	. . .	98	101	117	117	144	178
Paper and products	. . .	72	85	65	114	123	150	139	139	139
Tobacco products	72	88	96	79	106	109	120	133	125	136
Printing and publishing	. . .	92	104	74	106	112	127	111	101	108
Petroleum and coal products	. . .	76	96	69	110	120	135	185	247	235
Chemical products	. . .	70	89	68	112	130	176	384	324	284
Rubber products	. . .	80	100	64	113	123	163	228	234	215
Total	62	79	93	70	109	115	142	176	171	166
Total, durable and nondurable manufactures	72	95	110	57	109	126	168	258	252	214
Minerals										
Fuels	. . .	95	103	72	105	114	122	132	145	143
Metals	. . .	126	134	36	113	134	149	126	113	101
Total	71	100	107	67	106	117	125	132	140	137
Total, manufactures and minerals	72	96	110	58	109	125	162	239	235	203

[a] The production index makes it possible to measure production by industry with an arbitrarily selected period. The time selected, 1935–39, was during the Great Depression, although not at its lowest point. That point is revealed in the numbers for the year 1932.

Source: Board of Governors of the Federal Reserve System. Reproduced in *Information Please Almanac, 1948* (New York, 1948), 340.

TABLE 4.3 NATIONAL INCOME BY DISTRIBUTIVE SHARES (MILLIONS OF DOLLARS), 1929–1945

National income is the earnings of labor and property incurred in the production of goods and services.

Type of Share	1929	1930	1931	1932	1933	1934	1935	1936	1937	1938	1939	1940	1941	1942	1943	1944	1945
National income	87,355	75,003	58,873	41,690	39,584	48,613	56,789	66,941	73,627	67,375	72,532	81,347	103,834	136,486	168,262	182,260	182,808
Compensation of employees	50,786	46,515	39,470	30,826	29,330	34,067	37,107	42,675	47,696	44,747	47,820	51,786	64,280	84,689	109,102	121,184	122,872
Wages and salaries	50,165	45,894	38,886	30,284	28,825	33,520	36,508	41,754	45,948	42,812	45,745	49,587	61,708	81,681	105,537	116,944	117,551
Private	45,206	40,720	33,607	25,297	23,660	27,420	29,984	33,866	38,432	34,564	37,519	41,130	51,537	65,628	78,671	83,317	82,085
Military	312	315	308	295	270	271	306	338	358	370	398	591	1,862	6,285	14,478	20,782	22,438
Government civilian	4,647	4,859	4,971	4,692	4,895	5,829	6,218	7,550	7,158	7,878	7,828	7,866	8,309	9,768	12,388	12,845	13,028
Supplements to wages and salaries	621	621	584	542	505	547	599	921	1,748	1,935	2,075	2,199	2,572	3,008	3,565	4,240	5,321
Employer contributions for social insurance	101	106	111	126	133	147	171	418	1,234	1,423	1,540	1,624	1,983	2,302	2,677	2,936	3,805
Other labor income	520	515	473	416	372	400	428	503	514	512	535	575	589	706	888	1,304	1,516
Income of unincorporated enterprises and inventory valuation adjustment	13,927	10,963	8,214	4,921	5,207	6,603	9,858	12,164	12,249	10,768	11,282	12,660	16,504	22,724	25,951	27,690	30,165
Business and professional	8,262	7,032	5,316	3,206	2,925	4,276	4,987	6,074	6,630	6,347	6,776	7,720	9,566	12,112	14,128	15,310	16,700
Income of unincorporated enterprises	8,120	6,277	4,705	2,911	3,450	4,330	5,037	6,194	6,659	6,126	6,942	7,772	10,210	12,464	14,266	15,369	16,754
Inventory valuation adjustment	142	755	611	295	−525	−54	−50	−120	−29	221	−166	−52	−644	−352	−138	−59	−54
Farm	5,665	3,931	2,898	1,715	2,282	2,327	4,871	6,090	5,619	4,421	4,506	4,940	6,938	10,612	11,823	12,380	13,465
Rental income of persons	5,811	4,786	3,620	2,508	2,018	2,095	2,288	2,682	3,140	3,278	3,465	3,620	4,322	5,371	6,150	6,693	6,952
Corporate profits and inventory valuation adjustment	10,290	6,563	1,631	−1,995	−1,981	1,098	2,997	4,946	6,166	4,292	5,753	9,177	14,615	19,824	23,692	23,486	19,689
Corporate profits before tax	9,818	3,303	−783	−3,042	162	1,723	3,224	5,684	6,197	3,329	6,467	9,325	17,232	21,098	24,516	23,841	20,222
Corporate profits tax liability	1,398	848	500	382	524	746	965	1,411	1,512	1,040	1,462	2,878	7,846	11,665	14,153	13,913	11,283
Corporate profits after tax	8,420	2,455	−1,283	−3,424	−362	977	2,259	4,273	4,685	2,289	5,005	6,447	9,386	9,433	10,363	9,928	8,939
Dividends	5,823	5,500	4,098	2,574	2,066	2,596	2,872	4,557	4,693	3,195	3,796	4,049	4,465	4,297	4,477	4,689	4,765
Undistributed profits	2,597	−3,045	−5,381	−5,998	−2,428	−1,619	−613	−284	−8	−906	1,209	2,398	4,921	5,136	5,886	5,239	4,174
Inventory valuation adjustment	472	3,260	2,414	1,047	−2,143	−625	−227	−738	−31	963	−714	−148	−2,617	−1,274	−824	−355	−533
Net interest	6,541	6,176	5,938	5,430	5,010	4,750	4,539	4,474	4,376	4,290	4,212	4,104	4,113	3,878	3,367	3,207	3,130

Source: Bureau of the Census, Statistical Abstract of the United States, 1948 (Washington, D.C., 1948), 276.

TABLE 4.4   NATIONAL INCOME BY INDUSTRIAL ORIGIN (MILLIONS OF DOLLARS), 1929–1945

Industrial Division	1929	1930	1931	1932	1933	1934	1935	1936	1937	1938	1939	1940	1941	1942	1943	1944	1945
All industries, total	87,355	75,003	58,873	41,690	39,584	48,613	56,789	66,941	73,627	67,375	72,532	81,347	103,834	136,486	168,262	182,260	182,808
Agriculture, forestry, and fisheries	8,002	6,022	4,625	3,080	3,521	3,568	6,231	7,549	7,249	6,003	6,120	6,599	8,880	12,937	14,524	15,279	16,500
Mining, total	2,097	1,665	994	680	662	1,173	1,243	1,551	1,941	1,483	1,601	1,903	2,341	2,590	2,739	2,961	2,888
Anthracite	285	281	229	150	130	172	139	146	137	113	126	138	165	190	210	238	225
Bituminous and other soft coal	652	530	372	239	255	416	446	537	603	457	503	628	809	989	1,125	1,257	1,209
Contract construction	3,691	3,088	2,139	1,030	735	1,034	1,257	1,918	2,017	1,930	2,254	2,593	4,370	6,954	5,605	4,117	4,207
Manufacturing, total	22,012	18,270	12,434	7,196	7,563	10,922	13,336	16,183	19,304	14,997	17,936	22,368	32,897	45,144	57,567	59,749	51,754
Food and kindred products	2,157	2,395	1,865	1,408	1,335	1,600	1,882	2,077	2,400	2,255	2,280	2,483	2,683	3,593	4,328	4,994	5,046
Textile-mill products	1,797	1,404	1,147	713	697	1,100	1,200	1,356	1,597	1,093	1,259	1,511	2,036	2,829	3,024	2,920	2,988
Apparel and other finished fabric products	1,240	997	807	491	532	775	841	958	982	910	1,016	1,109	1,429	1,909	2,306	2,525	2,639
Paper and allied products	563	503	388	270	290	419	463	502	562	573	555	660	1,034	1,124	1,242	1,335	1,341
Printing and publishing	1,580	1,490	1,213	880	790	925	1,037	1,161	1,246	1,132	1,206	1,247	1,359	1,442	1,750	2,051	2,224
Chemicals and allied products	1,136	1,035	827	557	690	725	810	959	1,165	1,005	1,205	1,489	1,941	2,751	3,293	3,374	3,297
Iron and steel and their products	2,978	2,212	1,109	410	682	1,085	1,478	2,061	2,586	1,592	2,259	3,057	5,048	6,883	9,000	8,969	7,308
Nonferrous metals and their products	767	640	415	197	155	385	469	561	702	440	594	793	1,201	1,479	1,903	1,884	1,597
Machinery (except electrical)	1,903	1,485	755	298	426	735	1,021	1,398	1,759	1,247	1,492	2,181	3,850	5,379	5,917	5,794	5,110
Electrical machinery	1,048	824	502	244	276	376	526	708	908	659	850	1,136	1,915	2,492	3,328	3,714	3,133
Transportation equipment except automobiles	317	288	142	89	69	119	139	231	332	264	397	813	2,276	6,192	12,049	12,452	7,773
Wholesale and retail trade, total	13,090	11,998	9,604	6,290	5,375	7,892	9,006	10,319	11,938	11,652	12,126	13,748	15,903	18,186	21,363	23,807	26,551
Wholesale trade	3,955	3,777	2,963	1,994	1,631	2,297	2,726	3,005	3,693	3,507	3,558	4,108	4,708	5,460	6,067	6,777	7,458
Retail trade and auto. services	9,135	8,221	6,641	4,296	3,744	5,595	6,280	7,314	8,245	8,145	8,568	9,640	11,195	12,726	15,296	17,030	19,093
Finance, insurance, and real estate, total	13,098	10,693	8,511	6,452	5,681	5,861	6,294	7,165	7,943	8,026	8,216	8,489	9,523	10,969	12,183	13,124	13,771
Banking	1,960	1,478	984	728	493	541	665	776	892	842	876	973	1,088	1,174	1,379	1,619	1,713
Insurance carriers, agents and combination offices	1,321	1,222	1,094	924	881	991	1,075	1,168	1,321	1,329	1,345	1,328	1,395	1,519	1,614	1,712	1,806
Real estate	8,978	7,858	6,402	4,778	4,060	4,099	4,313	4,833	5,353	5,483	5,675	5,903	6,743	7,840	8,722	9,321	9,661
Transportation, total	6,562	5,513	4,285	3,133	2,958	3,326	3,612	4,168	4,530	3,961	4,543	4,915	6,188	8,459	10,593	11,184	10,821
Railroads	4,600	3,753	2,814	1,965	1,849	2,040	2,236	2,614	2,797	2,368	2,735	2,934	3,779	5,550	6,930	6,925	6,303
Communications and public utilties, total	2,878	2,787	2,625	2,281	2,000	2,195	2,285	2,478	2,713	2,713	2,863	3,039	3,313	3,660	3,915	4,008	4,244
Telephone and telegraph	1,130	1,097	991	794	692	740	779	841	923	948	1,008	1,022	1,135	1,367	1,546	1,641	1,809
Utilities: electric and gas	1,640	1,606	1,562	1,404	1,237	1,359	1,405	1,522	1,662	1,639	1,716	1,860	2,002	2,113	2,153	2,109	2,158
Services	10,168	9,019	7,714	6,006	5,447	6,106	6,526	7,316	8,049	7,728	8,080	8,637	9,709	10,950	12,242	13,439	14,515
Government and Government enterprises, total	5,114	5,336	5,447	5,171	5,349	6,295	6,747	8,130	7,795	8,548	8,550	8,796	10,479	16,399	27,272	34,366	37,344
Federal—general government	900	935	942	901	1,187	1,718	1,791	3,592	3,036	3,529	3,444	3,537	5,046	10,791	21,288	28,059	30,501
State and local—general government	3,456	3,630	3,737	3,565	3,531	3,884	4,178	3,696	3,889	4,121	4,185	4,280	4,368	4,442	4,622	4,883	5,324
Rest of the world	643	612	495	371	293	241	252	164	148	334	243	260	231	238	259	226	213

Source: Bureau of the Census, *Statistical Abstract of the United States, 1948*, 277.

TABLE 4.5 STEEL INDUSTRY OPERATING RATES, 1914–1945 CAPACITY, PRODUCTION (INGOTS AND CASTINGS), PERCENT OF OPERATIONS

Net tons

	Capacity Jan. 1	Production	Rates Percent
1914	44,451,977	26,334,594	59.2
1915	46,249,146	36,009,161	77.9
1916	51,282,314	47,906,522	93.4
1917	55,567,555	50,467,880	90.8
1918	58,846,418	49,797,923	84.6
1919	61,020,669	38,831,779	63.6
1920	62,313,591	47,188,886	75.7
1921	64,262,027	22,157,853	34.5
1922	65,426,682	39,875,277	60.9
1923	65,682,014	50,336,940	76.6
1924	66,563,515	42,483,772	63.8
1925	68,473,222	50,840,747	74.2
1926	64,750,035	54,089,014	83.5
1927	67,236,117	50,327,407	74.9
1928	68,840,912	57,729,481	83.9
1929	71,438,516	63,205,490	88.5
1930	72,985,406	45,583,421	62.5
1931	77,257,803	29,058,961	37.6
1932	78,780,913	15,322,901	19.5
1933	78,614,403	26,020,229	33.1
1934	78,128,416	29,181,924	37.4
1935	78,451,930	38,183,705	48.7
1936	78,164,300	53,499,999	68.4
1937	78,148,374	56,636,945	72.5
1938	80,185,638	31,751,990	39.6
1939	81,828,958	52,798,714	64.5
1940	81,619,496	66,982,686	82.1
1941	85,158,150	82,839,259	97.3
1942	88,886,550	86,031,931	96.8
1943	90,589,190	88,836,512	98.1
1944	93,854,420	89,641,600	95.5
1945	95,505,280	79,701,648	83.5

Source: American Metal Market, *Metal Statistics, 1955* (New York, 1955), 120.

TABLE 4.6 WORLD PRODUCTION OF STEEL

Net tons

1915	73,438,000
1920	79,856,000
1925	99,602,000
1930	104,272,000
1931	76,619,000
1932	55,888,000
1933	74,771,000
1934	90,272,000
1935	109,424,000
1936	136,640,000
1937	149,960,000
1938	119,840,000
1939	150,416,000
1940	155,113,544
1941	171,545,464
1942	168,551,080
1943	179,027,080
1944	169,836,592
1945	127,041,444

Source: American Metal Market, *Metal Statistics, 1955,* 255.

TABLE 4.7 YEARLY NEW HOUSING UNITS STARTED AND CONSTRUCTION COSTS

| | Number of Units Started in Thousands | | | | Construction Cost, Average Amount per Unit | | | |
| | | Privately Owned[a] | | Publicly Owned, Total | | Privately Owned[a] | | Publicly Owned, Total |
Year	Total	Total	1-unit Structures		Total	Total	1-unit Structures	
					Excluding Farm Housing			
1945	326	325	(NA)	1	4,625	4,625	(NA)	5,350
1944	142	139	115	3	3,500	3,475	3,450	4,125
1943	191	184	136	7	3,600	3,600	3,675	3,925
1942	356	301	252	55	3,775	3,775	3,900	3,825
1941	706	620	533	87	4,000	4,075	4,250	3,400
1940	603	530	448	73	3,825	3,925	4,075	3,125
1939	515	458	373	57	3,775	3,850	(NA)	3,250
1938	406	399	316	7	3,900	3,900	(NA)	3,325
1937	336	332	266	4	4,125	4,100	(NA)	4,600
1936	319	304	238	15	3,975	3,925	(NA)	5,225
1935	221	216	182	5	3,425	3,400	(NA)	4,700
1934	126	126	109	. . .	2,925	2,925	(NA)	. . .
1933	93	93	76	. . .	3,075	3,075	(NA)	. . .
1932	134	134	118	. . .	3,050	3,050	(NA)	. . .
1931	254	254	187	. . .	4,350	4,350	(NA)	. . .
1930	330	330	227	. . .	4,525	4,525	(NA)	. . .
1929	509	509	316	. . .	4,825	4,825	(NA)	. . .
1928	753	753	436	. . .	4,800	4,800	(NA)	. . .
1927	810	810	454	. . .	4,825	4,825	(NA)	. . .
1926	849	849	491	. . .	4,850	4,850	(NA)	. . .
1925	938	938	573	. . .	4,775	4,775	(NA)	. . .
1924	893	893	534	. . .	4,550	4,550	(NA)	. . .
1923	871	871	513	. . .	4,325	4,325	(NA)	. . .
1922	716	716	437	. . .	4,125	4,125	(NA)	. . .
1921	449	449	316	. . .	3,950	3,950	(NA)	. . .
1920	247	247	202	. . .	4,325	4,325	(NA)	. . .
1919	315	315	239	. . .	4,000	4,000	(NA)	. . .
1918	118	118	91	. . .	3,325	3,325	(NA)	. . .
1917	240	240	166	. . .	3,200	3,200	(NA)	. . .
1916	437	437	267	. . .	2,875	2,875	(NA)	. . .
1915	433	433	262	. . .	2,750	2,750	(NA)	. . .
1914	421	421	263	. . .	2,575	2,575	(NA)	. . .

[a]Privately owned units pertained to units constructed by persons or companies and sold to individuals. Publicly owned structures came from projects of the government, usually the national government, to deal with a pressing need for housing.
Source: Bureau of the Census, *Housing Construction Statistics, 1889–1964* (Washington, D.C., 1966), 25.

TABLE 4.8   FUEL PRODUCTION

The United States was a major producer of nearly all types of energy, and production as a rule followed the ups and downs of the economy. Although use of coal remained massive, there was a trend toward using less coal and relying more on natural gas. Production of petroleum increased steadily, even—except for one or two years—during the depression, as the United States moved more and more into the world of motor vehicles.

	Coke (millions of net tons)	Anthracite Coal (short tons)	Bituminous Coal (short tons)	Natural Gas (millions of cubic feet)	Crude Petroleum (thousands of 42-gal. barrels)
1945	67.3	54,933,909	577,617,327	3,918,686	1,713,655
1944	74.0	63,701,363	619,576,240	3,711,039	1,677,904
1943	71.7	60,643,620	590,177,069	3,414,689	1,505,613
1942	70.6	60,327,729	582,692,937	3,053,475	1,386,645
1941	65.2	56,368,267	514,149,245	2,812,658	1,402,228
1940	57.1	51,484,640	460,771,500	2,660,222	1,353,214
1939	44.3	51,487,377	394,855,325	2,476,756	1,264,962
1938	32.5	46,099,027	348,544,764	2,295,562	1,214,355
1937	52.4	51,856,433	445,531,449	2,407,620	1,279,160
1936	46.3	54,579,535	439,087,903	2,167,802	1,099,687
1935	35.1	52,158,783	372,373,122	1,916,595	996,596
1934	31.8	57,168,291	359,368,022	1,770,721	908,065
1933	27.6	49,541,344	333,630,533	1,555,474	905,656
1932	21.8	49,855,221	309,709,872	1,555,990	785,159
1931	33.5	59,645,652	382,089,396	1,686,436	851,081
1930	48.0	69,384,837	467,526,299	1,943,421	898,011
1929	59.9	73,828,195	534,988,593	1,917,693	1,007,323
1928	52.8	75,348,069	500,744,970	1,568,139	901,474
1927	51.1	80,095,564	517,763,352	1,445,428	901,129
1926	56.9	84,437,452	573,366,985	1,313,019	770,874
1925	51.3	61,817,149	520,052,741	1,188,571	763,743
1924	44.3	87,926,862	483,686,538	1,141,521	713,940
1923	57.0	93,339,009	564,564,662	1,006,976	732,407
1922	37.1	54,683,022	422,268,099	762,546	557,531
1921	25.3	90,473,451	415,921,950	662,052	472,183
1920	51.3	89,598,249	568,666,683	798,210	442,929
1919	44.2	88,092,201	465,860,058	745,916	378,367
1918	56.5	98,826,084	579,385,820	721,001	355,928
1917	55.6	99,611,811	551,790,563	795,110	335,316
1916	54.5	87,578,493	502,519,682	753,170	300,767
1915	41.6	88,995,061	442,624,426	628,579	281,104
1914	34.6	90,821,507	422,703,970	591,867	265,763

Source: Bureau of the Census, *Historical Statistics of the United States, 1789 to 1945* (Washington, D.C., 1949), 142, 145–146.

TABLE 4.9   VALUE OF MINERAL PRODUCTION (THOUSANDS OF DOLLARS)

| Year | All Mineral Products | Metallic | Nonmetallic | | |
			Total	Fuels[a]	Other
1945	8,140,000	1,974,000	6,166,000	5,212,000	954,000
1944	8,419,000	2,340,000	6,079,000	5,178,000	901,000
1943	8,071,800	2,488,000	5,583,800	4,608,300	975,500
1942	7,576,300	2,363,900	5,212,400	4,103,400	1,109,000
1941	6,878,000	2,132,000	4,746,000	3,708,100	1,037,900
1940	5,613,900	1,678,600	3,935,300	3,116,500	818,800
1939	4,914,200	1,291,700	3,622,500	2,834,300	788,200
1938	4,363,200	892,600	3,470,600	2,820,300	650,300
1937	5,413,400	1,468,200	3,945,200	3,200,500	744,700
1936	4,556,800	1,081,600	3,475,200	2,759,200	716,000
1935	3,650,000	733,130	2,916,870	2,330,000	586,870
1934	3,325,400	548,934	2,776,466	2,233,300	543,166
1933	2,555,100	417,065	2,138,035	1,683,400	454,635
1932	2,461,700	285,875	2,175,825	1,743,400	432,425
1931	3,166,600	569,790	2,596,810	1,892,400	704,410
1930	4,764,800	985,790	3,779,010	2,764,500	1,014,510
1929	5,887,600	1,480,390	4,407,210	3,190,527	1,216,683
1928	5,385,200	1,288,290	4,096,910	2,884,962	1,211,948
1927	5,530,000	1,220,633	4,309,367	3,060,047	1,249,320
1926	6,213,600	1,405,345	4,808,255	3,541,916	1,266,339
1925	5,677,630	1,382,155	4,295,475	3,058,680	1,236,795
1924	5,305,800	1,233,370	4,072,430	2,898,630	1,173,800
1923	5,986,500	1,511,930	4,474,570	3,317,100	1,157,470
1922	4,647,290	988,100	3,659,190	2,737,880	921,310
1921	4,138,500	654,700	3,483,800	2,703,470	780,330
1920	6,981,840	1,763,675	5,217,665	4,192,910	1,024,755
1919	4,623,770	1,361,099	3,262,671	2,510,894	751,777
1918	5,540,708	2,156,588	3,384,120	2,736,151	647,969
1917	4,992,496	2,088,914	2,903,582	2,237,837	665,745
1916	3,508,439	1,622,129	1,886,310	1,332,584	553,726
1915	2,394,644	993,353	1,401,291	972,617	428,674
1914	2,111,172	687,101	1,424,071	992,837	431,234

[a]Coal, natural gas, natural gasoline and allied products, and petroleum.
Source: Bureau of the Census, *Historical Statistics of the United States, 1789 to 1945,* 141.

The Special Case of Rubber

The importance of rubber to the American nation grew in conjunction with the motor vehicle industries, the period of the Great Depression—when production of many items declined—notwithstanding. Much natural rubber went into the construction of tires and tubes (in the days before tubeless tires, the air was contained in an all-rubber inner container called a tube). Virtually all rubber was imported. At the start of the Second World War, the United States faced a near crisis when the Japanese seized the principal sources of rubber in Southeast Asia. The nation dealt with the situation partly by conservation (very few tires were available for domestic consumption), partly by recycling old rubber, but largely by a crash program to develop a synthetic substitute. In production by 1943, the synthetic—called butadiene—represented one of the "miracles" of industry during the Second World War.

The nation sought to deal with wartime scarcity of rubber by conservation and re-using rubber already in service. These children in Chicago turn in old tires for recycling in 1942. (Library of Congress)

TABLE 4.10   NATURAL RUBBER

Year	Crude Rubber			Reclaimed Rubber			Automotive	
	Total Consumption	Consumption for Tires and Tubes	Imports, Including Latex and Guayule	Consumption	Production	Stocks End of Year	Tire Production	Tube Production
	Monthly Average in Long Tons						Monthly Average in Thousands	
1926	30,513	25,094	34,804	13,710	. . .	23,218	5,134	6,385
1927	31,083	24,947	35,937	15,792	. . .	24,980	5,370	5,844
1928	36,417	30,185	36,644	18,583	. . .	24,785	6,495	6,686
1929	38,950	31,430	47,091	18,085	17,857	27,000	5,727	5,736
1930	31,333	21,794	40,636	12,788	13,344	22,000	4,247	4,368
1931	29,599	20,976	41,816	10,250	10,807	21,714	4,062	4,028
1932	28,062	19,185	34,556	6,459	6,305	16,334	3,340	3,074
1933	34,364	23,630	34,908	7,084	7,799	17,780	3,775	3,546
1934	38,540	26,502	38,585	8,405	8,980	20,000	3,936	3,856
1935	40,962	27,571	38,929	9,794	10,246	17,000	4,113	3,990
1936	47,917	34,418	40,679	11,791	12,548	19,000	4,670	4,753
1937	45,300	32,492	50,040	13,500	15,417	28,800	4,442	4,364
1938	36,419	24,005	34,341	10,067	10,200	23,000	3,409	3,154
1939	49,333	33,829	41,635	14,167	15,500	25,250	4,801	4,221
1940	54,042	36,535	68,187	15,854	17,414	32,630	4,932	4,353
1941	64,583	41,058	85,751	20,936	22,850	41,750	5,128	4,786
1942	31,399	19,444	23,512	21,235	23,759	42,532	1,279	1,057
1943	26,470	13,688	4,993	24,257	25,333	46,201	1,702	1,251
1944	12,009	6,603	9,470	20,924	21,717	43,832	2,787	2,291
1945	8,786	5,582	12,440	20,086	20,276	28,155	3,710	3,478

Source: National Industrial Conference Board, *The Economic Almanac for 1950* (New York, 1950), 438.

TABLE 4.11   SYNTHETIC RUBBER

Long Tons

Period	Production	Consumption	Stocks End of Period	Used in Manufacture of Automotive Tires and Tubes
1943				
First quarter	10,486	7,696	6,693	19,137
Second quarter	28,373	17,526	16,139	17,588
Third quarter	71,217	50,421	31,342	22,346
Fourth quarter	121,523	95,248	47,295	27,913
Total	231,722	170,891	. . .	86,984
1944				
First quarter	159,603	116,887	64,548	54,059
Second quarter	198,905	130,080	98,536	58,677
Third quarter	193,602	150,092	127,849	71,174
Fourth quarter	210,520	169,611	150,032	84,932
Total	762,630	566,670	. . .	268,842
1945				
First quarter	227,865	189,184	170,024	97,813
Second quarter	237,857	180,901	208,933	92,334
Third quarter	212,107	152,489	245,656	88,983
Fourth quarter	142,544	171,006	203,454	102,512
Total	820,373	693,580	. . .	381,641

Source: National Industrial Conference Board, *Economic Almanac for 1950*, 438.

Corporate Earnings

Statistics on earnings of American corporations confirmed the ever recurring themes of the first half of the twentieth century: (1) The depression had a devastating effect—many, if not most, firms lost money; (2) What was lost during the depression was gained back and more during the Second World War.

TABLE 4.12   CORPORATE PROFITS BEFORE AND AFTER FEDERAL AND STATE INCOME AND EXCESS PROFITS TAXES, 1929–1945

Millions of Dollars

Year	All Industries, Total		Agriculture, Forestry and Fisheries		Mining		Contract Construction		Manufacturing		Wholesale Trade	
	Before	After	Before	After	Before	After	Before	After	Before	After	Before	After
1929	9,818	8,420	20	13	466	416	121	102	5,038	4,403	319	267
1930	3,303	2,455	−35	−39	125	101	93	75	1,704	1,327	−35	−64
1931	−783	−1,283	−68	−69	−122	−130	1	−8	−274	−480	−176	−193
1932	−3,042	−3,424	−69	−70	−89	−97	−88	−92	−1,291	−1,423	−243	−258
1933	162	−362	−29	−31	−12	−23	−51	−55	840	583	94	61
1934	1,723	977	−28	−33	179	154	−27	−32	1,388	1,056	217	158
1935	3,224	2,259	16	3	195	168	0	−9	2,234	1,742	257	193
1936	5,684	4,273	28	18	322	279	27	14	3,606	2,885	427	330
1937	6,197	4,685	14	5	469	404	42	26	3,711	2,936	366	273
1938	3,329	2,289	−7	−12	219	183	28	15	1,601	1,147	142	90
1939	6,467	5,005	9	2	318	272	32	18	3,712	2,958	358	276
1940	9,325	6,447	24	13	442	364	70	44	5,601	3,840	492	349
1941	17,232	9,386	63	38	622	464	188	97	11,140	5,713	1,028	567
1942	21,098	9,433	84	41	616	405	311	113	12,695	5,209	1,111	480
1943	25,052	10,646	117	50	536	357	240	73	14,615	5,752	1,280	514
1944	24,333	10,808	120	50	517	361	127	36	13,972	5,985	1,349	548
1945	19,717	8,502	119	49	422	291	94	28	10,437	4,277	1,347	572

Year	Retail Trade		Finance, Insurance and Real Estate		Transportation		Communication and Public Utilities		Services		Rest of the World
	Before	After	Before	After	Before	After	Before	After	Before	After	
1929	457	384	1,200	917	1,056	919	925	812	151	122	65
1930	18	−28	199	50	433	359	715	611	83	60	3
1931	−240	−280	−303	−384	−96	−132	587	496	−36	−47	−56
1932	−483	−509	−661	−727	−330	−357	451	357	−183	−192	−56
1933	−9	−53	−672	−728	−241	−269	383	303	−109	−118	−32
1934	192	133	−575	−670	−162	−212	558	457	−17	−32	−2
1935	287	214	−299	−422	−86	−138	569	469	7	−10	44
1936	485	375	22	−171	93	21	661	536	45	18	−32
1937	455	342	251	60	57	−20	785	635	66	37	−13
1938	259	172	295	141	−178	−238	728	578	47	18	195
1939	480	365	340	192	160	70	870	696	74	42	114
1940	624	436	487	276	332	179	1,012	748	104	61	137
1941	1,151	668	671	330	910	570	1,171	733	189	107	99
1942	1,513	680	871	458	2,092	1,095	1,370	701	337	153	98
1943	1,903	809	1,174	678	2,945	1,286	1,556	762	556	235	130
1944	2,080	828	1,447	852	2,452	1,038	1,588	768	585	246	96
1945	2,189	904	1,573	855	1,386	537	1,534	718	599	254	17

Source: National Industrial Conference Board, *Economic Almanac for 1950,* 122.

Corporations set records in production, income, and profits during the years 1942–45. Here workers at Boeing Aircraft in Seattle celebrate production in 1944 of the 5,000th B-17 bomber since the attack on Pearl Harbor. (The Boeing Historical Archives)

TABLE 4.13 MANUFACTURING CORPORATIONS— GROSS INCOME, NET PROFITS, AND NET INCOME

Amounts in Millions of Dollars

Year	Gross Income	Net Profit		Net Income	
		Amount	Percent of Gross Income	Amount	Percent of Gross Income
1922	44,683	2,918	6.5	2,641	5.9
1923	56,221	3,903	6.9	3,571	6.4
1924	53,911	3,079	5.7	2,763	5.1
1925	60,830	4,109	6.8	3,701	6.1
1926	62,495	4,225	6.8	3,708	5.9
1927	63,723	3,558	5.6	3,088	4.8
1928	67,273	4,480	6.7	3,911	5.8
1929	72,132	5,081	7.0	4,406	6.1
1930	60,900	1,741	2.9	1,118	1.8
1931	44,033	356d	0.8d	823d	1.9d
1932	31,977	1,516d	4.7d	1,806d	5.6d
1933	35,151	444	1.3	204	0.6
1934	41,093	1,432	3.5	980	2.4
1935	47,898	2,478	5.2	1,817	3.8
1936	56,955	3,724	6.5	3,702	6.5
1937	62,457	3,721	6.0	3,703	5.9
1938	51,128	1,605	3.1	1,590	3.1
1939	58,294	3,580	6.1	3,568	6.1
1940	66,980	5,317	7.9	5,307	7.9
1941	93,433	10,439	11.2	10,431	11.2
1942	119,432	13,660	11.4	13,652	11.4
1943	146,368	16,594	11.3	16,582	11.3
1944	154,202	14,864	9.6	14,851	9.6
1945	141,277	10,257	7.3	10,250	7.3

Note: d = deficit
Source: National Industrial Conference Board, *The Economic Almanac for 1950,* 414.

TABLE 4.14 RETAIL SALES, 1929–1945

(In Millions)

Year	All Retail Stores	Durable Goods Stores	Nondurable Goods Stores
1929	$48,459	$14,180	$34,279
1930	41,989	10,269	31,720
1931	34,752	7,372	27,380
1932	25,013	4,034	20,979
1933	24,517	4,844	19,673
1934	28,743	5,959	22,784
1935	32,791	7,626	25,165
1936	38,338	9,863	28,475
1937	42,150	11,071	31,079
1938	38,053	8,591	29,462
1939	42,042	10,379	31,663
1940	46,383	12,418	33,970
1941	55,490	15,604	39,886
1942	57,552	9,846	47,706
1943	63,680	9,339	54,341
1944	69,484	9,967	59,517
1945	76,572	11,493	65,074

Source: Bureau of Labor Statistics, *Handbook of Labor Statistics, 1947* (Washington, D.C., 1947), 216.

Money and Banking, 1914–1945

The most important change to the banking system during this era was the introduction of the Federal Reserve System. Created by law in December 1913, during the Woodrow Wilson administration, the Federal Reserve System constituted a central bank of the United States with branches spread throughout the nation in twelve districts. By controlling reserve requirements of member banks and setting the discount rate, the "Fed" had some influence over the economy, although, as it developed, not enough to keep it on an even course. The number of banks grew in the years following the First World War, a boom that was halted by the collapse of land speculation in Florida in 1926. After that point the number of banks slowly declined until the onset of the depression, which had a devastating effect on financial institutions. The number of banks in 1933 was half what it had been ten years earlier. Bank failure inspired numerous "runs" by citizens fearful of losing their deposits. In many cases they did. To halt this dreadful process, the administration of

Franklin D. Roosevelt produced the Glass-Steagall Act, which created the Federal Deposit Insurance Corporation to protect bank deposits. Thereafter the number of bank failures declined sharply and even temporarily came to a halt. The banking system then stabilized, with far fewer banks than there had been in the 1920s with—beginning in the 1940s—rapidly increasing resources.

Changes in the currency system included growth of the money in circulation, even during the 1930s; a reduced proportionate reliance on coined currency; and a sharp deflation of prices during the early 1930s that increased the value of money. In 1934 the government called in gold currency and stopped the coinage of gold. The entire period was marked with steady growth in the use of federal reserve notes, a new currency that appeared in 1915 as part of the new national banking system. By 1945 the federal note had become standard; most money in circulation was federal reserve notes.

TABLE 4.15 NUMBER OF BANKS AND TOTAL ASSETS OR LIABILITIES

(Amounts in thousands of dollars)

Year (Jun. 30)	Number of Banks	Total Assets or Liabilities (or Total Resources)
1945	14,587	163,026,979
1944	14,598	139,559,665
1943	14,661	117,252,406
1942	14,815	92,259,991
1941	14,919	87,828,719
1940	15,017	80,213,629
1939	15,146	73,601,320
1938	15,341	68,277,707
1937	15,580	68,924,757
1936	15,803	67,188,241
1935	16,053	60,386,863
1934	15,894	56,157,554
1933	14,624	51,293,912
1932	19,163	57,190,109
1931	22,071	69,757,104
1930	24,079	73,462,376
1929	25,330	71,718,679
1928	26,213	71,137,842
1927	27,061	67,922,039
1926	28,146	64,686,070
1925	28,841	61,898,134
1924	29,348	57,084,786
1923	30,178	53,905,293
1922	30,389	50,294,893
1921	30,812	49,584,788
1920	30,139	52,828,247
1919	29,123	47,615,447
1918	28,880	40,726,439
1917	27,923	37,126,763
1916	27,513	32,271,238
1915	27,062	27,804,130
1914	26,765	26,971,398

Source: Bureau of the Census, *Historical Statistics of the United States, 1789 to 1945*, 262.

TABLE 4.16 SHORT-TERM INTEREST RATES AND FEDERAL RESERVE DISCOUNT RATE

Year	Stock Exchange Time Loans 90 Days	Prime Commercial Paper, 4 to 6 Months	Federal Reserve Bank of New York Discount Rate Low	Federal Reserve Bank of New York Discount Rate High
1945	1.25	0.75	0.50	1.00
1944	1.25	0.73	0.50	1.00
1943	1.25	0.69	0.50	1.00
1942	1.25	0.66	0.50	1.00
1941	1.25	0.53	1.00	1.00
1940	1.25	0.56	1.00	1.00
1939	1.25	0.59	1.00	1.00
1938	1.25	0.81	1.00	1.00
1937	1.25	0.94	1.00	1.50
1936	1.16	0.75	1.50	1.50
1935	0.55	0.75	1.50	1.50
1934	0.90	1.02	1.50	2.00
1933	1.11	1.73	2.00	3.50
1932	1.87	2.73	2.50	3.50
1931	2.15	2.64	1.50	3.50
1930	3.26	3.59	2.00	4.50
1929	7.75	5.85	4.50	6.00
1928	5.86	4.85	3.50	5.00
1927	4.35	4.11	3.50	4.00
1926	4.60	4.34	3.50	4.00
1925	4.23	4.02	3.00	3.50
1924	3.64	3.98	3.00	4.50
1923	5.14	5.07	4.00	4.50
1922	4.53	4.52	4.00	4.50
1921	6.15	6.62	4.50	7.00
1920	8.06	7.50	6.00	7.00
1919	5.83	5.37	4.00	4.75
1918	5.90	6.02	3.50	4.00
1917	4.62	5.07	3.00	3.50
1916	3.25	3.84	3.00	4.00
1915	2.85	4.01	4.00	5.00
1914	4.37	5.47	5.00	6.00

Source: Bureau of the Census, *Historical Statistics of the United States, Colonial Times to 1957* (Washington, D.C., 1960), 654.

TABLE 4.17   BANK SUSPENSIONS[a]

Year	Total	National	State	Private	Member[b]	Non-member
1945	0	. . .	. . .	. . .	. . .	. . .
1944	1	. . .	1	. . .	. . .	1
1943	4	2	2	. . .	2	2
1942	9	. . .	9	. . .	. . .	9
1941	8	4	4	. . .	4	4
1940	22	1	21	. . .	1	21
1939	42	4	37	1	7	35
1938	55	1	52	2	2	53
1937	59	4	54	1	6	53
1936	44	1	42	1	1	43
1935	34	4	30	. . .	4	30
1934	57[c]	1	43	13	1	56
1933	4,004	1,101	2,794	109	1,275	2,729
1932	1,456	276	1,143	37	331	1,125
1931	2,294	409	1,805	80	516	1,778
1930	1,352	161	1,133	58	188	1,164
1929	659	64	564	31	81	578
1928	499	57	423	19	73	426
1927	669	91	545	33	122	547
1926	976	123	801	52	158	818
1925	618	118	461	39	146	472
1924	775	122	616	37	160	578
1923	646	90	533	23	122	524
1922	367	49	295	23	62	305
1921	505	52	409	44	71	434
1920	167	7	136	24	. . .	. . .
1919	62	2	59	1	. . .	. . .
1918	47	2	35	10	. . .	. . .
1917	49	5	29	15	. . .	. . .
1916	52	8	32	12	. . .	. . .
1915	152	20	93	39	. . .	. . .
1914	149	15	107	27	. . .	. . .

[a] Bank suspensions pertain to banks closed to the public temporarily or permanently; often they were permanent.
[b] The term *member* applies to membership in the Federal Reserve System.
[c] Note the effect of the Glass-Steagall Act of 1933.
Source: Bureau of the Census, *Historical Statistics of the United States, 1789 to 1945*, 273.

The Money Supply

Money stock means all bank deposits and currency in circulation and held in the United States Treasury and the Federal Reserve Banks. The amount of currency generally increased with growth of the population, but especially during the years of the Second World War, when inflation also created the need for more money.

TABLE 4.18   MONEY STOCK AND MONEY IN CIRCULATION (THOUSANDS OF DOLLARS)

Year (Jun. 30)	Total Money in U.S.	Money Held in Treasury	Money outside Treasury	
			In Federal Reserve Banks	In Circulation
1945	48,009,400	22,202,115	3,745,512	26,746,438
1944	44,805,301	28,173,693	3,811,797	22,504,342
1943	40,868,266	24,466,764	3,770,331	17,421,260
1942	35,840,908	24,783,526	3,520,465	12,382,866
1941	32,774,611	24,575,186	3,380,914	9,612,432
1940	28,457,960	21,836,936	3,485,695	7,847,501
1939	23,754,736	17,862,671	3,436,467	7,046,743
1938	20,096,865	14,535,627	3,503,576	6,460,891
1937	19,376,690	13,685,480	3,454,205	6,447,056
1936	17,402,493	11,851,635	3,360,854	6,241,200
1935	15,113,035	9,997,362	1,147,422	5,567,093
1934	13,634,381	8,408,392	1,305,985	5,373,470
1933	10,078,417	3,797,692	2,271,682	5,720,764
1932	9,004,505	3,493,122	1,795,349	5,695,171
1931	9,079,624	4,227,735	2,226,059	4,821,933
1930	8,306,564	4,021,937	1,741,087	4,521,988
1929	8,538,796	3,789,886	1,856,986	4,746,297
1928	8,118,091	3,725,650	1,582,576	4,796,626
1927	8,667,282	4,159,056	1,753,110	4,851,321
1926	8,428,971	4,210,358	1,473,118	4,885,266
1925	8,299,382	4,176,381	1,367,591	4,815,208
1924	8,846,542	4,248,438	1,376,935	4,849,307
1923	8,702,788	3,821,846	1,207,836	4,823,275
1922	8,276,070	3,515,583	1,297,893	4,463,172
1921	8,174,528	2,921,089	1,262,089	4,910,992
1920	8,158,496	2,379,664	1,015,881	5,467,589
1919	7,688,413	2,907,812	810,636	4,876,638
1918	6,906,237	2,976,251	855,984	4,481,697
1917	5,678,774	2,859,396	816,365	4,066,404
1916	4,541,730	2,356,536	593,345	3,649,258
1915	4,050,783	1,967,665	382,965	3,319,582
1914	3,797,825	1,845,570	. . .	3,459,434

Source: Bureau of the Census, *Historical Statistics of the United States, 1789 to 1945*, 279.

TABLE 4.19 AMOUNT COINED OF GOLD, SILVER, AND MINOR COIN, AND SILVER PRICES

The amount of currency coined dropped sharply during the depression of the 1930s. The government in 1934 withdrew all gold coin from circulation. A need for more coinage in the 1940s led to greater use of silver—the half-dollars, quarters, and dimes—and also to more paper money and bank deposits. The use of coins in no way approximated the years of the 1920s, when gold had reigned supreme.

| Year | Coinage | | | | Silver Prices | |
	Total	Gold	Silver	Minor Coin	Bullion Value of the Silver Dollar	Average Commercial Ratio of Silver to Gold
1945	$101,132,085	. . .	$ 75,871,300	$25,260,785	$0.40404	67.00
1944	120,928,430	. . .	90,781,100	30,142,330	0.34853	77.67
1943	136,237,136	. . .	105,772,800	30,464,336	0.34853	77.67
1942	119,283,799	. . .	102,054,773	17,229,026	0.29889	90.57
1941	102,209,510	. . .	76,120,483	26,089,027	0.27144	99.73
1940	50,157,850	. . .	29,359,834	20,798,017	0.27136	99.76
1939	38,289,170	. . .	27,913,498	10,375,672	0.30470	88.84
1938	12,718,179	. . .	8,998,493	3,719,686	0.33673	80.39
1937	31,128,993	. . .	22,035,562	9,088,432	0.34956	77.44
1936	46,388,101	. . .	34,656,955	11,731,147	0.35113	77.09
1935	38,580,924	. . .	31,237,224	7,343,700	0.49950	54.19
1934	25,951,751	. . .	22,091,840	3,859,910	0.37344	72.49
1933	18,136,225	$ 12,035,000	895,625	205,600	0.27068	59.06
1932	68,422,820	66,665,000	1,562,200	195,620	0.21814	73.29
1931	61,828,420	60,895,000	621,000	307,420	0.22440	71.25
1930	8,730,510	2,440,000	2,658,300	3,632,210	0.29751	53.74
1929	54,225,400	40,235,000	8,590,500	5,399,900	0.41229	38.78
1928	189,773,337	177,360,000	8,748,667	3,664,670	0.45237	35.34
1927	141,147,127	125,645,000	11,286,217	4,215,910	0.43838	36.47
1926	102,828,002	78,540,565	19,825,806	4,461,630	0.48284	33.11
1925	216,456,863	192,380,000	19,374,218	4,202,645	0.53681	29.78
1924	229,946,730	206,010,000	21,627,040	2,309,690	0.51906	30.80
1923	114,575,118	45,365,000	66,283,038	2,927,080	0.50458	31.69
1922	165,076,646	80,680,016	84,325,030	71,600	0.52543	30.43
1921	100,782,846	10,570,000	89,057,536	1,155,310	0.48801	32.76
1920	50,213,920	16,990,000	25,057,270	8,166,650	0.78844	20.28
1919	20,777,500	. . .	11,068,400	9,709,100	0.86692	18.44
1918	31,445,691	. . .	25,473,029	5,972,662	0.76142	21.00
1917	35,540,403	10,014	29,412,300	6,118,089	0.69242	24.61
1916	33,743,376	18,525,026	8,880,800	6,337,550	0.58094	30.78
1915	30,145,339	23,968,402	4,114,098	2,062,840	0.40135	40.48
1914	61,749,712	58,457,818	6,083,823	2,208,071	0.42780	37.37

Source: Bureau of the Census, *Historical Statistics of the United States, 1789 to 1945*, 277.

TABLE 4.20 FOREIGN EXCHANGE RATES, 1939

Country	Unit	U.S. Cents
Argentina	peso	31.21
Australia	pound	372.75
Belgium	belga	16.83
Brazil	milreis	5.86
Bulgaria	lev	1.21
Canada	dollar	99.52
Chile	peso	5.17
China	yuan	16.03
Colombia	peso	56.99
Cuba	peso	99.93
Denmark	krone	20.89
Finland	markka	2.05
France	franc	2.65
Germany	reichsmark	40.09
Greece	drachma	.86
Hong Kong	dollar	28.67
Hungary	pengo	19.60

Country	Unit	U.S. Cents
India	rupee	34.96
Italy	lira	5.26
Japan	yen	27.27
Mexico	peso	20.02
Netherlands	guilder	53.08
New Zealand	pound	374.37
Norway	krone	232.51
Poland	zloty	18.81
Portugal	escudo	4.24
Rumania	leu	.71
South Africa	pound	463.05
Spain	peso	12.50
Sweden	krona	24.09
Switzerland	franc	22.43
United Kingdom	pound	468.02
Uruguay	peso	61.58
Yugoslavia	dinar	2.26

Source: Saint Anthony's Guild, *The 1940 National Catholic Almanac* (Paterson, N.J., 1940), 663.

Coinage

Coinage continued to take on different appearances—partly as part of a general plan for occasional change, partly in response to contemporary pressures. The new "peace" silver dollar—to celebrate the end of the war—introduced in 1921 became known to some as the "flapper" dollar because of the youth of the coin's version of Miss Liberty and her trendy hairdo. The half-dollar with Liberty on one side and an eagle with spread wings on the other continued to be coined during the years 1916–45. The twenty-five-cent piece featuring a full-standing Liberty, first coined in 1916, had poor wearing qualities (the date often disappeared), and so the Treasury used the bicentennial of the birth of the first president to shift to a George Washington quarter in 1932. The mercury dime, named from the wings on the cap of Liberty, was coined during 1916–45. The familiar Indian-head nickel, with a buffalo on the reverse side, in service for twenty-five years, was replaced in 1938 with a five-cent piece honoring Thomas Jefferson. The penny continued to feature the likeness of Abraham Lincoln that had appeared in 1909. A shortage of copper during the Second World War led the government to introduce in 1943 a penny made of steel with zinc coating. Some critics called it the Roosevelt penny, implying that the president was forever changing things, in this case cheapening the currency. Between February and December, 1,093,838,670 of the unpopular coins were minted. The penny of 1944 again was copper, made from expended shell casings supplemented with a small amount of virgin copper. Of course, the prestigious gold coins had not circulated since 1934.

The New York Stock Exchange

The New York Stock Exchange was the focal point of a larger exchange system that helped fuel the American capitalist system. It also served as a barometer of the power and health of the economy. Heavy trading and rising prices on the New York Exchange symbolized the optimism and speculative nature of society in the 1920s, especially 1927 and 1928. The collapse of prices in October 1929 jolted the nation's financial system, ruined many investors, and set in motion the start of a great depression that would affect every citizen in the land. By suggesting dubious practices in the exchange system, the stock market crash helped provoke intervention by the national government—another theme of the new era—notably in the law of 1934 that created the Securities and Exchange Commission. The SEC undertook responsibility for making and supervising rules for operations of the market.

TABLE 4.22 CLOSINGS OF THE NEW YORK STOCK EXCHANGE

Listed below are the days on which the trading floor of the New York Stock Exchange has been regularly closed, and closings for special reasons. Excluded from the list are Saturday closings solely for the extension of holidays and partial closings announced in advance—such as for funerals and parades.

New Year's Day	Labor Day
Lincoln's Birthday	Columbus Day
Washington's Birthday	Election Day
Good Friday	Armistice Day—1921, 1934
Decoration Day	Thanksgiving Day
Independence Day	Christmas Day

Jul. 31, 1914 to Dec. 14	World War I
Jun. 5, 1917	Draft registration
Aug. 4, 1917	Heat
Jan. 28, Feb. 4, Feb. 11, 1918	Heatless days
Sep. 12, 1918	Draft registration
Nov. 7, 1918	Closed 2:30—false armistice
Nov. 11, 1918	Armistice signed
Mar. 25, 1919	Return of 27th Division
May 6, 1919	Parade, 77th Division
Jul. 19, 1919	Heat
Sep. 10, 1919	Return of General Pershing
May 1, 1920	Relocation of offices
Sep. 16, 1920	Closed at noon—Wall Street explosion
Aug. 3, 1923	Death, President Harding
Aug. 10, 1923	Funeral, President Harding
Jun. 13, 1927	Parade, Colonel Lindbergh
Apr. 21, May 5, 12, May 19, May 26, Nov. 24, 1928	Volume activity on prior days
Feb. 9, Nov. 1, 2, 9, 16, 29, 30, 1929	Volume activity on prior days
Jan. 7, 1933	Funeral, President Coolidge
Mar. 4 to Mar. 14, 1933	Banking moratorium
Jul. 29, 1933	Volume activity on prior day
Aug. 4, 1933	Closed at 12:30—gas fumes on floor
Aug. 5, 12, 19, 26, 1933	Volume activity, heavy office workload
Apr. 14, 1945	Funeral, President Roosevelt
Aug. 15, 1945	V-J Day
Aug. 16, 1945	End of World War II
Oct. 27, 1945	Navy Day
Dec. 24, 1945	Monday before Christmas

Source: New York Stock Exchange, Fact Book, 37.

TABLE 4.21 HISTORIC DATES, 1914–1945

Jul. 31, 1914	Exchange closed through Dec. 14—World War I.
Oct. 13, 1915	Stock prices quoted in dollars as against percent of par value.
Jan. 2, 1919	Separate ticker system for bonds installed.
Apr. 26, 1920	Stock Clearing Corporation established.
Jan. 3, 1927	Start of 10-share unit of trading for inactive stocks.
Jun. 12, 1928	First 5 million–share day—5,252,000 shares.
Oct. 29, 1929	Only 16 million–share day—16,410,000 shares.
Sep. 2, 1930	Faster ticker—500 characters a minute—installed.
Mar. 4, 1933	Exchange closed to March 14 for bank holiday.
Jun. 6, 1934	Enactment of Securities Exchange Act of 1934.
Jun. 30, 1938	First salaried exchange president elected—William McChesney Martin, Jr.

Source: New York Stock Exchange, Fact Book (New York, 1966), 36.

Investment Activity

After the brief recession following the First World War, investment activity picked up steadily, especially in stocks, whose prices rose accordingly. The pace increased markedly during the late 1920s until 1929, when volume and prices reached their highest point. Then came the crash and a decline that was both sharp and gradual; the lowest stock prices were not reached until 1932. Transactions in bonds followed a somewhat similar course, but being less speculative than those in stocks, the fluctuations were less sharp. Bond prices would rise considerably in the 1940s, but activity in stocks—the volume and the prices—would not come close to the levels reached in 1929.

TABLE 4.23   BOND AND STOCK PRICES

| Year | Bonds (Price per $100 Bond) | | | Index of Common Stocks (1941–43 = 10) | | | |
	U.S. Government	Municipal High Grade	Corporate High Grade	Total	Industry	Railroad	Utilities
1945	$102.0	$139.6	$121.6	15.16	14.72	18.21	16.84
1944	100.3	135.7	118.7	12.47	12.34	13.47	12.81
1943	100.5	131.8	118.3	11.50	11.49	11.81	11.34
1942	100.7	126.2	117.4	8.67	8.78	8.81	7.74
1941	109.5	130.9	117.7	9.82	9.72	9.39	10.93
1940	106.6	123.6	116.3	11.02	10.69	9.41	15.05
1939	104.5	119.0	114.7	12.06	11.77	9.82	16.34
1938	101.8	116.6	111.7	11.49	11.39	9.15	14.17
1937	100.1	113.3	110.2	15.41	14.97	16.86	19.07
1936	100.8	113.8	109.6	15.47	14.69	17.71	22.47
1935	99.5	108.6	105.5	10.60	10.13	11.78	15.15
1934	95.4	99.7	98.2	9.84	9.00	14.05	15.79
1933	93.1	91.0	91.2	8.96	7.61	12.75	19.72
1932	88.9	91.7	84.4	6.93	5.37	8.75	20.65
1931	92.8	100.0	92.8	13.66	10.51	23.72	37.18
1930	108.8	99.0	90.9	21.03	16.42	39.82	53.24
1929	104.8	96.5	89.1	26.02	21.35	46.15	59.33
1928	108.3	99.3	91.8	19.95	16.92	40.40	36.86
1927	108.1	100.3	91.6	15.34	12.53	38.17	27.63
1926	103.8	99.0	90.1	12.59	10.04	32.72	24.11
1925	101.7	98.8	88.3	11.15	8.69	29.21	23.28
1924	99.3	97.4	86.6	9.05	6.83	25.02	19.34
1923	95.9	96.7	85.0	8.57	6.54	23.45	18.11
1922	96.6	96.9	85.5	8.41	6.35	23.71	17.39
1921	88.2	86.5	76.6	6.86	5.07	20.15	14.18
1920	85.9	87.7	75.2	7.98	6.50	20.86	13.36
1919	91.9	93.9	81.9	8.78	7.13	22.94	14.79
1918	. . .	93.5	82.3	7.54	5.57	22.40	14.70
1917	. . .	97.3	87.6	8.50	6.15	24.89	18.24
1916	. . .	100.9	90.7	9.47	6.62	28.35	20.26
1915	. . .	97.8	89.5	8.31	5.22	26.38	18.65
1914	. . .	98.4	90.4	8.08	4.50	27.39	18.14

Source: Bureau of the Census, *Historical Statistics of the United States, Colonial Times to 1957*, 657.

TABLE 4.24   STOCK VOLUME, SHARES, AND TURNOVER RATE

| Year | Reported Stock Volume | Average of Shares Listed | Percent Turnover |
	millions	millions	
1914[a]	47.4	154.8	31%
1915	172.5	155.8	111
1916	232.6	160.2	145
1917	184.6	179.7	103
1918	143.3	193.9	74
1919	318.3	208.0	153
1920	227.6	251.1	91
1921	172.8	292.7	59
1922	260.9	337.2	77
1923	236.5	393.2	60
1924	284.0	424.8	67
1925	459.7	462.5	99
1926	451.9	538.6	84
1927	581.7	620.3	94
1928	930.9	706.2	132
1929	1,124.8	942.5	119

| Year | Reported Stock Volume | Average of Shares Listed | Percent Turnover |
	millions	millions	
1930	810.6	1,212.2	67
1931	576.8	1,307.8	44
1932	425.2	1,315.3	32
1933	654.8	1,302.6	50
1934	323.8	1,299.4	25
1935	381.6	1,311.6	29
1936	496.0	1,339.1	37
1937	409.5	1,386.2	30
1938	297.5	1,418.1	21
1939	262.0	1,429.8	18
1940	207.6	1,445.1	14
1941	170.6	1,459.0	12
1942	125.7	1,466.9	9
1943	278.7	1,479.9	19
1944	263.1	1,490.8	18
1945	377.6	1,542.2	24

[a]Exchange closed on Jul. 31, on outbreak of World War I, and remained closed until Dec. 15, 1914.
Source: New York Stock Exchange, *Fact Book*, 43.

TABLE 4.25 BOND VOLUME (PAR VALUE)

Values in millions

Year	Total Reported	Daily Average	High Day Amt.	High Day Date	Low Day Amt.	Low Day Date
1914	$ 461.7	$ 2.5	$ 7.4	1/22	$1.0	12/31
1915	961.7	3.5	9.7	4/28	1.4	6/1
1916	1,148.2	4.2	9.6	10/26	1.6	7/21
1917	1,034.7	3.8	8.8	4/10	1.1	8/3
1918	2,092.8	7.7	57.0	12/30	2.7	3/1
1919	3,676.1	13.6	42.5	12/30	7.4	6/25
1920	3,868.4	14.1	36.2	12/30	6.7	9/16
1921	3,386.2	12.4	26.6	11/29	5.6	8/16
1922	4,132.7	15.1	36.6	1/10	6.3	7/3
1923	2,745.0	10.0	16.2	5/9	5.4	8/31
1924	3,810.5	13.8	29.6	6/12	7.0	12/24
1925	3,427.0	12.4	20.6	2/5	7.0	8/31
1926	3,015.3	11.0	27.1	4/23	5.9	8/16
1927	3,308.0	12.0	21.1	1/13	7.1	8/26
1928	2,906.6	10.7	19.9	4/20	5.6	8/27
1929	2,996.4	11.4	28.8	10/29	6.0	12/24
1930	2,720.3	9.9	29.1	3/20	5.9	8/4
1931	2,969.8	10.8	22.6	9/24	5.7	4/20
1932	2,991.2	10.8	19.7	8/23	5.5	11/21
1933	3,355.6	12.9	25.5	7/7	6.4	9/1
1934	3,702.8	13.5	30.7	2/5	6.3	8/20
1935	3,339.5	12.1	26.8	1/11	6.2	2/11
1936	3,576.9	12.9	24.2	1/8	6.2	8/17
1937	2,792.5	10.2	35.2	3/12	3.7	8/30
1938	1,859.9	6.8	15.4	12/28	3.2	8/15
1939	2,046.1	7.5	83.1	9/6	2.5	7/3
1940	1,669.4	6.0	13.6	5/21	1.9	8/19
1941	2,111.8	7.7	19.9	1/9	3.8	5/26
1942	2,311.5	8.4	19.1	9/24	3.2	7/20
1943	3,254.7	11.8	32.2	3/3	3.8	8/30
1944	2,694.7	9.8	25.8	2/15	3.7	9/18
1945	2,262.0	8.5	23.3	1/11	3.0	9/17

Note: ☐ = series record.
Source: New York Stock Exchange, *Fact Book*, 45.

Foreign Trade, 1914–1945

Statistics for foreign trade during this period reflect the fact that the United States was the industrial and productive giant of the world. Even a giant, however, was at the mercy of national and international developments. Trade picked up during the First World War when European nations made heavy demands for goods from America's farms and factories. It leveled off during the 1920s, took a sharp nose-dive in the 1930s, and then soared—at least exports soared—during the Second World War. Europe remained the leading trading partner and America's largest customer, although trade with Canada became more important than with any other single nation. The United States consistently ran an unfavorable balance with Asia until the time of the Second World War. Conspicuous was the virtual stoppage of trade with Germany—part of the time it did stop—during 1915–19 and 1941–45 and with Japan in 1942–45. If one reckons foreign trade in terms of buying and selling general merchandise, the United States had a favorable balance every year of this period; in some years the excess of exports was substantial. In the end, however, it was necessary to take into account all transactions by the U.S. government or U.S. citizens abroad. Unusual circumstances, such as large purchases of gold in the 1930s and special U.S. assistance programs, such as Lend-Lease, during the Second World War led the country occasionally to experience an unfavorable balance of payments. Thus it was possible for the United States to have an annual favorable balance of trade and still experience an occasional unfavorable balance of payments.

TABLE 4.26 VALUE OF IMPORTS AND EXPORTS

(In millions of dollars)

Year	Total, Gold, Silver, and Merchandise Exports	Imports	Excess of Exports (+) or Imports (−)	Gold Exports	Gold Imports	Gold Excess of Exports (+) or Imports (−)	Silver Exports	Silver Imports	Silver Excess of Exports (+) or Imports (−)	Merchandise Exports and Reexports Total	Exports of U.S. Merchandise	Re-exports	General Imports	Excess of Exports (+) or Imports (−)
1945	10,097	4,280	+5,816	200	94	+106	91	27	+64	9,806	9,585	221	4,159	+5,646
1944	15,345	4,066	+11,279	959	114	+845	127	23	+104	14,259	14,162	97	3,929	+10,330
1943	13,028	3,511	+9,517	33	102	−69	31	28	+3	12,965	12,842	123	3,381	+9,583
1942	8,081	3,113	+4,968	. . .	316	−316	2	41	−39	8,079	8,003	76	2,756	+5,323
1941	5,153	4,375	+778	. . .	982	−982	6	47	−41	5,147	5,020	127	3,345	+1,802
1940	4,030	7,433	−3,403	5	4,749	−4,744	4	58	−55	4,021	3,934	87	2,625	+1,396
1939	3,192	5,978	−2,786	1	3,575	−3,574	15	85	−71	3,177	3,123	54	2,318	+859
1938	3,107	4,170	−1,063	6	1,979	−1,974	7	231	−223	3,094	3,057	37	1,960	+1,134
1937	3,407	4,807	−1,400	46	1,632	−1,586	12	92	−80	3,349	3,299	50	3,084	+265
1936	2,495	3,750	−1,254	28	1,144	−1,117	12	183	−171	2,456	2,419	37	2,423	+33
1935	2,304	4,143	−1,839	2	1,741	−1,739	19	355	−336	2,283	2,243	40	2,047	+235
1934	2,202	2,944	−742	53	1,187	−1,134	17	103	−86	2,133	2,100	33	1,655	+478
1933	2,061	1,703	+358	367	193	+173	19	60	−41	1,675	1,647	28	1,450	+225
1932	2,434	1,706	+729	810	363	+446	14	20	−6	1,611	1,576	35	1,323	+288
1931	2,918	2,731	+186	467	612	−145	26	29	−2	2,424	2,378	46	2,091	+334

Year	Total, Gold, Silver, and Merchandise Exports	Imports	Excess of Exports (+) or Imports (−)	Gold Exports	Imports	Excess of Exports (+) or Imports (−)	Silver Exports	Imports	Excess of Exports (+) or Imports (−)	Merchandise Exports and Reexports Total	Exports of U.S. Merchandise	Re-exports	General Imports	Excess of Exports (+) or Imports (−)
1930	4,013	3,500	+514	116	396	−280	54	43	+11	3,843	3,781	62	3,061	+782
1929	5,441	4,755	+686	117	292	−175	83	64	+19	5,241	5,157	84	4,399	+842
1928	5,776	4,328	+1,448	561	169	+392	87	68	+19	5,128	5,030	98	4,091	+1,037
1927	5,142	4,447	+695	201	208	−6	76	55	+21	4,865	4,759	107	4,185	+681
1926	5,017	4,714	+303	116	214	−98	92	70	+23	4,809	4,712	97	4,431	+378
1925	5,272	4,419	+852	263	128	+134	99	65	+35	4,910	4,819	91	4,227	+683
1924	4,763	4,004	+759	62	320	−258	110	74	+36	4,591	4,498	93	3,610	+981
1923	4,269	4,189	+79	29	323	−294	72	74	−2	4,167	4,091	77	3,792	+375
1922	3,931	3,459	+473	37	275	−238	63	71	−8	3,832	3,765	67	3,113	+719
1921	4,560	3,264	+1,297	24	691	−667	52	63	−12	4,485	4,379	106	2,509	+1,976
1920	8,664	5,784	+2,880	322	417	−95	114	88	+26	8,228	8,080	148	5,278	+2,950
1919	8,528	4,070	+4,457	368	77	+292	239	89	+150	7,920	7,750	171	3,904	+4,016
1918	6,443	3,165	+3,278	41	62	−21	253	71	+181	6,149	6,048	101	3,031	+3,118
1917	6,690	3,558	+3,131	372	552	−181	84	53	+31	6,234	6,170	64	2,952	+3,281
1916	5,709	3,110	+2,599	156	686	−530	71	32	+38	5,483	5,423	60	2,392	+3,091
1915	2,966	1,875	+1,091	146	172	−25	51	29	+22	2,769	2,716	52	1,674	+1,094
1914	2,532	1,991	+541	112	67	+46	55	30	+25	2,365	2,830	35	1,894	+471

Source: Bureau of the Census, *Historical Statistics of the United States, Colonial Times to 1957*, 557.

TABLE 4.27 VALUE OF IMPORTS AND EXPORTS BY AREAS

(In millions of dollars)

	Europe (total) Exports to	Imports from	UK Exports to	Imports from	Germany Exports to	Imports from	Rest of America Exports to	Imports from	Asia (total) Exports to	Imports from	Japan Exports to	Imports from
1914	1,486	896	594	294	345	190	654	650	141	305	51	107
1915	1,971	614	912	256	29	91	576	734	139	272	41	99
1916	3,813	633	1,887	305	2	6	1,145	1,086	388	551	109	182
1917	4,062	551	2,009	280	. . .	. . .	1,573	1,471	469	821	186	254
1918	3,859	318	2,061	149	. . .	. . .	1,628	1,585	498	939	274	302
1919	5,188	751	2,279	309	93	11	1,738	1,844	772	1,108	366	410
1920	4,466	1,228	1,825	514	311	89	2,553	2,424	872	1,397	378	415
1921	2,364	765	942	239	372	80	1,403	1,051	533	618	238	251
1922	2,083	991	856	357	316	117	1,142	1,181	449	827	222	354
1923	2,093	1,157	882	404	317	161	1,355	1,469	511	1,020	267	347
1924	2,445	1,096	983	366	440	139	1,404	1,461	515	931	253	340
1925	2,604	1,239	1,034	413	470	164	1,541	1,499	487	1,319	230	384
1926	2,310	1,278	973	383	364	198	1,620	1,580	565	1,409	261	401
1927	2,314	1,265	840	358	482	201	1,691	1,504	560	1,268	258	402
1928	2,375	1,249	847	349	467	222	1,802	1,530	655	1,169	288	384
1929	2,341	1,334	848	330	410	255	1,934	1,621	643	1,279	259	432
1930	1,838	911	678	210	278	177	1,357	1,195	448	854	165	279
1931	1,187	641	456	135	166	127	750	824	386	574	156	206
1932	784	390	288	75	134	74	462	539	292	362	135	134
1933	850	463	312	111	140	78	455	520	292	425	143	128
1934	950	490	383	115	109	69	648	628	401	489	210	119
1935	1,029	599	433	155	92	78	706	776	378	605	203	153
1936	1,043	718	440	200	102	80	821	910	399	708	204	172
1937	1,360	843	536	203	126	92	1,158	1,113	580	967	289	204
1938	1,326	567	521	118	107	65	1,040	753	517	570	240	127
1939	1,290	617	505	149	46	52	1,131	898	562	700	232	161
1940	1,645	390	1,011	155	. . .	5	1,501	1,089	619	981	227	158
1941	1,847	281	1,637	136	. . .	3	2,047	1,657	625	1,088	60	78
1942	4,009	220	2,529	134	. . .	. . .	2,205	1,762	688	340	. . .	. . .
1943	7,633	240	4,505	105	. . .	. . .	2,418	2,458	838	235	. . .	. . .
1944	9,364	289	5,243	84	. . .	. . .	2,627	2,965	996	322	. . .	. . .
1945	5,515	409	2,193	90	2	1	2,564	2,874	849	407	. . .	. . .

Source: Thelma Liesner, *Economic Statistics, 1900–1983* (New York, 1985), 59.

TABLE 4.28 EXPORTS OF SELECTED PRODUCTS

(In millions of units and dollars)

Year	Total Selected Commodities, Value	Cotton, Unmanufactured Quantity (lb.)	Cotton, Unmanufactured Value	Leaf Tobacco, Unmanufactured Quantity (lb.)	Leaf Tobacco, Unmanufactured Value	Wheat Quantity (60-lb. bu.)	Wheat Value	Wheat and Wheat Flour, Value	Cotton Manufactures, Value	Animal Fats and Oils, Value	Fruits and Nuts, Value	Meat Products, Value	Naval Stores, Gums, and Resins, Value	Automobiles, Incl. Engines and Parts, Value	Sawmill Products, Value	Other Wood Manufactures, Value	Coal and Related Fuels, Value	Petroleum and Products, Value	Iron and Steel Mill Products, Value	Machinery, Value	Copper and Manufactures, Value
1945	4,949	1,282	279	470	239	129	240	330	236	103	128	290	13	588	34	55	198	753	457	1,191	55
1944	5,398	531	115	280	146	10	16	76	232	163	126	535	14	643	31	43	182	960	551	1,478	103
1943	4,407	842	184	393	170	12	16	56	192	144	80	617	14	279	26	38	172	517	615	1,194	109
1942	3,266	539	99	237	68	7	7	28	131	95	51	358	13	433	27	24	152	350	592	763	82
1941	2,608	625	83	263	65	13	11	35	135	41	52	99	15	339	30	21	119	285	501	740	48
1940	2,456	2,046	213	217	44	14	11	33	76	14	36	22	12	254	37	21	87	310	516	671	110
1939	2,198	2,562	243	327	77	63	37	61	68	23	83	32	15	254	41	14	67	385	236	502	97
1938	2,226	2,442	229	473	155	87	78	101	57	20	99	28	12	270	38	14	56	390	184	486	87
1937	2,513	3,223	369	418	134	35	39	64	60	18	82	25	22	347	56	18	67	378	300	479	94
1936	1,821	2,974	361	407	137	2	2	19	44	16	81	25	19	240	45	14	57	265	112	335	51
1935	1,719	3,234	391	381	134	...	...	15	39	15	93	28	17	227	42	13	52	251	88	265	49
1934	1,612	3,149	373	419	125	17	10	27	43	31	74	35	15	190	44	13	57	228	89	218	50
1933	1,268	4,523	398	420	82	8	5	19	39	40	70	26	15	91	33	11	40	201	46	132	25
1932	1,200	4,803	345	388	65	55	33	51	46	38	77	19	12	76	27	9	45	209	29	131	21
1931	1,782	3,667	326	504	110	80	50	84	60	60	109	36	15	148	47	17	65	271	63	316	55
1930	2,905	3,492	497	561	145	88	88	157	89	88	111	66	23	279	82	26	90	495	139	513	105
1929	4,363	3,982	771	555	146	90	112	192	135	124	137	79	31	541	115	37	106	962	200	604	183
1928	3,861	4,579	920	575	154	96	120	194	135	119	129	68	26	502	113	33	100	527	180	491	170
1927	3,641	4,897	826	506	139	168	240	325	133	116	122	71	34	389	111	34	110	487	161	433	150
1926	3,683	4,692	814	479	137	138	202	285	129	135	112	107	37	320	102	33	204	555	174	398	141
1925	3,707	4,384	1,060	468	153	87	149	234	146	148	102	127	32	318	103	32	107	474	144	366	161
1924	3,496	3,483	951	547	163	166	237	328	131	158	98	121	25	210	106	28	116	444	150	310	157
1923	3,124	2,743	807	475	152	99	116	205	136	158	69	154	25	171	107	30	166	367	167	281	129
1922	2,711	3,153	673	431	146	165	206	292	137	116	76	140	19	103	70	23	96	346	136	234	104
1921	3,263	3,339	534	515	205	280	433	551	116	140	70	157	11	84	55	26	171	401	236	408	98
1920	5,848	3,179	1,136	468	245	218	597	821	398	192	84	279	35	303	114	60	360	593	498	588	142
1919	5,229	3,368	1,137	766	260	148	357	650	270	326	126	698	31	156	80	49	126	377	450	362	131
1918	4,155	2,118	674	404	123	111	261	505	179	181	32	668	10	101	57	25	120	371	632	270	207
1917	3,534	2,476	575	251	46	106	246	384	157	100	35	274	14	124	42	25	119	275	645	356	363
1916	2,746	3,645	545	477	63	154	227	313	127	85	37	198	16	123	35	19	73	221	376	278	237
1915	1,804	4,404	376	348	44	260	334	428	70	79	35	132	11	70	31	15	58	148	85	120	102
1914	1,822	4,761	610	447	54	92	88	142	49	81	32	68	20	35	71	25	63	162	91	168	151

Source: Bureau of the Census, Historical Statistics of the United States, Colonial Times to 1957, 546.

TABLE 4.29 IMPORTS OF SELECTED PRODUCTS

(In millions of units and dollars)

Year	Total Selected Commodities, Value	Coffee Quantity (lb.)	Coffee Value	Tea Quantity (lb.)	Tea Value	Sugar Quantity (lb.)	Sugar Value	Rubber, Crude Quantity (lb.)	Rubber, Crude Value	Raw Silk Quantity (lb.)	Raw Silk Value	Wool and Mohair, Value	Wool Manufactures (Including Rags, Noils, Waste), Value	Iron and Steel Manufactures, Value	Tin, Including Ore, Value	Cotton Manufactures, Value	Copper and Manufactures, Value	Hides and Skins, Value	Furs and Manufactures, Value	Fruits and Nuts, Value	Forest Products, Value	Petroleum and Products, Value
1945	2,005	2,717	346	84	29	6,574	202	312	99	a	1	241	25	a	42	38	195	50	144	110	331	152
1944	1,722	2,608	326	90	30	7,728	212	239	76	...	...	186	17	...	47	12	166	61	126	68	282	113
1943	1,577	2,200	273	89	29	6,684	184	117	33	a	a	296	16	...	38	12	157	66	91	41	256	85
1942	1,499	1,715	205	50	18	3,968	107	620	118	...	...	311	27	...	51	10	165	78	69	35	268	37
1941	1,974	2,255	177	107	29	5,807	117	2,294	418	23	62	205	28	...	177	23	142	83	109	62	260	82
1940	1,529	2,055	127	99	23	5,829	113	1,825	318	45	125	85	25	a	131	31	73	50	80	61	217	70
1939	1,243	2,014	140	98	21	5,807	125	1,114	178	52	121	50	26	...	71	40	44	47	55	58	223	44
1938	1,034	1,987	138	81	18	5,949	130	917	130	55	89	23	18	...	45	35	38	30	46	55	200	39
1937	1,560	1,697	151	95	21	6,395	166	1,339	248	58	107	96	32	...	104	57	53	71	86	67	256	45
1936	1,255	1,739	134	82	18	5,939	158	1,091	159	60	102	53	30	...	76	49	30	55	82	58	210	41
1935	1,063	1,756	137	86	17	5,910	133	1,045	119	68	96	30	20	a	70	41	33	46	53	55	175	38
1934	894	1,524	133	76	16	5,994	118	1,036	102	56	72	17	15	...	45	32	28	35	41	46	157	37
1933	820	1,586	124	97	14	5,669	105	938	46	67	103	21	16	...	51	32	18	46	38	37	143	26
1932	784	1,501	137	95	12	5,943	97	929	33	74	114	6	13	...	16	28	24	22	28	44	149	61
1931	1,207	1,742	175	87	19	6,353	113	1,124	74	84	191	22	23	...	37	41	49	50	56	60	204	93
1930	1,695	1,599	209	85	23	6,990	130	1,090	141	74	263	37	40	a	60	46	105	92	69	75	259	146
1929	2,477	1,482	302	89	26	9,777	209	1,263	241	87	427	87	79	...	92	69	154	137	126	87	296	145
1928	2,346	1,457	310	90	27	7,737	207	978	245	75	368	80	78	...	87	69	98	151	122	90	280	134
1927	2,430	1,433	264	89	28	8,431	258	955	340	74	390	83	79	...	101	66	85	113	138	85	285	115
1926	2,653	1,493	323	96	31	9,420	233	926	506	66	393	107	71	...	105	67	100	97	120	88	286	126
1925	2,534	1,284	286	101	31	8,920	246	888	430	64	396	142	74	a	95	79	84	97	117	89	259	109
1924	2,190	1,421	249	93	27	8,272	364	735	174	51	328	93	69	44	69	91	96	75	88	72	248	103
1923	2,302	1,410	190	105	30	7,709	380	692	185	49	392	130	69	54	63	100	134	119	89	70	255	80
1922	1,831	1,246	161	97	24	9,722	252	674	102	51	366	87	59	48	46	87	67	107	69	72	195	89
1921	1,429	1,341	143	76	14	5,967	235	415	74	45	259	60	51	29	22	75	46	68	41	74	159	79
1920	3,212	1,297	252	90	24	8,065	1,115	567	243	30	285	127	58	50	93	138	90	244	92	102	231	68
1919	2,309	1,334	261	81	20	7,020	393	536	216	45	329	217	19	27	63	53	86	307	76	79	130	33
1918	1,608	1,052	99	134	30	5,167	241	326	146	33	180	252	23	25	105	41	134	108	34	49	114	27
1917	1,692	1,287	123	127	26	4,941	222	406	233	37	184	172	23	28	68	56	138	210	29	45	113	22
1916	1,373	1,167	119	105	19	5,530	227	270	160	32	145	126	16	24	56	55	95	173	21	45	77	15
1915	908	1,119	107	97	18	5,093	166	172	83	26	81	68	30	23	31	46	32	104	10	41	57	11
1914	934	1,002	111	91	17	4,948	99	132	71	29	98	53	34	32	39	71	55	120	14	51	54	15

aNot available.
Source: Bureau of the Census, *Historical Statistics of the United States, Colonial Times to 1957*, 548.

TABLE 4.30 **VALUE OF EXPORTS AND IMPORTS BY ECONOMIC CLASS**

(In millions of dollars)

Year	Exports of U.S. Merchandise						Imports					
	Total	Crude Materials[a]	Crude Food-stuffs	Manufac-tured Foodstuffs	Semi-Manu-factures[b]	Finished Manufac-tures[c]	Total	Crude Materials	Crude Food-stuffs	Manufac-tured Foodstuffs	Semi-Manu-factures	Finished Manufac-tures
1945	9,585	871	432	1,246	780	6,257	4,098	1,183	693	462	928	832
1944	14,162	554	134	1,633	1,097	10,744	3,887	1,078	841	521	706	741
1943	12,842	662	109	1,551	1,089	9,431	3,390	1,037	584	421	678	670
1942	8,003	418	68	925	920	5,672	2,780	1,061	349	275	640	457
1941	5,020	362	84	418	771	3,385	3,222	1,376	376	322	724	423
1940	3,934	464	74	167	900	2,330	2,541	1,011	285	277	559	409
1939	3,123	545	111	202	599	1,667	2,276	745	291	313	487	440
1938	3,057	607	249	184	494	1,523	1,950	576	260	311	385	418
1937	3,299	731	105	178	669	1,617	3,010	971	413	440	634	551
1936	2,419	670	58	144	393	1,154	2,424	733	349	386	490	466
1935	2,243	683	59	157	350	394	2,039	582	322	319	410	406
1934	2,100	653	59	168	342	879	1,636	461	254	264	307	350
1933	1,647	591	48	155	237	617	1,450	418	216	201	292	322
1932	1,576	514	89	152	197	624	1,323	358	233	174	217	341
1931	2,378	567	127	247	318	1,120	2,091	642	305	222	372	549
1930	3,781	829	179	363	513	1,898	3,061	1,002	400	293	608	757
1929	5,157	1,142	270	484	729	2,532	4,399	1,559	539	424	885	994
1928	5,030	1,293	295	466	716	2,260	4,091	1,467	550	406	763	906
1927	4,759	1,193	421	463	700	1,982	4,185	1,601	505	451	750	879
1926	4,712	1,261	335	503	656	1,957	4,431	1,792	540	418	804	877
1925	4,819	1,422	318	574	662	1,843	4,227	1,748	495	433	755	796
1924	4,498	1,333	393	573	611	1,588	3,610	1,258	425	522	656	749
1923	4,091	1,208	257	583	564	1,478	3,792	1,407	363	530	721	771
1922	3,765	988	459	588	438	1,292	3,113	1,180	330	387	553	663
1921	4,379	984	673	685	410	1,627	2,509	859	300	368	362	620
1920	8,080	1,883	918	1,117	958	3,205	5,278	1,784	578	1,238	802	877
1919	7,750	1,623	678	1,963	922	2,564	3,904	1,701	545	556	609	493
1918	6,048	972	547	1,406	1,053	2,069	3,031	1,234	346	397	650	405
1917	6,170	833	509	807	1,315	2,706	2,952	1,286	386	352	537	392
1916	5,423	816	421	648	912	2,625	2,392	1,029	260	339	419	346
1915	2,716	591	507	455	356	807	1,674	591	224	286	237	336
1914	2,330	800	137	293	374	725	1,894	650	248	228	319	449

[a]Crude materials pertain to the unchanged produce, such as petroleum.
[b]Semimanufactures are products changed from the original, such as iron and steel plates or copper bars.
[c]Finished manufactures are the completed product: radios, automobiles, books.
Source: Bureau of the Census, *Historical Statistics of the United States, Colonial Times to 1957*, 544.

TABLE 4.31   BALANCE OF PAYMENTS

(In millions of dollars)

This table shows that while American exports exceeded imports every year (a favorable balance of trade) except one, the nation nonetheless occasionally had an unfavorable balance of payments—because of travel on foreign ships or other services and especially because of American assistance to other nations during the Second World War.

	Imports	Exports	Investment Income		Net Military Transactions	Net Travel & Transport	Other Services	Unilateral Transfers	Current Balance
			Receipts	Payments					
1914	1,815	2,230	145	200	. . .	−304	. . .	−170	−114
1915	1,813	3,686	200	136	. . .	−189	. . .	−150	1,598
1916	2,423	5,560	250	118	. . .	−167	. . .	−150	2,952
1917	3,006	6,398	350	100	. . .	−167	. . .	−205	3,270
1918	3,103	6,432	450	100	−1,018	−203	. . .	−268	2,190
1919	3,995	8,891	719	130	−757	224	−84	−1,044	3,824
1920	5,384	8,481	596	120	−123	148	−75	−679	2,844
1921	2,572	4,586	445	105	−65	−64	−103	−509	1,613
1922	3,184	3,929	670	105	−42	−237	−34	−352	645
1923	3,866	4,266	840	130	−33	−219	−16	−365	477
1924	3,684	4,741	762	140	−36	−272	−20	−364	987
1925	4,291	5,011	912	170	−39	−337	1	−403	684
1926	4,500	4,922	953	200	−43	−307	1	−381	445
1927	4,240	4,982	981	240	−38	−343	−29	−357	716
1928	4,159	5,249	1,080	275	−44	−415	−59	−365	1,012
1929	4,463	5,347	1,139	330	−50	−463	−32	−377	771
1930	3,104	3,929	1,040	295	−49	−486	−3	−342	690
1931	2,120	2,494	766	220	−48	−366	10	−319	197
1932	1,343	1,667	527	135	−47	−278	16	−238	169
1933	1,510	1,736	437	115	−41	−179	30	−208	150
1934	1,763	2,238	437	135	−34	−200	58	−172	429
1935	2,462	2,404	521	155	−41	−211	72	−182	−54
1936	2,546	2,590	569	270	−38	−269	79	−208	−93
1937	3,181	3,451	577	295	−41	−343	129	−235	62
1938	2,173	3,243	585	200	−41	−209	86	−182	1,109
1939	2,409	3,347	541	230	−46	−219	82	−178	888
1940	2,698	4,124	564	−210	−61	−27	27	−210	1,509
1941	3,416	5,343	544	−187	−162	77	211	−1,136	1,274
1942	3,499	9,187	614	−158	−953	353	969	−6,336	177
1943	4,599	15,115	509	−155	−1,763	678	1,253	−12,907	−1,869
1944	5,043	16,969	573	−161	−1,982	799	1,297	−14,142	−1,690
1945	5,245	12,473	589	−231	−2,434	741	148	−7,113	−1,072

Source: Liesner, *Economic Statistics*, 60.

The Workers

The labor force as a rule applied to those persons over fourteen years old who were employed, unemployed, or looking for work; the number did not include women at work in their own homes. The labor force mirrored the United States and American economic history. It increased, of course, as the population grew, whether or not the individuals could find a job. The number of people at work grew during the First World War, dropped off at war's end, and increased steadily during the prosperous 1920s. The number fell off sharply in the 1930s—the lowest number was reached in 1932–33—and began a slow and unsteady increase that continued until the start of the Second World War. The war produced record levels of employment, the number swelled by the admission (or readmission) into the employed work force of older people, women, and older children.

The work force grew markedly in manufacturing, in the various white-collar professions, and in trade. The number of people em-ployed in government increased steadily, especially during the Second World War. The areas that experienced a general decline included mining, construction, and, steadily, agriculture. Virtually all areas of economic activity dropped off during the depression of the 1930s.

Working conditions were less than ideal in the American workplace. The workweek in manufacturing usually ranged from forty-five to fifty hours until the time of the depression, when it dropped below forty, the average no doubt fostered by the many people who did not have full-time work. Wages changed remarkably little during the boom years of the 1920s. The total increase for production workers between 1923 and 1929 was only five cents per hour. During the depression nearly every worker faced a wage reduction. The period of largest gain in income was the Second World War. Boosted by a newly discovered unionism and by a government that was more or less friendly, production workers more than doubled

TABLE 4.32 THE LABOR FORCE, 1914–1945

In thousands

Year	Total Labor Force		Armed Forces	Civilian Labor Force	Employed		
	Number	Percent of Noninstitutional Population[a]			Total	Farm	Nonfarm
1945	65,290	61.9	11,430	53,860	52,820	8,580	44,240
1944	66,040	63.1	11,410	54,630	53,960	8,950	45,010
1943	64,560	62.3	9,020	55,540	54,470	9,080	45,390
1942	60,380	58.8	3,970	56,410	53,750	9,250	44,500
1941	57,530	56.7	1,620	55,910	50,350	9,100	41,250
1940	56,180	56.0	540	55,640	47,520	9,540	37,980
1939	55,588	56.0	370	55,218	45,738	9,710	36,028
1938	54,872	56.0	340	54,532	44,142	9,840	34,302
1937	54,088	55.9	320	53,768	46,068	10,000	36,068
1936	53,319	55.7	300	53,019	43,989	10,090	33,899
1935	52,553	55.6	270	52,283	41,673	10,110	31,563
1934	51,910	55.7	260	51,650	40,310	9,990	30,320
1933	51,132	55.6	250	50,882	38,052	10,090	27,962
1932	50,348	55.4	250	50,098	38,038	10,120	27,918
1931	49,585	55.2	260	49,325	41,305	10,240	31,065
1930	48,783	55.0	260	48,523	44,183	10,340	33,843
1929	48,017	55.1	260	47,757	46,207	10,541	35,666
1928	47,367	55.2	262	47,105	45,123	10,497	34,626
1927	46,634	55.2	259	46,375	44,856	10,529	34,327
1926	45,885	55.3	256	45,629	44,828	10,690	34,138
1925	45,431	56.4	262	45,169	43,716	10,662	33,054
1924	44,502	55.5	267	44,235	42,045	10,599	31,446
1923	43,699	55.8	255	43,444	42,395	10,621	31,774
1922	42,772	55.7	276	42,496	39,637	10,561	29,076
1921	42,341	55.9	362	41,979	37,061	10,443	26,618
1920	41,720	55.6	380	41,340	39,208	10,440	28,768
1919	41,239	56.4	1,543	39,696	39,150	10,498	28,652
1918	41,980	57.7	2,904	39,076	38,540	10,674	27,866
1917	40,742	56.6	719	40,023	38,175	10,788	27,387
1916	40,238	56.6	181	40,057	38,014	10,802	27,212
1915	39,774	56.8	174	39,600	36,223	10,953	25,270
1914	39,564	57.3	163	39,401	36,281	10,945	25,336

[a]Essentially means the entire population except certain groups—people under 14, students, wives and mothers at home—who were not counted as part of the work force and those who were institutionalized.
Source: Wattenberg, Statistical History, 126.

their earnings between 1934 and 1944. The explanation for the gain rested partly with a steady increase in hourly wages, especially after 1940, and the ability during the war to work more hours and be paid at overtime rates. Women's wages remained far behind the average for men throughout this period, and despite impressive gains in a few areas of activity during the Second World War, as a whole they caught up hardly at all.

TABLE 4.33 NONAGRICULTURAL EMPLOYMENT, BY INDUSTRIAL DIVISION, 1919–1945

In thousands

Year	Total	Mining	Contract Construction	Manufacturing	Transportation and Public Utilities	Wholesale and Retail Trade	Finance, Insurance, and Real Estate	Service and Miscellaneous	Government
1945	40,037	826	1,132	15,302	3,872	7,522	1,428	4,011	5,944
1944	41,534	883	1,094	17,111	3,798	7,260	1,409	3,934	6,043
1943	42,106	917	1,567	17,381	3,619	7,189	1,435	3,919	6,080
1942	39,779	983	2,170	15,051	3,433	7,333	1,469	3,857	5,483
1941	36,220	947	1,790	12,974	3,248	7,416	1,480	3,705	4,660
1940	32,058	916	1,294	10,780	3,013	6,940	1,436	3,477	4,202
1939	30,311	845	1,150	10,078	2,912	6,612	1,399	3,321	3,995
1938	28,902	882	1,055	9,253	2,840	6,453	1,347	3,196	3,876
1937	30,718	1,006	1,112	10,606	3,114	6,543	1,355	3,233	3,749
1936	28,802	937	1,145	9,653	2,956	6,076	1,313	3,060	3,662
1935	26,792	888	912	8,907	2,771	5,692	1,262	2,883	3,477
1934	25,699	874	862	8,346	2,736	5,552	1,247	2,784	3,298
1933	23,466	735	809	7,258	2,659	4,999	1,225	2,614	3,167
1932	23,377	722	970	6,797	2,804	4,907	1,270	2,682	3,225
1931	26,383	864	1,214	8,021	3,243	5,531	1,333	2,913	3,264
1930	29,143	1,000	1,372	9,401	3,675	6,064	1,398	3,084	3,149
1929	31,041	1,078	1,497	10,534	3,907	6,401	1,431	3,127	3,066
1928	29,710	1,041	1,606	9,786	3,822	6,137	1,360	2,962	2,996
1927	29,691	1,105	1,608	9,839	3,891	6,165	1,295	2,871	2,917
1926	29,539	1,176	1,555	9,997	3,940	6,033	1,235	2,755	2,848
1925	28,505	1,080	1,446	9,786	3,824	5,810	1,166	2,591	2,802
1924	27,770	1,092	1,321	9,523	3,806	5,626	1,163	2,516	2,723
1923	28,128	1,203	1,229	10,155	3,882	5,494	1,123	2,431	2,611
1922	25,569	920	1,185	8,986	3,505	5,084	1,079	2,268	2,542
1921	24,125	953	1,012	8,132	3,459	4,754	1,097	2,187	2,531
1920	27,088	1,230	848	10,534	3,998	4,623	1,110	2,142	2,603
1919	26,829	1,124	1,021	10,534	3,711	4,664	1,050	2,054	2,671

Source: Bureau of the Census, *Historical Statistics of the United States, Colonial Times to 1957*, 73.

TABLE 4.34 DETAILED OCCUPATION OF THE ECONOMICALLY ACTIVE POPULATION: 1910–1940

[In thousands. "n. e. c." means not elsewhere classified]

Occupation	1940	1930	1920	1910
Total	51,742	48,686	42,206	37,291
Professional, technical, and kindred workers	3,879	3,311	2,283	1,758
Accountants and auditors	288	192	118	39
Actors and actresses	21			
Athletes	9			
Dancers and dancing teachers	14	76	48	48
Entertainers (n. e. c.)	12			
Sports instructors and officials	25			
Airplane pilots and navigators	5	6	1	...
Architects	22	28	17	16
Artists and art teachers	66	57	35	34
Authors	14	12	7	4

Occupation	1940	1930	1920	1910
Professional, technical, and kindred workers				
Chemists	57	45	28	16
Clergymen	141	149	127	118
Religious workers	42			
Recreation and group workers	77	71	46	19
Social and welfare workers, except group				
College presidents, professors, & instructors (n. e. c.)	77	62	33	16
Dentists	71	71	56	40
Designers	32	98	67	45
Draftsmen	82			
Editors and reporters	66	61	39	36
Engineers, technical	297	217	134	77
Engineers, civil	97	88	56	40
Engineers, chemical	13			
Engineers, metallurgical and metallurgists	12	14	11	7
Engineers, mining				

TABLE 4.34   (continued)

Occupation	1940	1930	1920	1910
Professional, technical, and kindred workers				
Engineers, electrical	65	58	27	15
Engineers, industrial	13			
Engineers, aeronautical				
Engineers, mechanical	97	58	39	15
Engineers, (n. e. c.)				
Farm and home management advisors	12	4	3	1
Funeral directors and embalmers	40	34	24	21
Lawyers and judges	182	161	123	115
Librarians	39	30	15	7
Musicians and music teachers	167	165	130	139
Nurses, professional	377	294	149	82
Nurses, student professional				
Optometrists	10	8	7	1
Pharmacists	83	84	64	54
Photographers	38	33	29	30
Physicians and surgeons	168	157	146	
Osteopaths	6	6	5	152
Chiropractors	11	12	12	
Therapists and healers (n. e. c.)	18	14		5
Radio operators	7	5	5	4
Surveyors	17	15	9	8
Teachers (n. e. c.)	1,086	1,044	752	595
Technicians, medical and dental	73	20	4	. . .
Technicians, testing				
Technicians (n. e. c.)	11			
Veterinarians	11	12	13	12
Dietitians and nutritionists				
Foresters and conservationists				
Natural scientists (n. e. c.)				
Personnel and labor relations workers	153	73	32	20
Social scientists				
Professional, technical, and kindred workers (n. e. c.)				
Farmers and farm managers	**5,362**	**6,032**	**6,442**	**6,163**
Farmers (owners and tenants)	5,324	5,992	6,384	6,132
Farm managers	38	40	58	31
Managers, officials, and proprietors, exc. farm	**3,770**	**3,614**	**2,803**	**2,462**
Buyers and department heads, store	74	35	20	15
Buyers and shippers, farm products	43	42	48	51
Conductors, railroad	48	73	75	66
Credit men	30	22	14	2
Floormen and floor managers, store	7	6	4	4
Inspectors (n. e. c.) public administration	43	124	100	72
Officials (n. e. c.), public administration	122			
Inspectors (n. e. c.), Federal public administration and postal service	20			
Officials and administrators (n. e. c.), Federal public administration and postal service	40	40	42	20
Inspectors (n. e. c.), State public administration	11			
Officials & admins. (n. e. c.), State public admin.	21	15	9	7
Inspectors (n. e. c.), local public administration	12			
Officials & admins. (n. e. c.), local public admin.	61	70	49	44
Managers and superintendents, building	72	71	43	32
Officers, pilots, pursers, and engineers, ship	35	49	49	45
Officials, lodge, society, union, etc.	26	15	12	8
Postmasters	40	34	29	25
Purchasing agents and buyers (n. e. c.)	34	29	18	8

Occupation	1940	1930	1920	1910
Managers, officials, and proprietors, exc. farm				
Managers, officials, and proprietors (n. e. c.)	3,197	3,113	2,390	2,135
Construction	175	199	107	183
Manufacturing	432	447	406	350
Transportation	90	98	83	82
Telecommunications, & utilities & sanitary services	54	39	25	19
Wholesale trade	225	152	143	104
Retail trade	1,620	1,592	1,220	1,119
Eating and drinking places	270	165	106	129
Food & dairy products stores, & milk retailing	469	540	444	395
General merchandise and five and ten cent stores	111	184	162	167
Apparel and accessories stores	99	96	97	85
Motor vehicles and accessories retailing	65	62	29	5
Gasoline service stations	183	89	15	2
Furniture, home furnishings, and equipment stores	57			
Hardware, farm implement, & bldg. material retail	95	456	368	336
Other retail trade	271			
Banking and other finance	126	174	122	75
Insurance and real estate	65	66	38	29
Automobile repair services and garages	66	93	56	5
Miscellaneous repair services	14	9	8	7
Personal services	129	105	76	88
Business services				
All other industries (incl. not reported)	33	140	107	74
	169			
Clerical and kindred workers	**4,982**	**4,336**	**3,385**	**1,987**
Agents (n. e. c.)	78	102	64	28
Collectors, bill and account	45	43	31	36
Attendants and assistants, library	24	2	2	3
Attendants, physician's and dentist's office	35	28	14	6
Baggagemen, transportation	6	9	12	12
Bookkeepers	721	738	616	447
Cashiers				
Express messengers and railway mail clerks	23	26	25	22
Mail carriers	124	121	91	81
Stenographers, typists, and secretaries	1,223	1,097	786	387
Messengers and office boys	64	80	110	103
Telegraph messengers	17	16	9	9
Telegraph operators	42	68	75	66
Telephone operators	214	249	190	98
Ticket, station, and express agents	47	38	37	35
Office machine operators	66	38		
Shipping and receiving clerks	233			
Bank tellers		1,681	1,323	654
Dispatchers and starters, vehicle	2,026			
Clerical and kindred workers (n. e. c.)				
Sales workers	**3,450**	**3,059**	**2,058**	**1,755**
Advertising agents and salesmen	41	40	25	11
Auctioneers	4	4	5	4
Demonstrators	10	8	5	4
Hucksters and peddlers	55	57	50	80
Insurance agents and brokers	253	257	120	88
Newsboys	58	39	28	30

Occupation	1940	1930	1920	1910
Sales workers				
Real estate agents and brokers	119	150	89	78
Stock and bond salesmen	18	22	11	6
Salesmen and sales clerks (n. e. c.):				
Manufacturing				
Wholesale trade	2,893	2,482	1,724	1,454
Retail trade				
Other industries (incl. not reported)				
Craftsmen, foremen, and kindred workers	**6,203**	**6,246**	**5,482**	**4,315**
Bakers	139	141	98	90
Boilermakers	33	50	74	45
Bookbinders	19	19	19	17
Brickmasons, stonemasons, and tile setters	141	171	135	160
Cabinetmakers	60	63	50	43
Carpenters	776	917	885	815
Cement and concrete finishers	32	15	8	9
Electrotypers and stereotypers	8	8	5	4
Engravers, except photoengravers	9	28	23	22
Photoengravers and lithographers	23			
Compositors and typesetters	181	184	140	128
Pressmen and plate printers, printing	36	31	19	20
Decorators and window dressers	30	20	9	5
Electricians	221	253	192	108
Cranemen, derrickmen, and hoistmen	123			
Excavating, grading, and road machinery operators		294	258	219
Stationary engineers	201			
Blacksmiths	99	136	209	238
Forgemen and hammermen				
Foremen (n. e. c.)	585	551	485	318
Construction	79	43	14	15
Manufacturing	310	293	296	164
Metal industries				
Machinery, including electrical	112			
Transportation equipment				
Textiles, textile products, and apparel	53	293	296	164
Other durable goods				
Other nondurable goods (incl. not specified mfg.)	144			
Railroads and railway express service	51	83	81	69
Transportation, except railroad	15			
Telecommunications, & utilities & sanitary services	27	44	31	24
Other industries (incl. not reported)	104	88	63	45
Furriers	16	12	9	8
Painters, construction and maintenance	451	446	265	288
Glaziers	8			
Heat treaters, annealers, and temperers	11	6	3	2
Inspectors, scalers, and graders, log and lumber	17	7	7	7
Inspectors (n. e. c.)	82	78	77	53
Construction	9	7	3	4
Railroads and railway express service	30	39	43	28
Transp. exc. railroad, commun., & other pub. util.	14	14	10	8
Other industries (incl. not reported)	30	17	21	14
Jewelers, watchmakers, goldsmiths, and silversmiths	36	39	40	33
Linemen & servicemen, telegraph, telephone, & power	116	106	51	35
Locomotive engineers	67	104	113	99
Locomotive firemen	50	67	91	76
Loom fixers	25	19	16	13

Occupation	1940	1930	1920	1910
Craftsmen, foremen, and kindred workers				
Job setters, metal	535			
Machinists				
Mechanics and repairmen, airplane	28			
Mechanics and repairmen, automobile	448			
Mechanics and repairmen, railroad and car shop	46	1,387	1,168	520
Mechanics and repairmen, office machine				
Mechanics and repairmen, radio and television	436			
Mechanics and repairmen (n. e. c.)				
Toolmakers, and die makers and setters	100			
Millers, grain, flour, feed, etc.	16	16	23	23
Millwrights	44	42	38	17
Molders, metal	86	105	124	121
Motion picture projectionists	24	20	10	4
Opticians, and lens grinders and polishers	12	13	11	9
Paperhangers	31	28	19	26
Pattern and model makers, except paper	30	30	28	24
Piano and organ tuners and repairmen	5	7	7	7
Plasterers	53	70	38	48
Plumbers and pipe fitters	211	238	207	148
Rollers and roll hands, metal	33	31	25	18
Roofers and slaters	33	24	12	14
Shoemakers and repairers, except factory	68	76	79	70
Stone cutters and stone carvers	15	23	23	36
Structural metal workers	47	33	31	18
Tailors and tailoresses	120	169	192	205
Tinsmiths, coppersmiths, and sheet metal workers	91	83	75	60
Upholsterers	43	42	24	20
Craftsmen and kindred workers (n. e. c.)	47	43	66	73
Members of the Armed Forces	3	. . .	. . .	. . .
Operatives and kindred workers	**9,518**	**7,691**	**6,587**	**5,441**
Apprentice carpenters	8	4	5	6
Apprentice electricians	3	5	10	3
Apprentice plumbers and pipefitters	5	6	7	10
Apprentices, printing trades	10	11	12	12
Apprentice machinists and toolmakers	20	14	39	
Apprentice auto mechanics				
Apprentice bricklayers and masons				86
Apprentice mechanics, except auto	33			
Apprentices, building trade (n. e. c.)		49	66	
Apprentices, metalworking trades (n. e. c.)				
Apprentices, other specified trades				
Apprentices, trade not specified	12			
Asbestos and insulation workers	6	3	1	2
Attendants, auto service and parking	245	144	18	. . .
Blasters and powdermen	7	7	7	2
Boatmen, canalmen, and lock keepers	6	6	6	5
Brakemen, railroad	77	173	208	160
Switchmen, railroad	50			
Chainmen, rodmen, and axmen, surveying	11	4	3	4
Conductors, bus and street railway	18	37	64	57
Deliverymen and routemen	294	187	170	230
Dressmakers and seamstresses, except factory	172	198	259	467
Dyers	28	18	15	14
Filers, grinders, and polishers, metal	117	79	60	50
Fruit, nut, & veget. graders & packers, exc. factory	25	10	8	5
Furnacemen, smeltermen, and pourers	33	20	24	26
Heaters, metal	10	15	16	10
Laundry and dry cleaning operatives	314	265	142	132

(continued)

TABLE 4.34 (continued)

Occupation	1940	1930	1920	1910
Operatives and kindred workers				
Meat cutters, except slaughter and packing house	160	120	61	41
Milliners	15	25	50	100
Mine operatives and laborers (n. e. c.): Coal mining	345	892	995	907
Crude petroleum and natural gas extraction				
Mining and quarrying, except fuel				
Motormen, mine, factory, logging camp, etc	20	17	12	3
Motormen, street, subway, and elevated railway	39	58	63	56
Oilers and greasers, except auto	40	31	25	14
Painters, except construction and maintenance	104	83	61	49
Photographic process workers	15	8	3	2
Power station operators	22	29	21	12
Sailors and deckhands	47	65	55	47
Sawyers	50	36	34	43
Spinners, textile	113	81	83	74
Stationary firemen	128	127	144	111
Bus drivers				
Taxicab drivers and chauffeurs	1,515	972	285	46
Truck and tractor drivers				
Weavers, textile	109	225	219	202
Welders and flame-cutters	137	37	54	3
Operatives and kindred workers (n. e. c.)	4,654	3,634	3,284	2,451
Manufacturing	4,225	3,189	3,076	2,318
Sawmills, planing mills, and millwork	63	91	92	105
Miscellaneous wood products	36			
Furniture and fixtures	82	72	52	44
Glass and glass products	54	41	45	42
Cement & concrete, gypsum, & plaster products	13	11	8	9
Structural clay products	16	13	10	13
Pottery and related products	25	23	17	16
Miscellaneous nonmetallic mineral & stone prod	18	8	6	9
Motor vehicles and motor vehicle equipment	208	170	125	21
Ship and boat building and repairing	19	11	53	6
Blast furnaces, steelworks, and rolling mills	105			
Other primary iron and steel industries				
Fabricated steel products	209			
Office and store machines & devices	24			
Miscellaneous machinery	123	397	370	286
Not specified metal industries	12			
Agricultural machinery and tractors	21			
Aircraft and parts	27			
Railroad & miscellaneous transportation equipment	11			
Primary nonferrous industries				
Fabricated nonferrous metal products	48	34	32	27
Electrical machinery, equipment, & supplies	150	117	65	25
Professional equipment & supplies	29			
Photographic equipment & supplies				
Watches, clocks, & clockwork-operated devices		172	192	133
Miscellaneous manufacturing industries	172			

Occupation	1940	1930	1920	1910
Operatives and kindred workers				
Meat products	91	53	50	26
Canning & preserving fruits, veget., & seafood	52	26	18	8
Dairy products	36	26	19	12
Grain-mill products	17	7	8	4
Bakery products	45	28	20	9
Confectionery and related products	49	44	52	31
Beverage industries	36	7	10	20
Miscellaneous food preparations & kindred products				
Not specified food industries	29	30	21	16
Tobacco manufactures	86	104	145	152
Knitting mills	192	129	104	85
Dyeing and finishing textiles, except knit goods	24	20	18	16
Carpets, rugs, and other floor covering	21	17	14	15
Yarn, thread, and fabric mills	426	324	323	269
Miscellaneous textile mill products	35	35	46	48
Apparel and accessories	734	422	365	336
Miscellaneous fabricated textile products	53	15	21	18
Pulp, paper, and paperboard mills	87	64	55	36
Miscellaneous paper and pulp products	28	17	14	10
Paperboard containers and boxes	41	14	20	18
Printing, publishing, and allied industries	59	51	48	42
Synthetic fibers	31	21	. . .	. . .
Paints, varnishes, and related products	12	8	6	4
Drugs and medicines				
Miscellaneous chemicals and allied products	72	53	51	33
Petroleum refining	30	27	14	4
Miscellaneous petroleum and coal products	5	2	2	2
Rubber products	85	81	86	32
Leather: tanned, curried, and finished	35	29	32	34
Footwear, except rubber	228	210	206	181
Leather products, except footwear	44	26	33	29
Not specified manufacturing industries	74	139	207	93
Nonmanufacturing industries (incl. not reported)	429	445	208	132
Construction	40	15	4	8
Railroads and railway express service	73	98	111	61
Transportation, except railroad	24			
Telecommunications, & utilities & sanitary serv	24	57	30	19
Wholesale and retail trade	145	74	40	27
Business and repair services	38	30	8	6
Public administration	11	6	4	3
Personal services				
All other industries (incl. not reported)	75	165	12	9
Private household workers	**2,412**	**1,998**	**1,411**	**1,851**
Laundresses, private household—living in	203	344	375	513
Laundresses, private household—living out				

Occupation	1940	1930	1920	1910
Private household workers				
Housekeepers, private household—living in	} 410	} 1,654	1,036	1,338
Housekeepers, private household—living out				
Private household workers (n. e. c.)—living in	} 1,799			
Private household workers (n. e. c.)—living out				
Service workers, except private household	**3,657**	**2,774**	**1,901**	**1,711**
Attendants, hospital and other institution	102	} 198	157	133
Midwives	115			
Practical nurses				
Attendants, professional & personal service (n. e. c.)	42	4	3	2
Attendants, recreation and amusement	64	} 29	13	9
Ushers, recreation and amusement	22			
Barbers, beauticians, and manicurists	449	371	214	193
Bartenders	131	. . .	26	101
Boarding and lodging housekeepers	74	144	133	165
Bootblacks	16	19	15	14
Charwomen and cleaners	72	52	31	29
Cooks, except private household	349	292	200	174
Elevator operators	87	68	41	25
Firemen, fire protection	82	73	51	36
Guards, watchmen, and doorkeepers	216	148	116	78
Policemen and detectives, government	135	} 145	94	68
Policemen and detectives, private	21			
Marshals and constables	9	9	7	9
Housekeepers and stewards, except private household	90	61	52	45
Janitors and sextons	377	310	179	113
Porters	182	151	102	96
Sheriffs and bailiffs	16	15	11	7
Counter and fountain workers	636	415	242	200
Waiters and waitresses				
Watchmen (crossing) and bridge tenders	10	13	13	10
Service workers, except private household (n. e. c.)	360	259	203	203
Farm laborers and foremen	**3,632**	**4,290**	**4,948**	**5,370**
Farm foremen	17	28	35	19
Farm laborers, wageworkers	2,405	2,597	2,271	2,832
Farm laborers, unpaid family workers	1,208	1,660	2,633	2,514
Farm service laborers, self-employed	3	5	10	6
Laborers, except farm and mine	**4,875**	**5,335**	**4,905**	**4,478**
Fishermen and oystermen	64	73	53	68
Garage laborers, and car washers and greasers	63	77	33	4
Gardeners, except farm, and groundskeepers	163	168	71	65
Longshoremen and stevedores	74	74	86	63
Lumbermen, raftsmen, and woodchoppers	169	147	180	139
Teamsters	31	120	412	441
Laborers (n. e. c.)	4,312	4,675	4,070	3,696
Manufacturing	1,598	1,960	2,169	1,487
Sawmills, planing mills, and millwork	230	} 292	280	289
Miscellaneous wood products	27			
Furniture and fixtures	35	40	35	24
Glass and glass products	21	28	29	25

Occupation	1940	1930	1920	1910
Laborers, except farm and mine				
Cement & concrete, gypsum, & plaster products	26	39	30	36
Structural clay products	39	60	49	78
Pottery and related products	7	11	12	9
Miscellaneous nonmetallic mineral & stone prod	14	8	5	7
Motor vehicles and motor vehicle equipment	71	124	83	16
Ship and boat building and repairing	23	17	69	12
Blast furnaces, steelworks, and rolling mills	201	} 492	544	419
Other primary iron and steel industries	128			
Fabricated steel products				
Office and store machines and devices	2			
Miscellaneous machinery	46			
Not specified metal industries	6			
Agricultural machinery and tractors	11			
Aircraft and parts	4			
Railroad & miscellaneous transportation equipment	8			
Primary nonferrous industries	} 43	39	43	33
Fabricated nonferrous metal products				
Electrical machinery, equipment, and supplies	30	37	27	11
Professional equipment and supplies	} 4			
Photographic equipment and supplies				
Watches, clocks, and clockwork-operated devices	} 27	} 74	101	43
Miscellaneous manufacturing industries				
Meat products	47	43	60	34
Canning & preserving fruits, veget., & seafood	34	26	19	10
Dairy products	17	17	15	5
Grain-mill products	21	16	18	9
Bakery products	8	12	8	5
Confectionery and related products	8	6	7	3
Beverage industries	22	9	11	19
Miscellaneous food preparations & kindred prod	29	26	32	17
Not specified food industries				
Tobacco manufactures	17	21	35	16
Knitting mills	5	9	12	8
Dyeing and finishing textiles, except knit goods	5	8	11	10
Carpets, rugs, and other floor coverings	7	5	4	4
Yarn, thread, and fabric mills	71	94	120	59
Miscellaneous textile mill products	7	5	8	8
Apparel and accessories	10	14	12	8
Miscellaneous fabricated textile products	3	1	1	1
Pulp, paper, and paperboard mills	44	52	52	31
Miscellaneous paper and pulp products	6	4	3	2
Paperboard containers and boxes	10	3	3	1
Printing, publishing, and allied industries	10	11	3	5
Synthetic fibers	5	5	. . .	. . .
Paints, varnishes, and related products	6	6	5	3

TABLE 4.34 (continued)

Occupation	1940	1930	1920	1910
Laborers, except farm and mine				
Drugs and medicines	} 77	80	79	45
Miscellaneous chemical and allied products				
Petroleum, refining	28	41	32	11
Miscellaneous petroleum and coal products	8	5	9	11
Rubber products	20	29	51	14
Leather: tanned, curried, and finished	11	17	27	21
Footwear, except rubber	12	18	19	10
Leather products, except footwear	3	3	8	4
Not specified manufacturing industries	44	114	191	109
Nonmanufacturing industries (incl. not reported)	2,714	2,715	1,901	2,210
Construction	1,340	710	391	531

Occupation	1940	1930	1920	1910
Laborers, except farm and mine				
Railroads and railway express service	278	490	543	599
Transportation, except railroad	98	} 249	199	195
Telecommunications, & utilities & sanitary serv	103			
Wholesale and retail trade	250	253	182	152
Business and repair services	7	15	2	2
Public administration	52	134	93	56
Personal services	64	} 864	490	675
All other industries (incl. not reported)	520			

Source: Bureau of the Census, *Historical Statistics of the United States, Colonial Times to 1957*, 75–78.

TABLE 4.35 AVERAGE ANNUAL EARNINGS PER FULL-TIME EMPLOYEE, BY INDUSTRY: 1914 TO 1945

[In current dollars]

Year	Agriculture, Forestry, and Fisheries	Manufacturing	Mining				Construction	Transportation				Communications and Public Utilities		
			Total	Anthracite Coal	Bituminous Coal	Metal		Total	Railroad	Water	Local	Total	Gas and Electric	Telephone and Telegraph
1945	1,125	2,517	2,621	2,685	2,629	2,551	2,600	2,734	2,711	3,583	2,596	2,446	2,596	2,246
1944	1,021	2,517	2,499	2,525	2,535	2,458	2,602	2,679	2,714	3,624	2,458	2,276	2,467	2,035
1943	860	2,349	2,162	2,119	2,115	2,333	2,503	2,493	2,585	3,388	2,280	2,098	2,284	1,878
1942	669	2,023	1,796	1,753	1,715	2,045	2,191	2,183	2,303	2,729	1,990	1,891	2,040	1,715
1941	496	1,653	1,579	1,467	1,500	1,771	1,635	1,885	2,030	1,854	1,664	1,766	1,870	1,633
1940	407	1,432	1,388	1,297	1,235	1,610	1,330	1,756	1,906	1,648	1,559	1,717	1,795	1,610
1939	385	1,363	1,367	1,409	1,197	1,515	1,268	1,723	1,877	1,557	1,569	1,691	1,766	1,600
1938	369	1,296	1,282	1,315	1,050	1,453	1,193	1,676	1,849	1,299	1,529	1,673	1,749	1,580
1937	360	1,376	1,366	1,388	1,170	1,630	1,278	1,644	1,774	1,536	1,505	1,600	1,705	1,481
1936	308	1,287	1,263	1,408	1,103	1,380	1,178	1,582	1,724	1,373	1,433	1,520	1,615	1,420
1935	288	1,216	1,154	1,414	957	1,239	1,027	1,492	1,645	1,088	1,361	1,483	1,589	1,378
1934	253	1,153	1,108	1,500	900	1,133	942	1,393	1,505	1,055	1,310	1,424	1,510	1,338
1933	232	1,086	990	1,435	748	1,040	869	1,334	1,439	1,059	1,219	1,351	1,453	1,245
1932	250	1,150	1,016	1,452	723	1,060	907	1,373	1,461	1,038	1,328	1,440	1,542	1,335
1931	315	1,369	1,221	1,602	909	1,291	1,233	1,549	1,661	1,153	1,500	1,514	1,600	1,436
1930	388	1,488	1,424	1,750	1,119	1,551	1,526	1,610	1,717	1,214	1,587	1,499	1,603	1,410
1929	401	1,543	1,526	1,728	1,293	1,613	1,674	1,643	1,749	1,275	1,598	1,478	1,589	1,386
1928	385	1,534	1,478	1,825	1,342	1,516	1,719	1,607	1,720	1,255	1,553	1,474	1,591	1,378
1927	387	1,502	1,590	1,851	1,446	1,485	1,708	1,579	1,687	1,220	1,549	1,440	1,558	1,343
1926	386	1,476	1,597	2,124	1,434	1,463	1,664	1,562	1,671	1,238	1,530	1,427	1,571	1,317
1925	382	1,450	1,580	2,129	1,427	1,455	1,655	1,539	1,655	1,227	1,502	1,378	1,552	1,257
1924	375	1,427	1,703	2,117	1,621	1,378	1,620	1,509	1,627	1,219	1,472	1,371	1,544	1,250
1923	372	1,403	1,822	2,014	1,848	1,497	1,614	1,484	1,631	1,132	1,413	1,292	1,429	1,199
1922	331	1,283	1,300	1,814	1,165	1,345	1,297	1,461	1,630	1,088	1,394	1,265	1,423	1,176
1921	344	1,346	1,757	1,868	1,808	1,482	1,380	1,533	1,664	1,339	1,470	1,276	1,497	1,161
1920	528	1,532	1,684	1,777	1,633	1,639	1,710	1,645	1,807	1,499	1,435	1,238	1,489	1,115
1919	463	1,293	1,370	1,508	1,276	1,611	1,387	1,352	1,477	1,305	1,172	1,035	1,278	906
1918	401	1,107	1,399	1,426	1,427	1,499	1,191	1,265	1,393	1,086	938	866	1,081	753
1917	327	883	1,138	1,019	1,150	1,352	1,001	885	968	851	737	727	844	675
1916	259	751	889	711	884	1,152	882	768	848	669	674	640	672	647
1915	236	661	716	671	694	976	827	711	797	531	632	607	637	614
1914	234	696	666	636	640	923	838	695	778	484	623	579	644	557

Year	Wholesale and Retail Trade	Finance, Insurance, and Real Estate	Services						Government			
			Total	Personal	Medical and Other Health Services	Domestic	Nonprofit	Educational Services	Total	State and Local	Public Education	Federal Civilian
1945	2,114	2,347	1,688	1,709	1,401	1,312	1,876	1,641	2,052	1,962	1,882	2,646
1944	1,946	2,191	1,538	1,570	1,262	1,140	1,795	1,562	1,924	1,822	1,730	2,677
1943	1,781	2,041	1,347	1,384	1,127	919	1,679	1,469	1,777	1,713	1,608	2,628
1942	1,608	1,885	1,132	1,196	1,036	706	1,482	1,344	1,623	1,592	1,512	2,226
1941	1,478	1,777	1,020	1,075	955	601	1,379	1,264	1,388	1,534	1,462	1,970
1940	1,382	1,725	953	1,042	927	554	1,408	1,240	1,344	1,502	1,435	1,894
1939	1,360	1,729	952	1,034	908	544	1,546	1,234	1,337	1,476	1,403	1,843
1938	1,352	1,731	942	992	899	527	1,529	1,228	1,336	1,472	1,406	1,832
1937	1,352	1,788	938	978	876	558	1,497	1,211	1,355	1,441	1,367	1,797
1936	1,295	1,713	898	940	851	506	1,465	1,180	1,279	1,402	1,329	1,896
1935	1,279	1,632	873	915	829	485	1,435	1,162	1,292	1,290	1,293	1,759
1934	1,228	1,601	857	905	801	473	1,440	1,175	1,284	1,295	1,265	1,717
1933	1,183	1,555	854	889	810	460	1,442	1,189	1,328	1,338	1,300	1,673
1932	1,315	1,652	918	996	865	497	1,545	1,279	1,477	1,432	1,399	1,824
1931	1,495	1,858	1,008	1,136	919	584	1,653	1,323	1,547	1,500	1,463	1,895
1930	1,569	1,973	1,066	1,200	933	676	1,698	1,329	1,553	1,521	1,455	1,768
1929	1,594	2,062	1,079	1,219	925	731	1,712	1,312	1,551	1,504	1,445	1,933
1928	1,573	2,043	1,065	1,164	930	725	1,675	1,284	1,550	1,500	1,433	1,916
1927	1,480	2,019	1,046	1,095	931	756	1,647	1,252	1,531	1,488	1,393	1,907
1926	1,416	2,008	1,005	1,048	857	748	1,607	1,214	1,482	1,422	1,342	1,888
1925	1,359	1,997	984	1,006	916	741	1,578	1,173	1,425	1,377	1,299	1,762
1924	1,314	1,944	965	972	845	732	1,507	1,148	1,400	1,346	1,269	1,747
1923	1,272	1,896	942	941	845	711	1,454	1,130	1,378	1,336	1,239	1,704
1922	1,261	1,932	908	933	912	649	1,446	1,109	1,358	1,316	1,206	1,694
1921	1,260	1,860	905	932	983	649	1,392	1,022	1,317	1,296	1,109	1,683
1920	1,270	1,758	912	940	752	665	1,286	894	1,245	1,164	970	1,707
1919	1,070	1,589	757	780	606	538	1,104	784	1,156	1,022	852	1,609
1918	941	1,436	646	669	520	432	1,058	721	1,023	902	725	1,415
1917	828	1,439	571	580	451	389	953	679	880	832	682	1,318
1916	760	1,406	523	524	407	357	907	631	844	826	636	1,273
1915	720	1,399	493	490	381	342	876	623	753	804	608	1,224
1914	706	1,368	487	471	366	355	837	610	798	788	593	1,197

Source: Wattenberg, *Statistical History*, 166.

Employment in Manufacturing

The tables below reveal several significant themes: Changes in wages corresponded with the ups and downs of the economy; sharp differences existed between male and female wages; the workweek was more than fifty-two hours (for men) at the start of the period in 1914 and remained close to fifty during the 1920s, after which it dropped and started to rise again only during the Second World War. The graph traces economic change through employment and pay, and it measures both beside a common year, 1939, a time still affected by the depression. The most striking turns came in the early 1930s (downward) and during the Second World War, when payrolls reached more than 3½ times what they had been in 1939. The reasons? More people were working; they worked more hours, and they received more per hour.

TABLE 4.36   EARNINGS AND HOURS, MALE AND FEMALE PRODUCTION WORKERS, IN 25 MANUFACTURING INDUSTRIES, 1914–1945

Period	Male			Female		
	Average Hourly Earnings	Average Weekly Earnings	Avg. Actual Hours per Week	Average Hourly Earnings	Average Weekly Earnings	Avg. Actual Hours per Week
1914 July	$ .262	$13.65	52.2	$.155	$ 7.75	50.1
Annual Average						
1920	.642	31.69	49.2	.414	17.71	43.0
1921	.554	25.35	46.0	.362	15.63	43.2
1922	.520	25.90	50.0	.352	15.84	45.0
1923	.570	28.39	50.0	.383	17.24	45.0
1924	.592	28.27	47.8	.393	16.75	42.6

(continued)

TABLE 4.36 (continued)

Period	Male Average Hourly Earnings	Male Average Weekly Earnings	Male Avg. Actual Hours per Week	Female Average Hourly Earnings	Female Average Weekly Earnings	Female Avg. Actual Hours per Week
1925	.592	29.00	49.0	.389	17.17	44.1
1926	.601	29.51	49.1	.398	17.27	43.5
1927	.610	29.59	48.5	.398	17.37	43.7
1928	.614	29.95	48.8	.396	17.15	43.4
1929	.625	30.64	49.1	.398	17.61	44.2
1930	.622	27.66	44.5	.395	15.98	40.5
1931	.597	24.00	40.4	.371	14.69	39.8
1932	.526	17.96	34.4	.325	11.73	36.3
1933	.518	18.69	36.3	.340	12.35	36.6
1934	.607	21.07	34.8	.427	14.50	34.0
1935	.628	23.49	37.5	.437	15.37	35.2
1936	.651	26.02	40.1	.434	15.74	36.2
1937	.735	28.72	39.3	.473	17.02	36.1
1938	.758	26.07	34.6	.482	15.69	32.6
1939	.765	28.96	38.0	.475	17.02	35.8
1940	.784	30.64	39.2	.491	17.43	35.5
1941	.867	36.18	41.8	.533	20.29	38.0
1942	.987	43.46	43.9	.609	23.95	39.2
1943	1.103	51.05	46.2	.699	28.83	41.1
1944	1.164	54.65	46.9	.752	31.21	41.3
1945	1.185	53.47	45.2	.787	32.18	40.8

Note: Hourly earnings are not wage rates, because they include overtime and other monetary compensation.
Source: National Industrial Conference Board, *Economic Almanac for 1950,* 343.

GRAPH 4.1

Note: In this index of employment and payrolls, most vivid are the sharp turndown during the depression and upturn during the Second World War.
Source: Monthly Labor Review (February 1946), 335.

TABLE 4.37   WAGE RATES OF HIRED FARM WORKERS, TOTAL AND GEOGRAPHIC DIVISIONS, 1914–1945

| Period | United States Average Wage Rate | | | | Composite Wage Rate per Month | | | | | | | | | |
| | Per Day | | Per Month | | | | | | | | | | | |
	With Board	Without Board	With Board	Without Board	United States	New England	Middle Atlantic	East North Central	West North Central	South Atlantic	East South Central	West South Central	Mountain	Pacific
1914	1.17	1.43	22.62	29.74	25.13	32.10	28.10	28.50	30.30	18.40	18.30	22.70	34.80	39.00
1915	1.18	1.44	22.97	30.06	25.41	32.90	28.50	29.00	31.00	18.30	18.10	22.80	35.20	39.40
1916	1.31	1.58	25.17	32.84	27.93	37.40	32.90	32.00	33.50	20.20	19.50	24.60	37.90	41.50
1917	1.65	1.98	31.11	40.52	34.79	45.30	39.90	38.60	41.20	26.60	24.80	30.20	47.50	51.10
1918	2.15	2.54	37.96	48.80	43.73	54.90	47.70	46.00	52.00	33.20	32.20	38.90	59.00	64.20
1919	2.54	3.03	43.29	56.63	51.13	59.10	52.60	52.20	59.60	39.20	38.30	50.20	63.40	74.70
1920	2.98	3.46	51.73	65.40	59.88	69.30	64.60	62.70	70.20	44.60	43.10	55.40	73.90	87.70
1921	1.77	2.12	33.62	44.67	38.29	52.60	47.30	42.10	41.20	37.40	26.30	31.60	45.30	61.30
1922	1.73	2.07	32.75	43.33	37.47	51.20	47.10	40.60	39.30	26.30	26.40	30.50	42.90	61.10
1923	1.89	2.25	37.24	48.25	41.87	60.10	54.40	46.80	43.10	29.10	28.50	31.70	47.10	68.00
1924	1.94	2.29	37.92	49.32	42.91	61.90	55.40	47.40	43.70	31.70	29.90	34.70	48.30	63.70
1925	1.97	2.29	38.77	49.90	43.51	62.10	56.00	47.60	44.90	33.60	29.70	34.70	48.90	66.50
1926	1.98	2.31	39.87	50.83	44.36	64.00	57.20	48.90	45.10	33.50	30.00	35.80	50.40	68.30
1927	1.98	2.28	40.11	50.85	44.36	64.50	57.40	49.20	45.90	32.40	28.80	34.30	51.20	69.40
1928	1.98	2.27	40.11	50.72	44.28	64.80	55.90	48.60	46.40	32.20	29.00	34.60	52.20	68.50
1929	1.96	2.25	40.61	51.22	44.52	66.30	57.00	49.30	46.70	31.70	28.90	35.00	53.40	68.90
1930	1.76	2.06	37.59	48.10	41.25	63.20	53.60	43.60	42.80	28.80	26.40	31.30	49.30	67.00
1931	1.32	1.62	28.77	38.38	32.11	54.20	43.70	33.60	32.30	22.40	19.70	23.40	38.10	52.90
1932	.94	1.20	20.85	28.88	23.66	42.00	33.50	23.70	23.00	16.60	14.40	17.80	28.40	39.60
1933	.85	1.11	18.07	25.67	21.10	36.80	28.00	20.80	19.20	15.40	13.90	17.40	25.80	34.90
1934	.98	1.26	20.24	28.19	23.61	39.30	29.90	23.10	21.10	17.80	16.00	19.60	29.90	39.50
1935	1.07	1.33	22.42	30.24	25.53	40.60	31.10	25.70	25.00	13.60	17.10	20.70	32.90	43.40
1936	1.15	1.42	24.53	32.28	27.51	42.60	33.80	30.50	27.60	19.30	17.90	22.10	35.00	47.40
1937	1.33	1.61	23.00	36.32	31.25	46.20	38.40	35.70	31.00	21.60	19.90	24.50	38.60	53.50
1938	1.31	1.58	27.73	36.18	30.91	46.00	37.70	34.60	30.90	21.30	19.60	24.10	38.40	51.80
1939	1.30	1.56	27.39	35.82	30.56	47.10	37.10	34.40	30.70	21.40	19.80	23.70	38.30	51.40
1940	1.36	1.59	28.05	36.68	31.28	47.40	38.40	35.20	31.30	22.70	20.10	24.40	38.60	52.20
1941	1.69	1.93	34.85	43.64	38.14	54.30	47.70	44.80	42.10	25.10	22.40	28.30	51.00	64.40
1942	2.19	2.49	46.64	55.91	49.80	72.40	59.40	54.60	54.50	31.50	29.70	39.40	63.60	92.30
1943	2.87	3.27	61.91	72.51	65.35	87.80	73.00	68.30	72.90	40.10	37.80	52.70	84.50	127.00
1944	3.46	3.93	74.00	85.70	78.00	99.90	83.50	78.40	85.90	48.10	45.90	65.10	101.00	145.00
1945	3.80	4.34	82.30	95.40	86.60	107.00	91.10	85.80	96.00	54.40	49.60	72.90	111.00	154.00

Source: Bureau of Labor Statistics, *Handbook of Labor Statistics, 1947,* 98.

TABLE 4.38   AVERAGE NET INCOME IN SELECTED PROFESSIONS, 1929–1936

[In dollars]

Profession	1929	1930	1931	1932	1933	1934	1935	1936
Certified public accountants	7,154	6,601	5,480	4,308	3,968	4,364	4,573	4,992
Physicians	5,573	4,965	4,300	3,235	2,985	3,422	3,625	4,120
Dentists	4,176	3,920	3,350	2,473	2,178	2,387	3,400	4,100
Architects	4,500	3,600	2,600	1,800	1,540	1,400	1,600	2,450
College teachers	2,792	2,822	2,990	2,950	2,906	2,403	2,573	2,655
Engineers	5,000	4,350	4,000	3,220	2,900	2,820	3,500	4,200
Lawyers	5,100	4,600	4,125	3,500	3,550	3,700	4,150	4,300
Librarians	1,920	1,860	1,810	1,750	1,610	1,590	1,600	1,625
Ministers	2,200	1,950	1,750	1,600	1,450	1,500	1,560	1,625
Nurses	1,500	1,325	1,075	825	715	785	845	935
Public school teachers	1,392	1,420	1,440	1,417	1,316	1,222	1,226	1,266

Source: National Industrial Conference Board, *The Economic Almanac for 1940* (New York, 1940), 289.

Women in the Labor Force

The first half of the twentieth century was a time when women generally were expected to absorb themselves in duties at home. In common usage the term *working woman* referred—unjustly, of course—to a woman undertaking work activity beyond the family residence. In many circles a working wife stood as a mark of inadequacy on the part of her husband. Even so, women had always worked outside the home—because they had to support themselves, because they were needed, or in some cases because they insisted upon doing so. Until the time of the Second World War, women made up between 20% and 25% of the work force, and the number slowly increased. During the Great Depression women workers were particularly frowned upon, especially if their husbands had a job. Even so, the number of women at work and the percentage of women in the work force increased between 1930 and 1940. The most conspicuous change in behavior and in attitudes toward women working outside the home came during the two world wars, especially at the time of the Second World War. With the United States facing a labor shortage during the massive military buildup of the 1940s, women were actively recruited for defense factories. What previously had been viewed as brazen and unfeminine behavior now became a patriotic duty. By war's end more than one-third of all women were working; women made up nearly 30% of the labor force. Working women previously had been identified with certain types of activity, most of it involving low-paying jobs, but during the war women moved into numerous new areas of industrial work, including several jobs classified as heavy industry. The symbol of the female war worker of the 1940s was Rosie the Riveter. It remained to be seen if this remarkable change represented an expedient solution to the temporary problem—which was the standard interpretation at the time—or if the Second World War had opened a new era in the position of women in American society.

TABLE 4.39 WOMEN IN THE WORK FORCE, 1910–1945

Year	Women in the Work Force	Women as Percentage of the Total Work Force	Percentage of Working Women Who Were Married	Women Workers as Percentage of Female Population
1910	7,640,000	20.8	24.7	25.4
1920	8,347,000	20.4	23.0	23.7
1930	10,632,000	21.9	28.9	24.8
1940	13,007,000	24.6	35.9	25.8
1941	14,650,000	25.4	. . .	. . .
1942	16,120,000	26.7	. . .	. . .
1943	18,830,000	29.1	. . .	. . .
1944	19,390,000	29.2	45.7	35.0
1945	19,304,000	29.2	. . .	. . .

Source: Wattenberg, Statistical History, 133.

These women in Montana in 1918, during the First World War, take over "man's work" on a locomotive. (National Archives)

This woman helps produce 155mm shells at the Oldsmobile plant in Lansing, Michigan, during the Second World War. (Courtesy Oldsmobile History Center, Lansing)

Black People in the Labor Force

Throughout this period the majority of black people lived in the southern states, and during a great many of these years most southern blacks made their living from agriculture. Although farming provided blacks with a high percentage of employment, it offered little in the way of economic gain. Most black farmers were tenants or sharecroppers, as opposed to owners, and when the accounts were settled at harvest time, they found little to show for a year's work. Most proceeds from sale of the crop (probably cotton) were eaten up by demands made by the landowner to pay for advances of money, seed, or goods made earlier in the year. A year's profit of $200 was exceptional. Clearing less than $100 was common. Not

surprisingly, many left the farm. By the year 1940 the typical black person worked in a town or city, even in the South; in the North few black people had or sought employment in agriculture.

In the nonagricultural work force blacks were conspicuous in the types of activity in which they were most numerous and in their absence from other types of work. Blacks as a rule received the dirtiest, lowest-paying jobs. They dominated in such areas as fertilizer or turpentine factories, where work was hard, foul smelling, and altogether unpleasant. Very few black people were classified—North or South—as professional persons, and in general they were scarce in the white-collar professions. One change that moving north or

More black people continued to farm than to do anything else. These field workers are "chopping cotton" on rented land in 1941. (Library of Congress)

TABLE 4.40 **NUMBER AND PROPORTION OF PERSONS 10 YEARS OLD AND OVER GAINFULLY OCCUPIED, BY COLOR, NATIVITY, AND SEX, FOR THE UNITED STATES: 1930, 1920, AND 1910**

[Percent not shown where less than 1/10 of 1 percent, or where base is less than 100]

Class of Population	Total Number	Total — Gainfully Occupied: Number	Total — Gainfully Occupied: Percent	Male Total Number	Male — Gainfully Occupied: Number	Male — Gainfully Occupied: Percent	Female Total Number	Female — Gainfully Occupied: Number	Female — Gainfully Occupied: Percent	Percent Distribution of Gainfully Occupied: Total	Percent Distribution: Male	Percent Distribution: Female
1930	**98,723,047**	**48,829,920**	**49.5**	**49,949,798**	**38,077,804**	**76.2**	**48,773,249**	**10,752,116**	**22.0**	**100.0**	**100.0**	**100.0**
Negro	9,292,556	5,503,535	59.2	4,564,690	3,662,893	80.2	4,727,866	1,840,642	38.9	11.3	9.6	17.1
Native white	74,763,739	35,173,370	47.0	37,475,901	27,511,862	73.4	37,287,838	7,661,508	20.5	72.0	72.3	71.3
Foreign-born white	13,216,928	7,411,127	56.1	7,078,223	6,255,071	88.4	6,138,705	1,156,056	18.8	15.2	16.4	10.8
Other races	1,449,824	741,888	51.2	830,984	647,978	78.0	618,840	93,910	15.2	1.5	1.7	0.9
Mexican [a]	1,002,241	498,765	49.8	547,863	431,677	78.8	454,378	67,088	14.8	1.0	1.1	0.6
Indian	238,981	98,148	41.1	123,469	80,306	65.0	115,512	17,842	15.4	0.2	0.2	0.2
Chinese	63,392	47,106	74.3	53,650	45,547	84.9	9,742	1,559	16.0	0.1	0.1	. . .
Japanese	97,273	54,230	55.8	60,580	47,489	78.4	36,693	6,741	18.4	0.1	0.1	0.1
Filipino	42,964	39,615	92.2	41,128	39,073	95.0	1,836	542	29.5	0.1	0.1	. . .
All other	4,973	4,024	80.9	4,294	3,886	90.5	679	138	20.3	. . .	. . .	. . .
1920	**82,739,315**	**41,614,248**	**50.3**	**42,289,969**	**33,064,737**	**78.2**	**40,449,346**	**8,549,511**	**21.1**	**100.0**	**100.0**	**100.0**
Negro	8,053,225	4,824,151	59.9	4,009,462	3,252,862	81.1	4,043,763	1,571,289	38.9	11.6	9.8	18.4
Native white [a]	60,861,863	28,869,463	47.4	30,651,045	23,025,680	75.1	30,210,818	5,843,783	19.3	69.4	69.6	68.4
Foreign-born white [a]	13,497,886	7,746,460	57.4	7,419,691	6,627,997	89.3	6,078,195	1,118,463	18.4		20.0	13.1
Other races	326,341	174,174	53.4	209,771	158,198	75.4	116,570	15,976	13.7	0.4	0.5	0.2
Indian	176,925	63,326	35.8	91,546	53,478	58.4	85,379	9,848	11.5	0.2	0.2	0.1
Chinese	56,230	45,614	81.1	51,041	44,882	87.9	5,189	732	14.1	0.1	0.1	. . .
Japanese	84,238	57,903	68.7	58,806	52,614	89.5	25,432	5,289	20.8	0.1	0.2	0.1
All other	8,948	7,331	81.9	8,378	7,224	86.2	570	107	18.8	. . .	. . .	. . .
1910	**71,580,270**	**38,167,336**	**53.3**	**37,027,558**	**30,091,564**	**81.3**	**34,552,712**	**8,075,773**	**23.4**	**100.0**	**100.0**	**100.0**
Negro	7,317,922	5,192,535	71.0	3,637,386	3,178,554	37.4	3,680,536	2,013,981	54.7	13.6	10.6	24.9
Native white [a]	50,989,341	24,962,554	49.0	25,843,033	20,141,636	77.9	25,146,308	4,820,918	19.2	65.4	66.9	59.7
Foreign-born white [a]	12,944,529	7,811,502	60.3	7,321,196	6,588,711	90.0	5,623,333	1,222,791	21.7	20.5	21.9	15.1
Other races	328,478	200,745	61.1	225,943	182,663	80.8	102,535	18,082	17.6	0.5	0.6	0.2
Indian	188,758	73,916	39.2	96,582	59,206	61.3	92,176	14,710	16.0	0.2	0.2	0.2
Chinese	68,924	} 123,811	90.6	65,479	} 120,460	95.4	{ 3,445	} 3,351	32.5	0.3	0.4	. . .
Japanese	67,661			60,809			{ 6,852					
All other	3,135	3,018	96.3	3,073	2,997	97.5	62	21	. . .	. . .	. . .	. . .

[a] In 1920 and in 1910 Mexicans were included for the most part in the white population.
Source: Bureau of the Census, *Negroes in the United States, 1920–1932* (Washington, D.C., 1935), 288.

TABLE 4.41 NEGRO WORKERS IN BUSINESS, PROFESSIONAL, AND WHITE-COLLAR OCCUPATIONS, BY SEX: 1910, 1920, AND 1930

Sex and Occupation	Number of Negro Workers 1910	1920	1930	Negroes as a Percentage of All Workers 1910	1920	1930
Both Sexes						
Professional persons	64,648	77,118	115,765	4.0	3.8	3.9
Wholesale and retail dealers	20,894	23,593	28,343	1.7	1.7	1.6
Other proprietors, managers, and officials	19,102	17,610	27,648	1.6	1.3	1.5
Clerks and kindred workers	38,698	63,095	82,669	1.0	1.1	1.0
Males						
Professional persons	35,815	39,434	55,610	3.9	3.7	3.7
Wholesale and retail dealers	17,888	20,455	24,493	1.5	1.5	1.5
Other proprietors, managers, and officials	15,487	13,309	21,196	1.4	1.0	1.2
Clerks and kindred workers	31,926	48,046	62,138	1.2	1.4	1.3

Sex and Occupation	Number of Negro Workers 1910	1920	1930	Negroes as a Percentage of All Workers 1910	1920	1930
Females						
Professional persons	28,833	37,684	60,155	4.0	3.8	4.2
Wholesale and retail dealers	3,006	3,138	3,850	4.4	3.9	3.4
Other proprietors, managers, and officials	3,615	4,301	6,452	6.6	5.5	4.9
Clerks and kindred workers	6,772	15,048	20,531	0.6	0.7	0.7

Sources: Census reports; Gunnar Myrdal, *An American Dilemma* (New York, 1944), 1:306.

Industry and Service Group	Number of Negro Workers, 1930 (in Thousands)			Negro Workers as Percentage of All Workers, 1930	Percent Females among Negro Workers, 1930
	United States	The South	The North and West		
Forestry	26	25	1	13.3	1.2
Coal mines	58	46	12	8.4	0.1
Building industry	181	97	84	7.0	0.1
Chemical and allied industries	48	34	14	7.7	1.9
Fertilizer factories	17	a	a	60.4	0.7
Cigar and tobacco factories	34	31	3	22.9	54.0
Clay, glass and stone industries	29	15	14	7.8	2.6
Clothing industries	35	11	24	4.4	48.0
Suit, coat, and overall factories	15	a	a	4.8	16.7
Food and allied industries	57	31	26	6.2	20.8
Slaughter and packing houses	18	5	13	11.2	7.6
Iron, steel, vehicle and machinery industries	77	69	108	5.4	1.0
Automobile factories	26	3	23	4.0	1.1
Blast furnaces and steel rolling mills	53	15	38	8.5	0.6
Car and railroad shops	16	a	a	7.2	0.8
Lumber and furniture industries	139	132	7	16.1	2.4
Saw and planing mills	114	112	2	25.1	1.4
Paper, printing and allied industries	17	8	9	2.2	12.3
Textile industries	26	21	5	2.1	24.4
Cotton mills	16	15	1	3.9	18.0
Miscellaneous manufacturing industries	141	100	41	6.7	22.4
Independent hand trades	28	19	9	7.8	76.2
Turpentine farms and distilleries	33	a	a	75.2	0.9
Construction and maintenance of roads, streets, sewers and bridges	64	48	16	14.1	0.5
Garages, greasing stations and automobile laundries	44	19	25	10.4	0.4
Postal service	18	6	12	6.3	3.3
Steam railroads	163	105	58	10.3	1.1
Truck transfer and cab companies	41	a	a	8.5	0.6
Water transportation	45	a	a	15.0	0.7
Wholesale and retail trades, except automobiles	192	121	71	3.6	8.4
Public service (not elsewhere classified)	62	38	24	5.9	5.6
Recreation and amusement	35	16	19	7.9	16.0
Other professional and semiprofessional service	138	103	35	4.7	48.1
Hotels, restaurants, boarding houses	228	124	104	16.8	46.4
Laundries and cleaning, dyeing and pressing shops	78	43	35	18.6	65.3
Other domestic and personal service	1,174	806	368	38.6	83.6

ªData not available.

Sources: Census reports; Myrdal, *An American Dilemma,* 2:1081.

moving to the cities made was that it provided more opportunities for employment for black females. In those days when white wives mostly stayed at home, black females consistently had higher rates of employment than white females. Black women, however, were expected to content themselves with certain types of work, the most common example of which was domestic service.

Something of an exception to these themes took place during the two world wars. In both cases a shortage of labor created new opportunity for black workers and sparked movement of black workers to the urban North, to such cities as Detroit, Chicago, Cleveland, and Philadelphia. At the time of the Second World War, a second trail led from the South to the Pacific Coast states. During the Second World War the number of black people employed in defense factories rose from 3% to 8%, and in some cases black people were able to obtain higher-level positions. The changes did not come without considerable racial tension, notably in 1919 and again in 1943, and in either case they represented expediency—yielding to a temporary need—rather than recognition of a pressing national problem. At the end of each war black people became reacquainted with an old adage: They were the last hired and first fired.

TABLE 4.43 MAJOR INDUSTRY OF EMPLOYED PERSONS 14 YEARS OLD AND OVER: 1940

(Numbers in thousands)

Industry and Year	All Races	Black	Percent Black of All Races
1940			
Total employed	45,166	4,479	10
Percent	100	100	NA
Agriculture, forestry, and fisheries	19	33	18
Construction	5	3	7
Manufacturing	23	12	5
Wholesale and retail trade	17	8	5
Personal services	9	29	32
Professional and related services	7	4	5
Public administration	4	1	3
Other industries	15	9	6
Industry not reported	2	1	9

Source: Department of Commerce, *The Social and Economic Status of the Black Population in the United States, 1790–1978* (Washington, D.C., 1979), 77.

Black people discovered that war was an effective instrument in demanding more and better jobs. (Library of Congress)

TABLE 4.44   UNEMPLOYED IN LARGE CITIES, BY SEX AND RACE, 1940

City	Labor Force as a Percentage of All Persons, 14 Years of Age and Over				Unemployed (Exclusive of Emergency Workers) as a Percentage of Total Labor Force			
	Male		Female		Male		Female	
	Negro	White	Negro	White	Negro	White	Negro	White
New York	80.8	81.1	50.7	32.5	20.1	15.2	18.1	14.8
Philadelphia	78.5	80.8	43.6	31.9	33.1	15.4	23.7	14.6
Cleveland	79.5	81.4	33.0	30.3	16.7	12.4	22.4	11.3
Detroit	84.7	84.7	30.0	28.1	16.1	9.7	19.4	11.3
Chicago	77.9	82.4	35.7	33.3	17.2	11.1	23.2	9.5
St. Louis	81.6	82.9	37.4	32.8	19.6	10.5	20.4	9.2
Louisville	79.7	81.8	45.7	29.9	17.6	10.4	18.6	9.8
Baltimore	79.6	80.8	46.8	29.8	13.2	7.3	10.8	7.9
Washington, D.C.	81.0	80.7	51.7	43.0	10.6	5.4	11.3	5.1
Richmond	79.5	81.7	56.1	36.1	15.5	6.6	13.1	6.8
Atlanta	82.0	83.0	54.4	35.5	13.9	6.7	11.6	7.6
Birmingham	82.0	81.9	39.9	26.7	15.9	7.0	14.9	9.1
Memphis	85.4	82.5	44.8	30.9	14.5	6.8	15.5	7.4
New Orleans	80.7	81.1	43.4	28.9	15.3	10.2	15.2	9.6
Houston	84.0	83.8	53.7	28.7	11.9	7.2	9.7	7.0

Sources: Census reports; Myrdal, *An American Dilemma,* 1:300.

Symbols of the depression were apple sellers and soup and bread lines. This line of hungry, unemployed men formed in Chicago. (National Archives)

TABLE 4.45   MEDIAN INCOMES OF NEGRO AND NATIVE WHITE FAMILIES IN SELECTED CITIES: 1935–1936

Race	Normal Families[a]						Broken Families		
	New York, N.Y.	Chicago, Ill.	Columbus, Ohio	Atlanta, Ga.	Columbia, S.C.	Mobile, Ala.	Atlanta, Ga.	Columbia, S.C.	Mobile, Ala.
Negro families	$ 980	$ 726	$ 831	$ 632	$ 576	$ 481	$ 332	$ 254	$ 301
White families	1,930	1,687	1,622	1,876	1,876	1,419	940	1,403	784

[a] The term *normal* was intended to convey the idea that parents were present in the family.
Source: Myrdal, *An American Dilemma*, 1:365.

Unemployment: The Effect of War and Depression

The United States was in a recession at the start of the First World War in 1914. War production brought the recession to a halt, and by the time of the war's end in 1918 the nation enjoyed virtually full employment. The end of the war produced a sharp but brief rise in unemployment rates, to be followed by generally high employment for the rest of the 1920s. Unemployment statistics perhaps told the story of the depression of the 1930s better than any other numbers—more than 25% for the civilian work force and nearly 40% if one excluded farm workers—and yet even these statistics failed to give a full account of the suffering of the population. Once again, however, war turned the economy around. By the year 1944, unemployment virtually had come to an end. If anything, there was a labor shortage.

TABLE 4.46   UNEMPLOYMENT RATES, 1914–1945

[In thousands of persons 14 years old and over. Annual averages]

Year		Unemployed	
	Total	Percent of—	
		Civilian Labor Force	Nonfarm Employees
1945	1,040	1.9	2.7
1944	670	1.2	1.7
1943	1,070	1.9	2.7
1942	2,660	4.7	6.8
1941	5,560	9.9	14.4
1940	8,120	14.6	21.3
1939	9,480	17.2	25.2
1938	10,390	19.1	27.9
1937	7,700	14.3	21.3
1936	9,030	17.0	25.4
1935	10,610	20.3	30.2
1934	11,340	22.0	32.6
1933	12,830	25.2	37.6
1932	12,060	24.1	36.3
1931	8,020	16.3	25.2
1930	4,340	8.9	14.2
1929	1,550	3.2	5.3
1928	1,982	4.2	6.9
1927	1,519	3.3	5.4
1926	801	1.8	2.9
1925	1,453	3.2	5.4
1924	2,190	5.0	8.3
1923	1,049	2.4	4.1
1922	2,859	6.7	11.4
1921	4,918	11.7	19.5
1920	2,132	5.2	8.6
1919	546	1.4	2.4
1918	536	1.4	2.4
1917	1,848	4.6	8.2
1916	2,043	5.1	9.1
1915	3,377	8.5	15.6
1914	3,120	7.9	14.7

Source: Bureau of the Census, *Historical Statistics of the United States, Colonial Times to 1970* (Washington, D.C., 1976), 126.

Unemployment Relief, 1934

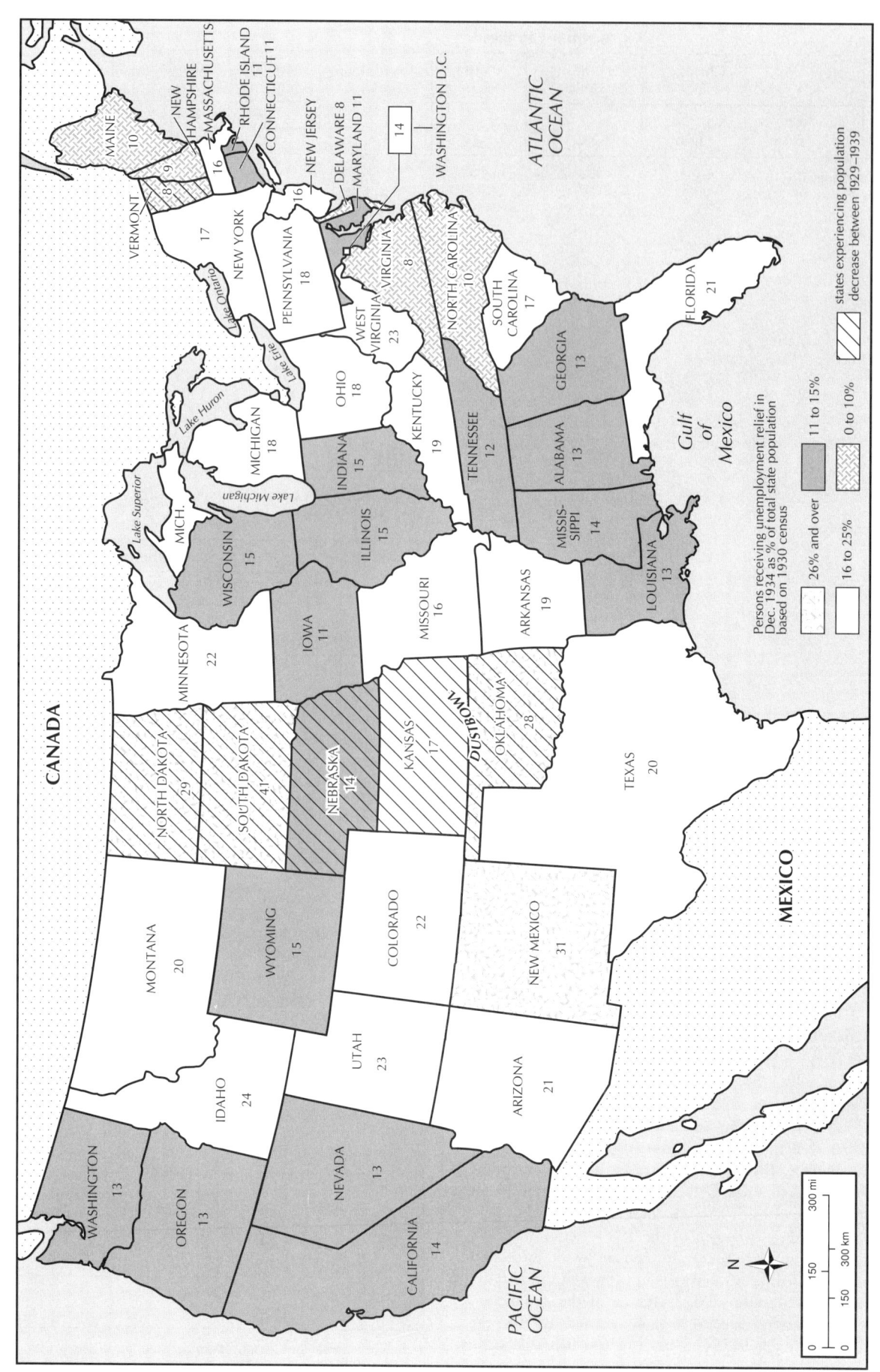

The intensity of the depression was suggested by the amount of unemployment and partly by unemployment relief. This map shows the percentage of people receiving some form of unemployment relief in 1934, not the worst year of the depression. It should be remembered that there was no regular, systematic unemployment relief service in 1934 but rather a number of stopgap programs of work relief or direct handouts such as those provided by the WPA and FERA. Many other people nominally employed but barely getting by received no assistance.

Map labels and values:

CANADA

MAINE 10
VERMONT 8
NEW HAMPSHIRE 9
MASSACHUSETTS 16
RHODE ISLAND 11
CONNECTICUT 11
NEW YORK 17
NEW JERSEY 16
PENNSYLVANIA 18
DELAWARE 8
MARYLAND 11
WASHINGTON D.C. 14
VIRGINIA 8
WEST VIRGINIA 23
NORTH CAROLINA 10
SOUTH CAROLINA 17
GEORGIA 13
FLORIDA 21
OHIO 18
KENTUCKY 19
TENNESSEE 12
ALABAMA 13
MISSISSIPPI 14
LOUISIANA 13
INDIANA 15
ILLINOIS 15
MICHIGAN 18
MICH.
WISCONSIN 15
MINNESOTA 22
IOWA 11
MISSOURI 16
ARKANSAS 19
NORTH DAKOTA 29
SOUTH DAKOTA 41
NEBRASKA 14
KANSAS 17
OKLAHOMA 28
TEXAS 20
DUST BOWL
MONTANA 20
WYOMING 15
COLORADO 22
NEW MEXICO 31
IDAHO 24
UTAH 23
ARIZONA 21
WASHINGTON 13
OREGON 13
NEVADA 13
CALIFORNIA 14

MEXICO

ATLANTIC OCEAN
Gulf of Mexico
PACIFIC OCEAN

Lake Superior, Lake Michigan, Lake Huron, Lake Erie, Lake Ontario

Persons receiving unemployment relief in Dec. 1934 as % of total state population based on 1930 census

26% and over
16 to 25%
11 to 15%
0 to 10%

states experiencing population decrease between 1929–1939

N
300 mi
0 150 300 km
0 150 300

102   Modern America, 1914 to 1945

Work Relief Projects of the New Deal

One of the most memorable aspects of the administration of Franklin D. Roosevelt was the participation of the national government during the depression in direct assistance to unemployed workers or to families in need of a means of simple subsistence. Although the government did provide some people with direct handouts of money or supplies, it for numerous reasons preferred to offer relief payments for work contributed to projects created for the occasion. The immediate purpose of the projects was to help people survive; a second purpose was to enhance national and individual morale through the effort extended. It also was hoped that such extensive activity would spark the economy and thus help promote recovery from the depression. The most important work relief programs of the New Deal were as follows:

1. Civil Works Administration. The Civil Works Administration was created in November 1933 to help people through the devastating first winter of the Roosevelt administration. Administered by Harry Hopkins, the CWA spent approximately $1 billion to employ some four million for a few weeks or months. It lasted only until spring 1934.

2. Civilian Conservation Corps. Perhaps the most popular of the relief agencies, the CCC was created by Congress in March 1933—one of the first measures of the New Deal. The first director was Robert Fechner. It was open to young men aged eighteen to twenty-five who agreed to live in a CCC camp. Their pay would be thirty dollars per month plus board, and they were expected to send most of the earnings back to their families. The work included building dams and planting trees as well as various efforts to end soil erosion and promote conservation in general. The term of service was from six months to two years. Up to 500,000 were employed at one time. Approximately 2.5 million had gone through the program when it ended in 1942; this number included 20,000 blacks and several thousand American Indians.

3. Public Works Administration. The Public Works Administration was created in June 1933 as part of the ambitious National Industrial Recovery Act. As much as any measure, it symbolized the heart and also the strategy of the new Roosevelt administration. Besides putting people to work, the PWA was to supply the financial spark (the government spending money) that would start the economic spiral upward. Directed by Harold Ickes, the PWA in 1933 was responsible for one-third of all construction in the United States. Although the organization was slow to get started and in time lost favor with the administration, it supplied work to several million unemployed people. The PWA spent some $6 billion on 34,000 projects that included building roads, bridges, power projects (it built Grand Coulee Dam), schools, and various other public buildings. In 1939 the PWA was incorporated into a Federal Works Agency.

4. Works Progress Administration. Created by Congress in June 1935, the Works Progress Administration developed into the largest and most creative effort by the government to supply people with work and give something back to the community. The original director was Harry Hopkins. Similar to the PWA in some respects, the WPA differed in scope. Between 1935 and June 1943 the WPA spent nearly $11.5 billion and employed some 8.5 million people at an average monthly wage of fifty dollars. The projects included work on roads and schools as well as a Federal Writers Project and a Federal Art, Theater, and Music Program for people of given specialties. Perhaps the most celebrated alumnus of the program was John Steinbeck. Although the organization was subjected to at least as much criticism as any work relief program—

WPA, critics said, meant We Piddle Around—it provided timely assistance for many people and left thousands of worthwhile accomplishments. It was a rare county in the United States that was unaffected by the WPA.

5. National Youth Administration. The National Youth Administration was created in 1935, originally a part of the WPA, to deal with the needs of American youth. It loosely represented America's response to the Hitler Youth and was to help keep young people democratic as opposed to radical and militant. During its tenure it gave part-time work to 600,000 college students, helping to keep them in school; 1.5 million high school students; and nearly 2.7 million youth not in school. The work included building roads, bridges, and public buildings; some enrollees received special technical training. Specific attention was given to the needs of black youth. After 1941 more than half the enrollees were women. In 1939 the NYA was shifted to the Federal Security Agency and in 1942 to the War Manpower Commission. It ended in September 1943.

The Depression: A Poet's View

Louise McNeill has been the poet laurate of West Virginia since 1979. Born in 1911, she observed, and wrote poems about, much of the history covered in this volume. The selection below offers a moving description of behavior during the depression of the 1930s.

The Great Depression

Who are these men tramping the roads
Day after day, packing their loads,
Looking for jobs, asking for chores?
Who are these men knocking on doors?

Who are these men standing in queues,
Waiting for soup, asking for news?

Who are these men sunburnt and worn
Out in the field, burning their corn?

Who are these men dumping our food
Into the sea—all of it good?

Who is this child, starving and pale?
What is the twist? Where did we fail?

Who are these men walking forlorn?
Who are these men burning their corn?
Who are these men dumping the wheat?
Who is this child—nothing to eat?
Who are these men hunting for jobs?
When will they turn, turning to mobs?
How is this land?

Rich as the plain,
Warm in the sun, sweet with the rain.

What is the twist?
Why is the pain?

Source: Louise McNeill, *Hill Daughter: New and Selected Poems* (Pittsburgh, 1991), 98; published with permission of Elderberry Books.

Men of the WPA clean up in Louisville after the flood of 1937. (Franklin D. Roosevelt Library)

Unionism

The movement for organized labor began the years 1914–45 on a tone of optimism. After some difficult times in the past, the advocates of unionism found reason for hope in the attitude of the presidency of Woodrow Wilson. The number of members grew during the First World War. The peak was reached in 1920, when there were more than five million members throughout the country, the bulk of them in the craft-union organization, the American Federation of Labor.

At the end of the war, however, the movement ran afoul of the Red Scare and other political and social stirrings of that time. The upshot was that unions became entangled—at least in popular perception—in the suspicion of radicalism and in the antiforeign mood that swelled at the start of the 1920s. Management in these years used various devices—company unions, "yellow dog" contracts, espionage, and even violence—to keep unions out of their places of business. Unions lost 1.5 million members by the year 1926, most of them formerly a part of the AFL. By 1932 there were barely three

million members in the entire United States.

The change in labor's fortunes was identified with the depression and the arrival of the presidency of Franklin D. Roosevelt. Somewhat sympathetic to the workers' plight and anxious for labor's support, the people of Roosevelt's New Deal produced the historic Wagner Act of 1935, which placed the national government behind the principle of unionism. A new National Labor Relations Board became responsible for supervising ground rules of labor-management relations. In 1938 the Roosevelt administration also produced a wages and hours law. The result was that the 1930s was labor's most productive decade. In less than ten years membership grew by more than seven million—to 10.5 million. The most dramatic change came in the emergence of the Congress of Industrial Organizations, the CIO, a new umbrella union headed by the dynamic John L. Lewis, who also headed the United Mine Workers.

The shift to unionism did not come without industrial strife, and thus the period of the late 1930s was marked with the largest number of work stoppages since the time of the First World War. Whereas most disputes in earlier years had been about wages and hours, the controversy now centered on the character of unionism—the nature of the unions' relations with management.

While most unions pledged not to strike during the Second World War, the work stoppages nonetheless were numerous between 1942 and 1945. They were, however, mostly of short duration, with a small portion of working time lost. The exception was the year 1945, and the strikes of that year reflected not the war but the end of the war. Most strikes came near year's end. The person most conspicuous in work stoppages of the war years was John L. Lewis, who showed willingness to place his coal miners on strike, war or no war. This man who earlier had been the darling of the labor movement became in many people's estimate the nation's scourge. Unionism by the mid-1940s had turned many people hostile, setting the stage for new legislation that likely would be less favorable to the workers than the revered Wagner Act.

Congestion at change of shift at Electric Boat Works (a producer of submarines) in Groton, Connecticut, 1941. (Library of Congress)

TABLE 4.47 LABOR UNION MEMBERSHIP, 1914–1945

| Year | American Federation of Labor | | Congress of Industrial Organizations | | Independent or Unaffiliated Unions | All Unions |
	Number of Affiliated Unions	Total Membership (Thousands)	Number of Affiliated Unions	Total Membership (Thousands)	Total Membership (Thousands)	Total Membership (Thousands)
1914	110	2,021	. . .	. . .	626	2,647
1915	110	1,946	. . .	. . .	614	2,560
1916	111	2,073	. . .	. . .	649	2,722
1917	111	2,371	. . .	. . .	605	2,976
1918	111	2,726	. . .	. . .	642	3,368
1919	111	3,260	. . .	. . .	786	4,046
1920	110	4,079	. . .	. . .	955	5,034
1921	110	3,907	. . .	. . .	815	4,722
1922	112	3,196	. . .	. . .	754	3,950
1923	108	3,926	. . .	. . .	703	3,629
1924	107	2,866	. . .	. . .	683	3,549
1925	107	2,877	. . .	. . .	689	3,566
1926	107	2,804	. . .	. . .	783	3,592
1927	106	2,813	. . .	. . .	787	3,600
1928	107	2,896	. . .	. . .	671	3,567
1929	105	2,934	. . .	. . .	691	3,625
1930	104	2,961	. . .	. . .	671	3,632
1931	105	2,890	. . .	. . .	636	3,526
1932	106	2,532	. . .	. . .	694	3,226
1933	108	2,127	. . .	. . .	730	2,857
1934	109	2,608	. . .	. . .	641	3,249
1935	109	3,045	. . .	. . .	683	3,723
1936	111	3,422	. . .	. . .	742	4,164
1937	100	2,861	32	3,718	639	7,218
1938	102	3,623	42	4,038	604	8,265
1939	104	4,006	45	4,000	974	8,080
1940	105	4,247	42	3,625	1,072	8,944
1941	106	4,569	41	5,000	920	10,439
1942	102	5,483	39	4,195	1,084	10,762
1943	99	6,564	40	5,285	1,793	13,642
1944	100	6,807	41	5,935	1,879	14,621
1945	102	6,931	40	6,000	1,865	14,796

Source: Bureau of Labor Statistics, *Handbook of Labor Statistics, 1947,* 130.

TABLE 4.48   WORK STOPPAGES, 1914–1945

Year	Work Stoppages and Man-days Idle						Major Issues				
	Stoppages Beginning in Year			Man-days Idle			Number of Stoppages				
		Workers Involved						Major Issues			Average Dura-tion of Stop-pages (Days)
	Number	Number (Thou-sands)	Percent of Employed Wage Earners	Number (Thou-sands)	Percent of Estimated Working Time	Per Worker Involved	Total	Wages and Hours	Union Organi-zation	Other and Not Reported	
1945	4,750	3,470	12.2	38,000	0.47	11.0	4,616	1,956	946	1,714	9.9
1944	4,956	2,120	7.0	8,720	0.09	4.1	4,958	2,146	808	2,004	5.6
1943	3,752	1,980	6.9	13,500	0.15	6.3	3,734	1,906	585	1,243	5.0
1942	2,968	840	2.8	4,180	0.05	5.0	3,026	1,423	943	670	11.7
1941	4,288	2,360	3.4	23,000	0.32	9.8	4,314	1,535	2,138	641	18.3
1940	2,508	577	2.3	6,700	0.10	11.6	2,493	753	1,243	497	20.9
1939	2,613	1,170	4.7	17,800	0.28	15.2	2,639	699	1,411	529	23.4
1938	2,772	688	2.8	9,150	0.15	13.3	2,772	776	1,385	611	23.6
1937	4,740	1,860	7.2	28,400	0.43	15.3	4,720	1,410	2,728	582	20.3
1936	2,172	789	3.1	13,900	0.21	17.6	2,156	756	1,083	317	23.3
1935	2,014	1,120	5.2	15,500	0.29	13.8	2,003	760	945	298	23.8
1934	1,856	1,470	7.2	19,600	0.38	13.4	1,817	717	835	265	19.5
1933	1,695	1,170	6.3	16,900	0.36	14.4	1,672	926	533	213	16.9
1932	841	324	1.8	10,500	0.23	32.4	852	560	162	130	19.6
1931	810	342	1.6	6,890	0.11	20.2	796	447	221	128	18.8
1930	637	183	0.8	3,320	0.05	18.1	651	284	207	160	22.3
1929	921	289	1.2	5,350	0.07	18.5	924	373	382	169	22.6
1928	604	314	1.3	12,600	0.17	40.2	620	222	226	172	27.6
1927	707	330	1.4	26,200	0.37	79.5	666	273	240	153	26.5
1926	1,035	330	1.5	. . .	. . .	. . .	1,035	478	206	351	. . .
1925	1,301	428	2.0	. . .	. . .	. . .	1,301	537	219	545	. . .
1924	1,249	655	3.1	. . .	. . .	. . .	1,249	537	244	468	. . .
1923	1,553	757	8.5	. . .	. . .	. . .	1,553	721	308	524	. . .
1922	1,112	1,610	8.7	. . .	. . .	. . .	1,112	583	208	321	. . .
1921	2,385	1,100	6.4	. . .	. . .	. . .	2,385	1,501	373	511	. . .
1920	3,411	1,460	7.2	. . .	. . .	. . .	3,411	2,038	622	751	. . .
1919	3,630	4,160	20.8	. . .	. . .	. . .	3,630	2,036	869	725	. . .
1918	3,353	1,240	6.2	. . .	. . .	. . .	3,353	1,869	584	900	. . .
1917	4,450	1,230	6.3	. . .	. . .	. . .	4,450	2,268	799	1,383	. . .
1916	3,789	1,600	8.4	. . .	. . .	. . .	3,789	2,036	721	1,032	. . .
1915	1,593	. . .	. . .	. . .	. . .	. . .	1,593	770	312	511	. . .
1914	1,204	. . .	. . .	. . .	. . .	. . .	1,204	403	253	548	. . .

Source: Bureau of the Census, Historical Statistics of the United States, 1789 to 1945, 73.

Working Accidents

In the broad range the workplace gradually became safer between 1914 and 1945, although in many areas it remained hazardous. The increase in industrial accidents between 1936 and 1945 was largely attributable to the fact that more people were working. The substantial growth in accidents in manufacturing is explainable in the same way. The deadliest profession in the country in absolute numbers was agriculture, partly because it employed so many people. Two traditionally dangerous places to work, the mines and the railroads, underwent a decrease in incidents that went beyond the decrease in people employed in each industry. Even so, both places remained hazardous. The mines, especially coal mines, remained synonymous with unsafe conditions at best and disaster at worst—given to cave-ins, explosions, and other accidents that caused multiple deaths. The lists of dead were not as large in 1945 as in 1914, but they were still substantial. In the mines as in other areas of industry, casualty lists failed to include victims of contaminated air—in coal mining they called it black lung—and other aspects of the workplace that could cause lifelong ailment and often eventual death.

This miner in western Pennsylvania used older and more dangerous equipment—carbide headlamp, not an electric light, and pony power instead of an electric railway. (Library of Congress)

TABLE 4.49　COAL MINE DISASTERS IN THE UNITED STATES

Date	Location of Mine	Killed
1914 Apr. 28	Eccles, W.Va.	181
1915 Mar. 2	Layland, W.Va.	112
1917 Apr. 27	Hastings, Colo.	121
1923 Feb. 8	Dawson, N.Mex.	120
1924 Mar. 8	Castle Gate, Utah	171
1924 Apr. 28	Benwood, W.Va.	119
1928 May 19	Mather, Pa.	195
1929 Mar. 21	Parnassus, Pa.	46
1929 Dec. 17	McAlester, Okla.	61
1930 Oct. 27	McAlester, Okla.	30
1930 Nov. 5	Millfield, Ohio	79
1931 Jan. 28	Dugger, Ind.	28
1932 Feb. 27	Boissevain. Va.	38
1932 Dec. 9	Yancey, Ky.	23
1932 Dec. 23	Moweaqua, Ill.	54
1937 Oct. 15	Birmingham, Ala.	34
1938 Apr. 22	Grundy, Va.	45
1939 Jul. 14	Providence, Ky.	28
1940 Jan. 10–12	Bartley, W.Va.	91
1940 Mar. 16	St. Clairsville, Ohio	73
1940 Jul. 15	Portage, Pa.	63
1940 Nov. 29	Cadiz, Ohio	31
1942 Jan. 27	Rout, Colo.	34
1942 May 12	Osage, W.Va.	56
1942 Jul. 9	Pursglove, W.Va.	20
1943 Feb. 27	Red Lodge, Mont.	75
1943 May 5	La Follette, Tenn.	10
1943 Aug. 29	Sayreton, Ala.	28
1944 Jul. 6	Bellaire, Ohio	66
1945 May 9	Sunnyside, Utah	23

Source: The World Almanac and Book of Facts for 1946 (New York, 1946), 654.

Coal Mine Owners

Coal miners had to deal with the hazards of their dangerous occupation, and they also often had to do battle with management. Mine ownership came in different forms, but some of the most demanding were large corporations, in essence absentee landlords who controlled nearly every aspect of the miner's life. Mine fields often became battlefields, especially during the 1920s and 1930s. Louise McNeill wrote a poem about the issue as it existed in her state, West Virginia, which was synonymous with coal mining.

The Company

The Company owned the houses,
And The Company owned the store;
The Company paid the Sheriff off,
And fixed the Schoolhouse door.

The Company owned the Baldwin-Felts,[*]
And opened up the bar;
And set the tipple on its stilts,
And lit the Christmas Star.

They owned the mountain and the mine,
The river and its fork;

They summered in the Byzantine
And wintered in New York.

[*]Baldwin-Felts were company police, almost a private army, on the order of the more famous Pinkerton detectives.
Source: McNeill, *Hill Daughter,* 90; published with permission of Elderberry Books.

TABLE 4.50   ESTIMATED NUMBER OF WORK INJURIES BY INDUSTRY GROUP, 1936–1945

Industry Group and Type of Disability	1936	1937	1938	1939	1940	1941	1942	1943	1944	1945
All industry groups: Total	1,407,200	1,838,000	1,375,600	1,603,500	1,889,700	2,180,200	2,267,700	2,414,000	2,230,400	2,020,300
Fatalities	16,000	19,600	16,400	16,400	18,100	19,200	18,100	18,400	15,900	16,500
Permanent—total	a	a	a	a	b	b	1,800	1,700	1,700	1,800
Permanent—partial	66,200	126,700	98,900	109,400	89,600	100,600	100,800	108,800	94,200	88,100
Temporary—total	1,325,000	1,691,700	1,260,300	1,477,700	1,782,000	2,060,400	2,147,000	2,285,900	2,118,400	1,913,900
Agriculture:[c] Total	264,600	270,500	267,400	257,300	270,400	270,400	283,700	311,900	311,900	305,600
Fatalities	5,500	4,500	4,400	4,300	4,500	4,500	4,500	4,800	4,800	4,500
Permanent—total	a	a	a	b	b	b	400	400	400	400
Permanent—partial	6,100	13,500	13,000	13,000	13,900	13,900	14,200	15,600	15,600	15,300
Temporary—total	253,000	252,500	250,000	240,000	252,000	252,000	264,000	291,100	291,100	285,400
Mining and quarrying:[d] Total	103,100	107,800	82,000	91,000	86,500	97,100	102,700	96,400	92,100	82,100
Fatalities	1,700	1,900	1,700	1,600	1,800	1,900	2,000	2,000	1,700	1,500
Permanent—total	a	a	a	b	b	b	200	200	200	200
Permanent—partial	3,400	3,300	2,500	2,700	2,900	3,700	4,500	4,200	4,000	3,600
Temporary—total	98,000	102,600	77,800	86,700	81,800	91,500	96,000	90,000	86,200	76,800
Construction:[e] Total	283,900	291,700	292,200	404,700	453,800	495,500	349,500	260,100	99,600	112,200
Fatalities	2,700	3,700	2,600	3,600	4,100	4,100	3,300	2,500	1,100	1,700
Permanent—total	a	a	a	b	b	b	300	200	100	100
Permanent—partial	154,00	20,600	14,600	18,100	20,900	21,800	17,100	12,800	3,600	3,400
Temporary—total	265,800	367,40	275,000	383,000	428,800	469,600	328,800	244,600	94,800	107,000
Manufacturing:[f] Total	311,600	364,400	220,800	286,200	316,000	452,700	635,200	802,500	786,900	591,600
Fatalities	2,100	2,500	1,900	1,600	1,900	2,400	2,500	3,100	2,900	2,700
Permanent—total	a	a	a	b	b	b	300	300	300	300
Permanent—partial	21,200	27,900	14,000	17,600	18,600	25,300	27,000	34,100	35,400	30,700
Temporary—total	288,300	334,000	204,900	267,000	295,500	425,000	605,400	765,000	748,300	557,900
Public utilities: Total	13,700	16,500	16,300	21,000	21,000	21,000	21,000	19,700	19,300	20,300
Fatalities	300	300	500	500	500	500	500	400	400	400
Permanent—total	a	a	a	b	b	b	g	g	g	g
Permanent—partial	400	700	700	500	500	500	500	500	500	600
Temporary—total	13,000	15,500	15,100	20,000	20,000	20,000	20,000	18,800	18,400	19,300
Trade:[e] Total	133,000	241,200	201,500	200,800	244,600	297,100	284,200	268,400	273,800	296,400
Fatalities	600	2,800	1,800	1,800	1,900	1,600	1,200	1,100	700	1,200
Permanent—total	a	a	a	b	b	b	100	100	100	100
Permanent—partial	1,700	32,000	39,700	39,000	8,700	7,500	7,000	6,600	6,000	7,100
Temporary—total	130,700	206,400	160,000	160,000	234,000	288,000	275,900	260,600	267,000	288,000
Railroads:[h] Total	37,800	40,100	30,300	34,500	33,700	48,200	60,800	85,400	92,400	94,100
Fatalities	800	800	600	800	700	1,100	1,100	1,300	1,200	1,100
Permanent—total	a	a	a	b	b	b	200	200	300	400
Permanent—partial	1,200	1,400	1,500	1,700	1,700	3,300	4,200	5,900	6,400	6,500
Temporary—total	35,800	37,900	28,200	32,000	31,300	43,800	55,300	78,000	84,500	86,100
Miscellaneous transportation:[e]										
Total	27,500	42,400	52,900	54,400	129,300	130,300	136,900	146,000	135,100	139,900
Fatalities	600	800	700	800	900	1,200	1,200	1,300	900	1,000
Permanent—total	a	a	a	b	b	b	100	100	100	100
Permanent—partial	1,100	2,200	1,000	1,600	3,400	3,600	3,800	4,100	4,100	4,200
Temporary—total	25,800	39,400	51,200	52,000	125,000	125,500	131,800	140,500	130,000	134,600
Service, government, and miscellaneous industries:[e]										
Total	232,000	363,400	212,200	253,600	334,400	367,900	393,700	423,600	419,300	378,100
Fatalities	1,700	2,300	2,200	1,400	1,800	1,900	1,800	1,900	2,200	2,400
Permanent—total	a	a	a	b	b	b	200	200	200	200
Permanent—partial	15,700	25,100	11,900	15,200	19,000	21,000	22,500	24,200	18,800	16,700
Temporary—total	214,600	336,000	198,100	237,000	313,600	345,000	369,200	397,300	398,100	358,800

[a] Permanent-total included in permanent-partial.
[b] Permanent-total included in fatalities.
[c] Based on fragmentary data.
[d] Based largely on Bureau of Mines data.
[e] Based on small sample studies.
[f] Based on comprehensive surveys.
[g] Less than 50.
[h] Based on Interstate Commerce Commission data.
Source: Bureau of Labor Statistics, *Handbook of Labor Statistics, 1947,* 164.

TABLE 4.51 FARMS AND FARM POPULATION, 1914–1945

[Census figures in italics]

Year	Farm Population Total (1,000)	Percentage of Total Population	Net Change through Migration (1,000)	Number of Farms (1,000)
1945	24,420	17.5	671	*5,859*
1944	24,815	18.0	−748	6,003
1943	26,186	19.2	−1,740	6,089
1942	28,914	21.5	−3,145	6,202
1941	30,118	22.6	−1,587	6,293
1940	30,547	23.2	−788	*6,102* [a]
1939	30,840	23.6	−703	6,441
1938	30,980	23.9	−545	6,527
1937	31,266	24.3	−661	6,636
1936	31,737	24.8	−834	6,739
1935	32,161	25.3	−799	*6,812*
1934	32,305	25.6	−537	6,776
1933	32,393	25.8	−463	6,741
1932	31,388	25.2	607	6,687
1931	30,845	24.9	156	6,608

Year	Farm Population Total (1,000)	Percentage of Total Population	Net Change through Migration (1,000)	Number of Farms (1,000)
1930	30,529	24.9	−61	*6,295* [a]
1929	30,580	25.2	−477	6,512
1928	30,548	25.4	−422	6,470
1927	30,530	25.7	−457	6,458
1926	30,969	26.5	−907	6,462
1925	31,190	27.0	−702	*6,372*
1924	31,177	27.5	−487	6,480
1923	31,490	28.2	−807	6,492
1922	32,109	29.3	−1,137	6,500
1921	32,123	29.7	−564	6,511
1920	31,974	30.1	−336	*6,454* [a]
1919	31,200	29.7	. . .	6,506
1918	31,950	30.6	. . .	6,488
1917	32,430	31.5	. . .	6,478
1916	32,530	32.0	. . .	6,463
1915	32,440	32.4	. . .	6,458
1914	32,320	32.8	. . .	6,447

[a] Includes Hawaii and Alaska.
Source: Wattenberg, *Statistical History,* 457.

TABLE 4.52 AVERAGE ACRES PER FARM, BY REGION AND STATE, 1910–1945

Division, Region, and State	1945	1940	1935	1930	1925	1920	1910
United States	**195**	**175**	**155**	**157**	**145**	**149**	**139**
Northeast	**98**	**97**	**93**	**102**	**92**	**99**	**96**
New England	96	99	98	114	99	109	104
Maine	109	108	113	119	103	113	105
N.H.	107	109	120	132	107	127	120
Vt.	148	156	149	157	141	146	143
Mass.	56	61	63	78	71	78	78
R.I.	74	74	71	84	79	81	84
Conn.	72	72	65	87	79	84	82
Middle Atlantic	99	97	92	98	90	95	92
N.Y.	118	112	106	113	102	107	102
N.J.	69	73	65	69	65	77	77
Pa.	87	86	83	89	81	87	85
North Central	**201**	**185**	**172**	**181**	**167**	**172**	**157**
East North Central	121	113	108	115	107	109	105
Ohio	99	94	90	98	91	92	89
Ind.	114	107	102	108	102	103	99
Ill.	155	145	137	143	136	135	129
Mich.	105	96	94	101	94	97	92
Wis.	133	123	117	120	113	117	119
West North Central	275	252	231	239	223	234	210
Minn.	175	165	161	167	160	169	177
Iowa	165	160	155	158	156	157	156
Mo.	145	136	126	132	125	132	125
N. Dak.	590	513	462	496	452	466	382
S. Dak.	626	545	445	439	403	464	335
Nebr.	427	391	349	345	329	339	298
Kans.	344	308	275	283	264	275	244
South	**131**	**123**	**110**	**106**	**104**	**109**	**114**
South Atlantic	93	91	84	82	80	84	93
Del.	99	100	89	93	88	93	96
Md.	102	100	99	101	91	99	103
Va.	95	94	89	98	89	100	106
W. Va.	89	90	90	90	107	110	104
N.C.	65	68	66	65	66	74	88
S.C.	75	82	75	66	62	65	77
Ga.	105	110	101	86	88	82	93
Fla.	214	134	83	85	99	112	105
East South Central	79	75	70	69	70	75	78
Ky.	83	80	74	81	77	80	86

Division, Region, and State	1945	1940	1935	1930	1925	1920	1910
Tenn.	76	75	70	73	71	77	82
Ala.	85	83	72	68	70	76	79
Miss.	74	66	63	55	62	67	68
West South Central	234	208	177	167	162	174	179
Ark.	88	83	70	66	70	75	81
La.	78	67	61	58	67	74	87
Okla.	219	194	166	166	157	166	152
Tex.	367	329	275	252	236	262	269
West	**639**	**504**	**414**	**434**	**373**	**364**	**300**
Mountain	1,151	822	641	653	564	481	325
Mont.	1,557	1,111	940	940	698	608	517
Idaho	301	236	221	224	200	199	172
Wyo.	2,533	1,866	1,610	1,469	1,203	750	778
Colo.	761	613	471	482	417	408	293
N. Mex.	1,671	1,139	832	982	879	818	316
Ariz.	2,881	1,389	745	743	1,024	582	135
Utah	392	287	203	207	192	197	157
Nev.	1,802	1,059	980	1,186	1,054	745	1,010
Pacific	(NA)	241	(NA)	238	(NA)	246	278
Wash.	209	186	174	191	172	200	208
Oreg.	313	291	268	300	253	270	257
Calif.	252	230	202	224	202	250	317

Source: Wattenberg, *Statistical History*, 461.

Farms and Farming

The trend of American agriculture between 1914 and 1945 was toward fewer farmers and fewer but larger agricultural establishments. The farm population experienced a net loss in nearly every year; the percentage of farmers in the nation in 1945 was slightly more than half that in 1914. Although the number of farms held steady until the 1940s, when it decreased, the amount of land in farms went up. Although the average size of farms seemed reasonable, if not impressive—150–190 acres—a closer examination suggested other themes. The largest number of farmers worked farms of less, often much less, than 100 acres. A good portion of the land was being cultivated by a small number of massive agricultural enterprises. The time of the individual family farm by no means had passed, but the trend clearly was toward agriculture strictly as a business. The number of farmers who were tenants remained high—never less than 30%. In the southern states tenants (including sharecroppers) outnumbered farm owners in every year. In the case of black farmers in the South, the ratio of tenants to owners was overwhelming. A reduction in the number of black tenant farmers under way since the 1920s was attributable less to an increase in black farm ownership than to black families deciding to give up on farming and leave the land.

TABLE 4.53   NUMBER OF FARMS BY COLOR AND TENURE OF OPERATOR, 1910–1945

Color and Tenure of Operator	1945	1940	1930	1920	1910
U.S.	**5,859,169**	**6,096,799**	**6,288,648**	**6,448,343**	**6,361,502**
Full owner	3,301,361	3,084,138	2,911,644	3,366,510	3,354,897
Part owner	660,502	615,039	656,750	558,580	593,825
Manager	38,885	36,351	55,889	68,449	58,104
Tenant	1,858,421	2,361,271	2,664,365	2,454,804	2,354,676
White	5,169,954	5,377,728	5,372,578	5,498,454	5,440,619
Full owner	3,126,212	2,916,562	2,752,787	3,174,109	3,159,088
Part owner	629,734	581,517	612,887	517,759	548,413
Manager	38,263	35,634	52,767	66,223	56,560
Tenant	1,375,745	1,844,015	1,954,137	1,740,363	1,676,558
Nonwhite	689,215	719,071	916,070	949,889	920,883
Full owner	175,149	167,576	158,857	192,401	195,809
Part owner	30,768	33,522	43,863	40,821	45,412
Manager	622	717	3,122	2,226	1,544
Tenant	482,676	517,256	710,228	714,441	678,118

(continued)

TABLE 4.53   (continued)

Color and Tenure of Operator	1945	1940	1930	1920	1910
South	2,881,135	3,007,170	3,223,816	3,206,664	3,097,547
Full owner	1,509,056	1,327,690	1,190,683	1,405,762	1,329,390
Part owner	193,607	216,607	224,992	191,463	215,121
Manager	13,193	13,580	17,358	18,318	16,284
Tenant	1,165,279	1,449,293	1,790,783	1,591,121	1,536,752
Croppers	446,556	541,291	776,278	561,091	. . .
White	2,215,722	2,326,904	2,342,129	2,283,750	2,207,406
Full owner	1,348,076	1,185,788	1,050,187	1,227,204	1,154,100
Part owner	165,355	185,246	183,469	152,432	171,944
Manager	12,751	13,215	16,529	16,548	15,084
Tenant	689,540	942,655	1,091,944	887,566	866,278
Croppers	176,260	242,173	383,381	227,378	. . .
Nonwhite	665,413	680,266	881,687	922,914	890,141
Full owner	160,980	141,902	140,496	178,558	175,290
Part owner	28,252	31,361	41,523	39,031	43,177
Manager	442	365	829	1,770	1,200
Tenant	475,739	506,638	698,839	703,555	670,474
Croppers	270,296	299,118	392,897	333,713	. . .

Source: Bureau of the Census, *Historical Statistics of the United States, Colonial Times to 1957,* 278.

Farm Size and Land Ownership

The two tables that follow indicate the course undertaken by American agriculture in the twentieth century. Although the vast majority of farmers operated small farms throughout this period, most of them comprising fewer than 100 acres, and while the number of very small farms did grow between 1920 and 1945, the bulk of acreage progressively was coming under control of what one must call landlords, each of whom had more than 1,000 acres. By 1945 fewer than 2% of farms contained more than 40% of land, and fewer than 5% of farms had 51% of the land. In sum, farming in the United States was becoming the domain of massive agricultural corporations and not the function of much-honored independent family farms.

TABLE 4.54   NUMBER OF FARMS BY SIZE, 1920 AND 1945

Size of Farm (Acres)	Number		Percentage of All Farms	
	1920	1945	1920	1945
Under 10	288,772	593,937	4.5	10.1
10–49	2,011,495	1,651,923	32.0	28.2
50–99	1,474,745	1,157,744	22.9	19.8
100–179[a]	1,449,630	1,200,859	22.5	20.5
180–259[a]	530,800	493,149	8.2	8.4
260–499	475,677	473,923	7.4	8.1
500–999	149,819	173,547	2.3	3.0
1,000 and over	67,405	113,807	1.0	1.9

[a]The census in 1920 measured farms of 100–174 (not 179) acres, and 175–259 acres (not 180).
Sources: Bureau of the Census, *United States Census of Agriculture for 1935, General Report* (Washington, D.C., 1937), 50, and *United States Census of Agriculture for 1945, General Report* (Washington, D.C., 1948), XXXII.

TABLE 4.55   LAND IN FARMS BY SIZE OF FARM, 1920 AND 1945

Size of Farm (Acres)	Number of Acres		Percentage of All Farm Land	
	1920	1945	1920	1945
Under 10	1,600,287	2,801,029	.2	.2
10–49	55,552,942	43,868,796	3.9	5.8
50–99	105,630,796	83,217,975	11.1	7.3
100–179[a]	194,681,260	162,541,154	20.4	14.2
180–259[a]	112,562,596	105,729,603	11.8	9.2
260–499	164,244,399	164,892,132	17.2	14.4
500–999	100,975,916	118,985,731	10.6	10.4
1,000 and over	220,635,519	466,647,557	23.1	40.6

[a]The census in 1920 measured farms of 100–174 (not 179) acres, and 175–259 (not 180) acres.
Source: Bureau of the Census, *Census of Agriculture for 1935,* 50, and *Census of Agriculture for 1945,* XXXII.

Farm Production and Earning

Agriculture remained the most persistently perplexing sector of the economy during the first half of the twentieth century. In the broad scope American farmers could do wonders. Agriculture as a whole became much more efficient. The ability to produce more goods with fewer people was attributable to such familiar factors as the use of modern equipment and scientific development in and management of seed, soil, and livestock. The power of American agriculture was one of the great forces of world affairs. Instead of a continuing agricultural prosperity, however, which one might expect increased production to bring, there was a continuing "farm problem." The problem was partly a consequence of the farmers' success; farm efficiency produced such an oversupply of some commodities that it brought down the price received for the items. In some measure farm economics followed the course of national economics. Farm income was high during the period of the First World War. It fell sharply in 1921, leveled off somewhat in the 1920s, underwent absolute disaster in the 1930s, began recovery in the 1940s, and achieved record high numbers during the Second World War. And yet, except possibly for brief periods during the two world wars, farm income was not what it needed to be. It did not keep pace in 1920s with improvement in other economic sectors. The decline in the 1930s was so devastating that the national government had to intervene to pay farm subsidies, try to increase farm prices, and stop the trend of farmers losing their land. By planting trees, damming up rivers, and other moves the government sought to deal with such natural problems as floods, dust storms, and soil erosion in general. And profits, when they did exist, mostly went to larger, more mechanized farm producers. Almost hidden behind general statistics was what one might call an agricultural underworld—millions of tenants, croppers, or small owners working with tired soil and outmoded methods. Located in every state but most numerous in the South and border areas, they were—whether black or white—staying alive but not really living, not a statistic of unemployment but not truly gainfully employed. And the world wars did not help these people's earnings much. They probably were more affected during 1917–19 or 1941–45 by having a son called to the army or by deciding to leave the farm for a defense plant.

TABLE 4.56 INDEXES OF AGRICULTURAL PRODUCTION, MAN-HOUR REQUIREMENTS, AND PRODUCTIVITY

(1935–1939 = 100)

The information below measures the increased efficiency of the American farmer. The table shows that absolute production for sale or home consumption increased, although not in every year, that the number of hours required to do a task as a rule decreased, and as a consequence the amount of production per hour of work increased sharply, especially during the Second World War. The explanation rests with the use of better equipment and increased use of scientific agricultural methods.

Year	Agricultural Production	Man-hour Requirements	Production per Man-hour
1914	86	113	76
1915	86	110	78
1916	83	110	75
1917	86	113	76
1918	90	114	79
1919	91	112	81
1920	92	114	81
1921	83	105	79
1922	91	109	84
1923	94	110	85
1924	98	111	88
1925	97	113	86
1926	100	114	88

Year	Agricultural Production	Man-hour Requirements	Production per Man-hour
1927	98	109	90
1928	102	111	92
1929	99	110	90
1930	98	109	90
1931	102	112	91
1932	96	108	89
1933	96	108	89
1934	93	106	88
1935	91	100	91
1936	94	97	97
1937	106	105	101
1938	103	99	104
1939	107	99	108
1940	110	98	112
1941	113	97	116
1942	124	101	123
1943	129	100	129
1944	137	100	137
1945	134	95	141

Source: Frederick J. Dewhurst and Associates, America's Needs and Resources (New York, 1947), 1080.

TABLE 4.57 PRODUCTION OF CHIEF CROPS

[Figures refer to crop or growth year. Weight of bushel of wheat, 60 pounds; bushel of corn, 56 pounds]

Year	Corn	Wheat	Rice	Sugar Beet (Chiefly Refined)	Sugar Cane (Chiefly raw)	Cotton Running Bales [a]	Cotton 500-Pound Bales	Tobacco
	1,000 Bushels	1,000 Bushels	1,000 Pounds	1,000 Pounds	1,000 Pounds	Thousands	Thousands	1,000 Pounds
1914	2,523,750	897,487	652,167	1,444,000	504,000	15,906	16,112	1,036,745
1915	2,829,044	1,008,637	725,194	1,748,000	282,000	11,068	11,172	1,157,425
1916	2,425,206	634,572	1,098,444	1,642,000	634,000	11,364	11,448	1,206,785
1917	2,908,242	619,790	964,278	1,530,000	502,000	11,248	11,284	1,325,530
1918	2,441,249	904,130	1,111,056	1,522,000	580,000	11,906	12,018	1,444,505
1919	2,678,541	952,097	1,191,972	1,452,000	250,000	11,326	11,411	1,444,206
1920	3,070,604	843,277	1,434,667	2,178,000	360,000	13,271	13,429	1,509,212

(continued)

TABLE 4.57 (continued)

[Figures refer to crop or growth year. Weight of bushel of wheat, 60 pounds; bushel of corn, 56 pounds]

| Year | Corn | Wheat | Rice | Sugar | | Cotton | | Tobacco |
| | | | | Beet (Chiefly Refined) | Cane (Chiefly raw) | Running Bales [a] | 500-Pound Bales | |
	1,000 Bushels	1,000 Bushels	1,000 Pounds	1,000 Pounds	1,000 Pounds	Thousands	Thousands	1,000 Pounds
1921	2,928,442	818,964	1,090,944	2,040,000	668,000	7,978	7,945	1,004,928
1922	2,707,306	846,649	1,157,306	1,350,000	604,000	9,729	9,755	1,254,304
1923	2,875,292	759,482	923,278	1,762,000	336,000	10,171	10,140	1,517,583
1924	2,223,123	841,617	906,750	2,180,000	180,000	13,639	13,630	1,244,928
1925	2,798,367	668,700	917,667	1,826,000	284,000	16,123	16,105	1,376,008
1926	2,546,972	832,213	1,167,361	1,794,000	96,000	17,755	17,978	1,289,272
1927	2,616,120	875,059	1,236,028	2,186,000	144,000	12,783	12,956	1,211,311
1928	2,665,516	914,373	1,217,611	2,122,000	272,000	14,297	14,477	1,373,214
1929	2,515,937	824,183	1,098,167	2,036,000	436,000	14,548	14,825	1,532,676
1930	2,080,130	886,522	1,248,028	2,416,000	430,000	13,756	13,932	1,648,037
1931	2,575,927	941,540	1,239,250	2,312,000	368,000	16,629	17,097	1,565,088
1932	2,930,352	756,307	1,156,083	2,714,000	530,000	12,710	13,003	1,018,011
1933	2,397,593	552,215	1,045,861	3,284,000	500,000	12,664	13,047	1,371,965
1934	1,448,920	526,052	1,084,639	2,320,000	534,000	9,472	9,636	1,084,589
1935	2,299,363	628,227	1,095,889	2,370,000	766,000	10,420	10,638	1,302,041
1936	1,505,689	629,880	1,383,889	2,608,000	874,000	12,141	12,399	1,162,838
1937	2,642,978	873,914	1,483,944	2,576,000	924,000	18,252	18,946	1,569,023
1938	2,548,753	919,913	1,458,500	3,370,000	1,166,000	11,623	11,943	1,385,573
1939	2,580,912	741,180	1,501,722	3,286,000	1,008,000	11,481	11,817	1,880,793
1940	2,462,320	813,305	1,512,028	3,546,000	664,000	12,298	12,566	1,462,080
1941	2,675,790	943,127	1,425,639	2,968,000	838,000	10,495	10,744	1,262,049
1942	3,131,518	974,176	1,793,028	3,226,000	920,000	12,438	12,817	1,408,717
1943	3,034,354	841,023	1,801,194	1,866,000	996,000	11,129	11,427	1,406,196
1944	3,203,310	1,072,177	1,893,361	1,974,000	874,000	11,839	12,230	1,956,896
1945	2,880,933	1,108,224	1,893,056	2,388,000	950,000	8,813	9,016	1,993,837

[a] A running bale is a bale as it came from the gin, weighing from 500 to 508 lbs.
Source: Bureau of the Census, *Statistical Abstract of the United States, 1947* (Washington, D.C., 1947), 637.

Livestock on Farms

A general, if unsteady, increase in the number of meat-producing animals suggested that Americans were eating more meat. The rise in the production of cattle largely reflected an increase in the number of beef (as opposed to dairy) cattle. The most marked change in livestock was the reduction of draft animals, the horses and mules, an indication that more and more farmers were acquiring tractors.

TABLE 4.58 LIVESTOCK ON FARMS, JANUARY 1

In Thousands

Jan. 1	Cattle	Sheep	Hogs	Horses	Mules
1914	59,461	43,089	52,853	21,308	4,870
1915	63,849	40,513	56,600	21,431	5,062
1916	67,438	40,010	60,596	21,334	5,200
1917	70,979	38,886	57,578	21,306	5,353
1918	73,040	39,664	62,931	21,238	5,485
1919	72,094	41,875	64,326	20,922	5,568
1920	70,400	40,743	60,159	20,091	5,651

Jan. 1	Cattle	Sheep	Hogs	Horses	Mules
1921	68,714	39,479	58,942	19,369	5,768
1922	68,795	36,922	59,849	18,764	5,824
1923	67,546	36,803	69,304	18,125	5,893
1924	65,996	37,139	66,576	17,378	5,907
1925	63,373	38,543	55,770	16,651	5,918
1926	60,576	40,363	52,105	16,083	5,903
1927	58,178	42,415	55,496	15,388	5,804
1928	57,322	45,258	61,873	14,792	5,656
1929	58,877	48,381	59,042	14,234	5,510
1930	61,003	51,565	55,705	13,742	5,382
1931	63,030	53,233	54,835	13,195	5,273
1932	65,801	53,902	59,301	12,664	5,148
1933	70,280	53,054	62,127	12,291	5,046
1934	74,369	53,503	58,621	12,052	4,945
1935	68,846	51,808	39,066	11,861	4,822
1936	67,847	51,136	42,975	11,598	4,628
1937	66,098	50,848	43,083	11,342	4,460
1938	65,249	51,063	44,525	10,995	4,250
1939	66,029	51,348	50,012	10,629	4,163
1940	68,309	52,107	61,165	10,444	4,034
1941	71,755	53,920	54,353	10,193	3,911
1942	76,025	56,213	60,607	9,873	3,782
1943	81,204	55,150	73,881	9,605	3,626
1944	85,334	50,782	83,741	9,192	3,421
1945	85,573	46,520	59,331	8,715	3,235

Source: National Industrial Conference Board, *Economic Almanac for 1950*, 205.

TABLE 4.59   COWS KEPT FOR MILK

(Census figures in italics)

| Year | Cows and Heifers 2 Years Old and Over Kept for Milk, Jan. 1 | |
	Number	Value per Head
1945	*22,803*	. . .
1945	27,770	99.40
1944	27,704	102.00
1943	27,138	99.50
1942	26,313	77.90
1941	25,453	60.90
1940	*21,937*	. . .
1940	24,940	57.30
1939	24,600	55.73
1938	24,466	54.52
1937	24,649	50.45
1936	25,196	49.32
1935	*24,582*	. . .
1935	26,082	30.17
1934	26,931	27.00
1933	25,936	29.18
1932	24,896	39.51
1931	23,820	57.03

| Year | Cows and Heifers 2 Years Old and Over Kept for Milk, Jan. 1 | |
	Number	Value per Head
1930	*21,124*	. . .
1930	23,032	82.70
1929	22,440	83.89
1928	22,231	73.38
1927	22,251	59.15
1926	22,410	54.65
1925	*20,900*	. . .
1925	22,575	48.34
1924	22,331	49.91
1923	22,138	48.65
1922	21,851	48.68
1921	21,456	61.19
1920	*19,675*	. . .
1920	21,455	81.51
1919	21,545	78.37
1918	21,536	70.63
1917	21,212	59.51
1916	20,752	53.81
1915	20,270	55.30
1914	19,821	53.91

Source: Wattenberg, *Statistical History*, 522.

Farm Earnings

The first table below indicates that after reasonably good times during the First World War, farm income dropped sharply at war's end and never recovered during the 1920s, normally thought of as a time of prosperity. Bad times became worse in the 1930s, as agricultural prices collapsed. Only during the Second World War did prosperity return to the farms. The second table suggests that from an economic point of view, an individual was better off—often much better off—doing something other than farming, even during the good times of the 1940s.

TABLE 4.60   CASH RECEIPTS FROM FARM MARKETINGS

[In millions of dollars]

| Year | Crops | | | | | | | | Livestock and Livestock Products | | | | | | | | |
	Cotton (Lint and Seed)	Tobacco	Food Grains	Oil-Bearing Crops	Feed Crops	Vege-tables	Fruits and Tree Nuts	Other	Hogs	Cattle and Calves	Sheep and Lambs	Wool	Dairy Products	Eggs	Broilers and Farm Chickens	Turkeys and Other Poultry	Other
1945	1,208	898	1,563	615	1,509	1,611	1,498	753	2,263	3,318	319	126	3,021	1,518	1,004	295	144
1944	1,548	690	1,375	590	1,271	1,484	1,528	699	2,800	2,605	300	144	2,915	1,365	862	241	119
1943	1,301	538	1,068	703	1,135	1,472	1,273	637	2,929	2,563	342	182	2,785	1,446	926	202	118
1942	1,272	476	977	525	839	1,028	844	565	2,198	2,263	306	133	2,330	1,018	538	170	83
1941	1,006	323	689	238	626	692	604	441	1,302	1,705	226	138	1,900	663	364	116	78
1940	638	242	479	126	600	559	446	379	836	1,375	180	106	1,521	468	268	92	67
1939	627	271	465	111	507	527	439	389	810	1,289	172	81	1,346	437	248	85	68
1938	655	294	468	92	444	471	403	373	870	1,163	157	69	1,388	485	235	79	77
1937	886	320	659	85	446	586	540	402	925	1,239	186	114	1,525	517	269	80	85
1936	904	243	500	77	473	597	473	382	991	1,114	166	95	1,478	481	262	74	81
1935	712	243	418	69	302	468	432	333	682	1,063	152	70	1,310	502	235	68	61
1934	863	236	348	53	355	468	398	300	520	813	132	81	1,146	373	190	54	27
1933	578	157	335	33	327	423	343	290	524	599	105	77	1,004	309	161	44	23
1932	461	115	220	30	245	347	321	257	445	620	93	30	986	324	190	45	19
1931	497	157	298	38	312	471	455	312	774	838	130	51	1,277	434	258	55	24
1930	826	244	500	73	557	687	577	404	1,135	1,184	162	68	1,608	606	333	59	32
1929	1,511	279	788	85	694	711	631	431	1,297	1,495	224	99	1,839	740	374	70	44
1928	1,453	247	840	84	757	514	633	428	1,218	1,556	221	114	1,755	709	350	64	48
1927	1,500	245	969	87	668	617	602	437	1,238	1,336	197	88	1,585	626	333	60	45
1926	1,222	240	901	65	668	708	618	453	1,407	1,271	205	92	1,566	696	340	59	47

(continued)

TABLE 4.60 (continued)

[In millions of dollars]

	Crops								Livestock and Livestock Products								
Year	Cotton (Lint and Seed)	Tobacco	Food Grains	Oil-Bearing Crops	Feed Crops	Vege-tables	Fruits and Tree Nuts	Other	Hogs	Cattle and Calves	Sheep and Lambs	Wool	Dairy Products	Eggs	Broilers and Farm Chickens	Turkeys and Other Poultry	Other
1925	1,762	260	910	87	776	677	619	454	1,318	1,252	207	100	1,515	682	306	51	45
1924	1,664	260	889	100	906	572	561	461	1,064	1,119	181	87	1,405	585	278	46	47
1923	1,569	276	679	61	692	553	559	476	1,027	1,042	160	91	1,425	583	262	44	46
1922	1,148	249	749	42	613	488	584	427	1,024	1,037	143	62	1,171	506	250	40	46
1921	852	253	907	36	634	477	514	433	857	876	108	42	1,200	528	251	41	49
1920	1,476	295	1,535	68	1,220	712	702	636	1,385	1,528	166	114	1,529	781	317	50	86
1919	2,282	500	1,743	92	1,166	593	632	595	1,911	1,921	213	134	1,522	762	296	48	128
1918	1,784	343	1,703	94	1,428	603	505	514	1,866	2,029	196	147	1,250	599	232	41	133
1917	1,604	242	1,187	75	1,043	660	403	428	1,299	1,651	159	98	1,030	523	184	32	118
1916	1,148	139	912	48	715	412	330	331	949	1,132	127	64	764	375	152	27	121
1915	830	93	822	32	618	286	297	285	691	966	111	53	686	341	134	24	123
1914	602	99	716	31	555	318	300	278	713	985	116	42	667	336	138	26	114

Source: Wattenberg, *Statistical History*, 485.

TABLE 4.61 FARM EMPLOYMENT AND WAGES

	Employment			Wage Rates				Farmers' Expenditures for Hired Labor ($1,000,000)
				Per Month		Per Day		
Year	Total Farm (1,000)	Family Workers (1,000)	Hired Workers (1,000)	With Board (Dollars)	Without Board (Dollars)	With Board (Dollars)	Without Board (Dollars)	
1945	10,000	7,881	2,119	79.00	101.00	3.85	4.35	2,299
1944	10,219	7,988	2,231	71.00	91.00	3.50	3.95	2,202
1943	10,446	8,010	2,436	59.00	77.00	2.90	3.30	2,027
1942	10,504	7,949	2,555	45,50	59.00	2.20	2.55	1,631
1941	10,669	8,017	2,652	34.50	44.50	1.65	1.95	1,249
1940	10,979	8,300	2,679	27.50	37.50	1.30	1.60	1,029
1939	11,338	8,611	2,727	27.00	36.00	1.25	1.55	988
1938	11,622	8,815	2,807	27.00	36.00	1.30	1.55	979
1937	11,978	9,054	2,924	27.50	36.50	1.35	1.65	988
1936	12,331	9,350	2,981	24.00	32.50	1.20	1.45	868
1935	12,733	9,855	2,878	22.00	30.50	1.10	1.35	775
1934	12,627	9,765	2,862	20.00	28.00	1.00	1.25	679
1933	12,739	9,874	2,865	18.00	25.50	.90	1.15	617
1932	12,816	9,922	2,894	20.50	29.00	.95	1.20	669
1931	12,745	9,642	3,103	28.50	38.00	1.30	1.65	914
1930	12,497	9,307	3,190	37.50	48.00	1.80	2.15	1,177
1929	12,763	9,360	3,403	40.00	51.00	2.00	2.30	1,300
1928	12,691	9,340	3,351	39.50	50.00	2.00	2.30	1,290
1927	12,642	9,278	3,364	39.50	50.00	2.00	2.35	1,302
1926	12,976	9,526	3,450	39.50	50.00	2.00	2.40	1,330
1925	13,036	9,715	3,321	38.50	49.00	2.00	2.35	1,267
1924	13,031	9,705	3,326	38.00	49.00	1.95	2.40	1,248
1923	13,162	9,798	3,364	37.50	47.50	1.95	2.35	1,251
1922	13,337	9,936	3,401	33.00	43.50	1.65	2.00	1,127
1921	13,398	10,001	3,397	33.50	44.50	1.65	2.05	1,170
1920	13,432	10,041	3,391	51.00	65.00	2.80	3.30	1,790
1919	13,243	9,968	3,275	43.00	56.00	2.40	2.90	1,515
1918	13,391	10,053	3,338	37.50	48.50	2.05	2.45	1,337
1917	13,568	10,121	3,447	31.00	40.50	1.55	1.90	1,127
1916	13,632	10,144	3,488	25.00	33.00	1.25	1.50	904
1915	13,592	10,140	3,452	22.50	30.00	1.10	1.40	815
1914	13,580	10,147	3,433	22.50	29.50	1.10	1.35	804

Source: Bureau of the Census, *Historical Statistics of the United States, Colonial Times to 1957*, 280.

TABLE 4.62 INCOME OF FARM OPERATORS FROM FARMING

[In millions of dollars, except as indicated]

Year	Realized Gross Income from Farming							Net Income of Farm Operators from Farming	
	Realized Gross Farm Income	Cash Receipts from Marketings			Government Payments	Value of Farm Products Consumed in Farm Households	Gross Rental Value of Farm Dwellings	Total Net Income	Average per Farm (dollars)
		Total	Crops	Livestock and Livestock Products					
1945	25,813	21,663	9,655	12,008	742	2,356	1,052	12,312	2,063
1944	24,448	20,536	9,185	11,351	776	2,181	955	11,705	1,950
1943	23,397	19,620	8,127	11,493	645	2,253	879	11,736	1,927
1942	18,794	15,565	6,526	9,039	650	1,758	821	9,853	1,588
1941	13,851	11,111	4,619	6,492	544	1,429	767	6,490	1,031
1940	11,059	8,382	3,469	4,913	723	1,210	744	4,482	706
1939	10,585	7,872	3,336	4,536	763	1,209	741	4,414	685
1938	10,149	7,723	3,200	4,523	446	1,235	745	4,361	668
1937	11,367	8,864	3,924	4,940	336	1,434	733	6,005	905
1936	10,756	8,391	3,649	4,742	278	1,394	693	4,308	639
1935	9,696	7,120	2,977	4,143	573	1,320	683	5,278	775
1934	8,568	6,357	3,021	3,336	446	1,125	640	2,923	431
1933	7,107	5,332	2,846	2,846	131	1,030	614	2,555	379
1932	6,405	4,748	1,996	2,752	. . .	993	664	2,032	304
1931	8,421	6,381	2,540	3,841	. . .	1,265	775	3,344	506
1930	11,472	9,055	3,868	5,187	. . .	1,552	865	4,259	651
1929	13,938	11,312	5,130	6,182	. . .	1,713	913	6,152	945
1928	13,598	10,991	4,956	6,035	. . .	1,724	883	5,981	924
1927	13,336	10,733	5,125	5,608	. . .	1,725	878	5,699	883
1926	13,302	10,558	4,875	5,683	. . .	1,875	869	5,937	919
1925	13,716	11,021	5,545	5,476	. . .	1,827	868	6,734	1,041
1924	12,785	10,225	5,413	4,812	. . .	1,706	854	4,855	749
1923	12,167	9,545	4,865	4,680	. . .	1,772	850	5,068	781
1922	11,059	8,575	4,300	4,275	. . .	1,717	767	4,343	668
1921	10,573	8,058	4,106	3,952	. . .	1,746	769	3,370	517
1920	15,944	12,600	6,644	5,956	. . .	2,509	835	7,795	1,196
1919	17,918	14,538	7,603	6,935	. . .	2,556	824	9,078	1,395
1918	16,547	13,467	6,974	6,493	. . .	2,341	739	8,887	1,370
1917	13,410	10,736	5,642	5,094	. . .	2,003	671	8,304	1,282
1916	9,744	7,746	4,035	3,711	. . .	1,384	614	4,570	707
1915	8,147	6,392	3,263	3,129	. . .	1,192	563	4,307	667
1914	7,793	6,036	2,899	3,137	. . .	1,228	529	4,181	649

Source: Wattenberg, Statistical History, 483.

TABLE 4.63 AVERAGE NET PER CAPITA INCOME ON FARMS FROM FARMING (ALL PERSONS ON FARMS) COMPARED WITH INCOME OF PERSONS NOT ON FARMS, 1929–1945

Year	Income per Person	
	On Farms from Farming	Not on Farms
	(Dollars)	(Dollars)
1929	223	871
1930	170	761
1931	114	605
1932	74	442
1933	93	419
1934	111	488
1935	159	540

Year	Income per Person	
	On Farms from Farming	Not on Farms
	(Dollars)	(Dollars)
1936	171	626
1937	197	671
1938	165	622
1939	173	663
1940	181	721
1941	253	840
1942	389	1,045
1943	523	1,248
1944	534	1,317
1945	544	1,314

Sources: Department of Agriculture, Agricultural Statistics, 1945 (Washington, D.C., 1945), 441, and 1947 (Washington, D.C., 1947), 538.

Establishment of a parity ratio represented an effort in the 1930s to identify a level at which prices paid by farmers were equitable in relation to prices received. It was established that an equitable relationship had existed during the years 1909–14. This level of equitability was called parity. The general objective was to keep prices at parity. Whenever the parity ratio went below 100, it meant that farm costs were high in relation to prices received. A parity above 100 meant that prices received were high in relation to prices paid. Farmers, of course, preferred a parity of more than 100.

TABLE 4.64   INDEXES OF PRICES PAID AND RECEIVED BY FARMERS AND PARITY RATIO

(1910–14 = 100)

Year	Prices Received by Farmers			Prices Paid by Farmers		Payable per Acre		Wage Rates	Prices Paid, Including Interest, Taxes, and Wage Rates	Parity Ratio
	All Farm Products	Crops	Livestock and Products	Living	Production	Interest Payable	Taxes Payable			
1945	207	202	211	182	176	75	192	359	190	109
1944	197	199	196	175	173	79	185	318	182	108
1943	193	187	198	166	164	84	185	262	171	113
1942	159	145	171	149	148	94	189	197	152	105
1941	124	108	138	130	130	98	187	151	133	93
1940	100	90	109	121	123	102	189	129	124	81
1939	95	82	107	120	121	106	185	127	123	77
1938	97	80	112	122	122	110	187	130	124	78
1937	122	118	126	128	132	117	181	129	131	93
1936	114	108	119	124	122	125	180	114	124	92
1935	109	103	114	124	122	135	178	107	124	88
1934	90	98	81	122	114	147	188	99	120	75
1933	70	71	70	108	99	164	220	88	109	64
1932	65	57	72	106	99	185	254	104	112	58
1931	87	75	98	124	113	197	277	139	130	67
1930	125	115	134	144	135	206	281	177	151	83
1929	148	135	159	154	146	213	279	186	160	92
1928	148	142	155	156	148	219	277	184	162	91
1927	140	134	146	155	141	223	271	184	159	88
1926	145	139	151	158	141	228	270	183	160	91
1925	156	164	149	161	145	236	265	181	164	95
1924	143	159	128	156	140	250	266	182	160	89
1923	142	156	128	156	138	261	261	172	159	89
1922	131	136	126	153	127	260	259	154	151	87
1921	124	121	127	164	128	248	244	156	155	80
1920	211	235	190	228	195	216	200	241	214	99
1919	217	230	206	202	195	180	160	206	197	110
1918	206	220	194	170	180	159	151	177	173	119
1917	178	191	165	143	156	145	136	141	148	120
1916	119	120	117	115	115	132	128	112	116	103
1915	99	96	102	104	104	122	118	101	105	94
1914	101	96	107	102	102	116	117	101	103	98

Source: Bureau of the Census, *Historical Statistics of the United States, Colonial Times to 1957*, 283.

TABLE 4.65 FARM-TO-RETAIL PRICE SPREADS OF FARM FOOD PRODUCTS

Market basket of farm food products

Year	Retail Cost	Farm Value	Farmer's Share of Consumer's Dollar
	Dollars	Dollars	Cents
1914	272	125	46
1915	267	120	45
1916	321	145	45
1917	442	210	48
1918	458	235	51
1919	513	250	49
1920	568	245	43
1921	427	172	40
1922	408	163	40
1923	413	166	40
1924	406	166	41
1925	442	191	43
1926	448	188	42
1927	434	180	41
1928	435	186	43
1929	435	183	42
1930	421	165	39
1931	339	121	36
1932	284	92	32
1933	276	89	32
1934	311	107	34
1935	347	138	40
1936	349	143	41
1937	362	156	43
1938	328	128	39
1939	316	122	39
1940	317	128	40
1941	347	154	44
1942	407	196	48
1943	458	236	52
1944	450	237	53
1945	459	247	54

Source: National Industrial Conference Board, *Economic Almanac for 1950,* 213.

Machinery and Equipment on Farms

The machinery and modern methods that gave American agriculture its force and prestige were not available to all people who lived on farms. Although clear trends were established with respect to modern methods of work and the use of new household devices, most rural folk during 1914–45 had to make do with older tools and methods. Most rural households lacked the appliances and devices that were contemporary to that age. Much of the agricultural produce came from farms that used modern machines, the best example of which was the tractor; after the mid-1930s it was the all-purpose, rubber-tire tractor. Most efficient farm equipment flowed from the modern tractor. As late as 1941, however, no more than one-fourth of American farms had tractors of any sort. The rest relied on horses and mules. Even so, it was clear that the future belonged to the machines.

Most farmers during 1914–45 used draft animals, not machines, to do their work. This farmer in Indiana in 1936 used an old but still common method of harvesting hay, or in this case, oats. (Library of Congress)

TABLE 4.66 FARM MACHINERY AND EQUIPMENT

Year	Motor Vehicles and Specified Machines on Farms (1,000)								Value of Farm Implements and Machinery ($1,000,000)
	Tractors[a]	Motor Trucks	Auto-mobiles	Grain Combines	Corn Pickers	Farms with Milking Machines	Pickup Balers	Field Forage Harvesters	
1945	2,354	1,490	4,148	375	168	365	42	20	6,291
1944	2,160	1,385	4,185	345	146	300	34	. . .	5,346
1943	2,055	1,280	4,350	320	138	275	31	. . .	4,906
1942	1,860	1,160	4,670	275	130	255	25	. . .	3,981
1941	1,665	1,095	4,330	225	120	210	. . .	. . .	3,254
1940	1,545	1,047	4,144	190	110	175	. . .	. . .	3,060
1939	1,445	1,020	4,030	. . .	. . .	. . .	. . .	. . .	3,036
1938	1,370	1,042	4,109	. . .	. . .	. . .	. . .	. . .	2,998
1937	1,230	990	3,962	. . .	. . .	. . .	. . .	. . .	2,648
1936	1,125	923	3,735	. . .	. . .	. . .	. . .	. . .	2,359
1935	1,048	890	3,642	. . .	. . .	. . .	. . .	. . .	2,217
1934	1,016	875	3,399	. . .	. . .	. . .	. . .	. . .	2,168
1933	1,019	865	3,399	. . .	. . .	. . .	. . .	. . .	2,464
1932	1,022	910	3,798	. . .	. . .	. . .	. . .	. . .	2,915
1931	997	920	4,077	. . .	. . .	. . .	. . .	. . .	3,217
1930	920	900	4,135	61	50	100	. . .	. . .	3,302
1929	827	840	3,970	. . .	. . .	. . .	. . .	. . .	3,178
1928	782	753	3,820	. . .	. . .	. . .	. . .	. . .	3,088
1927	693	662	3,820	. . .	. . .	. . .	. . .	. . .	3,126
1926	621	559	3,605	. . .	. . .	. . .	. . .	. . .	3,042
1925	549	459	3,283	. . .	. . .	. . .	. . .	. . .	2,955
1924	496	363	3,004	. . .	. . .	. . .	. . .	. . .	2,985
1923	428	316	2,618	. . .	. . .	. . .	. . .	. . .	2,832
1922	372	263	2,425	. . .	. . .	. . .	. . .	. . .	2,900
1921	343	207	2,382	. . .	. . .	. . .	. . .	. . .	3,551
1920	246	139	2,146	4	10	55	. . .	. . .	3,595
1919	158	111	1,760	. . .	. . .	. . .	. . .	. . .	3,345
1918	85	89	1,502	. . .	. . .	. . .	. . .	. . .	2,965
1917	51	60	966	. . .	. . .	. . .	. . .	. . .	2,338
1916	37	40	687	. . .	. . .	. . .	. . .	. . .	2,046
1915	25	25	472	. . .	. . .	. . .	. . .	. . .	1,849
1914	17	15	343	. . .	. . .	. . .	. . .	. . .	1,719

[a] Excludes steam or garden type.
Source: Bureau of the Census, *Historical Statistics of the United States, Colonial Times to 1957*, 284–285.

Women usually did not operate farm machinery (many did not drive cars), but if necessary they did. The steel wheels with lugs identify this woman's tractor as an older machine. Crawford County, Indiana, 1940. (Library of Congress)

National Income and National Product

Wealth and earnings in the United States underwent large changes in the first half of the twentieth century. Not only did the gross national product and national income increase substantially, but there was also a large rise in income per person. A per capita gross national product of $387 in 1914 had increased to more than $1,500 by 1945. The trend of growth, needless to say, halted during the depression. Not until 1941 did the nation again reach the level that had been reached in 1929. Other noticeable developments included a fluctuation in personal savings until the year 1929, when a profound drop began that would last until the years of the Second World War. Under the impetus of high wartime earnings, savings then set record highs. Americans were not a heavily taxed people—that is, until the time of the Second World War. Then taxes soared.

Not revealed in the table below are shifts in the distribution of income. The wealthiest people earned their largest share of national income during the First World War and the decade of the 1920s. The depression years of the 1930s produced a steady and immediate proportionate decline for the earnings of the wealthiest 1% of the population. For the top 5% the slide was delayed until 1933, and then it was continuous until 1945. Because of increased earnings by other segments of the population and because of steeply graduated income taxes, the relative loss for both the highest 1% and 5% was much more dramatic during the years of the Second World War. The same theme held true with respect to family income measured in fifths of earners. Beginning in 1929, the highest one-fifth suffered a proportionate loss, and each of the four-fifths beneath them experienced a proportionate gain. Even so, all rankings of wage earners, including the highest, experienced an absolute increase in earnings during the Second World War.

TABLE 4.67   NATIONAL INCOME AND NATIONAL PRODUCT AT CURRENT PRICES

(Dollar Amounts in Billions)

Year	Gross National Product	National Income	Personal Income	Personal Taxes	Disposable Personal Income	Personal Savings	Personal Consumption Expenditures	Personal Taxes and Savings as Percent of Personal Income	Personal Savings as Percent of Disposable Income	Est. Pop. on Jul. 1
1914	38.5	33.9	33.8	.6	33.2	3.4	29.8	11.8	10.2	99,117,567
1915	42.1	37.0	36.0	.6	35.4	6.9	28.5	20.8	19.5	100,549,013
1916	47.8	44.8	42.4	.8	41.6	6.8	34.8	17.9	16.3	101,965,984
1917	59.5	53.7	50.9	.9	50.0	9.6	40.4	20.6	19.2	103,413,743
1918	65.5	58.3	57.5	1.6	55.9	11.5	44.4	22.8	20.6	104,549,886
1919	76.5	68.2	65.5	2.0	63.5	10.8	52.7	19.5	17.0	105,062,747
1920	85.0	69.5	68.9	2.1	66.8	9.0	57.8	16.1	13.5	106,466,420
1921	68.5	51.7	54.9	2.1	52.8	2.3	50.5	8.0	4.4	108,541,489
1922	69.9	59.5	58.9	1.9	57.0	5.0	52.0	11.7	8.8	110,054,778
1923	81.6	69.5	68.3	2.4	65.9	8.1	57.8	15.4	12.3	111,949,945
1924	82.0	69.1	68.8	2.1	66.7	5.8	60.9	11.5	8.7	114,113,463
1925	86.4	73.7	72.8	2.2	70.6	7.6	63.0	13.5	10.8	115.831.963
1926	92.3	76.6	75.6	2.4	73.2	6.9	66.3	12.3	9.4	117,399,225
1927	90.9	75.9	76.0	2.5	73.5	7.5	66.0	13.2	10.2	119,038,062
1928	93.7	78.7	78.1	2.7	75.4	6.6	68.8	11.9	8.8	120,501,115
1929	103.8	87.4	85.1	2.6	82.5	3.7	78.8	7.4	4.5	121,769,939
1930	90.9	75.0	76.2	2.5	73.7	2.9	70.8	7.1	3.9	123,076,741
1931	75.9	58.9	64.8	1.9	63.0	1.8	61.2	5.7	2.9	124,039,648
1932	58.3	41.7	49.3	1.5	47.8	−1.4	49.2	.2	−2.9	124,840,471
1933	55.8	39.6	46.6	1.5	45.2	−1.2	46.3	.6	−2.7	125,578,763
1934	64.9	48.6	53.2	1.6	51.6	−.2	51.9	2.6	−.4	126,373,773
1935	72.2	56.8	59.9	1.9	58.0	1.8	56.2	6.2	3.1	127,250,232
1936	82.5	64.7	68.4	2.3	66.1	3.6	62.5	8.6	5.4	128,053,180
1937	90.2	73.6	74.0	2.9	71.1	3.9	67.1	9.2	5.5	128,824,829
1938	84.7	67.4	68.3	2.9	65.5	1.0	64.5	5.7	1.5	129,824,939
1939	91.3	72.5	72.6	2.4	70.2	2.7	67.5	7.0	3.8	130,879,718
1940	101.4	81.3	78.3	2.6	75.7	3.7	72.1	8.0	4.9	131,970,224
1941	126.4	103.8	95.3	3.3	92.0	9.8	82.3	13.7	10.7	133,202,873
1942	161.6	137.1	122.7	6.0	116.7	25.6	91.2	25.8	21.9	134,664,924
1943	194.3	169.7	150.3	17.8	132.4	30.2	102.2	31.9	22.8	136,497,049
1944	213.7	183.8	165.9	18.9	147.0	35.4	111.6	32.7	24.1	138,083,449
1945	215.2	182.7	171.9	20.9	151.1	28.0	123.1	28.4	18.5	139,585,518

Sources: Frederick J. Dewhurst and Associates, *America's Needs and Resources: A New Survey* (New York, 1955), 958; Bureau of the Census, *Statistical Abstract of the United States, 1947*, 9.

TABLE 4.68 WAGE OR SALARY WORKERS IN 1939, BY STATES

Division and State	Total Persons	Number with Wage or Salary Income of—								Median Wage or Salary Income
		$0	$1 to $399	$400 to $799	$800 to $1,199	$1,200 to $1,599	$1,600 to $1,999	$2,000 to $2,999	$3,000 and Over	
United States	38,322,420	2,673,440	7,911,640	8,131,260	6,582,960	5,318,060	2,737,200	2,811,440	1,269,740	$877
New England	2,984,160	173,220	436,960	694,780	637,500	454,920	197,000	217,960	90,920	940
Me.	255,820	11,380	61,260	73,860	50,560	27,320	10,780	10,700	3,920	715
N.H.	167,460	7,680	31,380	46,500	39,060	20,960	7,500	7,700	2,580	800
Vt.	101,160	4,720	25,000	27,860	18,800	11,020	4,000	4,980	1,680	714
Mass.	1,527,680	95,660	195,940	338,500	319,960	243,320	113,960	127,860	51,660	995
R.I.	268,780	15,680	42,660	71,560	59,500	36,180	14,220	16,300	6,840	858
Conn.	663,260	38,100	80,720	136,500	149,620	116,120	46,540	50,420	24,240	1,026
Middle Atlantic	9,688,860	794,060	1,374,420	1,977,240	1,813,860	1,490,060	713,680	817,820	429,400	1,010
N.Y.	4,922,560	394,900	646,780	982,980	917,340	760,980	369,520	457,720	261,320	1,048
N.J.	1,544,120	100,320	206,700	300,920	275,040	250,200	119,420	149,440	79,400	1,069
Pa.	3,222,180	298,840	520,940	693,340	621,480	478,880	224,740	210,660	88,680	930
East North Central	8,143,400	552,860	1,279,260	1,553,600	1,530,080	1,363,800	721,520	702,260	288,740	1,030
Ohio	2,117,820	146,280	325,620	403,940	399,500	364,400	188,500	174,340	75,180	1,937
Ind.	953,320	64,080	174,700	195,560	184,980	141,900	78,200	69,240	24,060	935
Ill.	2,603,880	174,980	383,380	521,000	498,300	412,860	208,720	244,860	110,400	1,023
Mich.	1,650,820	108,480	238,400	279,920	295,860	316,420	173,140	155,300	58,000	1,128
Wis.	817,560	59,040	157,160	153,180	151,440	128,220	72,960	58,520	21,100	948
West North Central	3,162,040	223,120	784,720	685,260	516,220	395,760	203,160	199,500	84,580	779
Minn.	701,160	48,800	154,600	137,140	117,260	103,780	55,320	49,220	21,820	887
Iowa	567,880	31,620	143,880	131,580	94,780	71,580	32,600	32,600	11,760	746
Mo.	1,001,780	75,220	235,460	224,660	165,520	119,580	60,140	66,520	32,440	787
N. Dak.	112,100	9,080	40,220	22,460	14,220	11,040	5,540	5,020	1,600	557
S. Dak.	110,280	9,420	34,540	23,680	15,820	10,760	6,400	5,200	1,820	639
Nebr.	275,180	19,680	74,460	61,620	44,120	32,260	15,760	16,380	6,640	729
Kans.	393,660	29,300	101,560	84,120	64,500	46,760	27,400	24,560	8,500	766
South Atlantic	4,975,560	287,740	1,489,140	1,273,200	711,920	479,460	243,000	240,980	122,640	651
Del.	93,880	4,720	18,220	19,440	16,420	12,960	7,200	7,400	4,260	924
Md.	635,000	34,780	120,920	147,580	114,840	86,020	42,040	46,780	22,400	875
D.C.	303,100	15,660	32,520	52,260	48,180	56,900	37,920	35,300	20,500	1,264
Va.	755,780	39,760	225,180	196,220	109,000	72,100	39,640	39,760	20,320	658
W. Va.	466,000	36,800	93,960	88,860	100,300	71,840	29,860	25,420	9,100	907
N.C.	859,640	49,280	270,020	269,000	122,660	56,860	24,180	22,920	12,960	599
S.C.	455,020	24,480	184,420	130,500	52,780	23,840	11,100	11,440	5,800	483
Ga.	808,500	49,820	338,620	209,420	74,920	47,820	25,760	27,820	15,180	458
Fla.	598,640	32,440	205,280	159,920	72,820	51,120	25,300	24,140	12,120	560
East South Central	2,196,560	163,900	777,880	537,680	280,440	171,700	81,280	84,280	36,860	555
Ky.	587,280	47,000	172,180	140,400	91,120	58,520	25,660	24,540	10,440	654
Tenn.	664,000	47,040	216,440	171,840	91,160	55,780	25,660	28,800	12,660	611
Ala.	601,360	41,800	231,940	148,300	69,620	38,480	20,320	21,380	9,260	500
Miss.	343,920	28,060	157,320	77,140	28,540	18,920	9,640	9,560	4,500	386
West South Central	2,962,220	216,809	1,051,460	617,380	365,600	267,520	171,600	153,300	68,700	591
Ark.	338,220	25,060	149,280	77,640	29,940	20,280	11,040	10,940	4,520	412
La.	566,600	38,380	217,440	128,680	67,320	45,200	26,400	25,160	13,060	538
Okla.	463,200	42,300	141,860	82,240	66,240	48,280	32,040	25,700	10,760	701
Tex.	1,594,200	111,060	542,880	328,820	202,100	153,760	102,120	91,500	40,360	630
Mountain	1,014,320	65,440	217,640	210,020	163,300	149,100	85,420	72,840	28,760	880
Mont.	143,240	8,100	29,760	29,680	21,860	22,240	13,120	11,740	3,680	907
Idaho	115,420	6,600	25,960	28,080	18,620	16,040	9,020	6,360	1,960	785
Wyo.	68,460	3,360	14,360	14,940	9,780	10,520	6,500	5,000	2,120	888
Colo.	288,120	19,220	59,920	59,820	49,800	42,880	20,720	20,780	8,880	884
N. Mex.	109,300	9,360	31,420	22,880	15,340	11,760	7,480	5,460	2,160	691
Ariz.	130,060	9,580	31,280	24,360	19,500	18,540	12,120	9,780	3,220	870
Utah	124,080	7,180	20,500	23,780	22,180	21,840	11,600	10,180	5,080	1,034
Nev.	35,640	2,040	4,440	6,480	6,220	5,280	4,860	3,540	1,660	1,135
Pacific	3,195,300	196,300	500,160	582,100	564,040	545,740	320,540	322,500	119,140	1,070
Wash.	531,180	31,360	94,820	97,500	88,880	96,640	51,360	46,560	15,660	1,028
Oreg.	329,040	18,240	65,300	62,460	60,720	50,800	28,260	26,340	9,500	953
Calif.	2,335,080	146,700	340,040	422,140	414,440	398,300	240,920	249,600	93,980	1,097

Source: Bureau of the Census, *Statistical Abstract of the United States, 1947,* 278.

Income During the Depression

TABLE 4.69 **MEDIAN MONEY INCOME IN 1939 OF ALL WORKERS WITH WAGE OR SALARY INCOME, BY OCCUPATION, COLOR, AND SEX**

Sex, color, and major occupation group in survey week (1939)

Male	
Color	
White	$1,112
Nonwhite	460
Major Occupation Group	
Professional, technical, and kindred workers	1,809
Farmers and farm managers	373
Managers, officials, and proprietors, except farm	2,136
Clerical and kindred workers	1,421
Salesworkers	1,277
Craftsmen, foremen, and kindred workers	1,309
Operatives and kindred workers	1,007
Service workers, except private household	833
Farm laborers and foremen	309
Laborers, except farm and mine	673
Female	
Color	
White	676
Nonwhite	246
Major Occupation Group	
Professional, technical, and kindred workers	1,023
Managers, officials, and proprietors, except farm	1,107
Clerical and kindred workers	966
Salesworkers	636
Craftsmen, foremen, and kindred workers	827
Operatives and kindred workers	582
Private household workers	296
Service workers, except private household	493

Source: Bureau of the Census, *Historical Statistics of the United States, Colonial Times to 1957,* 168.

TABLE 4.70 **PER CAPITA INCOME IN THE UNITED STATES IN 1938 AS COMPARED WITH VARIOUS EUROPEAN COUNTRIES**

	1938
United States	$521
Europe (excluding USSR)	207
Austria	179
Belgium-Luxembourg	275
Bulgaria	68
Czechoslovakia	176
Denmark	316
Finland	178
France	236
Germany	337
Greece	80
Hungary	112
Ireland	252
Italy	127
Netherlands	323
Norway	255
Poland	104
Sweden	367
Switzerland	367
United Kingdom	378

Source: Dewhurst and Associates, *America's Needs and Resources, A New Survey,* 896.

The low earnings of the American people during the Great Depression can be seen in the first table left, which shows earnings in the year 1939. While not the worst year of the depression, 1939 still was marked with hard times; the nation had moved only a short distance on the road to recovery. The largest number of workers made between $400 and $800 per year, although the number that earned less than $400 was almost as large. Many of these people made much less than $400. The richest parts of the United States were the upper Midwest, the Middle Atlantic states, and the Pacific Coast. The poorest part was the South. Wherever one lived, it was in any year more profitable—in 1939 nearly three times more profitable—to be white rather than nonwhite, and one's income as a male was almost twice the income of a female, whether black or white. Remarkably, the third table shows that despite the hard times of the 1930s, the United States remained in per capita income—using the year 1938 as an example—far ahead of the most prosperous European states.

Prices and Cost of Living

Prices began to rise because of the inflationary pressures created by the First World War. They reached their highest point in 1920, after the fighting had stopped, but that year was still influenced by the pressures of the war era. Prices dropped off sharply in 1921–22 as the country struggled to restore a peacetime economy. Then prices leveled off and proceeded to rise modestly during most of the boom years of the 1920s. A few selected food products cost more at the end of the 1920s than even during the inflationary year of 1920. The start of the Great Depression produced a sharp decline in most prices. This deflationary condition, normally greeted with joy by consumers, unfortunately was more than offset by the scarcity and expensive character of money. By comparing yearly prices with a common standard, a price index makes it easy to spot times in which prices might be termed low or high. Not surprisingly, the lowest point in the price index (after the year 1917) corresponded with the lowest point of the depression, in 1932–33. The recovery of prices, which began in the last half of the 1930s, was uneven and very slow until the start of the Second World War. The turnabout accelerated in 1942, after the United States became a direct participant.

The war produced new tendencies toward inflation that potentially were much stronger than during the previous conflict. Although prices did increase during the mid-1940s, they failed to achieve the level reached at the end of the First World War. That prices did not rise more during 1941–45 was perhaps the most remarkable aspect of the pricing structure in the first half of the twentieth century. The explanation rested partly with a novel and complicated system of rationing and price controls imposed by the government, partly by a spirit of cooperation and a willingness to save increased wartime earnings for the new world that remained ahead. Even so, many Americans were willing to engage in a separate, illegal pricing system—an economic underworld, so to speak—called the black market.

TABLE 4.71 CONSUMER PRICE INDEXES[a]

Year	Consumer Price Index (NICB), 1923=100	Consumers' Prices (BLS), 1935–1939=100						
		All Items	Food	Apparel	Rent	Fuel, Electricity, and Ice	House Furnishings	Miscel-laneous
1945	106.3	128.4	139.1	145.9	108.3	110.3	145.8	124.1
1944	104.6	125.5	136.1	138.8	108.2	109.8	136.4	121.3
1943	103.1	123.6	138.0	129.7	108.0	107.7	125.6	115.8
1942	97.7	116.5	123.9	124.2	108.5	105.4	122.2	110.9
1941	89.0	105.2	105.5	106.3	106.2	102.2	107.3	104.0
1940	85.3	100.2	96.6	101.7	104.6	99.7	100.5	101.1
1939	84.5	99.4	95.2	100.5	104.3	99.0	101.3	100.7
1938	85.7	100.8	97.8	102.2	104.1	99.9	103.3	101.5
1937	87.8	102.7	105.3	102.8	100.9	100.2	104.3	101.0
1936	84.1	99.1	101.3	97.6	96.4	100.2	96.3	98.7
1935	82.2	98.1	100.4	96.8	94.2	100.7	94.8	98.1
1934	79.4	95.7	93.7	96.1	94.4	101.4	92.8	97.9
1933	74.9	92.4	84.1	87.9	100.7	100.0	84.2	98.4
1932	77.9	97.6	86.5	90.8	116.9	103.4	85.4	101.7
1931	87.2	108.7	103.9	102.6	130.3	108.9	98.0	104.1
1930	96.7	119.4	126.0	112.7	137.5	111.4	108.9	105.1
1929	100.1	122.5	132.5	115.3	141.4	112.5	111.7	104.6
1928	100.6	122.6	130.8	116.5	144.8	113.4	113.1	103.8
1927	102.0	124.0	132.3	118.3	148.3	115.4	115.9	103.2
1926	104.3	126.4	137.4	120.6	150.7	117.2	118.8	102.6
1925	103.7	125.4	132.9	122.4	152.2	115.4	121.5	102.2
1924	101.3	122.2	122.8	124.9	151.6	113.7	124.0	101.4
1923	100.0	121.9	124.0	125.9	146.4	115.2	126.1	100.8
1922	97.4	119.7	119.9	125.6	142.7	113.1	117.5	101.2
1921	102.3	127.7	128.3	154.8	138.6	114.0	138.5	104.3
1920	118.2	143.3	168.8	201.0	120.7	106.9	164.6	100.5
1919	102.4	123.8	149.8	168.7	102.7	91.1	134.1	87.6
1918	90.5	107.5	134.4	127.5	94.9	84.2	106.4	77.8
1917	77.6	91.6	116.9	94.1	93.2	72.4	82.8	65.1
1916	65.4	77.9	90.8	78.3	94.0	65.0	70.9	56.3
1915	61.0	72.5	80.9	71.4	92.9	62.5	63.6	53.6
1914	61.3	71.8	81.8	69.8	92.2	62.3	60.7	51.9

[a]Indexes presented here measure prices by two groups: the National Industrial Conference Board (NICB) and the Bureau of Labor Statistics (BLS). Each used a different period as a basis for measurement. Both showed the same pattern of price fluctuation.
Source: Bureau of the Census, *Historical Statistics of the United States, 1789–1945,* 236.

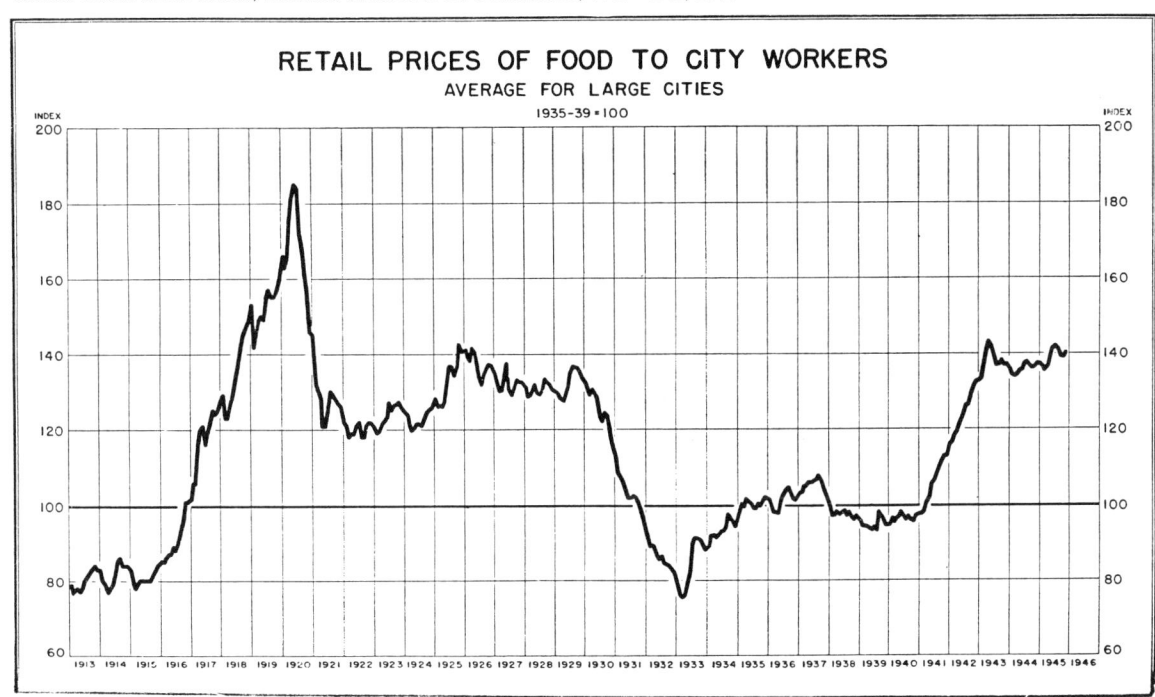

RETAIL PRICES OF FOOD TO CITY WORKERS
AVERAGE FOR LARGE CITIES
1935-39=100

GRAPH 4.2

This graph shows interesting changes in food prices. Perhaps most striking is the comparison between the two world wars.

Source: Monthly Labor Review (February 1946), 306.

Viewed from another, broader perspective, the purchasing power of the dollar by the mid-1980s had declined ten times beyond what it had been in 1914. The dollar of 1945 was more than five times as valuable as the dollar of 1982–84.

The table below confirms familiar trends in American economic behavior: the First World War elevated consumption to a new level. After the war, economic growth generally was the rule until the time of the depression, when consumption experienced a nosedive that would be reversed by the world war. Food, housing, and clothing made up the bulk of consumption, as they always did. Of interest is the small amount spent on medical care in this period. The money spent on education was tiny, in many years less than one-third the amount spent on recreation.

TABLE 4.72 CONSUMPTION EXPENDITURES BY MAJOR GROUPS

[Amount in billions, at current prices]

Year	Total	Food, Liquor, and Tobacco	Clothing, Accessories, and Personal Care	Housing and Utilities	Household Equipment and Operation	Consumer Transportation	Medical Care and Insurance	Recreation	Education (Private)	Religion	Welfare (Private)
1914	33.4	11.7	4.7	7.9	3.7	2.1	.9	1.0	.5	.3	.5
1919	60.6	22.0	9.6	10.2	7.3	4.9	2.1	2.2	.8	.6	.8
1921	55.8	16.8	9.3	12.3	6.7	4.8	1.5	2.1	.7	.6	.8
1923	66.6	19.1	11.1	13.8	9.0	6.5	2.2	2.6	.8	.7	.6
1925	71.8	21.1	11.0	14.2	10.0	7.6	2.5	2.8	.9	.8	.5
1927	74.6	21.7	11.8	14.4	11.0	7.2	2.7	3.1	1.0	.8	.6
1929	80.8	23.4	11.9	14.5	13.3	8.0	3.0	3.8	1.2	.9	.6
1930	72.4	21.1	10.4	14.1	11.0	6.6	2.9	3.5	1.1	.9	.6
1931	62.5	17.6	8.9	13.1	9.5	5.3	2.6	2.9	1.1	.8	.5
1932	50.1	13.6	6.6	11.6	7.6	4.2	2.2	2.1	.9	.7	.4
1933	46.3	12.8	5.9	10.5	7.3	4.1	2.0	1.9	.8	.7	.4
1934	51.9	15.6	7.1	10.3	7.8	4.7	2.2	2.1	.8	.6	.3
1935	56.2	17.7	7.6	10.4	8.5	5.4	2.3	2.3	.9	.6	.4
1936	62.5	20.0	8.3	10.9	9.7	6.3	2.5	2.6	1.0	.6	.4
1937	67.1	21.6	8.8	11.5	10.5	6.7	2.7	2.9	1.1	.6	.4
1938	64.5	20.7	8.7	11.7	9.8	5.8	2.7	2.8	1.1	.7	.4
1939	67.5	21.1	9.2	12.1	10.4	6.5	2.9	3.0	1.1	.7	.4
1940	72.1	22.6	9.7	12.7	11.1	7.1	3.1	3.3	1.1	.7	.5
1941	82.3	26.5	11.5	13.5	12.6	8.4	3.4	3.7	1.2	.7	.4
1942	91.1	32.8	14.3	14.6	12.7	5.6	3.9	4.2	1.4	.7	.6
1943	102.2	37.9	17.8	15.4	13.0	6.1	4.4	4.2	1.7	.7	.8
1944	111.6	41.5	19.7	16.1	14.1	6.7	4.9	4.8	1.7	.8	1.0
1945	123.1	45.9	22.0	16.8	15.7	8.2	5.1	5.4	1.8	.8	.9

Source: Dewhurst and Associates, *America's Needs and Resources, A New Survey,* 102.

TABLE 4.73 RETAIL PRICES OF SELECTED FOODS IN AMERICAN CITIES

[In cents per unit indicated]

Year	Flour	Bread	Meats Round Steak	Meats Chuck Roast	Meats Pork Chops	Meats Bacon	Dairy Products and Eggs Butter	Dairy Products and Eggs Eggs	Dairy Products and Eggs Milk, Delivered
	5 lb.	Lb.	Lb.	Lb.	Lb.	Lb.	Lb.	Doz.	Qt.
1945	32.1	8.8	40.6	28.1	37.1	41.1	50.7	58.1	15.6
1944	32.4	8.8	41.4	28.8	37.3	41.1	50.0	54.5	15.6
1943	30.6	8.9	43.9	30.2	40.3	43.1	52.7	57.2	15.5
1942	26.4	8.7	43.5	29.3	41.4	39.4	47.3	48.4	15.0
1941	22.6	8.1	39.1	25.5	34.3	34.3	41.1	39.7	13.6
1940	21.5	8.0	36.4	23.5	27.9	27.3	36.0	33.1	12.8
1939	19.0	7.9	36.0	23.4	30.4	31.9	32.5	32.1	12.2
1938	19.8	8.6	34.9	22.8	32.9	36.7	34.7	35.5	12.5
1937	24.0	8.6	39.1	25.7	36.7	41.3	40.7	36.2	12.5
1936	23.8	8.2	34.1	22.3	34.1	40.7	39.5	37.1	12.0
1935	25.3	8.3	36.0	24.0	36.1	41.3	36.0	37.6	11.7
1934	24.5	8.3	28.1	17.5	25.5	29.1	31.5	32.5	11.2
1933	19.5	7.1	25.7	16.0	19.8	22.6	27.8	28.8	10.4
1932	16.0	7.0	29.7	18.5	21.5	24.2	27.8	30.2	10.7
1931	18.0	7.7	35.4	22.7	29.6	36.6	35.8	35.0	12.6

| Year | Flour | Bread | Meats | | | | Dairy Products and Eggs | | |
| | | | Round Steak | Chuck Roast | Pork Chops | Bacon | Butter | Eggs | Milk, Delivered |
	5 lb.	Lb.	Lb.	Lb.	Lb.	Lb.	Lb.	Doz.	Qt.
1930	23.0	8.6	42.6	28.6	36.2	42.5	46.4	44.5	14.1
1929	25.5	8.8	46.0	31.4	37.5	43.9	55.5	52.7	14.4
1928	26.5	8.9	43.7	29.6	35.2	44.4	56.9	50.3	14.2
1927	27.5	9.2	38.7	25.2	37.2	47.8	56.3	48.7	14.1
1926	30.0	9.3	37.1	23.7	39.9	50.8	53.6	51.9	14.0
1925	30.5	9.3	36.2	22.8	37.0	47.1	55.2	55.4	13.9
1924	24.5	8.9	34.8	21.6	31.0	38.4	52.2	51.0	13.4
1923	23.5	8.8	34.3	20.8	30.3	39.7	55.8	49.9	13.9
1922	25.5	8.7	32.3	19.7	33.0	39.8	47.9	44.4	13.1
1921	29.0	9.9	34.4	21.2	34.9	42.7	51.7	50.9	14.6
1920	40.5	11.5	39.5	26.2	42.3	52.3	70.1	68.1	16.7
1919	36.0	10.0	38.9	27.0	42.3	55.4	67.8	62.8	15.5
1918	33.5	9.8	36.9	26.6	39.0	52.9	57.7	59.0	13.9
1917	35.0	9.2	29.0	20.9	31.9	41.0	48.7	48.1	11.2
1916	22.0	7.3	24.5	17.1	22.7	28.7	39.4	37.5	9.1
1915	21.0	7.0	23.0	16.1	20.3	26.9	35.8	34.1	8.8
1914	17.0	6.3	23.6	16.7	22.0	27.5	36.2	35.3	8.9

| Year | Fruits and Vegetables | | | | Other | | |
| | Oranges | Potatoes | Tomatoes, Canned | Navy Beans | Coffee | Margarine | Sugar |
	Doz.	10 lb.	15 oz. can	Lb.	Lb.	Lb.	5 lb.
1945	48.5	49.3	10.3	11.4	30.5	24.1	33.4
1944	46.0	46.5	10.1	10.7	30.1	24.1	33.6
1943	44.3	45.6	10.6	10.1	30.0	23.6	34.2
1942	35.7	34.2	9.9	9.0	28.3	22.1	34.1
1941	31.0	23.5	7.7	7.4	23.6	17.1	28.6
1940	29.1	23.9	7.2	6.6	21.2	15.9	26.0
1939	28.9	24.7	7.2	6.2	22.4	16.7	27.2
1938	26.7	21.3	7.5	6.3	23.2	17.5	26.6
1937	38.9	27.9	7.9	9.6	25.5	19.2	28.2
1936	33.6	31.9	8.0	6.7	24.3	18.5	27.9
1935	32.0	19.1	8.6	6.2	25.7	18.8	28.2
1934	34.1	23.0	8.8	6.1	26.9	13.5	27.5
1933	27.3	23.0	7.7	5.3	26.4	13.2	26.5
1932	30.2	17.0	7.8	5.2	29.4	15.4	25.0
1931	35.0	24.0	8.5	8.1	32.8	19.9	28.0
1930	57.1	36.0	10.2	11.7	39.5	25.0	30.5
1929	44.7	32.0	10.8	14.1	47.9	27.0	32.0
1928	58.6	27.0	9.9	11.8	48.2	27.3	34.5
1927	52.0	38.0	10.0	9.4	47.4	28.3	36.0
1926	51.6	49.0	9.9	9.4	50.2	30.1	34.0
1925	57.1	36.0	11.1	10.3	50.4	30.2	35.0
1924	44.8	28.0	10.8	9.9	42.6	29.3	45.0
1923	49.7	30.0	10.5	10.9	36.9	28.1	49.5
1922	57.4	28.0	11.3	9.9	36.1	28.0	36.5
1921	49.6	31.0	10.2	8.2	36.3	31.6	40.0
1920	63.2	63.0	12.5	11.4	47.0	42.3	97.0
1919	53.2	38.0	13.6	12.6	43.3	41.3	56.5
1918	. . .	32.0	. . .	17.3	30.5	. . .	48.5
1917	. . .	43.0	. . .	17.9	30.2	. . .	46.5
1916	. . .	27.0	. . .	11.0	29.9	. . .	40.0
1915	. . .	15.0	. . .	7.8	30.0	. . .	33.0
1914	. . .	18.0	. . .	. . .	29.7	. . .	29.5

Source: Bureau of the Census, *Historical Statistics of the United States, Colonial Times to 1957,* 128.

TABLE 4.74 PRICE INDEX AND PURCHASING POWER FOR URBAN CONSUMERS, 1914–1945, MEASURED IN 1980S DOLLARS (1982–84 = 100) [a]

Year	All Items	Food	Rent, Residential	Apparel and Upkeep	Purchasing Power of Consumer Dollar 1982–84 = $1.00
1914	10.0	10.2	21.0	15.0	9.942
1915	10.1	10.0	21.1	15.3	9.843
1916	10.9	11.3	21.3	16.8	9.152
1917	12.8	14.5	21.2	20.2	7.793
1918	15.1	16.7	21.5	27.3	6.635
1919	17.3	18.6	23.3	36.2	5.779
1920	20.0	21.0	27.4	43.1	4.989
1921	17.9	15.9	31.5	33.2	5.585
1922	16.8	14.9	32.4	27.0	5.962
1923	17.1	15.4	33.2	27.1	5.857
1924	17.1	15.2	34.4	26.8	5.845
1925	17.5	16.5	34.6	26.3	5.701
1926	17.7	17.0	34.2	25.9	5.647
1927	17.4	16.4	33.7	25.3	5.755
1928	17.1	16.3	32.9	25.0	5.833
1929	17.1	16.5	32.1	24.7	5.833
1930	16.7	15.6	31.2	24.2	5.986
1931	15.2	12.9	29.6	22.0	6.563
1932	13.7	10.7	26.5	19.5	7.317
1933	13.0	10.4	22.9	18.8	7.712
1934	13.4	11.6	21.4	20.6	7.464
1935	13.7	12.4	21.4	20.8	7.281
1936	13.9	12.6	21.9	21.0	7.213
1937	14.4	13.1	22.9	22.0	6.961
1938	14.1	12.1	23.7	21.9	7.093
1939	13.9	11.8	23.7	21.6	7.195
1940	14.0	12.0	23.7	21.8	7.126
1941	14.7	13.1	24.2	22.8	6.788
1942	16.3	15.4	24.7	26.7	6.132
1943	17.3	17.1	24.7	27.8	5.779
1944	17.6	16.9	24.8	29.8	5.680
1945	18.0	17.3	24.8	31.4	5.552

[a] This table indicates that a dollar in 1914 was worth nearly 10 times as much as a dollar in the mid-1980s; in 1945 it was 5.5 times as much. But people had far fewer dollars, and so the price index was important. All items combined cost in 1914 10% of what they would cost in 1984.
Source: Bureau of Labor Statistics, *Handbook of Labor Statistics, 1989.* (Washington, D.C., 1989), 475.

National Taxes

The most striking change to the tax obligations of the American citizen was the adoption of a national individual income tax, introduced in 1913 as a product of the Seventeenth Amendment. Beginning with a modest rate of 1% of incomes over $3,000—which few people had to pay—rates soon changed to meet the demands of

TABLE 4.75 TYPICAL MONTHLY ELECTRIC BILLS,[a] 1925–1945

Date	Average Bill in Dollars for[b]—			Average Bill in Cents per Kilowatt-hour for—			Index of Average Bill (Jan. 1, 1935 = 100) for—		
	25 kw.-hrs.	100 kw.-hrs.	250 kw.-hrs.	25 kw.-hrs.	100 kw.-hrs.	250 kw.-hrs.	25 kw.-hrs.	100 kw.-hrs.	250 kw.-hrs.
Oct. 1, 1925	1.88	6.00	12.95	7.5	6.0	5.2	119.7	134.8	144.5
Oct. 1, 1926	1.86	5.85	12.57	7.4	5.9	5.0	118.5	131.5	140.3
Oct. 1, 1927	1.81	5.58	11.94	7.2	5.6	4.8	115.3	125.4	133.3
Oct. 1, 1928	1.76	5.34	11.25	7.0	5.3	4.5	112.1	120.0	125.6
Oct. 1, 1929	1.73	5.13	10.69	6.9	5.1	4.3	110.2	115.3	119.3
Oct. 1, 1930	1.70	4.98	10.38	6.8	5.0	4.2	108.3	111.9	115.8
Oct. 1, 1931	1.69	4.72	9.58	6.8	4.7	3.8	107.6	106.1	106.9
Oct. 1, 1932	1.67	4.65	9.42	6.7	4.7	3.8	106.4	104.5	105.1
Oct. 1, 1933	1.63	4.58	9.26	6.5	4.6	3.7	103.8	102.9	103.3
Oct. 1, 1934	1.58	4.47	8.98	6.3	4.5	3.6	100.6	100.4	100.2
Jan. 1, 1935	1.57	4.45	8.96	6.3	4.5	3.6	100.0	100.0	100.0
Jan. 1, 1935	1.60	4.47	8.90	6.3	4.5	3.6	100.0	100.0	100.0
Jan. 1, 1936	1.53	4.21	7.85	6.1	4.2	3.1	95.6	94.2	88.2
Jan. 1, 1937	1.45	4.10	7.51	5.8	4.1	3.0	90.6	91.7	84.4
Jan. 1, 1938	1.43	4.03	7.34	5.7	4.0	2.9	89.4	90.2	82.5
Jan. 1, 1939	1.40	3.96	7.21	5.6	4.0	2.9	87.5	88.6	81.0
Jan. 1, 1940	1.36	3.88	7.05	5.4	3.9	2.8	85.0	86.8	79.2
Jan. 1, 1941	1.34	3.83	6.98	5.4	3.8	2.8	83.8	85.7	78.4
Jan. 1, 1942	1.34	3.80	6.95	5.4	3.8	2.8	83.8	85.0	78.1
Jan. 1, 1943	1.33	3.80	6.94	5.3	3.8	2.8	83.1	85.0	78.0
Jan. 1, 1944	1.33	3.78	6.92	5.3	3.8	2.8	83.1	84.6	77.8
Jan. 1, 1945	1.32	3.76	6.89	5.3	3.8	2.8	82.5	84.1	77.4

[a] For cities of population 50,000 or more.
[b] 25 kw.-hrs. for people who use lighting and small appliances only; 100 kw.-hrs. for use in lighting, small appliances, and refrigeration; 250 kw.-hrs. for use in lighting, small appliances, refrigeration, and cooking.
Source: Bureau of the Census, *Statistical Abstract of the United States, 1947,* 487.

TABLE 4.76 RETAIL PRICE OF GASOLINE IN FIFTY CITIES

[Cents per gallon]

Year	Retail Price
1919	. . .
1920	30.3
1921	25.6
1922	24.6
1923	20.7
1924	19.4
1925	20.3
1926	21.1
1927	18.0
1928	18.0
1929	17.9
1930	15.9
1931	12.8
1932	13.3
1933	12.6
1934	13.5
1935	13.6
1936	14.1
1937	14.6
1938	14.0
1939	13.3
1940	12.6
1941	13.5
1942	14.5
1943	14.6
1944	14.6
1945	14.5

Source: National Industrial Conference Board, *Economic Almanac for 1950*, 443.

financing the First World War. Income taxes decreased sharply during the 1920s, consistent with the business-oriented government of that era. Most noticeable were a steep decline in rates for highest incomes and the establishment in 1929 of a lowest rate of less than 0.5%. With the government accepting new obligations, rates nudged upward in the 1930s, and beginning in 1937 workers under the Social Security System had a new obligation: a 1% tax that by 1943 would grow to 2%. Employers, it should be noted, paid an identical rate. Taxes increased markedly in the Second World War. By 1943 virtually everyone who worked had to pay income taxes, and the top bracket exceeded 90%. To these rates were added a special victory tax of 5%, although only 3% was collected after July 1943. In 1943 the worker also began to face the new "pay-as-you-go" system whereby taxes were deducted at the workplace from one's wages.

TABLE 4.78 AVERAGE INCOME TAX PAYMENTS OF FAMILIES, 1939–1945[a]

Average Annual Income ($)	Average Income Tax Payments ($)						
	1939	1940	1941	1942	1943	1944	1945
1,000	. . .	. . .	. . .	. . .	9	12	12
1,500	. . .	. . .	. . .	. . .	22	26	26
2,000	. . .	. . .	. . .	. . .	35	39	39
2,500	. . .	. . .	3	71	120	102	102
3,000	. . .	. . .	41	158	219	206	206
3,500	. . .	7	86	244	319	310	310
4,000	3	26	131	331	419	413	413
4,500	20	44	176	427	528	518	518
5,000	37	63	221	528	642	630	630
8,000	148	207	637	1,196	1,389	1,353	1,353
10,000	291	376	993	1,734	1,980	1,915	1,915

[a]Family consisting of husband, wife, and two children.
Source: Bureau of Labor Statistics, *Handbook of Labor Statistics, 1947*, 219.

TABLE 4.77 INDIVIDUAL INCOME TAX EXEMPTIONS AND HIGHEST AND LOWEST BRACKETS

Income Year	Personal Exemptions					Tax Rates			
	Single ($)	Married				First Bracket		Top Bracket	
		Dependents					Amt. of Income ($)		Income Over ($)
		None	1	2	3	Rate		Rate	
1944–1945	500	1,000	1,500	2,000	2,500	23	2,000	94	200,000
1942–1943	500	1,200	1,550	1,900	2,250	19	2,000	88	200,000
1941	750	1,500	1,900	2,300	2,700	10	2,000	81	5,000,000
1940	800	2,000	2,400	2,800	3,200	4.4	4,000	81.1	5,000,000
1936–1939	1,000	2,500	2,900	3,300	3,700	4	4,000	79	5,000,000
1934–1935	1,000	2,500	2,900	3,300	3,700	4	4,000	63	1,000,000
1932–1933	1,000	2,500	2,900	3,300	3,700	4	4,000	63	1,000,000
1930–1931	1,500	3,500	3,900	4,300	4,700	1 1/8	4,000	25	100,000
1929	1,500	3,500	3,900	4,300	4,700	3/8	4,000	24	100,000
1925–1928	1,500	3,500	3,900	4,300	4,700	1 1/8	4,000	25	100,000
1924	1,000	2,500	2,900	3,300	3,700	1 1/2	4,000	46	500,000
1923	1,000	2,500	2,900	3,300	3,700	3	4,000	56	200,000
1922	1,000	2,500	2,900	3,300	3,700	4	4,000	56	200,000
1921	1,000	2,500	2,900	3,300	3,700	4	4,000	73	1,000,000
1919–1920	1,000	2,000	2,200	2,400	2,600	4	4,000	73	1,000,000
1918	1,000	2,000	2,200	2,400	2,600	6	4,000	77	1,000,000
1917	1,000	2,000	2,200	2,400	2,600	2	2,000	67	2,000,000
1916	3,000	4,000	4,000	4,000	4,000	2	20,000	15	2,000,000
1913–1915	3,000	4,000	4,000	4,000	4,000	1	20,000	7	500,000

Source: Bureau of the Census, *Historical Statistics of the United States, Colonial Times to 1957*, 703.

CHAPTER 5 Transportation and Communication

Transportation

Transportation in the United States underwent vast changes during the years 1914–45. On the whole people traveled more and over larger distances than ever before. The United States adopted a system of transport that was increasingly varied and competitive. New transportation industries came of age; others stood on the verge of doing so. Still others lost ground in proportion to the extent of gain by new industries. Transportation industries reacted sharply to the topsy-turvy course of national history. The Great Depression slowed commercial movement somewhat and slowed even more the production of vehicles of transport. The two world wars produced conflicting trends. If they stimulated an increase in the movement of people and goods that operated to the economic benefit of many agents of transport, especially railroads, the reordering of wartime priorities for raw materials and production stopped the making of cars almost completely. The wars laid a groundwork for a surge in national economic energy afterward, in which cases the automobile producers stood in the forefront.

Automobiles

The age of the automobile truly arrived in the first half of the twentieth century. Although there were fewer than two million motor vehicles in the United States in 1914, by 1929 the number had jumped to more than twenty-six million. The number of vehicle miles traveled increased from fifty-five million in 1921 to more than 333 million in 1941, after which time it dropped off because of the war. The innovative practices of Henry Ford led the way in changing a luxury item into a necessity, a symbol of freedom and of one's economic and social standing. In the process of development and weeding out competition, automobile companies came and went by the dozens; if in 1923 more than 100 firms produced cars, by the 1930s over 90% were sold by three companies. Changes in technology and design were even more numerous. The trend during the 1930s and 1940s was toward rounded, all-metal, closed-in bodies, powered by six- or eight-cylinder (although some cars had as many as sixteen) engines with other changes—many of them made with

TABLE 5.1 MOTOR VEHICLES—PRODUCTION, REGISTRATIONS, AND MOTOR FUEL USAGE: 1914 TO 1945

Year	Motor Vehicle Production				Motor Vehicle Registration				Motor Fuel Usage		
	Passenger Cars		Motor Trucks								
	Number	Value	Number	Value	Total	Automobiles	Buses	Trucks	Total	Highway	Nonhighway
		1,000 dollars		*1,000 dollars*					*1,000 gals.*	*1,000 gals.*	*1,000 gals.*
1945	69,532	60,603	655,683	1,219,957	30,638,429	25,691,434	112,253	4,834,742	22,046,727	19,148,968	2,897,759
1944	610	476	737,524	1,712,356	30,086,189	25,466,331	106,518	4,513,340	19,292,047	16,429,668	2,862,379
1943	139	109	699,689	1,453,467	30,499,608	25,912,730	106,702	4,480,176	18,642,773	16,004,250	2,638,523
1942	222,862	174,083	818,662	1,436,162	32,578,925	27,858,746	102,093	4,608,086	22,438,925	19,939,887	2,499,038
1941	3,779,682	2,673,957	1,060,948	1,087,592	34,472,145	29,524,101	88,800	4,859,244	26,429,441	24,192,397	2,237,044
1940	3,717,385	2,441,513	754,905	577,012	32,035,424	27,372,397	72,641	4,590,386	24,038,525	22,001,356	2,037,169
1939	2,866,796	1,816,435	710,496	502,422	30,615,087	26,139,526	68,859	4,406,702	22,571,837	20,714,352	1,857,485
1938	2,000,985	1,269,765	488,100	339,227	29,442,705	25,167,030	65,198	4,210,477	21,311,675	19,611,643	1,700,032
1937	3,915,889	2,304,349	893,085	542,921	29,706,158	25,390,773	66,166	4,249,219	21,115,444	19,455,454	1,659,990
1936	3,669,528	2,015,646	784,587	462,820	28,172,318	24,108,236	62,618	4,001,464	19,561,677	18,099,138	1,462,539
1935	3,252,244	1,709,426	694,690	379,408	26,229,743	22,494,884	58,994	3,675,865	17,637,580	16,344,697	1,292,883
1934	2,177,919	1,147,116	575,192	320,144	24,954,004	21,472,078	51,530	3,430,396	16,557,921	15,414,896	1,143,025
1933	1,573,512	762,737	346,545	186,069	23,876,707	20,586,284	44,918	3,245,505	15,367,905	14,348,152	1,019,753
1932	1,135,491	618,291	235,187	136,193	24,132,609	20,832,357	43,476	3,256,776	15,427,340	14,339,151	1,088,189
1931	1,973,090	1,111,274	416,648	262,418	25,862,038	22,330,402	41,880	3,489,756	16,621,261	15,456,662	1,164,599
1930	2,784,745	1,645,399	571,241	389,437	26,531,999	22,972,745	40,507	3,518,747	15,777,707	14,753,911	1,023,796
1929	4,587,400	2,847,119	771,020	566,030	26,502,508	23,060,421	33,999	3,408,088	15,051,036	14,139,301	911,735
1928	3,815,417	2,576,490	543,342	437,132	24,511,683	21,308,159	31,982	3,171,542	13,090,282	12,361,460	728,822
1927	2,936,533	2,164,671	464,793	420,131	23,139,559	20,142,120	27,659	2,969,780	11,936,896	11,331,326	605,570
1926	3,783,987	2,640,065	516,947	452,123	22,052,559	19,220,885	24,320	2,807,354	10,552,161	10,063,951	488,210
1925	3,735,171	2,458,370	530,659	458,400	19,940,724	17,439,701	17,808	2,483,215	9,143,965	8,749,075	394,890
1924	3,185,881	1,970,097	416,659	318,581	17,612,940	15,436,102	. . .	2,176,838	7,809,186	7,497,000	312,186
1923	3,624,717	2,196,272	409,295	308,538	15,102,105	13,253,019	. . .	1,849,086	6,313,177	6,078,000	235,177
1922	2,274,185	1,494,514	269,991	226,050	12,273,599	10,704,076	. . .	1,569,523	5,014,035	4,841,000	173,035
1921	1,468,067	1,038,191	148,052	166,071	10,493,666	9,212,158	. . .	1,281,508	4,064,824	3,935,000	129,824
1920	1,905,560	1,809,171	321,789	423,249	9,239,161	8,131,522	. . .	1,107,639	3,448,164	3,346,000	102,164
1919	1,651,625	1,365,395	224,731	371,423	7,576,888	6,679,133	. . .	897,755	2,747,030	2,672,000	75,030
1918	943,436	801,938	227,250	434,169	6,160,448	5,554,952	. . .	605,496	. . .	. . .	. . .
1917	1,745,792	1,053,506	128,157	220,983	5,118,525	4,727,468	. . .	391,057	. . .	. . .	. . .
1916	1,525,578	921,378	92,130	161,000	3,617,937	3,367,889	. . .	250,048	. . .	. . .	. . .
1915	895,930	575,978	74,000	125,800	2,490,932	2,332,426	. . .	158,506	. . .	. . .	. . .
1914	548,139	420,838	24,900	44,219	1,763,018	1,664,003	. . .	99,015	. . .	. . .	. . .

Source: Bureau of the Census, *Historical Statistics of the United States, 1789–1945* (Washington, D.C., 1949), 223.

SOUND-PROOFED LIKE A BROADCASTING STUDIO

NEW PLYMOUTH

IS COMPLETELY INSULATED — Steel Roof, Sides, Doors and Floor — to keep OUTSIDE Noises OUT! Body Cushioned on Rubber — Safety Interiors — Biggest Plymouth Yet!

HEAR A WATCH TICK at any speed...noise shut out by new sound-proofing and insulation.

STEEL FOR SAFETY... this big Plymouth body is all steel... roof, sides, doors and floor!

New 1937 Plymouth De Luxe 4-Door Sedan, $670 list*

HOW PLYMOUTH DID IT

Engineers tracked down all kinds of motoring noise that drum in your ears...wear your nerves.

Developed five kinds of insulating material...that absorb, shut out or deflect all kinds of noises.

They "sound-proofed" the steel roof, walls, floor and doors of the new Plymouth.

Noise now shut out or absorbed at every point . . . just like it's done in a modern broadcasting studio.

EASY TO BUY—Today, you'll find Plymouth is priced with the lowest... and offers convenient payment terms. You can buy a new Plymouth for as little as $25 a month. The Commercial Credit Company offers—through Chrysler, De Soto and Dodge dealers—terms that make Plymouth easy to buy.

EVERY PART of the new Plymouth body is sound-proofed ...with five kinds of insulation!

And talk about smooth riding! Huge AIRPLANE-TYPE shock-absorbers level out bumps. The body is pillowed on live rubber.

Double-action hydraulic brakes ...all-steel body...finger-tip steering...Hypoid rear axle—formerly in costly cars only...the sensational new SAFETY INTERIOR... Floating Power engine mountings.

Tests show this BIG, ROOMY Plymouth...is also the most economical...saves you more.

Drive the new Plymouth. See your Chrysler, De Soto or Dodge dealer now. — PLYMOUTH DIVISION OF CHRYSLER CORP.

PRICED WITH THE LOWEST!

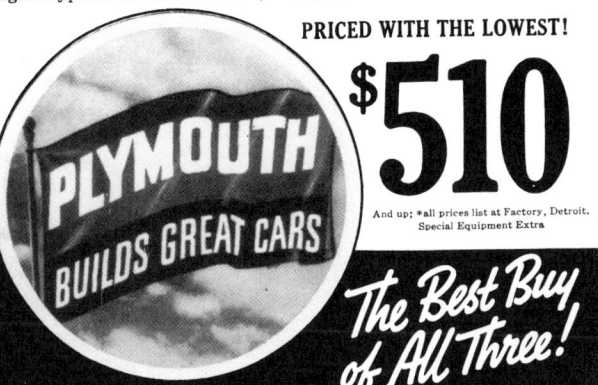

PLYMOUTH BUILDS GREAT CARS

$510

And up; *all prices list at Factory, Detroit. Special Equipment Extra

The Best Buy of All Three!

PLYMOUTH

The depression reduced auto sales and also auto prices. A new 1936 Plymouth could be had for $510. (*Life*, December 7, 1936)

women in mind—that eased the task of driving. By the 1940s automatic transmission had become popular optional equipment.

Managing the automobile culture largely fell within the domain of the states. The states built most of the roads—national highways excepted—and made the rules. Whether state or national, most roads were narrow passageways with one lane headed each way. If they happened to come to a city, the roads went on through, not around even the largest ones. Although the groundbreaking Pennsylvania Turnpike opened in 1940, the age of the dual-lane superhighway remained for the future. Speed limits in the 1930s ranged from 30 in Massachusetts to 60 in Colorado and Wyoming. Limits of 45 to 50 were common, and several states simply demanded "reasonable and proper" speed. The states undertook licensing of drivers, although most did not act until the 1930s and as late as 1945 it was possible to drive in three states, Louisiana, South Dakota, and Wyoming, without a license—a system that presumably placed no age limit on who could drive.

Perhaps more than any other major industry, automobiles followed the course of the national economic cycle. The grand year of 1929 produced a record in sales that would stand for many years. The depression years of the 1930s almost crushed the industry, and many firms had to pull out of competition. The period of the Second World War inspired a financial comeback for the remaining companies but not because of the production of cars. These firms had to make goods for the military establishment, and the production of cars virtually came to a halt between 1942 and 1945. The war years reversed an almost continuous trend of increase in traffic deaths, the explanation resting in a reduction of cars on the road, a shortage of gasoline, and a national speed limit of 35 miles per hour. The war also served to create large pent-up customer demand, and when the war ended in 1945, some dozen firms—led by the "Big Three" of Chrysler, Ford, and General Motors—stood poised to lead the charge into the new postwar world.

The war having stopped production of civilian automobiles, this last 1942 Olds comes down the line on February 10. (Courtesy Oldsmobile History Center)

TABLE 5.2   STATE TRAFFIC ENFORCEMENT AGENCIES

[As of June 1, 1938]

State	Name of Organization	Date Created	Number of Men in Service	Equipment		
				Number of Motorcycles	Number of Cars	Radio Equipped
Ala.	Highway Patrol	1935	144	87	35	yes
Ariz.	Highway Patrol	1928	43	none	47	yes
Ark.	State Police	1935	54	10	40	no
Calif.	Highway Patrol	1929	780	559	290	yes
Colo.	Highway Courtesy Patrol	1935	81	17	57	partially
Conn.	State Police	1903	225	170	190	no
Del.	State Police	1923	90	56	20	yes
Fla.	None	. . .	. . .	. . .	. . .	. . .
Ga.	State Patrol	1937	120	none	52	no
Idaho	Highway Patrol	1929	43	none	40	few sets
Ill.	State Police	1923	429	337	197	yes
Ind.	State Police	1929	234	50	171	yes
Iowa	Highway Patrol	1935	103	20	100	yes
Kans.	Highway Patrol	1937	47	2	31	yes (cars)
Ken.	Highway Patrol	1932	142	30	48	no
La.	State Police	1936	148	75	35	15
Maine	State Police	1925	108	15	95	no
Md.	State Police	1921	95	73	69[a]	yes
Mass.	State Police	1921	300	193	122	yes
Mich.	State Police	1919	312	65	155	125
Minn.	Highway Patrol	1929	109	60	63	yes
Miss.	Safety Patrol	1938	53	none	personal	no
Mo.	Highway Patrol	1931	126	11	84	yes
Mont.	Highway Patrol	1935	51	5	51	yes
Nebr.	Safety Patrol	1937	46	12	28	no short wave
Nev.	Highway Patrol	1923	5	none	5	yes
N.H.	State Police	1937	47	36	14	yes
N.J.	State Police	1921	257	70	87	teletype
N. Mex.	State Police	1929	42	36	5	no
N.Y.	State Police	1917	776	120	320	yes
N.C.	Highway Patrol	1927	121	103	113	yes
N. Dak.	Highway Patrol	1935	12	1	10	yes
Ohio	Highway Patrol	1933	120	65	55	yes
Okla.	Highway Patrol	1937	125	28	62	yes
Ore.	State Police	1931	164	none	147	yes
Penn.	Motor Police	1937	1,501	182	715	yes
R.I.	State Police	1925	70	36	46	yes
S.C.	Highway Patrol	1930	100	45	55	no
S. Dak.	Highway Patrol	1935	15	none	10	no
Tenn.	Highway patrol	1930	125	130	27	no
Tex.	(a) Highway Patrol	1927	235	none	95[*]	yes
	(b) Drivers' Lic. Div.	1935	107	none	60	no
Utah	Highway Patrol	1925	47	20	44	yes
Vt.	Highway Patrol	1919	37	none	37	no
Va.	State Police	1926	150	100	150	no
Wash.	State Patrol	1921	152	92	95	yes
W. Va.	State Police	1919	196	26	112	yes
Wisc.	Inspectors	1935	8	none	8	no
Wyo.	Highway Patrol	1933	18	5	18	no

[a] Including 1 trailer.
Source: Council of State Governments, *Book of the States, 1939–1940* (Chicago, 1939), 133.

TABLE 5.3   PRICES OF AUTOMOBILES, 1933

Listed below are prices for new automobiles on display at the New York Automobile Show in January 1933. The number immediately following the vehicle's name designated the number of cylinders in the engine. It should be noted that 1933 was perhaps the worst year of the depression, and so prices were some of the lowest in the history of automobile production. Ford Motor Company did not participate in the auto show.

Over $2,000			
Cadillac V-16	$6,250	Cadillac V-8	$2,695
Marmon 16	4,825	Stutz 8	2,495
Packard 12	3,720	Pierce-Arrow 8	2,385
Franklin 12	2,885	La Salle 8	2,245
Pierce-Arrow 12	2,785	Packard 8	2,150
Lincoln 12	2,700		
Over $1,000			
Franklin 6	$1,385	Dodge 8	$1,115
Hupmobile 8	1,195	Hudson 8	1,075
Auburn 12	1,145	Studebaker 8	1,000

Over $700			
Buick 8	$995	Nash 8	$830
Hupmobile 6	995	Hudson 6	765
Reo 6	995	Auburn 8	745
Studebaker 6	840	Graham 6	745
Chrysler 6	835	Oldsmobile 6	745
Over $500			
DeSoto 6	$695	Willys 6	$595
Nash 6	695	Pontiac 8	585
Essex 8	645	Rockne 6	585
Dodge 6	595		
Under $500			
Plymouth 6	$495	Willys 4	$395
Chevrolet 6	485	Continental 4	355
Continental 6	450	Austin 4	275
Essex 6	425		

Source: Time-Life Books, *Time Capsule, 1933* (New York, 1967), 204–205.

Vehicles produced during 1942–45 were almost entirely for military consumption. Ford workers here assemble the new durable and versatile Jeep. (Library of Congress)

TABLE 5.4 MOTOR VEHICLE ACCIDENTS—NUMBER AND DEATHS, BY TYPE OF ACCIDENT: 1914–1945

Year	Total Motor Vehicle Accidents (1,000)	Traffic Deaths						Traffic Death Rates	
		Total	Noncollision Accidents	Collision Accidents				Per 100,000 Population	Per 10,000 Motor Vehicles
				With Other Motor Vehicles	With Pedestrians	With Fixed Objects			
1945	5,500	28,076	6,600	7,150	11,000	800		21.2	9.1
1944	4,800	24,282	5,600	5,700	9,900	700		18.3	8.0
1943	4,400	23,823	5,690	5,300	9,900	700		17.8	7.7
1942	5,200	28,309	6,740	7,300	10,650	850		21.1	8.6
1941	7,000	39,969	9,450	12,500	13,550	1,350		30.0	11.5
1940	6,100	34,501	7,800	10,100	12,700	1,100		26.1	10.6
1939	5,700	32,386	7,900	8.700	12,400	1,000		24.7	10.4
1938	5,800	32,582	7,350	8,900	12,850	940		25.1	10.9
1937	7,000	39,643	9,690	10,320	15,500	1,160		30.8	13.2
1936	. . .	38,089	9,410	9,500	15,250	1,060		29.7	13.4
1935	. . .	36,369	9,720	8,750	14,350	1,010		28.6	13.7
1934	. . .	36,101	9,820	8,110	14,480	1,040		28.6	14.3
1933	. . .	31,363	8,680	6,470	12,840	900		25.0	13.0
1932	. . .	29,500	7,000	6,070	11,490	800		23.6	12.2
1931	. . .	33,700	7,850	6,820	13,370	870		27.2	13.0
1930	. . .	32,900	8,730	5,880	12,900	720		26.7	12.4
1929	. . .	31,200	8,430	5,400	12,250	620		25.7	11.8
1928	. . .	28,000	7,360	4,310	11,420	540		23.4	11.4
1927	. . .	25,800	7,280	3,430	10,820	500		21.8	11.2
1926	. . .	23,400	. . .	. . .	. . .	. . .		20.1	10.6
1925	. . .	21,900	. . .	. . .	. . .	. . .		19.1	11.0
1924	. . .	19,400	. . .	. . .	. . .	. . .		17.1	11.0
1923	. . .	18,400	. . .	. . .	. . .	. . .		16.5	12.2
1922	. . .	15,300	. . .	. . .	. . .	. . .		. . .	. . .
1921	. . .	13,900	. . .	. . .	. . .	. . .		. . .	. . .
1920	. . .	12,500	. . .	. . .	. . .	. . .		. . .	. . .
1919	. . .	11,200	. . .	. . .	. . .	. . .		. . .	. . .
1918	. . .	10,700	. . .	. . .	. . .	. . .		. . .	. . .
1917	. . .	10,200	. . .	. . .	. . .	. . .		. . .	. . .
1916	. . .	8,200	. . .	. . .	. . .	. . .		. . .	. . .
1915	. . .	6,600	. . .	. . .	. . .	. . .		. . .	. . .
1914	. . .	4,700	. . .	. . .	. . .	. . .		. . .	. . .

Source: Ben J. Wattenberg, *The Statistical History of the United States* (New York, 1976), 720.

TABLE 5.5   GASOLINE TAX RATES, 1930–1945

[Cents per gallon] [a]

Year	State Average	Federal Tax
1945	4.10	1.5
1944	4.06	1.5
1943	4.05	1.5
1942	3.99	1.5
1941	3.99	1.5
1940	3.96	1–1.5
1939	3.96	1
1938	3.96	1
1937	3.91	1
1936	3.85	1
1935	3.80	1
1934	3.66	1
1933	3.65	1–1.5
1932	3.60	0–1
1931	3.48	. . .
1930	3.35	. . .

[a]When two figures appear, the first is tax at start of the year, the second at year's end. By contrast, at the start of the 1990s the state tax ranged from 4 cents to 24, with most states receiving 15 cents or more; the federal tax was 14.1 cents per gallon.
Source: Bureau of the Census, *Historical Statistics of the United States, Colonial Times to 1957* (Washington, D.C., 1960), 463.

TABLE 5.6   MILEAGE OF RURAL ROADS AND MUNICIPAL STREETS: 1914–1945

Year	Total Existing Mileage						Existing Surfaced Mileage			Mileage Built by State Highway Departments				
		Rural Roads						Under State Control			Roads under State Control			
			State Administered		County Roads under Local Control	Municipal and Other Mileage								
	Total	Total	Primary	Secondary and County Roads			Total	High-type Roads[a]	Low-type Roads[a]	Total	Total	Earth Roads	High-type Surface	Low-type Surface
	1,000 miles	*1,000 miles*	*1,000 miles*	*1,000 miles*	*1,000 miles*	*1,000 miles*	*1,000 miles*	*1,000 miles*	*1,000 miles*	*Miles*	*Miles*	*Miles*	*Miles*	*Miles*
1945	3,319	2,939	339	202	2,398	380	1,721	168	312	15,278	14,827	250	3,971	10,606
1944	3,311	2,932	335	200	2,397	379	1,655	167	309	15,080	13,924	289	3,925	9,710
1943	3,311	2,930	333	200	2,397	381	1,646	166	306	15,971	14,692	458	4,446	9,788
1942	3,309	2,925	334	199	2,392	384	1,630	165	302	19,673	18,081	1,038	4,170	12,873
1941	3,309	2,926	332	196	2,398	383	1,607	162	296	32,634	30,554	1,343	6,304	22,907
1940	3,017	2,920	329	195	2,396	97	1,367	153	296	32,594	29,695	1,423	5,223	23,049
1939	3,007	2,913	328	194	2,391	94	1,318	151	286	32,996	30,671	1,720	5,021	23,930
1938	2,992	2,898	327	194	2,377	94	1,276	149	277	36,328	34,604	1,187	5,757	27,660
1937	2,982	2,894	327	189	2,378	88	1,232	144	265	35,627	28,945	1,828	6,532	20,585
1936	3,006	2,920	340	177	2,403	86	1,175	131	262	. . .	32,274	3,361	4,706	24,207
1935	3,050	3,032	332	173	2,527	18	1,080	128	246	. . .	26,814	3,284	3,806	19,724
1934	3,050	3,034	325	170	2,539	16	992	124	237	. . .	41,730	5,917	6,386	29,427
1933	. . .	3,029	346	135	2,548	. . .	914	116	195	. . .	33,471	6,258	7,412	19,801
1932	. . .	3,040	358	84	2,598	. . .	879	110	156	. . .	35,971	6,394	10,009	19,568
1931	. . .	3,036	329	45	2,662	. . .	830	96	146	. . .	44,634	10,095	12,513	22,026
1930	. . .	3,009	324	. . .	2,685	. . .	694	84	142	. . .	35,277	7,813	10,787	16,677
1929	. . .	3,024	314	. . .	2,710	. . .	662	75	133	. . .	32,522	7,451	8,847	16,224
1928	. . .	3,016	306	. . .	2,710	. . .	626	68	125	. . .	29,252	8,675	8,748	11,829
1927	. . .	3,013	293	. . .	2,720	. . .	589	60	117	. . .	26,723	7,151	6,733	12,839
1926	. . .	3,000	288	. . .	2,712	. . .	550	54	109	. . .	26,552	7,060	6,132	13,360
1925	. . .	3,006	275	. . .	2,731	. . .	521	48	97	. . .	23,152	5,316	6,686	11,150
1924	. . .	3,004	261	. . .	2,743	. . .	472	41	90	. . .	23,164	5,957	6,697	10,510
1923	. . .	2,996	252	. . .	2,744	. . .	439	34	78	. . .	20,311	5,814	5,628	8,869
1922	. . .	2,960	227	. . .	2,733	. . .	412	. . .	. . .	. . .	. . .	. . .	. . .	. . .
1921	. . .	2,925	203	. . .	2,722	. . .	387	. . .	. . .	. . .	. . .	. . .	. . .	. . .
1920	. . .	. . .	. . .	. . .	. . .	. . .	369	. . .	. . .	. . .	. . .	. . .	. . .	. . .
1919	. . .	. . .	. . .	. . .	. . .	. . .	350	. . .	. . .	. . .	. . .	. . .	. . .	. . .
1918	. . .	. . .	. . .	. . .	. . .	. . .	332	. . .	. . .	. . .	. . .	. . .	. . .	. . .
1917	. . .	. . .	. . .	. . .	. . .	. . .	313	. . .	. . .	. . .	. . .	. . .	. . .	. . .
1916	. . .	. . .	. . .	. . .	. . .	. . .	295	. . .	. . .	. . .	. . .	. . .	. . .	. . .
1915	. . .	. . .	. . .	. . .	. . .	. . .	276	. . .	. . .	. . .	. . .	. . .	. . .	. . .
1914	. . .	. . .	. . .	. . .	. . .	. . .	257	. . .	. . .	. . .	. . .	. . .	. . .	. . .

[a] High-type roads meant concrete or asphalt; low-type roads usually meant gravel.
Source: Bureau of the Census, *Historical Statistics of the United States, Colonial Times to 1957,* 458.

Besides contending with poor roads, this couple in Kentucky in 1940 had to change a wheel without a jack. (Library of Congress)

Developments in the Automobile Industry, 1914–1945

1914 Ford pays workers $5 for an eight-hour day; Cadillac introduces a V-8 engine; Horace and John Dodge begin making automobiles.

1915 Packard introduces a twelve-cylinder, "twin six," engine; several cars offer the "sociable" body with an aisle leading from the front to the back seats.

1916 The lightweight Marmon 34, weighing only 3,540 pounds, appears on the market; Charles W. Nash starts Nash Motors; eighteen companies now offer V-8s; Ford builds a tractor called Fordson.

1917 Hudson Motors organizes the Essex Motor Car Company; several closed cars appear, equipped with heaters; many auto and truck companies do work for the military.

1918 Production drops sharply because of demands of the war; White Motors stops producing cars to concentrate on trucks; Chevrolet joins General Motors Corporation.

1919 Ford produces 750,000 cars, one-third the industry's total; Studebaker stops making horse-drawn carriages; General Motors buys into Fisher Brothers Body Company.

1920 Closed cars dominate over open ones; Buick and McFarlan offer solid metal wheels; the Duesenberg appears, with straight-eight engine and hydraulic four-wheel brakes.

1921 Open touring cars are the hit of the National Automobile Show; Ford now has produced five million cars, more than 55% of total output; President Harding is the first president to ride in an auto to his inauguration: it is a Packard Twin Six; the General Motors building opens in Detroit.

1922 Balloon tires and air cleaners appear for the first time; Ford buys out Lincoln Motors at a receiver sale; Charles M. Schwab takes over Stutz Motors; some cars have a gas gauge on the instrument panel.

1923 Dodge offers steel closed bodies (no wood except on the roof); high-grade "ethyl" gasoline hits the market in Dayton, Ohio; Ford sells its lowest-priced Model T for $265.

1924 Packard, Duesenberg, Auburn, Hupmobile, Jordan, Rickenbacker, and several other makers produce straight-eight engines (eight cylinders placed consecutively in line); Maxwell-Chalmers offers a new Chrysler six-cylinder car; steamers and electric cars disappear completely from the auto show.

1925 More accessories, such as tire jacks, mirrors, and ashtrays, are now available; Maxwell-Chalmers becomes the Chrysler Corporation; front and rear bumpers become standard equipment; the national government adopts a method of numbering national highways: even numbers for east-west roads, odd numbers for those going north-south.

1926 Stutz and Rickenbacker offer a "shock-proof" glass with celluloid in between two sheets of glass; new cars at the auto show are Ajax, built by Nash, Moon's Diana, and Oakland's Pontiac; General Motors buys Fisher Body.

1927 New small cars on the market are the Little Marmon, Whippet Six by Willys, and Jordan's Little Playboy; Cadillac introduces the LaSalle V-8; Ford produces the last Model T, 15,007,033 since 1908; Ford introduces the Model A.

1928 Chrysler buys out Dodge Brothers; Studebaker buys Pierce-Arrow; Ford and Cadillac offer types of safety glass; Chrysler introduces the low-priced Plymouth and the more expensive line of DeSoto; Chevrolet shifts from the four-cylinder to the six-cylinder engine.

1929 Ford offers front-wheel drive; many cars now have tail lamps on both sides of the car; many cars now offer radio as optional equipment; Ford sets the minimum wage at seven dollars per day; motor vehicle production reaches 5,337,087, an all-time record that will stand for twenty years.

1930 Cadillac offers a V-12 and V-16 model; Studebaker introduces freewheeling (a method of coasting even with gears engaged); Chrysler offers its first eight-cylinder car; police cars are now being equipped with radios.

1931 Many firms offer large cars at reduced prices; General Motors stops production of the Oakland, in favor of the Pontiac; seventeen new cars turn to the freewheeling system.

1932 Although car sales are the worst since 1918, five makers still offer twelve-cylinder engines; Phaetons and coupes with disappearing tops, called convertibles, are popular; Ford introduces a new V-8 model to replace the Model A.

1933 More cars are streamlined with fender skirts, rounded bodies, sweeping lines, and slanted windshields; some firms place the starter button under or near the accelerator pedal.

1934 Chrysler features its streamlined "airflow" Chrysler and DeSoto models with independent front-wheel suspension and overdrive; Reo introduces an automatic transmission and tries putting a gearshift on the dashboard; all General Motors cars offer all-steel turret top.

1935 Most new cars carry lower price tags; Ford introduces a sleek new Lincoln Zephyr; Nash offers a model with seats that fold into twin beds.

1936 Reo stops making cars and starts to concentrate on trucks; many cars have built-in defrosters; Nash merges with Kelvinator of Detroit to become Nash-Kelvinator.

1937 Several makers place the gearshift on the steering column; Oldsmobile and Buick introduce an automatic shift called Automatic Safety Transmission; several companies place the storage battery under the hood; Studebaker offers a windshield washer; production of the classy Duesenberg stops.

1938 This is a bad year for sales; Ford introduces a new medium-priced Mercury with V-8 engine; Studebaker introduces the new low-priced Champion; Chevrolet introduces a vacuum-operated shift system; many cars have coil springs, instead of leafs, on the rear.

1939 Ford produces its twenty-seven millionth car, Chevrolet its fifteen millionth; Powell Crosley introduces a tiny vehicle called the Crosley; sealed-beam headlights are adopted for the following year's model; Oldsmobile offers "Hydramatic Drive"; many automobiles offer some variation of automatic shift; Packard offers the first air-conditioner unit.

1940 Willys Motors begins manufacture of a quarter-ton four-wheel-drive military vehicle called a Jeep; William Knudsen, president of General Motors, goes to Washington to direct defense production; many companies accept defense contracts; Chrysler offers a safety rim; running boards begin to disappear on the models produced for 1941; Cadillac discontinues production of the LaSalle.

1941 Sales pick up sharply; more factories turn to military goods; the 1942 models are introduced with much streamlining; the DeSoto has hidden headlights; the government begins to impose limits on automobile production.

1942 Production of all civilian cars stops on February 9, trucks on March 3, and car rationing starts March 2 (none are available for sale); nationwide gas rationing starts December 1—to save fuel and rubber.

1943 Twenty-five million gasoline ration books have been issued; shipbuilder Henry J. Kaiser announces his intent to build cars after the war.

1944 Willys-Overland says it will produce a civilian Jeep after the war; the basic gasoline ration is reduced from three to two gallons a week; the government authorizes some production of cars and trucks.

1945 Crosley announces an intent to resume building the little car; restrictions on production of replacement parts are lifted on May 22; the Willow Run Bomber Plant of Ford closes on June 23, after producing 8,685 planes; the Kaiser-Fraser Automobile Corporation is formed July 26; gasoline rationing ends August 15, one day after Japan surrenders; production of 1946 models begins; General Motors is struck by the United Auto Workers on November 21; in all, the automobile industry produced nearly $29 billion worth of war goods, 20% of total output. The following companies plan to produce cars for the postwar market:
Checker Motors
Chrysler (Plymouth, Dodge, DeSoto, Chrysler)
Crosley
Ford (Ford, Mercury, Lincoln, Continental)
General Motors (Chevrolet, Pontiac, Oldsmobile, Buick, Cadillac)
Hudson
Kaiser-Fraser
Nash-Kelvinator
Packard
Studebaker
Tucker
Willys-Overland

Source: Motor Vehicle Manufacturers Association, *Automobiles of America* (Detroit, 1974), 57–115.

Railroads

Although railroads remained a vital, even indispensable, part of the national transport system, the years 1914–45 showed a marked decline in several aspects of traffic by rail. The number of railroads went down, as did the miles of track; there were fewer passenger cars, fewer freight cars, and fewer locomotives in use in the 1940s than there had been at the start of the period. Railroads continued to carry much of the nation's freight. The sharp decline in the 1930s was only an expression of the decline in national economic activity and in all types of transport. Under heavy demand from the military effort, the period of the 1940s produced a substantial increase in the movement of freight tonnage.

As to the carrying of passengers, the trend for railroads was un-mistakable. The glory time was the period of the First World War; after that point railroads steadily lost out to other means of travel, largely automobiles. The period of the depression was exceptionally damaging. The number of passengers carried in 1933 was scarcely more than one-third the number carried in 1919. The growth in passenger travel during the Second World War was impressive, but it did not reach the level of freight traffic and the increase was not a result of choice but of restrictions placed on the use of motor vehicles. Even the switch in the 1930s and 1940s to streamlined, smooth-running diesel engines and better coaches—some of them air-conditioned—failed to brighten the prospect of the passenger business. Rather than freeing up railroad activity, the end of the war opened the door wider for competitors of travel by rail.

TABLE 5.7 RAILROAD MILEAGE, PASSENGER TRAFFIC, AND REVENUE

| Year Ending— | Number of Operating Railroads | Mileage | | | | | | | | Passenger Miles | | | | | Revenue | |
		Constructed	Abandoned	Road Owned	Track Operated Total	First Main Track	Other Main Tracks	Yard Tracks and Sidings	Road Operated Passenger Service	Passengers (1,000)	Total (Mil.)	Commutation (Mil.)	Coach (Mil.)	Parlor and Sleeping Car (Mil.)	Total ($1,000)	Per Passenger Mile (Cents)
Dec. 31																
1945	517	40	551	226,696	398,054	239,438	41,105	117,510	161,920	897,384	91,826	5,418	59,415	26,912	1,719,316	1.872
1944	524	46	705	227,335	398,437	240,215	41,178	117,044	162,290	915,817	95,663	5,344	63,288	26,944	1,793,322	1.875
1943	534	34	1,149	227,999	398,730	240,745	41,093	116,892	162,429	887,674	87,925	5,261	57,909	24,675	1,655,814	1.883
1942	543	38	2,886	229,174	399,627	241,737	41,137	116,753	163,658	672,420	53,747	4,761	30,910	17,853	1,030,486	1.917
1941	559	22	1,695	231,971	403,625	244,263	41,166	118,196	167,951	488,668	29,406	4,088	16,106	9,166	515,851	1.754
1940	574	19	1,284	233,670	405,975	245,740	41,373	118,862	170,175	456,088	23,816	3,997	12,485	7,288	417,955	1.755
1939	600	1	1,697	235,064	408,350	246,922	41,445	119,983	172,031	454,032	22,713	4,012	11,118	7,527	417,716	1.839
1938	611	35	1,621	236,842	411,324	248,474	41,589	121,261	173,616	454,508	21,657	4,032	10,247	7,354	406,406	1.877
1937	631	149	1,642	238,539	414,572	250,582	41,579	122,411	175,543	499,688	24,695	4,116	12,417	8,126	443,532	1.796
1936	641	38	1,577	240,104	416,381	251,542	41,731	123,108	178,403	492,493	22,460	4,188	. . .	. . .	413,189	1.840
1935	661	25	1,974	241,822	419,228	252,930	41,916	124,382	. . .	448,059	18,509	4,118	. . .	. . .	358,423	1.936
1934	678	33	1,784	243,857	422,401	254,882	42,109	125,410	. . .	452,176	18,069	4,163	. . .	. . .	346,870	1.920
1933	700	122	2,016	245,703	425,664	256,741	42,397	126,526	. . .	434,848	16,368	4,308	. . .	. . .	329,816	2.015
1932	709	321	1,370	247,595	428,402	258,869	42,556	126,977	. . .	480,718	16,997	4,986	. . .	. . .	377,511	2.221
1931	749	502	779	248,829	429,823	259,999	42,780	127,044	. . .	599,227	21,933	6,018	. . .	. . .	551,726	2.515
1930	775	460	954	249,052	429,883	260,440	42,742	126,701	. . .	707,987	26,876	6,669	. . .	. . .	730,766	2.719
1929	809	671	782	249,433	429,054	260,570	42,711	125,773	. . .	786,432	31,165	6,898	. . .	. . .	875,929	2.811
1928	849	946	710	249,309	427,750	260,546	42,432	124,772	. . .	798,476	31,718	6,626	. . .	. . .	905,271	2.854
1927	888	819	797	249,131	424,737	259,639	42,071	123,027	. . .	840,030	33,798	6,650	. . .	. . .	980,528	2.901
1926	929	881	892	249,138	421,341	258,815	41,686	120,840	. . .	874,589	35,673	6,605	. . .	. . .	1,049,210	2.941
1925	947	595	753	249,398	417,954	258,631	40,962	118,361	. . .	901,963	36,167	6,592	. . .	. . .	1,064,806	2.944
1924	995	635	617	250,156	415,028	258,238	39,916	116,874	. . .	950,459	36,368	6,407	. . .	. . .	1,085,672	2.985
1923	1,023	441	537	250,222	412,993	258,084	38,697	116,212	. . .	1,008,538	38,294	6,401	. . .	. . .	1,158,925	3.026
1922	1,041	318	1,188	250,413	409,359	257,425	37,888	114,046	. . .	989,509	35,811	6,132	. . .	. . .	1,087,516	3.037
1921	1,058	331	687	251,176	407,531	258,362	37,614	111,555	. . .	1,061,131	37,706	. . .	. . .	. . .	1,166,252	3.093
1920	1,085	. . .	. . .	252,845	406,580	259,941	36,894	109,744	. . .	1,269,913	47,370	. . .	. . .	. . .	1,304,815	2.755
1919	1,111	. . .	. . .	253,152	403,891	258,525	36,730	108,637	. . .	1,211,022	46,838	. . .	. . .	. . .	1,193,431	2.548
1918	1,131	. . .	. . .	253,529	402,343	258,507	36,228	107,608	. . .	1,122,963	43,212	. . .	. . .	. . .	1,046,166	2.421
1917	1,168	. . .	. . .	253,626	400,353	259,705	35,066	105,582	. . .	1,109,943	40,100	. . .	. . .	. . .	840,910	2.097
1916	1,216	. . .	. . .	254,037	397,014	259,705	34,325	102,984	. . .	1,048,987	35,220	. . .	. . .	. . .	722,359	2.051
June 30																
1916	1,243	. . .	. . .	254,251	. . .	259,211	33,864	101,869	. . .	1,015,338	34,309	. . .	. . .	. . .	689,627	2.010
1915	1,260	. . .	. . .	253,789	391,142	257,569	33,662	99,910	. . .	985,676	32,475	. . .	. . .	. . .	646,475	1.991
1914	1,297	. . .	. . .	252,105	387,208	256,547	32,376	98,285	. . .	1,063,249	35,357	. . .	. . .	. . .	703,484	1.990

Source: Bureau of the Census, *Historical Statistics of the United States, Colonial Times to 1957,* 429–430.

TABLE 5.8 RAILROAD EQUIPMENT

Year Ending— Dec. 31	Passenger-Train Cars in Service			Freight-Train Cars in Service		New Cars Delivered for Domestic Use		Locomotives in Service					
	Railroad Only	Class I Railroads and Pullman Co.		Number	Average Capacity (tons)	Freight Train	Passenger Train	Total	Steam	Electric	Diesel	Other	Average Tractive Effort
		Total	Air-conditioned										
1945	38,633	46,863	12,685	1,787,073	51.1	43,864	931	46,253	41,018	885	4,301	49	53,217
1944	38,217	46,588	13,175	1,797,012	50.8	43,003	1,003	46,305	41,921	902	3,432	50	52,822
1943	38,331	45,764	13,165	1,784,472	50.7	31,836	685	45,406	41,983	907	2,476	40	52,451
1942	38,446	. . .	. . .	1,773,735	50.5	62,873	418	44,671	41,755	892	1,978	46	51,811
1941	38,334	. . .	. . .	1,732,673	50.3	80,623	349	44,375	41,911	895	1,517	52	51,217
1940	38,308	. . .	. . .	1,684,171	50.0	62,341	257	44,333	42,410	900	967	56	50,905
1939	38,977	. . .	. . .	1,680,519	49.7	25,132	276	45,172	43,604	879	639	50	50,395
1938	39,931	. . .	. . .	1,731,096	49.4	16,470	434	46,544	45,210	882	403	49	49,803
1937	40,949	. . .	. . .	1,776,428	49.2	77,498	629	47,555	46,342	872	293	48	49,412
1936	41,390	. . .	. . .	1,790,043	48.8	46,612	191	48,009	46,923	858	175	53	48,972
1935	42,426	. . .	. . .	1,867,381	48.3	7,515	205	49,541	48,477	884	130	50	48,367
1934	44,884	. . .	. . .	1,973,247	48.0	25,176	275	51,423	50,465	805	104	49	47,712
1933	47,677	. . .	. . .	2,072,632	47.5	2,163	9	54,228	53,302	789	85	52	46,916
1932	50,598	. . .	. . .	2,184,690	47.0	3,252	77	56,732	55,831	764	80	57	46,299
1931	52,096	. . .	. . .	2,245,904	47.0	13,203	323	58,652	57,820	709	80	43	45,764
1930	53,584	. . .	. . .	2,322,267	46.9	74,920	1,534	60,189	59,406	663	77	43	45,225
1929	53,838	. . .	. . .	2,323,683	46.3	81,590	2,455	61,257	60,572	621	25	39	44,801
1928	54,800	. . .	. . .	2,346,751	45.8	46,060	1,571	63,318	62,642	617	. . .	52	43,838
1927	55,729	. . .	. . .	2,378,800	45.5	63,370	2,087	65,348	64,843	467	. . .	38	42,798
1926	56,855	. . .	. . .	2,403,967	45.1	88,862	2,814	66,847	66,381	435	11	20	41,886
1925	56,814	. . .	. . .	2,414,083	44.8	105,735	2,428	68,098	67,713	379	1	5	40,666
1924	57,451	. . .	. . .	2,411,627	44.3	113,711	2,517	69,486	69,114	372	. . .	. . .	39,891
1923	57,159	. . .	. . .	2,379,131	43.8	175,748	2,034	69,414	69,005	409	. . .	. . .	39,177
1922	56,827	. . .	. . .	2,352,483	43.1	66,289	977	68,518	68,121	397	. . .	. . .	37,441
1921	56,950	. . .	. . .	2,378,510	42.5	40,292	1,161	69,122	68,733	389	. . .	. . .	36,935
1920	56,102	. . .	. . .	2,388,424	42.4	60,955	831	68,942	68,554	388	. . .	. . .	36,365
1919	56,290	. . .	. . .	2,426,889	41.9	94,981	126	68,977	68,592	385	. . .	. . .	35,789
1918	56,611	. . .	. . .	2,397,943	41.6	67,063	750	67,936	67,563	373	. . .	. . .	34,995
1917	55,939	. . .	. . .	2,379,472	41.5	115,705	1,684	66,070	65,699	371	. . .	. . .	33,932
1916	55,193	. . .	. . .	2,329,475	40.9	111,516	1,344	65,595	65,253	342	. . .	. . .	32,840
June 30													
1916	54,774	. . .	. . .	2,313,378	40.5	. . .	. . .	65,314	65,021	293	. . .	. . .	32,380
1915	55,810	. . .	. . .	2,341,567	39.7	58,226	1,513	66,502	66,229	273	. . .	. . .	31,501
1914	54,492	. . .	. . .	2,349,734	39.1	97,626	3,589	67,012	. . .	. . .	. . .	. . .	31,006

Source: Bureau of the Census, *Historical Statistics of the United States, Colonial Times to 1957,* 429–430.

The Most Famous Train Competition for the passenger business prompted railroads to step up efforts to offer more in terms of comfort, service, and speed. The period of 1914–45 is memorable for the existence of distinctive trains with names designed to project an image of the best that railroads had to offer: the Chief and Super Chief; the Express trains; the City of San Francisco, Salina, and other cities; the Liners, Flyers, and Zephyrs. Of all the luxury trains, none carried the glamour of the Twentieth Century Limited. Flagship train of the New York Central Railroad, the Century in 1902 began the run between America's two largest cities, Chicago and New York, covering the distance in a speedy twenty hours. The train quickly caught on with the nation's most famous travelers. Movie stars from California might take the Santa Fe to Chicago and then board the Century for New York. They all liked its luxury, its catering to individual whim, its speed—in 1910 the trip was reduced to eighteen hours—but especially they liked the name. Traveling the Century became a status symbol of the first order.

In 1925 the Century earned a record $10 million, and the train's popularity necessitated using multiple sections. The record was reached in 1929 when seven identical trains, all marked Twentieth Century Limited, left Chicago's LaSalle Station for New York City on a single run. In 1938 New York Central introduced the new "all room" Century with salons, observation cars, and Pullmans but no open-berth cars. Designed by Henry Dreyfuss, the train was pulled by a massive hooded Hudson steam locomotive that whisked along at more than 80 miles per hour and made the trip in sixteen hours. The reign of the "Dreyfuss Century" lasted through the years of the Second World War. Although the future would hold a different fate, it appeared in 1945 that there always would be a Twentieth Century Limited.

YOU PAY—N. Y. C. GETS

Balance Sheet, One Manhattan-Chicago Run

Receipts

123 railroad fares @ $32.70...................................			$4,022.10
123 extra fares @ $9.60....................................			1,180.80
Pullman surcharges (one third of $927.75 accruing to the N. Y. C.)...............			309.25

Car	Style	No. passengers	Amount
James B. Eads	14 sections	15	$ 87.95
Star Island	14 sections	17	88.80
Star Valley	14 sections	13	81.60
New Winchester	14 sections	19	98.40
Glen Elm	6 compartments, 3 drawing-rooms	15	165.00
Glen Sunset	3 drawing-rooms	15	144.00
Willow Valley	7 drawing-rooms	11	126.00
Centlona	8 sections, 1 drawing-room, 2 compartments	14	103.00
Huron	1 drawing-room, 1 single room, and observation-lounge	4	33.00
Bay State	Composite		
		123	$927.75

Mail...	374.40
Dining-car receipts...................................	499.50
Total revenue..................................	$6,386.05

Expenditures

Wages...	$ 335.28

Operating personnel		Dining car		Others	
Enginemen	$ 67.69	Steward	$ 8.76	Stenographer	$ 5.84
Firemen	52.51	First cook	7.50	Barber	7.40
Conductor	46.03	Second cook	6.00	Maid	7.14
Brakemen	64.63	Third cook	5.01		$20.38
Baggagemen	29.68	Fourth cook	3.99		
	$260.54	Seven waiters	23.10		
			$54.36		

Food, linen, and menus for dining car.....................	548.30
Coal...	203.00

46 tons on at Harmon, Wayneport, and Air Line Junction..........	$204.72
Less a half ton left in tender at Chicago.....................	1.72
	$203.00

Depreciation.......................................	42.60

Equipment	Where Used	Cost	Depreciation per trip
Electric engine	New York-Harmon	$110,000	$ 6.77
Hudson steam locomotive	Harmon-Collinwood	86,000	10.60
Electric engine	Collinwood-Linndale	155,000	4.77
Hudson steam locomotive	Linndale-Chicago	86,000	10.60
Mail car	New York-Chicago	28,000	3.45
Dining car	New York-Chicago	52,000	6.41
		$517,000	$42.60

Lubrication (23 gallons of oil, 2 pounds of grease).....................	8.00
Overhead...	1,315.20

Maintenance of way and structures	960 miles @ .44..........		$ 422.40
Maintenance of equipment	960 " " .64..........		614.40
Traffic	960 " " .12..........		115.20
Miscellaneous and general	960 " " .17..........		163.20
			$1,315.20

Miscellaneous (magazines, newspapers, telephones)...................	6.41
Total expense..................................	$2,458.79

Summary

Total revenue, as above................................	$6,386.05
Total expense, as above................................	2,458.79
Net profit....................................	$3,927.26

¢ Excluded from this compilation is equipment owned and maintained by the Pullman Company as follows: Club car, observation-sleeper, and nine sleepers each costing $50,000, making a total of $550,000. This, with the cost of N. Y. Central equipment, makes train's total cost $1,067,000.

The balance sheet of one run of the Century in February 1932 shows that the Century was very profitable and that prices in 1932 were exceptionally low. (*World's Work*, February 1932)

TABLE 5.9 RAILROAD FREIGHT TRAFFIC AND REVENUE: 1914–1945

[In tons of 2,000 pounds]

Year Ending—	Revenue Freight Originated (Class I Railroads)								Freight and Revenue (Class I, II, and III Railroads)					
	All Tonnage	In Carloads						Less than Carload	Revenue Tons Originated	Ton-miles	Haul per Ton	Revenue		
		Total	Products of Agriculture	Animals and Products	Products of Mines	Products of Forests	Manufactures and Misc.					Total	Per Ton	Per Ton-mile
Dec. 31	1,000	1,000	1,000	1,000	1,000	1,000	1,000	1,000	Mil.	Mil.	Miles	$1,000	Dol.	Cents
1945	1,424,913	1,404,080	159,571	23,748	732,942	75,604	412,215	20,833	1,493	684,148	458.14	6,617,213	4.43	.967
1944	1,491,491	1,471,366	145,685	25,413	785,265	83,731	431,272	20,125	1,565	740,586	473.28	7,087,033	4.53	.957
1943	1,481,225	1,462,314	148,971	22,936	797,163	80,899	412,345	18,911	1,557	730,132	469.07	6,865,754	4.41	.940
1942	1,421,187	1,403,612	117,318	20,620	804,577	84,570	376,527	17,575	1,498	640,992	427.76	6,026,416	4.02	.940
1941	1,227,650	1,209,559	100,173	16,810	684,433	71,540	336,603	18,091	1,296	477,576	368.54	4,509,760	3.48	.944
1940	1,009,421	994,728	88,821	15,456	570,220	58,221	262,010	14,693	1,069	375,369	351.13	3,584,201	3.35	.955
1939	901,669	886,794	91,564	15,049	496,939	50,156	233,086	14,875	955	335,375	351.21	3,297,059	3.45	.983
1938	771,862	757,470	95,390	14,760	408,835	43,973	194,512	14,392	820	291,866	356.05	2,900,676	3.54	.994
1937	1,015,586	998,398	89,460	15,233	569,745	58,658	265,302	17,188	1,075	362,815	337.43	3,428,421	3.19	.945
1936	958,830	942,538	86,648	16,209	541,488	53,156	245,037	16,292	1,012	341,182	337.29	3,356,631	3.32	.984
1935	789,627	775,588	76,338	15,125	445,136	42,483	196,506	14,039	832	283,637	341.05	2,831,139	3.40	.998
1934	765,296	750,951	79,305	20,363	436,380	35,650	179,253	14,345	802	270,292	336.91	2,671,901	3.33	.989
1933	698,943	684,592	81,702	17,651	395,065	33,165	157,009	14,351	733	250,651	341.77	2,528,968	3.45	1.009
1932	646,223	630,989	80,917	18,055	362,226	26,109	143,682	15,234	679	235,809	346.63	2,485,475	3.66	1.056
1931	894,186	871,412	97,487	21,632	501,903	43,024	207,366	22,774	945	311,073	329.23	3,302,324	3.50	1.062
1930	1,153,197	1,123,530	110,728	23,129	642,537	69,371	277,765	29,667	1,220	385,815	316.21	4,145,015	3.40	1.074
1929	1,339,091	1,303,048	115,343	24,907	737,879	94,855	330,064	36,043	1,419	450,189	317.17	4,899,168	3.45	1.088
1928	1,285,943	1,248,989	118,022	25,634	696,583	96,737	312,013	36,954	1,371	436,087	318.00	4,771,562	3.48	1.094
1927	1,281,611	1,243,171	113,342	26,003	713,402	99,351	291,073	38,440	1,373	432,014	314.75	4,728,885	3.45	1.095
1926	1,336,142	1,296,651	111,787	26,244	757,703	104,851	296,066	39,491	1,440	447,444	310.81	4,905,981	3.41	1.096
1925	1,247,242	1,206,655	109,313	26,324	678,336	107,391	285,291	40,587	1,351	417,418	308.93	4,648,364	3.44	1.114
1924	1,187,296	1,146,747	116,587	27,747	637,582	108,094	256,737	40,549	1,287	391,945	304.44	4,437,380	3.45	1.132
1923	1,279,030	1,234,692	109,318	28,254	713,735	115,618	267,767	44,338	1,388	416,256	299.94	4,712,495	3.40	1.132
1922	1,023,745	980,516	111,787	26,230	532,998	89,059	220,442	43,229	1,112	342,188	307.77	4,085,742	3.67	1.194
1921	940,183	898,191	114,069	24,263	511,271	76,419	172,169	41,992	1,018	309,533	304.11	4,004,109	3.93	1.294
1920	1,255,421	1,202,219	110,840	26,595	712,155	100,765	251,864	53,202	1,363	413,699	303.52	4,420,833	3.24	1.069
1919	1,096,449	1,045,148	115,033	35,494	589,951	94,076	210,255	51,301	1,190	367,161	308.69	3,624,886	3.05	.987
1918	1,263,344	1,209,957	116,051	35,777	734,796	97,256	226,077	53,387	1,377	408,778	296.89	3,522,052	2.56	.862
1917	1,264,016	1,210,247	104,629	31,858	732,653	100,838	240,269	53,769	1,382	398,263	288.18	2,897,436	2.10	.728
1916	1,203,367	1,150,456	113,635	30,473	680,123	93,819	231,039	52,911	1,317	366,173	277.98	2,631,092	2.00	.719
June 30														
1916	. . .	. . .	. . .	. . .	. . .	. . .	. . .	. . .	1,263	343,477	271.98	2,469,027	1.96	.719
1915	925,697	878,761	109,483	26,001	507,250	76,674	157,085	46,936	1,024	277,135	270.69	2,037,926	1.99	.735
1914	1,023,131	982,892	98,825	26,352	574,000	91,094	177,950	40,239	1,130	288,637	255.43	2,126,717	1.88	.737

Source: Bureau of the Census, *Historical Statistics of the United States, Colonial Times to 1957*, 431.

TABLE 5.10 DEATHS IN STEAM RAILWAY ACCIDENTS, 1918 TO 1945

Year	Passengers on Trains		Travelers Not on Trains	Employees on Duty	Persons in Grade Crossing Accidents	Other Nontrespassers	Trespassers	Total
1918		521		3,566	1,979	501	3,423	9,194
1923		149		2,134	2,422	370	2,861	7,795
1928		104		1,357	2,768	363	2,532	7,002
1933	47		13	571	1,638	179	3,025	5,434
1938	79		9	549	1,679	190	2,428	4,879
1941	41		10	826	2,089	272	2,252	5,452
1942	98		21	1,043	2,117	322	2,040	5,559
1943	271		13	1,089	1,876	326	1,788	5,302
1944	259		14	1,087	2,000	315	1,549	5,146
1945	145		13	987	2,074	220	1,616	5,055

Note: For 1918, 1923, and 1928, numbers of deaths of passengers on trains and travelers not on trains are combined.
Sources: National Safety Council; *Information Please Almanac, 1948* (New York, 1948), 288.

Intracity Travel

The staple of urban transportation, the electric-powered railway, continued to be a major way of getting about in the cities. Whether called the streetcar, the elevated (or el), the subway, or the trolley, electric railway cars carried more passengers than any other form of public transport. In the small- and medium-sized cities and towns, however, the streetcar steadily lost ground. In many towns they were phased out altogether by the start of the Second World War.

In those places and to some extent in the large cities as well, other means of public transport took hold. The trolley coach or trolley bus—a bus powered by a "hot" electric-charged cable that ran overhead along the street—caught the fancy of some local officials. The clear trend of the 1930s and 1940s was toward use of a conventional gasoline- or diesel-powered motor bus.

This 1941 photo shows the "el" tracks in Manhattan. For many years a staple of urban transport, the elevated railways were still visible in the 1940s in such cities as Chicago and New York. (Library of Congress)

TABLE 5.11 PUBLIC TRANSIT MILEAGE, EQUIPMENT, PASSENGERS, AND PASSENGER REVENUE: 1917 to 1945

Year	Mileage (Dec. 31)			Equipment Owned (Dec. 31)			Revenue and Nonrevenue Passengers (millions)				Revenue Passengers (mil.)	Passenger Revenue (mil. dol.)
	Railway Track[a]	Trolley Coach[a]	Motor Bus[a]	Railway Cars[a]	Trolley Coaches	Motor Buses	Total	Railway	Trolley Coach	Motor Bus		
1945	17,702	2,313	90,400	36,377	3,711	49,670	23,254	12,124	1,244	9,886	18,982	1,313.7
1944	18,082	2,245	87,700	37,199	3,561	48,400	23,017	12,137	1,234	9,646	18,735	1,296.9
1943	18,181	2,248	87,000	37,505	3,501	47,100	22,000	11,806	1,175	9,019	17,918	1,235.6
1942	18,171	2,273	85,500	37,508	3,385	46,000	18,000	9,856	899	7,245	14,501	979.1
1941	18,342	2,041	82,100	37,670	3,029	39,300	14,085	8,502	652	4,931	11,302	758.8
1940	19,602	1,925	78,000	37,662	2,802	35,000	13,098	8,325	534	4,239	10,504	701.5
1939	20,600	1,543	74,300	40,372	2,184	32,600	12,837	8,539	445	3,853	10,252	681.5
1938	21,800	1,398	70,400	42,605	2,032	28,500	12,645	8,781	389	3,475	9,985	662.9
1937	23,770	1,166	67,000	45,312	1,655	27,500	13,246	9,468	289	3,489	10,436	689.7
1936	25,300	859	62,200	48,103	1,136	23,900	13,146	9,824	143	3,179	10,512	685.5
1935	26,700	548	58,100	50,466	578	23,800	12,226	9,512	96	2,618	9,782	642.3
1934	28,500	423	54,700	54,118	441	18,700	12,038	9,600	68	2,370	...	...
1933	...	...	...	58,124	310	17,200	11,327	9,207	45	2,075	...	...
1932	...	...	...	...	...	...	12,025	9,852	37	2,136	...	...
1931	...	...	...	...	...	...	13,924	11,583	28	2,313	...	...
1930	...	...	...	...	...	...	15,567	13,072	16	2,479	...	...
1929	...	...	...	...	...	...	16,985	14,358	5	2,622	...	...
1928	...	...	...	...	...	...	16,989	14,518	3	2,468	...	...
1927	...	...	...	...	...	...	17,201	14,901	...	2,300	...	...
1926	...	...	...	...	...	...	17,234	15,225	...	2,009	...	...
1925	...	...	...	...	...	...	16,651	15,167	...	1,484	...	...
1924	...	...	...	...	...	...	16,301	15,312	...	989	...	...
1923	...	...	...	...	...	...	16,311	15,650	...	661	...	...
1922	...	...	...	...	...	...	15,735	15,331	...	404	...	...
1921	...	...	...	...	...	...	...	14,574	...	...	...	...
1920	...	...	...	...	...	...	...	15,541	...	...	...	...
1919	...	...	...	...	...	...	...	14,916	...	...	...	...
1918	...	...	...	...	...	...	...	14,243	...	...	...	...
1917	...	...	...	...	...	...	...	14,507	...	...	...	...

[a]Railway track and railway cars apply to municipal travel by rail, usually powered by electricity, that involved elevated, subway, or surface operations—the trolley or the streetcar. The trolley coach was a bus powered by a hot line overhead. The motor bus was the bus driven by the gasoline or diesel engine.
Source: Bureau of the Census, *Historical Statistics of the United States, Colonial Times to 1957*, 464.

Aviation

Despite the fact that the First World War inspired increased interest in the use of airplanes, travel by air remained an infant enterprise at the start of this period. The development and popularity of airplanes grew during the 1920s—an age known for adventure and establishment of numerous "firsts" in air travel, the most sensational of which was the solo flight of Charles Lindbergh in 1927. Amelia Earhart acquired a reputation for skill and daring as a pilot. Airmail service was established between major cities in the 1920s, but passenger travel, though it did grow, was slowed by costs, by fear of flight, and by the absence of an efficient and reliable aircraft.

Douglas Aircraft's all-metal DC3 represented a breakthrough in 1936, and Boeing's massive seaplane, the Clipper, stood as progress of a different order. The Second World War produced revolutionary change. It created a need for numerous new and improved types of airplanes as well as thousands of new pilots. The war promoted public confidence in the safety and benefits of travel by air. The war multiplied the profits—the investment capital—and advanced the technical skills of aircraft companies, many of which were anxious to shift their attention to the production of civilian aircraft.

TABLE 5.12 AMERICAN AIRCRAFT PRODUCTION

Year	Number of Aircraft Produced — Total	For United States Military Services	Others	Value of All Products[a] (Thousands of Dollars)
1914	49	15	34	790
1915	178	26	152	n.a.
1916	411	142	269	n.a.
1917	2,148	2,013	135	n.a.
1918	14,020	13,991	29	n.a.
1919	780	682	98	14,373
1920	328	256	72	n.a.
1921	437	389	48	7,431
1922	263	226	37	n.a.
1923	743	687	56	13,142
1924	377	317	60	n.a.
1925	789	445	344	12,775
1926	1,186	478	708	17,695
1927	1,995	609	1,386	30,897
1928	4,346	847	3,499	64,662
1929	6,193	779	5,414	91,051
1930	3,437	836	2,601	60,846
1931	2,800	853	1,947	48,540
1932	1,396	500	896	34,861
1933	1,324	331	993	33,357
1934	1,615	393	1,222	43,892
1935	1,710	336	1,374	42,506
1936	3,010	858	2,152	78,149
1937	3,773	858	2,915	114,093
1938	3,623	925	2,698	198,293
1939	5,856	921	4,935	247,905
1940	12,794	6,019[b]	6,785	370,000[e]
1941	26,277[c]	19,433[b]	6,844	1,804,000[e]
1942	47,836[c]	47,836[b]	d	5,817,000[e]
1943	85,898[c]	85,898[b]	d	12,514,000[e]
1944	96,318[c]	96,318[b]	d	16,047,000[e]
1945	49,761[c]	47,714[b]	2,047	8,279,000[e]

[a]Value of aircraft, engines, parts, parachutes, etc.
[b]Includes military aircraft for lend-lease shipments.
[c]Includes United States–financed aircraft manufactured in Canada.
[d]No production other than military.
[e]Values are for military aircraft produced in the United States only. These data were computed by the War Production Board in terms of August 1943 unit costs. The values are not meant to measure output at current prices or expenditures. The 1940 figure is only for the second half of that year; the 1945 figure covers only the first 8 months.   n.a.—Not available
Source: National Industrial Conference Board, *The Economic Almanac for 1950* (New York, 1950), 274.

TABLE 5.13 AIR TRANSPORT—SCHEDULED AIR TRANSPORTATION, DOMESTIC ONLY: 1926 TO 1945

[All data reflect scheduled operations exclusively]

Year	Number of Operators	Aircraft in Service	Route Mileage	Average Passenger Revenue per Passenger Mile (Cents)	Number Persons Employed	Revenue Miles Flown	Revenue Passengers Carried — Duplicated[a]	Undupli-cated[b]	Revenue Passenger Miles Flown (1,000 Miles)	Ton-miles Flown Express and Freight	Mail
1945	20	421	48,516	0.0495	50,313	208,969,279	7,494,140	6,576,252	3,362,455	22,196,852	65,092,921
1944	19	288	47,384	0.0535	31,198	138,732,219	4,675,164	4,045,965	2,178,207	16,991,598	51,139,973
1943	19	204	42,537	0.0527	29,654	105,354,810	3,387,967	3,019,736	1,634,135	15,139,359	36,061,868
1942	19	186	41,596	0.0528	26,910	111,340,622	3,370,398	3,136,755	1,418,042	11,901,793	21,162,102
1941	19	370	45,163	0.0504	19,223	134,405,836	3,848,882	. . .	1,384,733	5,258,551	18,118,015
1940	19	369	42,757	0.0507	15,984	110,101,039	2,802,781	. . .	1,052,156	3,476,224	10,117,858
1939	18	276	36,654	0.0510	10,639	82,924,922	1,704,762	. . .	682,904	2,713,099	8,610,726
1938	16	260	34,879	0.0518	9,008	68,610,143	1,197,100	. . .	479,244	2,182,420	7,449,246
1937	22	291	32,006	0.056	7,586	66,791,079	985,084	. . .	411,545	2,162,488	6,698,230
1936	24	280	29,797	0.057	7,079	64,307,480	931,683	. . .	438,989	1,865,798	5,741,436
1935	26	363	29,190	0.057	5,945	55,918,151	678,549	. . .	316,336	1,097,602	4,132,708
1934	24	423	28,609	0.059	4,201	41,525,667	475,461	. . .	189,806	597,293	2,237,175
1933	25	418	28,283	0.061	4,369	49,256,320	502,218	. . .	174,820	422,860	2,567,949
1932	32	456	28,956	0.061	4,020	45,893,522	476,041	. . .	127,433	289,512	2,701,125
1931	39	490	30,857	0.067	4,314	43,109,166	472,438	. . .	106,952	220,657	3,140,205
1930	43	497	30,293	0.083	2,778	32,644,703	384,506	. . .	85,125	100,666	. . .
1929	38	442	. . .	0.12	1,958	22,728,869	161,933	. . .	. . .	69,898	. . .
1928	34	268	. . .	0.11	1,496	10,527,870	48,312	. . .	. . .	58,913	. . .
1927	18	. . .	. . .	0.106	. . .	5,856,189	8,679	. . .	. . .	12,841	. . .
1926	13	. . .	. . .	0.12	. . .	4,318,087	5,782	. . .	. . .	995	. . .

[a]Duplication exists where (a) the same passengers were carried on more than one route of an air carrier; and (b) where the same passengers were carried by more than one air carrier.
[b]Duplication has been eliminated where the same passengers were carried on more than one route of an air carrier, but still exists where the same passengers were carried by more than one air carrier.
Source: Bureau of the Census, *Historical Statistics of the United States, 1789–1945,* 224.

TABLE 5.14   AIR TRANSPORT—AIRPORTS, AIRCRAFT, PILOTS, AND MILES FLOWN: 1926 TO 1945

Year	Airports and Landing Fields — Total	Lighted	Total U.S. Civil Aircraft	Certificated Airplane Pilots[a] — Total	Airline Transport	Commercial	Private	Miles Flown in Civil Flying other than Scheduled Air Carrier
1945	4,026	1,007	37,789	296,895	5,815	162,873	128,207	b
1944	3,427	964	27,919	183,383	3,046	68,449	111,888	b
1943	2,769	859	27,180	173,206	2,315	63,940	106,951	b
1942	2,809	700	27,170	166,626	2,177	55,760	108,689	293,592,580
1941	2,484	662	26,013	129,947	1,587	34,578	93,782	346,303,400
1940	2,331	776	17,928	69,829	1,431	18,791	49,607	264,000,000
1939	2,280	735	13,772	33,706	1,197	11,677	20,832	177,868,157
1938	2,374	719	11,159	22,983	1,159	7,839	13,985	129,359,095
1937	2,299	720	10,836	17,681	1,064	6,411	10,206	103,196,355
1936	2,342	705	9,229	15,952	842	7,288	7,822	93,320,375
1935	2,368	698	9,072	14,805	736	7,362	6,707	84,755,630
1934	2,297	664	8,322	13,949	676	7,484	5,789	75,602,152
1933	2,188	626	9,284	13,960	554	7,635	5,771	71,222,845
1932	2,117	701	10,324	18,594	330	7,967	10,297	78,178,700
1931	2,093	680	10,680	17,739	c	8,513	9,226	94,343,115
1930	1,782	640	9,818	15,280	c	7,847	7,433	108,269,760
1929	1,550	d	9,922	10,287	c	6,053	4,162	110,000,000
1928	1,364	d	5,104	4,887	c	d	d	60,000,000
1927	1,036	d	2,740	1,572	c	d	d	30,000,000
1926	d	d	. . .	. . .	. . .	. . .	. . .	18,746,640

[a]The count of certificated pilots after 1941 is not directly comparable with the previous years as the Civil Aeronautics Regulations were amended to permit pilot certificates currently effective on April 1, 1942, to continue in effect indefinitely. This amendment expires on July 1, 1947.
[b]Not available. No surveys made during war years, because the Civil Air Regulations were amended and aircraft owners were not required to submit reports.
[c]Airline transport rating became effective May 5, 1932.
[d]Not available.
Source: Bureau of the Census, *Historical Statistics of the United States, 1789–1945*, 225.

TABLE 5.15   AIR TRANSPORT—ACCIDENTS: 1927 TO 1945

Year	Domestic Scheduled Air Carriers — Total Accidents	Number of Fatal Accidents	Total Passenger Fatalities	Plane Miles Flown per Fatal Accident	Passenger Fatalities per 100 Million Passenger Miles Flown	Non–Air-Carrier Flying Operations[a] — Total Accidents	Fatal Accidents	Fatalities	Miles Flown per Fatal Accident
1945	40	8	76	26,171,111	2.2	4,652	322	508	. . .
1944	30	5	48	27,768,033	2.2	3,343	169	257	. . .
1943	23	2	22	52,716,500	1.3	3,871	167	257	. . .
1942	23	5	55	22,354,936	3.7	3,324	143	220	2,053,095
1941	27	4	35	33,729,240	2.3	4,252	217	312	1,595,868
1940	30	3	35	36,837,890	3.0	3,471	232	359	1,137,931
1939	28	2	9	41,616,810	1.2	2,222	203	315	876,198
1938	23	5	25	13,818,740	4.5	1,861	176	274	734,995
1937	42	5	40	13,358,216	8.3	1,900	184	280	560,850
1936	65	8	44	8,038,435	10.0	1,674	155	261	602,067
1935	58	8	15	6,989,769	4.7	1,503	161	253	526,432
1934	71	8	17	5,190,708	9.0	1,491	184	323	410,881
1933	100	9	8	5,472,924	4.6	1,589	177	299	402,389
1932	108	16	19	2,868,345	14.9	1,936	207	318	377,675
1931	118	13	25	3,316,090	23.4	2,197	251	398	375,869
1930	88	9	24	3,627,189	28.2	2,029	300	504	360,899
1929	124	21	14	. . .	. . .	1,586	287	457	. . .
1928	85	11	14	. . .	. . .	1,036	215	362	. . .
1927	25	4	1	. . .	. . .	253	95	146	. . .

[a]Non–air-carrier pertains to private planes, company planes, business activities, such as aerial photography and crop dusting.
Source: Bureau of the Census, *Historical Statistics of the United States, 1789–1945*, 225.

Water Transport

The period produced a steady increase in transport by water, although the trend was interrupted during the Great Depression in the 1930s. The Second World War inspired recovery in foreign and, to a lesser extent, domestic activity. The bulk of American commerce continued to be carried in foreign bottoms, a trend that be-

TABLE 5.16 NET TONNAGE CAPACITY OF VESSELS ENTERED AND CLEARED: 1914–1945

[In thousands of net tons. Excludes domestic trade.]

| | Vessels Entered | | | Vessels Cleared | | |
| | All Ports | | | All Ports | | |
Year	Total	U.S. Vessels	Foreign Vessels	Total	U.S. Vessels	Foreign Vessels
1945	94,021	61,375	32,646	94,559	61,460	33,099
1944	81,860	48,071	33,789	87,385	53,050	34,335
1943	61,084	29,292	31,792	66,716	33,682	33,034
1942	43,942	13,611	30,331	47,706	16,354	31,352
1941	59,061	20,940	38,121	62,596	21,869	40,726
1940	58,544	19,220	39,324	62,171	20,248	41,923
1939	68,992	17,769	51,223	70,306	18,156	52,150
1938	70,516	19,020	51,496	71,286	18,829	52,456
1937	71,560	19,527	52,033	72,880	19,938	52,942
1936	65,972	20,682	45,290	66,066	20,069	45,997
1935	64,612	22,372	42,240	64,887	22,126	42,761
1934	63,787	23,192	40,594	63,702	22,799	40,903
1933	60,936	22,488	38,448	61,287	22,434	38,853
1932	64,837	24,278	40,559	64,446	23,865	40,582
1931	72,782	26,907	45,875	73,501	26,854	46,647
1930	81,253	31,866	49,387	81,307	31,550	49,747
1929	82,602	32,241	50,361	82,343	31,927	50,416
1928	80,211	31,285	48,926	80,667	31,734	48,933
1927	74,310	29,289	45,021	75,440	29,793	45,647
1926	76,933	26,890	50,043	79,041	28,532	50,509
1925	69,378	27,947	41,431	70,229	27,808	42,421
1924	68,292	29,628	38,664	68,910	30,092	38,818
1923	66,319	27,725	38,594	66,624	27,932	38,692
1922	65,191	31,738	33,453	64,839	31,759	33,080
1921	62,285	31,185	31,100	62,665	30,181	32,484
1920	64,104	32,119	31,985	67,817	34,053	33,764
1919	46,702	21,933	24,769	51,257	24,992	26,265
1918	45,456	19,284	26,173	46,014	19,206	26,808
1917	50,472	18,725	31,747	52,077	19,146	32,931
1916	51,550	17,928	33,622	52,423	17,902	34,521
1915	46,710	13,275	33,435	46,885	13,418	33,467
1914	53,389	13,730	39,659	53,183	13,740	39,443

Source: Bureau of the Census, Historical Statistics of the United States, Colonial Times to 1957, 450.

TABLE 5.17 WATERBORN CARGO TONNAGE, FOREIGN AND DOMESTIC: 1924–1945

[In thousands of short tons]

| | Foreign and Domestic Commerce | | Foreign Commerce | | | | | Domestic Commerce | | | | | | |
| | | | | Through Seaports | | Great Lakes Ports | | | | Between Ports | | Locale Traffic of Seaports and Great Lakes Ports | Between Seaports and River Ports | On Rivers, Canals, and Connecting Channels |
Year	Net Total	Unadjusted Total[a]	Total	Imports	Exports	Imports	Exports	Approximate Net Total	Unadjusted Total	Coastwise	Great Lakes			
1945	618,906	870,282	172,094	44,526	100,333	6,511	20,724	446,812	698,188	90,705	157,900	97,822	87,073	264,688
1944	605,928	859,954	153,736	39,441	82,613	8,055	23,627	452,192	706,218	70,806	164,971	106,194	95,821	268,426
1943	580,581	804,104	127,284	33,077	63,086	7,120	24,001	453,297	676,820	60,009	159,458	106,278	93,689	257,386
1942	589,900	827,624	99,221	25,974	46,023	4,488	22,736	490,679	728,403	74,016	172,606	104,189	92,748	284,844
1941	653,600	920,634	120,642	54,616	40,605	4,628	20,802	532,948	799,982	155,927	163,161	98,728	85,368	296,798
1940	607,900	836,416	111,255	40,740	49,568	4,118	16,829	496,645	725,161	157,027	141,103	97,632	70,217	259,182
1939	569,400	769,689	112,667	37,854	57,711	4,941	12,161	456,733	657,022	150,983	113,309	87,710	62,014	243,006
1938	466,900	664,751	105,182	33,886	55,476	5,110	10,710	361,718	559,569	138,545	72,846	76,216	56,034	215,928
1937	583,100	745,032	114,413	43,764	52,910	4,102	13,637	468,687	630,619	149,740	135,075	91,059	55,295	199,450
1936	525,842	649,860	90,247	37,507	37,154	5,423	10,163	435,595	559,613	132,515	115,250	88,024	44,337	179,487
1935	453,331	543,270	81,639	33,942	33,922	4,716	9,059	371,692	461,631	115,561	83,628	76,583	35,720	150,139
1934	414,308	480,893	77,898	30,553	33,570	4,287	9,488	336,410	402,995	113,349	71,685	60,998	34,894	122,069
1933	394,104	447,244	69,466	27,670	31,197	3,034	7,565	324,638	377,778	110,675	68,911	55,207	26,030	116,955
1932	342,489	390,323	70,429	29,843	30,039	3,072	7,475	272,060	319,894	94,434	39,544	54,845	27,242	103,829
1931	445,648	493,442	89,525	37,375	38,841	4,016	9,293	356,123	403,917	113,949	71,788	67,530	37,327	113,323
1930	520,280	591,331	114,110	46,448	48,148	7,590	11,924	406,170	477,221	117,821	109,791	79,414	37,591	132,604
1929	583,800	655,045	127,510	51,591	55,761	6,385	13,773	456,290	527,534	124,999	135,838	89,528	41,995	135,174
1928	539,200	608,001	126,768	46,690	56,151	8,548	15,379	412,432	481,233	119,254	119,301	75,728	39,870	127,080
1927	532,500	594,755	120,523	43,388	56,550	8,098	12,487	411,977	474,232	121,036	112,805	78,020	40,559	121,812
1926	540,500	602,196	131,293	44,834	69,859	6,424	10,176	409,207	470,903	108,023	115,791	88,270	36,798	122,021
1925	483,400	548,200	108,548	42,793	49,251	7,317	9,187	374,852	439,652	105,090	110,626	59,981	49,787	114,168
1924	453,700	487,167	101,562	36,425	49,008	4,962	11,167	352,138	385,605	88,554	92,563	77,270	34,101	93,117

[a] Unadjusted commerce refers to commerce counted in two locations.
Source: Bureau of the Census, Historical Statistics of the United States, Colonial Times to 1957, 453.

came more pronounced in the 1930s. During the last three years of the Second World War, when shipbuilding in the United States proceeded at fever pitch, American vessels began to take up a sharply increased share of commerce to foreign lands. Internal waterways—the rivers, lakes, and canals—continued to be important to transportation in the United States, and the outlay of money for river and harbor improvements steadily grew. A sharp increase in activity in the 1930s was tied in with various work relief, antidepression activity on the part of the national government. The decline in expendi-

tures during the Second World War suggested that during 1941–45 the priorities of the United States rested in other areas of activity.

The Age of the Transatlantic Liner The way to travel to and from Europe during the years 1914–45 was by sea. Alternative methods had either failed or not yet come of age. A brief experiment with a helium-filled airship called a dirigible, zeppelin, or blimp collapsed abruptly in the 1930s. Travel by airplane barely had started to surface by the 1940s. Even the numerous warplanes that traversed

TABLE 5.18 SOME FAMOUS LINERS

Ship	Line	Maiden Voyage	Length	Gross Tonnage	Normal Speed
Lusitania/Mauretania	Cunard (British)	1907	762 ft.	31,550/31,938	25 knots
Olympic/Titanic	White Star (British)	1911–1912	852	45,324/46,329	21 knots
Leviathan (Vaterland)	United States (Hamburg–America)	1914	907	59,956	23 knots
Ile de France	French	1927	764	43,153	23 knots
Bremen	North German Lloyd	1929	899	51,656	27 knots
Rex	Italia	1932	833	51,062	28 knots
Normandie	French	1935	981	82,799	29 knots
Queen Mary	Cunard–White Star	1936	975	80,774	29 knots
Queen Elizabeth	Cunard–White Star	1940	987	83,673	29 knots

Source: Byron S. Miller, *Sail, Steam, and Splendor: A Picture History of Life Aboard the Transatlantic Liners* (New York, 1977), 284.

Genuine queens of the sea, each displacing more than 80,000 tons, the *Normandie (left)*, *Queen Mary (center)*, and *Queen Elizabeth (right)* are docked together in New York. (Courtesy of the Mariners' Museum, Newport News, Virginia)

the Atlantic during 1942–45 were intended to transport the plane rather than the passengers. The soldiers who went to fight Hitler's army—and earlier the army of Kaiser Wilhelm—traveled by ship. Ships carried the millions of immigrants to America's shores. Except for rare exceptions late in the period, Americans who had any reason for going to Europe went by sea.

The most famous of these ships were the great transatlantic liners of the first half of the twentieth century. Although these vessels carried passengers of many kinds—most of them in fact crowded into steerage, later called third, or tourist, class—they were noted for pursuit of the first-class business. These ships became floating palaces that competed in size, luxury, and prestige, and in the 1930s they raced for the speed record in crossing the Atlantic. Admirers addressed them as grand ladies of the sea with personality unique to the vessel—this one elegant, this one gay and flighty. In times of peace they were symbols of national status; in times of war most of them became transporters of soldiers. Virtually every one had a storied existence and several—for example, *Titanic, Lusitania,* and *Normandie*—a storied death. Only one of the most famous vessels—the mammoth *Leviathan,* which in fact was the confiscated (1917) Ger-

man liner *Vaterland*—belonged to an American shipping line, but all were part of American history. They were built in Europe, and when they were fit to sail, all headed for New York.

TABLE 5.19 COMMERCIAL OCEAN TRAFFIC ON THE PANAMA CANAL: 1915 TO 1945

Year	Number of Transits	Tolls ($1,000)	Cargo (1,000 long tons)
1945	1,939	7,244	8,604
1944	1,562	5,456	7,003
1943	1,822	7,357	10,600
1942	2,688	9,752	13,607
1941	4,727	18,158	24,951
1940	5,370	21,145	27,299
1939	5,903	23,661	27,867
1938	5,524	23,170	27,387
1937	5,387	23,102	28,108
1936	5,382	23,479	26,506

(continued)

In wartime, passenger liners often became troopships, as in the case of America's *Leviathan* (a confiscated German vessel), here "dazzle-painted" to confuse German submarines. (National Archives)

TABLE 5.19 (continued)

Year	Number of Transits	Tolls ($1,000)	Cargo (1,000 long tons)
1935	5,180	23,307	25,310
1934	5,234	24,047	24,704
1933	4,162	19,602	18,161
1932	4,362	20,695	19,799
1931	5,370	24,625	25,065
1930	6,027	27,060	30,018
1929	6,289	27,111	30,648
1928	6,253	26,922	29,616
1927	5,293	24,212	27,734
1926	5,087	22,920	26,030
1925	4,592	21,394	23,957
1924	5,158	24,285	26,993
1923	3,908	17,504	19,566
1922	2,665	11,192	10,883
1921	2,791	11,269	11,596
1920	2,393	8,508	9,372
1919	1,948	6,164	6,910
1918	1,989	6,429	7,526
1917	1,738	5,621	7,055
1916[a]	724	2,403	3,093
1915[b]	1,058	4,367	4,888

[a]Canal closed about 7 months by slides.
[b]Canal opened Aug. 15, 1914.
Source: Bureau of the Census, *Historical Statistics of the United States, Colonial Times to 1957,* 454.

Communication

Postal Service

Use of the United States mail system remained the standard and most reliable method of written communication during the period 1914–45. The number of post offices decreased—there were 15,000 fewer in 1945 than in 1914—as offices in villages were phased out and consolidation took place in large cities. Although the pace of business steadily increased, the number of workers changed only slightly; the price of postage remained stable. Because of revenue earned from first-class mail—the other types consistently lost money—the postal service maintained a close relationship between revenue and expenditure, and occasionally it even turned a profit.

TABLE 5.20 POSTAL SERVICE OPERATIONS

[In thousands, except number of post offices]

Year	Post Offices	Revenues	Expenditures	Ordinary Postage Stamps Issued	Stamped Envelopes and Wrappers Issued	Postal Cards Issued	Pieces of Matter of All Kinds Handled
1945	41,792	1,314,240	1,145,002	20,239,986	2,064,773	2,282,280	37,912,067
1944	42,161	1,112,877	1,068,986	19,106,171	1,902,312	1,912,990	34,930,685
1943	42,654	966,227	952,529	19,123,977	1,797,400	2,316,990	32,818,261
1942	43,358	859,817	873,950	19,492,121	1,676,573	2,370,061	30,117,633
1941	43,739	812,827	836,858	16,381,321	1,645,254	2,400,188	29,235,791
1940	44,024	766,948	807,629	16,381,427	1,649,548	2,26,519	27,749,467
1939	44,327	745,955	784,549	15,073,795	1,605,075	2,170,572	26,444,846
1938	44,586	728,634	772,307	14,912,092	1,643,815	2,186,720	26,041,979
1937	44,877	726,201	772,743	15,108,639	1,663,818	2,226,153	25,801,278
1936	45,230	665,343	753,616	13,835,399	1,647,891	1,917,793	23,571,315
1935	45,686	630,795	696,503	13,610,497	1,617,677	1,754,030	22,331,752
1934	46,506	586,733	630,732	12,525,716	1,580,819	1,590,257	20,625,826
1933	47,641	587,631	699,887	11,917,442	1,644,993	1,389,523	19,868,455
1932	48,159	588,171	793,684	14,650,970	2,384,792	1,334,753	24,306,743
1931	48,733	656,463	802,484	15,559,164	2,847,439	1,531,245	26,544,352
1930	49,063	705,484	803,667	16,268,856	3,164,127	1,643,212	27,887,823
1929	49,482	696,947	782,343	16,917,274	3,228,586	1,783,897	27,951,548
1928	49,944	693,633	725,699	16,676,492	3,201,458	1,872,040	26,837,005
1927	50,266	683,122	714,577	15,999,701	3,145,946	1,834,456	26,686,555
1926	50,601	659,819	679,704	16,333,410	3,001,858	1,668,240	25,483,528
1925	50,957	599,591	639,281	17,386,555	2,997,177	1,497,366	. . .
1924	51,266	572,948	587,876	15,954,475	2,964,464	1,293,184	. . .
1923	51,613	532,827	556,851	15,478,095	2,721,475	1,253,196	23,054,831
1922	51,950	484,853	545,644	14,261,948	2,364,372	1,111,124	. . .
1921	52,168	463,491	620,993	13,869,934	2,738,934	1,081,206	. . .

Year	Post Offices	Revenues	Expenditures	Ordinary Postage Stamps Issued	Stamped Envelopes and Wrappers Issued	Postal Cards Issued	Pieces of Matter of All Kinds Handled
1920	52,641	437,150	454,322	13,212,790	2,350,073	986,156	. . .
1919	53,084	436,239	362,497	15,020,470	1,844,884	456,924	. . .
1918	54,347	388,976	324,833	13,065,784	1,819,307	707,111	. . .
1917	55,414	329,726	319,838	12,451,522	2,161,108	1,112,337	. . .
1916	55,935	312,057	306,204	11,671,842	1,853,791	1,047,894	. . .
1915	56,880	287,248	298,546	11,226,386	1,793,764	975,542	. . .
1914	56,810	287,934	283,543	11,112,254	1,864,713	962,072	. . .

Source: Bureau of the Census, *Historical Statistics of the United States, Colonial Times to 1957,* 496.

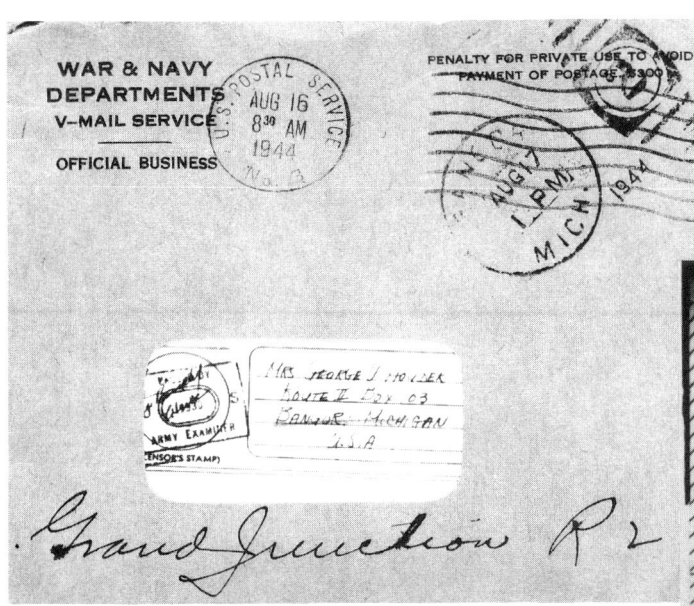

To save money, space, and labor during the Second World War, the government adopted a miniature "V-mail" for soldiers abroad to use. Shown here is the envelope, whose actual size was 4⁷⁄₈″ × 3½″. (Courtesy John T. Houdek)

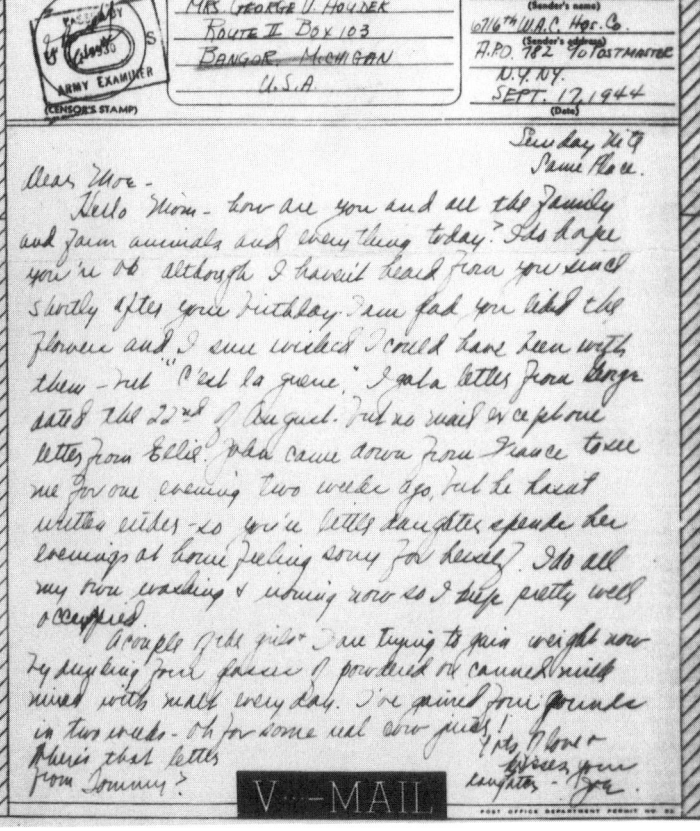

A V-mail letter. The actual size was 4″ × 5″. (Courtesy John T. Houdek)

TABLE 5.21 TYPES OF MAIL AND EMPLOYEES, 1926–1945

[In millions, except employees in thousands]

Year	First-class Mail			Second-class Mail			Third-class Mail			Fourth-class Mail			Airmail, Domestic			Post Office Employees
	Reve-nues	Ex-penses	Pieces	Reve-nues	Ex-penses	Pieces	Reve-nues	Ex-penses	Pieces	Reve-nues	Ex-penses	Pieces	Reve-nues	Ex-penses	Pieces	
1945	615	373	21,010	29	144	5,522	76	99	5,446	232	232	1,028	81	49	876	436
1944	540	369	20,760	29	137	4,635	62	87	4,409	202	216	961	79	49	1,092	389
1943	a	a	a	a	a	a	a	a	a	a	a	a	a	a	a	374
1942	459	293	16,972	26	112	4,571	74	98	5,435	150	168	779	33	37	463	369
1941	432	278	15,989	25	109	4,607	82	105	6,075	141	161	738	23	31	323	361
1940	413	267	15,224	24	110	4,577	75	101	5,556	133	155	712	19	28	259	353
1939	400	263	14,657	23	111	4,310	70	94	5,181	133	150	693	16	25	221	348
1938	389	259	14,226	24	114	4,377	71	94	5,272	129	146	670	15	22	210	345
1937	384	254	13,882	24	113	4,529	71	91	5,356	132	146	685	12	19	168	332
1936	355	246	12,731	22	112	4,353	63	86	4,674	121	139	618	9	16	134	323
1935	343	229	12,498	20	106	4,138	54	75	4,030	112	133	573	6	12	89	308
1934	325	205	11,557	21	98	3,956	50	67	3,612	101	121	531	5	15	57	314
1933	332	227	10,878	19	108	3,869	50	79	3,753	100	132	530	6	23	60	321
1932	310	276	14,598	23	125	4,552	50	79	3,641	113	146	617	6	23	89	332
1931	335	277	15,824	27	124	4,857	58	81	4,100	138	158	766	6	17	88	338
1930	359	278	16,832	30	120	4,968	61	83	4,325	151	167	837	5	15	69	339
1929	365	287	17,170	29	123	4,834	61	80	4,341	142	162	770	...	...	...	339
1928	355	268	16,706	34	119	4,678	66	72	3,838	143	150	752	...	...	...	336
1927	345	262	16,284	35	119	4,753	68	72	4,062	141	145	743	...	...	...	332
1926	321	247	15,266	34	117	4,658	69	71	3,962	144	147	770	...	...	...	329

[a]Not available.
Source: Bureau of the Census, *Historical Statistics of the United States, Colonial Times to 1957,* 498.

TABLE 5.22 POSTAL RATES

Postal Rates for First-class Mail, Letters, and Postcards		
Year of Rate Change	Letters, Nonlocal	Postcards
1940[a]	3¢ per oz.	1¢
1932	3¢ per oz.	1¢
1919	2¢ per oz.	1¢
1917	3¢ per oz.	2¢
1885 to 1917	2¢ per oz.	1¢

Postal Rates for Domestic Airmail	
Effective Date	Rate
1944, Mar. 26	8¢ per oz.
1934, Jul. 1	6¢ per oz.
1932, Jul. 6	8¢ first oz., 13¢ each additional oz.
1928, Aug. 1	5¢ first oz., 10¢ each additional oz.
1927, Feb. 1	10¢ per 1/2 oz., regardless of distance
1926, Feb. 15	Contract air routes: Under 1,000 miles, 10¢ per oz. 1,000–1,500 miles, 15¢ per oz. Over 1,500 miles, 20¢ per oz. An additional 5¢ per oz. for each airmail zone[b] Government Routes: Daytime zone rate, 8¢ per oz.[b] New York to Chicago (overnight), 10¢ per oz.

Postal Rates for Domestic Airmail	
Effective Date	Rate
1925, Jul. 1	Government operated: 8¢ per oz. daytime zone rate;[b] 10¢ per oz. New York to Chicago overnight
1924, Jul. 1	8¢ per oz., per zone[b]
1919, Jul. 18	2¢ per oz.[c]
1918, Dec. 15	6¢ per oz.
1918, Jul. 15	16¢ per oz. and 6¢ each additional oz., of which 10¢ was for special delivery
1918, May 15	24¢ per oz., of which 10¢ was for special delivery

[a]A change in 1940 specified that current rate did not apply to first-class local mail.
[b]Zones were: (1) New York–Chicago; (2) Chicago–Cheyenne; (3) Cheyenne–San Francisco.
[c]Between Jul. 18, 1919, and Jul. 1, 1924, there was no genuine airmail service. Some mail was carried on planes at the regular first-class rate.
Source: Wattenberg, *Statistical History,* 807.

More and more Americans relied on their telephones. The number of telephones doubled in the fifteen years after 1914, the bulk of them part of the vast Bell system. The number of telephones actually decreased in the 1930s. In the last half of that decade the government stepped up efforts to take the telephone to the countryside, where in many areas phones were scarce. Technology continued to improve, with a tendency toward greater automation and less need for operator-assisted calls. In rural areas, however, one often found people speaking into the wall-mounted box with a crank on the side, holding the separate receiver to the ear. The telephone took on added significance during the Second World War. A call home often carried a sad farewell from a soldier in transience, his station and his fate unknown. A telephone call to or from stations abroad was for the individual citizen virtually beyond reach: Such calls were very expensive; in addition, telephone lines were fully given over to wartime necessity. The telegraph remained an important means of communication, well suited to a period of war. Because the sender was charged per word, the messages were short, abrupt, and frequently impersonal. Arrival of a telegram almost always meant that one was about to learn very important news. The most dreaded telegram of wartime carried information about a family member who had fallen in action.

TABLE 5.23   TELEPHONES AND AVERAGE DAILY CALLS

[In thousands; census figures in italics]

| Year | Telephones | | | | | Average Daily Calls | | | |
| | Total | | Bell | Independent Companies | | Bell | | Independent Companies | |
	Number	Per 1,000 Population		Connecting with Bell	Not Connecting with Bell	Local Exchange	Toll	Local Exchange	Toll
1945	27,867	198.1	23,202	4,651	14	88,703	4,831	17,667	99
1944	26,859	192.9	22,309	4,534	16	84,493	4,373	17,227	107
1943	26,381	191.6	21,970	4,345	66	84,922	4,047	17,138	93
1942	24,919	183.4	20,694	4,159	66	86,239	3,552	17,141	68
1941	23,521	175.3	19,476	3,975	70	84,241	3,231	16,659	69
1940	21,928	165.1	18,066	3,795	67	79,040	2,844	16,110	306
1939	20,831	158.5	17,086	3,678	67	73,518	2,696	15,292	294
1938	19,953	153.0	16,287	3,598	68	69,591	2,587	14,739	283
1937	*19,453*	*150.*	*15,332*	. . .	. . .	. . .	. . .	. . .	. . .
1937	19,453	150.4	15,848	3,537	68	68,362	2,673	14,678	287
1936	18,433	143.5	14,940	3,422	71	64,516	2,579	14,124	281
1935	17,424	136.4	13,845	3,509	71	58,809	2,276	14,631	284
1934	16,969	133.8	13,458	3,437	74	56,648	2,142	14,332	278
1933	16,711	132.6	13,163	3,472	76	55,199	2,047	14,481	273
1932	*17,424*	*139.*	*13,793*	. . .	. . .	. . .	. . .	. . .	. . .
1932	17,424	139.1	13,793	3,548	84	58,813	2,251	15,637	299
1931	19,707	158.3	15,407	4,206	94	62,205	2,700	17,245	350
1930	20,202	163.4	15,682	4,416	103	62,365	2,933	17,860	362
1929	20,068	163.8	15,414	4,543	110	61,034	3,139	18,107	370
1928	19,341	159.6	14,525	4,672	144	56,196	2,839	17,895	370
1927	*18,523*	*155.*	*13,726*	. . .	. . .	. . .	. . .	. . .	. . .
1927	18,523	154.6	13,726	4,639	158	52,581	2,615	18,100	369
1926	17,746	150.0	12,816	4,758	172	49,980	2,375	18,453	372
1925	16,936	145.2	12,035	4,685	216	46,702	2,098	18,148	352
1924	16,073	139.7	11,242	4,581	250	43,981	1,835	18,260	324
1923	15,369	135.9	10,406	4,594	369	41,109	1,683	18,516	322
1922	*14,347*	*130.*	*9,515*	. . .	. . .	. . .	. . .	. . .	. . .
1922	14,347	129.2	9,515	4,401	432	36,831	1,523	18,329	317
1921	13,875	126.9	8,914	4,466	495	33,671	1,356	18,447	281
1920	13,329	123.9	8,334	4,268	727	31,836	1,327	18,371	280
1919	12,669	119.7	7,739	4,057	873	29,286	1,167	18,158	276
1918	12,078	115.2	7,202	3,864	1,012	30,001	1,067	18,753	285
1917	*11,717*	*112.*	*7,327*	*3,165*	. . .	. . .	. . .	. . .	. . .
1917	11,717	112.7	7,032	3,458	1,226	30,845	1,009	19,785	302
1916	11,241	109.5	6,545	3,348	1,348	28,530	890	19,856	302
1915	10,524	103.9	5,968	3,204	1,351	25,184	819	18,535	282
1914	10,046	100.6	5,585	3,074	1,388	22,775	799	17,198	262

Source: Bureau of the Census, *Historical Statistics of the United States, Colonial Times to 1957,* 480.

TABLE 5.24 TELEPHONE TOLL RATES BETWEEN NEW YORK CITY AND SELECTED CITIES: 1915–1945

[Rate for station-to-station, daytime, 3-minute call]

Effective Date	Between New York City and—			
	Philadelphia	Chicago	Denver	San Francisco
1945, Jul.	$0.45	$1.75	$2.35	$2.50
1941, Jul.	.45	1.75	3.25	4.00
1940, May	.45	1.90	3.25	4.00
1937, Jan.	.45	2.20	4.50	6.50
1936, Sep.	.50	2.50	5.25	7.50
1930, Jan.	.50	3.00	6.00	9.00
1929, Feb.	.60	3.00	6.00	9.00
1927, Dec.	.60	3.25	6.00	9.00
1926, Oct.	.60	3.40	7.25	11.30
1919, Jan.	.55	4.65	10.40	16.50
1917, Jun.	.75[a]	5.00[a]	11.25	18.50
1917, Mar.	[b]	[b]	11.25	19.80
1915, Jan.	[b]	[b]	11.25	20.70

[a]Rates in effect immediately prior to Jan. 21, 1919, according to an item in the *New York Times* for Jan. 23, 1919.
[b]Not available.
Source: Bureau of the Census, *Historical Statistics of the United States, Colonial Times to 1957,* 481.

TABLE 5.25 DOMESTIC TELEGRAPH INDUSTRY, 1916–1945

[In thousands, except employees, census figures in italics]

Year	Messages Handled	Private-Line Telegraph Service Revenues		Miles of Wire	Employees	
		Telegraph Companies	Telephone Companies		Number	Wages and Salaries
1945	236,169	3,572	23,627	2,247	63,446	126,662
1944	225,462	3,655	20,727	2,272	61,481	112,553
1943	231,692	3,688	17,590	2,303	61,037	111,872
1942	223,148	3,889	19,318	2,294	64,674	92,450
1941	210,928	3,079	14,830	2,281	65,363	84,267
1940	191,645	2,170	14,621	2,269	59,670	74,736
1939	189,055	2,185	15,744	2,277	57,513	71,287
1938	185,639	2,056	16,834	2,279	57,190	70,124
1937	200,711	1,981	19,098	2,275	64,084	77,745
1937	*206,987*	. . .	. . .	*2,302*	*64,254*	*77,928*
1936	193,566	1,897	18,538	2,270	67,862	71,155
1935	176,250	1,782	17,007	2,245	62,257	65,030
1934	155,215	1,749	19,131	2,247	62,839	65,810
1933	143,553	1,856	20,023	2,245	58,368	60,401
1932	143,075	1,830	21,284	2,239	60,997	64,760
1932	*147,941*	. . .	. . .	*2,260*	*60,933*	*66,988*
1931	183,373	1,787	25,245	2,250	72,916	90,084
1930	211,971	1,881	27,034	2,269	84,962	108,557
1929	234,050	1,947	25,197	2,251	87,435	113,928
1928	211,559	1,754	21,057	2,202	77,644	94,415
1927	203,365	1,853	18,016	2,095	76,183	91,493
1927	*215,595*	. . .	. . .	*2,138*	*74,903*	*89,984*
1926	203,035	1,899	16,548	1,977	79,755	101,003
1925	185,187	1,601	15,153	1,944	73,262	90,911
1924	162,700	1,510	13,207	1,884	68,451	80,692
1923	158,468	1,502	13,106	1,836	69,045	79,341
1922	149,219	1,689	12,145	1,807	62,576	70,497
1922	*181,519*	. . .	. . .	*1,845*	*62,299*	*68,737*
1921	139,544	1,873	11,270	1,787	64,395	71,942
1920	155,884	1,489	10,541	1,711	74,448	86,037
1919	139,435	1,318	7,969	1,686	64,181	66,351
1918	134,031	1,121	5,811	1,620	69,528	58,376
1917	129,273	1,300	5,202	1,863	60,122	46,953
1917	*151,725*	. . .	. . .	*1,889*	*60,376*	*40,512*
1916	. . .	1,365	4,162	1,877	. . .	. . .

Source: Bureau of the Census, *Historical Statistics of the United States, Colonial Times to 1957,* 484–485.

Radio and Television

Radio came to be most commonly thought of as entertainment, but it remained after its development at the start of the 1920s a unique and exceptionally important means of communication. Radio by the start of the 1940s passed newspapers as the primary supplier of news to the American people; it also carried weather and market reports and various types of information programs. Through advertisements, radio guided people in their purchases; it communicated how people communicated—how they used words—and even suggested what they should think. Radio grew so rapidly in the 1920s and 1930s that it reached almost every family in the country, even those that did not have a set. Even though television arrived on the American scene in the 1930s, it failed to make a major mark on communication before the end of the Second World War. There were probably fewer than 5,000 sets in existence and only two sending stations in 1941. Virtually all the activity was in the Northeast. Television remained synonymous with the bold, new postwar world.

Publications

Production of books, which might be counted as information, entertainment, or both, underwent modest growth during the years 1914–45, with two periods standing as important exceptions: the period of the early 1930s, when the cost of publication and of purchase were important considerations, and the period of the Second World War, when there was a paper shortage. In the early 1940s the inexpensive paperback editions began to appear on the scene, carrying signs of a publication revolution in the making. Newspapers were indispensable carriers of information. Some publishers—the "Hearst" press, or the *Chicago Tribune,* for example—sought to be deliberate molders of opinion. The number of daily and Sunday newspapers steadily declined during the period, although the amount of circulation did not. More and more cities had only one newspaper. Political observers often decried the absence of competing points of view in the press, but the effect was somewhat offset by the fact that more people received their news from radio.

TABLE 5.26   RADIO AND TELEVISION

Year	Radio Stations Standard (AM)	Frequency Modulation (FM)	Television Stations	Radio Sets Produced (thousands)	Families with Radio (thousands)
1921	1	. . .	. . .	. . .	. . .
1922	30	. . .	. . .	100	60
1923	556	. . .	. . .	500	400
1924	530	. . .	. . .	1,500	1,250
1923	571	. . .	. . .	2,000	2,750
1926	528	. . .	. . .	1,750	4,500
1927	681	. . .	. . .	1,350	6,750
1928	677	. . .	. . .	3,250	8,000
1929	606	. . .	. . .	4,428	10,250
1930	618	. . .	. . .	3,789	13,750
1931	612	. . .	. . .	3,594	16,700
1932	604	. . .	. . .	2,446	18,450
1933	599	. . .	. . .	4,157	19,250
1934	583	. . .	. . .	4,479	20,400
1935	585	. . .	. . .	6,030	21,456
1936	616	. . .	. . .	8,249	22,869
1937	646	. . .	. . .	8,083	24,500
1938	689	. . .	. . .	7,142	26,667
1939	722	. . .	. . .	10,763	27,500
1939	765	. . .	. . .	11,831	28,500
1941	831	5	2	13,642	29,300
1942	887	7	4	4,307[a]	30,600
1943	910	18	4	. . .[a]	30,800
1944	910	49	6	. . .[a]	32,500
1945	919	52	6	. . .[a]	33,100

[a]Production of commercial radio receivers stopped during the Second World War, from April 1942 until October 1945.
Source: Bureau of the Census, *Historical Statistics of the United States, Colonial Times to 1957,* 491.

TABLE 5.27   BOOKS—NEW BOOKS, NEW EDITIONS, AND PAMPHLETS PUBLISHED: 1914—1945

Year	Total	New Books	New Editions	Pamphlets
1945	6,548	5,386	1,162	. . .
1944	6,970	5,807	1,163	. . .
1943	8,325	6,764	1,561	. . .
1942	9,525	7,786	1,739	. . .
1941	11,112	9,337	1,775	. . .
1940	11,328	9,515	1,813	. . .
1939	10,640	9,015	1,625	. . .
1938	11,067	9,464	1,603	. . .
1937	10,912	9,273	1,639	. . .
1936	10,436	8,584	1,852	. . .
1935	8,766	6,914	1,852	. . .
1934	8,198	6,788	1,410	. . .
1933	8,092	6,813	1,279	. . .
1932	9,035	7,556	1,479	. . .
1931	10,307	8,506	1,801	. . .
1930	10,027	8,134	1,893	. . .
1929	10,187	8,342	1,845	. . .
1928	10,354	7,614	1,562	1,178
1927	10,153	7,450	1,449	1,254
1926	9,925	6,832	1,527	1,566
1925	9,574	6,680	1,493	1,401
1924	9,012	6,380	1,158	1,474
1923	8,863	6,257	921	1,685
1922	8,638	5,998	865	1,775
1921	8,329	5,438	1,008	1,883
1920	8,422	5,101	1,086	2,235
1919	8,594	7,625	969	(2,853)
1918	9,237	8,085	1,152	(2,876)
1917	10,060	8,849	1,211	(2,051)
1916	10,445	9,160	1,285	(1,941)
1915	9,734	8,349	1,385	(1,532)
1914	12,010	10,175	1,835	(1,662)

[a]During 1914–19 pamphlets were counted but not included in the total number of books published. During 1920–28 pamphlets were included in books published. After 1928 pamphlets were not counted.
Source: Bureau of the Census, *Historical Statistics of the United States, Colonial Times to 1957,* 499.

**TABLE 5.28   NEWSPAPERS—NUMBER AND
CIRCULATION OF DAILY AND SUNDAY
NEWSPAPERS: 1920–1945**

Year	Daily		Sunday	
	Number	Circulation	Number	Circulation
1945	1,749	48,384,188	484	39,860,036
1944	1,744	45,954,838	481	37,945,622
1943	1,754	44,392,829	467	37,291,832
1942	1,787	43,374,850	474	35,293,543
1941	1,857	42,080,391	510	33,435,575
1940	1,878	41,131,611	525	32,371,092
1939	1,888	39,670,682	524	31,519,009
1938	1,936	39,571,839	523	30,480,922
1937	1,993	41,418,730	539	30,956,916
1936	1,989	40,292,266	520	29,962,120
1935	1,950	38,155,540	518	28,147,343
1934	1,929	36,709,010	505	26,544,516
1933	1,911	35,175,238	506	24,040,630
1932	1,913	36,407,689	518	24,859,888
1931	1,923	38,761,187	513	25,701,798
1930	1,942	39,589,172	521	26,413,047
1929	1,944	39,425,615	528	26,879,536
1928	1,939	37,972,488	522	25,771,588
1927	1,949	37,966,656	526	25,469,037
1926	2,001	36,001,803	545	24,435,192
1925	2,008	33,739,369	548	23,354,622
1924	2,014	32,999,437	539	22,219,646
1923	2,036	31,453,683	547	21,463,289
1922	2,033	29,780,328	546	19,712,874
1921	2,028	28,423,740	545	19,041,413
1920	2,042	27,790,656	522	17,083,604

Source: Bureau of the Census, *Historical Statistics of the United States, Colonial Times to 1957,* 500.

CHAPTER 6 Vital Statistics

Births and Deaths

The trend of the birthrate for all groups generally was downward through this period until the 1930s, when the decline became more pronounced. The depression clearly affected all aspects of life. The birthrate turned modestly upward during the years of the Second World War, although it might be more proper to say that it returned to roughly what it had been during the first half of the 1920s, before the depression struck. By 1945 the general birthrate was approximately one-third lower than what it had been in 1915. The birthrate and fertility rate were significantly higher for nonwhites than for whites. Otherwise the trend for each category was similar: a gradual reduction of both, sharper decline in the 1930s, and a small increase in the 1940s. The rates of illegitimacy were higher for nonwhites than whites, although rates increased markedly for both

groups throughout the period. Slightly more males than females were born in 1915, and the number remained remarkably steady through all these years—approximately fifty-five more males per thousand. During no year did female births outnumber males, and the slight male majority was exactly the same in 1945 as it had been in 1915.

The sharpest change was in the excess of births over deaths, even with the declining birthrate. The death rate declined steadily, more for nonwhites than whites, more for females than males. Life expectancy lengthened considerably for all groups. Women lived 4.3 years longer than men in 1945, exactly what the gap had been in 1915. Causes of death were familiar. Heart disease, the largest killer in 1915, was an even greater danger in 1945. Pneumonia declined somewhat as a threat to life, and cancer increased in importance,

TABLE 6.1 BIRTHRATES AND FERTILITY RATES BY RACE

Year	Birthrate (Births per 1,000 Population[a])			Fertility Rate (Births per 1,000 Women Aged 15–44 Years)		
	Total	White	Nonwhite	Total	White	Nonwhite
1945	20.4	19.7	26.5	85.9	83.4	106.0
1944	21.2	20.5	27.4	88.8	86.3	108.5
1943	22.7	22.1	28.3	94.3	92.3	111.0
1942	22.2	21.5	27.7	91.5	89.5	107.6
1941	20.3	19.5	27.3	83.4	80.7	105.4
1940	19.4	18.6	26.7	79.9	77.1	102.4
1939	18.8	18.0	26.1	77.6	74.8	100.1
1938	19.2	18.4	26.3	79.1	76.5	100.5
1937	18.7	17.9	26.0	77.1	74.4	99.4
1936	18.4	17.6	25.1	75.8	73.3	95.9
1935	18.7	17.9	25.8	77.2	74.5	98.4
1934	19.0	18.1	26.3	78.5	75.8	100.4
1933	18.4	17.6	25.5	76.3	73.7	97.3
1932	19.5	18.7	26.9	81.7	79.0	103.0
1931	20.2	19.5	26.6	84.6	82.4	102.1
1930	21.3	20.6	27.5	89.2	87.1	105.9
1929	21.2	20.5	27.3	89.3	87.3	106.1
1928	22.2	21.5	28.5	93.8	91.7	111.0
1927	23.5	22.7	31.1	99.8	97.1	121.7
1926	24.2	23.1	33.4	102.6	99.2	130.3
1925	25.1	24.1	34.2	106.6	103.3	134.0
1924	26.1	25.1	34.6	110.9	107.8	135.6
1923	26.0	25.2	33.2	110.5	108.0	130.5
1922	26.2	25.4	33.2	111.2	108.8	130.8
1921	28.1	27.3	35.8	119.8	117.2	140.8
1920	27.7	26.9	35.0	117.9	115.4	137.5
1919	26.1	25.3	32.4	111.2	. . .	. . .
1918	28.2	27.6	33.0	119.8	. . .	. . .
1917	28.5	27.9	32.9	121.0	. . .	. . .
1916	29.1	28.5	. . .	123.4	121.8	. . .
1915	29.5	28.9	. . .	125.0	123.2	. . .
1914	29.9	29.3	. . .	126.6	124.6	. . .

[a]Birthrates were based on estimates compiled from statistics supplied by a changing number of states. Before 1915 it was only 10 states and Washington, D.C. Beginning with 1933 all states provided registration statistics.
Source: Department of Health, Education, and Welfare, *Vital Statistics Rates in the United States, 1940–1960* (Washington, D.C., 1968), 114.

As suggested by this family in Gee's Bend, Alabama, in 1937, there was a continuing "baby boom" in black America. (Arthur Rothstein, *The Depression Years*)

but both remained major killers. Tuberculosis stayed in the top five causes of death, owing in no small part to its threat to nonwhite people. The best chance for a long life came to white females, the worst to a black or to a Native-American male.

There were indications that in health and medical care the United States was entering the modern world during this era, but markings of an earlier age remained numerous and conspicuous. The trend of childbirth clearly was in the direction of physician-assisted births in hospitals. But doctors still delivered babies in the family homes frequently, and the use of midwives remained a familiar, if diminishing, practice. Medical insurance programs covered approximately 25% of the population in 1945—a small portion, to be sure, but considerably higher than in 1914, when such programs were virtually unheard of.

The impact of being something other than white in America was in no area more conspicuous or more meaningful than in vital statistics—numbers that related to life and death. Use by the Bureau of the Census of the term *nonwhite* was to considerable extent a measurement of the status of black people, inasmuch as approximately 96% of those people classified as nonwhite were black. A good portion of the remaining 4%–5% were Native Americans—a group of people who, incidentally, produced in some categories even more distressing statistics than African Americans. Even so, if the term *nonwhite* was not exactly synonymous with the term *black*, it was close enough to supply a good indication of the status of black peo-

TABLE 6.2 BIRTHS BY SEX, EXCESS OF BIRTHS OVER DEATHS

Year	Number of Births			Number of Male Births per 1,000 Female Births	Excess of Births over Deaths
	Total	Male	Female		
1915	776,304	398,615	377,689	1,055	339,711
1920	1,508,874	775,322	733,552	1,057	672,740
1925	1,878,880	966,973	911,907	1,060	848,362
1930	2,203,958	1,131,976	1,071,982	1,056	882,591
1935	2,155,105	1,105,489	1,049,616	1,053	762,353
1936	2,144,790	1,099,465	1,045,325	1,052	665,562
1937	2,203,337	1,130,641	1,072,696	1,054	752,910
1938	2,286,962	1,172,541	1,114,421	1,052	905,571
1939	2,265,588	1,162,600	1,102,988	1,054	877,691
1940	2,360,399	1,211,684	1,148,715	1,055	943,130
1941	2,513,427	1,289,734	1,223,693	1,054	1,115,785
1942	2,808,996	1,444,365	1,364,631	1,058	1,423,809
1943	1,934,860	1,506,959	1,427,901	1,055	1,475,316
1944	2,794,800	1,435,301	1,359,499	1,056	1,383,462
1945	2,735,456	1,404,587	1,330,869	1,055	1,333,737

Source: Bureau of the Census, *Statistical Abstract of the United States, 1947* (Washington, D.C., 1947), 68.

ple in society. That status was not enviable. One could document the difference between the standard of living of whites and blacks by looking at general death rates, rates of infant mortality, and the availability of doctors for childbirth. Although higher nonwhite birthrates and strikingly higher rates of illegitimate births represented a different sort of vital statistic, they also stood as a reflection of circumstance and a measurement of lifestyle and standard of living. Perhaps the statistic for life expectancy told the story best. Whites on the average could expect to live in excess of sixteen years longer than nonwhites in 1915. While life expectancy expanded for both groups with the passage of years, and while the gap between white and nonwhite narrowed, in 1945 it still stood at more than ten years. A long and healthy life was not as reachable for as many people during 1914–45 as later would be the case. The existence of two world wars and outbreak of an incomparable influenza epidemic did not help. But one stood a considerably better chance if one were white.

TABLE 6.3 MIDWIVES AND DOCTORS: ATTENDANCE AT BIRTH BY RACE, 1935 AND 1940–1945

| Year and Race | Percentage Attended by— | | |
	Physician in Hospital	Physician Not in Hospital	Midwife or Other
All Races			
1935	36.9	50.6	12.5
1940	55.8	35.0	9.3
1941	61.2	30.2	8.6
1942	67.9	24.7	7.4
1943	72.1	21.0	6.9
1944	75.6	17.7	6.7
1945	78.8	14.7	6.5
White			
1935	39.6	54.0	6.4
1940	59.9	36.5	3.6
1941	65.7	31.2	3.1
1942	72.7	24.8	2.5
1943	77.2	20.6	2.2
1944	81.0	16.9	2.1
1945	84.3	13.7	2.0
Nonwhite			
1935	18.2	26.4	55.4
1940	26.7	24.1	49.2
1941	29.0	23.3	47.7
1942	30.6	24.0	45.3
1943	33.3	24.0	42.7
1944	37.0	23.1	39.9
1945	40.2	21.7	38.1

Source: Department of Health, Education, and Welfare, *Vital Statistics of the United States, 1950,* Vol. I (Washington, D.C., 1954), 95.

Illegitimate Births

The statistics below represent only a partial report on illegitimate births in the country. Three states failed to issue reports in any of these years; other states failed to do so for certain years. Absence of complete statistics obviously affected the total report, although the numbers of births were more profoundly different than the ratio. Two sets of statistics stand out in this table: the large difference in ratio between whites and nonwhites (most of whom were black), and the fact that the number of illegitimate births steadily increased for each group. The ratio in 1945 for whites, for example, approached double what it had been in 1917. It also must be remembered that illegitimacy was a sensitive topic—more so for this period than for later years, and that births continued to take place beyond the reach of public health facilities. In every state, some illegitimate births were never reported.

TABLE 6.4 ILLEGITIMATE BIRTHS BY RACE: BIRTH REGISTRATION AREA, 1917–1945 [a]

[Ratios per 1,000 births]

| Year | Number | | | Ratio | | |
	Total	White	Nonwhite	Total	White	Nonwhite
1917	20,464	12,238	8,226	20.2	13.0	120.1
1919	23,660	12,360	11,300	23.6	13.6	121.9
1921	34,824	17,440	17,384	26.6	14.8	128.5
1923	35,040	18,139	16,901	25.2	14.4	126.2
1925	37,414	21,564	15,850	25.3	16.0	120.6
1927	52,022	26,124	25,898	29.0	16.9	131.6
1929	60,921	27,780	33,141	33.9	17.7	143.5
1931	65,952	30,137	35,815	37.5	19.8	150.5
1933	73,389	31,742	41,647	41.8	21.3	158.9
1935	75,141	33,685	41,456	41.1	21.4	163.6
1937	74,938	32,231	42,707	40.2	20.1	163.9
1939	74,941	31,330	43,611	40.4	19.4	169.3
1941	83,067	33,220	49,847	40.8	19.0	176.0
1943	82,568	31,755	50,831	40.4	19.6	166.1
1945	95,047	40,056	54,991	46.2	22.8	183.0

[a] The following states did not require a statement of legitimacy of child: California, Massachusetts, and New York for each year; Texas for 1938 and 1939; Maryland, Nebraska, New Hampshire, and Wyoming for 1940–45; Colorado, Connecticut, and New Mexico for 1943–45; Arizona, Idaho, and Nevada for 1945.
Source: United States Public Health Service, *Vital Statistics of the United States, 1945,* pt. 1 (Washington, D.C., 1947), xxiv.

TABLE 6.5   CONTRACEPTIVE ACTIVITY BY RELIGIOUS GROUP, 1939–1940

Practices	Total Urban		Protestant		Catholic		Jewish		Christian Science	
	Num.	Pct.	Num.	Pct.	Num.	Pct.	Num.	Pct.	Num.	Pct.
Do not practice	417	17	281	17	110	23	17	10	9	20
Practice "simpler" methods only	428	18	244	14	163	34	10	6	11	24
Practice other	1,544	65	1,177	69	202	43	139	84	26	26
Total Respondents	2,389	100	1,702	100	475	100	166	100	46	100

Source: John W. Riley and Matilda White, "The Use of Various Methods of Contraception," *American Sociological Review* (December 1940), 895.

TABLE 6.6   METHODS OF CONTRACEPTION BY RELIGION, 1939–1940

Method	Protestant		Catholic		Jewish		Christian Science	
	Num.	Pct.	Num.	Pct.	Num.	Pct.	Num.	Pct.
Antiseptic douche	467	33	95	26	29	19	11	30
Jelly	420	30	52	14	56	38	8	22
Diaphragm	316	22	46	13	59	40	5	14
Condom	277	19	44	12	60	40	8	22
Safe period	75	5	140	38	2	1	2	6
Suppository	103	7	11	3	3	2	2	6
Plain douche	203	14	45	12	9	6	9	24
Coitus interruptus	74	5	24	7	3	2	2	6
Total methods used	1,935	135	457	125	221	148	47	130
Total contraceptors	1,421	100	365	100	149	100	37	100

Source: Riley and White, "Methods of Contraception," 899.

Birth Control

Contraception was such a controversial subject at the start of the twentieth century that the foremost advocate of birth control, Margaret Sanger, left the country because of harassment encountered in her efforts to establish a clinic. Most states forebade the sale of instruments of contraception, and a few states did not permit distribution of information about ways to limit the number of children. The Roman Catholic Church was especially emphatic in disallowing all methods of "artificial" birth control. With the emergence of a women's movement, capped with approval of woman suffrage in 1920, with relaxation of moral restraints in the aftermath of the First World War, and with a clear indication of a wish for smaller families, the attitude toward contraception also changed. Planned Parenthood Federation of America, an offshoot of the activities of Sanger, had affiliations in thirty-seven states in the 1940s. It engaged in numerous projects, including distribution of a manual, *Techniques of Conception Control.* A national survey of 3,500 women, most of whom were married (515 were single), reported in 1940 by the Market Research Corporation of America revealed that some 83% of the individuals questioned made some attempt to control conception, and the bulk of the efforts involved "artificial" methods. The position of the Catholic Church did not change, but the behavior of Catholics did. Whereas Protestants and Jews practiced birth control more fre-

quently than Catholics, only 23% of Catholics claimed to honor the church's ban on contraception, and 43% admitted to using the most popular devices on sale at the drug store—condoms, douches, and jellies. Other Catholics reported using so-called simple methods, such as plain douche, identifying the woman's "safe" period, or coitus interruptus. There were no contraceptive pills. The tables below measured the attitude toward birth control in 1940 by religious grouping in urban areas, where most of the participants resided, and by popularity of the most common methods.

With respect to birth control after conception, the first antiabortion law was passed in New York in 1828. Other states followed, and in the first half of the twentieth century abortion was illegal in all states. The most common exception was to save the mother's life. The laws were partly a product of moral consideration and partly a fear that the abortion itself presented a considerable hazard to the mother. Abortion therefore belonged to the underworld of health, medicine, and social behavior, or at least to the underground. An estimate in 1940 placed the number of abortions at 500,000 per year, all of them illegal, some performed by the women themselves, many by self-styled abortionists, who often were ill trained, opportunistic, and predatory. There were reports, for example, of abortions being performed on women who were not pregnant.

TABLE 6.7   INFANT MORTALITY RATES BY RACE FOR BIRTH REGISTRATION STATES

(Rates per 1,000 births, exclusive of stillbirths)

Year	Total	White	Black	Other
1915	99.9	98.6	180.6	196.2
1917	93.8	90.5	148.6	142.5
1919	86.6	83.0	134.3	88.2
1921	75.6	72.5	110.7	78.8
1923	77.1	73.5	119.9	85.8
1925	71.7	68.3	112.0	95.6
1927	64.6	60.6	99.9	103.4
1929	67.6	63.2	101.5	119.3
1931	61.6	56.7	92.7	117.8
1933	58.1	52.8	85.4	127.5
1935	55.7	51.9	81.9	110.8
1937	54.4	50.3	82.0	108.9
1939	48.0	44.3	73.2	97.2
1941	45.3	41.2	74.1	88.8
1943	40.4	37.5	61.5	84.6
1945	38.3	35.6	56.2	74.3

Source: United States Public Service, *Vital Statistics of the United States, 1945,* Part I, xxxv.

Position of the Roman Catholic Church on Birth Control 1940

By the technical term "birth control" is meant the unlawful limitation of offspring. All such birth control is by its very nature evil. Because it is intrinsically evil, no reason, however great, can justify it. The prohibition against birth control is not a Church law, but is a dictate of the natural law which is God's law implanted in His creatures. The chief forms of birth control are: contraceptives, abortion and sterilization.

Contraceptives—The use of contraceptives, whether they be instruments or medicines, is to the married and unmarried alike mortally sinful. The malice of this type of birth control arises from the fact that while the faculty of generation is used, its primary purpose (the generation of offspring) is frustrated. When that primary purpose is frustrated, nature (God's law) is perverted. Such a perversion is nothing less than the sin of onanism, spoken of in Genesis, xxxviii, 9–10.

Abortion is the ejection of a living immature foetus from the womb of the mother at a time when the foetus cannot live outside the womb. Intentional or direct abortion is really murder. Hence it has the evil and sinfulness of murder. Moreover, all those who take part in an abortion, not excepting the mother, incur an excommunication reserved to the bishop, if the abortion really follows from the attempt to perform it (Canon 2350).

Closely allied to abortion is craniotomy which is that operation in which forceps are used to crush and kill the child in the womb. This also is murder.

Sterilization is an operation in which the tubes, destined to carry the seed, are cut or tied so that during the sexual act no seed will be ejected and no conception can take place. Sterilization frustrates and perverts nature in the same way as does the use of contraceptives. Hence sterilization, except when necessary to preserve the health of the whole body of the one sterilized, is gravely sinful.

The only legitimate method for limiting offspring is abstinence and self-control.

Source: Saint Anthony's Guild, *The 1940 National Catholic Almanac* (Paterson, N.J., 1940), 557.

TABLE 6.8   DEATH RATES, BY RACE AND SEX

[Per 1,000 population]

Year	All Races	White Total	White Male	White Female	Nonwhite Total	Nonwhite Male	Nonwhite Female
1915	13.2	12.9	13.7	12.0	20.2	20.8	19.5
1917[a]	14.0	13.5	14.6	12.4	20.4	21.4	19.4
1919	12.9	12.4	13.0	11.8	17.9	18.1	17.8
1921	11.5	11.1	11.6	10.6	15.5	15.7	15.4
1923	12.1	11.7	12.3	11.0	16.5	17.0	16.0
1925	11.7	11.1	11.8	10.4	17.4	18.2	16.6
1927	11.3	10.8	11.6	10.0	16.4	17.2	15.6
1929	11.9	11.3	12.2	10.4	16.9	18.0	15.8
1931	11.1	10.6	11.5	9.6	15.5	16.5	14.5
1933	10.7	10.3	11.2	9.3	14.1	15.1	13.1
1935	10.9	10.6	11.6	9.5	14.3	15.6	13.0
1937	11.3	10.8	12.0	9.6	14.9	16.4	13.4
1939	10.6	10.3	11.3	9.2	13.5	14.7	12.4
1941[b]	10.5	10.2	11.4	8.9	13.5	14.8	12.2
1943[b]	10.9	10.7	12.2	9.2	13.6	14.0	11.6
1945[b]	10.6	10.5	12.6	8.6	12.0	13.7	10.5

[a] The high number for 1917 suggests the effect of the great flu epidemic. Not appearing on the chart was the rate for 1918—18.1—by far the largest for any year, also attributable to the flu. See also Table 6.9.
[b] Excludes armed forces overseas.
Source: Bureau of the Census, *Historical Statistics of the United States, 1789 to 1945* (Washington, D.C., 1949), 47.

TABLE 6.9 LEADING CAUSES OF DEATH IN SELECTED YEARS

[Rates per 100,000 population] All races

Year	Cause of Death	Rate
1915	1. cardiovascular diseases	383.5
	2. influenza and pneumonia	145.9
	3. tuberculosis	140.1
	4. cancer, malignant tumors	80.7
	5. gastritis, duodenitis, colitis	67.5
1918	1. influenza and pneumonia	588.5
	2. cardiovascular diseases	387.0
	3. tuberculosis	149.8
	4. cancer, malignant tumors	80.8
	5. gastritis, duodenitis, colitis	72.2
1920	1. cardiovascular diseases	364.9
	2. influenza and pneumonia	207.3
	3. tuberculosis	113.1
	4. cancer, malignant tumors	83.4
	5. gastritis, duodenitis, colitis	53.7
1925	1. cardiovascular diseases	391.5
	2. influenza and pneumonia	121.7
	3. cancer, malignant tumors	92.0
	4. tuberculosis	84.8
	5. accidents, excluding falls and automobile	46.3
1930	1. cardiovascular diseases	414.4
	2. influenza and pneumonia	102.5
	3. cancer, malignant tumors	97.4
	4. tuberculosis	71.1
	5. accidents, excluding falls and automobile	38.4
1935	1. cardiovascular diseases	431.2
	2. cancer, malignant tumors	108.2
	3. influenza and pneumonia	104.2
	4. tuberculosis	55.1
	5. accidents, excluding falls and automobile	30.1
1940	1. cardiovascular diseases	485.7
	2. cancer, malignant tumors	120.3
	3. influenza and pneumonia	70.3
	4. tuberculosis	45.9
	5. diabetes mellitus	26.6
1945	1. cardiovascular diseases	508.2
	2. cancer, malignant tumors	134.0
	3. influenza and pneumonia	51.6
	4. tuberculosis	39.2
	5. accidents, excluding falls and automobile	33.2

Source: Ben J. Wattenberg, *The Statistical History of the United States* (New York, 1976), 58.

Suicides

A few trends stood out with respect to people taking their own lives. Although the rates fluctuated during the period, the trend was for higher rates rather than lower. The highest rate came during the Great Depression of the 1930s and the lowest during the Second World War, although the first half of the 1920s was second lowest. The huge preponderance of suicides was by males—at rates of three or four to one—although the margin narrowed slightly in the later years. The instrument of choice each year, 1915–45, was a firearm.

TABLE 6.10 SUICIDES, 1915–1945

[Rates per 100,000 population]

Year	Number	Rate	Male	Female
1915	10,011	16.2	7,712	2,299
1920	8,790	10.2	6,364	2,426
1925	12,209	12.0	9,297	2,912
1930	18,323	15.6	14,319	4,004
1935	18,214	14.3	13,942	4,272
1940	18,907	14.4	14,466	4,441
1945	14,782	11.2	10,754	4,028
Year of Highest Rate				
1932	20,646	17.4	16,453	4,193
Year of Lowest Rate				
1944	13,231	10.0	9,497	3,734

Source: Wattenberg, *Statistical History*, 44.

TABLE 6.11 EXPECTATION OF LIFE, BY RACE AND SEX

Year	Total Both Sexes	Total Male	Total Female	White Both Sexes	White Male	White Female	Nonwhite Both Sexes	Nonwhite Male	Nonwhite Female
1915	54.5	52.5	56.8	55.1	13.1	57.5	38.9	37.5	40.5
1917	50.9	48.4	54.0	52.0	49.3	55.3	38.8	37.0	40.8
1919	54.7	53.5	56.0	55.8	54.5	57.4	44.5	44.5	44.4
1921	60.8	60.0	61.8	61.8	60.8	62.9	51.5	51.6	51.3
1923	57.2	56.1	58.5	58.3	57.1	59.6	48.3	47.7	48.9

Year	Total			White			Nonwhite		
	Both Sexes	Male	Female	Both Sexes	Male	Female	Both Sexes	Male	Female
1925	59.0	57.6	60.6	60.7	59.3	62.4	45.7	44.9	46.7
1927	60.4	59.0	62.1	62.0	60.5	63.9	48.2	47.6	48.9
1929	57.1	55.8	58.7	58.6	57.2	60.3	46.7	45.7	47.8
1931	61.1	59.4	63.1	62.6	60.8	64.7	50.4	49.5	51.5
1933	63.3	61.7	65.1	64.3	62.7	66.3	54.7	53.5	56.0
1935	61.7	59.9	63.9	62.9	61.0	65.0	53.1	51.3	55.2
1937	60.0	58.0	62.4	61.4	59.3	63.8	50.3	48.3	52.5
1939	63.7	62.1	65.4	64.9	63.3	66.6	54.5	53.2	56.0
1941	64.8	63.1	66.8	66.2	64.4	68.5	53.8	52.5	55.3
1943	63.3	62.4	64.4	64.2	63.2	65.7	55.6	55.4	56.1
1945	65.9	63.6	67.9	66.8	64.4	69.5	57.7	56.1	59.6

Source: Bureau of the Census, Historical Statistics of the United States, Colonial Times to 1957 (Washington, D.C., 1960), 25.

TABLE 6.12   DEATH RATES IN THE UNITED STATES COMPARED WITH SELECTED OTHER COUNTRIES

[Death rates per 1,000 inhabitants in selected countries]

Period	United States[a]	England and Wales[a,b]	France[b]	Germany	Italy	Sweden	Canada[a]	Japan	Australia	Netherlands	New Zealand[a]	Chile
1911–1913	14.1	13.9	19.0	14.8	19.3	13.9	n.a.	20.2	10.9	13.1	9.2	31.0
1921–1925	11.8	12.2	17.2	13.3	17.4	12.1	11.2	21.8	9.5	10.4	8.6	30.3
1926–1930	11.8	12.1	16.8	11.8	16.0	12.1	11.1	19.3	9.3	9.9	8.6	25.8
1931–1935	10.9	12.0	15.7	11.2	14.1	11.6	9.7	17.9	9.0	8.9	8.2	24.4
1933	10.7	12.3	15.8	11.2	13.7	11.2	9.6	17.7	8.9	8.8	8.0	26.5
1934	11.1	11.8	15.1	10.9	13.3	11.2	9.5	18.1	9.3	8.4	8.5	26.3
1935	10.9	11.7	15.7	11.8	13.9	11.7	9.7	16.8	9.5	8.7	8.2	24.4
1936	11.6	12.1	15.3	11.8	13.8	12.0	9.8	17.6	9.4	8.7	8.7	24.4
1937	11.3	12.6	15.0	11.7	14.3	12.0	10.3	17.0	9.4	8.8	9.1	23.1
1938	10.6	11.8	15.4	12.0	14.1	11.5	9.6	17.7	9.6	8.5	9.7	23.5
1939	10.6	12.2	15.3	12.7	13.4	11.5	9.7	17.8	9.9	8.6	9.2	23.3
1940	10.7	14.0	18.7	13.0	13.6	11.4	9.8	16.4	9.8	9.9	9.2	21.6
1941	10.5	13.0	17.1	12.5	13.9	11.3	10.0	15.7	10.6	10.0	9.8	19.8
1942	10.4	11.6	16.8	12.4	14.3	9.9	9.7	15.8	12.0	9.5	10.6	20.3
1943	10.9	12.0	16.4	12.6	15.2	10.2	10.1	16.3	11.5	10.0	10.0	19.9
1944	10.6	11.7	20.2	15.8	15.9	11.0	9.7	17.4	10.8	11.8	9.9	19.5
1945	10.6	11.5	16.6	19.0	13.9	10.8	9.4	29.2	10.3	15.3	10.1	20.0

[a] Based on total population excluding armed forces overseas and deaths of the latter beginning 1940 for Canada, New Zealand, and the United States. Canada, however, computed on total population.
[b] Beginning 1937, data for United Kingdom (England, Wales, Scotland, and Northern Ireland).
Note: The data prior to 1937, with the exception of the Netherlands, exclude deaths of military persons. War losses are included in the Netherlands, and the rates for Italy, 1935–1939, include persons serving with the armed forces, killed in Africa and Spain.
Source: National Industrial Conference Board, The Economic Almanac for 1950 (New York, 1950), 19.

TABLE 6.13   INFANT MORTALITY COMPARED WITH OTHER COUNTRIES, 1930–1944

Country	Deaths per 1,000 Live Births among Children under 1 Year of Age
Iceland	28
New Zealand[a]	36
Netherlands	37
Norway	37
Australia[a]	38
Sweden	42
Switzerland	43
United States	51

[a] Excluding Aboriginal population.
Note: Based on statistics compiled by the Bureau of the Census during the years 1930–44 and reported in November 1945.
Source: Carl Malmberg, 100 Million Patients (New York, 1947), 4.

TABLE 6.14 MATERNAL MORTALITY COMPARED WITH OTHER COUNTRIES[a]

Country	Deaths per 1,000 Live Births
Japan	2.3
Sweden	2.4
Italy	2.4
Norway	2.5
Denmark	3.15
Uruguay	3.15
Venezuela	3.3
Argentina	3.4
England and Wales	3.4
Greece	3.6
Germany	3.7
Hungary	3.75
Iceland	3.8
Portugal	4.0
New Zealand	4.1
Ireland	4.1
Switzerland	4.2
Canada	4.2
Poland	4.2
Romania	4.3
Finland	4.3
United States	4.4

[a] Number given is for last available year before the Second World War. Based on statistics compiled by the Bureau of the Census during the years 1930–44 and reported in November 1945.
Source: Malmberg, 100 Million Patients, 5.

Number of Doctors

The table below indicates the following themes: while there was a modest increase in the number of doctors during the years 1914–45, the number of doctors per person declined. The number of medical schools dropped significantly, although these fewer schools turned out more graduates.

TABLE 6.16 NUMBER OF DOCTORS AND MEDICAL SCHOOLS

Year	Physicians		Medical Schools	
	Number	Rate per 100,000 pop.	Number	Graduates
1914	142,332	144	102	3,594
1916	145,241	142	95	3,518
1918	147,812	141	90	2,670
1921	145,404	134	83	3,186
1923	145,966	130	80	3,120
1925	147,010	127	80	3,974
1927	149,521	126	80	4,035
1929	152,503	125	80	4,262
1931	156,406	126	76	4,735
1934	161,359	128	77	5,035
1936	165,163	129	77	5,183
1938	169,628	131	77	5,194
1940	175,163	133	77	5,097
1942	180,496	134	77	5,163

Sources: Wattenburg, Statistical History, 76. There was, in addition, growth in the number of hospitals from 5,000 in 1914 to some 6,500 in 1945. The most striking change came in the growth of federal hospitals. Together with state institutions, these government hospitals provided two-thirds of patient capacity. See Bureau of the Census, Statistical Abstract of the United States, 1947, 84.

TABLE 6.15 NOTIFIABLE DISEASES—NUMBER OF CASES REPORTED IN A CONSTANT GROUP OF STATES, 1940 TO 1945

[States are excluded if they failed to report for any one of the 6 years]

Disease	Number of States[a]	1940	1941	1942	1943	1944	1945
Chicken pox	49	280,300	299,580	303,1076	304,203	319,902	286,507
Diphtheria	49	15,536	17,987	16,260	14,811	14,150	18,669
Dysentery, amebic	43	3,018	3,162	2,707	3,315	3,206	3,214
Dysentery, bacillary	41	17,482	18,955	22,762	30,988	37,427	33,452
Influenza	45	427,724	677,519	159,769	461,731	477,749	516,158
Malaria	49	78,130	68,075	60,071	54,555	57,629	62,763
Measles	49	291,162	894,134	547,393	633,627	630,291	146,002
Meningitis, meningococcus	49	1,665	2,032	3,826	18,221	16,315	8,190
Mumps	46	117,151	198,983	285,740	201,686	177,526	192,824
Pneumonia (all forms)	27	124,484	117,465	113,242	121,914	103,411	87,241
Poliomyelitis (infantile paralysis)	49	9,826	9,086	4,033	12,449	19,029	13,619
Rocky Mountain spotted fever	49	457	516	499	467	470	475
Scarlet fever	49	155,464	128,928	128,194	142,622	192,661	175,398
Smallpox	49	2,795	1,396	865	765	397	346
Tuberculosis (all forms)	41	97,266	100,317	109,514	108,051	111,423	104,967
Typhoid and paratyphoid fever	49	9,809	8,601	6,678	5,540	5,529	4,860
Typhus fever	49	1,882	2,787	3,736	4,530	5,401	5,193
Undulant fever	49	3,310	3,484	3,228	3,734	4,436	5,049
Venereal diseases:							
Gonorrhea	48	179,989	198,890	246,386	293,404	287,947	310,671
Syphilis	48	444,105	468,928	532,507	497,388	386,025	339,805
Whooping cough	49	183,866	222,202	191,383	191,890	109,873	133,792

[a] District of Columbia counted as a state.
Source: Bureau of the Census, Statistical Abstract of the United States, 1947, 84.

Agent of Death: The Outbreak of the Flu in 1918–1919

The nation's largest influenza epidemic, indeed the most deadly outbreak of any disease, took place in the years 1918 and 1919. Called the Spanish flu, it spread rapidly among the armies in Europe in spring and summer 1918, the latter stages of the First World War. Carried home by returning servicemen, it entered the United States through Boston; it affected the Northeast and eventually forty-six states. Influenza by itself normally did not cause death, but it led to numerous complications and frequently to pneumonia, which did kill. Of some 112,000 American soldiers who died during the war, more than half succumbed to disease. In all, more than 450,000 Americans died as a result of the flu, and close to 30% of the population was ill at one time or another. Life insurance companies folded from paying so many claims; hospitals and later graveyards ran out of space. No one seemed able to identify a cure or a cause, although evangelist Billy Sunday blamed it on the Germans. When President Woodrow Wilson was badly stricken in Paris in April 1919, his doctor said it was the flu, although there was some doubt about the accuracy of that diagnosis. Because the flu spread to many countries, it became a pandemic. In four months it killed more than died in four years of war. Estimates of total deaths worldwide varied widely, although a reasonable number was twenty million.

Agents of Life: Penicillin and Other Developments in American Health Care

Penicillin probably came one war too late. A powerful germicide produced by molds belonging to the genus *Penicillum,* it would not have stopped influenza but could have been effective against pneumonia and some other complications arising from the flu. Penicillin was discovered by Alexander Fleming in London in 1928 when he observed that germs around a mold were dying off. Further work was done in 1940 by Howard W. Florey of Australia and Ernst Chain of Germany. First used on a patient in 1941, penicillin was remarkably effective in killing harmful germs without endangering other body cells. The American contribution, perhaps fittingly, came in the area of mass production. Manufacture of the drug was transferred to the United States at the start of the Second World War. In 1943 discovery of a different mold on a cantaloupe in Peoria, Illinois, speeded up production rapidly at a time the germ killer was the object of growing demand. Taken orally or by injection, penicillin proved effective in attacking one disease after another: pneumonia, meningitis, trench mouth, gonorrhea, and syphillis, as well as dealing with infection that accompanied wounds. During the First World War, 70% of American soldiers wounded in the abdomen died; with penicillin and other antibiotic drugs available the number dropped to 20% during the Second World War. Penicillin ushered in a new family of medicines called antibiotics. While antibiotics did deserve to be called "miracle" or "wonder" drugs, their powers were not absolute. There were some diseases they could not treat: antibiotics, for example, had no effect on cancer.

Some Developments in Health Care, 1914–1940s

1914   Pasteurization of milk starts in several cities.

1915   Death certificates come into common usage.

1918–19   Enormous attention is devoted to the plague of influenza and pneumonia, but no cure is produced.

1921   Two Canadians, Frederick Banting and Charles Best, isolate insulin.

1922   Elmer V. McCollum, who had discovered vitamin A in 1913, discovers vitamin D.

1927   Bellevue Hospital in New York first uses an artificial respirator, an iron lung, to assist breathing for victims of polio.

1928   Alexander Fleming discovers penicillin in London.

1933   The first Blue Cross hospitalization plan is established. Elmer McCollum helps to find part of a B-complex called thiamin. Progress in vitamin research helps promote virtual elimination of such dietary-caused diseases as pellagra and beriberi.

1936   Sulfa drugs, useful in treating bacterial diseases, are introduced in the United States.

1937   The first blood bank is established by Bernard Fantus in Chicago. American scientists develop a vaccine for the yellow fever virus. American doctors relate lung cancer to smoking cigarettes.

1938   New York becomes the first state to require a blood test before receiving a marriage license—to halt spread of venereal disease.

1943   Selman Waksman discovers streptomycin, a different antibiotic (a "miracle" drug) that will later be found effective against tuberculosis.

1940s and period of the Second World War   After much research with diet and general conditions of poverty, hookworm, largely a plague on the southern states, is virtually eliminated. Aided by new developments, penicillin goes into mass production in the United States. Other antibiotics follow. The crippled condition of President Franklin D. Roosevelt dramatizes the continu-

TABLE 6.17   PERCENTAGE DISTRIBUTION OF EXPENDITURES FOR MEDICAL CARE IN THE UNITED STATES

Year	Total Medical Care	Physicians' Services	Hospitals	Drugs and Sundries	Dentists' Services	All Other Medical Care
1930	100.0%	31.8%	13.9%	19.5%	15.9%	18.9%
1935–39	100.0	31.1	16.9	20.7	13.0	18.3
1940	100.0	29.7	17.1	20.8	13.6	18.8
1945	100.0	26.1	17.9	22.7	12.6	20.7

Source: Oscar N. Serbein, Jr., *Paying for Medical Care in the United States* (New York, 1953), 49.

ing campaign against poliomyelitis, or infantile paralysis, but it still has not been successful. Americans entering military service receive, at least in many cases, their first comprehensive medical and dental attention. All these people receive a wide variety of shots and vaccinations; those destined for service abroad receive more. New substitutes are discovered for quinine to combat malaria, a problem of the war in the Pacific. Other wartime developments with respect to disease and infection, blood supply, and surgery are numerous.

Source: James Bordley III and A. McGehee Harvey, *Two Centuries of American Medicine* (Philadelphia, 1976), 792–795.

Medical Costs and Medical Payments

Medical costs as considered below included drugs and appliances, doctors, dentists, nurses, and privately controlled hospitals and sanitariums. They also included costs of accident and health insurance, although these expenses, if only because few people had them, were tiny. A broad survey by the Public Health Service in 1935–36 revealed, not surprisingly, that medical care was related to family income. Many people could not afford medical treatment, and deficiencies were especially acute in rural areas and in slum sections of cities. The need for a more comprehensive approach to medical care was recognized, but not a great deal of progress—at least, not enough—was made in that direction. Although private health insurance dated from the mid-nineteenth century, plans that covered significant groups of people did not begin to take hold until the 1930s. Before the 1940s, a vast majority of the people had no medical insurance of any kind. By the 1940s, only a small portion of the population could count on assistance in paying medical bills; the rest were expected to fend for themselves, hope for some aid from government, or do without. There were several reasons why the proportionate costs of medical care were low. The charges made by doctors and other agents of the medical system were lower in relation to other expenses of living than later would be the case. Many aspects of medical care—ranging from minute specialization on the part of practitioners, to elaborate hospital facilities, to expensive tests and procedures (not to mention malpractice litigation)—were not as available, or as well developed, as they later would be. Had they

been available, most people would not have been able to obtain them. Low relative medical costs were partly a reflection of inability to pay and, as compared with later years, of lower levels of medical care.

Home Remedies and Medical Superstitions

The basic standards of medical care were not available to all the American people. The limiting factors largely involved a shortage of money or of doctors, distance from medical facilities, and local attitudes with respect to what one could reasonably expect in care of the body. These limitations applied most frequently to rural areas. Conditions, however, did change. Distances were shortened by changes in transportation. The fighting of two wars brought many millions of young men into contact—often a first contact—with medical officials. Those who entered military service received care they needed, and many others who were not drafted received at least a physical exam. Expanded government activity during the Great Depression brought some medical attention into the public schools, if only in the form of visits by a county nurse. Even so, many people lived their lives without seeing, or very rarely seeing, a medical professional. In such circumstances the people relied on their own devices, called for divine intervention, or sought out local individuals who had acquired a reputation for providing medical service. The best example was the use of a midwife in time of childbirth. Granny Duff of Hyden, Kentucky, for example, claimed to have "cotched"—caught or delivered—700–800 babies, all without use of sedatives or anesthetics. All she needed was a butcher knife, a pair of scissors, newspapers, soap and water, and a few rags. What she knew she had learned from her mother and grandmother. Her fee was two to ten dollars, depending upon ability to pay. In other cases the people relied on home remedies or superstitions. Some examples of home remedies used in the hills of Kentucky are as follows:

1. For intense thirst brought on by fever, take a teaspoon of glycerine and lemon juice.
2. For old sores apply lye or red oak bark tea.
3. For poison oak and poison ivy use a mixture of gunpowder and milk.
4. For colds take a syrup made of boiled-down wild cherry bark and white sugar three times a day.
5. To "break out" a person with measles, give the patient "nannie tea" made of sheep droppings and boiling water.
6. For the mumps bind "hawg dung" on the jaws.
7. For shingles, drink blood (half a glass) of a black cat.
8. To cure a sty, apply an eyewash of fresh, undiluted urine.

Handed down through generations and taken half-seriously at best, the superstitions were less useful and also less risky:

1. To ward off the flu, put sulphur in your shoes.
2. To take off a corn, rub a snail over it between 7 and 11 A.M. for three consecutive days.
3. To stop a nosebleed, tie a red string around your finger or drop a key down the back of your neck.
4. To remove warts, steal a dishrag from a neighbor, rub it on the warts, and then hide the rag.
5. For rheumatism, cut a double slit in the skin of the arm and pull a horse's hair through it.
6. To cure a cold, kiss a horse on the nose.

TABLE 6.18   MEDICAL EXPENSES AS PERCENTAGE OF ALL CONSUMER EXPENSES

Year	Percentage
1914	2.70
1919	3.40
1921	2.75
1923	3.30
1925	2.47
1927	3.61
1929	3.74
1931	4.17
1933	4.35
1935	4.14
1937	4.06
1939	4.29
1941	4.14
1943	4.27
1945	4.18

Source: Frederick J. Dewhurst and Associates, *America's Needs and Resources: A New Survey* (New York, 1955), 990–992.

Source: John F. Day, *Bloody Ground* (New York, 1941), 273–280.

This poor sharecropper family in Hale County, Alabama, lacked even the simplest professional medical care. (Library of Congress)

TABLE 6.19 PERSONS COVERED BY PRIVATE HEALTH INSURANCE FOR HOSPITAL AND SURGICAL COSTS

[In thousands]

| Year | Hospitalization | | | Private Companies | | | Surgical | |
| | Persons Covered | | | | | | | |
	Number	Percentage of Population	Blue Cross	Group Policies	Indiv. Policies	Indiv. Plans	Persons Covered	Percentage of Population
1939	7,976	6.1	. . .	. . .	. . .	. . .	3,103	2.4
1940	12,312	9.3	6,072	2,500	1,200	2,250	5,350	4.0
1941	16,349	12.4	8,469	3,850	1,500	2,270	6,775	5.1
1942	19,695	15.2	10,295	5,080	1,800	2,290	8,140	6.3
1943	24,160	18.9	12,696	6,800	2,100	2,319	10,069	7.9
1944	29,232	22.9	15,828	8,400	2,400	2,495	11,713	9.2
1945	32,068	24.0	18,961	7,804	2,700	2,670	12,890	9.7

Source: Wattenberg, *Statistical History,* 82.

Marriage and Divorce

This was an age that believed in the bonds of matrimony. Marriage was proper and desirable during 1914–45, the logical conclusion of a romance, the ending point for movies, songs, and novels. Divorce in many circles was a mark of failure, even disgrace, and a barrier to professional advancement, not to mention the cause of financial disaster. The tables suggest, however, that both practices continued their course regardless of popular perception and notions about what they should be. Marriage rates fluctuated with the times: steady during much of the 1920s, a noticeable drop-off during the worst times of the depression. The start of war and the prospect of military service sparked a modest marriage boom (married men at first were not drafted), and then, as the conscription laws changed,

the rate declined in the middle years of the Second World War. The graph for divorce showed a smoother, more steady line. The rate nudged steadily upward, however, except for the early 1930s, and by 1940 the rate per 1,000 population was double what it had been in 1914. There was, moreover, growing concern that divorce was becoming halfway respectable and noticeably easier to obtain—with shorter waiting time and wider grounds for action. Nevada's reduction of the residency requirement to forty-two days enabled Reno to become famous as the divorce capital. One could "play and pay," as the saying went, while applicants waited for the time to pass. There even seemed to be competition for the business, when states sought to entice applicants—frequently women expecting a sizable

TABLE 6.20 MARRIAGES AND DIVORCES: NUMBERS

Year	Marriages		Divorces	
	Number	Per 1,000 Population	Number	Per 1,000 Population
1914	1,025,092	10.3	100,584	1.0
1915	1,007,595	10.0	104,298	1.0
1916	1,075,775	10.6	114,000	1.1
1917	1,144,200	11.1	121,564	1.2
1918	1,000,109	9.7	116,254	1.1
1919	1,150,186	11.0	141,527	1.3
1920	1,274,476	12.0	170,505	1.6
1921	1,163,863	10.7	159,580	1.5
1922	1,134,151	10.3	148,815	1.4
1923	1,229,784	11.0	165,096	1.5
1924	1,184,574	10.4	170,952	1.5
1925	1,188,334	10.3	175,449	1.5
1926	1,202,574	10.2	184,678	1.6
1927	1,201,053	10.1	196,292	1.6
1928	1,182,497	9.8	200,176	1.7
1929	1,232,559	10.1	205,876	1.7
1930	1,126,856	9.2	195,961	1.6
1931	1,060,914	8.6	188,003	1.5
1932	981,903	7.9	164,241	1.3
1933	1,098,000	8.7	165,000	1.3
1934	1,302,000	10.3	204,000	1.6
1935	1,327,000	10.4	218,000	1.7
1936	1,369,000	10.7	236,000	1.8
1937	1,451,296	11.3	249,000	1.9
1938	1,330,780	10.3	244,000	1.9
1939	1,403,633	10.7	251,000	1.9
1940	1,595,879	12.1	264,000	2.0
1941	1,695,999	12.7	293,000	2.2
1942	1,772,132	13.2	321,000	2.4
1943	1,577,050	11.8	359,000	2.6
1944	1,452,394	11.0	400,000	2.9
1945	1,603,139	12.1	494,000	3.5

Source: Bureau of the Census, *Statistical Abstract of the United States, 1948* (Washington, D.C., 1948), 89.

TABLE 6.21 MEDIAN AGE OF FIRST MARRIAGE, BY SEX

Year	Male	Female
1910	25.1	21.6
1920	24.6	21.2
1930	24.3	21.3
1940	24.3	21.5

Source: Wattenberg, *Statistical History,* 19.

settlement—to come, spend much money, and be rewarded with funds and freedom. Such states as Florida, Idaho, and Wyoming had entered the bidding by also reducing their requirement for residency.

The period of the Second World War produced turmoil as states moved to accommodate men in the service or recognize extraordinary wartime bases for marriages breaking up. One thus heard of a proxy wedding for someone overseas or a soldier obtaining a divorce in Illinois while stationed in Italy at the time. Some states refused to honor the laws of others, even though the courts said they must. Many states would not recognize "quickie" Mexican divorces, some of which could be acquired by mail. It was a mess. One theme did stand out: Divorces increased markedly at war's end, and by 1945 the rate was 3½ times what it had been in 1914.

Divorce

Even with the trend toward shortening residency requirements for divorce in the first half of the twentieth century, the process of breaking up a marriage generally was not simple and rarely anything but painful. In addition to feelings of failure and the prospect of loneliness and of living near the level of poverty, the procedure itself

For nearly every young American woman the objective was marriage, and to that end many (if they had the means to do so) began to accumulate a hope chest. (*Life,* May 26, 1941)

TABLE 6.22   MARITAL STATUS OF THE POPULATION 15 YEARS OLD AND OVER, BY SEX, TO 1940, AND BY URBAN AND RURAL, 1940

[1940 figures for "single" include unknown marital status]

Area and Class	Population 15 Years Old and Over						Percentage of Total		
	Total	Single	Married	Widowed	Divorced	Unknown	Single	Married	Widowed
Male									
1910	32,425,805	12,550,129	18,092,600	1,471,390	156,162	155,524	38.7	55.8	4.5
1920	36,920,663	12,967,565	21,849,266	1,758,308	285,284	110,240	35.1	59.2	4.8
1930	43,881,021	14,953,712	26,327,109	2,025,036	489,478	85,686	34.1	60.0	4.6
1940	49,335,632	16,376,595	30,191,087	2,143,552	624,398	. . .	33.2	61.2	4.3
Urban	28,312,463	9,218,434	17,488,846	1,195,146	410,037	. . .	32.6	61.8	4.2
Rural-nonfarm	9,965,457	3,129,750	6,250,430	456,080	129,197	. . .	31.4	62.7	4.6
Rural-farm	11,057,012	4,028,411	6,451,811	492,326	85,164	. . .	36.4	58.3	4.5
Female									
1890	19,602,178	6,233,316	11,124,785	2,154,598	71,883	17,596	31.8	56.8	11.0
1900	24,249,191	7,566,530	13,810,057	2,717,715	114,647	40,242	31.2	57.0	11.2
1910	30,047,325	8,933,170	17,684,687	3,176,228	185,068	68,172	29.7	58.9	10.6
1920	35,177,515	9,616,902	21,318,933	3,917,625	273,304	50,751	27.3	60.6	11.1
1930	42,837,149	11,306,653	26,170,756	4,734,207	573,148	52,385	26.4	61.1	11.1
1940	49,361,562	12,751,772	30,087,135	5,700,092	822,563	. . .	25.8	61.0	11.5
Urban	30,166,092	8,256,093	17,535,268	3,742,439	632,292	. . .	27.4	58.1	12.4
Rural-nonfarm	9,590,723	2,164,104	6,185,943	1,113,076	127,600	. . .	22.6	64.5	11.6
Rural-farm	9,604,747	2,331,575	6,365,924	844,577	62,671	. . .	24.3	66.3	8.8

Source: Bureau of the Census, *Statistical Abstract of the United States, 1947,* 42.

TABLE 6.23   MARRIAGE LAWS AS OF JANUARY 1, 1945

State	Legal Minimum Marriage Age		Common-law Marriages Valid	Blood Test	Waiting Period		Residence for Divorce
	Male	Female			For License	After License	
Ala.	17	14	Yes	a	None	None	1 yr.
Ariz.	18	16	No	No	None	None	1 yr.
Ark.	18	16	No	No	None	None	3 mo.[b]
Calif.	18	16	No	Yes	3 d.	3 d.	1 yr.
Colo.	18	18	Yes	Yes	None	None	1 yr.
Conn.	16	16	No	Yes	5 d.	None	3 yr.
Del.	18	16	No	No	None	Yes[c]	2 yr.[d]
Fla.	18	16	Yes	No	None	None	3 mo.
Ga.	17	14	Yes	No	5 d.	None	1 yr.
Idaho	14[e]	12[e]	Yes	Yes	None	None	6 wk.
Ill.	18	16	Yes	Yes	None	None	1 yr.
Ind.	18	16	Yes	Yes	None	None	1 yr.
Iowa	16	14	Yes	Yes	None	None	1 yr.
Kans.	18	16	Yes	No	None	None	1 yr.
Ky.	16	14	No	Yes	None	None	1 yr.
La.	18	16	No	a	None	None	1 yr.
Maine	16	16	Yes	Yes	5 d.	None	1 yr.
Md.	18	16	No	No	2 d.	None	1 yr.
Mass.	18	16	No	Yes	5 d.	None	5 yr.
Mich.	18	16	Yes	Yes	5 d.	None	1 yr.
Minn.	18	16	No	No	5 d.	None	1 yr.
Miss.	14[e]	12[e]	Yes	No	5 d.	None	1 yr.
Mo.	15	15	No	Yes	None	None	1 yr.
Mont.	18	16	Yes	No	None	None	1 yr.
Nebr.	18	16	No	No	None	None	2 yr.[f]
Nev.	18	16	No	No	None	None	6 wk.
N.H.	14	13	No	Yes	5 d.	None	1 yr.[g]
N.J.	14[e]	12[e]	No	Yes	2 d.	None	2 yr.
N.Mex.	18	16	No	No	None	None	1 yr.
N.Y.	16	14	No	Yes	3 d.	1 d.	h

| State | Legal Minimum Marriage Age | | Common-law Marriages Valid | Blood Test | Waiting Period | | Residence for Divorce |
	Male	Female			For License	After License	
N.C.	16	16	No	Yes	None	None	6 mo.
N.Dak.	18	15	No	Yes	None	None	1 yr.
Ohio	18	16	Yes	Yes	5 d.	None	1 yr.
Okla.	18	15	Yes	No	5 d.	None	1 yr.
Oreg.	18	15	No	Yes	3 d.	None	1 yr.
Pa.	16	16	Yes	Yes	3 d.	None	1 yr.
R.I.	18	16	Yes	Yes	None	None	2 yr.
S.C.	18	14	Yes	No	None	None	No divorce
S.Dak.	18	15	Yes	Yes	None	None	1 yr.
Tenn.	16	15	Yes	Yes	3 d.	None	2 yr.
Tex.	16	14	Yes	a	None	None	1 yr.
Utah	16	14	No	Yes	None	None	1 yr.
Vt.	18	16	No	Yes	None	None	6 mo.
Va.	18	16	No	Yes	3 d.	None	1 yr.
Wash.	14[e]	12[e]	No	No	3 d.	None	1 yr.
W.Va.	18	16	No	Yes	3 d.	None	2 yr.[f]
Wis.	18	15	No	Yes	5 d.	None	2 yr.
Wyo.	18	16	Yes	Yes	None	None	2 mo.

[a] Law adopted applying to male only; laboratory test authorized but not required.
[b] Divorce suits may be filed after 2 months' residence, but an additional month must elapse before a decree may be granted.
[c] Residents 24 hours, nonresidents 96 hours.
[d] One year's residence for divorce based on adultery or bigamy.
[e] Common-law marriage age.
[f] One year where the cause for divorce arose within the state.
[g] Three years on grounds of desertion.
[h] Parties must have married in the state or resided there when offense was committed.
Sources: Council of State Governments, *Book of the States, 1945–1946* (Chicago, 1945), 343–344, summarized in *Information Please Almanac, 1947* (Garden City, N.Y., 1947), 192.

seemed geared to promote acrimony, if not humiliation. Even though such vague terms as *extreme cruelty* had started to enter the lexicon of divorce undertakings, the grounds as a rule were specific. The primary cause in all states but South Carolina was adultery. Impotence, if unknown at time of marriage, ranked high on the list, as

did desertion and alcoholism. Beyond these points the states moved off into many differing directions. Whatever the ground, or the charge, it all had to be proved in court. The day of "irreconcilable differences" remained for the future.

TABLE 6.24   GROUNDS FOR DIVORCE, 1945

| State | Adultery | Cruelty | Desertion | Alcoholism | Impotence | Felony Conviction | Neglect to Provide | Insanity | Pregnancy at Marriage | Bigamy | Imprisonment | Fraudulent Contract | Felony before Marriage | Violence | Loathsome Disease | Period Before Parties May Remarry | |
																Plaintiff	Defendant
Ala.	yes	...	yes	yes	yes	yes	yes	yes[a]	yes	...	...	...	...	yes	...	2 mo.	2 mo.
Ariz.	yes	yes	yes	yes	yes	yes	yes	...	yes	...	...	...	yes	yes	...	1 yr.	1 yr.
Ark.	yes	yes	yes	yes	yes	yes[a]	...	...	...	yes	...	...	...	...	...	immediately	immediately
Calif.	yes	yes	yes	yes	...	yes	yes	yes	...	...	...	...	...	...	...	1 yr.	1 yr.
Colo.	yes	yes	yes	yes	yes	yes	yes	yes[a]	...	yes	...	...	...	...	...	6 mo.	6 mo.
Conn.	yes	yes	yes	yes	...	...	yes	yes[a]	...	...	yes	yes	...	...	...	immediately	immediately
Del.	yes	yes	yes	yes	...	...	yes	yes[a]	...	yes	yes[b]	...	...	...	...	1 yr.	1 yr.
D.C.	yes	yes	yes	...	...	yes	...	...	...	...	...	...	...	...	...	6 mo.	6 mo.
Fla.	yes	yes	yes	yes	yes	...	...	...	...	yes	...	...	...	...	...	immediately	immediately
Ga.	yes	yes[c]	yes	yes[c]	yes	yes	...	...	yes	...	...	yes	...	yes[c]	...	fixed by court	fixed by court

(continued)

TABLE 6.24 (continued)

State	Adultery	Cruelty	Desertion	Alcoholism	Impotence	Felony Conviction	Neglect to Provide	Insanity	Pregnancy at Marriage	Bigamy	Imprisonment	Fraudulent Contract	Felony before Marriage	Violence	Loathsome Disease	Period Before Parties May Remarry — Plaintiff	Period Before Parties May Remarry — Defendant
Idaho	yes	yes	yes	yes	...	yes	yes	yes[d]	...	...	...	...	...	...	...	6 mo.	6 mo.
Ill.	yes	yes	yes	yes	yes	yes	...	...	...	yes	...	...	...	yes	yes	immediately	immediately
Ind.	yes	yes	yes	yes	yes	yes	yes	yes[a]	...	...	...	...	...	...	...	immediately	immediately
Iowa	yes	yes	yes	yes	...	yes	...	...	yes	...	...	...	...	...	...	1 yr.	1 yr.
Kans.	yes	yes	yes	yes	yes	yes	...	yes[a]	yes	yes	...	yes	...	...	...	6 mo.	6 mo.
Ky.	yes	yes	yes	yes	yes	yes	...	...	yes	...	...	yes	...	yes	yes	immediately	immediately
La.	yes	yes	...	yes	...	...	...	...	...	...	...	...	...	yes	...	man, 1 yr.; wife, 22 mo.	man, 14 mo.; wife, 2 yr.
Maine	yes	yes	yes	yes	yes	...	yes	...	...	...	...	...	...	yes	...	immediately	immediately
Md.	yes	...	yes	...	yes	...	...	...	yes	...	yes	...	...	...	...	immediately	immediately
Mass.	yes	yes	yes	yes	yes	...	yes	...	...	...	yes[a]	...	...	...	...	6 mo.	2 yr.
Mich.	yes	...	yes	yes	yes	...	...	...	...	...	yes[e]	...	...	...	...	immediately	immediately
Minn.	yes	yes	yes	yes	yes	...	...	yes[a]	...	...	yes	...	...	...	...	6 mo.	6 mo.
Miss.	yes	yes	yes	yes	yes	...	...	yes[e]	...	...	yes	...	...	...	...	immediately	immediately
Mo.	yes	yes	yes	yes	yes	yes	yes	...	yes	yes	...	...	yes	...	...	immediately	immediately
Mont.	yes	yes	yes	yes	...	yes	yes	yes[a]	...	...	...	...	...	...	...	immediately	immediately
Nebr.	yes	yes	yes	yes	yes	...	yes	...	...	...	yes[e]	...	...	...	...	6 mo.	6 mo.
Nev.	yes	yes	yes	yes	yes	yes	yes	yes[b]	...	...	...	...	...	...	...	immediately	immediately
N.H.	yes	yes	yes	yes	yes	...	yes	...	...	...	yes	...	...	...	...	immediately	immediately
N.J.	yes	yes	yes	...	...	...	yes	...	...	...	...	...	...	...	...	3 mo.	3 mo.
N.Mex.	yes	yes	yes	yes	yes	yes	yes	yes	yes	...	...	...	...	...	...	immediately	immediately
N.Y.	yes	...	...	...	...	...	...	...	...	...	...	...	...	...	...	immediately	3 yr., consent of court
N.C.	yes	...	...	...	yes	...	...	...	yes	...	...	...	...	...	...	immediately	immediately
N.Dak.	yes	yes	yes	yes	...	yes	yes	yes[a]	...	...	...	...	...	...	...	immediately	immediately
Ohio	yes	yes	yes	yes	yes	...	yes	...	...	yes	yes	yes	...	...	...	immediately	immediately
Okla.	yes	yes	yes	yes	yes	yes	yes	...	yes	yes	...	yes	...	...	...	6 mo.	6 mo.
Oreg.	yes	yes	yes	yes	yes	yes	...	[a]	...	...	...	...	...	...	...	6 mo.	6 mo.
Pa.	yes	yes	yes	...	yes	yes	...	...	...	yes	...	yes	...	...	...	immediately	immediately
R.I.	yes	yes	yes	yes	yes	yes	yes	...	...	...	...	...	...	...	...	6 mo.	6 mo.
S.C.	...	...	...	...	...	...	...	...	...	...	...	...	...	...	...	...	...
S.Dak.	yes	yes	yes	yes	...	yes	yes	yes[a]	...	...	...	...	...	...	...	immediately	immediately
Tenn.	yes	yes	yes	yes	yes	yes	yes	...	yes	yes	...	...	...	yes	...	immediately	immediately
Tex.	yes	yes	yes	...	...	yes	...	yes	...	...	...	...	...	...	...	immediately; cruelty, 1 yr.	immediately; cruelty, 1 yr.
Utah	yes	yes	yes	yes	yes	yes	yes	yes[a]	...	...	...	...	...	...	...	6 mo.	6 mo.
Vt.	yes	...	yes	...	...	yes	...	yes[a]	...	...	yes[e]	...	...	...	...	6 mo.	2 yr.
Va.	yes	...	yes	...	yes	yes	...	...	yes	...	yes	...	...	...	...	6 mo.	6 mo.
Wash.	yes	yes	yes	yes	yes	...	yes	yes[a]	...	...	yes	yes	...	...	...	immediately	immediately
W.Va.	yes	yes	yes	yes	...	...	...	...	...	...	yes	...	...	...	...	2 mo.	2 mo.
Wis.	yes	yes	yes	yes	yes	...	yes	...	...	...	yes[e]	...	...	yes	...	1 yr.	1 yr.
Wyo.	yes	yes	yes	yes	...	yes	yes	yes[a]	yes	...	yes	...	yes	...	...	immediately	immediately
Alaska	yes	yes	yes	yes	yes	yes	yes	yes[e]	...	...	...	...	...	...	...	immediately	immediately
Hawaii	yes	yes	yes	yes	...	...	yes	yes[e]	...	...	yes[f]	...	...	...	yes	immediately— 1 mo.	immediately— 1 mo.
P.R.	yes	yes	yes	yes	yes	yes	...	...	...	...	...	...	...	...	...	immediately	immediately

[a] Five years.
[b] Two years.
[c] At discretion of jury.
[d] Six years.
[e] Three years.
[f] Seven years.
Source: U.S. Department of Labor; summarized in *Information Please Almanac, 1947,* 190–191.

TABLE 6.25 AMERICAN OPINION ON DIVORCE

The American Institute on Public Opinion asked on April 11, 1936, the following question: Should divorces be easier to obtain in your state? The responses are interesting in several respects. First, a large majority of people did not favor easier divorce. In Maine the vote was close to unanimous. In Massachusetts, with a large Catholic population, most people opposed easier divorce, despite a five-year residency requirement before filing. The two states that had the largest support for change were New York—the only state in which a majority favored more lenient laws—which recognized only adultery as legitimate grounds for divorce, and South Carolina, which had no divorce law. Even in this state, 55% opposed any change to make divorce easier. In another survey taken in 1945, only 34% believed that their state should recognize the famous "quickie" divorces being granted in Reno, Nevada.
(April 11, 1936) Should divorces be easier to obtain in your state? (AIPO)

	Yes	No
National total	23%	77%
By Size of Community		
Farmers	16%	84%
Small towns	16	84
Cities	23	77
State by State		
Ala.	15%	85%
Ariz.	33	67
Ark.	10	90
Calif.	23	77
Colo.	7	93
Conn.	29	71
Del.	14	86
Fla.	14	86
Ga.	24	76
Idaho	12	88
Ill.	16	84
Ind.	14	86
Iowa	10	90
Kans.	12	88
Ky.	22	78
La.	26	74
Maine	4	96
Md.	27	73
Mass.	15	85
Mich.	15	85
Minn.	16	84
Miss.	17	83
Mo.	10	90
Mont.	24	76
Nebr.	12	88
Nev.	11	89
N.H.	9	91
N.J.	39	61
N.Mex.	29	71
N.Y.	51	49
N.C.	24	76
N.Dak.	16	84
Ohio	14	86
Okla.	15	85
Oreg.	11	89
Pa.	20	80
R.I.	15	85
S.C.	45	55
S.Dak.	21	79
Tenn.	19	81
Tex.	14	86
Utah	15	85
Vt.	13	87
Va.	23	77
Wash.	15	85
W.Va.	24	76
Wis.	9	91
Wyo.	21	79

Source: Hadley Cantril, *Public Opinion, 1935–1946* (Princeton, 1951), 477.

CHAPTER 7 Religion

It is impossible to measure the religious behavior of the American people in the first half of the twentieth century. The most one can do is to list membership as reported by the institutions. Membership unfortunately was not the same as participation, and even if it was, the reliability of numbers varied from church to church. Some kept poor records; some did not report at all. The definition of membership varied. The Roman Catholic Church probably did the best, and it was the most opportunistic in identifying membership; it counted and registered every baby from birth. Many Protestant denominations dated membership from age thirteen, and membership generally was not to Protestants what it was to Catholics. Some of the most devout Protestants did not belong to a church. In 1916, statistics on Jews included only heads of families. Statistics in later years included all Jews who lived in a congregational area, falsely suggesting that they all were religious participants.

Religion took many diverse directions during this period—as it frequently has done in this nation with such a diverse population. Perhaps most striking were the efforts of the Ku Klux Klan and other organizations in the 1920s to equate American nationhood

TABLE 7.1 CHURCH MEMBERSHIP AND MEMBERSHIP AS PERCENTAGE OF THE TOTAL POPULATION

Year	Reported Membership	Percentage of Population
1916	41,926,854	41
1926	54,576,346	46.5
1936	55,872,366	43.5
1940	64,501,594	48.8
1945	72,492,669	52

Sources: Bureau of the Census, *Statistical Abstract of the United States, 1931* (Washington, D.C., 1931), 64; *1940* (Washington, D.C., 1941), 71; *1948* (Washington, D.C., 1948), 60.

with white, midwestern Protestantism, and the intense struggle during approximately the same years between modernism and fundamentalist Protestantism, as manifested in the debate over evolution that produced the Scopes trial (the "monkey trial") in Dayton, Tennessee, in 1925.

In absolute terms membership in religious organizations grew during this period, with the years 1916–26 showing the sharpest growth, if only because of different methods of accounting. The Great Depression was costly for religion, as it was for so many aspects of American life. Thousands of churches collapsed, and although membership increased slightly, the growth did not keep pace with the change in population. There was a modest recovery during the early 1940s. During virtually the entire period, churches, synagogues included, could claim but a minority of the American population—not a good record. Only in the mid-1940s did membership pass 50%. Even so, religion remained one of the most important forces in American society. It affected the way millions of people went about their daily lives, and it affected millions more, and the country as a whole, in other general ways. The United States remained the world's most populous Christian country, and it became the nation with the largest number of the world's Jews.

A devoted churchman and almost a minister, politician William Jennings Bryan had his swan song defending traditional religion in the Scopes trial in 1925. (National Archives)

TABLE 7.2 MAJOR RELIGIOUS BODIES, AS REPORTED BY THE YEAR 1945 [a]

Religious Group	Membership
Roman Catholic Church	23,419,701
Eastern Orthodox Churches	686,287
Jewish congregations	4,641,184
Protestant bodies over 50,000	41,943,104
Other bodies	1,802,393

[a] Reporting years for these statistics varied. For most churches it was 1944; for the Roman Catholic Church it was 1945 and for Jewish congregations 1936. The number for Protestants was smaller than the number of participants, because of different methods of identifying membership and because many Protestant organizations had fewer than 50,000 members.
Sources: Bureau of the Census, *Statistical Abstract of the United States, 1931*, 64; *1940*, 71; *1948*, 60.

TABLE 7.3 MEMBERSHIP IN RELIGIOUS ORGANIZATIONS, 1916, 1926, 1936

Denomination	Churches Reporting Members			Number of Members		
	1916	1926	1936	1916	1926	1936
All denominations	**226,718**	**232,154**	**199,302**	**41,926,854**	**54,576,346**	**55,872,366**
Adventists (5 bodies)	2,667	2,576		114,915	146,177	
Adventists (6 bodies)			2,536			165,815
Baptist bodies	**57,828**	**60,192**	**49,478**	**7,153,313**	**8,440,922**	**8,262,287**
Northern Baptist Convention	18,319	7,611	6,284	1,244,705	1,289,966	1,329,044
Southern Baptist Convention	23,580	23,374	13,815	2,708,870	3,524,378	2,700,155
American Baptist Association			1,064			115,022
Negro Baptists	21,071	22,081	23,093	2,938,579	3,196,623	3,782,464
Free Will Baptists	750	1,024	920	54,833	79,592	76,643
Primitive Baptists	2,142	2,267	1,726	80,311	81,374	69,157
All other (13 bodies)	1,966	3,835		126,015	268,989	
All other (15 bodies)			2,576			189,802
Brethren, German Baptist (Dunkers) (5 bodies)	1,283	1,279		133,626	158,248	
Brethren, German Baptist (Dunkers) (4 bodies)			1,381			188,290
Christian Church (Gen. Convention)	1,263	1,044		118,737	112,795	
Church of Christ Scientist		1,913	2,113		202,098	268,915
Church of the Nazarene	866	1,444	2,197	32,259	63,558	136,227
Churches of Christ	5,570	6,226	3,815	317,937	433,714	309,551
Congregational Churches	5,900	5,028		809,236	881,696	
Congregational and Christian Churches			5,300			976,388
Disciples of Christ	8,396	7,648	5,566	1,226,028	1,377,595	1,196,315
Eastern Orthodox Churches	**301**	**446**	**659**	**249,840**	**259,394**	**356,638**
Greek Orthodox Church	87	153	241	119,871	119,495	189,368
Russian Orthodox Church	169	199	229	99,681	95,134	89,510
All other (5 bodies)	45	94		30,288	44,765	
All other (9 bodies)			189			77,760
Evangelical Church	2,592	2,054	1,695	210,530	206,080	212,446
Evangelical Synod of North America	1,331	1,287		339,853	314,518	
Evangelical Congregational Church			160			23,894
Federated Churches		361	508		59,977	88,411
Evangelical and Reformed Church			2,875			723,877
Friends (4 bodies)	1,023	885	717	112,982	110,422	93,697
Jewish Congregations	1,619	3,118	3,728	357,135	4,081,242	4,706,184
Latter-Day Saints (2 bodies)	1,530	1,867		462,329	606,561	
Latter-Day Saints			**2,072**			**774,169**
Church of Jesus Christ of Latter-Day Saints			1,452			678,217
Reorganized Church of Jesus Christ of Latter-Day Saints			567			93,470
All other (4 bodies)			53			2,482
Luthern bodies	**13,921**	**15,102**	**14,788**	**2,467,516**	**3,966,003**	**4,244,890**
United Luth. Church in America	3,559	3,650	3,484	763,596	1,214,340	1,286,612
American Luth. Conference			5,855			1,424,442
Augustana Synod	1,165	1,180		204,417	311,425	
Evangelical Luth. Synodical Conference of North America			4,926			1,463,482
Synodical Conference of America	3,620	4,752		777,701	1,292,620	
Norwegian Luth. Church of America	2,740	2,554		318,650	496,707	
Joint Synod of Ohio and Other States	826	872		164,968	247,783	
Synod of Iowa and Other States	977	873		130,793	217,873	
All other (9 bodies)			523			70,354
All other (12 bodies)	1,034	1,221		107,391	185,255	
Mennonites (17 bodies)	835	826	913	79,363	87,164	114,337
Methodist bodies	**65,692**	**60,644**	**42,327**	**7,166,885**	**8,070,619**	**7,001,637**
Methodist Episcopal Church	29,315	26,130	18,349	3,717,785	4,080,777	3,509,763
Methodist Protestant Church	2,473	2,239	1,498	186,908	192,171	148,288
Methodist Episcopal, South	19,184	18,096	11,454	2,114,479	2,487,694	2,061,683
African Methodist Episcopal	6,633	6,708	4,578	548,355	545,814	493,357
African Methodist Episcopal Zion	2,716	2,466	2,252	257,169	456,813	414,244
Colored Methodist Episcopal	2,621	2,518	2,063	245,749	202,713	269,915
All other (13 bodies)	2,750	2,487		96,440	104,637	
All other (15 bodies)			2,133			104,387
Polish National Catholic Church	34	91	118	28,245	61,574	63,366

(continued)

TABLE 7.3 (continued)

Denomination	Churches Reporting Members			Number of Members		
	1916	1926	1936	1916	1926	1936
Presbyterian bodies	**15,840**	**14,848**	**12,685**	**2,255,626**	**2,625,284**	**2,513,653**
Presbyterian Church, U.S.A.	9,773	8,947	7,789	1,625,817	1,894,030	1,797,927
Cumberland Presbyterian Church	9,773	8,947	699	72,052	67,938	49,975
United Presbyterian Church	991	901	778	160,726	171,571	170,967
Presbyterian Church, U.S.	3,365	3,469	2,907	357,769	451,043	449,045
All other (5 bodies)	398	434		39,262	40,702	
All other (6 bodies)			452			45,739
Protestant Episcopal Church	7,345	7,299	6,407	1,092,821	1,859,086	1,735,335
Reformed bodies	**2,745**	**2,682**	**986**	**537,822**	**617,551**	**299,694**
Reformed Church in America	715	717	695	144,929	153,739	184,536
Reformed Church in the U.S.	1,758	1,709		344,374	361,286	
All other (2 bodies)	272	256	291	48,519	102,526	115,158
Roman Catholic Church	17,375	18,940	18,409	15,721,815	18,605,003	19,914,937
Salvation Army	742	1,052	1,088	35,954	74,768	103,038
Spiritualists	354	611		29,028	50,631	
Spiritualists (4 bodies)			424			27,352
Unitarians	411	353	305	82,515	60,152	59,228
United Brethren (3 bodies)	3,889	3,375	2,762	367,934	395,885	392,897
Universalist Church	643	498	339	58,566	54,957	45,853
All other denominations	4,723	8,465	12,951	364,044	592,672	873,045

Sources: Bureau of the Census, *Statistical Abstract of the United States, 1931*, 64; *1940*, 71.

TABLE 7.4 DETAILED LIST OF RELIGIOUS ORGANIZATIONS AS REPORTED BY THE YEAR 1945[a]

Denomination	Membership, 1945
All denominations	**72,492,669**
Adventist bodies:	
Advent Christian Church	30,547
Church of God (Adventist)	5,295
Life and Advent Union	288
Seventh-Day Adventist Denomination	194,832
Primary Advent Christian Church	538
African Orthodox Church	**5,200**
Amana Church Society	**880**
American Ethical Union	**2,875**
American Rescue Workers	**300**
Apostolic Overcoming Holy Church of God	**8,000**
Armenian Orthodox Church of Am.	**18,787**
Assemblies of God, General Council	**227,349**
Assyrian Jacobite Apostolic Church	**3,100**
Baha'ls	**4,489**
Baptist bodies:	
Northern Baptist Convention	1,555,914
Southern Baptist Convention	5,667,926
National Baptist Convention, U.S.A.	4,021,618
National Baptist Conv. of America	2,352,339
American Baptist Association	115,022
Christian Unity Baptist Association	418
Colored Primitive Baptists	43,897
Duck River (and Kindred) Association of Baptists	7,951
Evangelical Baptist Church	400
Free Will Baptists	118,871
General Baptists	39,600
General Six Principle Baptists	280
Independent Baptist Church of America	129
National Baptist Evangelical Life and Soul Saving Assembly of U.S.A.	59,743

Denomination	Membership, 1945
Primitive Baptists	69,157
Regular Baptists	17,186
General Association of Regular Baptist Churches, North	22,345
Separate Baptists	6,490
Seventh-Day Baptists	6,581
Seventh-Day Baptists (German, 1728)	125
Two-Seed-in-the-Spirit Predestinarian Baptists	201
United American Free Will Baptist Church	75,000
United Baptists	27,000
Bible Protestant Church	**2,000**
Brethren German Baptist (Dunkers)	
Brethren Church (Progressive Dunkers)	17,669
Church of the Brethren (Conservative Dunkers)	180,278
Church of God (New Dunkers)	526
Old German Baptist Brethren	3,271
Brethren Plymouth (8 bodies)	**25,806**
Brethren River:	
Old Order or Yorker Brethren	291
Brethren in Christ	5,171
United Zion's Children	1,025
Buddhist Churches of America	**70,000**
Catholic Apostolic Church	**2,577**
Christadelphians	**2,755**
Christian and Missionary Alliance	**40,283**
Christian Nation Church	**112**
Christian Union	**15,400**
Christ's Sanctified Holy Church	**831**
Church of Christ Holiness U.S.A.	**11,751**
Church of Christ, Scientist	**268,915**
Church of Eternal Life	**113**

Denomination	Member-ship, 1945
Churches of God:	
Church of God	67,138
Church of God (Anderson, Ind.)	83,875
Church of God. Seventh-Day	1,154
The (Original) Church of God	5,000
The Church of God	20,065
The Church of God	20,000
Church of God and Saints of Christ	**37,084**
Church of God in Christ	**300,000**
Church of the Gospel	**47**
Church of the Nazarene	**187,082**
Churches of Revelation	**879**
Churches of Christ	**309,551**
Churches of Christ in Christian Union of Ohio	**5,872**
Churches of God, Holiness	**5,872**
General Eldership of the Churches of God in North America	**33,563**
Churches of the Living God:	
Church of the Living God, (Christian Workers for Fellowship)	120
Church of the Living God. The Pillar and Ground of Truth	4,838
Church of the New Jerusalem:	
General Convention of the New Jerusalem in the U.S.A.	5,175
General Church of the New Jerusalem	1,387
Congregational and Christian Churches	**1,075,401**
Congregational Holiness Church	**2,849**
Disciples of Christ	**1,672,354**
Divine Science College and Church	**4,085**
Eastern Orthodox Churches:	
Albanian Orthodox Church	3,137
American Holy Orthodox Catholic Apostolic Eastern Church	1,325
Apostolic Episcopal Church	6,389
Bulgarian Orthodox Church	1,336
Greek Orthodox Church (Hellenic)	250,000
Holy Orthodox Church in America (Eastern Catholic and Apostolic)	1,300
Roumanian Orthodox Church	21,000
Russian Orthodox Church	300,000
Serbian Orthodox Church	42,000
Syrian Antiochian Orthodox Church	20,300
Ukrainian Orthodox Church of America	39,500
Erieside Church	**66**
Evangelical and Reformed Church	**675,958**
Evangelical Church	**255,881**
Evangelical Congregational Church	**25,952**
Evangelistic associations:	
The Apostolic Christian Church, Nazarean	1,663
Apostolic Christian Church of America	6,425
Apostolic Faith Mission	2,288
The Christian Congregation	3,820
Church of Daniel's Band	131
Church of God (Apostolic)	3,085
Church of God As Organized by Christ	2,192
Hephzibah Faith Missionary Association	350
Metropolitan Church Association	961
Missionary Bands of the World	190
Missionary Church Association	5,000
Pillar of Fire	4,044
Faith Tabernacle	**200**
Federated Churches	**88,411**
Fire Baptized Holiness Church	**6,000**
Free Christian Zion Church of Christ	**2,478**

Denomination	Member-ship, 1945
Friends:	
Primitive Friends	13
Religious Society of Friends (Conservative)	3,351
Religious Society of Friends (General Conference)	17,870
Religious Society of Friends (Five Years Meeting)	70,000
Religious Society of Friends (Philadelphia and Vicinity)	4,966
Religious Society of Friends (Kansas Yearly Meeting)	8,233
Oregon Yearly Meeting of the Friends Church	3,691
Ohio Yearly Meeting of the Friends Church	5,175
Religious Society of Friends (Central Yearly Meeting)	770
Holiness Church	**453**
Holiness Church of God, Inc.	**587**
House of David	**350**
House of God, Holy Church of the Living God, The Pillar and Ground of the Truth, House of Prayer for All People	**200**
House of the Lord	**302**
Church of Illumination	**5,000**
Independent Churches	**40,275**
Independent Fundamental Churches of America	**60,000**
Independent Negro Churches	**12,337**
International Church of the Four Square Gospel	**21,728**
Italian bodies:	
General Council of the Italian Pentecostal Assemblies of God	1,547
Unorganized Italian Christian Churches	9,567
Jewish Congregations	**4,770,647**
Kodesh Church of Immanuel	**562**
Latter-Day Saints:	
Church of Christ (Temple Lot)	2,179
Church of Jesus Christ (Bickertonites)	1,550
Church of Jesus Christ (Cuttlerites)	24
Church of Jesus Christ of Latter-Day Saints	870,346
Church of Jesus Christ (Strangites)	123
Reorganized Church of Jesus Christ of Latter-Day Saints	113,064
The Latter House of the Lord (Apostolic Faith)	29
Liberal Catholic Church	**2,002**
Lithuanian National Catholic Church	**3,325**
Lutheran bodies:	
American Lutheran Conference:	
American Lutheran Church	584,499
Evangelical Lutheran Augustana Synod of North America	373,163
Evangelical Lutheran Church	595,034
Lutheran Free Church	49,583
United Danish Evangelical Lutheran Church in America	34,628
Lutheran Synodical Conference of North America:	
Evangelical Lutheran Synod of Missouri, Ohio and Other States	1,356,655
Evangelical Lutheran Joint Synod of Wisconsin and Other States	324,492
Slovak Evangelical Lutheran Church	22,186
Norwegian Synod of the American Evangelical Lutheran Church	8,853
Negro Mission	11,521
United Lutheran Church in America	1,690,204
Church of the Lutheran Brethren of America	2,250
Evangelical Lutheran Church of America (Elelsen Synod)	1,400
Finnish Apostolic Lutheran Church	14,511

(continued)

TABLE 7.4 (continued)

Denomination	Member-ship, 1945
Finnish Evangelical Lutheran Church (Suomi Synod)	28,365
Finnish Evangelical Lutheran National Church of America	5,928
Icelandic Evangelical Lutheran Synod of North America	1,386
Danish Evangelical Lutheran Church in America	18,813
The Protestant Conference (Lutheran)	3,253
Independent Lutheran Churches	2,423
Mayan Temple	**2,916**
Mennonite bodies:	
Central Conference of Mennoites	3,216
Church of God in Christ (Mennonite)	3,000
Conference of the Defenseless Mennonites of North America	1,626
Evangelical Mennonite Brethren	1,240
Conservative Amish Mennonite Church	3,936
General Conference of the Mennonite Church of North America	40,000
Hutterian Brethren	265
Krimmer Mennonite Brethren Conference	1,558
Mennonite Brethren in Christ	10,061
Mennonite Brethren Church of North America	16,125
Mennonite Church	51,813
Mennonite Kleine Gemeinde	275
Old Order Amish Mennonite Church	13,408
Old Order Mennonite Church (Wisler)	2,975
Reformed Mennonite Church	1,500
Stauffer Mennonite Church	167
Unaffiliated Mennonite Congregations	422
Methodist bodies:	
African Methodist Episcopal Church	868,735
African Methodist Episcopal Zion Church	489,244
African Union First Colored Methodist Protestant Church	2,597
Apostolic Methodist Church	31
Colored Methodist Episcopal Church	382,000
Congregational Methodist Church	16,163
Congregational Methodist Church of America	6,593
Free Methodist Church of N.A.	46,783
Holiness Methodist Church	578
Independent A.M.E. Denomination	1,000
The Methodist Church	8,046,129
New Congregational Methodist Church	1,449
Primitive Methodist Church	12,185
Reformed Methodist Church	326
Reformed Methodist Union Episcopal Church	3,000
Reformed New Congregational Methodist Church	329
Reformed Zion Union Apostolic Church	3,000
Union American Methodist Episcopal Church	9,369
Wesleyan Methodist Connection of America	29,331
Moravian bodies:	
Bohemian and Moravian Brethren	250
Evangelical Unity of Bohemian and Moravian Brethren in North America	4,538
Moravian Church (Unitas Fratrum)	40,764
National David Spiritual Temple of Christ Church Union (Inc.) U.S.A.	**15,898**
New Apostolic Church	**5,535**
Old Catholic Churches in America:	
American Catholic Church, Archdiocese of N.Y.	1,400
American Catholic Church (Syro-Antlochean)	3,162
Old Catholic Church in America	6,274
Pentecostal assemblies:	
Pentecoastal Fire Baptized Holiness Church	1,900

Denomination	Member-ship, 1945
Church of God in Christ (Pentecostal)	210
Pentecostal Assemblies of Jesus Christ	17,000
International Pentecostal Assemblies	6,333
Pentecostal Assemblies of the World	5,713
Pentecostal Church of God of America	37,048
Pentecostal Church, Incorporated	20,000
Calvary Pentecostal Church, Inc.	20,000
Pentecostal Holiness Church	24,910
Pilgrim Holiness Church	**25,668**
Polish National Catholic Church	**250,000**
Presbyterian bodies:	
Associate Reformed Presbyterian Church (General Synod)	23,385
Associate Presbyterian Church of N.A.	250
Colored Cumberland Presbyterian Church	30,000
Cumberland Presbyterian Church	64,984
Presbyterian Church in the U.S.	565,853
Presbyterian Church in the U.S.A.	2,040,399
Reformed Presbyterian Church in North America, General Synod	1,559
Orthodox Presbyterian Church	7,084
Reformed Presbyterian Church of North America (Old School)	6,617
United Presbyterian Church of North America	193,637
Protestant Episcopal Church	**2,227,524**
Reformed bodies:	
Christian Reformed Church	128,914
Free Magyar Reformed Church in America	6,126
Reformed Church in America	169,390
Reformed Episcopal Church	**8,939**
Roman Catholic Church	**24,402,124**
Salvation Army	208,329
Scandinavian Evangelical bodies:	
Norwegian and Danish Evangelical Free Church Association of N.A.	10,033
Evangelical Free Church of America	11,052
Evangelical Mission Covenant Church of America	48,000
Schwenkfelders	**2,050**
Social Brethren	**521**
Spiritualists:	
International General Assembly of Spiritualists	100,000
National Christian Spiritual Alliance	5,487
National Spiritualist Association	11,266
Progressive Spiritualist Church	11,347
Triumph the Church and Kingdom of God in Christ	**30,000**
Unitarian Churches	**62,593**
United Brethren bodies:	
United Brethren in Christ	433,480
United Christian Church	676
Church of the United Brethren in Christ (Old Constitution)	15,401
United Holy Church of America, Inc.	**25,000**
Universal Emancipation Church	**18**
Universalist Church of America	**47,541**
Vedanta Society	**30**
Volunteers of America	**4,230**

[a]Jewish membership was for the year 1937, the latest available. The number of Roman Catholics was what appeared in the Catholic Directory of 1946.
Sources: Statistics from *Yearbook of American Churches, 1945,* reproduced in *The World Almanac and Book of Facts for 1946)* (New York, 1946), 308–309.

Black people in segregated urban areas often went to small storefront churches, such as this one in Chicago's Southside. (Library of Congress)

Women and the Church

When in 1929 the president of the Women's Mission Union of the Southern Baptist Convention was permitted to report to the convention, a group of men walked out in protest. Women were not supposed to appear at the pulpit. The Christian tradition of male dominance and female subservience remained strong until well into the twentieth century. There were a few exceptions: Evangeline Booth headed the Salvation Army in the early twentieth century; women were active in missionary work; black churches long had made use of females, including in the ministry. The number of Pentecostal and Holiness churches grew rapidly in the twentieth century, and several of these allowed women to preach from the beginning. Even so, the mainline churches and Christianity in general remained firm in their opposition to female leadership, and at anytime between 1914 and 1945 the number of female ministers was tiny—less than 5%. In the Roman Catholic Church the number was zero. At the same time, the people that the preachers and priests addressed were largely women, as statistics of church membership confirmed. The concept of man as leader and woman as follower was made in no place more clear than in the halls of Christendom.

TABLE 7.5 MEMBERSHIP IN REPRESENTATIVE CHURCHES AS MEASURED BY SEX, 1936

Church	Male Members	Female Members	Males per 100 Females
Assemblies of God	53,902	91,849	58.7
Northern Baptist Convention	493,998	740,293	66.7
Southern Baptist Convention	1,071,011	1,437,885	74.5
Negro Baptist Church	1,378,225	2,259,287	61.0
Church of the Nazarene	47,899	84,027	57.0
American Lutheran Conference	653,842	712,376	91.8
Mennonite (Conservative Amish)	1,205	1,118	101.4
Methodist Episcopal Church	1,309,508	1,923,547	68.1
Pentecostal Fire-Baptized Holiness Church	433	905	47.8
Pentecostal Holiness Church	4,049	8,490	47.7
Presbyterian Church	656,711	949,746	69.1
Roman Catholic Church	8,174,177	8,917,678	91.7

Source: Bureau of the Census, *Religious Bodies, 1936* (Washington, D.C., 1941), 63, 91, 114, 143, 858, 1020, 1086, 1354, 1385, 1528.

Protestant Evangelists

Although some Protestant organizations were almost as closely structured as the Roman Catholic Church, Protestantism in general occupied a broad range of territory. An individual could go to any church that seemed fitting, and if none were acceptable, one theoretically could get by without a church or even start a new one. Protestantism permitted wide differences in interpretation of the Bible and much individualism in worship and style of presentation of the Word. Even before the advent of television and at a time when radio was only emerging as a medium of communication, certain Protestant sects were marked with colorful preachers who demonstrated special talents in winning converts to the faith. A few of these individuals became national personalities, as much for their style as for their message. The more they experienced success, however, the more they opened themselves to the human temptations of power, wealth, and other attractions of the flesh. The better known they became, the more they opened themselves to public scrutiny and charges that they were charlatans, more interested in self-aggrandizement and private gain than in the salvation of their followers. Few escaped without at least a hint of scandal. Three of the most powerful evangelists of this era were Father Divine, Aimee Semple McPherson, and Billy Sunday.

Father Divine

Father Major Jealous Divine probably was the most famous black evangelist of the period between the two world wars. He also reflected the many contradictions inherent in such emotional, individualized exercise of Protestant theology. Was he a savior of people, or was he their exploiter? Of somewhat mysterious background, the man who called himself Father Divine preached and led various denominations in the New York City area—Brooklyn, Long Island, Harlem—from 1919 to 1942, at which time he moved to another city. A preacher of no small magnetism, Father Divine also provided significant poor relief for black people in the inner city. In his congregation he exercised total control, forbidding members to smoke or drink or have sexual relations, even between married people, or to engage in interracial marriage. These rules did not apply to him, however, as was suggested by his collection of "Rosebud" companions and by the fact that he eventually married a white woman. He also claimed to have "Godlike" power, a claim revealed in the case of his conviction in 1931 for being a public nuisance. When the judge who handed him an extraordinarily harsh sentence suddenly died, Father Divine reportedly remarked, "I sure hated to have to do that," or something to that effect. He later would lead a Peace Mission Movement, and in Philadelphia he continued his socioreligious activity until his death in 1965. Father Divine manifested the spontaneous, emotional aspect of the pentecostal approach. He reflected the conflict of working for the salvation of followers on the one hand while reserving special power and privilege for the leader on the other—giving all these themes a racial, inner-city flavor. Many white people doubtless viewed him as reflective of the peculiar characteristics of black religious behavior, if not of the character of black people in general.

Aimee Semple McPherson

Aimee Semple McPherson, "the world's most pulchritudinous evangelist," was born in Canada in surroundings of Pentecostal Holiness Protestantism. Converted as a teenager, she married a preacher named Semple, who died a few years later. She then married a man named McPherson. The second marriage did not work, but she kept both husbands' names. She began preaching in 1909, and after much travel in North America and beyond, she settled in Los Angeles in 1918. California became her base for revival tours across country and for establishment of her own localized ministry. Controversial for her style and because she was a woman in a man's business, she founded her own denomination, the International Church of the Foursquare Gospel, and her own church, massive Angelus Temple in Los Angeles, in 1923. Her gatherings were noted for her saintlike appearances in striking blond hair and long gowns, with Bible in one hand and a rose in the other, and for her claims to mystical powers of healing. There were at least sexual undertones to the activity. She symbolized, as much as any preacher, the many facets of evangelism in the 1920s, if not the contradictory aspects of that colorful decade. Her career was scandalized by her sudden disappearance in 1926, leaving clues suggesting a dramatic death, and her reappearance thirty-six days later, at which time she claimed to have been kidnapped. Evidence suggested mysterious goings-on, and her reputation never fully recovered from the blemish. She continued her ministry, however, wounded as it was, and Angelus Temple and the Church of the Foursquare Gospel lived on in California, even after her death in 1944.

Billy Sunday

William Ashley Sunday was probably the most popular American evangelist in the first half of the twentieth century. In his early years a major-league baseball player—a right fielder for the Chicago White Stockings and later for teams in Philadelphia and Pittsburgh—he finished an eight-year career with a decent batting average of .248 and 236 stolen bases. In 1891 he left baseball for Christian work, began preaching in 1898, and became an ordained Presbyterian minister in 1903. More flamboyant and individualist than many in the Presbyterian ministry, Billy filled his sermons with fundamentalist oratory attacking the evils of modern education, most entertainment—except, that is, for baseball—and especially demon rum. He had no small part in the campaign for prohibition. He became a specialist in the tent revival meeting, the sessions marked with frank and colorful speech and dramatic presentations with Billy playing all the parts: the society woman, the drunk, the "vile, iniquitous, low down, groveling, worthless, damnable, rotten, hellish, corrupt, miserable sinners." His career probably peaked with a dramatic ten-week series of meetings in the heart of Manhattan in 1917, where he consorted with famous people, attacked the Germans (war recently had started), and preached to hundreds of thousands. During the meetings some 98,264 reportedly "hit the trail," the "sawdust trail," coming forward to accept conversion. Some reporters seemed more interested in a report that "free will offerings" the final week amounted to $114,000. Increasingly criticized for loose financial dealings, later sued for plagiarism, Sunday moved his revivals to smaller population areas, but he continued to preach. He died in Indiana in 1935, leaving behind a considerable reputation and the huge Billy Sunday Tabernacle in Winona Lake, Indiana.

Religion in much of rural America during 1914–45 remained heavily traditional. Several sects, especially Baptists, insisted upon full immersion baptism. (Library of Congress)

The Roman Catholic Church in America

The Roman Catholic Church was the single largest religious body in the United States. Protestants, though more numerous, were split into many diverse organizations. The Catholic Church grew slowly during the years 1914–45, with the period of slowest increase occurring between the mid-1920s and the mid-1930s. During this time immigration from European Catholic countries was slowed by the Immigration Law of 1924. The Great Depression in the 1930s left the United States an unattractive place in which to settle. The church of this era was exceptionally traditionalist, with masses said in Latin and the priest standing with his back to the congregation. The Roman Church maintained a centralized authority reaching from the papacy in Rome through archbishops and bishops and down to the parish priest, who was a man of no small power and influence in the community. To remain in good standing, members were re-

quired to obey a set of rules that Catholics of a later era might have considered inconvenient, if not downright harsh. The requirement of "no meat on Fridays" was only the most familiar of these mandates.

TABLE 7.6   CATHOLICS AS PERCENTAGE OF THE POPULATION AND OF CHURCH MEMBERS

Year	Number of Catholics	Percentage of Total Population	Percentage of Church Members
1916	15,722,000	15.5	37
1926	18,605,000	15.8	34
1936	19,915,000	15.5	36
1940	21,285,000	16.0	32
1945	23,420,000	16.7	32

Sources: Bureau of the Census, *Statistical Abstract of the United States, 1931,* 64; *1940;* 71; *1948,* 60.

Rules of the Catholic Church, 1940

Major Commandments of the Catholic Church

1. To hear Mass on Sundays and holy days of obligation.
2. To fast and abstain on the days appointed.
3. To confess at least once a year.
4. To receive the Holy Eucharist during the Easter time.
5. To contribute to the support of our pastors.
6. Not to marry persons who are not Catholics, or who are related to us within the fourth degree of kindred, nor privately without witnesses, nor to solemnize marriage at forbidden times.

Source: Saint Anthony's Guild, *The 1940 National Catholic Almanac* (Paterson, N.J., 1940), 143.

Holy Days of Obligation

Every Catholic who has attained the age of reason, and is not prevented by sickness or other sufficient cause, is obliged to rest from servile work and attend Holy Mass on the following days:

All Sundays of the year.

The Circumcision of Our Lord (New Year's Day), January 1.

The Ascension of Our Lord 40 days after Easter.

The Assumption of the Blessed Virgin Mary, August 15.

All Saints' Day, November 1.

The Immaculate Conception of the Blessed Virgin Mary (Patronal Feast of the United States), December 8.

Christmas, the Nativity of Our Lord, December 25.

Source: Saint Anthony's Guild, *1940 National Catholic Almanac*, 18.

Roman Catholic Days of Fast and Abstinence, 1940

Days of Fast

Rules of fasting affected all Catholics in good health between the ages of twenty-one and sixty. They required that only one full meal be taken, with small additional amounts at two other times during the day. The fast days were:

1. Ember days (first week of Lent)
2. Pentecost week (May 15, 16, 17, 1940)
3. Third week in September (3 days)
4. Third week in December (3 days)
5. Vigil of Pentecost (May 11, 1940)
6. Vigil of Assumption (August 14)
7. Vigil of All Saints Day (October 31)
8. Vigil of Christmas (December 24)
9. All days of Lent to noon on Holy Saturday

The Law of Fast also required abstinence from food or drink before receiving the Eucharist; the Communion fast began at midnight—that is, Catholics taking Communion on Sunday morning were not to eat or drink anything after midnight Saturday night.

Days of Abstinence

The Law of Abstinence required that all the faithful who had reached age seven eat no meat on the assigned days. Otherwise, the amount of food remained open. The days of abstinence were:

1. All Fridays of the year
2. Wednesdays and Fridays of Lent
3. Ember days and vigil days listed under Fast Days.

Source: Saint Anthony's Guild, *1940 National Catholic Almanac*, 18.

TABLE 7.7 AMERICAN CARDINALS, 1914–1945

Cardinal	Office (City)	Years of Service
John Farley	New York	1911–18
William O'Connell	Boston	1911–44
Dennis Dougherty	Philadelphia	1921–
Patrick Hayes	New York	1924–38
George Mundelein	Chicago	1924–39
John Glennon [a]	St. Louis	1945–
Edward Mooney [a]	Detroit	1945–
Francis Spellman [a]	New York	1945–
Samuel Stritch [a]	Chicago	1945–

Note: No end dates are shown for those candinals whose terms continued past 1945.
[a] Appointed December 23, 1945.
Source: Saint Anthony's Guild, *The 1946 National Catholic Almanac* (Paterson, N.J., 1946), 75, 136.

TABLE 7.8 CATHOLIC ARCHDIOCESES OF THE UNITED STATES, 1945

See [a]	Formed	Archbishop
Baltimore, Md.	1789	Michael J. Curley
Boston, Mass.	1808	Richard J. Cushing
Chicago, Ill.	1843	Samuel Cardinal Stritch
Cincinnati, Ohio	1821	John T. McNicholas, O.P.
Denver, Colo.	1887	Urban J. Vehr
Detroit, Mich.	1833	Edward Cardinal Mooney
Dubuque, Iowa	1837	Henry P. Rohlman
Indianapolis, Ind.	1834	Paul C. Schulte
Los Angeles, Calif.	1840	John J. Cantwell
Louisville, Ky.	1808	John A. Floersh
Milwaukee, Wis.	1843	Moses E. Kiley
Newark, N.J.	1853	Thomas J. Walsh
New Orleans, La.	1793	Joseph F. Rummel
New York, N.Y.	1808	Francis Cardinal Spellman
Omaha, Nebr.	1885	James H. Ryan
Philadelphia, Pa.	1808	Dennis Cardinal Dougherty
Portland, Oreg.	1846	Edward D. Howard
St. Louis, Mo.	1826	Joseph E. Ritter
St. Paul, Minn.	1850	John G. Murray
San Antonio, Tex.	1874	Robert E. Lucey
San Francisco, Calif.	1853	John J. Mitty
Santa Fe, N. Mex.	1850	Edwin V. Byrne
Washington, D.C.	1939	Michael J. Curley

[a] A see was the jurisdiction of a bishop (or archbishop) as identified by the official seat of authority—the city.
Source: Saint Anthony's Guild, *1946 National Catholic Almanac*, 145.

Sociological Aspects of Religious Groups in the 1940s

Although the social status of religious groups continued to change, by the 1940s it remained true that members of such "elitist" denominations as Episcopalian, Presbyterian, and Congregational and,

TABLE 7.9 CLASS COMPOSITION OF CATHOLICS AND PROTESTANTS, 1939–1940

	Percentage Distribution		
	Upper Class	Middle Class	Lower Class
Protestants			
In U.S.	14	52	34
In South	8	48	44
In remainder of U.S.	17	54	29
Catholics			
In U.S.	9	50	41
In South	10	42	48
In remainder of U.S.	9	51	40

Source: Leo Rosten, *A Guide to the Religions of America* (New York, 1955), 273.

TABLE 7.10 CLASS COMPOSITION OF RELIGIOUS BODIES, 1945–1946

	Percentage Distribution		
Body	Upper Class	Middle Class	Lower Class
Entire Sample	*13*	*31*	*56*
Catholic	9	25	66
Jewish	22	32	46
Methodist	13	35	52
Baptist	8	24	68
Presbyterian	22	40	38
Lutheran	11	36	53
Episcopalian	24	34	42
Congregational	24	43	33

Source: Rosten, *Religions of America*, 273.

TABLE 7.11 EDUCATIONAL LEVELS IN RELIGIOUS BODIES, 1945–1946

	Percentage Distribution		
Body	High School Incomplete (or less)	High School Graduates (or more)	College Graduates
Entire Sample	*52*	*48*	*11*
Catholic	57	43	7
Jewish	37	63	16
Methodist	49	51	12
Baptist	65	35	6
Presbyterian	37	63	22
Lutheran	56	44	8
Episcopalian	35	65	22
Congregational	29	71	21

Source: Rosten, *Religions of America*, 274.

TABLE 7.12 OCCUPATIONAL CATEGORIES AND TRADE UNION MEMBERSHIP, IN MAJOR RELIGIOUS BODIES, 1945–1946

	Percentages by Occupational Categories				Percentage Belonging to Trade Unions
Body	Business and Professional	White Collar	Urban Manual Workers	Farmers	
Entire Sample	*19*	*20*	*44*	*17*	*19*
Catholic	14	23	55	8	28
Jewish	36	37	27	0.6	23
Methodist	19	19	39	23	14
Baptist	12	14	52	22	16
Presbyterian	31	21	31	17	13
Lutheran	13	18	43	26	20
Episcopalian	32	25	36	7	13
Congregational	33	19	28	20	12

Source: Rosten, *Religions of America*, 273.

TABLE 7.13 POLITICAL PREFERENCES IN RELIGIOUS BODIES, 1944

	Percentage Voting for Dewey	Percentage Voting for Roosevelt
Entire Sample	*32*	*42*
Catholic	20	54
Jewish	6	75
Methodist	38	37
Baptist	24	42
Presbyterian	48	32
Lutheran	42	35
Episcopalian	44	36
Congregational	56	26

Source: Rosten, *Religions of America*, 274.

in increasing numbers, Jews were likely to be in the upper or middle classes, while larger numbers of Baptists, Catholics, and Lutherans were in the lower classes. The adage that the lower the class, the more likely the individual would vote Democratic held true with religious groups, with the exception of the Jewish people, who voted overwhelmingly Democratic regardless of social class. In nearly all categories the Methodists were lodged as a whole in the center.

CHAPTER 8 Politics and Government

The period from 1914 to 1945 was a time of sharp turns in political attitudes and in the fortunes of traditional American political parties. The Progressive Era—the last phase of which was in 1912–16—produced close races. The Democrats fared somewhat better than their opponents, if only because the Republicans were weakened temporarily by the break-off of a reformist faction into a Progressive Party. The Democratic administration of Woodrow Wilson guided the United States through the First World War, although the potency of the Republican opposition showed itself at the war's end.

Republican political power came to the front as the United States moved away from the activism of progressivism and war and into the internally oriented period of the 1920s. Republican victories in the three presidential races of the 1920s were massive, the last one—Herbert Hoover's election in 1928—slightly less so. Republican margins in congressional races, though smaller than in the presidential elections, also were impressive. Even the fallout from the scandals of the Warren Harding administration failed to make a dent in the wall of support for the Republicans.

The coming of the Great Depression produced another large turnabout in political behavior. The people evidently blamed the depression on the Republicans, and they found reason for hope in the Democrats and especially in the Democrat leader Franklin D. Roosevelt. Easily the dominant political personage of this entire era, Roosevelt won four successive presidential elections, helped produce large Democratic majorities in Congress and in local elections, and did much to make the Democrats the majority party. The high point occurred with the landslide victory of 1936, when the Republican presidential candidate received the votes of but two states and the performance in congressional races was so meager as to create concern about continuation of the Republican Party. The Republicans hung on, however; they slowly regained strength, and although the Democrats continued to dominate through the period of the Second World War, the Republicans experienced increased optimism for future success, if only because of the knowledge that Franklin Roosevelt could not live forever.

During this period of tumultuous world politics and the emergence of various "-isms" and radical movements on both ends of the political spectrum, the United States remained loyal to its political system. An impressive performance by a third political party, the Progressives, in 1912 and 1924 was more a manifestation of personality than of a demand for something drastically different. The Socialist candidate made a somewhat respectable showing in 1912, in 1920, and early in the depression in 1932, but after that point the support dropped to a minuscule level. In 1944 the American Communist Party did not even run a candidate for president. In this time of shifting political currents, the Americans showed that what they meant by change in politics was from Democrats to Republicans and then back again.

Woodrow Wilson *(right),* president in 1913–21, poses with his close friend and adviser Edward M. (Colonel) House. (National Archives)

TABLE 8.1   1912 PRESIDENTIAL ELECTION

Total popular votes: 15,040,963
Wilson's plurality: 2,173,945

State	Woodrow Wilson (Democrat) Votes	%	Theodore Roosevelt (Progressive) Votes	%	William H. Taft (Republican) Votes	%	Eugene V. Debs (Socialist) Votes	%	Other Votes	%	Plurality
Ala.	82,438	69.9	22,680	19.2	9,807	8.3	3,029	2.6	5	. . .	59,758
Ariz.	10,324	43.6	6,949	29.3	2,986	12.6	3,163	13.4	265	1.1	3,375
Ark.	68,814	55.0	21,644	17.3	25,585	20.5	8,153	6.5	908	.7	43,229
Calif.	283,436	41.8	283,610	41.8	3,847	.6	79,201	11.7	27,783	4.1	174
Colo.	113,912	42.8	71,752	27.0	58,386	22.0	16,366	6.2	5,538	2.1	42,160
Conn.	74,561	39.2	34,129	17.9	68,324	35.9	10,056	5.3	3,334	1.8	6,237
Del.	22,631	46.5	8,886	18.3	15,997	32.9	556	1.1	620	1.3	6,634
Fla.	35,343	69.5	4,555	9.0	4,279	8.4	4,806	9.5	1,854	3.7	30,537
Ga.	93,087	76.6	21,985	18.1	5,191	4.3	1,058	.9	149	.1	71,102
Idaho	33,921	32.1	25,527	24.1	32,810	31.0	11,960	11.3	1,536	1.5	1,111
Ill.	405,048	35.3	386,478	33.7	253,593	22.1	81,278	7.1	19,776	1.7	18,570
Ind.	281,890	43.1	162,007	24.8	151,267	23.1	36,931	5.6	22,379	3.4	119,883
Iowa	185,322	37.6	161,819	32.9	119,805	24.3	16,967	3.5	8,440	1.7	23,503
Kans.	143,663	39.3	120,210	32.9	74,845	20.5	26,779	7.3	63	. . .	23,453
Ky.	219,484	48.5	101,766	22.5	115,510	25.5	11,646	2.6	4,308	1.0	103,974
La.	60,871	76.8	9,283	11.7	3,833	4.8	5,261	6.6	. . .	. . .	51,588
Maine	51,113	39.4	48,495	37.4	26,545	20.5	2,541	2.0	947	.7	2,618
Md.	112,674	48.6	57,789	24.9	54,956	23.7	3,996	1.7	2,566	1.1	54,885
Mass.	173,408	35.5	142,228	29.1	155,948	32.0	12,616	2.6	3,856	.8	17,460
Mich.	150,201	27.4	213,243	38.9	151,434	27.6	23,060	4.2	10,003	1.8	61,809
Minn.	106,426	31.8	125,856	37.7	64,334	19.3	27,505	8.2	10,098	3.0	19,430
Miss.	57,324	88.9	3,549	5.5	1,560	2.4	2,050	3.2	. . .	. . .	53,775
Mo.	330,746	47.4	124,375	17.8	207,821	29.8	28,466	4.1	7,158	1.0	122,925
Mont.	28,129	35.1	22,709	28.3	18,575	23.1	10,811	13.5	32	. . .	5,420
Nebr.	109,008	43.7	72,681	29.1	54,226	21.7	10,185	4.1	3,383	1.4	36,327
Nev.	7,986	39.7	5,620	27.9	3,196	15.9	3,313	16.5	. . .	. . .	2,366
N.H.	34,724	39.5	17,794	20.2	32,927	37.4	1,981	2.3	535	.6	1,797
N.J.	178,638	41.2	145,679	33.6	89,066	20.5	15,948	3.7	4,332	1.0	32,959
N. Mex.	20,437	41.9	8,347	17.1	17,164	35.2	2,869	5.9	. . .	. . .	3,273
N.Y.	655,573	41.3	390,093	24.6	455,487	28.7	63,434	4.0	23,728	1.5	200,086
N.C.	144,407	59.2	69,135	28.4	29,129	12.0	987	.4	118	.1	75,272
N. Dak.	29,549	34.2	25,726	29.8	22,990	26.6	6,966	8.1	1,243	1.4	3,823
Ohio	424,834	41.0	229,807	22.2	278,168	26.8	90,164	8.7	14,141	1.4	146,666
Okla.	119,143	47.0	. . .	. . .	90,726	35.8	41,630	16.4	2,195	.9	28,417
Oreg.	47,064	34.3	37,600	27.4	34,673	25.3	13,343	9.7	4,360	3.2	9,464
Pa.	395,637	32.5	444,894	36.5	273,360	22.5	83,614	6.9	20,231	1.7	49,257
R.I.	30,412	39.0	16,878	21.7	27,703	35.6	2,049	2.6	852	1.1	2,709
S.C.	48,355	95.9	1,293	2.6	536	1.1	164	.3	55	.1	47,062
S. Dak.	48,942	42.1	58,811	50.6	. . .	. . .	4,664	4.0	3,910	3.4	9,869
Tenn.	133,021	52.8	54,041	21.5	60,475	24.0	3,564	1.4	832	.3	72,546
Tex.	218,921	72.7	26,715	8.9	28,310	9.4	24,884	8.3	2,131	.7	190,611
Utah	36,576	32.6	24,174	21.5	42,013	37.4	8,999	8.0	510	.5	5,437
Vt.	15,350	24.4	22,129	35.2	23,303	37.1	928	1.5	1,094	1.7	1,174
Va.	90,332	66.0	21,776	15.9	23,288	17.0	820	.6	759	.6	67,044
Wash.	86,840	26.9	113,698	35.2	70,445	21.8	40,134	12.4	11,682	3.6	26,858
W. Va.	113,097	42.1	79,112	29.4	56,754	21.1	15,248	5.7	4,517	1.7	33,985
Wis.	164,230	41.1	62,448	15.6	130,596	32.7	33,476	8.4	9,225	2.3	33,634
Wyo.	15,310	36.2	9,232	21.8	14,560	34.4	2,760	6.5	421	1.0	750
Total	6,293,152	41.84	4,119,207	27.39	3,486,333	23.18	900,369	5.99	241,902	1.61	

Source: Congressional Quarterly, *Presidential Elections since 1789* (Washington, D.C., 1979), 86.

TABLE 8.2   1916 PRESIDENTIAL ELECTION

Total popular votes: 18,535,022
Wilson's plurality: 579,511

State	Woodrow Wilson (Democrat) Votes	%	Charles E. Hughes (Republican) Votes	%	Allan L. Benson (Socialist) Votes	%	J. Frank Hanly (Prohibition) Votes	%	Other Votes	%	Plurality
Ala.	99,116	76.0	28,662	22.0	1,916	1.5	741	.6	. . .	. . .	70,454
Ariz.	33,170	57.2	20,522	35.4	3,174	5.5	1,153	2.0	. . .	. . .	12,648
Ark.	112,211	66.0	48,879	28.7	6,999	4.1	2,015	1.2	. . .	. . .	63,332
Calif.	465,936	46.6	462,516	46.3	42,898	4.3	27,713	2.8	187	. . .	3,420
Colo.	177,496	60.8	101,388	34.7	9,951	3.4	2,793	1.0	409	.1	76,108
Conn.	99,786	46.7	106,514	49.8	5,179	2.4	1,789	.8	606	.3	6,728
Del.	24,753	47.8	26,011	50.2	480	.9	566	1.1	. . .	. . .	1,258
Fla.	55,984	69.3	14,611	18.2	5,353	6.6	4,786	5.9	. . .	. . .	41,373
Ga.	127,754	79.5	11,294	7.0	941	.6	. . .	. . .	20,692	12.9	107,062
Idaho	70,054	52.0	55,368	41.1	8,066	6.0	1,127	.8	. . .	. . .	14,686
Ill.	950,229	43.3	1,152,549	52.6	61,394	2.8	26,047	1.2	2,488	.1	202,320
Ind.	334,063	46.5	341,005	47.4	21,860	3.0	16,368	2.3	5,557	.8	6,942
Iowa	221,699	42.9	280,439	54.3	10,976	2.1	3,371	.7	2,253	.1	58,740
Kans.	314,588	50.0	277,658	44.1	24,685	3.9	12,882	2.1	. . .	. . .	36,930
Ky.	269,990	51.9	241,854	46.5	4,734	.9	3,039	.6	461	.1	28,136
La.	79,875	85.9	6,466	7.0	284	.3	. . .	. . .	6,349	6.8	73,409
Maine	64,033	47.0	69,508	51.0	2,177	1.6	596	.4	. . .	. . .	5,475
Md.	138,359	52.8	117,347	44.8	2,674	1.0	2,903	1.1	756	.3	21,012
Mass.	247,885	46.6	268,784	50.5	11,058	2.1	2,993	.6	1,102	.2	20,899
Mich.	283,993	43.9	337,952	52.2	16,012	2.5	8,085	1.3	831	.1	53,959
Minn.	179,155	46.3	179,544	46.4	20,117	5.2	7,793	2.0	758	.2	389
Miss.	80,422	93.3	4,253	4.9	1,484	1.7	. . .	. . .	520	. . .	76,169
Mo.	398,032	50.6	369,339	46.9	14,612	1.9	3,887	.5	903	.1	28,693
Mont.	101,104	56.8	66,933	37.6	9,634	5.4	. . .	. . .	338	.2	34,171
Nebr.	158,827	55.3	117,771	41.0	7,141	2.5	2,952	1.0	624	.2	41,056
Nev.	17,776	53.4	12,127	36.4	3,065	9.2	346	1.0	. . .	. . .	5,649
N.H.	43,781	49.1	43,725	49.1	1,318	1.5	303	.3	. . .	. . .	56
N.J.	211,018	42.7	268,982	54.4	10,405	2.1	3,182	.6	855	.2	57,964
N. Mex.	33,693	50.4	31,097	46.5	1,977	3.0	112	.2	. . .	. . .	2,596
N.Y.	759,426	44.5	879,238	57.5	45,944	2.7	19,031	1.1	2,666	.2	119,812
N.C.	168,383	58.1	120,890	41.7	509	.2	55	. . .	. . .	. . .	47,493
N. Dak.	55,206	47.8	53,471	46.3	5,716	5.0	997	.9	. . .	. . .	1,735
Ohio	604,161	51.9	514,753	44.2	38,092	3.3	8,085	.7	. . .	. . .	89,408
Okla.	148,123	50.7	97,233	33.3	45,091	15.4	1,646	.6	234	.1	50,890
Oreg.	120,087	45.9	126,813	48.5	9,711	3.7	4,729	1.8	310	.1	6,726
Pa.	521,784	40.2	703,823	54.3	42,638	3.3	28,525	2.2	419	. . .	182,039
R.I.	40,394	46.0	44,858	51.1	1,914	2.2	470	.5	180	.2	4,464
S.C.	61,845	96.7	1,550	2.4	135	.2	. . .	. . .	420	.7	60,295
S. Dak.	59,191	45.9	64,217	49.8	3,760	2.9	1,774	1.4	. . .	. . .	5,026
Tenn.	153,280	56.3	116,223	42.7	2,542	.9	145	.1	. . .	. . .	37,057
Tex.	287,415	77.0	64,999	17.4	18,960	5.1	1,936	.5	. . .	. . .	222,416
Utah	84,145	58.8	54,137	37.8	4,460	3.1	149	.1	254	.2	30,008
Vt.	22,708	35.2	40,250	62.4	798	1.2	709	1.1	10	. . .	17,542
Va.	101,840	67.0	48,384	31.8	1,056	.7	678	.5	67	. . .	53,458
Wash.	183,388	48.1	167,208	43.9	22,800	6.0	6,868	1.8	730	.2	16,180
W. Va.	140,403	48.5	143,124	49.4	6,144	2.1	. . .	. . .	. . .	. . .	2,721
Wis.	191,363	42.8	220,822	49.4	27,631	6.2	7,318	1.6	. . .	. . .	29,459
Wyo.	28,376	54.7	21,698	41.8	1,459	2.8	373	.7	. . .	. . .	6,678
Total	**9,126,300**	**49.24**	**8,546,789**	**46.11**	**589,924**	**3.18**	**221,030**	**1.19**	**50,979**	**.28**	

Source: Congressional Quarterly, *Presidential Elections,* 87.

TABLE 8.3 1920 PRESIDENTIAL ELECTION

Total popular votes: 26,753,786
Harding's plurality: 6,992,430

State	Warren G. Harding (Republican) Votes	%	James M. Cox (Democrat) Votes	%	Eugene V. Debs (Socialist) Votes	%	Parley P. Christensen (Farmer-Labor) Votes	%	Other Votes	%	Plurality
Ala.	74,719	31.9	156,064	66.7	2,402	1.0	. . .	. . .	766	.3	81,345
Ariz.	37,016	55.6	29,546	44.4	. . .	. . .	. . .	. . .	. . .	. . .	7,470
Ark.	71,107	38.7	107,406	58.5	5,108	2.8	. . .	. . .	. . .	. . .	36,299
Calif.	624,992	66.2	229,191	24.3	64,076	6.8	. . .	. . .	25,672	2.7	395,801
Colo.	171,709	59.4	103,721	35.9	7,860	2.7	2,898	1.0	2,807	1.0	67,988
Conn.	229,238	62.7	120,721	33.0	10,350	2.8	1,947	.5	3,262	.9	108,517
Del.	52,858	55.7	39,911	42.1	988	1.0	82	.1	1,025	1.1	12,947
Fla.	44,853	30.8	90,515	62.0	5,189	3.6	. . .	. . .	5,124	3.5	45,662
Ga.	42,981	28.7	106,112	70.9	558	.4	. . .	. . .	. . .	. . .	63,131
Idaho	88,975	65.6	46,579	34.3	38	. . .	. . .	. . .	32	. . .	42,396
Ill.	1,420,480	67.8	534,395	25.5	74,747	3.6	49,632	2.4	15,461	.8	886,085
Ind.	696,370	55.1	511,364	40.5	24,713	2.0	16,499	1.3	14,028	1.1	185,006
Iowa	634,674	70.9	227,924	25.5	16,981	1.9	10,321	1.2	5,185	.6	406,750
Kans.	369,268	64.8	185,464	32.5	15,511	2.7	. . .	. . .	75	. . .	183,804
Ky.	451,480	49.2	457,203	49.8	6,409	.7	. . .	. . .	3,250	.4	5,723
La.	38,539	30.5	87,355	69.2	. . .	. . .	. . .	. . .	342	.3	48,816
Maine	136,355	65.5	69,306	33.3	2,210	1.1	. . .	. . .	310	.2	67,049
Md.	236,117	55.1	180,626	42.2	8,876	2.1	1,645	.4	1,186	.3	55,491
Mass.	681,153	68.6	276,691	27.8	32,265	3.3	. . .	. . .	3,607	.4	404,462
Mich.	755,941	72.8	231,046	22.3	28,446	2.7	10,163	1.0	12,385	1.2	524,895
Minn.	519,421	70.6	142,994	19.4	56,106	7.6	. . .	. . .	17,317	2.4	376,427
Miss.	11,527	14.0	69,252	84.0	1,639	2.0	. . .	. . .	. . .	. . .	57,725
Mo.	727,252	54.6	574,799	43.2	20,342	1.5	3,108	.2	6,739	.5	152,453
Mont.	109,680	61.0	57,746	32.1	. . .	. . .	12,283	6.8	. . .	. . .	51,934
Nebr.	247,498	64.7	119,608	31.3	9,600	2.5	. . .	. . .	6,037	1.6	127,890
Nev.	15,479	56.9	9,851	36.2	1,864	6.9	. . .	. . .	. . .	. . .	5,628
N.H.	95,196	59.8	62,662	39.4	1,234	.8	. . .	. . .	. . .	. . .	32,534
N.J.	611,541	67.7	256,887	28.4	27,141	3.0	2,200	.2	6,114	.7	354,654
N. Mex.	57,634	54.7	46,668	44.3	. . .	. . .	1,097	1.0	. . .	. . .	10,966
N.Y.	1,871,167	64.6	781,238	27.0	203,201	7.0	18,413	.6	24,494	.9	1,089,929
N.C.	232,819	43.2	305,367	56.7	446	.1	. . .	. . .	17	. . .	72,548
N. Dak.	158,997	77.7	37,409	18.3	8,273	4.0	. . .	. . .	. . .	. . .	121,588
Ohio	1,182,022	58.5	780,037	38.6	57,147	2.8	. . .	. . .	2,447	.1	401,985
Okla.	243,465	50.2	215,798	44.5	25,698	5.3	. . .	. . .	. . .	. . .	27,667
Oreg.	143,592	60.2	80,019	33.6	9,801	4.1	. . .	. . .	5,110	2.2	63,573
Pa.	1,218,216	65.8	503,843	27.2	70,571	3.8	15,705	.9	44,282	2.4	714,373
R.I.	107,463	64.0	55,062	32.8	4,351	2.6	. . .	. . .	1,105	.7	52,401
S.C.	2,244	3.4	64,170	96.1	28	. . .	. . .	. . .	366	.6	61,926
S. Dak.	109,874	60.7	35,938	19.8	. . .	. . .	34,406	19.0	900	.5	73,936
Tenn.	219,229	51.2	206,558	48.3	2,249	.5	. . .	. . .	. . .	. . .	12,671
Tex.	114,384	23.5	288,933	59.4	8,122	1.7	. . .	. . .	75,010	15.4	174,549
Utah	81,555	55.9	56,639	38.8	3,159	2.2	4,475	3.1	. . .	. . .	24,916
Vt.	67,964	75.8	20,884	23.3	. . .	. . .	. . .	. . .	818	.9	47,080
Va.	87,456	37.9	141,670	61.3	808	.4	240	.1	826	.4	54,214
Wash.	223,137	56.0	84,298	21.1	8,913	2.2	77,246	19.4	5,111	1.3	138,839
W. Va.	282,010	55.3	220,789	43.3	5,609	1.1	. . .	. . .	1,526	.3	61,221
Wis.	498,576	71.1	113,196	16.2	80,635	11.5	. . .	. . .	8,648	1.2	385,380
Wyo.	35,091	64.2	17,429	31.9	. . .	. . .	2,180	4.0	. . .	. . .	17,662
Total	16,133,314	60.30	9,140,884	34.17	913,664	3.42	264,540	.99	301,384	1.13	

Source: Congressional Quarterly, *Presidential Elections,* 88.

TABLE 8.4   1924 PRESIDENTIAL ELECTION

Total popular votes: 29,075,959
Coolidge's plurality: 7,331,384

State	Calvin Coolidge (Republican) Votes	%	John W. Davis (Democrat) Votes	%	Robert M. La Follette (Progressive) Votes	%	Herman P. Faris (Prohibition) Votes	%	Other Votes	%	Plurality
Ala.	40,615	25.0	113,138	69.7	8,040	5.0	562	.4	...	...	72,523
Ariz.	30,516	41.3	26,235	35.5	17,210	23.3	...	...	...	...	4,281
Ark.	40,518	29.3	84,759	61.2	13,146	9.5	...	...	10	...	44,241
Calif.	733,196	57.2	105,514	8.2	424,649	33.1	18,436	1.4	122	...	308,547
Colo.	193,956	59.4	75,238	23.0	57,368	17.6	...	...	...	...	118,718
Conn.	246,322	61.5	110,184	27.5	42,416	10.6	...	...	1,373	.3	136,138
Del.	52,441	57.7	33,445	36.8	4,979	5.5	...	...	16	...	18,996
Fla.	30,633	28.1	62,083	56.9	8,625	7.9	5,498	5.0	2,315	2.1	31,450
Ga.	30,300	18.2	123,260	74.1	12,687	7.6	...	...	...	...	92,960
Idaho	72,084	48.1	24,217	16.2	53,664	35.8	...	...	...	...	18,420
Ill.	1,453,321	58.8	576,975	23.4	432,027	17.5	2,367	.1	5,377	.2	876,346
Ind.	703,042	55.3	492,245	38.7	71,700	5.6	4,416	.4	987	.1	210,797
Iowa	537,458	55.0	160,382	16.4	274,448	28.1	...	...	4,482	.5	263,010
Kans.	407,671	61.5	156,320	23.6	98,462	14.9	...	...	3	...	251,351
Ky.	396,758	48.8	375,543	46.1	38,465	4.7	...	...	3,093	.4	21,215
La.	24,670	20.2	93,218	76.4	...	...	...	...	4,063	3.3	68,548
Maine	138,440	72.0	41,964	21.8	11,382	5.9	...	...	406	.2	96,476
Md.	162,414	45.3	148,072	41.3	47,157	13.2	...	...	987	.3	14,342
Mass.	703,476	62.3	280,817	24.9	141,225	12.5	...	...	4,304	.4	422,659
Mich.	874,631	75.4	152,359	13.1	122,014	10.5	6,085	.5	5,330	.5	722,272
Minn.	420,759	51.2	55,913	6.8	339,192	41.3	...	...	6,282	.8	81,567
Miss.	8,384	7.5	100,057	89.4	3,448	3.1	...	...	...	...	91,673
Mo.	648,486	49.6	572,962	43.8	83,996	6.4	1,418	.1	1,231	.1	75,524
Mont.	74,246	42.5	33,867	19.4	65,985	37.8	...	...	370	.2	8,261
Nebr.	218,985	47.2	137,299	29.6	105,681	22.8	1,594	.3	...	...	81,686
Nev.	11,243	41.8	5,909	22.0	9,769	36.3	...	...	...	...	1,474
N.H.	98,575	59.8	57,201	34.7	8,993	5.5	...	...	...	...	41,374
N.J.	675,162	62.2	297,743	27.4	108,901	10.0	1,337	.1	2,936	.3	377,419
N. Mex.	54,745	48.5	48,542	43.0	9,543	8.5	...	...	...	...	6,203
N.Y.	1,820,058	55.8	950,796	29.1	474,913	14.6	...	...	18,172	.6	869,262
N.C.	190,754	39.6	284,190	59.0	6,651	1.4	13	...	...	...	93,436
N. Dak.	94,931	47.7	13,858	7.0	89,922	45.2	...	...	370	.2	5,009
Ohio	1,176,130	58.3	477,888	23.7	358,008	17.8	...	...	4,271	.2	698,242
Okla.	225,756	42.8	255,798	48.5	41,142	7.8	...	...	5,134	1.0	30,042
Oreg.	142,579	51.0	67,589	24.2	68,403	24.5	...	...	908	.3	74,176
Pa.	1,401,481	65.4	409,192	19.1	307,567	14.3	9,779	.5	16,700	.8	992,289
R.I.	125,286	59.6	76,606	36.5	7,628	3.6	...	...	596	.3	48,680
S.C.	1,123	2.2	49,008	96.6	623	1.2	...	...	1	...	47,885
S. Dak.	101,299	49.7	27,214	13.4	75,200	36.9	...	...	...	...	26,099
Tenn.	130,831	43.5	159,339	52.9	10,666	3.5	94		100		28,508
Tex.	130,794	19.8	485,443	73.7	42,879	6.5	...	...	...	...	354,649
Utah	77,327	49.3	46,908	29.9	32,662	20.8	...	...	...	...	30,419
Vt.	80,498	78.2	16,124	15.7	5,943	5.8	316	.3	5	...	64,374
Va.	73,328	32.8	139,717	62.5	10,369	4.6	...	...	189	.1	66,389
Wash.	220,224	52.3	42,842	10.2	150,727	35.8	...	...	7,709	1.8	69,497
W. Va.	288,635	49.5	257,232	44.1	36,723	6.3	...	...	1,072	.2	31,403
Wis.	311,614	37.1	68,096	8.1	453,678	54.0	2,918	.4	4,441	.5	142,064
Wyo.	41,858	52.4	12,868	16.1	25,174	31.5	...	...	...	...	16,684
Total	15,717,553	54.06	8,386,169	28.84	4,814,050	16.56	54,833	.19	103,354	.36	

Source: Congressional Quarterly, *Presidential Elections*, 89.

TABLE 8.5   1928 PRESIDENTIAL ELECTION

Total popular votes: 36,790,364
Hoover's plurality: 6,411,806

State	Herbert C. Hoover (Republican) Votes	%	Alfred E. Smith (Democrat) Votes	%	Norman M. Thomas (Socialist) Votes	%	William Z. Foster (Communist) Votes	%	Other Votes	%	Plurality
Ala.	120,725	48.5	127,796	51.3	460	.2	. . .	. . .	. . .	. . .	7,071
Ariz.	52,533	57.6	38,537	42.2	. . .	. . .	184	.2	. . .	. . .	13,996
Ark.	77,785	39.3	119,195	60.3	434	.2	317	.2	. . .	. . .	41,410
Calif.	1,147,929	63.9	614,365	34.2	19,595	1.1	112	. . .	14,655	.8	533,564
Colo.	252,924	64.8	132,747	34.0	2,630	.7	675	.2	1,092	.3	120,177
Conn.	296,614	53.6	252,040	45.6	3,019	.6	730	.1	622	.1	44,574
Del.	68,860	65.8	35,354	33.8	329	.3	58	.1	. . .	. . .	33,506
Fla.	144,168	57.1	100,721	39.9	4,036	1.6	3,704	1.5	. . .	. . .	43,447
Ga.	99,368	43.4	129,602	56.6	124	.1	64	. . .	. . .	. . .	30,234
Idaho	97,322	64.2	52,926	34.9	1,293	.9	. . .	. . .	. . .	. . .	44,396
Ill.	1,770,723	57.0	1,312,235	42.2	19,138	.6	3,581	.1	1,812	.1	458,488
Ind.	848,290	59.7	562,691	39.6	3,871	.3	321	. . .	6,141	.4	285,599
Iowa	623,570	61.8	379,011	37.6	2,960	.3	328	. . .	3,320	.3	244,559
Kans.	513,672	72.0	193,003	27.1	6,205	.9	319	. . .	. . .	. . .	320,669
Ky.	558,064	59.3	381,060	40.5	846	.1	307	. . .	354	. . .	177,004
La.	51,160	23.7	164,655	76.3	. . .	. . .	. . .	. . .	. . .	. . .	113,495
Maine	179,923	68.6	81,179	31.0	1,065	.4	. . .	. . .	. . .	. . .	98,744
Md.	301,479	57.1	223,626	42.3	1,701	.3	636	.1	906	.2	77,853
Mass.	775,566	49.2	792,758	50.2	6,262	.4	2,461	.2	776	.1	17,192
Mich.	965,396	70.4	396,762	28.9	3,516	.3	2,881	.2	3,527	.3	568,634
Minn.	560,977	57.8	396,451	40.8	6,774	.7	4,853	.5	1,921	.2	164,526
Miss.	26,202	17.3	124,445	82.2	. . .	. . .	. . .	. . .	788	.5	98,243
Mo.	834,080	55.6	662,684	44.2	3,739	.3	. . .	. . .	342	. . .	171,396
Mont.	113,472	58.4	78,638	40.5	1,690	.9	577	.3	. . .	. . .	34,834
Nebr.	345,745	63.2	197,950	36.2	3,433	.6	. . .	. . .	. . .	. . .	147,795
Nev.	18,327	56.5	14,090	43.5	. . .	. . .	. . .	. . .	. . .	. . .	4,237
N.H.	115,404	58.7	80,715	41.0	465	.2	173	.1	. . .	. . .	34,689
N.J.	925,285	59.8	616,162	39.8	4,866	.3	1,240	.1	642	. . .	309,123
N. Mex.	69,708	59.0	48,211	40.8	. . .	. . .	158	.1	. . .	. . .	21,497
N.Y.	2,193,344	49.8	2,089,863	47.4	107,332	2.4	10,876	.3	4,211	.1	103,481
N.C.	348,923	54.9	286,227	45.1	. . .	. . .	. . .	. . .	. . .	. . .	62,696
N. Dak.	131,419	54.8	106,648	44.5	842	.4	936	.4	. . .	. . .	24,771
Ohio	1,627,546	64.9	864,210	34.5	8,683	.4	2,836	.1	5,071	.2	763,336
Okla.	394,046	63.7	219,174	35.4	3,924	.6	. . .	. . .	1,283	.2	174,872
Oreg.	205,341	64.2	109,223	34.1	2,720	.9	1,094	.3	1,564	.5	96,118
Pa.	2,055,382	65.2	1,067,586	33.9	18,647	.6	4,726	.2	4,271	.1	987,796
R.I.	117,522	49.6	118,973	50.2	. . .	. . .	283	.1	416	.2	1,451
S.C.	5,858	8.5	62,700	91.4	47	.1	. . .	. . .	. . .	. . .	56,842
S. Dak.	157,603	60.2	102,660	39.2	443	.2	224	.1	927	.4	54,943
Tenn.	195,195	55.5	156,169	44.4	590	.2	70	. . .	. . .	. . .	39,026
Tex.	367,036	51.7	341,458	48.1	641	.1	209	. . .	. . .	. . .	25,578
Utah	94,485	53.5	80,985	45.9	954	.5	46	. . .	. . .	. . .	13,500
Vt.	90,404	66.9	44,440	32.9	. . .	. . .	. . .	. . .	347	.3	45,964
Va.	164,609	53.9	140,146	45.9	250	.1	179	.1	180	.1	24,463
Wash.	335,503	67.1	156,772	31.4	2,615	.5	1,083	.2	4,068	.8	178,731
W. Va.	375,551	58.4	263,784	41.0	1,313	.2	401	.1	1,703	.3	111,767
Wis.	544,205	53.5	450,259	44.3	18,213	1.8	1,528	.2	2,626	.3	93,946
Wyo.	52,748	63.7	29,299	35.4	788	1.0	. . .	. . .	. . .	. . .	23,449
Total	**21,411,991**	**58.20**	**15,000,185**	**40.77**	**266,453**	**.72**	**48,170**	**.13**	**63,565**	**.17**	

Source: Congressional Quarterly, *Presidential Elections,* 90.

TABLE 8.6   1932 PRESIDENTIAL ELECTION

Total popular votes: 39,749,382
Roosevelt's plurality: 7,066,619

State	Franklin D. Roosevelt (Democrat) Votes	%	Herbert C. Hoover (Republican) Votes	%	Norman M. Thomas (Socialist) Votes	%	William Z. Foster (Communist) Votes	%	Other Votes	%	Plurality
Ala.	207,732	84.7	34,647	14.1	2,060	.8	676	.3	13	. . .	173,085
Ariz.	79,264	67.0	36,104	30.5	2,618	2.2	256	.2	9	. . .	43,160
Ark.	186,829	86.3	27,465	12.7	1,166	.5	157	.1	952	.4	159,364
Calif.	1,324,157	58.4	847,902	37.4	63,299	2.8	. . .	. . .	30,464	1.3	476,255
Colo.	250,151	54.9	188,364	41.3	13,591	3.0	758	.2	2,824	.6	61,787
Conn.	281,632	47.4	288,420	48.5	20,480	3.5	1,364	.2	2,287	.4	6,788
Del.	54,319	48.1	57,073	50.6	1,376	1.2	133	.1	. . .	. . .	2,754
Fla.	206,307	74.9	69,170	25.1	. . .	. . .	. . .	. . .	. . .	. . .	137,137
Ga.	234,118	91.6	19,863	7.8	461	.2	23	. . .	1,125	.4	214,255
Idaho	109,479	58.7	71,312	38.2	526	.3	491	.3	4,660	2.5	38,167
Ill.	1,882,304	55.2	1,432,756	42.0	67,258	2.0	15,582	.5	10,026	.3	449,548
Ind.	862,054	54.7	677,184	42.9	21,388	1.4	2,187	.1	14,084	.9	184,870
Iowa	598,019	57.7	414,433	40.0	20,467	2.0	559	.1	3,209	.3	183,586
Kans.	424,204	53.6	349,498	44.12	18,276	2.3	. . .	. . .	. . .	. . .	74,706
Ky.	580,574	59.1	394,716	40.2	3,858	.4	275	. . .	3,663	.4	185,858
La.	249,418	92.8	18,853	7.0	. . .	. . .	. . .	. . .	533	.2	230,565
Maine	138,907	43.2	166,631	55.8	2,489	.8	162	.1	255	.1	37,724
Md.	314,314	61.5	184,184	36.0	10,489	2.1	1,031	.2	1,036	.2	130,130
Mass.	800,148	50.6	736,959	46.6	34,305	2.2	4,821	.3	3,881	.2	63,189
Mich.	871,700	52.4	739,894	44.4	39,205	2.4	9,318	.6	4,648	.3	131,806
Minn.	600,806	59.9	363,959	36.3	25,476	2.5	6,101	.6	6,501	.7	236,847
Miss.	140,168	96.0	5,170	3.5	675	.5	. . .	. . .	. . .	. . .	134,998
Mo.	1,025,406	63.7	564,713	35.1	16,374	1.0	568	. . .	2,833	.2	460,693
Mont.	127,476	58.8	78,134	36.0	7,902	3.7	1,801	.8	1,461	.7	49,342
Nebr.	359,082	63.0	201,177	35.3	9,876	1.7	. . .	. . .	. . .	. . .	157,905
Nev.	28,756	69.5	12,622	30.5	. . .	. . .	. . .	. . .	. . .	. . .	16,134
N.H.	100,680	49.0	103,629	50.4	947	.5	264	.1	. . .	. . .	2,949
N.J.	806,394	49.5	775,406	47.6	42,981	2.6	2,908	.2	1,811	.1	30,988
N. Mex.	95,089	62.8	54,146	35.7	1,771	1.2	133	.1	389	.3	40,943
N.Y.	2,534,959	54.1	1,937,963	41.3	177,397	3.8	27,956	.6	10,339	.2	596,996
N.C.	497,566	69.9	208,344	29.3	5,585	.8	. . .	. . .	. . .	. . .	289,222
N. Dak.	178,350	69.6	71,772	28.0	3,521	1.4	830	.3	1,817	.7	106,578
Ohio	1,301,695	49.9	1,227,319	47.0	64,094	2.5	7,231	.3	9,389	.4	74,376
Okla.	516,468	73.3	188,165	26.7	. . .	. . .	. . .	. . .	. . .	. . .	328,303
Oreg.	213,871	58.0	136,019	36.9	15,450	4.2	1,681	.5	1,730	.5	77,852
Pa.	1,295,948	45.3	1,453,540	50.8	91,223	3.2	5,659	. . .	12,807	.5	157,592
R.I.	146,604	55.1	115,266	43.3	3,138	1.2	546	.2	616	.2	31,338
S.C.	102,347	98.0	1,978	1.9	82	.1	. . .	. . .	4	. . .	100,369
S. Dak.	183,515	63.6	99,212	34.4	1,551	.5	364	.1	3,796	1.3	84,303
Tenn.	259,463	66.5	126,752	32.5	1,796	.5	254	.1	1,998	.5	132,711
Tex.	767,585	88.2	97,852	11.2	4,416	.5	204	. . .	387	.1	669,733
Utah	116,749	56.6	84,513	41.0	4,087	2.0	946	.5	. . .	. . .	32,236
Vt.	56,266	41.1	78,984	57.7	1,533	1.1	195	.1	2	. . .	22,718
Va.	203,979	68.5	89,634	30.1	2,382	.8	86	. . .	1,858	.6	114,345
Wash.	353,260	57.5	208,645	33.9	17,080	2.8	2,972	.5	32,844	5.3	144,615
W. Va.	405,124	54.5	330,731	44.5	5,133	.7	444	.1	2,342	.3	74,393
Wis.	707,410	63.5	347,741	31.2	53,379	4.8	3,105	.3	3,165	.3	359,669
Wyo.	54,370	56.1	39,583	40.8	2,829	2.9	180	.2	. . .	. . .	14,787
Total	22,825,016	57.42	15,758,397	39.64	883,990	2.22	102,221	.26	179,758	.45	

Source: Congressional Quarterly, *Presidential Elections*, 91.

TABLE 8.7 1936 PRESIDENTIAL ELECTION

Total popular votes: 45,642,303
Roosevelt's plurality: 11,068,093

State	Franklin D. Roosevelt (Democrat) Votes	%	Alfred M. Landon (Republican) Votes	%	William Lemke (Union) Votes	%	Norman M. Thomas (Socialist) Votes	%	Other Votes	%	Plurality
Ala.	238,131	86.4	35,358	12.8	543	.2	242	.1	1,397	.5	202,773
Ariz.	86,722	69.9	33,433	26.9	3,307	2.7	317	.3	384	.3	53,289
Ark.	146,756	81.8	32,049	17.9	. . .	. . .	446	.3	167	.1	114,707
Calif.	1,766,836	67.0	836,431	31.7	. . .	. . .	11,325	.4	23,794	.9	930,405
Colo.	294,599	60.3	181,267	37.1	9,962	2.0	1,594	.3	824	.2	113,332
Conn.	382,129	55.3	278,685	40.4	21,805	3.2	5,683	.8	2,421	.4	103,444
Del.	69,702	54.6	54,014	42.3	442	.4	172	.1	3,273	2.5	15,688
Fla.	249,117	76.1	78,248	23.9	. . .	. . .	. . .	. . .	. . .	. . .	170,869
Ga.	255,364	87.1	36,943	12.6	136	.1	68	. . .	660	.2	218,421
Idaho	125,683	63.0	66,232	33.2	7,677	3.9	. . .	. . .	. . .	. . .	59,451
Ill.	2,282,999	57.7	1,570,393	39.7	89,430	2.3	7,530	.2	5,362	.1	712,606
Ind.	934,974	56.6	691,570	41.9	19,407	1.2	3,856	.2	1,090	.1	243,404
Iowa	621,756	54.4	487,977	42.7	29,887	2.6	1,373	.1	1,944	.2	133,779
Kans.	464,520	53.7	397,727	46.0	497	.1	2,770	.3	. . .	. . .	66,793
Ky.	541,944	58.5	369,702	39.9	12,532	1.4	649	.1	1,472	.2	172,242
La.	292,802	88.8	36,697	11.1	. . .	. . .	. . .	. . .	93	. . .	256,105
Maine	126,333	41.6	168,823	55.6	7,581	2.5	783	.3	720	.2	42,490
Md.	389,612	62.4	231,435	37.0	. . .	. . .	1,629	.3	2,220	.4	158,177
Mass.	942,716	51.2	768,613	41.8	118,639	6.5	5,111	.3	5,278	.3	174,103
Mich.	1,015,794	56.3	699,733	38.8	75,795	4.2	8,208	.5	4,568	.3	317,061
Minn.	698,811	61.8	350,461	31.0	74,296	6.6	2,872	.3	3,535	.3	348,350
Miss.	157,333	97.0	4,467	2.8	. . .	. . .	342	.2	. . .	. . .	152,866
Mo.	1,111,043	60.8	697,891	38.2	14,630	.8	3,454	.2	1,617	.1	413,152
Mont.	159,690	69.3	63,598	27.6	5,539	2.4	1,066	.5	609	.3	96,092
Nebr.	347,445	57.1	247,731	40.7	12,847	2.1	. . .	. . .	. . .	. . .	99,714
Nev.	31,925	72.8	11,923	27.2	. . .	. . .	. . .	. . .	. . .	. . .	20,002
N.H.	108,460	49.7	104,642	48.0	4,819	2.2	. . .	. . .	193	.1	3,818
N.J.	1,083,549	59.6	719,421	39.6	9,405	.5	3,892	.2	2,860	.2	364,128
N. Mex.	105,848	62.7	61,727	36.5	924	.6	343	.2	104	.1	44,121
N.Y.	3,293,222	58.8	2,180,670	39.0	. . .	. . .	86,897	1.6	35,609	.6	1,112,552
N.C.	616,141	73.4	223,294	26.6	. . .	. . .	. . .	. . .	. . .	. . .	392,847
N. Dak.	163,148	59.6	72,751	26.6	36,708	13.4	552	.2	557	.2	90,397
Ohio	1,747,140	58.0	1,127,855	37.4	132,212	4.4	. . .	. . .	5,251	.2	619,285
Okla.	501,069	66.8	245,122	32.7	. . .	. . .	2,211	.3	1,328	.2	255,947
Oreg.	266,733	64.4	122,706	29.6	21,831	5.3	2,143	.5	608	.2	144,027
Pa.	2,353,987	56.9	1,690,200	40.8	67,478	1.6	14,599	.4	12,172	.3	663,787
R.I.	164,338	53.0	125,031	40.3	19,569	6.3	. . .	. . .	1,340	.4	39,307
S.C.	113,791	98.6	1,646	1.4	. . .	. . .	. . .	. . .	. . .	. . .	112,145
S. Dak.	160,137	54.0	125,977	42.5	10,338	3.5	. . .	. . .	. . .	. . .	34,160
Tenn.	328,083	68.9	146,520	30.8	296	.1	692	.2	960	.2	181,563
Tex.	730,843	86.9	104,728	12.5	3,193	.4	1,067	.1	772	.1	626,115
Utah	150,248	69.3	64,555	29.8	1,121	.5	432	.2	323	.2	85,893
Vt.	62,124	43.2	81,023	56.4	. . .	. . .	. . .	. . .	542	.4	18,899
Va.	234,980	70.2	98,336	29.4	233	.1	313	.1	728	.2	136,644
Wash.	459,579	66.4	206,885	29.9	17,463	2.5	3,496	.5	4,908	.7	252,694
W. Va.	502,872	60.6	325,486	39.2	. . .	. . .	832	.1	1,173	.1	177,386
Wis.	802,984	63.8	380,828	30.3	60,297	4.8	10,626	.8	3,825	.3	422,156
Wyo.	62,624	60.6	38,739	37.5	1,653	1.6	200	.2	166	.2	23,885
Total	27,747,636	60.79	16,679,543	36.54	892,492	1.96	187,785	.41	134,847	.30	

Source: Congressional Quarterly, *Presidential Elections*, 92.

TABLE 8.8 1940 PRESIDENTIAL ELECTION

Total popular votes: 49,840,443
Roosevelt's plurality: 4,927,188

State	Franklin D. Roosevelt (Democrat) Votes	%	Wendell Willkie (Republican) Votes	%	Norman M. Thomas (Socialist) Votes	%	Roger W. Babson (Prohibition) Votes	%	Other Votes	%	Plurality
Ala.	250.723	85.2	42,167	14.3	100	. . .	698	.2	509	.2	208,556
Ariz.	95,267	63.5	54,030	36.0	. . .	. . .	742	.5	. . .	. . .	41,237
Ark.	157,258	78.4	42,122	21.0	301	.2	793	.4	. . .	. . .	115,136
Calif.	1,877,618	57.4	1,351,419	41.3	16,506	.5	9,400	.3	13,848	.4	526,199
Colo.	265,364	48.4	279,022	50.9	1,899	.4	1,597	.3	378	.1	13,658
Conn.	417,621	53.4	361,819	46.3	. . .	. . .	. . .	. . .	2,062	.3	55,802
Del.	74,599	54.7	61,440	45.1	110	.1	187	.1	. . .	. . .	13,159
Fla.	359,334	74.0	126,158	26.0	. . .	. . .	. . .	. . .	. . .	. . .	233,176
Ga.	265,194	84.8	46,495	14.9	. . .	. . .	983	.3	14	. . .	218,699
Idaho	127,842	54.4	106,509	45.3	484	.2	. . .	. . .	276	.1	21,333
Ill.	2,149,934	51.0	2,047,240	48.5	10,914	.3	9,190	.2	. . .	. . .	102,694
Ind.	874,063	49.0	899,466	50.5	2,075	.1	6,437	.4	706	. . .	25,403
Iowa	578,802	47.6	632,370	52.0	. . .	. . .	2,284	.2	1,976	.2	53,568
Kans.	364,725	42.4	489,169	56.9	2,347	.3	4,056	.5	. . .	. . .	124,444
Ky.	557,312	57.4	410,384	42.3	1,062	.1	1,465	.2	. . .	. . .	146,928
La.	319,751	85.9	52,446	14.1	. . .	. . .	. . .	. . .	108	. . .	267,305
Maine	156,478	48.8	163,951	51.1	. . .	. . .	. . .	. . .	411	.1	7,473
Md.	384,552	58.3	269,534	40.8	4,093	.6	11	. . .	1,940	.3	115,018
Mass.	1,076,522	53.1	939,700	46.4	4,091	.2	1,370	.1	5,310	.3	136,822
Mich.	1,032,991	49.5	1,039,917	49.9	7,593	.4	1,795	.1	3,663	.2	6,926
Minn.	644,196	51.5	596,274	47.7	5,454	.4	. . .	. . .	5,264	.4	47,922
Miss.	168,267	95.7	7,363	4.2	193	.1	. . .	. . .	. . .	. . .	160,904
Mo.	958,476	52.3	871,009	47.5	2,226	.1	1,809	.1	209	. . .	87,467
Mont.	145,698	58.8	99,579	40.2	1,443	.6	664	.3	489	.2	46,119
Nebr.	263,677	42.8	352,201	57.2	. . .	. . .	. . .	. . .	. . .	. . .	88,524
Nev.	31,945	60.1	21,229	39.9	. . .	. . .	. . .	. . .	. . .	. . .	10,716
N.H.	125,292	53.2	110,127	46.8	. . .	. . .	. . .	. . .	. . .	. . .	15,165
N.J.	1,016,404	51.5	944,876	47.9	2,823	.1	852	. . .	9,260	.5	71,528
N. Mex.	103,699	56.6	79,315	43.3	143	.1	100	.1	. . .	. . .	24,384
N.Y.	3,251,918	51.6	3,027,478	48.0	18,950	.3	3,250	.1	. . .	. . .	224,440
N.C.	609,015	74.0	213,633	26.0	. . .	. . .	. . .	. . .	. . .	. . .	395,382
N. Dak.	124,036	44.2	154,590	55.1	1,279	.5	325	.1	545	.2	30,554
Ohio	1,733,139	52.2	1,586,773	47.8	. . .	. . .	. . .	. . .	. . .	. . .	146,366
Okla.	474,313	57.4	348,872	42.2	. . .	. . .	3,027	.4	. . .	. . .	125,441
Oreg.	258,415	53.7	219,555	45.6	398	.1	154	. . .	2,678	.6	38,860
Pa.	2,171,035	53.2	1,889,848	46.3	10,967	.3	. . .	. . .	6,864	.2	281,187
R.I.	182,182	56.7	138,653	43.2	. . .	. . .	74	. . .	239	.1	43,529
S.C.	95,470	95.6	4,360	4.4	. . .	. . .	. . .	. . .	. . .	. . .	91,110
S. Dak.	131,362	42.6	177,065	57.4	. . .	. . .	. . .	. . .	. . .	. . .	45,703
Tenn.	351,601	67.3	169,153	32.4	463	.1	1,606	.3	. . .	. . .	182,448
Tex.	861,390	80.9	201,866	19.0	628	.1	928	.1	215	. . .	659,524
Utah	153,833	62.2	92,973	37.6	198	.1	. . .	. . .	191	.1	60,860
Vt.	64,269	44.9	78,371	54.8	. . .	. . .	. . .	. . .	422	.3	14,102
Va.	235,961	68.1	109,363	31.6	282	.1	882	.3	120	. . .	126,598
Wash.	462,145	58.2	322,123	40.6	4,586	.6	1,686	.2	3,293	.4	140,022
W. Va.	495,662	57.1	372,414	42.9	. . .	. . .	. . .	. . .	. . .	. . .	123,248
Wis.	704,811	50.2	679,206	48.3	15,071	1.1	2,148	.2	4,263	.3	25,605
Wyo.	59,287	52.8	52,633	46.9	148	.1	172	.2	. . .	. . .	6,654
Total	**27,263,448**	**54.70**	**22,336,260**	**44.82**	**116,827**	**.23**	**58,685**	**.12**	**65,223**	**.13**	

Source: Congressional Quarterly, *Presidential Elections,* 93.

Dominant political figure—perhaps the dominant individual—of the years 1914–45, Franklin D. Roosevelt rides with his wife, Eleanor, to an unprecedented third inauguration, January 1941. (National Archives)

TABLE 8.9   1944 PRESIDENTIAL ELECTION

Total popular votes: 47,974,819
Roosevelt's plurality: 3,598,564

State	Franklin D. Roosevelt (Democrat) Votes	%	Thomas E. Dewey (Republican) Votes	%	Norman M. Thomas (Socialist) Votes	%	Claude A. Watson (Prohibition) Votes	%	Other Votes	%	Plurality
Ala.	198,904	81.3	44,478	18.2	189	.1	1,054	.4	. . .	. . .	154,426
Ariz.	80,926	58.8	56,287	40.9	. . .	. . .	421	.3	. . .	. . .	24,639
Ark.	148,965	70.0	63,556	29.8	438	.2	. . .	. . .	. . .	. . .	85,409
Calif.	1,988,564	56.5	1,512,965	43.0	2,515	.1	14,770	.4	2,061	.1	475,599
Colo.	234,331	46.4	268,731	53.2	1.977	.4	. . .	. . .	. . .	. . .	34,400
Conn.	435,146	52.3	390,527	46.9	5,097	.6	. . .	. . .	1,220	.2	44,619
Del.	68,166	54.4	56,747	45.3	154	.1	294	.2	. . .	. . .	11,419
Fla.	339,377	70.3	143,215	29.7	. . .	. . .	. . .	. . .	. . .	. . .	196,162
Ga.	268,187	81.7	56,507	17.2	6	. . .	35	. . .	3,373	1.0	211,680
Idaho	107,399	51.6	100,137	48.1	282	.1	503	.2	. . .	. . .	7,262
Ill.	2,079,479	51.5	1,939,314	48.1	180	. . .	7,411	.2	9,677	.2	140,165
Ind.	781,403	46.7	875,891	52.4	2,223	.1	12,574	.8	. . .	. . .	94,488
Iowa	499,876	47.5	547,267	52.0	1,511	.1	3,752	.4	193	. . .	47,391
Kans.	287,458	39.2	442,096	60.3	1,613	.2	2,609	.4	. . .	. . .	154,638
Ky.	472,589	54.5	392,448	45.2	535	.1	2,023	.2	317	. . .	80,141
La.	281,564	80.6	67,750	19.4	. . .	. . .	. . .	. . .	69	. . .	213,814
Maine	140,631	47.5	155,434	52.4	. . .	. . .	. . .	. . .	335	.1	14,803
Md.	315,983	52.0	292,150	48.0	. . .	. . .	. . .	. . .	. . .	. . .	23,833
Mass.	1,035,296	52.8	921,350	47.0	. . .	. . .	973	.1	3,046	.1	113,946
Mich.	1,106,899	50.2	1,084,423	49.2	4,598	.2	6,503	.3	2,800	.1	22,476
Minn.	589,864	52.4	527,416	46.9	5,048	.5	. . .	. . .	3,176	.3	62,448
Miss.	168,621	93.6	11,613	6.4	. . .	. . .	. . .	. . .	. . .	. . .	157,008
Mo.	807,804	51.4	761,524	48.4	1,751	.1	1,195	.1	220	. . .	46,280
Mont.	112,566	54.3	93,163	44.9	1,296	.6	340	.2	. . .	. . .	19,403
Nebr.	233,246	41.4	329,880	58.6	. . .	. . .	. . .	. . .	. . .	. . .	96,634
Nev.	29,623	54.6	24,611	45.4	. . .	. . .	. . .	. . .	. . .	. . .	5,012
N.H.	119,663	52.1	109,916	47.9	46	. . .	. . .	. . .	. . .	. . .	9,747
N.J.	987,874	50.3	961,335	49.0	3,358	.2	4,255	.2	6,939	.4	26,539
N. Mex.	81,338	53.5	70,559	46.4	. . .	. . .	147	.1	. . .	. . .	10,779
N.Y.	3,304,238	52.3	2,987,647	47.3	10,553	.2	. . .	. . .	14,352	.2	316,591
N.C.	527,408	66.7	263,155	33.3	. . .	. . .	. . .	. . .	. . .	. . .	264,253
N. Dak.	100,144	45.5	118,535	53.8	954	.4	549	.3	. . .	. . .	18,391
Ohio	1,570,763	49.8	1,582,293	50.2	. . .	. . .	. . .	. . .	. . .	. . .	11,530
Okla.	401,549	55.6	319,424	44.2	. . .	. . .	1,663	.2	. . .	. . .	82,125
Oreg.	248,635	51.8	225,365	46.9	3,785	.8	2,362	.5	. . .	. . .	23,270
Pa.	1,940,481	51.1	1,835,054	48.4	11,721	.3	5,751	.2	1,789	.1	105,427
R.I.	175,356	58.6	123,487	41.3	. . .	. . .	433	.1	. . .	. . .	51,869
S.C.	90,601	87.6	4,617	4.5	. . .	. . .	365	.4	7,799	7.5	82,802
S. Dak.	96,711	41.7	135,365	58.3	. . .	. . .	. . .	. . .	. . .	. . .	38,654
Tenn.	308,707	60.5	200,311	39.2	792	.2	882	.2	. . .	. . .	108,396
Tex.	820,048	71.4	191,372	16.7	592	.1	1,013	.1	135,661	11.8	628,676
Utah	150,088	60.5	97,833	39.4	340	.1	. . .	. . .	. . .	. . .	52,255
Vt.	53,806	43.0	71,420	57.0	. . .	. . .	. . .	. . .	14	. . .	17,614
Va.	242,276	62.4	145,243	37.4	417	.1	459	.1	90	. . .	97,033
Wash.	486,774	56.8	361,689	42.2	3,824	.5	2,396	.3	1,645	.2	125,085
W. Va.	392,777	54.9	322,819	45.1	. . .	. . .	. . .	. . .	. . .	. . .	69,958
Wis.	650,413	48.6	674,532	50.4	13,205	1.0	. . .	. . .	1,002	.1	24,119
Wyo.	49,419	48.8	51,921	51.2	. . .	. . .	. . .	. . .	. . .	. . .	2,502
Total	25,611,936	53.39	22,013,372	45.89	79,000	.16	74,733	.16	195,778	.41	

Source: Congressional Quarterly, *Presidential Elections*, 94.

A weary Roosevelt campaigns for a fourth term in 1944 with vice presidential candidate Harry S. Truman *(center)* and Vice President Henry A. Wallace *(right)*. (National Archives)

TABLE 8.10   POLITICAL MAKEUP OF CONGRESS, 1913–1946

Year	Congress	House Major Party	House Principal Minority Party	House Other (except vacancies)	Senate Major Party	Senate Principal Minority Party	Senate Other (except vacancies)	President
1945–1946	79th	D-242	R-190	2	D-56	R-38	1	D (Truman)
1943–1944	78th	D-218	R-208	4	D-58	R-37	1	D (F. Roosevelt)
1941–1942	77th	D-268	R-162	5	D-46	R-28	2	D (F. Roosevelt)
1939–1941	76th	D-261	R-164	4	D-69	R-28	4	D (F. Roosevelt)
1937–1938	75th	D-331	R-89	13	D-76	R-16	4	D (F. Roosevelt)
1935–1936	74th	D-319	R-103	10	D-69	R-25	2	D (F. Roosevelt)
1933–1934	73d	D-310	R-117	5	D-60	R-35	1	D (F. Roosevelt)
1931–1933	72d	D-220	R-214	1	R-48	D-47	1	R (Hoover)
1929–1931	71st	R-267	D-167	1	R-56	D-39	1	R (Hoover)
1927–1929	70th	R-237	D-195	3	R-49	D-46	1	R (Coolidge)
1925–1927	69th	R-247	D-183	4	R-56	D-39	1	R (Coolidge)
1923–1925	68th	R-225	D-205	5	R-51	D-43	2	R (Coolidge)
1921–1923	67th	R-303	D-131	1	R-59	D-37	. . .	R (Harding)
1919–1921	66th	R-240	D-190	3	R-49	D-47	. . .	D (Wilson)
1917–1919	65th	D-216	R-210	6	D-53	R-42	. . .	D (Wilson)
1915–1917	64th	D-230	R-196	9	D-56	R-40	. . .	D (Wilson)
1913–1915	63d	D-291	R-127	17	D-51	R-44	1	D (Wilson)

Source: Bureau of the Census, *Historical Statistics of the United States, 1789 to 1945* (Washington, D.C., 1949), 293.

TABLE 8.11   NATIONAL VOTER TURNOUT, 1912–1944 (IN PERCENT)

Year	President	U.S. Representative	U.S. Senator
1912	59.0	55.7	. . .
1914	. . .	50.4	54.4
1916	65.3	59.5	59.5
1918	. . .	40.1	37.8
1920	49.3	46.7	50.2
1922	. . .	35.7	37.6
1924	48.8	44.8	42.2
1926	. . .	32.8	35.7
1928	56.7	53.5	56.1
1930	. . .	36.6	34.5
1932	57.0	53.4	53.9
1934	. . .	44.6	48.4
1936	61.4	57.8	51.7
1938	. . .	46.8	50.2
1940	62.8	58.6	62.3
1942	. . .	34.0	30.0
1944	56.0	52.6	53.7

Source: Erik W. Austin, *Political Facts of the United States since 1789* (New York, 1986), 378–379.

Democratization of Politics and the Nomination Process: The Primary and the Convention

One of the most important themes of the Progressive movement was that politics could be improved by making it more democratic. In the first two decades of the twentieth century, such democratic devices as the initiative, referendum, and recall were widely adopted, as well as an amendment mandating that United States senators be elected by the people. The process extended to presidential elections through the direct primary, which permitted the people to vote on nominees. At the peak of the Progressive movement the primary seemed the wave of the future. President Woodrow Wilson in 1913 even proposed a national primary. As with many changes of the movement, however, the primary never lived up to expectation. At no time did a majority of states adopt the presidential primary, and the number that did declined after 1916. Doing well in the primary was no guarantee of success. The most important instrument for choosing presidential candidates remained the national party convention, which offered ample opportunity for individual wielding of power and brokered backroom deals. Party conventions could be exciting events, and they also could become laborsome. Until 1936 the Democrats held to the rule that the nominee must receive the endorsement of two-thirds of the delegates. It has been suggested that in several cases—notably the convention of 1924, which ran 103 ballots—a choice was made out of simple fatigue.

TABLE 8.12   VOTES CAST AND DELEGATES SELECTED IN PRESIDENTIAL PRIMARIES, 1912–1944

| Year | Democratic Party | | | Republican Party | | | Total | |
	Number of Primaries	Votes Cast	Delegates Selected through Primaries (%)	Number of Primaries	Votes Cast	Delegates Selected through Primaries (%)	Votes Cast	Delegates Selected through Primaries (%)
1912	12	974,775	32.9	13	2,261,240	41.7	3,236,015	37.3
1916	20	1,187,691	53.5	20	1,923,374	58.9	3,111,065	56.2
1920	16	571,671	44.6	20	3,186,248	57.8	3,757,919	51.2
1924	14	763,858	35.5	17	3,525,185	45.3	4,289,043	40.4
1928	16	1,264,220	42.2	15	4,110,288	44.9	5,374,508	43.5
1932	16	2,952,933	40.0	14	2,346,996	37.7	5,299,929	38.8
1936	14	5,181,808	36.5	12	3,319,810	37.5	8,501,618	37.0
1940	13	4,468,631	35.8	13	3,227,875	38.8	7,696,506	37.3
1944	14	1,867,609	36.7	13	2,271,605	38.7	4,139,214	37.7

Source: Congressional Quarterly, *The People Speak* (Washington, D.C., 1990), 5.

TABLE 8.13   DEMOCRATIC CONVENTIONS, 1912–1944

Year	City	Dates	Presidential Nominee	Vice Presidential Nominee	No. of Ballots
1912	Baltimore	Jun. 25–Jul. 2	Woodrow Wilson	Thomas R. Marshall	46
1916	St. Louis	Jun. 14–16	Woodrow Wilson	Thomas R. Marshall	1
1920	San Francisco	Jun. 28–Jul. 6	James M. Cox	Franklin D. Roosevelt	44
1924	New York	Jun. 24–Jul. 9	John W. Davis	Charles W. Bryan	103
1928	Houston	Jun. 26–29	Alfred E. Smith	Joseph T. Robinson	1
1932	Chicago	Jun. 27–Jul. 2	Franklin D. Roosevelt	John N. Garner	4
1936	Philadelphia	Jun. 23–27	Franklin D. Roosevelt	John N. Garner	Acclamation
1940	Chicago	Jul. 15–18	Franklin D. Roosevelt	Henry A. Wallace	1
1944	Chicago	Jul. 19–21	Franklin D. Roosevelt	Harry S. Truman	1

Source: Congressional Quarterly, *The People Speak*, 86.

TABLE 8.14   REPUBLICAN CONVENTIONS, 1912–1944

Year	City	Dates	Presidential Nominee	Vice Presidential Nominee	No. of Ballots
1912	Chicago	Jun. 18–22	William H. Taft	James S. Sherman Nicholas Murray Butler[a]	1
1916	Chicago	Jun. 7–10	Charles E. Hughes	Charles W. Fairbanks	3
1920	Chicago	Jun. 8–12	Warren G. Harding	Calvin Coolidge	10
1924	Cleveland	Jun. 10–12	Calvin Coolidge	Charles G. Dawes	1
1928	Kansas City	Jun. 12–15	Herbert Hoover	Charles Curtis	1
1932	Chicago	Jun. 14–16	Herbert Hoover	Charles Curtis	1
1936	Cleveland	Jun. 9–12	Alfred M. Landon	Frank Knox	1
1940	Philadelphia	Jun. 24–28	Wendell L. Willkie	Charles L. McNary	6
1944	Chicago	Jun. 26–28	Thomas E. Dewey	John W. Bricker	1

[a]The 1912 Republican convention nominated James S. Sherman, who died on October 30. The Republican National Committee subsequently selected Nicholas Murray Butler to receive the Republican electoral votes for vice president.
Source: Congressional Quarterly, *The People Speak*, 87.

Qualifications for Voting, 1930

Qualifications for voting varied from state to state, although all required that a voter be twenty-one years old and a citizen of the United States. Residents of Washington, D.C., were not permitted to vote. The use of some form of literacy test was not uncommon in 1930, and it was not exclusive of any section of the nation. Hidden from view in this requirement was the extent to which literacy was used in the southern states to prevent black people from voting. The states in 1930 found several interesting grounds for disqualifica-

TABLE 8.15 REQUIREMENTS FOR VOTING, 1930

State	Requirements other than Citizenship	In State	In County	In Town	In Precinct
			Previous Residence Required		
Ala.	Ability to read and write English, employment, payment of poll tax	2 years	1 year	3 months	3 months
Ari.	Ability to read U.S. Constitution and sign name	1 yer	30 days	30 days	30 days
Ark.	Payment of poll tax	1 year	6 months	1 month	1 month
Calif.	Ability to read Constitution and write name	1 year	90 days	. . .	40 days
Colo.	. . .	1 year	90 days	30 days	10 days
Conn.	Ability to read Constitution, good moral character	1 year	. . .	6 months	. . .
Del.	Ability to read Constitution and write name	1 year	3 months	. . .	30 days
Fla.	. . .	1 year	6 months	. . .	30 days
Ga.	Ability to read and write English	1 year	6 months	. . .	. . .
Idaho	Registration	6 months	30 days	. . .	. . .
Ill.	. . .	1 year	90 days	30 days	30 days
Ind.	. . .	6 months	60 days	. . .	30 days
Iowa	. . .	6 months	60 days	10 days	10 days
Kans.	. . .	6 months	30 days	30 days	10 days
Ky.	Registration	1 year	6 months	60 days	60 days
La.	General understanding of the Constitution, ability to read and write	2 years	1 year in parish	. . .	3 months
Maine	Ability to read Constitution and write name	6 months	6 months	6 months	6 months
Md.	. . .	1 year	6 months	6 months	1 day
Mass.	Ability to read Constitution and write name	1 year	. . .	6 months	. . .
Mich.	. . .	6 months	20 days	20 days	20 days
Minn.	. . .	6 months	30 days	30 days	30 days
Miss.	Ability to read or understand Constitution when read, payment of poll tax	2 years	1 year	1 year	1 year
Mo.	. . .	1 year	60 days	60 days	10 days
Mont.	. . .	1 year	30 days	30 days	30 days
Nebr.	. . .	6 months	40 days	10 days	10 days
Nev.	. . .	6 months	30 days	30 days	10 days
N.H.	Ability to read Constitution in English and write	6 months	6 months	6 months	6 months
N.J.	. . .	1 year	5 months	. . .	. . .
N. Mex.	. . .	1 year	90 days	30 days	30 days
N.Y.	Ability to read and write English	1 year	4 months	30 days	. . .
N.C.	Ability to read and write English, registration	1 year	. . .	. . .	4 months
N. Dak.	. . .	1 year	90 days	. . .	30 days
Ohio	. . .	1 year	30 days	. . .	20 days
Okla.	Ability to read and write English	1 year	6 months	30 days	30 days
Oreg.	Ability to read and write English, registration	6 months	No specified time		. . .
Pa.	. . .	1 year	. . .	. . .	2 months
R.I.	Registration or payment of a tax	2 years	. . .	6 months	. . .
S.C.	Ability to read and write for persons not registered before Jan. 1, 1898, payment of poll tax, and registration	2 years	1 year	6 months	6 months
S. Dak.	. . .	1 year	90 days	. . .	30 days
Tenn.	Payment of poll tax, registration in civil districts of over 2,500 population	1 year	6 months	. . .	. . .
Tex.	Payment of poll tax; in municipal elections only taxpayers vote on fiscal measures; ability to read and write English	1 year	6 months	6 months	6 months
Utah	Ability to read Constitution and write	1 year	4 months	. . .	60 days
Vt.	Good behavior; willingness to take prescribed oath	1 year	. . .	. . .	. . .
Va.	Payment of poll tax, registration, ability to read English	1 year	6 months	6 months	30 days
Wash.	Ability to read or speak English	1 year	90 days	30 days	30 days
W. Va.	. . .	1 year	60 days	. . .	. . .
Wis.	. . .	1 year	10 days	10 days	10 days
Wyo.	Ability to read Constitution in English unless physically disabled	1 year	60 days	10 days	10 days

Source: The Lincoln Library of Essential Information (Buffalo, N.Y., 1937), 1422.

tion. Dueling disqualified a person in many states, for example; Chinese could not vote in Nevada or California. Several states disqualified Native Americans for various reasons, the most common of which was that they were not required to pay taxes. Members of the Narraganset tribe could not vote in Rhode Island, and Minnesota denied the suffrage to American Indians who were "uncivilized."

The South: Politics of Race and of Democrats

Recalling the memory of the Civil War and a harsh Republican-directed Reconstruction, the southern states remained a Democratic stronghold during the years 1914–45. As a rule a Republican running for office was wasting his or her time. The practice extended to all levels of politics, including presidential elections, where the term *solid South* had much meaning. The principal exception was the election of 1928, when seven southern states reacted to the candidacy of Al Smith—a Roman Catholic, native of New York City, and opponent of prohibition—by voting Republican. None of these seven were truly states of the Deep South, however, and after 1928 the South returned to being safely in the Democratic fold.

The Democratic South was reserved for white voters and office-holders. Building on a system that had emerged in the 1890s, the southern states disfranchised virtually all black people in the Deep South and most in the border states. The method varied from state to state, but it usually made use of such devices as a poll tax, a literacy test, or complicated registration requirements. All applications were subject to the scrutiny of white administrators. States also employed the "white primary," which held that the Democratic Party was a private club, entitled to exclude anyone it chose from membership. Pervading the region was a universal understanding that white people did not want black people to vote.

Election Laws, 1930, Louisiana

The laws of Louisiana offered a good example of the devices used to deny suffrage to black people. Especially effective were "character" or "understanding" clauses or other phrases granting broad latitude to local officials.

Suffrage Qualifications

Residence   Two years in State, one year in parish, four months in municipality, three months in precinct.
Taxes   Poll tax, $1.00 annually, paid for two preceding years by 31 December. No proceedings to collect.
Property   Required only for participation in bond-issue elections.
Education   Applicant shall demonstrate his ability to read and write by written application for registration on prescribed form, under oath. Penalties for false swearing not clear, but range between six months' and five years' imprisonment, with or without hard labor. Character and understanding alternatives.
Character   Good character obligatory. But illiterate may qualify as of good character and reputation, and well disposed to the good order and happiness of the U.S. and the State, and must take special "understanding" test.

Understanding   Obligatory to understand duties and obligations of citizenship under a Republican form of government, and to read and give a reasonable interpretation of U.S. Constitution. But illiterate may qualify under "character" clause (above), and understanding, upon having any section of U.S. or Louisiana Constitution read to him.
(Note: The Constitution is not at all clear as to how far "character" and "understanding" is obligatory on all voters, and how far all requirements, including education, are alternatives.)
Appeals   Person denied registration may have two trials in district court, without costs.
Primary   Only registered voters may participate in primaries or conventions. Parties may prescribe other and additional requirements. Democratic party rule bars Negroes.

Registration Procedure

Officers   One registrar for each parish, appointed by parish authorities (elected). A State Board of Registration consists of Governor, Lt.-Governor, and Speaker of House. Any two of State Board may remove registrar at will. New Orleans registrar appointed by Governor.
Time   Registrar must keep office open at all times, save in New Orleans, where registration closes 30 days before election.
Term   Life; save in New Orleans, where new registration every four years.
Refusal   Registrar may refuse; see "Appeals" above.
Purging   By registrar, of own motion or on voter's appeal. Five days' notice given to show cause why name should not be stricken off. Challenged registrant may show qualifications by affidavit signed by three voters. Persons stricken off by a court order may appeal to usual next court.

Source: Paul Lewinson, Race, Class, and Party: A History of Negro Suffrage and White Politics in the South (New York, 1932), 230–231.

TABLE 8.16   **BLACK VOTERS IN SELECTED SOUTHERN STATES IN THE 1920S**

State	21-Yr.-Old, Literate Black Population in the 1920s	Black Voters 1920–1930
Ala.	269,847	3,500
Ga.	369,511	10,000
Miss.	290,782	850

Source: Lewinson, Race, Class, and Party, 218–219.

TABLE 8.17 HOW THE 13 SOUTHERN STATES CAST THEIR ELECTORAL VOTES IN PRESIDENTIAL ELECTIONS, 1912–1944

Year	President Elected	States Won by Republican Party	Electoral Votes Cast			
			Democratic Party	Republican Party	Other Parties	Total
1944	Roosevelt	None	148	. . .	. . .	148
1940	Roosevelt	None	146	. . .	. . .	146
1936	Roosevelt	None	146	. . .	. . .	146
1932	Roosevelt	None	146	. . .	. . .	146
1928	Hoover	Fla., Ky., N.C., Okla., Tenn., Tex., Va.	64	85	. . .	149
1924	Coolidge	Ky.	136	13	. . .	149
1920	Harding	Okla., Tenn.	127	22	. . .	149
1916	Wilson	None	149	. . .	. . .	149
1912	Wilson	None	149	. . .	. . .	149

Source: George Gallup, *The Political Almanac, 1952* (Garden City, N.Y., 1952), 75.

TABLES 8.18 THE PRESIDENTS AND THE CABINETS

The Wilson Administration

President	Woodrow Wilson	1913–1921
Vice President	Thomas R. Marshall	1913–1921
Secretary of State	William J. Bryan	1913–1915
	Robert Lansing	1915–1920
	Bainbridge Colby	1920–1921
Secretary of Treasury	William G. McAdoo	1913–1918
	Carter Glass	1918–1920
	David F. Houston	1920–1921
Secretary of War	Lindley M. Garrison	1913–1916
	Newton D. Baker	1916–1921
Attorney General	James C. McReynolds	1913–1914
	Thomas W. Gregory	1914–1919
	A. Mitchell Palmer	1919–1921
Postmaster General	Albert S. Burleson	1913–1921
Secretary of Navy	Josephus Daniels	1913–1921
Secretary of Interior	Franklin K. Lane	1913–1920
	John B. Payne	1920–1921
Secretary of Agriculture	David F. Houston	1913–1920
	Edwin T. Meredith	1920–1921
Secretary of Commerce	William C. Redfield	1913–1919
	Joshua W. Alexander	1919–1921
Secretary of Labor	William B. Wilson	1913–1921

The Harding Administration

President	Warren G. Harding	1921–1923
Vice President	Calvin Coolidge	1921–1923
Secretary of State	Charles E. Hughes	1921–1923
Secretary of Treasury	Andrew Mellon	1921–1923
Secretary of War	John W. Weeks	1921–1923
Attorney General	Harry M. Daugherty	1921–1923
Postmaster General	Will H. Hays	1921–1922
	Hubert Work	1922–1923
	Harry S. New	1923
Secretary of Navy	Edwin Denby	1921–1923
Secretary of Interior	Albert B. Fall	1921–1923
	Hubert Work	1923
Secretary of Agriculture	Henry C. Wallace	1921–1923
Secretary of Commerce	Herbert C. Hoover	1921–1923
Secretary of Labor	James J. Davis	1921–1923

The Coolidge Administration

President	Calvin Coolidge	1923–1929
Vice President	Charles G. Dawes	1925–1929
Secretary of State	Charles E. Hughes	1923–1925
	Frank B. Kellogg	1925–1929
Secretary of Treasury	Andrew Mellon	1923–1929
Secretary of War	John W. Weeks	1923–1925

The Coolidge Administration

	Dwight F. Davis	1925–1929
Attorney General	Henry M. Daugherty	1923–1924
	Harlan F. Stone	1924–1925
	John G. Sargent	1925–1929
Postmaster General	Harry S. New	1923–1929
Secretary of Navy	Edwin Derby	1923–1924
	Curtis D. Wilbur	1924–1929
Secretary of Interior	Hubert Work	1923–1928
	Roy O. West	1928–1929
Secretary of Agriculture	Henry C. Wallace	1923–1924
	Howard M. Gore	1924–1925
	William M. Jardine	1925–1929
Secretary of Commerce	Herbert C. Hoover	1923–1928
	William F. Whiting	1928–1929
Secretary of Labor	James J. Davis	1923–1929

The Hoover Administration

President	Herbert C. Hoover	1929–1933
Vice President	Charles Curtis	1929–1933
Secretary of State	Henry L. Stimson	1929–1933
Secretary of Treasury	Andrew Mellon	1929–1932
	Ogden L. Mills	1932–1933
Secretary of War	James W. Good	1929
	Patrick J. Hurley	1929–1933
Attorney General	William D. Mitchell	1929–1933
Postmaster General	Walter F. Brown	1929–1933
Secretary of Navy	Charles F. Adams	1929–1933
Secretary of Interior	Ray L. Wilbur	1929–1933
Secretary of Agriculture	Arthur M. Hyde	1929–1933
Secretary of Commerce	Robert P. Lamont	1929–1932
	Roy D. Chapin	1932–1933
Secretary of Labor	James J. Davis	1929–1930
	William N. Doak	1930–1933

The Franklin D. Roosevelt Administration

President	Franklin D. Roosevelt	1933–1945
Vice President	John Nance Garner	1933–1941
	Henry A. Wallace	1941–1945
	Harry S. Truman	1945
Secretary of State	Cordell Hull	1933–1944
	Edward R. Stettinius, Jr.	1944–1945
Secretary of Treasury	William H. Woodin	1933–1934
	Henry Morgenthau, Jr.	1934–1945
Secretary of War	George H. Dern	1933–1936
	Henry H. Woodring	1936–1940
	Henry L. Stimson	1940–1945
Attorney General	Homer S. Cummings	1933–1939

<table>
<tr><th colspan="3">The Franklin D. Roosevelt Administration</th></tr>
<tr><td></td><td>Frank Murphy</td><td>1939–1940</td></tr>
<tr><td></td><td>Robert H. Jackson</td><td>1940–1941</td></tr>
<tr><td></td><td>Francis Biddle</td><td>1941–1945</td></tr>
<tr><td>Postmaster General</td><td>James A. Farley</td><td>1933–1940</td></tr>
<tr><td></td><td>Frank C. Walker</td><td>1940–1945</td></tr>
<tr><td>Secretary of Navy</td><td>Claude A. Swanson</td><td>1933–1940</td></tr>
<tr><td></td><td>Charles Edison</td><td>1940</td></tr>
<tr><td></td><td>Frank Knox</td><td>1940–1944</td></tr>
<tr><td></td><td>James V. Forrestal</td><td>1944–1945</td></tr>
<tr><td>Secretary of Interior</td><td>Harold L. Ickes</td><td>1933–1945</td></tr>
<tr><td>Secretary of Agriculture</td><td>Henry A. Wallace</td><td>1933–1940</td></tr>
<tr><td></td><td>Claude R. Wickard</td><td>1940–1945</td></tr>
<tr><td>Secretary of Commerce</td><td>Daniel C. Roper</td><td>1933–1939</td></tr>
<tr><td></td><td>Harry L. Hopkins</td><td>1939–1940</td></tr>
<tr><td></td><td>Jesse Jones</td><td>1940–1945</td></tr>
<tr><td></td><td>Henry A. Wallace</td><td>1945</td></tr>
<tr><td>Secretary of Labor</td><td>Frances Perkins</td><td>1933–1945</td></tr>
</table>

<table>
<tr><th colspan="3">The Truman Administration (1945)</th></tr>
<tr><td>President</td><td>Harry S. Truman</td><td>1945–1953</td></tr>
<tr><td>Vice President</td><td>none</td><td></td></tr>
<tr><td>Secretary of State</td><td>Edward R. Stettinius, Jr.</td><td>1945</td></tr>
<tr><td></td><td>James F. Byrnes</td><td>1945–1947</td></tr>
<tr><td>Secretary of Treasury</td><td>Fred M. Vinson</td><td>1945–1946</td></tr>
<tr><td>Secretary of War</td><td>Robert P. Patterson</td><td>1945–1947</td></tr>
<tr><td>Attorney General</td><td>Tom C. Clark</td><td>1945–1949</td></tr>
<tr><td>Postmaster General</td><td>Frank C. Walker</td><td>1945</td></tr>
<tr><td></td><td>Robert E. Hannegan</td><td>1945–1947</td></tr>
<tr><td>Secretary of Navy</td><td>James V. Forrestal</td><td>1945–1947</td></tr>
<tr><td>Secretary of Interior</td><td>Harold L. Ickes</td><td>1945–1946</td></tr>
<tr><td>Secretary of Agriculture</td><td>Clinton P. Anderson</td><td>1945–1948</td></tr>
<tr><td>Secretary of Commerce</td><td>Henry A. Wallace</td><td>1945–1946</td></tr>
<tr><td>Secretary of Labor</td><td>Lewis B. Schwellenbach</td><td>1945–1948</td></tr>
</table>

Source: Mary Beth Norton et al., *A People and a Nation*, vol. 2 (Boston, 1990), A35–36.

TABLE 8.19   POLITICAL MAKEUP AND OFFICERS OF CONGRESS, 1914–1945

63d Congress, 1913–1915   (U.S. President: Wilson, D)

Senate   D-51 R-44 Other-1

President:	Thomas R. Marshall	
President Pro Tem:	James P. Clark (D, Ark.)	
Majority Leader:	John W. Kern (D, Ind.)	
Majority Whip:	J. Hamilton Lewis (D, Ill.)	
Minority Leader:	Jacob H. Gallinger (R, N.H.)	
Minority Whip:	James W. Wadsworth (R, N.Y.)	

House   D-291 R-127 Other-17

Speaker:	Champ Clark (D, Mo.)
Majority Leader:	Oscar W. Underwood (D, Ala.)
Majority Whip:	Thomas M. Bell (D, Ga.)
Minority Leader:	James R. Mann (R, Ill.)
Minority Whip:	Charles H. Burke (R, S. Dak.)

64th Congress, 1915–1917   (U.S. President: Wilson, D)

Senate   D-56 R-40

President:	Thomas R. Marshall
President Pro Tem:	James P. Clark (D, Ark.)
	Willard Saulsbury (D, Del.)
Majority Leader:	John W. Kern (D, Ind.)
Majority Whip:	J. Hamilton Lewis (D, Ill.)
Minority Leader:	Jacob H. Gallinger (R, N.H.)
Minority Whip:	Charles Curtis (R, Kans.)

House   D-230 R-196 Other-9

Speaker:	Champ Clark (D, Mo.)
Majority Leader:	Claude Kitchin (D, N.C.)
Majority Whip:	. . .
Minority Leader:	James R. Mann (R, Ill.)
Minority Whip:	Charles M. Hamilton (R, N.Y.)

65th Congress, 1917–1919   (U.S. President: Wilson, D)

Senate   D-53 R-42

President:	Thomas R. Marshall
President Pro Tem:	Willard Saulsbury (D, Del.)
Majority Leader:	Thomas S. Martin (D, Va.)
Majority Whip:	J. Hamilton Lewis (D, Ill.)
Minority Leader:	Henry C. Lodge (R, Mass.)
Minority Whip:	Charles Curtis (R, Kans.)

House   D-216 R-210 Other-6

Speaker:	Champ Clark (D, Mo.)
Majority Leader:	Claude Kitchin (D, N.C.)
Majority Whip:	. . .
Minority Leader:	James R. Mann (R, Ill.)
Minority Whip:	Charles M. Hamilton (R, N.Y.)

66th Congress, 1919–1921   (U.S. President: Wilson, D)

Senate   R-49 D-47

President:	Thomas R. Marshall
President Pro Tem:	Albert B. Cummins (R, Iowa)
Majority Leader:	Henry C. Lodge (R, Mass.)
Majority Whip:	Charles Curtis, (R, Kans.)
Minority Leader:	Thomas S. Martin (D, Va.)
	Oscar Underwood (D, Ala.)
Minority Whip:	Peter G. Gerry (D, R.I.)

House   R-240 D-190 Other-3

Speaker:	Frederick H. Gillett (R, Mass.)
Majority Leader:	Franklin W. Mondell (R, Wyo.)
Majority Whip:	Harold Knutson (R, Minn.)
Minority Leader:	Champ Clark (D, Mo.)
Minority Whip:	. . .

67th Congress, 1921–1923   (U.S. President: Harding, R)

Senate   R-59 D-37

President:	Calvin Coolidge
President Pro Tem:	Albert B. Cummins (R, Iowa)
Majority Leader:	Henry C. Lodge (R, Mass.)
Majority Whip:	Charles Curtis (R, Kans.)
Minority Leader:	Oscar Underwood (D, Ala.)
Minority Whip:	Peter G. Gerry (D, R.I.)

House   R-303 D-131 Other-1

Speaker:	Frederick H. Gillett (R, Mass.)
Majority Leader:	Franklin W. Mondell (R, Wyo.)
Majority Whip:	Harold Knutson (R, Minn.)
Minority Leader:	Claude Kitchin (D, N.C.)
Minority Whip:	William A. Oldfield (D, Ark.)

(continued)

TABLE 8.19 (continued)

68th Congress, 1923–1925 (U.S. President: Coolidge, R)

Senate R-51 D-43 Other-2		House R-225 D-205 Other-5	
President:	none	Speaker:	Frederick H. Gillett (R, Mass.)
President Pro Tem:	Albert B. Cummins (R, Iowa)	Majority Leader:	Nicholas Longworth (R, Ohio)
Majority Leader:	Henry C. Lodge (R, Mass.)	Majority Whip:	Albert H. Vestal (R, Ind.)
	Charles Curtis (R, Kans.)	Minority Leader:	Finis J. Garrett (D, Tenn.)
Majority Whip:	Charles Curtis (R, Kans.)	Minority Whip:	William A. Oldfield (D, Ark.)
	Wesley L. Jones (R, Wash.)		
Minority Leader:	Joseph T. Robinson (D, Ark.)		
Minority Whip:	Peter G. Gerry (D, R.I.)		

69th Congress, 1925–1927 (U.S. President: Coolidge, R)

Senate R-56 D-39 Other-1		House R-247 D-183 Other-4	
President:	Charles G. Dawes	Speaker:	Nicholas Longworth (R, Ohio)
President Pro Tem:	George H. Moses (R, N.H.)	Majority Leader:	John Q. Tilson (R, Conn.)
Majority Leader:	Charles Curtis (R, Kans.)	Majority Whip:	Albert H. Vestal (R, Ind.)
Majority Whip:	Wesley L. Jones (R, Wash.)	Minority Leader:	Finis J. Garrett (D, Tenn.)
Minority Leader:	Joseph T. Robinson (D, Ark.)	Minority Whip:	William A. Oldfield (D, Ark.)
Minority Whip:	Peter G. Gerry (D, R.I.)		

70th Congress, 1927–1929 (U.S. President: Coolidge, R)

Senate R-49 D-46 Other-1		House R-237 D-195 Other-3	
President:	Charles G. Dawes	Speaker:	Nicholas Longworth (R, Ohio)
President Pro Tem:	George H. Moses (R, N.H.)	Majority Leader:	John Q. Tilson (R, Conn.)
Majority Leader:	Charles Curtis (R, Kans.)	Majority Whip:	Albert H. Vestal (R, Ind.)
Majority Whip:	Wesley L. Jones (R, Wash.)	Minority Leader:	Finis J. Garrett (D, Tenn.)
Minority Leader:	Joseph T. Robinson (D, Ark.)	Minority Whip:	William A. Oldfield (D, Ark.)
Minority Whip:	Peter G. Gerry (D, R.I.)		John McDuffie (D, Ala.)

71st Congress, 1929–1931 (U.S. President: Hoover, R)

Senate R-56 D-39 Other-1		House R-267 D-167 Other-1	
President:	Charles Curtis	Speaker:	Nicholas Longworth (R, Ohio)
President Pro Tem:	George H. Moses (R, N.H.)	Majority Leader:	John Q. Tilson (R, Conn.)
Majority Leader:	James E. Watson (R, Ind.)	Majority Whip:	Albert H. Vestal (R, Ind.)
Majority Whip:	Simeon D. Fess (R, Ohio)	Minority Leader:	John N. Garner (D, Tex.)
Minority Leader:	Joseph T. Robinson (D, Ark.)	Minority Whip:	John McDuffie (D, Ala.)
Minority Whip:	Morris Sheppard (D, Tex.)		

72d Congress, 1931–1933 (U.S. President: Hoover, R)

Senate R-48 D-47 Other-1		House D-220 R-214 Other-1	
President:	Charles Curtis	Speaker:	John N. Garner (D, Tex.)
President Pro Tem:	George H. Moses (R, N.H.)	Majority Leader:	Henry T. Rainey (D, Ill.)
Majority Leader:	James E. Watson (R, Ind.)	Majority Whip:	John McDuffie (D, Ala.)
Majority Whip:	Simeon D. Fess (R, Ohio)	Minority Leader:	Bertrand H. Snell (R, N.Y.)
Minority Leader:	Joseph T. Robinson (D, Ark.)	Minority Whip:	Carl G. Bachmann (R, W.Va.)
Minority Whip:	Morris Sheppard (D, Tex.)		

73d Congress, 1933–1934 (U.S. President: F. Roosevelt, D)

Senate D-60 R-35 Other-1		House D-310 R-117 Other-5	
President:	John N. Garner	Speaker:	Henry T. Rainey (D, Ill.)
President Pro Tem:	Key Pittman (D, Nev.)	Majority Leader:	Joseph W. Byrns (D, Tenn.)
Majority Leader:	Joseph T. Robinson (D, Ark.)	Majority Whip:	Arthur H. Greenwood (D, Ind.)
Majority Whip:	J. Hamilton Lewis (D, Ill.)	Minority Leader:	Bertrand H. Snell (R, N.Y.)
Minority Leader:	Charles McNary (R, Oreg.)	Minority Whip:	Harry L. Englebright (R, Calif.)
Minority Whip:	Felix Hebert (R, R.I.)		

74th Congress, 1935–1936 (U.S. President: F. Roosevelt, D)

Senate D-69 R-25 Other-2		House D-319 R-103 Other-10	
President:	John N. Garner	Speaker:	Joseph W. Byrns (D, Tenn.)
President Pro Tem:	Key Pittman (D, Nev.)	Majority Leader:	William B. Bankhead (D, Ala.)
Majority Leader:	Joseph T. Robinson (D, Ark.)	Majority Whip:	Patrick J. Boland (D, Pa.)
Majority Whip:	J. Hamilton Lewis (D, Ill.)	Minority Leader:	Bertrand H. Snell (R, N.Y.)
Minority Leader:	Charles McNary (R, Oreg.)	Minority Whip:	Harry L. Englebright (R, Calif.)
Minority Whip:	Felix Hebert (R, R.I.)		

75th Congress, 1937–1938 (U.S. President: F. Roosevelt, D)			
Senate D-76 R-16 Other-4		House D-331 R-89 Other-13	
President:	John N. Garner	Speaker:	William B. Bankhead (D, Ala.)
President Pro Tem:	Key Pittman (D, Nev.)	Majority Leader:	Sam Rayburn (D, Tex.)
Majority Leader:	Joseph T. Robinson (D, Ark.)	Majority Whip:	Patrick J. Boland (D, Pa.)
	Alben W. Barkley (D, Ky.)	Minority Leader:	Bertrand H. Snell (R, N.Y.)
Majority Whip:	J. Hamilton Lewis (D, Ill.)	Minority Whip:	Harry L. Englebright (R, Calif.)
Minority Leader:	Charles McNary (R, Oreg.)		
Minority Whip:	Felix Hebert (R, R.I.)		

76th Congress, 1939–1940 (U.S. President: F. Roosevelt, D)			
Senate D-69 R-23 Other-4		House D-261 R-164 Other-4	
President:	John N. Garner	Speaker:	William B. Bankhead (D, Ala.)
President Pro Tem:	Key Pittman (D, Nev.)		Sam Rayburn (D, Tex.)
	William H. King (D, Utah)	Majority Leader:	Sam Rayburn (D, Tex.)
	Alben W. Barkley (D, Ky.)		John W. McCormack (D, Mass.)
Majority Leader:	Sherman Minton (D, Ind.)	Majority Whip:	Patrick J. Boland (D, Pa.)
Majority Whip:	Charles McNary (R, Oreg.)	Minority Leader:	Joseph W. Martin, Jr. (R, Mass.)
Minority Leader:	Felix Hebert (R, R.I.)	Minority Whip:	Harry L. Englebright (R, Calif.)
Minority Whip:			

77th Congress, 1941–1942 (U.S. President: F. Roosevelt, D)			
Senate D-66 R-28 Other-2		House D-268 R-162 Other-5	
President:	Henry A. Wallace	Speaker:	Sam Rayburn (D, Tex.)
President Pro Tem:	Pat Harrison (D, Miss.)	Majority Leader:	John W. McCormack (D, Mass.)
	Carter Glass (D, Va.)	Majority Whip:	Patrick J. Boland (D, Pa.)
Majority Leader:	Alben W. Barkley (D, Ky.)	Minority Leader:	Joseph W. Martin, Jr. (R, Mass.)
Majority Whip:	Lister Hill (D, Ala.)	Minority Whip:	Harry L. Englebright (R, Calif.)
Minority Leader:	Charles McNary (R, Oreg.)		
Minority Whip:	Felix Herbert (R, R.I.)		

78th Congress, 1943–1944 (U.S. President: F. Roosevelt, D)			
Senate D-58 R-37 Other-1		House D-218 R-208 Other-4	
President:	Henry A. Wallace	Speaker:	Sam Rayburn (D, Tex.)
President Pro Tem:	Carter Glass (D, Va.)	Majority Leader:	John W. McCormack (D, Mass.)
Majority Leader:	Alben W. Barkley (D, Ky.)	Majority Whip:	Robert Ramspeck (D, Ga.)
Majority Whip:	Lister Hill (D, Ala.)	Minority Leader:	Joseph W. Martin, Jr. (R, Mass.)
Minority Leader:	Charles McNary (R, Oreg.)	Minority Whip:	Leslie C. Arends (R, Ill.)
Minority Whip:	Kenneth Wherry (R, Nebr.)		

79th Congress, 1945–1946 (U.S. President: F. Roosevelt, Truman, D)			
Senate D-56 R-38 Other-1		House D-242 R-190 Other-2	
President:	Harry S. Truman	Speaker:	Sam Rayburn (D, Tex.)
President Pro Tem:	Kenneth McKellar (D, Tenn.)	Majority Leader:	John W. McCormack (D, Mass.)
Majority Leader:	Alben W. Barkley (D, Ky.)	Majority Whip:	John J. Sparkman (D, Ala.)
Majority Whip:	Lister Hill (D, Ala.)	Minority Leader:	Joseph W. Martin, Jr. (R, Mass.)
Minority Leader:	Wallace H. White, Jr. (R, Mass.)	Minority Whip:	(Leslie C. Arends (R, Ill.)
Minority Whip:	Kenneth Wherry (R, Nebr.)		

Sources: Bureau of the Census, *Historical Statistics of the United States, 1789 to 1945,* 293; Austin, *Political Facts of the United States,* 37–44.

TABLE 8.20   BLACK MEMBERS OF CONGRESS, 1914–1945

Black participation in national politics dated from the period of Reconstruction following the Civil War. During the period of domination of the South by Radical Republicans and later by conservative southerners, some twenty black men served in the House of Representatives and two served in the Senate—all from the South and all Republican. With widespread disfranchisement of blacks in the South after 1890, with few black people living in northern states and those few poorly organized for political action, black presence in Congress came to an end. None served between 1901 and 1929. The years that follow are scarcely more fruitful. Before the appearance of Adam Clayton Powell in 1945, only a single district in Chicago was represented by a black person. A revolution in national politics was still years away.

Blacks in the Senate, 1914–1945	
None	
Blacks in the House of Representatives, 1914–1945	
Oscar De Priest (R, Ill.)	1929–1935
Arthur W. Mitchell (D, Ill.)	1935–1943
William L. Dawson (D, Ill.)	1943–1970
Adam C. Powell (D, N.Y.)	1945–1967

Source: Congressional Quarterly, *Members of Congress since 1789* (Washington, D.C., 1981), 6.

TABLE 8.21   WOMEN MEMBERS OF CONGRESS, 1914–1945

The Course of Policy

The early part of the twentieth century marked a challenge to the proposition that politics was the exclusive domain of males. A few states granted women the right to vote before 1920, and in that year woman suffrage became national. Officeholding came not far behind. In one case, in fact, a woman—Jeannette Rankin of Montana—served in Congress before the passage of the Nineteenth Amendment. After 1920 the number of women in politics increased steadily. Several of the first congresswomen were individuals serving out terms of an expired husband. Although many, if not most, Americans continued to believe that politics was man's business, as years went on women showed a greater tendency to become involved and pursue their own course in politics.

Women in the Senate, 1914–1945	
Rebecca L. Felton (Independent Party affiliation, D, Ga.)	1922
Hattie W. Caraway (D, Ark.)	1931–45
Rose McConnell Long (D, La.)	1936–37
Dixie Bibb Graves (D, Ala.)	1937–38
Gladys Pyle (R, S.Dak.)	1938–39

Women in the House of Representatives, 1914–1945	
Jeannette Rankin (R, Mont.)	1917–19; 1941–43
Alice M. Robertson (R, Okla.)	1921–23
Winnifred S. M. Huck (R, Ill.)	1922–23
Mae E. Nolan (R, Calif.)	1923–25
Florence P. Kahn (R, Calif.)	1925–37
Mary T. Norton (D, N.J.)	1925–51
Edith N. Rogers (R, Mass.)	1925–60
Katherine G. Langley (R, Ky.)	1927–31
Ruth H. McCormick (R, Ill.)	1929–31
Pearl P. Oldfield (D, Ark.)	1929–31
Ruth B. Owen (D, Fla.)	1929–33
Ruth S. B. Pratt (R, N.Y.)	1929–33
Effiegene Wingo (D, Ark.)	1930–33
Willa M. B. Eslick (D, Tenn.)	1932–33
Marian W. Clarke (R, N.Y.)	1933–35
Virginia E. Jenckes (D, Ind.)	1933–39
Kathryn O'Loughlin McCarthy (D, Kans.)	1933–35
Isabella S. Greenway (D, Ariz.)	1934–37
Caroline L. G. O'Day (D, N.Y.)	1935–43
Nan W. Honeyman (D, Oreg.)	1937–39
Elizabeth H. Gasque (D, S.C.)	1938–39
Clara G. McMillan (D, S.C.)	1939–41
Jessie Sumner (R, Ill.)	1939–47
Frances P. Bolton (R, Ohio)	1940–69
Florence R. Gibbs (D, Ga.)	1940–41
Margaret Chase Smith (R, Maine)	1940–49
Katherine E. Byron (D, Md.)	1941–43
Veronica G. Boland (D, Pa.)	1942–43
Clare Boothe Luce (R, Conn.)	1943–47
Winifred C. Stanley (R, N.Y.)	1943–45
Willa L. Fulmer (D, S.C.)	1944–45
Emily T. Douglas (D, Ill.)	1945–47
Helen G. Douglas (D, Calif.)	1945–51
Chase G. Woodhouse (D, Conn.)	1945–47

Source: Congressional Quarterly, Members of Congress, 4.

In large measure changes in the pace and character of policy making corresponded with shifts in the strength of the political parties. In the twentieth century the Democrats came to be identified with utilization of the national government in dealing with large social and economic problems. The Republicans were more likely to favor leadership by private individuals or groups, which usually meant by businessmen—a perspective that necessarily encouraged a less active government. A Democratic president was more likely than a Republican to regard himself the nation's chief legislator. The Woodrow Wilson presidency took place during the last part of the Progressive Era, a movement that produced significant legislation dealing with regulation of big business, democratization of the political process, and, to lesser extent, growing social problems. There were progressive Republicans as well as progressive Democrats, although those people who called themselves conservatives were likely to be associated with the Republican Party.

The Republican era of the 1920s fittingly was not a time of activism in the making of public policy. The economy was expected to run itself. Social concerns were to be handled by individuals and private groups; if government had to get involved, it was expected to be on the state or local level. If Congress did seek to address a large issue, as in the case of hard times in agriculture, it ran into vetoes from Republican presidents. The most memorable legislation of the 1920s occurred in the areas of immigration and tariffs and in the lowering of taxes.

The stock market crash and the coming of the Great Depression served to discredit the Republicans and also the Republican approach to government. The period of the 1930s brought forth an avalanche of legislative activity not merely because the Democrats came back to power but because the people demanded that the national government take charge. The states seemed powerless to cope with the economic collapse. The New Deal of Franklin Roosevelt moved the national government into almost every aspect of American life. Many of the laws were temporary, designed to treat problems peculiar to the depression; others were either struck down by the Supreme Court or fell under their own weight. A significant number lived on to affect American society for years into the future. The best example was the Social Security Act of 1935.

The period of the Second World War brought an end to the social activism of the New Deal (as an agent for initiating social and economic change the New Deal ends in 1938), but it did not end broad activity on the national level. War in the United States is the responsibility of the national government, not the states. The war served to reinforce the concept of national leadership and national responsibility. For credit or for blame, Americans became accustomed to looking to Washington, D.C., not Sacramento, Albany, or Indianapolis.

TABLE 8.22 MAJOR BILLS AND TREATIES, 1914–1945

Party Abbreviations: Dem.—Democratic; Rep.—Republican; A.L.—American Labor; F.L.—Farmer-Labor; Ind.—Independent; Prog.—Progressive; Proh.—Prohibition; Soc.—Socialist

Bill or Treaty	Party	House Vote Yea	House Vote Nay	Senate Vote Yea	Senate Vote Nay	Date Enacted
Federal Trade Commission. Established to enforce antitrust laws.		No roll-call vote		53	16	Sep. 26, 1914
Clayton Antitrust Act. Prohibited monopolistic price discrimination, restrictive sales or leases, intercorporate stock holding, interlocking directorates of competing companies capitalized at $1,000,000 or more. Exempted labor from antitrust laws and declared peaceful picketing legal.		244	54	35	24	Oct. 15, 1914
Federal Farm Loan Act. Created system of land banks to lend money to farmers on their land and permanent improvements.		No roll-call vote		58	5	Jul. 17, 1916
Keating-Owen Law. Forbade shipping in interstate commerce of goods produced by children. (Declared unconstitutional in 1918.)		337	46	52	12	Sep. 1, 1916
Adamson Act. Limited working hours of railroad employees to 8 per day on interstate railroads.		259	36	43	28	Sep. 3–5, 1916[a]
Burnett Immigration Bill. Required literacy test for immigrants.		308	87	64	7	Vetoed, Jan. 29, 1917
		285 (Reconsideration vote)	106	62	19	Feb. 5, 1917
Armed Neutrality Act. Allowed American vessels to be armed in war zones.				Filibustered		Defeated, Mar. 4, 1917
Declaration of War. Against Germany (World War I).		373	50	82	6	Apr. 6, 1917
Volstead Act. Prohibited manufacture, transportation, and sale of beverages containing more than .5 percent alcohol.		321	70	Voice vote approval		Vetoed, Oct. 27, 1919
	Dem.	. . . (Reconsideration vote)	. . .	27	11	Oct. 28, 1919
	Rep.	. . .	. . .	38	9	
Treaty of Versailles.	Dem.	No vote required		4	42	Rejected, Nov. 19, 1919
	Rep.			35	13	
18th Amendment. Forbade manufacture, sale, and transportation of intoxicating liquors.	Dem.	141	64	36	12	Jan. 16, 1920
	Rep.	137	62	29	8	
	Ind.	2	. . .	. . .	. . .	
	Proh.	1	. . .	. . .	. . .	
	Prog.	1	1	. . .	. . .	
	Soc.	. . .	1	. . .	. . .	
Transportation Act. Reorganized ICC with 11 members and increased powers; authorized loans to railroads; created Railroad Labor Board; provided for consolidation of railroads.		250	150	47	17	Feb. 29, 1920
Treaty of Versailles.	Dem.	No vote required		21	23	Rejected, Mar. 19, 1920
	Rep.			28	12	
Federal Water Power Act. Created federal power commission to license citizens who use navigable streams for power; licenses limited to 50 years.				52	18	Jun. 18, 1920
19th Amendment. Gave women the right to vote.	Dem.	102	70	20	17	Aug. 26, 1920
	Rep.	200	19	36	8	
	Ind.	1	. . .	. . .	. . .	
	Prog.	1	. . .	. . .	. . .	
Emergency Quota Act. Limited annual number of immigrants from any country to 3 percent of that nationality living in U.S. in 1910. (Renewed in 1922 for two more years.)		No record vote		78	1	May 19, 1921
Emergency Tariff Act. Raised rates on agricultural articles, wool, sugar, chemicals, etc.	Dem.	. . .	. . .	7	27	May 27, 1921
	Rep.	. . .	. . .	56	1	
Capper-Volstead Act. Exempted farm cooperatives from antitrust laws.		264	49	58	1	Feb. 18, 1922
Washington Conference Treaties:						
Four Power Pacific Peace Pact. Related to Pacific island possessions of Britain, France, U.S., and Japan.	Dem.	No vote required		12	23	Mar. 24, 1922
	Rep.			55	4	
Five Power Limitation on Naval Armaments Treaty. Powers were U.S., Britain, France, Italy, and Japan.		No vote required		74	1	Mar. 29, 1922
Nine Power Treaty. Guaranteed the territorial integrity of China.		No vote required		65	0	Mar. 30, 1922
Fordney-McCumber Tariff. Highly protective, averaging 32.22 percent; gave tariff commission power to suggest that presidential increase or decrease rates not more than 50 percent of original rate on any item to meet competition.	Dem.	. . .	. . .	3	24	Sep. 21, 1922
	Rep.	. . .	. . .	45	1	
World Court Protocal.	Dem.	No vote required		23	3	Defeated, Mar. 3, 1923
	Rep.			1	46	

[a] As Sep. 3 was a Sunday, the validity of the president's signature was questioned. Therefore, the bill was re-signed on the following Tuesday.

(continued)

TABLE 8.22 (continued)

Party Abbreviations: Dem.—Democratic; Rep.—Republican; A.L.—American Labor; F.L.—Farmer-Labor; Ind.—Independent; Prog.—Progressive; Proh.—Prohibition; Soc.—Socialist

Bill or Treaty	Party	House Vote		Senate Vote		Date Enacted
		Yea	Nay	Yea	Nay	
Federal Intermediate Credit Act. Lent money to farmers to extent of 75 percent of value of harvested crops and livestocks.		277	3	No record vote		Mar. 4, 1923
Bonus Bill. Provided 20-year endowment policies for veterans.	Dem.	177	20	32	9	Vetoed, May 15, 1924
	Rep.	175	34	33	8	
	F.L.	1	. . .	2	. . .	
	Soc.	1	. . .	. . .	. . .	
	Ind.	1	. . .	. . .	. . .	
		(Reconsideration vote)				
	Dem.	145	21	27	9	May 19, 1924
	Rep.	166	57	30	17	
	F.L.	. . .	. . .	2	. . .	
	Soc.	1	. . .	. . .	. . .	
	Ind.	1	. . .	. . .		
Immigration Quota Law. Limited annual number of immigrants to 2 percent of each country's residents in U.S. in 1890. After 1927, the number was to be limited anually to 150,000. Did not apply to nations of Western Hemisphere.		308	58	69	9	May 26, 1924
World Court Membership.	Dem.	No vote required		36	2	Jan. 27, 1926
	Rep.			40	14	
	F.L.			. . .	1	
McNary-Haugen Bill. Lent money to farm cooperatives and paid farmers equalizing price on their products.	Dem.	97	70	22	17	Vetoed, Feb. 25, 1927; no. reconsideration vote
	Rep.	113	108	24	22	
	F.L.	2	. . .	1	. . .	
	Soc.	1	. . .	. . .	. . .	
	Ind.	1	. . .	. . .	. . .	
McNary-Haugen Bill. (Repassage of bill the following year.)	Dem.	100	53	28	9	Vetoed, May 23, 1928
	Rep.	101	68	24	14	
	F.L.	2	. . .	1	. . .	
	Soc.	1	. . .	. . .	. . .	
		(Reconsideration vote)				
	Dem.	No vote required		29	12	Defeated, May 25, 1928
	Rep.			20	19	
	F.L.			1	. . .	
Norris-Morin Resolution. Would have completed construction of Muscle Shoals for nitrates and power.		251	165	48	25	Pocket veto, Jun. 4, 1928
Kellogg-Briand Pact. Outlawed wars and prescribed arbitration of interntional disputes		No vote required		85	1	Jan. 15, 1929
Agricultural Marketing Act. Created federal farm board with power to lend money to farm cooperatives and to create stabilization corporations to buy farm surplus and to store and sell abroad to maintain prices.	Dem.	121	32	33	2	Jun. 15, 1929
	Rep.	245	2	21	32	
	F.L.	1	. . .	. . .	. . .	
Hawley-Smoot Tariff. Very high protective tariff, averaging 40.08 percent but giving president power to initiate reduction or increase in rates.	Dem.	14	132	5	30	Jun. 17, 1930
	Rep.	208	20	39	11	
	F.L.	. . .	1	. . .	1	
Bonus Loan Bill. Increased amount veterans might borrow and reduced interest rate.	Dem.	150	. . .	37	. . .	Vetoed, Feb. 26, 1931
	Rep.	212	39	34	12	
	F.L.	1	. . .	1	. . .	
		(Reconsideration vote)				
	Dem.	148	. . .	39	1	Feb. 27, 1931
	Rep.	179	79	36	16	
	F.L.	1	. . .	1	. . .	
Norris Resolution. Would have completed Muscle Shoals.	Dem.	128	3	35	2	Vetoed, Mar. 3, 1931; no reconsideration vote
	Rep.	87	150	20	26	
	F.L.	1	. . .	. . .	. . .	
War Debt Moratorium. Provided for moratorium on payment of interest and war debt installments by nations indebted to U.S.	Dem.	120	95	33	6	Dec. 23, 1931
	Rep.	196	5	36	6	
	F.L.	1	. . .	. . .	. . .	
Reconstruction Finance Corporation. Established with a working fund of $500,000,000 and power to borrow more to release frozen assets in banks and mortgage companies and to help bankrupt railroads.	Dem.	153	43	29	5	Jan. 22, 1932
	Rep.	182	12	34	3	
Norris-LaGuardia Act. Limited granting of injunctions against labor; required open testimony in open court and outlawed yellow dog contracts.		363	13	75	5	Mar. 23, 1932
Hawes-Cutting Bill. Granted Philippine independence but was rejected by the Philippine legislature because of its economic and immigration provisions.		No record vote		No record vote		Vetoed, Jan. 13, 1933
		(Reconsideration vote)				
	Dem.	191	1	45	1	
	Rep.	82	93	20	25	
	F.L.	1	. . .	1	. . .	

Bill or Treaty	Party	House Vote Yea	House Vote Nay	Senate Vote Yea	Senate Vote Nay	Date Enacted
20th Amendment. Changed date of meeting of Congress to Jan. 3 and date of presidential inauguration to Jan. 20; authorized procedure for selection of filling vacancies in presidency.		335	56	73	3	Jan. 23, 1933
3.2 Percent Liquor Law. Legalized manufacture and sale of 3.2 wines and beers.	Dem. Rep.	No record vote		33 10	19 17	Mar. 22, 1933
Civilian Conservation Corps. Created to relieve unemployment and to work at reforestation, road building and flood control.		No roll-call vote		No roll-call vote		Mar. 31, 1933
Agricultural Adjustment Act. Created the AAA, which was authorized to limit acreage on specified crops at farmers' option and to pay benefits to farmers; money for this purpose to be raised by a process tax, which was declared unconstitutional Jan. 16, 1936.		315	98	52	31	May 12, 1933
Tennessee Valley Authority. Established to develop and sell electric power, to serve as yardstick for electricity rates, to develop rural electrification, to establish flood control, and to produce fertilizer.	Dem. Rep. F.L.	284 17 5	2 89 . . .	48 14 1	3 17 . . .	May 18, 1933
Federal Securities Act. Required that all stock and bond issues be registered and approved.		No roll-call vote		No roll-call vote		May 27, 1933
Home Owners Refinancing Act. Established the HOLC, which took over mortgages in exchange for bonds in order to save home owners from losing homes.		383	4	No record vote		Jun. 13, 1933
Glass-Steagall Banking Act. Created Federal Deposit Insurance Corporation to insure deposits up to $5,000; required that private banks be either investment or deposit banks, but not both.		No record vote		No roll-call vote		Jun. 16, 1933
National Industrial Recovery Act. Created NRA; authorized establishment of trade associations; suspended antitrust laws; authorized drawing-up of codes of Fair Competition to be accepted by president; guaranteed collective bargaining and required employers to accept approved maximum and minimum wage provisions. (Declared unconstitutional in 1935.)	Dem. Rep. F.L.	266 53 4	25 50 . . .	46 10 1	4 20 . . .	Jun. 16, 1933
21st Amendment. Repealed prohibition.	Dem. Rep. F.L.	179 109 1	32 89 . . .	33 29 1	9 14 . . .	Dec. 5, 1933
Gold Reserve Act. Gave president power to devalue gold and to impound for treasury all gold in Federal System and to establish Exchange Stabilization Fund.	Dem. Rep. F.L.	287 68 5	2 38 . . .	55 10 1	1 22 . . .	Jan. 30, 1934
Farm Mortgage Refinancing Act. Created Federal Farm Mortgage Corporation to assist farmers in payment of mortgages on easier interest terms.		No record vote		No record vote		Jan. 31, 1934
Tydings-McDuffie Act. Gave the Philippine Islands independence.	Dem. Rep. F.L.	No roll-call vote		51 16 1	. . . 8 . . .	Mar. 24, 1934
Johnson Debt Default Bill. Forbade sale in this country of securities of defaulting countries.		No record vote		No record vote		Apr. 13, 1934
Home Owners Loan Act. Supplemented Home Owners Refinancing Act.		337	1	35	34	Apr. 28, 1934
Securities and Exchange Act. Established Securities and Exchange Commission; required licensing of stock exchanges; made certain speculative practices illegal; gave Federal Reserve Board power to fix margins; required full financial statements from registered companies.	Dem. Rep. F.L.	254 22 4	11 73 . . .	47 15 . . .	1 12 . . .	Jun. 6, 1934
Trade Agreements Act. Authorized president to reduce tariffs by as much as 50 percent of prevailing rates for those countries which granted the U.S. most favored nation treatment without the need for senatorial ratification for three years.	Dem. Rep. F.L.	No record vote		51 5 1	5 28 . . .	Jun. 12, 1934
National Housing Act. Created Federal Housing Administration to administer funds for modernizing homes and for lending for new construction.		176	19	No record vote		Jun. 28, 1934
Federal Farm Bankruptcy Act (Frazier-Lemke Act). Declared moratorium on farm mortgage foreclosures. (Declared unconstitutional in May, 1935.)		No record vote		60	16	Jun. 28, 1934
World Court Ratification.	Dem. Rep. F.L. Prog.	No vote required		43 9	20 14 1 1	Defeated, Jan. 29, 1935
Soldiers' Bonus Bill. Would have paid off veterans compensation certificates.		318	90	55	33	Vetoed, May 2, 1935
(Reconsideration vote)		322	98	40	54	Defeated, May 23, 1935
National Labor Relations Act (Wagner-Connery Act). Created the NLRB with power to determine appropriate collective bargaining unit sub-	Dem. Rep.	No record vote		49 12	4 8	Jul. 5, 1935

(continued)

TABLE 8.22   (continued)

Party Abbreviations: Dem.—Democratic; Rep.—Republican; A.L.—American Labor; F.L.—Farmer-Labor; Ind.—Independent; Prog.—Progressive; Proh.—Prohibition; Soc.—Socialist

Bill or Treaty	Party	House Vote		Senate Vote		Date Enacted
		Yea	Nay	Yea	Nay	
ject to elections they supervised at request of the workers; to certify the duly chosen trade union and to take testimony about unfair employer practices and issue cease and desist orders.	F.L. Prog.		1 1	. . . . . .		
Social Security Act. Created social security board to administer old-age benefits based on earnings before the age of 65; unemployment administered under state laws and grants to states to aid the needy aged, blind, orphans, widows, etc.		372	33	76	6	Aug. 14, 1935
Glass-Steagall Banking Act. Increased power of Federal Reserve Board of Governors over open market and credit transactions.		No record vote		No record vote		Aug. 23, 1935
Public Utilities Act (Wheeler-Rayburn Act). Required all public utilities to register with the SEC and limited utility holding corporations to first degree unless necessity required greater complexity.	Dem. Rep. F.L. Prog.	203 7 3 6	59 83 . . .	No record vote		Aug. 26, 1935
Farm Mortgage Moratorium Act. Allowed three-year moratorium on foreclosures with court permission upon payment of reasonable rental.		No record vote		No record vote		Aug. 29, 1935
Soldiers, Bonus Bill. Made 9-year 3 percent bonds redeemable on demand.	Dem. Rep. F.L. Prog.	265 72 3 6	29 30	56 15 2 1	9 7	Vetoed, Jan. 24, 1936
		(Reconsideration vote)				
	Dem. Rep. F.L. Prog.	248 66 3 7	32 29	57 16 2 1	12 7	Jan. 27, 1936
Soil Conservation and Domestic Allotment Act. Granted payments to farmers who let their land lie fallow or planted cover crops.	Dem. Rep. F.L. Prog.	246 20 1 . . .	25 64 1 7	49 5 1 1	90 11	Mar. 2, 1936
Reciprocal Trade Agreement Act. Extended to Jun. 1940, period during which president is authorized to negotiate foreign trade under Trade Agreements Act of 1934.		284	0	58	24	Mar. 1, 1937
Neutrality Act. Forbade export of arms and ammunition to belligerents, the sale in this country of belligerents' securities, the use of American ships for carrying munitions; required belligerents to pay upon purchase and carry all purchases in their own ships (cash and carry clause).		377	12	41	15	May 1, 1937
Judiciary Act. Allowed voluntary retirement of Supreme Court justices and other federal court judges on full pension at age of 70.		No roll-call vote		Unanimous, no roll-call vote		Aug. 25, 1937
National Housing Act. Established the U.S. Housing Authority to administer loans to local communities and states for rural and urban construction. (Amended in 1938.)		275	86	64	16	Sep. 2, 1937
National Housing Act Amendment.	Dem. Rep. F.L. Prog. Ind.	No record vote		41 1	25 13 1 1 . . .	Feb. 4, 1938
Agricultural Adjustment Act. Continued soil conservation program; provided parity payments and commodity loans to farmers; established crop insurance corporations and ever-normal granary plan.	Dem. Rep. F.L. Prog. Ind.	243 14 5 1 . . .	54 74 . . . 7 . . .	53 2 1	17 11 2 1 . . .	Feb. 16, 1938
Wage and Hours Act. Provided minimum wage of 25 cents to rise to 40 cents after 6 yers; limited hours from 44 per week the first year to 40 after the third year; goods produced by "oppressive child labor" could not be shipped in interstate commerce.	Dem. Rep. F.L. Prog.	247 31 5 7	41 48	No record vote		Jun. 25, 1938
Reciprocal Trade Agreement Act. Extended Trade Agreements Act of 1937 three more years.	Dem. Rep. F.L. Prog. Ind. A.L.	212 5 1	20 146 1 1	41 . . . . 1 . . .	15 20 2	Apr. 12, 1940
Selective Service Act. Established system for compulsory service in armed forces. (Extended in 1941.)	Dem. Rep. F.L.	211 52 . . .	33 112 1	50 8 . . .	17 10 2	Sep. 16, 1940

Bill or Treaty	Party	House Vote Yea	House Vote Nay	Senate Vote Yea	Senate Vote Nay	Date Enacted
	Prog.	. . .	2	. . .	1	
	Ind.	. . .	. . .	. . .	1	
	A.L.	. . .	1	. . .	. . .	
Lend-Lease. Provided system whereby U.S. lent goods and munitions to democratic nations in return for services and goods.		260	165	60	31	Mar. 11, 1941
Selective Service Act Extension. Extended period of service to not more than 30 months in time of peace and eliminated 900,000-man limit of army.	Dem.	182	65	38	16	Aug. 18, 1941
	Rep.	21	133	7	13	
	Prog.	. . .	3	. . .	1	
	A.L.	. . .	1	. . .	. . .	
Declarations of World War II: Against Japan.	Dem.	235	. . .	56	. . .	Dec. 8, 1941
	Rep.	149	1	24	. . .	
	Prog.	3	. . .	1	. . .	
	Ind.	. . .	. . .	1	. . .	
	A.L.	1	. . .	. . .	. . .	
Against Germany.		393	0	88	0	Dec. 11, 1941
U.N. Charter Ratification.	Dem.	No vote required		53	. . .	Jul. 28, 1945
	Rep.			35	2	
	Prog.			1	. . .	

Source: Compiled by The Information Please Almanac, 1948 (New York, 1948), 93–98.

TABLE 8.23 GOVERNMENT AGENCIES OF THE NEW DEAL ERA

A characteristic of the administration of Franklin D. Roosevelt was the expansion of the national government into numerous areas of activity. This activity called for the creation of many new government agencies. Listed below are many of the "alphabet agencies," each with an acronym, created during the 1930s, the period of the New Deal.

AAA Agricultural Adjustment Administration	**FSRC** Federal Surplus Relief Corporation
BPA Bonneville Power Administration	**FTP** Federal Theatre Project
CAA Civil Aeronautics Authority	**FWA** Federal Works Agency
CCC Civilian Conservation Corps	**FWP** Federal Writers' Project
CWA Civil Works Administration	**HOLC** Home Owners' Loan Corporation
EHFA Electric Home and Farm Authority	**NBCC** National Bituminous Coal Commission
EIB Export-Import Bank	**NLB** National Labor Board
FAP Federal Art Project	**NLRB** National Labor Relations Board
FCA Farm Credit Administration	**NRA** National Recovery Administration
FCC Federal Communications Commission	**NRPB** National Resources Planning Board
FCIC Federal Crop Insurance Corporation	**NRS** National Reemployment Service
FDIC Federal Deposit Insurance Corporation	**NSLRB** National Steel Labor Relations Board
FDP Federal Dance Project	**NYA** National Youth Administration
FEPC Fair Employment Practices Committee	**PWA** Public Works Administration
FERA Federal Emergency Relief Administration	**PWAP** Public Works of Art Project
FFMC Federal Farm Mortgage Corporation	**RA** Resettlement Administration
FHA Federal Housing Administration	**REA** Rural Electrification Administration
FNMA Federal National Mortgage Association	**SEC** Securities and Exchange Commission
FSA Farm Security Administration	**TVA** Tennessee Valley Authority
FSLIC Federal Savings and Loan Insurance Corporation	**USHA** United States Housing Authority
	WPA Works Progress Administration

Source: James S. Olson, ed., Historical Dictionary of the New Deal (Westport, Conn., 1985), 587–588.

The Supreme Court, 1914–1945

The Supreme Court moved in various directions during the years 1914–45. Much of the time it assumed conservative positions on economic issues, taking a dim view of regulation by the national government and closely scrutinizing laws passed by the states. Some state legislation was sustained, especially dealing with working conditions for women and children. On civil liberties the Court was inconsistent, permitting sharp limits on freedoms of the First Amendment during the era of First World War and protecting the rights of religious minorities in the years that followed. For the most part it allowed segregation to stand in the South. Until the end of the period most of the justices were appointed by Republican presidents, which is perhaps one explanation why the Court in the mid-1930s sparked such controversy by striking down many laws of a new Democratic administration. The behavior of the "nine old men" of 1934–36 provoked Franklin D. Roosevelt's "court-packing plan" of 1937, which rightly failed to pass Congress. In time, however, Roosevelt was able to appoint no fewer than eight justices. Driven by a philosophy called "judicial restraint," the Court of the late 1930s and early 1940s permitted the national government broad latitude in dealing with economic issues. While the "Roosevelt Court" sustained the internment of Japanese Americans during the period of the Second World War, it also belatedly began to address the social and political structure of the southern and border states, the long-standing system of segregation known as Jim Crow.

TABLE 8.24 JUSTICES OF THE SUPREME COURT, 1914–1945

Name	From	Term of Service	Years of Service	Appointed by
Joseph McKenna	Calif.	1898–1925	26	McKinley
Oliver W. Holmes, Jr.	Mass.	1902–1932	30	T. Roosevelt
William R. Day	Ohio	1903–1922	19	T. Roosevelt
Horace H. Lurton	Tenn.	1910–1914	4	Taft
Charles E. Hughes	N.Y.	1910–1916	5	Taft
Willis Van Devanter	Wyo.	1911–1937	26	Taft
Joseph R. Lamar	Ga.	1911–1916	5	Taft
Edward D. White[a]	La.	1910–1921	11	Taft
Mahlon Pitney	N.J.	1912–1922	10	Taft
James C. McReynolds	Tenn.	1914–1941	26	Wilson
Louis D. Brandeis	Mass.	1916–1939	22	Wilson
John H. Clarke	Ohio	1916–1922	6	Wilson
William H. Taft[a]	Ohio	1921–1930	8	Harding
George Sutherland	Utah	1922–1938	15	Harding
Pierce Butler	Minn.	1923–1939	16	Harding
Edward T. Sanford	Tenn.	1923–1930	7	Harding
Harlan F. Stone[b]	N.Y.	1925–1946	21	Coolidge
Charles E. Hughes[a]	N.Y.	1930–1941	11	Hoover
Owen J. Roberts	Pa.	1930–1945	15	Hoover
Benjamin N. Cardozo	N.Y.	1932–1938	6	Hoover
Hugo L. Black	Ala.	1937–1971	34	F. Roosevelt
Stanley F. Reed	Ky.	1938–1957	19	F. Roosevelt
Felix Frankfurter	Mass.	1939–1962	23	F. Roosevelt
William O. Douglas	Conn.	1939–1975	36	F. Roosevelt
Frank Murphy	Mich.	1940–1949	9	F. Roosevelt
James F. Byrnes	S.C.	1941–1942	1	F. Roosevelt
Robert H. Jackson	N.Y.	1941–1954	13	F. Roosevelt
Wiley B. Rutledge	Iowa	1943–1949	6	F. Roosevelt
Harold H. Burton	Ohio	1945–1958	13	Truman

[a]Chief justice.
[b]Appointed by Coolidge, Harlan Stone was elevated to chief justice in 1941 by F. Roosevelt.
Source: Congressional Quarterly, *Guide to the U.S. Supreme Court* (Washington, D.C., 1979), 947–948.

Major Cases of the Supreme Court

Arver v. U.S. (1918) In this and subsequent decisions the Supreme Court upheld the conscription law of the First World War, ruling that the power to require military service grew out of the principle of national sovereignty. The government had the right to draft men.

Hammer v. Dagenhart (1918) The Court struck down a law passed by Congress that sought to use the commerce clause to restrict work by children. In a second case in 1922 the Court invalidated a national law that regulated child labor by taxation. In essence the Court was saying that restrictions on child labor, if they were to exist at all, were to come from the states.

Schenck v. U.S. (1919) Here the Court upheld a broadly worded, wartime Espionage Act. Justice Holmes issued his "clear and present danger" doctrine as a means of measuring freedom of speech in wartime, but this decision authorized broad limits on speech.

Missouri v. Holland (1920) The Supreme Court ruled that the power of the national government is very broad when exercised through the instrument of a treaty.

Adkins v. Children's Hospital (1923) The Court invalidated an act of Congress that authorized the fixing of wages for women in the District of Columbia. A majority ruled that the measure violated freedoms in the Fifth Amendment.

Gitlow v. New York (1925) In this and several subsequent decisions, the Supreme Court defined the Fourteenth Amendment as encompassing many of the restrictions on government specified in the Bill of Rights. The decisions, which restrained state governments from encroaching on individual liberties, vastly broadened the meaning of the Fourteenth Amendment.

Schechter v. U.S. (1935) In this famous "sick chicken" case, the Supreme Court struck down the heart of the New Deal's recovery program, the NIRA or NRA, by a vote of 9–0. The Court ruled in sum that Congress had interpreted its powers too broadly. The case was one of numerous decisions in 1935–36 that seemed to render the New Deal powerless to deal with the depression.

Ashwander v. TVA (1936) The Court upheld the authority of the national government to build dams on the Tennessee River, a step toward upholding the TVA as a whole.

National Labor Relations Board v. Jones and Laughlin Steel Corporation (1937) In sustaining the New Deal's pro-labor Wagner Act, the Court took a much broader view of the power of the national government than it had done in several previous cases. The decision suggested that under heavy attack the Court might be changing its view.

Missouri Ex. Rel. Gaines v. Canada (1938) In this "Gaines" case the Court chipped away at the system of segregation in the southern states by ruling that a black person had to be admitted to a "whites only" law school in this state, where no law school for blacks existed.

West Virginia State Board of Education v. Barnette (1943) The Supreme Court overturned an earlier ruling by invalidating a state law that required school children to salute the flag. The law was said to violate free speech and possibly religious freedom.

Korematsu v. U.S. (1944) Here the Supreme Court upheld the government's controversial policy of detaining Japanese Americans in special camps during the Second World War. At the same time, however, the same Court ruled in *Ex parte Endo* that a person could not be held in detention if his or her loyalty to the United States had been proven.

Smith v. Allwright (1944) In this case dealing with civil rights of black people, the Court struck down the "white primary" as a means of excluding black people from voting in the segregated South. The Court ruled that the Democratic party was not a private club but, through use of the party primary, an integral part of the electoral system.

Source: Congressional Quarterly, *Guide to the U.S. Supreme Court,* 889–893.

TABLE 8.25 STATE GOVERNORS, 1914–1945

Alabama	Arizona	Arkansas	California
Emmett O'Neal (D) 1911–1915	George W. P. Hunt (D) 1912–1917	George W. Hays (D) 1913–1917	Hiram W. Johnson (R) 1911–1917
Charles Henderson (D) 1915–1919	Thomas E. Campbell (R) 1917	Charles H. Brough (D) 1917–1921	William D. Stephens (R) 1917–1923
Thomas E. Kirby (D) 1919–1923	George W. P. Hunt (D) 1917–1919	Thomas C. McRae (D) 1921–1925	Friend William Richardson (R) 1923–1927
William D. Brandon (D) 1923–1927	Thomas E. Campbell (R) 1919–1923	Tom J. Terral (D) 1925–1927	Clement C. Young (R) 1927–1931
Bibb Graves (D) 1927–1931	George W. P. Hunt (D) 1923–1929	John E. Martineau (D) 1927–1928	James Rolph, Jr. (R) 1931–1934
Benjamin M. Miller (D) 1931–1935	John C. Phillips (R) 1929–1931	Harvey Parnell (D) 1928–1933	Frank F. Merriam (R) 1934–1939
Bibb Graves (D) 1935–1939	George W. P. Hunt (D) 1931–1933	J. M. Futrell (D) 1933–1937	Culbert L. Olson (D) 1939–1943
Frank M. Dixon (D) 1939–1943	Benjamin B. Moeur (D) 1933–1937	Carl E. Bailey (D) 1937–1941	Earl Warren (R) 1943–1953
Chauncey M. Sparks (D) 1943–1947	Rawleigh C. Stanford (D) 1937–1939	Homer M. Adkins (D) 1941–1945	
	Robert T. Jones (D) 1939–1941	Ben T. Laney (D) 1945–1949	
	Sidney P. Osborn (D) 1941–1948		

Colorado	Connecticut	Delaware	Florida
Elias M. Ammons (D) 1913–1915	Simeon E. Baldwin (D) 1911–1915	Charles R. Miller (R) 1913–1917	Park Trammell (D) 1913–1917
George A. Carlson (R) 1915–1917	Marcus H. Holcomb (R) 1915–1921	John G. Townsend, Jr. (R) 1917–1921	Sidney J. Catts (Prohibition) 1917–1921
Julius C. Gunter (D) 1917–1919	Everett J. Lake (R) 1921–1923	William D. Denney (R) 1921–1925	Cary A. Hardee (D) 1921–1925
Oliver H. Shoup (R) 1919–1923	Charles A. Templeton (R) 1923–1925	Robert P. Robinson (R) 1925–1929	John W. Martin (D) 1925–1929
William E. Sweet (D) 1923–1925	Hiram Bingham (R) 1925	C. Douglas Buck (R) 1929–1937	Doyle E. Carlton (D) 1929–1933
Clarence J. Morley (R) 1925–1927	John H. Trumbull (R) 1925–1931	Richard C. McMullen (D) 1937–1941	Dave Sholtz (D) 1933–1937
William H. Adams (D) 1927–1933	Wilbur L. Cross (D) 1931–1939	Walter W. Bacon (R) 1941–1949	Fred P. Cone (D) 1937–1941
Edwin C. Johnson (D) 1933–1937	Raymond E. Baldwin (R) 1939–1941		Spessard L. Holland (D) 1941–1945
Ray H. Talbot (D) 1937	Robert A. Hurley (D) 1941–1943		Millard F. Caldwell (D) 1945–1949
Teller Ammons (D) 1937–1939	Raymond E. Baldwin (R) 1943–1946		
Ralph L. Carr (R) 1939–1943			
John C. Vivian (R) 1943–1947			

Georgia	Idaho	Illinois	Indiana
John M. Slaton 1913–1915	John M. Haines (R) 1913–1915	Edward F. Dunne (D) 1913–1917	Samuel M. Ralston (D) 1913–1917
Nathaniel E. Harris (D) 1915–1917	Moses Alexander (D) 1915–1919	Frank O. Lowden (R) 1917–1921	James P. Goodrich (R) 1917–1921
Hugh M. Dorsey (D) 1917–1921	D. W. Davis (R) 1919–1923	Len Small (R) 1921–1929	Warren T. McCray (R) 1921–1924
Thomas W. Hardwick (D) 1921–1923	C. C. Moore (R) 1923–1927	Louis L. Emmerson (R) 1929–1933	Emmett Forest Branch (R) 1924–1925
Clifford Walker (D) 1923–1927	H. C. Baldridge (R) 1927–1931	Henry Horner (D) 1933–1940	Ed Jackson (R) 1925–1929
Lamartine G. Hardman (D) 1927–1931	C. Ben Ross (D) 1931–1937	John H. Stelle (D) 1940–1941	Harry G. Leslie (R) 1929–1933
Richard B. Russell, Jr. (D) 1931–1933	Barzilla W. Clark (D) 1937–1939	Dwight H. Green (R) 1941–1949	Paul V. McNutt (D) 1933–1937
Eugene Talmadge (D) 1933–1937	C. A. Bottolfsen (R) 1939–1941		M. Clifford Townsend (D) 1937–1941
Eurith D. Rivers (D) 1937–1941	Chase A. Clark (D) 1941–1943		Henry F. Schricker (D) 1941–1945
Eugene Talmadge (D) 1941–1943	C. A. Bottolfsen (R) 1943–1945		Ralph F. Gates (R) 1945–1949
Ellis Arnall (D) 1943–1947	Charles C. Gossett (D) 1945		
	Arnold Williams (D) 1945–1947		

Iowa	Kansas	Kentucky	Louisiana
George W. Clarke (R) 1913–1917	George Hartshorn Hodges (D) 1913–1915	James B. McCreary (D) 1911–1915	Luther E. Hall (D) 1912–1916
William L. Harding (R) 1917–1921	Arthur Capper (R) 1915–1919	Augustus O. Stanley (D) 1915–1919	Ruffin G. Pleasant (D) 1916–1920
N. E. Kendall (R) 1921–1925	Henry J. Allen (R) 1919–1923	James D. Black (D) 1919	John M. Parker (D) 1920–1924
John Hammill (R) 1925–1931	Jonathan M. Davis (D) 1923–1925	Edwin P. Morrow (R) 1919–1923	Henry L. Fuqua (D) 1924–1926
Daniel W. Turner (R) 1931–1933	Ben S. Paulen (R) 1925–1929	William J. Fields (D) 1923–1927	Oramel H. Simpson (D) 1926–1928
Clyde L. Herring (D) 1933–1937	Clyde M. Reed (R) 1929–1931	Flem D. Sampson (R) 1927–1931	Huey P. Long (D) 1928–1932
Nelson G. Kraschel (D) 1937–1939	Harry H. Woodring (D) 1931–1933	Ruby Laffoon (D) 1931–1935	Alvin O. King (D) 1932
George A. Wilson (R) 1939–1943	Alfred M. Landon (R) 1933–1937	Albert B. Chandler (D) 1935–1939	Oscar K. Allen (D) 1932–1936
Bourke B. Hickenlooper (R) 1943–1945	Walter A. Huxman (D) 1937–1939	Keen Johnson (D) 1939–1943	James A. Noe (D) 1936
Robert D. Blue (R) 1945–1949	Payne Ratner (R) 1939–1943	Simeon S. Willis (R) 1943–1947	Richard W. Leche (D) 1936–1939
	Arthur F. Schoeppel (R) 1943–1947		Earl K. Long (D) 1939–1940
			Sam H. Jones (D) 1940–1944
			James H. Davis (D) 1944–1948

Maine	Maryland	Massachusetts	Michigan
William T. Haines (R) 1913–1915	Phillips Lee Goldsborough (R) 1912–1916	Eugene N. Foss (D) 1911–1914	Woolbridge N. Ferris (D) 1913–1916
Oakley C. Curtis (D) 1915–1917	Emerson C. Harrington (D) 1916–1920	David I. Walsh (D) 1914–1916	Albert E. Sleeper (R) 1917–1920
Carl E. Milliken (R) 1917–1921	Albert C. Ritchie (D) 1920–1935	Samuel W. McCall (R) 1916–1919	Alexander J. Grobeck (R) 1921–1926
Frederic H. Parkhurst (R) 1921	Harry W. Nice (R) 1935–1939	Calvin Coolidge (R) 1919–1921	Fred W. Green (R) 1927–1930
Percival R. Baxter (R) 1921–1925	Herbert R. O'Conor (D) 1939–1947	Channing H. Cox (R) 1921–1925	Wilber M. Brucker (R) 1931–1932
Ralph O. Brewster (R) 1925–1929		Alvin T. Fuller (R) 1925–1929	William A. Comstock (D) 1933–1934

(continued)

TABLE 8.25 (continued)

Maine	Maryland	Massachusetts	Michigan
William Tudon Gardiner (R) 1929–1933 Louis J. Brann (D) 1933–1937 Lewis O. Barrows (R) 1937–1941 Sumner Sewall (R) 1941–1945 Horace A. Hildreth (R) 1945–1949		Frank G. Allen (R) 1929–1931 Joseph B. Ely (D) 1931–1935 James M. Curley (D) 1935–1937 Charles F. Hurley (D) 1937–1939 Leverett Saltonstall (R) 1939–1945 Maurice J. Tobin (D) 1945–1947	Frank D. Fitzgerald (R) 1935–1936 Frank Murphy (D) 1937–1938 Frank D. Fitzgerald (R) 1939 Luren D. Dickinson (R) 1939–1940 Murray D. Van Wagoner (D) 1941–1942 Harry F. Kelly (R) 1943–1946

Minnesota	Mississippi	Missouri	Montana
Adolph O. Eberhart (R) 1914–1915 Winfield S. Hammond (D) 1915 Joseph A. A. Burnquist (R) 1915–1921 Jacob A. O. Preus (R) 1921–1925 Theodore Christianson (R) 1925–1931 Floyd B. Olson (Farmer-Labor) 1931–1936 Hjalmar Petersen (Farmer-Labor) 1936–1937 Elmer A. Benson (Farmer-Labor) 1937–1939 Harold E. Stassen (R) 1939–1943 Edward J. Thye (R) 1943–1947	Earl L. Brewer (D) 1912–1916 Theodore G. Bilbo (D) 1916–1920 Lee M. Russell (D) 1920–1924 Henry L. Whitfield (D) 1924–1927 Dennis Murphree (D) 1927–1928 Theodore G. Bilbo (D) 1928–1932 Martin Sennett Connor (D) 1932–1936 Hugh L. White (D) 1936–1940 Paul B. Johnson (D) 1940–1943 Dennis Murphree (D) 1943–1944 Thomas L. Bailey (D) 1944–1946	Elliot W. Major (D) 1913–1917 Frederick D. Gardner (D) 1917–1921 Arthur M. Hyde (R) 1921–1925 Sam A. Baker (R) 1925–1929 Henry S. Caulfield (R) 1929–1933 Guy B. Park (D) 1933–1937 Lloyd C. Stark (D) 1937–1941 Forrest C. Donnell (R) 1941–1945 Phil M. Donnelly (D) 1945–1949	Sam V. Stewart (D) 1913–1921 Joseph M. Dixon (R) 1921–1925 John E. Erickson (D) 1925–1933 Frank H. Cooney (D) 1933–1935 W. Elmer Holt (D) 1935–1937 Roy E. Ayres (D) 1937–1941 Sam C. Ford (R) 1941–1949

Nebraska	Nevada	New Hampshire	New Jersey
John Henry Morehead (D) 1913–1917 Keith Neville (D) 1917–1919 Samuel Roy McKelvie (R) 1919–1923 Charles Wayland Bryan (D) 1923–1925 Adam McMullen (R) 1925–1929 Arthur J. Weaver (R) 1929–1931 Charles Wayland Bryan (D) 1931–1935 Robert LeRoy Cochran (D) 1935–1941 Dwight Palmer Griswold (R) 1941–1947	Tasker L. Oddie (R) 1911–1915 Emmet D. Boyle (D) 1915–1923 James G. Scugham (D) 1923–1927 Frederick B. Balzar (R) 1927–1934 Morley Griswold (R) 1934–1935 Richard Kirman Sr. (R) 1935–1939 Edward P. Carville (D) 1939–1945 Vail Pittman (D) 1945–1951	Samuel D. Felker (D) 1913–1915 Rolland H. Spaulding (R) 1915–1917 Henry W. Keyes (R) 1917–1919 John H. Bartlett (R) 1919–1921 Albert O. Brown (R) 1921–1923 Fred H. Brown (D) 1923–1925 John G. Winnant (R) 1925–1927 Huntley N. Spaulding (R) 1927–1929 Charles W. Tobey (R) 1929–1931 John G. Winant (R) 1931–1935 Styles Bridges (R) 1935–1937 Francis P. Murphy (R) 1937–1941 Robert O. Blood (R) 1941–1945 Charles M. Dale (R) 1945–1949	Leon R. Taylor (D) 1913–1914 James F. Fielder (D) 1914–1917 Walter E. Edge (R) 1917–1919 William N. Runyan (R) 1919–1920 Clarence E. Case (R) 1920 Edward I. Edwards (D) 1920–1923 George S. Silzer (D) 1923–1926 A. Harry Moore (D) 1926–1929 Morgan F. Larson (R) 1929–1932 A. Harry Moore (D) 1932–1935 Clifford R. Powell (R) 1935 Horace G. Prall (R) 1935 Harold G. Hoffman (R) 1935–1938 A. Harry Moore (D) 1938–1941 Charles Edison (D) 1941–1944 Walter E. Edge (R) 1944–1947

New Mexico	New York	North Carolina	North Dakota
William C. McDonald (D) 1912–1917 Ezequiel Cabeza da Baca (D) 1917 Washington E. Lindsey (R) 1917–1919 Octaviano A. Larrazolo (R) 1919–1921 Merritt C. Mechem (R) 1921–1923 James F. Hinkle (D) 1923–1925 Arthur T. Hannett (D) 1925–1927 Richard C. Dillon (R) 1927–1931 Arthur Seligman (D) 1931–1933 A. W. Hockenhull (D) 1933–1935 Clyde Tingley (D) 1935–1939 John E. Miles (D) 1939–1943 John J. Dempsey (D) 1943–1947	Martin H. Glynn (D) 1913–1914 Charles S. Whitman (R) 1915–1918 Alfred E. Smith (D) 1919–1920 Nathan L. Miller (R) 1921–1922 Alfred E. Smith (D) 1923–1928 Franklin D. Roosevelt (D) 1929–1932 Herbert H. Lehman (D) 1933–1942 Charles Poletti (D) 1942 Thomas E. Dewey (R) 1943–1954	Locke Craig (D) 1913–1917 Thomas W. Bickett (D) 1917–1921 Cameron Morrison (D) 1921–1925 Angus W. McLean (D) 1925–1929 O. Max Gardner (D) 1929–1933 J. C. B. Ehringhaus (D) 1933–1937 Clyde R. Hoey (D) 1937–1941 Joseph M. Broughton (D) 1941–1945 R. Gregg Cherry (D) 1945–1949	Louis B. Hanna (R) 1913–1917 Lynn J. Frazier (Nonpartisan) 1917–1921 Ragnvald A. Nestos (R) 1921–1925 Arthur G. Sorlie (R) 1925–1928 Walter Maddock (Nonpartisan) 1928–1929 George F. Shafer (R) 1929–1933 William Langer (Nonpartisan) 1933–1934 Ole H. Olson (R) 1934–1935 Thomas H. Moodie (D) 1935 Walter Welford (R) 1935–1937 William Langer (Independent) 1937–1939 John Moses (D) 1939–1945 Fred G. Aandahl (R) 1945–1951

Ohio	Oklahoma	Oregon	Pennsylvania
James D. Cox (D) 1913–1915 Frank B. Willis (R) 1915–1917 James D. Cox (D) 1917–1921 Harry L. Davis (R) 1921–1923 A. V. Donahey (D) 1923–1929 Myers V. Cooper (R) 1929–1931 George White (D) 1931–1935 Martin L. Davey (D) 1935–1939	Lee Cruce (D) 1911–1915 Robert L. Williams (D) 1915–1919 James B. A. Robertson (D) 1919–1923 John C. Walton (D) 1923 Martin E. Trapp (D) 1923–1927 Henry S. Johnston (D) 1927–1929 William J. Holloway (D) 1929–1931 William H. Murray (D) 1931–1935	Oswald West (D) 1911–1915 James Withycombe (R) 1915–1919 Ben W. Olcott (R) 1919–1923 Walter M. Pierce (D) 1923–1927 Ussac Lee Patterson (R) 1927–1929 Albin W. Norblad (R) 1929–1931 Julius L. Meier (Independent) 1931–1935	John K. Tener (R) 1911–1915 Martin G. Brumbaugh (R) 1915–1919 William G. Sproul (R) 1919–1923 Gifford Pinchot (R) 1923–1927 John S. Fisher (R) 1927–1931 Gifford Pinchot (R) 1931–1935 George H. Earle (D) 1935–1939 Arthur H. James (R) 1939–1943

Ohio	Oklahoma	Oregon	Pennsylvania
John W. Bricker (R) 1939–1945 Frank J. Lauche (D) 1945–1947	Earnest W. Marland (D) 1935–1939 Leon C. Phillips (D) 1939–1943 Robert S. Kerr 1943–1947	Charles H. Martin (D) 1935–1939 Charles A. Sprague (R) 1939–1943 Earl Snell (R) 1943–1947	Edward Martin (R) 1943–1947

Rhode Island	South Carolina	South Dakota	Tennessee
Aram J. Pothier (R) 1909–1915 R. Livingston Beeckman (R) 1915–1921 Emery J. San Souci (R) 1921–1923 William S. Flynn (D) 1923–1925 Aram J. Pothier (R) 1925–1928 Norman S. Case (R) 1928–1933 Theodore F. Green (D) 1933–1937 Robert E. Quinn (D) 1937–1939 William H. Vanderbilt (R) 1939–1941 J. Howard McGrath (D) 1941–1945 John O. Pastore (D) 1945–1951	Coleman L. Blease (D) 1911–1915 Charles A. Smith (D) 1915 Richard I. Manning (D) 1915–1919 Robert A. Cooper (D) 1919–1922 Wilson G. Harvey (D) 1922–1923 Thomas A. McLeod (D) 1923–1927 John A. Richards (D) 1927–1931 Ubra C. Blackwood (D) 1931–1935 Olin D. Johnston (D) 1935–1939 Burnet R. Maybank (D) 1939–1941 J. Emile Harley (D) 1941–1942 R. M. Jeffries (D) 1942–1943 Olin D. Johnston (D) 1943–1945 R. J. Williams (D) 1945–1947	Frank M. Byrne (R-Progressive) 1913–1917 Peter Norbeck (R) 1917–1921 William H. McMaster (R) 1921–1925 Carl Gunderson (R) 1925–1927 William J. Bulow (D) 1927–1931 Warren E. Green (R) 1931–1933 Thomas Berry (D) 1933–1937 Leslie Jensen (R) 1937–1939 Harlan J. Bushfield (R) 1939–1943 Merrell Q. Sharpe (R) 1943–1947	Ben W. Hooper (R) 1911–1915 Thomas C. Rye (D) 1915–1919 Albert H. Roberts (D) 1919–1921 Alfred A. Taylor (R) 1921–1923 Austin Peay (D) 1923–1927 Henry H. Horton (D) 1927–1933 Hill McAlister (D) 1933–1937 Gordon Browning (D) 1937–1939 Prentice Cooper (D) 1939–1945 Jim Nance McCord (D) 1945–1949

Texas	Utah	Vermont	Virginia
Oscar B. Colquitt (D) 1911–1915 James E. Ferguson (D) 1915–1917 William P. Hobby (D) 1917–1921 Pat M. Neff (D) 1921–1925 Miriam A. Ferguson (D) 1925–1927 Dan Moody (D) 1927–1931 Ross Sterling (D) 1931–1933 Miriam A. Ferguson (D) 1933–1935 James V. Allred (D) 1935–1939 W. Lee O'Daniel (D) 1939–1941 Coke R. Stevenson (D) 1941–1947	William Spry (R) 1909–1917 Simon Bamberger (D) 1917–1921 Charles R. Mabey (R) 1921–1925 George H. Dern (D) 1925–1933 Henry H. Blood (D) 1933–1941 Herbert B. Maw (D) 1941–1949	Allen M. Fletcher (R) 1912–1915 Charles W. Gates (R) 1915–1917 Horace F. Graham (R) 1917–1919 Percival W. Clement (R) 1919–1921 James Hartness (R) 1921–1923 Redfield Proctor (R) 1923–1925 Franklin S. Billings (R) 1925–1927 John E. Weeks (R) 1927–1931 Stanley C. Wilson (R) 1931–1935 Charles M. Smith (R) 1935–1937 George D. Aiken (R) 1937–1941 William H. Wills (R) 1941–1945 Mortimer R. Proctor (R) 1945–1947	William H. Mann (D) 1910–1914 Henry C. Stuart (D) 1914–1918 Westmoreland Davis (D) 1918–1922 E. Lee Trinkle (D) 1922–1926 Harry Flood Byrd, Sr. (D) 1926–1930 John Garland Pollard (D) 1930–1934 George C. Peery (D) 1934–1938 James H. Price (D) 1938–1942 Colgate W. Darden, Jr. (D) 1942–1946

Washington	West Virginia	Wisconsin	Wyoming
Ernest Lister (D) 1913–1919 Louis Folwell Hart (R) 1919–1925 Roland H. Hartley (R) 1925–1933 Clarence D. Martin (D) 1933–1941 Arthur B. Langlie (R) 1941–1945 Monrad C. Wallgren (D) 1945–1949	Henry D. Hatfield (R) 1913–1917 John J. Cornwell (D) 1917–1921 Ephraim F. Morgan (R) 1921–1925 Howard M. Gore (R) 1925–1929 William G. Conley (R) 1929–1933 H. Guy Kump (D) 1933–1937 Homer A. Holt (D) 1937–1941 M. Mansfield Neely (D) 1941–1945 Clarence W. Meadows (D) 1945–1949	Francis E. McGovern (R) 1911–1915 Emanuel L. Philipp (R) 1915–1921 John J. Blaine (R) 1921–1927 Fred R. Zimmerman (R) 1927–1929 Walter J. Kohler, Sr. (R) 1929–1931 Philip F. La Follette (R) 1931–1933 Albert G. Schmedeman (D) 1933–1935 Philip F. La Follette (Progressive) 1935–1939 Julius P. Heil (R) 1939–1943 Walter S. Goodland (R) 1943–1947	Joseph M. Carey (D) 1911–1915 John B. Kendrick (D) 1915–1917 Frank L. Houx (D) 1917–1919 Robert D. Carey (R) 1919–1923 William B. Ross (D) 1923–1924 Frank E. Lucas (R) 1924–1925 Nellie Tayloe Ross (D) 1925–1927 Frank C. Emerson (R) 1927–1931 Alonzo M. Clark (R) 1931–1933 Leslie A. Miller (D) 1933–1939 Nels H. Smith (R) 1939–1943 Lester C. Hunt (D) 1943–1949

Sources: Joseph and Jessamine Kallenbach, *American State Governors, 1776–1976* (3 vols., Dobbs Ferry, N.Y. 1977–1982), numerous pages; *World Book Encyclopedia* (New York, 1973), numerous pages.

Finances of the National Government

The financial status of the national government changed in proportion to shifts in the need for government activity. The First World War created need for more spending, more employees, more revenue, and still greater indebtedness. The period of the 1920s found the government earning less, spending much less than during the peak of the war years (but considerably more than in the prewar period), and still balancing the budget and reducing the public debt.

Demands made on government during the depression produced a string of unbalanced budgets that appeared large until one compared them with the years of the Second World War that followed. During the war the United States experienced striking growth in expenditures, number of employees, and budget deficits. The revolutionary source of income throughout this period was the income tax, which went into effect in 1913.

TABLE 8.26   SUMMARY OF FINANCES

(In thousands of dollars)

Year	Receipts	Expenditures	Surplus or deficit (−)
1945	44,475,304	98,416,220	−53,940,916
1944	43,635,315	95,058,708	−51,423,393
1943	21,986,701	79,407,131	−57,420,430
1942	12,555,436	34,045,679	−21,490,243
1941	7,102,931	13,262,204	−6,159,272
1940	5,144,013	9,062,032	−3,918,019
1939	4,996,300	8,858,458	−3,862,158
1938	5,615,221	6,791,838	−1,176,617
1937	4,978,601	7,756,021	−2,777,421
1936	4,068,937	3,493,486	−4,424,549
1935	3,729,914	6,520,966	−2,791,052
1934	3,064,268	6,693,900	−3,629,632
1933	2,021,213	4,622,865	−2,601,652
1932	1,923,913	4,659,203	−2,785,290
1931	3,115,557	3,577,434	−461,877
1930	4,177,942	3,440,269	737,673
1929	4,033,250	3,298,859	734,391
1928	4,042,348	3,103,265	939,083
1927	4,129,394	2,974,030	1,155,366
1926	3,962,756	3,097,612	365,144
1925	3,780,149	3,063,105	717,043
1924	4,012,045	3,048,678	963,367
1923	4,007,135	3,294,628	712,508
1922	4,109,104	3,372,608	736,496
1921	5,624,933	5,115,928	509,005
1920	6,694,565	6,403,344	291,222
1919	5,152,257	18,514,880	−13,362,623
1918	3,664,583	12,696,702	−9,032,120
1917	1,124,825	1,977,682	−853,357
1916	782,535	734,056	48,478
1915	697,911	760,587	−62,676
1914	734,673	735,081	−408

Source: Bureau of the Census, *Historical Statistics of the United States, Colonial Times to 1957* (Washington, D.C., 1960), 711.

TABLE 8.27   PUBLIC DEBT OF THE GOVERNMENT

Year	Total Gross Debt	
	Amount	Per Capita
	1,000 Dollars	Dollars
1945	258,682,187	1,848.60
1944	201,003,387	1,452.44
1943	136,696,090	999.83
1942	72,422,445	537.13
1941	48,961,444	367.09
1940	42,967,531	325.23
1939	40,439,532	308.98
1938	37,164,740	286.27
1937	36,424,614	282.75
1936	33,778,543	263.79
1935	28,700,393	225.55
1934	27,053,141	214.07
1933	22,538,673	179.48
1932	19,487,002	156.10
1931	16,801,281	135.45
1930	16,185,310	131.51
1929	16,931,088	139.04
1928	17,604,293	146.09
1927	18,511,907	155.51
1926	19,643,216	167.32
1925	20,516,194	177.12
1924	21,250,813	186.23
1923	22,349,707	199.64
1922	22,963,382	208.65
1921	23,977,451	220.91
1920	24,299,321	228.23
1919	25,484,506	242.56
1918	12,455,225	119.13
1917	2,975,619	28.77
1916	1,225,146	12.04
1915	1,191,264	11.85
1914	1,188,235	11.99

Source: Bureau of the Census *Historical Statistics of the United States, Colonial Times to 1957*, 720–721.

TABLE 8.28   PAID CIVILIAN EMPLOYMENT OF THE GOVERNMENT

Year	Employees			Competitive Civil Service Employees (classified)[a]	Executive Branch				Legislative Branch	Judicial Branch
	Total	Washington, D.C.	All Other Areas		Total	Defense	Post Office	Other		
1945	3,816,310	264,770	3,551,540	. . .	3,786,645	2,634,575	416,314	735,756	26,959	2,706
1944	3,332,356	276,758	3,055,598	. . .	3,304,379	2,246,454	374,758	683,167	25,314	2,663
1943	3,299,414	284,665	3,014,749	. . .	3,273,887	2,200,064	339,005	734,818	22,903	2,624
1942	2,296,384	276,352	2,020,032	. . .	2,272,082	1,291,093	338,090	642,899	21,657	2,645
1941	1,437,682	190,588	1,247,094	990,233	1,416,444	556,073	335,008	525,368	18,712	2,526
1940	1,042,420	139,770	902,650	726,895	1,022,853	256,025	323,481	443,347	17,099	2,468
1939	953,891	129,314	824,577	662,832	935,797	195,997	314,478	425,322	15,802	2,292
1938	882,226	120,744	761,482	562,909	864,534	163,457	311,440	389,637	15,609	2,083
1937	895,993	117,020	778,973	532,073	878,214	160,737	304,852	412,625	15,609	2,170
1936	867,432	122,937	744,495	498,725	950,395	148,369	281,314	420,712	14,976	2,061
1935	780,582	108,673	671,909	455,229	765,712	147,188	275,483	343,041	12,970	1,900
1934	698,649	94,244	604,405	450,592	685,108	133,092	281,770	270,246	11,667	1,874
1933	603,587	70,261	533,326	456,096	590,984	101,228	286,935	202,821	10,847	1,756
1932	605,496	73,455	532,041	467,161	592,560	100,420	296,136	196,004	11,159	1,777
1931	609,746	76,303	533,443	468,050	596,745	107,980	297,159	191,606	11,192	1,809
1930	601,319	73,032	528,287	462,083	588,951	103,462	297,895	187,594	10,620	1,748
1929	579,559	68,266	511,293	445,957	567,721	103,098	295,695	168,928	10,240	1,598
1928	560,772	65,506	495,266	431,763	549,238	94,005	293,023	162,210	9,894	1,640
1927	547,127	63,814	483,313	422,998	535,599	85,717	291,249	158,633	9,848	1,680
1926	548,713	64,722	483,991	422,300	537,251	92,208	288,573	156,470	9,742	1,720
1925	553,045	67,563	485,482	423,538	541,792	94,772	284,550	162,470	9,493	1,760
1924	543,484	68,000	475,484	415,593	532,048	92,331	279,679	160,038	9,636	1,800
1923	536,900	70,062	466,838	411,398	525,746	94,001	268,951	162,794	9,314	1,840
1922	543,507	73,645	469,862	420,688	532,210	107,126	260,100	164,984	9,417	1,880
1921	561,142	82,416	478,726	448,112	550,020	138,293	251,300	160,427	9,202	1,920
1920	655,265	94,110	561,155	497,603	645,408	237,212	242,400	165,796	7,897	1,960
1919	794,271	106,073	688,198	592,961	784,180	. . .	. . .	. . .	8,091	2,000
1918	854,500	120,835	733,665	642,432	844,480	. . .	. . .	. . .	7,980	2,040
1917	438,500	48,313	390,187	326,899	429,727	91,982	215,883	121,862	6,693	2,080
1916	399,381	41,804	357,577	296,926	391,133	63,395	212,215	115,523	6,128	2,120
1915	395,429	41,281	354,148	292,291	387,294	58,286	212,012	116,996	5,975	2,160
1914	401,887	40,016	361,871	292,460	393,555	57,989	212,973	122,593	6,132	2,200

[a]This category pertained to all positions covered under the civil service system—a large majority of civilian employees of the national government except those excluded by law. The government did not release statistics for the years of the Second World War.
Source: Bureau of the Census, *Historical Statistics of the United States, Colonial Times to 1957*, 710.

Finances of the States

In this period marked with emphasis on the national government, the states also found more reason to spend. The largest sums went for schools, highways, and, beginning in the 1930s, public welfare. The leading provider of revenue for the states was various forms of sales taxes.

TABLE 8.29   STATE GOVERNMENTS, GENERAL EXPENDITURES

[In millions of dollars. Because of rounding, detail does not always add to total. Includes all expenditures susceptible of classification by function; hence, excludes debt service and contributions to trust funds and to enterprises.]

Year	Total	General Control	Public Safety	Highways	Sanitation and Health	Hospitals and Institutions for the Handicapped	Public Welfare	Correction	Schools	Natural Resources	Other
1945	4,405	189	134	833	96	297	955	85	1,214	148	458
1944	4,277	172	135	854	70	278	944	81	1,208	135	400
1943	4,223	172	138	992	58	261	917	79	1,125	125	358
1942	4,322	172	131	1,146	55	258	916	79	1,071	130	363
1941	4,136	175	118	1,044	52	246	906	81	1,053	124	335
1940	4,097	172	135	1,134	50	268	947	85	939	107	261
1939	4,099	186	135	1,133	50	281	895	83	957	110	271
1938	3,887	168	131	1,141	45	241	799	84	927	97	253
1937	3,555	161	112	1,151	36	227	613	75	867	83	229
1932	2,597	138	92	1,071	30	186	128	86	621	79	166
1927	1,878	111	68	720	20	151	66	63	482	72	125
1923	1,361	86	55	433	16	118	79	66	382	53	74
1919	678	56	35	120	10	72	47	55	195	26	63
1915	470	50	30	77	6	55	34	32	157	18	11

Source: Bureau of the Census, *Historical Statistics of the United States, 1789 to 1945*, 316.

TABLE 8.30   STATE TAX COLLECTIONS, 1915–1945

[In millions of dollars. Because of rounding, detail does not always add to total. Data include local shares of state collected taxes.]

	Total		General Sales, Use, and Gross Receipts	Motor Vehicle Fuels Sales	Tobacco Products Sales	Alcoholic Beverage Sales and Licenses	Motor Vehicle and Operators' Licenses	Income			Property	Death and Gift	Severance	Unemployment Compensation	Other
	Including Unemployment Compensation	Excluding Unemployment Compensation						Total	Individual	Corporation					
1945	5,603	4,349	776	696	145	368	414	810	357	453	276	136	83	1,254	643
1944	5,425	4,105	721	685	160	322	413	762	316	446	247	114	71	1,319	608
1943	5,132	3,961	671	776	141	335	414	633	293	340	259	109	75	1,172	547
1942	5,015	3,939	633	942	131	312	451	518	249	269	271	112	62	1,076	504
1941	4,507	3,606	575	913	106	272	434	422	225	197	268	118	53	901	445
1940	4,157	3,313	499	839	97	255	387	361	206	155	260	113	53	844	449
1939	3,884	3,085	440	801	60	228	364	331	197	134	259	133	47	799	422
1938	3,834	3,132	447	777	55	227	359	383	218	165	244	142	58	702	440
1937	3,360	3,013	434	722	54	221	349	356	199	157	292	116	49	347	420
1936	2,641	2,618	364	687	44	166	360	266	153	113	228	117	34	23	354
1935	. . .	2,217	284	617	29	143	323	159	105	54	248	100	26	. . .	288
1934	. . .	1,979	173	565	25	81	305	129	80	49	273	93	21	. . .	314
1933	. . .	1,724	16	518	20	10	303	121	64	57	285	127	14	. . .	311
1932	. . .	1,890	7	527	19	1	335	153	74	79	328	148	19	. . .	353
1931	. . .	2,042	8	536	15	1	344	201	86	115	371	187	27	. . .	352

[In millions of dollars. Because of rounding, detail does not always add to total. Data include local shares of state collected taxes.]

	Total		General Sales, Use, and Gross Receipts	Motor Vehicle Fuels Sales	Tobacco Products Sales	Alcoholic Beverage Sales and Licenses	Motor Vehicle and Operators' Licenses	Income			Property	Death and Gift	Severance	Unemployment Compensation	Other
	Including Unemployment Compensation	Excluding Unemployment Compensation						Total	Individual	Corporation					
1930	. . .	2,108	1	495	12	. . .	356	233	. . .	. . .	345	183	. . .	. . .	482
1929	. . .	1,951	. . .	431	. . .	. . .	348	204	. . .	. . .	350	149	. . .	. . .	469
1928	. . .	1,756	. . .	305	. . .	. . .	323	184	. . .	. . .	381	128	. . .	. . .	436
1927	. . .	1,608	. . .	259	. . .	. . .	301	162	. . .	. . .	370	106	. . .	. . .	409
1926	. . .	1,465	. . .	188	. . .	. . .	288	134	. . .	. . .	376	91	. . .	. . .	388
1925	. . .	1,305	. . .	148	. . .	. . .	261	103	. . .	. . .	359	86	. . .	. . .	349
1924	. . .	1,139	. . .	80	. . .	. . .	226	101	. . .	. . .	352	79	. . .	. . .	301
1923	. . .	1,020	. . .	39	. . .	. . .	189	93	. . .	. . .	353	75	. . .	. . .	272
1922	. . .	947	. . .	13	. . .	. . .	152	98	. . .	. . .	348	66	. . .	. . .	271
1919	. . .	594	. . .	1	. . .	14	65	50	. . .	. . .	237	46	. . .	. . .	182
1915	. . .	368	. . .	. . .	. . .	21	15	2	. . .	. . .	186	29	. . .	. . .	115

Source: Bureau of the Census, *Historical Statistics of the United States, 1789 to 1945*, 317.

TABLE 8.31   GOVERNMENT FINANCES—TREASURY EXPENDITURES

[Figures are rounded to nearest dollar and will not necessarily add to totals]

		Expenditures, Excluding Debt Retirements									
Year	Total Expenditures, Excluding Debt Retirements	War Department (including rivers and harbors, and Panama Canal)	Navy Department	Interest on Public Debt	Other Expenditures					Statutory Debt Retirements (sinking fund, etc.)
					Total	Indians	Veterans' Pensions	Postal Deficiencies	Civil and Miscellaneous	
1945	$100,404,594,686	$50,490,101,935	$30,047,152,135	$3,616,686,048	$16,250,654,567	$29,679,512	$772,190,347	$649,769	$15,448,134,939	$2,000
1944	93,743,513,214	49,438,330,158	26,537,633,877	2,608,979,806	15,158,569,373	31,266,494	494,959,142	− 28,999,995	14,603,343,742	1,650
1943	78,178,885,241	42,525,562,523	20,888,349,026	1,808,160,396	12,956,813,297	24,665,410	442,393,770	14,620,875	12,475,133,242	3,463,400
1942	32,396,585,098	14,325,508,098	8,579,588,976	1,260,085,336	8,231,402,688	31,838,510	431,294,492	18,308,869	7,749,960,817	94,722,300
1941	12,710,629,824	3,938,943,048	2,313,057,956	1,110,092,812	5,347,936,008	33,587,984	433,147,890	30,064,048	4,851,136,086	64,260,500
1940	8,998,189,706	907,160,151	891,484,523	1,040,935,697	6,158,609,335	37,821,090	429,178,230	40,870,336	5,650,739,679	129,184,100
1939	8,707,091,581	695,256,481	672,722,327	940,539,764	6,398,473,009	46,964,171	416,720,951	41,237,263	5,893,650,624	58,246,450
1938	7,238,822,158	644,263,842	596,129,739	926,280,714	5,072,147,863	33,378,889	402,779,083	44,258,861	4,591,731,530	65,464,950
1937	8,177,408,756	628,104,285	445,674,066	866,384,331	6,126,246,074	36,933,148	396,047,400	41,896,945	5,651,368,581	103,971,200
1936	8,665,645,422	618,587,184	528,882,143	749,396,802	6,768,779,293	28,875,773	399,065,694	86,038,862	5,254,798,964	403,240,150
1935	7,009,875,312	487,995,220	436,265,532	820,926,353	5,264,688,207	27,918,899	373,804,501	63,970,405	4,798,994,402	573,558,250
1934	6,011,083,254	408,586,783	296,927,490	756,617,127	4,548,951,854	23,372,905	319,322,034	52,003,296	4,154,253,619	359,864,093
1933	3,863,544,922	434,620,860	349,372,794	689,365,106	2,300,186,162	22,722,347	234,990,427	117,380,192	2,015,093,196	461,604,800
1932	4,535,147,138	476,305,311	357,517,834	599,276,631	3,102,047,362	26,125,092	232,521,292	202,876,341	2,640,524,637	412,629,750
1931	3,651,515,712	478,418,974	354,071,004	611,559,704	2,207,466,030	26,778,585	234,402,722	145,643,613	1,800,641,110	440,082,000
1930	3,440,268,884	464,853,515	374,165,639	659,347,613	1,941,902,117	32,066,628	220,608,931	91,714,451	1,597,512,107	553,883,603
1929	3,298,859,486	425,947,194	364,561,544	678,330,400	1,830,020,348	34,086,586	229,781,079	94,699,744	1,471,452,939	549,603,704
1928	3,103,264,855	400,989,683	331,335,492	731,764,476	1,639,175,204	36,990,808	229,401,462	32,080,202	1,340,702,732	540,255,020
1927	2,974,020,674	369,114,122	318,909,096	787,019,578	1,498,986,878	36,791,649	230,556,065	27,263,191	1,204,375,973	519,554,845
1926	3,097,611,823	364,089,945	312,743,410	831,937,700	1,588,840,768	48,442,120	207,189,622	39,506,490	1,293,702,536	487,376,051
1925	3,063,105,332	370,980,708	346,142,001	881,806,662	1,464,175,961	38,755,457	218,321,424	23,216,784	1,183,882,296	466,538,114
1924	3,048,677,965	357,016,878	332,249,137	940,602,913	1,418,809,037	46,754,026	228,261,555	12,638,850	1,131,154,606	457,999,750
1923	3,294,627,529	397,050,596	333,201,362	1,055,923,690	1,508,451,881	45,142,763	264,147,869	32,526,915	1,166,634,334	402,850,491
1922	3,372,607,900	457,756,139	476,775,194	991,000,759	1,447,075,808	38,500,413	252,576,848	64,346,235	1,091,652,312	422,694,600
1921	5,115,927,690	1,118,076,423	650,373,836	999,144,731	2,348,332,700	41,470,808	260,611,416	130,128,458	1,916,122,018	422,281,500
1920	6,403,343,841	1,621,953,095	786,021,456	1,020,251,622	3,025,117,668	40,516,832	213,344,204	114,854	2,771,141,778	78,746,350
1919	18,514,879,955	9,009,075,789	2,002,310,785	619,215,569	6,884,277,812	34,593,257	221,614,781	343,511	6,627,726,263	8,014,750
1918	12,696,702,471	4,869,955,286	1,278,840,487	189,743,277	6,358,163,421	30,888,400	181,137,754	2,221,095	6,143,916,172	1,134,234
1917	1,977,681,761	377,940,870	239,632,757	24,742,702	1,335,365,422	30,598,093	160,318,406	. . .	1,144,448,923	. . .
1916	734,056,202	183,176,439	153,853,567	22,900,869	374,125,327	17,570,284	159,302,351	5,500,000	191,752,692	. . .
1915	760,586,802	202,160,134	141,835,654	22,902,897	393,688,117	22,130,351	164,387,942	6,636,593	200,533,231	. . .
1914	735,081,431	208,349,746	139,682,186	22,863,957	364,185,542	20,215,076	173,440,231	. . .	170,530,235	. . .

Source: Bureau of the Census, *Historical Statistics of the United States, 1789 to 1945*, 299.

TABLE 8.32 GOVERNMENT RECEIPTS

[In thousands of dollars]

Year	Net	Total	Customs	Internal Revenue	Other Receipts Total	Sales of Public Lands
1945	44,475,304	47,750,306	354,776	43,902,002	3,493,529	184
1944	43,635,315	45,441,049	431,252	41,684,987	3,324,810	99
1943	21,986,701	23,402,322	324,291	22,143,969	934,063	129
1942	12,555,436	13,676,680	388,948	12,993,118	294,614	90
1941	7,102,931	7,995,612	391,870	7,361,675	242,067	178
1940	5,144,013	5,893,368	348,591	5,303,134	241,643	117
1939	4,996,300	5,667,824	318,837	5,161,221	187,765	248
1938	5,615,221	6,241,661	359,187	5,674,318	208,156	96
1937	4,978,601	5,293,590	486,357	4,597,140	210,094	71
1936	4,068,937	4,115,957	386,812	3,512,852	216,293	74
1935	3,729,914	3,800,467	343,353	3,277,690	179,424	87
1934	3,064,268	3,115,554	313,434	2,640,604	161,516	99
1933	2,021,213	2,079,697	250,750	1,604,424	224,523	103
1932	1,923,913	2,005,725	327,755	1,561,006	116,964	170
1931	3,115,557	3,189,639	378,354	2,429,781	381,504	230
1930	. . .	4,177,942	587,001	3,039,295	551,646	396
1929	. . .	4,033,250	602,263	2,938,019	492,968	315
1928	. . .	4,042,348	568,986	2,794,971	678,391	385
1927	. . .	4,129,394	605,500	2,869,414	654,480	621
1926	. . .	3,962,756	579,430	2,337,639	545,686	754
1925	. . .	3,780,149	547,561	2,589,176	643,412	624
1924	. . .	4,012,045	545,638	2,795,157	671,250	522
1923	. . .	4,007,135	561,929	2,624,473	820,734	657
1922	. . .	4,109,104	356,443	3,213,253	539,408	895
1921	. . .	5,624,933	308,564	4,596,426	719,943	1,530
1920	. . .	6,694,565	322,903	5,405,032	966,631	1,910
1919	. . .	5,152,257	184,458	4,315,285	652,514	1,405
1918	. . .	3,664,583	179,998	3,186,034	298,550	1,969
1917	. . .	1,124,325	225,962	809,366	88,996	1,893
1916	. . .	782,535	213,186	512,702	56,647	1,888
1915	. . .	697,911	209,787	415,670	72,455	2,167
1914	. . .	734,673	292,320	380,041	62,312	2,572

Source: Bureau of the Census, Historical Statistics of the United States, Colonial Times to 1957, 712.

CHAPTER 9 Military Forces and World Wars

It is possible to detect broad outlines of the history of the United States by tracing the status of its military forces. The arrival of the United States as a world power was observable less in raw numbers at the start of this period—what with an army in 1914 of fewer than 100,000—than in ship construction, especially battleships, which was the clearest mark of power, or pretensions of power, in that age. Entry into the First World War in 1917 produced a major change in the military forces, suggesting perhaps that the United States had decided to enter into competition with the giants of world affairs on their terms. Large as they were, the military statistics of the First World War failed to give a full picture of how much the relative power of the United States had advanced in a short time. The nation's armed forces—substantially enlarged by 1918—could have been made even larger, if need be, and behind these forces stood a financial and industrial base of uncomparable proportion. If one factors in the extent to which the war had weakened America's competitors, it developed that military domination by the United States was only a matter of will.

The reluctance of the nation to accept that status was reflected in the speed with which the armed forces shrank after 1918–19. The army dropped to fewer than 150,000 by 1922, and the navy had to accept the enormous reductions mandated in the Washington Naval Conference. The size of the military forces suggested that in the 1920s the Americans wished to avoid paying large taxes, go about their business, stay out of other people's troubles—all this while maintaining a force adequate to national security. Protection in the 1920s still emphasized the navy, still the battleships, and even with the reductions accepted in the treaty of 1922 the battleship fleet remained one of the two largest in the world and thus anything but insignificant.

The coming of the Second World War produced another swing in the pendulum of American history and in the size and character of military forces. Military statistics revealed that, as in the case of the First World War, the United States entered the war later than other major participants, but otherwise the comparison faded. The United States constructed a military force during the years 1941–45

TABLE 9.1 MILITARY PERSONNEL ON ACTIVE DUTY

Year	Grand Total	Army			Navy			Marines		
		Total	Officers	Enlisted	Total	Officers	Enlisted	Total	Officers	Enlisted
1914	165,919	98,544	5,033	93,511	56,989	3,406	53,583	10,386	336	10,050
1915	174,112	106,754	4,948	101,806	57,072	3,593	53,479	10,286	338	9,948
1916	179,376	108,399	5,175	103,224	60,376	4,022	56,354	10,601	348	10,253
1917	643,833	421,467	34,224	387,243	194,617	8,383	186,234	27,749	776	26,973
1918	2,897,167	2,395,742	130,485	2,265,257	448,606	23,631	424,975	52,918	1,503	51,316
1919	1,172,602	851,624	91,975	759,649	272,144	19,357	252,787	48,834	2,270	46,564
1920	343,302	204,292	18,999	185,293	121,845	10,642	111,203	17,165	1,104	16,061
1921	386,542	230,725	16,501	214,224	132,837	9,979	122,848	22,990	1,087	21,903
1922	270,207	148,763	15,667	133,096	100,211	8,334	91,877	21,233	1,135	20,098
1923	247,011	133,243	14,021	119,222	94,094	8,410	85,684	19,674	1,141	18,533
1924	261,189	142,673	13,784	128,889	98,184	8,651	89,533	20,332	1,157	19,175
1925	251,756	137,048	14,594	122,454	95,230	8,918	86,312	19,478	1,168	18,310
1926	247,396	134,938	14,143	120,795	93,304	9,091	84,213	19,154	1,178	17,976
1927	248,943	134,829	14,020	120,809	94,916	9,440	85,476	19,198	1,198	18,000
1928	250,907	136,084	14,019	122,065	95,803	9,401	86,402	19,020	1,198	17,822
1929	255,031	139,118	14,047	125,071	97,117	9,434	87,683	19,380	1,181	17,615
1930	255,648	139,378	14,151	125,227	96,890	9,540	87,350	19,380	1,208	18,172
1931	252,605	140,516	14,159	126,357	93,307	9,849	83,458	18,782	1,196	17,586
1932	244,902	134,957	14,111	120,846	93,384	9,967	83,417	16,561	1,196	15,365
1933	243,845	136,547	13,896	122,651	91,230	9,947	81,283	16,068	1,192	14,876
1934	247,137	138,464	13,761	124,703	92,312	9,972	82,340	16,361	1,187	15,174
1935	251,799	139,486	13,471	126,015	95,053	10,115	84,938	17,260	1,163	16,097
1936	291,356	167,816	13,512	154,304	106,292	10,247	96,045	17,248	1,208	16,040
1937	311,808	179,968	13,740	166,228	113,617	10,367	103,250	18,223	1,312	16,911
1938	322,932	185,488	13,975	171,513	119,088	10,739	108,349	18,356	1,359	16,997
1939	334,473	189,839	14,486	175,353	125,202	12,023	113,179	19,432	1,380	18,052
1940	458,365	269,023	18,326	250,697	160,997	13,604	147,393	28,345	1,800	25,545
1941	1,801,101	1,462,315	99,536	1,362,779	284,427	29,092	255,335	54,359	3,339	51,020
1942	3,858,791	3,075,608	206,422	2,869,186	640,570	69,564	571,006	142,613	7,138	135,475
1943	9,044,745	6,994,472	579,576	6,414,896	1,741,750	179,676	1,562,174	308,523	21,384	187,139
1944	11,541,719	7,994,750	776,980	7,217,770	2,981,365	276,153	2,705,212	475,604	32,788	442,816
1945	12,123,455	8,267,958	891,663	7,376,295	3,380,817	331,379	3,049,438	474,680	37,067	437,613

Source: Bureau of the Census, *Historical Statistics of the United States, Colonial Times to 1957* (Washington, D.C., 1960), 736.

TABLE 9.2 SELECTED CHARACTERISTICS OF THE ARMED FORCES, BY WAR

Characteristic		World War I	World War II
Military personnel	1,000	4,744	16,354
Army	1,000	4,057	11,260
Air Force	1,000	. . .	. . .
Navy	1,000	599	4,183
Marines	1,000	79	669
Coast Guard	1,000	9	241
Draftees:			
Classified	1,000	24,234	36,677
Examined	1,000	3,764	17,955
Rejected	1,000	803	6,420
Inducted	1,000	2,820	10,022
Average duration of service	months	12	33
Officers	months	14	39
Enlisted	months	12	33
Overseas service:			
Percent of total who served overseas		53	73
Average months served overseas[a]		5.5	16.2
Occupation of enlisted personnel	percent	100.0[b]	100.0
Technical and scientific	percent	3.7	10.4
Administrative and clerical	percent	8.0	12.6
Mechanics and repairment	percent	8.5	16.6
Craftsmen	percent	13.0	5.9
Service workers	percent	12.5	9.6
Operators and laborers	percent	20.2	6.1
Military-type occupations, not elsewhere classified	percent	34.1	38.8
Casualties, number:			
Total deaths		116,516	405,399
Battle deaths		53,402	291,557
Other deaths		63,114	113,842
Wounds not mortal		204,002	670,846
Annual rate per 1,000 average strength:			
Total deaths		35.5	11.6
Battle deaths		17.1	8.6
Other deaths		18.4	3.0
Medical care:			
Army:			
Admissions for care, all causes:			
Number	1,000	4,039	17,919
Annual rate per 1,000 average strength		978	704
Noneffectiveness, total:			
Man-days lost	1,000	86,947	413,393
Daily rate per 1,000 average strength		57.7	44.5
Wounded who died subsequently	percent	8.1	4.5
Annual nonbattle death rate per 1,000 average strength		15.4	3.0
Navy and Marine Corps:			
Admissions for care, all causes:			
Number	1,000	1,073	5,514
Annual rate per 1,000 average strength		1,024	553
Noneffectiveness, total:			
Man-days lost	1,000	12,705	115,700
Daily rate per 1,000 average strength		33.2	31.8
Wounded who died subsequently	percent	9.0	3.2
Annual nonbattle death rate per 1,000 average strength		11.6	2.8

Characteristic		World War I	World War II
Military pay (current dol.):			
Basic pay (annual rate):			
All personnel	dollars	510	1,017
Officers	dollars	2,141	2,442
Enlisted	dollars	417	856
Pay and allowances (annual rate):			
All personnel	dollars	968	1,811
Officers	dollars	2,698	3,777
Enlisted	dollars	870	1,587

[a] During hostilities only.
[b] Army personnel only.
Source: Bureau of the Census, *Historical Statistics of the United States, Colonial Times to 1970* (Washington, D.C., 1976), 2:1140.

that was massive in both absolute and relative terms, larger than any nation save the Soviet Union and the best equipped in the world. American casualties, though much smaller than those of most other major belligerents, were much larger than in the war of 1917–18.

The two world wars were large wars and national wars, affecting nearly the entire population. Virtually anyone who was old enough and physically able had something to do in both wars. The males who were the most fit with respect to age and health probably went into the military service. Since not enough young men volunteered for these wars of great magnitude, the government in both cases began to force men into service through conscription, and in both cases, as the war progressed, the draft reached deeper into the reservoir of able men. It involved people of all ethnic backgrounds and races. Women contributed to both wars in various ways, ranging from doing factory work in large numbers to small numbers being permitted to enter special military forces. Military necessity had social effects, very few of which were planned. Changes produced by special circumstances did not quickly vanish once the circumstances had passed. Bringing women and minority groups into the wartime military and economic mainstream, for example, established a foundation—and incentive—for more lasting changes in years to come.

The world wars were conventional wars in the sense that both involved large armies meeting in the field. As technology changed in this conventional setting, the combatants were able to remain farther apart and rely on larger and more devastating weapons, such as artillery, machine guns, poison gas, bombs, and tanks. As a consequence more people could be killed in a shorter period of time.

Although the admirals throughout this period remained enthralled with large ships with big guns and thick armor, technological change gradually moved these forces into obsolescence. The First World War produced few battles between the British and German fleets and none for the Americans. A more effective naval weapon was the submarine. Submarines vastly increased in importance to the navies of all major belligerents in the Second World War, with the exception of the Soviet Union. The most striking change of the Second World War came in the emergence of airpower as a weapon for all seasons and all fronts. The war started with an air attack at Pearl Harbor and ended with air attacks on Hiroshima and Nagasaki, and in between came the naval battles of the Pacific, the saturation bombing of German and Japanese cities, and numerous other expressions of warfare from the air. If the atomic bomb represented technological change of the first order, truly a new departure in warfare, its use also stands as America's last air strike in the war.

TABLE 9.3   ESTIMATES OF TOTAL COST OF U.S. WARS

[In millions of dollars, except percent]

War	Estimated Total War Costs	Original War Costs	Veteran's Benefits			Estimated Interest Payments on War Loans	
			Total Costs under Present Laws[a]	Percent of Original War Costs	Total Costs to 1970	Total	Percent of Original War Costs
World War II	664,000	288,000	290,000	100	87,445	86,000	30
World War I	112,000	26,000	75,000	290	45,585	11,000	42

[a]Estimates are based on those of the 1956 report of the President's Commission on Veterans' Pensions plus 25 percent—the increase in the average value of benefits (up to 1970) since the commission made its report.
Source: Bureau of the Census, *Historical Statistics of the United States, Colonial Times to 1970*, 1140.

TABLE 9.4   COSTS OF THE ARMY

Fiscal Year	Expenditures
1914	115,566,000
1915	115,410,000
1916	122,392,000
1917	401,418,000
1918	5,632,731,000
1919	8,915,974,000
1920	1,008,300,000
1921	462,866,000
1922	322,682,000
1923	277,060,000
1924	246,092,000
1925	251,870,000
1926	267,260,000
1927	265,595,000
1928	292,699,000
1929	315,374,000
1930	328,739,000
1931	345,274,000
1932	344,611,000
1933	298,417,000
1934	269,170,000
1935	365,861,000
1936	340,804,000
1937	381,456,000
1938	432,499,000
1939	496,075,000
1940	668,586,000
1941	3,775,896,589
1942	14,805,138,600
1943	42,573,034,116
1944	49,288,936,346
1945	49,749,550,599

Source: Gordon R. Young, ed., *The Army Almanac* (Harrisburg, Pa., 1959), 419.

TABLE 9.5   COSTS OF THE NAVY

Fiscal Year	Amount Expended
1915	144,956,199
1916	147,598,136
1917	231,671,137
1918	1,169,447,554
1919	1,721,098,608
1920	838,485,576
1921	963,449,978
1922	485,583,028
1923	308,943,019
1924	316,716,719
1925	323,940,534
1926	317,495,316
1927	320,553,753
1928	336,441,214
1929	366,443,933
1930	375,291,828
1931	357,806,219
1932	353,628,362
1933	342,176,417
1934	303,639,404
1935	440,604,669
1936	518,625,222
1937	539,030,790
1938	587,945,491
1939	660,206,184
1940	885,769,793
1941	2,257,597,451
1942	8,163,157,579
1943	19,356,047,886
1944	25,872,717,527
1945	29,380,421,832

Source: *The World Almanac and Book of Facts for 1947* (New York, 1947), 812.

Commanding Officers of the Military Services

Leonard Wood was the first commanding general of the army to have the title chief of staff. The navy had no senior commander until 1915. George Dewey was senior by virtue of a special rank created for him. The air force during this period was not a separate service but a part of the army.

TABLE 9.6 CHIEF OFFICERS OF THE MILITARY SERVICES

Army		
Leonard Wood	(chief of staff)	Apr. 1910–Apr. 1914
William W. Wotherspoon		Apr. 1914–Nov. 1914
Hugh L. Scott		Nov. 1914–Sep. 1917
Tasker H. Bliss		Sep. 1917–May 1918
Peyton C. March		May 1918–Jun. 1921
John J. Pershing		Jul. 1921–Sep. 1924
John L. Hines		Sep. 1924–Nov. 1926
Charles P. Summerall		Nov. 1926–Nov. 1930
Douglas MacArthur		Nov. 1930–Oct. 1935
Malin Craig		Oct. 1935–Aug. 1939
George C. Marshall		Sep. 1939–Nov. 1945
Dwight D. Eisenhower		Nov. 1945–Feb. 1948

Navy		
George Dewey	(admiral of the navy)	Mar. 1899–Jan. 1917
William S. Benson	(chief of naval operations)	May 1915–Sep. 1919
Robert E. Coontz		Oct. 1919–Jul. 1923
Edward W. Eberle		Jul. 1923–Nov. 1927
Charles F. Hughes		Nov. 1927–Sep. 1930
William V. Pratt		Sep. 1930–Jul. 1933
William H. Standley		Jul. 1933–Jan. 1937
William D. Leahy		Jan. 1937–July 1939
Harold R. Stark		Aug. 1939–Mar. 1942
Ernest J. King		Mar. 1942–Dec. 1945
Chester W. Nimitz		Dec. 1945–Dec. 1947

Air Force		
George P. Scriven	(chief signal officer; Aviation Section, Signal Corps, created Jul. 18, 1914)	Feb. 1913–Feb. 1917
George O. Squier	(chief signal officer)	Feb. 1917–May 1918
William L. Kenly	(director of Bureau of Military Aeronautics, created May 20, 1918; director of Air Service, comprising Bureau of Military Aeronautics and Bureau of Aircraft Production from Aug. 28, 1918)	May 1918–Dec. 1918
Charles T. Menoher	(director of Air Service; chief of reorganized Air Service, line of the army, from Jun. 4, 1920)	Jan. 1919–Oct. 1921
Mason M. Patrick	(chief of Air Service; chief of Army Air Corps from Jul. 2, 1926)	Oct. 1921–Dec. 1927
James E. Fechet	(chief, AAC)	Dec. 1927–Dec. 1931
Benjamin D. Foulois		Dec. 1931–Dec. 1935
Oscar Westover		Dec. 1935–Sep. 1938
Henry H. Arnold	(chief, AAC; chief Army Air Forces from Jul. 20, 1941; commanding general, AAF, from Mar. 9, 1942)	Sep. 1938–Mar. 1946

Marine Corps		
William P. Biddle	(commandant, U.S. Marine Corps)	Feb. 1911–Feb. 1914
George Barnett		Feb. 1914–Jun. 1920
John A. Lejeune		Jun. 1920–Mar. 1929
Wendell C. Neville		Mar. 1929–Jul. 1930
Ben H. Fuller		Jul. 1930–Mar. 1934
John H. Russell		Mar. 1934–Nov. 1936
Thomas Holcomb		Nov. 1936–Dec. 1943
Alexander A. Vandegrift		Jan. 1944–Jan. 1948

Source: G. and C. Webster Co., *Webster's American Military Biographies* (Springfield, Mass., 1978), 504, 528, 540, 542–543.

Raising the Troops: The United States and the Draft

The First World War

It quickly was determined that to raise an army of the size needed in the First World War, the United States would have to resort to conscription. The measure calling for a draft passed Congress on May 17, 1917, albeit not without opposition, and creation of the drafting mechanism soon followed. Approximately 10 million men aged twenty-one to thirty-one participated in the first registration on June 5, 1917; some 3,000 "slackers" fled to Mexico. Two additional registrations extended eligibility ages to eighteen and to thirty-five. In all, some 24 million registered; approximately 6.5 million were declared eligible after various forms of weeding out—taking into account deferment and physical deficiency—and then nearly 2.7 million young men were drafted. Another 2 million enlisted. Nearly 350,000 sought to evade the draft. Approximately 57,000 were classified as conscientious objectors. Of these, 21,000 were still drafted for noncombat duty; many others—notably Alvin York, who became one of America's most famous wartime heroes—changed their mind and agreed to enter service as a combatant. Some 4,000 who refused any kind of government activity were imprisoned or otherwise punished. The draft was a large undertaking for the United States, by far the largest since the Civil War and an unprecedented exercise in compulsory service, but the demands of the draft still stood a considerable distance from the nation's full potential for constructing a massive military force.

Sources: Young, *The Army Almanac*, 139; Randall Gray, *Chronicle of the First World War* (New York, 1991), 2:55.

TABLE 9.7 WORLD WAR I INDUCTIONS, BY STATE OR TERRITORY AND COLOR, SEP. 5, 1917–NOV. 11, 1918

State or Territory	Total	Negro	White
U.S.	2,666,867	367,710	2,299,157
Ala.	59,755	25,874	33,881
Ariz.	8,113	77	8,036
Ark.	49,312	17,544	31,768
Calif.	67,067	919	66,148
Colo.	22,858	317	22,487
Conn.	32,539	941	31,598
Del.	4,993	1,365	3,628
D.C.	9,631	4,000	5,631
Fla.	24,916	12,904	12,012
Ga.	66,841	34,303	32,538
Idaho	12,566	95	12,471
Ill.	177,483	8,754	168,729
Ind.	69,749	4,579	65,170
Iowa	66,864	929	65,935
Kans.	41,905	2,127	39,778
Ky.	58,330	11,320	47,010
La.	56,205	28,711	27,494
Maine	15,266	50	15,216
Md.	33,867	9,212	24,655
Mass.	76,567	1,200	75,367
Mich.	96,480	2,395	94,085
Minn.	73,680	511	73,169
Miss.	43,362	24,066	19,296
Mo.	92,843	9,219	83,624
Mont.	27,340	198	27,142
Nebr.	29,807	642	29,165
Nev.	3,164	26	3,138
N.H.	8,404	27	8,377
N.J.	71,390	4,863	66,527
N. Mex.	8,862	51	8,811
N.Y.	253,589	6,193	247,396
N.C.	58,441	20,082	38,359
N. Dak.	18,595	87	18,508
Ohio	138,148	7,861	130,287
Okla.	64,941	5,694	59,247
Oreg.	16,158	68	16,090
Pa.	201,211	15,392	185,819
R.I.	11,176	291	10,885
S.C.	44,059	25,798	18,261
S. Dak.	21,255	62	21,193
Tenn.	59,878	17,774	42,104
Tex.	117,395	31,506	85,889
Utah	10,788	77	10,711
Vt.	6,629	22	6,607
Va.	58,337	23,541	34,796
Wash.	28,686	173	28,513
W. Va.	45,355	5,492	39,863
Wis.	70,982	224	70,758
Wyo.	7,923	95	7,828
Alaska	1,962	5	1,957
Hawaii	5,466	. . .	5,466
P.R.	15,734	. . .	15,734

Source: Young, The Army Almanac, 140.

TABLE 9.8 WORLD WAR I CAMPS AND CANTONMENTS (ZONE OF THE INTERIOR)

Camp and Location	Capacity
National Guard Camps	
Beauregard, Alexandria, La.	29,121
Bowie, Fort Worth, Tex.	41,879
Cody, Deming, N. Mex.	44,959
Doniphan, Fort Sill, Okla.	46,183
Fremont, Palo Alto, Calif.	30,000
Greene, Charlotte, N.C.	48,305
Hancock, Augusta, Ga.	45,099
Kearney, Linda Vista, Calif.	32,066
Logan, Houston, Tex.	44,899
MacArthur, Waco, Tex.	45,074
McClellan, Anniston, Ala.	57,746
Sevier, Greenville, S.C.	41,693
Shelby, Hattiesburg, Miss.	36,010
Sheridan, Montgomery, Ala.	41,593
Wadsworth, Spartanburg, S.C.	56,249
Wheeler, Macon, Ga.	43,011
National Army Cantonments	
Custer, Battle Creek, Mich.	49,014
Devens, Ayer, Mass.	36,832
Dix, Wrightstown, N.J.	42,806
Dodge, Des Moines, Iowa	49,229
Funston, Fort Riley, Kans.	42,806
Gordon, Atlanta, Ga.	46,612
Grant, Rockford, Ill.	62,675
Jackson, Columbia, S.C.	44,009
Lee, Petersburg, Va.	60,335
Lewis, American Lake, Wash.	46,232
Meade, Admiral, Md.	52,575
Pike, Little Rock, Ark.	55,010
Sherman, Chillicothe, Ohio	49,112
Taylor, Louisville, Ky.	45,424
Travis, San Antonio, Tex.	42,809
Upton, Yaphank, N.Y.	43,567
Special Camps Built during the War	
Benning, Columbus, Ga. (Infantry School)	5,040
Bragg, Fayetteville, N.C. (Field Artillery)	11,831
Colt, Gettysburg, Pa. (Tank Corps)	4,000
Eustis, Lee Hall, Va. (Coast Artillery)	16,759
Forrest, Ft. Oglethorpe, Ga. (Engineers)	24,457
Franklin, Camp Meade, Md. (Signal Corps)	11,000
Holabird, Baltimore, Md. (Motor Transport)	7,500
Humphreys, Belvoir, Va. (Engineers)	32,434
Johnston, Jacksonville, Fla. Quartermaster)	18,265
Knox, Stithton, Ky. (Field Artillery)	27,805
Las Casas, San Juan, P.R. (Training Center)	13,265
Meigs, Washington, D.C. (Quartermaster)	3,774
Merritt, Dumont, N.J. (Embarkation)	39,079
Mills, Garden City, N.Y. (Embarkation)	25,000
Polk, Raleigh, N.C. (Tank Corps)	4,820
Raritan, Metuchen, N.J. (Ordnance)	6,250
Stuart, Newport News, Va. (Embarkation)	30,086

Source: Young, The Army Almanac, 552–553.

By the time the United States entered the war, the government could draw not only on the experience of raising troops in the First World War but also on some fifteen months in peacetime of creating a "new army." The Selective Service Act of September 16, 1940, provided for what would become a vast system of 6,442 local draft boards, staffed by 182,509 individuals, 95% of whom served without pay. The law of 1940 called for a year of military service, a term that was extended by eighteen months before the year had ended. In the original measure men aged twenty-one to thirty-six were eligible for the draft, and there were liberal terms for deferment; physical requirements were rigorous. The most familiar classifications were 1-A, ready for induction, and 4-F, physically or mentally unfit, with other classes in between. With an expected induction of no more than a million men, the government could afford to be liberal in excluding people from immediate induction. In that first year, the government learned much about which rules could be followed and which would have to be changed.

The government and the nation also learned much about a people still coming out of a depression. Of those deemed eligible for induction, more than 40% failed to pass the physical and mental requirements. If one adds to that number the large group who merited deferment—including nearly all married men—it developed that more than twelve million out of seventeen million who registered were not available for duty. The army in that period would induct 921,722 men.

The start of war produced many changes. The registration age stretched from eighteen to sixty-five, although the army was not supposed to draft men over thirty-eight and it clearly preferred much younger men, from eighteen to the mid-twenties. Physical requirements loosened somewhat, and many deferments ended—for husbands and for fathers as well. Treatment of conscientious objectors borrowed from the First World War. Men so classified—there

President Roosevelt looks on while Secretary of War Henry L. Stimson is blindfolded before selecting the first number in the draft lottery, October 29, 1940. (Franklin D. Roosevelt Library)

were 42,793—could accept noncombat military service (such as medical corpsman) or alternate nonmilitary service. Approximately 12,000 chose duty in Civilian Public Service Camps. Most conscientious objectors came from such pacifist religious denominations as Quakers, Amish, and Mennonites. Most of those men who refused any kind of government service, as well as those who failed to receive classification as COs, went to prison for sentences of four to five years. The bulk of these individuals belonged to the Jehovah's Witnesses sect and were not given classification as conscientious objectors.

The military forces did not knowingly take homosexuals, and a young man might avoid induction by convincing the examining official that he was a homosexual. Some straight men evaded the draft in this fashion, and some homosexuals got into service by lying about their sexual preferences. An uncounted number of homosexuals lived out their military careers by staying in the closet. For those who

TABLE 9.9 REGISTRANTS INDUCTED, BY STATE OR TERRITORY, AND RACE (AS OF OCT. 31, 1946)[a]

State or Territory	Total	White	Negro
U.S. and Territories	10,110,104	9,027,565	1,082,539
U.S. Continental	10,023,599	8,948,304	1,075,295
Ala.	210,599	144,193	66,406
Ariz.	39,609	37,979	1,630
Ark.	143,682	112,909	30,773
Calif.	500,920	486,313	14,607
Colo.	73,786	72,752	1,034
Conn.	139,629	135,351	4,278
Del.	22,330	18,198	4,132
D.C.	64,243	40,127	24,116
Fla.	138,619	90,568	48,051
Ga.	209,589	147,017	62,572
Idaho	39,220	39,135	85
Ill.	629,516	582,617	46,899
Ind.	261,079	249,332	11,747
Iowa	154,603	153,422	1,181
Kans.	122,470	116,688	5,782

(continued)

Soldiers on maneuvers in 1941 receive a helping hand in aiming a field piece from a citizen in a southern town. (National Archives)

TABLE 9.9 (continued)

State or Territory	Total	White	Negro
Ky.	220,619	201,574	19,045
La.	179,029	111,489	67,540
Maine	59,815	59,733	82
Md.	158,121	126,480	31,641
Mass.	292,439	288,508	3,931
Mich.	424,335	402,817	21,518
Minn.	191,238	190,584	654
Miss.	172,136	88,037	84,099
Mo.	272,180	250,407	21,773
Mont.	38,820	38,771	49
Nebr.	82,735	81,534	1,201
Nev.	10,289	10,215	74
N.H.	32,920	32,873	47
N.J.	345,236	319,058	26,178
N. Mex.	39,944	39,494	450
New York City	659,081	602,937	56,144
New York (except New York City)	449,718	437,288	12,430
N.C.	262,942	194,360	68,582
N. Dak.	39,895	39,881	14
Ohio	576,622	540,002	36,620
Okla.	151,883	138,245	13,638
Oreg.	72,800	72,511	289
Pa.	866,264	816,909	49,355
R.I.	53,602	52,579	1,023
S.C.	137,969	85,486	52,483
S. Dak.	39,707	39,684	23
Tenn.	233,993	194,275	39,718
Tex.	438,323	364,276	74,047
Utah	41,061	40,939	122
Vt.	21,456	21,434	22
Va.	216,060	159,051	57,009
Wash.	113,451	112,926	525
W. Va.	158,533	148,065	10,468
Wis.	203,235	202,111	1,124
Wyo.	17,254	17,170	84
Alaska	3,564	3,564	. . .
Hawaii	31,899	31,899	. . .
P.R.	50,235	42,991	7,244
V.I.[b]	807	807	. . .

[a] It should be remembered that these numbers represent the individuals brought in through the conscription system, not the total number that served.
[b] White and Negro combined on report.
Source: Young, The Army Almanac, 142.

TABLE 9.10   REJECTION RATES[a]

By year of birth and race, per 100 registrants examined Sep. 1942–June 1943.

Age in 1943	Local Board and Induction Station		
	Total	White	Negro
All ages	36.4	33.6	52.9
18	27.6	26.3	45.4
19	25.2	23.2	43.7
20	25.5	23.5	42.4
21	26.2	24.0	38.8
22	27.6	25.3	37.7
23	31.0	28.6	42.8
24	37.4	34.0	53.1
25	37.0	33.8	54.3
26	38.0	35.0	55.5
27	39.4	36.2	57.5
28	40.3	37.1	59.8
29	41.8	38.6	59.1
30	43.5	40.3	60.5
31	45.4	42.0	62.8
32	46.9	43.4	64.6
33	48.9	45.7	64.9
34	50.7	47.9	66.2
35	52.0	49.2	68.0
36	54.7	51.8	69.1
37	55.4	53.0	69.4
38	59.1	56.0	73.0
39	54.1	50.8	68.8
40	54.4	51.4	68.8
41	57.4	54.0	71.5
42	59.6	57.2	73.7
43	61.3	58.0	73.5
44	63.2	61.2	75.4
45	66.3	64.4	77.4
46	67.5	65.2	80.8

[a] The rates are conspicuous in that they are high for all categories. Most striking is the high rate for black men, most of whom came from the South. The rates were a consequence of diet, lack of education and health care, and a testimony on living conditions in general.
Source: The Information Please Almanac, 1947 (Garden City, N.Y., 1947), 361.

TABLE 9.11   CONVICTIONS INVOLVING PROFESSED RELIGIOUS OR CONSCIENTIOUS OBJECTION, OCT. 16, 1940, TO JUNE 30, 1945

Sect	Violation						
	Total	Failure to Register	Failure to Return Questionnaire	Failure to Report for Physical Examination	Failure to Report for Induction	Failure to Report for Work of National Importance	Refusal to Comply with Civilian Work Assignment	Counseling or Aiding Evasion
Total	5,516	266	49	70	3,331	1,539	233	28
Jehovah's Witnesses	3,992	1	1	13	2,519	1,373	83	2
Negro, "Moslems," "Hebrews," etc.	166	100	9	5	30	5	. . .	17
Large sects	462	43	10	10	264	67	68	. . .
Small sects	267	25	4	7	160	44	22	5
No sect	291	52	18	15	163	25	15	3
Rationalist	250	43	5	14	146	16	25	1
Not yet classified	88	. . .	2	6	49	9	20	. . .

Source: Director of Selective Service, Selective Service and Victory: The 4th Report of the Director of Selective Service (Washington, D.C., 1948), 186.

were found out the treatment varied. In some units they were tolerated and assigned to duty deemed appropriate to their perceived personal characteristics. Others were tried for sodomy and sent to "queer stockades." More commonly, the recognized homosexuals were branded as undesirable and discharged. The army and navy released approximately 9,000 men from service with *homosexual* placed on their military record.

All in all the Selective Service System provided the foundation for America's armed forces in the Second World War. Approximately 66% of the people in military service during the war were drafted. Many of those who enlisted or sought out commission as officers did so because of their belief that they were about to be drafted.

Sources: Young, *The Army Almanac,* 141; Normal Polmar and Thomas B. Allen, *World War II: Americans at War, 1941–1945* (New York, 1991), 393, 725–726.

Prisoners of War: Two World Wars

These numbers include enemy personnel held by the United States during each of the two world wars. The captured Americans are army and army air force personnel only. The individuals not counted include a small number of marine ground soldiers in both wars and a few marine and navy aviators and various other naval personnel.

TABLE 9.12 PRISONERS OF WAR—WORLD WAR I

United States Army Personnel Held by Germany	
Captured	4,457
Died	41
Repatriated	4,416
German Prisoners Held by the United States	
In France	49,969
In the United States	5,888 [a]
	55,857

[a]Of German prisoners in the United States, 1,346 were members of crews of German auxiliary cruisers in American ports when the war started. They were interned. The rest probably were enemy aliens in the United States who for some reason created suspicion and who were taken into custody after the United States went to war in 1917.
Source: Young, *The Army Almanac,* 382.

The army's new 28-ton tank—the M 3 medium—was too heavy for this bridge in Monroe, North Carolina. (National Archives)

TABLE 9.13   U.S. PRISONERS OF WAR—WORLD WAR II

United States Army Personnel (including army air forces) who were prisoners of war at any time during the period December 7, 1941–December 31, 1946

				Theater of Operations			
Distribution by Theaters							
	Total	Officers	Enlisted Men	European	Mediterranean	Pacific[a]	Other[b]
Captured or Interned	124,079	21,593	102,486	73,759	20,182	27,465	2,673
Died	12,653	1,726	10,927	950	171	11,107	425
Returned	111,426	19,867	91,559	72,809	20,011	16,358	2,248

	Total	Air Corps (incl. flight Officers)	Infantry	Field Artillery	Corps of Engineers	All Others[c]
Distribution by Branches						
Captured or Interned	124,079	41,057	56,212	5,966	3,518	17,326
Died	12,653	2,763	3,913	835	639	4,503
Returned	111,426	38,294	52,299	5,131	2,879	12,823

[a]Excludes Alaskan Department, U.S. Army Strategic Air Forces, and China-Burma-India theater.
[b]Includes unreported theaters (theater unknown), and en route personnel not chargeable to any command.
[c]Includes general officers, warrant officers, and female personnel.
Source: Young, *The Army Almanac,* 382.

TABLE 9.14   ENEMY PRISONERS OF WAR—WORLD WAR II

Enemy army personnel who were at any time prisoners of war of the United States

European Theater:	About 2,000,000 were held in Europe by the United States at the end of the war.[a]
Mediterranean Theater:	In May 1943, with the surrender of the remaining German and Italian forces in Tunisia, 252,415 prisoners were captured. In September 1943, approximately 82,000 Italian POWs were held in North Africa and Sicily.
Pacific Theater	
20,000	Maximum number held (on Aug. 20, 1945) in southwest Pacific area. These were held in the Philippines. Prior to the capture of the Philippines, enemy were evacuated to Australia for interment by that country.
1,000	Italian POWs were sent to Hawaii in Jun. 1944 as a labor force.
1,073	Koreans
17	Japanese } Number of Pacific area prisoners interned in Hawaii, Apr. 1945
15	Civilian internees from Japanese possessions
1,200	Japanese POWs interned on Saipan and Guam at end of war (Sep. 2, 1945).
23,305	Maximum number of prisoners held by the United States in the Pacific theater by the end of World War II. In addition, many other prisoners were received as a result of the unconditional surrender. This amounted to an influx of over 260,000 in the Philippines alone.
CBI Theater:[b]	About 100 enemy prisoners were captured and were turned over to the British for internment.

[a]It must be remembered that German forces were subject to a general unconditional surrender, thus the estimate of 2,000,000 prisoners in American hands. Technically, all German forces were prisoner at the end, as were all Japanese. Many enemy prisoners were brought to the United States, partly to facilitate guarding and provisioning them, partly to make use of their labor. At its peak in May 1945 the number reached 425,871, of which there were 371,683 Germans, 50,273 Italians, and 3,915 Japanese. All prisoners had been repatriated by Jun. 30, 1946, except 162 who were serving prison sentences and those who had died during their period of incarceration.
[b]Pertains to China-India-Burma theater of war, where only a small number of Americans were engaged.
Source: Young, *The Army Almanac,* 383.

Army Slang

Men in the army did indeed use the terms as publicized by *The Army Almanac,* but it is only fair to add that these were the words considered suitable to print. Soldiers, and in fact members of all the military services, also had another vocabulary made up of coarser and more vulgar words and terms that hardly ever made it to the printed page.

World War I Slang

The following slang terms were in general use in the army, or at least in the AEF (American Expeditionary Forces in Europe), in World War I.

Airnat   a member or flyer of the American Air Service.

Archie   an antiaircraft gun; a term borrowed from the British.

Basket case   a soldier who has lost both arms and both legs.

Beaucoup   the French word for "much" or "many," adopted by the American soldier. (Also used in World War II.)

Big Bertha   a famous German long-range railroad artillery piece; later, any large gun. (Supposedly named after Bertha Krupp, of the well-known family of German steel and munition makers.)

Blimp   see "sausage."

Boche   a German or German soldier; originally French army slang.

Cootie   the ordinary body louse of man, which was a constant irritation to soldiers living in the trenches.

Corn willie   corned beef, issued as a standard ration.

Devil dogs   the United States Marines; said to have been originated by a German soldier who had encountered them in action and called them "Teufel Hunde."

Didonk   a French soldier; from the common French exclamation, "Dis donc!"

Dog robber   a soldier who takes care of an officer's personal equipment; also called a "striker."

Doughboy   an American soldier; especially, an infantry soldier.

Go west   to die; especially, to die in action or from wounds.

Goldfish   canned salmon, issued as a standard ration. (The American soldier placed it on the "hated" list, along with "corn willie.")

Hun   a German or German soldier.

IC   initial form of the words "inspected and condemned," the stamp put on Government equipment that has been worn out and is to be destroyed.

Liberty cabbage   the patriotic name of sauerkraut.

Limey   a British sailor; later broadened to include the British soldier. (Also used in World War II.)

Monkey meat   canned beef of the French ration, shipped in from Madagascar. Its peculiar flavor caused it to be disliked.

Sausage   an observation balloon, used in rear of the front line to see into enemy territory; also called "blimp."

Slum   meat stew. (This term is still in use in a variety of forms, such as "slum burner" for an army cook. Better rations are now causing the word to fade from use.)

Striker   see "dog robber."

Yank   the American soldier; a term used by the British, but generally disliked by our men.

Source: Young, *The Army Almanac,* 399.

Slang of World War II

AWOL   absent without leave.

Blitz   to shine shoes, or brass, or equipment, so that they have a high polish.

Bolo   to fail to qualify, especially in weapons firing.

Brass or Brass hat   the commander or staff of a higher echelon.

Break   (1) to cease work for a short period of time; (2) to reduce a soldier in grade or position.

Buck   (1) to work hard to achieve a personal goal; (2) to work against.

Chicken   (1) to be afraid; (2) to adhere strictly to regulations.

Clue (him)   to inform another person about some situation.

Chow   food, a meal; used also as an adjective, as in "chow time." "chow wagon."

Crash (project)   a project of extreme urgency and immediacy, usually generated by pressure from above.

Dog-face   an infantry soldier.

Dog it   to lack effort in doing a job.

Dog tag   the identification tag worn about the neck of a soldier.

Dough-foot   an infantry soldier.

Flap   a situation requiring very rapid action to arrive at a solution to a problem.

Fruit salad   the ribbons, representing awards and decorations, worn on the uniform coat or shirt.

GI   (1) "Government issue" equipment; (2) to scrub equipment clean; (3) to conduct oneself strictly according to regulations; (4) an intestinal upset; (5) an American soldier, especially a private.

Goof off   to avoid an assigned duty.

Highball   to render the military hand salute.

G2 ("to G2 something")   to evaluate a situation: to predict results; from the term "A. C. of S. G2," meaning the assistant chief of staff of a command who collects information and disseminates military intelligence.

Jeep   a small passenger-carrying military vehicle.

KP   kitchen police, i.e., some task, other than cooking, connected with preparing or cleaning up after meals.

NCO   a noncommissioned officer.

No sweat   ability to get results without great effort.

Old man   the commanding officer.

Over the hill (go over the hill)   to desert.

Panic button   feverish activity to find a solution to a problem ("push the panic button").

Police   to tidy or to put in correct order.

Poop   information obtained from an authoritative source.

Pot   the steel helmet worn by a soldier for protection.

PX   post exchange, a store on an army post for the use of soldiers.

Sack   sleeping bag or bed; also used in combination with other words, such as "sack time" to denote time for sleep.

"See the chaplain"   a phrase used to tell a complainant that his problem is of no concern to anyone except the spiritual adviser of his unit.

Shavetail   a second lieutenant.

Ship out   to leave one's place of duty as the result of formal orders.

Short-stop   to stop an action prior to its completion.

Six-by   an army truck, usually of 2½-ton capacity, having six wheels all geared to the power train.

Sky pilot   an army chaplain.

Stay loose   to remain flexible in action; to be ready for an unexpected turn of events.

Straight leg   term used by airborne troops to describe nonparachutists.

Trooper   (1) an airborne soldier; (2) a horse cavalry soldier; (3) any soldier of the combat arms; (4) sometimes a general term for a soldier whose name is not known.

Twenty-per-cent man   a soldier who loans other soldiers money at usurious rates.

White side-walls   a haircut extremely short on the sides, making a light skin contrast with the lower sunburned portion of the face.

Source: Young, *The Army Almanac,* 398–399.

The Age of the Battleship

The arrival of the battleship corresponded with the emergence of the United States as a world power. It was the age of sea power when the dreadnoughts, as the British called them, served as the agent of military might as well as the symbol of national strength and greatness. To have one, one had to have the other. Theodore Roosevelt belonged to that era—he helped make it—and it was no accident that the Roosevelt era corresponded with a period of American battleship construction. Another wave of battleship building during the period of the First World War (one also might regard it as an extension of the first movement) ended in the war's aftermath when the major nations found themselves agreeing in the Washington treaties of 1921–22 to slow down this dangerous business. Proponents of naval disarmament doubtless felt no satisfaction in noting that an absence for nearly twenty years of battleship construction failed to produce an absence of international tension or even of war. As the Second World War approached, the United States reentered the business in a large way. The war inspired the construction of several new dreadnoughts; more and larger vessels were on the way when two forces intervened. First, the war abruptly came to an end. Second, the war had produced a remarkable message: Airplanes and aircraft carriers had made the battlewagon obsolete; at least its much-reduced function did not warrant the great cost of construction and operation. The continued interest of the United States in military power after 1945 did not include any new battleships.

In the end the battleships compiled a record that was skimpy and sketchy, as compared with their glamour and expectation, not to

TABLE 9.15   COMPLETE LIST OF AMERICAN BATTLESHIPS

Hull No.	Name	Length	Design Displacement	Launched	Commissioned	Main Armament
[a]	Maine	319'	6,682	10-17-88	9-17-95	4 × 10"
[a]	Texas	308'10"	6,315	6-1-89	8-15-95	2 × 12"
BB-1	Indiana	350'11"	10,288	5-17-91	11-20-95	4 × 13"
BB-2	Massachusetts	350'11"	10,288	6-25-91	6-10-96	4 × 13"
BB-3	Oregon	351'	10,288	11-19-91	7-15-96	4 × 13"
BB-4	Iowa	362'5"	11,410	8-5-93	6-16-97	4 × 12"
BB-5	Kearsarge	375'4"	11,540	6-30-96	2-20-00	4 × 13"
BB-6	Kentucky	375'4"	11,540	6-30-96	5-15-00	4 × 13"
BB-7	Illinois	375'4"	11,565	2-10-97	9-16-01	4 × 13"
BB-8	Alabama	374'	11,565	12-2-96	10-16-00	4 × 13"
BB-9	Wisconsin	373'10"	11,653	2-9-97	2-4-01	4 × 13"
BB-10	Maine [b]	393'11"	12,846	2-15-99	12-29-02	4 × 12"
BB-11	Missouri [b]	393'11"	12,362	2-7-00	12-1-03	4 × 12"
BB-12	Ohio	393'10"	12,723	4-22-99	10-4-04	4 × 12"
BB-13	Virginia [b]	441'3"	14,948	5-21-02	5-7-06	4 × 12"
BB-14	Nebraska [b]	441'3"	14,948	7-4-02	7-1-07	4 × 12"
BB-15	Georgia [b]	441'3"	14,948	8-31-01	9-24-06	4 × 12"
BB-16	New Jersey [b]	441'3"	14,948	4-2-02	5-12-06	4 × 12"
BB-17	Rhode Island [b]	441'3"	16,000	5-1-02	2-19-06	4 × 12"
BB-18	Connecticut [b]	456'4"	16,000	3-10-03	9-29-06	4 × 12"
BB-19	Louisiana [b]	456'4"	16,000	2-7-03	6-2-06	4 × 12"
BB-20	Vermont [b]	456'4"	16,000	5-21-04	3-4-07	4 × 12"
BB-21	Kansas [b]	456'4"	16,000	2-10-04	4-18-07	4 × 12"
BB-22	Minnesota [b]	456'4"	16,000	10-27-03	3-9-07	4 × 12"
BB-23	Mississippi [b]	382'	13,000	5-12-04	2-1-08	4 × 12"
BB-24	Idaho	382'	13,000	5-12-04	4-1-08	4 × 12"
BB-25	New Hampshire [b]	456'4"	16,000	6-1-05	3-19-08	4 × 12"
BB-26	South Carolina [b]	452'9"	16,000	12-18-06	3-1-10	8 × 12"
BB-27	Michigan [b]	452'9"	16,000	12-17-06	1-4-10	8 × 12"
BB-28	Delaware [b]	518'9"	20,380	11-11-07	4-4-10	10 × 12"
BB-29	North Dakota [b]	518'9"	20,000	12-16-07	4-11-10	10 × 12"
BB-30	Florida	521'6"	21,825	3-9-09	9-15-11	10 × 12"
BB-31	Utah [c]	521'6"	21,825	3-15-09	8-31-11	10 × 12"
BB-32	Wyoming	562'	26,000	2-9-10	9-25-12	12 × 12"
BB-33	Arkansas	562'	26,000	1-25-10	9-17-12	12 × 12"

Hull No.	Name	Length	Design Displacement	Launched	Commissioned	Main Armament
BB-34	*New York*	573'	27,000	9-11-11	4-15-14	10 × 14"
BB-35	*Texas*	573'	27,000	4-17-11	3-12-14	10 × 14"
BB-36	*Nevada*[c]	583'	27,500	11-4-12	3-11-16	10 × 14"
BB-37	*Oklahoma*[c]	583'	27,500	10-26-12	5-2-16	10 × 14"
BB-38	*Pennsylvania*[c]	608'	31,400	10-27-13	6-12-16	12 × 14"
BB-39	*Arizona*[c]	608'	31,400	3-16-14	10-17-16	12 × 14"
BB-40	*New Mexico*	624'	32,000	10-14-15	5-20-18	12 × 14"
BB-41	*Mississippi*	624'	32,000	4-5-15	12-18-17	12 × 14"
BB-42	*Idaho*	624'	32,000	1-20-15	3-24-19	12 × 14"
BB-43	*Tennessee*[c]	624'6"	32,300	5-14-17	6-3-20	12 × 14"
BB-44	*California*[c]	624'6"	32,300	10-25-16	8-10-21	12 × 14"
BB-45	*Colorado*	624'6"	32,600	5-29-19	8-30-23	8 × 16"
BB-46	*Maryland*[c]	624'6"	32,600	4-24-17	7-21-21	8 × 16"
BB-47	*Washington*[b]	624'	32,600	6-30-19	(canceled 2-8-22)	
BB-48	*West Virginia*[c]	624'	32,600	4-12-20	12-1-23	8x16"
BB-49	*South Dakota*[b]	624'	32,600	3-15-20	(canceled 2-8-22)	
BB-50	*Indiana*[b]	624'	32,600	11-1-20	(canceled 2-8-22)	
BB-51	*Montana*[b]	624'	32,600	9-1-20	(canceled 2-8-22)	
BB-52	*North Carolina*[b]	624'	32,600	1-12-20	(canceled 2-8-22)	
BB-53	*Iowa*[b]	624'	32,600	5-17-20	(canceled 2-8-22)	
BB-54	*Massachusetts*[b]	624'	32,600	4-4-21	(canceled 2-8-22)	
BB-55	North Carolina	728'9"	35,000	10-27-37	4-9-41	9 × 16"
BB-56	Washington	729'	35,000	6-14-38	5-15-41	9 × 16"
BB-57	South Dakota	680'	35,000	7-5-39	3-20-42	9 × 16"
BB-58	Indiana	680'	35,000	11-20-39	4-30-42	9 × 16"
BB-59	Massachusetts	680'10"	35,000	7-20-39	5-12-42	9 × 16"
BB-60	Alabama	680'	35,000	2-1-40	8-16-42	9 × 16"
BB-61	Iowa	887'3"	45,000	6-27-40	2-22-43	9 × 16"
BB-62	New Jersey	887'7"	45,000	9-16-40	5-23-43	9 × 16"
BB-63	Missouri	887'3"	45,000	1-6-41	6-11-44	9 × 16"
BB-64	Wisconsin	887'3"	45,000	1-25-41	4-16-44	9 × 16"
BB-65	Illinois	887'3"	45,000	1-15-41	(canceled 8-12-45)	
BB-66	Kentucky	887'3"	45,000	12-6-44	(never completed, stricken 6-9-58)	
BB-67	Montana	925'	60,500		(ord. 7-19-40 canc. 7-21-43)	
BB-68	Ohio	925'	60,500		(ord. 7-19-40 canc. 7-21-43)	
BB-69	Maine	925'	60,500		(ord. 7-19-40 canc. 7-21-43)	
BB-70	New Hampshire	925'	60,500		(ord. 7-19-40 canc. 7-21-43)	
BB-71	Louisiana	925'	60,500		(ord. 7-19-40 canc. 7-21-43)	

[a] Because the *Maine* and the *Texas* were not first-class battleships, they were not given a hull number.

[b] Ships destroyed (dismantled or construction abandoned on) as a result of agreement at the Washington Naval Conference in 1922. In addition to these twenty-four vessels, the United States also stopped construction on six battle cruisers. Thus in one sweep, the United States eliminated thirty capital ships. The British destroyed twenty-two vessels and the Japanese fifteen.

[c] Battleships sunk or damaged in the Japanese attack on Pearl Harbor on December 7, 1941. In fact, all battleships based at Pearl were sunk or damaged. Because the aged *Utah*, used as a target ship, no longer was classified as a battleship, the official number involved was eight.

Sources: Norman Friedman, *U.S. Battleships: An Illustrated Design History* (Annapolis, 1984), various pages, especially 419–450; Department of State, *Papers Relating to the Foreign Relations of the United States, 1922, Vol. I* (Washington, D.C., 1938), 253–254, 259; Michael Slackman, *Target: Pearl Harbor* (Honolulu, 1990), 263–271.

mention the cost. The big ships had virtually nothing to do in the First World War, although some were sent to European waters. Their function in the Second World War was—with a few notable exceptions—peripheral to the main course of action. Airplanes (and their carriers) and submarines were far more important. Battleships of course provided the primary attraction in the Japanese attack on Pearl Harbor, and while that event continues to be labeled a disaster, the consequences for battleships—as for U.S. forces in general—

were not nearly as damaging as they might have been. Five battleships were classified as sunk, but the water of the harbor was so shallow that none was fully submerged. Three could be raised and repaired. Three other battleships were so lightly damaged that they could be ready for action within two weeks. Only two vessels—the *Oklahoma*, which capsized, and the *Arizona*, which blew up—were put permanently out of service.

Seven battleships are visible under attack by the Japanese. The *Arizona* is on the inside of the second row from the left; the *Oklahoma* is on the outside of the second row from the right, not counting the *California*, parked in the inlet on the extreme right. (National Archives)

In the full sweep of battleship history the United States lost but two to hostile action, both at Pearl Harbor, unless one chooses to count the destruction of the *Maine* in Cuba in February 1898. In their half century of life American dreadnoughts participated in the destruction of four enemy (all Japanese) battleships, although other types of forces assisted in the same action. Of course, one should not discount the impact that the mere possession of capital ships had on the position of the United States in world affairs. American battleships would sail the seas for a few years after the Second World War, but their standing as the pride and strength of national military power—indeed, the age of the battleship—had ended by 1945.

Naming of Vessels

Naming of Vessels. The following system has been adopted for naming naval vessels—

Battleships   States of the Union.
Cruisers, heavy and light   cities of the United States.
Cruisers, large   territories or insular possessions of the United States.
Aircraft carriers   names of famous ships formerly on the Navy list, or of important battles.
Aircraft carriers, escort   islands, bays or sounds of the United States, or important battles.
Destroyers   deceased persons who were (1) distinguised Navy, Marine, or Coast Guard officers; or (2) Secretaries or Assistant Secretaries of the Navy; or (3) Members of Congress closely identified with naval affairs; or (4) inventors.
Destroyer escort vessels   personnel of the Navy, Marine Corps, or Coast Guard killed in action in World War II.
Landing ships   places of historic interest.
Submarines   names of fish or other sea animals.

Similar rules apply to the naming of other types of vessels.

Source: Young, *The Army Almanac,* 425.

Women in War

Inasmuch as the wars of the first half of the twentieth century were national wars that in some fashion involved the entire national population, it was inevitable that demands would be made on, and opportunities opened for, America's women, who made up nearly half the population. Changing notions about women's capabilities, not to mention their rights, contributed to the process. The First World War established a foundation. As gaps in the work force opened up, some 2,250,000 women answered the call. Many of them held such traditional female jobs as clerks and secretaries, but others joined the dirtier and more dangerous process of producing arms and munitions. Approximately 13,000 women served in the U.S. Navy and the Marine Corps. These "yeomanettes" mostly held clerical jobs. Another 1,000 women went abroad as civilian contract workers, serving as translators and as telephone and telegraph operators for the American Expeditionary Force, the American army in Europe.

It was the Second World War that truly inspired the support and participation of American women on a massive scale. Most conspicuous and most significant was the entry of women into the work force. Some six million women went to work during the years 1942–45. Most of the new workers were married, most had children, and many were beyond age thirty-five. Nearly a half million were black women who left domestic service—often the only work they could find—for higher-paying jobs in industry. The new workers served in various capacities; some taught school or served as secretaries or clerks—jobs traditionally regarded as suited for women. Most striking, however, was the large number of women who performed heavier and dirtier work normally considered the domain of males. Under pressure of a growing labor shortage, lured by higher wages and simply by the challenge, women drove tractors and operated cranes, grinders, drill presses, and large equipment.

Women could not join the regular military forces during the First World War. (National Archives)

During the First World War a few women did go abroad to serve the American Expeditionary Force as telephone and telegraph operators. (National Archives)

They welded at shipyards, and above all—at shipyards and airplane factories—they became riveters. "Rosie the Riveter" became the symbol of the female war worker.

Other women served in jobs much closer to military operations. Women were serving as army or navy nurses when the war began. Several dozen were in the Philippine Islands when the Japanese attacked in December 1941; sixty-six were captured and lived out the conflict as prisoners of war. Demand for more military nurses was so unrelenting that the government in 1943 created a cadet nurse corps designed to train professional nurses at government expense. By war's end, membership in the cadet corps reached 117,000. The need for nurses was so acute that President Roosevelt in 1945 recommended, and Congress came within a hair of passing, a draft bill for female nurses. The measure surely would have become law but for the fact that war ended in Europe, causing pressure to subside somewhat. By the end of 1945 some 1,000 army and navy nurses—most of them with the army—had received military citations.

Women were not drafted into the armed forces during the Second World War, but they were given the opportunity to serve. Beginning with the army in 1942, each branch created its female unit. Although most did clerical work in the United States, female military personnel served in many different roles worldwide. They received numerous, and some of the most prestigious, military commendations. Millions of other women who stayed home supported the war in a wide range of activities, ranging from preparing bandages to entertaining soldiers to handling various aspects of a civil defense system. These dozens of volunteer organizations encompassed females of nearly all ages. Women were not drafted and were not required (or permitted) to go into combat, but in all other respects the Second World War was a woman's war.

Women's Military (or Semimilitary) Organizations in the Second World War

Women's Army Corps (Women's Army Auxiliary Corps)—WAC or WAAC. Created by Congress as an auxiliary unit in May 1942, the WACs became a regular part of the army in July 1943. The peak strength in April 1945 was slightly more than 99,000. A stubborn Congress refused to authorize a star, and so commander Oveta Culp Hobby carried the rank of colonel.

Women Accepted for Volunteer Emergency Service—WAVES. Created as a part of the navy in July 1942, the WAVES grew to 86,000 by August 1945. With higher qualifications than the army's counterpart, with higher morale and higher prestige, the WAVES faced no difficulty with recruitment. Sexual innuendo followed all the female military units, and the suggestion for a young man to "join the navy and ride the waves" suggested the difficulty in accepting the concept of women in military uniform.

Women's Coast Guard. Called the SPARS after the motto *Semper Paratus* ("always ready"), this unit was created in November 1942. It reached 10,000 by the end of the war.

Women's Marines. Created in February 1943, this organization never received a catchy nickname or acronym. Consistent with the sexism of that age, it was suggested that female marines might be called "leatherteats" or BAM, "broad-assed marines." Neither name caught on. By war's end there were 18,460 who served as drivers, mechanics, and photographers, as well as in the familiar secretarial roles.

Women's Auxiliary Ferrying Squadron—WAFS. This small group of experienced women pilots was formed in September 1942 to ferry military aircraft from factory to base.

Women's Airforce Service Pilots—WASP. These women were less experienced pilots, also hired in 1942 to ferry military aircraft. In August 1943, WAFS merged with WASP. Some 1,800 women participated. To the end WASP remained a civilian group that performed military functions, such as flying planes to destination, towing targets, teaching, and repair service.

Sources: Encyclopedia Britannica Yearbook, 1946 (Chicago, 1946), 829–831; Polmar and Allen, *World War II*, 753, 869–870, 887–889; Doris Weatherford, *American Women and World War II* (New York, 1990), 31–32, 41–44.

Domestic Volunteer Organizations in the Second World War

Aerial Nurse Corps of America

Air Rifle Corps of Tulsa, Okla.

American Relief Society

American WAC Mothers

American Women's Hospitals Reserve Corps

American Women's Volunteer Services (AWVS)

Association of Army and Navy Wives

Blue Star Mothers

Citizens Committee for the Army and Navy

Crop Corps

Daughters of the Defenders of the Republic

Friends of Democracy

Gold Star Mothers

Green Guards of Washington

Home Guard of Kalamazoo, Mich.

Junior American Nurses

Liberty Belles of San Antonio, Tex.

Mothers of Men in Service (MOMS)

National Security Women's Corps

National Women's Republic Club

Navy Mothers Club of America

Navy Wives Club of America

New York Women's Defense Corps

Powder Puff Platoon of Joplin, Mo.

Red Cross

    Production

    Nurses Aides

    Gray Ladies

    Motor Corps

    Blood Bank

Rifle Corps of Prescott, Ariz.

United Service Organization (USO)

Victory Farm Volunteers

Women's Ambulance and Defense Corps of America

Women's Defense School of Boston

Women's Hospital Reserve Corps

Women in Airline Maintenance (WAMS)

Women in National Service (WINS)

Women in Radio and Electric Service (WIRES)

Women's Land Army

Women's Ordnance Workers (WOWS)

Women's Overseas Service League

Source: Weatherford, *American Women and World War II,* numerous pages, especially 228–234.

War and Minority Groups

The impact of American minority groups on the military forces and their general involvement in two world wars can be put fairly simply: Whether their minority status was based on race or on ethnicity that could be traced to another country, they overwhelmingly gave their allegiance to the United States. Through participation in the nation's military forces and in the mobilization effort at home, they helped bring about victory in both conflicts. The impact of the wars on the minority groups provided a more complex proposition. All groups, with one possible exception, benefited from enlarged opportunities in the military forces and in domestic employment. In degrees that varied with each minority group, the gains did not come without cost; they often proved to be of short duration. The groups that profited most from both wars were white ethnic groups that had faced discrimination in the past (though some of these groups continued to face discrimination). Although one ordinarily did not think of German Americans as objects of discrimination, a sentiment did exist during the First World War that caused some individuals to suffer in various forms; many more German Americans were careful about their behavior lest they be branded disloyal. The story is better told in the examples of Irish, Italians, Poles, Jews, and other white groups that found better jobs and encountered more mixing with what one might call native white stock on the home front. For these people the military forces acted as a force for assimilation. The impact of the Second World War was more pronounced—more widespread and more lasting—than the conflict of 1917–18.

Nonwhite minority groups faced a much different situation. Small numbers of Japanese, Chinese, and Native Americans served in the military forces in the First World War without noticing any change in their standing in society. Changes produced by the Second World War were more profound, if in the long run little more encouraging. The Japanese-American experience had two outstanding parts: the painful and costly internment of nearly the entire continental population; and the participation of several thousand Nisei—persons of Japanese descent born and raised in the United States—in the U.S. armed forces. In February 1943 the government reversed an earlier policy and began to take Nisei volunteers. In June 1944 these young men became subject to the draft. In November 1944 the government authorized enlistment by Japanese aliens. It was from this reservoir of men, but mostly from the Nisei volunteers, that the army created the much-decorated 442d Regimental Combat Team. By bearing these dual burdens with determination and honor, Japanese Americans earned credits that the general society—however slowly—would have to honor.

Many American Indians fought in the First World War, and in the war of 1941–45 the number grew to nearly 30,000. Although some 300 Navajo code talkers later received much attention and acclaim, the typical Native-American soldier found war making anything but glamorous. His prewar status and shortage of education destined him, for the most part, for the lower ranks of the military forces. Temporary wartime gains through the military or civilian work force were mostly canceled at war's end.

The largest minority group, African Americans, always had played

Two of the Navajo code talkers in the Second World War who, by speaking their native language, confounded Japanese seeking to intercept American messages. (National Archives)

The army often assigned African-American soldiers to rear echelon duty, such as this coffin detail. (National Archives)

a part in American military forces, and the contribution grew substantially in both world wars. This participation came despite a profound prejudice by the white leadership about the competence of black soldiers and a policy lasting through both wars that blacks were to serve in separate units, officered in large measure by white men. Black men in the First World War served almost exclusively in the army, and in the Second World War most of them did, although the other services, the navy and marines, opened slightly to admit some black members.

Approximately 400,000 blacks entered military service during the First World War, a proportion of the army (9.5%) that approximated the number of black people in general society. In familiar military style, the bulk of these soldiers were placed in various types of labor and service units. The army did form two African-American combat divisions, the 92d and the 93d, both of which were sent to France. The 92d on the whole fared badly, was little motivated, and saw little combat duty. Portions of the 93d division, by contrast, remained at the front most of the summer of 1918 and performed very well. Especially noteworthy was the 369th regiment, the "Fighting 369th," which earned several citations for its distinguished performance in engaging the Germans.

At the start the Second World War seemed to offer a duplicate of the first, differing primarily by the larger numbers. Segregation

remained a fact of life, as did racial discrimination of many forms. These were little changed by the war. Black servicemen mostly performed labor work—for example, in the Transportation Corps, one unit of which formed the famous Red Ball Express that supplied the soldiers fighting Hitler's *Wehrmacht*. The army reformed the 92d and 93d divisions, and curiously, while the 93d helped conquer the Philippine Islands and other Pacific outposts, the 92d again compiled a less than admirable record. Before war's end, however, changes had started to surface. Black pilots formed the 99th Fighter Squadron, the Black Eagles, which flew many combat missions in Europe. Other squadrons were added to form the 332d Fighter Group, and a black Bomber Group had formed before the war ended. An all-black unit, the 761st Tank Battalion, received the praise of Gen. George Patton. Fostered by demands of the battlefield, a tiny measure of integration even crept into the armies in Europe. Other military services opened at least a crack, and so in the end, of approximately one million blacks who saw military service, most were in the army, but blacks were represented in all the military branches, and some 4,000 black women joined the various women's military services.

Long-range changes, however, were exceedingly disappointing. Black people who found work in the military or in military-related places usually became the "first fired" in either war, although a

Members of the 93d Division return home in 1919 displaying medals from the French government, earned in combat. (National Archives)

Members of the 99th Fighter Squadron, the first African-American pilots in the Second World War. (National Archives)

TABLE 9.16 MINORITY GROUPS INDUCTED INTO THE ARMY DURING THE SECOND WORLD WAR[a]

Chinese	13,311
Filipinos	11,506
Hawaiians	1,320
Indians	19,567
Japanese	24,085
Puerto Ricans	51,438
African Americans	893,796 (1,064,698 in all services)

[a]Through Dec. 31, 1945. Except for African Americans, statistics for the navy or marines are not included.
Source: Director of Selective Service, *Selective Service and Victory,* 885, 945.

growing number of black men chose to remain in the military service. Both wars prompted large movements of black people out of the South to the industrial North and to the Pacific Coast states. Both wars produced widespread racial tension in the military forces and in the "home fronts," including major riots in 1919 in Chicago and East St. Louis and in 1943 in Detroit. Profound change seemed so slow as to be nonexistent. If the attitude of white people remained much as it had been, the attitude of black people did not. The world wars had much to do with changes in the racial status quo that would come in the second half of the twentieth century.

Sources: Harry A. Ploski and James Williams, eds., *Reference Library of Black America* (5 vols., New York, 1990), 3:844–848; Polmar and Allen, *World War II,* 439–440, 723–724; Young, *The Army Almanac,* 140–142.

The United States and the First World War

The United States entered the First World War late. If one considers that war started in Europe in July–August 1914, that the United States entered in April 1917, and that the war ended in November 1918, it develops that approximately two-thirds of the war went on without direct American participation. Thus a large portion of the American association with that war involved a long period of official neutrality during which time the Americans tried to maintain a strong connection to the European belligerents without having to become a belligerent themselves. Americans had strong emotional and intellectual ties to both sides, although the largest number sympathized with the Allies, especially Britain and France. In the long run it was an economic connection, and ramifications of that connection, that had the largest impact on bringing America into the war. The United States set out to trade with both sides, but because of need, geography, and circumstance, most American trade soon went to the British and French. The most important factor in determining the course of American commerce was the British fleet. Within a year there had emerged a trade that was vital not only to British and French prosecution of the war but also to a booming American wartime economy. Unwilling to see its enemies supplied from abroad, Germany set out to stop this traffic. Unequipped to use the British method of stopping ships at sea, the Germans began to utilize submarines against commerce, which represented a new departure in warfare on the high seas. The American government objected to the effect of submarine warfare on American property and especially on American lives, especially after the sinking of the passenger liner *Lusitania* on May 7, 1915, a sensational event that caused the death of 128 Americans. There followed a long diplomatic struggle between Germany and the United States that lasted nearly two years. Although the German government made temporary concessions to avoid provoking American intervention, in the end Germany decided that if it had any chance of winning this war of "attrition," it would have to use submarines without restriction, even if the action did bring the Americans in. President Woodrow Wilson severed diplomatic relations, and when evidence proved that Germany intended to attack American shipping, he asked Congress for war on April 2, 1917. In that message Wilson explained his decision in high moral terms. He chose to see submarine warfare as more of a moral issue than economic, and Germany's willingness to use that

American soldiers receive additional training in Le Mans, France, before going to the front in the First World War. (National Archives)

weapon as an indication of the danger and brutality in German leadership that no longer could be tolerated. Many factors influenced America's going to war with Germany, but submarine warfare was the immediate precipitant, and American trade with the Allies brought it about. Congress passed the declaration of war on April 6.

U.S. participation in the war thus came late, but it was not small in terms of people involved, and it certainly was not insignificant. As the Germans had predicted, it took approximately a year for the Americans to raise an army and get it to France. Although the United States did create a large military force and did contribute heavily with supplies of many kinds and especially in the financial aspects of the war, other major belligerents provided much more in terms of modern weaponry. American forces, for example, had to rely heavily on Britain and France for such weapons as artillery and aircraft. The most striking expression of differences in the extent of combat between the United States and the European giants was in terms of casualties. When the Americans did get to France in the summer of 1918, they were instrumental in determining the outcome of the war. The United States entered a conflict marked with two sides nearly evenly balanced—although by 1918 the tide had shifted in favor of the Germans. Both sides were war-weary, if not on the edge of demoralization. Fresh American troops tipped the balance in favor of the Allies. It is, of course, false to claim—as many Americans later were wont to do—that the United States won the First World War, but had the Americans not been involved, the war would have ended differently.

TABLE 9.17   FIRST WORLD WAR MILITARY COMMANDERS

Army		
American Expeditionary Forces	John J. Pershing	May 1917–Nov. 1918
First Army	John J. Pershing	Aug. 1918–Oct. 1918
	Hunter Liggett	Oct. 1918–Nov. 1918
Second Army	Robert L. Bullard	Oct. 1918–Nov. 1918
Third Army	John T. Dickman	Nov. 1918
became Army of Occupation		Dec. 1918–Jan. 1923
I Corps	H. Liggett	Jan. 1918–Oct. 1918
	J. T. Dickman	Oct. 1918–Nov. 1918
II Corps	G. W. Read	Jun. 1918–Nov. 1918
III Corps	W. M. Wright	Jun. 1918–Jul. 1918
	R. L. Bullard	Jul. 1918–Oct. 1918
	J. L. Hines	Oct. 1918–Nov. 1918
IV Corps	J. T. Dickman	Aug. 1918–Oct. 1918
	C. H. Muir	Oct. 1918–Nov. 1918
V. Corps	W. M. Wright	Jul. 1918–Aug. 1918
	G. H. Cameron	Aug. 1918–Oct. 1918
	C. P. Summerall	Oct. 1918–Nov. 1918
VI Corps	O. Bundy	Aug. 1918–Sep. 1918
	C. C. Ballou	Oct. 1918–Nov. 1918
	C. T. Menoher	Nov. 1918
VII Corps	W. M. Wright	Aug. 1918–Sep. 1918
	O. Bundy	Sep. 1918–Oct. 1918

(continued)

Members of the 132d Infantry in combat, October 3, 1918. (National Archives)

TABLE 9.17 (continued)

Navy		
Atlantic Fleet	Henry T. Mayo	. . .
U.S. naval forces in Europe	William S. Sims	. . .
Battleships (Battle Squadron 6)	Hugh Rodman	. . .
Patrol Force, later U.S. naval forces in France	Henry B. Wilson	. . .
Convoys	Albert Gleaves	. . .
Asiatic Fleet	Austin M. Knight	. . .

Marines		
4th Marine Brigade	J. G. Harbord, J. A. Lejeune, W. C. Neville, J. T. Boone (USN), T. Holcomb	Oct. 1917–Nov. 1918

Source: G. and C. Webster Co., *Webster's American Military Biographies*, 523–524, 537, 541.

TABLE 9.19 POISON GAS: CASUALTIES AND PRODUCTION, 1915–1918

	Total casualties	Deaths	Production (tons)	Used (tons)
British Empire	188,706	8,109	25,735	14,000
France	190,000	8,000	36,955	26,000
Italy	60,000	4,627	6,300	6,300
Russia	419,340	56,000	4,700	4,700
U.S.	72,807	1,462	6,215	1,000
Austria	100,000	3,000	7,900	7,900
Germany	200,000	9,000	68,100	52,000
Others	10,000	1,000	. . .	. . .

Source: Gray, *Chronicle of the First World War*, 2:288.

TABLE 9.20 AMERICANS ENGAGED IN VARIOUS CAMPAIGNS, 1918

Belleau Wood, Jun.	2d Infantry Division (army), 4th marine brigade
Amiens, Aug.	2 regiments (33d division), 2,070 guns, 430 tanks, 12 armored cars, 800 aircraft
St. Mihiel, Aug.	1st army—500,000 men in 18 divisions (4 French), 3,019 guns (1,329 French manned), 267 tanks (113 French manned)
Hindenberg Line, Sept.	39 divisions—more than 1,000,000 men, 320 tanks
Meuse-Argonne, Sept.	1st army—300,000 men in 16 divisions, 189 tanks, 842 aircraft

Source: Gray, *Chronicle of the First World War*, 2:184, 284.

TABLE 9.18 MILITARY STATISTICS, FIRST WORLD WAR

Casualties—by nation

	Total Mobilized Forces	Killed and Died[a]	Wound Casualties	Prisoners and Missing	Total Casualties	Total Casualties in Percent of Total Mobilized
Allies						
Russia	12,000,000	1,700,000	4,950,000	2,500,000	9,150,000	76.3
France[b]	8,410,000	1,357,800	4,266,000	537,000	6,160,800	73.3
Brit. Emp.[b]	8,904,467	908,371	2,090,212	191,642	3,190,235	35.8
Italy	5,615,000	650,000	947,000	600,000	2,197,000	39.1
U.S.[c]	4,355,000	126,000[d]	234,300[d]	4,500	350,300	8.0
Japan	800,000	300	907	3	1,210	.2
Rumania	750,000	335,706	120,000	80,000	535,706	71.4
Serbia	707,343	45,000	133,148	152,958	331,106	46.8
Belgium	267,000	13,716	44,686	34,659	93,061	34.9
Greece	230,000	5,000	21,000	1,000	27,000	11.7
Portugal	100,000	7,222	13,751	12,318	33,291	33.3
Montenegro[e]	50,000	3,000	10,000	7,000	20,000	40.0
Total	42,188,810	5,152,115	12,831,004	4,121,090	22,089,709	52.3
Central Powers						
Germany	11,000,000	1,773,700	4,216,058	1,152,800	7,142,558	64.9
Austro-Hungary	7,800,000	1,200,000	3,620,000	2,200,000	7,020,000	90.0
Turkey	2,850,000	325,000	400,000	250,000	975,000	34.2
Bulgaria	1,200,000	87,500	152,390	27,029	266,919	22.2
Total	22,850,000	3,386,200	8,388,448	3,629,829	15,404,477	67.4
G. Total	64,038,810	8,538,315	21,219,452	7,750,919	37,494,186	57.6

[a] Includes deaths from all causes.
[b] Official figures.
[c] Includes marines serving with the army.
[d] Includes "Died of Wounds" (14,500).
[e] A tiny independent kingdom that would be incorporated into a new Yugoslavia.
Source: *Encyclopedia Britannica* (Chicago, 1962), 23:775.

TABLE 9.21 ALLIED STRENGTH, WESTERN FRONT, NOVEMBER 1918 (ARMISTICE DAY)

	France	Britain	U.S.
Total strength	2,600,000	1,966,727	1,981,701
Combat strength	1,554,000	1,202,000	1,078,222
Infantry divisions	102[a]	58	31
Cavalry divisions	6	3	. . .
Horses	630,000	388,000	151,000
Field guns	6,000	4,202	2,400
Heavy guns	5,600	2,204	406
Trench mortars	1,600	2,500	750
Light machine guns	50,000	20,000	18,000
Machine guns	30,000	5,000	6,000
Tanks	2,300	610	90
Aircraft	3,600	1,576/1,799 serviceable	740
Motor vehicles	96,000	57,051	
Length of front	214 miles	70 miles	83 miles

[a]Includes 1 Czechoslovak and 2 Polish divisions.
Source: Gray, *Chronicle of the First World War,* 2:184.

America's most celebrated hero of the First World War, Sgt. Alvin York stands near the place where in 1918 he performed his renowned military deed: the shooting of fifteen enemy soldiers and inducing the surrender of 132 more. (National Archives)

Losses of Ships

The record of losses of combat vessels reflected once again the fact that the United States was in the First World War a shorter time than other belligerents. America's naval losses were minuscule compared with Britain's. Except for Britain and Germany, however, naval losses generally were small—a fact that confirmed that the First World War was essentially a land conflict. When it came to merchant vessels, American losses, while much smaller than those of Great Britain, were anything but insignificant. Before the United States became heavily involved in the fighting, it was a major participant in the business of supply. These losses were largely a reflection of the effect of the German submarine campaign, a major force in bringing America into the war and a force on which Germany depended heavily for victory.

TABLE 9.22 WARSHIP LOSSES—BY NATION

	Great Britain	France	Italy	Japan	United States	Russia	Turkey	Austria	Germany Losses	Germany Surrendered
Dreadnoughts	2[a]	. . .	1[a]	1[a]	. . .	2[a]	. . .	2	. . .	18
Pre-dreadnoughts	11[a]	4	3	. . .	. . .	2	1	1	1	. . .
Battle cruisers	3	. . .	. . .	1[a]	. . .	. . .	. . .	. . .	1	6
Cruisers	13[a]	5	1	. . .	1	2	. . .	. . .	6	. . .
Light cruisers	12	. . .	2	2	. . .	. . .	1	3	17[a]	23
Destroyers	67	12	8	1	2	20	3	6	66	92[c]
Submarines	54	14	8	. . .	. . .	20	. . .	14[b]	199	All

[a]One lost by accidental internal explosion.
[b]By the peace terms Austria was left without coastline and its navy ceased to exist.
[c]Also 50 of the newest torpedo boats.
Source: Encyclopedia Britannica (1962 edition), 23:788.

TABLE 9.23   ALLIED AND NEUTRAL MERCHANT SHIPPING LOSSES, 1914–1918

Belgium	105,000t	
Brazil	31,000t	
Britain	7,759,090t	(2,479 ships)
Denmark	245,000t	
France	891,000t	(500 ships to U-boats)
Greece	415,000t	
Holland	230,000t	
Italy	872,341t	(633 ships)
Japan	128,000t	
Norway	1,177,001t	
Portugal	28,637t	
Rumania	n/a	
Russia	183,000t	
Spain	260,000t	
Sweden	264,000t	
U.S.	531,000t	

Note: t = tons.
Source: Gray, *Chronicle of the First World War,* 2:290.

Financing the War

If the United States contributed far less than several other nations in terms of troops and certain types of weaponry, such was not the case with respect to the financial costs of the war. America's war expenses were high in relation to the period of direct involvement and in fact came reasonably close to the expenses of other major combatants that fought a much longer war. One of the reasons for the high costs was the large amount of money loaned to Allied and other European countries during and shortly after the war. Payment of these war loans would become a major source of controversy during the 1920s. The United States paid approximately one-third of its war expenses on a pay-as-you-go basis, by taxation; two-thirds came from borrowing through five popular loan drives (four Liberty Loans and one Victory Loan). All were oversubscribed.

The United States and the Treaty of Versailles

The First World War ground to a merciful halt in the armistice of November 11, 1918, and leaders of the warring powers—Germany conspicuously excluded—assembled in Paris to prepare a permanent settlement. Negotiations, which proceeded during the greater part of the period from December 1918 to June 1919, were marked with large and detailed controversies over geographic and territorial issues, politics, and economics. Many of the major quarrels pitted the position of the French leader—Georges Clemenceau—who favored harsh and crippling treatment of Germany, with proposals of the American president, Woodrow Wilson, who supported a more lenient treaty. Wilson wanted a settlement that would stand on its own merits, and he was convinced that for a peace that would last far into the future, it was necessary to create new machinery for nations dealing with one another. Thus on Wilson's insistence the covenant of the new League of Nations became an integral part—the first twenty-six articles—of the settlement with Germany, the Treaty of Versailles, signed on June 28, 1919. Subsequent treaties with other defeated nations also contained the covenant of the league. To accept the Treaty of Versailles, one had to accept the league. Wilson believed that the treaty would facilitate acceptance of the League of Nations and that through the league it would be possible to remove flaws in the treaty and advance the world toward lasting peace. Acceptance of the League of Nations, he was convinced, was absolutely indispensable for the future of humankind.

Other people in the United States had different ideas. Criticism of the treaty surfaced even before Wilson brought it home in early July 1919. While it was impossible to measure the extent to which opposition grew out of political partisanship, one could not ignore the fact that the treaty was the handiwork of a Democratic president being placed before a Senate that contained a majority of Republicans. The Republican leader was Henry Cabot Lodge of Massachusetts, a political rival and personal foe of the president. Most of the senators who opposed the treaty and the League of Nations were Republican, and most of the senators who favored the settlement intact were Democratic. The public thrust of the opposition centered on the proposition that membership in the League of Nations would compromise American sovereignty, that decisions on American policy would be handed over to a league council dominated by European nations. Critics of the league mustered harshest criticism for Article X of the league's covenant, which they claimed created an opening for decisions binding on all member states. The debate that followed produced fourteen changes in the treaty (mostly in the league), sponsored by Lodge. Known as the Lodge Reservations, they had two major objectives: (1) to protect the power of the United States to make decisions in foreign affairs; and (2) to promote the authority of the legislative branch as regarding the power of the president. The reservations passed the Senate one by one by majority vote. (The treaty itself needed approval of two-thirds of the senators.)

TABLE 9.24   FINANCIAL AND ECONOMIC COSTS, 1914–1918 (millions)

Allied	
Belgium	$10,195
Britain	39,260
British Empire	51,975
France	49,877
Greece	556
Italy	18,143
Japan	. . .
Portugal	300–400
Rumania	2,601
Russia	21,600
Serbia	2,400
U.S.	32,320
Central Powers	
Austria	23,706
Bulgaria	1,015
Germany	58,072
Turkey	3,445
Neutrals	
Denmark	90
Holland	672
Norway	130
Sweden	4,298
Switzerland	250

Note: These figures include government spending, loans, and material damage valuation. They can only be taken as an approximate relative guide.
Sources: Gray, *Chronicle of the First World War,* 2:292; *The Lincoln Library of Essential Information* (Buffalo, N.Y., 1937), 1266.

Flowers are thrown at the feet of President Wilson as he arrives in Dover, England, en route to the fateful Paris Peace Conference of 1918–19. (National Archives)

In an effort to salvage support for his floundering treaty, a beleaguered president undertook an extensive speaking tour. In the course of that exhausting undertaking Wilson collapsed and suffered a stroke; he was seriously ill for eight months and never experienced full recovery, although he lived on until 1924. When during that period the Senate voted three times on the Treaty of Versailles, the weakened president remained adamant: There must be no change, at least nothing of substance, in the League of Nations. In fact, neither side compromised, and so the United States turned down the treaty that ended the Great War and in so doing refused to accept membership in Woodrow Wilson's grand parliament of the world, the League of Nations. The United States would sign a separate treaty with Germany that very much resembled the Treaty of Versailles, without including the covenant of the League of Nations.

Article X of the Covenant of the League of Nations

Although opponents of the League of Nations focused criticism on Article X, the article in fact was general, and it might leave the reader to doubt that it carried the danger that its critics claimed.

> The Members of the League undertake to respect and preserve as against external aggression the territorial integrity and existing political independence of all Members of the League. In case of any such aggression or in case of any threat or danger of such aggression the Council shall advise upon the means by which this obligation shall be fulfilled.

Source: Robert H. Ferrell, ed., *America as a World Power, 1882–1945.* (New York, 1971), 179.

TABLE 9.25 VOTES IN THE SENATE ON THE TREATY OF VERSAILLES

Nov. 19, 1919		
1. On the treaty with fourteen Lodge Reservations		
	Yes	No
Republicans	35	13
Democrats	4	42
	39	55
2. On the treaty (Wilson's Treaty) with no change		
	Yes	No
Republicans	1	46
Democrats	37	7
	38	53
Mar. 19, 1920		
1. On the treaty with slightly modified Lodge Reservations		
	Yes	No
Republicans	28	12
Democrats	21	23
	49	35

Note: Sixty-three votes were needed for approval of the treaty on Mar. 19. A change of seven votes would have placed the United States in the League of Nations.
Source: Albert Castel and Scott Gibson, *The Yeas and the Nays: Key Congressional Decisions, 1774–1945* (Kalamazoo, Mich., 1975), 142–143.

America and the World Between Two World Wars

American rejection of the League of Nations signaled a rejection of Wilsonian internationalism and revealed a popular intent to steer an independent course in world affairs, clear of foreign entanglement. The American posture in the 1920s might be called isolationist only to the extent that it involved political problems, for in other respects, and especially in economics, the United States remained a part of the world. The nation even participated in ways of its own choosing in the treatment of world issues, always taking care to remain apart from the League of Nations. The Americans led the way in pursuing peace through disarmament. In accordance with agreement at the Washington Naval Conference of 1921–22, the United States proceeded to destroy—by scrapping or stopping construction on—no fewer than thirty capital ships, a massive arms reduction that was to be matched by an appropriate destruction of British and Japanese vessels (see table 9.15, American Battleship Registry). The United States also provided leadership in seeking peace another way: a treaty that outlawed war. What followed was the Kellogg-Briand Pact, also called the Pact of Paris of 1928, signed first by the United States and France and eventually by most nations. Needless to say, the treaty to outlaw war did not become the treaty that prevented war. It had no teeth, no enforcement provisions, as

observers at the time quickly detected, but the Pact of Paris stood as a mark of the American approach to foreign policy in the 1920s.

The issue that came to cause the most friction in dealing with European nations was settlement of war debts. The problem grew out of more than $10 billion loaned to European nations during and immediately after the First World War (see Financing the War). The largest debtors were America's former allies, notably Britain and France. The United States chose to treat the loans as a business deal to be paid with interest, but the Europeans found numerous ways, including pleading poverty, to explain why they could not comply. War debts became entangled with the larger issue of the requirement of Germany to pay reparations. The full scope of international indebtedness vastly complicated diplomacy in the 1920s and surely delayed—possibly prevented—recovery from the war. In the face of an international financial crisis in 1923–24, the United States made what it regarded as a magnanimous gesture. In signing individual agreements with the debtor nations, the Americans canceled none of the principal of the debts, but they spread payment over sixty-two years and reduced interest rates drastically. They calculated that the interest reduction, reckoned over such a long period, amounted to cancellation of 60% of the entire obligation. Even so, the move did

TABLE 9.26   WAR AND POSTWAR FOREIGN LOANS OF U.S. GOVERNMENT

	Pre-Armistice [Cash]	Post-Armistice [Cash & Supplies]	Total Indebtedness
To Allies			
Great Britain	$3,696,000,000	$ 581,000,000.00	$ 4,277,000,000.00
France	1,970,000,000	1,434,818,945.01	3,404,818,945.01
Italy	1,031,000,000	617,034,050.90	1,648,034,050.90
Belgium	171,780,000	207,307,200.43	379,087,200.43
Russia	187,729,750	4,871,547.37	192,601,297.37
Romania	. . .	37,911,152.92	37,911,152.92
Greece	. . .	27,167,000.00	27,167,000.00
Cuba	10,000,000	. . .	10,000,000.00
Nicaragua	. . .	431,849.14	431,849.14
Liberia	. . .	26,000.00	26,000.00
To Countries Formed Out of Allied Territory			
Esthonia	. . .	13,999,145.60	13,999,145.60
Finland	. . .	8,281,926.17	8,281,926.17
Latvia	. . .	5,132,287.14	5,132,287.14
Lithuania	. . .	4,981,628.03	4,981,628.03
To Areas or Countries Formed Partially or Wholly Out of Enemy Territory			
Poland	. . .	159,666,972.39	159,666,972.39
Czechoslovakia	. . .	91,879,671.03	91,879,671.03
Yugoslavia	10,605,000	41,153,486.55	51,758,486.55
Austria	. . .	24,055,708.92	24,055,708.92
Armenia	. . .	11,959,917.49	11,959,917.49
Hungary	. . .	1,685,835.61	1,685,835.61
	$7,077,114,750	$3,273,364,324.70	$10,350,479,074.70

Source: Thomas A. Bailey, *A Diplomatic History of the American People* (New York, 1968), 657.

not solve the problem. Payment of war debts and of reparations proceeded in good faith after 1925, but the coming of the world depression in 1929 canceled all that had been gained. Payments stopped and for the most part never would start again. This turn of events deeply angered those Americans who had agreed with the remark of President Calvin Coolidge: "They hired the money, didn't they?" The war debts question worsened American relations with its former allies into the 1930s, by which time those same nations, Britain and France, were nudging toward another war with another Germany and again were in need of help.

TABLE 9.27   THE DEBT AGREEMENTS

Debtor	Funding Agreement Signed	Average Interest Rate over 62-Year Repayment Period	Reduction of Entire Debt on 5% Basis
Finland	May 1, 1923	3.3	29.8
Great Britain	Jun. 19, 1923	3.3	30.1
Hungary	Apr. 25, 1924	3.3	30.0
Lithuania	Sep. 22, 1924	3.3	30.5
Poland	Nov. 14, 1924	3.3	30.0
Belgium	Aug. 18, 1925	1.8	60.3
Latvia	Sep. 24, 1925	3.3	29.8
Czechoslovakia	Oct. 13, 1925	3.3	37.0
Esthonia	Oct. 28, 1925	3.3	29.9
Italy	Nov. 14, 1925	0.4	80.2
Romania	Dec. 4, 1925	3.3	37.1
France	Apr. 29, 1926	1.6	60.3
Yugoslavia	May 3, 1926	1.0	75.9
Greece	May 10, 1929	0.3	72.1

Source: Bailey, *Diplomatic History of the American People*, 663.

The Second World War

There is something to be said for the proposition that the Second World War in fact consisted of two separate wars going on at the same time. Although links existed between the two from the beginning, the principal connecting factor was that the United States became a major participant in both. Fighting started first in Asia, between Japan and China in July 1937, but the war that began in Europe in September 1939 attracted most of the attention of the United States. From the start the administration of Franklin D. Roosevelt took the position that the United States had much at stake in this conflict that at first pitted Germany against Britain and France. While the Americans wished to not become an active participant, most did support the government's efforts to find ways of assisting the nations fighting the forces of Adolf Hitler. To this end the Roosevelt administration took several steps between September 1939 and December 1941:

1. September 1939: It pressed for a change (passed in November) in previous neutrality laws that authorized sale of military goods to Britain and France.

TABLE 9.28   WORLD WAR I DEBT OWED THE U.S. AS OF JULY 1, 1944

Country	Total Indebtedness	Principal Unpaid	Interest Postponed and Payable under Moratorium Agreements	Interest Accrued and Unpaid under Funding and Moratorium Agreements
Funded debts:				
Belgium	$495,263,077.60	$400,680,000.00	$3,750,000.00	$90,833,077.60
Czechoslovakia	170,484,850.31	165,241,108.90	. . .	5,243,741.41
Estonia	23,919,170.81	16,466,012.87	492,360.20	6,960,797.74
Finland	8,704,800.15	7,941,403.92	763,396.23	. . .
France	4,529,589,934.38	3,863,650,000.00	38,636,500.00	627,303,434.38
Germany (Austrian indebtedness)	26,024,539.59	25,980,480.66	. . .	44,058.93
Great Britain	6,263,764,782.58	4,368,000,00.00	131,520,000.00	1,764,244,782.58
Greece	36,437,695.10	31,516,000.00	449,080.00	4,472,615.10
Hungary	2,674,567.89	1,908,560.00	57,072.75	708,935.14
Italy	2,047,231,659.34	2,004,900,000.00	2,506,125.00	39,825,534.34
Latvia	9,875,762.05	6,879,464.20	205,989.96	2,790,307.89
Lithuania	8,848,573.28	6,197,682.00	185,930.46	2,464,960.82
Poland	299,332,204.20	206,057,000.00	6,161,835.00	87,113,369.20
Rumania	73,111,160.13	63,860,560.43	. . .	9,250,599.70
Yugoslavia	63,088,593.78	61,625,000.00	. . .	1,463,593.78
Total	**$14,058,351,371.19**	**$11,230,903,272.98**	**$184,728,289.60**	**$2,642,719,808.61**
Unfunded debts:				
Armenia	26,793,083.46	11,959,917.49	. . .	14,833,165.97
Russia	438,449,173.08	192,601,297.37	. . .	245,847,875.71
Total	**$465,242,256.54**	**$204,561,214.86**	**. . .**	**$260,681,041.68**
Grand total	**$14,523,593,627.73**	**$11,435,464,487.84**	**$184,728,289.60**	**$2,903,400,850.29**

Source: *The World Almanac and Book of Facts for 1946* (New York, 1946), 30.

2. September 1940: The president signed an executive agreement that transferred fifty American warships (destroyers) to Great Britain. Britain at this time stood alone, facing a likely invasion from Germany.

3. January 1941: Roosevelt proposed a measure called the Lend-Lease Bill—passed in March—that authorized sending vast amounts of war matériel to Britain at government expense. Some goods later went to Russia.

4. April 1941: Roosevelt sent destroyers into the Atlantic on "patrols"; in fact the ships were seeking out hostile German submarines.

5. August 1941: Roosevelt met secretly with Prime Minister Winston Churchill of Great Britain; he signed the Atlantic Charter and in a general way planned the defeat of Germany.

6. September 1941: After a submarine attack on the American destroyer *Greer,* Roosevelt ordered the navy to "shoot on sight," to attack any German submarine encountered on the high seas.

Thus by the fall of 1941, though the United States and Germany were not officially at war, they were shooting at each other. In his efforts to assist the enemies of Hitler, Roosevelt faced bitter opposition from isolationists, both inside Congress and outside. Although most Americans preferred to avoid war with anybody, they continued to give Roosevelt support, even as relations with Germany became increasingly perilous. Despite the so-called Undeclared War on the Atlantic, open hostilities came only in the aftermath of the Japanese attack on Pearl Harbor. Germany (and Italy) declared war on the United States on December 11, 1941.

Trouble between the United States and Japan grew out of Japanese expansion in Asia, which the United States believed threatened its interests in that area. The Americans became especially distressed at the Japanese conquests in China, a beleaguered and vulnerable nation that, as many Americans believed, merited special sympathy and assistance from the United States. After war began in Europe in September 1939, the Roosevelt administration increasingly found similarities between the militaristic right-wing regimes of Japan and Germany. The connection became hardfast in September 1940, when these Axis nations signed a military alliance called the Tripartite Pact (Italy was the third partner). Although the principal American focus

remained on Europe, Roosevelt continued to seek ways to encourage resistance from the Chinese government, to discourage the Japanese from their course, if not punish them absolutely. He moved the Pacific Fleet from California to Pearl Harbor, Hawaii, and took the first steps toward fortification of American bases in east Asia; in fall 1940 he began a program of piecemeal embargo of goods sold to Japan. In the meantime the American secretary of state, Cordell Hull, gave Japanese negotiators no reason to expect a more compliant American attitude on anything, and above all not on China. The Americans wanted the Japanese out. The final blow came in July 1941, when, after Japanese occupation of French Indochina, Roosevelt stopped all trade. Japanese officials concluded that unless they could get the policy changed—which they did not—Japan would have to go to war with the United States to protect and preserve its position in Asia. In view of Japan's vastly smaller size, population, resources, and productive power, for there to be any chance of success, the war had to start with a considerable Japanese advantage—such was the thinking of the Japanese regime. Japan expected to receive that advantage by destroying the Pacific Fleet based at Pearl Harbor.

The largest differences between American participation in the First and Second World Wars, if one excludes technological change, were in size and length of commitment. The Second World War was much longer for the United States and involved much larger military forces and more time in combat. It involved the total population in a larger way. During 1941–45 the United States had more military forces than all nations but the Soviet Union; it spent more money than any belligerent and easily produced the most military goods. In the war against Germany the United States could count on major assistance, mostly from the Soviet Union and Britain. The war against Japan was essentially an American project.

Faced in December 1941 with two wars, the United States decided to concentrate first on Europe. Japan could wait. Even so, the war proceeded on such a course that within one year after intervention, by the end of 1942, the Americans could begin to think in terms of two simultaneous offensive wars. In either case the Americans largely fought their way: placing large armies in the field (although more so in Europe than in Asia), using advanced technology—the larger the weapons the better. The war in Europe belonged to the army (bearing in mind that the air force then was

TABLE 9.29   COSTS OF THE SECOND WORLD WAR, BY NATION[a]

Nations	Total Forces Mobilized (million)	Military Dead	Military Wounded	Civilian Dead	Economic and Financial Costs ($ billion)
United States	14.9	292,100[b]	571,822	Negligible	350
United Kingdom	6.2	397,762	475,000	65,000	150
France	6	210,671	400,000	108,000	100
Soviet Union	20	7,500,000	14,012,000	10–15,000,000	200
China[c]	6–10	500,000	1,700,000	1,000,000	No estimate
Germany	12.5	2,850,000	7,250,000	500,000	300
Italy	4.5	77,500	120,000	40–100,000	50
Japan	7.4	1,506,000	500,000	300,000[d]	100
All other participants	20	1,500,000	No estimate	14–17,000,000[e]	350
Total	100	15,000,000	No estimate	26–34,000,000	1,600

[a]Many of these figures are approximations or estimates, since official figures are misleading, missing, or contradictory in many instances.
[b]This number represents only battle deaths. Deaths from all causes including accidents, sickness, etc., were 405,399. See Table 9.2.
[c]Statistics for China are the least reliable of any nation. Other estimates put military deaths at 1,500,000 and possibly much more. Estimates of civilian deaths range from 700,000 to 10,000,000.
[d]Other estimates place Japanese civilian deaths much higher—as many as 670,000 from American air raids alone.
[e]This includes approximately 6,000,000 Jews of Germany and all occupied European nations, and approximately 4,500,000 Poles.
Source: R. Ernest Dupuy and Trevor N. Dupuy, *The Encyclopedia of Military History from 3500 B.C. to the Present* (New York, 1970), 1198.

the army air force). The army bombed German cities and engaged German armies in the field—in Italy beginning in 1943 and in France starting in June 1944. The job of the navy was to protect (from submarine and air attack) the transport of men and supplies to the battlefronts. It should be noted that the largest forces that fought the Germans were Russian.

The war in the Pacific drew heavily on the navy and marines, although substantial army troops participated in the largest land campaigns, as in the Philippines, and bombing of Japan mostly was undertaken by the army air force. Although there were cases of ship-to-ship engagements—notably in the Solomon campaign of 1942–43 and the Philippine campaign of 1944—the most effective naval forces were submarines and carrier-based aircraft. The Pacific war rested on three basic strategies: (1) the use of carrier task forces to carry the war to the enemy in various ways; (2) the selective "island-hopping" offensive, landings on Pacific islands, mostly undertaken by marines; and (3) the devastating program, after summer 1944, of saturation bombing of Japan.

If American casualties appeared large in comparison with the First World War, they were very small compared with those of China, German, Japan, and the Soviet Union. The reasons included numerical and technological (in many cases) superiority of weaponry. American goods were not always the best, but there usually were much more of them. If a ship was sunk or a plane shot down, the

American Military Commanders, Second World War

TABLE 9.30   ARMY COMMANDERS

Alaska Defense Command	Simon B. Buckner	Feb. 1941–Oct. 1943
redesignated		
Alaskan Department	Simon B. Buckner	Nov. 1943–Mar. 1944
	Delos C. Emmons	Jun. 1944–Jun. 1946
Hawaiian Department	Walter C. Short	Jan. 1941–Dec. 1941
	Delos C. Emmons	Dec. 1941–May 1943
	Robert C. Richardson	Jun. 1943–Aug. 1943
Far East	Douglas MacArthur	Jul. 1941–Mar. 1942
	Jonathan M. Wainwright	Mar. 1942–Jun. 1942
Central Pacific Area	Robert C. Richardson	Aug. 1943–Aug. 1944
merged into		
Pacific Ocean Areas	Robert C. Richardson	Aug. 1944–Jun. 1945
South Pacific Area	Millard F. Harmon	Jan. 1942–Aug. 1944
Southwest Pacific Area	Douglas MacArthur	Apr. 1942–Sept. 1945
Pacific	Douglas MacArthur	Apr. 1945–Dec. 1946
China-Burma-India	Joseph W. Stilwell	Mar. 1942–Oct. 1944
split into		
China	Claire L. Chennault	Oct. 1944
	Albert C. Wedemeyer	Oct. 1944–May 1946
and		
India-Burma	Daniel I. Sultan	Oct. 1944–Jun. 1945
European Theater	Dwight D. Eisenhower	Jun. 1942–Feb. 1943
	Frank M. Andrews	Feb. 1943–May 1943
	William S. Key	May 1943
	Jacob L. Devers	May 1943–Jan. 1944
	Dwight D. Eisenhower	Jan. 1944–Jul. 1945
redesignated		
U.S. Forces, European Theater		
	Dwight D. Eisenhower	Jul. 1945–Nov. 1945
	George S. Patton	Nov. 1945
	Joseph T. MacNarney	Nov. 1945–Mar. 1947
North African Theater	Dwight D. Eisenhower	Feb. 1943–Jan. 1944
	Jacob L. Devers	Jan. 1944–Oct. 1944
	Joseph T. McNarney	Oct. 1944–Nov. 1944
redesignated		

Mediterranean Theater	Joseph T. McNarney	Nov. 1944–Nov. 1945
	John C. H. Lee	Dec. 1945–Sep. 1947
Supreme Headquarters, Allied Expeditionary Force	Dwight D. Eisenhower	Feb. 1944–Jul. 1945
First U.S. Army Group	Omar N. Bradley	Oct. 1943–Aug. 1944
superseded by		
12th Army Group	Omar N. Bradley	Aug. 1944–Jul. 1945
15th Army Group	Sir H. R. L. G. Alexander	Jul. 1943–Dec. 1944
	Mark W. Clark	Dec. 1944–Jul. 1945
6th Army Group	Jacob L. Devers	Sep. 1944–Jun. 1945
First Army	Omar N. Bradley	Jan. 1944–Aug. 1944
	Courtney H. Hodges	Aug. 1944–Mar. 1949
Third Army	Courtney H. Hodges	Feb. 1943–Jan. 1944
	George S. Patton	Jan. 1944–Nov. 1945
	Lucian K. Truscott	Nov. 1945–May 1946
Fourth Army	John L. DeWitt	Dec. 1941–Sep. 1943
	William H. Simpson	Oct. 1943–Apr. 1944
	John P. Lucas	Apr. 1944–Jul. 1945
	Alexander M. Patch	Jul. 1945–Jun. 1946
Fifth Army	Mark W. Clark	Dec. 1942–Dec. 1944
	Lucian K. Truscott	Dec. 1944–Oct. 1945
Sixth Army	Walter Krueger	Feb. 1943–Jan. 1946
Seventh Army	George S. Patton	Jul. 1943–Jan. 1944
	Mark W. Clark	Jan. 1944–Mar. 1944
	Alexander M. Patch	Mar. 1944–Jun. 1945
Eighth Army	Robert L. Eichelberger	Sep. 1944–Sep. 1948
Ninth Army	William H. Simpson	May 1944–Oct 6, 1945
Tenth Army	Simon B. Buckner	Jun. 1944–Jun. 1945
	Roy S. Geiger (USMC)	Jun. 1945
	Joseph W. Stilwell	Jun. 1945–Oct. 1945
Fifteenth Army	Leonard T. Gerow	Jan. 1945–Oct. 1945
	George S. Patton	Nov. 1945–Dec. 1945
First Allied Airborne Army	Lewis H. Brereton	Aug. 1944–May 1945
Women's Army Corps	Oveta C. Hobby	May 1942–Jul. 1945
	Westray B. Boyce	Jul. 1945–May 1947

Source: G. and C. Webster Co., *Webster's American Military Biographies,* 526–527.

Americans could replace them, often many times over. The nations that lost the most were countries that had the war brought to their soil. The Americans fought their war on other people's land. Alone among the major participants the United States was not bombed or attacked in any effective way. In sum, the United States fought the Second World War on its own terms.

TABLE 9.31   NAVY COMMANDERS

U.S. Fleet	Husband E. Kimmel	Feb. 1941–Dec. 1941
	Ernest J. King	Dec. 1941–Oct. 1945
Atlantic Fleet	Ernest J. King	Feb. 1941–Jan. 1942
	Royal E. Ingersoll	Jan. 1942–Nov. 1944
	Jonas H. Ingram	Nov. 1944–Apr. 1947
Amphibious Force	H. Kent Hewitt	Apr. 1942–Feb. 1943
	Alan G. Kirk	Feb. 1943–Oct. 1944
Pacific Fleet	Husband E. Kimmel	Feb. 1941–Dec. 1941
	Chester W. Nimitz	Dec. 1941–Nov. 1945
Asiatic Fleet	Thomas C. Hart	Jul. 1939–Jan. 1942
merged into		
American-British-Dutch-Australian Command (ABDACOM)	Thomas C. Hart	Jan. 1942–Feb. 1942
U.S. Naval Forces, Europe	Harold R. Stark	Mar. 1941–Aug. 1945
Pacific Ocean Areas	Chester W. Nimitz	Apr. 1942–Sep. 1945
North Pacific Area	Thomas C. Kinkaid	Jan. 1943–Nov. 1943
Central Pacific Area	Raymond A. Spruance	Aug. 1943–Sep. 1945
subsequently Fifth Fleet		
V Amphibious Force	R. Kelly Turner	Aug. 1943–Apr. 1945
Task Force 58 (38)	Marc A. Mitscher	Jan. 1944–Jul. 1945

(continued)

TABLE 9.31 (continued)

South Pacific Area	Robert L. Ghormley	Apr. 1942–Oct. 1942
	William F. Halsey	Oct. 1942–Jun. 1944
Amphibious Force	R. Kelly Turner	Jul. 1942–Jul. 1943
	Theodore S. Wilkinson	Jul. 1943–Jun. 1944
subsequently Third Fleet	William F. Halsey	Jun. 1944–Sep. 1945
III Amphibious Force	Theodore S. Wilkinson	Jun. 1944–Sep. 1945
Task Force 38 (58)	Marc A. Mitscher	Jan. 1944–Jul. 1945
Southwest Pacific Area	Arthur S. Carpender	Mar. 1943–Nov. 1943
subsequently Seventh Fleet	Thomas C. Kinkaid	Nov. 1943–Sep. 1945
VII Amphibious Force	Daniel E. Barbey	Jan. 1943–Sep. 1945
Eighth Fleet	H. Kent Hewitt	Feb. 1943–Aug. 1945
Tenth Fleet	Ernest J. King	May 1943–Jun. 1945
Construction Battalions (Seabees)	Ben Moreell	Dec. 1941–Sep. 1945
Women Accepted for Volunteer Emergency Service (WAVES)	Mildred H. (McAfee) Horton	Aug. 1942–Feb. 1946
Coast Guard	Russell R. Waesche	Nov. 1941–Dec. 1945
Coast Guard Auxiliary (SPARS)	Dorothy C. Stratton	Nov. 1942–Feb. 1946

Source: G. and C. Webster Co., *Webster's American Military Biographies*, 539.

TABLE 9.32 (ARMY) AIR FORCE COMMANDERS

American Volunteer Group (Flying Tigers)	C. L. Chennault, G. Boyington, R. L. Scott	. . . .
Fifth Air Force	Lewis H. Brereton	Nov. 1941–Jan. 1942
	George H. Brett	Feb. 1942–Aug. 1942
	George C. Kenney	Sep. 1942–Jun. 1944
	Ennis C. Whitehead	Jun. 1944–Dec. 1945
Seventh Air Force	Frederick L. Martin	Nov. 1940–Dec. 1941
	Clarence L. Tinker	Dec. 1941–Jun. 1942
	Howard C. Davidson	Jun. 1942
	Willis H. Hale	Jun. 1942–Apr. 1944
	Robert W. Douglass	Apr. 1944–Jun. 1945
	Thomas D. White	Jun. 1945–Oct. 1946
Eighth Air Force	Asa N. Duncan	Jan. 1942–May 1942
	Carl Spaatz	May 1942–Dec. 1942
	Ira C. Eaker	Dec. 1942–Jan. 1944
	James H. Doolittle	Jan. 1944–May 1945
	William E. Kepner	May 1945–Jun. 1945
	Westside T. Larson	Jun. 1945–Jul. 1945
	James H. Doolittle	Jul. 1945–Sep. 1945
Ninth Air Force	Lewis H. Brereton	Jun. 1942–Aug. 1944
	Hoyt S. Vandenberg	Aug. 1944–May 1945
Tenth Air Force	Lewis H. Brereton	Mar. 1942–Jun. 1942
	Earl L. Naiden	Jun. 1942–Aug. 1942
	Clayton L. Bissell	Aug. 1942–Aug. 1943
	Howard C. Davidson	Aug. 1943–Aug. 1945
	Albert F. Hegenberger	Aug. 1945–Nov. 1945
Eleventh Air Force	Everett S. Davis	Feb. 1942
	Lionel H. Dunlap	Feb. 1942–Mar. 1942
	William O. Butler	Mar. 1942–Sep. 1943
	Davenport Johnson	Sep. 1943–Jul. 1945
	John B. Brooks	Jul. 1945–Nov. 1945
Twelfth Air Force	James H. Doolittle	Sep. 1942–Mar. 1943
	Carl Spaatz	Mar. 1943–Dec. 1943
	John K. Cannon	Dec. 1943–Apr. 1945
	Benjamin W. Chidlaw	Apr. 1945–May 1945
Thirteenth Air Force	Nathan F. Twining	Jan. 1943–Dec. 1943
	Ray L. Owens	Dec. 1943–Jan. 1944
	Hubert R. Harmon	Jan. 1944–Jun. 1944
	George L. Usher	Jun. 1944
	St. Clair Streett	Jun. 1944–Feb. 1945
	Paul B. Wurtsmith	Feb. 1945–Jul. 1946

Fourteenth Air Force	Claire L. Chennault	Mar. 1943–Aug. 1945
	Charles B. Stone	Aug. 1945–Jan. 1946
Fifteenth Air Force	James H. Doolittle	Nov. 1943–Jan. 1944
	Nathan F. Twining	Jan. 1944–May 1945
Twentieth Air Force	Henry H. Arnold	Apr. 1944–Jul. 1945
	Curtis E. LeMay	Jul. 1945–Aug. 1945
	Nathan F. Twining	Aug. 1945–Oct. 1945
WAC director, AAF	Geraldine P. May	Mar. 1943–Oct. 1946
Women's Airforce Service Pilots (WASP)	Jacqueline Cochran	Jul. 1943–Dec. 1944

Source: G. and C. Webster Co., *Webster's American Military Biographies*, 543–544.

TABLE 9.33 MARINE COMMANDERS

Guadalcanal assault	A. Vandegrift, C. B. Cates	Aug. 7, 1942
Makin Island raid	E. F. Carlson	Aug. 1942
Henderson Field, Guadalcanal	L. B. Puller	Oct. 23–25, 1942
Guadalcanal air war	J. J. Foss	Oct.–Nov. 1942
Bougainville	A. Vandegrift, R. S. Geiger	Nov. 1, 1942
Cape Gloucester, New Britain		Dec. 26, 1942
Central Solomons air war	G. Boyington	Aug. 1943–Jan. 1944
Tarawa	H. M. Smith	Nov. 20–23, 1943
Betio	D. M. Shoup	Nov. 20–22, 1943
Makin atoll	H. M. Smith	Nov. 22–24, 1943
Kwajalein	H. M. Smith	Jan. 31–Feb. 7, 1944
Eniwetok	H. M. Smith	Feb. 17–21, 1944
Saipan	H. M. Smith, C. B. Cates	June 15, 1944
Guam assault	R. S. Geiger	July 21, 1944
Tinian assault	H. M. Smith, C. B. Cates	July 24, 1944
Peleliu	R. S. Geiger	Sept. 15, 1944
Iwo Jima	H. M. Smith, C. B. Cates, I. H. Hayes	Feb. 19–March 27, 1945
Okinawa	R. S. Geiger	April 1–July 3, 1945
Women's Reserve (WR)	Ruth C. Streeter	Feb. 1943–Dec. 1945

Source: G. and C. Webster Co., *Webster's American Military Biographies*, 541–542.

TABLE 9.34 U.S. ACTIVE MILITARY PERSONNEL (1939–1945)

(Enlisted and Officers)

	Army	Navy	Marines	Total
1939	189,839	125,202	19,432	334,473
1940	269,023	160,997	28,345	458,365
1941	1,462,315	284,427	54,359	1,801,101
1942	3,075,608	640,570	142,613	3,858,791
1943	6,994,472	1,741,750	308,523	9,044,745
1944	7,994,750	2,981,365	475,604	11,451,719
1945	8,267,958	3,380,817	474,680	12,123,455

Source: Robert Goralski, *World War II Almanac, 1931–1945* (New York, 1981), 422.

PROFILE OF U.S. SERVICEMEN (1941–1945)

- 38.8 percent (6,332,000) of U.S. servicemen and women were volunteers.
- 61.2 percent (11,535,000) were draftees. Of the 17,955,000 men examined for induction, 35.8 percent (6,420,000) were rejected as physically or mentally unfit.
- Average duration of service: 33 months.
- Overseas Service: 73 percent served overseas, with an average of 16.2 months abroad.
- Combat Survivability (out of 1,000): 8.6 were killed in action, 3 died from other causes, and 17.7 received nonmortal combat wounds.
- Noncombat Jobs: 38.8 percent of the enlisted personnel had rear echelon assignments—administrative, technical, support, or manual labor.
- Average Base Pay: Enlisted: $71.33 per month; Officer: $203.50 per month.

Source: Goralski, *World War II Almanac, 1931–1945,* 422.

TABLE 9.35   AMERICAN CASUALTIES BREAKDOWN[a]

Military killed		292,131
Army and Air Force	234,874	
Navy	36,950	
Marines	19,733	
Coast Guard	574	
Military wounded		671,278
Army and Air Force	565,861	
Navy	37,778	
Marines	67,207	
Coast Guard	432	
Merchant Marine dead		5,662
Killed at sea	845	
Died as POWs	37	
Missing and presumed dead	4,780	

[a]Statistics vary in accordance with reporting agency, differences in period being covered, and in what is being counted. This table lists only those killed in action. There were from all causes a total of 405,399 deaths.
Sources: Goralski, *World War II Almanac, 1931–1945,* 428; Ben J. Wattenberg, *The Statistical History of the United States* (New York, 1976), 1140.

TABLE 9.36   CASUALTIES IN PACIFIC ISLAND CAMPAIGN[a]

Some of the most vicious fighting for U.S. troops took place in the various small Pacific islands. Most of these engagements were a part of the long American "island-hopping" offensive against Japan. Though American deaths might seem small, they were considerable in proportion to the number of men committed to these small places. The intensity of battle can best be seen in comparing Japanese deaths with the number of soldiers in the engagements.

Dates	Island	Strength of Japanese Garrison	Japanese Killed	Americans Killed
Aug. 1942–Feb. 1943	Guadalcanal	36,000	25,000	1,592
May 1943	Attu (N. Pacific)	2,650	2,622	549
Nov. 1943	Tarawa	4,600	4,580	1,090
Jun.–Aug. 1944	Saipan	32,000	30,000	3,426
Sep.–Dec. 1944	Peleliu	10,500	10,000	1,500
Oct.–Dec. 1944	Leyte	70,000	65,000	3,593
Feb.–Mar. 1945	Iwo Jima	23,000	21,900	4,554
Apr.–Jun. 1945	Okinawa	80,000	73,000	7,613

[a]Ground fighting only
Source: Chris Cook and John Stevenson, *The Longman Handbook of World History since 1914* (New York, 1991), 108.

The American Arsenal

The key to the American military effort in the Second World War was its vast industrial establishment, which needed only to be unleashed and shifted over to production of military goods. Only in the United States could the factories continue to turn out their goods unhampered by enemy attack. Industry produced weapons

TABLE 9.37   WEAPONS AND MUNITIONS DELIVERED TO U.S. ARMY AND AIR FORCE (1942–1945)

Combat aircraft	129,255
Support aircraft	80,930
240-mm howitzers	315
155-mm field guns	6,389
8-inch field guns	1,193
105-mm howitzers	18,269
90-mm guns	4,853
76-mm guns	14,952
75-mm guns	58,342
3-inch guns	9,325
57-mm guns	16,999
37-mm guns	62,397
Antiaircraft artillery pieces	49,100
Rocket launchers	476,628
Aircraft machine guns	1,575,114
Ground machine guns	945,989
Antiaircraft machine guns	72,777
Rifles	6,174,363
Carbines	6,117,822
Submachine guns	1,790,847
Ammunition	
240-mm and 8-inch	3,126,000
155-mm	27,340,000
105-mm	93,081,000
90-mm	16,386,000
75-mm	75,244,000
37-mm	100,500,000
Mortar	97,174,000
Bombs (all types)	37,701,000
Tanks	
Heavy	2,464
Medium	55,560
Light	26,003
Jeeps	631,873

Source: Goralski, *World War II Almanac, 1931–1945,* 443.

TABLE 9.38   WARSHIP CONSTRUCTION: JAPAN AND THE UNITED STATES

		Battleships	Aircraft Carriers	Cruisers
1937–1940	Japan	2	5	4
	U.S.	2	2	7
1941	Japan	0	3	2
	U.S.	3	9	6
1942	Japan	0	6	3
	U.S.	3	35	10
1943	Japan	0	7	0
	U.S.	1	51	11
1944	Japan	0	5	1
	U.S.	1	44	20
1945	Japan	0	0	0
	U.S.	0	20	11

Source: Cook and Stevenson, *Longman Handbook of World History,* 109.

This 1942 poster urged Americans on the home front to "keep 'em firing" by producing more military goods. (R. E. Olds Museum, Lansing, Michigan)

Air Power

Perhaps the clearest evidence of the industrial supremacy of the United States, and the fact that the Americans were spared enemy attack, came in the production of aircraft. By 1942 the United States had passed all other powers in producing airplanes, and by 1945 the Americans approached being able to equal all other combatants—enemy or ally—combined. American factories turned out vast numbers of varied and ever improving aircraft as the war progressed. In some cases the United States obtained technological superiority—as in the case of long-range bombers—but if American planes were not always the best, the United States could count on overpowering the enemy with sheer numbers.

Air power made it possible to carry the war directly to the enemy nations and people. While the dropping of atomic bombs on two Japanese cities has received the most attention—and in some quarters, the most condemnation—America's so-called conventional bombing of German and Japanese cities was far more deadly and destructive. In conjunction with the RAF—the British air force—the American air war against Germany went on almost continuously between 1942 and 1945. It was so devastating that by 1945 American and British airmen had almost run out of targets. Air raids on Japan started much later, in 1944, and were an exclusive American operation, but the result was no less devastating. In both theaters of war the bombing included both precision assaults on specific military targets and general bombing—saturation bombing—of general population areas. As a consequence most German cities suffered massive damage, and Japan's industrial centers, Tokyo, Nagoya, Kobe, Osaka, and Yokohama, were all but destroyed. The most violent assaults came in the incendiary raids, the firebombing, of Hamburg, Germany, in July 1943, which caused 80,000 casualties; Dresden, Germany, in February 1945, in which at least 100,000 died; and Tokyo on March 9–10, 1945, which killed or injured 125,000. To the Germans and Japanese these raids went beyond military necessity and represented an Allied counterpart to their charges of enemy atrocities of war.

that increased with every year and improved in quality. During its first year in the war, the United States passed all other combatants in military production. By 1943 American factories could turn out more aircraft than Germany and Japan put together. Beginning in 1941, the United States easily outpaced Japan in production of major warships, which were so important in the conflict between those two nations. Most significant was the vast lead that the United States established in aircraft carriers.

TABLE 9.39 AMERICAN TANK PRODUCTION

	Weight (tons)	Length	Speed (mph)	Range (in miles)	Armament	Crew	No. Built
M3 "Lee" and "Grant"	31	18'6"	22	146	1 75-mm 1 37-mm 4 mg	6	4,924
M3A1 "Stuart"	14.3	14'10"	36	60	1 37-mm	4	4,621
M4A3 "Sherman"	37.1	19'3"	30	120	1 76-mm 3 mg	5	49,000
M26 "Pershing"	41.1	28'10"	20	92	1 90-mm 2 mg	5	2,428

Source: Goralski, *World War II Almanac, 1931–1945*, 438.

TABLE 9.40 MILITARY AIRCRAFT PRODUCTION

(Includes All Types)

	1939	1940	1941	1942	1943	1944	1945[a]
Britain	7,940	15,049	20,094	23,672	26,263	26,461	12,070
Soviet Union	10,382	10,565	15,735	25,436	34,900	40,300	20,900
U.S.	2,141	6,086	19,433	47,836	85,898	96,318	46,001
Germany	8,295	10,826	12,401	15,409	24,807	40,593	7,540
Japan	4,467	4,768	5,088	8,861	16,693	28,180	8,263

[a]Through end of war.
Source: Goralski, *World War II Almanac, 1931–1945,* 438.

TABLE 9.41 MILITARY AIRCRAFT LOSSES (1939–1945)

Germany	95,000
U.S.	59,296
Japan	49,485
Britain	33,090
Australia	7,160
Italy	4,000
Canada	2,389
France	2,100
New Zealand	684
India	527
Sweden[a]	272
Denmark	154

[a]Neutral
Note: Russian losses were extremely high, but they were undisclosed by the Soviet government.
Source: Goralski, *World War II Almanac, 1931–1945,* 442.

TABLE 9.43 U.S. FIGHTERS

	Max. Speed (mph)	Service Ceiling (feet)	Max. Range (miles)	Armament	No. Built
F4F Wildcat	318	35,000	900	4 × .50	. . .
F4U Corsair	415	37,000	1,015	6 × .50	12,571
F6F Hellcat	376	37,500	1,090	6 × .50	12,272
P-38L Lightning	414	44,000	460	1 × 20-mm 4 × .50	9,942
P-39D Airacobra	335	29,500	600	1 × .37 2 × .50 2 × .30	4,900
P-40F Kittyhawk	364	30,000	610	6 × .50	13,738
P-47D Thunderbolt	428	40,000	1,000	8 × .50	15,579
P-51D Mustang	437	41,900	2,300	6 × .50	14,490
P-61B Black Widow	366	33,100	3,000	4 × .50	976
P-63A Kingcobra	410	43,000	2,200	1 × .37 3 × .50	332

Source: Goralski, *World War II Almanac, 1931–1945,* 440.

TABLE 9.42 LEADING AMERICAN COMBAT ACES[a]

U.S. Army Air Force	
Major Richard I. Bong	(P)40
Major Thomas B. McGuire	(P)38
Colonel Frances S. Gabreski	(E)31
Lieutenant Colonel Robert S. Johnson	(E)28
Colonel Charles H. MacDonald	(P)27
Major George E. Preddy	(E)26
Colonel John C. Meyer	(E)24
Captain Ray S. Whetmore	(E)22
Colonel David C. Schilling	(E)22
Lieutenant Colonel Gerald R. Johnson	(P)22
Major Neel E. Kearby	(P)22
Lieutenant Colonel Jay T. Robbins	(P)22

U.S. Navy	
Captain David McCampbell	34
Lieutenant Cecil E. Harris	24
Commander Eugeane A. Valencia	23

U.S. Marine Corps	
Lieutenant Colonel Gregory Boyington (including six as a Flying Tiger)	28
Major Joseph J. Foss	26
First Lieutenant Robert M. Hanson	25
Major Kenneth A. Walsh	21
Captain Donald M. Aldrich	20

[a]Impressive as these numbers appeared, they paled in comparison with German pilots, who flew many more missions. Erich Hartmann, for example, had 352 kills. Ten Germans had more than 200. Twenty-five others had at least 150.
Note: (P)*Pacific*   (E)*Europe*
Source: Goralski, *World War II Almanac, 1931–1945,* 423.

TABLE 9.44   U.S. BOMBERS

	Max. Speed (mph)	Service Ceiling (feet)	Max. Range (miles)	Bomb Load (pounds)	Crew	No. Built
B-17E (Boeing)	317	35,000	1,100	6,000	6/10	12,731
B-24J (Consolidated Vultee)	290	28,000	2,200	5,000	10	19,203
B-25J (North American)	275	24,000	1,500	4,000	4/6	9,816
B-26E (Martin)	310	23,000	1,150	3,000	5/7	5,157
B-29 (Boeing)	357	36,000	3,250	10,000	10/14	3,000

Source: Goralski, *World War II Almanac, 1931–1945*, 441.

TABLE 9.45   U.S. ATTACK AIRCRAFT

	Max. Speed (mph)	Service Ceiling (feet)	Max. Range (miles)	Bomb Load (pounds)	Crew	No. Built
A-20 Boston, Havoc (Douglas)	351	25,000	1,000	4,000	2/3	7,385
A-26 Invader (Douglas)	355	22,100	1,400	8,000	3	1,355
A-29 Hudson (Lockheed)	261	24,500	2,160	750	4	2,584
A-30 Baltimore (Martin)	320	24,000	1,060	1,000	4	1,975
SBD Dauntless (Douglas)	252	24,300	456	1,000	2	5,936
SB2C Helldiver (Curtiss)	281	24,700	1,100	1,000	2	7,200
TBM Avenger (Grumman)	267	30,100	2,530	2,000	3	9,839

Source: Goralski, *World War II Almanac, 1931–1945*, 442.

TABLE 9.46   BRITISH AND U.S. AIRCRAFT DELIVERIES TO RUSSIA

Hurricanes	2,000
Spitfires	
MK VB	143
LF 9s	1,186
P-39 Airacobras	4,746[a]
P-63 Kingcobras	2,400[a]
P-47 Thunderbolts	195[a]
B-25 Mitchells	862[a]
C-47s	700[a]
All others	6,633
Total	18,865
Lost in transit	638

[a]Designates American aircraft.
Source: Goralski, *World War II Almanac, 1931–1945*, 442.

TABLE 9.47   AMERICAN BOMBING OF JAPANESE CITIES

Japanese killed in air raids on home islands	668,000
Private homes destroyed	2,251,928
Private homes damaged	1,270,000
Heaviest-hit cities:[a]	
Tokyo homes destroyed or severely damaged	709,906
Osaka homes destroyed	328,237
Nagoya homes destroyed	136,557
Kobe homes destroyed	131,528

[a]To these names one might add the two cities struck by atomic bombs: Hiroshima, Aug. 6, 1945—70,000 buildings damaged or destroyed, 140,000 dead by Dec. 1945; and Nagasaki, Aug. 9, 1945—70,000 dead by Dec., 140,000 in 5 years.
Sources: Goralski, *World War II Almanac, 1931–1945*, 427; Polmar and Allen, *World War II*, 385, 571.

American Naval Losses

Losses of ships were major events, and sinkings of large vessels often had familiar stories describing the circumstances of their destruction—the battleships at Pearl Harbor, the *Lexington* at Coral Sea and the *Yorktown* at Midway, the cruiser *Indianapolis* after delivering the atomic bomb to Tinian, and the sinking of the cruiser *Juneau*, which carried the five Sullivan brothers to their deaths. The list of vessels that follows reveals that naval warfare largely took place in the Asian theater of war. None of the ships named below went down in European waters. The list also reveals the deadly nature of the long Solomons campaign, which centered on the island of Guadalcanal, early in the war. American wartime losses were substantial, but losses by the enemy were proportionately much worse. The Japanese lost eleven battleships, fifteen aircraft carriers and five escort carriers, and thirty-six cruisers. By 1945 virtually the entire Japanese navy was gone.

TABLE 9.48   AMERICAN NAVAL SHIP LOSSES

Battleships			
	Location	Agent	Date
Arizona	Pearl Harbor	Aircraft	Dec. 7, 1941
Oklahoma	Pearl Harbor	Aircraft	Dec. 7, 1941
Aircraft Carriers			
Hornet	Off Solomon Islands	Aircraft	Oct. 26, 1942
Lexington	Coral Sea	Aircraft	May 8, 1942
Princeton	Off Philippines	Aircraft	Oct. 24, 1944
Wasp	Off Espiritu Santo	Submarine	Sep. 15, 1942
Yorktown	Off Midway	Aircraft	Jun. 7, 1942

Escort Carriers

Bismarck Sea	Off Iwo Jima	Kamikaze	Feb. 21, 1945
Block Island	Off Madeira Islands	Submarine	May 29, 1944
Gambier Bay	Off Timor Island	Surface ships	Oct. 25, 1944
Liscome Bay	Off Tarawa	Submarine	Nov. 24, 1943
Ommaney Bay	Off Panay, Philippines	Kamikaze	Jan. 4, 1945
St. Lo	Off Leyte, Philippines	Kamikaze	Oct. 25, 1944

Heavy Cruisers

Astoria	Off Savo, Solomons	Surface ships	Aug. 9, 1942
Chicago	Off Guadalcanal	Surface ships	Jan. 30, 1943
Houston	Off Java	Surface ships	Mar. 1, 1942
Indianapolis	Off Leyte, Philippines	Submarine	Jul. 29, 1945
Northampton	Off Savo, Solomons	Surface ships	Nov. 30, 1942
Quincy	Off Savo, Solomons	Surface ships	Aug. 9, 1942
Vincennes	Off Savo, Solomons	Surface ships	Aug. 9, 1942

Light Cruisers

Atlanta	Off Guadalcanal	Surface ships	Nov. 13, 1942
Helena	Kula Gulf, Solomons	Surface ships	July 6, 1943
Juneau	Off Guadalcanal	Surface ships	Nov. 13, 1942

Other U.S. Naval Ship Losses

Destroyers	71	Destroyer escorts	11
Submarines	52	Minelayers	3
Mine sweepers	24	Submarine chasers	18
Gunboats	12	Coast Guard vessels	15
Seaplane tenders	3	Motor torpedo boats	68
Landing ships–tank (LST)	40	Landing ships–medium (LSM)	9
Landing craft–tank (LCT)	67		
Landing craft–support (LCS)	6	Landing craft–infantry (LCI)	22
Tankers	27	Tugs	10
Miscellaneous district craft	179	District patrol craft (YP)	36

Source: Goralski, *World War II Almanac, 1931–1945,* 449–454.

Poem about a Boy Who Died

It was a scene repeated in thousands of cities, towns, and villages: the telegram from the government, the mourning, a gold star replacing a blue one in the window of the family home, some form of community recognition. Another young man in his early twenties, perhaps, or even still in his teens had paid the price of war. The army and navy called them men, but to the folks back home they all were boys. Louise McNeill described how it went in her area of West Virginia, and then—perhaps to ease the pain—she added a touch of humor.

Ballad of Joe Bittner

Joe Bittner, he was a mountain lad,
And he went to the second war—
Joined the navy for good or bad
And sailed where the bloodbills are—

Solomon Islands—the place he died
When his burning ship sucked deep—
And the letter came, and his mother cried,
And he slept where the war whales sleep.

We held his wake at his mother's house—
In the churchyard held his prayer—
And we wrote his name on the golden board
That sits in our courthouse square.

It was fourteen years, on a summer day,
When I looked at my yard fence stile,
And I saw the ghost of a sailor's sway
And Joe Bittner's cocky smile.

"Joe Bittner! Joe Bittner! Where have you been?
When your ship went down that night—
And we thought—we heard"—Then he grinned at me:
"Well—I never was much to write."

Source: Louise McNeill, *Hill Daughter: New and Selected Poems* (Pittsburgh, 1991), 33; published with permission of the West Virginia University Press.

CHAPTER 10 States

This chapter contains basic information about the forty-eight states in the nation before 1945. The material is confined to the states as they existed at that time. If emblems—state tree, flower, etc.—do not appear for some states, it is because these states had not officially adopted such emblems by 1945. Seemingly low population statistics for many states in 1945 can be explained largely in the fact that more than twelve million servicemen (and several thousand servicewomen) were away from their homes at that time, many of them serving outside the United States. Sources are: Bureau of the Census, *Historical Statistics of the United States, 1789 to 1945* (Washington, D.C., 1949); Bureau of the Census, *Historical Abstract of the United States, 1947* (Washington, D.C., 1947) and *1948* (Washington, D.C., 1948); Council of State Governments, *Book of the States, 1945–1946* (Chicago, 1945) and *1948–1949* (Chicago, 1948); The Encyclopedia Americana, *Americana Annual, 1947* (New York, 1947); The Encyclopaedia Britannica, *Yearbooks, 1935–47* (Chicago, 1935–47); Joseph N. Kane, et al., *Facts About the States* (New York, 1989); *World Book Encyclopedia*, (1973 ed.), (New York, 1973).

Alabama

Various American Indian groups, including the Alabama and the Creek, inhabited the area that later became Alabama. Spanish and French explorers visited the area. Britain acquired claim over the territory from France in 1763. The United States took control in the Treaty of 1783. Native Americans of the area were gradually pushed out—by treaty and by force. The Alabama Territory was organized in 1817. Alabama became the twenty-second state on December 22, 1819. Its capital is Montgomery. The state's name came from Choctaw, meaning "thicket cleaners" or "vegetation gatherers." Nickname: the Cotton State. Motto: "We Dare Defend Our Rights." Flower: goldenrod. Bird: yellowhammer. Song: "Alabama."

Land

Area: 52,078 sq. mi. (28th in area). Rivers: Alabama, Chattahoochee, Mobile, Tennessee, Tensaw, Tombigbee. Mountains: Cumberland, Lookout, Racoon, Sand. Cities (with 1940 pop.): Birmingham (267,583), Mobile (78,720), Montgomery (78,084), Gadsden (36,975), Tuscaloosa (27,493).

People

Population, 1910: 2,138,093; 1945 (est.): 2,812,301 (17th in population). Breakdown, 1940: 1,849,097 white, 983,090 black, 574 other, 30.2% urban, 69.8% rural. Famous natives: Tallulah Bankhead (actress), Hugo Black (jurist), W. C. Handy (songwriter), Jesse Owens (athlete), Leroy "Satchell" Paige (baseball player).

Economics

State personal income, 1940: $801 million; per capita, $282. Leading crops: corn, oats, cotton, potatoes, peanuts. Manufactured goods: cotton textiles, iron and steel, electricity. Minerals: pig iron, coal, coke, iron ore, cement, stone.

Major Developments, 1914–1945

Alabama was the leading industrial state of the South. Birmingham was the "Pittsburgh of the South," and after 1917 Mobile became a shipbuilding center. Even so, the state remained essentially rural and agricultural and generally poor. Cotton was devastated by the boll weevil in the 1920s, and the entire state suffered from the depression in the 1930s. Floods devastated land along the Alabama and Tombigbee Rivers in 1929. The long and celebrated case of the "Scottsboro Boys," involving race relations in the South, started in 1931. The government approved the Tennessee Valley Authority in 1933 and started the project with the great power plant at Muscle Shoals. The army's Redstone Arsenal was established at Huntsville in 1941, and many other war-related enterprises followed.

Arizona

The home of numerous American Indian tribes, notably Apache, Hopi, and Navajo, Arizona was a site of conflict between rival European settlers and later between the United States and Mexico. The United States took most of the area after the war with Mexico in 1848, and the rest was acquired in the Gadsden Purchase of 1853. Railroads brought settlers and conflict with the Native Americans until 1886. Settlement was slowed because of the extreme heat and dryness. After a quarrel with the national government over the recall of judges, Arizona joined the Union on February 14, 1912, the last of the original forty-eight states. Its capital is Phoenix. The origin of the state's name is from an Indian word, probably Pima or Papago, meaning "little spring." Nickname: the Grand Canyon State. Motto: *Ditat Deus* (God Enriches). Flower: saguaro cactus. Bird: cactus wren. Song: "Arizona."

Land

Area: 113,956 sq. mi. (5th in area). Rivers: Colorado, Gila, Little Colorado, Salt, Zumi. Mountains: Black, Gila, Hualpai, Mohawk, San Francisco. Cities (with 1940 pop.): Phoenix (65,414), Tucson (36,818), Douglas (8,623), Mesa (7,224), Globe (6,141).

People

Population, 1910: 204,353; 1945 (est.): 630,298 (37th in population). Breakdown, 1940: 426,792 white, 14,993 black, 57,476 other (55,076 American Indian), 34.4% urban, 65.6% rural. Famous natives: Geronimo (Indian leader), Sharlot M. Hall (author, poet), William C. Barnes (soldier, geographer), George P. Hunt (politician).

Economics

State personal income, 1940: $248 million; per capita, $497. Leading agricultural produce: citrus fruits, cotton, lettuce, cattle. Manufacturing (very little): food, textiles, lumber, metals. Minerals: copper (the national leader), gold, silver.

Major Developments, 1914–1945

A miner's strike at Brisbee in 1917 was crushed when more than 1,200 people were placed in boxcars and deposited in the desert. The nation's newest state grew as the population pushed west and as irrigation facilities increased. When people took to the road in the 1920s, Arizona was a feature attraction, with its large Indian population and such magnificent scenery as the Painted Desert, Petrified Forest, and especially the Grand Canyon. The Grand Canyon National Park was established in 1919. The Great Depression sent

The United States with State Capitals, 1914–45

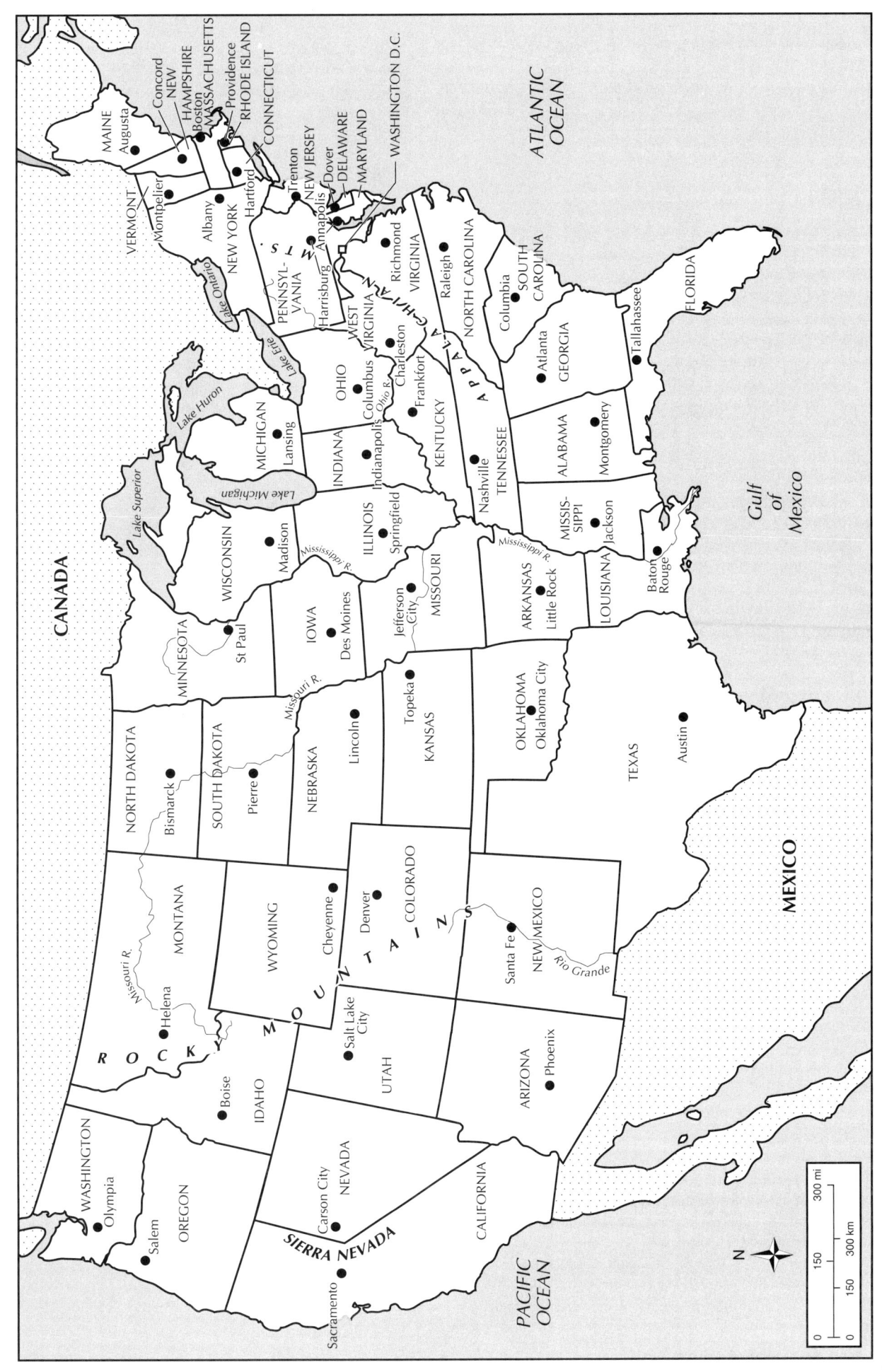

With admission of Arizona into the Union in 1912, the map of the 48 continental states (excluding of course Alaska) became complete and permanent. There were no changes in states or capitals during 1914–45.

more people into the state, despite the fact that many copper mines had to close in the 1930s. Parker Dam was completed in 1934 and massive Boulder (Hoover) Dam in 1935, both on the Colorado River. The start of the Second World War did much to revive activity in the copper mines. Arizona's flat land and sunny skies attracted many airfields during the war.

Arkansas

The land that is now Arkansas was originally inhabited by the Caddo and Quapaw Indians. French explorers crossed the territory west of the Mississippi River. The area was settled by the French as part of the Louisiana Territory, which the Spanish held from 1763 to 1800. France sold it to the United States in 1803. Arkansas became part of the Louisiana Territory, the Missouri Territory, and then the Arkansas Territory. Arkansas became the twenty-fifth state on June 15, 1836. Its capital is Little Rock. The state's name is from the French name for the Quapaw tribe. Nickname: the Wonder State. Motto: *Regnat Populus* (The People Rule). Flower: flower blossom. Bird: mockingbird. Tree: pine. Song: "Arkansas."

Land

Area: 53,335 sq. mi. (25th in area). Rivers: Arkansas, Mississippi, Ouachita, Red, White. Mountains: Ozark, Ouchita. Cities (with 1940 pop.): Little Rock (88,039), Fort Smith (36,584), Hot Springs (21,370), Pine Bluff (21,290), North Little Rock (21,137).

People

Population, 1910: 1,574,449; 1945 (est.): 1,779,817 (29th in population). Breakdown, 1940: 1,466,084 white, 482,578 black, 725 other, 22.2% urban, 77.8% rural. Famous natives: Hattie Caraway (politician), Alan Ladd (actor), Dick Powell (actor), Douglas MacArthur (general), Maya Angelou (author).

Economics

State personal income, 1940: $501 million; per capita, $256. Agricultural produce: cotton, corn, rice. Industry: wood products, petroleum refining, baked goods, newspaper printing. Minerals: petroleum, coal, bauxite, manganese, gas.

Major Developments, 1914–1945

Oil was discovered near El Dorado in 1921. The first hydroelectric plant was constructed on the Arkansas River at Halvern in 1924. In 1927 the Mississippi River flooded 20% of the state. In 1928 the state passed a law forbidding the teaching of evolution in public schools. In 1929 a state income tax was adopted. Hattie W. Caraway became in 1932 the first woman elected to the United States Senate (she had been appointed to the Senate in 1931). World War II sparked the growth of mining, especially of bauxite, as well as agriculture and some industry.

California

In 1542, the Spanish arrived in this land, which was then home to more than forty different Indian tribes. The Spanish set up many missions. California became part of an independent Mexico in 1821. American settlers moved in, especially after the discovery of gold between 1842 and 1848. California was part of the Mexican cession to the United States in 1848. The state entered the Union on September 9, 1850, as part of the pre–Civil War Compromise of 1850. The capital is Sacramento. The state's name came from the book *Las sergas de esplandian* by Garcia Ordonez de Montalvo. Nickname: the Golden State. Motto: *Eureka* (I Have Found It). Flower: golden poppy. Bird: California Valley quail. Tree: California redwood. Song: "I Love You, California."

Land

Area: 158,693 sq. mi. (2d in area). Rivers: American, Colorado, Eel, Klamath, Russian, Sacramento, Salinas, San Joaquin. Mountains: Coast Ranges, Klamath, Sierra Nevada, Lassen Peak. Cities (with 1940 pop.): Los Angeles (1,504,277), San Francisco (634,536), Oakland (302,163), San Diego (203,341), Long Beach (164,271).

People

Population, 1910: 2,377,549; 1945 (est.): 8,822,688 (3d in population). Breakdown, 1940: 6,596,763 white, 124,306 black, 186,318 other (93,717 Japanese, 18,675 American Indian), 71% urban, 29% rural. Famous natives: Walt Disney (film producer), William Randolph Hearst (publisher), Shirley Temple (actress), Earl Warren (politician), Joe DiMaggio (baseball player).

Economics

State personal income, 1940: $5,839,000,000; per capita, $840. The state was rich in many areas of economic activity. Agricultural produce: oranges, grapes, cotton, lettuce, beans, tomatoes. Industry: aircraft, shipbuilding, food products, iron and steel goods, chemical products. Minerals: petroleum, gold, quicksilver, tungsten, silver, copper.

Major Developments, 1914–1945

Lassen Peak erupted in 1914–17. Shipyards and factories grew up after 1917. Irrigation made California a major agricultural state. Completion of Hoover Dam on the Colorado River in 1935 reduced floods, supplied electric power, and increased irrigation. The magnificent Golden Gate Bridge was completed in 1937. The glamour of the film center in Hollywood, pleasant climate, and economic opportunity made California the fastest-growing state. Millions moved there during the depression and World War II. The United Nations Charter was approved in San Francisco in 1945.

Colorado

The home of the Ute and Arapaho, Colorado was part of the huge Louisiana area that was exchanged between colonial powers and then sold by France to the United States in 1803. Among the people exploring the territory were Zebulon Pike, Kit Carson, and John C. Fremont. Gold was discovered at Pikes Peak in 1858. The arrival of settlers and the railroad produced many conflicts with Native Americans in the 1860s and 1870s. Colorado became the thirty-eighth state on August 1, 1876. Its capital is Denver. The state's name originated with a Spanish word meaning "red" or "ruddy." Nickname: the Centennial State. Motto: *Nil Sine Numine* (Nothing without the Diety). Flower: Rocky Mountain columbine. Bird: lark bunting. Tree: Colorado blue spruce. Song: "Where the Columbines Grow."

Land

Area: 103,948 sq. mi. (7th in area). Rivers: Arkansas, Colorado, Green, Platte, Rio Grande. Mountains: Front Range, Laramie, Sangre de Cristo, San Juan, Sawatch Range. Cities (with 1940 pop.): Denver (122,412), Pueblo (42,162), Colorado Springs (36,789), Greeley (15,995), Trinidad (13,223).

People

Population, 1910: 799,024; 1945 (est.): 1,120,595 (34th in population). Breakdown, 1940: 1,106,502 white, 12,126 black, 4,618 other, 56.6% urban, 47.4% rural. Famous natives: Douglas Fairbanks (actor), Lowell Thomas (newsman), Jack Dempsey (boxer), Paul Whiteman (musician), Molly Brown (social leader).

Economics

State personal income, 1940: $617 million; per capita, $546. Agricultural produce: wheat, corn, hay, potatoes, livestock. Industry: meatpacking, baked goods, butter, publishing material. Minerals: gold, silver, lead, zinc, copper, coal, oil.

Major Developments, 1914–1945

A miners' strike at Ludlow in 1914 led to the death of twenty miners and a virtual civil war for ten days. Rocky Mountain National Park was established in 1915. Many tourists visited the state in the 1920s. In 1927 the Moffat Railroad Tunnel through the mountains was completed. In the 1920s oil became the most valuable mineral. The depression of the 1930s was worsened by huge dust storms between 1932 and 1937. Many air bases and army camps were established during the Second World War. By 1943 an ordnance plant in Denver employed 20,000 making small-arms ammunition.

Connecticut

Originally home to Pequot and Mohegan Indians, the area was claimed by the Dutch and settled by the English in 1633. Mostly made up of dissenters from Massachusetts Bay, many of them led by Thomas Hooker, Connecticut became a separate colony in 1636 when three towns joined together. Connecticut was a leading state in the Revolution, with a history of production of firearms. On January 9, 1788, it became the fifth state to ratify the new Constitution. Its capital is Hartford. The origin of the state's name is a Mohican word meaning "beside the long tidal river." Nickname: the Constitution State. Motto: *Qui Transtulit Sustinet* (He Who Transplanted Continues to Sustain). Flower: mountain laurel. Bird: robin.

Land

Area: 5,004 sq. mi. (46th in area). Rivers: Connecticut, Housatonic, Mianus, Naugatuck, Thames. Cities (with 1940 pop.): Hartford (166,267), Bridgeport (147,121), New Haven (160,605), Waterbury (99,314), New Britain (68,685).

People

Population, 1910: 1,114,756; 1945 (est.): 1,786,300 (28th in population). Breakdown, 1940: 1,675,407 white, 32,992 black, 843 other, 67.8% urban, 32.2% rural. Famous natives: J. P. Morgan (financier), Katharine Hepburn (actress), Charles Goodyear (manufacturer), Wilbur Cross (politician), Raymond E. Baldwin (politician).

Economics

State personal income, 1940: $1,566,000,000; per capita, $917. Agricultural produce: dairy goods, poultry, tobacco. Industry: firearms and ammunition, sewing machines, cutlery, typewriters, machinery, ships.

Major Developments, 1914–1945

Groton became a submarine base in 1917, adding to the Coast Guard Academy already established at New London. The First World War boosted the arms industry. A huge blizzard struck the state in 1934. The depression was devastating, and this normally Republican state voted Democratic in the 1930s. Wilbur Cross was elected governor four times. The Second World War produced an economic boom in the specialized manufacturing industries. Most conspicuous was the Electric Boat Company at Groton, which produced submarines.

Delaware

Home to the Delaware Indian tribe, the territory was settled by the Dutch and Swedes in the 1630s. It was captured from the Dutch by the British in 1664. Delaware was part of the territory granted to William Penn in 1682. It broke off and became a separate colony. Delaware was the first state to ratify the Constitution (on December 7, 1787) and thus the first state in the Union. Its capital is Dover. The origin of the state's name is Sir Thomas West—Lord De La Warr. Nickname: the Diamond State. Motto: Liberty and Independence. Flower: peach blossom. Bird: blue hen chicken. Song: "Our Delaware."

Land

Area: 2,370 sq. mi. (47th in area). Rivers: Chesapeake and Delaware Canal, Delaware, Nanticoke. Cities (with 1940 pop.): Wilmington (112,504), Dover (5,517), Newark (4,502), New Castle (4,414).

People

Population, 1910: 202,332; 1945 (est.): 286,832 (46th in population). Breakdown, 1940: 230,538 white, 35,876 black, 100 other, 52.3% urban, 47.7% rural. Famous natives: Du Pont family (manufacturing), Edward Squibb (physician), Walter W. Bacon (politician).

Economics

State personal income, 1940: $270 million; per capita, $1,004. Agricultural produce: fruits and vegetables. Industry: ammunition and explosives, chemicals, machine tools, vulcanized fiber, leather and special items. Fishing was important in the bay area.

Major Developments, 1914–1945

Throughout the period the Du Pont family was powerful in politics and economics. During 1916–18 the Du Pont firm employed more than 100,000, making explosives for the Allies. In the 1920s Delaware created a state board of welfare and a highway department, and it utilized an income tax. The Du Pont family donated money to enhance the school system. In 1941 the state repealed blue laws that forbade many practices on Sunday. The arms factories again operated at rapid pace during the Second World War, with Wilmington the largest wartime producer.

Florida

The area that later became Florida was inhabited by several American Indian groups, including the Apalachee, Timucua, Ais, and Calusa. Ponce de Leon explored the area and claimed it for Spain. Florida was as a sparsely settled, little-developed Spanish colony for more than 200 years; most of its inhabitants were Seminole Indians. Spain ceded Florida to the United States in 1819, and the Native Americans were mostly dealt with during the Seminole Wars of 1835–42. Florida entered the Union on March 3, 1845, as the twenty-seventh state and then departed—or tried to—in 1861. Its capital is Tallahassee. The state's name originated with a Spanish word meaning "feast of flowers." Nickname: the Peninsula State. Motto: In God We Trust. Flower: orange blossom. Bird: mockingbird. Song: "The Suwannee River."

Land

Area: 58,666 sq. mi. (21st in area). Rivers: Apalachicola, Caloosahatchee, Indian, Kissimmee, Perdido, St. Johns, St. Marys, Suwannee, Withlacoochee. Cities (with 1940 pop.): Jacksonville (173,065), Miami (172,172), Tampa (108,391), St. Petersburg (60,812), Pensacola (37,448).

People

Population, 1910: 752,619; 1945 (est.): 2,385,917 (21st in population). Breakdown, 1940: 1,381,986 white, 514,198 black, 1,230 other, 55.1% urban, 44.9% rural. Famous natives: Mary M. Bethune (reformer), Colin Kelly (pilot), Joseph Stilwell (general), A. Philip Randolph (black activist).

Economics

State personal income, 1940: $982, million; per capita, $513. Agricultural produce: corn, tobacco, fruit, potatoes, sugar cane, livestock. Industry: lumber, naval stores, cigars. Minerals: phosphate rock, stone, sand and gravel, lime. Tourism also was a growing industry.

Major Developments, 1914–1945

People and speculators poured into the state during the great land boom of 1920–25. The bubble burst in 1926 when a separate depression hit the state. A state law of 1925 required reading of the Bible in public schools. Deadly hurricanes hit Florida in 1926, 1928, 1935, and 1941. An assassination attempt on President-elect Franklin D. Roosevelt in Miami in February 1933 killed instead Mayor Anton Cermak of Chicago. During the Second World War many factories and land and naval bases were established in the state.

Georgia

Home to the Creek, Hitchiti, Yamasee, Guale Indians, and others, the area was explored by Hernando De Soto, and the Spanish won out over French claims in the 1560s. The English also claimed the land, but not until the 1730s did they establish a colony of Georgia—to be used as a haven for debtors. Georgia became the fourth state to enter the Union, on January 2, 1788. Its capital is Atlanta. The state's name originated as an honor to King George II of England. Nickname: the Cracker State. Motto: Wisdom, Justice, and Moderation. Flower: Cherokee rose. Bird: brown thrasher. Tree: live oak. Song: "Georgia."

Land

Area: 59,265 sq. mi. (20th in area). Rivers: Altamaha, Apalachicola, Chattachoochee, Flint, Ocmulgee, Oconee, Savannah, Suwannee. Mountains: Blue Ridge. Cities (with 1940 pop.): Atlanta (302,288), Savannah (95,996), Augusta (65,919), Macon (57,865), Columbus (53,280).

People

Population, 1910: 2,609,121; 1945 (est.): 3,191,766 (13th in population). Breakdown, 1940: 2,038,278 white, 1,084,927 black, 518 other, 34.4% urban, 65.6% rural. Famous natives: Erskine Caldwell (author), Ty Cobb (baseball player), W. E. B. Du Bois (reformer), Margaret Mitchell (author).

Economics

State personal income, 1940: $1,060,000,000; per capita, $340. Agricultural produce: cotton, corn, peanuts, tobacco, hay, vegetables, peaches. Industry: cotton goods, paper products, fertilizer, meatpack-

ing. Minerals: stone, clay, cement.

Major Developments, 1914–1945

The Leo Frank case of 1913–15 ended with the lynching of a Jewish man convicted of murder. The Ku Klux Klan was revived near Atlanta in 1915. In 1922 Rebecca L. Felton became the first woman United States senator (she was appointed to the office). In the 1920s the boll weevil devastated the cotton crop. Atlanta, which became a major transportation and communication center of the South, hosted the premier of Gone With the Wind in 1939. In 1943 Georgia became the first state to allow eighteen-year-olds to vote. In April 1945 President Franklin D. Roosevelt died at Warm Springs.

Idaho

The Nez Percé, Kalispel, Coeur d'Alene, and Bannoch lived in what later became Idaho. Lewis and Clark explored this territory of the Northwest in 1805. American control of the area was confirmed in the Oregon Treaty with Britain in 1846. A gold rush in 1860 was followed by a series of wars with local Native Americans, notably the Nez Percé. On July 3, 1890, Idaho became the forty-third state; it was known as a so-called silver state. Its capital is Boise. The state's name came from the Shoshone word meaning "sunup." Nickname: the Gem State. Motto: Esto Perpetua (Mayest Thou Endure Forever). Flower: syringa. Bird: mountain bluebird. Tree: white pine. Song: "Here We Have Idaho."

Land

Area: 83,888 sq. mi. (12th in area). Rivers: Bear, Clearwater, Payette, Salmon, Snake. Mountains: Bitterroot, Centennial, Wasatch Range. Cities (with 1940 pop.): Boise (26,130), Pocatello (18,133), Idaho Falls (15,024), Nampa (12,149), Twin Falls (11,851).

People

Population, 1910: 325,594; 1945 (est.): 500,109 (42d in population). Breakdown, 1940: 519,595 white, 595 black, 4,986 other (3,638 American Indian), 33.7% urban, 66.3% rural. Famous natives: Ezra Pound (poet), Lana Turner (actress), William E. Borah (politician).

Economics

State personal income, 1940: $242 million; per capita, $464. Agricultural produce: wheat, corn, oats, sugar beets, potatoes. Industry: aircraft, food products. Minerals: silver, lead, zinc, gold, copper.

Major Developments, 1914–1945

Moses Alexander in 1914 became the first Jewish governor of a state. In 1915 the Arrorock Dam on the Boise River became the highest dam in the world. Farmers prospered during World War I and then overexpanded, leading to a postwar depression. The American Falls Dam on the Snake River was finished in 1927. In 1938 Sun Valley was created as a ski resort by officials of the Union Pacific Railroad. A paved highway connected the northern and southern parts of the state in 1938. Idaho supplied foodstuffs, airplanes, and other goods during the Second World War.

Illinois

Several Indian tribes, including the Peoria, Kaskaskia, and Illinois, lived here. French explorers Jacques Marquette and Louis Joliet visited the area and claimed it for France. The French surrendered their claim to Britain in 1763. After American independence, Virginia relinquished claim to the land in 1784, and Illinois became part of the Northwest Territory. On December 3, 1818, Illinois became the twenty-first state. Its capital is Springfield. The state's name came from the tribal name, meaning "men." Nickname: the Prairie State. Motto: State Sovereignty—National Union. Flower: native violet. Bird: cardinal. Tree: oak. Song: "Illinois."

Land

Area: 56,400 sq. mi. (23d in area). Rivers: Fox, Illinois, Kankakee, Kaskaskia, Mississippi, Ohio, Rock, Vermillion, Wabash. Cities (with 1940 pop.): Chicago (3,396,808), Peoria (105,087), Rockford (84,637), East St. Louis (75,609), Springfield (75,503).

People

Population, 1910: 5,638,591; 1945 (est.): 7,721,099 (4th in population). Breakdown, 1940: 7,504,202 white, 387,446 black, 5,593 other, 73.6% urban, 26.4% rural. Famous natives: Jane Addams (reformer), Benny Goodman (musician), Archibald MacLeish (poet), Gloria Swanson (actress), Clarence Darrow (lawyer), Carl Sandburg (poet), Ernest Hemingway (author).

Economics

State personal income, 1940: $5,964,000,000; per capita, $754. The state stood large in all economic areas. Agricultural produce: soybeans (national leader), corn, wheat, livestock. Industry: machinery of many kinds, railroad cars, furniture, iron and steel, chemicals, meatpacking. Minerals: oil, coal, sand and gravel (2d in nation).

Major Developments, 1914–1945

Illinois supplied a complete division, the 33d, Prairie Division, in the First World War. The Naval Training Center at Great Lakes and Ft. Sheridan operated during the war. Race riots in East St. Louis (1917) and Chicago (1919) killed nearly 140. Chicago and suburban Cicero became centers of crime and violence during the 1920s. The Illinois Waterway in 1933 linked Lake Michigan with the Mississippi River system. An oil boom in the late 1930s made Illinois the nation's fourth largest producer of oil. The first controlled atomic chain reaction took place in Chicago in 1942. Illinois developed thousands of war-related establishments during the Second World War.

Indiana

The home of ancient Mound Builder civilizations and later other American Indian tribes, including the Miami and the Kickapoo, Indiana was explored and in a few places settled by French colonists. Britain received control of the land after the French and Indian War. The area became part of the Northwest Territory in 1887. After numerous battles between whites and Indians, Indiana became a state on December 11, 1816, the nineteenth state to enter the Union. Its capital is Indianapolis. The state's name came from a Latinized form of the word *Indian*. Nickname: the Hoosier State. Motto: The Crossroads of America. Flower: zinnia. Bird: cardinal. Tree: tulip tree. Song: "On the Banks of the Wabash Far Away."

Land

Area: 36,555 sq. mi. (37th in area). Rivers: Kankakee, Ohio, Tippecanoe, Wabash, White, Whitewater. Cities (with 1940 pop.): Indianapolis (386,972), Ft. Wayne (118,410), Gary (111,719), South Bend (101,268), Evansville (97,062).

People

Population, 1910: 2,700,876; 1945 (est.): 3,437,745 (12th in pop-

ulation). Breakdown, 1940: 3,305,323 white, 121,916 black, 557 other, 51.5% urban, 48.9% rural. Famous natives: Cole Porter (songwriter), Ernie Pyle (reporter), Wendell Willkie (politician), Theodore Dreiser (author), John Dillinger (criminal).

Economics

State personal income, 1940: $1,898,000,000; per capita, $553. Agricultural produce: soybeans, corn, wheat, oats, tomatoes, tobacco. Industry: the northern part of the state was a major industrial center—iron and steel, farm machinery, automobiles, airplane parts. Minerals: coal, clay, sand and gravel, limestone, petroleum.

Major Developments, 1914–1945

The Gary area became a major center of steel production in the early twentieth century. By 1923 there were 300,000 members of the Ku Klux Klan in Indiana. In 1933 the state government was reorganized, giving large new power to the governor. Indiana was the home of many auto firms, but by the 1940s only Studebaker in the South Bend area held on. Great floods along the Ohio River in 1937 submerged entire towns. Many cities and towns established military plants after 1940. Evansville, on the Ohio River, even had a shipyard.

Iowa

The area that is now Iowa was home for ancient Mound Builders and later other American Indian tribes, such as the Iowa. France claimed the area as a result of exploration. It was part of the Louisiana Purchase of 1803, part of the Missouri Territory in 1812–21, site of the Black Hawk wars of the 1830s, and part of the Iowa Territory. Iowa became the twenty-ninth state on December 28, 1846. Its capital is Des Moines. The state's name originated from the tribal name. Nickname: the Hawkeye State. Motto: Our Liberties We Prize and Our Rights We Will Maintain. Flower: wild rose. Bird: eastern goldfinch. Song: "Iowa."

Land

Area: 56,280 sq. mi. (24th in area). Rivers: Big Sioux, Des Moines, Mississippi, Missouri. Cities (with 1940 pop.): Des Moines (159,819), Sioux City (82,364), Davenport (66,039), Cedar Rapids (62,120), Waterloo (51,743).

People

Population, 1910: 2,224,771; 1945 (est.): 2,259,526 (22d in population). Breakdown, 1940: 2,520,691 white, 16,694 black, 883 other, 49.8% urban, 50.2% rural. Famous natives: Herbert Hoover (president), Grant Wood (painter), George Gallup (pollster), John L. Lewis (labor leader), Harry Hopkins (presidential adviser).

Economics

State personal income, 1940: $1,272,000,000; per capita, $501. With 25% of the nation's best farmland, Iowa ranked first in production of corn, oats, and livestock, second in soybeans, high in other farm produce. Industry: chemicals, food processing, metals, insurance.

Major Developments, 1914–1945

A leader in the temperance movement, Iowa became a dry state in 1915. Iowa's farmland sold for high prices during the First World War, and many farmers overextended to get it. By 1935 more than half of the state's farmers had lost their land. Women were admitted to the state legislature in 1926. Farm cooperatives became popular in the 1930s. The Second World War produced demand for all farm goods, and Iowa prospered.

Kansas

Home primarily to the Kansa Indians, the area was explored by the Spaniard Francisco Coronado and later by the French. Kansas was part of the Louisiana Purchase in 1803, and it became a battleground in the period leading up to the Civil War. Statehood followed the start of war—on January 29, 1861, the thirty-sixth state in the Union. Its capital is Topeka. The state's name came from the tribal name meaning "people of the south wind." Nickname: the Sunflower State. Motto: *Ad Astra per Aspera* (To the Stars through Difficulties). Flower: sunflower. Bird: western meadowlark. Tree: cottonwood. Song: "Kansas, We're Proud of You."

Land

Area: 82,158 sq. mi. (13th in area). Rivers: Arkansas, Kansas, Missouri, Republican, Saline, Smoky Hill, Solomon. Cities (with 1940 pop.): Kansas City (121,458), Wichita (114,966), Topeka (67,833), Hutchinson (30,013), Salina (21,073).

People

Population, 1910: 1,690,949; 1945 (est.): 1,740,397 (30th in population). Breakdown, 1940: 1,734,496 white, 65,138 black, 1,394 other, 41.9% urban, 58.1% rural. Famous natives: Amelia Earhart (pilot), Walter P. Chrysler (manufacturer), Dwight D. Eisenhower (general), William Allen White (newsman), Alfred Landon (politician).

Economics

State personal income, 1940: $762 million; per capita, $426. Agricultural produce: wheat, corn, hay, oats, sorghums. Industry: meatpacking, petroleum refining, flour, chemicals. Minerals: petroleum, natural gas, zinc, cement, coal, stone.

Major Developments, 1914–1945

Oil was discovered at El Dorado in 1915. Wheat profits soared during the First World War. In 1931 the state produced a record wheat crop of 240 million bushels. Great dust storms devastated the area in 1934–35. Drought and the Great Depression forced many people from the land in the 1930s. Kansas produced a presidential candidate, Alfred Landon, in 1936. The Second World War created large demand for farm products and minerals from Kansas.

Kentucky

Home to the Shawnee, the "land over the mountains" was explored by English colonists moving west. The territory was part of the area officially ceded by France to Britain in 1763. Daniel Boone led exploration and settlement before and after the American Revolution. Virginia relinquished claim to the land, and Kentucky became the fifteenth state on June 1, 1792. Its capital is Frankfort. The state's name came from the Wyandot word *ken-tah-teh,* which means "land of tomorrow." Nickname: the Bluegrass State. Motto: United We Stand, Divided We Fall. Flower: goldenrod. Bird: cardinal. Song: "My Old Kentucky Home."

Land

Area: 40,598 sq. mi. (36th in area). Rivers: Cumberland, Kentucky, Licking, Ohio, Tennessee. Mountains: Appalachian, Cumber-

land. Cities (with 1940 pop.): Louisville (319,077), Covington (62,018), Lexington (49,304), Paducah (33,765), Newport (30,631).

People

Population, 1910: 2,289,905; 1945 (est.): 2,578,179 (36th in population). Breakdown, 1940: 2,631,425 white, 214,031 black, 171 other, 29.8% urban, 70.2% rural. Famous natives: Louis Brandeis (jurist), D. W. Griffith (filmmaker), Alben Barkley (politician), Robert Penn Warren (poet), Fred Vinson (jurist).

Economics

State personal income, 1940: $914 million; per capita, $320. Agricultural produce: tobacco, corn, barley, horses. Industry: furniture, aluminum goods, lumber products, textiles, iron and steel, whiskey. Minerals: coal, oil, stone, gas.

Major Developments, 1914–1945

The state continued as leading producer of race horses and whiskey. The coal industry experienced ups and downs, and the mine fields became places of bloody conflict in the 1920s, 1930s, and 1940s. The sensational episode of Floyd Collins trapped in a cave ended tragically in 1925. Mammoth Cave National Park was established in 1926. In 1932 Camp Knox became a permanent military base called Ft. Knox. In 1936 it became the government's gold depository. The state remained one of the poorest in the land, although the Second World War promoted some improvement in the economy.

Louisiana

Originally inhabited by various Indians, including the Chitimacha, Chawash, and Natchez, this territory on the lowest reaches of the Mississippi River was settled and influenced by the French. The United States acquired the land in 1803, although French influence lingered. Louisiana entered the Union on April 8, 1812, the eighteenth state, with French institutions and using two languages. The capital is Baton Rouge. The state's name came from King Louis XIV of France. Nickname: the Pelican State. Motto: Union, Justice, and Confidence. Flower: magnolia. Bird: eastern brown pelican. Song: "Song of Louisiana."

Land

Area: 48,506 sq. mi (30th in area). Rivers: Atchafalaya, Mississippi, Ouachita, Pearl, Red, Sabine. Cities (with 1940 pop.): New Orleans (494,537), Shreveport (98,167), Baton Rouge (34,719), Monroe (28,309), Alexandria (27,066).

People

Population, 1910: 1,656,388; 1945 (est.): 2,465,057 (20th in population). Breakdown, 1940: 1,511,739 white, 849,303 black, 2,838 other (1,801 American Indian), 41.5% urban, 58.5% rural. Famous natives: Huey Long (politician), Louis Armstrong (musician), Lillian Hellman (writer), Clyde Cessna (manufacturer), Mahalia Jackson (singer).

Economics

State personal income, 1940: $861 million; per capita, $363. Wildlife was plentiful in this state, with many game birds and other birds, and many people engaged in fur-related enterprises, dealing with mink, muskrat, racoon, and opossum. Major agricultural produce: sugarcane, rice, sweet potatoes, cotton. Industry: petrochemicals, oil refining, paper goods, chemicals, shipbuilding. Minerals:

petroleum, gas, salt.

Major Developments, 1914–1945

Oil and natural gas was discovered in 1916. Especially bad floods damaged the state in 1927. Huey Long became governor in 1928. He struck a deal with the petrochemical industry that brought jobs, roads, improved schools, and much power for Governor Long. Later elected to the United States Senate, Long was assassinated in 1935. The Second World War sparked shipbuilding and gas and oil industries. Country singer Jimmy Davis was governor during the years 1940–44.

Maine

Many explorers, including the Vikings, touched this rugged and distant part of New England where the Passamaquoddy, Penobscot, and Abnahi lived. Claimed by the English, it would be attached to Massachusetts Bay Colony in 1652. Massachusetts relinquished claim after the American Revolution, and on March 15, 1820, Maine became the twenty-third state to enter the Union. Its capital is Augusta. The state's name originated with the French province of Mayne. Nickname: the Pine State. Motto: *Dirigo* (I Guide). Flower: pine cone and tassel. Bird: chickadee. Tree: white pine. Song: "State of Maine Song."

Land

Area: 33,040 sq. mi. (38th in area). Rivers: Alagash, Androscoggin, Aroostook, Kennebec, Machias, Penobscot, Piscataqua, Salmon Falls, St. John. Mountains: Longfellow. Cities (with 1940 pop.): Portland (76,643), Lewiston (38,598), Bangor (29,822), Auburn (19,817), Biddeford (19,790).

People

Population, 1910: 742,371; 1945 (est.): 785,913 (35th in population). Breakdown, 1940: 844,543 white, 1,304 black, 1,379 other (1,251 American Indian), 40.5% urban, 59.5% rural. Famous natives: Nelson Rockefeller (industrialist), John K. Paine (composer), Edna St. Vincent Millay (poet), Margaret Chase Smith (politician), Thomas B. Reed (politician).

Economics

State personal income, 1940: $444 million; per capita, $523. Agricultural goods: potatoes (a major producer), blueberries, hay. Most lobsters came from the state's fishermen. Industry: wood pulp and wood products, boots and shoes, world leader in tins for sardines, ships, textiles.

Major Developments, 1914–1945

Maine's shipyards supplied vessels for the navy in World War I. State farms became more specialized during the 1920s. Textiles declined in importance, but wood products gained. Bank failures in 1933 caused suffering in rural areas, as did the worst floods in history in 1936. Maine was but one of two states to vote against Franklin D. Roosevelt in 1936. The state economy revived during the Second World War with growth in business for mills and factories.

Maryland

The area that later became Maryland was used by coastal Indian tribes. Explored by English settlers from Jamestown, the land was granted by the king of England to Cecilius Calvert, Lord Baltimore, in 1632. It was to serve as a haven for Roman Catholics. One of the original colonies, Maryland entered the Union on April 28, 1788, the seventh state to do so. Maryland was a border state during the Civil War. Its capital is Annapolis. The state's name originated with Henrietta Maria, queen of Charles I. Nickname: the Old Line State. Motto: *Scuto Bonae Voluntatis Tuae Coronasti Nos* (With the Shield of Thy Good-will Thou Hast Covered Us). Flower: black-eyed Susan. Bird: Baltimore oriole. Tree: white oak. Song: "Maryland, My Maryland."

Land

Area: 12,327 sq. mi. (41st in area). Rivers: Chester, Choptank, Nanticoke, Patapsco, Patuxent, Potomac, Susquehanna. Mountains: Allegheny, Blue Ridge. Cities (with 1940 pop.): Baltimore (859,100), Cumberland (39,483), Hagerstown (32,491), Frederick (15,802), Salisbury (13,313).

People

Population, 1910: 1,295,346; 1945 (est.): 2,125,419 (23d in population). Breakdown, 1940: 1,518,481 white, 301,931 black, 832 other, 59.3% urban, 40.7% rural. Famous natives: Billie Holiday (singer), H. L. Mencken (newsman), Charles Willson Peale (artist), Babe Ruth (baseball player), Upton Sinclair (writer).

Economics

State personal income, 1940: $1,308,000,000; per capita, $712. Cut in two by Chesapeake Bay, Maryland had much waterfront and seafood activities: fish, crabs, oysters. Agricultural produce: corn, tobacco, vegetables, dairy goods. Industry: baked goods, canned goods, shipbuilding, aircraft, chemicals. Minerals: coal, sand and gravel, clay, cement.

Major Developments, 1914–1945

Industry and shipbuilding grew during World War I; the government established the military's Aberdeen Proving Grounds in 1917. Gov. Albert Ritchie in 1919 refused to enforce prohibition, and Maryland became known as the Free State. Floods of the Potomac River did much damage in 1924 and 1936. The New Deal city, Greenbelt, was completed in 1941. In 1945 Maryland's Board of Censors banned the film *Birth of a Nation.*

Massachusetts

Massachusetts was home to several Native American tribes, including the Pequot, Nipmuc, and the Massachuset. The territory was rich in history, ranging from such historic places as Plymouth Rock, where the Pilgrims landed in 1620, and Massachusetts Bay Colony to historic events such as the Boston Tea Party in 1770 and early battles of the Revolutionary War. Massachusetts joined the Union on February 6, 1788, the sixth state. Its capital is Boston. The state's name originated from Algonquian words meaning "great mountain place." Nickname: the Bay State. Motto: *Ense Petit Placidam Sub Libertate Quietem* (By the Sword We Seek Peace, but Peace Only under Liberty). Flower: mayflower. Bird: chickadee. Tree: American elm. Song: "Massachusetts."

Land

Area: 7,839 sq. mi. (44th in area). Rivers: Cape Cod Canal, Connecticut, Merrimack, Taunton. Cities (with 1940 pop.): Boston (770,816), Worcester (193,694), Springfield (149,554), Fall River (115,428), Cambridge (110,879).

People

Population, 1910: 3,366,416; 1945 (est.): 4,183,179 (9th in population). Breakdown, 1940: 4,257,596 white, 55,391 black, 3,734 other, 89.4% urban, 10.6% rural. Famous natives: Bette Davis (actress), Oliver Wendell Holmes (jurist), Joseph P. Kennedy (financier), Henry Cabot Lodge (politician), Joseph Martin, Jr. (politician), Samuel E. Morison (historian).

Economics

State personal income, 1940: $4,385,000,000; per capita, $1,662. Agricultural produce: tobacco, cranberries, apples, corn, potatoes. Industry: textiles, shoes, cotton goods, printing goods, baked goods, shipbuilding. Minerals: coke, lime, stone, sand and gravel.

Major Developments, 1914–1945

Cape Cod Canal opened in 1914. World War I boosted the state's shipbuilding and other industries. The Boston police strike of 1919 enhanced the political reputation of Gov. Calvin Coolidge. The long-drawn-out case of Sacco and Vanzetti lasted from 1920 to 1927. In the 1920s the textile industry faced competition from southern and western states. In 1938 the first hurricane in more than 100 years caused much damage. World War II led to the construction of many factories and expansion of coastal shipyards in the state.

Michigan

Michigan was home to the Potawatomi and Menominee. French explorers traversed large portions of the land, and so such places as Marquette and Detroit received French names. England obtained control in 1763, and the United States took over the land in 1783. A part of the Northwest Territory, Michigan became the twenty-sixth state on January 26, 1837. Its capital is Lansing. The state's name came from the Ojibwa words meaning "great lake." Nickname: the Wolverine State. Motto: *Si Quaeris Peninsulam Amoenam Circumspice* (If You Seek a Pleasant Peninsula Look around You). Flower: apple blossom. Bird: robin. Song: "Michigan My Michigan."

Land

Area: 57,980 sq. mi. (22d in area). Rivers: Brule, Detroit, Kalamazoo, Menominee, Montreal, Muskegon, St. Joseph, St. Marys. Cities (with 1940 pop.): Detroit (1,623,452), Grand Rapids (164,292), Flint (151,543), Saginaw (82,794), Lansing (78,753).

People

Population, 1910: 2,810,173; 1945 (est.): 5,471,774 (7th in population). Breakdown, 1940: 5,039,643 white, 208,345 black, 8,118 other (6,282 American Indian), 65.7% urban, 34.3% rural. Famous natives: Henry Ford (manufacturer), William Knudsen (industrialist), Charles Lindbergh (pilot), Thomas E. Dewey (politician), Edgar Guest (poet), Joe Louis (boxer).

Economics

State personal income, 1940: $3,610,000,000; per capita, $679. Divided into two parts and surrounded by the Great Lakes, Michigan developed a lively tourist industry. The Detroit area became a massive manufacturing center. Agricultural produce: grapes, peaches, apples, corn, potatoes, sugar beets. Industry: automobiles, aircraft, refrigerators, paper, steel products. Minerals: iron ore, pig iron, petroleum, copper, natural gas.

Major Developments, 1914–1945

Michigan became headquarters of the automobile industry and Detroit a major manufacturing center. Henry Ford announced major innovations in 1914, including opening of the Highland Park assembly plant. The depression devastated the state, with 43% of the nonfarm labor force unemployed in 1932. Major labor disputes in 1936 and 1937 produced victories for organized labor, notably the new CIO. Michigan rebounded during the Second World War with the construction of large numbers of military factories. The largest one, perhaps, was the bomber plant built by Ford at Willow Run. A major race riot in Detroit in 1943 left thirty-four dead and hundreds injured.

Minnesota

Santee Sioux and Ojibwa lived in the area that was to become Minnesota. Numerous French explorers visited the area in the seventeenth century, and it was claimed by France in 1679. Britain controlled part of the area between 1763 and 1783; the western part was acquired by the United States in the Louisiana Purchase of 1803. On May 11, 1858, Minnesota became the thirty-second state. Wars with the Sioux Indians followed. The capital is Saint Paul. The state's name originated from the Dakota Indian word meaning "sky-tinted water." Nickname: the Gopher State. Motto: *L'Etoile du Nord* (The Star of the North). Flower: moccasin flower. Bird: American goldfinch. Tree: red pine. Song: "Hail! Minnesota."

Land

Area: 84,286 sq. mi. (11th in area). Rivers: Minnesota, Mississippi, Red River of the North, St. Croix. Cities (with 1940 pop.): Minneapolis (492,370), St. Paul (287,736), Duluth (101,065), Rochester (26,312), St. Cloud (24,173).

People

Population, 1910: 2,075,708; 1945 (est.): 2,497,485 (19th in population). Breakdown, 1940: 2,768,982 white, 9,928 black, 13,390 other (12,528 American Indian), 49.8% urban, 50.2% rural. Famous natives: F. Scott Fitzgerald (writer), Judy Garland (singer), Sinclair Lewis (writer), William and Charles Mayo (physicians) Frank B. Kellogg (diplomat).

Economics

State personal income, 1940: $1,467,000,000; per capita, $526. Mesabi, Cuyuna, and Vermillion Ranges produced much of the nation's iron ore. Agricultural products: potatoes, corn, wheat, grains, dairy products, livestock. Industry: meatpacking, flour and grain milling, baked goods, printing. Minerals: iron ore, coke, sand and gravel, stone. The lakes attracted many fishermen.

Major Developments, 1914–1945

World War I produced great demand for Minnesota's minerals and farm goods. Huge forest fires in 1918 destroyed much timber and killed 400. The depression of the 1930s devastated farmers and the iron industry, leading to a political revolt by the Farmer-Labor Party, which merged in 1944 with the Democrats. World War II promoted much recovery, and the iron ranges remained very important.

Mississippi

The Choctaw, Biloxi, Yazoo, Chakchiuma, and other Indian tribes originally lived in Mississippi. Hernando De Soto explored the area, and Rene-Robert Cavelier de la Salle claimed it for France in 1682. Britain acquired control in 1763, and it was part of the United States' original territory. Mississippi became the twentieth state on

December 10, 1817. Its capital is Jackson. The state name came from an Algonquian word meaning "big river." Nickname: the Magnolia State. Motto: *Virtute et Armis* (By Valor and Arms). Flower: magnolia. Bird: mockingbird. Song: "Mississippi."

Land

Area: 46,865 sq. mi. (31st in area). Rivers: Big Black, Mississippi, Pearl, Tennessee, Yazoo. Cities (with 1940 pop.): Jackson: (62,107), Meridian (35,481), Vicksburg (24,460), Hattiesburg (21,026), Greenville (20,892).

People

Population, 1910: 1,797,114; 1945 (est.): 2,080,377 (25th in population). Breakdown, 1940: 1,106,327 white, 1,074,578 black, 2,891 other (2,134 American Indian), 19.8% urban, 80.2% rural. Famous natives: William Faulkner (writer), Richard Wright (writer), Tennessee Williams (playwright), John Rankin (politician), Theodore Bilbo (politician).

Economics

State personal income, 1940; $474 million; per capita, $218. The state remained rural, agricultural, and poor. Agricultural produce: cotton, corn, peanuts, rice, soybeans, pecans. Industry: cotton goods, lumber products. Minerals: natural gas, petroleum, clay, sand and gravel.

Major Developments, 1914–1945

Numerous army camps were built during World War I. The boll weevil harmed cotton crops of the 1920s. Poor economic conditions and harsh racial laws caused many black people to leave the state in 1920s to 1940s. Flooding of the Mississippi River valley in 1927 was very harmful. Petroleum was discovered in 1939. Pasagoula became a major ship-assembly center in the 1940s, and other military-related establishments grew up.

Missouri

This area was originally home to the Missouri Indians. French explorers traveled along the Mississippi River, established St. Louis, and claimed the area for France. The land was acquired by the United States in the Louisiana Purchase of 1803. Missouri became the twenty-fourth state on August 10, 1821, as part of the historic compromise over slavery. It remained a border state. Its capital is Jefferson City. The state's name came from the Indian tribal name, meaning "muddy water." Nickname: the Show-Me State. Motto: *Salus Populi Suprema Lex Esto* (Let the Welfare of the People Be the Supreme Law). Flower: hawthorn. Bird: bluebird.

Land

Area: 69,420 sq. mi (18th in area). Rivers: De Moines, Mississippi, Missouri, Osage, St. Francis. Mountains: Ozark. Cities (with 1940 pop.): St. Louis (816,048), Kansas City (399,178), St. Joseph (75,711), Springfield (61,238), Joplin (37,144).

People

Population, 1910: 3,784,664; 1945 (est.): 3,556,393 (10th in population). Breakdown, 1940: 3,539,187 white, 244,386 black, 1,091 other, 51.8% urban, 48.2% rural. Famous natives: John J. Pershing (general), George Washington Carver (scientist), Ginger Rogers (actress), Omar Bradley (general), Harry S. Truman (president).

Economics

State personal income, 1940: $1,982,000,000; per capita, $524. Agricultural produce: corn, cotton, hay, oats, wheat. Industry: meatpacking, iron and steel, shoes, malt liquor, drugs. Minerals: coal, lead, lime, stone, clay.

Major Developments, 1914–1945

Missouri remained the gateway to the West and a state influenced by the huge Mississippi and Missouri river systems, with midwestern prairie in the north and the rugged Ozarks in the south. A Missourian, John J. Pershing, led army troops in France in 1917–18. Completion of Bagnell Dam on the Missouri River in 1931 created the large Lake of the Ozarks. The depression was very costly to the state citizenry. Recovery occurred during World War II when many new industries came to the state, notably to St. Louis. A native son, Harry S. Truman, became president in 1945.

Montana

The home of numerous Native American tribes such as the Crow and Flathead, visited by trappers and various explorers, Montana was part of the territory acquired from France in 1803. There followed more exploration, changes in territorial status, discovery of gold, and numerous conflicts between whites and Indians in the 1860s and 1870s. Discovery of copper deposits preceded statehood; Montana became the forty-first state on November 8, 1889. Its capital is Helena. The state's name originated in a Mexican variation of a Spanish word. Nickname: the Treasure State. Motto: *Aro y Plata* (Gold and Silver). Flower: bitterroot. Bird: meadowlark. Song: "Montana."

Land

Area: 146,997 sq. mi. (3d in area). Rivers: Kootenai, Milk, Missouri, Musselshell, Powder, Yellowstone. Mountains: Absaroka, Beartooth, Big Belt, Bitterroot, Centennial, Crazy, Lewis Range, Little Belt. Cities (with 1940 pop.): Butte (37,081), Great Falls (29,928), Billings (23,261), Missoula (18,449), Helena (15,056).

People

Population, 1910: 376,053; 1945 (est.): 457,624 (43d in population). Breakdown, 1940: 540,468 white, 1,120 black, 17,868 other (16,841 American Indian) 37.8% urban, 62.2% rural. Famous natives: Gary Cooper (actor), Myrna Loy (actress), Jeannette Rankin (politician), Charles M. Russell (artist), Burton K. Wheeler (politician).

Economics

State personal income, 1940: $318 million; per capita, $570. The state was dominated by its production of minerals, notably copper. Agricultural produce: hay, oats, sugar beets, corn, potatoes. Industry: baked goods, flour, lumber, malt liquor. Minerals: copper, gold, silver, zinc, lead, coal, petroleum.

Major Developments, 1914–1945

Anaconda Copper was dominant after 1915 in economics and in politics. World War I created a large demand for copper. Oil production started in 1915. Jeannette Rankin in 1916 became the first woman elected to Congress. In 1923 Montana was one of two states to pass an old-age pension law. Ft. Peck Dam was completed in 1940. World War II produced a boom in demand for meat, grain, and Montana's minerals. Many people left the farms.

Nebraska

Originally home to the Pawnee, the land that would become Nebraska was in the area purchased from France in 1803. It was set aside as a Native American domain in 1834, but whites entered anyway, and in 1854 Nebraska became a separate territory. Railroads and the Homestead Act fostered settlement, and Nebraska became the thirty-seventh state on March 1, 1867. Its capital is Lincoln. The state's name came from Siouan words meaning "flat water." Nickname: the Cornhusker State. Motto: Equality before the Law. Flower: goldenrod. Bird: western meadowlark. Tree: American elm.

Land

Area: 77,510 sq. mi. (15th in area). Rivers: Missouri, North Platte, Republican, South Platte. Cities (with 1940 pop.): Omaha (223,844), Lincoln (81,984), Grand Island (19,130), Hastings (15,145), Scottsbluff (12,057).

People

Population, 1910: 1,192,214; 1945 (est.): 1,198,492 (33d in population). Breakdown, 1940: 1,297,624 white, 14,171 black, 4,039 other (3,401 American Indian), 39.1% urban, 60.9% rural. Famous natives: Fred Astaire (dancer), Henry Fonda (actor), William J. Bryan (politician), Edward J. Flanning (reformer), George W. Norris (politician).

Economics

State personal income, 1940: $578 million; per capita, $439. Nebraska relied on agriculture and ranching, often with harsh results. Agricultural produce: corn, wheat, oats, barley, potatoes, sugar beets. Industry: meatpacking, butter, flour, poultry. Minerals: (very little) petroleum.

Major Developments, 1914–1915

Nebraska suffered from the great dust storms during the mid-1930s. Many people in rural areas left the state. It became in 1937 the only state to have a unicameral legislature. Oil was discovered in 1939. World War II sparked industry and the establishment of army airfields, but grains and cattle remained the basic enterprises.

Nevada

Nevada was originally home to the Shoshone. It was explored by Spaniards, English, and such Americans as John C. Fremont, but settlement was delayed by extreme aridity. The United States acquired the land from Mexico in 1848. Discovery of the Comstock Lode in 1857 inspired migration, and on October 31, 1864, Nevada became the thirty-sixth state. Its capital is Carson City. The state's name comes from the Spanish words meaning "snowcapped." Nickname: the Sagebrush State. Motto: All for Our Country. Flower: sagebrush. Bird: mountain bluebird. Tree: aspen.

Land

Area: 110,690 sq. mi. (6th in area). Rivers: Colorado, Humboldt. Cities (with 1940 pop.): Reno (21,317), Las Vegas (8,422), Sparks (5,318), Ely (4,140), Elko (4,094).

People

Population, 1910: 81,875; 1945 (est.): 159,804 (48th in population). Breakdown, 1940: 104,030 white, 644 black, 5,553 other (4,747 American Indian), 39.3% urban, 60.7% rural. Famous natives: John W. McKay (miner), Patrick A. McCarran (politician), Key Pittman (politician).

Economics

State personal income, 1940: $99 million; per capita, $876. The state relied on minerals, irrigation, and special social attractions. Agricultural produce: grains, hay, potatoes, fruit. Industry: iron and steel, clay and brick, auto parts. Minerals: goal, silver, copper, lead, zinc.

Major Developments, 1914–1945

Nevada passed an old-age pension law in 1923. A law of 1927 reduced the residency requirement for divorce to three months, and another in 1931 changed it to six weeks. Reno became a divorce capital. Gambling became legal in 1931. Gold and silver mining slowed, but extraction of copper, lead, zinc, and manganese increased in the 1940s.

New Hampshire

Home to the Pennacook Indians, New Hampshire was explored by the French but claimed by the English. Several Englishmen received land grants, and the land remained a part of Massachusetts Bay Colony until 1680. New Hampshire became the ninth state on June 21, 1788. Its capital is Concord. The state's name came from Hampshire County in England. Nickname: the Granite State. Motto: Live Free or Die. Flower: purple lilac. Bird: purple finch. Song: "Old New Hampshire."

Land

Area: 9,210 sq. mi. (43d in area). Rivers: Connecticut, Merrimack, Piscataqua, Saco, Salmon Falls. Mountains: White. Cities (with 1940 pop.): Manchester (77,685), Nashua (32,927), Concord (27,171), Berlin (19,084), Dover (14,990).

People

Population, 1910: 430,572; 1945 (est.): 452,174 (44th in population). Breakdown, 1940: 490,989 white, 414 black, 121 other, 57.6% urban, 42.4% rural. Famous natives: Robert Frost (poet), Styles Bridges (politician), Mary Baker Eddy (religious leader).

Economics

State personal income, 1940: $285 million; per capita, $579. Agricultural produce: corn, oats, wheat, hay potatoes, poultry, dairy products. Industry: machinery, leather goods, textiles, paper products. Minerals: clay products, feldspar, mica, stone.

Major Developments, 1914–1945

Portsmouth shipyard built vessels in World War I. Long a producer of textiles, New Hampshire shifted to producing shoe and leather goods in the 1920s. The depression years were harsh, but World War II sparked production of submarines and ship repair. A major International Monetary Conference was held at Bretton Woods in 1944.

New Jersey

New Jersey's history was closely tied to that of New York. While inhabited by American Indians, it was explored by Giovanni de Verrazano and Henry Hudson and settled by the Dutch. It was taken by the British and established as a separate colony in 1665. New Jersey was the site of several battles during the Revolutionary War. On December 3, 1787, it became the third state to enter the Union.

Its capital is Trenton. The state was named for the English island of Jersey. Nickname: the Garden State. Motto: Liberty and Prosperity. Flower: violet. Bird: eastern goldfinch. Song: "Ode to New Jersey."

Land

Area: 8,224 sq. mi. (45th in area). Rivers: Delaware, Hackensack, Hudson, Passaic, Raritan. Mountains: Ramapo. Cities (with 1940 pop.): Newark (429,760), Jersey City (301,173), Paterson (139,656), Trenton (124,697), Camden (117,536).

People

Population, 1910: 2,537,167; 1945 (est.): 4,200,941 (8th in population). Breakdown, 1940: 3,931,087 white, 226,973 black, 2,105 other, 81.6% urban, 18.4% rural. Famous natives: Joyce Kilmer (poet), Paul Robeson (singer), William Halsey (admiral), Frank Sinatra (singer).

Economics

State personal income, 1940: $3,433,000,000; per capita, $822. Although heavily urbanized and industrialized, New Jersey had numerous truck farms. Agricultural produce: vegetables, fruits, poultry, dairy goods. Industry: chemicals, machinery, leather, paper goods. Minerals: zinc, clay, sand and gravel. Atlantic City and the coastal area attracted tourism.

Major Developments, 1914–1945

A resident of New Jersey, Woodrow Wilson served as president from 1913 to 1921. Hoboken was a point of departure for troops in 1917–18, and training camps were located at Camp Dix and Merrit. The *Morro Castle* cruise ship burned offshore in 1934. The German airship *Hindenburg* exploded and burned at Lakehurst in 1937. The electronics and chemical industries and the state economy in general grew in the 1940s.

New Mexico

Many American Indians lived here—Apache, Navajo, Ute, Zuni. The area was explored by Francisco Coronado and other Spaniards; it became part of Mexico and after 1848 the property of the United States. The remote location and lack of rainfall delayed statehood, which did not come until January 6, 1912, making New Mexico the forty-seventh state. Its capital is Santa Fe. The state's name is of Spanish-Mexican origin. Nickname: the Sunshine State. Motto: *Crescit Eundo* (It Grows As It Goes). Flower: yucca flower. Bird: roadrunner. Song: "O, Fair New Mexico."

Land

Area: 122,634 sq. mi. (4th in area). Rivers: Gila, Pecos, Rio Grande, Zuni. Mountains: Chuska, Guadalupe, Sacramento, San Andres, Sangre de Cristo. Cities (with 1940 pop.): Albuquerque (35,449), Santa Fe (20,325), Roswell (13,482), Hobbs (10,619), Clovis (10,065).

People

Population, 1910: 327,301; 1945 (est.): 535,220 (40th in population). Breakdown, 1940: 492,312 white, 4,672 black, 34,834 other (34,510 American Indian), 33.2% urban, 66.8% rural. Famous natives: William C. McDonald (politician), John F. Dempsey (politician).

Economics

State personal income, 1940: $199 million; per capita, $375. The state relied on minerals. Irrigation was necessary for farming. Agricultural produce: grains, corn, sorghums, beans, cotton. Industry: petroleum refining, lumber goods, baked goods, newspapers. Minerals: copper, zinc, silver, gold, lead.

Major Developments, 1914–1945

In 1916 the Mexican revolutionary Pancho Villa raided Columbus, killing sixteen. Oil was discovered in the south in 1922. Carlsbad Caverns became a national park in 1930. Many soldiers from New Mexico were lost in the defeat in the Philippines in 1942. Los Alamos became a research center in 1942. In 1945 the first atomic bomb test took place near Alamogordo.

New York

The home of several Native American Indian tribes, including those of the powerful Iroquois Confederacy, New York was visited by the Italian explorer Giovanni de Verrazano and founded as a colony by the Dutch, led by English explorer Henry Hudson. England forcibly acquired New Amsterdam in 1664 and renamed it New York. Many New Yorkers joined the American Revolution; many others, loyalists, left the state. New York entered the Union on July 26, 1788, as the eleventh state. Its capital is Albany. The state is named for the duke of York, who later became King James II. Nickname: the Empire State. Motto: *Excelsior* (Higher, or Ever, Upward). Flower: rose.

Land

Area: 49,576 sq. mi. (29th in area). Rivers: Allegheny, Delaware, Genesee, Hudson, Mohawk, Niagara, St. Lawrence, Susquehanna. Mountains: Adirondack, Allegheny, Berkshire Hills, Catskill. Cities (with 1940 pop.): New York City (7,454,995), Buffalo (575,901), Rochester (324,975), Syracuse (205,967), Yonkers (142,598).

People

Population, 1910: 9,113,614; 1945 (est.): 12,584,913 (1st in population). Breakdown, 1940: 12,879,546 white, 571,221 black, 28,375 other (8,651 American Indian), 82.8% urban, 17.2 rural. Famous natives: George Gershwin (songwriter), Humphey Bogart (actor), Elizabeth Cady Stanton (reformer), Eugene O'Neill (playwright), Franklin D. Roosevelt (president), Theodore Roosevelt (president), Eleanor Roosevelt (reformer).

Economics

State personal income, 1940: $11,713,000,000; per capita, $870. New York remained a major industrial area, the center of national commerce and finance. Agricultural produce: vegetables, potatoes, grapes, corn, dairy products. Industry: clothing, chemicals, drugs, paper goods, locomotives, iron and steel products. Minerals: coke, ferroalloys, petroleum, pig iron, cement, stone and gravel.

Major Developments, 1914–1945

To the extent that the United States had a dominant state, it was New York, a giant in population and many economic areas, entry point for most immigration. Soldiers left New York for Europe and returned there during the two world wars. New Yorkers ran for the presidency in 1916, 1928, 1932, 1936, 1940, and 1944. Yankee Stadium opened in 1923. The Empire State Building was completed in 1931. The New York World's Fair was held in 1939–40. A bomber struck the Empire State Building in 1945. The headquarters of the new United Nations was established in New York City in 1945.

North Carolina

Originally home to the Cherokee and other Indian tribes, North Carolina grew out of a land grant to eight English noblemen by King Charles II in 1663. The northern part became a royal province in 1729 when the proprietors sold their rights to the Crown. Many in North Carolina strongly supported the independence movement. The state entered the Union on November 21, 1789, the twelfth state to do so. Its capital is Raleigh. The state was named in honor of Charles I of England. Nickname: the Tarheel State. Motto: *Esse Quam Videri* (To Be Rather Than to Seem). Flower: dogwood. Bird: cardinal. Song: "The Old North State."

Land

Area: 52,426 sq. mi. (27th in area). Rivers: Albemarle, Pee Dee, Roanoke, Yadkin. Mountains: Black, Blue Ridge, Great Smoky, Unaka. Cities (with 1940 pop.): Charlotte (100,899), Winston-Salem (79,815), Durham (60,195), Greensboro (59,315), Raleigh (46,897).

People

Population, 1910: 2,206,287; 1945 (est.): 3,504,626 (11th in population). Breakdown, 1940: 2,567,635 white, 981,298 black, 22,690 other (22,546 American Indian), 27.3% urban, 72.7% rural. Famous natives: Jonathan Daniels (newsman), Walter Hines Page (diplomat), Thomas Nelson Page (author), Edward R. Murrow (newsman), Josephus Daniels (politician).

Economics

State personal income, 1940: $1,171,000,000; per capita, $328. Agricultural produce: tobacco, cotton, corn, hay, peanuts, potatoes. Industry: textiles, tobacco products, lumber and furniture. Minerals: stone, clay, feldspar, sand and gravel.

Major Developments, 1915–1945

As with all southern states, North Carolina maintained a policy of segregation with its black citizenry. In 1918 Ft. Bragg was established for training in specialized warfare. By 1920 tobacco passed cotton as the chief money crop. In 1926 Great Smoky Mountain National Park was established. The state government took over full support of the public schools in 1933. In 1942, marine bases were established at Le Jeune and Cherry Point. Fontana Dam was completed in 1945.

North Dakota

Formerly the land of the Sioux Indians, the eastern half of this area was part of the Louisiana Purchase from France in 1803. The western part became American through agreement with Britain in 1818. Settlement by whites was slowed by lack of good transportation and fear of Indians who lived there. The railroad and Indian Wars of the 1870s helped pave the way for statehood on November 2, 1889, when North Dakota became the thirty-ninth state. Its capital is Bismarck. The state's name came from the Dakota Indian tribal name. Nickname: the Sioux State. Motto: Liberty and Union, Now and Forever, One and Inseparable. Flower: wild prairie rose. Bird: western meadowlark. Song: "North Dakota State Song."

Land

Area: 70,837 sq. mi (16th in area). Rivers: Missouri, Red River of the North. Cities (with 1940 pop.): Fargo (32,580), Grand Forks (20,228), Minot (16,577), Bismarck (15,496), Jamestown (8,700).

People

Population, 1910: 577,056; 1945 (est.): 520,935 (41st in population). Breakdown, 1940: 631,464 white, 201 black, 10,270 other (10,114 American Indian), 20.6% urban, 79.4% rural. Famous natives: Peggy Lee (singer), Eric Sevareid (newsman), Lawrence Welk (band leader), Gerald Nye (politician).

Economics

State personal income, 1940: $224 million; per capita, $350. Agriculture prevailed. Agricultural produce: wheat, rye, barley, corn, potatoes. Industry: mostly dairy goods, especially butter, and flour. Minerals: oil, gas, salt, clay, gravel.

Major Developments, 1914–1945

In 1915 the Non-Partisan League was formed to challenge private interests, especially in grain milling. In 1916 Lynn J. Frazier, a non-Partisan candidate, was elected governor. In 1919 a state-owned bank opened, and in 1922 a state-owned mill and elevator began operation. The state capitol in Bismarck burned in 1930. The depression and severe drought in the mid-1930s caused a sharp drop in population. World War II created demand for foodstuffs and promoted economic revival.

Ohio

Ohio was part of the territory dominated by the Iroquois, and other tribes occupied parts of the area. Ohio was in the territory claimed by several colonial powers. It became part of British America in 1763 (France yielded claim) and in 1783 was included in the original United States of America. Many settlers followed the Ohio River west after the Revolution, and on February 19, 1803, Ohio entered the Union as the seventeenth state. Its capital is Columbus. The state's name came from the Iroquoian word meaning "beautiful." Nickname: the Buckeye State. Flower: scarlet carnation. Bird: cardinal.

Land

Area: 41,122 sq. mi. (35th in area). Rivers: Cuyahoga, Maumee, Miami, Muskigum, Ohio, Sandusky, Scioto. Mountains: Allegheny. Cities (with 1940 pop.): Cleveland (878,336), Cincinnati (455,610), Columbus (306,087), Toledo (282,349), Akron (244,791).

People

Population, 1910: 4,767,121; 1945 (est.): 6,873,448 (5th in population). Breakdown, 1940: 6,566,531 white, 339,461 black, 1,620 other, 66.8% urban, 33.2 rural. Famous natives: Sherwood Anderson (author), Thomas Edison (inventer), Zane Grey (author), William Howard Taft (politician), Robert A. Taft (politician).

Economics

State personal income, 1940: $4,606,000,000; per capita, $665. Ohio had numerous manufacturing centers as well as areas of good farmland and mineral wealth. Agricultural produce: corn, soybeans, wheat, grapes, dairy produce. Industry: iron and steel, tires, refrigerators, automobiles, radios. Minerals: coal, oil, sand and gravel.

Major Developments, 1914–1945

Large floods caused the state in 1914 to begin work on a flood control system. State factories produced many goods for the First World War. An Ohioan, Warren Harding, became president in 1921. Iron and steel became the state's largest industry in the 1920s, but it dipped sharply during the 1930s. Many factories underwent strikes in 1936–37, notably in Akron and Youngstown. The Second

World War induced recovery in numerous areas of the economy.

Oklahoma

This area was home to the Kiowa and Kiowa-Apache Indians. Explored mostly by the French, it was acquired by the United States in the Louisiana Purchase of 1803. In 1830, the territory was set aside for the "Five Civilized Indian Tribes" (as whites referred to the Creek, Cherokee, Chicasaw, Choctaw, and Seminole), whom the government was forcing west from their traditional homes. But in 1889 the land was opened to settlers—50,000 "boomers" rushed in during one day. Oil was discovered in the 1890s and would dominate economics for many years, although large Indian lands remained. Oklahoma became the forty-sixth state on November 16, 1907. Its capital is Oklahoma City. The state's name came from Choctaw words meaning "red people." Nickname: the Sooner State. Motto: *Labor Omnia Vincit* (Labor Conquers all Things). Flower: mistletoe. Bird: bobwhite. Song: "Oklahoma: A Toast."

Land

Area: 70,057 sq. mi. (17th in area). Rivers: Arkansas, Canadian, Cimarron, Red. Mountains: Ozark, Ouachita, Wichita. Cities (with 1940 pop.): Oklahoma City (204,424), Tulsa (142,157), Muskogee (32,332), Enid (28,081), Shawnee (22,053).

People

Population, 1910: 1,657,155; 1945 (est.): 2,034,460 (26th in population). Breakdown, 1940: 2,104,228 white, 168,849 black, 63,357 other (63,125 American Indian), 37.6% urban, 62.4% rural. Famous natives: Woody Guthrie (singer), Wiley Post (flier), Will Rogers (humorist), Jim Thorpe (athlete), Patrick Hurley (politician).

Economics

State personal income, 1940: $867 million; per capita, $373. Oil dominated the state economy for many years. Agricultural produce: corn, wheat, soybeans, oats, sorghums, cattle. Industry: petroleum refining, meatpacking, milling, baked goods, publishing. Minerals: petroleum, natural gas, zinc, gasoline, coal, lead.

Major Developments, 1914–1945

Oklahoma produced oil and foodstuffs during the First World War. Large new oil fields opened in 1918 and in 1926. The Ku Klux Klan became powerful in the early 1920s, leading to the impeachment in 1923 of Gov. John C. Walton, who challenged the Klan. Gov. William ("Alfalfa Bill") Murray closed the oil fields in 1931, hoping to stabilize prices. A severe drought and huge dust storms in 1934–35 caused many "Okies" to depart, heading west. The Second World War restored some prosperity, if only temporarily.

Oregon

This area was home to several different Indian tribes. Explored by Sir Francis Drake, James Cook, Meriwether Lewis, and James Clark, the Oregon territory was claimed by Britain and the United States. Britain relinquished claim to the part that became Oregon in the Treaty of 1846. Statehood followed on February 14, 1859, when Oregon became the thirty-third state. Its capital is Salem. The origin of the state's name is unknown. Nickname: the Beaver State. Motto: The Union. Flower: Oregon grape. Bird: western meadowlark. Tree: Douglas fir. Song: "Oregon, My Oregon."

Land

Area: 96,981 sq. mi. (9th in area). Rivers: Columbia, Snake, Willamette. Mountains: Cascade, Coast Ranges, Klamath. Cities: (with 1940 pop.): Portland (305,394), Salem (30,908), Eugene (20,838), Klamath Falls (16,497), Medford (11,281).

People

Population, 1910: 672,765; 1945 (est.): 1,206,322 (32d in population). Breakdown, 1940: 1,075,731 white, 2,565 black, 11,388 other, 48.8% urban, 51.2% rural. Famous natives: John Reed (author), William A. U'Ren (reformer), Edwin Markham (poet), Charles McNary (politician).

Economics

State personal income, 1940: $677 million; per capita, $623. The state's economy stood out for lumber products, fishing, and special farm produce. Agricultural goods: corn, oats, barley, Blue Lake beans, cranberries, holly, peppermint. Industry: lumber goods, sawmills, paper mills, meatpacking, fisheries. Minerals: gold, stone, sand and gravel.

Major Developments, 1914–1945

The Weyerhauser Company held huge plots of pine and fir timberlands. A law in 1923 prohibited aliens ineligible for citizenship (Chinese and Japanese) from owning land. A fire in 1933 burned more than 300,000 acres of forest along the northern coast. Owyhee Dam was completed in 1932 and the great Bonneville Dam on the Columbia River in 1937. Many people moved to the state in the 1940s to find work. Portland became a major port and shipbuilding center during the Second World War.

Pennsylvania

Early explorers who came to the Pennsylvania area found numerous Native-American tribes, most of them belonging to the Algonquian and Iroquois groups. Charles II of England granted a charter to William Penn, a Quaker, in 1681, and so Pennsylvania became a proprietary colony. It was known for religious toleration and opposition to slavery. Philadelphia was a leader of colonial cities and a center of revolutionary political activity. On December 12, 1787, Pennsylvania became the second state to enter the Union. Its capital is Harrisburg. The state's name honored Adm. Sir William Penn, father of the proprietor. Nickname: the Keystone State. Motto: Virtue, Liberty, and Independence. Flower: mountain laurel. Bird: ruffed grouse. tree: Hemlock.

Land

Area: 45,333 sq. mi. (32d in area). Rivers: Allegheny, Delaware, Juniata, Monongahela, Ohio, Schuylkill, Susquehanna. Mountains: Allegheny, Kittatinny, Laurel Hills, Pocono. Cities (with 1940 pop.): Philadelphia (1,931,334), Pittsburgh (671,659), Scranton (140,404), Erie (116,955), Reading (110,568).

People

Population, 1910: 7,665,111; 1945 (est.): 9,193,957 (2d in population). Breakdown, 1940: 9,426,989 white, 470,172 black, 3,019 other, 66.5% urban, 33.5% rural. Famous natives: George C. Marshall (general), Robert E. Peary (explorer), Maxwell Anderson (playwright), Louisa May Alcott (author), John Weismuller (athlete and actor).

Economics

State personal income, 1940: $6,417,000,000; per capita, $648. The state was a leader in heavy and light industry and in production of coal. Agricultural produce: corn, grains, tobacco, fruit, mushrooms, potatoes. Industry: metals, aircraft, machinery, batteries, explosives, leather. Minerals: anthracite and bituminous coal, pig iron, petroleum, natural gas.

Major Developments, 1914–1945

The state was a giant in munitions production during World War I. The Hog Island naval shipyard started work in 1918. The first radio station (KDKA) broadcast from Pittsburgh in 1920. Many coal and steel workers lost their jobs in the 1930s. Large floods damaged Pittsburgh and Johnstown in 1936. The first part of the first superhighway, the Pennsylvania Turnpike, was completed in 1940. The state's mines and factories boomed during World War II.

Rhode Island

The land that is now Rhode Island was originally inhabited by Narraganset Indians. The first white settlers followed Roger Williams, a Baptist, in protest of intolerance by Puritans in Massachusetts Bay Colony. Other dissenters, including Anne Hutchinson, founded other settlements. Four joined together in 1647 and made Rhode Island a separate colony. Rhode Island was the first colony to declare independence in 1776, and it became on May 29, 1790, the thirteenth and last of the original states to enter the Union. Even then the vote was close: 34–32. The capital is Providence. The state's name came from the Greek island of Rhodes. Nickname: Little Rhody. Motto: Hope. Flower: violet. Tree: red maple.

Land

Area: 1,300 sq. mi. (48th in area). Rivers: Blackstone, Pawcatuck, Providence, Sakonnet. Cities (with 1940 pop.): Providence (253,504), Pawtucket (75,797), Woonsocket (49,303), Cranston (47,085), Newport (30,532).

People

Population, 1910: 542,610; 1945 (est.): 758,222 (36th in population). Breakdown, 1940: 701,805 white, 11,024 black, 517 other, 91.6% urban, 8.4% rural. Famous natives: George M. Cohan (songwriter), Theodore F. Green (politician), J. Howard McGrath (politician).

Economics

State personal income, 1940: $534 million; per capita, $743. This densely populated urbanized state relied heavily on manufacturing. Agricultural produce: dairy products, fruits and vegetables, corn, potatoes. Industry: textiles (cotton and rayon), machinery and metal goods, rubber. Minerals: (very little) stone, sand and gravel.

Major Developments, 1914–1945

World War I boosted industrial development, notably in Newport and Providence. In 1920 Rhode Island declined to ratify the Eighteenth Amendment (prohibition) but did endorse the Nineteenth Amendment (woman suffrage). The textile industries slid in the 1920s; the state turned more to iron and steel, and these industries declined in the 1930s. A hurricane and tidal wave in 1938 killed 300 and caused $100 million in damage. World War II restored prosperity, especially in the shipyards at Providence. Newport remained the home of the Naval War College, and in 1941 the navy established an air station at Quonset Point.

South Carolina

The home of many Indian tribes, this territory was visited by French and Spanish explorers but claimed by the English. King Charles II granted the land to eight proprietors in 1663, and the first settlers arrived near Charleston in 1670. South Carolina thus was an original colony, and on May 23, 1788, it became the eighth state to enter the Union. The capital is Columbia. In 1860 it became the first state to leave—or attempt to leave—the Union. The state's name honored King Charles II of England. Nickname: the Palmetto State. Motto: *Animis Opibusque Parati* (Ready in Soul and Resource). Flower: yellow jessamine. Bird: mockingbird. Tree: palmetto tree. Song: "Carolina."

Land

Area: 30,989 sq. mi. (39th in area). Rivers: Congaree, Edisto, Pee Dee, Savannah, Tugalos, Wateree. Mountains: Blue Ridge. Cities (with 1940 pop.): Charlestown (71,275), Columbia (62,396), Greenville (34,734), Spartanburg (32,249), Anderson (19,424).

People

Population, 1910: 1,515,400; 1945 (est.): 1,905,597 (27th in population). Breakdown, 1940: 1,084,308 white, 814,164 black, 1,332 other, 24.5% urban, 75.5% rural. Famous natives: Benjamin Tillman (politician), James F. Byrnes (jurist, administrator), Dizzy Gillespie (musician), Strom Thurmond (politician).

Economics

State personal income, 1940: $584 million; per capita, $307. Textiles and agriculture dominated. Agricultural produce: cotton, corn, tobacco, peanuts, sweet potatoes. Industry: textiles, asbestos, steel, pulp and wood products. Minerals: stone, clay, gold.

Major Developments, 1914–1945

Textile mills boomed during World War I. In 1916 the legislature raised the minimum age for child labor from twelve to fourteen. The boll weevil damaged the cotton crops of the 1920s, and the Great Depression caused more hardship in the 1930s. Throughout this era South Carolina retained Jim Crow legislation and other restrictions on African Americans. In 1941 the Santee-Cooper project was completed; it provided power and helped industry to expand during the Second World War.

South Dakota

The French explored and claimed the area. It was ceded to the United States in the Louisiana Purchase of 1803. White settlers generally stayed away from this land, which was the home of numerous Indians, until the discovery of gold in the Black Hills in the 1870s. The rush of whites to the area produced many battles with Sioux and other Native Americans. Deadwood became a famous town. South Dakota became the fortieth state on November 2, 1889, shortly before the last substantial conflict between whites and Sioux at Wounded Knee in 1890. The capital is Pierre. The state's name came from the Indian word meaning "allies." Nickname: the Coyote State. Motto: Under God the People Rule. Flower: pasqueflower. Bird: ring-necked pheasant. Song: "Hail, South Dakota."

Land

Area: 77,615 sq. mi. (15th in area). Rivers: Cheyenne, James, Missouri, Moreau, White. Mountains: Black Hills. Cities (with 1940 pop.): Sioux Falls (40,832), Aberdeen (17,015), Rapid City (13,844),

Huron (10,843), Mitchell (10,633).

People

Population, 1910: 583,888; 1945 (est.): 555,347 (39th in population). Breakdown, 1940: 619,075 white, 474 black, 23,412 others (23,387 American Indian), 24.6% urban, 75.4% rural. Famous natives: Karl Mundt (politician), Ernest O. Lawrence (physicist), Joe Foss (pilot).

Economics

State personal income, 1940: 230 million; per capita, $359. Agricultural produce: wheat, corn, oats, barley, bluegrass, livestock. Industry: meatpacking, butter, baked goods, poultry. Minerals: gold, iron, beryllium, sand and gravel.

Major Developments, 1914–1945

In 1917 the state began extending loans to farmers. In 1919 the state provided hail insurance and acquired a coal mine and cement plant. These state enterprises—except for the cement plant—failed in 1928 and in the 1930s. By 1930 land values fell to half the price of 1921. The depression, drought, and a grasshopper plague caused foreclosures to soar and many farmers to leave the state. The Mount Rushmore Memorial, with carved images of four presidents, was finished in 1941. The Second World War and approval of the Missouri Basin Project in 1944 encouraged economic recovery.

Tennessee

This land of Cherokee, Chickasaw, and other Native American tribes was explored by Hernando De Soto of Spain and claimed for France by Sieur de la Salle. A rival English claim was confirmed at the end of the French and Indian War. Settlers fought the British and Indians in the 1770s. In 1789 North Carolina relinquished claim to the land, and on June 1, 1796, Tennessee became the sixteenth state. Its capital is Nashville. The state's name came from Cherokee. Nickname: the Volunteer State. Motto: Agriculture and Commerce. Flower: iris. Bird: mockingbird. Song: "My Homeland, Tennessee."

Land

Area: 42,246 sq. mi. (34th in area). Rivers: Clinch, Cumberland, Mississippi, Tennessee. Mountains: Cumberland, Great Smoky, Unaka. Cities (with 1940 pop.): Memphis (292,942), Nashville (167,402), Chattanooga (128,163), Knoxville (111,580), Johnson City (25,332).

People

Population, 1910: 2,184,799; 1945 (est.): 2,878,777 (16th in population). Breakdown, 1940: 2,406,906 white, 508,735 black, 199 other, 35.2% urban; 64.8% rural. Famous natives: Cordell Hull (diplomat), Alvin York (soldier), James Agee (author), E. H. Crump (politician), Roy Acuff (singer).

Economics

State personal income, 1940: $995 million; per capita, $339. Agricultural produce: cotton, tobacco, corn, wheat, potatoes. Industry: chemicals, aluminum, textiles, shoes, wood products. Minerals: coal, stone, cement, marble, sand and gravel.

Major Developments, 1914–1945

In 1925 the Scopes trial was held in Dayton. In 1925 WSM inaugurated the "Barn Dance," a predecessor to the "Grand Ole Opry," and Nashville became a center of country music. Great

Smoky National Park was created in 1926. Work began on the TVA in 1933. In 1942 work began on the atomic energy project at Oak Ridge.

Texas

Home of many Indian tribes, Texas was part of Spanish America and then of Mexico before it wrested independence from Mexico in 1836. After nine years as a nation, Texas joined the United States in 1845. It officially became the twenty-eighth state on December 29, 1846. Its capital is Austin. The state's name came from an Indian word meaning "friends." Nickname: the Lone Star State. Motto: Friendship. Bird: mockingbird. Tree: pecan. Song: "Texas, Our Texas."

Land

Area: 265,896 sq. mi. (1st in area). Rivers: Brazos, Colorado, Red, Rio Grande, Trinity. Mountains: Guadalupe. Cities (with 1940 pop.): Houston (384,514), Dallas (294,734), San Antonio (253,854), Ft. Worth (177,662), El Paso (96,810).

People

Population, 1910: 3,896,542; 1945 (est.): 6,786,740 (6th in population). Breakdown, 1940: 5,487,545 white, 924,391 black, 2,888 other (1,103 American Indian), 45.4% urban, 54.6% rural. Famous natives: Audie Murphy (soldier and actor), Sam Rayburn (politician), Mildred "Babe" Didriksen Zaharias (athlete), Chester Nimitz (admiral), Edward M. House (political operative).

Economics

State personal income, 1940: $2,776,000,000; per capita, $432. Long identified as cattle country, Texas in the twentieth century profited much from its oil. Agricultural produce: cotton, wheat, corn, oats, sorghum, cattle. Industry: oil refining, metals, meatpacking, oil field machinery, baked goods. Minerals: oil, natural gas, gasoline, sulfur, cement.

Major Developments, 1914–1945

The state passed a compulsory education law in 1915. Many military camps were established after 1917. In 1925 Texas elected the second woman governor, Miriam (Ma) Ferguson. A new eastern oil field was discovered in 1930. In 1936 the state celebrated its centennial. Many military establishments were developed during 1940–45. Audie Murphy of Farmersville became the most decorated American soldier of the Second World War.

Utah

Mormon leader Brigham Young took his followers to the Salt Lake area in 1847 and established the state of Deseret. The people the Mormans encountered were the Ute Indians who had settled there. The land became American after the Mexican War ended in 1848. Statehood was delayed by the Mormon practice of polygamy. After Utah became the forty-fifth state on January 4, 1896, polygamy ended, but dominance by Mormons continued. The capital is Salt Lake City. The state's name came from the Ute Indians and means "people of the mountains." Nickname: the Beehive State. Motto: Industry. Flower: sego lily. Bird: seagull. Song: "Utah We Love Thee."

Land

Area: 84,990 sq. mi. (10th in area). Rivers: Bear, Colorado, Green, Sevies. Mountains: La Sal, Uinta, Wasatch Range. Cities (with

1940 pop.): Salt Lake City (149,934), Ogden (43,688), Provo (18,071), Logan (11,868), Murray (5,740).

People

Population, 1910: 373,351; 1945 (est.): 616,989 (38th in population). Breakdown, 1940: 542,920 white, 1,235 black, 6,155 other (3,611 American Indian), 55.5% urban, 44.5% rural. Famous natives: Loretta Young (actress), John M. Browning (inventor).

Economics

State personal income, 1940: $269 million; per capita, $487. Utah was largely a mining state. Agriculture depended on irrigation. Agricultural produce: sugar beets, onions, potatoes, fruits and vegetables. Industry: (very little) metals. Minerals: gold, silver, copper, zinc, lead, lime, coal.

Major Developments, 1914–1945

Utah's mines produced much nonferrous metal after 1917. Copper mining became especially important. Irrigation produced sharp expansion of agriculture in the early 1920s. A coal mine explosion at Castle Gate killed 172 in 1924. In 1928 Bryce Canyon National Park was established. By 1932 more than one-third of the work force was unemployed, and by 1934, 21% of the population was on relief. Despite Mormon opposition to alcohol, the state supported an end to prohibition in 1933. The Second World War brought several military bases and some steelworks to the state.

Vermont

This home of Iroquois Indians was explored by the French and settled by English from Massachusetts Bay Colony. It was a site of battles in the Revolutionary War, notably by Ethan Allen and the Green Mountain Boys. Vermont was quick to abolish slavery and provide for full male suffrage in 1777. After neighboring areas relinquished claims to the land, Vermont entered the Union on March 4, 1791, as the fourteenth state. Its capital is Montpelier. The state's name originated in the French words meaning "green mountain." Nickname: the Green Mountain State. Motto: Freedom and Unity. Flower: red clover. Bird: hermit thrush. Song: "Hail, Vermont."

Land

Area: 9,564 sq. mi. (42d in area). Rivers: Connecticut, Lamoille, Otter Creek, Poultney, White, Winooski. Mountains: Green, Taconic. Cities (with 1940 pop.): Burlington (27,686), Rutland (17,082), Barre (10,909), Brattleboro (9,622), St. Albans (8,037).

People

Population, 1910: 355,956; 1945 (est.): 310,352 (45th in population). Breakdown, 1940: 385,806 white, 384 black, 41 other, 34.3% urban, 65.7% rural. Famous natives: John Dewey (philosopher), Rudy Vallee (singer), Calvin Coolidge (president), George Dewey (admiral), George Aiken (politician).

Economics

State personal income, 1940: $184 million; per capita, $507. Vermont led the nation in producing certain types of stone. The terrain did not encourage extensive farming. Agricultural produce: dairy products, corn, potatoes, fruit, maple syrup. Industry: machinery, lumber products, military items. Minerals: granite, marble.

Major Developments, 1914–1945

A native, Calvin Coolidge, became president in 1923 and was reelected in 1924. The worst flood on record killed sixty in 1927.

In 1931 the state adopted an income tax. A major hurricane in 1938 caused heavy damage. Vermont declared war on Germany in September 1941, months before the nation did. The state's factories resumed work during the period 1941–45.

Virginia

The settlers encountered Native Americans of three major language groups—the Algonquian, Siouian, and Iroquoian—who made up many different tribes. Perhaps the Powhatan were best known. Jamestown was the site of the first permanent English settlement in North America in 1607. Virginia colony was a leader in economics and government, and the state of Virginia led in the early years of the Republic. From Virginia came a dynasty of presidents, but Virginia also was a key to the Union's breakup in 1860–61. Statehood came on June 25, 1788, when Virginia became the tenth state. Its capital is Richmond. The state's name honored Elizabeth, the "Virgin Queen." Nickname: the Old Dominion. Motto: *Sic Temper Tyrannis* (This Ever to Tyrants). Flower: dogwood. Song: "Carry Me Back to Old Virginny."

Land

Area: 39,899 sq. mi. (33d in area). Rivers: James, Potomac, Rappahannock, Roanoke, Shenandoah, York, Allegheny. Mountains: Blue Ridge, Cumberland, Unaka. Cities (with 1940 pop.): Richmond (193,042), Norfolk (144,332), Roanoke (69,287), Portsmouth (50,745), Lynchburgh (44,541).

People

Population, 1910: 2,061,612; 1945 (est.): 3,079,706, (14th in population). Breakdown, 1940: 2,015,583 white, 661,449 black, 741 other, 35.3% urban, 64.7% rural. Famous natives: Booker T. Washington (educator), Walter Reed (army surgeon), Richard E. Byrd (explorer), Bill "Bojangles" Robinson (entertainer), Carter Glass (politician).

Economics

State personal income, 1940: $1,267,000,000; per capita, $466. This state with a long tradition in agriculture turned more to industry. Agricultural produce: tobacco, fruits, peanuts, vegetables, cotton, dairy produce. Industry: textiles, lumber, furniture, shipbuilding, tobacco products. Minerals: coal, coke.

Major Developments, 1914–1945

Woodrow Wilson, born in Virginia, served as president from 1913 to 1921. The Norfolk Naval Base was founded in 1917. John D. Rockefeller restored Colonial Williamsburg during 1926–29. Many Virginians left the state in the 1920s. The Norfolk base expanded in the 1940s, as did the Newport News shipyards and military bases at Ft. Lee, Ft. Belvoir, and other places. The Pentagon was completed in Arlington in 1943.

Washington

Home to many American Indian tribes, the land was noted for its fur-bearing animals, heavy forestation, and rain along the coast. It was part of the disputed Oregon Territory, of which the United States legitimized control in 1846. Gold in the general area brought in settlers in the 1860s. Washington became the forty-second state on November 11, 1889. Its capital is Olympia. The state was named for the nation's first president. Nickname: the Evergreen State. Motto: *Alki* (By and By). Flower: western rhododendron. Bird: willow goldfinch. Song: "Washington Beloved."

Land

Area: 69,127 sq. mi. (19th in area). Rivers: Chehalis, Columbia, Pend, Oreille, Snake, Yakima. Mountains: Cascades, Coast Ranges, Kettle River Range, Olympic. Cities (with 1940 pop.): Seattle (368,302), Spokane (122,001), Tacoma (109,408), Everett (30,224), Bellingham (29,314).

People

Population, 1910: 1,141,990; 1945 (est.): 2,088,574 (24th in population). Breakdown, 1940: 1,698,147 white, 7,424 black, 30,620 other (11,394 American Indian), 53.1% urban, 46.9% rural. Famous natives: Bing Crosby (singer), Jonathan M. Wainwright (soldier), Bob Crosby (bandleader).

Economics

State personal income, 1940: $1,152,000,000; per capita, $662. The state led in all wood products and grew in heavy industry. Agricultural produce: apples, wheat, hay, potatoes, oats, pears. Industry: lumber and wood products, paper, airplanes, military goods. Minerals: copper, magnesium.

Major Developments, 1914–1945

The state of war in 1917 inspired development of the area of Puget Sound. Ft. Lewis expanded. Seattle faced a general strike in 1919. The capitol at Olympia was completed in 1928. Bonneville Dam was finished in 1937 and Grand Coulee Dam in 1941—both on the Columbia River. Some 14,000 people of Japanese ancestry were moved out in 1942. Washington produced warships, and the Boeing plant in Seattle produced many B-17 and B-29 bombers during 1935–45.

West Virginia

Several Indian tribes, including the Cherokee, Delaware, and Shawnee, used the area that became West Virginia as a hunting ground, although none claimed it as a home. Originally part of Virginia colony and then the state, West Virginia was the rugged western part of Virginia that refused to follow the state into secession in 1861. Separate statehood came during the Civil War on June 20, 1863, when West Virginia became the thirty-fifth state. The state was named for Elizabeth, the "Virgin Queen." Nickname: the Panhandle State. Motto: *Montani Semper Liberi* (Mountaineers Are Always Freemen). Flower: rhododendron. Bird: tufted titmouse. Song: "West Virginia Hills."

Land

Area: 24,282 sq. mi. (40th in area). Rivers: Big Sandy, Guayandotte, Kanahwa, Monongahela, Ohio, Potomac. Mountains: Allegheny, Blue Ridge, Cumberland. Cities (with 1940 pop.): Huntington (78,836), Charleston (67,914), Wheeling (61,099), Clarksburg (30,579), Parkersburg (30,103).

People

Population, 1910: 1,221,119; 1945 (est.): 1,724,677 (35th in population). Breakdown, 1940: 1,784,102 white, 117,754 black, 118 other, 28.9% urban, 71.9% rural. Famous natives: Pearl Buck (author), Newton D. Baker (politician), Dwight W. Morrow (ambassador), Walter Reuther (labor leader), John W. Davis (politician).

Economics

State personal income, 1940: $777 million; per capita, $407. The state was a leader in production of coal; industry also grew. Agricultural produce (difficult in poor and hilly land): corn, wheat, oats, potatoes, dairy products. Industry: chemicals, steel, aluminum, lumber. Minerals: coal, petroleum, natural gas, coke, salt.

Major Developments 1914–1945

The Supreme Court ruled in 1915 that the state owed Virginia a debt of over $12 million from the time of separation. The debt was paid by 1939. As coal became the primary industry, bitter labor battles raged in 1920–21, especially in Logan and Mingo Counties, and again in 1924–27, the 1930s, and 1941. The capitol at Charleston burned in 1921, and a new building was dedicated in 1932. Locks and dams on state rivers eased movement of chemicals and coal in the 1930s and 1940s. The first synthetic rubber plant opened at Charleston during the Second World War.

Wisconsin

This area was originally inhabited by the Sauk, Fox, and Winnebago. It was explored and sparsely settled by the French. The British took control in 1763. American control was not firm and final until after the War of 1812. Settlers, many of them German, Dutch, Swedish, and Norwegian, clashed with Native Americans in the Black Hawk Wars of the 1830s. Wisconsin became the thirtieth state on May 29, 1848. Its capital is Madison. The name represented a French variation of an Ojibwa word that meant "gathering of waters." Nickname: the Badger State. Motto: Forward. Flower: violet. Bird: robin.

Land

Area: 56,066 sq. mi. (25th in area). Rivers: Black, Chippewa, Menominee, Mississippi, St. Croix, Wisconsin. Cities (with 1940 pop.): Milwaukee (587,472), Madison (67,447), Racine (67,195), Kenosha (48,765), Green Bay (46,235).

People

Population, 1910: 2,333,860; 1945 (est.): 2,952,205 (15th in population). Breakdown, 1940: 3,112,752 white, 12,158 black, 12,677 other (12,265 American Indian), 53.5% urban, 46.5% rural. Famous natives: Orson Welles (actor/director), Frank Lloyd Wright (architect), Robert M. La Follette (politician), Harry Houdini (escape artist), Thorstein Veblen (author).

Economics

State personal income, 1940: $1,740,000,000; per capita, $554. A leading dairy state, Wisconsin also developed manufacturing. Agricultural produce: dairy products, corn, wheat, fruits, and vegetables. Industry: furniture, processed food, farm machinery, automobiles. Minerals: stone, iron ore, sand and gravel.

Major Developments, 1914–1945

The state led in progressive reforms of the early twentieth century. Robert La Follette was a major leader. Forest fires killed many people in 1918. In 1921 women received full civil and property rights. The Packers, one of the earliest professional football teams, were started in Green Bay in 1921. Robert La Follette received almost five million votes for the presidency in 1924. He died in 1925, and his son, Robert Jr., became senator. A second son, Philip, was elected governor in 1930. The La Follettes dominated politics for many years.

Wyoming

Indians had hunted in the Wyoming area for hundreds of years and when the whites arrived, they found Arapaho, Crow, Nez Percé, Sioux and other tribes living there. This formerly French territory was part of the Louisiana Purchase by the United States in 1803. Settlement by whites was slow. Bitter struggles with Native Americans of this area occurred in the 1850s and 1860s. Territorial status was achieved in 1868; Wyoming joined the Union with five other states on July 10, 1890, and became the forty-fourth state. Its capital is Cheyenne. The state's name originated with Indian words meaning "mountains and valleys alternating." Nickname: the Equality State. Motto: *Cedant Arma Togae* (Let Arms Yield to the Gown). Flower: Indian paintbrush. Bird: meadowlark.

Land

Area: 97,914 sq. mi (8th in area). Rivers: Bighorn, Green, North Platte, Powder, Snake, Yellowstone. Mountains: Abaroka, Bighorn, Black Hills, Laramie, Owl Creek, Teton, Wind River Range, Wyoming Range. Cities (with 1940 pop.): Cheyenne (22,474), Casper (17,964), Laramie (10,627), Sheridan (10,529), Rock Springs (9,827).

People

Population, 1910: 145,964; 1945 (est.): 246,766 (47th in population). Breakdown, 1940: 246,597 white, 956 black, 3,189 other (2,349 American Indian), 37.3% urban, 62.7% rural. Famous natives: Nellie Tayloe Ross (politician).

Economics

State personal income, 1940: $152 million; per capita, $608. The state produced much cattle and had significant mineral wealth. Agricultural produce: cattle, sheep, hogs, hay, sugar beets, beans, corn. Industry: petroleum refining, baked goods. Minerals: coal, petroleum, iron ore, bentonite.

Major Developments, 1914–1945

An oil boom starting in 1918 caused Casper to become a state commercial center. The lease of Teapot Dome oil reserves in 1922 began a long political scandal. Hard times on the farms caused many banks to close in 1924. In 1925 Nellie Tayloe Ross became the first woman governor of a state. Completion of dams on the North Platte River in 1938 and 1939 aided irrigation and production of electricity. All aspects of the economy grew in 1941–45. Heart Mountain became a relocation center for Japanese Americans in 1942.

CHAPTER 11 Possessions and Dependencies of the United States

During the years 1914–45 the United States went about clarifying a relationship with, and considering the future of, several non–self-governing pieces of territory, the bulk of them acquired only a few years earlier. The country had to determine the status of these areas and consider what was to become of them, as well as reach conclusions about who was to make the decisions. The Second World War affected the status of several of these places. Evidence showed that by 1945 no single conclusion had been reached, no single policy applied. The issue of the Philippine Islands, for example, was about to be resolved with independence; Hawaii by contrast seemed moving toward full statehood. The status of Puerto Rico was marked with much indecision. The following material is designed to provide brief introductory information about what one might call the "American empire" (the District of Columbia excepted), note changes during the first half of the twentieth century, and identify the status of each territory as of the end of the year 1945.

Sources are the Bureau of the Census, *Statistical Abstract of the United States, 1946* (Washington, D.C., 1946); Council of State Government, *The Book of the States, 1945–1946* (Chicago, 1945); The Encyclopaedia Britannica, *Yearbooks, 1935–47* (Chicago, 1935–47); and *The Information Please Almanac, 1948* (New York, 1948).

The United States and Its Empire, 1914–45

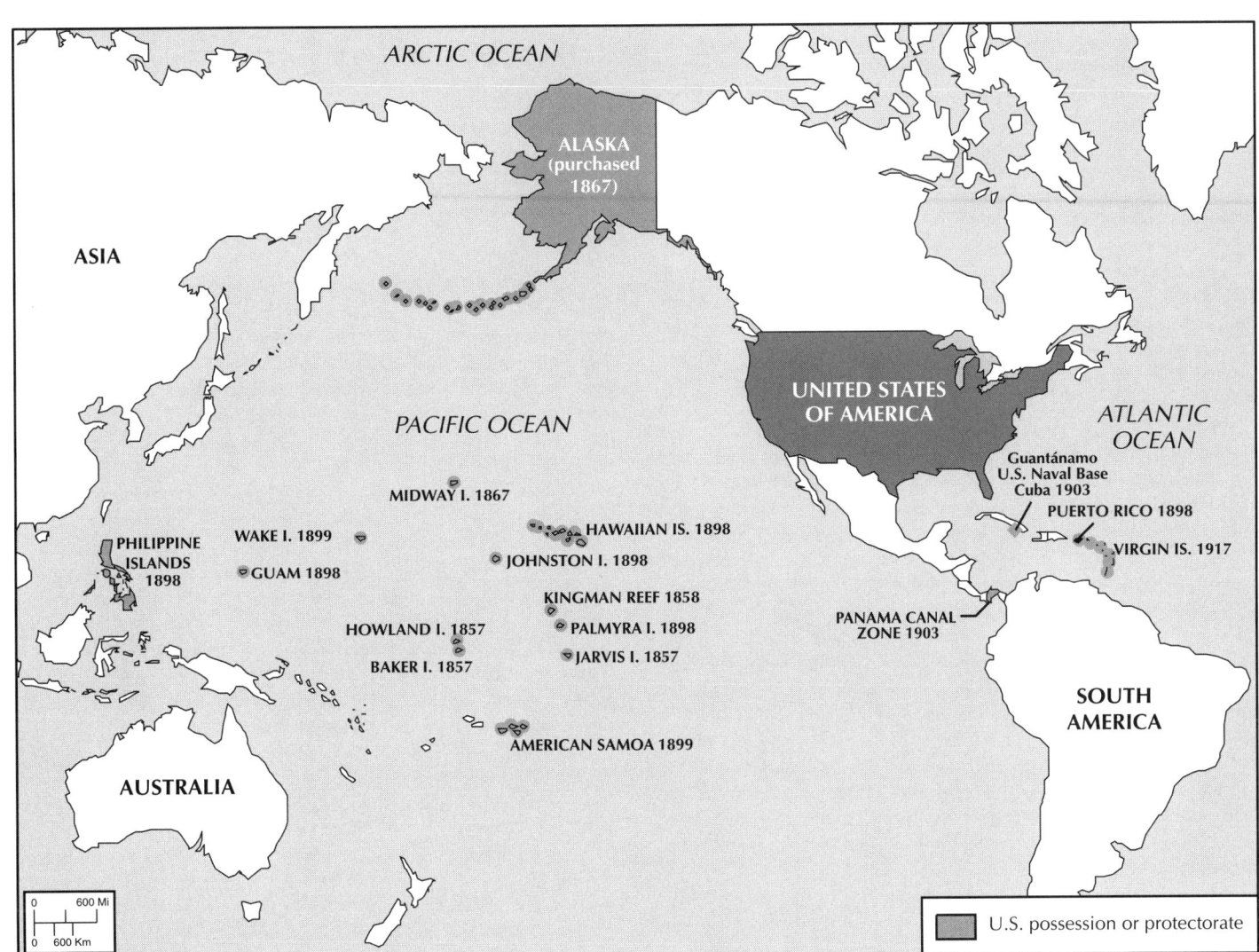

Dates of acquisition accompany the territories. What one might call the "American empire" was at its peak in terms of territory controlled during the years 1914–45. Except for the addition of the Virgin Islands in 1917, the territory did not change during the period. As the year 1945 neared an end, however, it was clear that change was about to take place—with the impending independence of the Philippine Islands, the indefinite status of several territories in the Pacific in the wake of the Second World War, and growing pressure for a reevaluation of the political position of Alaska and the Hawaiian Islands.

District of Columbia

Profile

Area: 69.2 sq. mi.
Population (est. 1945): 926,260
Elevation: 30 ft. above sea level
County: no county (independent)
Average temperature: January, 33.4°F; July, 76.8°F; annual average, 55°F
Average liquid precipitation: 42.6 inches (snowfall: 21.8 inches)

History and Development

The District of Columbia, better known as the city of Washington, D.C., is the capital of the United States. Situated on the north bank of the Potomac River, nearly surrounded by Maryland and bordered by Virginia, it is not part of any state. Washington is the property of the government of the United States.

The district and city were created after Congress decided in 1790 to find a new site for the national capital. The strip chosen originally also included 30 square miles on the Virginia side of the Potomac River, but this land was retroceded to Virginia in 1846. A French engineer and veteran of the American Revolution, Pierre Charles L'Enfant, planned and began work on the city's layout. The project was finished by Maj. Andrew Endicott. Enough work was done on streets and buildings to allow the government, and President John Adams, to move in on December 1, 1800. In 1814, during the War of 1812, British forces burned the Capitol, the president's home, and other buildings. White paint applied to cover the fire damage caused the president's home to be called the White House.

Washington grew in population and significance as the nation developed and as the United States emerged as a great nation of the world. The city was dominated by two imposing structures of the nineteenth century, the Capitol, sitting on an 88-foot-high hill, and the obelisk of the Washington Monument, 555 feet high. Other buildings, museums, and monuments were added over the years. The Lincoln Memorial was dedicated in 1922, the National Gallery of Art opened in 1941, and the massive Pentagon, technically in Arlington, Virginia, opened in 1943.

Washington was site of countless historic developments. It was almost attacked by Confederate troops in 1861; Abraham Lincoln was shot there in 1865; Woodrow Wilson died on S Street in 1924. Here the United States declared war in 1917 and 1941; here the Senate rejected a League of Nations in 1919–20; here the Bonus Army marched in 1932; here people wept as the caisson carrying Franklin D. Roosevelt rolled by in April 1945.

Washington was the fastest growing city in the United States during the Second World War. The population soared to more than one million in 1943, by which time all aspects of city facilities—the streetcars and buses, the availability of housing and eating establishments—were stretched to unbelievable lengths. Even so, Washington did not rule itself. The city was administered by three commissioners appointed by the president. The citizens of Washington still could not vote for president; they were not represented in Congress (although many residents retained these rights in their home state). When the war ended in 1945, Washington's population shrank slightly, to approximately 925,000.

Alaska

With 888,811 square miles of territory, nearly one-fifth the size of the United States, Alaska was by far the nation's largest posses-

sion. Synonymous with barren landscape and frigid temperatures, Alaska had a sparse population. The census of 1939 reported only 72,524 residents, of whom 39,000 were white, 5,600 Aleut, 15,600 Eskimo, and 11,300 Indian. Sitka was the capital until 1906. After 1912 it was Juneau.

Alaska was discovered in 1741 by Vitus Bering, a Dane in the employ of Russia. Russia retained nominal control until 1867, when a farsighted American secretary of state, William H. Seward, purchased the land for the United States for $7.2 million. The acquisition was deemed by many an act of folly—"Seward's Icebox," "Walrussia," and "Frigidia" were terms frequently used—but the land would pay for itself many times over. Alaska became, and remained, a valuable source for beaver, muskrat, otter, mink, and the Alaskan fur seal. Mineral wealth included gold (after discovery in 1898), tin, copper, gypsum, and later oil. Alaska was a major fishery, a world leader in the canning of salmon.

The land is a plump peninsula with a long, narrow panhandle extending for hundreds of miles south along the Canadian coast and the Aleutian Islands and running 1,200 miles into the Pacific Ocean. The Japanese captured two Aleutian Islands, Kiska and Attu, during the Second World War. American forces retook them in 1943. With bears of many kinds, including polar and grizzly, with caribou, moose, and mountain sheep, Alaska had an array of wildlife seldom found anywhere. With glaciers, active volcanoes, and North America's highest peak—Mt. McKinley at 20,300 feet—it was a land of breathtaking beauty.

Formally a territory of the United States since 1912, Alaska was administered by a locally elected legislature and a governor appointed by the president of the United States. The governor in 1945 was Ernest Gruening. Alaska's representative in Washington had no vote in the House of Representatives. Sentiment mounted for statehood sometime in the future (which was finally achieved in 1959).

Guam

Thirty miles long, 4 to 8 miles wide, with a total land area of 209 square miles, Guam is the largest of the Mariana Islands in the western Pacific Ocean. It is more than 5,000 miles southwest of California and 1,500 miles east of the Philippines. The population in 1940 was 22,290, mostly native Chamorros, although in the 1940s the island came under assault by various groups of outsiders.

Chamorros from the Malay Peninsula had lived in Guam for hundreds of years before the arrival of the Spanish explorer Ferdinand Magellan in 1521. Colonization by Spain began in the seventeenth century, and Spanish control lasted until the last part of the nineteenth century. The United States acquired control in 1898–99, more or less by conquest, although Spanish on the island, who did not know a war was on, offered no resistance. Guam was placed under the administration of the department of the U.S. Navy, and so it remained until the 1940s. For unforeseen years into the future, Guam was a territory of the United States.

The climate of Guam was rainy (69 inches per year) and hot, usually ranging between 70 and the low 90s. Local produce was largely tropical agricultural goods. Exports, which amounted to less than $85,000 in 1941, were made up of coconut oil and copra (dried coconut meat). English was the official language, but outside Agana, the capital, one heard many dialects. The Americans in the twentieth century introduced a modern school system.

The Japanese seized Guam on December 12, 1941—the first U.S. territory to fall to the enemy—and they held the island until July 1944, at which time the Americans took it back. Before Guam could fully reassume its status as an unincorporated territory of the United States, issues created by the war would have to be attended to, including recovery from the extensive damage done by the fighting.

Guantanamo Bay, Cuba

Guantanamo Bay is a small, pear-shaped indention on the underside of Cuba near the eastern end of the island. In the aftermath of the Spanish-American War, the United States decided to build a naval base there—the decision rationalized by the Americans assuming a "protector" status over the new nation of Cuba. A treaty in 1903 legalized lease of some 30 square miles for a sum of $2,000 a year. A new Cuban-American treaty in 1934 canceled the protectorate but reaffirmed U.S. control of Guantanamo. The base was useful to the navy during the Second World War; later it served as a station for the fleet's winter maneuvers. Cubans who became disturbed with America's control of their land had no reason to hope for a better day, for the original treaty of 1903—and subsequent agreements—carried no time limit. The Americans could rent the land, evidently, forever.

Hawaii

Hawaii is made up of a group of islets and eight main islands, comprising 6,454 square miles, stretching over a distance of nearly 400 miles. The eight islands are Kahoolawe, Maui, Lanai, Oahu, Kauai, Molokai, Niihau, and Hawaii. The largest island is Hawaii and the most famous is Oahu, where one finds the modern, bustling city of Honolulu (population in 1944: 217,692). The Hawaiian chain is approximately 2,400 miles southwest of California. The population of Hawaii in 1940 was 423,330, of which 14,000 were native Hawaiian, 50,000 Hawaiian/mixed, 29,000 Chinese, 53,000 Filipino, 104,000 white, and 158,000 Japanese.

Originally named the Sandwich Islands by the English seaman James Cook, Hawaii was ruled by native chieftains and monarchs, the last of whom was Queen Liliuokalani, who served until the 1890s. Native domination steadily receded in the face of immigration from Asia and America, most significantly Japanese and Americans who were interested in the islands' economic potential and in the fine port facilities at Pearl Harbor on Oahu. Annexation to the United States in 1898 was maneuvered by expansionist-minded politicians and by Americans active in Hawaii's various economic enterprises, especially sugar. In 1900 Hawaii officially became a territory of the United States.

For its small size, Hawaii in the twentieth century took on an exceptional appeal to its mother country. The pleasant climate—normally between the high 50s and high 80s—the beautiful scenery, and exotic wildlife (which included no snakes) made it a growing tourist spot. Waikiki Beach on Oahu became familiar to many Americans, as did native Hawaiian ways, such as the soothing music, the hula-hula dance, and charming use of flower garlands called leis. The islands also produced many tropical foodstuffs, including 50% of the world's pineapple and a good share of its cane sugar. The United States made Pearl Harbor its principal naval base in the Pacific in the 1940s.

Hawaii became permanently etched in the American memory as the target for the sudden Japanese attack on December 7, 1941, which provoked the United States' entry into the Second World War. Thereafter Oahu served as the primary base for fighting the Pacific War. The Honolulu area was taken over by people in military uniform. Not surprising, the island's population grew—to more than 500,000 by 1945. Hawaii still functioned as a territory, with a locally elected legislature and a governor appointed by the American president. The governor in 1945 was Ingram M. Stainback. Its delegate to the national House of Representatives had no vote. Fostered no doubt by the cry of "Remember Pearl Harbor," momentum was

well under way in 1945 for the admission of Hawaii as the forty-ninth state.

Panama Canal Zone

The Panama Canal Zone is a strip of land 10 miles wide and 50 miles long, stretching across the Republic of Panama at its narrowest point. In the center of the zone—in effect, cutting the country in two—was the Panama Canal, an artificial waterway that linked together the Atlantic and Pacific Oceans. The zone took up 553 square miles of land and water in a hot, rainy part of Central America. The population in 1940 was 51,827, of whom 32,856 were white and 18,524 were black or mixed.

The United States acquired rights to the territory under somewhat curious circumstances. Having decided to construct a canal in Central America, the Americans were disappointed when negotiations with Colombia, the nation that then owned the Isthmus of Panama, did not produce an agreement acceptable to both sides. With American encouragement, especially from President Theodore Roosevelt, Panamanian nationalists rose up in November 1903 and created the new nation of Panama. The United States then negotiated with Panama and received a treaty, ratified in 1904, that offered exceptionally generous terms. In return for a payment of $10 million and an annual rental fee of $250,000 (later raised to $430,000), the United States leased the 10-mile-wide Canal Zone (an earlier proposal had suggested only 6 miles) and received the right to build and operate the canal. Although the property technically remained Panamanian, American power was to be absolute and the treaty was to be in effect "in perpetuity."

Work on the canal began almost immediately and was finished in 1914—one of the great engineering feats of the twentieth century. What emerged was a complicated but highly effective system of locks 110 feet wide and 1,000 feet long and artificial lakes. The minimum depth was 40 feet. Vessels that passed through paid tolls based on size and weight. In 1929 an average of seventeen ships a day used the canal. Tolls for the year brought in more than $27 million.

The Canal Zone was the exclusive domain of the U.S. government. No private citizen of any country could own land there. It was administered by the Panama Canal Company, an agency of the U.S. government. The governor of the Canal Zone, also the president of the company, was appointed by the president of the United States.

Congress in 1939 authorized the construction of larger locks that would permit the handling of larger vessels. Work, which began in 1940, had to stop because of the start of the world war. The war swelled the local population when numerous military people arrived to assure protection of the canal. Although it was possible to detect rumblings of discontent among Panamanians about foreigners controlling their land, the Americans remained content with terms of the original treaty of 1903–4. Other than raising the rent, they gave no indication in the 1940s of being willing to change the status of the Canal Zone.

The Philippine Islands

Almost 7,000 miles from California, the Philippine Islands are part of the Malay Archipelago. The 7,100 islands make up a territory encompassing 115,600 square miles in a hot, moist part of east Asia. The temperature in winter averages 78°F, in summer 84°F. The population in 1939 was 16,000,304, made up of 15,758,637 Filipinos, 141,811 Japanese and Chinese, 29,157 black, 19,300 white, and

50,519 mixed. The capital is Manila, on the largest island of Luzon.

The Philippines were discovered by Ferdinand Magellan in 1521, conquered by the Spanish in 1565, and remained a Spanish colony for more than 300 years. The United States acquired control as a consequence of the Spanish-American War of 1898. American naval and land forces defeated the Spanish at Manila, and the American government demanded the islands in the treaty that followed in December 1898. Before the Americans could assert control, however, they had to suppress an uprising of native nationalists who wanted an independent state. The brutal war in the Philippines lasted until 1902.

Under its new master the Philippines began to take on American ways, which now mixed with older Spanish influence and various native patterns of living. Perhaps four million Filipinos came to speak the English language, although more understood Spanish, and numerous dialects still circulated. Two-thirds of the people were Roman Catholic. The United States gradually allowed home rule, especially in the Jones Act of 1916, although highest authority remained in the hands of an American high commissioner, appointed by the president of the United States. Congress in 1934 provided for Philippine independence ten years after the Filipinos approved it, which they did in 1936. In 1935 a new locally written constitution was approved by President Franklin D. Roosevelt and by Philippine voters. Manuel Quezon became president.

Japan conquered the Philippine Islands in early 1942 despite legendary resistance by combined Philippine and American forces at Bataan Peninsula and the tiny offshore island of Corregidor. Commanding American general Douglas MacArthur, who departed before the defeat, promised to return. President Quezon took up residence in the United States, and a guerrilla resistance movement of Americans and Filipinos continued to operate throughout the war.

The American government in 1944 approved two resolutions pertaining to the Philippine Islands. The first announced an intent to drive out the "treacherous invading Japanese" and then carry through with the promise of independence. The second called for keeping U.S. military bases on the islands. Reconquest of the Philippines began in October 1944; MacArthur proclaimed the islands liberated on July 5, 1945. As 1945 ended, the Philippines faced a huge task of political and economic reconstruction. In that year Paul V. McNutt was appointed for a second tour as high commissioner, and everyone knew he would be the last, for eyes of the people and the American government remained fixed on July 4, 1946, the anticipated date of Philippine independence.

Puerto Rico

Puerto Rico is an island 95 miles long and 35 miles wide at the northeastern end of the Caribbean Sea. The island's 3,435 square miles in 1940 contained a population of 1,869,255, of which about 75% were white and 25% black. The people spoke English and Spanish and mostly followed the Roman Catholic faith. The United States acquired Puerto Rico from Spain at the conclusion of the Spanish-American War in 1898—a consequence of conquest but virtually without opposition. As of the year 1945 the island remained a dependency of the United States, headed by a governor appointed by the American president. The governor in 1945 was Rexford G. Tugwell.

The semitropical climate and plentiful rainfall in the island fostered the production and export of sugar, citrus fruits, coffee, rum, molasses, coconuts, pineapples, and tobacco. The intense population density—550 per square mile—created difficulty in finding employment for all and produced growing interest in the 1930s in methods of birth control. The period of the Second World War was generally

a time of high employment—at home, on the mainland, or in the U.S. Army—but the end of war and the return of many people to Puerto Rico raised much concern about future economic conditions.

President Harry S. Truman recommended in October 1945 that the Puerto Rican people be allowed to vote on any change of status that Congress might legislate. Alternatives included giving Puerto Ricans more political rights, including the right to elect their governor, and some form of dominion status, statehood, or complete independence. The people seemed to be sharply split.

American Samoa

What is regarded as American Samoa is made up of seven coral or volcanic islands in the South Pacific, some 2,400 miles south of Hawaii. The total land area of the islands is approximately 76 square miles (about the same as Cincinnati), and the population in 1940 was 12,908. The best-known island is Tutuila, the capital of which is Pago-Pago.

American interest in the area dated from the 1870s, at which time the United States faced competition for coaling stations and stopping-off places from Germany and Great Britain. A treaty signed with these two powers in 1899 sanctioned American control of part of Samoa (Germany received another part—which it lost during the First World War). Between 1900 and 1904 local Polynesian chiefs ceded their islands to the United States. In 1929 Congress formally approved American sovereignty over the land and authorized administration by the president. Administration of Samoa through 1945 remained with the department of the U.S. Navy.

The islands produced products typical of the tropical climate: citrus fruits, coconuts, breadfruit, copra, and hula skirts. Samoa remained an unincorporated, unorganized territory of the United States. Although the final authority rested in a naval officer, local chiefs exercised much influence over local issues. Foreigners were forbidden to purchase land. Many Samoans converted to various denominations of Christianity. Of more than forty schools on the islands in the 1940s, six were operated by missionaries.

Virgin Islands

The Virgin Islands comprise three main islands, St. Croix, St. Thomas, and St. John, and approximately fifty uninhabited islets. East of Puerto Rico in the northwestern Caribbean, the islands have a total area of approximately 132 square miles. The population in 1940 was 24,889, the bulk of them black.

Columbus in 1493 discovered and gave the islands their name. The Spanish later drove out the local Indians and thinly settled the territory, although claim was contested by other nations. The Danes asserted control in 1671. In 1917 the United States purchased the islands from Denmark for $25 million, an act influenced by the recent completion of the Panama Canal. The United States placed the islands under control of the navy until 1931, at which time the Department of the Interior assumed authority. Although Virgin Islanders received American citizenship in 1927, the islands remained a dependency of the United States. Local councils were elected, but the governor was appointed by the U.S. president. The governor in 1945 was Charles Harwood. English was the dominant language.

Once the hideaway of pirates, the Virgin Islands in the 1940s were noted for tropical agricultural produce but especially for sandy beaches and the production of rum, including a then-popular cosmetic liquid called bay rum.

Other Pacific Territories

This group includes Baker, Canton, Enderbury, Howland, Jarvis, Johnston, Midway, Wake, and other outlying islands, together making up only a few square miles of land. These tiny outposts in the central Pacific were claimed by the United States at various times in the nineteenth and twentieth centuries and became non–self-governing territories. Thinly populated, if they had any native population at all, they took on added significance, if only temporarily, during the American war with Japan. Amelia Earhart was heading for Howland—1½ miles by ½—when her plane vanished in 1937. Japanese aircraft bombed Midway in June 1942, and then the forces withdrew in defeat after the momentous naval engagement that bore the island's name. Wake, captured by the Japanese in December 1941, was recaptured by the Americans on September 4, 1944. The United States retained its claim to these areas at the end of the Second World War. The relationship to the United States of numerous other islands, such as the Marshalls, Caroline, and Marianas—whose status had been changed by the war in the Pacific—remained pending as 1945 came to an end. They were headed toward a position of trusteeship.

CHAPTER 12 Cities of the United States

The information provided here includes a list of American cities of 100,000 people or more in 1940 and 1945, ranked according to size, and a description of the nation's ten largest cities, ranked in order, based on population estimates for the year 1945. Material on the ten largest cities is designed to give a brief description of the origin of the cities, basic characteristics, and their development up to the year 1945, with emphasis on the years 1914–45. Although Washington, D.C., moved into the ranks of the ten most populous cities in the 1940s, it here is treated as a special, separate entity and not in the group of ten.

Sources for the cities include: Bureau of the Census, *Sixteenth Census of the United States, 1940* (Washington, D.C., 1942); Bureau of the Census, *Statistical Abstract of the United States, 1946* (Washington, D.C., 1946); *1947* (Washington, D.C., 1947); *The Encyclopedia Americana* (1963 edition) (New York, 1963); *Encyclopaedia Britannica Yearbooks, 1935–1947* (Chicago, 1935–1947); *World Book Encyclopedia* (1973 edition), (New York, 1973).

TABLE 12.1 POPULATION OF CITIES HAVING 100,000 PEOPLE OR MORE, 1940 AND 1930, ARRANGED ACCORDING TO SIZE

City	Population		Increase 1930–40	Percentage of Increase	
	1940	1930		1930–40	1920–30
1. New York, N.Y.	7,454,995	6,930,446	524,549	7.6	23.3
2. Chicago, Ill.	3,396,808	3,376,438	20,370	0.6	25.0
3. Philadelphia, Pa.	1,931,334	1,950,961	−19,627	−1.0	7.0
4. Detroit, Mich.	1,623,452	1,568,662	54,790	3.5	47.9
5. Los Angeles, Calif.	1,504,277	1,238,048	266,229	21.5	114.7
6. Cleveland, Ohio	878,336	900,429	−22,093	−2.5	13.0
7. Baltimore, Md.	859,100	804,874	54,226	6.7	9.7
8. St. Louis, Mo.	816,048	821,960	−5,912	−0.7	6.3
9. Boston, Mass.	775,816	781,188	−10,372	−1.3	4.4
10. Pittsburgh, Pa.	671,659	669,817	1,842	0.3	13.8
11. Washington, D.C.	663,091	486,869	176,222	36.2	11.3
12. San Francisco, Calif.	634,536	634,394	142	a	25.2
13. Milwaukee, Wis.	587,472	578,249	9,223	1.6	26.5
14. Buffalo, N.Y.	575,901	573,076	2,825	0.5	13.1
15. New Orleans, La.	494,537	458,762	35,775	7.8	18.5
16. Minneapolis, Minn.	492,370	464,356	28,014	6.0	22.0
17. Cincinnati, Ohio	455,610	451,160	4,450	1.0	12.4
18. Newark, N.J.	429,760	442,337	−12,577	−2.8	6.7
19. Kansas City, Mo.	399,178	399,746	−568	−0.1	23.2
20. Indianapolis, Ind.	386,972	364,161	22,811	6.3	15.9
21. Houston, Tex.	384,514	292,352	92,162	31.5	111.4
22. Seattle, Wash.	368,302	365,583	2,719	0.7	15.9
23. Rochester, N.Y.	324,975	328,132	−3,157	−1.0	10.9
24. Denver, Colo.	322,412	287,861	34,551	12.0	12.2
25. Louisville, Ky.	319,077	307,745	11,332	3.7	31.0
26. Columbus, Ohio	306,087	290,564	15,523	5.3	22.6
27. Portland, Oreg.	305,394	301,815	3,579	1.2	16.9
28. Atlanta, Ga.	302,288	270,366	31,922	11.8	34.8
29. Oakland, Calif.	302,163	284,063	18,100	6.4	31.4
30. Jersey City, N.J.	301,173	316,715	−15,542	−4.9	6.2
31. Dallas, Tex.	294,734	260,475	34,259	13.2	63.8
32. Memphis, Tenn.	292,942	253,143	39,799	15.7	55.9
33. St. Paul, Minn.	287,736	271,606	16,130	5.9	15.7
34. Toledo, Ohio	282,349	290,718	−8,369	−2.9	19.6
35. Birmingham, Ala.	267,583	259,678	7,905	3.0	45.2
36. San Antonio, Tex.	253,854	231,542	22,312	9.6	43.5
37. Providence, R.I.	253,504	252,981	523	0.2	6.5
38. Akron, Ohio	244,791	255,040	−10,249	−4.0	22.4
39. Omaha, Nebr.	273,844	214,006	9,838	4.6	11.7
40. Dayton, Ohio	210,718	200,982	9,736	4.8	31.7

City	Population		Increase 1930–40	Percentage of Increase	
	1940	1930		1930–40	1920–30
41. Syracuse, N.Y.	205,967	209,326	− 3,359	− 1.6	21.9
42. Oklahoma City, Okla.	204,424	185,389	19,035	10.3	103.1
43. San Diego, Calif.	203,341	147,995	55,346	37.4	99.0
44. Worcester, Mass.	193,694	195,311	− 1,617	− 0.8	8.7
45. Richmond, Va.	193,042	182,929	10,113	5.5	6.6
46. Fort Worth, Tex.	177,662	163,447	14,215	8.7	53.5
47. Jacksonville, Fla.	173,065	129,549	43,516	33.6	41.5
48. Miami, Fla.	172,172	110,637	61,535	55.6	274.1
49. Youngstown, Ohio	167,720	170,002	− 2,282	− 1.3	28.4
50. Nashville, Tenn.	167,402	153,866	13,536	8.8	30.0
51. Hartford, Conn.	166,267	164,072	2,195	1.3	18.9
52. Grand Rapids, Mich.	164,292	168,592	− 4,300	− 2.6	22.5
53. Long Beach, Calif.	164,271	142,032	22,239	15.7	155.5
54. New Haven, Conn.	160,605	162,655	− 2,050	− 1.3	0.1
55. Des Moines, Iowa	159,819	142,559	17,260	12.1	12.7
56. Flint, Mich.	151,543	156,492	− 4,949	− 3.2	70.8
57. Salt Lake City, Utah	149,934	140,267	9,667	6.9	18.8
58. Springfield, Mass.	149,554	149,900	− 346	− 0.2	15.7
59. Bridgeport, Conn.	147,121	146,716	405	0.3	2.2
60. Norfolk, Va.	144,332	129,710	14,622	11.3	12.0
61. Yonkers, N.Y.	142,598	134,646	7,952	5.9	34.4
62. Tulsa, Okla.	142,157	141,258	899	0.6	96.0
63. Scranton, Pa.	140,404	143,433	− 3,029	− 2.1	4.1
64. Paterson, N.J.	139,656	138,513	1,143	0.8	1.9
65. Albany, N.Y.	130,577	127,412	3,165	2.5	12.4
66. Chattanooga, Tenn.	128,163	119,798	8,365	7.0	106.9
67. Trenton, N.J.	124,697	123,356	1,341	1.1	3.4
68. Spokane, Wash.	122,001	115,514	6,487	5.6	10.6
69. Kansas City, Kans.	121,458	121,857	− 399	− 0.3	20.4
70. Fort Wayne, Ind.	118,410	114,946	3,464	3.0	32.8
71. Camden, N.J.	117,536	118,700	− 1,164	− 1.0	2.1
72. Erie, Pa.	116,955	115,967	988	0.9	24.2
73. Fall River, Mass.	115,428	115,274	154	0.1	− 4.3
74. Wichita, Kans.	114,966	111,110	3,856	3.5	53.9
75. Wilmington, Del.	112,504	106,597	5,907	5.5	− 3.2
76. Gary, Ind.	111,719	100,426	11,293	11.2	81.3
77. Knoxville, Tenn.	111,580	105,802	5,778	5.5	36.0
78. Cambridge, Mass.	110,879	113,643	− 2,764	− 2.4	3.6
79. Reading, Pa.	110,568	111,171	− 603	− 0.5	3.1
80. New Bedford, Mass.	110,341	112,597	− 2,256	− 2.0	− 7.1
81. Elizabeth, N.J.	109,912	114,589	− 4,677	− 4.1	19.6
82. Tacoma, Wash.	109,408	106,817	2,591	2.4	10.2
83. Canton, Ohio	108,401	104,906	3,495	3.3	20.5
84. Tampa, Fla.	108,391	101,161	7,230	7.1	96.0
85. Sacramento, Calif.	105,958	93,750	12,208	13.0	42.2
86. Peoria, Ill.	105,087	104,969	118	0.1	37.9
87. Somerville, Mass.	102,177	103,908	− 1,731	− 1.7	11.6
88. Lowell, Mass.	101,389	100,234	1,155	1.2	− 11.1
89. South Bend, Ind.	101,268	104,193	− 2,925	− 2.8	46.8
90. Duluth, Minn.	101,065	101,463	− 398	− 0.4	2.6
91. Charlotte, N.C.	100,899	82,675	18,224	22.0	78.4
92. Utica, N.Y.	100,518	101,740	− 1,222	− 1.2	8.1

aLess than 0.1%.
Note: Two cities on the list in 1940, Sacramento, Calif. and Charlotte, N.C., did not have 100,000 in 1930, and three on the list in 1930, El Paso, Tex., Lynn, Mass., and Evansville, Ind., by 1940 had dropped below 100,000.
Source: Bureau of the Census, Sixteenth Census of the United States: 1940, Vol. I: Number of Inhabitants (Washington, D.C., 1942), 32.

Ten Largest Cities of the United States
New York City

Profile

Founded: 1613, incorporated 1653

Population (est. 1945): 7,730,383

Rank in 1945: 1st

Area: 365.4 sq. mi.

Elevation: 55 ft. above sea level

Counties: Bronx, Kings, New York, Queens, Richmond

Average temperature: January, 30.9°F; July, 73.8°F; annual average, 52.3°F

Average liquid precipitation: 42.99 inches (snowfall: 31.9 inches)

Type of government: mayor-council; mayor in 1945: Fiorello H. La Guardia

History and Development

Originally the land of Algonquian Indians, the area of New York was explored in 1524 by Giovanni da Verrazano, an Italian sailing for France. Henry Hudson, an Englishman employed by the Dutch, sailed up the river that bears his name. The Netherlands claimed the land and built a fort named New Amsterdam. In 1626, so the story goes, the Dutch bought Manhattan Island from the Indians for items worth approximately twenty-four dollars. The English seized the colony in 1664 and renamed it after the duke of York, the future King James II. New York became a major city of colonial America and a leader in the revolt against Great Britain. In the nineteenth century New York's growth to supremacy among American cities was based on its excellent location with respect to entry into the hinterland, as well as its fine harbor, which made it a natural center for business and commerce, all this activity fostered by the ongoing American association with Europe. In the twentieth century New York became the premier city of not merely the United States but also the world—the focal point of business, finance, art, and culture. It was the major point of entry for most immigrants from Europe (at a time when most immigrants came from Europe), and so New York was the first city of immigrants, noted especially for large numbers of Italians, Irish, Jews, and Germans. It was principal point of departure and return for millions of American troops who fought two

A portion of New York's skyline in the early 1940s. (Library of Congress)

world wars in Europe.

Made up of the five boroughs of Manhattan, the Bronx, Brooklyn, Queens, and Staten Island, New York City in the early twentieth century could boast of countless "firsts" and scientific and cultural developments and a growing list of famous structures. The Port Authority of New York, created in 1921, produced the Holland Tunnel (1927), George Washington Bridge (1931), and Triborough Bridge (1936). Radio City Music Hall opened in 1932, and Rockefeller Center was finished in 1940. The massive Chrysler Building (1930) was surpassed as the world's tallest by the Empire State Building, finished in 1931. Yankee Stadium baseball park opened in 1933. The New York World's Fair opened in 1939 and reopened the following year. With the Yankees, the Giants, the Brooklyn Dodgers, and the Rangers in hockey, with Carnegie Hall, Madison Square Garden, and the theaters of Broadway, with headquarters of the radio networks and most of the television sets then in existence, New York was the starting place for American entertainment.

New York's turbulent, often corrupt, immigrant-influenced political setting was dominated by the colorful reformist mayor Fiorello H. La Guardia during the years 1933–45. On La Guardia's decision to step down in 1945, a Democrat, William V. O'Dwyer, was elected and prepared to take office the next year. In 1945 the capital of the new United Nations organization, New York City stood poised to defend its title as the informal capital of the world.

Chicago

Profile

Founded: 1803, incorporated 1837
Population (est. 1945): 3.5 million
Rank in 1945: 2d
Area: 211.3 sq. mi.
Elevation: 595 ft. above sea level

County: Cook
Average temperature: January, 23.7°F; July, 72.5°F; annual average, 49.1°F
Average liquid precipitation: 32.86 inches (snowfall: 33.4 inches)
Type of government: mayor-council; mayor in 1945: Edward J. Kelly

History and Development

Wyandot Indians occupied the territory before the arrival of the whites, and the area that became Chicago was a crossroads for Native Americans moving from one waterway to another. After defeat at the Battle of Fallen Timbers in 1794, the Indians ceded to the United States a 6-mile tract of land at the mouth of the Chicago River on the southern shore of Lake Michigan, where soldiers proceeded to build Ft. Dearborn. Slow at first to take hold, the area around the fort began to grow as the nation moved west. Chicago's location on the Great Lakes and on the Chicago River promoted its establishment as a national commercial center and in time a hub for the expanding railway system. After the Civil War it became a manufacturing city as well and the center of the meatpacking industry that was pointed toward the major markets in the East.

Reborn and rebuilt after the great fire of 1871, Chicago truly became an American metropolis as it grew in business and commerce, attracting many immigrants who managed to travel beyond the cities of the Atlantic Coast, as well as large numbers of migrants from states of the Midwest and South.

In the period following the First World War, Chicago added reasons for notoriety that its citizens would have preferred not to have. Black migration from the South produced destructive racial tension, especially during the "Red Summer" of 1919. In the era of prohibition Chicago became world famous as a hotbed of brutal gangland rivalry over power and profits from the sale of illegal alcohol, the home of the notorious chieftain Al Capone, and the site of the St. Valentine's Day Massacre in 1929.

Often heralded in song and verse, the city continued to accumu-

All large cities had slums, and most black people in large cities lived in slums. Residents called Chicago's black district Bronzeville. (Library of Congress)

A view of large buildings in Chicago, the city of skyscrapers and "big shoulders." (Library of Congress)

late distinctions of a more proper sort. Midway Airport began business in 1927 and soon became the nation's busiest. The World's Fair opened in 1933. Chicago liked things big—such as the Wrigley Building, built in 1924, and the Tribune Tower and Union Station (both 1925). Merchandise Mart, which opened in 1930, was the largest building in floor area before the Pentagon was finished in 1943. The first leg of Chicago's subway opened in 1943. A massive center of manufacturing during the Second World War, with two major-league baseball teams and two professional football teams, with excellent museums, zoos, and other attractions, Chicago at the time of the war's end in 1945 claimed with ease and confidence its title as the nation's Second City.

Philadelphia

Profile

Founded: 1682, chartered 1701
Population (est. 1945): 2.1 million
Rank in 1945: 3d
Area: 135 sq. mi.
Elevation: 100 ft. above sea level
County: Philadelphia
Average temperature: January, 34.4°F; July, 76.7°F; annual average, 56°F
Average liquid precipitation: 41.86 inches (snowfall: 20 inches)
Type of government: mayor-council; mayor in 1945: Bernard Samuel.

History and Development

Situated in southeastern Pennsylvania, 90 miles from New York and 135 miles from Washington, D.C., Philadelphia is the largest city in the state. The Delaware River runs on two sides of the city, and the Schuylkill River runs through it.

Originally called New Sweden and controlled briefly by the Dutch, Philadelphia was officially founded in 1682 by William Penn.

A Quaker and a pacifist, Penn named it the City of Brotherly Love. It grew rapidly as a center of commerce, business, and culture. Partly because of the guidance of a popular native, Benjamin Franklin, it developed into a bustling location of colonial education and the arts. Franklin participated in the founding of the University of Pennsylvania. Philadelphia was home of the Continental Congress and capital of the United States during the Revolutionary War. The city had many historic sites, such as Carpenter's Hall, Old Christ Church, and Benjamin Franklin's tomb. Independence Hall, which remained home of the Liberty Bell, was the place where the Founding Fathers signed the Declaration of Independence and in 1787 the Constitution. The city retained a reputation for orderly arrangement of streets and a lack of tall buildings. Policy decreed that no structure could be taller than city hall (548 feet) with a 37-foot statue of William Penn on top.

In the twentieth century Philadelphia continued to grow as a center of oil refining and of many types of manufacturing, especially of defense-related goods. Philadelphia supplied vast amounts of military goods during the First World War. Work started in 1917 on the shipyard at Hog Island, although production proceeded slowly. The national government took over the police department in 1918 as part of an anti-vice campaign. In 1924, during the era of prohibition, local authorities closed 973 saloons. The Delaware Bridge that connected Philadelphia and Camden, New Jersey, was finished in 1926, and the North Broad Street subway opened in 1928. In 1934 two famous newspapers, the *Inquirer* and the *Public Ledger,* merged. The city experienced a racially inspired riot in the local transit company in 1944. Philadelphia's factories boomed again during the Second World War, and its trademark magazine, the *Saturday Evening Post,* founded by Benjamin Franklin and still selling for five cents a copy, continued to be popular throughout the nation.

Los Angeles

Profile

Founded: 1781, incorporated 1850
Population (est. 1945): 1,855,000
Rank in 1945: 4th
Area: 452.2 sq. mi.
Elevation: 275 ft. above sea level
County: Los Angeles
Average temperature: January, 54.6°F; July, 70.2°F; annual average, 62.4°F
Average liquid precipitation: 15.23 inches (snowfall: trace)
Type of government: mayor-council; mayor in 1945: Fletcher Bowron

History and Development:

Located on the Pacific coast in southern California (130 miles north of Mexico), Los Angeles is one of the largest cities of the United States in terms of territory. Many groups of American Indians lived in the area before the first appearance of whites in 1542. Spanish colonists arrived in some number in 1769, at which time a priest among them gave the place its name—the City of Angels. The area remained a Spanish mission and town (pueblo) until 1821, when, with the recession of the Spanish empire, it became part of the new state of Mexico. A growing American interest in the western lands reached fruition in 1848, at the end of the American war with Mexico, when the United States acquired control of all the area of California. Arrival of the railroad from points east in the 1870s opened the city to many new residents from the rest of the United States and its western territories.

In the twentieth century several forces merged to make Los Angeles a vibrant city and perhaps the nation's most rapidly growing metropolis. Oil production continued to be a major enterprise. Completion of a harbor in 1914 made the city a port. Expansion of irrigation facilities in the surrounding territory made Los Angeles a location for the processing and distribution of foodstuffs. One by one the movie companies established themselves in the area, and the attraction of Hollywood reached large and unique dimensions. During the 1920s many new industries settled in the area, and even the depression years of the 1930s drove more people to Los Angeles, seeking work or at least a pleasant climate in which to spend idle time.

The city retained a reputation as a location of strange people and bizarre developments, many of them associated with Hollywood or with the area's lack of a solid tradition. Social change continued at a steady pace. In 1917 the Tournament of Roses Association decided to use a football game instead of a chariot race to celebrate New Year's Day. In 1923 Angelus Temple was established by the colorful evangelist and faith healer Aimee Semple McPherson, and in the same year the massive Los Angeles Coliseum was finished. Huntington Library and Art Gallery opened in 1928. In 1932 Los Angeles

hosted the Olympic Games. The city experienced the racially motivated "zoot-suit" riots in 1943, largely involving white sailors and Mexican Americans. The opening of many new defense factories and other considerations made Los Angeles a virtual magnet for the rest of the country in the 1940s, and by the end of the Second World War it had passed Detroit and become the nation's fourth largest city in population.

Detroit

Profile

Founded: 1701, incorporated 1806
Population (est. 1945): 1,685,000
Rank in 1945: 5th
Area: 142 sq. mi.
Elevation: 581 ft. above sea level
County: Wayne
Average temperature: January, 24.4°F; July, 72.1°F; annual average, 48.5°F
Average liquid precipitation: 32.05 inches (snowfall: 41.7 inches)
Type of government: mayor-council; mayor in 1945: Edward J. Jeffries

In western cities slum areas were more likely to be inhabited by Hispanics than by African Americans. (Library of Congress)

History and Development

Detroit is situated on the north bank of the Detroit River, on Lake Saint Claire and near the Great Lakes of Erie and Huron. It was thus a natural crossroads for commerce. It was the home of Wyandot and other Indian tribes before the arrival of French explorers and fur traders. Founded in 1701 by Sieur de Cadillac, Detroit became the site of a fort and fur-trading station. The name in French means "strait." The French controlled the area until 1760; the British held the land until 1796, when in fact as well as legally it became part of the new United States (it had become American in the peace treaty of 1783, but the British held on to it until 1796). In 1796 the surrounding territory was named Wayne County in honor of "Mad Anthony" Wayne, a Revolutionary War hero. Detroit was Michigan's capital during the years 1837–47. Development in the nineteenth century was aided by resources of the surrounding territory and the Great Lakes. Abundant transport advantages were given a large new boost with opening of the Erie Canal in 1825.

Already a manufacturing center by the start of the twentieth century, Detroit became a true industrial giant with the blossoming of the new automobile industry, a development that was much the work of Henry Ford, Ransom E. Olds, and the Dodge brothers. Not surprisingly, the city turned to military production in 1916–18, during the First World War. Returning to automobile production in a large way, Detroit grew to be the nation's third largest city in 1925, with a population of more than 1,250,000, half of them foreign-born. The largest number came from Poland. Despite a substantial movement of black people from the South into the city, the black population then made up only 6.5% of the total.

Making cars was a mixed blessing, however, and the Great Depression was devastating for the city. Automobile production dropped from 5.3 million in 1929 to 1.3 million in 1932. Perhaps the only reason for celebration in the mid-1930s was in sports, as in 1935 the local teams in baseball (Tigers), football (Lions), and hockey (Red Wings, 1935–36) won championships. The road to recovery was strewn with major strikes in the late 1930s. Big business for Detroit had also come to mean big labor. In 1943 the city experienced a major race riot that left thirty-four dead and more than 700 injured. By that time Detroit was engaged in a boom of massive proportions caused by the start of the Second World War. The Motor City became America's "arsenal of democracy." With the end of war in 1945 Detroit was impatient to start a headlong rush into production of civilian goods. It would not come without the now-familiar disputes between labor and management. The strikes started even before the year was out.

Baltimore

Profile

Founded: 1729, incorporated 1797
Population (est. 1945): 930,000
Rank in 1945: 6th
Area: 85.6 sq. mi.
Elevation: 155 ft. above sea level
County: none (independent)
Average temperature: January, 32.3°F; July, 74.8°F; annual average, 58°F
Average liquid precipitation: 46.6 inches (snowfall: 22 inches)
Type of government: mayor-council; mayor in 1945: Thomas R. McKeldin

History and Development

Baltimore was established in 1729 in a harbor near the Patappsco River 14 miles from Chesapeake Bay. The city was named after Charles Calvert, the fifth Lord Baltimore and a part of the family that founded the colony of Maryland. The town quickly became connected with the tobacco trade from the Piedmont region, and it functioned as an important colonial port. The downtown area expanded along the first two streets, Baltimore and Charles, and in the 1800s the city grew around the harbor area—the so-called inner core—where one found many historic buildings and monuments. Here, in Baltimore Harbor, Francis Scott Key wrote "The Star-Spangled Banner" in 1814. The city served as a gateway into the interior. The National Road ran from Baltimore, and the Baltimore and Ohio Railroad, the B & O, started in 1827, remained a major east-west route to the Midwest in the twentieth century.

The city grew as a center of manufacturing, especially shipbuilding, and of commerce. A new business district was built after a huge fire in 1904. Baltimore served as an important port and shipbuilding location in the two world wars. In 1914, true to the spirit of its blue laws, Baltimore refused to legalize playing baseball on Sunday. In that year the city celebrated the centennial of the writing of "The Star-Spangled Banner," an event that highlighted the city's most important tourist attraction: Fort McHenry. William Jennings Bryan, the secretary of state, was featured speaker. In 1916 the city held a major preparedness parade. Baltimore in 1919 banned the sale of gasoline on Sunday. In 1921 a statue of poet Edgar Allan Poe was unveiled. The *Baltimore American* newspaper merged in 1928 with the *News*. In 1931 the state legislature at last gave the city home rule with respect to blue laws, the Sunday closings. The new municipal airport opened in 1941. During the Second World War, in 1943, Theodore R. McKeldin defeated Howard Johnson—who was running for a third term—and became mayor.

Cleveland

Profile

Founded: 1796, incorporated 1836
Population (est. 1945): 900,000
Rank in 1945: 7th
Area: 73.1 sq. mi.
Elevation: 660 ft. above sea level
County: Cuyahoga
Average temperature: January, 26.5°F; July, 71.4°F; annual average, 49.2°F
Average liquid precipitation: 33.82 inches (snowfall: 40.4 inches)
Type of government: mayor-council; mayor in 1945: Thomas A. Burke, Jr.

History and Development

The largest city in Ohio, Cleveland is situated on the shore of Lake Erie, at the mouth of the Cuyahoga River, some 575 miles from New York City and 350 from Chicago. The Cuyahoga River divides the city in half as it runs to Lake Erie. Erie, Chippewa, and Iroquois Indians preceded whites to the area. Moses Cleaveland surveyed the land for the Connecticut Land Company in 1796 in a site called the Western Reserve of Connecticut land. It was established as a village in 1814.

Cleveland profited from its location in the interior, on the Great Lakes system, and close to the coalfields of Ohio, Pennsylvania, and the Appalachian region in general. The opening of the Erie Canal in 1825 helped the city become a commercial center, with a population growing from movement inside the country and from European immigration. One of the places where Appalachian coal and iron ore from the Minnesota region came together, Cleveland became active in the production of iron and steel. Close to the Detroit area, the city also profited in the twentieth century from expansion of the automobile industry.

New residents moved to the city in the 1920s, notably black people from the South seeking work. The Republican National Convention met in Public Auditorium in 1924 and renominated President Calvin Coolidge. Many new structures were built in the period between the two world wars. The Museum of Art was finished in 1916, the Union Commerce Building in 1924, and the Public Library the following year. Completed in 1928, Terminal Tower was, at 708 feet, the tallest building in Ohio. Union Station opened in 1930, Main Avenue Bridge in 1939. The Cleveland Health and Education Center became in 1940 the first permanent health museum. Massive Municipal Stadium was host for the professional baseball team (the Indians) and for sporting and cultural events. Lakeview Cemetery on Euclid Avenue was resting place for such famous people as President James A. Garfield, John Hay, and John D. Rockefeller. A beehive of activity during the Second World War, Cleveland was expected to enjoy continued prosperity long afterward.

St. Louis

Profile

Founded: 1764, incorporated 1822
Population (est. 1945): 845,000
Rank in 1945: 8th
Area: 65 sq. mi.
Elevation: 455 ft. above sea level
County: none (not in a county)
Average temperature: January, 31.1°F; July, 78.8°F; annual average, 56.2°F
Average liquid precipitation: 37.44 inches (snowfall: 19 inches)
Type of government: mayor-council; mayor in 1945: Aloys P. Kaufman

History and Development

The key to the development of St. Louis was its location on the west bank of the Mississippi River, some 4 miles south of the confluence of the Mississippi and Missouri Rivers. In time the border of the city stretched some 20 miles along the shore of the Mississippi. It was in all ways a river city.

First visited by Jesuits in 1700 and then abandoned, St. Louis was permanently settled by French fur traders, beginning in 1784. It was named after King Louis IX of France. Spanish property between 1768 and 1801 and then regained by France, it was sold to the United States in 1803, a part of the vast Louisiana Territory. The first steamboat on the Mississippi reached the town in 1817. St. Louis gradually became a center of trade and business activity and was starting point for people heading into the West. People moved to the area from Virginia, Kentucky, and Tennessee. Large numbers of Irish and German immigrants arrived between 1830 and 1870. St. Louis took on an identity as a city of Germans, perhaps most conspicuously marked by its many breweries with German names. A part of St. Louis County until 1876, it then became a separate entity. A home-rule charter was approved in 1914.

In the twentieth century the city grew as a center of commerce and manufacturing, with specialization in the metal industries. Local businessmen in 1927 financed Charles A. Lindbergh's historic flight across the Atlantic Ocean in an airplane appropriately named the *Spirit of St. Louis.* When prohibition in the 1920s caused hardship in

the breweries, local producers turned to making malt, yeast, and various types of corn products. St. Louis, more than most cities, cheered the end of the Eighteenth Amendment. Even so, the depression of the 1930s was devastating. St. Louis could boast of two fine newspapers, the *Post-Dispatch* and *Globe-Democrat,* two good universities, and two major-league baseball teams in the 1940s. In 1944 the baseball teams played each other in the World Series, and the Cardinals of the National League defeated the Browns of the American League. In 1941 a thirty-seven-block area of the waterfront was cleared to make room for a memorial to Thomas Jefferson and the Louisiana Purchase, but construction was delayed. The first public housing project was completed in 1943, by which time the city was in the midst of a wartime economic boom.

Boston

Profile

Founded: 1630, chartered 1822
Population (est. 1945): 780,000
Rank in 1945: 9th
Area: 65.9 sq. mi.
Elevation: 21 ft. above sea level
County: Suffolk
Average temperature: January, 27.9°F; July, 71.7°F; annual average, 49.6°F
Average liquid precipitation: 40.14 inches (snowfall: 42.8 inches)
Type of government: mayor-council; mayor in 1945: John E. Kerrigan

History and Development

Located at the mouth of the Charles River on Boston Harbor, Boston is made up of three land areas—East Boston, Charlestown, and Boston Proper. Parts of the inner city include Old Boston, a peninsula that reaches into the harbor; Boston Common, 50 acres in the center of the city, which is the oldest public park in the United States; and such other areas as Beacon Hill, the Market District, and the Back Bay District.

Although other Englishmen had visited the area, Boston was settled by the people of the Massachusetts Bay Company—at Charlestown in 1629 and Boston in 1630. Puritan colonists, led by Gov. John Winthrop, followed, and in September 1630 the territory was named in honor of Boston in Lincolnshire, England, whence many of the settlers came. Under control by a Puritan theocracy, Boston grew, not without provoking protest from those people left out of the political/religious system. Some left to live in another colony. Puritan control ended with revocation of the colony's charter in 1684.

Boston became a major colonial port and in time a center of revolutionary activity without peer—the site of protests, acts of defiance to the throne of England, home of famous revolutionaries, and finally location of the first battles of the Revolution at Lexington and Concord. The city's numerous attractions thus included exceptional historic sites. In the nineteenth century Boston stood out as a literary center, the home of poets and writers, of Harvard University and other institutions, and such distinguished publications as the *Atlantic Monthly.* Immigration changed the character of the population, as large numbers of European immigrants, notably Irish, produced a heavily Roman Catholic city.

Many changes took place in the twentieth century. The Boston City Planning Board, created in 1914, prepared a zoning plan that became law in 1924. The plan limited the height of new buildings, and the only structures piercing the skyline were church steeples and the tower of the Custom House, a federal building not bound by the mandate of a maximum height of 125 feet. A Metropolitan District commission was created in 1919 to deal with services for the greater Boston area. In the 1920s much money was spent on streets, parks, and the harbor. A police strike in 1919 received much national attention and boosted the political career of Gov. Calvin Coolidge of Massachusetts. The Irish began to assert themselves in politics. John "Honey Fitz" Fitzgerald, the first Irish mayor, served until 1914. Others would follow. Blessed with a fine natural harbor, Boston was an Atlantic port second only to New York. With a naval base and a shipyard—the colonial frigate *Constitution,* "Old Ironsides," remained permanently docked there—and with a growing industrial base, Boston bustled with production and commerce during the two world wars of the twentieth century.

Pittsburgh

Profile

Founded: 1758, incorporated 1816
Population (est. 1945): 675,000
Rank in 1945: 10th
Area: 55.1 sq. mi.
Elevation: 745 ft. above sea level
County: Allegheny
Average temperature: January, 30.7°F; July, 74.6°F; annual average, 52.8°F
Average liquid precipitation: 36.17 inches (snowfall: 32.1 inches)
Type of government: mayor-council; mayor in 1945: Cornelius D. Scully

History and Development

Pittsburgh is in southwestern Pennsylvania, where the Allegheny and Monongahela Rivers merge to form the Ohio River—the Three Rivers or Golden Triangle area. It became a major center for the production of steel, in time taking on such names as Iron City, Steel City, and Smoky City.

This wilderness area was explored by Sieur de la Salle for France, John Cabot for the English, and others. George Washington later surveyed the land for the British government. France and Britain claimed the area. A French fortress in the three rivers area, Fort Duquesne, was attacked by British troops in 1754 and 1755. On departure of the French in 1758, the British built a fort at the fork of the Allegheny and Monongahela Rivers and named it Ft. Pitt, after William Pitt, the British prime minister. The village outside the fort became Pittsburgh. After the Revolution, Pittsburgh became an early gateway to the West as the new nation expanded—the distinction fostered by the excellent river and rail transport facilities.

Pittsburgh was well situated for a marriage of the coal from the nearby Appalachian fields and iron ore from the upper Midwest. Natural gas also was available in abundant supply. The city produced goods for the Union army during America's Civil War and later became a part of Andrew Carnegie's vast empire of steel. Oil from Pennsylvania's fields was refined there. Into the twentieth century it continued to attract immigrants from Europe and later black and white settlers from the American South.

The overwhelming presence of the rivers left many marks. Pittsburgh became a city of bridges, more than 200. It was susceptible to floods. The large flood at the Golden Triangle in 1936 caused forty-five deaths and property damage worth $25 million. In 1920 the first commercial radio broadcast (the election returns) beamed from the first commercial station, KDKA, Pittsburgh. Heavy industrialization led to numerous labor disputes, to polluted air and water, and to the economic ups and downs of the economic cycle of the First World War, the 1920s, 1930s, and 1940s. The cycle went up during 1940–45, at which time Pittsburgh had its special claim to being an arsenal of the United States. The city produced one-third of the steel used by the American army.

CHAPTER 13 Profiles of Prominent Individuals

This chapter contains profiles of prominent people from an age that produced many such individuals. All the presidents are included, and there are enough military leaders to suggest that this was indeed a time of war and rumor of war. The selection of other individuals represents an effort to touch many areas of activity, various groups, and diverse points of view. They are only examples. Dozens of individuals omitted had as much—if not more—claim to prominence as many of those whose profiles appear here.

Irving Berlin

Irving Berlin was born Isidore Baline of Russian-Jewish parents in Temun, Russia, on May 11, 1888. Arriving in New York in 1893, he had only two years of schooling and scarcely any training in anything. He nonetheless showed talent for writing popular music, especially for the stage. In 1911 "Alexander's Ragtime Band" became his first hit. Never a musical innovator, Berlin showed himself to be flexible, adept, and remarkably prolific at detecting popular American moods and writing songs that fit. His music was pleasant, often dreamy and frequently patriotic. His show music was performed in the Ziegfield Follies, in *Face the Music, Top Hat, Annie Get Your Gun, Easter Parade,* and many other movies and plays. His popular songs include "Blue Skies," "Remember," "Always," "A Pretty Girl Is Like a Melody," "What'll I Do?" "Easter Parade," and many others. His "God Bless America," written in 1917 but released in 1938, and "White Christmas," released in 1942, became American standards. Many believe that no other person has contributed as much music for the general American population. Berlin had a very long time in which to work. He died in 1989 at age 101.

Mary McLeod Bethune

Mary McLeod was born in South Carolina on July 10, 1875, one of seventeen children in a family little removed from slavery. Her

Two prominent and influential women of the Roosevelt years and after—Eleanor Roosevelt *(left)* and Mary McLeod Bethune *(right).*
(Franklin D. Roosevelt Library)

early years were marked with hard work and dedication to education and religion. Mary McLeod graduated from Moody Bible Institute in 1895 and hoped to become a missionary. Marriage to Albert Bethune provided her with little beyond a single child and an additional name. Her life for more than a half century was given over to working with whites and other blacks to advance the status of black people in America, especially black women. In 1904 she founded Daytona Normal and Industrial Institute, which later became Bethune-Cookman College. In the 1920s she became the leader of the National Association of Colored Women. In the 1930s and 1940s she was the most influential black woman in public affairs. A strong supporter of Franklin Roosevelt and a close friend and colleague of Eleanor Roosevelt, she worked through the National Youth Administration and as general adviser to the Roosevelt administration. She was in many ways the leader of the "black cabinet." Forceful and idealistic, yet conciliatory and practical, she used her considerable talents as educator, orator, negotiator, even singer—always within the confines of her Christian faith—to promote the standing of her people in America, to urge government and private individuals and institutions to create conditions that would allow black people to help themselves. She died in Daytona Beach in 1955.

Margaret Bourke-White

Margaret Bourke White was born in New York City on June 14, 1904, and despite two marriages she continued to use this name, adding only a hyphen. She studied at Columbia University, the University of Michigan, and Western Reserve and Cornell Universities and then became a professional photographer, doing work for *World's Work, Fortune,* and *Life.* Her efforts produced some of the most moving pictures of depression-ridden America. The collection *You Have Seen Their Faces* (1937) probably was best known. During the Second World War she accompanied the air force and army on missions and produced in 1945 *The Living Dead of Buchenwald,* about a concentration camp in Germany. She went on several assignments for *Life* after the Second World War until Parkinson's disease caused her to slow down. One of the most important photojournalists of her era, mostly the 1930s and 1940s, she died in 1971.

Louis Brandeis

Born on November 13, 1856, in Louisville, Kentucky, Louis Dembitz Brandeis studied abroad in the 1870s and returned to receive a law degree from Harvard University in 1877. In private practice in the late nineteenth century, he established an identity as the "people's attorney," much troubled about the huge accumulation of wealth and power in the hands of large corporations. His endorsement of a "living law," the concept that political institutions had to adjust to economic reality, was manifested in the "Brandeis Brief" in the case of *Muller v. Oregon* (1908), which favored legislation limiting women's working hours. Part of Woodrow Wilson's New Freedom program, he was appointed by President Wilson in 1916 to the Supreme Court, the first Jewish justice to serve on the High Court. For more than thirty years Brandeis distinguished himself on the Court as a critic of big business and a friend of most social legislation. In the 1920s he often joined Oliver Wendell Holmes in dissent of conservative Court decisions; in the 1930s he usually, but not in every case, voted to allow the government of Franklin D. Roosevelt broad latitude in dealing with huge social and economic problems. Brandeis also was one of the Americans most prominent in the emerging Zionist movement and remained so until his death in 1941.

Pearl S. Buck

Pearl Comfort Sydenstricker was born on June 26, 1892, in Hillsboro, West Virginia, while her parents were home on leave from missionary work in China. Because the family soon returned to Asia, Pearl grew up in two cultures, with two types of education. She received degrees from Randolph-Macon College and Columbia University. Marriage to John Buck in 1917 gave her a name she used the rest of her life. Dividing time between China and the United States, Buck would establish an identity in humanitarian work, especially in the care of Asian-American children, and above all as a writer. The novel *The Good Earth,* published in 1931, gave her an international reputation as an interpreter of Chinese society. Buck was awarded the 1938 Nobel Prize for literature. *Dragon Seed,* also about China, followed in 1942. Although she produced more than 100 books and many other works on numerous subjects, when she died at 81 in 1973, people remembered her as the lady of *The Good Earth* (the book and the movie) and an important component of what one might call the romantic era of America's relationship with China.

Al Capone

Alphonse Capone was born in Naples, Italy, on January 17, 1899. Settling with his family in Brooklyn, he briefly attended school before entering New York's underworld. Nicknamed "Scarface Al" from a gangland wound, he accompanied Johnny Torio to Chicago in 1920, intent on controlling the city's rackets. Through bribing public officials and brutal wars against such competitors as Dion O'Banion, Capone became the dominant figure in Chicago's crime by the mid-1920s, reaping huge profits from various illegal activity but mostly from selling bootleg booze. His men executed the St. Valentine's Day Massacre in 1929. Finally in 1931 he was convicted of income tax evasion and sentenced to eleven years in the national prison at Alcatraz. By the time of his release in 1939 he was seriously crippled, suffering from lasting effects of syphilis. When he died in 1947, he still existed in many people's minds a symbol of the bygone age of prohibition and organized crime, if not of evil in general in the United States.

George Washington Carver

The son of slave parents, George Washington Carver was born near Diamond Grove, Missouri, in 1864. After earning two degrees from Iowa State College, he became in 1896 head of agricultural research at Tuskegee Institute in Alabama. At Tuskegee Carver became a foremost scientist in his chosen area of interest. Seeking to help poor southern farmers, he urged planting less soil-depleting cotton and more peanuts, soybeans, and sweet potatoes. In his laboratory he produced from these and other products new types of dyes, face creams—more than 400 items in all. He also developed a new durable cotton that became known as Carver's Hybrid. A modest, gentle man, Carver refused to use his success for financial enrichment. What money he did make he donated in 1940 to the George Washington Carver Foundation, with instruction that it be used to further his research. He died in January 1943, in his beloved Tuskegee.

Carrie Chapman Catt

The former Carrie Lane took the name of both her first husband, Leo Chapman, and her second husband, George W. Catt. Born in Ripon, Wisconsin, on January 9, 1859, Carrie Chapman Catt went to college in Iowa, worked as an administrator in the Iowa school system, and became a convert to the state's movement for woman suffrage. An heir of Elizabeth Cady Stanton and Susan B. Anthony, she was—unlike the other two leaders—on the scene when the movement reached its climax in the second decade of the twentieth century. As head of the National American Woman Suffrage Association, in 1915 she drew apart from the more militant—and abrasive—suffragettes and placed the movement on a more moderate, practical, middle-class course. Although concerned with social problems and all aspects of the status of women, she focused on the vote, reminding President Woodrow Wilson and members of Congress that even after casting their ballots, women would be no less wives and mothers. She probably was the single individual most significant in persuading Congress to pass a woman suffrage amendment in 1919 and having the states accept the Nineteenth Amendment the following summer, in time for the election of 1920. In years that followed, Carrie Chapman Catt continued to be active in politics—founding what would become the League of Women Voters—in the peace movement, and in refugee activity in the 1930s. She died in 1947.

Calvin Coolidge

Calvin Coolidge was born in Plymouth, Vermont, on July 4, 1872. He graduated from Amherst College, practiced law in Northampton, Massachusetts, and then held many state offices. As governor of Massachusetts, his position on the Boston police strike in 1919 helped place him on the Republican national ticket with Warren Harding the following year. Assuming the presidency in 1923 (the thirtieth president) on the death of Harding, he handled the Republican scandals competently and was easily reelected in 1924. He remained to the end a low-profile, business-oriented chief executive at a time when such an individual was tolerable—quick to veto proposals he believed would cause the government to do too much or spend too much. His decision not to run in 1928 enabled him to get out just in time before the system—his system—came crashing down in 1929. He died in 1933.

John Dewey

John Dewey was first and foremost a philosopher. He was born on October 20, 1859. After being educated at the University of Vermont and the Johns Hopkins University (Ph.D., 1884), he taught at the Universities of Michigan, Minnesota, and Chicago and in 1904 settled in for a long tenure at Columbia University. In years to come he would produce many volumes advocating a school of thought called "pragmatism," "instrumentalism," or the "Chicago School." Perhaps best known of these works was *The School and Society* (1899), which helped establish his identity as a foremost exponent of "progressive education," loosely described as learning by doing and giving attention to the social development of the student. When Dewey died in 1952, his name was perhaps more commonly associated with educational method than with either his many works on philosophy or his association with many left-of-center political causes.

John Dillinger

John Dillinger created a brief sensation in an America mired in depression. A killer and habitual criminal, he ended up a virtual folk hero. Born in Indianapolis on June 28, 1902, Dillinger would become a deserter from the navy, and after bungling his first bank job he spent nine years in prison in Indiana. On being paroled in 1933 he began a sensational crime spree that lasted approximately a year. People knew that he was wrong, but in these desperate times many could not avoid admiration for Dillinger's sense of humor, his daring, and his creativity in robbing banks, outwitting his pursuers even to the point of raiding police stations to acquire new weaponry. Most dashing was an escape from an "escapeproof" jail in Crown Point, Indiana—accomplished, legend had it, with a wooden pistol fashioned by his own hand. He became public enemy number one. Betrayed by a woman companion, the famous "lady in red," he was shot down by federal agents outside the Biograph Theater in Chicago on July 22, 1934. A major media event, Dillinger's dramatic demise had the additional effect of enhancing the prestige of the FBI, of agent Melvin Purvis, and of director J. Edgar Hoover.

Amelia Earhart

Amelia Earhart was born in Atchison, Kansas, on July 24, 1897, and she spent much of her early life in transience. An adventurous young woman, she was drawn to aviation when flying was a supreme mark of daring and adventure. Becoming the first woman to fly the Atlantic in 1928 (with two companions) established her in some measure as the female counterpart of Charles A. Lindbergh. Fame eased her passage into new ventures, such as marriage to publisher George Putnam in 1931 and the post of aviation editor for *Cosmopolitan*. It was as a pilot, however, that she continued to make a reputation and establish records for speed and distance in the mid-1930s. The end to her life contributed heavily to the mystique of Amelia Earhart. She and her navigator, Fred Noonan, were on the last leg of an around-the-world flight when on July 2, 1937, their twin-engine Lockheed Electra vanished en route to Howland Island in the central Pacific. No proof exists as to their fate. One of the most famous and admired people of her age, she was by example a genuine trailblazer in new roles for women and in a broader understanding of what women were capable of doing.

Albert Einstein

Born in Ulm, Germany, on March 14, 1879, Albert Einstein attended school in Germany and Switzerland. He received a Ph.D. in physics at Zurich in 1905. Thereafter he taught at universities in Zurich and Berlin and attracted international attention for his research. In 1915 he published his general theory of relativity; in 1921 he received the Nobel Prize for physics for work on the photoelectric effect of light. A Jew and a dedicated Zionist (a supporter of a Jewish national home in Palestine), he left Germany in 1933 as the anti-Semitic Adolf Hitler regime came to power. He accepted a position at the Institute for Advanced Study at Princeton University. He informed President Franklin D. Roosevelt in 1939 of the possibility of someone developing an atomic bomb—a move that helped set the Manhattan Project in motion—and advised the government in other ways. He continued to do research at Princeton and to work for Zionism and for world government and control of atomic energy until his death in New Jersey on April 18, 1955. Einstein's name still stands as the symbol of the scientist-intellectual, of extreme brilliance of the mind, and it deserves the distinction. His work in

President Franklin D. Roosevelt meets Gen. Dwight D. Eisenhower in Sicily, December 8, 1943. (Franklin D. Roosevelt Library)

physics allows him to rank in a small elite of people who have probed the mysteries of the universe.

Dwight Eisenhower

Although Dwight David Eisenhower had two careers, the one that occupied most of his adult life and constituted his true profession was in the military. Born in Denison, Texas, on October 14, 1890, and raised in Abilene, Kansas, he attended the military academy at West Point because, as he frequently said, it provided a free education. A mediocre student, he graduated in 1915 and then entered into many years of routine assignments and army schools. It was the Second World War that made the career of Eisenhower. Lacking the flair and color of a George Patton, he impressed army chief of staff George Marshall as dedicated, intelligent, and exceptionally clear-thinking. The support of Marshall helped him get his first star in 1941 and then to be catapulted by Franklin D. Roosevelt over hundreds of generals to command U.S. troops in Europe and finally to head all Allied forces in Operation Overlord, the invasion of France in 1944. A competent strategist, he better distinguished himself as manager of a large, complex, multinational military opera-

tion. He returned to the United States in 1945 with five stars on his shoulder, a gigantic victory to his credit, and claim to being probably the country's foremost military hero. After brief terms as army chief of staff, president of Columbia University (1948–51), and first commander of NATO, he was elected the thirty-fifth president in 1952 (on the Republican ticket). Although his time in office was not a period of vigorous social action, the assessment of his leadership of Cold War America in 1953–61 seems to improve with passing years. Eisenhower also wrote *Crusade in Europe* (1948) and, after retiring, two volumes of memoirs. These accomplishments notwithstanding, Americans at the time of his death in 1969 still preferred to think of him fondly as General Ike with the friendly grin, leader of their victory over Nazi Germany and a man they were willing to have stand as representative of the nation's character and qualities.

Henry Ford

Henry Ford was a big businessman, to be sure, but one with a different touch. Born on July 30, 1863, in Dearborn, Michigan, he acquired little formal schooling but much practical experience: in farming and lumber, in the electrical business, and even shipbuilding in Detroit. He made his first automobile in 1896, briefly produced racers (the "Ford 999"), and formed Ford Motor Company in 1903. Ford eventually established an international reputation as a down-to-earth innovator who was determined to bring the automobile within reach of the average citizen. To that end he began producing the Model T—the "flivver"—on a moving assembly line in Highland Park (1914), paid workers the exceptional wage of five dollars a day (1914), and lowered the car's price to less than $300 (1924). Except for offering the V-8 engine, his innovations had come by the end of the 1920s. In later years he became fad-ridden and prejudiced on many issues, and he was bitterly opposed to labor unions. Bullheaded and resistant to change, he almost ran Ford Motors into the ground in the 1930s. By the time of his death in 1947, time had passed him by. Nonetheless, no single individual contributed as much to the automobile industry as did Ford; he transformed the business. No name is more deservedly synonymous with cars than is Henry Ford.

Clark Gable

William Clark Gable was born on February 1, 1901, in Cadiz, Ohio. Joining an acting company at age nineteen, he received his first bit part in *What Price Glory?* in 1924. His first major film role came in 1930 in *The Painted Desert.* Then his career took off. Despite having huge ears, he was handsome and suave, the symbol of the matinee idol, with enormous masculine sex appeal. Countless men began wearing the pencil-thin mustache in an attempt to look like Gable, and countless women wished their men could be like him too. The most popular of his many movies included *It Happened One Night* (1934), for which he received an Academy Award; *Mutiny on the Bounty* (1935); and especially *Gone with the Wind* (1939). Of modest acting talent and less than an innovative artist, he was still the long-acclaimed "King of Hollywood," probably the most popular performer for a quarter century, the best representative of the thrust of the movie business in the 1930s and 1940s, and a good representative of American tastes. He died in 1960, shortly after doing *The Misfits,* with Marilyn Monroe.

Judy Garland

Frances Ethel Gumm, born on June 10, 1922, in Grand Rapids, Minnesota, seemed destined for show business almost from the beginning. There were three members of the singing Gumm Sisters, but any listener could tell that the talent—the style and especially the range—belonged to Frances, the youngest. Pressed by an ambitious mother, she sang at countless engagements, changed her name to Judy Garland, and attracted the attention of Louis B. Mayer in 1935. After a slow start with M-G-M she hit her stride in 1939 appearing as Dorothy in *The Wizard of Oz.* The film's theme song, "Over the Rainbow," became her trademark. In years to come she contributed mightily to the golden age of Hollywood, especially to the musical films of the 1940s, appearing first as a teenage star and then as the attractive but not beautiful, wholesome girl who could sing exceptionally well. *For Me and My Gal* (1942), *Meet Me in St. Louis* (1944), and *Easter Parade* (1948) were examples. She also reminded Americans that Hollywood was indeed a land of make-believe. The Garland one saw on screen was not the Garland that existed. Her life continued to be a roller coaster of personal triumph—notably a performance at Carnegie Hall in 1961—interspersed with broken marriages, struggles with drugs, and emotional problems. Her death on June 22, 1969, at age forty-seven did nothing to minimize the paradox. Her passing if anything added to the strength of her considerable following. Perhaps some of her fans had hoped to make it

big, as Garland had done; some identified with her elusive quest for happiness; many simply adored that booming and feeling voice. For all of them she remained Dorothy, still looking over the rainbow.

Marcus Garvey

Marcus Garvey was one of the more original and lively advocates of a black awakening in the period between the two world wars. Born in Jamaica on August 17, 1887, he came to New York City in 1916, bringing his concept of a Universal Negro Improvement Association. In his efforts to promote black pride, independence, and a vigorous activism, he founded numerous businesses, including a black flying corps and a steamship company, the Black Star Line. Always grandiose, he attracted millions of followers, and a convention in New York in 1921 named him "Provisional President General of Africa." Not long after announcing his "Back to Africa" movement—for black emigration to Liberia—he was convicted of mail fraud and sentenced to prison in 1923. Pardoned four years later and deported to Jamaica, he died in 1940. Most of his projects were poorly managed; his Back to Africa plan never got off the ground; he was bitterly attacked by many black intellectuals. Even so, Garvey offered something different and meaningful to American blacks seemingly confined to a life of subservience. He would stand as a forerunner to the militant activism of the 1960s and 1970s.

Freeman Gosden and Charles Correll

Freeman F. Gosden and Charles J. Correll were much better known as Amos and Andy. Gosden was born in Virginia in 1899, and Correll came from Peoria, Illinois (born February 2, 1890), and as early as 1920 they began to experiment as a comedy team. Calling themselves Sam and Henry, in January 1926 they brought to WGN (Chicago) a new type of radio show. When they moved to WMAQ in 1928 and to NBC in 1929, they adopted the name Amos and Andy, and so it remained for more than twenty years: two white men playing parts of allegedly typical blacks in Harlem—sounding as blacks were thought by many to sound, with Correll and Gosden supplying voices for five characters. Until 1943 the show ran fifteen minutes five nights a week; then it changed to a half-hour weekly and later moved to television. It was far and away the most popular radio show during the early years of the depression and, relative to its competition, possibly the most popular radio show ever produced. The show was piped into stores; theaters scheduled movies around the 7 to 7:15 time slot. People from the president on down were familiar with Amos Jones, Andrew H. Brown, Kingfish Stevens, Lightnin', and the rest of the cast. Although the show was drenched in racial stereotypes and suggested how many white people looked upon blacks in the prewar era, it was possible to listen without taking offense, and evidently many people of both races did. Predictably such tactics would face assaults from civil rights activists of the postwar period. When a much-changed program left the air for good in 1960, among the people who fondly remembered the golden years of the 1930s were many blacks as well as millions of white people.

D. W. Griffith

Born on January 22, 1875, in La Grande, Kentucky, David Lewelyn Wark Griffith tried numerous types of activity before entering filmmaking during its infant stage. He directed his first film, *The Adventures of Dollie,* in 1908. His most famous work, the silent movie *Birth of a Nation,* premiered in 1915. Long assailed as an expression of racism in American society, the film also broke ground in many areas. It was the first film spectacular, the first epic. On an investment of $100,000 it produced earnings of nearly $50 million. In 1919 Griffith joined with Douglas Fairbanks, Charlie Chaplin, and Mary Pickford to form United Artists Corporation. Continuing to make such silent movies as *True Heart Susie* and *America,* he established himself as an innovative giant of the new medium, pioneering such devices as fade-in, fade-out, angle shots, and the moving camera. He retired in 1932 and pulled out of UAC in 1933. He died in Hollywood in 1948.

Warren G. Harding

Warren Gamaliel Harding was born in Blooming Grove (earlier known as Corsica), Ohio, on November 2, 1865. After trying several undistinguished ventures, he married a wealthy widow, Florence Kling DeWolfe, in 1891, a move that made possible the purchase of the *Marion Star.* Ownership of the newspaper, along with striking good looks and identification as a likable supporter of regular Republicanism, facilitated his rise in state politics and his election to the United States Senate in 1914. His selection in 1920 as the twenty-ninth president was more a reflection of the relaxed self-indulgence of the post–First World War era than of Harding's strengths of character and political competence. Although he appointed a few good men to office, such as Herbert Hoover, and was capable of an occasional courageous act, such as the pardon of Eugene Debs, Harding would be better known for what went wrong during his time in office. Many of his appointees were friends and cronies, members of the "Ohio Gang," who proceeded to splatter the administration with corruption and other marks of scandal. Such names as Albert Fall and Teapot Dome are only the best known. Harding soon realized he was out of his league, indeed that he had failed, and for that reason his death of unclear causes on August 2, 1923, after less than three years in office, might be seen by some as merciful. Virtually every survey rating the American presidents places Harding at or near the bottom of the list.

Ernest Hemingway

Ernest Hemingway was one of the most popular American writers of the 1920s through the 1950s; he was surely the most imitated American author of the twentieth century. He was born on July 21, 1899, in Oak Park, Illinois. Just as his life was marked with pursuit of adventure, excitement, and danger, his novels and short stories dealt with war, challenge, courage, and sex. His writing style was simple, clear, almost devoid of adjectives, and still so remarkably moving and effective that thousands worldwide tried to copy it as they also copied his lifestyle. His works include *The Sun Also Rises* (1926), *A Farewell to Arms* (1929), *To Have and Have Not* (1937), *For Whom the Bell Tolls* (1940), and many other books and short stories. After the success of *The Old Man and the Sea* (1952) he won the Nobel Prize for literature in 1954. As Hemingway wrote and lived, he also died. Conscious that writing was becoming more difficult and aware of shortcomings in his mental and physical capabilities, he shot himself in July 1961.

Herbert Hoover

For much of his life, Herbert Clark Hoover stood as a clear representative of the merits of hard work and clean, honest, and caring living. Born in West Branch, Iowa, on August 10, 1874, he

worked his way through Stanford University and became a highly successful international mining engineer. During the First World War he gave effective service as food administrator and head of various relief operations in Europe. As secretary of commerce during 1921–28 he advanced the Republican idea of self-policing of industry through trade associations. Scoring a huge victory over Al Smith in 1928, he was inaugurated thirty-second president in 1929 and seemed the high priest of a humane and sensible business-dominated system of private enterprise. Unfortunately, the stock market crashed a few months later, and he lived out his presidency in a time of devastating economic decline. Although he came to accept a limited program of public works, he remained ever fearful of tampering with basic capitalism. The speed with which his successor, Franklin D. Roosevelt, supported change after 1933 seemed to harden Hoover's image as a defender of orthodox economics. A decent, honest, intelligent individual, he was the most qualified of the three Republican presidents of the 1920s. Even so, when he died in 1964, people still equated the name Hoover with depression, and they would do so for years to come. Many even falsely believed that he caused it.

Fiorello H. La Guardia

Born in New York City on December 11, 1882, dying in the same place in 1947, Fiorello Henry La Guardia would become almost synonymous with his city. Even so, he traveled widely as a young man, as a correspondent, a diplomatic official, and member of the army. He received a law degree from New York University in 1910. A man with ties to several ethnic minority groups, he paved a path in politics for others to follow, starting with service as a Republican congressman during 1917 and 1923–33. La Guardia would be best known as the tireless, colorful, incorruptible mayor of New York for three terms (1933–45) with the backing of several parties. During much of that time he also led the opposition to Hitler (and Mussolini) and served as national head of Civil Defense. He could not please everyone in New York, but he did set a high standard for politics in a very difficult place. He was short and stocky and even resembled comedian Lou Costello, and people loved his riding fire engines, his reading funnies over the radio during a newspaper strike, his optimism and honest efforts at reform. He was their Fiorello, their "Little Flower."

John L. Lewis

John Llewellyn Lewis was born in Lucas, Iowa, on February 12, 1880. The son of a coal miner and a worker in the pits as a teenager, he rose rapidly in union organization until he became president of the United Mine Workers in 1920. As head of this union for forty years he would score remarkable gains in membership, wages, and working conditions in an industry in which work was exceptionally dangerous and labor issues fiercely fought out. In the 1930s he was the prime mover behind a new general union for unskilled workers, the Congress of Industrial Organizations (CIO), which officially broke off from the American Federation of Labor (AFL) in 1938. As with Samuel Gompers, Lewis accepted capitalism and concentrated on practical gains for his charges, but he showed no hesitation to urge the miners into various forms of direct action. Tough-looking and aggressively independent, he engaged in numerous bitter quarrels with President Franklin D. Roosevelt. His willingness to have his miners strike in the critical times before, during, and after the Second World War led many to accuse him of greed and irresponsibility and made him a hated man in America. Nevertheless, no person was more responsible than Lewis for the growth in size and strength of the union movement in the twentieth century. Though coal miners and many union people would sing his praises, his reputation among the general population was mixed. He died in June 1969.

Charles A. Lindbergh

Charles Augustus Lindbergh, Jr., was first and foremost a man of flight. Born in Detroit on February 4, 1902, Lindbergh briefly attended the University of Wisconsin and then joined that small group of people who devoted themselves to the new frontier of aviation. Lindbergh's fame was established forever by his carefully planned solo flight from New York to Paris on May 20–21, 1927. Tall, good-looking, and modest, he was the perfect hero to people of an era looking for something to celebrate and an American to honor. Thereafter nothing associated with Lindbergh escaped attention of the press, ranging from his story-book marriage to Anne Morrow in 1929, to the brutal slaying of his baby in 1932, to his entanglement in national and international politics of the 1930s and 1940s. Basically shy, he did not appreciate his loss of privacy, although he continued to act in ways that would attract attention. His reputation was tarnished by his advocacy of isolationism in the debate over foreign policy in 1940–41, when critics sought to label him as anti-Semitic and an apologist of the Nazi regime in Germany. In the final decades of his life he continued to advise the government on aviation and established a reasonable reputation as an author, mostly of autobiography, and as a conservationist. Still somewhat marked by the

Charles A. Lindbergh and the airplane that carried him across the Atlantic in 1927. (National Archives)

controversies of his life, the man known as "Slim" or the "Lone Eagle" died in 1974.

Huey Long

Huey Pierce Long was an exceptionally colorful and effective politician. Born on September 10, 1893, in Winnfield, Louisiana, he studied law and moved quickly into politics in his native state. As governor during the years 1928–32, he headed a regime marked by high taxes and extensive internal improvements, especially in education and highway construction. Although charged with dictatorial practices and other political misconduct, he remained a hero to the masses, a genuine populist. As a U.S. senator, he appeared as a rural radical, author in 1934 of a simplistic but appealing program called "Share Our Wealth," which called for the confiscation of large fortunes and their distribution to the people—enough for a car, home, and radio and for other purposes. He clearly had larger goals in mind and was mentioned as a presidential candidate—if not as a challenger to Franklin D. Roosevelt in 1936, at least in an election soon to come. In September 1935 he was killed by gunfire from a member of an opposition faction in Louisiana. His memory lived on, however, as did the power of the Long family in the politics of the state.

Joe Louis

Joe Louis was more than a skilled boxer and superb athlete. He was the most popular and possibly the most important African American in the first half of the twentieth century. Born Joe Louis

Arguably the best heavyweight of them all, Joe Louis appears here in 1935, before he became champion. (State of Michigan Historical Archives)

Barrow on May 13, 1914, in Alabama, he moved at age seven to Detroit, where he briefly attended school. After several years as an amateur boxer, he turned professional in 1934 and won the heavyweight championship three years later. Fighting as Joe Louis, the Brown Bomber, he held the title for twelve years; his bouts included a stunning defeat of German challenger Max Schmeling in 1938 and a thrilling contest with Billy Conn in 1941, and for a time he met one challenger a month. After service in the army during the Second World War, he returned to boxing for a while. Coming out of retirement twice, he quit permanently after losing to Rocky Marciano in October 1951. In the opinion of many observers, he was the most skilled person to hold the crown. Radio helped Louis leave an influence that went beyond sports. He helped to bring long-overdue attention and respectability to blacks. Though not exactly a civil rights activist, he did draw attention to the plight of black people in the United States. Among blacks he was a source of pride, accomplishment, and encouragement beyond peer—the first truly national black hero. Personal problems he would experience in his later years did nothing to diminish his legacy. Joe Louis died in April 1981.

Douglas MacArthur

Douglas MacArthur provoked strong opinion during his long career in the U.S. Army. The criticism usually included a charge of

arrogance that probably was traceable to a life of being at or near the top. Born in Little Rock, Arkansas, on January 26, 1880, he was the son of a general, highest in his class at West Point (1903), aide to his father, aide to President Theodore Roosevelt, and a participant in the expedition into Mexico and in the First World War. He also was commander at West Point, chief of staff of the army, head of army forces in Asia during the Second World War and a five-star general, commander of the American occupation of Japan, and commander of United Nations forces in Korea. Supporters found him brilliant as a strategist, charismatic as a leader, right-headed in his view of national and world politics. Opponents saw him as a supreme egotist, given to frequent tactical mistakes for which he refused to accept responsibility. MacArthur is best remembered as one of the two most popular military leaders of the Second World War (along with Dwight D. Eisenhower) and for his willingness to challenge President Harry Truman's policy in Korea, for which he was fired in 1951. He served as chairman of Remington Rand until his death in 1964, still a hero of anticommunists and the right in American politics and of those who favored a policy of "Asia First."

George C. Marshall

Born in Uniontown, Pennsylvania, on December 31, 1880, George Catlett Marshall decided at early age on a career as a profes-

Roosevelt confers with Gen. Douglas MacArthur *(left)*, Adm. Chester Nimitz *(center)*, and presidential aide Adm. William D. Leahy *(right)* in Hawaii on July 28, 1944. (Franklin D. Roosevelt Library)

sional soldier. After graduating from the Virginia Military Institute in 1901, he served in the Philippines (twice) and in China and as an aide to John J. Pershing, as chief of war plans (1938), and as chief of staff of the army from 1939 to 1945—virtually everything a military man could hope for save command of a large force in combat. He was denied this honor because Franklin D. Roosevelt could not spare him from Washington. Aloof, dedicated, and disciplined, with a commanding demeanor, he became a five-star general, superior in rank to Eisenhower, MacArthur, everyone except William D. Leahy. His ability to supervise the raising of a vast army and the strategy for the Second World War in Europe and Asia, to deal with the egos and idiosyncrasies of the generals beneath him, and still retain respect from president and Congress earned him placement as one of America's greatest military leaders. Marshall also had a second career—as a diplomat in China (1945–46), secretary of state (1947–49), and secretary of defense (1950–51). These efforts would attract treacherous attacks by Joseph McCarthy and others of his ilk, but they also would bring him a Nobel Peace Prize in 1953. Harry S. Truman called Marshall the "greatest living American." He died in October 1959.

Mike Masaoka

Mike Masaru Masaoka was born on October 15, 1915, in Fresno, California, of Japanese descent. He was a Nisei—a second-generation Japanese American and a citizen of the United States. After graduation from the University of Utah in 1937, he became a member of the Japanese American Citizens League. In 1940 he wrote the creed of that organization, stressing loyal American citizenship, and in 1941 he became the national secretary. Although he opposed the internment of Japanese Americans in 1941–42, he continued to urge cooperation and patriotism, going so far as to insist that Nisei be allowed to be drafted. When the army started to take Nisei volunteers, Masaoka was the first to sign up; four Masaoka brothers followed. All five received war wounds; one was killed and one permanently disabled. The brothers earned some thirty medals. After the war Mike Masaoka remained active with the JACL—still urging patriotism and also seeking fair compensation for losses suffered during the internment. He was frequently honored for his work. Masaoka was at no time a household name in the United States, but he was the closest to being a spokesperson for his people. He reflected perhaps more than any person what a mistake the wartime internment policy had been.

Glenn Miller

Alton Glenn Miller was born in Clarinda, Iowa, on March 1, 1904. Frequently moving with his family, he attended high school in Fort Morgan, Colorado, where he learned to play the trombone. Thereafter he began playing professionally in such groups as the orchestra of Ben Pollack (1925), where he joined Benny Goodman, and Red Nichols and His Five Pennies, where he played with Jimmy and Tommy Dorsey. He also demonstrated talent as an organizer and musical arranger. His first effort at forming his own band failed in 1937, but the second a year later did not, the mellow "Miller sound" marked with lead coming from saxophone and clarinet. His band became one of the most successful of the "swing" or big-band era. His most popular selections included "In the Mood," "Little Brown Jug," and "I Got a Gal in Kalamazoo." Although nearly forty, he joined the army in 1942, during the Second World War, and was assigned to head up an air force band to entertain the troops. Planning to play for soldiers who recently had invaded Hitler's Europe,

Miller departed England en route to France on December 15, 1944. His plane vanished over the English Channel. Although Miller was considered not as creative as some of his colleagues, his music has stood the test of time, and he remains to many who grew up in the era the best-known representative of the big-band era of the 1930s and 1940s.

Chester W. Nimitz

Chester William Nimitz was born in Fredericksburg, Texas, on February 23, 1885. After graduation from the Naval Academy in 1903, he served several years as a submarine officer. In the 1930s he worked in the Bureau of Navigation and then as a commander of cruisers and battleships. When Husband Kimmel fell from grace in wake of the disaster at Pearl Harbor, Nimitz in December 1941 became commander of the Pacific Fleet. The war against Japan was in no small measure a naval war, and the man in charge throughout was Chet Nimitz. Commanding the largest fleet in history, he helped devise the special tactics—the carrier task force, the island invasions—suited to the far-flung Pacific theater. A deliberate, soft-spoken, and unspectacular man, his approach in some ways resembled that of Dwight D. Eisenhower. He was especially effective in choosing men and getting the most from them. A five-star admiral in September 1945, he and Douglas MacArthur accepted the surrender of the Japanese. After two years as head of Naval Operations, Nimitz left the navy in 1947. He died in 1966.

Eugene O'Neill

Born on October 16, 1888, in New York City, Eugene Gladstone O'Neill experienced a life marked with pain and tumult, starting with his rearing in a show-business family and extending to wandering and drunkenness, three marriages, an attempt at suicide, and tuberculosis and other physical problems. When he found his calling as a playwright, it is not surprising that his plays focused on tragedy. His first Broadway play, *Beyond the Horizon,* won a Pulitzer Prize in 1920. Other prominent plays of the 1920s included *The Emperor Jones* (1921), *Anna Christie* (1922), *All God's Chillun Got Wings* (1924), *Desire under the Elms* (1924), and *Strange Interlude* (1928). He won three Pulitzer Prizes and became in 1936 the second American to receive a Nobel Prize for literature. The foremost American dramatist of his era, O'Neill would acquire even greater status after his death in 1953. Perhaps his best-known work, the autobiographical *Long Day's Journey into Night* was published three years later.

Jesse Owens

Trackman Jesse Owens was a premier athlete of the 1930s and one of the few blacks to receive attention and acclaim in America at that time. Born in Danville, Alabama, on September 12, 1913, he went to school in Cleveland and then attended Ohio State University. On one day in 1935 he broke three world records and tied a fourth in the dashes, hurdles, and long jump. His star shone brightest at the Olympics of 1936 in Berlin when, in games generally dominated by the Germans, he acquired four gold medals in sprints and long jump. The feat received heightened attention when Adolf Hitler reportedly refused to greet Owens and thus confront a black man's challenge to Hitler's notion of Aryan supremacy. Owens, however, happened to excel in a field that brought fame but not fortune, and so after graduating from Ohio State in 1937, he gave up participatory sports and tried show business and other activities, spending many of his years working in sports-related positions for the state of Illinois.

George S. Patton

George Smith Patton, Jr., became one of America's most colorful and popular military leaders of the twentieth century. Born on November 11, 1885, in San Gabriel, California, he graduated from West Point in 1909 and served on the staff of John J. Pershing in Mexico and during the First World War. He was badly wounded in the battle of Meuse-Argonne. By war's end he probably was the American officer most knowledgeable in the new area of armored warfare. The Second World War revived a need for Patton's special skills as a tank commander. He performed brilliantly in command of armored forces in North Africa in 1942 and of the 7th Army in Sicily and the 3d Army in France and Germany—successes that earned him the fourth star of a full general. Multitalented—he competed in the Olympic Games in 1912—and flamboyant, an inspiring leader of offensive warfare, he also had a capacity for false steps off the battlefield, such as the slapping of shell-shocked soldiers in Sicily in 1943. He died as a result of a vehicle accident on December 21, 1945, near Heidelberg, Germany.

John J. Pershing

John Joseph Pershing was America's first great military hero of the twentieth century. Born near Laclede, Missouri, on September 13, 1860, he attended West Point, finishing as president of the class of 1886. Thereafter he fulfilled numerous military assignments,

Commander of the American forces in Europe in the First World War, John J. Pershing *(right)* is pictured here with French general Ferdinand Foch. (National Archives)

Roosevelt lunches with Gen. Mark Clark *(left)* and Gen. George S. Patton *(right)* in French Morocco, January 21, 1943. Adviser Harry Hopkins has his back to the camera. (Franklin D. Roosevelt Library)

fighting Indians in the West and seeing combat in Cuba and the Philippine Islands, along the way earning the nickname "Black Jack" for his service with black soldiers. President Theodore Roosevelt provided the high honor of promoting him from captain to brigadier general in 1906, passing over many senior officers in the process. Pershing led U.S. forces in pursuit of Pancho Villa in Mexico during 1916–17. As commander of U.S. forces in Europe in 1917–18, he contributed significantly to the war against the Germans, and his name became identified with victory in the First World War. Before retirement in 1924, he reached the zenith of his profession, serving as chief of staff and general of the armies. He died in 1948.

Eleanor Roosevelt

Anna Eleanor Roosevelt was born in New York City on October 11, 1890, the niece of future president Theodore Roosevelt. The security of a strong and loving family life—which might have taken over her energies—was not to be for her, neither in her immediate family nor in her marriage after 1905 to a distant cousin, Franklin D. Roosevelt. She moved quickly into various reform movements of the turn of the century and into efforts to advance the political career of her husband. Producing six children, one of whom died in infancy, slowed her only temporarily. After Franklin's election to the presidency in 1932, she became the nation's most independent and active first lady, writing columns, traveling apart from her husband, and involving herself in the causes of black people, young people, and women and the concerns of the underprivileged in general. She was a more dedicated social reformer and advocate of civil rights than her famous husband, who would acquire a considerable reputation for being both. Not all Americans, however, approved of this sort of independent action from the president's—especially this president's—wife. After Franklin's death in 1945, she continued her activity. As a delegate to the United Nations, she was the dominant force in the movement to promote human rights in the world. By the time of her death in 1962, most of the cruel jokes and harsh criticism, largely from the White House years, were forgotten, and Americans recognized her as being one of the most dedicated, enlightened, courageous social leaders of her century.

Franklin D. Roosevelt

Franklin Delano Roosevelt is destined to stand as one of the most significant American presidents. Elected four times, he is—and ever will be—the only person to win more than twice. He presided over the country during its greatest depression and its largest war. He was, in the judgment of many specialists, the most effective leader to hold the office. He was born in Hyde Park, in upstate New York, on January 30, 1882, and like his distant cousin, Theodore Roosevelt, he came from patrician Dutch stock. After studies at Harvard University and Columbia law school, he entered New York politics on the Democratic side and later served in the administration of Woodrow Wilson. He bounced back from a serious attack of polio in the early 1920s to be elected governor of New York in 1928 and 1930 and easily defeated Herbert Hoover for the presidency in 1932, during the depth of the depression. His domestic program, called the New Deal, did not accomplish its primary goal of ending the depression, but it did leave a large legacy of expanded government activity, much of it beneficial, including such worthy programs as the Social Security System, started in 1935. Concerned after 1938 mostly with world affairs, he quickly expressed hostility to totalitarian movement in Europe and Asia. Without his resistance to Hitler during 1939–41, it is difficult to know what the course of Europe might have

been. During the years 1941–45 he was leader of the Grand Alliance against Germany, Italy, and Japan. His death of a cerebral hemorrhage on April 12, 1945, reminded scholars of the fate of Abraham Lincoln. Two presidents were denied a victory on their fingertips. Germany would surrender in May.

Roosevelt was never a profound thinker about economic or political systems. He left these matters to others. He was a specialist in politics, and politics of his age called for action. As with many politicians, he preferred to bring good news rather than bad. He was sometimes misleading, occasionally deceptive, even untruthful. People who followed him, and there were many, found him a source of direction, trust, and hope. People who disliked him believed him capable of the most devious personal and political action. Perhaps his most appealing personal characteristic was the optimism and sunny good cheer with which he faced work and challenge in the wake of his dreaded disease—this from a man who could not walk on his own the last twenty-three years of his life.

Babe Ruth

Babe Ruth was born George Herman Ruth on February 6, 1895, in Baltimore, Maryland. A large young man, he soon demonstrated special talents in baseball, even then a familiar participatory and spectator American sport. The Boston Red Sox introduced him into the major leagues in 1915 as a left-handed pitcher, and he was excellent, winning World Series games in 1916 and 1918. The New York Yankees, who purchased Ruth in 1920, were more impressed with

George Herman Ruth was perhaps the most popular player in the history of baseball and one of the most familiar personages of his era. His major-league career (1914–35) spanned almost this entire period. (National Baseball Library, Cooperstown, New York)

his ability as a batter. The Yankees took him from the mound and placed him permanently in right field, allowing him to play every day. He transformed the game: adding immensely to its popularity, vastly enhancing the appeal of hitting (or trying to hit) home runs, and showing that it could be profitable; he earned $80,000 in a year (1930) when President Hoover made $75,000. His grandiose, undisciplined style on and off the field fit and symbolized the extravagant mood often associated with the 1920s. He led the American League in home runs twelve times; when he retired in 1935, he left a batting average of .342, remarkable for a power hitter. Even after his most memorable records of sixty home runs in one season and grand total of 714 were broken, he would continue to stand as the foremost giant of the game, if not of all American sports. For years to come Babe Ruth was the only baseball player's name that many individuals—inside or outside the United States—knew. He died of cancer in 1947.

Carl Sandburg

Born in Galesburg, Illinois, on January 6, 1878, Carl Sandburg tried the army, college, and politics before moving to Chicago to work for a newspaper and write poetry. His interest in the welfare of the working man, especially in Illinois and the Midwest, appeared in his first poems, published in 1914. His collection *Chicago Poems* (1916) included poems that would become some of his best known. Many more followed. In 1926 he published a biography, *Abraham Lincoln: The Prairie Years.* His *Abraham Lincoln: The War Years* (4 vols., 1939) won a Pulitzer Prize for history in 1940. A second Pulitzer, in poetry, came in 1951 for *Complete Poems,* most of which had been written much earlier. He died in July 1967, beloved by many, mostly for his poetry but also for other literary work and for his folk songs.

Margaret Sanger

Margaret Louise Higgins was born in Corning, New York, on September 14, 1883, the daughter of a freethinking father and a Catholic mother who bore eleven children and died at forty-nine. A freethinker herself, Margaret tried college (Claverack College in Hudson, New York), nursing, and an eighteen-year marriage to William Sanger, which produced three children. After a brief flirtation with radical politics she found her cause: the need for women's reproductive freedom, or to use her phrase, "birth control." Controlling conception would permit women to preserve their bodies and still participate in liberal sexual expression, of which she heartily approved. To the goal of planned, safe contraception she devoted her long life—traveling, publishing, opening clinics (the first in Brownsville, New York, in 1916), challenging the law, fighting off numerous critics. An organization she founded in 1928 provided a nucleus for what would become the Planned Parenthood Federation of America. She died in 1966 in Tucson, not long after having had an indirect part in the development of a contraceptive pill. A genuine pioneer in birth control, perhaps its most persistent publicist, she fostered significantly the objective of personal control of the body.

Henry L. Stimson

Henry Louis Stimson was an example of aristocracy in the American government. There were several such people, but virtually none with the record he would accumulate in the service of five presidents. Born in New York City on September 21, 1867, he graduated from Yale University and Harvard law school before becoming active in Republican politics. Thereafter he would serve as secretary of war under William Howard Taft, as colonel of artillery in France during the First World War, as special envoy to Nicaragua and governor-general of the Philippines under Calvin Coolidge, as secretary of state under Herbert Hoover and secretary of war under Democrat Franklin D. Roosevelt and briefly under Harry S. Truman. In 1932 he authored the "Stimson Doctrine," condemning Japanese action in Manchuria. During 1940–45 he was one of Franklin D. Roosevelt's principal wartime advisers, and he urged Truman to drop the atomic bomb on Japan. He died in 1950, two years after producing a successful memoir, entitled *On Active Service.*

Jim Thorpe

Born near Shawnee, Oklahoma, on May 28, 1888, of Sac and Fox Indian heritage, Jim Thorpe grew to be a young man six feet tall with strong body and exceptional speed, power, and coordination. He received national attention as an athlete at Carlisle Indian School in Pennsylvania and in 1911–12 was named to what was a forerunner to the All American football team. In Stockholm in 1912 he won the decathlon and pentathlon, the most demanding events at the Olympic Games, although a technical ruling forced him to return the gold medals. He then played major-league baseball from 1913 to 1919 (batting .252 as a part-time outfielder) and was a star in an infant National Football League during 1917–29. The rest of his life was taken up with sports and Indian affairs and a relationship between the two. He died in 1953, not long after supervising his film biography, a feature movie with Burt Lancaster. Thorpe was in many ways to Native Americans what Joe Louis was to African Americans, an enormous—and much overdue—example of accomplishment and source of group pride. In the case of the American Indians, he was virtually the only one. The decision of the Associated Press in 1950 to call him the "Greatest Athlete of the Century" might have been premature, but he was by all counts an exceptionally gifted performer. He also represented the fact that when seemingly nothing else worked for members of suppressed and underprivileged minority groups, participatory sports provided an avenue for recognition in American society.

Harry S. Truman

Harry S. Truman was born on May 8, 1884, into a modest agricultural family in Lamar (near Independence), Missouri. He did not attend college; he worked as a farmer and in various business enterprises and served during the First World War in France as an artillery officer in the Missouri National Guard. He rose in politics in the 1920s and 1930s as a member of the Pendergast Machine of Kansas City, and yet he stayed clear of the corruption associated with that organization. He was elected to the U.S. Senate in 1934 and 1940. His placement on the Democratic national ticket with Franklin D. Roosevelt in 1944 was a simple expression of practical politics. On Roosevelt's death, Truman became the thirty-third president on April 12, 1945, with little preparation for the job. He grew rapidly in office, however, and was elected to a full term in 1948. His time in the presidency was a period of great change and momentous decisions, which Truman made with little hesitation. He ordered the dropping of the atomic bomb in 1945, committed the United States to a long-term anticommunist alliance in 1949, sent troops to Korea in 1950, and fired popular general Douglas MacArthur in 1951. Although he was much criticized as president and left office widely unpopular, his reputation has stood up well with the passage of time. His major decisions have been viewed as correct for

Harry S. Truman saw combat in the First World War as an officer of Battery D (artillery) of the Missouri National Guard. (Harry S. Truman Library)

apprenticeship as governor of New Jersey, and then, running as a Democrat, he defeated Theodore Roosevelt and William Howard Taft in 1912 and became the twenty-eighth president. He was re-elected in 1916. His administration produced several important pieces of legislation, notably the Federal Reserve Act and other measures to curb big business. Nearly six of his eight years in office were taken up with the First World War. After struggling for two and one-half years with difficult problems of American neutrality, in April 1917 he led the nation into war against Germany. He placed the war, and the peace that followed, on a high moral plane, suggesting that properly managed, this war could be the last major conflict. Wilson's personal negotiation of the Treaty of Versailles in 1919 was equally high minded, but he antagonized many people abroad and in the United States. In this country his opponents objected to his self-righteousness, his personal control of policy, and his demand that the United States join the new League of Nations. He lost that battle. His treaty, and his league, lost in the Republican-dominated Senate in 1919–20. In the process Wilson almost lost his life. He suffered a stroke in September 1919, and though he lived on until February 1924, he was a man broken in spirit as well as health. Although Wilson continues to obtain high marks for vision, dedication, and leadership—he consistently ranks among the top ten of presidents—his presidency has been viewed by many as a tragedy.

Frank Lloyd Wright

Frank Lloyd Wright was one of the most recognizable and influential American architects of the first half of the twentieth century. Born in Richland Center, Wisconsin, on June 8, 1869, and getting his professional footing in Chicago, Wright always showed a bias toward the Midwest and West. A follower of Louis H. Sullivan, he believed that form needed to follow function, that usefulness of a structure was preferable to mere beauty. He was best known as a designer of residences, including his "Taliesin" houses in Wisconsin, but he also produced such public structures as the Imperial Hotel in Tokyo in the 1920s, the Johnson Wax Building in Wisconsin, and the Guggenheim Museum in New York. In a long career he executed approximately 300 projects and near its end brought forth many radically new structural proposals. In the ten years before his death in 1959, he also produced numerous books and articles about architecture in the years ahead.

Richard Wright

Born in poverty on a plantation in Mississippi on September 4, 1908, Richard Wright left the South at age seventeen. He lived briefly in Nashville and in 1927 moved to Chicago, where he worked, began writing fiction and poetry, and became an active convert to the American Communist Party. Moving to New York in 1937, he contributed to Communist publications and to the Federal Writers' Project. His first novel and best-known work, *Native Son,* published in 1940, would have a run on Broadway and on the screen. *Twelve Million Black Voices* (1941) and *Black Boy* (1945) helped establish his identity as one of the more angry and militant critics of the racial status quo, a person pleased to call himself *black* when many others felt more comfortable with *Negro* or *colored*. Wright left the United States permanently in 1947, and from his home base in Paris he lectured, wrote, and traveled over much of the world. When he died in Paris in 1960, he was internationally known and honored as a writer and spokesperson of the status of black people in America and worldwide.

the most part; his basic decency and honesty and his direct and open manner of dealing with people and problems have been taken as desirable characteristics of a leader of the United States. He died on December 26, 1972, fittingly in humble circumstances, in the same place in Missouri from which he came.

Woodrow Wilson

Thomas Woodrow Wilson was perhaps America's best-educated president. He was born in Staunton, Virginia, on December 28, 1856, and grew up in the post–Civil War South. After receiving an undergraduate degree from Princeton University, a law degree from the University of Virginia, and a Ph.D. in political science from the Johns Hopkins University, he spent the bulk of his adult life teaching college and in scholarly research activity, finally serving as president of Princeton between 1902 and 1910. He spent a two-year political

CHAPTER 14 Education

The attitude toward education in the United States was consistent with the perception of the nation as a land of liberty and opportunity. The people needed to be educated to protect their freedom and develop their opportunities—so reasoned the Founding Fathers, and the idea was passed along from one generation to another. Government in the first instance must provide education for the people.

When one compared American literacy rates with those of other countries during the years 1914–45, it appeared that the country had accomplished the goal. The United States had a literacy rate higher than those of all but a few countries, and the rates moved higher with passage of each decade. The statistics were less impressive when one considered that they measured not education but the

TABLE 14.1 PUBLIC ELEMENTARY AND SECONDARY SCHOOLS

School Year Ending—	Average Length of School Term (days)	Average Days Attended by Students	Annual Expenditures per Pupil Enrolled (current dollars)	Annual Expenditures per Capita (current dollars)
1914	158.7	117.8	$ 29	$ 5.60
1915	159.4	121.2	31	6.03
1916	160.3	120.9	31	6.29
1918	160.7	119.8	37	7.40
1920	161.9	121.2	48	9.91
1922	164.0	130.6	68	14.37
1924	168.3	132.5	75	16.25
1926	169.3	135.9	82	17.26
1928	171.5	140.4	87	18.12
1930	172.7	143.0	90	18.87
1932	171.2	144.9	83	17.42
1934	171.6	145.8	65	13.54
1936	173.0	146.3	75	15.38
1938	173.9	149.3	86	17.15
1940	175.0	151.7	92	17.77
1942	174.7	149.6	95	17.23
1944	175.5	147.9	105	17.76

Source: Ben J. Wattenberg, The Statistical History of the United States (New York, 1976), 373–375.

TABLE 14.3 PUBLIC ELEMENTARY AND SECONDARY SCHOOLS: STAFF

School Year Ending—	Classroom Teachers and Other Nonsupervisory Staff			Average Annual Salary[a] (current dollars)	Principals (1,000)
	Total (1,000)	Male (1,000)	Female (1,000)		
1914	580	115	465	$ 525	. . .
1915	604	118	486	543	. . .
1916	622	123	499	563	. . .
1918	651	105	546	635	. . .
1920	680	96	584	871	13.6
1922	723	118	605	1,166	18.6
1924	761	129	633	1,227	17.9
1926	814	139	675	1,277	26.9
1928	832	138	694	1,364	28.8
1930	854	142	712	1,420	30.9
1932	872	154	718	1,417	23.9
1934	847	162	685	1,227	28.1
1936	871	179	692	1,283	29.6
1938	877	185	692	1,374	36.4
1940	875	195	681	1,441	31.5
1942	859	183	676	1,507	33.1
1944	828	127	701	1,728	31.6

[a]Before 1920, salaries were computed only on teaching positions; beginning with 1920, the numbers also include supervisors and principals.
Source: Wattenberg, Statistical History, 375.

TABLE 14.2 PUBLIC ELEMENTARY AND SECONDARY SCHOOLS: ENROLLMENT

School Year Ending—	Total (1,000)	Kindergarten (1,000)	Elementary[a]		Secondary	
			Students (1,000)	Student/Teacher Ratio	Students (1,000)	Student/Teacher Ratio
1914	19,154	. . .	17,935	. . .	1,219	. . .
1915	19,704	. . .	18,375	. . .	1,329	. . .
1916	20,352	. . .	18,896	. . .	1,456	. . .
1918	20,854	. . .	18,920	32.6	1,934	23.0
1920	21,578	481	18,897	33.6	2,200	21.6
1922	23,239	529	19,837	34.3	2,873	22.2
1924	24,289	610	20,289	33.9	3,390	23.5
1926	24,741	673	20,311	32.6	3,757	22.2
1928	25,180	695	20,573	33.1	3,911	20.7
1930	25,678	723	20,566	33.2	4,399	20.9
1932	26,275	701	20,434	33.0	5,140	22.2
1934	26,434	602	20,163	33.5	5,669	24.9
1936	26,367	607	19,786	33.8	5,975	22.3
1938	25,975	607	19,141	33.2	6,227	22.0
1940	25,434	595	18,237	32.7	6,601	22.0
1942	24,562	626	17,549	32.5	6,388	21.3
1944	23,267	697	17,016	32.9	5,542	19.2

[a]The reader might be struck by the fact that there were more elementary students in 1914 than there were twenty years later, in the 1940s. The answer rests with the exceptionally low birthrate during the years of the depression. Immigration also was unusually low during the 1930s.
Source: Wattenberg, Statistical History, 368.

TABLE 14.4 HIGH SCHOOL GRADUATES, BY SEX

(In thousands, except percentage)

Year	Total	Percentage of Persons 17 Years Old[a]	Male	Female
1914	219	11.7	90	129
1915	240	12.8	99	140
1916	259	13.8	108	151
1917	272	14.5	110	162
1918	285	15.1	112	173
1919	298	16.0	118	180
1920	311	16.3	124	188
1921	334	17.1	137	198
1922	357	17.8	150	207
1923	426	20.8	181	244
1924	494	23.4	213	281
1925	528	24.4	230	298
1926	561	25.5	246	315
1927	579	25.8	256	323
1928	597	26.2	266	330
1929	632	27.5	283	349
1930	667	28.8	300	367
1931	747	32.1	337	409
1932	827	35.5	375	452
1933	871	37.3	403	468
1934	915	39.2	432	483
1935	965	41.1	459	506
1936	1,015	42.7	486	530
1937	1,068	44.2	505	563
1938	1,120	45.6	524	596
1940	1,221	49.0	579	643
1942	1,242	51.3	577	666
1944	1,019	42.7	424	595

[a]This statistic was designed to give a rough idea of the rate at which America's students graduated from high school. Most encouraging was the fact that the percentage of the age group—dreadfully low at the start—increased every year until the time of the Second World War.
Source: Wattenberg, *Statistical History*, 379.

ability to read or write—or worse yet, a claim to be able to do so. The numbers were less impressive in the case of individual states and in literacy for nonwhites.

During the period from 1914 to 1945, enrollment went up steadily in public schools, as one would expect; the students faced longer school years with the passage of time; more money was being spent virtually every year per pupil enrolled. These trends were reversed during several years of the Great Depression. One of the most impressive statistics was that the percentage of people who graduated from high school increased from less than 12% of the age group in 1914 to more than 50% in 1942. The percentage then slid slightly because of the Second World War. There were more males than females at the start of the school experience, but females always outnumbered males in graduation. Young men dropped out to help on the farm, join the army, or take some other job, or simply because they did not like school. In some circles, schooling was not considered a manly undertaking. Although many people continued to believe that girls did not need education—at least not much of it—in the end they received more "learning" than the boys. Teachers in the public schools were paid barely passable salaries; they were overwhelmingly female, the vast majority of whom were unmarried. The stereotype of the "old maid" school teacher was not totally removed from fact, as this was one of the few "respectable" occupations open to women at that time. For all the gains in education after 1914, by the 1940s the median experience in school for Americans over age twenty-four—the normal years for schooling—was barely past eighth grade.

TABLE 14.5 SUBJECTS STUDENTS TOOK IN PUBLIC HIGH SCHOOLS, 1910–1922

	1910		1915		1922[a]	
	Students	Percentage of Total	Students	Percentage of Total	Students	Percentage of Total
Students in schools reporting on studies	739,143	. . .	1,165,495	. . .	2,155,460	. . .
Students in—						
Latin	362,548	49.05	434,925	37.32	593,086	27.52
Greek	5,511	.75	3,351	.29	1,873	0.09
French	73,161	9.90	102,516	8.80	333,162	15.46
German	175,083	23.69	284,294	24.39	13,918	0.65
Spanish	4,920	.67	31,743	2.39	242,715	11.26
Algebra	420,207	56.85	569,215	48.84	865,515	40.15
Geometry	228,170	30.87	309,383	26.55	488,825	22.68
Trigonometry	13,812	1.87	17,220	1.48	32,930	1.53
Astronomy	3,915	.53	3,224	.28	1,474	0.07
Physics	107,988	14.61	165,854	14.23	192,380	8.93
Chemistry	50,923	6.89	86,031	7.38	159,413	7.40
Physical geography	142,948	19.34	169,911	14.58	92,146	4.28
Zoology	59,253	8.02	37,456	3.21	32,956	1.53
Botany	124,380	16.83	106,520	9.14	82,241	3.82
General biology	. . .	. . .	80,403	6.90	189,288	8.78

(continued)

TABLE 14.5   (continued)

	1910		1915		1922[a]	
	Students	Percentage of Total	Students	Percentage of Total	Students	Percentage of Total
Students in schools reporting on studies	739,143	. . .	1,165,495	. . .	2,155,460	. . .
Students in—						
Geology	8,538	1.16	5,558	.48	3,520	0.16
Physiology	113,252	15.32	110,541	9.48	109,519	5.08
Psychology	7,109	.96	13,626	1.17	18,748	0.87
Rhetoric	422,051	57.10	680,871	58.42	. . .	. . .
English literature	421,980	57.09	650,613	55.82	1,693,928[b]	78.59[b]
History	406,784	55.03	589,067	50.54	[c]	[c]
Civil government	114,965	15.55	100,736	8.64	416,329[d]	19.32[d]
Civics	. . .	. . .	82,558	7.08	. . .	. . .
Agriculture	34,418	4.66	83,573	7.17	110,242	5.11
Domestic economy	27,933	3.78	150,276	12.89	307,553	14.27
Industrial	. . .	. . .	9,424	.81	. . .	. . .
Manual training	. . .	. . .	130,155	11.17	226,023	10.49
Drawing	. . .	. . .	266,492	22.87	317,825	14.75
Music	. . .	. . .	367,188	31.50	544,764	25.27
Bookkeeping	. . .	. . .	39,816	3.42	270,517	12.55

[a]Subjects regarding which statistics for 1922 only are available include general science, students 393,885, percentage 18.27; typewriting, students 281,524, percentage 13.06; arithmetic, students 226,918, percentage 10.53.
[b]Includes rhetoric.
[c]American history, students 329,565, percentage 15.29; English history, students 61,766, percentage 2.87; ancient history, students 371,392, percentage 17.23; medieval and modern history, students 330,836, percentage 15.35.
[d]Includes civics.
Source: The Lincoln Library of Essential Information (Buffalo, N.Y., 1937), 1,671.

Illiteracy in the United States and Abroad

Identification of illiteracy was an inexact undertaking. Until the year 1930 the process involved census takers' asking individuals over ten years old if they could read or write any language. Those who answered no were deemed illiterate. Statistics for 1940 came from a

TABLE 14.6   ILLITERACY IN THE UNITED STATES (PERCENTAGE)

Year	Total	White			Nonwhite[a]
		Total	Native	Foreign-born	
1910	7.7	5.0	3.0	12.7	30.5
1920	6.0	4.0	2.0	13.1	23.0
1930	4.3	3.0	1.6	10.8	16.4
1940	2.9	2.0	1.1	9.0	11.5

[a]Nonwhite in large measure (more than 95%) applied to African Americans. The bulk of the remainder were Native Americans.
Source: Wattenberg, Statistical History, 382.

TABLE 14.7   ILLITERACY BY STATE, 1930

States	Percentage
United States	**4.3**
New England	**3.7**
Maine	2.7
N.H.	2.7
Vt.	2.2
Mass.	3.5
R.I.	4.9
Conn.	4.5

States	Percentage
United States	**4.3**
Middle Atlantic	**3.5**
N.Y.	3.7
N.J.	3.8
Pa.	3.1
East North Central	**2.1**
Ohio	2.3
Ind.	1.7
Ill.	2.4
Mich.	2.0
Wis.	1.9
West North Central	**1.4**
Minn.	1.3
Iowa	0.8
Mo.	2.3
N. Dak.	1.5
S. Dak.	1.2
Nebr.	1.2
Kans.	1.2
South Atlantic	**8.3**
Del.	4.0
Md.	3.8
D.C.	1.6
Va.	8.7
W. Va.	4.3
N.C.	10.0
S.C.	14.9
Ga.	9.4
Fla.	7.1
East South Central	**9.6**
Ky.	6.6
Tenn.	7.2
Ala.	12.6
Miss.	13.1

States	Percentage
United States	**4.3**
West South Central	**7.2**
Ark.	6.8
La.	13.5
Okla.	2.8
Tex.	6.8
Mountain	**4.2**
Mont.	1.7
Idaho	1.1
Wyo.	1.6
Colo.	2.8
N. Mex.	13.3
Ariz.	10.1
Utah	1.2
Nev.	4.4
Pacific	**2.1**
Wash.	1.0
Oreg.	1.0
Calif.	2.6

Source: The Encyclopedia Americana (New York, 1945), 698.

TABLE 14.8   ILLITERACY IN VARIOUS COUNTRIES

Country	Year	Percentage Illiterate
Austria	1930	16.4
Belgium	1930	11.0
Bulgaria	1930	58.1
England and Wales	1931	4.4
France	1931	11.5
Germany	1933	0.9
Greece	1928	43.0
Hungary	1930	22.0
Ireland	1926	7.5
Italy	1931	26.3
Malta	1931	49.5
Netherlands	1933	3.7
Portugal	1930	65.0
Rumania	1930	54.4
Russia	1935	30.0
Scotland	1931	3.14
Serbia	1900	78.9
Spain	1930	44.0
Switzerland	1931	0.3
United States	1930	4.3
Native white, native parents, U.S.	1930	2.1
Native white, foreign parents, U.S.	1930	3.1
Foreign-born white	1930	10.2
Negro, U.S.	1930	20.5
Argentina	1933	44.0
Brazil	1930	67.0
Canada	1931	3.79
Chile	1933	38.5
Cuba	1930	28.0
Mexico	1930	59.3
Australia	1931	1.1
India	1931	34.0
Philippine Islands	1930	47.4
Union of South Africa	1931	52.5

Source: The Encyclopedia Americana (1945 ed.), 697.

system of estimates. One suspects that in either case the number of functional illiterates was considerably higher than the statistics suggested. Literacy in other nations was determined by various methods of finding whether people over a certain age, differing in the countries from five to twelve, were able to read or write.

The States and Education

There was no national education policy in the United States. The national government had virtually nothing to do with the day-to-day, year-by-year conduct of the education process. Virtually all education was the responsibility of the states individually, and although there was some tendency for trends to become national—the minimum age limit of sixteen years before quitting school, for example—the states varied widely in their willingness and ability to support education. State control also permitted local or regional attitudes to enter into the education process—to the benefit of some groups and the detriment of others. The most striking set of statistics in measuring education on a state-by-state basis was the position of the South and so-called border states. In virtually every means of measuring progress in education, the South lagged far behind, and below the Mason-Dixon line a distinct attitude marked the organization and operation of the schools.

TABLE 14.9   EDUCATIONAL RANKING OF STATES, 1930[a]

State	Rank in Education	Percentage of Illiteracy, 10 Years and Over	Ratio of Average Daily Attendance to Population of School Age	Percentage Enrollment in High School	Average Daily Attendance by Each Pupil Enrolled	Average Number of Days School in Session	Ratio of Students Training for Teaching to Teachers Employed	Total Cost (ex. salaries) per Pupil in Average Daily Attendance	Average Annual Salary of Teachers, Principals, and Supervisors	Total Amount Spent per Child of School Age	Percentage of High School Graduates Continuing Education
	1	2	3	4	5	6	7	8	9	10	11
Ala.	46	45	46	47	44	44	27	44	46	46	18
Ariz.	27	44	34	35	37	24	3	8	8	12	22
Ark.	47	38	43	46	47	47	44	48	45	48	15
Calif.	4	21	2	5	12	9	32	5	4	3	44
Colo.	18	25	13	28	33	10	30	10	17	8	28
Conn.	19	33	25	23	7	6	43	11	6	17	31
Del.	11	31	35	30	15	15	12	9	13	13	2
D.C.	5	11	8	15	26	21	47	2	2	2	3
Fla.	41	39	20	38	43	41	45	39	43	37	7
Ga.	48	42	41	42	45	46	23	49	49	49	43
Idaho	21	4	12	4	34	28	5	30	29	26	39
Ill.	7	20	24	7	2	2	19	14	10	18	32
Ind.	10	13	5	6	13	31	1	29	20	21	29
Iowa	17	1	9	10	23	26	38	17	28	10	40
Kans.	22	8	7	8	29	33	33	20	27	16	30
Ky.	40	36	47	43	38	34	25	42	34	44	5
La.	44	48	48	41	39	42	10	40	38	41	37
Maine	29	22	18	19	5	18	13	35	37	34	33
Md.	31	29	45	34	9	5	20	26	15	33	45
Mass.	12	27	30	17	8	7	6	13	5	19	46
Mich.	6	16	6	27	3	32	11	12	9	9	13
Minn.	28	9	22	24	24	17	41	22	25	23	23
Miss.	43	46	21	49	49	49	21	47	48	43	9
Mo.	20	18	23	16	6	23	17	33	24	31	17
Mont.	2	14	15	13	16	14	4	7	26	7	14
Nebr.	30	5	16	9	32	20	28	27	31	25	49
Nev.	13	32	1	11	22	30	39	3	16	1	25
N.H.	23	23	40	20	10	19	9	28	22	30	12
N.J.	9	30	27	33	11	3	2	4	3	5	48
N. Mex.	39	47	42	39	36	29	35	34	30	35	16
N.Y.	3	28	29	18	1	4	46	1	1	4	1
N.C.	38	43	32	40	42	40	18	41	40	40	4
N. Dak.	32	10	14	26	27	37	24	25	42	22	38
Ohio	8	19	17	12	4	11	15	16	7	14	35
Okla.	37	24	31	31	48	45	26	38	33	38	24
Oreg.	14	2	10	3	31	25	31	19	12	15	42
Pa.	16	26	33	32	14	8	8	23	11	28	19
R.I.	34	35	49	36	17	1	48	15	19	29	36
S.C.	49	49	44	45	46	48	49	46	47	47	8
S. Dak.	26	7	19	21	21	16	36	24	36	24	21
Tenn.	42	40	37	48	40	39	22	45	44	45	11
Tex.	36	37	38	29	41	43	29	37	39	39	6
Utah	15	6	3	2	19	27	40	31	21	20	26
Vt.	33	17	26	25	18	35	37	32	35	32	27
Va.	45	41	39	44	35	36	34	43	41	42	41
Wash.	1	3	4	1	28	13	7	18	14	11	20
W. Va.	35	34	28	37	25	38	14	36	32	36	10
Wis.	25	15	36	22	20	12	16	21	18	27	34
Wyo.	24	12	11	14	30	22	42	6	23	6	47

[a] Based on a system worked out by Frank M. Phillips in 1930. Column one shows the ranking of the states based on standings in columns two through eleven.
Source: Lincoln Library of Essential Information, 1,666.

TABLE 14.10   EDUCATIONAL DIFFERENTIALS IN THE UNITED STATES, 1940

State	Average Number of Days in School Session[a]	Average Number of Days Attended by Each Pupil Enrolled[a]	Value of School Property per Enrolled Pupil	Average Salary of Teachers (Including Principals and Supervisors)[a]	Current Expense (Excluding interest) per Enrolled Pupil[a]	Percentage of Adults 25 Years of Age and Over Who Had Not Completed More Than 4 Years of School
United States	175	152	$300	$1,441	$ 88	14
The North						
Maine	178	161	217	894	64	7
N.H.	176	157	326	1,258	91	8
Vt.	179	156	241	981	85	6
Mass.	180	162	447	2,037	115	10
R.I.	180	157	390	1,809	105	14
Conn.	183	167	433	1,861	109	11
N.Y.	184	159	526	2,604	157	12
N.J.	185	164	499	2,093	136	12
Pa.	182	164	355	1,640	92	12
Ohio	181	167	287	1,587	96	8
Ind.	170	149	304	1,433	96	8
Ill.	185	162	452	1,700	115	10
Mich.	183	163	377	1,576	92	10
Wis.	180	164	473	1,379	91	9
Minn.	173	154	390	1,276	100	7
Iowa	177	153	270	1,017	86	4
Mo.	179	153	252	1,159	80	10
N. Dak.	173	154	315	745	69	11
S. Dak.	175	154	305	807	86	7
Nebr.	176	155	298	829	74	6
Kans.	172	152	315	1,014	83	6
The South						
Del.	182	163	504	1,684	109	13
Md.	188	168	301	1,642	84	15
D.C.	179	154	552	2,350	132	8
Va.	180	157	156	899	48	23
W. Va.	176	160	187	1,170	64	16
N.C.	164	147	134	946	41	26
S.C.	163	130	110	743	40	35
Ga.	162	128	109	770	42	30
Fla.	167	148	228	1,112	58	18
Ky.	159	130	124	826	47	20
Tenn.	166	138	80	862	44	22
Ala.	154	127	84	744	36	29
Miss.	146	116	98	559	31	30
Ark.	159	127	93	584	31	23
La.	169	142	154	1,006	57	36
Okla.	176	139	160	1,014	63	13
Tex.	172	144	215	1,079	66	19
The West						
Mont.	172	157	352	1,184	109	7
Idaho	175	153	244	1,057	78	5
Wyo.	177	149	235	1,169	109	7
Colo.	172	155	303	1,393	92	9
N. Mex.	175	140	143	1,144	76	27
Ariz.	169	136	212	1,544	96	19
Utah	175	159	309	1,394	78	5
Nev.	171	150	364	1,557	131	9
Wash.	179	148	312	1,706	105	6
Oreg.	174	153	332	1,333	97	5
Calif.	177	157	369	2,351	142	8

[a] Public schools only.
Sources: U.S. Office of Education; Frederick J. Dewhurst and Associates, *America's Needs and Resources* (New York, 1947), 310–311.

Rural Education

One of the most striking conditions of American education was the large difference that existed between urban and rural areas. Education in the countryside lagged behind that in cities and towns in almost every means of measurement: in all aspects of the physical plant, in equipment available, in the number of days spent in school. There were fewer teachers per student in the countryside, and rural teachers received about half as much pay as their counterparts in the cities. Rural children often walked or rode long distances; they had virtually no opportunity to go to kindergarten. The reader might be struck by the continued existence of so many one-teacher schools, better known as the "one-room schools," where a single person often did everything, from starting a fire in the stove to teaching several grades. Although the number of such schools dropped sharply in the twentieth century, by the end of the Second World War there still were close to 100,000. Equally significant was the large number of schools staffed by a small number of people—usually two to four—which means that each taught more than one grade in the same room. As one class "recited" or was receiving the teacher's attention, other classes in the room did their work, presumably oblivious to what else went on about them. Movements for consolidation of rural schools grew, but they continued to face opposition from many quarters: the people who feared increased costs or the necessity of transporting children even greater distances; many feared the possible loss of a territorial identity. In Indiana many people objected to the prospect of losing the local basketball team.

TABLE 14.11   URBAN-RURAL PUBLIC SCHOOL DIFFERENCES, 1940

	Urban	Rural
Number of school buildings	37,700	189,062
Pupils enrolled per school building	353	63
Teachers[a] per school building	11.8	2.4
Number enrolled as percentage of population aged 5–17	90	81
Average days in school session	182	167
Average days attended by each pupil enrolled	158	145
Average teacher[a] salary	$1,937	$967
Current expenses[b] per pupil in average daily attendance	$105	$70
Value of school property per pupil enrolled	$405	$185

[a] Including principals and supervisors.
[b] Excluding interest.
Source: Statistical Summary of Education, 1939–1940, U.S. Office of Education, published in Dewhurst and Associates, *America's Needs and Resources,* 312.

Although their number was in decline, one-room schools remained commonplace in rural America throughout this period. (Western Michigan University, Archives and Regional History Collections)

TABLE 14.12   ONE-TEACHER PUBLIC SCHOOLS

1916	200,000
1918	196,000
1920	190,700
1922	180,800
1924	169,700
1926	162,800
1928	156,100
1930	149,300
1932	143,400
1934	139,200
1936	131,100
1938	121,200
1940	113,600
1942	107,700
1944	96,300

Source: Wattenberg, *Statistical History,* ix.

Education and Race

Statistics on education suggested clear themes about racial prejudice in the United States, and yet the numbers were not totally a product of racial attitudes and policy on education. The individuals measured in some racial minority groups were born in foreign lands and came to the United States as adults. In some measure the groups brought their illiteracy with them. Language presented a problem for the foreign-born. Mexicans, counted separately in the census of 1930, encountered both of these difficulties.

Native Americans frequently had the highest illiteracy rate of all. It was a consequence of the unique status of American Indians, segregated in ways that black people were not. Native Americans were torn more than any group between the benefits of assimilation and the wish to remain separate (although most ended up staying on the reservation). Low levels of education were both an indication of the status of Indians and a cause of it. Education revealed perhaps as much as any theme the dilemma of the Native American. To accept the white man's education was to accept white man's ways and move toward assimilation; to reject a general education carried, as the statistics showed, dismal consequences. If it can be said that the government failed in the program of educating Indians, the efforts that were put forth were often attacked as an effort at forced assimilation.

It was in the case of African Americans that discrimination in education was most conspicuous and widespread, a consequence not of immigration or language but of public policy and attitudes that were steeped in history and tradition. The factor that most determined the status of black people's education is that it took place largely in the South. Illiteracy rates for blacks outside the South were not vastly higher than the national average. In the South all the forces were present to drive down the quantity and quality of

Although this setting (a home school) was not typical of black schools in the South, segregated education for blacks operated under enormous handicaps. (Library of Congress)

TABLE 14.13 ILLITERACY RATES OF RACIAL MINORITY GROUPS, 1910–1930

| Group | Percentage by Decade | | |
	1910	1920	1930
African Americans	30.4	22.9	16.3
Native Americans	45.3	34.9	25.7
Mexicans	NA	NA	27.5
Chinese	15.8	20.0	20.4
Japanese	9.2	11.0	9.2
Filipinos	35.9	5.4	6.6
Hindus	45.0	32.2	26.6
Koreans	12.6	8.1	12.7
All others	NA	4.4	5.9
National rate	7.7	6.0	4.3

Source: Bureau of the Census, *Negroes in the United States, 1920–1932* (Washington, D.C., 1935), 231.

black people's education. It was largely a rural area, and education in the countryside nationally lagged behind the cities. It was the poorest area with the poorest education for all races. The South had less money to spend on teaching its children. Most significant was the fact that education was an expression of a social system. Segregated education stood as a cornerstone of the system of Jim Crow, and it was virtually inevitable that segregated schools were unequal schools. The situation shows itself in statistics of many kinds—literacy rates, teachers' salaries, money spent on schools. People in power in the South asserted that black people as a whole were incapable of sophisticated learning, and their management of education made the notion a self-fulfilling prophecy.

TABLE 14.14 ILLITERACY RATES OF BLACK PEOPLE BY SECTION, 1910–1930

| Section | Percentage by Decade | | |
	1910	1920	1930
North	10.5	7.0	4.7
West	7.0	4.9	3.3
South	33.3	26.5	19.7

Source: Bureau of the Census, *Negroes in the United States, 1920–1932,* 233.

TABLE 14.16 VALUE OF SCHOOL PROPERTY IN SOUTH, BY RACE, 1935–1936

| State | Value of Sites, Buildings, and Equipment | | Amount per Negro for Each $1.00 per White |
	Per White Pupil	Per Negro Pupil	
10 States	**$183**	**$ 36**	**$0.19**
Tex.	282	63	.22
Md.	273	151	.55
Fla.	248	49	.20
N.C.	158	46	.29
Miss.	147	11	.07
Va.	146	44	.30
S.C.	145	24	.17
Ala.	111	20	.19
Ga.	103	22	.21
Ark.	103	24	.23

Source: Doxey A. Wilkerson, *Special Problems of Negro Education* (Washington, D.C., 1939), 31.

TABLE 14.15 LEVEL OF SCHOOLING COMPLETED FOR PERSONS 25 YEARS OLD AND OVER, BY RACE AND BY REGION: 1940

| Race and Region | Total Population (thousands) | Percentage of Total Population | | | | Median School Years Completed |
| | | Elementary School | | 4 Years of High School or More | | |
		Less than 5 Years	8 Years	Total	4 Years or More of College	
Nonwhite[a]						
United States	6,491	42	12	7	1	5.7
North and West	1,776	22	23	13	2	7.6
South	4,716	49	7	5	1	5.0
White						
United States	68,000	11	30	26	5	8.8
North and West	51,567	9	34	27	5	8.8
South	16,432	16	17	25	5	8.5

[a]Although the term *nonwhite* referred here to several racial groups, it was largely made up of black people, and the statistics provide a fair representation of the level of education of black people.
Source: Department of Commerce, *The Social and Economic Status of the Black Population in the United States, 1790–1978* (Washington, D.C., 1979), 93.

TABLE 14.17   SALARIES OF TEACHERS IN SOUTH, BY RACE

State	1931–32			1935–36		
	White	Negro	Amount per Negro for Each $1.00 per White	White	Negro	Amount per Negro for Each $1.00 per White
States reporting Both years	$951	$451	$0.47	$907	$450	$0.50
Each year	937	462	.49	833	510	.61
Ala.	830	351	.42	709	328	.46
Ark.	652	341	.52	550	316	.57
Del.	1,662	1,433	.86	1,538	1,664	1.08
D.C.	a	a	a	2,376	2,376	1.00
Fla.	987	462	.47	1,030	493	.48
Ga.	844	301	.36	709	282	.40
Ky.	a	a	a	802	607	.76
La.	1,050	442	.42	931	403	.43
Md.	1,589	1,211	.76	1,515	1,187	.78
Miss.	422	175	.41	783	247	.32
Mo.	a	a	a	1,031	1,332	1.29
N.C.	904	504	.56	811	543	.67
Okla.	1,048	843	.80	926	821	.89
S.C.	879	275	.31	825	302	.37
Tenn.	873	559	.64	752	520	.69
Tex.	951	629	.66	991	604	.61
Va.	960	528	.55	901	520	.58
W. Va.	1,090	1,008	.92	a	a	a

[a] Data not available.
Source: Wilkerson, *Special Problems of Negro Education*, 25.

TABLE 14.18   WHITE AND NEGRO STATISTICS IN SELECTED STATES, 1944

State	Enrollment[a]		Average Days Attended by Each Pupil		Instructional Staff		Average Annual Salary of Teachers[b]	
	White	Negro	White	Negro	White	Negro	White	Negro
Ala.	413,567	228,468	138.4	137.9	13,983	6,001	$1,158	$ 661
Ark.	300,898	99,999	132.7	111.8	9,833	2,6544	924	555
Del.	34,356	6,876	158.4	152.0	1,401	253	1,953	1,814
D.C.	54,132	38,055	146.2	151.1	2,085	1,243	2,610	2,610
Fla.	257,004	98,648	152.7	145.3	10,066	3,341	1,530	970
Ga.	426,126	256,023	143.9	127.2	15,524	7,642	1,123	515
Ky.	488,278	37,166	125.4	138.0	16,628	1,412	. . .	. . .
La.	269,347	163,248	149.8	131.5	10,171	4,360	1,683	828
Md.	222,800	59,247	164.4	156.8	7,165	1,757	2,085	2,002
Miss.	275,097	272,495	135.8	104.6	9,188	6,499	1,107	342
Mo.	584,004	47,814	154.0	152.5	22,137	1,560	1,397	1,590
N.C.	568,919	256,634	161.4	152.7	18,519	7,410	1,380	1,249
Okla.	427,418	36,474	140.3	150.4	15,660	1,475	1,428	1,438
S.C.	249,042	204,942	145.9	124.2	9,306	6,007	1,203	615
Tenn.	503,686	102,734	134.6	139.7	17,256	2,980	1,071	1,010
Tex.	1,043,438	199,547	141.9	128.6	38,512	6,590	1,395	946
Va.	391,937	142,841	155.3	151.1	13,870	4,370	1,364	1,129
W. Va.	383,549	25,531	151.3	157.1	14,325	999	. . .	. . .
Total	6,893,598	2,276,742	145.0	133.4	245,629	66,553	c	c

[a] Elementary and secondary schools.
[b] Includes supervisors, principals, and teachers.
[c] Average salary for 15 states and D.C.: white, $1,349; negro, $895.
Source: U.S. Office of Education, published in *The Information Please Almanac, 1948* (New York, 1948), 320.

Signing with a Mark: Draft Registrants, 1940–1941

One of the more compelling pictures of American education appeared in the registration of young men aged twenty-one to thirty-six for the military draft in the period before the United States entered the Second World War. During 1940 and 1941 more than seventeen million registered. The table below shows the number and location of those registrants who had to sign their name with an X.

TABLE 14.19 DRAFT REGISTRANTS WHO SIGNED WITH A MARK, 1940–1941

State	Total	Percentage of Registration	White	Percentage of Registration	Negro	Percentage of Registration
Continental United States	**347,038**	**2.0**	**126,986**	**0.8**	**220,052**	**12.0**
Ala.	30,708	8.4	7,635	3.2	23,073	18.4
Ariz.	963	1.5	928	1.5	35	1.4
Ark.	12,629	5.1	4,380	2.4	8,249	12.9
Calif.	741	.1	685	.1	56	.3
Colo.	157	.1	155	.1	2	.1
Conn.	179	.1	139	.1	40	.8
Del.	360	1.0	117	.4	243	4.0
D.C.	733	.6	72	.1	661	1.7
Fla.	13,354	5.0	2,226	1.2	11,128	12.8
Ga.	47,560	11.3	11,950	4.4	35,610	23.6
Idaho	73	.1	72	.1	1	.8
Ill.	1,508	.1	1,025	.1	483	.8
Ind.	942	.2	826	.2	116	.6
Iowa	299	.1	296	.1	3	.1
Kans.	288	.1	253	.1	35	.5
Ky.	13,496	3.9	12,331	3.8	1,165	4.1
La.	30,407	9.3	8,932	4.3	21,475	18.2
Maine	351	.4	351	.4	0	0
Md.	2,536	1.0	734	.4	1,802	3.8
Mass.	505	.1	481	.1	24	.4
Mich.	829	.1	684	.1	145	.4
Minn.	319	.1	318	.1	1	.1
Miss.	38,221	13.8	4,011	2.8	34,210	25.2
Mo.	3,336	.7	2,487	.6	849	2.4
Mont.	54	.1	54	.1	0	0
Nebr.	148	.1	146	.1	2	.1
Nev.	15	.1	14	.1	1	.9
N.H.	100	.2	98	.2	2	2.3
N.J.	1,073	.2	536	.1	537	1.5
N. Mex.	1,083	1.6	1,076	1.6	7	.8
N.Y.	1,893	.1	1,205	.1	688	.7
N.C.	34,806	7.3	12,003	3.5	22,803	16.8
N. Dak.	89	.1	89	.1	0	0
Ohio	1,602	.2	1,257	.1	345	.7
Okla.	2,034	.7	1,644	.6	390	1.8
Oreg.	76	.1	75	.1	1	.3
Pa.	2,506	.2	1,671	.1	835	1.2
R.I.	130	.1	129	.1	1	.1
S.C.	34,959	13.8	5,803	4.0	29,156	27.1
S. Dak.	70	.1	70	.1	0	0
Tenn.	20,796	5.3	13,077	4.1	7,719	10.7
Tex.	18,870	2.2	12,303	1.7	6,567	4.9
Utah	126	.2	126	.2	0	0
Vt.	75	.2	75	.2	0	0
Va.	20,964	5.7	9,744	3.6	11,220	11.7
Wash.	118	.1	110	0	8	.7
W. Va.	4,381	1.7	4,036	1.7	345	2.1
Wis.	539	.1	520	.1	19	1.1
Wyo.	37	.1	37	.1	0	0

Source: Director of Selective Service, *Selective Service in Peacetime: First Report of the Director of Selective Service, 1940–1941* (Washington, D.C., 1942), 402.

TABLE 14.20 NONPUBLIC SCHOOLS ENROLLMENT

Year	Total (1,000)	Elementary Students (1,000)	Elementary Student/ Teacher Ratio	Secondary Students (1,000)	Secondary Student/ Teacher Ratio
1920	1,699	1,456	. . .	214	12.3
1922	1,581	. . .	. . .	. . .	. . .
1924	1,727	. . .	. . .	. . .	. . .
1926	2,439	. . .	. . .	. . .	. . .
1928	2,631	2,235	. . .	341	. . .
1930	2,651	2,255	. . .	341	14.0
1932	2,786	2,384	. . .	403	NA
1934	2,729	2,371	. . .	360	NA
1936	2,639	2,253	34.0	387	15.3
1938	2,687	2,252	33.4	437	16.0
1940	2,611	2,096	33.2	458	15.2
1942	2,617	2,085	32.6	483	15.3
1944	2,491	2,022	NA	421	NA

Source: Wattenberg, *Statistical History*, 368.

The results of this registration, revealing as they were, did not measure the full extent of illiteracy—only those who could not sign their names. In view of the fact that some people could write only their names, it developed that illiteracy, the inability to read or write, was higher than the numbers indicated here. The table brings together the three factors most conducive to a retarded level of education: being in the South, being rural, and being black. Very few people outside the South, black or white, could not write their name.

Private Schools

Private schools were in certain cases alternatives to public education in the United States. Private schools during this period took between 7.5% and 9.5% of enrollment in elementary and secondary schools. Private schooling largely meant religious schools, and religious schooling in large measure meant schools of the Roman Catholic Church, which provided a major portion of them. Although the church made education in religion an article of faith for its member-

TABLE 14.21 TEACHERS AND ENROLLMENT IN PRIVATE SCHOOLS BY RELIGIOUS AFFILIATION, 1940–1941

Religious Affiliation or Control	Number of Schools	Teachers Men	Teachers Women	Teachers Total	Enrollment Male	Enrollment Female	Enrollment Total
Elementary Schools							
Baptist	18	6	30	36	476	457	933
Brethren	2	1	4	5	75	52	127
Congregational	10	6	37	43	444	510	954
Friends	25	20	159	179	1,574	1,466	3,040
Jewish	4	26	16	42	982	27	1,009
Lutheran	890	1,107	312	1,419	28,248	26,564	54,812
Methodist	26	8	47	55	608	874	1,482
Presbyterian	26	19	72	91	1,026	1,079	2,105
Protestant Episcopal	100	99	184	283	2,873	2,317	5,190
Reformed	6	4	11	15	406	97	503
Roman Catholic	7,944	1,183	58,898	60,081	1,108,694	1,016,488	2,035,182
Seventh-Day Adventist	62	12	84	96	1,595	1,484	3,079
Other denominations	43	17	81	98	1,125	1,200	2,325
Nonsectarian	566	536	1,839	2,375	20,970	21,184	42,154
Total	**9,730**	**3,047**	**61,800**	**64,847**	**1,169,252**	**1,074,027**	**2,243,279**
Secondary Schools							
Baptist	24	154	91	245	1,754	1,309	3,063
Brethren	4	8	13	21	106	128	234
Church of the Nazarene	2	8	6	14	132	151	283
Congregational	9	28	53	81	592	674	1,266
Friends	19	140	138	278	1,284	1,212	2,496
Lutheran	25	102	42	144	1,322	1,040	2,362
Mennonite	2	8	4	12	74	83	157
Methodist	28	132	148	280	1,481	1,470	2,951
Moravian	2	6	23	29	48	135	183
Pilgrim Holiness	2	. . .	12	12	87	90	177
Presbyterian	27	90	122	212	1,672	1,560	3,232
Protestant Episcopal	101	591	453	1,044	5,498	3,025	8,523
Reformed	8	102	20	122	1,681	296	1,977
Roman Catholic	2,105	6,536	14,440	20,976	157,583	203,540	361,123
Seventh-Day Adventist	70	213	181	394	2,212	2,500	4,712
Unitarian	2	5	9	14	87	. . .	87
Other denominations	23	181	141	322	1,708	1,511	3,219
Nonsectarian	536	3,226	2,669	5,895	37,034	24,520	61,554
Total	**2,997**	**11,547**	**18,583**	**30,130**	**214,463**	**243,305**	**457,768**

Source: *Information Please Almanac*, 1948, 314.

ship and strongly urged that Catholic children go to Catholic schools, the realities of the situation made it impossible. Inasmuch as parochial schools were denied public funds, the costs of constructing schools or of paying tuition were often too great. Only approximately 40% of Catholic children went to church schools in the early 1940s. The rest had to go to public schools and get their religious training separately. Many Catholic politicians continued to argue for help from the public treasury, but the prospect of receiving a share of tax revenue did not look promising.

Position of the Roman Catholic Church on Education

1 Parents are responsible for the training of their children.

2 Parents may be assisted by the Church, the State, private societies or individuals in fulfilling this duty.

3 Teachers have their authority to teach by delegation from the parents.

4 The Church has the right to demand of the parents that their children be trained in religion and morality.

5 Since such training is not given in non-Catholic schools, parents who send their children to such schools are bound under pain of mortal sin to supply such training fully and adequately.

6 Since most parents are unable to supply full and adequate religious training to their children, it becomes in most cases their obligation to send the children to Catholic schools.

7 Parents may send their children to non-Catholic schools only when such practice is tolerated by the bishop of the diocese.

8 The State has the right to demand that the child be prepared for his duties as a citizen. Such training is given in parochial as well as public schools.

Source: Saint Anthony's Guild, *The 1940 National Catholic Almanac* (Paterson, N.J., 1940), 277.

College Education

The number of Americans who went to college during these years was small—only about 3% of people of standard "college age" at the start of the period—but it increased every year until the worst part of the depression of the 1930s, when the number dropped. The number moved up again as early as 1936 and was on the way toward 10% of the age group when the Second World War intervened. During the early 1940s young people were expected to be either in the armed forces or engaged in some form of work for the defense effort, and so fewer were in college. More men went to college than women, and more men graduated during nearly the entire period. The gap steadily narrowed, however, and during the mid-1940s, when millions of young men were under arms, women passed men

TABLE 14.22 AMERICANS IN COLLEGE

[Resident students in thousands, except percentage]

Year	Number	Undergraduate	Graduate	Percentage of Population Aged 18–24
1914	379	NA[a]	NA	2.9
1915	404	NA	NA	3.1
1916	441	NA	NA	3.3
1918	441	NA	NA	3.6
1920	598	582	16	4.7
1922	681	NA	NA	5.1
1924	823	NA	NA	5.9
1926	941	NA	NA	6.6
1928	1,054	NA	NA	7.1
1930	1,101	1,054	47	7.2
1932	1,154	1,082	78	7.4
1934	1,055	983	71	6.6
1936	1,208	1,129	79	7.5
1938	1,351	1,270	91	8.3
1940	1,494	1,388	106	9.1
1942	1,404	1,319	85	8.4
1944	1,155	1,100	59	6.8

[a]NA = not available.
Source: Wattenberg, *Statistical History*, 383.

TABLE 14.23 INSTITUTIONS OF HIGHER EDUCATION—NUMBER AND FACULTY

| School Year Ending— | Number of Institutions | | | | | | | Faculty | | | |
| | Total | Junior Colleges | | | 4-Year Colleges | Medical Schools | Dental Schools | Total | Male | Female | Resident Instructional Staff |
		Total	Public	Private							
1944	1,650	413	210	203	1,237	77	39	150,980	106,254	44,726	105,841
1942	1,769	461	231	230	1,308	77	39	151,066	109,309	41,757	114,693
1940	1,708	456	217	239	1,252	77	39	146,929	106,328	40,601	110,885
1938	1,690	453	209	244	1,237	77	39	135,989	97,362	38,627	102,895
1936	1,628	415	187	228	1,213	77	39	121,036	86,567	34,469	92,580
1934	1,418	322	152	170	1,096	77	39	108,873	78,369	30,504	86,914
1932	1,478	342	159	183	1,136	76	38	100,789	71,680	29,109	88,172
1930	1,409	277	129	148	1,132	76	38	82,386	60,017	22,369	82,386
1928	1,410	248	114	134	1,162	80	40	(NA)	(NA)	(NA)	76,080
1926	1,377	153	47	106	1,224	79	44	(NA)	(NA)	(NA)	70,674
1924	1,295	132	39	93	1,163	79	43	(NA)	(NA)	(NA)	63,999
1922	1,162	80	17	63	1,082	81	45	(NA)	(NA)	(NA)	56,486
1920	1,041	52	10	42	989	85	46	48,615	35,807	12,808	. . .
1918	980	46	14	32	934	90	46	(NA)	(NA)	(NA)	. . .
1916	(NA)	. . .	. . .	. . .	. . .	95	49	(NA)	(NA)	(NA)	. . .

Source: Wattenberg, *Statistical History*, 382–383.

TABLE 14.24 INSTITUTIONS OF HIGHER EDUCATION—DEGREES CONFERRED, BY SEX

School Year Ending—	Total All Degrees	Bachelor's or First Professional					Master's or Second Professional				Doctor's or Equivalent				Lapse Time in Years, Bachelor's-to-Doctor's
		Total	Male	Female	Per 1,000 Persons 23 Years Old	Per 100 High School Graduates 4 Years Earlier	Total	Male	Female	Per 100 Bachelor's Degrees 2 Years Earlier	Total	Male	Female	Per 1,000 Bachelor's Degrees X-Years Earlier	
1944	141,582	125,863	55,865	69,998	52	10	13,414	5,711	7,703	7	2,305	1,380	425	13.8	9.4
1942	213,491	185,346	103,889	81,457	78	16	24,648	14,179	10,469	15	3,497	3,036	461	24.9	8.8
1940	216,521	186,500	109,546	76,954	81	18	26,731	16,508	10,223	19	3,290	2,861	429	23.5	9.4
1938	189,503	164,943	97,678	67,265	72	18	21,628	13,400	8,228	16	2,932	2,502	430	22.3	9.5
1936	164,197	143,125	86,067	57,058	63	17	18,302	11,503	6,799	13	2,770	2,370	400	24.7	9.2
1934	157,279	136,156	82,341	53,815	61	20	18,293	11,516	6,777	15	2,830	2,456	374	27.7	8.5
1932	160,084	138,063	83,271	54,792	63	23	19,367	12,210	7,157	17	2,654	2,247	407	29.0	9.1
1930	139,752	122,484	73,615	48,869	57	22	14,969	8,925	6,044	15	2,299	1,946	353	33.4	8.7
1928	124,995	111,161	67,659	43,502	55	22	12,387	7,727	4,660	15	1,447	1,249	198	33.2	8.4
1926	108,407	97,263	62,218	35,045	49	27	9,735	6,202	3,533	16	1,409	1,216	193	37.3	8.6
1924	92,097	82,783	54,908	27,875	43	27	8,216	5,515	2,701	17	1,098	939	159	24.8	8.4
1922	68,488	61,668	41,306	20,362	33	22	5,984	4,304	1,680	16	836	708	128	17.6	7.8
1920	53,516	48,622	31,980	16,642	26	19	4,279	2,985	1,294	9	615	522	93	14.2	7.7
1918	42,041	38,585	26,269	12,316	22	18	2,900	1,806	1,094	7	556	491	65	15.0	...
1916	49,823	45,250	31,852	13,398	24	25	3,906	2,934	972	9	667	586	81	18.1	...
1915	48,100	43,912	31,417	12,495	23	26	3,577	2,638	939	8	611	549	62	17.2	...
1914	48,097	44,268	32,183	12,085	24	28	3,270	2,256	1,014	8	559	486	73	15.7	...

Source: Wattenberg, Statistical History, 385–386.

TABLE 14.25 NUMBER OF DOCTORATES, BY FIELD: 1920 TO 1945

Year	Total, All Fields	Physics-Astronomy	Chemistry	Earth Sciences	Mathematics	Engineering	Basic Medical Sciences	Medical Sciences	Agricultural Sciences	Other Biological Sciences	Psychology
1945	1,621	43	288	23	36	68	121	31	54	96	64
1944	1,954	64	474	18	43	64	173	38	46	128	68
1943	2,585	131	511	43	44	53	227	43	75	218	92
1942	3,402	157	589	66	76	98	271	60	101	297	126
1941	3,481	179	647	64	95	122	244	53	93	273	113
1940	3,276	144	534	59	103	107	260	47	94	303	129
1939	2,948	160	467	62	93	69	242	36	69	266	117
1938	2,756	156	409	70	61	75	220	51	68	258	116
1937	2,749	155	504	54	74	98	162	26	59	255	112
1936	2,712	138	444	71	76	70	150	45	60	274	114
1935	2,521	132	365	66	75	111	126	47	80	233	122
1934	2,696	124	415	68	91	119	175	64	91	246	128
1933	2,460	133	382	74	75	92	153	44	75	203	92
1932	2,401	115	328	55	74	68	132	40	83	202	105
1931	2,340	112	333	42	82	67	130	52	62	225	118
1930	2,071	106	302	66	76	64	103	46	61	169	101
1929	1,913	97	251	48	68	41	107	38	60	164	122
1928	1,628	95	255	31	42	51	97	20	56	154	84
1927	1,539	81	216	45	51	33	103	24	42	121	76
1926	1,442	87	252	42	48	27	78	33	29	120	74
1925	1,206	51	211	27	28	16	69	30	36	110	71
1924	1,133	62	224	44	29	14	50	34	32	100	54
1923	1,062	60	185	40	34	14	67	28	45	102	65
1922	780	55	140	22	17	15	42	19	27	69	34
1921	661	37	125	12	15	10	34	27	15	57	28
1920	560	31	76	21	19	7	38	12	17	66	35

(continued)

TABLE 14.25   (continued)

Year	Economics	Anthropology and Sociology	Political Science	Other Social Sciences	History	English and American Language and Literature	Foreign Language and Literature	Other Arts and Humanities	Professional Fields	Education	Other and Unspecified Fields
1945	59	33	26	5	71	72	70	62	107	291	1
1944	61	39	36	14	60	74	69	66	103	316	...
1943	82	58	48	13	122	124	115	81	105	399	1
1942	138	77	70	13	168	177	150	126	148	493	1
1941	158	91	71	13	182	189	178	127	111	478	...
1940	125	73	81	25	167	174	180	107	94	470	...
1939	112	75	60	14	177	173	164	106	109	377	...
1938	125	61	56	10	159	159	172	84	83	363	...
1937	108	73	64	10	144	161	169	80	80	357	4
1936	103	56	53	12	135	144	185	98	103	354	27
1935	90	52	59	26	156	136	174	81	133	250	17
1934	113	52	65	24	148	137	166	74	103	280	13
1933	108	52	68	27	148	114	140	109	103	261	7
1932	122	58	58	20	123	129	137	115	123	309	5
1931	119	50	57	18	118	108	102	125	107	303	10
1930	107	44	33	27	128	96	95	96	74	268	9
1929	103	58	37	24	107	69	94	113	85	211	16
1928	85	25	51	11	94	70	68	83	77	173	6
1927	91	29	45	17	88	63	64	88	88	170	4
1926	81	26	33	13	71	71	55	76	64	161	1
1925	64	29	28	13	63	55	57	60	56	128	4
1924	52	20	29	5	60	57	65	47	52	102	1
1923	40	15	22	8	61	44	48	69	45	68	2
1922	33	14	17	3	56	34	45	44	32	59	3
1921	38	13	24	7	38	30	42	40	34	33	2
1920	22	15	12	3	23	23	42	31	18	48	1

Source: Wattenberg, *Statistical History,* 387–388.

in graduation. The wartime drop in traditional student population was partly offset by the armed forces' use of the colleges to offer specialized training to certain individuals. Without these special programs the decline in the campus population would have been severe indeed. The number of nonmilitary students in 1943–44 was 44% fewer than in 1939. Of that total 225,440 were men and 506,190 were women: a more than 2–1 ratio.

A virtual educational—and in some measure social—revolution was on the way, however. Congress in 1944 passed the Serviceman's Readjustment Act, better known as the "GI Bill of Rights." The measure offered government-subsidized college education and other kinds of special training to men and women who served in the armed forces during the Second World War. With this development, college now was being opened to—and economically feasible for—millions of young people who otherwise would not have considered it.

CHAPTER 15 Science, Invention, and Technology

The pace of scientific and technological change increased considerably in the first half of the twentieth century. Change at any time is built on change that had come before, and some of the most significant developments were of the agents—the tools—of scientific and technological advance. A better telescope, for example, facilitated acquisition of new knowledge in astronomy. Many of the technological developments of the twentieth century would have been impossible without greater availability of electric power. Although the years 1914–45 probably had more in common with the last half of the twentieth century than with the last half of the nineteenth, the period in fact provided a bridge between the two. One still found a few individual giants of American scientific and technological development. Alexander Graham Bell lasted until 1922, and Thomas A. Edison, perhaps the greatest of them all, lived until 1931, although the great discoveries of both men came at an earlier time. Henry Ford, a leading technological innovator, remained alive through the period. It was Ford who led the way in the technology of mass production, using the moving assembly line and interchangeable parts to bring, as much of American industry after the First World War sought to do, more goods within reach of more people. The 1920s were important for the work of Frederick W. Taylor, who argued that principles of science could be applied to organization and management.

Increasingly, discovery, invention, and change were due not to one person but to teams and organizations, with corporations, universities, and foundations leading the way. Because the nation fought two major wars in this period, the government became more involved in scientific development. The number of patents issued to individuals reached a peak in 1932 and then underwent a general decline. The number issued in 1945 was substantially lower—by some 14,000—than in 1914. The number of patents issued to corporations generally increased, although it did drop off during the Second World War. Research increasingly was connected with money. The greater availability of money from various sources and the general political and intellectual climate in the United States, which offered incentive, inspiration, and free pursuit of ideas, were important reasons why Americans stood in the forefront of scientific and technological development. The grand New York World's Fair of 1939, entitled "The World of Tomorrow," indicated the extent to which Americans equated science and technology with progress, as well as the extent to which technological change was equated with the United States. Technology indeed had become worldwide an American trademark.

Major Developments in American Science and Technology

The list that follows includes only a few of the most significant developments in American science and technology. There were hundreds more during the years 1914–45 that were of lesser—or in some cases equal—magnitude.

1914: Alexis Carrel announced a successful heart operation on an animal by suspending blood circulation.

1915: Joseph Goldberger discovered that pellagra came from a vitamin deficiency.

Irving Langmuir developed a tungsten filament electric light bulb.

1916: Gen. John T. Thompson invented a submachine gun appropriately called a "Tommy" gun.

1917: Clarence Birdseye found freezing to be an effective means of preserving food.

1920: The first graduate school of geography was established at Clark University.

Station KDKA, Pittsburgh (of the Westinghouse Company), began the first regular radio broadcast. It was of the national election returns.

1922: Herbert T. Kalmus produced the first process of colored motion pictures.

Alexis Carrel of the Rockefeller Institute discovered white corpuscles—blood agents that prevent the spread of infection.

1923: After purchasing the patent from a Swiss firm, Du Pont began producing "cellophane" film.

Colonel Jacob Schick received a patent for an electric shaver.

Arthur H. Compton discovered changes in X-ray wavelengths.

1924: Ford produced its ten millionth automobile. A new Model T without a self-starter sold for $290.

Vladimir K. Zworykin developed the iconoscope, a beginning of modern television.

1925: The Prest-Air Company of New York produced the first commercial dry ice.

Robert A. Millikan discovered cosmic rays in the upper atmosphere.

John T. Scopes was tried in Dayton, Tenn., for violation of a law forbidding the teaching of the theory of evolution.

1926: Robert H. Goddard fired the first liquid-fueled rocket.

1927: Charles A. Lindbergh completed the first solo nonstop flight from New York to Paris.

Warner Brothers produced the first "talkie" motion picture: *The Jazz Singer*.

John D. and Mack D. Rust invented a mechanical cotton picker.

Louis Shaw and Phillip Drinker introduced the first electric respirator, the "iron lung," at Bellevue Hospital in New York City.

The Holland Tunnel, carrying vehicular traffic under the Hudson River from New York to New Jersey, was completed.

The center of many living rooms and rapidly available to much of the population, radio was one of the half dozen most important technological developments of 1914–45. (Library of Congress)

1928: George Eastman showed his first colored motion pictures in Rochester, N.Y.

The *New York Times* placed its first moving electric sign at Times Square in New York City. The sign first gave the election results.

Amelia Earhart became the first female to fly the Atlantic Ocean; she flew as a passenger and had two companions.

1929: Sebastiano Lando received the first patent for a coin-operated vending machine.

1930: Scientists at Lowell Observatory in Flagstaff, Ariz. discovered Pluto.

Ernest O. Lawrence developed the cyclotron.

1931: The Empire State Building, the world's tallest, opened in New York City on May 1.

Harold C. Urey discovered heavy hydrogen.

The George Washington Bridge, connecting New York and New Jersey, opened.

Vannevar Bush at the Massachusetts Institute of Technology

(MIT) completed a "differential analyzer," a first computer machine with electronic components.

1932: Charles Anderson discovered the positron—a positive analogue of the electron.

1933: *Ranger,* the first American aircraft carrier, was launched.

The Muscle Shoals Bill, signed by President Franklin D. Roosevelt, marked the beginning of the Tennessee Valley Authority.

Edwin H. Armstrong discovered frequency modulation (FM) in radio.

1934: Wallace H. Carothers, a chemist at Du Pont, created a tough synthetic fiber he called "polymer 66," later called nylon.

1936: Boulder (renamed Hoover) Dam on the Colorado River was completed, creating Lake Mead.

Alexis Carrel introduced a perfusion pump, a type of artificial heart, at Rockefeller Institute in New York.

1937: The army's coast artillery demonstrated a system of radar at Ft. Monmouth, N.J.

Bonneville Dam on the Columbia River was dedicated.

Chester Carlson invented xerography, the first photocopier.

The Golden Gate Bridge in California was dedicated.

1938: To prevent the spread of venereal disease, New York became the first state to require medical tests—a blood test—before people could obtain a marriage license.

1939: The New York World's Fair opened in Queens in April. With the theme of "The World of Tomorrow," it heralded such scientific wonders as television.

Rufus Stetson and Philip Levine discovered the Rh factor in human blood.

Igor Sikorsky made the first helicopter.

1940: Edwin M. McMillan and Philip H. Abelson discovered neptunium, the first element with an atomic number higher than uranium.

Peter Carl Goldmark demonstrated the first color television system.

1941: The "Manhattan Project," research into a possible atomic weapon, secretly began.

Edwin M. McMillan, Glenn T. Seaborg, and Arthur C. Wahl produced plutonium.

The Grand Coulee Dam, on the Columbia River in Washington, opened.

Rationing of rubber started at the end of the year. Finding a substitute was imperative.

By executive order President Roosevelt created an Office of Scientific Research and Development. Its function was to coordinate work in military areas. Vannevar Bush was chairman.

1942: Enrico Fermi built the first continuous nuclear reactor at the University of Chicago.

America's first jet aircraft, the XP-59 produced by Bell Aircraft, was tested by pilot Robert Stanley.

Manufacturer Henry J. Kaiser perfected a technique for speedy construction of cargo ships (Liberty ships).

1943: The "Big Inch," an oil pipeline stretching 1,254 miles from Texas to Pennsylvania, which crossed thirty rivers, went into service.

Chicago's first subway opened.

1944: Now produced in large quantities in the United States, penicillin continued to amaze as a "wonder drug," effective against growing numbers of diseases and against infection.

A new insecticide, DDT, used as a dust or spray, was found effective against body parasites and thus reduced typhus among soldiers and civilians.

The rubber crisis was essentially ended with production of a synthetic called butadiene.

American industry continued to utilize numerous recycled commodities, making special use of wastepaper, scrap iron, tin cans, fats, and rags.

1945: The Federal Communications Commission (FCC) allocated thirteen channels for commercial television.

The atomic bomb was successfully tested at Los Alamos, New Mexico, on July 16. The first bomb was dropped on Hiroshima on August 6. The second bomb was dropped on Nagasaki on August 9.

TABLE 15.1 PATENTS FILED AND ISSUED

Year	Patent Applications Filed		Patents Issued						
	Inventions	Designs	Inventions						Designs
			Total	Individuals	Corporations		U.S. Government		
					U.S.	Foreign			
1914	67,774	2,454	39,892	. . .	. . .	. . .	. . .		1,711
1916	68,075	2,684	43,892	31,742	11,540	610	. . .		1,745
1918	57,343	2,234	38,452	. . .	. . .	. . .	. . .		1,206
1920	81,915	4,660	37,060	. . .	. . .	. . .	. . .		2,481
1922	83,962	4,763	38,369	27,369	10,300	700	. . .		1,609
1924	76,987	3,635	42,574	29,174	12,400	1,000	. . .		2,670
1926	81,365	4,343	44,733	28,633	15,200	900	. . .		5,103
1928	87,603	4,761	42,357	23,357	17,800	1,200	. . .		5,218
1930	89,554	4,182	45,226	23,726	19,700	1,800	. . .		2,710
1932	67,006	4,345	53,458	26,274	24,822	2,325	37		2,942
1934	56,643	4,399	44,420	19,731	22,529	2,131	29		2,919
1936	62,599	6,478	39,782	16,639	21,207	1,903	33		4,556
1938	66,874	8,084	38,061	16,304	19,635	2,063	59		5,026
1940	60,863	8,530	42,238	17,627	22,165	2,406	40		6,145
1942	45,549	4,218	38,449	14,534	22,019	1,286	62		3,728
1944	54,190	5,063	28,053	9,636	16,769	645	106		2,914
1945	67,846	8,066	25,695	8,981	15,665	580	87		3,524

Source: Ben J. Wattenberg, *Statistical History of the United States* (New York, 1976), 958.

Even with the emergence of sleek diesel locomotives in the 1930s and 1940s, the chugging, puffing steam engine remained the backbone of rail transport during 1914–45 for both freight and passenger service. (Library of Congress)

As rationing ended, item by item, and the war came to a halt, American industry began to wind down from the vast military programs and to shift its attention and technology acquired during the war to the production of domestic goods.

Sources: Gordon Carruth and Associates, *The Encyclopedia of American Facts and Dates* (New York, 1987), numerous pages; Richard Morris, *Encyclopedia of American History* (New York, 1982), 184–186, 797–800, 810–812.

American Winners of Nobel Prizes in the Sciences

The Nobel Prizes grew out of the will of Alfred B. Nobel, a Swedish scientist who, on his death in 1896, left a fund the interest of which was to be divided each year among persons who made the largest contributions in the area of chemistry, physics, and medicine or physiology, as well as the individual who produced the most distinguished literary work and the person who contributed the most to world peace. The prizes for chemistry and physics were awarded by the Swedish Academy of Science and the prize for medicine by the Caroline Medical Institute, both of which were in Stockholm. The value of the prize changed with the income from the fund.

Between 1936 and 1945 each prize earned approximately 8,000 British pounds, or approximately (in the exchange rate of 1939) $38,000. In the early 1990s, by contrast, each Nobel Prize was worth approximately $1 million. That Americans in the twentieth century began to receive increased numbers of these prestigious awards was traceable to many factors, among them improvements in American college education, especially in the research aspects; better funding from public and private sources for research activity; and the fact that American scientific inquiry was aided by movement to the United States of talented people seeking to escape Hitler's Europe. Listed here are the American winners in the sciences from 1914 to 1944:

1914 Theodore W. Richards (chemistry) for determining atomic weight of chemical elements.

1923 Robert A. Millikan (physics) for work on elementary charge of electricity and photoelectric phenomena.

1927 Arthur H. Compton (physics) for discovery of the Compton phenomenon.

1930 Karl Landsteiner (medicine) for discovery of human blood groups.

1932 Edgar D. Adrian (medicine) for discovery of the function of the neuron.

1932 Irving Langmuir (chemistry) for work in the realm of surface chemistry.

1934 Harold C. Urey (chemistry) for discovery of heavy hydrogen.

1934 George R. Minot, William P. Murphy, and George H. Whipple (medicine) for discovery of liver therapy against anemias.

1936 Carl D. Anderson (physics) for discovery of the positron.

1937 Clinton J. Davisson (physics) for discovery of diffraction of electrons by crystals.

1939 Ernest Orlando Lawrence (physics) for development of the cyclotron.

1943 Edward A. Doisy (medicine) for analysis of vitamin K.

1943 Otto Stern (physics) for detecting the magnetic momentum of protons.

1944 Joseph Erlanger and Herbert Spencer Gasser (medicine) for work on the function of nerve threads.

1944 Isidor Isaac Rabi (physics) for work on the magnetic movement of atomic particles.

Source: The Information Please Almanac, 1948 (New York, 1948), 741–743.

Science Museums in the United States

The museums listed below include the major establishments in existence in the year 1945 that were devoted to some aspect of science or technology. The list gives the name of the establishment, its location by city and state, and the date of its opening.

Academy of Natural Sciences of Philadelphia, Philadelphia, Pa., 1812

Adler Planetarium, Chicago, Ill., 1930

Alabama Museum of Natural History, Tuscaloosa, Ala., 1831

Alaska Historical Library and Museum, Juneau, Alaska, 1920

American Geographical Society, New York, N.Y., 1852

American Museum of Natural History, New York, N.Y., 1869

Arizona State Museum, Tucson, Ariz., 1893

Army Institute of Pathology, Washington, D.C., 1862

Buffalo Museum of Science, Buffalo, N.Y., 1929

Buhl Planetarium and Institute of Popular Science, Pittsburgh, Pa., 1939

California Academy of Sciences, San Francisco, Calif., 1853

Carnegie Institute, Pittsburgh, Pa., 1896

Chicago Academy of Sciences, Chicago, Ill., 1857

Chicago Natural History Museum (Field Museum), Chicago, Ill. 1893

Cleveland Health Museum, Cleveland, Ohio, 1940

Cleveland Museum of Natural History, Cleveland, Ohio, 1920

Colorado Museum of Natural History, Denver, Colo., 1900

Franklin Institute, Philadelphia, Pa., 1824

Griffith Observatory and Planetarium, Los Angeles, Calif., 1935

Hayden Planetarium in the American Museum of Natural History, New York, N.Y., 1935

Mariner's Museum, Hampton Roads, Va., 1930

Marine Studios, Marineland, Fla., 1938

Mellon Institute, Pittsburgh, Pa., 1913

Museum of Natural History (University of Oregon), Eugene, Oreg., 1935

Museum of Science and Industry, Chicago, Ill., 1926

Museum of Vertebrate Zoology, Berkeley, Calif., 1908

National Academy of Sciences, Washington, D.C., 1919

National Geographic Society, Washington, D.C., 1888

Newark Museum, Newark, N.J., 1909

New England Museum of Natural History, Boston, Mass., 1830

New York Botanical Garden, New York, N.Y., 1891

New York Museum of Science and Industry, New York, N.Y., 1927

New York State Museum, Albany, N.Y., 1870

Peabody Museum of Archaeology and Ethnology, Cambridge, Mass., 1866

Peabody Museum of Natural History, New Haven, Conn., 1866

San Diego Natural History Museum, San Diego, Calif., 1933

Smithsonian Institution (United States National Museum), Washington, D.C., 1846

Southwest Museum, Los Angeles, Calif., 1907

Sources: The American Association of Museums, The Official Museum Directory (New York, 1970), 1000–1003; The World Almanac and Book of Facts for 1947 (New York, 1947), 289, 314.

Science and Technology: A Blessing and a Curse

The period between 1914 and 1945 was an age of damming the major waterways—such rivers as the Colorado, Columbia, and Tennessee, nearly all of them except the mighty Mississippi. The purposes of these projects of technology were to stop floods, to relieve the distress caused by rivers overflowing, and to generate electricity, thus illuminating and generally improving the lives of people in the area. War was a major precipitant of change in these years, and although military goods were created for the dubious purpose of killing, the knowledge obtained in their production often could be transferred to production of goods for domestic consumption. The basic thrust of American technological development was to change the lifestyle, to make life longer, easier, and more enjoyable. It was in pursuit of these ends that Americans sought out discoveries and new products or expanded on or improved the items that were created or discovered in the years before 1914. Technological creations that had a great effect on life during 1914–45 were radio, movies, automobiles, and the modern farm tractor. None of them would have been possible without expanded use of electricity.

If the United States was to no small extent a creation of technology, Americans had learned long before 1914 that American problems were traceable to technology. So it continued. Automobiles led to traffic accidents and deaths and the huge costs of roads and bridges; they changed the character of cities and fouled the air. Technological and industrial development in fact raised many questions about clean water and air and the general welfare of the planet, although environmental concerns received dreadfully little attention in this age marked with so many reasons for producing more goods. Availability of better medical facilities meant higher medical costs

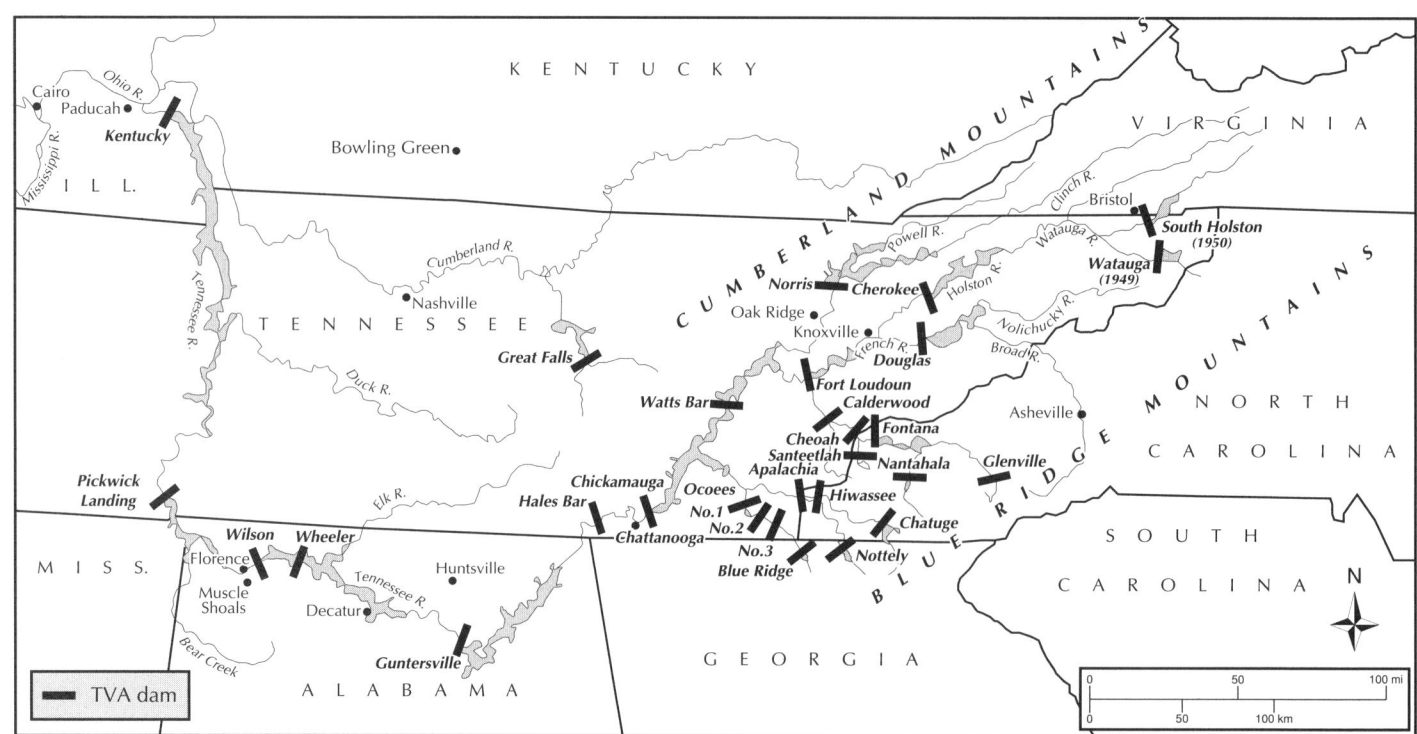

The TVA was to become a technological showcase for the United States somewhat on the order of the Panama Canal. The social and economic effects were even greater than the canal. Once developed, the project would produce a virtual revolution in one of the poorest areas of the United States. By slowing floods, providing inexpensive electric power (in many cases to places that had no electricity) and cheap fertilizer, reforesting eroded land, and creating recreation areas, the TVA enhanced social and economic conditions for people in parts of seven states.

The modern, rubber-tired, all-purpose tractor that appeared in the mid-1930s revolutionized the tractor almost as much as the tractor revolutionized agriculture. (Library of Congress)

and higher expectations, as well as more decisions on how to spend one's money. Better technology produced a need to relate industrial and agricultural production to the markets. Failure to do so sharpened the economic cycle and helped cause the Great Depression of 1929–41. Demand begot supply, to be sure, but it also worked the other way around. Availability of new goods and services generated a need to find a way to produce the demand, leading to a new problem and new decisions with respect to work, lifestyle, and personal relationships. An additional problem at the end of 1945 was the bomb. What was one to do with the bomb? It was impossible to know. One could say, however, that the previous three decades had been a time of great change. If Rip Van Winkle had fallen asleep in 1914 and awakened in 1945, he might have concluded—looking at how people traveled from one place to another, how they spent their spare time, how the United States fought its wars—that he had awakened in a different world.

TABLE 15.2 EXAMPLES OF ITEMS DISCOVERED, CREATED, OR MADE AVAILABLE FOR WIDESPREAD USE DURING 1914–1945

Domestic Goods	Military Goods
radio television talking motion pictures colored motion pictures air-conditioning (for trains and businesses)	bolt-action rifle (Enfield, Winchester) semiautomatic rifle (Garand) submachine gun (Thompson) automatic rifle (Browning) gas and chemical agents
electric refrigerators electric ranges electric washing machines electric sewing machines electric vacuum cleaners	gas masks zeppelins bombs, shells, torpedoes pursuit (fighter) planes, many kinds horizontal bombers (2 and 4 engines)
computer (crude and elementary) frozen foodstuffs wristwatches rayon, nylon, other synthetic fabrics plastics	dive bombers torpedo bombers jet aircraft antiaircraft artillery (land and naval) parachutes
penicillin sulfa drugs blood plasma vitamins time clocks	bomb sight (Norden) proximity fuse aircraft carriers submarines Liberty (cargo) ships

Domestic Goods	Military Goods
synthetic rubber diesel locomotives streamlined railway cars automobile technology enclosed bodies	LST (landing ship) LSD (landing ship) tanks and tank technology steel helmets (2 styles) land mines (anti-tank, personnel)
all-metal bodies streamlined body styles hydraulic brakes hypoid gears synchronized transmission	military trucks jeeps half-tracks flamethrowers radio (land, sea, air)
gearshift on steering column automatic transmission independent front suspension sealed-beam headlights curved windshields	radar (many kinds) sonar napalm bazooka, other rockets portable bridges (pontoon, etc.)
freewheeling safety rims ethyl gasoline coil springs self-starter	atomic bombs
start button on dashboard safety glass engines: 4-cylinder, 6-cylinder, straight 8, V-8, V-12, V-16	

Military technology, 1941, before radar. The technology was prompted by another innovation of the twentieth century: air power. (National Archives)

CHAPTER 16 Art and Architecture

Art

American painters continued to be children of European art in the first half of the twentieth century, although by the 1940s there were signs of an emerging American leadership. The period began with a "realist" revolt against the sentimentalism, the pretty pictures long associated with the impressionists. The revolt was manifested by an independent showing by eight American artists in 1908 and by the opening in 1913 of the Armory Show in New York featuring works of contemporary American and European artists—an event heralded by many as America's true introduction to modern art. The works exhibited suggested nothing less than a reexamination of what art was.

In the period between the two world wars, the continued quest for social realism produced more pictures about the hard challenges of life. Work scenes and city scenes were popular, and there were paintings of the local bar or of grisly prizefights. The eight artists who had surfaced in 1908, now deemed the "Ashcan school," often led the way in their selection of topics. Still much affected by European trends, American painters dabbled in all the current styles—in postimpressionism or expressionism or the cubism that had become associated with Pablo Picasso. Portrait painting, almost a lost art, managed to stay alive in the last works of John Singer Sargent or in the painting of Eugene Speicher and a few others.

The years of the depression produced several themes. One was the popularity of a small number of regionalists, including Andrew Wyeth, who painted New England landscapes; Thomas Hart Benton; John S. Curry; and Grant Wood, whose painting *American Gothic* was one of the most familiar in the United States. The expansion of art collecting, begun earlier, continued in public museums, highlighted

McSorley's Bar by John Sloan (1912). Probably best known of "The Eight" American individualists was John Sloan, whose work reflected modernism more in subject than in style. (The Detroit Institute of Arts, Founders Society Purchase)

In *Cradling Wheat* (1938), Thomas Hart Benton reveals a fondness for sturdy rural stock characteristic of most regionalist painters. (The Saint Louis Art Museum)

by the opening of the Museum of Modern Art in 1929, and in private collections. In 1935 the government created the Federal Art Project—a branch of the work relief agency, the WPA—that made it possible for unemployed artists to continue to paint, for $23.86 per week. The Art Project continued the theme of social realism, and it virtually revived the practice of mural painting. If critics considered much of the work second-rate, the project gave formal sanction to the worth of painting and provided work for such soon-to-be-famous artists as Jackson Pollock and Willem de Kooning. In the 1930s and 1940s many foreign artists fled Hitler's Europe for the United States. In New York they mixed with American artists and began to coalesce around a striking new form called abstract expressionism.

Even with the swirl of artistic currents and the growth of museums and art collections, Americans were not an art-oriented people. Millions could not name a single living American artist; of those who could, many would identify Wyeth and Benton and Wood—painters cast aside by art's inner circles as hopeless provincialists. Asked to name their favorite artist, a remarkable number of Americans probably would say Norman Rockwell, the popular painter of covers for the *Saturday Evening Post*.

Major American Painters, 1914–1945

Malvin Albright
Cecelia Beaux
George W. Bellows
Thomas Hart Benton
F. A. Bridgman
John S. Curry
*Arthur B. Davies
Arthur Dove
Lyonel Feininger
*William J. Glackens
William Gropper
Philip L. Hale
*Robert Henri
Edward Hopper
William H. Howe
George Inness
Bernard Karfiol
Rockwell Kent
Walter Kuhn
William Lathrop

*Ernest Lawson
*George Luks
John Marin
Alfred Maurer
Charles H. Miller
Thomas Moran
Anna Mary (Grandma) Moses
Jerome Myers
Georgia O'Keeffe
William Paxton
*Maurice Prendergast
Abraham Rattner
Edward Redfield
Paul Sample
John S. Sargent
Ben Shahn
Charles Sheeler
*Everett Shinn
*John Sloan
Eugene Speicher
Robert Spencer
Maurice Sterne
Max Weber
Grant Wood
Andrew Wyeth

*Members of "The Eight," famous for the "revolt" of 1908.
Source: E. P. Richardson, Painting in America, from 1502 to the Present (New York, 1965), numerous pages.

Art Museums in the United States

Listed below are major establishments in operation in the year 1945 that were devoted partially or wholly to art, essentially painting. It is significant to note that of the places listed, nearly 50% opened during the first four decades of the twentieth century. The list provides the name of the institution, its location, and the date of its opening.

Art Institute of Chicago, Chicago, Ill., 1879

Brooklyn Museum, Brooklyn, N.Y., 1889

Buffalo Academy—Albright Art Gallery, Buffalo, N.Y., 1905

California Palace of the Legion of Honor, San Francisco, Calif., 1924

Carnegie Institute, Pittsburgh, Pa., 1896

Cincinnati Art Museum, Cincinnati, Ohio, 1880

City Art Museum, St. Louis, Mo., 1912

Cleveland Museum of Art, Cleveland, Ohio, 1913

Corcoran Gallery of Art, Washington, D.C., 1869

Currier Gallery of Art, Manchester, N.H., 1915

Denver Art Museum, Denver, Colo., 1917

Detroit Institute of Arts, Detroit, Mich., 1884

Fine Arts Gallery of San Diego, San Diego, Calif., 1925

Freer Gallery of Art, Washington, D.C., 1923

Frick Collection, New York, N.Y., 1935

Henry E. Huntington Library and Art Gallery, San Marino, Calif., 1919

Hispanic Society of America, New York, N.Y., 1904

John Herron Art Museum, Indianapolis, Ind., 1883

Los Angeles County Museum of History, Science, and Art, Los Angeles, Calif., 1911

Metropolitan Museum of Art, New York, N.Y., 1870

Milwaukee Art Center, Milwaukee, Wis., 1888

Museum of Fine Arts, Boston, Mass., 1870

Museum of Modern Art, New York, N.Y., 1929

Museum of the City of New York, New York, N.Y., 1923

National Collection of Fine Arts, Washington, D.C., 1906

National Gallery of Art, Washington, D.C., 1937

Newark Museum, Newark, N.J., 1909

New-York Historical Society, New York, N.Y., 1804

New York State Historical Association, Cooperstown, N.Y., 1899

Pennsylvania Academy of the Fine Arts, Philadelphia, Pa., 1805

Philadelphia Museum of Art, Philadelphia, Pa., 1875

San Francisco Museum of Art, San Francisco, Calif., 1921

Toledo Museum of Art, Toledo, Ohio, 1901

Virginia Museum of Fine Arts, Richmond, Va., 1910

Walters Art Gallery, Baltimore, Md., 1931

Whitney Museum of American Art, New York, N.Y., 1930

William H. Fogg Art Museum, Cambridge, Mass., 1895

William Rockhill Nelson Gallery of Art, Kansas City, Mo., 1915

Worcester Art Museum, Worcester, Mass., 1896

Sources: The American Association of Museums, The Official Museum Directory (New York, 1970), numerous pages; Encyclopedia Britannica (New York, 1962), 15:975.

Architecture

In its broadest sense architecture pertains to the designing and building of objects, and while there are various types of architecture, the term as commonly used applies to buildings. Needless to say, architecture of buildings has followed various trends. When the twentieth century began, American architecture was in an age of elegance, with ornate, grandiose public structures and homes built for the wealthy and business elite that almost resembled Gothic cathedrals. At approximately the same time there had emerged another philosophy that form, or design, should be determined by function (what the building was supposed to do) and by the surroundings in which the structure was to exist. This approach became known as the "Chicago school." It came to be associated with the skyscraper, so visible a part of Chicago's growing skyline, and with the architect associated with the skyscraper, Louis Sullivan. A unique American contribution to world architecture, the skyscraper represented an effort to maximize space in a crowded urban setting. Made possible by the development of the steel or iron skeleton and by the invention of the electric elevator, the skyscraper came to symbolize size, strength, and power. Doubts that might have lingered about the sturdiness of these elongated structures should have been put to rest at last in 1945, when a twin-engine B-25 bomber smashed into the Empire State Building, the tallest of them all. The crash produced havoc in the affected area, the seventy-eighth and seventy-ninth floors, but the structure itself stood rock solid.

It was possible, of course, that the two approaches could blend. Skyscrapers could be built in classical, decorative style, as was indicated in 1913 with completion of the Woolworth Building in New York. Although the classical approach was on the decline by 1914, its influence reached at least through the 1920s, as could be seen in the design of the Wrigley Building (1921) and Tribune Tower (1923–25), both in Chicago. Louis Sullivan, who lived until 1924, spent his last years designing banks in midwestern towns, not large

The Empire State Building, 1930s. Completed in Manhattan in 1931, the Empire State Building was not only the tallest and most famous skyscraper but also an expression of sleek modern architecture with stepped-back design required by construction codes. (The Empire State Building)

metropolitan structures. By then the brilliance of Sullivan's most famous pupil, Frank Lloyd Wright, had surfaced, but Wright received little attention in the 1920s. His most noted projects of the era were his own house in Wisconsin and the Imperial Hotel in Tokyo.

By the 1930s, however, the classicists had run their course, and the modernists who favored simpler, more functional designs began to prevail. They were boosted by architects from abroad, who favored designs even simpler than those of the Americans. In the late 1930s several European members of what had become known as the "International school" fled to the United States. Foremost among them were two Germans, Walter Gropius and Ludwig Mies van der Rohe. Examples of the modernist victory indicated a continuing American romance with the skyscraper. They included the New York Daily News Building (1930), McGraw-Hill Building (1931), and Rockefeller Center (1931–39), all in New York. Wright began to receive the attention that would make him America's most famous architect with such structures as "Falling Water," a private residence near Pittsburgh (1936), and the Johnson Wax Building in Racine, Wisconsin (1939), both of which embodied Wright's supreme principle that buildings must harmonize with their surroundings. By the start of the 1940s there had begun to emerge a reaction against the modernists as being too structured, even sterile—too much glass and too many steel posts. The more architects stressed individualism and the importance of region and environment, the more the influence of Frank Lloyd Wright—who certainly was no opponent of creativity—continued to rise.

Of course the building, or rebuilding, of America during these years went far beyond the stars of the small, even elitist, field of architecture. Movie houses had to be built to meet the demands of a new industry and then modified as the industry changed. Factories were being built all the time, and though most were not designed by professionals, some were, and probably the busiest architect in the 1930s was Albert Kahn, noted for buildings that served the automobile industry in Michigan. Growth of the urban population produced growth of demand for urban housing. Two world wars created special, albeit temporary, demands, ranging from housing for troops to buildings to make war materiel. Henry Ford built a mile-long bomber factory at Willow Run, Michigan, in 1941 and then abruptly shut it down in 1945. Perhaps the most original architectural design of the 1940s was a prefabricated, intended to be temporary, structure of corrugated metal called a Quonset hut.

American Architects, 1914–1945

Henry Bacon
Marcel Breuer
Barry Byrne
Harvey W. Corbett
Ralph Adams Cram
George G. Elmslie
Cass Gilbert

TABLE 16.1   AMERICA'S TALLEST BUILDINGS, 1945

City	Building	No. of Stories	Height in Feet
New York	Empire State	102	1,250
New York	Chrysler	77	1,046
New York	60 Wall Tower	66	950
New York	Bk. of Manhattan	90	927
New York	R.C.A.	70	850
New York	Woolworth	60	792
Cleveland	Terminal	52	708
New York	Met. Life	50	700
New York	500 Fifth Ave.	60	697
New York	City Bank	54	686
New York	Chanin	50	680
New York	Lincoln	53	673
New York	Irving Trust	50	646
New York	Waldorf-Astoria	47	625
New York	10 E. 40th	48	620
New York	Sherry Netherlands	43	620
New York	General Electric	50	616
New York	Singer	47	612
Chicago	Board of Trade	44	612
New York	New York Life	40	610
New York	U.S. Court House	37	590
Pittsburgh	Gulf	43	584
New York	Municipal	24	580
Cincinnati	Carew Tower	48	574
New York	Carlyle	40	570
Chicago	Temple	21	569
New York	Continental Bank	48	562
New York	N.Y. Central	35	560
Detroit	Penobscot	47	557
Chicago	Pittsfield	38	557
Chicago	Civic Opera	45	555
Chicago	Medinah	42	555
Columbus	Citadel	46	555
Chicago	Palmolive	37	551

Source: The Information Please Almanac, 1947 (New York, 1947), 623.

Charles and Henry Greene
Walter Burley Griffin
Walter Gropius
Arthur Harmon
Thomas Hastings
Raymond Hood
J. M. Howells
Philip C. Johnson
Albert Kahn
Christopher LaFarge
George Maher
Bernard Maybeck
Ludwig Mies van der Rohe
Benjamin Morris
Dwight Perkins
John Russell Pope
William G. Purcell
R. N. Schindler
Clarence Stein
Louis Sullivan
Samuel B. P. Trowbridge
Frank Lloyd Wright

Source: Wayne Andrews, *Architecture, Ambition, and Americans* (New York, 1978), numerous pages.

Bridges

If the architecture of bridges was vastly different from the designing of buildings, it was no less a precise and sophisticated art that produced results fully as spectacular and, in terms of the numbers who used them, probably more helpful for society. Big bridges no less than big buildings were a mark of a vigorous, productive society, and an international and especially a national American competition existed over which place could build the largest bridge. New York had captured the prize in 1931 with the George Washington Bridge only to lose it six years later with the completion of the Golden Gate Bridge in San Francisco. The style of bridges continued to vary, but the most dramatic design was the suspension bridge. Both the George Washington and the Golden Gate were suspension bridges.

As with any other bridge, it was necessary to build suspension bridges to proper specifications. If not, the result could be disaster, as was demonstrated with the Tacoma Narrows Bridge at Puget Sound. When completed in 1940, it was the world's third longest bridge and the pride of the Northwest. Flexible and poorly anchored, however, the bridge from the start showed a troublesome inclination toward twisting in the wind. In a gale only four months after its opening, the oscillation became so severe that the bridge—now called "Galloping Gertie"—broke up and fell into the sound. Newer and longer bridges, however, could do nothing to diminish the popularity of the grandest of them all, the Brooklyn Bridge. A suspension bridge across the East River in New York, this magnificent structure remained on reaching age fifty in 1941 the world's most famous bridge.

The George Washington Bridge. Connecting New York and New Jersey, the George Washington Bridge (pictured here in a later photograph) was the nation's longest when completed in 1931. (Port of New York and New Jersey Authority)

TABLE 16.2   NOTABLE AMERICAN BRIDGES, 1945

Length of Channel Span. Feet	Name	Location	Type[a]	Year Completed
4,200	Golden Gate	San Francisco	S	1937
3,500	George Washington	New York City	S	1931
2,310	Transbay	San Francisco	S	1936
2,300	Bronx-Whitestone	New York City	S	1939
1,850	Ambassador	Detroit, Mich.	S	1929
1,750	Delaware River	Philadelphia, Pa.	S	1926
1,652	Kill Van Kull	Bayonne, N.J.	SA	1931
1,632	Bear Mountain	Peekskill, N.Y.	S	1924
1,600	Williamsburg	New York City	S	1903
1,595.5	Brooklyn	New York City	S	1883
1,500	Mid-Hudson	Poughkeepsie, N.Y.	S.	1930
1,470	Manhattan	New York City	S	1909
1,400	Transbay	Oakland, Calif.	C	1936
1,380	Triborough	New York City	S	1936
1,207	St. Johns	Portland, Oreg.	S	1931
1,200	Longview	Longview, Wash.	C	1930
1,200	Mt. Hope	Near Bristol, R.I.	S	1929
1,182	Queensboro	New York City	C	1909
1,100	Carquinez Strait	Near San Francisco	C	1927
1,080	Deer Isle	Deer Isle, Maine	S	1939
1,057	Cincinnati	Cincinnati, Ohio	S	1867
1,050	Cooper River	Charleston, S.C.	C	1929
1,010	Wheeling	Wheeling, W.Va.	S	1849
977.5	Hell Gate	New York City	SA	1917
950	Rainbow	Niagara Falls, N.Y.	SA	1941
930	Peace River	Alaska Highway	S	1943
875	Natchez	Natchez, Miss.	C	1940
871	Blue Water	Port Huron, Mich.	C	1938
845	Dubuque	Dubuque, Iowa	CT	1942
800	Thousand Islands	Alexandria Bay, N.Y.	S	1938
800	Waldo-Hancock	Bucksport, Maine	S	1931
800	Rip Van Winkle	Catskill, N.Y.	C	1935
800	Henry Hudson	New York City	SA	1936
790	Huey P. Long	Near New Orleans, La.	C	1935

[a]C—Cantilever. S—Suspension. SA—Steel arch. CT—Continuous truss.
Source: The Information Please Almanac, 1955 (New York, 1955), 735.

"Galloping Gertie": the Tacoma Narrows Bridge. One of the longest bridges when completed in 1940, the Tacoma Narrows Bridge did not last one year. Here the bridge starts to twist in the wind before falling into Puget Sound. (Washington State Historical Society)

CHAPTER 17 Agents of Lifestyle

Instruments of Modern Living: Household Goods

The United States participated in a revolution in household commodities that brought about changes in lifestyle for many Americans and lightened somewhat the burdens of the person responsible for running the household: in nearly all cases the wife and mother of the home. The keys to this fledgling revolution were electricity, running water, and of course the money to obtain the new commodities. From these foundations flowed most of the changes in domestic lifestyle. Most urban areas had water and electricity throughout the period, but the process of inventing the household devices and developing them into usable, affordable form and the perfection of marketing techniques came gradually and in some cases slowly. The fact that this period included two world wars and the Great Depression did not in the short run aid the process of modernization. Both wars changed national priorities and thus affected practices of development and production. Both wars stressed military goods and not consumer items. The depression discouraged production in many areas of enterprise because it discouraged demand. Thus, as remarkable as the fact that a domestic revolution had begun was that it reached so few people—at least at the start. Most electrical devices, other than lights, were virtually unheard of in 1914, and as late as 1940 nearly half of America's families were without refrigerators or electric washing machines. One-third of the population lacked running water, and nearly two-thirds lacked central heating. Very few kitchens included an electric range. If the Second World War seemed to stall the revolution in domestic goods, in some ways it established a foundation for a new thrust forward. Wartime shortages prompted innovations that later would be useful to the housewares industry. Plastics are a good example. The war also produced large individual earnings and savings and created a huge pent-up consumer demand. Americans in 1945 were anxious to spend their money on goods that would make their lives easier and happier.

Before refrigerators came into widespread use, people purchased ice (for an icebox) at a store or from a delivery man. During the First World War the iceman was sometimes a woman. (National Archives)

TABLE 17.1 SERVICES AVAILABLE TO URBAN AREAS IN THE UNITED STATES, 1926

Size of Community	Percentage of Families Having							
	Public Garbage Collection	Water Piped into House	Gas	Stationary Bathtub	Stationary Kitchen Sink	Flush Toilet	Electric Lights	Electric Iron
Under 1,000	10.1	52.7	3.6	26.1	42.7	26.3	72.1	49.2
1,000 to 2,500	17.3	87.3	11.9	40.6	57.1	44.2	77.3	55.0
2,500 to 5,000	39.9	97.2	34.4	51.0	66.6	61.0	77.3	57.0
5,000 to 10,000	48.9	100.0	74.0	61.0	72.3	72.3	79.3	58.9
10,000 to 25,000	56.3	100.0	95.6	66.9	79.1	78.1	78.6	61.2
25,000 to 50,000	88.4	100.0	98.8	70.5	81.5	80.8	78.4	60.2
50,000 to 100,000	88.1	100.0	100.0	74.5	79.9	85.7	77.0	54.7
Over 100,000	95.3	100.0	100.0	75.5	93.7	90.3	81.5	67.8

Source: Margaret G. Reid, *Economics of Household Production* (New York, 1934), 87.

You can barely hear it !

WHEN a proud owner of a General Electric Refrigerator takes her friends in to see it, the first comment is apt to be "Why it's *so* quiet—you can barely hear it."

The thing which seems to impress everyone is the extreme quietness with which these refrigerators operate. Their unique construction has indeed established a new standard for quiet operation.

This design, however, accomplishes something even more important. It makes possible the top-unit arrangement—a distinctive feature found only in the General Electric Refrigerator. Placing the unit on top makes it possible to enclose all the machinery—

together with a permanent supply of metal protecting oil—in an hermetically sealed steel casing. There the hidden machinery, always oiled, remains safe from dust and difficulties. No one can tinker with it—no one needs to.

Quietly, automatically, the General Electric Refrigerator gives you the perfect refrigeration that does away with food spoilage and safeguards health. It provides a generous supply of ice, makes menu-planning so much easier, permits you to serve the sort of food that your guests will instantly recognize as perfect . . . crisp lettuce, well-chilled beverages, smart desserts. For further details, drop us a card for Booklet Y-3.

GENERAL ⊕ ELECTRIC
Refrigerator

ELECTRIC REFRIGERATION DEPARTMENT · OF GENERAL ELECTRIC COMPANY · HANNA BUILDING · CLEVELAND, OHIO

Refrigerators became more widely available in the 1920s, but the styles often were bulky, as this model of 1929 indicated. (*World's Work,* March 1929)

Household Commodities That Came into Popular Usage, 1914–1945

radio

telephone

flush toilet

central heating (marginal)

stainless steel cookware

electric lights

refrigerator (marginal)

vacuum cleaner

electric iron

toaster

electric washing machine (marginal)

electric or gas range (marginal)

electric percolator

electric fan

Household Commodities Not in Popular Usage by 1945

television

air-conditioning

automatic clothes washer

automatic clothes dryer

automatic dishwasher

mixer

home freezer

waffle iron

electric can opener

electric fry pan

electric toothbrush

electric hair dryer

microwave oven

plastic housewares (until World War II)

blender

TABLE 17.2 ESTIMATES OF APPLIANCES IN THE UNITED STATES, 1931

Appliance	Total	Percentage of Families Having
Vacuum cleaner	6,415,000	21.5
Washing machine	4,925,000	16.5
Refrigerator	2,569,000	8.6
Range	952,000	3.2
Ironing machine	560,000	1.9

Source: Reid, *Economics of Household Production,* 87.

TABLE 17.3 ELECTRICAL APPLIANCES IN WIRED HOMES,[a] 1925–1945

End of Year	Number of Wired Homes (Thousands)	Percentage of Wired Homes Owning:			
		Mechanical Refrigerators	Washing Machines	Vacuum Cleaners	Electric Ranges
1925	14,965	. . .	21	31	3
1926	16,458	2	27	37	. . .
1927	17,951	4	28	39	3
1928	19,090	6	30	41	4
1929	19,967	9	33	44	4
1930	20,332	13	35	44	5
1931	20,151	17	41	45	5
1932	19,850	22	39	47	6
1933	20,004	25	44	49	6
1934	20,694	29	46	48	6
1935	21,235	34	49	48	7
1936	22,030	41	53	49	8
1937	22,939	49	56	49	9
1938	23,517	52	58	49	10
1939	24,599	57	60	51	11
1940	25,638	64	63	52	12
1941	27,012	73	65	53	13
1942	27,716	72	63	51	13
1943	28,000	71	62	49	13
1944	28,436	70	61	48	12
1945	29,215	67	59	47	12

[a] It should be noted that these numbers apply to wired homes only. As late as 1945 approximately 50% of farm homes—perhaps 3 million residences—were not wired and thus had no electrical appliances.
Source: Frederick J. Dewhurst and Associates, *America's Needs and Resources: A New Survey* (New York, 1955), 1041.

Although urban people as a whole had living facilities more modern than those of people in the countryside, conditions in the cities differed in accordance with race and location. Whites in nearly all sizes of cities had indoor toilet facilities. Black people in large northern cities probably did, but only a small portion of the nation's blacks lived in these areas. Most black people in southern cities had neither private nor communal indoor facilities. Except in the very largest cities most black people went to an outhouse, and even in such cities as Atlanta, Dallas, and Washington, D.C., a goodly number of African Americans continued to do so. For heating, black people in southern cities at best had a stove (as opposed to central heating); many used a fireplace for their major source of heat. In the case of southern whites the situation differed widely from city to city, although access to central heating was much more prevalent than in the case of blacks. These statistics provided an indication of the distinctions between living conditions for blacks and whites, but they stopped far short of a full description of the conditions in which most black people lived in urban America. There were white slums and black slums in the cities, but the proportion of urban blacks who lived in these places was much higher than white residents of the cities.

The line that separated places with "modern" living facilities from those without them commonly corresponded with a line separating urban and rural America. City people who lacked the modern devices—and there were many—did so mostly because of a shortage of money or because of the industries' slowness in developing an effective and affordable commodity. In rural areas these shortcomings applied to most people, and there were other fundamental problems. Rural America as a whole lacked the basic foundations of "modern living": electricity, common supply of water and natural gas, and a common system of waste disposal, although these conditions did change with passage of time and in accordance with differences in location.

The keys to lifestyle in much of rural America were a shortage of money and especially the absence of electric power. At the start of the period, when most urban areas had electricity, rural America had virtually none. Expansion of power lines proceeded steadily in some parts of the nation, but in others they hardly moved at all. By the year 1940 only in the Far West did the number of electrified farms reach 50%. In the South, where progress was slowest, the number scarcely reached 20%, even after the Tennessee Valley Authority had begun to carry electricity to parts of the area. Another

TABLE 17.4   HEATING FACILITIES IN SELECTED CITIES, BY RACE AND TENURE, 1933

City	Percentage of Dwelling Units with Specified Type of Heating											
	Negro Owners			Negro Tenants			White Owners			White Tenants		
	Heating Stove	Central Heating Plant[a]	Other [b]	Heating Stove	Central Heating Plant[a]	Other [b]	Heating Stove	Central Heating Plant[a]	Other [b]	Heating Stove	Central Heating Plant[a]	Other [b]
Trenton, N.J.	t	t	t	68.9	28.5	2.6	19.1	80.8	0.1	36.8	63.0	0.2
Cleveland, Ohio	31.1	68.9	. . .	74.7	24.8	0.5	13.6	86.3	0.1	24.9	74.8	0.3
Topeka, Kans.	76.5	23.5	. . .	92.0	8.0	. . .	36.0	63.6	0.4	49.4	50.5	0.1
Richmond, Va.	96.0	3.6	0.4	99.2	0.5	0.3	29.1	69.9	1.0	41.7	57.1	1.2
Wheeling, W.Va.	t	t	t	77.6	2.0	20.4	35.6	55.1	9.3	57.0	30.6	12.4
Asheville, N.C.	t	t	t	88.0	3.3	8.7	36.4	60.1	3.5	44.6	46.5	6.9
Greensboro, N.C.	t	t	t	84.4	. . .	15.6	29.5	63.5	7.0	41.3	29.8	28.9
Columbia, S.C.	52.2	2.6	45.2	22.8	3.7	73.5	37.6	42.7	19.7	39.6	23.2	37.2
Charleston, S.C.	90.3	0.9	8.8	83.5	. . .	16.5	76.3	10.2	13.5	84.8	1.8	13.4
Atlanta, Ga.	58.8	6.2	35.0	45.1	0.8	54.1	34.1	48.9	17.0	28.6	47.0	24.4
Jacksonville, Fla.	64.2	. . .	35.8	50.6	0.3	49.1	73.8	8.7	17.5	67.7	7.3	25.0
Paducah, Ky.	94.9	2.2	2.9	89.4	0.3	10.3	69.0	25.5	5.5	66.9	21.0	10.1
Birmingham, Ala.	38.2	1.1	60.7	12.3	0.2	87.5	34.1	40.1	25.8	27.2	36.9	35.9
Jackson, Miss.	t	t	t	11.1	. . .	88.9	90.4	5.4	4.2	87.5	5.1	7.4
Little Rock, Ark.	98.2	. . .	1.8	100.0	. . .	. . .	94.9	3.1	2.0	97.8	0.3	1.9
Baton Rouge, La.	14.3	0.9	84.8	26.6	. . .	73.4	79.4	4.0	16.6	74.2	5.3	20.5
Oklahoma City, Okla.	97.2	. . .	2.8	96.0	. . .	4.0	84.9	12.2	2.9	93.3	5.0	1.7
Austin, Tex.	98.5	. . .	1.5	100.0	. . .	. . .	91.9	5.7	2.4	96.7	0.9	2.4
Dallas, Tex.	83.4	16.6	. . .	100.0	. . .	. . .	96.7	3.2	0.1	98.7	1.2	0.1

[a] Includes warm-air furnaces, steam or vapor, and hot-water heating plants.
[b] Probably fireplace.
Note: t = Fewer than 100 cases.
Sources: Department of Commerce; Richard Sterner, *The Negro's Share: A Study of Income, Consumption, Housing, and Public Assistance* (New York, 1943), 403.

TABLE 17.5 PERCENTAGE OF FARMS REPORTING ELECTRIC LIGHTS, 1920–1945

	1920	1930	1940	1945
United States	7	13	33	48
West	12	39	50	71
North	10	20	43	60
South	1.5	2	20	31

Sources: Department of Agriculture; David E. Lindstrom, *American Rural Life* (New York, 1948), 133.

agency of the New Deal, the Rural Electrification Administration (REA), was created to aid in the establishment of electrification for farms. Even so, at the end of the period in 1945, more than half of America's farms still lacked electricity.

Except for the telephone and a supply of natural gas, nearly every aspect of the household was tied to electric power. For those without electricity, modern conveniences were useless. Instead of electric lights one had to use kerosene lamps or some other, older illumina-

tion device. Instead of using a washing machine, the homemaker probably had to do all aspects of the laundry by hand. Without a refrigerator, the household might have an icebox, if there was any cooling device at all. Running water beyond the reaches of a city supply depended upon an electric pump, and so without electricity one did not have running water and every aspect of life that related to it. Deprived of a bathroom, for example—which relied on running water—one could not have a faucet and lavatory, a permanent bathtub and a toilet, and so one went to an outdoor privy, even in winter. Because the outhouse often was an eyesore on the rural landscape, one of the more memorable activities of work relief agencies of the New Deal was construction of sturdy, sanitary outdoor privies. People of that generation called them the WPA toilets or even the "Roosevelt toilets." Families who obtained a Roosevelt toilet in the 1930s probably viewed the move as a step upward in lifestyle, replacing as it usually did a rickety, rotting, smelly old structure, but the outhouse still stood as a symbol of rural backwardness. For this set of circumstances rural people had an absence of electricity—and of money—to blame.

Without running water and a stationary porcelain tub, people took a bath, if at all, many ways, including in this different version of a bathtub. (Library of Congress)

TABLE 17.6 FACILITIES IN FARMHOUSES, BY REGION, 1934

Item	United States	New England	East North Central	West North Central	South Atlantic	East South Central	West South Central	Mountain	Pacific
Number of houses surveyed	595,855	12,826	83,808	116,184	131,847	93,626	96,548	31,225	27,756
Percentage of farmhouses									
By age of house									
Under 10 years	15.3	5.6	7.4	11.3	14.8	17.6	22.1	20.7	25.6
10–24 years	29.9	6.7	17.0	27.4	30.6	31.6	37.6	47.3	42.4
25–49 years	35.6	12.5	38.0	44.4	35.5	34.6	33.4	27.6	26.3
50 years and over	19.2	75.2	37.6	16.9	19.1	16.2	6.9	4.4	5.7
Unpainted frame	35.7	7.6	11.1	8.7	54.6	56.7	55.7	24.3	21.5
Having bathrooms	14.5	33.0	16.8	16.6	7.8	4.8	11.3	20.2	57.1
Having water supplied to house									
Hand pump in dwelling	14.0	28.9	34.9	23.7	10.1	2.7	1.9	5.9	5.6
Piped cold only	8.7	28.9	9.3	7.8	4.9	1.9	11.4	13.6	24.2
Piped hot and cold	7.7	26.3	8.8	8.0	4.0	2.2	1.7	13.2	45.7
Having indoor toilet									
Chemical	0.5	2.5	1.2	1.1	0.1	0.1	0.1	0.3	0.2
Flush	8.5	29.4	10.3	8.8	4.9	2.5	3.6	11.9	41.5
Having kitchen sink with drain	28.4	96.1	55.1	37.5	12.4	5.4	10.9	31.1	75.0
Having electricity									
Home plant	3.9	2.5	6.2	8.0	2.4	1.4	2.5	3.6	2.0
Power line	13.9	55.0	20.5	10.2	8.0	3.6	4.1	24.3	71.0
Having central heating system	8.6	29.9	23.4	17.0	1.5	1.0	0.3	4.8	5.7
Having specified cooking stoves									
Kerosene or gasoline	24.4	24.0	43.3	45.5	9.2	6.7	23.0	19.2	15.4
Gas or electric	4.2	5.5	7.1	2.9	2.2	0.7	2.3	6.9	24.6
Having specified refrigeration									
Ice	22.7	54.3	18.8	22.5	22.1	18.7	26.4	22.5	24.9
Mechanical	2.4	10.6	2.3	2.3	1.8	1.1	1.6	3.9	8.5
Not reporting screens	26.8	4.3	8.2	7.0	50.6	44.1	32.2	12.4	13.9
Not reporting exterior paint	40.0	8.9	14.8	12.2	59.9	62.2	58.4	34.7	22.9

Sources: Department of Agriculture; Sterner, Negro's Share, 168.

TABLE 17.7 REFRIGERATORS AND WASHING MACHINES IN SOUTHERN FARMHOUSES, BY RACE, 1934

State	Percentage of Dwellings Occupied by Nonwhite Farm Operators with			Percentage of Dwellings Occupied by White Farm Operators with		
	Refrigeration		Power Washing Machine	Refrigeration		Power Washing Machine
	Ice	Mechanical		Ice	Mechanical	
11 states, total	9.6	0.1	0.1	24.8	2.1	3.6
Owners	18.6	0.1	0.2	31.7	3.4	5.3
Nonowners	7.2	0.1	a	17.3	0.7	1.8
Md.	38.0	. . .	1.7	41.6	4.5	26.9
Va.	20.1	0.1	0.2	32.8	4.3	10.2
N.C.	9.8	0.1	0.2	24.3	1.5	2.5
S.C.	6.2	a	. . .	21.2	1.1	0.2
Ga.	9.9	0.2	a	24.0	0.9	0.1
Fla.	22.5	a	0.1	50.0	8.8	6.2
Tenn.	10.8	0.1	0.1	21.4	1.0	1.6
Ala.	4.5	. . .	a	12.8	0.6	0.2
Miss.	6.9	0.1	. . .	28.2	1.0	0.2
Ark.	7.7	a	a	15.0	1.8	3.5
La.	3.7	a	. . .	15.0	1.3	0.3

a Less than 0.05 percent.
Source: Sterner, Negro's Share, 175.

Race and Living Facilities in the Rural South

Limited as modern living facilities were for rural people throughout the South, the conditions worsened even more when one added the factor of race. Very few southern rural people, and virtually no blacks, had a refrigerator or washing machine in the 1930s. Except in two or three states, only a tiny minority of black families and—outside Florida—a minority of whites as well had even an icebox. Almost no blacks and—outside Florida—only a tiny portion of whites had a flush toilet of any kind.

Many families in rural America had no washing machine, even into the 1940s; this woman in Oklahoma in 1939 uses a washboard. (Library of Congress)

TABLE 17.8 TOILET FACILITIES IN SOUTHERN FARMHOUSES, BY RACE, 1934

State	Percentage of Dwellings Occupied by Non-white Farm Operators with Specified Facilities			Percentage of Dwellings Occupied by White Farm Operators with Specified Facilities		
	Indoor Toilet		Septic Tank	Indoor Toilet		Septic Tank
	Chemical	Flush		Chemical	Flush	
11 states, total	a	0.2	0.1	0.1	5.5	3.1
Owners	a	0.4	0.2	0.2	8.1	4.7
Nonowners	a	0.1	0.1	a	2.6	1.4
Md.	. . .	1.1	0.5	0.3	16.4	5.0
Va.	a	0.5	0.3	0.2	9.5	4.1
N.C.	. . .	0.1	0.3	0.1	4.2	2.9
S.C.	. . .	a	a	a	3.1	2.6
Ga.	a	a	a	0.1	2.2	0.9
Fla.	. . .	2.1	1.5	0.2	24.6	20.2
Tenn.	a	0.1	. . .	0.1	2.4	1.2
Ala.	a	0.1	a	a	1.4	0.6
Miss.	a	0.1	a	0.1	3.5	1.3
Ark.	a	0.1	a	0.1	1.8	1.3
La.	. . .	0.1	a	0.1	3.0	0.5

[a] Less than 0.05 percent.
Source: Sterner, *Negro's Share,* 369.

Instruments of Lifestyle Used in Absence of Electricity

Heating and Lighting
kerosene lamp
candle
wood and coal-burning range
wood and coal-burning stove
fireplace
bottled gas stove (rare)

Water Supply, Laundry, Bath and Toilet
open (dug) well
drilled well
cistern
hand suction pump
gasoline pump (rare)
portable bathtub
enamel washpan
water bucket and dipper
washtub
hand wringer
corrugated washboard
clothesline
cast iron stove-heated iron (sad iron)
combinet (a type of portable, overnight toilet)
toilet pans and jars
outdoor privy (outhouse)
Sears, Roebuck catalog (as toilet paper)

Food Preparation and Preservation
icebox
root cellar
smokehouse
Ball, Mason jars
other canning facilities
cast iron, enamel, aluminium pots and pans
hand food grinder
potato masher
hand mixer
tea kettle
ice cream maker

Cleaning
manual carpet sweeper
carpet beater
broom
mop
duster

Smoking and Drinking

Consumption Expenditures

The portion of income given over to alcoholic beverages fluctuated more than with tobacco products. Such changes are not surprising in view of the sharp changes that took place with respect to public policy and public attitudes toward the use of alcohol. Relative expenditure for alcohol dropped after 1914 as the nation gradually moved toward the grand experiment of prohibition. Although the official statistics remained low during the dozen or so years of prohibition, it must be remembered that much consumption took place beyond the eye of public count. Even though an end to prohibition produced a sharp increase in relative expenditure on liquors, the portion spent in 1945 surpassed by only a tiny margin that spent at the start of the period in 1914. Proportionate expenditure on tobacco products of all kinds remained steady, although the period as a whole produced a modest increase. Perhaps the most striking change came in the growth during the depression and early 1940s, which suggested that people continued to smoke (and more people smoked) at a time when there was less money to spend for anything.

TABLE 17.9 PERCENTAGE OF TOTAL CONSUMPTION EXPENDITURE SPENT ON LIQUOR AND TOBACCO PRODUCTS

	Alcohol	Tobacco
1914	5.99	2.19
1919	3.30	2.36
1921	2.51	2.66
1923	2.25	2.22
1925	2.37	2.12
1927	2.41	2.17
1929	2.48	2.10
1931	2.08	2.39
1933	1.35	2.67
1935	4.54	2.56
1937	5.13	2.50
1939	5.09	2.63
1941	5.15	2.52
1943	5.86	2.52
1945	6.31	2.38

Source: Dewhurst and Associates, *America's Needs and Resources: A New Survey,* 96.

Cigarette companies over the years made many claims—directly or by implication—about the benefits of smoking. A familiar approach was to associate cigarettes with actresses and the glamorous movie industry. (*Life,* May 5, 1941)

The Cigarette Takes Over

Smoking practices underwent marked changes during the years 1914–45. A steady decline in such traditional, almost exclusively male-oriented forms of tobacco usage as cigars, pipe smoking, snuff, and especially chewing tobacco was easily offset by a surge in the popularity of cigarettes. Cigarette smoking, which began in the nineteenth century, came of age in the first half of the twentieth century. The introduction in 1913 of Camels, a new blend in a neat packet of twenty for ten cents, accompanied by a vast advertising campaign, began the trend. The success of Camels, produced by R. J. Reynolds, sparked the introduction of Lucky Strike, by American Tobacco, and Chesterfield, by Liggett and Myers. This "Big Three" would dominate cigarette production throughout the period; in some years Camels alone captured more than 40% of cigarette sales.

In the 1920s the cigarette companies aggressively went after the female market and with much success. The cigarette became part of the image of the adventuresome young female of the era, the Flapper. Lucky Strike and other brands promoted the idea of smoking to enhance beauty and even health. "Reach for a Lucky instead of a sweet" became a popular slogan. The quest for the female market in the 1930s and 1940s carried the notion of smoking as an indication of being smart, trendy, sociable, and sophisticated. Manipulation of a cigarette bolstered the performance of many an actress, not to mention actor, in the films of that age.

If the depression produced a lag in consumption in the early 1930s, it did not last long. By the middle of the thirties the increase had resumed, and it proceeded at an accelerated pace until the end of the Second World War. Even though the Big Three continued to dominate, more people turned during the depression to cheaper brands, such as Marvels, Twenty Grand, and Wings, and some smokers—mostly men—reverted to an older practice of "rolling your own." The Second World War created a setting almost ideal for the

TABLE 17.10 PER CAPITA CONSUMPTION OF CIGARETTES

Year	Consumption
1914	166
1916	248
1917	337
1919	426
1921	469
1923	576
1925	690
1927	817
1929	977
1932	915
1933	890
1935	1,058
1937	1,263
1939	1,318
1941 [a]	1,580
1943 [a]	2,166
1945 [a]	2,334

[a] Includes tax-free cigarettes for the armed forces. During the war, cigarettes for the military were not only tax-free but, as a result of various programs by the industry or by government, free as well.
Sources: Bureau of the Census, *Statistical Abstract of the United States, 1951* (Washington, D.C., 1951), 776; Robert, *Story of Tobacco,* 269; Dewhurst and Associates, *America's Needs and Resources: A New Survey,* 95.

Chief officer Harry Manning says:

"Reach for a Lucky instead of a sweet."

"WHEN I climbed aboard the 'America' after those cold, strenuous hours getting the men off the freighter 'Florida,' there was nothing I wanted so much as a Lucky — 'By George,' it tasted wonderful! A Lucky is always refreshing. My tense nerves relaxed, my aching throat was soothed and the whole thrilling adventure just seemed a part of the day's work. As time goes by, and I look back to that memorable night, I'll always remember the wonderful taste of that welcome Lucky. As I went around to visit the men we'd rescued, I found many of them enjoying Luckies, too. We really couldn't wait to get back to our ship and 'Luckies.' As an actual fact in returning to the 'America' I noticed one of our men* rowing with one hand and lighting a 'Lucky' with the other. There's no flavor to equal toasted tobaccos, and I always prefer Lucky Strikes. There's wisdom in the saying: 'Reach for a Lucky instead of a sweet.' It helps a man to keep physically fit and we who follow the sea must always be prepared for any emergency."

*The man mentioned by Chief Officer Manning was Boatswain's Mate Aloys A. Wilson.

H Manning
Harry Manning
Chief Officer, who as a result of his heroism was appointed Acting Captain, "S. S. America."
© 1929, The American Tobacco Co. Manufacturers

"REACH FOR A LUCKY INSTEAD OF A SWEET."

Note: Authorities attribute the enormous increase in Cigarette smoking to the improvement in the process of Cigarette manufacture by the application of heat. It is true that during the year 1928, Lucky Strike Cigarettes showed a greater increase than all other Cigarettes combined. This confirms in no uncertain terms the public's confidence in the superiority of Lucky Strike.

According to this 1929 advertisement, smoking Luckies helped make one physically fit, thus facilitating heroism on the high seas. (*World's Work*, March 1929)

tobacco industry. The atmosphere of war produced an excuse—smoking as a means of handling tension, "war nerves"—and numerous new social settings for males and females conducive to lighting up a cigarette. The government seemed to encourage smoking by military personnel: "Smoke 'em if you got 'em," the men were told at break time, and some military rations included a small packet of cigarettes. Various wartime forces combined to produce a shortage of cigarettes on the home front. While cigarettes were never rationed to the domestic population, they were often in short supply, and many dealers devised individual systems of distribution to preferred customers. Small cigarettes outsold large ones hundreds of times over throughout the period. Kool cigarettes, a rare mentholated brand, were one of the very few makes that used a filter. Camels, Luckies, Chesterfield, and most others did not.

Sources: Joseph C. Robert, *The Story of Tobacco in America* (New York, 1949), 230–265; Bureau of the Census, *Statistical Abstract of the United States, 1947* (Washington, D.C., 1947), 845.

TABLE 17.11   TOBACCO USED IN MANUFACTURE OF TOBACCO PRODUCTS

(In thousands of pounds)

Yearly Average	Total	Tobacco and Snuff	Cigars	Cigarettes
1911–15	578,283	374,186	151,890	52,207
1916–20	650,460	364,828	155,312	130,320
1921–25	672,077	322,588	151,421	198,069
1926–30	762,540	300,767	149,240	312,533
1931–35	740,934	282,652	112,296	345,985
1936–40	878,722	261,726	124,700	492,296
1941–45	1,182,914	228,221	133,383	821,311

Source: Bureau of the Census, *Statistical Abstract of the United States, 1951,* 776.

Good digestion helps bring a sense of well-being and contentment—so

FOR DIGESTION'S SAKE SMOKE CAMELS

COSTLIER TOBACCOS

Camels are made from finer, MORE EXPENSIVE TOBACCOS – Turkish and Domestic—than any other popular brand.

This ad claimed that smoking Camels calmed the nerves and aided the process of digestion. (*Life,* December 7, 1936)

Consumption of Alcohol

Government statistics for the consumption of alcoholic beverages fell far short of measuring drinking during the years 1914–45. The weak spot occurred in the unique era of prohibition, at which time the government counted only the authorized production of alcoholic beverages. Inasmuch as no beer was authorized, no beer was counted at a time when the sale of booze, mostly beer, was one of the most lucrative activities of organized crime. The numbers nonetheless did supply meaningful information. Americans had become fairly heavy drinkers, especially of beer, in the period immediately preceding the prohibition era of 1920–33. Per capita consumption rose sharply in all categories, as expected, when prohibition was abolished as national policy. Although consumption continued to increase to the end of the period, and although the period included the Second World War—which perhaps provided a new rationale, or excuse, for drinking—drinking as a rule did not return to practices of the preprohibition era. Only in the consumption of wine did drinking reach or go beyond the levels established in the years before the First World War.

TABLE 17.12 PER CAPITA CONSUMPTION OF ALCOHOLIC BEVERAGES

(In gallons, except distilled spirits, which is shown in tax gallons)

Fiscal Year	Distilled Spirits			Malt Liquors			Wines		
	Total	Domestic	Imported	Total	Domestic	Imported	Total	Domestic	Imported
1914	1.44	1.40	.04	20.69	20.62	.07	.53	.46	.07
1915	1.26	1.23	.03	18,40	18.37	.03	.33	.27	.06
1916	1.37	1.33	.04	17.78	17.76	.02	.47	.42	.05
1917	1.62	1.59	.03	18.17	18.15	.02	.41	.36	.05
1918	.87	.86	.01	14.77	14.76	.01	.49	.46	.03
1919	.79	.79	a	8.00	8.00	a	.51	.49	.02
1920	.22	.22	a	2.61	2.61	a	.12	.12	a
1921	.32	.32	a	. . .	. . .	. . .	.19	.18	.01
1922	.18	.18	a	. . .	. . .	. . .	.06	.05	.01
1923	.11	.11	a	. . .	. . .	. . .	.13	.13	a
1924	.10	.10	a	. . .	. . .	. . .	.08	.08	a
1925	.09	.09	a	. . .	. . .	. . .	.03	.03	a
1926	.09	.09	a	. . .	. . .	. . .	.05	.05	a
1927	.08	.08	a	. . .	. . .	. . .	.04	.04	a
1928	.09	.09	a	. . .	. . .	. . .	.04	.04	a
1929	.09	.09	a	. . .	. . .	. . .	.09	.09	a
1930	.08	.08	a	. . .	. . .	. . .	.03	.03	a
1931	.07	.07	a	. . .	. . .	. . .	.05	.05	a
1932	.06	.06	a	. . .	. . .	. . .	.04	.04	a
1933	.05	.05	a	1.56	1.55	.01	.01	.01	a
1934	.33	.30	.03	7.90	7.89	.01	.14	.12	.02
1935	.70	.67	.03	10.45	10.44	.01	.30	.28	.02
1936	.81	.73	.08	11.93	11.92	.01	.39	.37	.02
1937	1.03	.90	.13	13.47	13.45	.02	.52	.49	.03
1938	1.00	.89	.11	13.02	13.00	.02	.51	.48	.03
1939	.93	.84	.09	12.41	12.39	.02	.55	.52	.03
1940	1.02	.93	.09	12.58	12.57	.01	.66	.63	.03
1941	1.04	.96	.08	12.42	12.41	.01	.70	.68	.02
1942	1.13	1.06	.07	14.18	14.17	.01	.79	.78	.01
1943	1.11	1.00	.11	15.96	15.93	.03	.84	.83	.01
1944	1.03	.72	.31	17.97	17.92	.05	.73	.66	.07
1945	1.22	1.05	.17	18.86	18.79	.07	.73	.70	.03

ª Less than .005.
Source: Bureau of the Census, *Statistical Abstract of the United States, 1947,* 843.

CHAPTER 18 Entertainment and Sports

It seemed that almost everything was fashioned to make the first half of the twentieth century a period of expansion and creativity in the entertainment industries, creating in many areas a genuine golden age. The nation grew rapidly in numbers, wealth, and confidence. There was more money to spend, the period of the depression notwithstanding, and more people to entertain. The growth of cities fostered the establishment of urban entertainment centers, and many people who did not live in cities now found it possible with automobiles to get into town to see what was going on.

The American political and economic system fostered creative activity in popular culture. In America an idea need not be socially the most useful; it did not need to be intellectually the most penetrating. It only needed to be accepted. It was a system that tolerated the fanciful and the frivolous if it would sell. The American Dream as it was recognized worldwide focused on making it big, and in the twentieth century there was no more conspicuous expression of instantaneous success than in entertainment. In some areas they called it being "discovered." It was not surprising that many people in entertainment, especially in filmmaking, were foreign-born.

The growing attractiveness of professional entertainment encouraged technological change, and the technology, in turn, further hastened the growth. The character and quality of movies underwent many changes—to full-length films, to talkies, to color movies. These areas fed each other; they all were interrelated. Popular music benefited from the advances in recording devices, from the development of sound in film, and from the introduction of radio. Film performers often appeared on radio. A few people—Bing Crosby is the best example—established themselves in three major areas: Crosby was a popular recording artist; he had his own radio show and appeared regularly in films.

Even though two world wars and a depression drained the national energy, they did little to slow the swell in popular culture. Fortunately, the mass means of entertainment were mostly inexpensive. Newspapers of the period cost a few pennies (less than ten and often less than five), and movies cost only a few more, about the same as a seat in the bleachers at a major-league baseball game. Radio came free if one already had the set. Wars and depression produced new topics for movies, books, and radio shows, new

TABLE 18.1   PERSONAL CONSUMPTION EXPENDITURES FOR RECREATION, 1914–1945

(In millions of dollars)

Year	Total	Nondurable Toys and Sport Supplies	Wheel Goods, Durable Toys, Sports Equipment, Boats, and Pleasure Aircraft	Radio and Television Receivers, Records, and Musical Instruments	Radio and Television Repair	Admission to Specified Spectator Amusements — Total	Motion Picture Theaters	Theater Entertainment (plays, operas, etc.) of Nonprofit Institutions, except Athletics	Spectator Sports	Clubs and Fraternal Organizations, except Insurance	Commercial Participant Amusements	Parimutuel, Net Receipts	Books and Maps	Magazines, Newspapers, and Sheet Music	Flowers, Seeds, and Potted Plants	Other
1945	6,139	553	400	344	88	1,714	1,450	148	116	281	284	153	520	965	378	459
1944	5,422	459	323	311	72	1,563	1,341	142	80	236	241	131	450	880	327	429
1943	4,961	393	271	403	60	1,455	1,275	118	62	217	215	79	366	838	274	390
1942	4,677	404	306	634	46	1,204	1,022	92	90	205	213	69	291	703	241	361
1941	4,239	362	314	607	36	995	809	79	107	203	210	65	255	636	229	327
1940	3,761	306	254	494	32	904	735	71	98	203	197	55	234	599	201	292
1939	3,452	285	228	420	28	821	659	64	98	199	183	41	226	554	191	276
1938	3,241	268	210	339	25	816	663	58	95	200	164	44	221	514	176	264
1937	3,381	269	210	385	23	818	676	53	89	203	194	38	243	518	186	294
1936	3,020	242	171	333	21	759	626	50	83	198	165	29	208	490	159	245
1935	2,630	216	136	248	21	672	556	44	72	197	141	26	183	456	130	204
1934	2,441	200	118	229	17	625	518	42	65	199	135	19	165	441	116	177
1933	2,202	181	93	195	14	573	482	41	50	208	121	6	152	419	90	150
1932	2,442	207	110	268	19	631	527	57	47	242	132	4	153	428	89	159
1931	3,302	266	159	478	24	854	719	78	57	277	175	6	253	479	134	197
1930	3,990	281	172	921	27	892	732	95	65	294	203	7	264	512	190	227
1929	4,331	336	219	1,012	26	913	720	127	66	302	207	8	309	538	221	240
1927	3,120	470		713		769	526	195	48	283	159		349		183	...
1925	2,835	411		739		588	367	174	47	275	145		318		182	...
1923	2,620	455		637		528	336	146	46	242	148		270		176	...
1921	2,055	338		439		412	301	81	30	242	128		239		128	...
1919	2,189	377		667		...		336[a]	...	242	55		204		135	...
1914	1,000	186		193		...		191[a]	...	140	25		131		56	...

[a]Before 1920, motion pictures were classified with other types of theater entertainment.
Source: Ben J. Wattenberg, *The Statistical History of the United States* (New York, 1976), 401.

moods and themes to write songs about, new reasons for escapist activity. While there might have been slow years during the early 1930s and at times during the Second World War, the long-range trend was growth in all major areas of the entertainment media. In at least one way, however, the depression and war did interrupt the evolution that had marked the first third of the century. Virtually all areas of popular culture were affected by the status of television— perhaps one should say an absence of television. Television was developed during the 1920s and 1930s, but it was not perfected before the start of the Second World War. Only two stations sent television signals in 1941; few homes had sets. By reordering national priorities, the war stalled the development of television a few more years and thus helped give expression to a classical era, in some thinking a golden age, of movies, radio, and other entertainment existing at that time.

Entertainment in the twentieth century went far beyond being a means of passing the time. It became the source of major new industries, affecting manufacturing, construction, automobiles, and many other areas of the economy. The entertainment industries became setters of standards and of trends. How many young women did not want to be actresses or nightclub singers? How many young men did not want to appear in movies or a radio show or play in a big band

or professional baseball? How many young blacks did not want to emulate Joe Louis? For better or for worse, the entertainment media offered a powerful vision of what America was, or what Americans wanted to be.

Movies

Already a blooming industry by the time of the First World War, American moviemaking truly came of age in the years that followed. From the nickelodeon and the Keystone comedies, movies shifted to the full-length feature, starting with *Birth of a Nation* by D. W. Griffith in 1915. The romance of the silent screen followed, with hundreds of movies produced each year and a full bevy of handsome, vigorous males and female beauties to suit each viewer's taste. In the 1920s the industry began to police its activity, to impose a tight censorship through its Hays Office, and in 1927 it started to recognize a professional nobility in what came to be called the Academy Awards. Sound movies arrived in some measure with *Don Juan* in 1926 and fully with *The Jazz Singer* in 1927, the first movie with soundtrack on the film. The silent movie was largely dead by 1930, although a few holdouts remained, notably Charlie Chaplin, who

Children went to movies too, especially on Saturday. Theaters, like most of American life, were segregated. Chicago, 1941. (Library of Congress)

continued to succeed with *City Lights* (1931) and *Modern Times* (1936). The coming of the talkies shocked the industry, causing some performers to drop from sight and others to take speaking lessons; studios sought out actors who could speak, mostly people with experience on stage. Although a few people made the transition from silent movies to sound films, talkies for the most part called for a new generation of stars.

The 1930s and 1940s marked bountiful years of the golden age of Hollywood. Movies were still mostly made in California. The studios controlled their performers; the stars seemed larger than life—people to be envied and imitated. Except for some slow times in the first half of the 1930s, when money was exceptionally tight for the general populace, attendance held up well, with more than eighty million going to theaters each week. (In 1960 by contrast the number would be forty million and in 1970 less than eighteen million). The technical quality of films continued to improve; Technicolor movies arrived in the 1930s. In many of its movies Hollywood offered escapism—glamour, heroism, and happy endings. Sound made possible the development of the musical film, which turned out to be another form of fantasy. Moviemakers quickly fell in stride with the coming of the Second World War. Many movies made between 1940 and 1945 were war movies. Films about war are not normally regarded as escapism, but movies about heroism can be, and many of them came close to being fantasy. Fewer movies were produced, but the numbers who watched them increased. By 1945 weekly attendance reached ninety million. People involved in the industry hoped that it would last but feared it would not. They knew that with the end of the war much would have to change, and they could think of many reasons—the arrival of television not being the least—why the golden age of Hollywood was near an end.

Aspects of the American Movie Industry, 1917–1945

TABLE 18.2 NUMBER OF FILMS RELEASED, 1917–1945

Year	U.S. Produced	Imported	Total
1917	687	. . .	687
1918	841	. . .	841
1919	646	. . .	796
1920	796	. . .	796
1921	854	. . .	854
1922	748	. . .	748
1923	576	. . .	576
1924	579	. . .	579
1925	579	. . .	579
1926	740	. . .	740

Left to right: Douglas Fairbanks, Mary Pickford, Charlie Chaplin, D. W. Griffith—makers of silent films who joined together in 1920 to form United Artists. (Film Stills Archive, Museum of Modern Art, New York)

Year	U.S. Produced	Imported	Total
1927	678	65	743
1928	641	193	884
1929	562	145	707
1930	509	86	595
1931	501	121	622
1932	489	196	685
1933	507	137	644
1934	480	182	662
1935	525	241	766
1936	522	213	735
1937	538	240	778
1938	455	314	769
1939	483	278	761
1940	477	196	673
1941	492	106	598
1942	488	45	533
1943	397	30	427
1944	401	41	442
1945	350	27	377

Source: Cobbett S. Steinberg, *Film Facts* (New York, 1980), 42–43.

TABLE 18.3 AVERAGE WEEKLY ATTENDANCE, 1926–1945

Year	Average Weekly Attendance
1926	50,000,000
1927	57,000,000
1928	65,000,000
1929	95,000,000
1930	90,000,000
1931	75,000,000
1932	60,000,000
1933	60,000,000
1934	70,000,000
1935	75,000,000
1936	88,000,000
1937	85,000,000
1938	85,000,000
1939	85,000,000
1940	80,000,000
1941	80,000,000
1942	85,000,000
1943	85,000,000
1944	85,000,000
1945	90,000,000

Source: Steinberg, *Film Facts*, 40–41.

TABLE 18.4 AVERAGE PRICE OF A TICKET, 1933–1945

Year	Admission Price
1933	23¢
1934	23¢
1935	24¢
1936	25¢
1937	23¢
1938	23¢
1939	23¢
1940	24.1¢
1941	25.2¢
1942	27.3¢
1943	29.4¢
1944	31.7¢
1945	35.2¢

Source: Steinberg, *Film Facts*, 40–41.

TABLE 18.5 ANNUAL BOX-OFFICE RECEIPTS, 1929–1945

Year	U.S. Box-Office Receipts (in millions $)	% of U.S. Personal Spending	% of U.S. Recreational Spending	% of U.S. Spectator Recreational Spending
1929	720	0.93	16.62	78.86
1930	732	1.05	18.35	82.06
1931	719	1.19	21.77	84.19
1932	527	1.08	21.58	83.52
1933	482	1.05	21.89	84.12
1934	518	1.01	21.22	82.88
1935	566	1.00	21.14	82.74
1936	626	1.01	20.73	82.48
1937	676	1.02	19.99	82.64
1938	663	1.04	20.46	81.25
1939	659	0.99	19.09	80.27
1940	735	1.04	19.54	81.31
1941	809	1.00	19.08	81.31
1942	1,022	1.15	21.85	84.88
1943	1,275	1.28	25.70	87.63
1944	1,341	1.24	24.73	85.80
1945	1,450	1.21	23.62	84.60

Source: Steinberg, *Film Facts*, 40–41.

TABLE 18.6 NUMBER OF MOVIE THEATERS, 1926–1945

Year	Wired for Sound	Silent	Total
1926	. . .	19,489	19,489
1927	20	21,644	21,664
1928	100	22,204	22,304
1929	800	22,544	23,344
1930	8,860	14,140	23,000
1931	13,128	8,865	21,993
1932	13,880	4,835	18,715
1933	14,405	4,128	18,553
1934	14,381	2,504	16,885
1935	15,273	. . .	15,273
1936	15,858	. . .	15,858
1937	18,192	. . .	18,192
1938	18,182	. . .	18,182
1939	17,829	. . .	17,829
1940	19,032	. . .	19,042
1941	19,645	95	19,750
1942	20,281	99	20,380
1943	20,196	97	20,293
1944	20,277	96	20,375
1945	20,355	102	20,457

Source: Steinberg, *Film Facts*, 40–41.

TABLE 18.7   POPULAR SILENT MOVIES, 1914–1929

1914	1915	1916	1917
Home Sweet Home Neptune's Daughter Sampson The Perils of Pauline The Spoilers Tillie's Punctured Romance	A Night Out Mistress Nell The Arab The Birth of a Nation The Eternal City The Yankee Girl	Less than the Dust Poor Little Peppina The Daughter of the Gods The Good, Bad Man To Have and to Hold The Kiss of Hate	Broadway Jones Cleopatra Glory Rebecca of Sunnybrook Farm Tom Sawyer The Poor Little Rich Girl

1918	1919	1920	1921
Eye for Eye Over the Top Tarzan of the Apes The Beast of Berlin The Savage Woman To Hell with the Kaiser	A Day's Pleasure Broken Blossoms Daddy Long Legs Test of Honor The Girl Who Stayed Home Victory	Pollyanna Polly with a Past The Flapper The Kid The Last of the Mohicans Treasure Island	Disraeli Little Lord Fauntleroy The Four Horsemen of the Apocalypse The Lotus Eater The Queen of Sheba The Sheik

1922	1923	1924	1925
Blood and Sand Foolish Wives Robin Hood Tess of the Storm Country The Prisoner of Zenda The Young Rajah	Bluebeard's Eighth Wife Down to the Sea in Ships The Covered Wagon The Hunchback of Notre Dame The Ten Commandments The Trail of the Lonesome Pine	Abraham Lincoln Forbidden Pleasure Manhandled Monsieur Beaucaire The Sea Hawk The Thief of Baghdad	Little Annie Rooney Stella Dallas The Charmer The Gold Rush The Merry Widow The Phantom of the Opera

1926	1927	1928	1929
Beau Geste Ben-Hur Let's Get Married Son of the Sheik Sparrows The Black Pirate	Flesh and the Devil It Seventh Heaven Sunrise The King of Kings Wings	Abie's Irish Rose Excess Baggage Just Married Laugh, Clown, Laugh The Last Command The Wind	Bulldog Drummond Disraeli The Kiss West of Zanzibar Why Be Good? Wild Orchids

Source: Daniel Blum, *A Pictorial History of the Silent Screen* (New York, 1953), numerous pages.

TABLE 18.8   STARS OF THE SILENT SCREEN[a]

The Top 15 Female Performers of 1921	The Top 10 Performers of 1924 (*Photoplay* magazine)
Norma Talmadge Constance Talmadge Mary Pickford Anita Stewart Dorothy Gish Clara Kimball Young Gloria Swanson Mary Miles Minter Katherine MacDonald Pearl White Marguerite Clark Ethel Clayton Elsie Ferguson Elaine Hammerstein Enid Bennett	Thomas Meighan Norma Talmadge Harold Lloyd Tom Mix Mary Pickford Douglas Fairbanks Gloria Swanson Pola Negri Jackie Coogan Rudolph Valentino

Source: Blum, *History of the Silent Screen*, 205, 265.

TABLE 18.9   THE *NEW YORK TIMES* ANNUAL LISTS OF "TEN BEST" MOVIES, 1930–1945

1930	1931	1932	1933
With Byrd at the South Pole	The Guardsman	Mädchen in Uniform	Cavalcade
All Quiet on the Western Front	City Lights	Trouble in Paradise	Reunion in Vienna
Journey's End	The Smiling Lieutenant	Der Raub der Mona Lisa	Morgenroth
Lightnin'	Arrowsmith	Grand Hotel	State Fair
The Devil to Pay	Tabu	Dr. Jekyll and Mr. Hyde	Dinner at Eight
Outward Bound	Bad Girl	The Mouthpiece	Berkeley Square
Tom Sawyer	Frankenstein	One Hour with You	The Private Life of Henry VIII
Holiday	Skippy	A Bill of Divorcement	Little Women
Abraham Lincoln	Private Lives	The Doomed Battalion	The Invisible Man
Anna Christie	A Connecticut Yankee	Reserved for Ladies	His Double Life

1934	1935	1936	1937
It Happened One Night	The Informer	(Eleven films this year)	The Life of Emile Zola
The House of Rothschild	Ruggles of Red Gap	La Kermesse Héroique	The Good Earth
The Battle	David Copperfield	(Carnival in Flanders)	Stage Door
The Thin Man	Lives of a Bengal Lancer	Fury	Captains Courageous
Catherine the Great	Les Miserables	Dodsworth	They Won't Forget
The First World War	The Scoundrel	Mr. Deeds Goes to Town	Make Way for Tomorrow
One Night of Love	Chapayev	Winterset	I Met Him in Paris
The Lost Patrol	The Man Who Knew Too Much	Romeo and Juliet	A Star Is Born
Man of Aran	Sequoia	The Green Pastures	Camille
Our Daily Bread	Love Me Forever	The Ghost Goes West	Lost Horizon
		The Story of Louis Pasteur	
		These Three	
		The Great Ziegfeld	

1938	1939	1940	1941
Snow White and the Seven Dwarfs	Made for Each Other	The Grapes of Wrath	The Lady Eve
The Citadel	Stagecoach	The Baker's Wife	Citizen Kane
To the Victor	Wuthering Heights	Rebecca	Major Barbara
Pygmalion	Dark Victory	Our Town	Sergeant York
A Slight Case of Murder	Juarez	The Mortal Storm	The Stars Look Down
Three Comrades	Goodbye, Mr. Chips	Pride and Prejudice	Here Comes Mr. Jordan
The Lady Vanishes	The Women	The Great McGinty	Target for Tonight
The Adventures of Robin Hood	Mr. Smith Goes to Washington	The Long Voyage Home	Dumbo
A Man to Remember	Ninotchka	The Great Dictator	How Green Was My Valley
Four Daughters	Gone with the Wind	Fantasia	One Foot in Heaven

1942	1943	1944	1945
In Which We Serve	Air Force	Destination Tokyo	A Tree Grows in Brooklyn
Journey for Margaret	Desert Victory	The Miracle of Morgan's Creek	The Way Ahead
Casablanca	The Ox-Bow Incident	The Purple Heart	Anchors Aweigh
One of Our Aircraft Is Missing	The More the Merrier	Going My Way	Pride of the Marines
Wake Island	For Whom the Bell Tolls	Wilson	The House on Ninety-Second Street
Mrs. Miniver	Report from the Aleutians	Hail the Conquering Hero	Story of G.I. Joe
Yankee Doodle Dandy	Watch on the Rhine	Thirty Seconds Over Tokyo	Spellbound
The Gold Rush	Corvette K-225	None But the Lonely Heart	The Last Chance
Woman of the Year	Sahara	Meet Me in St. Louis	The Lost Weekend
Sullivan's Travels	Madame Curie	National Velvet	They Were Expendable

Source: Steinberg, Film Facts, 170–172.

TABLE 18.10   MOST POPULAR MOVIE STARS, 1932–1945

Based on a poll by Quigley Publications that asked film exhibitors each year to list the top box-office attractions.

1932	1933	1934	1935
Marie Dressler	Marie Dressler	Will Rogers	Shirley Temple
Janet Gaynor	Will Rogers	Clark Gable	Will Rogers
Joan Crawford	Janet Gaynor	Janet Gaynor	Clark Gable
Charles Farrell	Eddie Cantor	Wallace Beery	Fred Astaire/Ginger Rogers
Greta Garbo	Wallace Beery	Mae West	Joan Crawford
Norma Shearer	Jean Harlow	Joan Crawford	Claudette Colbert
Wallace Beery	Clark Gable	Bing Crosby	Dick Powell
Clark Gable	Mae West	Shirley Temple	Wallace Beery
Will Rogers	Norma Shearer	Marie Dressler	Jeanette MacDonald
Joe E. Brown	Joan Crawford	Norma Shearer	James Cagney

(continued)

TABLE 18.10   **(continued)**

Based on a poll by Quigley Publications that asked film exhibitors each year to list the top box-office attractions.

1936	1937	1938	1939
Shirley Temple	Shirley Temple	Shirley Temple	Mickey Rooney
Clark Gable	Clark Gable	Clark Gable	Tyrone Power
Fred Astaire/Ginger Rogers	Robert Taylor	Sonja Henie	Spencer Tracy
Robert Taylor	Bing Crosby	Mickey Rooney	Clark Gable
Joe E. Brown	William Powell	Spencer Tracy	Shirley Temple
Dick Powell	Jane Withers	Robert Taylor	Bette Davis
Joan Crawford	Fred Astaire/Ginger Rogers	Myrna Loy	Alice Faye
Claudette Colbert	Sonja Henie	Jane Withers	Errol Flynn
Jeannette MacDonald	Gary Cooper	Alice Faye	James Cagney
Gary Cooper	Myrna Loy	Tyrone Power	Sonja Henie

1940	1941	1942	1943
Mickey Rooney	Mickey Rooney	Abbott & Costello	Betty Grable
Spencer Tracy	Clark Gable	Clark Gable	Bob Hope
Clark Gable	Abbott & Costello	Gary Cooper	Abbott & Costello
Gene Autry	Bob Hope	Mickey Rooney	Bing Crosby
Tyrone Power	Spencer Tracy	Bob Hope	Gary Cooper
James Cagney	Gene Autry	James Cagney	Greer Garson
Bing Crosby	Gary Cooper	Gene Autry	Humphrey Bogart
Wallace Beery	Bette Davis	Betty Grable	James Cagney
Bette Davis	James Cagney	Greer Garson	Mickey Rooney
Judy Garland	Judy Garland	Spencer Tracy	Clark Gable

1944	1945		
Bing Crosby	Bing Crosby		
Gary Cooper	Van Johnson		
Bob Hope	Greer Garson		
Betty Grable	Betty Grable		
Spencer Tracy	Spencer Tracy		
Greer Garson	Humphrey Bogart/Gary Cooper		
Humphrey Bogart	Bob Hope		
Abbott & Costello	Judy Garland		
Cary Grant	Margaret O'Brien		
Bette Davis	Roy Rogers		

Source: Steinberg, *Film Facts,* 57–58.

Actress Ingrid Bergman and actor Gary Cooper flank director Sam Wood during the filming in 1943 of *For Whom the Bell Tolls,* taken from the famous novel by Ernest Hemingway. (National Archives)

TABLE 18.11   THE ACADEMY AWARDS

Members of the film industry in 1927 founded the Academy of Motion Picture Arts and Sciences, a move designed to raise the "cultural, educational, and scientific standards of the industry." Members of the academy proceeded to honor its best participants by presenting annually, starting officially with 1928, its "Academy Awards," or Oscars, in various categories. The number of categories was increased in 1934. The ceremony of presentation became a major media event.

Year	Best Picture	Best Director	Best Actor	Best Actress	Best Cinematographer
1928	*Wings*	Frank Borzage *Seventh Heaven* Lewis Milestone *2 Arabian Knights*	Emil Jannings *The Way of All Flesh, The Last Command*	Janet Gaynor *Seventh Heaven, Sunrise, Street Angel*	Charles Rosher, Karl Struss *Sunrise*
1929	*Broadway Melody*	Frank Lloyd *The Divine Lady*	Warner Baxter *In Old Arizona*	Mary Pickford *Coquette*	Clyde DeVinna *White Shadows, in the South Seas*
1930	*All Quiet on the Western Front*	Lewis Milestone	George Arliss *Disraeli*	Norma Shearer *The Divorcee*	Joseph T. Rucker, Willard Van Der Veer *With Byrd at the South Pole*
1931	*Cimarron*	Norman Taurog *Skippy*	Lionel Barrymore *A Free Soul*	Marie Dressler *Min and Bill*	Floyd Crosby *Tabu*
1932	*Grand Hotel*	Frank Borzage *Bad Girl*	Wallace Beery *The Champ* Fredric March *Dr. Jekyll and Mr. Hyde*	Helen Hayes *The Sin of Madelon Claudet*	Lee Garmes *Shanghai Express*
1933	*Cavalcade*	Frank Lloyd	Charles Laughton *The Private Life of Henry VIII*	Katharine Hepburn *Morning Glory*	Charles Bryant Lang, Jr. *A Farewell to Arms*

Year	Best Picture	Best Director	Best Actor	Best Actress	Best Supporting Actor	Best Supporting Actress	Best Song (from film)	Original Score	Best Cinematographer
1934	*It Happened One Night*	Frank Capra	Clark Gable *It Happened One Night*	Claudette Colbert *It Happened One Night*	. . .	. . .	"The Continental" *The Gay Divorcee*	Louis Silvers *One Night of Love*	Victor Milner *Cleopatra*
1935	*Mutiny on the Bounty*	John Ford *The Informer*	Victor McLaglen *The Informer*	Bette Davis *Dangerous*	. . .	. . .	"Lullaby of Broadway" *Lullaby of Broadway*	Max Steiner *The Informer*	Hal Mohr *A Midsummer Night's Dream*
1936	*The Great Ziegfeld*	Frank Capra *Mr. Deeds Goes to Town*	Paul Muni *The Story of Louis Pasteur*	Luise Rainer *The Great Ziegfeld*	Walter Brennan *Come and Get It*	Gale Sondergaard *Anthony Adverse*	"The Way You Look Tonight" *Swing Time*	Leo Forbstein *Anthony Adverse*	Gaetano Gaudio *Anthony Adverse*
1937	*The Life of Emile Zola*	Leo McCarey *The Awful Truth*	Spencer Tracy *Captains Courageous*	Luise Rainer *The Good Earth*	Joseph Schildkraut *The Life of Emile Zola*	Alice Brady *In Old Chicago*	"Sweet Leilani" *Waikiki Wedding*	Charles Previn *100 Men and a Girl*	Karl Freund *The Good Earth*
1938	*You Can't Take It with You*	Frank Capra	Spencer Tracy *Boys Town*	Bette Davis *Jezebel*	Walter Brennan *Kentucky*	Fay Bainter *Jezebel*	"Thanks for the Memory" *Big Broadcast of 1938*	Alfred Newman *Alexander's Ragtime Band* Erich Wolfgang Korngold *The Adventures of Robin Hood*	Joseph Ruttenberg *The Great Waltz*
1939	*Gone with the Wind*	Victor Fleming	Robert Donat *Goodbye, Mr. Chips*	Vivien Leigh *Gone with the Wind*	Thomas Mitchell *Stagecoach*	Hattie McDaniel *Gone with the Wind*	"Over the Rainbow" *The Wizard of Oz*	Herbert Stothart *The Wizard of Oz* Richard Hageman, Frank Haring, John Leipold, Leo Shuken *Stagecoach*	Gregg Toland *Wuthering Heights* Ernest Haller, Ray Rennahan *Gone with the Wind*

(continued)

TABLE 18.11   (continued)

Members of the film industry in 1927 founded the Academy of Motion Picture Arts and Sciences, a move designed to raise the "cultural, educational, and scientific standards of the industry." Members of the academy proceeded to honor its best participants by presenting annually, starting officially with 1928, its "Academy Awards," or Oscars, in various categories. The number of categories was increased in 1934. The ceremony of presentation became a major media event.

Year	Best Picture	Best Director	Best Actor	Best Actress	Best Supporting Actor	Best Supporting Actress	Best Song (from film)	Original Score	Best Cinematographer
1940	*Rebecca*	John Ford *The Grapes of Wrath*	James Stewart *The Philadelphia Story*	Ginger Rogers *Kitty Foyle*	Walter Brennan *The Westerner*	Jane Darwell *The Grapes of Wrath*	"When You Wish upon a Star" *Pinocchio*	Alfred Newman *Tin Pan Alley* Leigh Harline, Paul J. Smith, Ned Washington *Pinocchio*	George Barnes *Rebecca* George Perinal *Thief of Bagdad*
1941	*How Green Was My Valley*	John Ford	Gary Cooper *Sergeant York*	Joan Fontaine *Suspicion*	Donald Crisp *How Green Was My Valley*	Mary Astor *The Great Lie*	"The Last Time I Saw Paris" *Lady Be Good*	Bernard Herrmann *All That Money Can Buy* Frank Churchill, Oliver Wallace *Dumbo*	Arthur Miller *How Green Was My Valley* Ernest Palmer, Ray Rennahan *Blood and Sand*
1942	*Mrs. Miniver*	William Wyler	James Cagney *Yankee Doodle Dandy*	Greer Garson *Mrs. Miniver*	Van Heflin *Johnny Eager*	Teresa Wright *Mrs. Miniver*	"White Christmas" *Holiday Inn*	Max Steiner *Now, Voyager* Ray Heindorf, Heinz Roemheld *Yankee Doodle Dandy*	Joseph Ruttenberg *Mrs. Miniver* Leon Shamroy *The Black Swan*
1943	*Casablanca*	Michael Curtiz	Paul Lukas *Watch on the Rhine*	Jennifer Jones *The Song of Bernadette*	Charles Coburn *The More the Merrier*	Katina Paxinou *For Whom the Bell Tolls*	"You'll Never Know" *Hello, Frisco, Hello*	Alfred Nedwman *The Song of Bernadette* Ray Heindorf *This is the Army*	Arthur Miller *The Song of Bernadette* Hal Mohr, W. Howard Greene *The Phantom of the Opera*
1944	*Going My Way*	Leo McCarey	Bing Crosy *Going My Way*	Ingrid Bergman *Gaslight*	Barry Fitzgerald *Going My Way*	Ethel Barrymore *None but the Lonely Heart*	"Swinging on a Star" *Going My Way*	Max Steiner *Since You Went Away* Carmen Dragon, Morris Stoloff *Cover Girl*	Joseph LaShelle *Laura* Leon Shamroy *Wilson*
1945	*The Lost Weekend*	Billy Wilder	Ray Milland *The Lost Weekend*	Joan Crawford *Mildred Pierce*	James Dunn *A Tree Grows in Brooklyn*	Anne Revere *National Velvet*	"It Might As Well Be Spring" *State Fair*	Miklos Rozsa *Spellbound* Georgie Stoll *Anchors Aweigh*	Harry Stradling *The Picture of Dorian Gray* Leon Shamroy *Leave Her to Heaven*

Source: Mike Kaplan, ed., *Variety Presents: The Complete Book of Major U.S. Show Business Awards* (New York, 1985), 3–26.

Popular Music

Popular music benefited from continued urbanization and especially from technological change. Much music in the first part of the twentieth century was written for the stage, mostly in New York City, and circulated as sheet music. Improvement in the phonograph record offered a new means of circulation and a new incentive for producing music. Development of radio in the 1920s made the musical industry nationwide. Americans everywhere could hear the same music at the same time. The film musical of the 1930s and 1940s completed the story—putting Broadway music, and other types of music, on the screen, making it fully a part of the glamorous entertainment industry.

Although many types of music could be heard at all times throughout the period, the emphasis shifted from ragtime to jazz and blues in the 1920s to swing music in the 1930s and 1940s. Musical themes that often originated with black musicians were taken up—and often cooled down—by whites. The period produced a list of composers and lyricists possibly second to no other time in American history: Irving Berlin, Sigmund Romberg, Duke Ellington,

TABLE 18.12   POPULAR SONGS, 1914–1945

(Songs are listed in random order.)

1914	1915	1916	1917
By the Beautiful Sea A Little Bit of Heaven, Sure They Call It Ireland Love's Own Sweet Song Missouri Waltz St. Louis Blues Twelfth Street Rag When You Wore a Tulip and I Wore a Big Red Rose	Don't Bite the Hand That's Feeding You Keep the Home Fires Burning The Old Grey Mare Memories Down among the Sheltering Palms Pack Up Your Troubles in Your Old Kit Bag M-O-T-H-E-R, a Word That Means the World to Me	He May Be Old, but He's Got Young Ideas Li'l Liza Jane Mother Nola Poor Butterfly I Ain't Got Nobody Pretty Baby	The Bells of St. Mary's For Me and My Gal Bring My Daddy Back to Me Hail, Hail, the Gang's All Here MacNamara's Band Oh Johnny, Oh Jonny, Oh! Over There Swing Low, Sweet Chariot

1918	1919	1920	1921
After You've Gone Beautiful Ohio Hinky-Dinky Parlez-vous I'm Always Chasing Rainbows K-K-K-Katy Every Day Will Be Sunday When the Town Goes Dry Till We Meet Again	Alice Blue Gown I'm Forever Blowing Bubbles Let the Rest of the World Go By My Isle of Golden Dreams A Pretty Girl Is Like a Melody Swanee How Ya Gonna Keep 'Em Down on the Farm? (After They've Seen Paree)	I'll Be with You in Apple Blossom Time Look for the Silver Lining Mary Rose of Washington Square When My Baby Smiles at Me That Old Irish Mother of Mine	Ain't We Got Fun April Showers I'm Just Wild about Harry Ma—He's Making Eyes at Me Say It with Music Second Hand Rose

1922	1923	1924	1925
Carolina in the Morning Chicago (That Toddling Town) Do It Again Georgia I Wish I Could Shimmy Like My Sister Kate Three O'Clock in the Morning Way Down Yonder in New Orleans	Charleston (Runnin' Wild) I Cried for You It Ain't Gonna Rain No Mo' Mexicali Rose Who's Sorry Now? Yes! We Have No Bananas Swingin' Down the Lane That Old Gang of Mine	Amapola Charley My Boy Deep in My Heart, Dear I'll See You in My Dreams The Man I Love Rose Marie Tea for Two Fascinating Rhythm	Always Cecilia Dinah Drifting and Dreaming Five Foot Two, Eyes of Blue I'm Sitting on Top of the World Moonlight and Roses Sleepy Time Gal Sweet Georgia Brown Yes Sir, That's My Baby If You Knew Susie—Like I Know Susie

1926	1927	1928	1929
Are You Lonesome Tonight? Baby Face The Birth of the Blues Breezin' Along with the Breeze Bye, Bye, Blackbird Someone to Watch over Me When Day Is Done Gimme a Little Kiss, Will Ya Huh?	The Best Things in Life Are Free Blue Skies Can't Help Loving Dat Man Make Believe My Heart Stood Still Ol' Man River Side by Side Why Do I Love You? The Song Is Ended, but the Memory Lingers On	Button Up Your Overcoat Carolina Moon I Wanna Be Loved by You I'll Get By Let's Do It Let's Misbehave Makin' Whoopee Marie When You're Smiling	Happy Days Are Here Again Honeysuckle Rose I've Got a Feeling I'm Falling Louise More Than You Know Singin' in the Rain Stardust With a Song in my Heart You Do Something to Me I'll Always Be in Love with You

1930	1931	1932	1933
Body and Soul Beyond the Blue Horizon Can This Be Love? Embraceable You Georgia on My Mind I Got Rhythm Three Little Words What Is This Thing Called Love?	Dancing in the Dark Between the Devil and the Deep Blue Sea Dream a Little Dream of Me I Found a Million Dollar Baby in a Five and Ten Cent Store Mood Indigo The Thrill Is Gone When the Moon Comes over the Mountain	Brother, Can You Spare a Dime? Granada How Deep Is the Ocean? I've Told Every Little Star The Song Is You You're an Old Smoothie You're Getting to Be a Habit with Me Night and Day	Don't Blame Me Easter Parade We're in the Money It's Only a Paper Moon It's the Talk of the Town Maria Elena The Last Round-up Stormy Weather

1934	1935	1936	1937
Blue Moon Deep Purple I Get a Kick out of You I Only Have Eyes for You Tumbling Tumbleweeds Winter Wonderland You Oughta Be in Pictures	Begin the Beguine Cheek to Cheek I'm in the Mood for Love I Got Plenty o' Nuthin' It Ain't Necessarily So Just One of Those Things Lullaby of Broadway	I'm an Old Cowhand I Can't Get Started with You I've Got You Under My Skin Moonlight and Shadows The Night Is Young and You're So Beautiful Stompin' at the Savoy Pennies from Heaven	Harbor Lights I've Got My Love to Keep Me Warm I Can Dream, Can't I? The Lady Is a Tramp Sweet Leilani Thanks for the Memory Whistle While You Work Nice Work If You Can Get It

(continued)

TABLE 18.12 (continued)

(Songs are listed in random order.)

1938	1939	1940	1941
Falling in Love with Love I'll Be Seeing You Franklin D. Roosevelt Jones September Song Two Sleepy People You Go to My Head You Must Have Been a Beautiful Baby	God Bless America I'll Never Smile Again Do I Love You? Over the Rainbow South of the Border Three Little Fishes	All or Nothing at All The Breeze and I I Hear a Rapsody The Last Time I Saw Paris The Nearness of You You Stepped out of a Dream You Are My Sunshine	Bewitched Blues in the Night Chattanooga Choo Choo Deep in the Heart of Texas I Don't Want to Set the World on Fire Jersey Bounce The White Cliffs of Dover

1942	1943	1944	1945
Be Careful! It's My Heart Don't Get Around Much Anymore I Left My Heart at the Stage Door Canteen Paper Doll Serenade in Blue White Christmas You'd Be So Nice to Come Home To Praise the Lord and Pass the Ammunition This Is the Army, Mr. Jones	Besame Mucho Coming In on a Wing and a Prayer A Lovely Way to Spend an Evening Oh! What a Beautiful Morning Oklahoma People Will Say We're in Love Pistol Packin' Mama The Surrey with the Fringe on Top	Ac-cent-tchu-ate the Positive Close as Pages in a Book Don't Fence Me In Dream I'll Walk Alone A Little on the Lonely Side Long Ago and Far Away Sentimental Journey Spring Will Be a Little Late This Year	For Sentimental Reasons If I Loved You It's Been a Long, Long Time Laura June Is Bustin' Out All Over On the Atchison, Topeka and the Santa Fe Let It Snow, Let It Snow, Let It Snow Oh, What It Seemed to Be Waitin' for the Train to Come In

Sources: Julius Mattfeld, *Variety Music Cavalcade, 1620–1969* (Englewood Cliffs, N.J., 1971), 327–558; *Webster's Guide to American History* (New York, 1971), 781–82.

George and Ira Gershwin, Harold Arlen, Jerome Kern, Cole Porter, Lorenz Hart, Richard Rodgers, Oscar Hammerstein II, Johnny Mercer, and many others. Probably the most original, though not the most popular, was George Gershwin. Virtually all the composers were men, but much of the music was about women. Some of the best music continued to be show tunes. Each of the two world wars inspired music that temporarily moved the spirit and then faded quickly to insignificance. Berlin's "God Bless America" is an exception. In the 1940s Latin-American music with its numerous lively beats mingled easily with the tempo of the big bands.

Songs of War

The following songs were popular in World War I:

I Didn't Raise My Boy to Be a Soldier (1915)

Pack Up Your Troubles in Your Old Kit Bag and Smile, Smile, Smile (1915)

Keep the Home Fires Burning (1915)

Bring Back My Daddy to Me (1917)

Goodbye Broadway, Hello France (1917)

When Yankee Doodle Learns to Parlez Vous Francais (1917)

Over There (1917)

When Alexander Takes His Ragtime Band to France (1918)

They Were All out of Step but Jim (1918)

Bing! Bing! Bing 'Em on the Rhine (1918)

Oh! How I Hate to Get Up in the Morning (1918)

If He Can Fight Like He Can Love, Good Night, Germany (1918)

The Rose of No-Man's Land (1918)

I'm Gonna Pin My Medal on the Girl I Left Behind (1918)

How Ya Gonna Keep 'Em Down on the Farm? (After They've Seen Paree) (1919)

The songs listed below were popular in World War II:

I'll Be Back in a Year Little Darling (1940)

The Boogie Woogie Bugle Boy of Company B (1941)

The White Cliffs of Dover (1941)

Remember Pearl Harbor! (1941)

You're a Sap, Mr. Jap (1941)

We Did It Before and We Can Do It Again (1941)

Praise the Lord and Pass the Ammunition (1942)

Blitzkrieg Baby (1942)

Don't Sit under the Apple Tree (1942)

Coming in on a Wing and a Prayer (1943)

Don't Get Around Much Anymore (1943)

They're Either Too Young or Too Old (1943)

No Love, No Nothin' (Until My Baby Comes Home) (1944)

I'll Be Seeing You (1944)

It's Been a Long, Long Time (1945)

Waitin' for the Train to Come In (Waitin' for My Man to Come Home) (1945)

Sources: Mattfeld, *Variety Music Cavalcade,* 535, 558; *Webster's Guide to American History,* 781–782.

The Era of the Big Bands

Although band and orchestra music was popular in the United States throughout the twentieth century, the age of the great dance bands was from the early 1930s to the late 1940s, until shortly after the Second World War. These were musical organizations named after the leader and made up mostly of brass instruments, with drums and guitar and bass; later on some added strings. There were hundreds of these bands—black and white with not a great deal of mixture between the two, although there was some. Many black bands played almost exclusively for black audiences, but the most popular black bands—those of Count Basie, Duke Ellington, Louis Armstrong, Cab Calloway, Jimmie Lunceford, and several others—

While on maneuvers before the Second World War, men of the 2d Army get together for a jam session, playing either jazz or swing music. (National Archives)

were truly national bands, listened to partly, if not largely, by whites. The bands competed with and imitated one another; they differed in size, quality, prestige, and emphasis. Some played mostly sweet music; others played jazz or later bebop. All played some variation of the fast dance music called swing. It was the age of swing.

Fifty Nationally Popular Big Bands (White or Mostly White)

Charlie Barnet
Bunny Berigan
Les Brown
Frankie Chester
Bob Chester
Larry Clinton
Bob Crosby
Xavier Cugat
Sam Donahue
Jimmy Dorsey
Tommy Dorsey
Eddy Duchin
Jan Garber
Benny Goodman
Horace Heidt
Woody Herman
Eddy Howard
Ina Ray Hutton
Harry James
Dick Jurgens
Art Kassel
Sammy Kaye
Hal Kemp
Stan Kenton
Wayne King
Gene Krupa
Kay Kyser
Guy Lombardo
Johnny Long
Freddy Martin
Hal McIntyre
Ray McKinley
Glenn Miller
Vaughn Monroe
Russ Morgan
Ozzie Nelson
Red Nichols
Ray Noble
Tony Pastor
Ben Pollack
Alvino Rey
Buddy Rich
Artie Shaw
Charlie Spivak
Jack Teagarden
Claude Thornhill
Fred Waring
Ted Weems
Lawrence Welk
Paul Whiteman

Sources: Bruce Crowther, *The Big Band Years* (New York, 1988), numerous pages; George T. Simon, *The Big Bands* (New York, 1974), numerous pages.

Thirty Black Bands

Louis Armstrong
Walter Barnes
Count Basie
Cab Calloway
Benny Carter
Billy Eckstine
Duke Ellington
Dizzy Gillespie
Lionel Hampton
Erskine Hawkins
Fletcher Henderson
Teddy Hill
Earl Hines
Les Hite
James Jeter-Hayes Pillars

Andy Kirk
Milt Larkins
Harlan Leonard
Sabby Lewis
Jimmie Lunceford
Jay McShann
Lucky Millinder
Bennie Moten
Walter Page
Don Redman
Nat Towles
Alphonso Trent
Fats Waller
Chick Webb
Fess Williams

Source: Crowther, *Big Band Years,* 116–142.

Twenty Most Popular Bands, 1942: Poll by WNEW, New York

1. Harry James
2. Glenn Miller
3. Tommy Dorsey
4. Jimmy Dorsey
5. Vaughn Monroe
6. Benny Goodman
7. Woody Herman
8. Kay Kyser
9. Charlie Spivak
10. Sammy Kaye
11. Alvino Rey
12. Claude Thornhill
13. Gene Krupa
14. Count Basie
15. Artie Shaw
16. Charlie Barnet
17. Johnny Long
18. Freddy Martin
19. Guy Lombardo
20. Hal McIntyre

Source: Simon, *The Big Bands,* 29.

TABLE 18.13   THIRTY-FIVE POPULAR SINGERS OF THE BIG BAND ERA

Singer	Sang for
Bonnie Baker	Orin Tucker
Mildred Bailey	P. Whiteman, R. Norvo
Georgia Carroll	Kay Kyser
June Christy	Stan Kenton
Rosemary Clooney	Tony Pastor
Perry Como	Ted Weems
Chris Connor	Stan Kenton
Don Cornell	Sammy Kaye
Doris Day	B. Crosby, L. Brown
Gloria DeHaven	B. Crosby
Ray Eberle	G. Miller
Bob Eberly	J. Dorsey
Skinnay Ennis	Hal Kemp
Dale Evans	Anson Weeks
Ella Fitzgerald	Chick Webb
Helen Forrest	Goodman, Shaw, James
Maxine Gray	Hal Kemp
Connie Haines	T. Dorsey
Dick Haymes	H. James
Billie Holiday	A. Shaw
Lena Horne	C. Barnet
Betty Hutton	Vincent Lopez
Marion Hutton	G. Miller
Peggy Lee	B. Goodman
Mary Ann McCall	T. Dorsey, Barnet, Herman
Helen O'Connell	J. Dorsey
Anita O'Day	G. Krupa
Betty Roche	D. Ellington
Ginny Sims	K. Kyser
Frank Sinatra	H. James, T. Dorsey
Jo Stafford	T. Dorsey
Kay Starr	C. Barnet, Joe Venuti
Mel Torme	A. Shaw
Sarah Vaughan	Earl Hines
Bea Wain	Larry Clinton

Source: Simon, *The Big Bands,* numerous pages, especially 33–39.

Much entertainment was noncommercial. This family celebrated the Fourth of July with a makeshift picnic. (Library of Congress)

Radio

When the big bands played, young people danced the fox-trot, lindy, or jitterbug. (Arthur Rothstein, *The Depression Years*)

Radio was the most important new agent of entertainment of the first half of the twentieth century. After the first broadcast in 1920, radio grew with astonishing speed in numbers and type of activity. The first national network (NBC) appeared in 1926, and Columbia followed the next year. By 1930 almost fifteen million homes had radio; by 1940 the number doubled. By the time of the Second World War it appeared that everyone in the United States had a radio, although we know they did not. While radio devoted some time to public affairs and its coverage of news expanded with the expanding international crisis, it remained mostly a means of entertainment. A commercial operation from the start, radio offered programs that would attract the most listeners because a large audience bolstered a demand for more revenue from advertising. Thus radio offered a full slate of daytime and evening programming of comedy, music, and drama carefully geared to the anticipated audience. In the evening the variety shows usually dominated. Radio clearly benefited from the delay in the perfection of television. When television did appear in large numbers, it borrowed heavily from patterns that radio had established. Radio did not vanish but underwent a change in mission. Until the end of the Second World War, however, the king of the airwaves, providing almost universal entertainment for the American people, was radio.

TABLE 18.14 RADIO AND TELEVISION STATIONS, RADIOS PRODUCED, AND FAMILIES WITH RADIO, 1921–1945

Year	Radio Stations		Television Stations	Radio Sets Produced (thousands)	Families with Radio (thousands)
	AM	FM			
1921	1	...	...	...	...
1922	30	...	...	100	60
1923	556	...	...	500	400
1924	530	...	...	1,500	1,250
1925	571	...	...	2,000	2,750
1926	528	...	...	1,750	4,500
1927	681	...	...	1,350	6,750
1928	677	...	...	3,250	8,000
1929	606	...	...	4,428	10,250
1930	618	...	...	3,789	13,750
1931	612	...	...	3,594	16,700
1932	604	...	...	2,446	18,450
1933	599	...	...	4,157	19,250
1934	583	...	...	4,479	20,400
1935	585	...	...	6,030	21,456
1936	616	...	...	8,249	22,869
1937	646	...	...	8,083	24,500
1938	689	...	...	7,142	26,667
1939	722	...	...	10,763	27,500
1940	765	...	...	11,831	28,500
1941	831	5	2	13,642	29,300
1942	887	7	4	4,307[a]	30,600
1943	910	18	4	...[a]	30,800
1944	910	49	6	...[a]	32,500
1945	919	52	6	...[a]	33,100

[a]Production of commercial radio receivers stopped during the Second World War, from Apr. 1942 until October 1945.
Source: Bureau of the Census, *Historical Statistics of the United States, Colonial Times to 1957* (Washington, D.C., 1960), 491.

TABLE 18.15 MOST POPULAR RADIO PROGRAMS

The first significant effort to rate radio programs came in the early 1930s in the Cooperative Analysis of Broadcasting, the CAB or Crossley ratings, which called people and asked what they had listened to during that day. During the season of 1935–36 the C. E. Hooper service introduced a new, more complex, and more accurate system of calling listeners. From that season until 1949 the Hooperatings would prevail. Listed below are the programs that ranked highest for each year's radio season. They are listed in order of rank.

1930–31	1931–32	1932–33	1933–34
Amos 'n' Andy	Amos 'n' Andy	Eddie Cantor Program	Eddie Cantor Program
Rudy Vallee Varieties	Eddie Cantor Show	Jack Pearl–Baron Munchausen	Maxwell House Show Boat
Atwater Kent Hour	The Goldbergs	Ed Wynn, Fire Chief	Rudy Vallee Varieties
Lucky Strike Dance Orchestra	Rudy Vallee Varieties	Maxwell House Show Boat	Joe Penner Program
Camel Pleasure Hour	Sunday at Seth Parkers	Rudy Vallee Varieties	Ed Wynn, Fire Chief
Colliers Hour	Eno Crime Club	Ben Bernie Orchestra	Amos 'n' Andy
RKO Theater	Firestone Concert	George Burns & Gracie Allen	George Burns & Gracie Allen
General Motors Program	Lucky Strike Orchestra	Amos 'n' Andy	Paul Whiteman Revue
House of Magic	Paul Whiteman's Orchestra	Myrt and Marge	First Nighter
Palmolive Hour	Mary and Bob	Cities Service Orchestra	Phil Baker Program

1934–35	1935–36	1936–37	1937–38
Rudy Vallee Varieties	Major Bowes Amateur Hour	Eddie Cantor Program	Charlie McCarthy/Edgar Bergen
Maxwell House Show Boat	Rudy Vallee Varieties	Jack Benny	Jack Benny Program
Jack Benny Program	Jack Benny Program	Lux Radio Theater	George Burns & Gracie Allen
Fred Allen	March of Time	George Burns & Gracie Allen	Lux Radio Theater
Joe Penner Program	George Burns & Gracie Allen	Bing Crosby Show	Al Jolson
Ed Wynn, Fire Chief	Amos 'n' Andy	Fred Allen	Eddie Cantor Program
Beauty Box Theater	Fred Allen	Hollywood Hotel	Bing Crosby Show
Hoover Sentinels	First Nighter	Al Jolson	Major Bowes Amateur Hour
Guy Lombardo Orchestra	Maxwell House Show Boat	Phil Baker Program	Rudy Vallee Varieties
Lowell Thomas News	Al Jolson	Amos 'n' Andy	Fred Allen

1938–39	1939–40	1940–41	1941–42
Charlie McCarthy/Edgar Bergen	Charlie McCarthy/Edgar Bergen	Jack Benny	Charlie McCarthy/Edgar Bergen
Jack Benny	Jack Benny	Charlie McCarthy/Edgar Bergen	Fibber McGee and Molly
Lux Radio Theater	Fibber McGee and Molly	Bob Hope	Walter Winchell Commentary
Bing Crosby Show	One Man's Family	Fibber McGee and Molly	Bob Hope Show
Frank Morgan–Fanny Rice	Lux Radio Theater	Lux Radio Theater	Jack Benny
Major Bowes Amateur Hour	Bob Hope Show	Aldrich Family	Aldrich Family
Big Town (Edward G. Robinson)	Bing Crosby Show	Walter Winchell Commentary	Lux Radio Theater
George Burns & Gracie Allen	Fitch Bandwagon	Frank Morgan–Fanny Brice	Frank Morgan–Fanny Brice
Fred Allen	Kay Kyser's Kollege of Musical	Major Bowes Amateur Hour	Red Skelton
Kay Kyser's Kollege of Musical	Knowledge	Kay Kyser's Kollege	Kay Kyser's Kollege
Knowledge	Pot o' Gold		

1942–43	1943–44	1944–45	1945–46
Bob Hope Show	Fibber McGee and Molly	Bob Hope	Fibber McGee and Molly
Red Skelton	Bob Hope	Fibber McGee and Molly	Bob Hope
Fibber McGee and Molly	Red Skelton	Bing Crosby Show	Lux Radio Theater
Charlie McCarthy/Edgar Bergen	Charlie McCarthy/Ed Bergen	Walter Winchell Commentary	Charlie McCarthy/Edgar Bergen
Aldrich Family	Jack Benny	Mr. District Attorney	Red Skelton
Frank Morgan–Fanny Brice	Aldrich Family	Jack Benny	Jack Benny
Lux Radio Theater	Joan Davis–Jack Haley	Charlie McCarthy/Edgar Bergen	Screen Guild Players
Kay Kyser's Kollege	Mr. District Attorney	Lux Radio Theater	Fred Allen
Abbott and Costello Program	Frank Morgan–Fanny Brice	Joan Davis–Jack Haley	Mr. District Attorney
Rudy Vallee Variety	Walter Winchell Commentary	Screen Guild Players	Walter Winchell Commentary

Source: Harrison B. Summers, *A Thirty-Year History of Programs Carried on National Radio Networks in the United States, 1926–1956* (1958; reprint, New York, 1971), numerous pages.

Literature

Reading was the primary means of communication and entertainment at the start of the years 1914–45 and the development of movies and then radio did not slow production and sale of books. The period represented a golden age in American literature, with such writers as F. Scott Fitzgerald, Ernest Hemingway, Sinclair Lewis, Richard Wright, and Eugene O'Neill being some of the most admired and honored authors in American literary history. In the effort to reach a mass audience for both fiction and nonfiction works, important innovations included the Book-of-the-Month Club, started in 1926, and in the early 1940s came introduction of the inexpensive paperback version of hardbound books. The effect of the Great Depression, which produced hard times for the book industry, was offset by two world wars that created new subjects for writers and sparked new interest in reading. A paper shortage during the

TABLE 18.16   MOST POPULAR BOOKS 1914–1945

1914	1915	1916	1917
Fiction 1. *The Eyes of the World*, by Harold Bell Wright. 2. *Pollyanna*, by Eleanor H. Porter. 3. *The Inside of the Cup*, by Winston Churchill. 4. *The Salamander*, by Owen Johnson. 5. *The Fortunate Youth*, by William J. Locke.	**Fiction** 1. *The Turmoil*, by Booth Tarkington. 2. *A Far Country*, by Winston Churchill. 3. *Michael O'Halloran*, by Gene Stratton Porter. 4. *Pollyanna Grows Up*, by Eleanor H. Porter. 5. *K*, by Mary Roberts Rinehart.	**Fiction** 1. *Seventeen*, by Booth Tarkington. 2. *When a Man's a Man*, by Harold Bell Wright. 3. *Just David*, by Eleanor H. Porter. 4. *Mr. Britling Sees It Through*, by H. G. Wells. 5. *Life and Gabriella*, by Ellen Glasgow.	**Fiction** 1. *Mr. Britling Sees It Through*, by H. G. Wells. 2. *The Light in the Clearing*, by Irving Bacheller. 3. *The Red Planet*, by William J. Locke. 4. *The Road to Understanding*, by Eleanor H. Porter. 5. *Wildfire*, by Zane Grey. **General Nonfiction** 1. *Rhymes of a Red Cross Man*, by Robert W. Service. 2. *The Plattsburg Manual*, by O. O. Ellis and E. B. Garey. 3. *Raymond*, by Sir Oliver Lodge. 4. *Poems of Alan Seeger*. 5. *God the Invisible King*, by H. G. Wells.

1918	1919	1920	1921
Fiction 1. *The U. P. Trail*, by Zane Grey. 2. *The Tree of Heaven*, by May Sinclair. 3. *The Amazing Interlude*, by Mary Roberts Rinehart. 4. *Dere Mable*, by Edward Streeter. 5. *Oh, Money! Money!* by Eleanor H. Porter. **General Nonfiction** 1. *Rhymes of a Red Cross Man*, by Robert W. Service. 2. *Treasury of War Poetry*, by G. H. Clark. 3. *With the Colors*, by Everard J. Appleton. 4. *Recollections*, by Viscount Morley. 5. *Laugh and Live*, by Douglas Fairbanks.	**Fiction** 1. *The Four Horsemen of the Apocalypse*, by V. Blasco Ibañez. 2. *The Arrow of Gold*, by Joseph Conrad. 3. *The Desert of Wheat*, by Zane Grey. 4. *Dangerous Days*, by Mary Roberts Rinehart. 5. *The Sky Pilot in No Man's Land*, by Ralph Connor. **Nonfiction** 1. *The Education of Henry Adams*, by Henry Adams. 2. *The Years Between*, by Rudyard Kipling. 3. *Belgium*, by Brand Whitlock. 4. *The Seven Purposes*, by Margaret Cameron. 5. *In Flanders Fields*, by John McCrae.	**Fiction** 1. *The Man of the Forest*, by Zane Grey. 2. *Kindred of the Dust*, by Peter B. Kyne. 3. *The Re-Creation of Brian Kent*, by Harold Bell Wright. 4. *The River's End*, by James Oliver Curwood. 5. *A Man for the Ages*, by Irving Bacheller. **Nonfiction** 1. *Now It Can Be Told*, by Philip Gibbs. 2. *The Economic Consequences of the Peace*, by John M. Keynes. 3. *Roosevelt's Letters to His Children*, ed. by Joseph B. Bishop. 4. *Theodore Roosevelt*, by William Roscoe Thayer. 5. *White Shadows in the South Seas*, by Frederick O'Brien.	**Fiction** 1. *Main Street*, by Sinclair Lewis. 2. *The Brimming Cup*, by Dorothy Canfield. 3. *The Mysterious Rider*, by Zane Grey. 4. *The Age of Innocence*, by Edith Wharton. 5. *The Valley of Silent Men*, by James Oliver Curwood. **Nonfiction** 1. *The Outline of History*, by H. G. Wells. 2. *White Shadows in the South Seas*, by Frederick O'Brien. 3. *The Mirrors of Downing Street*, by a Gentleman with a Duster (Harold Begbie). 4. *Mystic Isles of the South Seas*, by Frederick O'Brien. 5. *The Autobiography of Margot Asquith*.

1922	1923	1924	1925
Fiction 1. *If Winter Comes*, by A. S. M. Hutchinson. 2. *The Sheik*, by Edith M. Hull. 3. *Gentle Julia*, by Booth Tarkington. 4. *The Head of the House of Coombe*, by Frances Hodgson Burnett. 5. *Simon Called Peter*, by Robert Keable. **Nonfiction** 1. *The Outline of History*, by H. G. Wells. 2. *The Story of Mankind*, by Hendrik Willem Van Loon. 3. *The Americanization of Edward Bok*, by Edward Bok. 4. *Diet and Health*, by Lulu Hunt Peters. 5. *The Mind in the Making*, by James Harvey Robinson.	**Fiction** 1. *Black Oxen*, by Gertrude Atherton. 2. *His Children's Children*, by Arthur Train. 3. *The Enchanted April*, by "Elizabeth." 4. *Babbitt*, by Sinclair Lewis. 5. *The Dim Lantern*, by Temple Bailey. **Nonfiction** 1. *Etiquette*, by Emily Post. 2. *The Life of Christ*, by Giovanni Papini. 3. *The Life and Letters of Walter H. Page*, ed. by Burton J. Hendrick. 4. *The Mind in the Making*, by James Harvey Robinson. 5. *The Outine of History*, by H. G. Wells.	**Fiction** 1. *So Big*, by Edna Ferber. 2. *The Plastic Age*, by Percy Marks. 3. *The Little French Girl*, by Anne Douglas Sedgwick. 4. *The Heirs Apparent*, by Philip Gibbs. 5. *A Gentleman of Courage*, by James Oliver Curwood. **Nonfiction** 1. *Diet and Health*, by Lulu Hunt Peters. 2. *The Life of Christ*, by Giovanni Papini. 3. *The Boston Cooking School Cook Book*; new ed. by Fannie Farmer. 4. *Etiquette*, by Emily Post. 5. *Ariel*, by André Maurois.	**Fiction** 1. *Soundings*, by A. Hamilton Gibbs. 2. *The Constant Nymph*, by Margaret Kennedy. 3. *The Keeper of the Bees*, by Gene Stratton Porter. 4. *Glorious Apollo*, by E. Barrington. 5. *The Green Hat*, by Michael Arlen. **Nonfiction** 1. *Diet and Health*, by Lulu Hunt Peters. 2. *The Boston Booking School Cook Book*; new ed. by Fannie Farmer. 3. *When We Were Very Young*, by A. A. Milne. 4. *The Man Nobody Knows*, by Bruce Barton. 5. *The Life of Christ*, by Giovanni Papini.

(continued)

TABLE 18.16 (continued)

1926	1927	1928	1929
Fiction 1. *The Private Life of Helen of Troy*, by John Erskine. 2. *Gentlemen Prefer Blondes*, by Anita Loos. 3. *Sorrell and Son*, by Warwick Deeping. 4. *The Hounds of Spring*, by Sylvia Thompson. 5. *Beau Sabreur*, by P. C. Wren. **Nonfiction** 1. *The Man Nobody Knows*, by Bruce Barton. 2. *Why We Behave Like Human Beings*, by George A. Dorsey. 3. *Diet and Health*, by Lulu Hunt Peters. 4. *Our Times*, Vol. I. by Mark Sullivan. 5. *The Boston Cooking School Cook Book;* new ed. by Fannie Farmer.	**Fiction** 1. *Elmer Gantry*, by Sinclair Lewis. 2. *The Plutocrat*, by Booth Tarkington. 3. *Doomsday*, by Warwick Deeping. 4. *Sorrell and Son*, by Warwick Deeping. 5. *Jalna*, by Mazo de la Roche. **Nonfiction** 1. *The Story of Philosophy*, by Will Durant. 2. *Napoleon*, by Emil Ludwig. 3. *Revolt in the Desert*, by T. E. Lawrence. 4. *Trader Horn*, Vol. I, by Alfred Aloysius Horn and Ethelreda Lewis. 5. *We*, by Charles A. Lindbergh.	**Fiction** 1. *The Bridge of San Luis Rey*, by Thornton Wilder. 2. *Wintersmoon*, by Hugh Walpole. 3. *Swan Song*, by John Galsworthy. 4. *The Greene Murder Case*, by S. S. Van Dine. 5. *Bad Girl*, by Viña Delmar. **Nonfiction** 1. *Disraeli*, by André Maurois. 2. *Mother India*, by Katherine Mayo. 3. *Trade Horn*, Vol. I, by Alfred Aloysius Horn and Ethelreda Lewis. 4. *Napoleon*, by Emil Ludwig. 5. *Strange Interlude*, by Eugene O'Neill.	**Fiction** 1. *All Quiet on the Western Front*, by *Erich Maria Remarque.* 2. *Dodsworth*, by *Sinclair Lewis.* 3. *Dark Hester*, by *Anne Douglas Sedgwick.* 4. *The Bishop Murder Case*, by *S. S. Van Dine.* 5. *Roper's Row*, by *Warwick Deeping.* **Nonfiction** 1. *The Art of Thinking*, by Ernest Dimnet. 2. *Henry the Eighth*, by Francis Hackett. 3. *The Cradle of the Deep*, by Joan Lowell. 4. *Elizabeth and Essex*, by Lytton Strachey. 5. *The Specialist*, by Chic Sale.

1930	1931	1932	1933
Fiction 1. *Cimarron*, by Edna Ferber. 2. *Exile*, by Warwick Deeping. 3. *The Woman of Andros*, by Thornton Wilder. 4. *Years of Grace*, by Margaret Ayer Barnes. 5. *Angel Pavement*, by J. B. Priestley. **Nonfiction** 1. *The Story of San Michele*, by Axel Munthe. 2. *The Strange Death of President Harding*, by Gaston B. Means and May Dixon Thacker. 3. *Byron*, by André Maurois. 4. *The Adams Family*, by James Truslow Adams. 5. *Lone Cowboy*, by Will James.	**Fiction** 1. *The Good Earth*, by Pearl S. Buck 2. *Shadows on the Rock*, by Willa Cather. 3. *A White Bird Flying*, by Bess Streeter Aldrich. 4. *Grand Hotel*, by Vicki Baum. 5. *Years of Grace*, by Margaret Ayer Barnes. **Nonfiction** 1. *Education of a Princess*, by Grand Duchess Marie. 2. *The Story of San Michele*, by Axel Munthe. 3. *Washington Merry-Go-Round*, Anonymous (Drew Pearson and Robert S. Allen) 4. *Boners.* 5. *Culbertson's Summary*, by Ely Culbertson.	**Fiction** 1. *The Good Earth*, by Pearl S. Buck 2. *The Fountain*, by Charles Morgan. 3. *Sons*, by Pearl S. Buck. 4. *Magnolia Street*, by Louis Golding. 5. *The Sheltered Life*, by Ellen Glasgow. **Nonfiction** 1. *The Epic of America*, by James Truslow Adams. 2. *Only Yesterday*, by Frederick Lewis Allen. 3. *A Fortune to Share*, by Vash Young. 4. *Culbertson's Summary*, by Ely Culbertson. 5. *Van Loon's Geography*, by Hendrik Willem Van Loon.	**Fiction** 1. *Anthony Adverse*, by Hervey Allen. 2. *As the Earth Turns*, by Gladys Hasty Carroll. 3. *Ann Vickers*, by Sinclair Lewis. 4. *Magnificent Obsession*, by Lloyd C. Douglas 5. *One More River*, by John Galsworthy. **Fiction** 1. *Life Begins at Forty*, by Walter B. Pitkin. 2. *Marie Antoinette*, by Stefan Zweig. 3. *British Agent*, by R. H. Bruce Lockhart. 4. *100,000,000 Guinea Pigs*, by Arthur Kallet and F. J. Schlink. 5. *The House of Exile*, by Nora Waln.

1934	1935	1936	1937
Fiction 1. *Anthony Adverse*, by Hervey Allen. 2. *Lamb in His Bosom*, by Caroline Miller. 3. *So Red the Rose*, by Stark Young. 4. *Good-Bye, Mr. Chips*, by James Hilton. 5. *Within This Present*, by Margaret Ayer Barnes. **Nonfiction** 1. *While Rome Burns*, by Alexander Woollcott. 2. *Life Begins at Forty*, by Walter B. Pitkin. 3. *Nijinsky*, by Romola Nijinsky. 4. *100,000,000 Guinea Pigs*, by Arthur Kallet and F. J. Schlink. 5. *The Native's Return*, by Louis Adamic.	**Fiction** 1. *Green Light*, by Lloyd C. Douglas. 2. *Vein of Iron*, by Ellen Glasgow. 3. *Of Time and the River*, by Thomas Wolfe. 4. *Time Out of Mind*, by Rachel Field. 5. *Good-Bye, Mr. Chips*, by James Hilton. **Nonfiction** 1. *North to the Orient*, by Anne Morrow Lindbergh. 2. *While Rome Burns*, by Alexander Woollcott. 3. *Life with Father*, by Clarence Day. 4. *Personal History*, by Vincent Sheean. 5. *Seven Pillars of Wisdom*, by T. E. Lawrence.	**Fiction** 1. *Gone with the Wind*, by Margaret Mitchell 2. *The Last Puritan*, by George Santayana. 3. *Sparkenbroke*, by Charles Morgan. 4. *Drums Along the Mohawk*, by Walter D. Edmonds. 5. *It Can't Happen Here*, by Sinclair Lewis **Nonfiction** 1. *Man the Unknown*, by Alexis Carrel. 2. *Wake Up and Live!* by Dorothea Brande. 3. *The Way of a Transgressor*, by Negley Farson. 4. *Around the World in Eleven Years*, by Patience, Richard, and Johnny Abbe. 5. *North to the Orient*, by Anne Morrow Lindbergh.	**Fiction** 1. *Gone with the Wind*, by Margaret Mitchell. 2. *Northwest Passage*, by Kenneth Roberts. 3. *The Citadel*, by A. J. Cronin. 4. *And So—Victoria*, by Vaughan Wilkins. 5. *Drums Along the Mohawk*, by Walter D. Edmonds. **Nonfiction** 1. *How to Win Friends and Influence People*, by Dale Carnegie. 2. *An American Doctor's Odyssey*, by Victor Heiser. 3. *The Return to Religion*, by Henry C. Link. 4. *The Arts*, by Hendrik Willem Van Loon. 5. *Orchids on Your Budget*, by Marjorie Hillis.

1938	1939	1940	1941
Fiction 1. *The Yearling*, by Marjorie Kinnan Rawlings. 2. *The Citadel*, by A. J. Cronin. 3. *My Son, My Son!* by Howard Spring. 4. *Rebecca*, by Daphne du Maurier. 5. *Northwest Passage*, by Kenneth Roberts. **Nonfiction** 1. *The Importance of Living*, by Lin Yutang. 2. *With Malice Toward Some*, by Margaret Halsey. 3. *Madame Curie*, by Eve Curie. 4. *Listen! the Wind!* by Anne Morrow Lindbergh. 5. *The Horse and Buggy Doctor*, by Arthur E. Hertzler.	**Fiction** 1. *The Grapes of Wrath*, by John Steinbeck. 2. *All This, and Heaven Too*, by Rachel Field. 3. *Rebecca*, by Daphne du Maurier. 4. *Wickford Point*, by John P. Marquand. 5. *Escape*, by Ethel Vance. **Nonfiction** 1. *Days of Our Years*, by Pierre van Paassen. 2. *Reaching for the Stars*, by Nora Waln. 3. *Inside Asia* by John Gunther. 4. *Autobiography with Letters*, by William Lyon Phelps. 5. *Country Lawyer*, by Bellamy Partridge.	**Fiction** 1. *How Green Was My Valley*, by Richard Llewellyn. 2. *Kitty Foyle*, by Christopher Morley. 3. *Mrs. Miniver*, by Jan Struther. 4. *For Whom the Bell Tolls*, by Ernest Hemingway. 5. *The Nazarene*, by Sholem Asch. **Nonfiction** 1. *I Married Adventure*, by Osa Johnson. 2. *How to Read a Book*, by Mortimer Adler. 3. *A Smattering of Ignorance*, by Oscar Levant. 4. *Country Squire in the White House*, by John T. Flynn. 5. *Land Below the Wind*, by Agnes Newton Keith.	**Fiction** 1. *The Keys of the Kingdom*, by A. J. Cronin. 2. *Random Harvest*, by James Hilton. 3. *This Above All*, by Eric Knight. 4. *The Sun Is My Undoing*, by Marguerite Steen. 5. *For Whom the Bell Tolls*, by Ernest Hemingway. **Nonfiction** 1. *Berlin Diary*, by William L. Shirer. 2. *The White Cliffs*, by Alice Duer Miller. 3. *Out of the Night*, by Jan Valtin. 4. *Inside Latin America*, by John Gunther. 5. *Blood, Sweat and Tears*, by Winston S. Churchill

1942	1943	1944	1945
Fiction 1. *The Song of Bernadette*, by Franz Werfel. 2. *The Moon Is Down*, by John Steinbeck. 3. *Dragon Seed*, by Pearl S. Buck. 4. *And Now Tomorrow*, by Rachel Field. 5. *Drivin' Woman*, by Elizabeth Pickett. **Nonfiction** 1. *See Here, Private Hargrove*, by Marion Hargrove. 2. *Mission to Moscow*, by Joseph E. Davies. 3. *The Last Time I Saw Paris*, by Elliot Paul. 4. *Cross Creek*, by Marjorie Kinnan Rawlings. 5. *Victory Through Air Power*, by Major Alexander P. de Seversky.	**Fiction** 1. *The Robe*, by Lloyd C. Douglas. 2. *The Valley of Decision*, by Marcia Davenport. 3. *So Little Time*, by John P. Marquand. 4. *A Tree Grows in Brooklyn*, by Betty Smith. 5. *The Human Comedy*, by William Saroyan. **Nonfiction** 1. *Under Cover*, by John Roy Carlson. 2. *One World*, by Wendell L. Willkie. 3. *Journey Among Warriors*, by Eve Curie. 4. *On Being a Real Person*, by Harry Emerson Fosdick. 5. *Guadalcanal Diary*, by Richard Tregaskis.	**Fiction** 1. *Strange Fruit*, by Lillian Smith. 2. *The Robe*, by Lloyd C. Douglas 3. *A Tree Grows in Brooklyn*, by Betty Smith. 4. *Forever Amber*, by Kathleen Winsor. 5. *The Razor's Edge*, by W. Somerset Maugham. **Nonfiction** 1. *I Never Left Home*, by Bob Hope. 2. *Brave Men*, by Ernie Pyle. 3. *Good Night, Sweet Prince*, by Gene Fowler. 4. *Under Cover*, by John Roy Carlson. 5. *Yankee from Olympus*, by Catherine Drinker Bowen.	**Fiction** 1. *Forever Amber*, by Kathleen Winsor. 2. *The Robe*, by Lloyd C. Douglas. 3. *The Black Rose*, by Thomas B. Costain. 4. *The White Tower*, by James Ramsey Ullman. 5. *Cass Timberlane*, by Sinclair Lewis. **Nonfiction** 1. *Brave Men*, by Ernie Pyle. 2. *Dear Sir*, by Juliet Lowell. 3. *Up Front*, by Bill Mauldin. 4. *Black Boy*, by Richard Wright. 5. *Try and Stop Me*, by Bennett Cerf.

Source: Alice P. Hackett, *Seventy Years of Best Sellers, 1895–1965* (New York, 1967), 112–72.

Second World War did handicap the distribution of books in 1944–45. The lists below give in ranked order the best-selling volumes, taken for the most part from information in the trade magazine, *Publishers Weekly*. The lists for 1914–16 give only works of fiction and after that point there are separate lists for fiction and nonfiction. Not included for the years 1917–18 is a separate category for war books.

The Pulitzer Prizes

The Pulitzer Prizes, some of the nation's most prestigious literary awards, stem from the generosity of Joseph Pulitzer, a journalist, born in Hungary, who went on to found a newspaper empire in the late nineteenth century. His newspapers, which included the *New York World* and *St. Louis Post-Dispatch*, were noted for their efforts to appeal to a broad readership. Pulitzer made a gift of $2 million that was used to establish the School of Journalism at Columbia University. Starting in 1917, trustees of the school began to make awards for excellence in journalism, the number of categories changing over the years. Perhaps even more attention was paid to the award granted in letters; there would eventually be five categories.

TABLE 18.17 PULITZER PRIZES IN JOURNALISM

Meritorious Public Service		
Year	Winner	Theme
1917	No award	. . .
1918	*New York Times*	First World War
1919	*Milwaukee Journal*	Americanism
1920	No award	. . .
1921	*Boston Post*	Activities of Charles Ponzi
1922	*New York World*	Activities of Ku Klux Klan
1923	*Memphis Commercial Appeal*	Ku Klux Klan
1924	*New York World*	Peonage in Florida
1925	No award	. . .
1926	*Columbus (Ga.) Enquirer Sun*	Corruption, evolution, Ku Klux Klan
1927	*Canton (Ohio) Daily News*	Corruption in city government
1928	*Indianapolis Times*	Corruption in legal system
1929	*New York Evening World*	Corruption in legal system
1930	No award	. . .
1931	*Atlanta Constitution*	Corruption
1932	*Indianapolis News*	Waste in city government
1933	*New York World-Telegram*	Various city issues
1934	*Medford (Ore.) Mail Tribune*	Politics in Jackson County
1935	*Sacramento (Ca.) Bee*	Politics and judiciary
1936	*Cedar Rapids Gazette*	Corruption in Iowa
1937	*St. Louis Post-Dispatch*	Vote fraud in St. Louis

(continued)

TABLE 18.17 (continued)

Meritorious Public Service

Year	Winner	Theme
1938	*Bismarck (N.Dak.) Tribune*	The "dust bowl"
1939	*Miami Daily News*	Recall of city commission
1940	*Waterbury (Conn.) Republican & American*	Municipal corruption
1941	*St. Louis Post-Dispatch*	City pollution
1942	*Los Angeles Times*	Freedom of press
1943	*Omaha World-Herald*	Scrap metal campaign
1944	*New York Times*	Teaching history
1945	*Detroit Free Press*	Corruption in Lansing

Reporting

Year	Winner, Newspaper
1917	Herbert Bayard Swope, *New York World*
1918	Harold A. Littledale, *New York Evening Post*
1919	No award
1920	John J. Leary, Jr., *New York World*
1921	Louis Seibold, *New York World*
1922	Kirke L. Simpson, Associated Press
1923	Alva Johnston, *New York Times*
1924	Magner White, *San Diego Sun*
1925	James W. Mulroyand, Alvin H. Goldstein, *Chicago Daily News*
1926	William Burke Miller, *Louisville Courier-Journal*
1927	John T. Rogers, *St. Louis Post-Dispatch*
1928	No award
1929	Paul Y. Anderson, *St. Louis Post-Dispatch*
1930	Russell D. Owen, *New York Times*
1931	A. B. MacDonald, *Kansas City Star*
1932	W. C. Richards, D. D. Martin, J. S. Pooler, F. D. Webb, and J. N. W. Sloan, *Detroit Free Press*
1933	Francis A. Jameson, Associated Press
1934	Royce Brier, *San Francisco Chronicle*
1935	William H. Taylor, *New York Herald Tribune*
1936	Lauren D. Lyman, *New York Times*
1937	John J. O'Neill, *New York Herald Tribune*
	William L. Laurence, *New York Times*
	Howard W. Blakeslee, Associated Press
	Gobind Behari Lal, Universal Service
	David Dietz, Scripps-Howard Newspaper Alliance
1938	Raymond Sprigle, *Pittsburgh Post-Gazette*
1939	Thomas Lunsford Stokes, Scripps-Howard Newspaper Alliance (articles published in *New York World-Telegram*)
1940	S. Burton Heath, *New York World-Telegram*
1941	Westbrook Pegler, *New York World-Telegram*
1942	Stanton Delaplane, *San Francisco Chronicle*
1943	George Weller, *Chicago Daily News*
1944	Paul Schoenstein and Associates, *New York Journal-American*
1945	Jack S. McDowell, *San Francisco Call-Bulletin*
	William Leonard Laurence, *New York Times*
	Frederick Wollman, *New York World-Telegram*

Editorial Writing

Year	
1917	*Lusitania* editorial article, *New York Tribune*
1918	War editorials and articles, *Louisville Courier Journal*
1919	No award
1920	Harvey E. Newbranch, *Evening World Herald*
1921	No award
1922	Frank M. O'Brien, *New York Herald*
1923	William Allen White, *Emporia (Kans.) Gazette*
1924[1]	Collidge editorial *Boston Herald*
1925	"Plight of the South" editorial, *Charleston (S.C.) News and Courier*
1926	Edward M. Kingsbury, *New York Times*
1927	F. Lauriston Bullard, *Boston Herald*
1928	Grover Cleveland Hall, *Montgomery (Ala.) Advertiser*
1929	Louis Isaac Jaffe, *Norfolk Virginian-Pilot*
1930	No award
1931	Charles S. Ryckman, *Fredmont (Nebr.) Tribune*
1932	No award
1933	Series of editorials. *Kansas City Star*

1934	E. P. Chase, *Atlantic (Iowa) News-Telegraph*
1935	No award
1936	Felix Morley, *Washington Post*
	George B. Parker, Scripps-Howard Newspapers
1937	John W. Owens, *Baltimore Sun*
1938	William Wesley Waymack, *Des Moines Register and Tribune*
1939	Ronald G. Callvert, *Portland Oregonian*
1940	Bart Howard, *St. Louis Post-Dispatch*
1941	Reuben Maury, *New York Daily News*
1942	Geoffrey Parsons, *New York Herald Tribune*
1943	Forrest W. Seymour, *Des Moines Register and Tribune*
1944	Henry J. Haskell, *Kansas City Star*
1945	George W. Potter, *Providence Journal-Bulletin*

Editorial Cartooning

1922	Rollin Kirby, *New York World*
1923	No award
1924	Jay Norwood Darling, *Des Moines Register and Tribune*
1925	Rollin Kirby, *New York World*
1926	Daniel R. Fitzpatrick, *St. Louis Post-Dispatch*
1927	Nelson Harding, *Brooklyn Daily Eagle*
1928	Nelson Harding, *Brooklyn Daily Eagle*
1929	Rollin Kirby, *New York World*
1930	Charles R. Macauley, *Brooklyn Daily Eagle*
1931	Edmund Duffy, *Baltimore Sun*
1932	John T. McCutcheon, *Chicago Tribune*
1933	H. M. Talburt, *Washington Daily News*
1934	Edmund Duffy, *Baltimore Sun*
1935	Ross A. Lewis, *Milwaukee Journal*
1936	No award
1937	C. D. Batchelor, *New York Daily News*
1938	Vaughn Shoemaker, *Chicago Daily News*
1939	Charles G. Werner, *Daily Oklahoman*
1940	Edmund Duffy, *Baltimore Sun*
1941	Jacob Burck, *Chicago Times*
1942	Herbert L. Block ("Herblock"), NEA Service
1943	Jay Norwood Darling, *Des Moines Register and Tribune*
1944	Clifford K. Berryman, *Evening Star* (D.C.)
1945	Sgt. Bill Mauldin, United Feature Syndicate, Inc.

Correspondence

1929	Paul Scott Mowrer, *Chicago Daily News*
1930	Leland Stowe, *New York Herald Tribune*
1931	H. R. Knickerbocker, *Philadelphia Public Ledger* and *New York Evening Post*
1932	Walter Duranty, *New York Times*
	Charles G. Ross, *St. Louis Post-Dispatch*
1933	Edgar Ansel Mowrer, *Chicago Daily News*
1934	Frederick T. Birchall, *New York Times*
1935	Arthur Krock, *New York Times*
1936	Wilfred C. Barber (posthumous), *Chicago Tribune*
1937	Anne O'Hare McCormick, *New York Times*
1938	Arthur Krock, *New York Times*
1939	Louis P. Lochner, Associated Press
1940	Otto D. Tolischus, *New York Times*
1941	Group Award[a]
1942	Carlos P. Romulo, *Philippines Herald*
1943	Hanson W. Baldwin, *New York Times*
1944	Ernest Taylor Pyle, Scripps-Howard Newspaper Alliance
1945	Harold V. (Hal) Boyle, Associated Press

Telegraphic Reporting (National)

1942	Louis Stark, *New York Times*
1943	No award
1944	Dewey L. Fleming, *Baltimore Sun*
1945	James B. Reston, *New York Times*

Telegraphic Reporting (International)

1942	Larence Edmund Allen, Associated Press
1943	Ira Wollert, North American Newspaper Alliance, Inc.
1944	Daniel DeLuce, Associated Press
1945	Mark S. Watson, *Baltimore Sun*

[a] For achievements of American reporters in the war zones.
Source: The 1988 Information Please Almanac, Atlas & Yearbook (Boston, 1988), 699–702.

TABLE 18.18 PULITZER PRIZES IN LETTERS

The Pulitzer Prize for the Novel		The Pulitzer Prize for Drama	
Year	Author/Title	Year	Author/Title
1918	Ernest Poole, *His Family*	1918	Jesse Lynch Williams, *Why Marry*
1919	Booth Tarkington, *The Magnificent Ambersons*	1919	No award
1920	No award	1920	Eugene O'Neill, *Beyond the Horizon*
1921	Edith Wharton, *The Age of Innocence*	1921	Zona Gale, *Miss Lulu Bett*
1922	Booth Tarkington, *Alice Adams*	1922	Eugene O'Neill, *Anna Christie*
1923	Willa Cather, *One of Ours*	1923	Owen Davis, *Icebound*
1924	Margaret Wilson, *The Able McLaughlins*	1924	Hatcher Hughes, *Hell-Bent fer Heaven*
1925	Edna Ferber, *So Big*	1925	Sidney Howard, *They Knew What They Wanted*
1926	Sinclair Lewis, *Arrowsmith*	1926	George Kelly, *Craig's Wife*
1927	Louis Bromfield, *Early Autumn*	1927	Paul Green, *In Abraham's Bosom*
1928	Thornton Wilder, *The Bridge of San Luis Rey*	1928	Eugene O'Neill, *Strange Interlude*
1929	Julia Peterkin, *Scarlet Sister Mary*	1929	Elmer L. Rice, *Street Scene*
1930	Oliver LaFarge, *Laughing Boy*	1930	Marc Connelly, *The Green Pastures*
1931	Margaret Ayer Barnes, *Years of Grace*	1931	Susan Glaspell, *Alison's House*
1932	Pearl S. Buck, *The Good Earth*	1932	George S. Kaufman, Morrie Ryskind, and Ira Gershwin, *Of Thee I Sing*
1933	T. S. Stribling, *The Store*	1933	Maxwell Anderson, *Both Your Houses*
1934	Caroline Miller, *Lamb in His Bosom*	1934	Sidney Kingsley, *Men in White*
1935	Josephine Winslow Johnson, *Now in November*	1935	Zoe Akins, *The Old Maid*
1936	Harold L. Davis, *Honey in the Horn*	1936	Robert E. Sherwood, *Idiot's Delight*
1937	Margaret Mitchell, *Gone with the Wind*	1937	Moss Hart and George S. Kaufman, *You Can't Take It with You*
1938	John Phillips Marquand, *The Late George Apley*	1938	Thornton Wilder, *Our Town*
1939	Marjorie Kinnan Rawlings, *The Yearling*	1939	Robert E. Sherwood, *Abe Lincoln in Illinois*
1940	John Steinbeck, *The Grapes of Wrath*	1940	William Saroyan, *The Time of Your Life*
1941	No award	1941	Robert E. Sherwood, *There Shall Be No Night*
1942	Ellen Glasgow, *In This Our Life*	1942	No award
1943	Upton Sinclair, *Dragon's Teeth*	1943	Thornton Wilder, *The Skin of Our Teeth*
1944	Martin Flavin, *Journey in the Dark*	1944	No award
1945	John Hersey, *A Bell for Adano*	1945	Mary Chase, *Harvey*

Source: *The 1988 Information Please Almanac*, 704–05.

TABLE 18.19 THE PULITZER PRIZE FOR POETRY

Year	Author/Title
1922	Edward Arlington Robinson, *Collected Poems*
1923	Edna St. Vincent Millay, *The Ballad of the Harp-Weaver; A Few Figs from Thistles; Eight Sonnets in American Poetry, 1922, A Miscellany*
1924	Robert Frost, *New Hampshire: A Poem with Notes and Grace Notes*
1925	Edward Arlington Robinson, *The Man Who Died Twice*
1926	Amy Lowell, *What's O'Clock*
1927	Leonora Speyer, *Fiddler's Farewell*
1928	Edward Arlington Robinson, *Tristram*
1929	Stephen Vincent Benét, *John Brown's Body*
1930	Conrad Aiken, *Selected Poems*
1931	Robert Frost, *Collected Poems*
1932	George Dillon, *The Flowering Stone*
1933	Archibald MacLeish, *Conquistador*
1934	Robert Hillyer, *Collected Verse*
1935	Audrey Wurdemann, *Bright Ambush*
1936	Robert P. Tristram Coffin, *Strange Holiness*
1937	Robert Frost, *A Further Range*
1938	Marya Zaturenska, *Cold Morning Sky*
1939	John Gould Fletcher, *Selected Poems*
1940	Mark Van Doren, *Collected Poems*
1941	Leonard Bacon, *Sunderland Capture*
1942	William Rose Benét, *The Dust Which Is God*
1943	Robert Frost, *A Witness Tree*
1944	Stephen Vincent Benét, *Western Star*
1945	Karl Shapiro, *V-Letter and Other Poems*

Source: *The 1988 Information Please Almanac*, 707.
Note: Pulitzer Prizes in poetry were first awarded in 1922.

TABLE 18.20 THE PULITZER PRIZE FOR HISTORY

Year	Author/Title
1917	His Excellency J. J. Jusserand, French ambassador to the U.S., *With Americans of Past and Present Days*
1918	James Ford Rhodes, *A History of the Civil War, 1861–1865*
1919	No award
1920	Justin H. Smith, *The War with Mexico*
1921	William Sowden Sims, with Burton J. Hendrick, *The Victory at Sea*
1922	James Truslow Adams, *The Founding of New England*
1923	Charles Warren, *The Supreme Court in United States History*
1924	Charles Howard McIlwain, *The American Revolution—A Constitutional Interpretation*
1925	Frederic L. Paxson, *A History of the American Frontier*
1926	Edward Channing, *The History of the United States*
1927	Samuel Flagg Bemis, *Pinckney's Treaty*
1928	Vernon Louis Parrington, *Main Currents in American Thought*
1929	Fred Albert Shannon, *The Organization and Administration of the Union Army, 1861–1865*
1930	Claude H. Van Tyne, *The War of Independence*
1931	Bernadotte E. Schmitt, *The Coming of the War: 1914*
1932	John J. Pershing, *My Experiences in the World War*
1933	Frederick J. Turner, *The Significance of Sections in American History*
1934	Herbert Agar, *The People's Choice*
1935	Charles McLean Andrews, *The Colonial Period of American History*
1936	Andrew C. McLaughlin, *The Constitutional History of the United States*
1937	Van Wyck Brooks, *The Flowering of New England*
1938	Paul Herman Buck, *The Road to Reunion, 1856–1900*
1939	Frank Luther Mott, *A History of American Magazines*
1940	Carl Sandburg, *Abraham Lincoln: The War Years*
1941	Marcus Lee Hansen, *The Atlantic Migration, 1607–1860*
1942	Margaret Leech, *Reveille in Washington*
1943	Esther Forbes, *Paul Revere and the World He Lived In*
1944	Merle Curti, *The Growth of American Thought*
1945	Stephen Bonsal, *Unfinished Business*

Source: *The 1988 Information Please Almanac*, 705.

TABLE 18.21 THE PULITZER PRIZE FOR BIOGRAPHY OR AUTOBIOGRAPHY

Year	Author/Title
1917	Laura E. Richards and Maude Howe Elliott, with Florence Howe Hall, *Julia Ward Howe*
1918	William Cabell Bruce, *Benjamin Franklin, Self-Revealed*
1919	Henry Adams, *The Education of Henry Adams*
1920	Albert J. Beveridge, *The Life of John Marshall*
1921	Edward Bok, *The Americanization of Edward Bok*

(continued)

TABLE 18.21   (continued)

Year	Author/Title
1922	Hamlin Garland, *A Daughter of the Middle Border*
1923	Burton J. Hendrick, *The Life and Letters of Walter H. Page*
1924	Michael Idvorsky Pupin, *From Immigrant to Inventor*
1925	M. A. DeWolfe Howe, *Barrett Wendell and His Letter*
1926	Harvey Cushing, *The Life of Sir William Osler*
1927	Emory Holloway, *Whitman*
1928	Charles Edward Russell, *The American Orchestra and Theodore Thomas*
1929	Burton J. Hendrick, *The Training of an American: The Earlier Life and Letters of Walter H. Page*
1930	Marquis James, *The Raven*
1931	Henry James, *Charles W. Eliot*
1932	Henry F. Pringle, *Theodore Roosevelt*
1933	Allan Nevins, *Grover Cleveland*
1934	Tyler Dennett, *John Hay*
1935	Douglas S. Freeman, *R. E. Lee*
1936	Ralph Barton Perry, *The Thought and Character of William James*
1937	Allan Nevins, *Hamilton Fish*
1938	Odell Shepard, *Pedlar's Progress*
	Marquis James, *Andrew Jackson*
1939	Carl Van Doren, *Benjamin Franklin*
1940	Ray Stannard Baker, *Woodrow Wilson, Life and Letters*, vols. 7 & 8
1941	Ola Elizabeth Winslow, *Jonathan Edwards*
1942	Forrest Wilson, *Crusader in Crinoline*
1943	Samuel Eliot Morison, *Admiral of the Ocean Sea*
1944	Carleton Mabee, *The American Leonardo: The Life of Samuel F. B. Morse*
1945	Russell Blaine Nye, *George Bancroft: Brahmin Rebel*

Source: The 1988 Information Please Almanac, 705.

Sports, 1914–1945

Baseball

Although there was increased activity in several areas of professional sports during the period 1914–45, baseball led the way. Baseball was truly a national game and the game that occupied most attention on the sports page of the nation's newspapers. Boys and men and some women and girls played the game over all the United States. It was the sport best organized professionally. Except for some decreases during the worst years of the depression and in the midst of the Second World War, attendance at major-league parks grew. To stimulate attendance even more, the teams turned to playing games at night during the late 1930s and early 1940s. For those who did not attend, interest could be maintained through the developing medium of radio. A game or two even had been televised before the Second World War.

The baseball played during these years was essentially the same game as exists at the end of the twentieth century. There were several modifications in the system of scoring plays, but the only substantive rule change came in 1920 with outlawing of the "spitter" and other methods pitchers used to alter the ball. The ball was enlivened in the 1920s as, thanks mostly to Babe Ruth, teams turned more to hitting home runs. Allowing fans to keep foul balls, rather than throwing them back, kept newer and more lively balls in play at all times. Batters wore soft caps, and "beanball"—a batter struck on the head by a pitched ball—was a dreaded term. Uniforms were baggy, all of them white or gray; spikes were sharp, and cutting ("spiking") an infielder, especially at second base, was common. Not all professional baseball players were white, but they certainly were not black. A few Indians played professional ball, and there were several players from Latin America. But up to the year 1945, no blacks were allowed into the professional major and minor leagues. Paradoxically, however, for some minority groups—such as Italians and Jews—the game served as an agent of assimilation.

People from the past often appear larger than life, and so it was with the baseball players. They were giants and they left giant records. These were days when a batter might hit .400—as with Ty Cobb or Rogers Hornsby—and a pitcher might win thirty games in a season. Not many people accomplished these feats, but a rare individual did one or the other more than once. Some people left truly unique records: Joe DiMaggio hit safely in fifty-six straight games in 1940–41; John Vandermeer pitched two consecutive no-hit games in 1938. The giant of giants of course was Babe Ruth. It was a time of domination by the American League, as manifested by its winning eight out of the first twelve All-Star Games. In the American League it was a time of domination by the New York Yankees—only another fitting expression, it would seem, of New York City's domination of the nation. In the thirty-two-year period from 1914 to 1945, the Yankees won fourteen pennants in the American League and in ten of those years won the World Series. The Yankees of 1927 still stand as the most famous of all baseball teams, and many people

This photo is from downtown Chicago, but all cities had burlesque, striptease, or other establishments of risqué entertainment. These places helped introduce many young men to the world of sexuality. (Library of Congress)

believe it was the best. The team had only one twenty-game–winning pitcher, Waite Hoyt, but with batters such as the Yankees had, who needed pitching? Five players batted more than .300, led by the two hitting stars. Ruth batted .356, drove in 164 runs, and hit a legendary sixty home runs. First baseman Lou Gehrig had, if anything, an even better year, with an average of .373, forty-seven home runs and 175 runs batted in. It was not surprising that the team won 110 games and lost only forty-four.

If the Yankees of 1927 marked a high point in baseball history, one of the darkest moments came in the year 1919 when several members of the Chicago White Sox were accused of "throwing" the World Series to the Cincinnati Reds for money. Even though a jury in 1921 failed to find enough evidence to convict the accused players, Commissioner K. M. Landis went on to ban eight of them for life: L. Williams, E. Cicotte, C. Gandil, H. Felsch, J. Jackson, F. McMullin, S. Risberg, and B. Weaver. The people involved included two twenty-game–winning pitchers (Cicotte won twenty-nine) and virtually the entire starting lineup, the most famous member of which was Shoeless Joe Jackson. Jackson batted .351 in 1919 and .382 the following year before he was banned and ended his career with a lifetime average of .356. The disgrace handed the "Black Sox" of 1919 eclipsed the fact that it was one of the better teams of the modern era.

There was some question about the professional season continuing during the Second World War. The war seemed to come first in every way. President Franklin D. Roosevelt urged that baseball go on, but he suggested that more games be played at night. The season did continue uninterrupted during 1942–45, although with many young men called to military service, quality declined. The use of a

Walter Johnson of the Washington Senators was the most successful pitcher of the period 1914–45. In all baseball's history he had the most shutouts (110). With lifetime earned run average of 2.17, he ranked second in wins (416) only to Cy Young. (National Baseball Library, Cooperstown, New York)

TABLE 18.22   THE MAJOR-LEAGUE TEAMS

Although the history of major-league baseball is marked with change, with teams often changing cities and occasionally names, the years 1914–45 produced remarkable stability. Throughout the period there were two eight-team leagues, with the pennant going to the team in each league with the best record. League playoffs came only in case of a tie. Except for two teams in St. Louis, all major-league squads represented cities north of the Ohio River and east of the Mississippi. The cities that had teams in 1945 were exactly the same as they had been in 1914.

League Standings, 1914							
National League				American League			
Team	Wins	Losses	Games Back	Team	Wins	Losses	Games Back
Boston Bees	94	59		Philadelphia Athletics	99	53	
New York Giants	84	70	10.5	Boston Red Sox	91	62	8.5
St. Louis Cardinals	81	72	13.0	Washington Senators	81	73	19.0
Chicago Cubs	78	76	16.5	Detroit Tigers	80	73	19.5
Brooklyn Dodgers	75	79	19.5	St. Louis Browns	71	82	28.5
Philadelphia Phillies	74	80	20.5	Chicago White Sox	70	84	30.0
Pittsburgh Pirates	69	85	25.5	New York Yankees	70	84	30.0
Cincinnati Reds	60	94	34.5	Cleveland Indians	51	102	48.5
League Standings, 1945							
National League				American League			
Team	Wins	Losses	Games Back	Team	Wins	Losses	Games Back
Chicago Cubs	98	56		Detroit Tigers	88	65	
St. Louis Cardinals	95	59	3	Washington Senators	87	67	1.5
Brooklyn Dodgers	87	67	11	St. Louis Browns	81	70	6.0
Pittsburgh Pirates	82	72	16	New York Yankees	81	71	6.5
New York Giants	78	74	19	Cleveland Indians	73	72	11.0
Boston Braves	67	85	30	Chicago White Sox	71	78	15.0
Cincinnati Reds	61	93	37	Boston Red Sox	71	83	17.5
Philadelphia Phillies	46	108	52	Philadelphia Athletics	52	98	34.5

Source: Joseph L. Reichler, ed., *The Baseball Encyclopedia* (New York, 1985), 246, 248, 373, 375.

TABLE 18.23 ATTENDANCE AT MAJOR-LEAGUE BASEBALL GAMES

| Year | Major-League Baseball Attendance | | |
	American League	National League	World Series
	1,000	1,000	1,000
1945	5,580	5,261	333
1944	4,798	3,975	207
1943	3,697	3,769	277
1942	4,200	4,353	277
1941	4,912	4,778	236
1940	5,434	4,390	282
1939	4,271	4,707	184
1938	4,446	4,561	201
1937	4,736	4,204	238
1936	4,179	3,904	303
1935	3,688	3,657	287
1934	3,764	3,200	282
1933	2,926	3,163	163
1932	3,133	3,841	192
1931	3,883	4,584	232
1930	4,686	5,447	213
1929	4,662	4,926	190
1928	4,221	4,881	199
1927	4,613	5,310	202
1926	4,913	4,920	328
1925	5,187	4,354	283
1924	5,255	4,341	284
1923	4,603	4,070	301
1922	4,874	3,942	186
1921	4,620	3,987	270
1920	5,084	4,037	174
1919	3,654	2,878	237
1918	1,708	1,372	186
1917	2,859	2,361	129
1916	3,452	3,052	163
1915	2,435	2,430	143
1914	2,748	1,707	111

Source: Wattenberg, *Statistical History,* 399–400.

Baseball Champions, 1914–1945

TABLE 18.24 NATIONAL LEAGUE PENNANT WINNERS

Year	Club	Manager	Won	Lost	Pct.
1914[a]	Boston	George T. Stallings	94	59	.614
1915	Philadelphia	Patrick J. Moran	90	62	.592
1916	Brooklyn	Wilbert Robinson	94	60	.610
1917	New York	John J. McGraw	98	56	.636
1918	Chicago	Fred L. Mitchell	84	45	.651
1919[a]	Cincinnati	Patrick J. Moran	96	44	.686
1920	Brooklyn	Wilbert Robinson	93	61	.604
1921[a]	New York	John J. McGraw	94	59	.614
1922[a]	New York	John J. McGraw	93	61	.604
1923	New York	John J. McGraw	95	58	.621
1924	New York	John J. McGraw	93	60	.608
1925[a]	Pittsburgh	William B. McKechnie	95	58	.621
1926[a]	St. Louis	Rogers Hornsby	89	65	.578
1927	Pittsburgh	Donie Bush	90	60	.610
1928	St. Louis	William B. McKechnie	95	59	.617

Year	Club	Manager	Won	Lost	Pct.
1929	Chicago	Joseph V. McCarthy	98	54	.647
1930	St. Louis	Gabby Street	92	62	.595
1931[a]	St. Louis	Gabby Street	101	53	.656
1932	Chicago	Charles J. Grimm	90	64	.584
1933[a]	New York	William H. Terry	91	61	.599
1934[a]	St. Louis	Frank F. Frisch	95	58	.621
1935	Chicago	Charles J. Grimm	100	54	.649
1936	New York	William H. Terry	92	62	.597
1937	New York	William H. Terry	95	57	.625
1938	Chicago	Gabby Hartnett	89	63	.586
1939	Cincinnati	William B. McKechnie	97	57	.630
1940[a]	Cincinnati	William B. McKechnie	100	53	.654
1941	Brooklyn	Leo E. Durocher	100	54	.649
1942[a]	St. Louis	William H. Southworth	106	48	.688
1943	St. Louis	William H. Southworth	105	49	.682
1944[a]	St. Louis	William H. Southworth	105	49	.682
1945	Chicago	Charles J. Grimm	98	56	.636

[a]World Series winner.
Source: Dan Golenpaul, ed., *The New Information Please Almanac, Atlas and Yearbook, 1967* (New York, 1966), 835.

TABLE 18.25 AMERICAN LEAGUE PENNANT WINNERS

Year	Club	Manager	Won	Lost	Pct.
1914	Philadelphia	Connie Mack	99	53	.651
1915[a]	Boston	William F. Carrigan	101	50	.669
1916[a]	Boston	William F. Carrigan	91	63	.591
1917[a]	Chicago	Clarence H. Rowland	100	54	.649
1918[a]	Boston	Ed Barrow	75	51	.595
1919	Chicago	William Gleason	88	52	.629
1920[a]	Cleveland	Tris E. Speaker	98	56	.636
1921	New York	Miller J. Huggins	98	55	.641
1922	New York	Miller J. Huggins	94	60	.610
1923[a]	New York	Miller J. Huggins	98	54	.645
1924[a]	Washington	Stanley R. Harris	92	62	.597
1925	Washington	Stanley R. Harris	96	55	.636
1926	New York	Miller J. Huggins	91	63	.591
1927[a]	New York	Miller J. Huggins	110	44	.714
1928[a]	New York	Miller J. Huggins	101	53	.656
1929[a]	Philadelphia	Connie Mack	104	46	.693
1930[a]	Philadelphia	Connie Mack	102	52	.662
1931	Philadelphia	Connie Mack	107	45	.704
1932[a]	New York	Joseph V. McCarthy	107	47	.695
1933	Washington	Joseph E. Cronin	99	53	.651
1934	Detroit	Mickey Cochrane	101	53	.646
1935[a]	Detroit	Mickey Cochrane	93	58	.616
1936[a]	New York	Joseph V. McCarthy	102	51	.667
1937[a]	New York	Joseph V. McCarthy	102	52	.662
1938	New York	Joseph V. McCarthy	99	53	.651
1939[a]	New York	Joseph V. McCarthy	106	45	.702
1940	Detroit	Delmar D. Baker	90	64	.584
1941[a]	New York	Joseph V. McCarthy	101	53	.656
1942	New York	Joseph V. McCarthy	103	51	.669
1943[a]	New York	Joseph V. McCarthy	98	56	.635
1944	St. Louis	Luke Sewell	89	65	.578
1945[a]	Detroit	Steve O'Neill	88	65	.575

[a]World Series winner.
Source: New Information Please Almanac, 1967, 834.

TABLE 18.26 MOST VALUABLE PLAYER AWARDS 1914–1945

The Most Valuable Player award began somewhat casually in 1911 with the presentation of an automobile to the player deemed most outstanding in each league. The so-called Chalmers Award lasted until 1914. In 1922 a special committee in the American League began naming a most valuable player. The National League took up the practice in 1924. Starting in 1931, the task was turned over to the Baseball Writers Association of America. The writers have made the selection ever since.

National League		American League	
Chalmers			
1914	Johnny Evers, Boston (2B)	1914	Eddie Collins, Philadelphia (2B)
League			
1922	No Selection	1922	George Sisler, St. Louis (1B)
1923	No Selection	1923	Babe Ruth, New York (OF)
1924	Dazzy Vance, Brooklyn (P)	1924	Walter Johnson, Washington (P)
1925	Rogers Hornsby, St. Louis (2B)	1925	Roger Peckinpaugh, Washington (SS)
1926	Bob O'Farrell, St. Louis (C)	1926	George Burns, Cleveland (1B)
1927	Paul Waner, Pittsburgh (OF)	1927	Lou Gehrig, New York (1B)
1928	Jim Bottomley, St. Louis (1B)	1928	Mickey Cochrane, Philadelphia (C)
1929	Rogers Hornsby, Chicago (2B)	1929	No Selection
Baseball Writers Association of America			
1931	Frankie Frisch, St. Louis (2B)	1931	Lefty Grove, Philadelphia (P)
1932	Chuck Klein, Philadelphia (OF)	1932	Jimmie Foxx, Philadelphia (1B)
1933	Carl Hubbell, New York (P)	1933	Jimmie Foxx, Philadelphia (1B)
1934	Dizzy Dean, St. Louis (P)	1934	Mickey Cohrane, Detroit (C)
1935	Gabby Hartnett, Chicago (C)	1935	Hank Greenberg, Detroit (1B)
1936	Carl Hubbell, New York (P)	1936	Lou Gehrig, New York (1B)
1937	Joe Medwick, St. Louis (OF)	1937	Charlie Gehringer, Detroit (2B)
1938	Ernie Lombardi, Cincinnati (C)	1938	Jimmie Foxx, Boston (1B)
1939	Bucky Walters, Cincinnati (P)	1939	Joe DiMaggio, New York (OF)
1940	Frank McCormick, Cincinnati (1B)	1940	Hank Greenberg, Detroit (1B)
1941	Dolph Camilli, Brooklyn (1B)	1941	Joe DiMaggio, New York (OF)
1942	Mort Cooper, St. Louis (P)	1942	Joe Gordon, New York (2B)
1943	Stan Musial, St. Louis (OF)	1943	Spud Chandler, New York (P)
1944	Marty Marion, St. Louis (SS)	1944	Hal Newhouser, Detroit (P)
1945	Phil Cavarretta, Chicago (1B)	1945	Hal Newhouser, Detroit (P)

Source: Reichler, *The Baseball Encyclopedia,* 29, 33.

one-armed outfielder, Pete Gray, in 1944 by the St. Louis Browns of the American League was only the most exceptional example of a shortage of capable personnel. The American League batting champion in 1945, Snuffy Sternweiss, barely batted .300.

The end to the Second World War left many questions to be answered about the future of professional baseball. The first involved expansion. The major leagues were confined to sixteen cities of the Northeast and Midwest at a time when the population was moving west. California and Texas, at the least, deserved major-league baseball. How would baseball respond to television once it was better developed? Why would people go to games if they could watch them at home? The answer to one question for baseball—and for the United States—was given dramatically before the year 1945 was out. On August 28 general manager Branch Rickey signed Jackie Robinson, a black infielder, to a professional contract in the Brooklyn Dodger organization.

TABLE 18.27 NATIONAL LEAGUE BATTING CHAMPIONS

Year		Avg.
1914	Jake Daubert, Bklyn.	.329
1915	Larry Doyle, N.Y.	.320
1916	Hal Chase, Cin.	.339
1917	Edd Roush, Cin.	.341
1918	Zach Wheat, Bklyn.	.335
1919	Edd Roush, Cin.	.321
1920	Rogers Hornsby, St. L.	.370
1921	Rogers Hornsby, St. L.	.397
1922	Rogers Hornsby, St. L.	.401
1923	Rogers Hornsby, St. L.	.384
1924	Rogers Hornsby, St. L.	.424
1925	Rogers Hornsby, St. L.	.403
1926	Gene Hargrave, Cin.	.353
1927	Paul Waner, Pitts.	.380
1928	Rogers Hornsby, Bost.	.387
1929	Lefty O'Doul, Phila.	.398
1930	Bill Terry, N.Y.	.401
1931	Chick Hafey, St. L.	.349
1932	Lefty O'Doul, Bklyn.	.368
1933	Chuck Klein, Phila.	.368
1934	Paul Waner, Pitts.	.362
1935	Arky Vaughan, Pitts.	.385
1936	Paul Waner, Pitts.	.373
1937	Joe Medwick, St. L.	.374
1938	Ernie Lombardi, Cin.	.342
1939	John Mize, St. L.	.349
1940	Debs Garms, Pitts.	.355
1941	Pete Reiser, Bklyn.	.343
1942	Ernie Lombardi, Bost.	.330
1943	Stan Musial, St. L.	.357
1944	Dixie Walker, Bklyn.	.357
1945	Phil Cavarretta, Chi.	.355

Source: New Information Please Almanac, 1967, 837.

TABLE 18.28 NATIONAL LEAGUE HOME RUN CHAMPIONS

Year		No.
1914	Cliff Cravath, Phila.	19
1915	Cliff Cravath, Phila.	24
1916	Davis Robertson, N.Y., and Fred Williams, Chi.	12
1917	Davis Robertson, N.Y., and Cliff Cravath, Phila.	12
1918	Cliff Cravath, Phila.	8
1919	Cliff Cravath, Phila.	12
1920	Cy Williams, Phila.	15
1921	George Kelly, N.Y.	23
1922	Rogers Hornsby, St. L.	42
1923	Cy Williams, Phila.	41
1924	Jacques Fournier, Bklyn.	27
1925	Rogers Hornsby, St. L.	39
1926	Hack Wilson, Chi.	21
1927	Hack Wilson, Chi., and Cy Williams, Phila.	30
1928	Hack Wilson, Chi., and Jim Bottomley, St. L.	31
1929	Chuck Klein, Phila.	43
1930	Hack Wilson, Chi.	56
1931	Chuck Klein, Phila.	31
1932	Chuck Klein, Phila., and Mel Ott, N.Y.	38
1933	Chuck Klein, Phila.	28
1934	Mel Ott, N.Y., and Rip Collins, St. L.	35
1935	Wally Berger, Bost.	34
1936	Mel Ott, N.Y.	33
1937	Mel Ott, N.Y., and Joe Medwick, St. L.	31
1938	Mel Ott, N.Y.	36
1939	John Mize, St. L.	28
1940	John Mize, St. L.	43
1941	Dolph Camilli, Bklyn.	34
1942	Mel Ott, N.Y.	30
1943	Bill Nicholson, Chi.	29
1944	Bill Nicholson, Chi.	33
1945	Tommy Holmes, Bost.	28

Source: New Information Please Almanac, 1967, 837.

TABLE 18.29 AMERICAN LEAGUE BATTING CHAMPIONS

Year		Avg.
1914	Ty Cobb, Det.	.368
1915	Ty Cobb, Det.	.369
1916	Tris Speaker, Cleve.	.386
1917	Ty Cobb, Det.	.383
1918	Ty Cobb, Det.	.382
1919	Ty Cobb, Det.	.384
1920	George Sisler, St. L.	.407
1921	Harry Heilmann, Det.	.394
1922	George Sisler, St. L.	.420
1923	Harry Heilmann, Det.	.403
1924	Babe Ruth, N.Y.	.378
1925	Harry Heilmann, Det.	.393
1926	Heinie Manush, Det.	.378
1927	Harry Heilmann, Det.	.398
1928	Goose Goslin, Wash.	.379

Year		Avg.
1929	Lew Fonseca, Cleve.	.369
1930	Al Simmons, Phila.	.381
1931	Al Simmons, Phila.	.390
1932	Dale Alexander, Det. Bost.	.367
1933	Jimmy Foxx, Phila.	.356
1934	Lou Gehrig, N.Y.	.363
1935	Buddy Myer, Wash.	.349
1936	Luke Appling, Chi.	.388
1937	Charles Gehringer, Det.	.371
1938	Jimmy Foxx, Bost.	.349
1939	Joe DiMaggio, N.Y.	.381
1940	Joe DiMaggio, N.Y.	.352
1941	Ted Williams, Bost.	.406
1942	Ted Williams, Bost.	.356
1943	Luke Appling, Chi.	.328
1944	Lou Boudreau, Cleve.	.327
1945	George Sternweiss, N.Y.	.309

Source: New Information Please Almanac, 1967, 836.

TABLE 18.30 AMERICAN LEAGUE HOME RUN CHAMPIONS

Year		Avg.
1914	Franklin Baker, Phila., and Sam Crawford, Det.	8
1915	Robert Roth, Chi.-Cleve.	7
1916	Wally Pipp, N.Y.	12
1917	Wally Pipp, N.Y.	9
1918	Babe Ruth, Bost., and Clarence Walker, Phils.	11
1919	Babe Ruth, Bost.	29
1920	Babe Ruth, N.Y.	54
1921	Babe Ruth, N.Y.	59
1922	Ken Williams, St. L.	39
1923	Babe Ruth, N.Y.	41
1924	Babe Ruth, N.Y.	46
1925	Bob Meusel, N.Y.	33
1926	Babe Ruth, N.Y.	47
1927	Babe Ruth, N.Y.	60
1928	Babe Ruth, N.Y.	54
1929	Babe Ruth, N.Y.	46
1930	Babe Ruth, N.Y.	49
1931	Babe Ruth, N.Y., and Lou Gehrig, N.Y.	46
1932	Jimmy Foxx, Phila.	58
1933	Jimmy Foxx, Phila.	48
1934	Lou Gehrig, N.Y.	49
1935	Jimmy Foxx, Phila., and Hank Greenberg, Det.	36
1936	Lou Gehrig, N.Y.	49
1937	Joe DiMaggio, N.Y.	46
1938	Hank Greenberg, Det.	58
1939	Jimmy Foxx, Phila.	35
1940	Hank Greenberg, Det.	41
1941	Ted Williams, Bost.	37
1942	Ted Williams, Bost.	36
1943	Rudy York, Det.	34
1944	Nick Etten, N.Y.	22
1945	Vern Stephens, St. L.	24

Source: New Information Please Almanac, 1967, 836.

TABLE 18.31 MAJOR-LEAGUE ALL-STAR GAMES

Year	Date	Winning League and Manager	Runs	Losing League and Manager	Runs	Winning Pitcher	Losing Pitcher	Site	Paid Attendance
1933	July 6	A.L. (Mack)	4	N.L. (McGraw)	2	Gomez	Hallahan	Chicago A.L.	47,595
1934	July 10	A.L. (Cronin)	9	N.L. (Terry)	7	Harder	Mungo	New York N.L.	48,363
1935	July 8	A.L. (Cochrane)	4	N.L. (Frisch)	1	Gomez	Walker	Cleveland A.L.	69,831
1936	July 7	N.L. (Grimm)	4	A.L. (McCarthy)	3	J. Dean	Grove	Boston N.L.	25,556
1937	July 7	A.L. (McCarthy)	8	N.L. (Terry)	3	Gomez	J. Dean	Washington A.L.	31,391
1938	July 6	N.L. (Terry)	4	A.L. (McCarthy)	1	Vander Meer	Gomez	Cincinnati N.L.	27,067
1939	July 11	A.L. (McCarthy)	3	N.L. (Hartnett)	1	Bridges	Lee	New York A.L.	62,892
1940	July 9	N.L. (McKechnie)	4	A.L. (Cronin)	0	Derringer	Ruffing	St. Lous N.L.	32,373
1941	July 8	A.L. (Baker)	7	N.L. (McKechnie)	5	E. Smith	Passeau	Detroit A.L.	54,674
1942	July 6	A.L. (McCarthy)	3	N.L. (Durocher)	1	Chandler	Cooper	New York N.L.	34,178
1943	July 13[a]	A.L. (McCarthy)	5	N.L. (Southworth)	3	Leonard	Cooper	Philadelphia A.L.	31,938
1944	July 11[a]	N.L. (Southworth)	7	A.L. (McCarthy)	1	Raffensberger	Hughson	Pittsburgh N.L.	29,589

[a] Night game.
Note: No game in 1945.
Source: New Information Please Almanac, 1967, 839.

TABLE 18.32 RECORD OF WORLD SERIES GAMES

[Figures in parentheses indicate number of victories for each club. Pitchers named are winner and loser, respectively.]

1914—Boston N.L. (4) vs. Philadelphia A.L. (0)

Managers—
George T. Stallings, Boston; Connie Mack, Philadelphia.

Oct. 9—Boston (Rudolph)	7	Philadelphia (Bender)	1	At Philadelphia
Oct. 10—Boston (James)	1	Philadelphia (Plank)	1	At Philadelphia
Oct. 12—Boston (James)	5	Philadelphia (Bush)	4	At Boston (12 inn.)
Oct. 13—Boston (Rudolph)	3	Philadelphia (Shawkey)	1	At Boston

1915—Boston A.L. (4) vs. Philadelphia N.L. (1)

Managers—
William Carrigan, Boston; Patrick J. Moran, Philadelphia.

Oct. 8—Philadelphia (Alexander)	3	Boston (Shore)	1	At Philadelphia
Oct. 9—Boston (Foster)	2	Philadelphia (Mayer)	1	At Philadelphia
Oct. 11—Boston (Leonard)	2	Philadelphia (Alexander)	1	At Boston
Oct. 12—Boston (Shore)	2	Philadelphia (Chalmers)	1	At Boston
Oct. 13—Boston (Foster)	5	Philadelphia (Rixey)	4	At Philadelphia

1916—Boston A.L. (4) vs. Brooklyn N.L. (1)

Managers—
William Carrigan, Boston; Wilbert J. Robinson, Brooklyn.

Oct. 7—Boston (Shore)	6	Brooklyn (Marquard)	5	At Boston
Oct. 9—Boston (Ruth)	2	Brooklyn (Smith)	1	At Boston (14 inn.)
Oct. 10—Brooklyn (Coombs)	4	Boston (Mays)	3	At Brooklyn
Oct. 11—Boston (Leonard)	6	Brooklyn (Marquard)	2	At Brooklyn
Oct. 12—Boston (Shore)	4	Brooklyn (Pfeffer)	1	At Boston

1917—Chicago A.L. (4) vs. New York N.L. (2)

Managers—
Clarence H. Rowland, Chicago; John J. McGraw, New York.

Oct. 6—Chicago (Cicotte)	2	New York (Sallee)	1	At Chicago
Oct. 7—Chicago (Faber)	7	New York (Anderson)	2	At Chicago
Oct. 10—New York (Benton)	2	Chicago (Cicotte)	0	At New York
Oct. 11—New York (Schupp)	5	Chicago (Faber)	0	At New York
Oct. 13—Chicago (Faber)	8	New York (Sallee)	5	At Chicago
Oct. 15—Chicago (Faber)	4	New York (Benton)	2	At New York

1918—Boston A.L. (4) vs. Chicago N.L. (2)

Managers—
Ed Barrow, Boston; Fred Mitchell, Chicago.

Sep. 5—Boston (Ruth)	1	Chicago (Vaughn)	0	At Chicago
Sep. 6—Chicago (Tyler)	3	Boston (Bush)	1	At Chicago
Sep. 7—Boston (Mays)	2	Chicago (Vaughn)	1	At Chicago
Sep. 9—Boston (Ruth)	3	Chicago (Douglas)	2	At Boston
Sep. 10—Chicago (Vaughn)	3	Boston (Jones)	0	At Boston
Sep. 11—Boston (Mays)	2	Chicago (Tyler)	1	At Boston

1919—Cincinnati N.L. (5) vs. Chicago A.L. (3)

Managers—
Patrick J. Moran, Cincinnati; William Gleason, Chicago.

Oct. 1—Cincinnati (Ruether)	9	Chicago (Cicotte)	1	At Cincinnati

(continued)

TABLE 18.32 (continued)

1919—Cincinnati N.L. (5) vs. Chicago A.L. (3)

Oct. 2—Cincinnati (Sallee)	4	Chicago (Williams)	2	At Cincinnati
Oct. 3—Chicago (Kerr)	3	Cincinnati (Fisher)	0	At Chicago
Oct. 4—Cincinnati (Ring)	2	Chicago (Cicotte)	0	At Chicago
Oct. 6—Cincinnati (Eller)	5	Chicago (Williams)	0	At Chicago
Oct. 7—Chicago (Kerr)	5	Cincinnati (Ring)	4	At Cincinnati
Oct. 8—Chicago (Cicotte)	4	Cincinnati (Sallee)	1	At Cincinnati
Oct. 9—Cincinnati (Eller)	10	Chicago (Williams)	5	At Chicago (10 inn.)

1920—Cleveland A.L. (5) vs. Brooklyn N.L. (2)

Managers—
Tris Speaker, Cleveland; Wilbert J. Robinson, Brooklyn.

Oct. 5—Cleveland (Coveleskie)	3	Brooklyn (Marquard)	1	At Brooklyn
Oct. 6—Brooklyn (Grimes)	3	Cleveland (Bagby)	0	At Brooklyn
Oct. 7—Brooklyn (Smith)	2	Cleveland (Cladwell)	1	At Brooklyn
Oct. 9—Cleveland (Coveleskie)	5	Brooklyn (Cadore)	1	At Cleveland
Oct. 10—Cleveland (Bagby)	8	Brooklyn (Grimes)	1	At Cleveland
Oct. 11—Cleveland (Mails)	1	Brooklyn (Smith)	0	At Cleveland
Oct. 12—Cleveland (Coveleskie)	3	Brooklyn (Grimes)	0	At Cleveland

1921—New York N.L. (5) vs. New York A.L. (3)

Managers—
John J. McGraw, New York N.L.; Miller J. Huggins,
New York A.L.

Oct. 5—New York A (Mays)	3	New York N (Nehf)	0	At Polo Grounds
Oct. 6—New York A (Hoyt)	3	New York N (Douglas)	0	At Polo Grounds
Oct. 7—New York N (Barnes)	13	New York A (Quinn)	5	At Polo Grounds
Oct. 9—New York N (Douglas)	4	New York A (Mays)	2	At Polo Grounds
Oct. 10—New York A (Hoyt)	3	New York N (Nehf)	1	At Polo Grounds
Oct. 11—New York N (Barnes)	8	New York A (Shawkey)	5	At Polo Grounds
Oct. 12—New York N (Douglas)	2	New York A (Mays)	1	At Polo Grounds
Oct. 13—New York N (Nehf)	1	New York A (Hoyt)	0	At Polo Grounds

1922—New York N.L. (4) vs. New York A.L. (0)

Managers—
John J. McGraw, New York N.L.; Miller J. Huggins,
New York A.L.

Oct. 4—New York N (Ryan)	3	New York A (Bush)	2	At Polo Grounds
Oct. 5—New York N (tie)	3	New York A (tie)	3	At Polo Grounds (10 inn.)
Oct. 6—New York N (Scott)	3	New York A (Hoyt)	0	At Polo Grounds
Oct. 7—New York N (McQuillan)	4	New York A (Mays)	3	At Polo Grounds
Oct. 8—New York N (Nehf)	5	New York A (Bush)	3	At Polo Grounds

1923—New York N.L. (4) vs. New York A.L. (2)

Managers—
Miller J. Huggins, New York A.L.; John J. McGraw,
New York N.L.

Oct. 10—New York N (Ryan)	5	New York A (Bush)	4	At Yankee Stadium
Oct. 11—New York A (Pennock)	4	New York N (McQuillan)	2	At Polo Grounds
Oct. 12—New York N (Nehf)	1	New York A (Jones)	0	At Yankee Stadium
Oct. 13—New York A (Shawkey)	8	New York N (Scott)	4	At Polo Grounds
Oct. 14—New York A (Bush)	8	New York N (Bentley)	1	At Yankee Stadium
Oct. 15—New York A (Pennock)	6	New York N (Nehf)	4	At Polo Grounds

1924—Washington A.L. (4) vs. New York N.L. (3)

Managers—
Stanley R. Harris, Washington; John J. McGraw, New York.

Oct. 4—New York (Nehf)	4	Washington (Johnson)	3	At Washington (12 inn.)
Oct. 5—Washington (Zachary)	4	New York (Bentley)	3	At Washington
Oct. 6—New York (McQuillan)	6	Washington (Marberry)	4	At New York
Oct. 7—Washington (Mogridge)	7	New York (Barnes)	4	At New York
Oct. 8—New York (Bentley)	6	Washington (Johnson)	2	At New York
Oct. 9—Washington (Zachary)	2	New York (Nehf)	1	At Washington
Oct. 10—Washington (Johnson)	4	New York (Bentley)	3	At Washington (12 inn.)

1925—Pittsburgh N.L. (4) vs. Washington A.L. (3)

Managers—
William B. McKechnie, Pittsburgh; Stanley R. Harris,
Washington.

Oct. 7—Washington (Johnson)	4	Pittsburgh (Meadows)	1	At Pittsburgh
Oct. 8—Pittsburgh (Aldridge)	3	Washington (Coveleskie)	2	At Pittsburgh
Oct. 10—Washington (Ferguson)	4	Pittsburgh (Kremer)	3	At Washington
Oct. 11—Washington (Johnson)	4	Pittsburgh (Yde)	0	At Washington
Oct. 12—Pittsburgh (Aldridge)	6	Washington (Coveleskie)	3	At Washington
Oct. 13—Pittsburgh (Kremer)	3	Washington (Ferguson)	2	At Pittsburgh
Oct. 15—Pittsburgh (Kremer)	9	Washington (Johnson)	7	At Pittsburgh

1926—St. Louis N.L. (4) vs. New York A.L. (3)

Managers—
Rogers Hornsby, St. Louis; Miller J. Huggins, New York.

Oct. 2—New York (Pennock)	2	St. Louis (Sherdel)	1	At New York
Oct. 3—St. Louis (Alexander)	6	New York (Shocker)	2	At New York
Oct. 5—St. Louis (Haines)	4	New York (Ruether)	0	At St. Louis
Oct. 6—New York (Hoyt)	10	St. Louis (Reinhart)	5	At St. Louis
Oct. 7—New York (Pennock)	3	St. Louis (Sherdel)	2	At St. Louis (10 inn.)
Oct. 9—St. Louis (Alexander)	10	New York (Shawkey)	2	At New York
Oct. 10—St. Louis (Haines)	3	New York (Hoyt)	2	At New York

1927—New York A.L. (4) vs. Pittsburgh N.L. (0)

Managers—
Miller J. Huggins, New York; Donie Bush, Pittsburgh.

Oct. 5—New York (Hoyt)	5	Pittsburgh (Kremer)	4	At Pittsburgh
Oct. 6—New York (Pipgras)	6	Pittsburgh (Aldridge)	2	At Pittsburgh
Oct. 7—New York (Pennock)	8	Pittsburgh (Meadows)	1	At New York
Oct. 8—New York (Moore)	4	Pittsburgh (Miljus)	3	At New York

1928—New York A.L. (4) vs. St. Louis N.L. (0)

Managers—
Miller J. Huggins, New York; William B. McKechnie, St. Louis.

Oct. 4—New York (Hoyt)	4	St. Louis (Sherdel)	1	At New York
Oct. 5—New York (Pipgras)	9	St. Louis (Alexander)	3	At New York
Oct. 7—New York (Pennock)	8	Pittsburgh (Meadows)	1	At New York
Oct. 9—New York (Hoyt)	7	St. Louis (Sherdel)	3	At St. Louis

1929—Philadelphia A.L. (4) vs. Chicago N.L. (1)

Managers—
Connie Mack, Philadelphia; Joseph V. McCarthy, Chicago.

Oct. 8—Philadelphia (Ehmke)	3	Chicago (Root)	1	At Chicago
Oct. 9—Philadelphia (Earnshaw)	9	Chicago (Malone)	3	At Chicago
Oct. 11—Chicago (Bush)	3	Philadelphia (Earnshaw)	1	At Philadelphia
Oct. 12—Philadelphia (Rommel)	10	Chicago (Blake)	8	At Philadelphia
Oct. 14—Philadelphia (Walberg)	3	Chicago (Malone)	2	At Philadelphia

1930—Philadelphia A.L. (4) vs. St. Louis N.L. (2)

Managers—
Connie Mack, Philadelphia; Gabby Street, St. Louis.

Oct. 1—Philadelphia (Grove)	5	St. Louis (Grimes)	2	At Philadelphia
Oct. 2.—Philadelphia (Earnshaw)	6	St. Louis (Rhem)	1	At Philadelphia
Oct. 4—St. Louis (Hallahan)	5	Philadelphia (Walberg)	0	At St. Louis
Oct. 5—St. Louis (Haines)	3	Philadelphia (Grove)	1	At St. Louis
Oct. 6—Philadelphia (Grove)	2	St. Louis (Grimes)	0	At St. Louis
Oct. 8—Philadelphia (Earnshaw)	8	St. Louis (Hallahan)	1	At Philadelphia

1931—St. Louis N.L. (4) vs. Philadelphia A.L. (3)

Managers—
Gabby Street, St. Louis; Connie Mack, Philadelphia.

Oct. 1—Philadelphia (Grove)	6	St. Louis (Derringer)	2	At St. Louis
Oct. 2—St. Louis (Hallahan)	2	Philadelphia (Earnshaw)	0	At St. Louis
Oct. 5—St. Louis (Grimes)	5	Philadelphia (Grove)	2	At Philadelphia
Oct. 6—Philadelphia (Earnshaw)	3	St. Louis (Johnson)	0	At Philadelphia
Oct. 7—St. Louis (Hallahan)	5	Philadelphia (Hoyt)	1	At Philadelphia
Oct. 9—Philadelphia (Grove)	8	St. Louis (Derringer)	1	At St. Louis

1931—St. Louis N.L. (4) vs. Philadelphia A.L. (3)

Managers—
Gabby Street, St. Louis; Connie Mack, Philadelphia.

Oct. 10—St. Louis (Grimes)	4	Philadelphia (Earnshaw)	2	At St. Louis

1932—New York A.L. (4) vs. Chicago N.L. (0)

Managers—
Joseph V. McCarthy, New York; Charles J. Grimm, Chicago.

Sep. 28—New York (Ruffing)	12	Chicago (Bush)	6	At New York
Sep. 29—New York (Gomez)	5	Chicago (Warneke)	2	At New York
Oct. 1—New York (Pipgras)	7	Chicago (Root)	5	At Chicago
Oct. 2—New York (Moore)	13	Chicago (May)	6	At Chicago

1933—New York N.L. (4) vs. Washington A.L. (1)

Managers—
William H. Terry, New York; Joseph E. Cronin, Washington.

Oct. 3—New York (Hubbell)	4	Washington (Stewart)	2	At New York
Oct. 4—New York (Schumacher)	6	Washington (Crowder)	1	At New York
Oct. 5—Washington (Whitehill)	4	New York (Fitzsimmons)	0	At Washington
Oct. 6—New York (Hubbell)	2	Washington (Weaver)	1	At Washington (11 inn.)
Oct. 7—New York (Luque)	4	Washington (Russell)	3	At Washington (10 inn.)

1934—St. Louis N.L. (4) vs. Detroit A.L. (3)

Managers—
Frank Frisch, St. Louis; Mickey Cochrane, Detroit.

Oct. 3—St. Louis (J. Dean)	8	Detroit (Crowder)	3	At Detroit
Oct. 4—Detroit (Rowe)	3	St. Louis (W. Walker)	2	At Detroit (12 inn.)
Oct. 5—St. Louis (P. Dean)	4	Detroit (Bridges)	1	At St. Louis
Oct. 6—Detroit (Auker)	10	St. Louis (W. Walker)	4	At St. Louis
Oct. 7—Detroit (Bridges)	3	St. Louis (J. Dean)	1	At St. Louis
Oct. 8—St. Louis (P. Dean)	4	Detroit (Rowe)	3	At Detroit
Oct. 9—St. Louis (J. Dean)	11	Detroit (Auker)	0	At Detroit

1935—Detroit A.L. (4) vs. Chicago N.L. (2)

Managers—
Mickey Cochrane, Detroit; Charles J. Grimm, Chicago.

Oct. 2—Chicago (Warneke)	3	Detroit (Rowe)	0	At Detroit
Oct. 3—Detroit (Bridges)	8	Chicago (Root)	3	At Detroit
Oct. 4—Detroit (Rowe)	6	Chicago (French)	5	At Chicago (11 inn.)
Oct. 5—Detroit (Crowder)	2	Chicago (Carleton)	1	At Chicago
Oct. 6—Chicago (Warneke)	3	Detroit (Rowe)	1	At Chicago
Oct. 7—Detroit (Bridges)	4	Chicago (French)	3	At Detroit

(continued)

TABLE 18.32 (continued)

[Figures in parentheses indicate number of victories for each club. Pitchers named are winner and loser, respectively.]

1936—New York A.L. (4) vs. New York N.L. (2)

Managers—
Joseph V. McCarthy, New York A.L.; William H. Terry, New York N.L.

Sep. 30—New York N (Hubbell)	6	New York A (Ruffing)	1	At Polo Grounds
Oct. 2—New York A (Gomez)	18	New York N (Schumacher)	4	At Polo Grounds
Oct. 3—New York A (Hadley)	2	New York N (Fitzsimmons)	1	At Yankee Stadium
Oct. 4—New York A (Pearson)	5	New York N (Hubbell)	2	At Yankee Stadium
Oct. 5—New York N (Schumacher)	5	New York A (Malone)	4	At Yankee Stadium (10 inn.)
Oct. 6—New York A (Gomez)	13	New York N (Fitzsimmons)	5	At Polo Grounds

1937—New York A.L. (4) vs. New York N.L. (1)

Managers—
Joseph V. McCarthy, New York A.L.; William H. Terry, New York N.L.

Oct. 6—New York A (Gomez)	8	New York N (Hubbell)	1	At Yankee Stadium
Oct. 7—New York A (Ruffing)	8	New York N (Melton)	1	At Yankee Stadium
Oct. 8—New York A (Pearson)	5	New York N (Schumacher)	1	At Polo Grounds
Oct. 9—New York N (Hubbell)	7	New York A (Hadley)	3	At Polo Grounds
Oct. 10—New York A (Gomez)	4	New York N (Melton)	2	At Polo Grounds

1938—New York A.L. (4) vs. Chicago N.L. (0)

Managers—
Joseph V. McCarthy, New York; Gabby Hartnett, Chicago.

Oct. 5—New York (Ruffing)	3	Chicago (Lee)	1	At Chicago
Oct. 6—New York (Gomez)	6	Chicago (Dean)	3	At Chicago
Oct. 8—New York (Pearson)	5	Chicago (Bryant)	2	At New York
Oct. 9—New York (Ruffing)	8	Chicago (Lee)	3	At New York

1939—New York A.L. (4) vs. Cincinnati N.L. (0)

Managers—
Joseph V. McCarthy, New York; William B. McKechnie, Cincinnati.

Oct. 4—New York (Ruffing)	2	Cincinnati (Derringer)	1	At New York
Oct. 5—New York (Pearson)	4	Cincinnati (Walters)	0	At New York
Oct. 7—New York (Hadley)	7	Cincinnati (Thompson)	3	At Cincinnati
Oct. 8—New York (Murphy)	7	Cincinnati (Walters)	4	At Cincinnati (10 inn.)

1940—Cincinnati N.L. (4) vs. Detroit A.L. (3)

Managers—
William B. McKechnie, Cincinnati; Del Baker, Detroit.

Oct. 2—Detroit (Newsom)	7	Cincinnati (Derringer)	1	Cincinnati
Oct. 3—Cincinnati (Walters)	5	Detroit (Rowe)	3	At Cincinnati
Oct. 4—Detroit (Bridges)	7	Cincinnati (Turner)	4	At Detroit
Oct. 5—Cincinnati (Derringer)	5	Detroit (Trout)	2	At Detroit
Oct. 6—Detroit (Newsom)	8	Cincinnati (Thompson)	0	At Detroit
Oct. 7—Cincinnati (Walters)	4	Detroit (Rowe)	0	At Cincinnati
Oct. 8—Cincinnati (Derringer)	2	Detroit (Newsom)	1	At Cincinnati

1941—New York A.L. (4) vs. Brooklyn N.L. (1)

Managers—
Joseph V. McCarthy, New York; Leo Durocher, Brooklyn.

Oct. 1—New York (Ruffing)	3	Brooklyn (Davis)	2	At New York
Oct. 2—Brooklyn (Wyatt)	3	New York (Chandler)	2	At New York
Oct. 4—New York (Russo)	2	Brooklyn (Casey)	1	At Brooklyn
Oct. 5—New York (Murphy)	7	Brooklyn (Casey)	4	At Brooklyn
Oct. 6—New York (Bonham)	3	Brooklyn (Wyatt)	1	At Brooklyn

1942—St. Louis N.L. (4) vs. New York A.L. (1)

Managers—
William Southworth, St. Louis; Joseph V. McCarthy, New York.

Sep. 30—New York (Ruffing)	7	St. Louis (M. Cooper)	4	At St. Louis
Oct. 1—St. Louis (Beazley)	4	New York (Bonham)	3	At St. Louis
Oct. 3—St. Louis (White)	2	New York (Chandler)	0	At New York
Oct. 4—St. Louis (Lanier)	9	New York (Donald)	6	At New York
Oct. 5—St. Louis (Beazley)	4	New York (Ruffing)	2	At New York

1943—New York A.L. (4) vs. St. Louis N.L. (1)

Managers—
Joseph V. McCarthy, New York; William Southworth, St. Louis.

Oct. 5—New York (Chandler)	4	St. Louis (Lanier)	2	At New York
Oct. 6—St. Louis (M. Cooper)	4	New York (Bonham)	3	At New York
Oct. 7—New York (Borowy)	6	St. Louis (Brazle)	2	At New York
Oct. 10—New York (Russo)	2	St. Louis (Brecheen)	1	At St. Louis
Oct. 11—New York (Chandler)	2	St. Louis (M. Cooper)	0	At St. Louis

1944—St. Louis N.L. (4) vs. St. Louis A.L. (2)

Managers—
William Southworth, St. Louis N.L.; Luke Sewell, St. Louis A.L.

Oct. 4—St. Louis A (Galehouse)	2	St. Louis N (M. Cooper)	1	At Sportsman's Park
Oct. 5—St. Louis N (Donnelly)	3	St. Louis A (Muncrief)	2	At Sportsman's Pk. (11 inn.)
Oct. 6—St. Louis A (Kramer)	6	St. Louis N. (Wilks)	2	At Sportsman's Park
Oct. 7—St. Louis N (Brecheen)	5	St. Louis A (Jakucki)	1	At Sportsman's Park
Oct. 8—St. Louis N (M. Cooper)	2	St. Louis A (Galehouse)	0	At Sportsman's Park
Oct. 9—St. Louis N (Lanier)	3	St. Louis A (Potter)	1	At Sportsman's Park

1945—Detroit A.L. (4) vs. Chicago N.L. (3)					
Managers— Steve O'Neill, Detroit; Charles J. Grimm, Chicago.					
Oct. 3—Chicago (Borowy)	9	Detroit (Newhouser)	0	At Detroit	
Oct. 4—Detroit (Trucks)	4	Chicago (Wyse)	1	At Detroit	
Oct. 5—Chicago (Passeau)	3	Detroit (Overmire)	0	At Detroit	
Oct. 6—Detroit (Trout)	4	Chicago (Prim)	1	At Chicago	
Oct. 7—Detroit (Newhouser)	8	Chicago (Borowy)	4	At Chicago	
Oct. 8—Chicago (Borowy)	8	Detroit (Trout)	7	At Chicago (12 inn.)	
Oct. 10—Detroit (Newhouser)	9	Chicago (Borowy)	3	At Chicago	

Sources: Reichler, The Baseball Encyclopedia, 2593–2624; New Information Please Almanac, 1967, 827–831.

Black Professional Baseball

Black people were barred from participating in professional baseball until after the Second World War, and so they formed their own teams. The first teams dated from the nineteenth century; in 1920 came the first effort to form the Negro Leagues, usually patterned after the major leagues. The exercise had a storied existence. Leagues came and went; teams came and went and often departed to barnstorm the country. Contracts were loosely honored, and so players often changed teams or left to play in Latin America. Teams were strapped for cash; they rarely owned their parks and thus had to rent playing facilities. Unfortunately, records were poorly kept. Although clowning often accompanied the games—in those days it was expected of blacks—the Negro Leagues produced some good

TABLE 18.33   STANDINGS OF 1940

Negro National League			
	W	L	Pct.
Homestead Grays	28	13	.683
Baltimore Elite Giants	25	14	.641
Newark Eagles	25	17	.595
New York Cubans	12	19	.387
Philadelphia Stars	16	31	.340
New York Black Yankees	10	22	.313

Negro American League			
First Half			
	W	L	Pct.
Kansas City Monarchs	12	7	.632
Cleveland Bears	10	10	.500
Memphis Red Sox	12	12	.500
Birmingham Black Barons	9	9	.500
Chicago American Giants	9	15	.429
Indianapolis Crawfords	3	5	.375
Second Half			

No final standings were published. The Kansas City Monarchs were declared pennant winners.

Note: No World Series was played.
Sources: Robert Peterson, Only the Ball Was White: A History of Legendary Black Players and All-Black Professional Teams (New York, 1992), numerous pages, especially 275; Jules Tygiel, Baseball's Great Experiment: Jackie Robinson and His Legacy (New York, 1983), 3–28.

baseball. The teams as a whole probably were not as good, not as balanced, as major-league teams, but some of the players matched the best the whites had to offer. When black all-star teams played teams of major-league players, the whites usually lost. The outcome of a league season was never predictable, as the leagues' standings of 1940 indicate. Starting in 1933, the highlight of every season was the East-West All-Star Game, always played in Comiskey Park in Chicago.

TABLE 18.34   PARTICIPANTS IN AND LINE SCORE OF EAST-WEST ALL-STAR GAME OF 1942

East				
	AB	R	H	E
Dan Wilson (N.Y. Black Yankees), lf	4	3	2	0
Sam Bankhead (Homestead Grays), 2b-cf	5	1	2	0
Willie Wells (Newark Eagles), ss	5	0	1	0
Josh Gibson (Homestead Grays), c	3	0	2	0
Bill Wright (Baltimore Elite Giants), rf	5	0	2	0
Jim West (Philadelphia Stars), 1b	4	0	0	0
Pat Patterson (Philadelphia Stars), 3b	3	0	0	2
Tetelo Vargas (N.Y. Cubans), cf	3	0	1	0
Herberto Blanco (N.Y. Cubans), 2b[a]	0	0	0	0
Jonas Gaines (Baltimore Elite Giants), p	1	0	0	0
Vic Harris (Homestead Grays)[b]	1	0	0	0
Lennie pearson (Newark Eagles)[c]	1	1	1	0
Dave Barnhill (N.Y. Cubans), p	0	0	0	0
Barney Brown (Philadelphia Stars), p	0	0	0	0
Leon Day (Newark Eagles), p	1	0	0	0
	36	5	11	2

West				
	AB	R	H	E
Cool Papa Bell (Chicago American Giants), cf	4	0	1	0
Parnell Woods (Cincinnati Buckeyes), 3b	3	1	1	0
Marlin Carter (Memphis Red Sox), 3b	1	0	0	0
Ted Strong (Kansas City Monarchs), rf	3	0	1	0
Willard Brown (Kansas City Monarchs), lf	4	0	1	0
Joe Greene (Kansas City Monarchs), c	4	0	0	0
John O'Neil (Kansas City Monarchs), 1b	4	0	0	1
Tommy Sampson (Birmingham Black Barons), 2b	3	0	0	1
Art Pennington (Chicago American Giants)[d]	1	0	0	0
T. J. Brown (Memphis Red Sox), ss	3	0	0	0
Lloyd Davenport (Birmingham Black Barons)[e]	1	0	0	0
Hilton Smith (Kansas City Monarchs), p	1	0	0	0
Fred Bankhead (Memphis Red Sox)[f]	0	1	0	0
Porter Moss (Memphis Red Sox), p	0	0	0	0
Eugene Bremmer (Cincinnati Buckeyes), p	0	0	0	0
Satchel Paige (Kansas City Monarchs), p	1	0	1	0
Sam Jethroe (Cincinnati Buckeyes)[g]	1	0	0	0
	34	2	5	2

Game Summary

East   001   010   102—5
West   001   001   000—2
RBI—Wright (2), Bankhead (2), Gibson, Greene. 2B—Wilson, Bankhead, W. Brown, Pearson. 3B—Woods. SH—Wells. SB—Patterson, Wilson (2), Wells, Vargas. LOB—East, 8; West, 6. DP—Sampson, T. Brown, and O'Neil (2). SO—by H. Smith, 2; Moss, 1; Barnhill, 4; Bremmer, 1; Paige, 2; Day, 5. BB—off Moss, 2; Barnhill, 1; Paige, 1. Hits—off Smith, 4 in 3 innings; Moss, 2 in 2; Bremmer, 0 in 1; Paige, 5 in 3; Gaines, 1 in 3; Barnhill, 2 in 3; B. Brown, 2 in ²/₃; Day, 0 in 2¹/₃.
     Winning pitcher—Day; loser–Paige.
     Attendance—48,400.

[a] Ran for Vargas in 8th.
[b] Batted for Gaines in 4th.
[c] Batted for Barnhill in 7th.
[d] Batted for Sampson in 9th.
[e] Batted for T. Brown in 9th.
[f] Ran for Smith in 3rd.
[g] Batted for Moss in 5th.
Source: Peterson, Only the Ball Was White, 298–299.

The period between the world wars was a nostalgic era for college football. Football was the popular sport of the colleges. It was a time of legends in the same way that Babe Ruth was a legend of baseball, of names that in retrospect appear larger than they truly were—the age of Red Grange, Knute Rockne, Notre Dame's Four Horsemen of the 1920s, and Tom Harmon of Michigan in the 1940s. It was the time of the development of the forward pass and the T formation, the time of stadiums, beginning with the Yale Bowl, that would accommodate upwards of 100,000 people. The national championship then, as now, was mythical, based on various awards and polls. Until 1923 the Citizens Savings–Helms Athletic Foundation offered an award; from 1924 through 1930 there was a Rissman Trophy; the Knute Rockne Trophy was awarded by the Associated Press during 1931–40, and after that year came the various polls, notably by the Associated Press and the United Press.

TABLE 18.35   MYTHICAL MAJOR COLLEGE CHAMPIONS

Year	Team (Coach)	Record
1914	Army (Charles D. Daly)	9-0-0
1915	Cornell (Albert H. Sharpe)	9-0-0
1916	Pittsburgh (Glenn S. Warner)	8-0-0
1917	Georgia Tech (John W. Heisman)	9-0-0
1918	Pittsburgh (Glenn S. Warner)	4-1-0
1919	Harvard (Robert T. Fisher)	9-0-1
1920	California (Andrew L. Smith)	9-0-0
1921	Cornell (Gilmour Dobie)	8-0-0
1922	Cornell (Gilmour Dobie)	8-0-0
1923	Illinois (Robert C. Zuppke)	8-0-0
1924	Notre Dame (Knute Rockne)	9-0-0
1925	Alabama (Wallace Wade)	10-0-0
	Dartmouth (Jess Hawley)	8-0-0
1926	Alabama (Wallace Wade)	9-0-1
	Dartmouth (Glenn S. Warner)	10-0-1
1927	Illinois (Robert C. Zuppke)	7-0-1
1928	Georgia Tech (William A. Alexander)	10-0-0
1929	Notre Dame (Knute Rockne)	9-0-0
1930	Notre Dame (Knute Rockne)	10-0-0
1931	So. California (Howard H. Jones)	10-1-0
1932	So. California (Howard H. Jones)	10-0-0
1933	Michigan (Harry G. Kipke)	7-0-1
1934	Minnesota (Bernard W. Bierman)	8-0-0
	Alabama (Frank Thomas)	10-0-0
1935	Minnesota (Bernard W. Bierman)	8-0-0
	Southern Methodist (Madison Bell)	12-1-0
1936	Minnesota (Bernard W. Bierman)	7-1-0
1937	Pittsburgh (John B. Sutherland)	9-0-1
1938	Texas Christian (Dutch Meyer)	11-0-0
	Tennessee (Robert R. Newland)	11-0-0
1939	Texas A&M (Homer H. Norton)	11-0-0
1940	Minnesota (Bernard W. Bierman)	8-0-0
1941	Minnesota (Bernard W. Bierman)	8-0-0
	Georgia (Wally Butts)	11-1-0
1942	Wisconsin (Harry Stuldreher)	8-1-1
	Ohio State (Paul E. Brown)	9-1-0
1943	Notre Dame (Frank Leahy)	9-1-0
1944	Army (Earl "Red" Blaik)	9-0-0
1945	Army (Earl "Red" Blaik)	9-0-0

Source: Ralph Hickok, *New Encyclopedia of Sports* (New York, 1977), 214.

Perhaps the most famous football player of the 1920s, Red Grange of the University of Illinois helped make college football nationally popular. (Courtesy of Division of Intercollegiate Athletics, University of Illinois)

TABLE 18.36   HEISMAN TROPHY WINNERS

(Outstanding College Player of the Year)

Year	Player, Team, Position
1935	Jay Berwanger, Chicago, halfback
1936	Larry Kelley, Yale, end
1937	Clint Frank, Yale, halfback
1938	Davey O'Brien, TCU, quarterback
1939	Nile Kinnick, Iowa, halfback
1940	Tom Harmon, Michigan, halfback
1941	Bruce Smith, Minnesota, halfback
1942	Frank Sinkwich, Georgia, halfback
1943	Angelo Bertelli, Notre Dame, quarterback
1944	Les Horvath, Ohio State, quarterback
1945	Felix "Doc" Blanchard, Army, fullback

Source: Hickok, *New Encyclopedia of Sports*, 214.

TABLE 18.37   COLLEGE COACH OF THE YEAR

(American Football Coaches Assn.)

Year	Coach, Team
1935	Lynn O. Waldorf, Northwestern
1936	Richard Harlow, Harvard
1937	E. E. "Hooks" Mylin, Lafayette
1938	William F. Kern, Carnegie Tech
1939	Dr. Edward N. Anderson, Iowa
1940	Clark Shaughnessy, Stanford
1941	Frank Leahy, Notre Dame
1942	William Alexander, Georgia Tech
1943	Amos Alonzo Stagg, Pacific
1944	Carroll Widdoes, Ohio State
1945	Alvin "Bo" McMillin, Indiana

Source: Hickok, *New Encyclopedia of Sports*, 218.

TABLE 18.38 RECORD OF ANNUAL MAJOR BOWL FOOTBALL GAMES

Rose Bowl (At Pasadena, Calif.)

1916	Washington State 14, Brown 0
1917	Oregon 14, Pennsylvania 0
1918	Mare Island Marines 19, Camp Lewis 7
1919	Great Lakes 17, Mare Island Marines 0
1920	Harvard 7, Oregon 6
1921	California 28, Ohio State 0
1922	Washington and Jefferson 0, California 0
1923	So. California 14, Penn State 3
1924	Navy 14, Washington 14
1925	Notre Dame 27, Stanford 10
1926	Alabama 20, Washington 19
1927	Alabama 7, Stanford 7
1928	Stanford 7, Pittsburgh 6
1929	Georgia Tech 8, California 7
1930	So. California 47, Pittsburgh 14
1931	Alabama 24, Washington State 0
1932	So. California 21, Tulane 12
1933	So. California 35, Pittsburgh 0
1934	Columbia 7, Stanford 0
1935	Alabama 29, Stanford 13
1936	Stanford 7, S.M.U. 0
1937	Pittsburgh 21, Washington 0
1938	California 13, Alabama 0
1939	So. California 7, Duke 3
1940	So. California 14, Tennessee 0
1941	Stanford 21, Nebraska 13
1942	Oregon State 20, Duke 16
1943	Georgia 9, U.C.L.A. 0
1944	So. California 29, Washington 0
1945	So. California 25, Tennessee 0

Orange Bowl (At Miami)

1933	Miami 7, Manhattan 0
1934	Duquesne 33, Miami 7
1935	Bucknell 26, Miami 0
1936	Catholic 20, Mississippi 19
1937	Duquesne 13, Mississippi State 12
1938	Alabama Poly. 6, Michigan State 0
1939	Tennessee 17, Oklahoma 0
1940	Georgia Tech 21, Missouri 7
1941	Mississippi State 14, Georgetown 7
1942	Georgia 40, Texas Christian 26
1943	Alabama 37, Boston College 21
1944	Louisiana State 19, Texas A&M 14
1945	Tulsa 26, Georgia Tech 12

Sugar Bowl (At New Orleans)

1935	Tulane 20, Temple 14
1936	Texas Christian 3, Louisiana State 2
1937	Santa Clara 21, Louisiana State 14
1938	Santa Clara 6, Louisiana State 0
1939	Texas Christian 15, Carnegia Tech 7
1940	Texas A&M 14, Tulane 13
1941	Boston College 19, Tennessee 13
1942	Fordham 2, Missouri 0
1943	Tennessee 14, Tulsa 7
1944	Georgia Tech 20, Tulsa 18
1945	Duke 29, Alabama 26

Cotton Bowl (At Dallas)

1937	Texas Christian 16, Marquette 6
1938	Rice 28, Colorado 14
1939	St. Mary's (Calif.) 20, Texas Tech. 13
1940	Clemson 6, Boston College 3
1941	Texas A&M 13, Fordham 12
1942	Alabama 29, Texas A&M 21
1932	Texas 14, Georgia Tech 7
1944	Randolph Field 7, Texas 7
1945	Oklahoma A&M 34, Texas Christian 0

Source: Hickok, New Encyclopedia of Sports, 216–217.

TABLE 18.39 TWO TOP TEAMS OF 1920

California was recognized as the national champion in 1920. The first team from the Far West to be so honored, California stunned Ohio State in the Rose Bowl. Notre Dame was second. The Irish completed a second consecutive undefeated season under Knute Rockne. Notre Dame was led by its somewhat roguish backfield star, George Gipp, who would die of strep infection before the year had ended.

California (9-0-0)			Notre Dame (9-0-0)		
Calif. Score	Opponent	Opponent Score	N.D. Score	Opponent	Opponent Score
21	Olympic Club	0	39	Kalamazoo	0
88	Mare Island Marines	0	42	Western Michigan	0
127	St. Mary's	0	16	Nebraska	7
79	Nevada	7	28	Valparaiso	3
63	Utah	0	27	Army	17
17	Oregon State	7	28	Purdue	0
49	Washington State	0	13	Indiana	10
38	Stanford	0	33	Northwestern	7
28	Ohio State (Rose Bowl)	0	25	Michigan State	0
510		14	251		44

Source: Tom Perrin, Football: A College History (Jefferson, N.C., 1987), 102.

This backfield of the early 1920s helped promote the legend of Notre Dame, under coach Knute Rockne, as a college football power. (Courtesy the University of Notre Dame)

Ill-fated (he died of strep infection in 1920) football star of the University of Notre Dame, George Gipp would undergo a posthumous rebirth of fame after Ronald Reagan played "the Gipper" in a movie. (Courtesy the University of Notre Dame)

Professional Football
TABLE 18.40   LEAGUE CHAMPIONSHIPS

National Football League		
Year	Team (Coach)	Record
1919	Canton Bulldogs (Jim Thorpe)	. . .
1920	Akron Pros (Elgie Tobin)	. . .
1921	Chicago Staleys (George Halas)	10-1-1
1922	Canton Bulldogs (Guy Chamberlin)	10-0-2
1923	Canton Bulldogs (Guy Chamberlin)	11-0-1
1924	Cleveland Indians (Guy Chamberlin)	7-1-1
1925	Chicago Cardinals (Norman Barry)	11-2-1
1926	Frankford Yellowjackets (Guy Chamberlin)	14-1-1
1927	New York Giants (Earl Potteiger)	11-1-1
1928	Providence Steamrollers (Jim Conzelman)	8-1-2
1929	Green Bay Packers (Curly Lambeau)	12-0-1
1930	Green Bay Packers (Curly Lambeau)	10-3-1
1931	Green Bay Packers (Curly Lambeau)	12-2-0
1932	Chicago Bears (Ralph Jones)	7-1-6
1933	East—New York Giants (Steve Owens)	11-3-0
	West—Chicago Bears (George Halas)	10-2-1
	Championship—Chicago 23, New York 21	
1934	East—New York Giants (Steve Owen)	8-5-0
	West—Chicago Bears (George Halas)	10-2-1
	Championship—New York 30, Chicago 13	
1935	East-New York Giants (Steve Owen)	9-3-0
	West—Detroit Lions ("Potsy" Clark)	7-3-2
	Championship—Detroit 26, New York 7	
1936	East—Boston Redskins (Ray Flaherty)	7-5-0
	West—Green Bay Packers (Curly Lambeau)	10-1-1
	Championship—Green Bay 21, Boston 6	

1937	East—Washington Redskins (Ray Flaherty)	8-3-0
	West—Chicago Bears (George Halas)	9-1-1
	Championship—Washington 28, Chicago 21	
1938	East—New York Giants (Steve Owen)	8-2-1
	West—Green Bay Packers (Curly Lambeau)	
	Championship—New York 23, Green Bay 17	
1939	East—New York Giants (Steve Owen)	9-1-1
	West—Green Bay Packers (Curly Lambeau)	9-2-0
	Championship—Green Bay 27, New York 0	
1940	East—Washington Redskins (Ray Flaherty)	9-2-0
	West—Chicago Bears (George Halas)	8-3-0
	Championship—Chicago 73, Washington 0	
1941	East—New York Giants (Steve Owen)	8-3-0
	West—Chicago Bears (George Halas)	8-3-0[a]
	Championship—Chicago 37, New York 9	
1942	East—Washington Redskins (Ray Flaherty)	10-1-0
	West—Chicago Bears (George Halas)	11-0-0
	Championship—Washington 14, Chicago 6	
1943	East—Washington Redskins (Dutch Bergman)	6-3-1[b]
	West—Chicago Bears (Luke Johnsos, Hunk Anderson)	10-1-0
	Championship—Chicago 41, Washington 21	
1944	East—New York Giants (Steve Owen)	8-1-1
	West—Green Bay Packers (Curly Lambeau)	8-2-0
	Championship—Green Bay 14, New York 7	
1945	East—Washington Redskins (Dudley DeGroot)	8-2-0
	West—Cleveland Rams (Adam Walsh)	9-1-0
	Championship—Cleveland 15, Washington 14	

[a]Beat Green Bay Packers, 33–14, in division playoff.
[b]Beat New York Giants, 28–0, in division playoff.
Source: Hickok, *New Encyclopedia of Sports,* 207.

TABLE 18.41   PASSING AND RUSHING LEADERS

Passing					
Year	Leader	Att.	Com.	Yd.	TD
1932	Arnie Herber, Green Bay	101	37	639	9
1933	Harry Newman, New York Giants	132	53	963	8
1934	Arnie Herber, Green Bay	115	42	799	8
1935	Ed Danowski, New York Giants	113	57	795	9
1936	Arnie Herber, Green Bay	173	77	1,239	9
1937	Sammy Baugh, Washington	171	81	1,127	7
1938	Ed Danowski, New York Giants	129	70	848	8
1939	Parker Hall, Cleveland Rams	208	106	1,227	9
1940	Sammy Baugh, Washington	177	111	1,367	12
1941	Cecil Isbell, Green Bay	207	117	1,479	15
1942	Cecil Isbell, Green Bay	268	146	2,021	24
1943	Sammy Baugh, Washington	239	133	1,754	23
1944	Frank Filchock, Washington	147	84	1,139	13
1945	Sammy Baugh, Washington	182	128	1,669	11

Rushing				
Year	Leader	Att.	Yd.	Av.
1932	Bob Campiglio, Stapleton	104	504	4.8
1933	Cliff Battles, Boston	146	737	5.0
1934	Beattie Feathers, Chicago Bears	101	1,004	9.9
1935	Doug Russell, Chicago Cardinals	140	499	3.6
1936	Alphonse Leemans, New York Giants	206	880	4.0
1937	Cliff Battles, Washington	216	874	4.0
1938	Byron White, Pittsburgh	152	567	3.7
1939	Bill Osmanski, Chicago Bears	121	699	5.8
1940	Byron White, Detroit	146	514	3.5
1941	Clarence Manders, Brooklyn	111	586	4.4
1942	Bill Dudley, Pittsburgh	164	696	4.3
1943	Bill Paschal, New York Giants	147	572	3.9
1944	Bill Paschal, New York Giants	196	737	3.8
1945	Steve Van Buren, Philadelphia	143	832	5.8

Source: Hickok, *New Encyclopedia of Sports,* 209–210.

Basketball

Basketball dates from 1891; by the time of the First World War the game was played nationally. High schools increasingly turned to basketball as a way of enlivening the long school year. Several forces came together in the 1930s to contribute to a burst of popularity for basketball in the nation's colleges. Basketball offered an outlet for a competition between schools that probably already existed. The rivalry between Purdue University, with its star John Wooden, and Indiana University led by Branch McCracken, was an example. A rules change of 1937–38 that eliminated the center jump after every basket speeded up the game, as did increased use of the one-hand shot and the jump shot (as opposed to the traditional two-hand set shot). Schools and towns, especially in the Midwest, constructed huge gymnasiums. Sportswriter Ned Irish in New York promoted college competition in huge Madison Square Garden. Irish and other writers in 1938 organized the first major basketball tournament, called the National Invitational Tournament, played at the Garden, then with six teams. Success of the NIT moved the National Collegiate Athletic Association, the NCAA in 1939 to arrange its own tournament that purportedly would produce a national basketball champion. The first tournament had eight teams, selected by a special committee.

The first successful professional team was the Buffalo Germans. Then came the popular New York Celtics, later renamed the Original Celtics. Perhaps the best professional team of the 1930s was the Renaissance Big Five, a barnstorming all-black team from New York. In the 1930s a localized American Basketball League existed in the East, and a National Basketball League took root in small cities of the Midwest. For the most part, basketball as a professional enterprise had to wait for a future day. With teams in the 1940s increasingly turning to very tall centers, and with the two most publicized tall men—George Mikan of DePaul (6' 9") and Bob Kurland of Oklahoma State (7')—about to leave college, the start of the National Basketball Association, the NBA was not far away.

TABLE 18.42   NATIONAL INVITATIONAL TOURNAMENT (NIT) CHAMPIONS

1938	Temple
1939	Long Island University
1940	Colorado
1941	Long Island University
1942	West Virginia
1943	St. John's
1944	St. John's
1945	De Paul

Source: William G. Mokray, *Ronald Encyclopedia of Basketball* (New York, 1963), 9.

TABLE 18.44   HELMS COLLEGE BASKETBALL PLAYER OF THE YEAR

1924	Charles Black, Kansas
1925	Earl Mueller, Colorado State
1926	John Cobb, North Carolina
1927	Victor Hanson, Syracuse
1928	Victor Holt, Oklahoma
1929	John A. Thompson, Montana State
1930	John Hyatt, Pittsburgh
1931	Bart Carlton, E. Central Oklahoma
1932	John Wooden, Purdue
1933	Forrest Sale, Kentucky
1934	Wesley Bennet, Westminster (Pa.)
1935	Leroy Edwards, Kentucky
1936	John Moir, Notre Dame
1937	Angelo Luisetti, Stanford
1938	Angelo Luisetti, Stanford
1939	Chester Jaworski, Rhode Island
1940	George Glamack, North Carolina
1941	George Glamack, North Carolina
1942	Stan Modzelewski, Rhode Island
1943	George Senesky, St. Joseph (Pa.)
1944	George Mikan, De Paul (Chicago)
1945	George Mikan, De Paul (Chicago)

Source: Hickok. *New Encyclopedia of Sports.* 96.

All-American at Indiana University in the mid-1930s—John Wooden at Purdue was a rival—Branch McCracken helped make college basketball a rising spectator sport. (Courtesy Indiana University)

TABLE 18.43   NCAA BASKETBALL CHAMPIONSHIPS

Year	Champion	Score	Runner-up	Winning Coach	Outstanding Player
1939	Oregon	46–43	Ohio State	Howard Hobson	None
1940	Indiana	60–42	Kansas	Branch McCracken	Harvin Huffman—Indiana
1941	Wisconsin	39–34	Washington St.	Harold Foster	John Kotz—Wisconsin
1942	Stanford	53–38	Dartmouth	Everett Dean	Howard Dallmar—Stanford
1943	Wyoming	46–34	Georgetown	Everett Shelton	Ken Sailors—Wyoming
1944	Utah	42–40	Dartmouth	Vadal Peterson	Arnold Ferrin—Utah
1945	Oklahoma St.	49–45	New York U.	Henry Iba	Bob Kurland—Oklahoma St.

Source: Hickok, *New Encyclopedia of Sports*, 96.

TABLE 18.45 **NATIONAL BASKETBALL LEAGUE CHAMPIONS**

1937–38	Akron Goodyears
1938–39	Akron Firestones
1939–40	Akron Firestones
1940–41	Oshkosh All-Stars
1941–42	Oshkosh All-Stars
1942–43	Ft. Wayne Pistons
1943–44	Ft. Wayne Pistons
1944–45	Ft. Wayne Pistons
1945–46	Rochester Royals

Source: Mokray, *Encyclopedia of Basketball*, Section 8, 30–32.

Boxing

While not popular with all Americans, professional boxing at given moments could rival the best agents of entertainment in attracting national attention. The reasons have to do with the appearance of popular performers in the heavyweight class, such people as Jack Dempsey and Gene Tunney in the 1920s and especially the emergence of Joe Louis in the 1930s. Louis attracted attention because he was a superb athlete; he held the title many years and defended it many times. He was a black man in a sport previously dominated by whites and thus added a sociological dimension to

TABLE 18.46   BOXING CHAMPIONS

Heavyweights		Light Heavyweights	
Year	Name	Year	Name
1908–15	Jack Johnson	1912–16	Jack Dillon
1915–19	Jess Willard	1916–20	Battling Levinsky
1919–26	Jack Dempsey	1920–22	Georges Carpentier
1926–28	Gene Tunney	1922–23	Battling Siki
1928–30	vacant	1923–25	Mike McTigue
1930–32	Max Schmeling	1925–26	Paul Berlenbach
1932–33	Jack Sharkey	1926–27	Jack Delaney
1933–34	Primo Carnera	1927–29	Tommy Loughran
1934–35	Max Baer	1930–34	Maxie Rosenbloom
1935–37	James J. Braddock	1934–35	Bob Olin
1937–49	Joe Louis	1935–39	John Henry Lewis
		1939	Melio Bettina
		1939–41	Billy Conn
		1941	Anton Christoforidis
		1941–48	Gus Lesnevich, Freddie Mills

Middleweights		Featherweights	
Year	Name	Year	Name
1914–17	Al McCoy	1912–23	Johnny Kilbane
1917–20	Mike O'Dowd	1923	Eugene Criqui, Johnny Kilbane
1920–23	Johnny Wilson		
1923–26	Harry Greb	1923–25	Johnny Dundee
1926–31	Tiger Flowers, Mickey Walker	1925–27	Kid Kaplan
		1927–28	Benny Bass, Tony Canzoneri
1931–32	Gorilla Jones		
1932–37	Marcel Thil	1928–29	Andre Routis
1938	Al Hostak,	1929–32	Battling Tattalino

Middleweights		Featherweights	
Year	Name	Year	Name
1939–40	Sonny Krieger	1932–34	Tommy Paul
1941–47	Al Hostak	1933–36	Freddie Miller
	Tony Zale	1936–37	Petey Sarron
		1937–38	Henry Armstrong
		1938–40	Joey Archibald
		1940–41	Harry Jeffra
		1942–48	Willie Pep

Welterweights		Lightweights	
Year	Name	Year	Name
1911–15	vacant	1912–14	Willie Ritchie
1915–19	Ted Lewis	1914–17	Freddie Welsh
1919–22	Jack Britton	1917–25	Benny Leonard
1922–26	Mickey Walker	1925	Jimmy Goodrich, Rocky Kansas
1926	Pete Latzo		
1927–29	Joe Dundee	1926–30	Sammy Mandell
1929	Jackie Fields	1930	Al Singer
1930	Jack Thompson, Tommy Freeman		Tony Canzoneri
		1930–33	Tony Canzoneri
1931	Tommy Freeman, Jack Thompson, Lou Brouillard	1933–35	Barney Ross
		1935–36	Tony Canzoneri
		1936–38	Lou Ambers
1932	Jackie Fields	1938	Henry Armstrong
1933	Young Corbett, Jimmy McLarnin	1939	Lou Ambers
		1940	Lew Jenkins
1934	Barney Ross, Jimmy McLarnin	1941–43	Sammy Angott
		1944	Sammy Angott, J. Zurita
1935–38	Barney Ross		
1938–40	Henry Armstrong	1945–51	Ike Williams
1940–41	Fritzie Zivic		
1941–46	Fred Cochrane		

Bantamweights		Flyweights	
Year	Name	Year	Name
1910–14	Johnny Coulon	1916–23	Jimmy Wilde
1914–17	Kid Williams	1923–25	Pancho Villa
1917–20	Pete Herman	1925	Frankie Genaro
1920–21	Joe Lynch	1925–27	Fidel La Barba
1921	Pete Herman	1927–31	disputed claims by several fighters
1921–22	Johnny Buff	1932–33	Jackie Brown
1922–24	Joe Lynch	1935–38	Benny Lynch
1924	Abe Goldstein	1939	Peter Kane
1924–25	Eddie (Cannonball) Martin	1943–47	Jackie Paterson
1925	Charlie Rosenberg		
1927–28	Bud Taylor		
1929–35	Al Brown		
1929–36	Baltazar Sangchili		
1936	Tony Marino		
1936–37	Sixto Escobar		
1937–38	Harry Jeffra		
1938–40	Sixto Escobar		
1940–42	Lou Salica		
1942–47	Manuel Ortiz		

Source: *New Information Please Almanac*, 1967, 880–882.

boxing. Louis was of immeasurable importance for arousing interest and admiration from black people in the United States. The popularity of boxing also grew with the development of radio. Audiences that listened to the fights of Joe Louis exceeded those of virtually anything that radio had to offer.

TABLE 18.47 HEAVYWEIGHT CHAMPIONSHIP FIGHTS

Year	Date	Fight
1914	Jun. 27	Jack Johnson won from Frank Moran, 20 rounds, Paris.
1915	Apr. 5	Jess Willard knocked out Jack Johnson, 26 rounds, Havana, Cuba.
1916	Mar. 25	Jess Willard and Frank Moran, 10 rounds (no decision), New York City.
1919	Jul. 4	Jack Dempsey knocked out Jess Willard, Toledo, Ohio (Willard failed to answer bell for fourth round.)
1920	Sep. 6	Jack Dempsey knocked out Billy Miske, 3 rounds, Benton Harbor, Mich.
1920	Dec. 14	Jack Dempsey knocked out Bill Brennan, 12 rounds, New York City.
1921	Jul. 2	Jack Dempsey knocked out Georges Carpentier, 4 rounds, Boyle's Thirty Acres, Jersey City, N.J.
1923	Jul. 4	Jack Dempsey won on points from Tom Gibbons, 15 rounds, Shelby, Mont.
1923	Sep. 14	Jack Dempsey knocked out Luis Firpo, 2 rounds, New York City.
1926	Sep. 23	Gene Tunney beat Jack Dempsey, 10 rounds, decision, Philadelphia.
1927	Sep. 22	Gene Tunney beat Jack Dempsey, 10 rounds, decision, Chicago.
1928	Jul. 26	Gene Tunney knocked out Tom Heeney, 11 rounds, Yankee Stadium, New York; soon afterward he announced his retirement.
1930	Jun. 12	Max Schmeling of Germany defeated Jack Sharkey in fourth round when Sharkey fouled Schmeling in a bout that was generally considered to have resulted in the election of a successor to Gene Tunney, New York City.
1931	Jul. 3	Max Schmeling knocked out W. L. Stribling, another contender for the title, in 15 rounds in Cleveland.
1932	Jun. 21	Jack Sharkey defeated Max Schmeling, 15 rounds, decision, New York City.
1933	Jun. 29	Primo Carnera knocked out Jack Sharkey, six rounds, New York City.
1933	Oct. 22	Primo Carnera defeated Paulino Uzcudun, heavyweight challenger, 15 rounds, Rome.
1934	Mar. 1	Primo Carnera defeated Tommy Loughran in 15 rounds, Miami.
1934	Jun. 14	Max Baer knocked out Primo Carnera, 11 rounds, New York City.
1935	Jun. 13	James J. Braddock defeated Max Baer, 15 rounds, New York City (judges' decision).
1937	Jun. 22	Joe Louis knocked out James J. Braddock, 8 rounds, Chicago.
1937	Aug. 30	Joe Louis defeated Tommy Farr, 15 rounds, decision, New York City.
1938	Feb. 23	Joe Louis knocked out Nathan Mann, 3 rounds, New York City.
1938	Apr. 1	Joe Louis Louis knocked out Harry Thomas, 5 rounds, New York City.
1938	Jun. 22	Joe Louis knocked out Max Schmeling, 1 round, New York City.
1939	Jan. 25	Joe Louis knocked out John H. Lewis, 1 round, New York City.
1939	Apr. 17	Joe Louis knocked out Jack Roper, 1 round, Los Angeles.
1939	Jun. 28	Joe Louis knocked out Tony Galento, 4 rounds, New York City.
1939	Sep. 20	Joe Louis knocked out Bob Pastor, 11 rounds, Detroit.
1940	Feb. 9	Joe Louis defeated Arturo Godoy, 15 rounds, decision, New York City.
1940	Mar. 29	Joe Louis knocked out Johnny Paychek, 2 rounds, New York City.
1940	Jun. 20	Joe Louis knocked out Arturo Godoy, 8 rounds, New York City.
1940	Dec. 16	Joe Louis knocked out Al McCoy, 6 rounds, Boston.
1941	Jan. 31	Joe Louis knocked out Red Burman, 5 rounds, New York City.
1941	Feb. 17	Joe Louis knocked out Gus Dorazio, 2 rounds, Philadelphia.
1941	Mar. 21	Joe Louis knocked out Abe Simon, 13 rounds, Detroit.
1941	Apr. 8	Joe Louis knocked out Tony Musto, 9 rounds, St. Louis.
1941	May 23	Joe Louis beat Buddy Baer, 7 rounds, Washington, D.C., on a disqualification.
1941	Jun. 18	Joe Louis knocked out Billy Conn, 13 rounds, New York City.
1941	Sep. 29	Joe Louis knocked out Lou Nova, 6 rounds, New York City.
1942	Jan. 9	Joe Louis knocked out Buddy Baer, 1 round, New York City.
1942	Mar. 27	Joe Louis knocked out Abe Simon, 6 rounds, New York City.

Note: No fights after 1942 because of the Second World War. They were resumed in Jun. 1946 with a rematch between Joe Louis and Billy Conn.
Source: John D. McCallum, *The Encyclopedia of World Boxing Champions since 1882* (Radnor, Pa., 1975), 324.

Tennis

Lawn tennis, which originated in Wales in 1873, spread to the United States a few months later. Order and organization of the sport came with the creation in 1881 of the United States Lawn Tennis Association, a forerunner of the United States Tennis Association (the USTA), which held its first national tournament in that year. While many Americans considered tennis an elitist sport, its popularity continued to grow in the early 20th century—aided, no doubt, by modern means of communication, especially radio, and better means of travel. Even before the Second World War tennis was a leading meeting ground for international competition. By that time four major tennis tournaments had been established: the French Open, the Australian Open, the United States Open, and the British Open, better known as Wimbledon. To win all four in the same year was called the Grand Slam of Tennis. To the year 1945, only one person—Don Budge, an American—had won the Grand Slam of tennis.

Winners of Major Tennis Tournaments

TABLE 18.48 WINNERS OF THE U.S. OPEN

USLTA Champions—Men's Singles			
Year	Winner	Runner-up	Score
1914	R. N. Williams	M. E. McLoughlin	6–3, 8–6, 10–8
1915	Wm. M. Johnson	M. E. McLoughlin	1–6, 6–0, 7–5, 10–8
1916	R. N. Williams	Wm. M. Johnston	4–6, 6–4, 0–6, 6–2, 6–4
1917	R. L. Murray	N. W. Niles	5–7, 8–6, 6–3, 6–3
1918	R. L. Murray	Wm. T. Tilden II	6–3, 6–1, 7–5
1919	Wm. M. Johnston	Wm. T. Tilden II	6–4, 6–4, 6–3
1920	Wm. T. Tilden II	Wm. M. Johnston	6–1, 1–6, 7–5, 5–7, 6–3
1921	Wm. T. Tilden II	Wallace F. Johnson	6–1, 6–3, 6–1
1922	Wm. T. Tilden II	Wm. M. Johnston	4–6, 3–6, 6–2, 6–3, 6–4
1923	Wm. T. Tilden II	Wm. M. Johnston	6–4, 6–1, 6–4
1924	Wm. T. Tilden II	Wm. M. Johnston	6–1, 9–7, 6–2
1925	Wm. T. Tilden II	Wm. M. Johnston	4–6, 11–9, 6–3, 4–6, 6–3
1926	Jean Rene Lacoste	Jean Borotra	6–4, 6–0, 6–4
1927	Jean Rene Lacoste	Wm. T. Tilden II	11–9, 6–3, 11–9
1928	Henri Cochet	Francis T. Hunter	4–6, 6–4, 3–6, 7–5, 6–3

(continued)

TABLE 18.48   (continued)

USLTA Champions—Men's Singles			
Year	Winner	Runner-up	Score
1929	Wm. T. Tilden II	Francis T. Hunter	3–6, 6–3, 4–6, 6–2, 6–4
1930	John H. Doeg	Francis X. Shields	10–8, 1–6, 6–4, 10–14
1931	H. Ellsworth Vines, Jr.	George M. Lott, Jr.	7–9, 6–3, 9–7, 7–5
1932	H. Ellsworth Vines Jr.	Henri Cochet	6–4, 6–4, 6–4
1933	Frederick J. Perry	John H. Crawford	6–3, 11–13, 4–6, 6–0, 6–1
1934	Frederick J. Perry	Wilmer L. Allison	6–4, 6–3, 3–6, 1–6, 8–6
1935	Wilmer L. Allison	Sidney B. Wood	6–2, 6–2, 6–3
1936	Fred Perry	J. Donald Budge	2–6, 6–2, 8–6, 1–6, 10–8
1937	J. Donald Budge	Baron G. von Cramm	6–1, 7–9, 6–1, 3–6, 6–1
1938	J. Donald Budge	C. Gene Mako	6–3, 6–8, 6–2, 6–1
1939	Robert Riggs	S. Welby Van Horn	6–4, 6–2, 6–4
1940	Donald McNeill	Robert L. Riggs	4–6, 6–8, 6–3, 6–3, 7–5
1941	Robert L. Riggs	Francis Kovacs II	5–7, 6–1, 6–3, 6–3
1942	Frederick R. Schroeder, Jr.	Frank Parker	8–6, 7–5, 3–6, 4–6, 6–2
1943	Lt. Joseph R. Hunt	Seaman John A. Kramer	6–3, 6–8, 10–8, 6–0
1944	Sgt. Frank A. Parker	William F. Talbert	6–4, 3–6, 6–3, 6–3
1945	Sgt. Frank A. Parker	William F. Talbert	14–12, 6–1, 6–2

USLTA Champions—Women's Singles			
Year	Winner	Runner-up	Score
1914	Mary K. Browne	Marie Wagner	6–2, 1–6, 6–1
1915	Molla Bjurstedt	H. Wightman	4–6, 6–2, 6–0
1916	Molla Bjurstedt	E. Raymond	6–0, 6–1
1917	Molla Bjurstedt	Marion Vanderhoef	4–6, 6–9, 6–2
1918	Molla Bjurstedt	Eleanor E. Goss	6–4, 6–3
1919	H. Wightman	Marion Zinderstein	6–1, 6–2
1920	M. Mallory	Marion Zinderstein	6–3, 6–1
1921	M. Mallory	Mary K. Browne	4–6, 6–4, 6–2
1922	M. Mallory	Helen Wills	6–3, 6–1
1923	Helen Wills	M. Mallory	6–2, 6–1
1924	Helen Wills	M. Mallory	6–1, 6–2
1925	Helen Wills	Kathleen McKane	3–6, 6–0, 6–2
1926	M. Mallory	Elizabeth Ryan	4–6, 6–4, 9–7
1927	Helen Wills	Betty Nuthall	6–1, 6–4
1928	Helen Wills	Helen H. Jacobs	6–2, 6–1
1929	Helen Wills	M. Watson	6–4, 6–2
1930	Betty Nuthall	L. A. Harper	6–4, 6–1
1931	Helen Wills Moody	E. B. Whittingstall	6–4, 6–1
1932	Helen H. Jacobs	Carolin A. Babcock	6–2, 6–2
1933	Helen H. Jacobs	Helen Wills Moody	8–6, 3–6, 3–0, default
1934	Helen H. Jacobs	Sarah H. Palfrey	6–1, 6–4
1935	Helen H. Jacobs	Sarah P. Pabyan	6–1, 6–4
1936	Alice Marble	Helen H. Jacobs	4–6, 6–3, 6–2

USLTA Champions—Women's Singles			
Year	Winner	Runner-up	Score
1937	Anita Lizana	Jadwiga Jedrzejowska	6–4, 6–2
1938	Alice Marble	Nancy Wynne	6–0, 6–3
1939	Alice Marble	Helen H. Jacobs	6–0, 8–10, 6–4
1940	Alice Marble	Helen H. Jacobs	6–2, 6–3
1941	Sarah Palfrey Cooke	Pauline Betz	6–1, 6–4
1942	Pauline Betz	A. Louise Brough	4–6, 6–1, 6–4
1943	Pauline Betz	A. Louise Brough	6–3, 5–7, 6–3
1944	Pauline Betz	Margaret Osborne	6–3, 8–6
1945	Sarah P. Cooke	Pauline Betz	3–6, 8–6, 6–4

Source: United States Lawn Tennis Association (USLTA), *Official Encyclopedia of Tennis* (New York, 1972), 222, 228.

TABLE 18.49   WINNERS OF THE BRITISH OPEN

All-England Championships—Men's Singles (Wimbledon)		
	Winner	Runner-Up
1914	Norman E. Brookes	Anthony F. Wilding
1915–18	not held	
1919	Gerald L. Patterson	Norman E. Brookes
1920	William T. Tilden II	Gerald L. Patterson
1921	William T. Tilden II	Brian I. C. Norton
1922	Gerald L. Patterson	Randolph Lycett
1923	William M. Johnston	Francis T. Hunter
1924	Jean Borotra	Jean Rene Lacoste
1925	Jean Rene Lacoste	Jean Borotra
1926	Jean Borotra	Howard Kinsey
1927	Henri Cochet	Jean Borotra
1928	Jean Rene Lacoste	Henri Cochet
1929	Henri Cochet	Jean Borotra
1930	William T. Tilden II	Wilmer Allison
1931	Sidney Wood	Frank X. Shields
1932	Ellsworth Vines	Wilfred Austin
1933	Jack Crawford	Ellsworth Vines
1934	Fred C. Perry	Jack Crawford
1935	Fred J. Perry	Gottfried von Cramm
1936	Fred J. Perry	Gottfried von Cramm
1937	Donald Budge	Gottfried von Cramm
1938	Donald Budge	Wilfred Austin
1939	Bobby Riggs	Elwood Cooke
1940–45	not held	

All-England Championships—Women's Singles (Wimbledon)		
	Winner	Runner-Up
1914	Dorothea Douglas Lambert Chambers	E. W. Thomson Larcombe
1915–18	not held	
1919	Suzanne Lenglen	Dorothea Douglas Lambert Chambers
1920	Suzanne Lenglen	Dorothea Douglas Lambert Chambers
1921	Suzanne Lenglen	Elizabeth Ryan
1922	Suzanne Lenglen	Molla Mallory
1923	Suzanne Lenglen	Kitty McKane
1924	Kitty McKane	Helen Wills
1925	Suzanne Lenglen	Joan Fry
1926	Kitty McKane Godfree	Lili Alvarez
1927	Helen Wills	Lili Alvarez
1928	Helen Wills	Lili Alvarez
1929	Helen Wills	Helen Jacobs
1930	Helen Wills Moody	Elizabeth Ryan
1931	Cilly Aussem	Hilda Krahwinkel
1932	Helen Wills Moody	Helen Jacobs
1933	Helen Wills Moody	Dorothy Round
1934	Dorothy Round	Helen Jacobs
1935	Helen Wills Moody	Helen Jacobs

TABLE 18.50   WINNERS OF THE FRENCH OPEN

French Championships—Men's Singles		French Championships—Women's Singles	
1914	Max Décugis	1914	M. Broquedis
1915–19	no competition	1915–19	no competition
1920	A. H. Gobert	1920	Suzanne Lenglen
1921	J. Samazeuith	1921	Suzanne Lenglen
1922	Henri Cochet	1922	Suzanne Lenglen
1923	P. Blanchy	1923	Suzanne Lenglen
1924	Jean Borotra	1924	D. Vlasto
1925	Jean René Lacoste	1925	Suzanne Lenglen
1926	Henri Cochet	1926	Suzanne Lenglen
1927	Jean René Lacoste	1927	K. Bouman
1928	Henri Cochet	1928	Helen Wills
1929	Jean René Lacoste	1929	Helen Wills
1930	Henri Cochet	1930	H. Wills Moody
1931	Jean Borotra	1931	C. Aussem
1932	Henri Cochet	1932	H. Wills Moody
1933	John H. Crawford	1933	M. C. Scriven
1934	G. von Cramm	1934	M. C. Scriven
1935	Fred J. Perry	1935	H. Sperling
1936	G. von Cramm	1936	H. Sperling
1937	H. Henkel	1937	H. Sperling
1938	J. Donald Budge	1938	R. Mathieu
1939	W. Donald McNeill	1939	R. Mathieu
1940	no competition	1940	no competition
1941	Bernard Destreman	1941	A. Weiwers
1942	Bernard Destreman	1942	A. Weiwers
1943	Yvon Petra	1943	N. Lafargue
1944	Yvon Petra	1944	L. Veber
1945	Yvon Petra	1945	L. Dodille Payot

Source: USLTA, *Encyclopedia of Tennis*, 296–297.

TABLE 18.51   WINNERS OF THE AUSTRALIAN OPEN

Australian Championships—Men's Singles		Australian Championships—Women's Singles	
1914	Pat O'Hara Wood	1922	M. Molesworth
1915	F. G. Lowe	1923	M. Molesworth
1916–18	no competition	1924	S. Lance
1919	R. F. Kingscote	1925	D. Akhurst
1920	Pat O'Hara Wood	1926	D. Akhurst
1921	R. G. Gemmell	1927	E. F. Boyd
1922	James Anderson	1928	D. Akhurst
1923	Pat O'Hara Wood	1929	D. Akhurst
1924	James Anderson	1930	D. Akhurst
1925	James Anderson	1931	C. Buttsworth
1926	John Hawkes	1932	C. Buttsworth
1927	Gerald Patterson	1933	J. Hartigan
1928	Jean Borotra	1934	J. Hartigan
1929	J. C. Gregory	1935	D. Round
1930	E. F. Moon	1936	J. Hartigan
1931	Jack Crawford	1937	Nancye Wynne
1932	Jack Crawford	1938	D. M. Bundy
1933	Jack Crawford	1939	V. Westacott
1934	Fred Perry	1940	Nancye Wynne
1935	Jack Crawford	1941–45	no competition
1936	Adrian Quist		
1937	Viv McGrath		
1938	Don Budge		

Australian Championships—Men's Singles		Australian Championships—Women's Singles
1939	John Bromwich	
1940	Adrian Quist	
1941–45	no competition	

Source: USLTA, *Encyclopedia of Tennis*, 290–291.

Golf

Golf came to the United States from Europe in the nineteenth century. Growing popularity in the early twentieth century increased the number of golf professionals. The Professional Golfers' Association of America (PGA) was formed in 1916. Tournament play increased, with contests specially for professionals, others for amateurs, and the "open" tournaments available to both. The greatest accomplishment of the era came at the hands of an amateur, Bobby Jones of Atlanta, who in a single year, 1930, won the British Amateur, the U.S. Amateur, the British Open, and the U.S. Open.

Winners of Major Golf Tournaments
TABLE 18.52   UNITED STATES OPEN

Year	Winner	Venue
1914	Walter Hagen	Midlothian, Ill.
1915	Jerome Travers	Baltusrol, N.J.
1916	Charles Evans	Minikahda, Minn.
1917–18	No championships	
1919	Walter Hagen	Brae Burn, Mass.
1920	Edward Ray	Inverness, Ohio
1921	Jim Barnes	Columbia, Md.
1922	Gene Sarazen	Skokie, Ill.
1923	R. T. Jones	Inwood, N.Y.
1924	Cyril Walker	Oakland Hills, Mich.
1925	Willie MacFarlane	Worcester, Mass.
1926	R. T. Jones	Scioto, Ohio
1927	Tommy Armour	Oakmont, Pa.
1928	Johnny Farrell	Olympia Fields, Ill.
1929	R. T. Jones	Winged Foot, N.Y.
1930	R. T. Jones	Interlachen, Minn.
1931	Billy Burke	Inverness, Ohio
1932	Gene Sarazen	Fresh Meadow, N.Y.
1933	Johnny Goodman	North Shore, Ill.
1934	Olin Dutra	Merion, Pa.
1935	Sam Parks	Oakmont, Pa.
1936	Tony Manero	Baltusrol, N.J.
1937	Ralph Guldahl	Oakland Hills, Mich.
1938	Ralph Guldahl	Cherry Hills, Colo.
1939	Byron Nelson	Philadelphia, Pa.
1940	W. Lawson Little	Canterbury, Ohio
1941	Craig Wood	Colonial, Tex.
1942–45	No championships	

Source: Webster Evans, *Encyclopedia of Golf* (New York, 1974), 276–277.

TABLE 18.53   BRITISH OPEN CHAMPIONSHIPS

Year	Winner	Venue
1914	Harry Vardon	Prestwick
1915–19	No championships	
1920	George Duncan	R. Cinque Ports
1921	Jock Hutchison	St. Andrews
1922	Walter Hagen	R. St. George's
1923	Arthur Havers	Troon
1924	Walter Hagen	R. Liverpool
1925	Jim Barnes	Prestwick
1926	R. T. Jones	R. Lytham
1927	R. T. Jones	St. Andrews
1928	Walter Hagen	R. St. George's
1929	Walter Hagen	Muirfield

(continued)

TABLE 18.53 (continued)

Year	Winner	Venue
1930	R. T. Jones	R. Liverpool
1931	Tommy Armour	Carnoustie
1932	Gene Sarazen	Prince's
1933	Densmore Shute	St. Andrews
1934	Henry Cotton	R. St. George's
1935	Alfred Perry	Muirfield
1936	Alfred Padgham	R. Liverpool
1937	Henry Cotton	Carnoustie
1938	Reg Whitcombe	R. St. George's
1939	Dick Burton	St. Andrews
1940–45	No championships	

Source: Evans, Encyclopedia of Golf, 41–42.

TABLE 18.54 PROFESSIONAL GOLFERS' ASSOCIATION OF AMERICA

Year	Winner	Runner-up	Venue
1916	Jim Barnes	Jock Hutchison	Siwanoy, N.Y.
1917–18	No championships		
1919	Jim Barnes	Fred McLeod	Engineers', N.Y.
1920	Jock Hutchison	Douglas Edgar	Flossmoor, Ill.
1921	Walter Hagen	Jim Barnes	Inwood, N.Y.
1922	Gene Sarazen	Emmet French	Oakmont, Pa.
1923	Gene Sarazen	Walter Hagen	Pelham, N.Y.
1924	Walter Hagen	Jim Barnes	French Lick Springs, Ind.
1925	Walter Hagen	Bill Mehlhorn	Olympia Fields, Ill.
1926	Walter Hagen	Leo Diegel	Salisbury, N.Y.
1927	Walter Hagen	Joe Turnesa	Cedar Crest, Tex.
1928	Leo Diegel	Al Espinosa	Five Farms, Mich.
1929	Leo Diegel	Johnny Farrell	Hillcrest, Calif.
1930	Tommy Armour	Gene Sarazen	Fresh Meadow, N.Y.
1931	Tom Creavy	Densmore Shute	Wannamoisett, R.I.
1932	Olin Dutra	Frank Walsh	Keller, Minn.
1933	Gene Sarazen	Bill Goggin	Blue Mound, Wis.
1934	Paul Runyan	Craig Wood	Park Club, N.Y.
1935	Johnny Revolta	Tommy Armour	Twin Hills, Okla.
1936	Densmore Shute	Jimmy Thompson	Pinehurst, N.C.
1937	Densmore Shute	Harold McSpaden	Pittsburgh, Pa.
1938	Paul Runyan	Sam Snead	Shawnee, Pa.
1939	Henry Picard	Byron Nelson	Pomonok, N.Y.
1940	Byron Nelson	Sam Snead	Hershey, Pa.
1941	Vic Ghezzi	Byron Nelson	Cherry Hills, Colo.
1942	Sam Snead	Jim Turnesa	Seaview, N.J.
1943	No championship		
1944	Bob Hamilton	Byron Nelson	Manito, Wash.
1945	Byron Nelson	Sam Byrd	Moraine, Ohio

Source: Evans, Encyclopedia of Golf, 174.

TABLE 18.55 MASTERS

Year	Winner
1934	Horton Smith
1935	Gene Sarazen
1936	Horton Smith
1937	Byron Nelson
1938	Henry Picard
1939	Ralph Guldahl
1940	Jimmy Demaret
1941	Craig Wood
1942	Byron Nelson
1943–45	No tournament

Source: John W. Wright, The Universal Almanac, 1991 (New York, 1991), 625.

TABLE 18.56 UNITED STATES LADIES' CHAMPIONSHIP

Year	Winner	Runner-up	Venue
1914	H. A. Jackson	Elaine Rosenthal	Nassau, N.Y.
1915	C. H. Vanderbeck	W. A. Gavin	Onwentsia, Ill.
1916	Alexa Stirling	Mildred Caverly	Belmont, Mass.
1917–18	No championships		
1919	Alexa Stirling	W. A. Gavin	Shawnee, Pa.
1920	Alexa Stirling	J. V. Hurd	Mayfield, Ohio
1921	Marion Hollins	Alexa Stirling	Hollywood, N.J.
1922	Glenna Collett	W. A. Gavin	Greenbrier, Va.
1923	Edith Cummings	Alexa Stirling	Westchester, N.Y.
19244	J. V. Hurd	Mary K. Browne	Rhode Island, R.I.
1925	Glenna Collett	Alexa Fraser	St. Louis, Mo.
1926	G. H. Stetson	W. G. Goss	Merion, Pa.
1927	Miriam Horn	Maureen Orcutt	Cherry Valley, N.Y.
1928	Glenna Collett	Virginia Van Wie	Hot Springs, Va.
1929	Glenna Collett	L. Pressler	Oakland Hills, Mich.
1930	Glenna Collett	Virginia Van Wie	Los Angeles, Calif.
1931	Helen Hicks	Glenna Vare	Buffalo, N.Y.
1932	Virginia Van Wie	Glenna Vare	Salem, Mass.
1933	Virginia Van Wie	Helen Hicks	Exmoor, Ill.
1934	Virginia Van Wie	Dorothy Traung	Whitemarsh, Pa.
1935	Glenna Vare	Patty Berg	Interlachen, Mich.
1936	Pamela Barton	J. D. Crews	Canoe Brook, N.J.
1937	Julius Page	Patty Berg	Memphis, Tenn.
1938	Patty Berg	Julius Page	Westmoreland, Ill.
1939	Betty Jameson	Dorothy Kirby	Wee Burn, Conn.
1940	Betty Jameson	Jane Cochran	Pebble Beach, Calif.
1941	Mrs. Frank Newell	Helen Sigel	Brookline, Mass.
1942–45	No championships		

Source: Evans, Encyclopedia of Golf, 274.

Hockey

Ice hockey, developed in Canada in the 1870s, spread to the United States in the 1890s. Professional hockey started in Michigan and then truly took root in Canada. The National Hockey League, with four Canadian teams, began in 1917. Boston became in 1924 the first U.S. city to join the league. By the year 1945 four of the six teams in the NHL were in the large population centers of the northeastern and northern midwestern United States. But appeal of hockey in the United States was localized—outside those cities most people did not know the rules of the game—and the vast majority of professional players were Canadian.

TABLE 18.57 STANLEY CUP WINNERS (CHAMPIONS OF NATIONAL HOCKEY LEAGUE)

Season	Champions	Manager	Coach
1913–14	Toronto Blue Shirts	Jack Marshall	Scotty Davidson
1914–15	Vancouver Millionaires	Frank Patrick	Frank Patrick
1915–16	Montreal Canadiens	George Kennedy	George Kennedy
1916–17	Seattle Metropolitans	Pete Muldoon	Pete Muldoon
1917–18	Toronto Arenas	Charlie Querrie	Dick Carroll
1918–19	No decision.		
1919–20	Ottawa Senators	Tommy Gorman	Pete Green
1920–21	Ottawa Senators	Tommy Gorman	Pete Green
1921–22	Toronto St. Pats	Charlie Querrie	Eddie Powers
1922–23	Ottawa Senators	Tommy Gorman	Pete Green
1923–24	Montreal Canadiens	Leo Dandurand	Leo Dandurand
1924–25	Victoria Cougars	Lester Patrick	Lester Patrick
1925–26	Montreal Maroons	Eddie Gerard	Eddie Gerard
1926–27	Ottawa Senators	Dave Gill	Dave Gill
1927–28	New York Rangers	Lester Patrick	Lester Patrick
1928–29	Boston Bruins	Art Ross	Cy Denneny
1929–30	Montreal Canadiens	Cecil Hart	Cecil Hart
1930–31	Montreal Canadiens	Cecil Hart	Cecil Hart
1931–32	Toronto Maple Leafs	Conn Smythe	Dick Irvin
1932–33	New York Rangers	Lester Patrick	Lester Patrick

Season	Champions	Manager	Coach
1933–34	Chicago Black Hawks	Tommy Gorman	Tommy Gorman
1934–35	Montreal Maroons	Tommy Gorman	Tommy Gorman
1935–36	Detroit Red Wings	Jack Adams	Jack Adams
1936–37	Detroit Red Wings	Jack Adams	Jack Adams
1937–38	Chicago Black Hawks	Bill Stewart	Bill Stewart
1938–39	Boston Bruins	Art Ross	Art Ross
1939–40	New York Rangers	Lester Patrick	Frank Boucher
1940–41	Boston Bruins	Art Ross	Cooney Weiland
1941–42	Toronto Maple Leafs	Conn Smythe	Hap Day
1942–43	Detroit Red Wings	Jack Adams	Jack Adams
1943–44	Montreal Canadiens	Tommy Gorman	Dick Irvin
1944–45	Toronto Maple Leafs	Conn Smythe	Hap Day
1945–46	Montreal Canadiens	Tommy Gorman	Dick Irvin

Source: Zander Hollander and Hal Bock, *The Complete Encyclopedia of Ice Hockey* (Englewood Cliffs, N.J., 1970), 209–10.

TABLE 18.58   HART MEMORIAL TROPHY

[Awarded annually to the league's Most Valuable Player—based on vote by writers and broadcasters]

1923–24	Frank Nighbor, Ottawa	1936–37	Babe Siebert, Montreal C.
1924–25	Billy Burch, Hamilton	1937–38	Eddie Shore, Boston
1925–26	Nels Stewart, Montreal M.	1938–39	Toe Blake, Montreal C.
1926–27	Herb Gardiner, Montreal C.	1939–40	Ebbie Goodfellow, Detroit
1927–28	Howie Morenz, Montreal C.	1940–41	Bill Cowley, Boston
1928–29	Roy Worters, New York A.	1941–42	Tommy Anderson, New York A.
1929–30	Nels Stewart, Montreal M.		
1930–31	Howie Morenz, Montreal C.	1942–43	Bill Cowley, Boston
1931–32	Howie Morenz, Montreal C.	1943–44	Babe Pratt, Toronto
1932–33	Eddie Shore, Boston	1944–45	Elmer Lach, Montreal C.
1933–34	Aurel Joliat, Montreal C.	1945–46	Max Bentley, Chicago
1934–35	Eddie Shore, Boston		
1935–36	Eddie Shore, Boston		

Source: Hollander and Bock, *Encyclopedia of Ice Hockey*, 311.

Automobile Racing

Automobile racing started almost as soon as there were cars. The first recorded race took place in France in 1894 and in the following year in the United States. With the development of a genuine automobile age in the early 20th century, it was inevitable that popularity of automobile competition would grow correspondingly, and that machines would be built specially for racing. Road-racing continued to dominate in Europe, but the Americans wanted to be able to watch the cars race; besides, several states banned racing on open roads. Thus emerged the concept of the closed-circuit race, and by far the most popular such contest was the Indianapolis 500, which began competition in 1911. Trends in the race at the "old brickyard" in Indianapolis included faster, not necessarily safer, machines, and as foreign participants dropped out, a domination by American drivers and American automobiles.

TABLE 18.59   INDIANAPOLIS "500" WINNERS

(No races, 1917–18, 1942–45)

Year	Winner	Car	Time	Average mph
1911	Ray Harroun	Marmon	6:42:08	74.59
1912	Joe Dawson	National	6:21:06	78.72
1913	Jules Goux	Peugeot	5:35:05	75.93
1914	Rene Thomas	Delage	6:03:45	82.47
1915	Ralph De Palma	Mercedes	5:33:55	89.84
1916	Davis Resta	Peugeot	3:34:17	84.00
1917–18	No competition			

Year	Winner	Car	Time	Average mph
1919	Howard Wilcox	Peugeot	5:40:42.87	88.05
1920	Gaston Chevrolet	Monroe	5:38:32.00	88.62
1921	Tommy Milton	Frontenac	5:34:44.65	89.62
1922	Jimmy Murphy	Murphy Special	5:17:30.79	94.48
1923	Tommy Milton	H.C.S. Special	5:29:50.17	90.95
1924	L. L. Corum and Joe Boyer	Duesenberg Special	5:05:23.51	98.23
1925	Peter De Paolo	Duesenberg Special	4:56:39.46	101.13
1926	Frank Lockhart	Miller Special	4:10:14.95	95.90
1927	George Souders	Duesenberg	5:07:33.08	97.54
1928	Louis Meyer	Miller Special	5:01:33.75	99.48
1929	Ray Keech	Simplex Special	5:07:25.42	97.58
1930	Billy Arnold	Hartz-Miller	4:58:39.72	100.44
1931	Louis Schneider	Bowes Special	5:10:27.93	96.62
1932	Fred Frame	Miller Special	4:48:03.79	104.14
1933	Louis Meyer	Miller Special	4:48:00.75	104.16
1934	Bill Cummings	Miller Special	4:46:05.20	104.86
1935	Kelly Petillo	Gilmore Special	4:42:22.71	106.24
1936	Louis Meyer	Ring Free Special	4:35:03.39	109.06
1937	Wilbur Shaw	Shaw-Gilmore Special	4:24:07.80	113.58
1938	Floyd Roberts	Burd Piston Reg. Special	4:15:58.40	117.20
1939	Wilbur Shaw	Boyle Special	4:20:47.39	115.03
1940	Wilbur Shaw	Boyle Special	4:22:31.17	114.27
1941	Mauri Rose and Floyd Davis	Noc-Out Hose Clamp Special	4:20:36.24	115.11
1942–45	No competition			

Source: Hickok, *New Encyclopedia of Sports*, 23.

Horse Racing

Horse racing began in America in the seventeenth century, and partly because at an early date it became associated with betting, it remained a popular sport over the centuries. Organized horse racing by the early twentieth century had several sides: producing and raising the registered animals, the thoroughbreds, was a science, an art and a special economic enterprise; betting on races produced temporary excitement for many and became a way of life for a few; the prestigious races were major social events. Although horse racing took many forms, the most spectacular and popular was by three-year-old thoroughbreds. The most famous race, the Kentucky Derby, was a yearly national sporting tradition, somewhat on the order of the World Series and Indianapolis 500. The most legendary horse of the years 1914–45, despite the fact that he did not run in the Kentucky Derby, was Man o' War.

TABLE 18.60   KENTUCKY DERBY

[3-yr.-olds—Churchill Downs, Lexington, Kentucky; distance: 1¼ miles.]

Year	Horse	Jockey	Time
1914	Old Rosebud	J. McCabe	2:03⅖
1915	Regret	Joseph Notter	2:05⅖
1916	George Smith	John Loftus	2:04
1917	Omar Khayyam	C. Borel	2:04⅗
1918	Exterminator	William Knapp	2:10⅘
1919	Sir Barton	John Loftus	2:09⅘
1920	Paul Jones	T. Rice	2:09
1921	Behave Yourself	C. Thompson	2:04⅕
1922	Morvich	Albert Johnson	2:04⅗
1923	Zev	Earl Sande	2:05⅖
1924	Black Gold	J. D. Mooney	2:05⅕
1925	Flying Ebony	Earl Sande	2:07⅗

(continued)

TABLE 18.60   (continued)

Year	Horse	Jockey	Time
1926	Bubbling Over	Albert Johnson	2:03⁴/₅
1927	Whiskery	Linus McAtee	2:06
1928	Raleigh Count	Chick Lang	2:10²/₅
1929	Clyde Van Dusen	Linus McAtee	2:10⁴/₅
1930	Gallant Fox	Earl Sande	2:07³/₅
1931	Twenty Grand	Charles Kurtsinger	2:01⁴/₅
1932	Burgoo King	E. James	2:05¹/₅
1933	Brokers Tip	Donald Meade	2:06⁴/₅
1934	Cavalcade	Mack Garner	2:04
1935	Omaha	W. Saunders	2:05
1936	Bold Venture	I. Hanford	2:03³/₅
1937	War Admiral	Charles Kurtsinger	2:03¹/₅
1938	Lawrin	Eddie Arcaro	2:04⁴/₅
1939	Johnstown	Jimmy Stout	2:03²/₅
1940	Gallahadion	C. Bierman	2:05
1941	Whirlaway	Eddie Arcaro	2:01²/₅
1942	Shut Out	W. D. Wright	2:04²/₅
1943	Count Fleet	John Longden	2:04
1944	Pensive	Conn McCreary	2:04¹/₅
1945	Hoop, Jr.	Eddie Arcaro	2:07

Source: Hickok, *New Encyclopedia of Sports*, p. 281–282.

TABLE 18.61   PREAKNESS

[3-yr. olds—Pimlico Racetrack, Baltimore, Maryland; distance: 1³/₁₆ miles (since 1925).]

Year	Horse	Jockey	Time
1914	Holiday	A. Schuttinger	1:53⁴/₅
1915	Rhine Maiden	D. Hoffman	1:58
1916	Damrosch	Linus McAtee	1:54⁴/₅
1917	Kalitan	E. Haynes	1:54³/₅
1918	War Cloud,	John Loftus	1:53³/₅
	Jack Hare Jr.	C. Peak	1:53²/₅
1919	Sir Barton	John Loftus	1:53
1920	Man o' War	Clarence Kummer	1:51³/₅
1921	Broomspun	Frank Coltiletti	1:54¹/₅
1922	Pillory	L. Morris	1:51³/₅
1923	Vigil	B. Marinelli	1:53¹/₅
1924	Nellie Morse	J. Merimee	1:57¹/₅
1925	Coventry	Clarence Kummer	1:59
1926	Display	John Maiben	1:59⁴/₅
1927	Bostonian	A. Abel	2:01³/₅
1928	Victorian	Raymond Workman	2:00¹/₅
1929	Dr. Freeland	L. Schaefer	2:01³/₅
1930	Gallant Fox	Earl Sande	2:00³/₅
1931	Mate	G. Ellis	1:59
1932	Burgoo King	E. James	1:59⁴/₅
1933	Head Play	Charles Kurtsinger	2:02
1934	High Quest	R. Jones	1:58¹/₅
1935	Omaha	W. Sanders	1:58²/₅
1936	Bold Venture	Gold Woolf	1:59
1937	War Admiral	Charles Kurtsinger	1:58²/₅
1938	Dauber	Maurice Peters	1:59⁴/₅
1939	Challedon	G. Seabo	1:59⁴/₅
1940	Bimelech	F. A. Smith	1:58³/₅
1941	Whirlaway	Eddie Arcaro	1:58⁴/₅
1942	Alsab	Basil James	1:57
1943	Count Fleet	John Longden	1:57²/₅
1944	Pensive	Conn McCreary	1:59¹/₅
1945	Polynesian	W. D. Wright	1:58⁴/₅

Source: Hickok, *New Encyclopedia of Sports*, p. 282.

TABLE 18.62   BELMONT STAKES

[3-yr.-olds—Belmont Park, New York; distance: 1¹/₂ miles.]

Year	Horse	Jockey	Time
1914	Luke McLuke	M. Buxton	2:20
1915	The Finn	G. Byrne	2:18²/₅
1916	Friar Rock	E. Haynes	2:22
1917	Hourless	J. Butwell	2:17³/₅
1918	Johren	Frank Robinson	2:20²/₅
1919	Sir Barton	John Loftus	2:17²/₅
1920	Man o' War	Clarence Kummer	2:14¹/₅
1921	Grey Lag	Earl Sande	2:16⁴/₅
1922	Pillory	C. H. Miller	2:18⁴/₅
1923	Zev	Earl Sande	2:19
1924	Mad Play	Earl Sande	2:18⁴/₅
1925	American Flag	Albert Johnson	2:16⁴/₅
1926	Crusader	Albert Johnson	2:32¹/₅
1927	Chance Shot	Earl Sande	2:32²/₅
1928	Vito	Clarence Kummer	2:33¹/₅
1929	Blue Larkspur	Mack Garner	2:32⁴/₅
1930	Gallant Fox	Earl Sande	2:32³/₅
1931	Twenty Grand	Charles Kurtsinger	2:29³/₅
1932	Faireno	T. Malley	2:32⁴/₅
1933	Hurryoff	Mack Garner	2:32³/₅
1934	Peace Chance	W. D. Wright	2:29¹/₅
1935	Omaha	W. Saunders	2:30⁴/₅
1936	Granville	Jimmy Stout	2:30
1937	War Admiral	Charles Kurtsinger	2:28⁴/₅
1938	Pasteurized	Jimmy Stout	2:29²/₅
1939	Johnstown	Jimmy Stout	2:29³/₅
1940	Bimelech	F. A. Smith	2:29³/₅
1941	Whirlaway	Eddie Arcaro	2:31
1942	Shut Out	Eddie Arcaro	2:29¹/₅
1943	Count Fleet	John Longden	2:28¹/₅
1944	Bounding Home	G. L. Smith	2:32¹/₅
1945	Pavot	Eddie Arcaro	2:30¹/₅

Source: Hickok, *New Encyclopedia of Sports*, p. 283.

TABLE 18.63   TRIPLE CROWN WINNERS

[Winners of Kentucky Derby, Preakness, Belmont Stakes]

Horse	Year
Sir Barton	1919
Gallant Fox	1930
Omaha	1935
War Admiral	1937
Whirlaway	1941
Count Fleet	1943

Source: Hickok, *New Encyclopedia of Sports*, p. 281–283.

TABLE 18.64   HORSE OF THE YEAR

1936	Granville
1937	War Admiral
1938	Seabiscuit
1939	Challedon
1940	Challedon
1941	Whirlaway
1942	Whirlaway
1943	Count Fleet
1944	Twilight Tear
1945	Busher

Source: Hickok, *New Encyclopedia of Sports*, p. 284.

National Parks, 1914–45

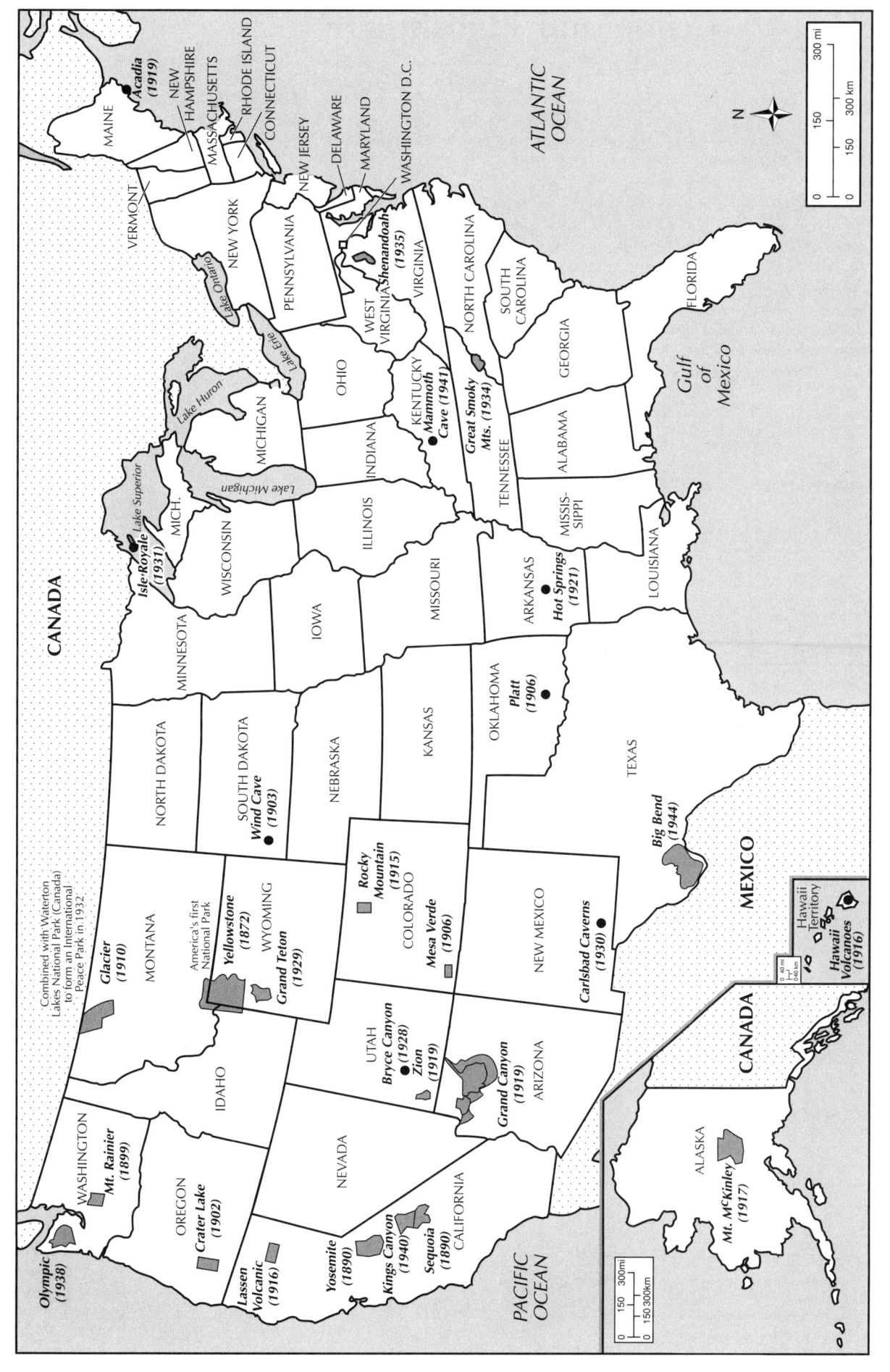

This map shows the national park system as it was developed by the end of the year 1945, with the date of each park's establishment. The park system was created to preserve sites of historical, scenic, or scientific importance. Congress establishes the parks, and the National Park Service, in the Department of the Interior, administers them. The first park was Yellowstone, in Wyoming, created in 1872. Favorite playgrounds of the American people, the parks were especially attractive in the 1920s, a time of prosperity and of broad use of the automobile.

CHAPTER 19 Crime and Punishment

Crimes and Criminals

The proposition that hard times promote lawlessness was borne out by the experience of the years 1914–45, a period of exceptionally severe economic want and also of high prosperity. The number of homicides was remarkably high in the prosperous 1920s—a statistic related in some measure to the peculiar consequences of prohibition—but the highest numbers were reached during the first half of the 1930s, the hardest time of the Great Depression. At any time the murder weapon of choice was usually a firearm. The theme remained even more consistent with respect to people incarcerated

in state or national prison. The numbers of homicides and most other crimes were lowest during the period of the Second World War, partly because of the high employment rates of that era, partly because the United States as a whole had at that time a different set of concerns and priorities. America's criminals were overwhelmingly male, and though the largest portion of prisoners were white, it was because most of the people in the United States were white. The percentage of nonwhite—mostly black—inmates was disproportionately high. Statistics for selected crimes in urban areas in 1945 re-

TABLE 19.1   HOMICIDES

[Refers only to deaths occurring within the United States. Rates per 100,000 resident population.]

Year	Number	Rate	Male[a]	Female[a]	Assault by— Firearms and Explosives	Assault by— Cutting and Piercing Instruments	Assault by— Other Means
1945	7,547	5.7	5,969	1,578	4,029	1,837	1,681
1944	6,675	5.0	5,251	1,424	3,449	1,741	1,485
1943	6,823	5.1	5,363	1,460	3,444	1,849	1,530
1942	7,890	5.9	6,266	1,624	4,204	2,120	1,566
1941	8,048	6.0	6,408	1,640	4,525	2,034	1,489
1940	8,329	6.3	6,647	1,682	4,655	2,064	1,610
1939	8,394	6.4	6,657	1,737	4,799	2,048	1,547
1938	8,799	6.8	6,935	1,864	5,055	2,018	1,726
1937	9,811	7.6	7,731	2,080	5,701	2,192	1,918
1936	10,232	8.0	8,134	2,098	6,106	2,151	2,065
1935	10,587	8.3	8,554	2,033	6,506	2,018	2,063
1934	12,055	9.5	9,850	2,205	7,702	2,122	2,231
1933	12,124	9.7	9,874	2,250	7,863	2,065	2,196
1932	10,722	9.0	8,646	2,076	7,252	1,578	1,892
1931	10,862	9.2	8,761	2,101	7,335	1,662	1,865
1930	10,331	8.8	8,233	2,098	6,995	1,553	1,783
1929	9,637	8.4	7,644	1,993	6,362	1,539	1,736
1928	9,780	8.6	7,889	1,891	6,668	1,409	1,703
1927	8,997	8.4	7,168	1,829	6,004	1,376	1,617
1926	8,740	8.4	7,057	1,683	6,035	1,239	1,466
1925	8,440	8.3	6,823	1,617	5,908	1,130	1,402
1924	8,014	8.1	6,408	1,606	5,736	920	1,358
1923	7,557	7.8	6,096	1,461	5,422	884	1,251
1922	7,381	8.0	5,996	1,385	5,430	763	1,188
1921	7,090	8.1	5,682	1,408	5,178	687	1,225
1920	5,815	6.8	4,661	1,154	4,178	587	1,050
1919	5,973	7.2	4,820	1,153	4,247	632	1,094
1918	5,113	6.5	4,107	1,006	3,475	603	1,035
1917	4,864	6.9	3,904	960	3,205	621	1,038
1916	4,237	6.3	3,419	818	2,708	546	983
1915	3,633	5.9	2,829	804	2,213	483	937
1914	3,776	6.2	3,000	776	2,366	511	388

[a]Refers to victims (as opposed to perpetrators).
Source: Ben J. Wattenberg, *The Statistical History of the United States* (New York, 1976), 414.

vealed that rates were lowest for the New England area and substantially higher for the South and border states.

Some Familiar Names in Crime and Punishment, 1914–1945

Alcatraz Federal maximum-security prison in San Francisco Harbor. Opened in January 1934 as a "superprison" for "superprisoners." The most famous inmate of the "Rock" was Al Capone, 1934–39.

Roscoe "Fatty" Arbuckle Rotund (300 lbs.) comedy actor of silent films, given to sordid private behavior. Accused of rape-slaying of Virginia Rappe in September 1921. Three sensational trials ended with acquittal. Blackballed by the film industry, he died of a heart attack in 1933.

Clarence Darrow Most famous criminal lawyer of the era with special skills in picking a jury. Often defended unpopular clients, such as Leopold and Loeb. Participated in the Scopes "Monkey" trial in 1925. Died at eighty-one in 1938.

Thomas E. Dewey Acquired a reputation as a "racket buster," pursuer of organized crime as U.S. attorney and district attorney for New York in the 1930s. Publicity received from these efforts helped propel him to the governorship of New York in 1942 and to the Republican presidential nomination in 1944 and 1948.

John Dillinger Perhaps the most famous individual gangster of the early depression years. A brutal robber and killer, he nonetheless became a folk hero for his creativity and skill in outwitting authorities. His death was part of the legend. Betrayed by the "woman in red," he was gunned down by FBI agents in Chicago in 1934.

TABLE 19.2 NUMBER AND RATE PER 100,000 OF STATE AND FEDERAL PRISONERS RECEIVED FROM COURT

Year	Number	Rate per 100,000
1910	29,710	32.5
1923	38,628	34.6
1926	48,108	42.3
1927	41,936	45.1
1928	55,746	47.7
1929	58,906	51.4
1930	66,013	56.2
1931	71,520	60.8
1932	67,477	57.8
1933	62,801	52.8
1934	62,251	51.9
1935	65,723	54.3
1936	60,925	50.0
1937	63,552	49.3
1938	68,326	52.6
1939	66,024	50.4
1940	73,104	55.5
1941	68,700	52.3
1942	58,858	45.5
1943	50,082	39.4
1944	50,162	39.5
1945	53,212	40.0

Source: Margaret Werner Cahalan, *Historical Correction Statistics in the United States, 1850–1984* (Rockville, Md., 1986), 36.

Bruno Richard Hauptmann The man convicted of kidnapping and murdering in March 1932 Charles A. Lindbergh, Jr., twenty-month-old son of America's most famous hero. Apprehended more than two years later, Hauptmann was tried in a carnival atmosphere in 1935 and convicted despite numerous doubts. His execution came on April 3, 1936, with newsman Gabriel Heatter providing play-by-play commentary.

J. Edgar Hoover An attorney who joined the Department of Justice in 1917, he became head of the Bureau of Investigation in 1924. He transformed the FBI and gave it vast publicity. He was perhaps America's most famous crime fighter of the 1930s and 1940s. His "public enemies" list mostly included small-time hoods—Dillinger, the Barkers, Pretty-Boy Floyd—not the people in organized crime.

Nathan Leopold and Richard Loeb Two young men from families of considerable means who confessed to the thrill-slaying of a little boy, Bobby Frank, in 1924, setting the stage for a sensational trial befitting the atmosphere of the 1920s. Skillful work by Clarence Darrow produced a sentence of life imprisonment, not execution.

Eliot Ness Headed at age twenty-six a ten-man prohibition detail, starting in 1928. They became known as the "untouchables" because of their determination to stay free of corruption. Ness received extravagant publicity for harassment of Capone and others involved in illegal alcohol, but he and his men stayed clean in a dirty era.

Bonnie Parker and Clyde Barrow Bonnie and Clyde were among the most famous small-time gangsters of the depression period. With various associates they robbed and killed for a few months in the Midwest and Southwest. As with Dillinger, they pursued publicity and were colorful and somewhat original. The pair was riddled with bullets from the Texas state police in 1934.

Nicola Sacco and Bartolomeo Vanzetti Italian immigrants accused of being part of a gang that robbed a factory in South Braintree, Mass., and killed two men on April 19, 1920. They were convicted under highly dubious circumstances—some said because of their radical political beliefs and even because of their physical appearance as immigrants from southern Europe. After years of appeals and investigation, they were executed in August 1927. Their names later would be cleared.

Scottsboro Boys A much celebrated case of race relations in the 1930s and 1940s, perhaps reflective of the fearful nature of southern society at the time. Nine young black youths—aged twelve to twenty—were convicted of raping two white women in Scottsboro, Ala., in 1931 and sentenced to death. Many appeals followed, and most people probably doubted the justice of the verdict or even of the trial. Later, sentences were reduced, and some were paroled.

David Curtis Stephenson Grand Dragon of the powerful Ku Klux Klan in Indiana, he was convicted of killing and sexually assaulting an Indianapolis secretary, Madge Oberholtzer, on March 15, 1924. This bizarre case placed Stephenson in jail for life and helped cause the decline of the Klan in Indiana.

Joseph Zangara An Italian immigrant and anarchist, enemy of all "bosses," he shot at President-elect Franklin D. Roosevelt in Miami on February 15, 1933. His bullets hit four bystanders, not Roosevelt, and Mayor Anton J. Cermak of Chicago, who died. Zangara was executed in the electric chair.

Sources: Carl Sifakis, *The Encyclopedia of American Crime* (New York, 1982), various pages; Jay Robert Nash, *Crime Chronology: A Worldwide Record, 1900–1983* (New York, 1984), various pages.

TABLE 19.3 CHARACTERISTICS OF PRISONERS RECEIVED IN STATE AND FEDERAL PRISONS AND REFORMATORIES BY AGE, SEX, AND RACE

| | Median Age | | Percentage 18 and Under | Percentage White | Percentage Nonwhite | Percentage Male | Percentage Female |
	Male	Female					
1910	26.1 [a,f]		14	66	34	95	5
1923	27.7	25.2	10	74 [b]	25 [b]	94	6
1926	26.6	24.2	10	76	24	94	6
1927	26.6 [c]	24.5 [c]	10	76 [b]	24 [b]	94	6
1928	26.5 [c]	25.0 [c]	10	76	24	94	6
1929	26.8 [c]	27.9 [c]	10	78 [d]	22	94	6
1930	26.7 [c]	28.8 [c]	10	77 [d]	23	95	5
1931	26.6 [a,c]		10	76	24	96	4
1932	26.9 [c]	27.2 [c]	9	75	25	96	4
1933	27.2 [c]	26.8 [c]	9	74	26	96	4
1934	27.2 [c]	27.6 [c]	9	72	28	95	5
1935	27.6 [c]	28.2 [c]	8	74 [b]	27 [b]	95	5
1936	28.1 [c]	28.1 [c]	8	73	27	95	5
1937	29.9 [a]	28.9 [a]					
	35.4 [f]	24.9 [f]	9	73	27	95	5
1938	27.7 [c]	28.9 [c]					
	36.7 [f]	24.5 [f]	9	73	27	95	5
1939	27.6 [c]	29.2 [c]					
	36.4 [f]	25.0 [f]	9	73	27	95	5
1940	28.6	28.4	9	70	30	95	5
1941	29.0	28.2	9	71	29	95	5
1942 [g]	29.0	27.3	10	70	30	94	6
1943 [g]	27.2	27.6	12	69	31	95	5
1944 [g]	27.1	26.0	12	69	31	95	5
1945 [g]	26.9	25.8	12	68	32	94	6

[a] Age not given by sex.
[b] Totals do not equal 100 percent due to rounding.
[c] Calculated from data grouped into age categories.
[d] Only races categorized are white and black.
[e] For felons.
[f] For misdemeanors.
[g] 1942, 1943, and 1945 exclude Mississippi, Georgia, and Michigan; 1944 excludes Mississippi and Georgia.
Source: Cahalan, *Historical Correction Statistics*, 66.

TABLE 19.4 DISTRIBUTION OF OFFENSES: STATE AND FEDERAL PRISONS [a]

[In percentages]

Category and Offense	Total 1910	Total 1923	Total 1933	Total 1940	Felonies Only 1940
Person					
Homicide, Manslaughter	9.7	9.5	6.2	4.4	5.2
Assault	9.9	5.2	5.7	5.5	3.2
Rape	3.9	4.1	2.3	2.6	3
Total	23.5	18.8	14.2	12.5	13.4
Property					
Robbery	4.8	8.1	12.4	7.3	8.5
Embezzlement, Forgery, Fraud	7.8	9	9	10.6	11.9
Burglary	22.1	17.4	23.5	16.8	19.5
All larceny	25.7	19.2	21.4	20.7	22.6
Arson	b	b	1	. . .	b
Stolen property	b	b	b	0.8	0.8
Total	60.4	53.7	67.3	56.2	63.3
Morals, Order, Government Charges					
Other sex-related crimes	1.1	1.2	3.3	2.8	3.1
Liquor-law violations	1.2	7.5	5.5	11.3	10.5
Drunkenness, Disorderly Conduct, vagrancy	2.1	1	1.6	6.6	b
Drug-law violations	0.1	6	2.4	2.5	2.8
Traffic violations	b	0.1	0.5	0.9	0.5
Carrying and possessing weapons	0.5	0.7	0.6	0.6	0.5
Nonsupport	0.5	0.8	0.8	0.9	1
Total	5.5	17.3	14.7	25.6	18.4
Other	10.9	11.1	3.8	5.8	4.9
Total reported	27,404	36,336	62,792	73,456	62,692
Unknown or unclear	328	1,279	9	b	b

[a] Before 1937, felony and misdemeanor commitments to state and federal prisons were categorized together by offense. From 1937 to 1942 separate and combined listings were provided. After 1942, state institutions reported only felonies. Using 1940 as an example, since this represents a high point in the percentage of misdemeanor commitment to state and federal prisons, the difference in the distribution produced by excluding all misdemeanors is shown.
[b] Not categorized.
Source: Cahalan, *Historical Corrections Statistics*, 45.

TABLE 19.5 **MEDIAN TIME SERVED IN MONTHS IN STATE INSTITUTIONS BY OFFENSE BY RACE: 1937**

Offense	Male Felons, Southern States Only 1937	
	White	Nonwhite
All offenses	16.4	19.5
Murder	58.0	72.8
Manslaughter	21.8	34.5
Homicide	a	a
Robbery	37.3	37.3
Aggravated assault	14.5	16.0
Burglary	18.1	20.8
Larceny	12.0	12.4
Auto theft	24.0	20.3
Embezzlement and fraud	b	b
Forgery	14.0	17.6
Rape	26.4	33.4
Other sex offenses	15.6	18.0
Drug laws	a	a
Weapons	a	a
All other offenses	11.1	10.6

[a] Information not available or not separately categorized.
[b] Larceny includes fraud and stolen property.
Source: Cahalan, *Historical Corrections Statistics*, 61.

TABLE 19.6 **CRIME RATES—OFFENSES KNOWN TO THE POLICE IN URBAN COMMUNITIES, BY CLASS, BY STATES: 1945**

[Based on monthly crime reports received from 2,267 urban communities representing a combined population of 67,608,610, except for burglary and larceny, which are based on reports from 2,265 urban communities with combined population of 58,222,281.]

Division and State	Murder Nonnegligent Manslaughter	Robbery	Aggravated Assault	Burglary— Breaking or Entering	Larceny—Theft (except auto theft)	Auto Theft
	Rate per 100,000 Population					
United States	**5.49**	**54.3**	**59.8**	**359.3**	**889.9**	**241.5**
New England	**1.17**	**16.7**	**12.8**	**260.5**	**515.0**	**162.5**
Maine	1.02	15.6	11.9	279.0	679.3	190.2
N.H.	.40	3.6	4.9	142.7	428.2	72.4
Vt.	. . .	3.9	2.6	174.6	793.3	102.9
Mass.	1.22	17.6	10.4	249.4	446.1	165.7
R.I.	.85	18.4	16.3	283.2	592.5	195.5
Conn.	1.46	16.8	22.2	314.1	667.0	151.1
Middle Atlantic	**2.95**	**23.1**	**31.7**	**218.6**	**427.9**	**156.5**
N.Y.	3.05	15.8	29.2	178.1	482.7	160.8
N.J.	2.69	30.4	46.8	278.8	477.1	172.3
Pa.	2.91	33.2	29.2	211.8	342.8	140.7
East North Central	**4.50**	**68.6**	**49.0**	**342.5**	**842.4**	**189.2**
Ohio	5.43	64.2	40.7	383.1	896.5	214.7
Ind.	5.12	53.5	60.5	379.4	1,038.8	260.5
Ill.	4.74	86.2	46.8	302.3	542.3	127.3
Mich.	4.11	81.1	77.3	426.0	1,193.2	244.5
Wis.	1.31	11.5	8.2	154.5	775.3	138.9
West North Central	**3.35**	**31.9**	**24.8**	**255.6**	**694.0**	**182.6**
Minn.	1.26	19.1	8.5	189.8	577.4	141.9
Iowa	1.64	15.0	7.7	245.1	673.0	160.3
Mo.	6.93	57.7	51.8	276.8	697.3	188.5
N. Dak.	1.64	5.8	4.1	159.5	513.8	120.8
S. Dak.	1.47	7.3	5.1	200.9	744.1	163.5
Nebr.	1.93	22.3	29.4	312.2	915.3	326.8
Kans.	2.38	31.5	17.1	336.7	817.7	196.2

(continued)

TABLE 19.6   (continued)

Division and State	Murder Nonnegligent Manslaughter	Robbery	Aggravated Assault	Burglary— Breaking or Entering	Larceny—Theft (except auto theft)	Auto Theft
	Rate per 100,000 Population					
United States	**5.49**	**54.3**	**59.8**	**359.3**	**889.9**	**241.5**
South Atlantic[a]	**13.96**	**61.5**	**190.8**	**419.8**	**1,041.7**	**304.8**
Del.	4.81	90.9	19.2	439.0	1,236.9	244.3
Md.	9.74	51.6	126.1	226.0	533.6	299.1
Va.	14.59	89.0	219.0	508.4	1,309.9	347.9
W. Va.	7.72	68.1	59.7	294.1	643.1	213.7
N.C.	13.47	43.4	483.0	436.3	897.7	207.4
S.C.	23.04	53.3	136.9	329.8	1,340.0	309.1
Ga.	23.24	58.7	159.6	455.2	1,281.8	328.8
Fla.	15.91	73.3	200.6	694.5	1,525.0	386.8
East South Central	**16.90**	**75.0**	**157.9**	**465.7**	**879.1**	**309.1**
Ky.	13.95	112.1	127.1	580.4	1,001.2	414.2
Tenn.	18.75	69.1	114.0	384.2	741.6	322.6
Ala.	18.12	58.4	225.7	515.0	890.8	222.0
Miss.	15.85	40.9	209.6	322.6	964.1	211.7
West South Central	**12.82**	**48.7**	**92.5**	**444.8**	**1,211.5**	**305.4**
Ark.	12.09	97.9	153.8	334.0	1,024.7	294.7
La.	12.27	26.5	93.8	162.8	530.1	242.9
Okla.	8.43	51.5	40.8	458.9	1,344.0	303.7
Tex.	14.42	50.2	100.3	557.7	1,445.1	330.1
Mountain	**4.10**	**58.5**	**41.5**	**486.2**	**1,424.7**	**299.4**
Mont.	1.13	30.5	9.6	230.2	1,045.5	174.3
Idaho	.70	28.8	14.1	412.8	1,468.5	353.8
Wyo.	6.02	57.8	37.3	446.5	1,624.7	310.5
Colo.	4.15	62.7	28.8	580.5	1,213.7	212.0
N. Mex.	9.09	42.4	92.4	313.5	1,029.1	305.9
Ariz.	8.57	107.5	110.8	572.3	2,326.2	520.2
Utah	1.54	50.1	39.7	461.9	1,594.6	373.2
Nev.	6.68	121.9	45.1	868.6	1,974.3	442.6
Pacific	**5.52**	**159.5**	**76.6**	**640.4**	**1,842.9**	**638.0**
Wash.	5.18	111.5	27.7	643.1	1,759.7	609.8
Oreg.	3.41	115.9	43.6	733.3	1,799.1	506.0
Calif.	5.79	172.9	89.0	630.3	1,862.8	656.8

[a] Includes District of Columbia.
Source: Bureau of the Census, *Statistical Abstract of the United States, 1947* (Washington, D.C., 1947), 96.

Capital Punishment

Execution was deemed an appropriate response to certain offenses, notably murder, throughout the United States, even in those states that did not have a death penalty. Methods of execution varied, although there was a clear trend toward death by electrocution, in the "electric chair." Several western states retained the older method of hanging. Even though the death penalty existed in all parts of the country, it increasingly became a southern phenomenon. In the South, capital punishment had distinct racial overtones. Not only did most executions in the 1930s and 1940s take place in the South, but most southern executions were of black men. So it was also with an illegal form of capital punishment, lynching. What once had been a means of dealing with horse thieves and other bad men in the crude and poorly organized western territories, most of them white men, became in the early twentieth century a subsidiary southern device for keeping the black population in place. Efforts to take the issue from the states and make lynching a national offense floundered in Washington. The fact that lynching declined in the last part of the period and by 1945 had almost died out represented less a softening of the racial line than of a tendency to allow the legal system to proceed to a roughly comparable conclusion. As lynchings decreased in the southern states in the 1930s and 1940s, legal executions increased.

TABLE 19.7   EXECUTIONS PER DECADE UNDER CIVIL AUTHORITY

	1910s	1920s	1930s	1940s
Total under state authority	636	1,038	1,523	1,177
Race				
Number nonwhite	286	481	745	706
Percent nonwhite	47%	49%	52%	63%
Race unknown	(26)	(51)	(79)	(55)
Offense				
Murder	570	961	1,383	980
Rape	40	69	112	172
Other	26	8	28	23
Offense unknown	(0)	(0)	(0)	(2)
Total under local authority	406	131	147	110
Total under civil authority (state and local)	1,042	1,169	1,670	1,287

Source: Cahalan, *Historical Corrections Statistics,* 10.

TABLE 19.8 **REGIONAL COMPARISON OF TOTAL PERSONS EXECUTED UNDER STATE AUTHORITY BY DECADE**

	1910s	1920s	1930s	1940s
Total number of executions	636	1,038	1,523	1,177
Northeast	260	325	301	184
North Central	34	120	195	106
South	254	453	836	733
West	88	140	191	154
Percentage of total executions				
Northeast	41	31	20	16
North Central	5	12	13	9
South	40	44	55	63
West	14	14	13	13
Rate per 100,00				
Total U.S.	.69	.98	1.24	.89
Northeast	1.0	1.10	.87	.51
North Central	.11	.35	.50	.26
South	.86	1.37	2.21	1.76
West	1.29	1.57	1.61	1.11

Source: Cahalan, *Historical Corrections Statistics*, 14.

TABLE 19.9 **REGIONAL COMPARISON OF NONWHITE PERSONS EXECUTED UNDER STATE AUTHORITY BY DECADE**

	1910s	1920s	1930s	1940s
Total known nonwhite executions	286	481	744	703
Northeast	43	85	56	66
North Central	16	44	51	43
South	212	326	601	553
West	15	26	36	41
Nonwhite percentage of total executions in which race is known	47	49	52	63
Northeast	17	27	20	40
North Central	47	37	28	46
South	84	72	72	76
West	20	26	24	30
Rate per 100,000 Nonwhite per decade	2.79	4.42	5.96	5.23
Northeast	8.46	12.07	4.73	4.68
North Central	2.63	5.14	3.78	2.86
South	2.40	3.62	6.34	5.53
West	5.34	7.74	7.58	7.68

Source: Cahalan, *Historical Corrections Statistics*, 15.

TABLE 19.10 **WOMEN EXECUTED UNDER CIVIL AUTHORITY IN THE UNITED STATES, 1930–1945**

Year	Total	Offense		Race		State in Which Executed
		Murder	Other	White	Black	
1945	1	1	. . .	. . .	1	Ga.
1944	3	3	. . .	. . .	3	Miss., N.Y., N.C.
1943	3	3	. . .	1	2	S.C., Miss., N.C.
1942	1	1	. . .	1	. . .	La.
1941	1	1	. . .	1	. . .	Calif.

Year	Total	Offense		Race		State in Which Executed
		Murder	Other	White	Black	
1938	2	2	. . .	2	. . .	Ill., Ohio
1937	1	1	. . .	. . .	1	Miss.
1936	1	1	. . .	1	. . .	N.Y.
1935	3	3	. . .	2	1	Del.
1934	1	1	. . .	1	. . .	N.Y.
1931	1	1	. . .	1	. . .	Pa.
1930	2	2	. . .	1	1	Ariz., Ala.

Source: Cahalan, *Historical Corrections Statistics*, 25.

TABLE 19.11 **METHODS OF EXECUTION IN THE UNITED STATES, 1945**

State	Method
Ala.	Electrocution
Ariz.	Lethal gas
Ark.	Electrocution
Calif.	Lethal gas
Colo.	Lethal gas
Conn.	Electrocution
Del.	Hanging
D.C.	Electrocution
Fla.	Electrocution
Ga.	Electrocution
Idaho	Hanging
Ill.	Electrocution
Ind.	Electrocution
Iowa	Hanging
Kans.	Hanging
Ky.	Electrocution
La.	Electrocution
Maine	No death penalty
Md.	Hanging
Mass.	Electrocution
Mich.	No death penalty
Minn.	No death penalty
Miss.	Electrocution
Mo.	Lethal gas
Mont.	Hanging
Nebr.	Electrocution
Nev.	Lethal gas
N.H.	Hanging
N.J.	Electrocution
N. Mex.	Electrocution
N.Y.	Electrocution
N.C.	Lethal gas
N. Dak.	No death penalty
Ohio	Electrocution
Okla.	Electrocution
Oreg.	Lethal gas
Pa.	Electrocution
R.I.	No death penalty
S.C.	Electrocution
S. Dak.	Electrocution
Tenn.	Electrocution
Tex.	Electrocution
Utah	Hanging or shooting
Vt.	Electrocution
Va.	Electrocution
Wash.	Hanging[a]
W. Va.	Hanging
Wis.	No death penalty

(continued)

TABLE 19.11 (continued)

State	Method
Wyo.	Lethal gas
U.S. (Fed. Gov't)	Hanging
Alaska	Hanging
Canal Zone	Hanging
Hawaii	Hanging
P.R.	No death penalty
V.I.	Hanging

[a]Jury can specify whether sentence shall be death or life imprisonment.
Source: The Information Please Almanac, 1948 (New York, 1948), 289.

TABLE 19.12 STATES THAT ABOLISHED THE DEATH PENALTY—TEMPORARY OR CONTINUING

State	Period of Abolition
Mich.[a]	1846–
R.I.[b]	1852–
Wis.	1853–
Maine	1887–
Kans.	1907–35
Minn.	1911–
Wash.	1913–19
Oreg.	1914–20
N. Dak.[c]	1915–
S. Dak.	1915–39
Tenn.[d]	1915–16
Ariz.	1916–18
Mo.	1917–19

[a]Death penalty retained for treason.
[b]Death penalty restored in 1882 for any life-term convict who commits murder.
[c]Death penalty retained for murder by a prisoner serving a life term for murder.
[d]Death penalty retained for rape.
Source: Cahalan, Historical Corrections Statistics, 13.

TABLE 19.13 AMERICAN OPINION ON CAPITAL PUNISHMENT

Random surveys on April 18, 1936, November 30, 1936, and November 30, 1937, asked Americans the following question: Are you in favor of the death penalty for murder? The results are as follows:

	Favor	Oppose	Undecided or No Opinion
April 1936	65%	35% = 100%	5%
November 1936	61	39 = 100	...
November 1937	65	35 = 100	7

American Opinion in November 1936 State by State

	Favor	Oppose
States having no capital punishment		
Wis.	49%	51% = 100%
R.I.	52	48
S. Dak.	52	48
Mich.	53	47
Minn.	55	45
Maine	56	44
N. Dak.	58	42
States having capital punishment		
Ind.	54%	46%
Colo.	56	44

States having capital punishment		
Okla.	59	41
Oreg.	59	41
Del.	60	40
Iowa	61	39
Ohio	62	38
Md.	62	38
N. Mex.	62	38
Kans.	63	37
Calif.	64	36
Mont.	64	36
Tex.	65	35
Va.	65	35
Nebr.	66	34
Pa.	67	33
N.Y.	67	33
Conn.	67	33
Mass.	67	33
N.C.	67	33
S.C.	68	32
Ky.	68	32
La.	68	32
Wash.	68	32
Mo.	69	31
Ala.	69	31
N.J.	69	31
Tenn.	69	31
Vt.	70	30
Ill.	70	30
W. Va.	71	29
N.H.	72	28
Ariz.	73	27
Ga.	75	25
Fla.	75	25
Ark.	76	24
Idaho	76	24
Wyo.	77	23
Miss.	79	21
Utah	82	18
Nev.	84	16

(Nov. 30, 1936) Are you in favor of it [the death penalty] for persons under twenty-one? Asked of a national cross-section of people who favored capital punishment—61% of the sample is represented. (AIPO)

	Yes	No
National total	46%	54%
By Geographical Section		
New England	31%	69%
Middle Atlantic	50	50
East Central	48	52
West Central	50	50
South	46	54
Mountain	41	59
Pacific Coast	46	54

(Nov. 30, 1937) Are you in favor of it [death penalty] for women? Asked of a national cross-section of people who favored capital punishment—65% of the sample is represented. (AIPO)

Yes 58%   No 42%

American Opinion on the Death Penalty in November 1937

	Favor	Oppose
Men	69%	31%
Women	57	43

Source: Hadley Cantril, Public Opinion, 1935–1946 (Princeton, 1951), 94.

Lynching

Lynching of white people was by no means unheard of in the United States. There was a time in the nineteenth century when a majority of lynching was of whites, with the explanation that this was an expression of vigilante justice in the development of the American West. By the start of the twentieth century, however, lynching had become a white man's method of dealing with black people in the southern states. The practice began to taper off in the 1920s, and by 1945 it had almost died out.

Crime and Prohibition

The Eighteenth Amendment to the Constitution went into effect on January 16, 1920, and so the sale of alcoholic beverages became illegal—indeed, unconstitutional—throughout the United States. In the Volstead Act of 1919 Congress had approached prohibition ruthlessly: Anything containing more than 1/2 of 1% alcohol was an alcoholic beverage. Exceptions, mostly for medicinal or religious purposes, generally were rare. Most drinking in the United States was criminal activity. It nonetheless went on, and there developed an entire subculture associated with prohibition. Some 200,000 speakeasies replaced saloons and cocktail lounges, and such terms as *bootleggers, rumrunners,* and *hipflasks* applied to clandestine efforts to circumvent the Eighteenth Amendment. The massive new effort to supply illegal booze ranged from the innovator at home to the still operator in the Appalachian hills to organized gangs in America's largest cities. In fact, one of the most reprehensible features of prohibition was the opening it provided for expanded activity of organized crime. The name Al Capone was of course synonymous with that theme. Much of Capone's profits came from the sale of illegal beer, and much of the brutality of gangland wars was a result of contests for power or rivalries over territory in which to operate. Prohibition ended in 1933 with an amendment to the Volstead Act that permitted sale of beverages containing as much as 3.2% alcohol and with passage later in the year of the Twenty-first Amendment. Organized criminal activity obviously did not then end, but the gangs had to move into different forms of activity.

Records of the consumption of alcohol before the era of prohibition are based on statistics published by the government in Statistical Abstracts. Consumption of alcohol after the start of prohibition was based on estimates from three sources: materials used in production, estimates from death rates related to alcohol, and from arrests. The

TABLE 19.14 LYNCHINGS BY RACE AND YEAR

Year	Whites	Blacks	Total
1914	4	51	55
1915	13	56	69
1916	4	50	54
1917	2	36	38
1918	4	60	65
1919	7	76	83
1920	8	53	61
1921	5	59	64
1922	6	51	57
1923	4	29	33
1924	0	16	16
1925	0	17	17
1926	7	23	30
1927	0	16	16
1928	1	10	11
1929	3	7	10
1930	1	20	21
1931	1	12	13
1932	2	6	8
1933	4	24	28
1934	0	15	15
1935	2	18	20
1936	0	8	8
1937	0	8	8
1938	0	6	6
1939	1	2	3
1940	1	4	5
1941	0	4	4
1942	0	6	6
1943	0	3	3
1944	0	2	2
1945	0	1	1

Source: Harry A. Ploski and James Williams, *The Negro Almanac: A Reference Work on the Afro-American* (New York, 1983), 348.

TABLE 19.15 CAUSES OF LYNCHINGS CLASSIFIED

Year	Homicides	Felonious Assault	Rape	Attempted Rape	Robbery and Theft	Insult to White Persons	All Other Causes
1914	31	9	6	1	2	1	5
1915	27	9	11	6	9	3	4
1916	21	7	3	9	8	2	4
1917	7	3	7	6	1	6	8
1918	27	3	10	6	5	2	11
1919	29	8	9	10	1	7	19
1920	23	9	15	3	0	3	8
1921	19	8	16	3	0	3	15
1922	15	5	14	5	4	2	12
1923	5	5	6	1	1	2	13
1924	4	2	5	2	0	3	0
1925	8	1	4	2	0	1	1
1926	13	3	2	3	1	1	7
1927	7	2	2	3	0	0	2

(continued)

TABLE 19.15 (continued)

Year	Homicides	Felonious Assault	Rape	Attempted Rape	Robbery and Theft	Insult to White Persons	All Other Causes
1928	5	2	3	0	0	0	1
1929	1	3	3	0	0	2	1
1930	5	0	8	2	3	0	3
1931	5	3	0	5	0	0	0
1932	1	2	1	1	0	1	2
1933	8	4	3	3	1	1	8
1934	2	2	2	4	1	3	1
1935	8	1	3	3	0	1	4
1936	1	0	3	3	0	1	0
1937	4	2	1	0	1	0	0
1938	3	0	1	0	0	1	1
1939	2	0	0	0	0	0	1
1940	0	0	0	1	0	1	3
1941	0	0	0	1	1	0	2
1942	1	1	0	3	0	0	1
1943	1	0	0	0	0	1	1
1944	2	0	0	0	0	0	0
1945	0	0	0	1	0	0	0

Source: Ploski and Williams, *Negro Almanac*, 349.

TABLE 19.16 PER CAPITA CONSUMPTION OF ALCOHOLIC BEVERAGES IN THE UNITED STATES, 1840 TO 1922

Year Ending June 30	Spirits (proof gallons)	Wine (gallons)	Beer (gallons)	Total Pure Alcohol (gallons)
1840	2.52	.29	1.36	1.36
1850	2.23	.27	1.58	1.22
1860	2.86	.34	3.22	1.62
1870	2.07	.32	5.31	1.31
1880	1.27	.56	8.26	1.06
1890	1.39	.46	13.56	1.34
1900	1.28	.39	16.06	1.38
1901	1.31	.36	15.95	1.38
1902	1.34	.62	17.15	1.49
1903	1.43	.47	17.64	1.53
1904	1.44	.52	17.88	1.55
1905	1.41	.41	17.99	1.53
1906	1.47	.53	19.51	1.64
1907	1.58	.65	20.53	1.75
1908	1.39	.58	20.23	1.64
1909	1.32	.67	19.04	1.56
1910	1.42	.65	19.77	1.64
1911	1.46	.67	20.69	1.70
1912	1.45	.58	20.02	1.66
1913	1.51	.56	20.72	1.71
1914	1.44	.53	20.69	1.67
1915	1.26	.33	18.40	1.46
1916	1.37	.47	17.78	1.51
1917	1.62	.41	18.17	1.64
1918	.85	.49	14.87	1.13
1919	.77	.51	8.00	.80
1920	.26	.12	2.45	.25
1921	.32	.19	. . .	.19
1922	.17	.09	. . .	.10

Source: Clark Warburton, *The Economic Results of Prohibition* (New York, 1932), 24.

term *pure alcohol* pertains to the alcohol content in beverages. It was assumed during prohibition that wine consisted of 10% alcohol and beer 4%. The estimates suggested that while prohibition caused a considerable drop in the consumption of beer, a great deal continued to be consumed and there was an absolute increase in the per capita consumption of wine and spirits.

Some Individuals Prominent in Organized Crime, 1914–1945

Joe Adonis
Albert Anastasia
Louis Lepke Buchalter
Alphonse ("Scarface Al") Capone
James ("Big Jim") Colosimo
Frank Costello
Carlo Gambino
Genna Brothers (the "Terrible Gennas")
Vito Genovese
Meyer Lansky
Charles ("Lucky") Luciano
Tommy Lucchese
Salvatore Marazano

Giuseppe ("Joe the Boss") Masseria
George ("Bugs") Moran
Willie Moretti
Frank Nitti
Dion O'Banion
Spike O'Donnell
Frank ("Don Chreech") Scalice
Dutch Schultz (Arthur Flegenheimer)
Benjamin ("Bugsy") Siegel
Ciro Terranova
Johnny Torrio
Umberto Valenti
Hymie Weiss

Source: Sifakis, *Encyclopedia of American Crime*, 792–793.

Crime and Popular Culture

Stories of mystery and criminal activity had long been subjects for popular consumption in the United States, and the dissemination of such stories had largely involved the use of the printed word. The twentieth century produced new reasons and devices for observing criminal behavior as entertainment. The film industry lent itself to subjects of crime not long after it started. People in the 1920s were fascinated with sensational trials and stories about organized crime. It was the decade of the 1930s, however, that brought together a number of forces to move the entertainment media into subjects of crime in a large way. The depression focused attention on an expan-

TABLE 19.17 ESTIMATES OF THE CONSUMPTION OF ALCOHOLIC BEVERAGES IN THE UNITED STATES, 1920 TO 1930

[Gallons per capita]

| Year | Spirits | | | Beer | | Wine |
	Estimate from Sources of Production	Estimate from Death Rates	Estimate from Arrests	Estimate from Sources of Production	Estimate from Death Rates	Estimate from Sources of Production
1920	. . .	.45	.15	. . .	5.63	. . .
1921	.30	.87	.38	1.26	6.13	.44
1922	1.54	1.01	.72	1.71	6.21	.57
1923	1.96	1.23	.93	2.24	6.12	.95
1924	1.75	1.27	.93	2.84	6.55	.90
1925	1.80	1.35	.94	3.46	6.61	.86
1926	1.91	1.36	.98	4.21	6.80	1.05
1927	1.53	1.45	1.02	5.03	7.37	1.08
1928	1.75	1.41	1.10	6.05	8.52	1.07
1929	1.86	1.38	1.04	7.11	7.26	.89
1930	1.33	. . .	. . .	6.90	. . .	.87

Source: Warburton, *Economic Results of Prohibition,* 106.

TABLE 19.18 ESTIMATES OF THE CONSUMPTION OF PURE ALCOHOL IN THE UNITED STATES, 1920 TO 1930

[Gallons per capita]

Year	Estimate from Sources of Production	Estimate from Death Rates	Estimate from Arrests for Drunkenness	Final Estimate	Index of Consumption of Alcohol, 1911–14 = 100
1920	. . .	.64	.16	. . .	. . .
1921	.26	.82	.43	.54	32.0
1922	.90	.92	.81	.91	53.8
1923	1.17	.97	1.05	1.07	63.3
1924	1.08	1.02	1.05	1.05	62.1
1925	1.13	1.07	1.06	1.10	65.1
1926	1.24	1.11	1.11	1.18	69.8
1927	1.08	1.15	1.15	1.12	66.3
1928	1.23	1.13	1.25	1.18	69.8
1929	1.31	1.09	1.18	1.20	71.0
1930	1.03	1.09	. . .	1.06	62.7

Source: Warburton, *Economic Results of Prohibition,* 104.

sion of crime and the number of well-known criminals; the modern devices of communication, especially film and radio, were well suited to featuring action and suspense; the instability of the time—on both a national and international level—created a following for strong leadership, for someone to take control, if not for some form of exceptional individual.

TABLE 19.19 THE CONSUMPTION OF ALCOHOLIC BEVERAGES IN THE UNITED STATES BEFORE AND AFTER THE ADOPTION OF PROHIBITION

[Gallons per capita]

Period	Spirits	Beer	Wine	Pure Alcohol
1911–14	1.47	20.53	.59	1.69
1921–22	.92	1.49	.51	.73
1927–30	1.62	6.27	.98	1.14

Source: Warburton, *Economic Results of Prohibition,* 107.

TABLE 19.20 ARRESTS FOR DRUNKENNESS, 1910–1919, BEFORE PROHIBITION

Year	Arrests for Drunkenness per 10,000 Population, 383 Cities
1910	175
1911	179
1912	185
1913	191
1914	187
1915	182
1916	192
1917	180
1918	138
1919	102

Source: Warburton, *Economic Results of Prohibition,* 101.

TABLE 19.21

ARRESTS FOR DRUNKENNESS, 1920–1929, AFTER START OF PROHIBITION

Year	Arrests for Drunkenness per 10,000 Population 383 Cities
1920	71
1921	92
1922	122
1923	141
1924	141
1925	142
1926	146
1927	149
1928	157
1929	151

Source: Warburton, Economic Results of Prohibition, 102.

Movies in the 1930s featured the activity of the Thin Man (in a series of movies), Sherlock Holmes (1939), the various Charlie Chan mysteries, and such films as *Little Caesar* (1930), *The Big House* (1930), and *The Maltese Falcon* (1931 and a popular remake in 1941). The era encouraged the emergence of movie "tough guys"—such actors as George Raft, Edward G. Robinson, Sydney Greenstreet, James Cagney, and Humphrey Bogart—whose characters might be on either side of the law, or, as in the case of numerous private detectives, the private eyes, somewhere in between.

The theme was even more conspicuous with respect to radio. Sherlock Holmes came to radio, as did another crime fighter, "The Shadow," in 1930. The noisy and violent show "Gangbusters" appeared in 1935 and ran for many years; the "Green Hornet" came in 1936, "Big Town" in 1937, "Captain Midnight" in 1939. "Mr. District Attorney," which began in 1939, was based on the career of Attorney Thomas E. Dewey. "Bulldog Drummond" arrived in 1941, "Nick Carter" and "Perry Mason" in 1943, and "This Is Your F.B.I." in 1945. All these shows and many others were involved in some

TABLE 19.22 ACTIVITIES BY FEDERAL AGENTS, 1920–1929, DURING THE PERIOD OF NATIONAL PROHIBITION

	Period from Jan. 17 to Jun. 30, 1920	1921[a]	1922[a]	1923	1924	1925	1926[a]	1927[a]	1928	1929
Illicit distilleries seized	4,645	9,746	8,313	12,219	10,392	12,023	12,227	14,514	16,220	15,794
Illicit stills seized	4,888	10,991	10,994	14,000	15,853	17,854	12,248	11,881	18,980	11,542
Illicit still worms seized	2,218	5,182	10,203	7,512	8,211	7,850	6,974	8,024	9,133	7,982
Illicit fermenters seized	21,111	70,014	81,640	124,401	124,720	134,810	130,530	173,656	217,278	211,924
Gallons of distilled spirits seized	137,722.38	413,987.32	382,390.44	457,365.25	1,672,743.81	1,102,787.65	1,247,520.08	1,462,532.76	1,048,636.84	1,185,654.88
Gallons of malt liquor seized	1,637,483.00	4,963,005.27	4,187,625.67	4,803,872.92	5,379,528.03	7,040,537.30	14,220,551.93	5,971,903.35	4,254,029.58	3,312,491.28
Gallons of wine, cider, mash, and pomace seized	95,672.90	428,303.88	4,052,213.88	9,085,411.34	8,774,916.80	10,572,933.50	13,273,738.10	21,736,395.24	27,171,567.06	26,393,410.74
Number of automobiles seized	209	706	1,886	3,977	5,214	6,089	5,935	7,137	6,934	7,299
Number of boats and launches seized	3	23	74	134	236	182	187	353	81	89
Total appraised value of property seized	$1,262,196.67	$8,181,866.70	$5,872,092.09	$11,478,277.53	$10,843,881.83	$11,199,664.46	$13,835,524.85	$24,540,338.03	$23,204,345.20	$25,726,357.14
Number of agents injured	0	13	28	45	28	39	50	59	89	94
Number of agents killed	0	14	9	11	2	7	6	6	10	6
Number of persons arrested	10,548	34,175	42,223	66,936	68,116	62,474	58,391	64,986	75,307	66,878

[a] Fiscal year ended June 30.
Source: Charles Merz, The Dry Decade (Garden City, N.Y., 1931), 330–331.

TABLE 19.23 CRIMINAL PROSECUTIONS IN THE NATIONAL COURTS UNDER THE PROHIBITION ACT, 1920–1929

	Jan.–Jun. 1920	1921	1922	1923	1924	1925	1926	1927	1928	1929
Commenced during the year	7,291	29,14	34,984	49,021	45,878	50,743	44,492	50,250	73,034	74,723
Terminated during the same period	5,095	21,297	28,743	42,730	45,609	47,925	48,529	51,945	77,799	75,298
Convictions	4,315	17,962	22,749	34,067	37,181	38,498	37,018	36,546	58,813	56,546
Acquittals	125	765	1,195	1,770	1,754	1,805	1,303	1,557	2,722	2,666
Nol pros or dismissed	655	2,570	4,799	6,893	7,674	7,622	7,580	13,842	17,264	16,086
Pleas of guilty	4,109	16,610	20,571	30,654	33,834	35,034	34,233	33,430	54,325	51,651
Trials by jury	322	2,075	3,346	4,835	5,217	5,389	4,090	4,399	7,072	4,622
Pending close of year	2,196	10,365	16,713	23,060	22,329	24,684	20,749	20,173	18,005	19,468
Fines and penalties imposed	$605,314.42	$2,360,298.46	$4,041,456.03	$5,832,389.18	$7,497,235.19	$7,681,947.28	$7,494,557.09	$5,775,225.48[b]	$7,031,109.66[b]	$7,363,492.22[b]
Realized on fines, forfeitures, etc.	$507,482.70	$2,418,117.55	$2,376,305.20	$4,366,056.00	$5,682,719.87	$5,312,719.87	$5,231,130.90	. . .	. . .	. . .
Average fine	. . .	. . .	. . .	. . .	. . .	. . .	. . .	$157.90[b]	$120.00[b]	$130.00[b]
Collected without prosecution	[a]	[a]	$846.95	$144,528.63	$84,052.65	$65,430.10	$97,417.88	. . .	. . .	. . .
Number of jail sentences imposed	. . .	. . .	. . .	. . .	. . .	. . .	. . .	11,818[b]	15,793[b]	19,074[b]

	Jan.–Jun. 1920	1921	1922	1923	1924	1925	1926	1927	1928	1929
Average sentence (based on every conviction) days	. . .	. . .	. . .	. . .	. . .	. . .	. . .	44[b]	34.4[b]	47.3[b]
Average sentence (based on number of jail sentences given) days	. . .	. . .	. . .	. . .	. . .	. . .	. . .	136.4[b]	120.7[b]	140.4[b]
Percentage of jail sentences	. . .	. . .	. . .	. . .	. . .	. . .	. . .	32.3[b]	28.5[b]	33.7[b]
Percentage of convictions	. . .	. . .	. . .	. . .	. . .	. . .	. . .	70.3[b]	75.5[b]	75.0[b]

[a] No record.
[b] Suspended, paroled, and probated sentences not included.
Source: Merz, The Dry Decade, 332–333.

fashion in the pursuit of justice as it was defined in that day and in proving, as promised in "Gangbusters," that crime does not pay.

Paralleling the action and probably exceeding the idealism of radio was crime fighting in the comics. The "funnies" increasingly were not funny anymore, and the theme especially applied to the soaring popularity of the sixty-four-page, 10- by 7-inch comic books (as opposed to the newspaper comic "strips") that came of age in the late 1930s. The edition of *Detective Comics* that appeared in March 1937 was the first comic "book" (really a magazine) that contained all stories about crime fighters. The concept of the superhuman hero truly emerged with Superman, the "man of steel," who appeared in *Action Comics* in June 1938. Batman, a mere mortal but with advanced technology and superb crime-fighting talents, came to *Detective Comics* in May 1939, to be accompanied later that year by his assistant and protege, Robin. *Thrill Comics* in January 1940 introduced Captain Thunder, a speciman on the order of Superman who came to life by uttering the word *shazam*. This publication soon would be changed to *Whiz Comics* and the superhero to Captain Marvel. In future issues he would be joined by Captain Marvel, Jr., and even Mary Marvel. The concept of the female superhero also extended to Wonder Woman, beginning in 1942. In the 1940s the comic book heroes had to give some attention to the world war and the notion of an enemy abroad, but it was clear that even then they were most comfortable at home fighting robbers and killers, the mad scientists and wacky professors, the hoods and hoodlums, or any kind of enemy of American society. Although the comics were ordinarily regarded as designed for youngsters, mostly boys, there was good reason to believe that the readership extended much further, that comics and comic books provided reading material for many millions of people of many ages.

CHAPTER 20 Selected Documents

This chapter focuses on major turns in the course of the American nation—and of its people—as revealed largely in essential public documents: additions to the Constitution, laws, speeches that signaled a change in course. The chapter also offers a small sampling, hopefully representative, of the standing of individual groups of people. A list of such samples of course could be made much longer. Some documents appear in full, as in the case of the constitutional amendments, but in several cases portions have been deleted.

President Wilson's War Message April 2, 1917

By the year 1917 it became clear to the German government that it had no chance of winning the First World War unless it could prevent foreign supplies—most of them American—from reaching its enemies, Britain and France. The German decision to resume unrestricted submarine warfare in January 1917 represented a retraction of earlier promises made to the United States and threatened American lives and property. President Woodrow Wilson thus broke relations with Germany on February 3, 1917. When during the latter part of March German U-boats struck three U.S. ships, Wilson called Congress into special session on April 2. On that date the president gave an eloquent war message that defined the First World War and American participation in high moral terms. After a period of spirited debate, Congress on April 6 voted the War Resolution by 82–6 in the Senate and 373–50 in the House.

I have called the Congress into extraordinary session because there are serious, very serious, choices of policy to be made, and made immediately, which it was neither right nor constitutionally permissible that I should assume the responsibility of making.

On the third of February last I officially laid before you the extraordinary announcement of the Imperial German Government that on and after the first day of February it was its purpose to put aside all restraints of law or of humanity and use its submarines to sink every vessel that sought to approach either the ports of Great Britain and Ireland or the western coasts of Europe or any of the ports controlled by the enemies of Germany within the Mediterranean. That had seemed to be the object of the German submarine warfare earlier in the war, but since April of last year the Imperial Government had somewhat restrained the commanders of its undersea craft in conformity with its promise then given to us that passenger boats should not be sunk and that due warning would be given to all other vessels which its submarines might seek to destroy, when no resistance was offered or escape attempted, and care taken that their crews were given at least a fair chance to save their lives in their open boats. The precautions taken were meager and haphazard enough, as was proved in distressing instance after instance in the progress of the cruel and unmanly business, but a certain degree of restraint was observed. The new policy has swept every restriction aside. Vessels of every kind, whatever their flag, their character, their cargo, their destination, their errand, have been ruthlessly sent to the bottom without warning and without thought of help or mercy for those on board, the vessels of friendly neutrals along with those of belligerents. Even hospital ships and ships carrying relief to the sorely bereaved and stricken people of Belgium, though the latter were provided with safe conduct through the proscribed areas by the German Government itself and were dis-

tinguished by unmistakable marks of identity, have been sunk with the same reckless lack of compassion or of principle.

I was for a little while unable to believe that such things would in fact be done by any government that had hitherto subscribed to the humane practices of civilized nations. International law had its origin in the attempt to set up some law which would be respected and observed upon the seas, where no nation had right of dominion and where lay the free highways of the world. . . . This minimum of right the German Government has swept aside under the plea of retaliation and necessity and because it had no weapons which it could use at sea except these which it is impossible to employ as it is employing them without throwing to the winds all scruples of humanity or of respect for the understandings that were supposed to underlie the intercourse of the world. I am not now thinking of the loss of property involved, immense and serious as that is, but only of the wanton and wholesale destruction of the lives of non-combatants, men, women, and children, engaged in pursuits which have always, even in the darkest periods of modern history, been deemed innocent and legitimate. Property can be paid for; the lives of peaceful and innocent people cannot be. The present German submarine warfare against commerce is a warfare against mankind.

It is a war against all nations. American ships have been sunk, American lives taken, in ways which it has stirred us very deeply to learn of, but the ships and people of other neutral and friendly nations have been sunk and overwhelmed in the waters in the same way. There has been no discrimination. The challenge is to all mankind. Each nation must decide for itself how it will meet it. The choice we make for ourselves must be made with a moderation of counsel and a temperateness of judgment befitting our character and our motives as a nation. We must put excited feeling away. Our motive will not be revenge or the victorious assertion of the physical might of the nation, but only the vindication of right, of human right, of which we are only a single champion.

When I addressed the Congress on the twenty-sixth of February last I thought that it would suffice to assert our neutral rights with arms, our right to use the seas against unlawful interference, our right to keep our people safe against unlawful violence. But armed neutrality, it now appears, is impracticable. Because submarines are in effect outlaws when used as the German submarines have been used against merchant shipping, it is impossible to defend ships against their attacks as the law of nations has assumed that merchantmen would defend themselves against privateers or cruisers, visible craft giving chase upon the open sea. It is common prudence in such circumstances, grim necessity indeed, to endeavor to destroy them before they have shown their own intention. They must be dealt with upon sight, if dealt with at all. The German Government denies the right of neutrals to use arms at all within the areas of the sea which it has proscribed, even in the defense of rights which no modern publicist has ever before questioned their right to defend. The intimation is conveyed that the armed guards which we have placed on our merchant ships will be treated as beyond the pale of law and subject to be dealt with as pirates would be. Armed neutrality is ineffectual enough at best; in such circumstances and in the face of such pretensions it is worse than ineffectual: it is likely only to produce what it was meant to prevent; it is practically certain to draw us into the war without either the rights or the effectiveness of belligerents. There is one choice we cannot make, we are incapable of making: we will not choose the path of submission and suffer the most sacred rights of our Nation and our people to be ignored or violated. The wrongs against which we now array ourselves are no common wrongs; they cut to the very roots of human life.

With a profound sense of the solemn and even tragical character of the step I am taking and of the grave responsibilities which it involves, but in unhesitating obedience to what I deem my constitutional duty, I advise that the Congress declare the recent course of the Imperial German Government to be in fact nothing less than war against the government and people of the United States; that it formally accept the status of belligerent which has thus been thrust upon it; and that it take immediate steps not only to put the country in a more thorough state of defense but also to exert all its power and employ all its resources to bring the Government of the German Empire to terms and end the war.

What this will involve is clear. It will involve the utmost practicable cooperation in counsel and action with the governments now at war with Germany, and, as incident to that, the extension to those governments of the most liberal financial credits, in order that our resources may so far as possible be added to theirs. It will involve the organization and mobilization of all the material resources of the country to supply the materials of war and serve the incidental needs of the Nation in the most abundant and yet the most economical and efficient way possible. It will involve the immediate full equipment of the navy in all respects but particularly in supplying it with the best means of dealing with the enemy's submarines. It will involve the immediate addition to the armed forces of the United States already provided for by law in case of war at least five hundred thousand men, who should, in my opinion, be chosen upon the principle of universal liability to service, and also the authorization of subsequent additional increments of equal force so soon as they may be needed and can be handled in training. It will involve also, of course, the granting of adequate credits to the Government, sustained, I hope, so far as they can equitably be sustained by the present generation, by well conceived taxation. . . .

While we do these things, these deeply momentous things, let us be very clear, and make very clear to all the world what our motives and our objects are. My own thought has not been driven from its habitual and normal course by the unhappy events of the last two months, and I do not believe that the thought of the Nation has been altered or clouded by them. I have exactly the same things in mind now that I had in mind when I addressed the Senate on the twenty-second of January last; the same that I had in mind when I addressed the Congress on the third of February and on the twenty-sixth of February. Our object now, as then, is to vindicate the principles of peace and justice in the life of the world as against selfish and autocratic power and to set up amongst the really free and self-governed peoples of the world such a concert of purpose and of action as will henceforth insure the observance of those principles. Neutrality is no longer feasible or desirable where the peace of the world is involved and the freedom of its peoples, and the menace to that peace and freedom lies in the existence of autocratic governments backed by organized force which is controlled wholly by their will, not by the will of their people. We have seen the last of neutrality in such circumstances. We are at the beginning of an age in which it will be insisted that the same standards of conduct and of responsibility for wrong done shall be observed among nations and their governments that are ob-

served among the individual citizens of civilized states.

We have no quarrel with the German people. We have no feeling towards them but one of sympathy and friendship. It was not upon their impulse that their government acted in entering this war. It was not with their previous knowledge or approval. It was a war determined upon as wars used to be determined upon in the old, unhappy days when peoples were nowhere consulted by their rulers and wars were provoked and waged in the interest of dynasties or of little groups of ambitious men who were accustomed to use their fellow men as pawns and tools. . . .

We are accepting this challenge of hostile purpose because we know that in such a Government, following such methods, we can never have a friend; and that in the presence of its organized power, always lying in wait to accomplish we know not what purpose, there can be no assured security for the democratic Governments of the world. We are now about to accept gauge of battle with this natural foe to liberty and shall, if necessary, spend the whole force of the nation to check and nullify its pretensions and its power. We are glad, now that we see the facts with no veil of false pretense about them, to fight thus for the ultimate peace of the world and for the liberation of its peoples, the German peoples included: for the rights of nations great and small and the privilege of men everywhere to choose their way of life and of obedience. The world must be made safe for democracy. Its peace must be planted upon the tested foundations of political liberty. We have no selfish ends to serve. We desire no conquest, no dominion. We seek no indemnities for ourselves, no material compensation for the sacrifices we shall freely make. We are but one of the champions of the rights of mankind. We shall be satisfied when those rights have been made as secure as the faith and the freedom of nations can make them.

Just because we fight without rancor and without selfish object, seeking nothing for ourselves but what we shall wish to share with all free peoples, we shall, I feel confident, conduct our operations as belligerents without passion and ourselves observe with proud punctilio the principles of right and of fair play we profess to be fighting for.

I have said nothing of the Governments allied with the Imperial Government of Germany because they have not made war upon us or challenged us to defend our right and our honor. The Austro-Hungarian Government has, indeed, avowed its unqualified indorsement and acceptance of the reckless and lawless submarine warfare adopted now without disguise by the Imperial German Government, and it has therefore not been possible for this Government to receive Count Tarnowski, the Ambassador recently accredited to this Government by the Imperial and Royal Government of Austria-Hungary; but that Government has not actually engaged in warfare against citizens of the United States on the seas, and I take the liberty, for the present at least, of postponing a discussion of our relations with the authorities at Vienna. We enter this war only where we are clearly forced into it because there are no other means of defending our rights.

It will be all the easier for us to conduct ourselves as belligerents in a high spirit of right and fairness because we act without animus, not in enmity towards a people or with the desire to bring any injury or disadvantage upon them, but only in armed opposition to an irresponsible government which has thrown aside all considerations of humanity and of right and is running amuck. We are, let me say again, the sincere friends of the German people, and shall desire nothing so much as the early reestablishment of intimate relations of mutual advantage between us,—however hard it may be for them, for the time being, to believe that this is spoken from our hearts. We have borne with their present Government through all these bitter months because of that friendship,—exercising a patience and forbearance which would otherwise have been impossible. We shall, happily, still have an opportunity to prove that friendship in our daily attitude and actions towards the millions of men and women of German birth and native sympathy who live amongst us and share our life, and we shall be proud to prove it towards all who are in fact loyal to their neighbors and to the Government in the hour of test. They are, most of them, as true and loyal Americans as if they had never known any other fealty or allegiance. They will be prompt to stand with us in rebuking and restraining the few who may be of a different mind and purpose. If there should be disloyalty, it will be dealt with with a firm hand of stern repression; but, if it lifts its head at all, it will lift it only here and there and without countenance except from a lawless and malignant few.

It is a distressing and oppressive duty, Gentlemen of the Congress, which I have performed in thus addressing you. There are, it may be, many months of fiery trial and sacrifice ahead of us. It is a fearful thing to lead this great peaceful people into war, into the most terrible and disastrous of all wars, civilization itself seeming to be in the balance. But the right is more precious than peace, and we shall fight for the things which we have always carried nearest our hearts,—for democracy, for the right of those who submit to authority to have a voice in their own Governments, for the rights and liberties of small nations, for a universal dominion of right by such a concert of free peoples as shall bring peace and safety to all nations and make the world itself at last free. To such a task we can dedicate our lives and our fortunes, everything that we are and everything that we have, with the pride of those who know that the day has come when America is privileged to spend her blood and her might for the principles that gave her birth and happiness and the peace which she has treasured. God helping her, she can do no other.

Source: Department of State, Foreign Relations of the United States, 1917, Supplement I: The World War (Washington, D.C., 1931), 195–203.

Amendments to the Constitution (XVIII, XIX, XX, XXI)

The four amendments added to the Constitution during the years 1914–45 all reflected the period that produced them. The Eighteenth and Nineteenth dealt with old issues in American history—prohibition of alcoholic beverages and woman suffrage—that received a new spark in the early part of the twentieth century. Both wore marks of the reformist mood in the Progressive movement (prohibition less so than woman suffrage); both benefited from changes and attitudes that came from the First World War. Granting women the vote was a reform that was long overdue; prohibition helped set the tone for the period of the 1920s. The Twentieth Amendment treated the old problem of a "lame duck" national government—the fact that after being elected, a president did not take office for three months. The Great Depression added a touch of urgency to the issue. It revealed an impatience with having to wait so long for a new government pledged to deal with the economic collapse. The Twenty-first Amendment, which canceled the Eighteenth and thus repealed prohibition as national policy, represented a reaction against a failed policy—and a failed political administration—of the recent past. It revealed the thinking that with the coming of a new government in 1933 there needed to be a new course for the United States. Prohibition, one might add, had deprived government of tax revenue, which in these desperate times it dearly needed.

AMENDMENT XVIII

[PROPOSED 18 DECEMBER 1917; DECLARED RATIFIED 29 JANUARY 1919]

After one year from the ratification of this article, the manufacture, sale, or transportation of intoxicating liquors within, the importation thereof into, or the exportation thereof from the United States and all territory subject to the jurisdiction thereof for beverage purposes is hereby prohibited.

The Congress and the several States shall have concurrent power to enforce this article by appropriate legislation.

This article shall be inoperative unless it shall have been ratified as an amendment to the Constitution by the legislatures of the several States, as provided in the Constitution, within seven years from the date of the submission thereof to the States by Congress.

AMENDMENT XIX

[PROPOSED 4 JUNE 1919; DECLARED RATIFIED 26 AUGUST 1920]

The right of citizens of the United States to vote shall not be denied or abridged by the United States or by any State on account of sex.

The Congress shall have power by appropriate legislation to enforce the provisions of this article.

AMENDMENT XX

[PROPOSED 2 MARCH 1932; DECLARED RATIFIED 6 FEBRUARY 1933]

Section 1. The terms of the President and Vice-President shall end at noon on the twentieth day of January, and the terms of Senators and Representatives at noon on the third day of January, of the years in which such terms would have ended if this article had not been ratified; and the terms of their successors shall then begin.

Section 2. The Congress shall assemble at least once in every year, and such meeting shall begin at noon on the third day of January, unless they shall by law appoint a different day.

Section 3. If, at the time fixed for the beginning of the term of the President, the President-elect shall have died, the Vice-President-elect shall become President. If a President shall not have been chosen before the time fixed for the beginning of his term, or if the President-elect shall have failed to qualify, then the Vice-President-elect shall act as President until a President shall have qualified; and the Congress may by law provide for the case wherein neither a President-elect nor a Vice-President-elect shall have qualified, declaring who shall then act as President, or the manner in which one who is to act shall be selected, and such person shall act accordingly until a President or Vice-President shall have qualified.

Section 4. The Congress may by law provide for the case of the death of any of the persons from whom the House of Representatives may choose a President whenever the right of choice shall have devolved upon them, and for the case of the death of any of the persons from whom the Senate may choose a Vice-President whenever the right of choice shall have devolved upon them.

Section 5. Sections 1 and 2 shall take effect on the 15th day of October following the ratification of this article.

Section 6. This article shall be inoperative unless it shall have been ratified as an amendment to the Constitution by the legislatures of three-fourths of the several States within seven years from the date of its submission.

AMENDMENT XXI

[PROPOSED 20 FEBRUARY 1933; DECLARED RATIFIED 5 DECEMBER 1933]

Section 1. The eighteenth article of amendment to the Constitution of the United States is hereby repealed.

Section 2. The transportation or importation into any State, Territory or possession of the United States for delivery or use therein of intoxicating liquors, in violation of the laws thereof, is hereby prohibited.

Section 3. This article shall be inoperative unless it shall have been ratified as an amendment to the Constitution by convention in the several States, as provided in the Constitution, within seven years from the date of the submission thereof to the States by the Congress.

The Volstead Act
October 28, 1919

The Eighteenth Amendment, which went into effect on January 16, 1920, merely forbade the production and sale of intoxicating liquor. It became the responsibility of Congress to provide for enforcement, a responsibility that included defining what legally constituted an alcoholic beverage. It has been suggested that if Congress had authorized the use of light wine and beer within the confines of the amendment, prohibition might have had a decent chance of working. The legislature instead was ruthless; by defining an intoxicant as a beverage with one-half of 1% alcohol or more, it permitted virtually nothing alcoholic. Any exceptions, mostly for religious or medicinal purposes, had to conform with specific conditions.

Be it Enacted. . . . That the short title of this Act shall be the "National Prohibition Act."

TITLE I.

TO PROVIDE FOR THE ENFORCEMENT OF WAR PROHIBITION.

The term "War Prohibition Act" used in this Act shall mean the provisions of any Act or Acts prohibiting the sale and manufacture of intoxicating liquors until the conclusion of the present war and thereafter until the termination of demobilization, the date of which shall be determined and proclaimed by the President of the United States. The words "beer, wine, or other intoxicating malt or vinous liquors" in the War Prohibition Act shall be hereafter construed to mean any such beverages which contain one-half of 1 per centum or more of alcohol by volume: . . .

TITLE II.

PROHIBITION OF INTOXICATING BEVERAGES.

SEC. 3. No person shall on or after the date when the eighteenth amendment to the Constitution of the United States goes into effect, manufacture, sell, barter, transport, import, export, deliver, furnish or possess any intoxicating liquor except as authorized in this Act, and all the provisions of this Act shall be liberally construed to the end that the use of intoxicating liquor as a beverage may be prevented.

Liquor for nonbeverage purposes and wine for sacramental purposes may be manufactured, purchased, sold, bartered, transported, imported, exported, delivered, furnished and possessed, but only as herein provided, and the commissioner may, upon application, issue permits therefor. . . .

All permits to manufacture, prescribe, sell, or transport liquor, may be issued for one year, and shall expire on the 31st day of December next succeeding the issuance thereof: . . . Permits to purchase liquor shall specify the quantity and kind to be purchased and the purpose for which it is to be used. . . .

No person to whom a permit may be issued to manufacture, transport, import, or sell wines for sacramental purposes or like religious rites shall sell, barter, exchange, or furnish any such to any person not a rabbi, minister of the gospel, priest, or an officer duly authorized for the purpose by any church or congregation, nor to any such except upon an application duly subscribed by him. . . .

SEC. 7. No one but a physician holding a permit to prescribe liquor shall issue any prescription for liquor. And no physician shall prescribe liquor unless after careful physical examination of the person for whose use such prescription is sought, or if such examination is found impracticable, then upon the best information obtainable, he in good faith believes that the use of such liquor as a medicine by such person is necessary and will afford relief to him from some known ailment. Not more than a pint of spiritous liquor to be taken internally shall be prescribed for use by the same person within any period of ten days and no prescription shall be filled more than once. Any pharmacist filling a prescription shall at the time indorse upon it over his own signature the word "canceled," together with the date when the liquor was delivered, and then make the same a part of the record that he is required to keep as herein provided. . . .

SEC. 29. Any person who manufactures or sells liquor in violation of this title shall for a first offense be fined not more than $1,000, or imprisoned not exceeding six months, and for a second or subsequent offense shall be fined not less than $200 nor more than $2,000 and be imprisoned not less than one month nor more than five years. . . .

SEC. 33. After February 1, 1920, the possession of liquors by any person not legally permitted under this title to possess liquor shall be prima facie evidence that such liquor is kept for the purpose of being sold, bartered, exchanged, given away, furnished, or otherwise disposed of in violation of the Provisions of this title. . . . But it shall not be unlawful to possess liquors in one's private dwelling while the same is occupied and used by him as his dwelling only and such liquor need not be reported, provided such liquors are for use only for the personal consumption of the owner thereof and his family residing in such dwelling and of his bona fide guests when entertained by him therein; and the burden of proof shall be upon the possessor in any action concerning the same to prove that such liquor was lawfully acquired, possessed, and used. . . .

Source: United States Congress, *United States Statutes at Large,* vol. 41, October 28, 1919 (Washington, D.C., 1919), 305–323.

Social Practices in 1924

The period of the 1920s was a time of revolution in manners and social behavior that extended to sexual behavior, as reflected in the passage that follows. The article dealt with a summer conference of college women in 1924 that focused on female behavior during dates. The passage indicated that new terms had surfaced to describe behavior in courtship, notably necking *and* petting, *and that interest in social adventurism had become much more open than in previous years and a great deal more widespread. It appeared that more lax and liberal female sexual practices had spread from the general society to the campus, rather than the other way around.*

Last summer I was at a student conference of young women comprised of about eight hundred college girls from the middle western states. The subject of petting was very much on their minds, both as to what attitude they should take toward it with the younger girls, (being upperclassmen themselves) and also how much renunciation of this pleasurable pastime was required of them. If I recall correctly, two entire mornings were devoted to discussing the matter, two evenings, and another overflow meeting.

So far as I could judge from their discussion groups, the girls did not advise younger classmen not to pet—they merely advised them to be moderate about it, not lose their heads, not go too far—in fact the same line of conduct which is advised for moderate drinking. Learn temperance in petting, not abstinence.

Before the conference I made it my business to talk to as many college girls as possible. I consulted as many, both in groups and privately, as I had time for at the conference. And since it is all to be repeated in another state this summer, I have been doing so, when opportunity offered, ever since. Just what does petting consist in? What ages take it most seriously? Is it a factor in every party? Do "nice" girls do it, as well as those who are not so "nice"? Are they "stringing" their elders, by exaggerating the prevalence of petting, or is there more of it than they admit? These are samples of the questions I have asked, and have heard them ask each other in the discussions where I have listened in.

One fact is evident, that whether or not they pet, they hesitate to have anyone believe that they do not. It is distinctly the *mores* of the time to be considered as ardently sought after, and as not too priggish to respond. As one girl said—"I don't particularly care to be kissed by some of the fellows I know, but I'd let them do it any time rather than think I wouldn't dare. As a matter of fact, there are lots of fellows I don't kiss. It's the very young kids that never miss a chance."

That petting should lead to actual illicit relations between the petters was not advised nor countenanced among the girls with whom I discussed it. They drew the line quite sharply. That it often did so lead, they admitted, but they were not ready to allow that there were any more of such affairs than there had always been. School and college scandals, with their sudden departures and hasty marriages, have always existed to some extent, and they still do. But only accurate statistics, hard to arrive at, can prove whether or not the sex carelessness of the present day extends to an increase of sex immorality, or whether since so many more people go to college, there is an actual decrease in the amount of it, in proportion to the number of students. The girls seemed to feel that those who went too far were more fools than knaves, and that in most cases they married. They thought that hasty and secret marriages, of which most of them could report several, were foolish, but after all about as likely to turn out well as any others. Their attitude toward such contingencies was disapproval, but it was expressed with a slightly amused shrug, a shrug which one can imagine might have sat well on the shoulders of Voltaire. In fact the writer was torn, in her efforts to sum up their attitude, between classifying them as eighteenth century realists and as Greek nymphs existing before the dawn of history!

I sat with one pleasant college Amazon, a total stranger, beside a fountain in the park, while she asked if I saw any harm in her kissing a young man whom she liked, but whom she did not want to marry. "It's terribly exciting. We get such a thrill. I think it is natural to want nice men to kiss you, so why not do what is natural?" There was no embarrassment in her manner. Her eyes and her conscience were equally untroubled. I felt as if a girl from the Parthenon frieze had stepped down to ask if she might not sport in the glade with a handsome faun. Why not indeed? Only an equally direct forcing of twentieth century science on primitive simplicity could bring us even to the same level in our conversation, and at that, the stigma of impropriety seemed to fall on me, rather than on her. It was hard to tell whether her infantilism were real, or half-consciously assumed in order to have a child's license and excuse to do as she pleased. I am inclined to think that both with her and with many others, it is assumed. One girl said, "When I have had a few nights without dates I nearly go crazy. I tell my mother she must expect me to go out on a fearful necking party." In different parts of the country, *petting* and *necking* have opposite meanings. One locality calls necking (I quote their definition) "petting only from the neck up." Petting involves anything else you please. Another section reverses the distinction, and the girl in question was from the latter area. In what manner she announces to her mother her plans to neck, and in what manner her mother accepts the announcement, I cannot be sure. . . .

The sex manners of the large majority of uncultivated and uncritical people have become the manners for all, because they have prospered, they are getting educated, and there are so many of them. They are not squeamish, and they never have been. But their children can set a social standard as the parents could not. The prudent lawyer's child has no idea of letting the gay daughter of the broad-joking workman get the dates away from her. If petting is the weapon Miss Workman uses, then petting it must be, and in nine cases out of ten, not only Mrs. Workman, but also Mrs. Lawyer agree not to see too much. At heart both women are alike. Neither one can bear to see her daughter take a back seat in the struggle for popularity, and neither woman has any other ambition for her daughter but a successful husband. If by any chance, petting led *away* from popularity and possible husbands instead of *to* them, the mothers would be whole-heartedly against it, and if they were—petting, as a recognized recreation, would stop.

Source: Eleanor Rowland Wembridge, "Petting and the Campus," *Survey* (July 1, 1925): 393–395.

Franklin D. Roosevelt's First Inaugural Address
March 4, 1933

This first speech as president by Franklin D. Roosevelt became one of his most memorable addresses, with early signs of Roosevelt's flair for catchy phrases and an ability to communicate with the people. Coming at a time when the Great Depression was near its lowest point, the speech carried a message of hope, optimism, and dedication. The memorable passages included the new president's remark that "the only thing we have to fear is fear itself," and a heartening pledge to action, regardless of whether or not Congress decided to move.

President Hoover, Mr. Chief Justice, my friends:

This is a day of national consecration, and I am certain that my fellow-Americans expect that on my induction into the Presidency I will address them with a candor and a decision which the present situation of our nation impels.

This is pre-eminently the time to speak the truth, the whole truth, frankly and boldly. Nor need we shrink from honestly facing conditions in our country today. This great nation will endure as it has endured, will revive and will prosper.

So first of all let me assert my firm belief that the only thing we have to fear is fear itself—nameless, unreasoning, unjustified terror which paralyzes needed efforts to convert retreat into advance.

In every dark hour of our national life a leadership of frankness and vigor has met with that understanding and support of the people themselves which is essential to victory. I am convinced that you will again give that support to leadership in these critical days.

In such a spirit on my part and on yours we face our common difficulties. They concern, thank God, only material things. Values have shrunken to fantastic levels; taxes have risen; our ability to pay has fallen, government of all kinds is faced by serious curtailment of income; the means of exchange are frozen in the currents of trade; the withered leaves of industrial enterprise lie on every side; farmers find no markets for their produce; the savings of many years in thousands of families are gone.

More important, a host of unemployed citizens face the grim problem of existence, and an equally great number toil with little return. Only a foolish optimist can deny the dark realities of the moment.

Yet our distress comes from no failure of substance. We are stricken by no plague of locusts. Compared with the perils which our forefathers conquered because they believed and were not afraid, we have still much to be thankful for. Nature still offers her bounty and human efforts have multiplied it. Plenty is at our doorstep, but a generous use of it languishes in the very sight of the supply.

Primarily, this is because the rulers of the exchange of mankind's goods have failed through their own stubbornness and their own incompetence, have admitted their failure and abdicated. Practices of the unscrupulous money changers stand indicted in the court of public opinion, rejected by the hearts and minds of men.

True, they have tried, but their efforts have been cast in the pattern of an outworn tradition. Faced by failure of credit, they have proposed only the lending of more money.

Stripped of the lure of profit by which to induce our people to follow their false leadership, they have resorted to exhortations, pleading tearfully for restored confidence. They know only the rules of a generation of self-seekers.

They have no vision, and when there is no vision the people perish.

The money changers have fled from their high seats in the temple of our civilization. We may now restore that temple to the ancient truths.

The measure of the restoration lies in the extent to which we apply social values more noble than mere monetary profit.

Happiness lies not in the mere possession of money; it lies in the joy of achievement, in the thrill of creative effort.

The joy and moral stimulation of work no longer must be forgotten in the mad chase of evanescent profits. These dark days will be worth all they cost us if they teach us that our true destiny is not to be ministered unto but to minister to ourselves and to our fellow-men.

Recognition of the falsity of material wealth as the standard of success goes hand in hand with the abandonment of the false belief that public office and high political position are to be valued only by the standards of pride of place and personal profit; and there must be an end to a conduct in banking and in business which too often has given to a sacred trust the likeness of callous and selfish wrongdoing.

Small wonder that confidence languishes, for it thrives only on honesty, on honor, on the sacredness of obligations, on faithful protection, on unselfish performance. Without them it cannot live.

Restoration calls, however, not for changes in ethics alone. This nation asks for action, and action now.

Our greatest primary task is to put people to work. This is no unsolvable problem if we face it wisely and courageously.

It can be accomplished in part by direct recruiting by the government itself, treating the task as we would treat the emergency of a war, but at the same time, through this employment, accomplishing greatly needed projects to stimulate and reorganize the use of our natural resources.

Hand in hand with this, we must frankly recognize the overbalance of population in our industrial centers and, by engaging on a national scale in the redistribution, endeavor to provide a better use of the land for those best fitted for the land.

The task can be helped by definite efforts to raise the values of agricultural products and with this the power to purchase the output of our cities.

It can be helped by preventing realistically the tragedy of the growing loss, through foreclosure, of our small homes and our farms.

It can be helped by insistence that the Federal, State and local governments act forthwith on the demand that their cost be drastically reduced.

It can be helped by the unifying of relief activities which today are often scattered, uneconomical and unequal. It can be helped by national planning for and supervision of all forms of transportation and of communications and other utilities which have a definitely public character.

There are many ways in which it can be helped, but it can never be helped merely by talking about it. We must act, and act quickly.

Finally, in our progress toward a resumption of work we require two safeguards against a return of the evils of the old order; there must be a strict supervision of all banking and credits and investments; there must be an end to speculation with other people's money, and there must be provision for an adequate but sound currency.

These are the lines of attack. I shall presently urge upon a new Congress in special session detailed measures for their fulfillment, and I shall seek the immediate assistance of the several States.

Through this program of action we address ourselves to putting our own national house in order and making income balance outgo.

Our international trade relations, though vastly important, are, in point of time and necessity, secondary to the establishment of a sound national economy.

I favor as a practical policy the putting of first things first. I shall spare no effort to restore world trade by international economic readjustment, but the emergency at home cannot wait on that accomplishment.

The basic thought that guides these specific means of national recovery is not narrowly nationalistic.

It is the insistence, as a first consideration, upon the

interdependence of the various elements in, and parts of, the United States—a recognition of the old and permanently important manifestation of the American spirit of the pioneer.

It is the way to recovery. It is the immediate way. It is the strongest assurance that the recovery will endure.

In the field of world policy I would dedicate this nation to the policy of the good neighbor—the neighbor who resolutely respects himself and, because he does so, respects the rights of others—the neighbor who respects his obligations and respects the sanctity of his agreements in and with a world of neighbors.

If I read the temper of our people correctly, we now realize as we have never before, our interdependence on each other; that we cannot merely take, but we must give as well; that if we are to go forward we must move as a trained and loyal army willing to sacrifice for the good of a common discipline, because, without such discipline, no progress is made, no leadership becomes effective.

We are, I know, ready and willing to submit our lives and property to such discipline because it makes possible a leadership which aims at a larger good.

This I propose to offer, pledging that the larger purposes will bind upon us all as a sacred obligation with a unity of duty hitherto evoked only in time of armed strife.

With this pledge taken, I assume unhesitatingly the leadership of this great army of our people, dedicated to a disciplined attack upon our common problems.

Action in this image and to this end is feasible under the form of government which we have inherited from our ancestors.

Our Constitution is so simple and practical that it is possible always to meet extraordinary needs by changes in emphasis and arrangement without loss of essential form.

That is why our constitutional system has proved itself the most superbly enduring political mechanism the modern world has produced. It has met every stress of vast expansion of territory, of foreign wars, of bitter internal strife, of world relations.

It is to be hoped that the normal balance of executive and legislative authority may be wholly adequate to meet the unprecedented task before us. But it may be that an unprecedented demand and need for undelayed action may call for temporary departure from that normal balance of public procedure.

I am prepared under my constitutional duty to recommend the measures that a stricken nation in the midst of a stricken world may require.

These measures, or such other measures as the Congress may build out of its experience and wisdom, I shall seek, within my constitutional authority, to bring to speedy adoption.

But in the event that the Congress shall fail to take one of these two courses, and in the event that the national emergency is still critical, I shall not evade the clear course of duty that will then confront me.

I shall ask the Congress for the one remaining instrument to meet the crisis—broad executive power to wage a war against the emergency as great as the power that would be given me if we were in fact invaded by a foreign foe.

For the trust reposed in me I will return the courage and the devotion that befit the time. I can do no less.

We face the arduous days that lie before us in the warm courage of national unity; with the clear consciousness of seeking old and precious moral values; with the clean satisfaction that comes from the stern performance of duty by old and young alike.

We aim at the assurance of a rounded and permanent national life.

We do not distrust the future of essential democracy. The people of the United States have not failed. In their need they have registered a mandate that they want direct, vigorous action.

They have asked for discipline and direction under leadership. They have made me the present instrument of their wishes. In the spirit of the gift I take it.

In this dedication of a nation we humbly ask the blessing of God. May He protect each and every one of us! May He guide me in the days to come!

Source: Samuel I. Rosenman, *The Public Papers and Addresses of Franklin D. Roosevelt,* vol. 2 (New York, 1938), 11–16.

The National Labor Relations Act July 5, 1935

The National Labor Relations Act, probably better known as the Wagner Act, was the most important piece of labor legislation in American history. It came during the depression, when workers in general needed a helping hand and when the union movement had dropped to its lowest point in many years. The act placed the power of the national government behind the right of workers to organize, be recognized by management, and bargain on a basis of equality—needless to say, a move without precedent in American government and economic policy. A new Labor Relations Board undertook responsibility for supervising these rights. The Wagner Act helped make the 1930s the most productive decade for labor's becoming a potent force in American society and cemented a relationship between the labor movement and the Democratic Party.

An Act to diminish the causes of labor disputes burdening or obstructing interstate and foreign commerce, to create a National Labor Relations Board, and for other purposes.
    Be it enacted,

FINDINGS AND POLICY

SECTION 1. The denial by employers of the right of employees to organize and the refusal by employers to accept the procedure of collective bargaining lead to strikes and other forms of industrial strife or unrest, which have the intent or the necessary effect of burdening or obstructing commerce by (a) impairing the efficiency, safety, or operation of the instrumentalities of commerce; (b) occurring in the current of commerce; (c) materially affecting, restraining, or controlling the flow of raw materials or manufactured or processed goods from or into the channels of commerce, or the prices of such materials or goods in commerce; or (d) causing diminution of employment and wages in such volume as substantially to impair or disrupt the market for goods flowing from or into the channels of commerce. . . .

It is hereby declared to be the policy of the United States to eliminate the causes of certain substantial obstructions to the free flow of commerce and to mitigate and eliminate these obstructions when they have occurred by encouraging the practice and procedure of collective bargaining and by protecting the exercise by workers of full freedom of association, self-organization, and designation of representatives of their own choosing, for the purpose of negotiating the terms and conditions of their employment or other mutual aid or protection. . . .

NATIONAL LABOR RELATIONS BOARD

SEC. 3. (a) There is hereby created a board, to be known as the "National Labor Relations Board," which shall be composed of three members, who shall be appointed by the President, by and with the advice and consent of the Senate. One of the original members shall be appointed for a term of one year, one for a term of three years, and one for a term of five years, but their successors shall be appointed for terms of five years each, except that any individual chosen to fill a vacancy shall be appointed only for the unexpired term of the member whom he shall succeed. The President shall designate one member to serve as chairman of the Board. Any member of the Board may be removed by the President, upon notice and hearing, for neglect of duty or malfeasance in office, but for no other cause. . . .

SEC. 6. (a) The Board shall have authority from time to time to make, amend, and rescind such rules and regulations as may be necessary to carry out the provisions of this Act. Such rules and regulations shall be effective upon publication in the manner which the Board shall prescribe.

RIGHTS OF EMPLOYEES

SEC. 7. Employees shall have the right of self-organization, to form, join, or assist labor organizations, to bargain collectively through representatives of their own choosing, and to engage in concerted activities, for the purpose of collective bargaining or other mutual aid or protection.

SEC. 8. It shall be an unfair labor practice for an employer—

(1) To interfere with, restrain, or coerce employees in the exercise of the rights guaranteed in section 7.

(2) To dominate or interfere with the formation or administration of any labor organization or contribute financial or other support to it. . . .

(3) By discrimination in regard to hire or tenure of employment or any term or condition of employment to encourage or discourage membership in any labor organization. . . .

(4) To discharge or otherwise discriminate against an employee because he has filed charges or given testimony under this Act.

(5) To refuse to bargain collectively with the representatives of his employees, subject to the provisions of Section 9 (a).

REPRESENTATIVES AND ELECTIONS

SEC. 9. (a) Representatives designated or selected for the purposes of collective bargaining by the majority of the employees in a unit appropriate for such purposes, shall be the exclusive representatives of all the employees in such unit for the purposes of collective bargaining in respect to rates of pay, wages, hours of employment, or other conditions of employment: *Provided,* That any individual employee or a group of employees shall have the right at any time to present grievances to their employer. . . .

(b) The Board shall decide in each case whether, in order to insure to employees the full benefit of their right to self-organization and to collective bargaining, and otherwise to effectuate the policies of this Act, the unit appropriate for the purposes of collective bargaining shall be the employer unit, craft unit, plant unit, or subdivision thereof. . . .

PREVENTION OF UNFAIR LABOR PRACTICES

SEC. 10. (a) The Board is empowered, as hereinafter provided, to prevent any person from engaging in any unfair labor practice (listed in section 8) affecting commerce. This power shall be ex-

clusive, and shall not be affected by any other means of adjustment or prevention that has been or may be established by agreement, code, law, or otherwise. . . .

LIMITATIONS

SEC. 13. Nothing in this Act shall be construed so as to interfere with or impede or diminish in any way the right to strike. . . .

Source: United States Congress, *United States Statutes at Large,* vol. 49, pt. 1 (Washington, D.C., 1936), 449–457.

The Social Security Act
August 14, 1935

It was not until the mid-1930s, in the midst of the Great Depression, that the national government began to inquire into the multiple issues of financial and social security in the United States—such old problems as unemployment, old-age retirement, disability, and dependency now worsened by the depression and by the nation's steady march toward an urban and industrial nation. Up to this point the problems had been left up to the states or to private individuals and families. The Social Security Act emerged as a part of the second phase of Franklin D. Roosevelt's New Deal, the part that came in 1935–36. In the end it became one of the most significant moves of the Roosevelt years. The measure of 1935 to be sure had many shortcomings: Millions of people were excluded from coverage; stipends were small for those who did qualify. The imposition of new taxes to fund the program did nothing to combat the depression. Even with these limitations the Social Security Act still stands as landmark legislation in American social history, a foundation on which future generations could build. The measure also stood as an expression of the trend—prominent in the 1930s and perhaps ever since that time— toward problem solving through the central government. If the excerpts below provide only introductions to the sections of a detailed and complicated measure, they at least offer a hint of the new social responsibilities undertaken by the national government.

An Act to provide for the general welfare by establishing a system of Federal old-age benefits, and by enabling the several States to make more adequate provision for aged persons, blind persons, dependent and crippled children, maternal and child welfare, public health, and the administration of their unemployment compensation laws; to establish a Social Security Board; to raise revenue; and for other purposes.

Be it enacted by the Senate and House of Representatives of the United States of America in Congress assembled,

TITLE I—GRANTS TO STATES FOR OLD AGE ASSISTANCE

APPROPRIATION

SECTION 1. For the purpose of enabling each State to furnish financial assistance, as far as practicable under the conditions in such State, to aged needy individuals, there is hereby authorized to be appropriated for the fiscal year ending June 30, 1936, the sum of $49,750,000, and there is hereby authorized to be appropriated for each fiscal year thereafter a sum sufficient to carry out the purposes of this title. The sums made available under this section shall be used for making payments to States which have submitted, and had approved by the Social Security Board established by Title VII, State plans for old-age assistance. . . .

TITLE II—FEDERAL OLD-AGE BENEFITS

OLD-AGE RESERVE ACCOUNT

SECTION 201. (a) There is hereby created an account in the Treasury of the United States to be known as the "Old-Age Reserve Account." . . .

OLD-AGE BENEFIT PAYMENTS

SEC. 202. (a) Every qualified individual shall be entitled to receive, with respect to the period beginning on the date he attains the age of sixty-five, or on January 1, 1942, whichever is the later, and ending on the date of his death, an old-age benefit. . . .

TITLE III—GRANTS TO STATES FOR UNEMPLOYMENT COMPENSATION ADMINISTRATION

APPROPRIATION

SECTION 301. For the purpose of assisting the States in the administration of their unemployment compensation laws, there is hereby authorized to be appropriated, for the fiscal year ending June 30, 1936, the sum of $4,000,000, and for each fiscal year thereafter the sum of $49,000,000, to be used as hereinafter provided. . . .

TITLE IV—GRANTS TO STATES FOR AID TO DEPENDENT CHILDREN

APPROPRIATION

SECTION 401. For the purpose of enabling each State to furnish financial assistance, as far as practicable under the conditions in such State, to needy dependent children, there is hereby authorized to be appropriated for the fiscal year ending June 30, 1936, the sum of $24,750,000, and there is hereby authorized to be appropriated for each fiscal year thereafter a sum sufficient to carry out the purposes of this title. The sums made available under this section shall be used for making payments to States which have submitted, and had approved by the Board, State plans for aid to dependent children. . . .

TITLE V—GRANTS TO STATES FOR MATERNAL AND CHILD WELFARE

PART 1—MATERNAL AND CHILD HEALTH SERVICES

APPROPRIATION

SECTION 501. For the purpose of enabling each State to extend and improve, as far as practicable under the conditions in such State, services for promoting the health of mothers and children, especially in rural areas and in areas suffering from severe economic distress, there is hereby authorized to be appropriated for each fiscal year, beginning with the fiscal year ending June 30, 1936, the sum of $3,800,000. The sums made available under this section shall be used for making payments to States which have submitted, and had approved by the Chief of the Children's Bureau, State plans for such services. . . .

PART 2—SERVICES FOR CRIPPLED CHILDREN

APPROPRIATION

SEC. 511. For the purpose of enabling each State to extend and improve (especially in rural areas and in areas suffering from severe economic distress), as far as practicable under the conditions in such State, services for locating crippled children, and for providing medical, surgical, corrective, and other services and care, and facilities for diagnosis, hospitalization, and aftercare, for children who are crippled or who are suffering from conditions which lead to crippling, there is hereby authorized to be appropriated for each fiscal year, beginning with the fiscal year ending June 30, 1936, the sum of $2,850,000. . . .

PART 3—CHILD-WELFARE SERVICES

SEC. 521. (a) For the purpose of enabling the United States, through the Children's Bureau, to cooperate with State public-welfare agencies in establishing, extending, and strengthening, especially in predominantly rural areas, public-welfare services (hereinafter in this section referred to as "child-welfare-services") for the protection and care of homeless, dependent, and neglected children, and children in danger of becoming delinquent, there is hereby authorized to be appropriated for each fiscal year, beginning with the fiscal year ending June 30, 1936, the sum of $1,500,000. . . .

PART 4—VOCATIONAL REHABILITATION

SEC. 531. (a) In order to enable the United States to cooperate with the States and Hawaii in extending and strengthening their programs of vocational rehabilitation of the physically disabled, and to continue to carry out the provisions and purposes of the Act entitled "An Act to provide for the promotion of vocational rehabilitation of persons disabled in industry or otherwise and their return to civil employment," approved June 2, 1920, . . . there is hereby authorized to be appropriated for the fiscal years ending June 30, 1936, and June 30, 1937, the sum of $841,000 for each such fiscal year in addition to the amount of the existing authorization, and for each fiscal year thereafter the sum of $1,938,000.

TITLE VI—PUBLIC HEALTH WORK

APPROPRIATION

SECTION 601. For the purpose of assisting States, counties, health districts, and other political subdivisions of the States in establishing and maintaining adequate public-health services, including the training of personnel for State and local health work, there is hereby authorized to be appropriated for each fiscal year, beginning with the fiscal year ending June 30, 1936, the sum of $8,000,000 to be used as hereinafter provided. . . .

TITLE VIII—TAXES WITH RESPECT TO EMPLOYMENT

INCOME TAX ON EMPLOYEES

SECTION 801. In addition to other taxes, there shall be levied, collected, and paid upon the income of every individual a tax equal to the following percentages of the wages (as defined in section 811) received by him after December 31, 1936, with respect to employment (as defined in section 811) after such date:

(1) With respect to employment during the calendar years 1937, 1938, and 1939, the rate shall be 1 per centum.

(2) With respect to employment during the calendar years 1940, 1941, and 1942, the rate shall be 1 1/2 per centum.

(3) With respect to employment during the calendar years 1943, 1944, and 1945, the rate shall be 2 per centum.

(4) With respect to employment during the calendar years 1946, 1947, and 1948, the rate shall be 2 1/2 per centum.

(5) With respect to employment after December 31, 1948, the rate shall be 3 per centum.

DEDUCTION OF TAX FROM WAGES

Sec. 802. (a) The tax imposed by section 801 shall be collected by the employer of the taxpayer, by deducting the amount of the tax from the wages as and when paid. . . .

EXCISE TAX ON EMPLOYERS

Sec. 804. In addition to other taxes, every employer shall pay an excise tax, with respect to having individuals in his employ, equal to the following percentages of the wages (as defined in section 811) paid by him after December 31, 1936, with respect to employment (as defined in section 811) after such date:

(1) With respect to employment during the calendar years 1937, 1938, and 1939, the rate shall be 1 per centum.

(2) With respect to employment during the calendar years 1940, 1941, and 1942, the rate shall be 1 1/2 per centum.

(3) With respect to employment during the calendar years 1943, 1944, and 1945, the rate shall be 2 per centum.

(4) With respect to employment during the calendar years 1946, 1947, and 1948, the rate shall be 2 1/2 per centum.

(5) With respect to employment after December 31, 1948, the rate shall be 3 per centum. . . .

DEFINITIONS

Sec. 811. When used in this title— . . .

(b) The term "employment" means any service, of whatever nature, performed within the United States by an employee for his employer except—

(1)–Agricultural labor;

(2)–Domestic service in a private home;

(3)–Casual labor not in the course of the employer's trade or business;

(4)–Service performed by an individual who has attained the age of sixty-five;

(5)–Service performed as an officer or member of the crew of a vessel documented under the laws of the United States or of any foreign country;

(6)–Service performed in the employ of the United States Government or of an instrumentality of the United States;

(7)–Service performed in the employ of a State, a political subdivision thereof, or an instrumentality of one or more States or political subdivisions;

(8)–Service performed in the employ of a corporation, community chest, fund, or foundation, organized and operated exclusively for religious, charitable, scientific, literary, or educational purposes, or for the prevention of cruelty to children or animals, no part of the net earnings of which inures to the benefit of any private shareholder or individual. . . .

TITLE X—GRANTS TO STATES FOR AID TO THE BLIND

APPROPRIATION

Section 1001. For the purpose of enabling each State to furnish financial assistance, as far as practicable under the conditions in such State, to needy individuals who are blind, there is hereby authorized to be appropriated for the fiscal year ending June 30, 1936, the sum of $3,000,000, and there is hereby authorized to be appropriated for each fiscal year thereafter a sum sufficient to carry out the purposes of this title. The sums made available under this section shall be used for making payments to States which have submitted, and had approved by the Social Security Board, State plans for aid to the blind. . . .

Source: United States Congress, *United States Statutes at Large,* vol. 49, pt. 1, 620–648.

The Okies, 1939

Among the most familiar photographs of the era of the Great Depression were those of poor families from the Southwest traveling in broken-down vehicles packed with all their belongings toward, hopefully, better times in the West. The Okies, as they were called regardless of whether they were from Oklahoma or not, were victims of a double plague: The depression, which continued throughout the 1930s, had been worsened in their locality by the great dust storms of the middle part of the decade. Their destination for the most part was California, and in one way or another most of them made it, often to encounter—at least at first—conditions little better than what they had left behind. The following passage was from testimony by Carey McWilliams before a congressional committee about the status of Okies in California in 1939.

The most characteristic of all housing in California in which migrants reside at the moment is the shacktown or cheap subdivision. Most of these settlements have come into existence since 1933 and the pattern which obtains is somewhat similar throughout the State. Finding it impossible to rent housing in incorporated communities on their meager incomes, migrants have created a market for a very cheap type of subdivision of which the following may be taken as being representative:

In Monterey County, according to a report of Dr. D. M. Bissell, county health officer, under date of November 28, 1939, there are approximately three well-established migrant settlements. One of these, the development around the environs of Salinas, is perhaps the oldest migrant settlement of its type in California. In connection with this development I quote a paragraph of the report of Dr. Bissell:

"This area is composed of all manners and forms of housing without a public sewer system. Roughly, 10,000 persons are renting or have established homes there. A chief element in this area is that of refugees from the Dust Bowl who inhabit a part of Alisal called Little Oklahoma. Work in lettuce harvesting and packing and sugar beet processing have attracted these people who, seeking homes in Salinas without success because they aren't available, have resorted to makeshift adobes outside the city limits. Complicating the picture is the impermeable substrata which makes septic tanks with leaching fields impractical. Sewer wells have resulted with the corresponding danger to adjacent water wells and to the water wells serving the Salinas public. Certain districts, for example, the Airport Tract and parts of Alisal, have grown into communities with quite satisfactory housing, but others as exemplified by the Graves district are characterized by shacks and lean-tos which are unfit for human habitation." . . .

Typical of the shacktown problem are two such areas near the city limits of Sacramento, one on the east side of B Street, extending from Twelfth Street to the Sacramento city dump and incinerator; and the other so-called Hoovertown, adjacent to the Sacramento River and the city filtration plant. In these two areas there were on September 17, 1939, approximately 650 inhabitants living in structures that, with scarcely a single exception, were rated by the inspectors of this division as "unfit for human occupancy." The majority of the inhabitants were white Americans, with the exception of 50 or 60 Mexican families, a few single Mexican men, and a sprinkling of Negroes. For the most part they are seasonally employed in the canneries, the fruit ranches, and the hop fields of Sacramento County. Most of the occupants are at one time or another upon relief, and there are a large number of occupants in these shacktowns from the Dust Bowl area. Describing the housing, an inspector of this division reports:

"The dwellings are built of brush, rags, sacks, boxboard, odd bits of tin and galvanized iron, pieces of canvas and whatever other material was at hand at the time of construction."

Wood floors, where they exist, are placed directly upon the ground, which because of the location of the camps with respect to the Sacramento River, is damp most of the time. To quote again from the report:

"Entire families, men, women, and children, are crowded into hovels, cooking and eating in the same room. The majority of the shacks have no sinks or cesspools for the disposal of kitchen drainage, and this, together with garbage and other refuse, is thrown on the surface of the ground."

Because of the high-water table, cesspools, where they exist, do not function properly; there is a large overflow of drainage and sewage to the surface of the ground. Many filthy shack latrines are located within a few feet of living quarters. Rents for the houses in these shacktowns range from $3 to $20 a month. In one instance a landlord rents ground space for $1.50 to $5 a month, on which tenants are permitted to erect their own dugouts. The Hooverville section is composed primarily of tents and trailers, there being approximately 125 tent structures in this area on September 17, 1939. Both areas are located in unincorporated territory. They are not subject at the present time to any State or county building regulation. In Hooverville, at the date of the inspection, many families were found that did not have even a semblance of tents or shelters. They were cooking and sleeping on the ground in the open and one water tap at an adjoining industrial plant was found to be the source of the domestic water supply for the camp. . . .

Source: United States Congress, *Hearings, 1941, House Select Committee to Investigate the Interstate Migration of Destitute Citizens* (Washington, D.C., 1941), 2543–2544.

Living Conditions in Black Districts of Northern Cities

Richard Wright

Born in Mississippi of sharecropper parents, Richard Wright moved to Chicago in 1927 and to New York in 1937. Author of Native Son *(1940) and many other works, he went on to become a successful writer and critic of white America's treatment of its black citizens. The following passage from* Twelve Million Black Voices *(1941) may have been inspired by Wright's experience in Chicago in the 1920s and 1930s, but it stood as an indictment of the black districts of any large northern city at any time during 1914–45 and beyond.*

When the white folks move, the Bosses of the Buildings let the property to us at rentals higher than those the whites paid. And the Bosses of the buildings take these old houses and convert them into "kitchenettes," and then rent them to us at rates so high that they make fabulous fortunes before the houses are too old for habitation. What they do is this: they take, say, a seven-room apartment, which rents for $50 a month to whites, and cut it up into seven small apartments, of one room each; they install one small gas stove and one small sink in each room. The Bosses of the Buildings rent these kitchenettes to us at the rate of, say, $6 a week. Hence, the same apartment for which white people—who can get jobs anywhere and who receive higher wages than we—pay $50 a month is rented to us for $42 a week! And because there are not enough houses for us to live in, because we have been used to sleeping several in a room on the plantations in the South, we rent these kitchenettes and are glad to get them. . . . Sometimes five or six of us live in a one-room kitchenette, a place where simple folk such as we should never be held captive. . . .

The kitchenette is our prison, our death sentence without a trial, the new form of mob violence that assaults not only the lone individual, but all of us, in its ceaseless attacks. The kitchenette, with its filth and foul air, with its one toilet for thirty or more tenants, kills our black babies so fast that in many cities twice as many of them die as white babies. The kitchenette is the seed bed for scarlet fever, dysentery, typhoid, tuberculosis, gonorrhea, syphilis, pneumonia, and malnutrition. The kitchenette scatters death so widely among us that our death rate exceeds our birth rate, and if it were not for the trains and autos bringing us daily into the city from the plantations, we black folks who dwell in northern cities would die out entirely over the course of a few years.

The kitchenette, with its crowded rooms and incessant bedlam, provides an enticing place for crimes of all sort—crimes against women and children or any stranger who happens to stray

Victims of the dust bowl or of poverty in general, these Oklahomans arrived in California, seeking work in the pea fields. (Franklin D. Roosevelt Library)

into its dark hallways. The noise of our living, boxed in stone and steel, is so loud that even a pistol shot is smothered. The kitchenette throws desperate and unhappy people into an unbearable closeness of association, thereby increasing latent friction, giving birth to never-ending quarrels of recrimination, accusation, and vindictiveness, producing warped personalities. The kitchenette injects pressure and tension into our individual personalities, making many of us give up the struggle, walk off and leave wives, husbands, and even children behind to shift as best they can.

The kitchenette creates thousands of one-room homes where our black mothers sit, deserted, with their children about their knees. The kitchenette blights the personalities of our growing children, disorganizes them, blinds them to hope, creates problems whose effects can be traced in the characters of its child victims for years afterward. The kitchenette jams our farm girls, while still in their teens, into rooms with men who are restless and stimulated by the noise and lights of the city; and more of our girls have bastard babies than the girls in any other sections of the city. The kitchenette fills our black boys with longing and restlessness, urging them to run off from home, to join together with other restless black boys in gangs, that brutal form of city courage.

The kitchenette piles up mountains of profits for the Bosses of the Buildings and makes them more determined to keep things as they are. The kitchenette reaches out with fingers full of golden bribes to the officials of the city, persuading them to allow old firetraps to remain standing and occupied long after they should have been torn down. The kitchenette is the funnel through which our pulverized lives flow to ruin and death on the city pavements, at a profit. . . .

Source: Richard Wright, *Twelve Million Black Voices* (New York, 1941; reprint, 1969), 104–111. Published with permission of Arno Press.

This woman cooks on a gas stove in an apartment on Chicago's Southside in the early 1940s. (Library of Congress)

African-American Schools in the South

The Swedish sociologist Gunnar Myrdal published in 1944 a massive work on the status of black people in America entitled An American Dilemma: The Negro Problem and Modern Democracy. *In the excerpt that follows, the author failed to date his visit to a southern black school, although it probably occurred during 1939–42, when most of the research took place. Nor does the passage indicate if the researcher was Myrdal or one of his assistants. What was clear was the state of black education in a segregated system.*

The present writer has gone into many one-room, one-teacher Negro schools and hardly believed his eyes and his ears when he ascertained the primitive school building, the lack of practically all equipment, the extreme lack of contact with modern American civilization on the part of the untrained, poorly paid, Negro woman serving as teacher, and the bottomless ignorance of the pupils. I once visited such a school in a rural county of Georgia, not far from Atlanta. The building was an old Rosenwald school, dilapidated but far better than many other school buildings in the region. The students were in all age groups from 6 to 7 years upward to 16 to 17. There was also an imbecile man of about 20 staying on as a steady student veteran. (The lack of institutions for old Negro mental defectives makes the great majority of them stay in their homes, and the homes find it often convenient to send them to school. There they are, of course, a great danger from several viewpoints.) The teacher, a sickly girl about 20 years old, looked shy and full of fear; she said she had had high school training.

The students seemed to enjoy the visit and it was easy to establish a human contact with them. No one could tell who was President of the United States or even what the President was. Only one of the older students knew, or thought he knew, of Booker T. Washington. He said that Washington was "a big white man," and intimated that he might be the President of the United States. This student, obviously a naturally very bright boy, was the only one who knew anything about Europe and England; they were "beyond the Atlantic," he informed me, but he thought that Europe was in England. No one had ever heard about Walter White, John Hope, Du Bois, or Morton. No one had heard of the N.A.A.C.P. One boy identified Carver as a "colored man who makes medicine." Several could identify Joe Louis, Ella Fitzgerald, and Henry Armstrong. Asked if they knew what the Constitution of the United States was and what it meant to them, all remained in solemn silence, until the bright boy helped us out, informing us that it was a "newspaper in Atlanta."

When telling such a horror story it must, at once, be added that it is not typical, though a large portion of rural Negro schools are at, or near, this cultural level. But it is remarkable, and a significant characteristic of the whole system, that it can exist even as an isolated case. It should also be said that there are a few white schools in some regions of the South which do not reach much higher. I recollect that some white school children in Louisiana believed that Huey Long was still living (autumn, 1938) and was the President of the United States.

A further reflection is that the usual measures of school efficiency . . . are inadequate when the problem is to sound the bottom of ignorance in many Negro schools.

Source: Gunnar Myrdal, *An American Dilemma* (New York, 1944), 2:902—903.

The Lend-Lease Act
March 11, 1941

President Franklin D. Roosevelt proposed the Lend-Lease bill in January 1941, at a time when Britain, while still standing alone against Germany, had lost its ability to purchase the goods necessary for survival. Although he used different language in the proposal, Roosevelt wished to give the British what they needed. When after a bitter debate the measure passed in March, the president had essentially what he needed to continue resisting Hitler. Lend-Lease was the most important part of U.S. policy toward the European war in 1941—possibly in the entire prewar period—and a vital force in helping Britain stay alive. The measure permitted the president to send American war material abroad, primarily to Britain but later also to other nations.

Be it enacted by the Senate and House of Representatives of the United States of America in Congress assembled, That this Act may be cited as "An Act to Promote the Defense of the United States."

SEC. 3 (a) Notwithstanding the provisions of any other law, the President may, from time to time, when he deems it in the interest of national defense, authorize the Secretary of War, the Secretary of the Navy, or the head of any other department or agency of the Government—

(1) To manufacture in arsenals, factories, and shipyards under their jurisdiction, or otherwise procure, to the extent to which funds are made available therefore, or contracts are authorized from time to time by the Congress, or both, any defense article for the government of any country whose defense the President deems vital to the defense of the United States.

(2) To sell, transfer title to, exchange, lease, lend, or otherwise dispose of, to any such government any defense article, but no defense article not manufactured or procured under paragraph (1) shall in any way be disposed of under this paragraph, except after consultation with the Chief of Staff of the Army or the Chief of Naval Operations of the Navy, or both. The value of defense articles disposed of in any way under authority of this paragraph, and procured from funds heretofore appropriated, shall not exceed $1,300,000,000. The value of such defense articles shall be determined by the head of the department or agency concerned or such other department, agency or officer as shall be designated in the manner provided in the rules and regulations issued hereunder. Defense articles procured from funds hereafter appropriated to any department or agency of the Government, other than from funds authorized to be appropriated under this Act, shall not be disposed of in any way under authority of this paragraph except to the extent hereafter authorized by the Congress in the Acts appropriating such funds or otherwise.

(3) To test, inspect, prove, repair, outfit, recondition, or otherwise to place in good working order, to the extent to which funds are made available therefor, or contracts are authorized from time to time by the Congress, or both, any defense article for any such government, or to procure any or all such services by private contract.

(4) To communicate to any such government any defense information, pertaining to any defense article furnished to such government under paragraph (2) of this subsection.

(5) To release for export any defense article disposed of in any way under this subsection to any such government.

(b) The terms and conditions upon which any such foreign government receives any aid authorized under subsection (a) shall be those which the President deems satisfactory, and the benefit to the United States may be payment or repayment in kind or property, or any other direct or indirect benefit which the President deems satisfactory.

(c) After June 30, 1943, or after the passage of a concurrent resolution by the two Houses before June 30, 1943, which declares that the powers conferred by or pursuant to subsection (a) are no longer necessary to promote the defense of the United States, neither the President nor the head of any department or agency shall exercise any of the powers conferred by or pursuant to subsection (a); except that until July 1, 1946, any of such powers may be exercised to the extent necessary to carry out a contract or agreement with such a foreign government made before July 1, 1943, or before the passage of such concurrent resolution, whichever is the earlier.

(d) Nothing in this Act shall be construed to authorize or to permit the authorization of convoying vessels by naval vessels of the United States.

(e) Nothing in this Act shall be construed to authorize or to permit the authorization of the entry of any American vessel into a combat area in violation of section 3 of the Neutrality Act of 1939. . . .

SEC. 5. (b) The President from time to time, but not less frequently than once every ninety days, shall transmit to the Congress a report of operations under this Act except such information as he deems incompatible with the public interest to disclose. Reports provided for under this subsection shall be transmitted to the Secretary of the Senate or the Clerk of the House of Representatives, as the case may be, if the Senate or the House of Representatives, as the case may be, is not in session.

SEC. 6. (a) There is hereby authorized to be appropriate from time to time, out of any money in the Treasury not otherwise appropriated, such amounts as may be necessary to carry out the provisions and accomplish the purposes of this Act. . . .

SEC. 8. The Secretaries of War and of the Navy are hereby authorized to purchase or otherwise acquire arms, ammunition, and implements of war produced within the jurisdiction of any country to which section 3 is applicable, whenever the President deems such purchase or acquisition to be necessary in the interests of the defense of the United States.

SEC. 9. The President may, from time to time, promulgate such rules and regulations as may be necessary and proper to carry out any of the provisions of this Act; and he may exercise any power or authority conferred on him by this Act through such department, agency, or officer as he shall direct.

SEC. 10. Nothing in this Act shall be construed to change existing law relating to the use of the land and naval forces of the United States, except insofar as such use relates to the manufacture, procurement, and repair of defense articles, the communication of information and other noncombatant purposes enumerated in this Act.

Source: United States Congress, *United States Statutes at Large,* vol. 55, pt. 1 (Washington, D.C., 1942), 31–33.

Prelude to Pearl Harbor
America's Reply to Japan,
November 26, 1941

With Japanese-American relations on a dangerous course in the fall and winter of 1941, the Franklin D. Roosevelt administration considered a conciliatory reply to a recent Japanese dispatch, a major part of which would have authorized partial lifting of trade restrictions imposed in July. For a variety of reasons the U.S. government decided instead to stand firm. This final comprehensive dispatch from Secretary of State Cordell Hull thus stood out for its rigidity. Any mention of compromise and trade concession faded beside the preconditions stipulated in item three, which insisted that Japan withdraw from China and Indochina—a harsh demand by almost anyone's reckoning. Japan's formal reply was delivered to Hull one hour after the attack on Pearl Harbor had started. The real answer, one might say, came in the attack itself.

SECTION II

Steps To Be Taken by the Government of the United States and by the Government of Japan

The Government of the United States and the Government of Japan propose to take steps as follows:

1. The Government of the United States and the Government of Japan will endeavor to conclude a multilateral non-aggression pact among the British Empire, China, Japan, the Netherlands, the Soviet Union, Thailand and the United States.

2. Both Governments will endeavor to conclude among the American, British, Chinese, Japanese, the Netherland and Thai Governments an agreement whereunder each of the Governments would pledge itself to respect the territorial integrity of French Indochina and, in the event that there should develop a threat to the territorial integrity of Indochina, to enter into immediate consultation with a view to taking such measures as may be deemed necessary and advisable to meet the threat in question. Such agreement would provide also that each of the Governments party to the agreement would not seek or accept preferential treatment in its trade or economic relations with Indochina and would use its influence to obtain for each of the signatories equality of treatment in trade and commerce with French Indochina.

3. The Government of Japan will withdraw all military, naval, air and police forces from China and from Indochina.

4. The Government of the United States and the Government of Japan will not support—militarily, politically, economically—any government or regime in China other than the National Government of the Republic of China with capital temporarily at Chungking.

5. Both Governments will give up all extraterritorial rights in China, including rights and interests in and with regard to international settlements and concessions, and rights under the Boxer Protocol of 1901.

Both Governments will endeavor to obtain the agreement of the British and other governments to give up extraterritorial rights in China, including rights in international settlements and in concessions and under the Boxer Protocol of 1901.

6. The Government of the United States and the Government of Japan will enter into negotiations for the conclusion between the United States and Japan of a trade agreement, based upon reciprocal most-favored-nation treatment and reduction of trade barriers by both countries, including an undertaking by the United States to bind raw silk on the free list.

7. The Government of the United States and the Government of Japan will, respectively, remove the freezing restrictions on Japanese funds in the United States and on American funds in Japan.

8. Both Governments will agree upon a plan for the stabilization of the dollar-yen rate, with the allocation of funds adequate for this purpose, half to be supplied by Japan and half by the United States.

9. Both Governments will agree that no agreement which either has concluded with any third power or powers shall be interpreted by it in such a way as to conflict with the fundamental purpose of this agreement, the establishment and preservation of peace throughout the Pacific area.

10. Both Governments will use their influence to cause other governments to adhere to and to give practical application to the basic political and economic principles set forth in this agreement.

Source: Department of State, *Papers Relating to the Foreign Relations of the United States, Japan, 1931–1941* (Washington, D.C., 1943), 2:769–770.

President Roosevelt's War Message
December 8, 1941

The Japanese attacked Pearl Harbor on December 7, 1941, and on the following day President Franklin D. Roosevelt spoke to a special session of Congress. In an address that took only ten minutes to deliver, a message marked with the passage "a date which will live in infamy," Roosevelt only asked the legislature to formalize what already had taken place, that the United States was at war with Japan. The shortness of the speech indicated that the president in truth did not have to make a case. It was a time of high drama and excitement, of expressions of patriotism and desire for revenge. The remarkable feature of Congress's response was not that the vote was overwhelming but that there was any opposition at all. One person, Congresswoman Jeanette Rankin of Montana, voted no.

Yesterday, December 7, 1941—a date which will live in infamy—the United States of America was suddenly and deliberately attacked by naval and air forces of the Empire of Japan.

The United States was at peace with that nation and, at the solicitation of Japan, was still in conversation with its government and its Emperor looking toward the maintenance of peace in the Pacific. Indeed, one hour after Japanese air squadrons had commenced bombing in Oahu, the Japanese ambassador to the United States and his colleague delivered to the Secretary of State a formal reply to a recent American message. While this reply stated that it seemed useless to continue the existing diplomatic negotiations, it contained no threat or hint of war or armed attack.

It will be recorded that the distance of Hawaii from Japan makes it obvious that the attack was deliberately planned many days or even weeks ago. During the intervening time the Japanese Government has deliberately sought to deceive the United States by false statements and expressions of hope for continued peace.

The attack yesterday on the Hawaiian Islands has caused severe damage to American naval and military forces. Very many American lives have been lost. In addition American ships have been reported torpedoed on the high seas between San Francisco and Honolulu.

Yesterday the Japanese government also launched an attack against Malaya.

Last night Japanese forces attacked Hong Kong.

Last night Japanese forces attacked Guam.

Last night Japanese forces attacked the Philippine Islands.

Last night the Japanese attacked Wake Island.

This morning the Japanese attacked Midway Island.

Japan has, therefore, undertaken a surprise offensive extending throughout the Pacific area. The facts of yesterday speak for themselves. The people of the United States have already formed their opinions and well understand the implications to the very life and safety of our nation.

As Commander-in-Chief of the Army and Navy, I have directed that all measures be taken for our defense.

Always will we remember the character of the onslaught against us.

No matter how long it may take us to overcome this premeditated invasion, the American people in their righteous might will win through to absolute victory.

I believe I interpret the will of the Congress and of the people when I assert that we will not only defend ourselves to the uttermost but will make very certain that this form of treachery shall never endanger us again.

Hostilities exist. There is no blinking at the fact that our people, our territory and our interests are in grave danger.

With confidence in our armed forces—with the unbounding determination of our people—we will gain the inevitable triumph—so help us God.

I ask that the Congress declare that since the unprovoked and dastardly attack by Japan on Sunday, December 7th, a state of war has existed between the United States and the Japanese Empire.

Source: Department of State, Papers Relating to the Foreign Relations of the United States, Japan, 1931–1941, 2:793–794.

Recommendation for Japanese Internment February 14, 1942

The decision in 1942 to intern virtually all people of Japanese origin in the United States grew out of an atmosphere of suspicion, fear, and near panic in the period immediately following the Japanese attack on Pearl Harbor. It was influenced by numerous other factors, not the least of which were racial conclusions and presumptions based on the Japanese being a nonwhite, Asian people. The order of removal by President Franklin D. Roosevelt came after much pressure from state and local officials, California-based interest groups, and other quarters. The following report by the commanding officer of the Western Defense Command, Gen. John L. DeWitt, based the policy on military necessity, but it also carried much in the way of racial implication.

February 14, 1942

014.31 (DCS)

Memorandum for: The Secretary of War

               (Thru: The Commanding General,
               Field Forces, Washington, D.C.)

Subject: Evacuation of Japanese and other Subversive Persons
         from the Pacific Coast. . . .

(1) Any estimate of the situation indicates that the following are possible and probable enemy activities:

    (a) Naval attack on shipping in coastal waters;

    (b) Naval attack on coastal cities and vital installations;

    (c) Air raids on vital installations, particularly within two hundred miles of the coast;

    (d) Sabotage of vital installations throughout the Western Defense Command.

Hostile Naval and air raids will be assisted by enemy agents signaling from the coastline and the vicinity thereof; and by supplying and otherwise assisting enemy vessels and by sabotage.

Sabotage, (for example, of airplane factories), may be effected not only by destruction within plants and establishments, but by destroying power, light, water, sewer and other utility and other facilities in the immediate vicinity thereof or at a distance. Serious damage or destruction in congested areas may readily be caused by incendiarism.

(2) The area lying to the west of the Cascade and Sierra Nevada Mountains in Washington, Oregon and California, is highly critical not only because the lines of communication and supply to the Pacific theater pass through it, but also because of the vital industrial production therein, particularly aircraft. In the war in which we are now engaged racial affinities are not severed by migration. The Japanese race is an enemy race and while many second and third generation Japanese born on United States soil, possessed of United States citizenship, have become "Americanized," the racial strains are undiluted. To conclude otherwise is to expect that children born of white parents on Japanese soil sever all racial affinity and become loyal Japanese subjects, ready to fight and, if necessary, to die for Japan in a war against the nation of their parents. That Japan is allied with Germany and Italy in this struggle is no ground for assuming that any Japanese, barred from assimilation by convention as he is, though born and raised in the United States, will not turn against this nation when the final test of loyalty comes. It, therefore, follows that along the vital Pacific Coast over 112,000 potential enemies, of Japanese extraction, are at large today. There are indications that these are organized and ready for concerted action at a favorable opportunity. The very fact that no sabotage has taken place to date is a disturbing and confirming indication that such action will be taken.

  c. Disposition of the Japanese.

(1) Washington. As the term is used herein, the word "Japanese" includes alien Japanese and American citizens of Japanese ancestry. In the State of Washington the Japanese population, aggregating over 14,500, is disposed largely in the area lying west of the Cascade Mountains and south of an eastwest line passing through Bellingham, Washington, about 70 miles north of Seattle and some 15 miles south of the Canadian border. The largest concentration of Japanese is in the area, the axis of which is along the line Seattle, Tacoma, Olympia, Willapa Bay and the mouth of the Columbia River, with the heaviest concentration in the agricultural valleys between Seattle and Tacoma, viz., the Green River and the Puyallup Valleys. The Boeing Aircraft factory is in the Green River Valley. The lines of communication and supply including power and water which feed this vital industrial installation, radiate from this plant for many miles through areas heavily populated by Japanese. Large numbers of Japanese also operate vegetable markets along the Seattle and Tacoma water fronts, in Bremerton, near the Bremerton Navy Yard, and inhabit islands in Puget Sound opposite vital naval ship building installations. Still others are engaged in fishing along the

southwest Washington Pacific Coast and along the Columbia River. Many of these Japanese are within easy reach of the forests of Washington State, the stock piles of seasoning lumber and the many sawmills of southwest Washington. During the dry season these forests, mills and stock piles are easily fired.

(2) Oregon. There are approximately 4,000 Japanese in the State of Oregon, of which the substantial majority reside in the area in the vicinity of Portland along the south bank of the Columbia River, following the general line Bonneville, Oregon City, Astoria, Tillamook. Many of these are in the northern reaches of the Willamette Valley and are engaged in agricultural and fishing pursuits. Others operate vegetable markets in the Portland metropolitan area and still others reside along the northern Oregon sea coast. Their disposition is in intimate relationship with the northwest Oregon sawmills and lumber industry, near and around the vital electric power development at Bonneville and the pulp and paper installations at Camas (on the Washington State side of the Columbia River) and Oregon City (directly south of Portland).

(3) California. The Japanese population in California aggregates approximately 93,500 people. Its disposition is so widespread and so well known that little would be gained by setting it forth in detail here. They live in great numbers along the coastal strip, in and around San Francisco and the Bay Area, the Salinas Valley, Los Angeles and San Diego. Their truck farms are contiguous to the vital aircraft industry concentration in and around Los Angeles. They live in large numbers in and about San Francisco, now a vast staging area for the war in the Pacific, a point at which the nation's lines of communication and supply converge. Inland they are disposed in the Sacramento, San Joaquin and Imperial Valleys. They are engaged in the production of approximately 38% of the vegetable produce of California. Many of them are engaged in the distribution of such produce in and along the waterfronts at San Francisco and Los Angeles. Of the 93,500 in California, about 25,000 reside inland in the mentioned valleys where they are largely engaged in vegetable production cited above, and 54,600 reside along the coastal strip, that is to say, a strip of coast line varying from eight miles in the north to twenty miles in width in and around the San Francisco bay area, including San Francisco, in Los Angeles and its environs, and in San Diego. Approximately 13,900 are dispersed throughout the remaining portion of the state. In Los Angeles City the disposition of vital aircraft industrial plants covers the entire city. Large numbers of Japanese live and operate markets and truck farms adjacent to or near these installations. . . .

b. I now recommend the following:

(1) That the Secretary of War procure from the President direction and authority to designate military areas in the combat zone of the Western Theater of Operations, (if necessary to include the entire combat zone), from which, in his discretion, he may exclude all Japanese, all alien enemies, and all other persons suspected for any reason by the administering military authorities of being actual or potential saboteurs, espionage agents, or fifth columnists. Such executive order should empower the Secretary of War to requisition the services of any and all other agencies of the Federal Government, with express direction to such agencies to respond to such requisition, and further empowering the Secretary of War to use any and all federal facilities and equipment, including Civilian Conservation Corps Camps, and to accept the use of State facilities for the purpose of providing shelter and equipment for evacuees. Such executive order to provide further for the administration of military areas for the purposes of this plan by appropriate military authorities acting with the requisitioned assistance of the other federal agencies and the cooperation of State and local agencies. The executive order should further provide that by reason of military necessity the right of all persons, whether citizens or aliens, to reside, enter, cross or be within any military areas shall be subject to revocation and shall exist on a pass and permit basis at the discretion of the Secretary of War and implemented by the necessary legislation imposing penalties for violation.

(2) That, pursuant to such executive order, there be designated as military areas all areas in Washington, Oregon and California, recommended by me to date for designation by the Attorney General as Category "A" areas and such additional areas as it may be found necessary to designate hereafter.

(3) That the Secretary of War provide for the exclusion from such military areas, in his discretion, of the following classes of persons, viz:

(a) Japanese aliens.

(b) Japanese-American citizens.

(c) Alien enemies other than Japanese aliens.

(d) Any and all other persons who are suspected for any reason by the administering military authorities to be actual or potential saboteurs, espionage agents, fifth columnists, or subversive persons.

(4) That the evacuation of classes (a), (b), and (c) from such military areas be initiated on a designated evacuation day and carried to completion as rapidly as practicable.

That prior to evacuation day all plans be complete for the establishment of initial concentration points, reception centers, registration, rationing, guarding, transportation to internment points, and the selection and establishment of internment facilities in the Sixth, Seventh, and Eighth Corps Areas.

That persons in class (a) and (c) above be evacuated and interned at such selected places of internment, under guard.

That persons in class (b) above, at the time of evacuation, be offered an opportunity to accept voluntary internment, under guard, at the place of internment above mentioned.

That persons in class (b) who decline to accept voluntary internment, be excluded from all military areas, and left to their own resources, or, in the alternative, be encouraged to accept resettlement outside of such military areas with such assistance as the State governments concerned or the Federal Security Agency may be by that time prepared to offer.

That the evacuation of persons in class (d) be progressive and continuing, and that upon their evacuation persons in class (d) be excluded from all military areas and left in their own resources outside of such military areas, or, in the alternative, be offered voluntary internment or encouraged to accept voluntary resettlement as above outlined, unless the facts in a particular case shall warrant other action.

(5) The Commanding General, Western Defense Command and Fourth Army, to be responsible for the evacuation, administration, supply and guard, to the place of internment; the Commanding Generals of the Corps Areas concerned to be responsible for guard, supply and administration at the places of internment.

(6) That direct communication between the Commanding General, Western Defense Command and Fourth Army and the Corps Area Commanders concerned for the purpose of making necessary arrangements be authorized.

(7) That the Provost Marshal General coordinate all phases of the plan between the Commanding General, Western Defense Command and Fourth Army, on the one hand, and the Corps Area Commanders on the other hand.

(8) That all arrangements be accomplished with the utmost secrecy.

(9) That adult males (above the age of 14 years) be interned separately from all women and children until the establishment of family units can be accomplished.

(10) No change is contemplated in Category "B" areas.

3. Although so far as the Army is concerned, such action is not an essential feature of the plan, but merely incident thereto, I, nevertheless, recommend that mass internment be considered as largely a temporary expedient pending selective resettlement, to be accomplished by the various Security Agencies of the Federal and State Governments.

4. The number of persons involved in the recommended evacuation will be approximately 133,000. . . .

J. L. DeWitt

Lieutenant General,
U.S. Army, Commanding.

Source: Masako Herman, ed., *The Japanese in America, 1843–1973* (Dobbs Ferry, N.Y., 1973), 56–61.

Women Shipyard Workers 1943–1944

Inasmuch as the United States faced a possible labor shortage during the Second World War, women went to work in droves. The most significant wartime change in the pattern of female employment had to do with the large number of married women who entered the work force and the type of jobs they held. Women participated in the construction of guns, tanks, planes, ships, anything involved in the war effort, and they often took jobs previously held by men. The program of placing women in the defense industries was put into place rapidly, a product of wartime expediency, and it ended with even greater haste, not to the satisfaction of everyone concerned. The following article offers at least a hint of the speed with which the program developed, some of the problems of adjustment on the part of males and females, and goals for the proper placement of women within the factories and shipyards.

Recent and Unprecedented Employment of Women

Just a little over 2 years ago the subject and purpose of this bulletin would have been considered as fanciful as a tale from the Arabian Nights. That American women should take active part in the man's job of building and repairing ships was almost inconceivable. As recently as July 1941 an outstanding periodical made sport of the extreme anti-feminine attitude of what is now one of the most publicized woman-employing ship building and repair corporations in the country. At that time, nearly 2 years after war began in Europe and but 5 months before Pearl Harbor, women were not accepted by the firm even as office secretaries, and the lone women telephone operators were, as it was facetiously reported, "kept under lock and key."

Times have changed with lightning speed. By late 1943, thousands of women along both coasts and on the Gulf, Great Lakes, and inland waterways were actively engaged in almost every phase of ship building and repair work, and it is anticipated that it will be necessary to recruit thousands more before the war is over. Though the introduction of women into the shipyards did not begin in earnest until the fall of 1942, by January 1943 as many as 4 per cent of all the production wage earners in the industry were women. The proportion had risen to a little over

5 per cent by March, and by September to 9.5 per cent. In January 1944 it was 10 per cent. These figures include the 8 navy yards engaged in ship construction and repair, in which women have made extensive gains and comprised in September nearly one-fourth of the women wage earners in the industry.

Many Adjustments Required in an Expanding Industry

The unprecedented influx of women into the shipyards has been the inevitable accompaniment of this country's tremendous war ship-building program, for which it has been necessary to recruit hundreds of thousands of additional workers since Pearl Harbor. The first 17 months of wartime production witnessed an increase of 189 per cent in shipyard personnel. Old-established yards employing from 3,000 to 10,000 workers in 1939 and 1940 had 5 to nearly 8 times that many late in 1943, and there are some shipyards for which ground had not even been broken in 1940 that employed 20,000 to 40,000 workers in the spring of 1943 when the peak had not yet been reached. Expansion on so gigantic a scale in competition with other war industries and Selective Service brought shipbuilders face to face with the necessity of employing women to help to produce the enormous tonnage so urgently needed.

Such rapid development alone carries with it innumerable problems of administration and plant adjustment, but coupled with the necessity for drawing on a labor element never before tried in the industry, the problems became extremely numerous and complex. Organized training programs had to be set up within the shipyards to provide instruction for the thousands of workers, men as well as women, who had never held tools before, much less seen a ship under construction. Special training was necessary for the supervisors who had never had so many workers under them, many having themselves only recently been promoted from the ranks. Rapid upgrading of men into the skilled and leadership jobs became a practical necessity for the most economical utilization of labor. As the nucleus of skilled and experienced workers has become dispersed and proportionately smaller, the training structure has grown in size and importance. In many yards now the training director helps to control the rate of accession and allocation of the labor force.

But the need to draw from the woman labor force often was not realized and accepted till the very last moment, leaving little time for study and planning. In many cases the management plunged headlong even before essential and obvious provision had been made to accommodate the newcomers. This was not surprising in view of acute manpower shortages in shipbuilding areas, yet it was nothing less than daring in an industry so bound in the tradition of dirt, sweat, and rough and tumble, so thoroughly male that any woman who ventured into a yard was greeted with hooting and whistling. The physical and administrative adaptations that should be introduced to insure women's efficient performance and necessary comfort on the job frequently are as nothing compared with the mental hurdles that must be overcome. Problems that are brought to the attention of those interested in women's success often stem as much from attitudes toward women workers in the man's world of shipbuilding as from the actual situation. Yet women frequently were taken on before the human or psychological adaptations necessary to avoid confusion, discontent, and waste, much less the physical and sometimes administrative changes necessary, had been attempted.

When field representatives of the Women's Bureau made visits to 41 shipyards between the beginning and the early fall of 1943, few yards had employed women for as long as a year; many had begun hiring women to do production work only a few months before; 6 had not yet hired any women for production work. Though the yards with women workers still were feeling their way, over half already were employing hundreds of women, some of them thousands, and in many cases expecting to hire hundreds or thousands more. While building more ships than ever before and servicing the Fleet, not a few were functioning under inadequate arrangements, hoping gradually to arrive at a satisfactory solution of their personnel problems with women. To be sure, some had already made excellent progress. Most had forged ahead in at least some phases, such as securing good safety observance, satisfactory rest- and wash-room facilities, and productively efficient distribution of the women on jobs; others were struggling with these aspects of the situation but had mastered other aspects. Many, aware of inadequacies, sought advice. Women's Bureau field representatives were asked in several of the yards visited to submit formal recommendations based on analysis and study of individual yard conditions and problems.

It is clear, then, that the shipyards are charting new seas in the utilization of the woman labor force, and the mistakes or successes that result may have a profound effect not only on the production and repair of ships, but on the cost and efficiency of such production and the health, work, and life histories of thousands of women. It is important to take stock now. Misconceptions should be dispelled, well-founded facts pooled, and the fund of information available from industries with longer histories in the employment of women disseminated. It is with these objects in view that the present report is submitted. It is the aim of the Women's Bureau through the recommendations and suggestions made here to promote conditions for the woman shipyard worker conducive to her most efficient and productive employment and her well-being as a member of society and the labor force....

1. Secure the cooperation of men supervisors and workers.

2. Select and place women carefully.

3. Employ women only in jobs found to be suitable.

4. Pay women and upgrade them on the same basis as men.

5. Schedule an 8-hour day and a 48-hour 6-day week; allow a lunch period of at least 30 minutes, and rest periods of 10 to 15 minutes in each work spell of as much as 4 hours. Rotate shifts no more frequently than every two months.

6. Set up an effective woman employee counselor system.

7. Give new women workers preliminary induction into the work and environment of the shipyard before putting them on the job.

8. Provide personal-service, food, and medical facilities that meet approved standards of adequacy and quality.

9. Study and expand the safety program to adapt it to women workers, and instruct women thoroughly in safe work practice.

Source: Dorothy K. Newman, "Employing Women in Shipyards," in Department of Labor, *Bulletin of the Women's Bureau, No. 192-6* (Washington, D.C., 1944), 1–6.

Japanese officials prepare to sign documents of surrender, September 2, 1945, ending the Second World War. (National Archives)

Surrender of Japan
September 2, 1945

The dropping of atomic bombs on Hiroshima on August 6, 1945, and Nagasaki on August 9, 1945, ended the war against Japan. The Japanese announced an intent to surrender—a decision made in this rare instance by the emperor himself—on August 14, but the formal ceremony did not take place until two and one-half weeks later. Although the Americans gave a vague verbal pledge to permit the Japanese to retain their emperor, the stipulation appeared in no place in the document of surrender. It was an unconditional surrender. On September 2, 1945, aboard the battleship Missouri *in Tokyo Bay, the Second World War officially came to an end.*

INSTRUMENT OF SURRENDER

We, acting by command of and in behalf of the Emperor of Japan, the Japanese Government and the Japanese Imperial General Headquarters, hereby accept the provisions set forth in the declaration issued by the heads of the Governments of the United States, China and Great Britain on 26 July 1945, at Potsdam, and subsequently adhered to by the Union of Soviet Socialist Republics, which four powers are hereafter referred to as the Allied Powers.

We hereby proclaim the unconditional surrender to the Allied Powers of the Japanese Imperial General Headquarters and of all Japanese armed forces and all armed forces under Japanese control wherever situated.

We hereby command all Japanese forces wherever situated and the Japanese people to cease hostilities forthwith, to preserve and save from damage all ships, aircraft, and military and civil property and to comply with all requirements which may be imposed by the Supreme Commander for the Allied Powers or by agencies of the Japanese Government at his direction.

We hereby command the Japanese Imperial General Headquarters to issue at once orders to the Commanders of all Japanese forces and all forces under Japanese control wherever situated to surrender unconditionally themselves and all forces under their control.

We hereby command all civil, military and naval officials to obey and enforce all proclamations, orders and directives deemed by the Supreme Commander for the Allied Powers to be proper to effectuate this surrender and issued by him or under his authority and we direct all such officials to remain at their posts and to continue to perform their non-combatant duties unless specifically relieved by him or under his authority.

We hereby undertake for the Emperor, the Japanese Government and their successors to carry out the provisions of the Potsdam Declaration in good faith, and to issue whatever orders and take whatever action may be required by the Supreme Commander for the Allied Powers or by any other designated representative of the Allied Powers for the purpose of giving effect to that Declaration.

We hereby command the Japanese Imperial Government and the Japanese Imperial General Headquarters at once to liberate all Allied prisoners of war and civilian internees now under Japanese control and to provide for their protection, care, maintenance and immediate transportation to places as directed.

The authority of the Emperor and the Japanese Government to rule the state shall be subject to the Supreme Commander for the Allied Powers who will take such steps as he deems proper to effectuate these terms of surrender.

Signed at Tokyo Bay, Japan at 9.04 I on the Second day of September, 1945.

(Signed) Mamoru Shigemitsu
By Command and in Behalf of the Emperor of Japan and the Japanese Government

(Signed) Yoshijiro Umezu
By Command and in behalf of the Japanese Imperial General Headquarters

Accepted at Tokyo Bay, Japan at 0908 I on the Second day of September, 1945. *for the United States, Republic of China, United Kingdom and the Union of Soviet Socialist Republics, and in the interests of the other United Nations at war with Japan*

(Signed) Douglas MacArthur
Supreme Commander for the Allied Powers

(Signed) C. W. Nimitz
United States Representative

(Signed) Hsu Yung-Chang
Republic of China Representative

(Signed) Bruce Fraser
United Kingdom Representative

(Signed) Kuzma Derevyanko
Union of Soviet Socialist Republics Representative

(Signed) T. A. Blamey
Commonwealth of Australia Representative

(Signed) L. Moore Cosgrave
Dominion of Canada Representative

(Signed) Leclerc
Provisional Government of the French Republic Representative

(Signed) E. L. Helfrich
Kingdom of the Netherlands Representative

(Signed) Leonard M. Isitt
Dominion of New Zealand Representative

Source: Department of State, *Bulletin,* vol. 13, September 9, 1945 (Washington, D.C.), 364–365.

Bibliography

Publications of the National Government

Bureau of Labor Statistics. *Handbook of Labor Statistics, 1947.* Washington, D.C.: U.S. Government Printing Office, 1947.

———. *Handbook of Labor Statistics, 1989.* Washington, D.C.: U.S. Government Printing Office, 1989.

———. *The Negroes in the United States: Their Economic and Social Situation.* Washington, D.C.: U.S. Government Printing Office, 1966.

Bureau of the Census. *Historical Statistics of the United States, 1789 to 1945.* Washington, D.C.: U.S. Government Printing Office, 1949.

———. *Historical Statistics of the United States, Colonial Times to 1957.* Washington, D.C.: U.S. Government Printing Office, 1960.

———. *Historical Statistics of the United States, Colonial Times to 1970.* Washington, D.C.: 2 vols., U.S. Government Printing Office, 1976.

———. *Housing Construction Statistics, 1889–1964.* Washington, D.C.: U.S. Government Printing Office, 1966.

———. *Negroes in the United States, 1920–1932.* Washington, D.C.: U.S. Government Printing Office, 1935.

———. *Religious Bodies, 1936.* Washington, D.C.: U.S. Government Printing Office, 1941.

Bureau of the Census, *Sixteenth Census of the United States: 1940,* Vol. I: *Number of Inhabitants.* Washington, D.C.: U.S. Government Printing Office, 1942.

———. *Statistical Abstract of the United States,* annual editions, 1914–52. Washington, D.C.: U.S. Government Printing Office, 1914–52.

———. *United States Census of Agriculture for 1935, General Report.* Washington, D.C.: U.S. Government Printing Office, 1937.

———. *United States Census of Agriculture for 1945, General Report.* Washington, D.C.: U.S. Government Printing Office, 1948.

Department of Agriculture. *Agriculture Statistics, 1943.* Washington, D.C.: U.S. Government Printing Office, 1943.

———. *Agriculture Statistics, 1945.* Washington, D.C.: U.S. Government Printing Office, 1945.

———. *Agriculture Statistics, 1947.* Washington, D.C.: U.S. Government Printing Office, 1947.

Department of Commerce. *The Social and Economic Status of the Black Population in the United States, 1790–1978.* Washington, D.C.: U.S. Government Printing Office, 1979.

Department of Health, Education, and Welfare. *Vital Statistics Rates in the United States, 1950, Vol. I.* Washington, D.C.: U.S. Government Printing Office, 1954.

———. *Vital Statistics Rates in the United States, 1940–1960.* Washington, D.C.: U.S. Government Printing Office, 1968.

Department of State. *Bulletin.* Vol. 13. Washington, D.C.: U.S. Government Printing Office, September 9, 1945.

———. *Foreign Relations of the United States, 1917, Supplement I: The World War.* Washington, D.C.: U.S. Government Printing Office, 1931.

———. *Papers Relating to the Foreign Relations of the United States, 1922. Vol. 1.* Washington, D.C.: U.S. Government Printing Office, 1938.

———. *Papers Relating to the Foreign Relations of the United States, Japan, 1931–1941.* 2 vols., Washington, D.C.: U.S. Government Printing Office, 1943.

———. *Peace and War: United States Foreign Policy, 1931–1941.* Washington, D.C.: U.S. Government Printing Office, 1943.

Department of War. *Final Report—Japanese Evacuation from the West Coast, 1942.* Washington, D.C.: U.S. Government Printing Office, 1943.

Director of Selective Service. *Selective Service in Peacetime: First Report of the Director of Selective Service, 1940–1941.* Washington, D.C.: U.S. Government Printing Office, 1942.

———. *Selective Service and Victory: The Fourth Report of the Director of Selective Service.* Washington, D.C.: U.S. Government Printing Office, 1948.

Immigration and Naturalization Service. *Annual Reports.* Washington, D.C.: U.S. Government Printing Office, 1976.

Newman, Dorothy K. "Employing Women in Shipyards." In Department of Labor, *Bulletin of the Women's Bureau, No. 192-6.* Washington, D.C.: U.S. Government Printing Office, 1944.

United States Congress. *Biographical Directory of the American Congress, 1774–1971.* Washington, D.C.: U.S. Government Printing Office, 1971.

———. *Hearings, 1941, House Select Committee to Investigate the Interstate Migration of Destitute Citizens.* Washington, D.C.: U.S. Government Printing Office, 1941.

———. *United States Statutes at Large.* Vol. 41. Washington, D.C.: U.S. Government Printing Office, 1919; vol. 49, pt. 1, 1936; vol. 55, pt. 1, 1942.

United States Public Health Service. *Vital Statistics of the United States, 1945. Pt. 1.* Washington, D.C.: U.S. Government Printing Office, 1947.

War Relocation Authority. *The Evacuated People: A Quantitative Description.* Washington, D.C.: U.S. Government Printing Office, 1946.

Publications of the State Governments

Council of State Governments, *Book of the States, 1939–1940.* Chicago: Council of State Governments, 1939.

———. *Book of the States, 1945–1946.* Chicago: Council of State Governments, 1945.

———. *Book of the States, 1948–1949.* Chicago: Council of State Governments, 1948.

General Almanacs, Encyclopedias and Other Works

Bailey, Thomas A. and David M. Kennedy. *The American Pageant.* New York: D.C. Heath, 1991.

Carruth, Gorton, and Associates. *The Encyclopedia of American Facts and Dates.* New York: Harper & Row, 1987.

Cook, Chris, and John Stevenson. *The Longman Handbook of World History since 1914.* New York: Longman, 1991.

Dewhurst, Frederick J. and Associates. *America's Needs and Resources.* New York: The Twentieth Century Fund, 1947.

———. *America's Needs and Resources: A New Survey.* New York: The Twentieth Century Fund, 1955.

Encyclopaedia Britannica, 1962 ed. Chicago: The Encyclopaedia Britannica Company, 1962.

Encyclopaedia Britannica Yearbook, 1935–47 yearbooks. Chicago: The Encyclopaedia Britannica Company, 1935–47.

The Encyclopedia Americana Annual, 1947. New York: Grolier, 1947.

The Encyclopedia Americana, 1945 and 1963 eds. New York: Grolier, 1945, 1963.

Henretta, James A., et al. America's History. New York: Worth Publishers, Inc., 1993.

The Information Please Almanac, 1947. Garden City, N.Y.: Doubleday and Co., 1947.

The Information Please Almanac, 1948. New York: Doubleday and Co., 1948.

The Information Please Almanac, 1955. New York: MacMillan, 1955.

The Information Please Almanac, Atlas and Yearbook, 1988. Boston: Houghton Mifflin, 1987.

Leonard, Thomas A. Day-by-Day: The Forties. New York: Facts On File, 1977.

The Lincoln Library of Essential Information, 1937 ed. Buffalo, N.Y.: The Frontier Press Company, 1937.

Linton, Calvin D. The Bicentennial Almanac. Nashville: T. Nelson, 1975.

Morris, Richard. Encyclopedia of American History. New York: Harper & Row, 1982.

The New Information Please Almanac, Atlas, and Yearbook, 1967. New York: Simon and Schuster, 1966.

Norton, Mary Beth, et al. A People and a Nation, Vol. 2. Boston: Houghton Mifflin, 1990.

Schlesinger, Arthur M., Jr. The Almanac of American History. New York: Putnam, 1983.

Time-Life Books. Time Capsule. Volumes for the years 1923, 1925, 1927, 1929, 1932, 1933, 1939, 1941, 1942, 1943, 1944, 1945. New York: Time-Life Books, 1967, 1968.

Wallechinsky, David, and Irving Wallace. The People's Almanac. Garden City, N.Y.: Doubleday, 1975.

Wattenberg, Ben J. The Statistical History of the United States, from Colonial Times to the Present. New York: Basic Books, 1976.

Webster's Guide to American History. Springfield, Mass.: C. Merriam, Co., 1971.

The World Almanac and Book of Facts for 1946. New York: New York World Telegram, 1946.

The World Almanac and Book of Facts for 1947. New York: New York World Telegram, 1947.

World Book Encyclopedia, 1973 ed. New York: World Book, Inc., 1973.

Wright, John W. The Universal Almanac, 1991. Kansas City, Mo.: Andrews and McMeel, 1991.

Topical Reference Works and Special Studies

American Association of Museums. The Official Museum Directory. New York: American Association of Museums, 1970.

American Metal Market. Metal Statistics, 1955. New York: American Metal Market, 1955.

Andrews, Wayne. Architecture, Ambition, and Americans. New York: The Free Press, 1978.

Austin, Erik W. Political Facts of the United States since 1789. New York: Columbia University Press, 1986.

Bailey, Thomas A. A Diplomatic History of the American People. New York: Appleton-Century-Crofts, 1968.

Beebe, Lucius. The Twentieth Century: The Greatest Train in the World. Berkeley: Howell-North, 1962.

Bernard, William S. American Immigration Policy: A Reappraisal. Port Washington, N. Y.: Kennikat Press, 1969.

Blum, Daniel. A Pictorial History of the Silent Screen. New York: Putnam, 1953.

Bordley, James, III, and A. McGehee Harvey. Two Centuries of American Medicine. Philadelphia: Saunders, 1976.

Cahalan, Margaret Werner. Historical Correction Statistics in the United States, 1850–1984. Rockville, Md.: Westat Inc., 1986.

Cantril, Hadley. Public Opinion, 1935–1946. Princeton: Princeton University Press, 1951.

Castel, Albert, and Scott Gibson. The Yeas and the Nays: Key Congressional Decisions, 1774–1945. Kalamazoo, Mich.: New Issues Press, 1975.

Commager, Henry Steele. Documents of American History. Vol. 2. New York: Appleton-Century-Crofts, 1968.

Congressional Quarterly. Guide to the U.S. Supreme Court. Washington, D.C.: Congressional Quarterly, Inc. 1979.

———. Members of Congress since 1789. Washington, D.C.: Congressional Quarterly, Inc., 1981.

———. The People Speak. Washington, D.C.: Congressional Quarterly, Inc., 1990.

———. Presidential Elections since 1789. Washington, D.C.: Congressional Quarterly, Inc., 1979.

Crowther, Bruce. The Big Band Years. New York: Facts On File, 1988.

Day, John F. Bloody Ground. New York: Doubleday Doran, 1941.

Dubin, Arthur D. Some Classic Trains. Milwaukee: Kalmbach Publishing, 1964.

Duffy, John. The Healers: A History of American Medicine. Urbana, Ill.: University of Illinois Press, 1979.

Dupuy, R. Ernest, and Trevor N. Dupuy. The Encyclopedia of Military History from 3500 B.C. to the Present. New York: Harper & Row, 1970.

Evans, Walker. Photographs for the Farm Security Administration, 1935–1938. New York: Da Capo Press, 1973.

Evans, Webster. Encyclopedia of Golf. New York: St. Martin's Press, 1974.

Ferrell, Robert H. ed. America as a World Power, 1872–1945. New York: Harper & Row, 1971.

Ferrell, Robert H., and Richard Natkiel. Atlas of American History. New York: Facts on File, 1987.

Flora, Snowden D. Tornadoes of the United States. Norman, Okla.: University of Oklahoma Press, 1954.

Friedman, Norman. U.S. Battleships: An Illustrated Design History. The Naval Institute Press, Annapolis: 1984.

Gallup, George. The Political Almanac, 1952. Garden City, N.Y.: Doubleday, 1952.

G. and C. Webster Co., Webster's American Military Biographies. Springfield, Mass.: G & C. Merriam Co., 1978.

Garcia, Richard. The Chicanos in America, 1540–1974. Dobbs Ferry, N.Y.: Oceana Publications, 1977.

Garraty, John A. Encyclopedia of American Biography. New York: Harper & Row, 1974.

Goralski, Robert. World War II Almanac, 1931–1945. New York: Putnam, 1981.

Gray, Randall. Chronicle of the First World War. 2 vols. New York: Facts On File, 1991.

Hackett, Alice P. Seventy Years of Best Sellers, 1895–1965. New York: R. R. Bowker, 1967.

Herman, Masako. The Japanese in America, 1843–1973. Dobbs Ferry, N.Y.: Oceana Publications, 1974.

Hickok, Ralph. New Encyclopedia of Sports. New York: McGraw-Hill, 1977.

Hollander, Zander, and Hal Bock. The Complete Encyclopedia of Ice Hockey. Englewood Cliffs, N.J.: Prentice-Hall, 1970.

Hosokawa, Bill. Nisei: The Quiet Americans. New York: W. Morrow, 1969.

Hurt, Douglas R. The Dust Bowl. Chicago: Nelson-Hall, 1981.

Kallenbach, Joseph and Jessamine. *American State Governors, 1776–1976.* Dobbs Ferry, N.Y.: Oceana Publications, 1977.

Kane, Joseph N., et al. *Facts about the States.* New York: H. W. Wilson, 1989.

Kaplan, Mike. ed., *Variety Presents: The Complete Book of Major U.S. Show Business Awards.* New York: Garland, 1985.

Kranz, Rachel. *The Biographical Dictionary of Black Americans.* New York: Facts On File, 1992.

Lewinson, Paul. *Race, Class, and Party: A History of Negro Suffrage and White Politics in the South.* New York: Oxford, 1932.

Liesner, Thelma. *One Hundred Years of Economic Statistics, 1900–1983.* New York: Facts On File, 1985.

Lifshey, Earl. *The Housewares Story: A History of the American Housewares Industry.* Chicago: National Housewares Manufactures Association, 1973.

Lindstrom, David E. *American Rural Life.* New York: Ronald Press, 1948.

MacDonald, J. Fred. *Don't Touch That Dial: Radio Programming in American Life, 1920–1960.* Chicago: Nelson-Hall, 1979.

Maddocks, Melvin. *The Seafarers: The Great Liners.* Alexandria, Va.: Time-Life Books, 1978.

Malmberg, Carl. *100 Million Patients.* New York: Reynal & Hitchcock, 1947.

Mattfeld, Julius. *Variety Music Cavalcade, 1620–1969.* Englewood Cliffs, N.J.: Prentice-Hall, 1971.

McCallum, John D. *The Encyclopedia of World Boxing Champions since 1882.* Radnor, Pa.: Chilton Book Co., 1975.

McLanthan, Richard. *The American Tradition in the Arts.* New York: Harcourt, Brace & World, 1968.

McNeill, Louise. *Hill Daughter: New and Selected Poems.* Pittsburgh: University of Pittsburgh Press, 1991.

Merz, Charles. *The Dry Decade.* Garden City, N.Y.: Doubleday, Doran 1931.

Miller, Byron S. *Sail, Steam, and Splendor: A Picture of Life aboard the Transatlantic Liners.* New York: Times Books, 1977.

Mokray, William G. *Ronald Encyclopedia of Basketball.* New York: Ronald Press, 1963.

Monthly Labor Review (February 1946).

Morris, Richard B. *400 Notable Americans.* New York: Harper & Row, 1953.

Motor Vehicle Manufacturers Association. *Automobiles of America.* Detroit: Automobile Manufacturers Association, 1974.

Myrdal, Gunnar. *An American Dilemma.* 2 Vols. New York: Harper & Row, 1944.

Nash, Jay Robert. *Crime Chronology: A Worldwide Record, 1900–1983.* New York: Facts On File, 1984.

National Industrial Conference Board. *The Economic Almanac for 1940.* New York: National Industrial Conference Board, 1940.

———. *The Economic Almanac for 1950.* New York: National Industrial Conference Board, 1950.

New York Stock Exchange. *Fact Book.* New York: New York Stock Exchange, 1966.

O'Brien, David J., and Fugita, Stephen. *The Japanese Experience.* Bloomington, Ind.: Indiana University Press, 1991.

Olson, James S. ed., *Historical Dictionary of the New Deal.* Westport, Conn.: Greenwood Press, 1985.

Packard, William. *Evangelism in America: From Tents to T.V.* New York: Paragon House, 1988.

Perrin, Tom. *Football: A College History.* Jefferson, N.C.: McFarland, 1987.

Peterson, Robert. *Only the Ball Was White: A History of Legendary Black Players and All-Black Professional Teams.* New York: Oxford, 1992.

Ploski, Harry A., and Williams, James eds. *The Negro Almanac: A Reference Work on the Afro-American.* New York: Wiley, 1983.

———. *Reference Library of Black America.* 5 Vols., New York: Gale Research, 1990.

Polmar, Norman, and Allen, Thomas B. eds. *World War II: Americans at War, 1941–1945.* New York: Random House, 1991.

Reichler, Joseph L., ed. *The Baseball Encyclopedia.* New York: Macmillan, 1985.

Reid, Margaret G. *Economics of Household Production.* New York: J. Wiley and Sons, 1934.

Reid, Robert L. *Back Home Again: Indiana in the Farm Security Administration Photographs, 1935–1943.* Bloomington, Ind.: Indiana University Press, 1987.

Reid, Robert L., and Larry A. Viskochil. *Chicago and Downstate: Illinois As Seen by the Farm Security Administration Photographers, 1936–1943.* Urbana: University of Illinois Press, 1989.

Richardson, E. P. *Painting in America, from 1502 to the Present.* New York: Crowell, 1965.

Riley, John W., and Matilda White. "The Use of Various Methods of Contraception." *American Sociological Review* (December 1940), 890–903.

Robert, Joseph C. *The Story of Tobacco in America.* New York: A. A. Knopf, 1949.

Rosenman, Samuel I. *The Public Papers and Addresses of Franklin D. Roosevelt.* Vol. 2. New York: Random House, 1938.

Rosten, Leo. *A Guide to the Religions of America.* New York: Simon and Schuster, 1955.

Rothstein, Arthur. *The Depression Years As Photographed by Arthur Rothstein.* New York: Dover Press, 1978.

Saint Anthony's Guild. *The 1940 National Catholic Almanac.* Paterson, N.J.: Saint Anthony's Guild, 1940.

———. *The 1946 National Catholic Almanac.* Paterson, N.J.: Saint Anthony's Guild, 1946.

Serbein, Oscar N., Jr. *Paying for Medical Care in the United States.* New York: Columbia University Press, 1953.

Sicherman, Barbara, and Carol Hurd Green. *Notable American Women: The Modern Period.* Cambridge: Belknap Press, 1980.

Sifakis, Carl. *The Encyclopedia of American Crime.* New York: Facts On File, 1982.

Simon, George T. *The Big Bands.* New York: MacMillan, 1974.

Slackman, Michael. *Target: Pearl Harbor.* Honolulu: University of Hawaii Press, 1990.

Steinberg, Cobbett S. *Film Facts.* New York: Facts On File, 1980.

Sterner, Richard. *The Negro's Share: A Study of Income, Consumption, Housing, and Public Assistance.* New York: Harper & Brothers, 1943.

Stryker, Roy E., and Nancy Wood. *In This Proud Land: America 1935–1943, As Seen in the FSA Photographs.* Greenwich, Conn.: New York Graphic Society, 1973.

Stuart, Paul. *Nations within a Nation: Historical Statistics of American Indians.* New York: Greenwood Press, 1987.

Summers, Harrison B. *A Thirty-Year History of Programs Carried on National Radio Networks in the United States, 1926–1956.* 1958. Reprint, New York: Arno, 1971.

Tannehill, Ivan Ray. *Hurricanes.* Princeton: Princeton University Press, 1952.

Thernstrom, Stephen, ed. *Harvard Encyclopedia of American Ethnic Groups.* Cambridge: Harvard University Press, 1988.

Thornton, Russell. *The American Indian: Holocaust and Survival.* Norman, Okla.: University of Oklahoma Press, 1987.

Tygiel, Jules. *Baseball's Great Experiment: Jackie Robinson and His Legacy.* New York: Oxford, 1983.

United States Lawn Tennis Association (USLTA). *Official Encyclopedia of Tennis.* New York: Harper & Row, 1972.

Warburton, Clark. *The Economic Results of Prohibition.* New York: AMS Press, 1932.

Weatherford, Doris. *American Women and World War II.* New York:

Facts On File, 1990.

Weisberger, Bernard A. *They Gathered at the River.* Chicago: Quadrangle Books, 1966.

Wembridge, Eleanor Rowland. "Petting and the Campus." *Survey* (July 1, 1925), pp. 393–395.

Wilkerson, Doxey A. *Special Problems of Negro Education.* Washington, D.C.: U.S. Government Printing Office, 1939.

Wood, Nancy. *Heartland New Mexico: Photographs from the Farm Security Administration, 1935–1943.* Albuquerque: University of New Mexico Press, 1989.

Wright, Richard. *Twelve Million Black Voices.* 1941. Reprint, New York: Arno, 1969.

Young, Gordon R., ed. *The Army Almanac.* Harrisburg, Pa.: Stackpole Co., 1959.

APPENDIX: LIST OF TABLES

Index

This index is arranged alphabetically letter by letter. Page numbers in *italic* indicate illustrations or captions.
Page numbers followed by *t* indicate tables; by *m* indicate maps; by *n* indicate notes; and by *b* indicate biographical profiles.

Deer Isle, Maine 326t
de Forest, Lee 44
DeGroot, Dudley 370t
DeHaven, Gloria 350t
de Kooning, Willem 323
Delaney, Jack 372t
Delaplane, Stanton 356t
de la Roche, Mazo 354t
Delaware 257
    crime and law enforcement:
        crime rates 384t; death pen-
        alty 385t, 386t
    divorce: grounds for 171t; pub-
        lic opinion regarding 173t
    economy: farm size 110t; wage
        and salary workers 123t
    education: illiteracy 302t, 310t;
        racial comparisons 309t;
        school comparisons 304t, 305t
    marriage laws 170t
    military draft 223t, 225t
    politics and government: gov-
        ernors 211t; presidential elec-
        tions 185t–192t, 194t; voting
        requirements 198t
    population 3t; migration
        to/from other states 4t; Na-
        tive American 10t
    traffic enforcement agencies
        133t
Delaware (U.S. battleship) 230t
Delaware Indians 11t
Delmar, Viña 354t
DeLuce, Daniel 356t
Demaret, Jimmy 376t
Democracy and Education (John
    Dewey) 39
Democratic Party
    congressional composition 196t
    conventions 197t
    policy making 204
    presidential elections 200t
    presidential primaries 197t
    Roosevelt's revival of 184
    Southern politics 199
    Versailles Treaty vote 243t
Dempsey, Jack 42, 44, 46, 257,
    372, 372t, 373t
Dempsey, John J. 212t, 265
Denby, Edwin 200t
Denison Dam (Oklahoma/Texas)
    34t
Denmark
    exchange rate 75t
    immigration to U.S. from 19t
    maternal mortality 164t
    per capita income 124t
    in World War I 242t
    in World War II 251t
Denneny, Cy 376t
Dennett, Tyler 358t
Denney, William D. 211t
dentists 93t
Denver, Colorado 256
    population 278t
    Roman Catholic archdiocese
        182t
    telephone rates 154t
    weather and climate: humidity
        27t; precipitation 28t, 29t;
        temperature 23t, 25t, 26t
De Palma, Ralph 377t

De Paolo, Peter 377t
deportations 22t
Depression *see* Great Depression
De Priest, Oscar 203t
Derby, Edwin 200t
Dere Mable (Edward Streeter)
    353t
Dern, George H. 200t, 213t
Der Raub der Mona Lisa (film) 343t
Desert of Wheat, The (Zane Grey)
    353t
Desert Victory (film) 343t
de Seversky, Alexander P. 355t
Des Moines, Iowa
    humidity 27t
    population 259, 279t
    precipitation 28t, 29t
    temperature 23t, 25t, 26t
DeSoto (automobile) 134t, 138
Destination Tokyo (film) 343t
Destreman, Bernard 375t
Detective Comics (comic book) 391
Detroit, Michigan 283–284
    bridges 326t
    buildings 325t
    population 262, 278t
    race riots 59
    Roman Catholic archdiocese
        182t
    unemployment 100t
    weather and climate: humidity
        27t; precipitation 28t, 29t;
        temperature 24t, 25t, 26t
Detroit Free Press (newspaper)
    356t
Detroit Red Wings (ice hockey
    team) 377t
Detroit Tigers (baseball team)
    359t
Devers, Jacob L. 247t
"devil dogs" 229
Devil to Pay, The (film) 343t
DeVinna, Clyde 345t
Dewey, George 222, 222t, 270
Dewey, John 39, 270, 289b
Dewey, Thomas E.
    home state 262
    presidential elections 59, 60,
        183t, 194t, 197t
    as "racket buster" 381
    as state governor 57, 212t
DeWitt, John L. 247t, 406
diabetes mellitus 162t
Diana (automobile) 138
Dickinson, Luren D. 212t
Dickman, John T. 239t
"Didonk" (army slang) 229
Diegel, Leo 376t
Dies, Martin 53
Diet and Health (Lulu Hunt Pe-
    ters) 353t, 354t
Dietz, David 356t
Dillinger, John 52, 259, 289b, 381
Dillon, George 357t
Dillon, Jack 372t
Dillon, Richard C. 212t
DiMaggio, Joe 55, 256, 358, 361t,
    362t
Dim Lantern, The (Temple Bailey)
    353t
Dimnet, Ernest 354t
"Dinah" (song) 347t

Dinner at Eight (film) 343t
Dionne quintuplets 52
diphtheria 164t
Disciples of Christ 175t, 177t
discount rate 73t
diseases, notifiable 164t
Disney, Walt 47, 256
Display (horse) 378t
Disraeli (1921 film) 342t
Disraeli (1929 film) 342t, 345t
Disraeli (André Maurois) 354t
Distinguished Service Medal 40
District of Columbia *see* Wash-
    ington, D.C.
Divine Lady, The (film) 345t
Divine Science College and
    Church 177t
divorce *see* marriage and divorce
"divorce capital" 168
Divorcee, The (film) 345t
Dixon, Frank M. 211t
Dixon, Joseph M. 212t
Doak, William N. 200t
Dobie, Gilmour 368t
doctorates 313t–314t
doctors 159t, 164, 164t
Dodge (automobile) 134t, 137
Dodge, Horace and John 137
Dodge Brothers (automobile com-
    pany) 138
Dodsworth (film) 343t
Dodsworth (Sinclair Lewis) 354t
Doeg, John H. 374t
Doering, William 59
"dog-face" 229
"dog it" 229
"dog robber" 229
"dog tag" 229
"Do I Love You?" (song) 348t
Doisy, Edward A. 319
"Do It Again" (song) 347t
domestic goods *see* household
    goods
Dominican Republic 39
Donahey, A. V. 212t
Donahue, Sam 349
Donat, Robert 345t
Don Juan (film) 46, 339
Donnell, Forrest C. 212t
Donnelly, Phil M. 212t
"Don't Bite the Hand That's Feed-
    ing You" (song) 347t
"Don't Blame Me" (song) 347t
"Don't Fence Me In" (song) 348t
"Don't Get Around Much Any-
    more" (song) 348, 348t
"Don't Sit under the Apple Tree"
    (song) 348
Doolittle, James H. 44, 48, 57,
    248t
Doomed Battalion, The (film) 343t
Doomsday (Warwick Deeping)
    354t
Dorazio, Gus 373t
Dorsey, George A. 354t
Dorsey, Hugh M. 211t
Dorsey, Jimmy 349, 350, 350t
Dorsey, Tommy 349, 350, 350t
Dos Passos, John 45, 53
"doughboy" 229
Dougherty, Dennis Cardinal 182t
"dough-foot" 229

Douglas, Arizona 254
Douglas, Emily T. 204t
Douglas, Helen G. 204t
Douglas, Lloyd C. 354t, 355t
Douglas, William O. 210t
Douglas Dam (Tennessee) 35t
Douglass, Robert W. 248t
Dove, Arthur 323
Dover, Delaware 257
Dover, New Hampshire 264
"Down among the Sheltering Palms"
    (song) 347t
Down to the Sea in Ships (film) 342t
Doyle, Larry 361t
Dr. Freeland (horse) 378t
Dr. Jekyll and Mr. Hyde (film) 343t, 345t
draft *see* World War I; World War II
Dragon, Carmen 346t
Dragon Seed (Pearl S. Buck) 355t
Dragon's Teeth (Upton Sinclair) 357t
"Dream" (song) 348t
"Dream a Little Dream of Me" (song)
    347t
Dreiser, Theodore 45, 259
Dressler, Marie 343t, 345t
Dreyfuss, Henry 140
"Drifting and Dreaming" (song) 347t
Drinker, Phillip 315
drinking *see* alcohol
Drivin' Woman (Elizabeth Pickett) 355t
Drums Along the Mohawk (Walter D.
    Edmonds) 354t
Dry Tortugas (Florida islands) 31t
Du Bois, W. E. B. 258
Dubuque, Iowa 182t, 326t
Duchin, Eddy 349
Dudley, Bill 370t
dueling 199
Duesenberg (automobile) 137, 138
Duff, "Granny" 166
Duffy, Edmund 356t
Dugger, Indiana 108t
Duke, James Buchanan 45
Duke University (Durham, North
    Carolina) 45
Duluth, Minnesota 262, 279t
du Maurier, Daphne 355t
Dumbarton Oaks Conference (August
    21, 1944) 59
Dumbo (film) 343t, 346t
Duncan, Asa N. 248t
Duncan, George 375t
Dundee, Joe 372t
Dundee, Johnny 372t
Dunlap, Lionel H. 248t
Dunn, James 346t
Dunne, Edward F. 211t
duodenitis 162t
Du Pont family 257
Durant, Will 354t
Duranty, Walter 356t
Durham, North Carolina 266
Durocher, Leo E. 360t, 366t
dust bowl 52
dust storms 36, *36*
Dust Which Is God, The (William Rose
    Benét) 357t
Dutra, Olin 375t, 376t
dysentery 164t

E
Eaker, Ira C. 248t

"I'm Sitting on Top of the World" (song) 347*t*

In Abraham's Bosom (Paul Green play) 357*t*

incomes
  in agriculture *see* agriculture
  corporate earnings *see* corporate earnings
  during Depression 124
  by industry 90*t*–91*t*
  national income *see* national income
  by occupation, color and sex 124*t*
  for production workers 91*t*–92*t*
  for professionals 93*t*
  state-by-state 123*t*
  in telegraph industry 154*t*
  United States versus European countries (1938) 124*t*
  for urban African Americans 101*t*

income tax 38, 128–129, 129*t*, 214

Independent Churches 177*t*

Independent Fundamental Churches of America 177*t*

Independent Negro Churches 177*t*

India
  exchange rate 75*t*
  illiteracy 303*t*
  immigration to U.S. from 18*t*
  in World War II 251*t*

Indiana 259
  crime and law enforcement: crime rates 383*t*; death penalty 385*t*, 386*t*
  divorce: grounds for 172*t*; public opinion regarding 173*t*
  economy: farm size 110*t*; wage and salary workers 123*t*
  education: illiteracy 302*t*, 310*t*; school comparisons 304*t*, 305*t*
  marriage laws 170*t*
  military draft 223*t*, 225*t*
  politics and government: governors 211*t*; presidential elections 185*t*–192*t*, 194*t*; voting requirements 198*t*
  population 3*t*; migration to/from other states 4*t*; Native American 10*t*
  traffic enforcement agencies 133*t*
  weather and climate: humidity 27*t*; precipitation 28*t*, 29*t*; temperature 23*t*, 25*t*, 26*t*; tornadoes 32*t*

Indiana (U.S. battleship) 230*t*, 231*t*

Indianapolis (U.S. heavy cruiser) 252, 253*t*

Indianapolis, Indiana
  humidity 27*t*
  population 259, 278*t*
  precipitation 28*t*, 29*t*
  Roman Catholic archdiocese 182*t*
  temperature 23*t*, 25*t*, 26*t*

Indianapolis "500" 377*t*, 377*t*

Indianapolis News (newspaper) 355*t*

Indianapolis Times (newspaper) 355*t*

Indians, American *see* Native Americans

industrial production indexes 62*t*

Industrial Workers of the World 40

I Never Left Home (Bob Hope) 355*t*

infantile paralysis *see* poliomyelitis

infant mortality 161*t*, 163*t*

In Flanders Fields (John McCrae) 353*t*

influenza 41, 162*t*, 164*t*, 165

Informer, The (film) 343*t*, 345*t*

Ingersoll, Royal E. 247*t*

Ingram, Jonas H. 247*t*

Inness, George 323

In Old Arizona (film) 345*t*

In Old Chicago (film) 345*t*

Inside Asia (John Gunther) 355*t*

Inside Latin America (John Gunther) 355*t*

Inside of the Cup, The (Winston Churchill) 353*t*

Institute for Advanced Study (Princeton, New Jersey) 49

insulin 165

interest rates 73*t*

International Church of the Four Square Gospel 177*t*

"International school" 325

In This Our Life (Ellen Glasgow) 357*t*

inventions *see* science and technology

investment activity 76–78

Invisible Man, The (film) 343*t*

In Which We Serve (film) 343*t*

"I Only Have Eyes for You" (song) 347*t*

Iowa 259–260
  crime and law enforcement: crime rates 383*t*; death penalty 385*t*, 386*t*
  divorce: grounds for 172*t*; public opinion regarding 173*t*
  economy: farm size 110*t*; wage and salary workers 123*t*
  education: illiteracy 302*t*, 310*t*; school comparisons 304*t*, 305*t*
  marriage laws 170*t*
  military draft 223*t*, 225*t*
  politics and government: governors 211*t*; presidential elections 185*t*–192*t*, 186*t*, 187*t*, 188*t*, 189*t*, 190*t*, 191*t*, 192*t*, 194*t*; voting requirements 198*t*
  population 3*t*; migration to/from other states 4*t*; Native American 10*t*
  traffic enforcement agencies 133*t*
  weather and climate: humidity 27*t*; precipitation 28*t*, 29*t*; temperature 23*t*, 25*t*, 26*t*; tornadoes 32*t*

Iowa (U.S. battleship) 59, 230*t*, 231*t*

Ireland (Eire)
  illiteracy 303*t*
  immigration to U.S. from 17*t*, 19*t*, 20*t*
  maternal mortality 164*t*
  per capita income 124*t*
  U.S. population born in 14*t*

Irish, Ned 371

Irish Americans 14*t*

iron 80*t*, 81*t*

ironing machines 329*t*

iron lung 165

Iroquois Indians 11*t*

Irvin, Dick 376*t*, 377*t*

Isbell, Cecil 370*t*

"island-hopping" 247, 249*t*

Issei (first-generation Japanese Americans) 11, 11*t*

It (film) 342*t*

"It Ain't Gonna Rain No Mo'" (song) 347*t*

"It Ain't Necessarily So" (song) 347*t*

Italy
  economy: exchange rate 75*t*; per capita income 124*t*
  illiteracy 303*t*
  immigration to U.S. from 17*t*, 19*t*, 20, 20*t*
  U.S. population born in 14*t*
  vital statistics: death rates 163*t*; maternal mortality 164*t*
  in World War I 240*t*, 241*t*, 242*t*, 244*t*, 245*t*
  in World War II 246, 246*t*, 247, 251*t*

It Can't Happen Here (Sinclair Lewis) 354*t*

It Happened One Night (film) 343*t*, 345*t*

"It Might As Well Be Spring" (song) 346*t*

"It's Been a Long, Long Time" (song) 348, 348*t*

"It's Only a Paper Moon" (song) 347*t*

"It's the Talk of the Town" (song) 347*t*

"I've Got a Feeling I'm Falling" (song) 347*t*

"I've Got My Love to Keep Me Warm" (song) 347*t*

"I've Got You Under My Skin" (song) 347*t*

"I've Told Every Little Star" (song) 347*t*

"I Wanna Be Loved by You" (song) 347*t*

"I Wish I Could Shimmy Like My Sister Kate" (song) 347*t*

J

Jack Benny Program (radio show) 352*t*

Jack Hare Jr. (horse) 378*t*

Jack Pearl–Baron Munchausen (radio show) 352*t*

Jackson, Ed 211*t*

Jackson, H. A. 376*t*

Jackson, J. 359

Jackson, Mahalia 260

Jackson, Mississippi 263, 330*t*

Jackson, Robert H. 201*t*, 210*t*

Jackson, "Shoeless Joe" 359

Jacksonville, Florida
  home heating systems 330*t*
  humidity 27*t*
  Ku Klux Klan parade 43
  population 258, 279*t*
  precipitation 28*t*, 29*t*
  temperature 23*t*, 25*t*, 26*t*

Jacobs, Helen H. 374*t*, 375*t*

Jaffe, Louis Isaac 356*t*

Jalna (Mazo de la Roche) 354*t*

James, Arthur H. 212*t*

James, Basil 378*t*

James, E. 378*t*

James, Harry 349, 350, 350*t*

James, Henry 38, 358*t*

James, Marquis 358*t*

James, Will 354*t*

Jameson, Betty 376*t*

Jameson, Francis A. 356*t*

Jamestown, North Dakota 266

Jannings, Emil 345*t*

Japan
  economy: exchange rate 75*t*; foreign trade 79*t*
  immigration to U.S. from 11*t*, 18*t*
  vital statistics: death rates 163*t*; maternal mortality 164*t*
  in World War I 240*t*, 241*t*, 242*t*
  in World War II 60, 246–252, 405, 409, 409–410

Japanese Americans 11–13
  employment 97*t*
  illiteracy 308*t*
  in military forces 235, 238*t*
  population 2*t*, 11*t*
  World War II internment 12*t*, 13, 57, 406–408

Jardine, William M. 200*t*

Jaworski, Chester 371*t*

Jazz Singer, The (film) 47, 315, 339

Jedrzejowska, Jadwiga 374*t*, 375*t*

Jeep 134, 138, 229

Jeffra, Harry 372*t*

Jeffries, R. M. 213*t*

Jehovah's Witnesses 59, 225, 226*t*

Jenckes, Virginia E. 204*t*

Jenkins, Lew 372*t*

Jensen, Leslie 213*t*

Jerome (war relocation center) 12*t*

"Jersey Bounce" (song) 348*t*

Jersey City, New Jersey 39, 265, 278*t*

Jethroe, Sam 367*t*

Jews
  attitudes toward 14*t*
  birth control practices 160*t*
  class composition 183*t*
  educational levels 183*t*
  immigration to U.S. 14, 17, 20*t*
  occupations 183*t*
  political preferences 183*t*
  private schools 311*t*
  religious membership 174, 174*t*, 175*t*, 177*t*

Jezebel (film) 345*t*

Joan Davis–Jack Haley (radio show) 352*t*

Joe Penner Program (radio show) 352*t*

John Brown's Body (Stephen Vincent Benét) 357*t*

John Hay (Tyler Dennett) 358*t*

Johnny Eager (film) 346*t*

Mundelein, George 182*t*
Mundt, Karl 269
Muni, Paul 345*t*
Munthe, Axel 354*t*
mural painting 323
murder *see* homicide
Murphree, Dennis 212*t*
Murphy, Audie 269
Murphy, Francis P. 212*t*
Murphy, Frank 201*t*, 210*t*, 212*t*
Murphy, Jimmy 377*t*
Murphy, William P. 319
Murray, Utah 270
Murray, John G. 182*t*
Murray, Philip 55
Murray, R. L. 373*t*
Murray, William H. 212*t*
Murrow, Edward R. 266
Musial, Stan 361*t*
music, popular 346–350
Muskogee, Oklahoma 267
Mussolini, Benito 59
Musto, Tony 373*t*
Mutiny on the Bounty (film) 345*t*
Myer, Buddy 362*t*
Myers, Jerome 324
My Experiences in the World War (John J. Pershing) 357*t*
"My Heart Stood Still" (song) 347*t*
"My Isle of Golden Dreams" (song) 347*t*
Mylin, E. E. ("Hooks") 368*t*
Myrdal, Gunnar 403
Myrt and Marge (radio show) 352*t*
My Son, My Son! (Howard Spring) 355*t*
Mysterious Rider, The (Zane Grey) 353*t*
Mystic Isles of the South Seas (Frederick O'Brien) 353*t*

N

Nagasaki bombing (August 9, 1945) 60
Naiden, Earl L. 248*t*
Nampa, Idaho 258
Napoleon (Emil Ludwig) 354*t*
Nash, Charles W. 137
Nash-Kelvinator (automobile company) 138
Nash Motors (automobile company) 134*t*, 137, 138
Nashua, New Hampshire 264
Nashville, Tennessee
    humidity 27*t*
    population 269, 279*t*
    precipitation 28*t*, 29*t*
    temperature 24*t*, 25*t*, 26*t*
Natchez, Mississippi 326*t*
National Basketball League 372*t*
National Collegiate Athletic Association (NCAA) 371
National Collegiate Athletic Association (NCAA) Basketball Championships 371*t*
National David Spiritual Temple of Christ Church Union (Inc.) U.S.A. 178*t*
National Defense Act (1916) 39
National Football League 370*t*
National Guard 223*t*

National Hockey League (NHL) 376
National Housing Act (1934) 207*t*
National Housing Act (1937) 208*t*
National Housing Act Amendment (1938) 208*t*
national income 63*t*, 64*t*, 122, 122*t*
National Industrial Recovery Act (1933) 51, 207*t*
National Invitational Tournament (NIT) (basketball) 371, 371*t*
National Labor Relations Act (Wagner-Connery Act) (1935) 52, 207*t*–208*t*, 398–399
National Labor Relations Board 104
National Labor Relations Board v. Jones and Laughlin Steel Corporation (1937) 210
National League (baseball)
    attendance 360*t*
    batting champions 361*t*
    home run champions 362*t*
    major-league teams 359*t*
    Most Valuable Player awards 361*t*
    pennant winners 360*t*
National Origins Act (1924) 45
national parks 379*m*
National Velvet (film) 343*t*, 346*t*
National Youth Administration (NYA) 103
Native Americans *see also specific group (e.g.,* Navajo Indians)
    education 307
    employment 97*t*
    illiteracy 308*t*
    lands 10*t*
    in military forces 235, 238*t*
    population 2*t*, 8–11, 10*t*, 11*t*
    vital statistics 158
    voting qualifications 199
Native Son (Richard Wright) 55
Native's Return, The (Louis Adamic) 354*t*
naturalization 20–21, 21*t*
Navajo code talkers 10, 235, *235*
Navajo Indians 11*t*
Navajo Reservation (Arizona/New Mexico/Utah) 11*t*
Navy, U.S. 220*t*
    active personnel 219*t*, 248*t*
    battleships 230–232, 230*t*–231*t*
    casualties 249*t*
    combat aces 251*t*
    commanders and chief officers 222*t*, 240*t*, 247*t*–248*t*
    costs 221*t*
    ship losses 252, 252*t*–253*t*
    women's participation in 234
    World War II Pacific campaign 247
Nazarene, The (Sholem Asch) 355*t*
NCAA *see* National Collegiate Athletic Association
NCO (noncommissioned officer) 229
"Nearness of You, The" (song) 348*t*
Nebraska 264

crime and law enforcement:
    crime rates 383*t*; death penalty 386*t*
divorce: grounds for 172*t*; public opinion regarding 173*t*
economy: farm size 110*t*; wage and salary workers 123*t*
education: illiteracy 302*t*, 310*t*; school comparisons 304*t*, 305*t*
marriage laws 170*t*
military draft 223*t*, 226*t*
politics and government: governors 212*t*; presidential elections 185*t*–192*t*, 194*t*; voting requirements 198*t*
population 3*t*; migration to/from other states 4*t*; Native American 10*t*
traffic enforcement agencies 133*t*
weather and climate: humidity 27*t*; precipitation 28*t*, 29*t*; temperature 24*t*, 25*t*, 26*t*
Nebraska (U.S. battleship) 230*t*
Neely, M. Mansfield 213*t*
Neff, Pat M. 213*t*
Negri, Pola 342*t*
Negro American League (baseball) 367*t*
Negro Baptist Church 179*t*
Negro National League 367*t*
Nellie Morse (horse) 378*t*
Nelson, Byron 375*t*, 376*t*
Nelson, Donald 56
Nelson, Ozzie 349
Neptune's Daughter (film) 342*t*
Ness, Eliot 381
Nestos, Ragnvald A. 212*t*
Netherlands
    death rates 163*t*
    exchange rate 75*t*
    illiteracy 303*t*
    immigration to U.S. from 19*t*, 20*t*
    infant mortality 163*t*
    per capita income 124*t*
    in World War I 242*t*
Neutrality Act (1935) 52
Neutrality Act (1937) 53, 208*t*
Nevada 264
crime and law enforcement:
    crime rates 384*t*; death penalty 385*t*, 386*t*; gambling legalized 49
divorce: grounds for 172*t*; public opinion regarding 173*t*; residency requirement reduced 38, 168
economy: farm size 111*t*; old-age pensions 44; wage and salary workers 123*t*
education: illiteracy 303*t*, 310*t*; school comparisons 304*t*, 305*t*
marriage laws 170*t*
military draft 223*t*, 226*t*
politics and government: governors 212*t*; presidential elections 185*t*–192*t*, 194*t*; voting requirements 198*t*
population 3*t*; migration to/from other states 4*t*; Native American 10*t*

traffic enforcement agencies 133*t*
weather and climate: humidity 27*t*; precipitation 28*t*, 29*t*; temperature 24*t*, 25*t*, 26*t*; weather and climate 23
Nevada (U.S. battleship) 231*t*
Neville, Keith 212*t*
Neville, Wendell C. 222*t*, 240*t*
Nevins, Allan 358*t*
New, Harry S. 200*t*
New Apostolic Church 178*t*
Newark, Delaware 257
Newark, New Jersey
    population 265, 278*t*
    Roman Catholic archdiocese 182*t*
New Bedford, Massachusetts 279*t*
Newbranch, Harvey E. 356*t*
New Britain, Connecticut 257
New Castle, Delaware 257
New Deal 51–54
    economy 61
    government agencies 209*t*
    policy making 204
    work relief projects 103
Newell, Frank 376*t*
Newfoundland 14*t*, 18*t*
New Hampshire 264
crime and law enforcement: crime rates 383*t*; death penalty 385*t*, 386*t*
divorce: grounds for 172*t*; public opinion regarding 173*t*
economy: farm size 110*t*; wage and salary workers 123*t*
education: illiteracy 302*t*, 310*t*; school comparisons 304*t*, 305*t*
marriage laws 170*t*
military draft 223*t*, 226*t*
politics and government: governors 212*t*; presidential elections 185*t*–192*t*, 194*t*; voting requirements 198*t*
population 3*t*; migration to/from other states 4*t*; Native American 10*t*
traffic enforcement agencies 133*t*
New Hampshire (U.S. battleship) 230*t*, 231*t*
New Hampshire: A Poem with Notes and Grace Notes (Robert Frost) 357*t*
New Haven, Connecticut 257, 279*t*
Newhouser, Hal 361*t*
New Jersey 264–265
    ammunition depot explosion 46
crime and law enforcement: crime rates 383*t*; death penalty 385*t*, 386*t*
divorce: grounds for 172*t*; public opinion regarding 173*t*
economy: farm size 110*t*; wage and salary workers 123*t*
education: illiteracy 302*t*, 310*t*; school comparisons 304*t*, 305*t*
marriage laws 170*t*
military draft 223*t*, 226*t*
politics and government: governors 212*t*; presidential elections 185*t*–192*t*, 194*t*; voting requirements 198*t*
population 3*t*; migration to/from other states 4*t*; Native American 10*t*
traffic enforcement agencies 133*t*

"Stardust" (song) 347t
Star Is Born, A (film) 343t
Stark, Harold R. 222t, 247t
Stark, Lloyd C. 212t
Stark, Louis 356t
Starr, Kay 350t
Stars and Stripes (army newspaper) 40
Stars Look Down, The (film) 343t
"Star-Spangled Banner, The" (national anthem) 49
Stassen, Harold E. 212t
State Fair (film) 343t, 346t
states
    crime and law enforcement:
        crime rates 383t–384t; death
        penalty and executions
        385t–386t, 386t
    economy: farm size 110t; unemployment relief 102m;
        wage or salary workers 123t
    education 303–305; educational comparisons 304t, 305t;
        illiteracy 302t–303t
    entertainment and sports: national parks 379m
    maps 255m
    military forces and world
        wars: military draft 223t,
        225t–226t
    politics and government: expenditures 216t; finances
        216–217; governors
        211t–213t; tax collections
        216t–217t
    population: density 2m; interstate movement 4t; Native
        American 10t; rural and urban 3t
    road building 132
    weather and climate: average
        daily maximum temperature
        25t; average daily minimum
        temperature 26t; average precipitation 28t; average relative humidity 27t; average
        snowfall 29t; mean temperature 23t, 24t
"stay loose" 229
Steamboat Willie (film) 47
steel 61, 65t, 80t, 81t
Steen, Marguerite 355t
Stein, Clarence 326
Steinbeck, John 53, 54, 103, 355t,
    357t
Steiner, Max 345t, 346t
Stella Dallas (film) 342t
Stelle, John H. 211t
Stephens, Vern 362t
Stephens, William D. 211t
Stephenson, David Curtis 381
Sterling, Ross 213t
Stern, Otto 319
Sterne, Maurice 324
Sternweiss, George 362t
Sternweiss, Snuffy 361
Stetson, G. H. 376t
Stetson, Rufus 317
Stettinius Jr., Edward R. 200t,
    201t
Stevenson, Coke R. 213t
Stewart, Anita 342t

Stewart, Bill 377t
Stewart, James 346t
Stewart, Nels 377t
Stewart, Sam V. 212t
Stilwell, Joseph W. 247t, 258
Stimson, Henry L. 48, 49, 200t,
    224, 298b
Stirling, Alexa 376t
Stockbridge Indians 11t
Stock Clearing Corporation 76t
stocks 77t
Stokes, Thomas Lunsford 356t
Stoll, Georgie 346t
Stoloff, Morris 346t
"Stompin' at the Savoy" (song)
    347t
Stone, Charles B. 248t
Stone, Harlan F. 45, 200t, 210t
Stone Mountain, Georgia 38
Store, The (T. S. Stribling) 357t
storms 30–32
"Stormy Weather" (song) 347t
Story of G.I. Joe (film) 343t
Story of Louis Pasteur, The (film)
    343t, 345t
Story of Mankind, The (Hendrik
    Willem Van Loon) 353t
Story of Philosophy, The (Will
    Durant) 354t
Story of San Michele, The (Axel
    Munthe) 354t
Stothart, Herbert 345t
Stout, Jimmy 378t
Stowe, Leland 356t
Strachey, Lytton 354t
Stradling, Harry 346t
*Strange Death of President Harding,
    The* (Gaston B. Means and May
    Dixon Thacker) 354t
Strange Fruit (Lillian Smith) 355t
Strange Holiness (Robert P. Tristram Coffin) 357t
Strange Interlude (Eugene O'Neill
    play) 354t, 357t
Stratton, Dorothy C. 248t
Street, Gabby 360t, 365t
Street Angel (film) 345t
streetcars 143
Streeter, Edward 353t
Streeter, Ruth C. 248t
streets 136t
Street Scene (Elmer L. Rice play)
    357t
Streett, St. Clair 248t
streptomycin 165
Stribling, T. S. 357t
Stribling, W. L. 373t
"striker" *see* "dog robber"
Stritch, Samuel Cardinal 182t
Strong, Ted 367t
Struss, Karl 345t
Struther, Jan 355t
Stuart, Henry C. 213t
Studebaker (automobile company) 134t, 137, 138
Student Prince, The (Sigmund
    Romberg play) 45
Stuldreher, Harry 368t
Stutz Motors (automobile company) 134t, 137, 138
submarines 220, 238–239

subways 143
suffragette movement 40
sugar 81t, 113t–114t, 127t
Sugar Bowl (football game) 369t
suicides 162, 162t
sulfa drugs 165
Sullivan, Louis 324, 326
Sullivan, Mark 354t
Sullivan's Travels (film) 343t
Sultan, Daniel I. 247t
Summerall, Charles P. 222t, 239t
Sumner, Jessie 204t
Sun Also Rises, The (Ernest Hemingway) 46
Sunday, Billy 165, 180
Sunday at Seth Parkers (radio
    show) 352t
Sunderland Capture (Leonard Bacon) 357t
Sun Is My Undoing, The (Marguerite Steen) 355t
Sunnyside, Utah 108t
Sunrise (film) 342t, 345t
Superman (comic book hero) 53,
    391
superstitions, medical 166
Supreme Court, U.S. 209–210,
    210t
Supreme Court in United States History, The (Charles Warren) 357t
"Surrey with the Fringe on Top,
    The" (song) 348t
Suspicion (film) 346t
Sussex attack (March 24, 1916) 39
Sutherland, George 210t
Sutherland, John B. 368t
"Swanee" (song) 347t
Swanson, Claude A. 201t
Swanson, Gloria 259, 342t
Swan Song (John Galsworthy)
    354t
Sweden
    death rates 163t
    exchange rate 75t
    immigration to U.S. from 19t
    infant mortality 163t
    maternal mortality 164t
    per capita income 124t
    U.S. population born in 14t
    in World War I 242t
    in World War II 251t
Swedish Americans 14t
Sweet, William E. 211t
"Sweet Georgia Brown" (song)
    347t
"Sweet Leilani" (song) 345t, 347t
"Swingin' Down the Lane"
    (song) 347t
"Swinging on a Star" (song) 346t
"Swing Low, Sweet Chariot"
    (song) 347t
swing music 349
Swing Time (film) 345t
Switzerland
    exchange rate 75t
    illiteracy 303t
    immigration to U.S. from 19t
    infant mortality 163t
    maternal mortality 164t
    per capita income 124t
    in World War I 242t
Swope, Herbert Bayard 356t

syphilis 164t
Syracuse, New York 265, 279t

T

Tabu (film) 343t, 345t
Tacoma, Washington 271, 279t
Tacoma Narrows Bridge (Washington) 326, 327
Taft, Robert A. 266
Taft, William Howard 44, 48, 185t,
    197t, 210t, 266
Talbert, William F. 374t
Talbot, Ray H. 211t
Talburt, H. M. 356t
Talmadge, Constance 342t
Talmadge, Eugene 211t
Talmadge, Norma 342t
Tampa, Florida
    hurricanes 31t
    population 258, 279t
tanks 227, 250t
Target for Tonight (film) 343t
Tarkington, Booth 38, 42, 353t, 354t,
    357t
Tarzan of the Apes (Edgar Rice Burroughs) 38
Tarzan of the Apes (film) 342t
Tattalino, Battling 372t
Taurog, Norman 345t
taxes *see also* income tax
    on gasoline 135t
    government receipts 218t
    state collection of 216t–217t
Taylor, Alfred A. 213t
Taylor, Bud 372t
Taylor, Frederick W. 315
Taylor, Leon R. 212t
Taylor, Robert 344t
Taylor, William H. 356t
tea 81t
teachers 309t
"Tea for Two" (song) 347t
Teagarden, Jack 349
Teapot Dome Scandal 44, 45, 47
technology *see* science and technology
Teheran Conference (November 28-December 1, 1943) 59
telegraphs 153–154, 154t
telephones 153–154, 153t, 154t, 329
television 351t
temperature 23t–26t
Temple, Shirley 256, 343t, 344t
Templeton, Charles A. 211t
Ten Commandments, The (film) 342t
Tener, John K. 212t
Tennessee 269
    crime and law enforcement: crime
        rates 384t; death penalty 385t, 386t
    divorce: grounds for 172t; public
        opinion regarding 173t
    economy: farm size 111t; wage and
        salary workers 123t
    education: illiteracy 302t, 310t; racial comparisons 309t; school comparisons 304t, 305t
    home appliances 332t
    marriage laws 171t
    military draft 223t, 226t
    politics and government: governors
        213t; presidential elections
        185t–192t, 194t, 200t; voting requirements 198t

unemployment 100*t*, 101, 101*t*, 102*m*

Unfinished Business (Stephen Bonsal) 357*t*

unionism 104–107, 106*t*, 183*t*

Unitarians
   membership 176*t*, 178*t*
   private schools 311*t*

United Auto Workers 55, 60, 138

United Brethren 176*t*, 178*t*

United Holy Church of America, Inc. 178*t*

United Kingdom *see* Great Britain

United Mine Workers 54

United Nations 60

United Nations Charter Ratification (1945) 209*t*

United States Open (golf) 375*t*

United States Steel Corporation 49, 53

United Steel Workers 53

Universal Emancipation Church 178*t*

Universalist Church 176*t*, 178*t*

universities *see* colleges and universities

"Untouchables" 381

Up Front (Bill Mauldin) 355*t*

U. P. Trail, The (Zane Grey) 353*t*

urban areas *see* cities and urban areas

U'Ren, William A. 267

Urey, Harold C. 316, 319

Uruguay 75*t*, 164*t*

U.S.A. (John Dos Passos) 53

Usher, George L. 248*t*

U.S. Open (tennis) 373*t*–374*t*

U.S.S.R. *see* Soviet Union

Utah 269–270
   crime and law enforcement: crime rates 384*t*; death penalty 386*t*
   divorce: grounds for 172*t*; public opinion regarding 173*t*
   economy: farm size 111*t*; wage and salary workers 123*t*
   education: illiteracy 303*t*, 310*t*; school comparisons 304*t*, 305*t*
   marriage laws 171*t*
   military draft 223*t*, 226*t*
   politics and government: governors 213*t*; presidential elections 185*t*–192*t*, 194*t*; voting requirements 198*t*
   population 3*t*; migration to/from other states 4*t*; Native American 10*t*
   traffic enforcement agencies 133*t*
   weather and climate: humidity 27*t*; precipitation 28*t*, 29*t*; temperature 24*t*, 25*t*, 26*t*

Utah (U.S. battleship) 230*t*

Ute Indians 11*t*

Utica, New York 279*t*

utilities 126*t*

Uzcudun, Paulino 373*t*

V

vacuum cleaners 329, 329*t*

Valencia, Eugeane A. 251*t*

Valenti, Umberto 388

Valentino, Rudolph 342*t*

Vallee, Rudy 270

Valley of Decision, The (Marcia Davenport) 355*t*

Valley of Silent Men, The (James Oliver Curwood) 353*t*

Valtin, Jan 355*t*

Van Buren, Steve 370*t*

Vance, Dazzy 361*t*

Vance, Ethel 355*t*

Vancouver Millionaires (ice hockey team) 376*t*

Vandegrift, Alexander A. 222*t*, 248*t*

Vandenberg, Hoyt S. 248*t*

Vanderbeck, C. H. 376*t*

Vanderbilt, William H. 213*t*

Vanderhoef, Marion 374*t*

Vandermeer, John 53, 358

Van Der Veer, Willard 345*t*

Van Devanter, Willis 53, 210*t*

Van Dine, S. S. 354*t*

Van Doren, Carl 358*t*

Van Doren, Mark 357*t*

Van Horn, S. Welby 374*t*

Van Loon, Hendrik Willem 353*t*, 354*t*

Van Loon's Geography (Hendrik Willem Van Loon) 354*t*

van Paassen, Pierre 355*t*

Van Tyne, Claude H. 357*t*

Van Wagoner, Murray D. 212*t*

Van Wie, Virginia 376*t*

Vanzetti, Bartolomeo 43, 47, 381

Vardon, Harry 375*t*

Vare, Glenna 376*t*

Vargas, Tetelo 367*t*

Vaughan, Arky 361*t*

Vaughan, Sarah 350*t*

Veber, L. 375*t*

Veblen, Thorstein 271

Vedanta Society 178*t*

V-E (Victory in Europe) Day (May 7, 1945) 60

vegetables 115*t*–116*t*

Vehr, Urban J. 182*t*

Vein of Iron (Ellen Glasgow) 354*t*

venereal disease 164*t*, 165

Venezuela 164*t*

Venuti, Joe 350*t*

Vermont 270
   crime and law enforcement: crime rates 383*t*; death penalty 385*t*, 386*t*
   divorce: grounds for 172*t*; public opinion regarding 173*t*
   economy: farm size 110*t*; wage and salary workers 123*t*
   education: illiteracy 302*t*, 310*t*; school comparisons 304*t*, 305*t*
   marriage laws 171*t*
   military draft 223*t*, 226*t*
   politics and government: governors 213*t*; presidential elections 185*t*–192*t*, 194*t*; voting requirements 198*t*
   population 3*t*; migration to/from other states 4*t*; Native American 10*t*
   traffic enforcement agencies 133*t*

weather and climate: humidity 27*t*; precipitation 28*t*, 29*t*; temperature 24*t*, 25*t*, 26*t*

Vermont (U.S. battleship) 230*t*

Versailles, Treaty of (1919) 41, 42, 43, 205*t*, 242–243, 243*t*

Vestal, Albert H. 202*t*

Vicksburg, Mississippi
   humidity 27*t*
   population 263
   precipitation 28*t*, 29*t*
   temperature 24*t*, 25*t*, 26*t*

Victoria Cougars (ice hockey team) 376*t*

Victorian (horse) 378*t*

Victory (film) 342*t*

Victory at Sea, The (William Sowden Sims, with Burton J. Hendrick) 357*t*

Victory Through Air Power (Alexander P. de Seversky) 355*t*

Vigil (horse) 378*t*

Villa, Pancho 39, 372*t*

Vincennes (U.S. heavy cruiser) 253*t*

Vines Jr., H. Ellsworth 374*t*

Vinson, Fred M. 201*t*, 260

Virginia 270
   crime and law enforcement: crime rates 384*t*; death penalty 385*t*, 386*t*
   divorce: grounds for 172*t*; public opinion regarding 173*t*
   economy: farm size 110*t*; wage and salary workers 123*t*
   education: illiteracy 302*t*, 310*t*; racial comparisons 308*t*, 309*t*; school comparisons 304*t*, 305*t*
   home appliances 332*t*
   marriage laws 171*t*
   military draft 223*t*, 226*t*
   politics and government: governors 213*t*; presidential elections 185*t*–192*t*, 194*t*, 200*t*; voting requirements 198*t*
   population 3*t*; migration to/from other states 4*t*; Native American 10*t*
   traffic enforcement agencies 133*t*
   weather and climate: humidity 27*t*; precipitation 28*t*, 29*t*; temperature 24*t*, 25*t*, 26*t*

Virginia (U.S. battleship) 230*t*

Virgin Islands 39, 226*t*, 276, 386*t*

vital statistics 157–173

vitamin research 165

Vito (horse) 378*t*

Vivian, John C. 211*t*

Vlasto, D. 375*t*

V-Letter and Other Poems (Karl Shapiro) 357*t*

V-mail *151*

Volstead Act (1919) 42, 205*t*, 395–396

Volstead Act (1933) 51

Volunteers of America 178*t*

von Cramm, Baron G. 374*t*

voting 196*t*, 198–199, 198*t*, 199*t*

W

WAC *see* Women's Army Corps

Wade, Wallace 368*t*

Wadsworth, James W. 201*t*

Waesche, Russell R. 248*t*

WAFS *see* Women's Auxiliary Ferrying Squadron

Wage and Hours Act (1938) 208*t*

wages *see* income

Wagner, Marie 374*t*

Wagner-Connery Act (1935) 104, 207*t*–208*t*

Wahl, Arthur C. 317

Waikiki Wedding (film) 345*t*

Wain, Beau 350*t*

Wainwright, Jonathan M. 57, 247*t*, 271

"Waitin' for the Train to Come In" (song) 348, 348*t*

Wake Island (film) 343*t*

Wake Up and Live! (Dorothea Brnde) 354*t*

Waksman, Selman 165

Waldorf, Lynn O. 368*t*

Walker, Clarence 362*t*

Walker, Clifford 211*t*

Walker, Cyril 375*t*

Walker, Dixie 361*t*

Walker, Frank C. 201*t*

Walker, James J. 45, 50

Walker, Mickey 372*t*

Wallace, DeWitt 44

Wallace, Henry A. (prominent Democrat) 55, *195*, 197*t*, 200*t*, 201*t*, 203*t*

Wallace, Henry C. (prominent Republican) 200*t*

Wallace, Oliver 346*t*

Waller, Fats 350

Wallgren, Monrad C. 213*t*

Waln, Nora 354*t*, 355*t*

Walpole, Hugh 354*t*

Walsh, Adam 370*t*

Walsh, David I. 211*t*

Walsh, Frank 376*t*

Walsh, Kenneth A. 251*t*

Walsh, Thomas J. 182*t*

Walsh-Healey Act (1936) 53

Walters, Bucky 361*t*

Walter Winchell Commentary (radio show) 352*t*

Walton, John C. 44, 212*t*

Waner, Paul 361*t*

War Admiral (horse) 378*t*

War Cloud (horse) 378*t*

War Debt Moratorium (1931) 206*t*

war debts 244–245, 244*t*, 245*t*

Waring, Fred 349

Warner, Glenn S. 368*t*

Warner Company 54

"war nerves" 336

War of Independence, The (Claude H. Van Tyne) 357*t*

War of the Worlds radio broadcast (October 30, 1938) 54

war relocation centers 12*t*

Warren, Charles 357*t*

Warren, Earl 211*t*, 256

Warren, Robert Penn 260

War Revenue Act (1917) 40

warships 249*t*

War with Mexico, The (Justin H. Smith) 357*t*

washboards *333*

washing machines 329*t*, 332*t*

Washington (U.S. battleship) 231*t*